HANDBOOK OF RESEARCH ON
Educational Administration

Second Edition

HANDBOOK OF RESEARCH ON

Educational Administration

Second Edition

A Project of the
American Educational Research Association

JOSEPH MURPHY
Vanderbilt University

KAREN SEASHORE LOUIS
University of Minnesota

Editors

Jossey-Bass Publishers • San Francisco

Jossey-Bass books and products are available through most
bookstores. To contact Jossey-Bass directly, call (888) 378-
2537, fax to (800) 605-2665, or visit our website at
www.josseybass.com.

Substantial discounts on bulk quantities of Jossey-Bass
books are available to corporations, professional associations, and other organizations. For details and discount information, contact the special sales department at
Jossey-Bass.

Manufactured in the United States of America.

Library of Congress Cataloging-in-Publication Data
Handbook of research on educational administration : a project of the
   American Educational Research Association / Joseph Murphy, Karen
   Seashore Louis, editors.—2nd ed.
      Includes bibliographical references and index.
      ISBN 0-7879-4340-1 (alk. paper)
      1. School management and organization—United States
   2. Educational change—United States.   I. Murphy, Joseph, date.
   II. Louis, Karen Seashore.   III. American Educational Research
   Association.   IV. Title: Educational administration.
   LB2805.H2864   1999
   371 . . 2'00973—dc21   98-54762

FIRST EDITION
HB Printing   10 9 8 7 6 5 4 3 2 1

To the memory of Linda S. Lotto—my star.

J. M.

For my father, Stanley E. Seashore,
who taught me to be a social observer
and a scholar and never to take myself too seriously.

K. S. L.

CONTENTS

PART II THE CHANGING NATURE OF EDUCATION AND SCHOOLING: EMERGING FOUNDATIONS FOR THE NEW PROFESSION

INTRODUCTION

EVOLVING VIEWS OF LEARNING AND TEACHING

EVOLVING VIEWS OF SCHOOL ORGANIZATIONS

EVOLVING VIEWS OF SCHOOL-ENVIRONMENT RELATIONS

PART III   RETHINKING THE CHALLENGES OF EDUCATIONAL LEADERSHIP

THE EDITORS

Joseph Murphy is Professor and Chair of the Department of Leadership and Organizations at Peabody College of Vanderbilt University. Prior to moving to the university, he served as a school administrator at the school, district, and state levels. His most recent experience was as Executive Assistant to the Chief Deputy Superintendent of Public Instruction in California.

He currently chairs the Interstate School Leaders Licenser Consortium and is a former Vice President of the American Educational Research Association (Division A, Administration).

He won the Jack A. Culbertson Research Award from the University Council of Educational Administration in 1986 and the Professional Service Award for outstanding contribution relating research to practice from the American Educational Research Association in 1998. He has been recognized for writing the outstanding articles in the *Journal of Vocational Education Research* in 1987 (with Linda S. Lotto) and in *The Journal of Educational Administration* in 1995 (with Philip Hallinger).

Murphy's primary interest is in school improvement, with emphasis in the areas of policy and leadership. He has authored or co-authored nine books in these areas. He has edited another seven volumes. He has presented more than 100 papers at national and international conferences. In addition, Murphy has written more than 150 book chapters and articles.

Karen Seashore Louis is currently Director of the Center for Applied Research and Educational Improvement and Professor of Educational Policy and Administration at the University of Minnesota. She received her B.A. from Swarthmore College (1967) and her Ph.D. in Sociology from Columbia University (1974), and before coming to the University of Minnesota held academic and research positions at Tufts, Abt Associates, the University of Massachusetts, and Harvard University. Her research and teaching interests focus on educational reform, knowledge use in schools and universities, and educational institutions as workplaces.

Her research in K–12 education has focused on school improvement, educational reform, and knowledge use in schools. Recent publications address the development of teachers' work in schools, the role of the district in school reform, urban education, comparative educational reform policies, the changing role of the principalship, and organizational learning. She is active in several divisions of AERA, served on the board of the University Council for Educational Administration for six years, and is a member of the Curriculum Committee of the NASSP.

THE CONTRIBUTORS

Jacob E. Adams, Jr., Assistant Professor, Peabody College, Vanderbilt University

David N. Aspin, Professor of Philosophy, Faculty of Education, Monash University

Lynn G. Beck, Professor and Chair, Administration and Educational Leadership, University of Alabama

William Lowe Boyd, Distinguished Professor of Education, Pennsylvania State University

Judith D. Chapman, Dean of the Faculty, Australian Catholic University

James G. Cibulka, Professor and Chair, Department of Education Policy, Planning, and Administration, University of Maryland

Robert L. Crowson, Professor of Education, Department of Educational Leadership, Peabody College, Vanderbilt University

Robert Donmoyer, Professor and Director, The School of Educational Policy and Leadership, Ohio State University

Mary Erina Driscoll, Associate Professor of Educational Administration, New York University, School of Education

Daniel L. Duke, Professor and Director of the Thomas Jefferson Center for Educational Design, University of Virginia

William A. Firestone, Professor, Graduate School of Education, Rutgers University

Patrick B. Forsyth, Executive Director, University Council for Educational Administration

William Foster, Professor, Indiana University

Lance D. Fusarelli, Assistant Professor, Fordham University

Ellen B. Goldring, Professor, Peabody College, Vanderbilt University

James W. Guthrie, Director, Peabody Center for Education Policy and Professor, Public Policy and Education, Vanderbilt University

Philip Hallinger, Professor, Peabody College, Vanderbilt University

Andy Hargreaves, Professor, Ontario Institute for Studies in Education at the University of Toronto

Ann Weaver Hart, Provost and Dean of Faculty, Claremont Gradute University

Ronald H. Heck, Professor, University of Hawaii at Manoa

Paul T. Hill, Research Professor, Graduate School of Public Affairs, University of Washington

Charles Taylor Kerchner, Professor, Claremont Graduate University

Michael W. Kirst, Professor of Education, School of Education, Stanford University

Kenneth Leithwood, Professor and Head, Centre for Leadership Development, Ontario Institute for Studies in Education, University of Toronto

Martha M. McCarthy, Chancellor Professor and Chair, Educational Leadership, Indiana University

Hanne B. Mawhinney, Associate Professor, College of Education, University of Maryland, College Park.

Cecil G. Miskel, Professor, University of Michigan

David H. Monk, Professor and Chair, Department of Education, Cornell University

Rodney T. Ogawa, Professor and Associate Dean, School of Education, University of California, Riverside

Penelope L. Peterson, Dean of the School of Education and Social Policy and John Evans Professor, Northwestern University

Margaret L. Plecki, Assistant Professor, University of Washington, Seattle

Richard S. Prawat, Professor of Teacher Education and Educational Psychology and Chair of the Department of Counseling, Educational Psychology and Special Education, Michigan State University

Pedro Reyes, Professor and Associate Dean, University of Texas at Austin

Brian Rowan, Professor of Education, University of Michigan

Larry E. Sackney, Professor, Department of Educational Administration, University of Saskatchewan, Canada

Charol Shakeshaft, Professor, Administration and Policy Studies, Hofstra University

Robert O. Slater, Professor, Texas A & M University

Claire E. Smrekar, Associate Professor, Peabody College, Vanderbilt University

Mark A. Smylie, Professor of Education, University of Illinois at Chicago

Gary Sykes, Professor, College of Education, Michigan State University

James Toole, President, Compass Institute, St. Paul, Minnesota

Lonnie H. Wagstaff, M. K. Hage Centennial Professor, University of Texas at Austin

Donald J. Willower, Distinguished Professor of Education, Pennsylvania State University

THE REVIEWERS

Paul V. Bredeson

Edwin M. Bridges

Ursula Casanova

Judith D. Chapman

David L. Clark (deceased)

David T. Conley

Sharon C. Conley

A. Reynaldo Contreras

Gary M. Crow

Larry Cuban

Philip A. Cusick

Joyce L. Epstein

Frances C. Fowler

Adam Gamoran

Naftaly Glasman

William D. Greenfield

Daniel E. Griffiths

Willis D. Hawley

Shirley M. Hord

Valerie Lee

Henry M. Levin

Martha M. McCarthy

Lorraine M. McDonnell

Betty Malen

Hermine Marshall

Mary H. Metz

John Meyer

Matthew B. Miles (deceased)

Jeffrey Mirel

Douglas E. Mitchell

Gary Natriello

Fred M. Newmann

George W. Noblit

Nel Noddings

Allan R. Odden

Laurence Parker

Diana G. Pounder

Kathryn A. Riley

Richard A. Rossmiller

Barbara L. Schneider

Thomas J. Sergiovanni

Charol Shakeshaft

Paula M. Short

C. John Tarter

Frons van Wieringen

Priscilla Wohlstetter

Kenneth Wong

EDITORIAL ADVISORY BOARD

INTRODUCTION

Framing the Project

Joseph Murphy and Karen Seashore Louis

In this introduction to the second edition of the *Handbook of Research on Educational Administration*, we undertake four assignments. We begin with a few notes that reveal the focus of the volume. We then expose the intellectual infrastructure that shaped the overall design of the Handbook. From there, we outline conceptions of leadership that guided the formation of the volume. In the final section, we acknowledge debts to colleagues who made this project possible.

Notes on the Focus

Developing a handbook that reveals the full research landscape in educational administration is not an easy task. Most important, almost all decisions in the development process are accompanied by opportunity costs, some quite significant. The central decision centered on the selection of an organizing framework for the volume. We treat that issue in some detail below. Another decision dealt with the question of target audience. Although we do not gainsay the connections between higher education administration and K-12 management, given the intellectual scaffolding of the book, limiting the focus to elementary and secondary education seemed most appropriate. As was the case with the first Handbook (Boyan, 1988), the audience for this volume is the research community. While a good deal of the material is accessible to practitioners of school administration, the volume was designed for those in the academic arm of the profession.

On the matter of contributors to the volume, two guiding principles were established early in the development process. First, we would rely primarily upon senior schol-

ars in both the writing and the review of the chapters. Second, we would encourage collaborative writing. Equally important, in a number of cases, we would attempt to forge collaboration among scholars with important lines of research who had not worked together previously. While a couple of these partnerships never blossomed and when others did manuscript development often took much longer than we anticipated, we believe that the process has produced more comprehensive and insightful chapters than would have been created otherwise.

The manuscript assessment process was organized to bring four reviewers into the development of each chapter. Two established scholars were assigned as consultant reviewers for each chapter. In seeking these analysts, we looked primarily at expertise but also heavily weighed diversity of perspectives. In addition, one member of the Editorial Advisory Board and one of the editors were assigned to each chapter. While the overall review process would earn a passing grade, it was far from perfect. A number of colleagues who volunteered as reviewers disappeared on us. And our efforts to provide a more substantive role for members of the Advisory Board through the review process was only partially successful.

The Framework

Setting the Stage

The selection of a framework to anchor the volume was paramount. We desired a structure that would be robust but parsimonious, allow for the integration of research across traditional domains of educational administration, privilege the educational as well as the organizational and managerial dimensions of our profession, and allow for both the accumulation of research findings and the foreshadowing of the nature of education and school leadership in a post-industrial world. Using these benchmarks led us early on to discard what, given the developmental and scholarly history of our profession, might be viewed as the logical organizational frameworks for such a project. For example, we viewed the three dominant frames used in the profession—roles (e.g., the principalship, the superintendency), functions (e.g., student personnel, teacher supervision), and disciplines (e.g., economics, political science)—as inadequate for the task at hand. We actually concluded that these designs would be dysfunctional. We also determined that an infrastructure based on the evolution of the profession and its scholarly foundations (e.g., structural, human relations, political, cultural) would not be helpful. We rejected the idea of levels of the educational system (e.g., federal, state) as too limiting. Finally, while we liked parts of the categorical framework that Professor Boyan employed in the first Handbook, we were troubled by its lack of explicit attention to the core technology of education and its seeming inability to facilitate greater integration of research findings.

Our resolution was to borrow a simple yet powerful framework provided by Parsons (1960) and to couple it to important shifts afoot in the movement from an industrial to a post-industrial world and to a post-industrial educational system. Before saying a bit more about the framework itself, we should acknowledge some of the costs that accompany our choice. By highlighting some aspects of the profession, the framework, by design, moves other ones to the background. For example, there is no chapter that examines research on the principalship. Topics, whether of long-standing interest (e.g., urban education, evaluation, the federal role in education) or of more recent vintage (e.g., critical theory, ethics) are not featured. Neither are important disciplinary areas such as law spotlighted. While we worked hard to ensure integration of material from the more traditional organizational frames into the various chapters, it would be disingenuous to suggest that they occupy as much space as they would have under alternate designs.

Some colleagues may also be uneasy about the foreshadowing dimension of many of these reviews. We were explicit in our request that authors attempt to capture emerging central trends in the educational, organizational, and institutional domains of schooling and in the larger contexts that set the stage for those discussions. In short, we viewed the archival function of the Handbook as necessary but insufficient. In following this path, we advantaged large-scale, macro-level analyses. In so doing, we allowed for a broader definition of scholarship than might be found in more traditional empirical reviews. We acknowledge that others would make different choices. In-

deed, at the outset of the project we heard from colleagues who encouraged us to do so.

Examining the Framework[1]

The framework laid out by Parsons describes three fundamental levels of an organization—technical, managerial, and institutional. In education, the technical level is concerned with the learning-teaching process. The managerial level refers to the leadership, administration, and organization of schooling. The institutional level attends to relations between the school and its external environment—both close-in relations, such as those with parents, and more distal relations, such as those with the economic, political, and social dimensions of society. As noted previously, this volume is concerned both with understanding what we know and with tracking important shifts at each of these organizational levels in education.

Technical Level

Some evidence points out that a more robust understanding of the education production function is beginning to be translated into new ways of thinking about learning and teaching. The strongest theoretical and disciplinary influence on education—behavioral psychology—is being pushed off center stage by constructivist psychology and newer sociological perspectives on learning. Underlying this change are radically different ways of thinking about the educability of children. Those who are at the forefront of transforming schools that were historically organized to produce results consistent with the normal curve, to sort youth into the various strata needed to fuel the economy, see education being transformed to ensure equal opportunity for all learners.

At the center of this newly forming vision about schooling for tomorrow are fairly important changes in assumptions about intelligence and knowledge. The prevailing conception of knowledge as an external entity is breaking down. A new view, one that holds that knowledge is internal and subjective, that it is closely connected to the learner and the situational context, is receiving serious consideration. Learning is seen as a social phenomenon and considerable attention is devoted to the social origins of cognition.

New views about what is worth learning also characterize emerging perspectives on the core technology of schooling. The traditional emphasis on acquiring information is being replaced by a focus on learning to learn and on the ability to use knowledge. New perspectives on the context of learning are also being developed, directing attention to active learning. A century-old concern for independent work and competition—a focus on the individual dimension of human existence, especially on individual ability—is slowly receding in favor of more cooperative learning relationships—a focus on the social dimensions of human existence.

New ways of thinking about learning are also beginning to redefine the technical level of schooling. Vigorous attacks on the practice of tracking are accompanied by calls for a core curriculum for all students. Educators involved in the redesign of the technical core are also tackling the traditional emphasis in schools on content coverage, rote learning of basic skills, and reliance on textbooks as the primary source of knowledge. They promulgate an alternative image of a core technology that (a) reflects an interdisciplinary vision, (b) features a curriculum that is more vertical and less horizontal—that covers fewer topics in more depth, (c) highlights higher-order thinking skills for all students, (d) spotlights the use of technology and original source documents in lieu of textbooks, (e) underscores the use of a broadened evaluation system that highlights authentic measures of assessment, and (f) pushes service learning closer to center stage.

Learner-centered pedagogy is featured in post-behavioral conceptions of the core technology. The model of the teachers as content specialists who possess relevant knowledge that they transmit to students through telling is replaced by an approach in which teaching is more of a guiding function. The student becomes the primary actor. Substantive conversation replaces conventional classroom talk and didactic instruction. Learning is seen as the construction of understanding, and teaching is viewed as facilitating this development. The focus is on learning, not on the delivery system.

Managerial Level

There is a growing sentiment that the existing managerial and organization structures are failing, that the reformers of the last century have produced "bureaucratic arteriosclerosis, insulation from parents and patrons, and the low productivity of a declining industry protected as a quasi monopoly" (Tyack, 1993, p. 3). It is increasingly being concluded that the existing bureaucratic system of administration is incapable of addressing the problems of the public education system.

In particular, the current bureaucratic system of management and governance has come under sharp criticism from: (1) those who argue that schools are so covered with bureaucratic sediment that initiative, creativity, and professional judgement have all been paralyzed; (2) reviewers who maintain that the current administrative structures are distorting the educational process, that they are paralyzing American education and interfering with learning; (3) analysts who believe that bureaucracy is counterproductive to the needs and interests of professionals within the schools; (4) educators who suggest that bureaucratic management is inconsistent with the sacred values and purposes of education; (5) scholars who view bureaucracy as a form of operation that inherently forces attention away from the core technology of schooling; (6) analysts who hold that the existing organizational structure of schools is neither sufficiently flexible nor sufficiently robust to meet the needs of students in a postindustrial society; and (7) reviewers who believe that the rigidities of bureaucracy impede the ability of parents and citizens to govern and reform schooling.

This tremendous attack on the bureaucratic infrastructure of schools has led to demands to develop alternative methods of operating that are grounded on new values and principles. Concomitantly, new forms of school organization and management are emerging. The basic organizing and management principles of schooling are giving way to more proactive attempts to govern educational systems. In addition, there is enhanced attention to issues of social capital. The hierarchical, bureaucratic organizational structures that have defined schools over the past 80 years are giving way to more decentralized and more professionally controlled systems that create new designs for school management. In these new postindustrial educational organizations, there are important shifts in roles, relationships, and responsibilities: traditional patterns of relationships are altered; authority flows are less hierarchical; role definitions are both more general and more flexible; leadership is connected to competence for needed tasks rather than to formal position; and independence and isolation are replaced by cooperative work. Furthermore, a traditional structural orientation is being overshadowed by a focus on the human element. The operant goal is no longer maintenance of the organizational infrastructure but rather the development of human resources. Developing learning climates and organizational adaptivity are being substituted for the more traditional emphasis on uncovering and applying the one best model of performance.

Institutional Level

Many analysts of the institutional level of schooling—the interface of the school with its larger environment—argue that the public monopoly approach to education led to the "almost complete separation of schools from the community and, in turn, discouragement of local community involvement in decision making related to the administration of schools." (Burke, 1992, p. 33). Indeed, a considerable body of literature suggests that one of the major functions of bureaucracy is the buffering of the school from the environment, especially from parents and community members.

Many chroniclers of the changing institutional arrangements envision the demise of schooling as a sheltered government monopoly heavily controlled by professionals. In its stead, they forecast the emergence of a system of schooling and improvement designs driven by economic and political forces that substantially increase the saliency of the market and the viability of forms of direct democracy. Embedded in this conception are a number of interesting dynamics, many of which gain force from a realignment of power and influence between professional educators and consumers. The most important is that the traditional dominant relationship —with professional educators on the playing field and parents on the sidelines acting as cheerleaders or agitators, or, more likely, passive spectators—is replaced by rules that advantage the consumer.

Four elements of this emerging portrait of transformed governance for consumers are most prevalent: choice in selecting a school, voice in school governance, partnership in the education of their children, and enhanced membership in the school community. Central to all four is a blurring of the boundaries between the home and the school, between the school and the community, and between professional staff and lay constituents. Collectively, these components lend support to the grassroots political and competitive economic arguments that support the calls for more locally controlled organizations and to market-anchored conceptions of schooling.

Leadership Foundations

In all countries—no matter whether they are developed or developing and irrespective of their hemispherical location —provision is made for leadership in schools. Position titles and specific responsibilities vary, and there is enormous diversity in the agencies and administrative positions that regulate schools from the outside. Nevertheless, we can conclude that designating one or more individuals to bear responsibility for organizing teaching and learning for a specified group of students and teachers is an institutionalized feature of schooling. Although this volume is intended largely for an academic audience, our framework speaks to issues that should engage school leaders in multiple positions—superintendents, principals, teacher leaders, staff in state education agencies, and school board members, for example. Much of the focus of the chapters is on schools as the critical organizational unit in education. Insofar as we agree that schools are the center of action, the role of the designated school leader becomes central. While all other school leaders can learn from the chapters in this volume, we argue that our focus must continue to be on strengthening leadership in the school.

A Principal Is a Principal—But Is the Role Changing?

Today's school leaders express concerns about the changes, demands, and ambiguities that accompany their daily work. We believe that we are in a period of such rapid change that much of our previous experience in providing leadership in education can be discounted. But, we must also remember that neither are sudden changes in the social context of education new, nor has the role of the school leader been stable and pre-

dictable through time. Today, Canada and the United States, as well as many other countries, are experiencing the dislocations of global migration/immigration that flood schools with new students with different cultures and languages, but these are no greater than the migrations from Europe that we witnessed at the beginning of the 20th century. New technologies are revolutionizing communications and teaching, but the advent of commercially published, subject-specific textbooks created a change of comparable magnitude years ago, displacing the Bible and the all-purpose McGuffy Readers. Demands on schools to meet social goals are weighty but hardly greater than the tremendous pressure to increase the availability of publicly funded education through high school that occurred nearly 100 years ago. The fact that ambiguity is not new is amply demonstrated by one of the first educational administration textbooks, published more than a century ago:

> [T]he organization of the school must be kept mobile to its inner life. To one who is accustomed to wind up the machine and to trust it to run itself for fixed periods, this constantly shifting shape of things will seem unsafe and troublesome. And troublesome it is; for no fixed plan can be followed; no two schools are alike; and the same school is shifting, requiring constant attention and nimble judgment on the part of the [school leader] (Tompkins, 1895, p. 124).

There are, however, new demands on administrators resulting from the current shifting context. Previous generations of school leaders were expected to balance the demands for managing internal turbulence, but the emphasis was typically on making sure that all schools looked somewhat similar. What was "real school" was defined and idealized. In the latter part of the 20th century, on the other hand, educators face many competing definitions of how schools should be organized. On the one hand, there is pressure toward national and/or state standards, with more uniformity in both internal school procedures and expectations about student performance—in other words, the principal and the superintendent become the interpreters of policies that are largely identified elsewhere. On the other hand, there is an expectation that school governance and organization should be decentralized, and local committees composed of teachers and parents should determine how schools are run and what they should teach. Under these circumstances, the role of the principal is less administrative than executive (in the political sense). Finally, there is an alternative image of the future educational system that is market driven and responsive to the demands of consumers—whether these are funders or parents. Because none of these images of the future organization of schooling is dominant, school leaders must manage the ambiguity of all three. This involves rethinking the technical, managerial, and institutional levels of administrative work through very different lenses. We cannot capture the complexity of this reality in our introduction. We offer, however, a few observations on the current effects of multiple meanings on the central problem of administration: the management of and adaptation to change.

Leading for Change

The educational leadership literature continues to emphasize the importance of "transformational leadership," which is often defined as the ability to guide the school toward a fundamental reconsideration of its work. Transformational leadership, according to current wisdom, requires operating effectively in the technical, managerial, and institutional spheres. The specific roles and responsibilities that have been frequently discussed include

- *Concentrating on system or organization-wide efforts that support teaching and learning and teacher development.* Since the 1960s, research on schools as organizations has pointed to the grim finding that they were poorly designed to support teachers as vital professionals. Over the past decades, teacher unions and advocates for teacher professionalism have successfully lobbied for higher pay and increased qualifications. Yet teachers still report that they become bored or burned out after a decade "in the trenches." We know from decades of research in education and other areas that motivation and continued vitality is dependent on a variety of factors, but one of the most important is the individual's belief that one's job setting provides one with opportunities to grow and try out new roles as well as new practices. The "institutional system" outside the school barely recognizes this reality. The pressures are, if anything, in the opposite direction. Parental demands that teachers not take "time off," the lack of availability of substitute teachers, the increasing complexity of school organizations and schedules, and the demands for constant response to externally designed standards and programs mitigate against serious professional development. The responsibility for carving out time and space for revitalization of the teaching force thus falls heavily on school leaders.

- *Playing the role of the "intellectual."* Few school leaders currently regard themselves as intellectuals. Yet with the continuing changes in the research base underlying improved practice, who is better placed to sift through the available information about "what works" than a school leader? And, if school leaders are to help support instructional excellence, where should they turn if not to the increasingly robust literature that systematically documents research- and practice-based efforts to make a difference? "Principals as technical experts" is a new configuration for a role that was, until recently, largely focused on management, discipline, and public relations. We expect that this volume will provide an introduction to what school leaders need to know today, and one of our goals is to provide a short-

cut entry for practicing and prospective school leaders into the best technical information about how schools and learning work. The perspectives on instruction, learning, and school organization that are outlined in the chapters to follow will provide, we believe, a framework for organizing technical information over a fairly long period—but inevitably our organization will be replaced as new, high-quality research and practice-based information becomes available. However, in the shorter term, principals and other school leaders must prepare themselves for the important role of scanning and screening for the best of the new.

- *Focusing on vision and strategy.* School leaders help people think through "how to do it" as well as "what to do." The school leader as intellectual can assist members of the school community to discuss how the best knowledge on practice relates to what the school "wants to be." Broadening the discussion from the effective teaching and schooling research base, however, involves asking larger questions that bring in the institutional elements of schooling. Articulating and affirming core values and beliefs is important—although, in a democratic setting, always contentious and subject to critical review and the persistent voices of minority perspectives. However, equally important is guiding staff members from the articulation of a vision (such as blurring the boundaries between the home and school or enabling children from high poverty settings to be academically successful) to a set of practices that will work in the community in question and that have some practical bases, drawing on applied research. Most school improvement efforts begin with a reasonable vision and high commitment; more founder on the inability of the school to imagine a way of "getting there" that takes into account the institutional factors that make school improvement efforts more or less likely to succeed. As persistent observers of the educational system have observed for decades, there are more predictable (but ignored) obstacles to change than facilitators.

- *Embracing the complexity of school reform and "letting go" of the need to control.* The hardest thing for any leader or leadership group to do is to acknowledge that they are not in control. Our images of leadership stem from pyramidal organization charts and from epic myths, from Ulysses to John Wayne. But schools are not unique or self-contained bureaucracies or entrepreneurial enterprises; they are part of a larger, messy political world that has more potential for affecting the success of a school than any individual. Understanding the technical, managerial and institutional complexities will help school leaders to balance their hopes and drive with the realistic assessment that, no matter how charismatic, they are "one of many" and need to manage their responsibilities within shifting fields of influence.

Guiding Change

Current studies of educational administrators are equally insistent that administrators must not let go of their significant responsibilities for directing the day-to-day aspects of change. Delegation may be important, but the role of district administrators and principals as "problem finders" and "expert problem solvers" resonates throughout the studies of school reform, whether these occur in new schools or in existing schools that are making serious efforts to find their way to a new reality of schooling. The organizational literature occasionally belittles the need to provide oversight to the change process and to organizational relations, by assuming that "transactional leadership," or the ability to get things done on a day-to-day basis, is less significant. We disagree and find little research evidence to support this assumption. Instead, we find that research suggests that quotidian activities are central to effective steering of the educational enterprise. These include

- *Continuing to play an instructional leadership role.* The "effective schools" research, which began in the 1970s and has become increasingly methodologically sophisticated, indicates that school leaders who provide both support for instructional innovation and pressure for improvement are instrumental in enabling teachers to do their best. Emphasizing the role of instructional leadership in today's schools is, however, a difficult job. Once appointed, principals are soon out of touch with the realities of day-to-day classroom practice; they are not necessarily "master teachers," and, except in primary school, their experience is subject-matter specialized so that they lack credibility as craft experts in other areas. In the current context of pressures toward instructional improvement, effective principals are reorganizing their role to focus on providing the managerial support and technical direction that permit teachers to continue their own learning. Rather than "having the knowledge," they help teachers to "get the knowledge" that will result in real change in instruction.
- *Spending time on the details of school life; motivating through daily behavior.* The centrality of the culture of the school to its performance—and to what Sarason (1990) refers to as "the predictable failure of school reform"—is well buttressed in research. Qualitative and quantitative studies of school leader behavior draw attention to the role of individuals and small groups in encouraging cultural vitality. This occurs not through dramatic strategic efforts but through "small behaviors" that are critical in setting and/or reinforcing expectations about norms and values that are appropriate or unacceptable. In particular, the role of the school leader in creating and maintaining a sense of trust and voice is paramount, as is modeling effective conflict resolution and mentoring. We are far from a solid theory

about how school leaders can help to form an effective school culture, but what is clear is that leadership involvement in the daily life of the school is critical.
- *Using positive "micro-politics."* Much of the initial micropolitical research in schools emphasized organizational settings as win-lose environments and arenas for coalition and interest group formation. More recently, this perspective has shifted to acknowledge that politics can be both professional and valuable. Effective school leaders see themselves as actively involved in micro-politics within the school and between school and community, mediating between managerial, technical, and institutional arenas. The micro-political perspective involves a balance between buffering the technical core of the school and opening it to outside influence by arguing for a focus on students and learning first. School leaders—whether principals or others—balance the need to resolve tensions that arise when individual and group interests diverge and when the legitimate concerns of educational stakeholders suggest the need for new directions. Balancing the competing benefits of decentralized initiatives, organizational coherence, and responsiveness to the community is a quotidian but essential managerial task.
- *Playing a major role in creating "professional community" and school networks.* It is safe to say that when schools are not working well, one of the major complaints of all involved is "poor communication." Poor communication is, however, often a shorthand expression for anomie—the collective sense that the social expectations are not clear and that personal success is not possible in the setting. The need is not for more of the same kind of communication but for reassessing relationships more fundamentally. "Poor communication" occurs within the school and between the schools and their immediate communities of parents and other teachers and educational professionals when there are few conversations about issues of fundamental importance, usually those related to how well the partners are doing in nurturing the intellectual, social, and personal development of students. It also occurs when individuals and groups feel isolated and unable to reach others in safe contexts to discuss hopes and fears and the technical and institutional changes that could be made to move forward. There is ample evidence to suggest that safe networks for communication can arise in the most troubled educational settings, but in the absence of strong leadership, they will remain fragmented and isolated from the functioning of the school.

Leadership Foundations and the Handbook Framework

The preceding discussion of how school leader roles are enacted in today's shifting educational settings is cursory and incomplete. The authors of the individual chapters in this volume were all invited to conclude their reviews with implications for their peers—scholars in multiple disciplines and those who are involved in the preparation and professional development of administrators. Most authors accepted the challenge and so, scattered throughout the book, there are significant reflections on the meaning of research in school organization and administration for practice. The emphasis that we place in this introduction on leading and managing change is consistent with our own beliefs but is clearly justified by the many authors who have pointed to the fluid demands and need for new understandings that emerge from the research. We thus hope and expect that this Handbook will provide sustenance for the continued development of leadership preparation programs that are linked to the ambiguous and shape-shifting future of education that was gracefully pointed to by Mr. Tompkins as being inherent.

Acknowledgments

We would like to close by recognizing our debt to the numerous participants in the Handbook project. First and foremost, we would like to thank the authors of the chapters. All of them made major investments of intellectual capital to ensure completion of the volume. We owe a special debt of gratitude to those authors who were teamed with colleagues with whom they had not worked previously. We would also like to acknowledge the contributions of the consultant reviewers whose work strengthened the quality of each chapter. The Editorial Advisory Board deserves kudos both for helping to shape the design of the Handbook and for serving as consultant reviewers on selected chapters.

On the administrative end, we owe a debt of gratitude to William Russell, Executive Director of AERA, who gave us considerable freedom in the management of the project. At The University of Minnesota, Cheryl Morgan performed all the needed administrative functions with competence and alacrity. At Vanderbilt, special recognition is afforded to Ruby Fisher and Martha Morrissey. Mrs. Fisher, in her role as administrative assistant, helped open up a considerable amount of time for Murphy to work on this project. Mrs. Morrissey was responsible for the technical management of all aspects of the Handbook, a responsibility that she completed superbly.

Finally, we would like to recognize colleagues who helped us form our thoughts about the design of the Handbook and our ideas about its role in defining the history and development of our profession. We acknowledge that our work rests on the labors of many scholars who preceded us and on the labors of many colleagues still active in the quest of creating a better profession. We thank them for their oftentimes unseen contributions to this volume.

NOTE

1. The material in this section is adapted from Murphy (1991).

REFERENCES

Boyan, N. J. (Ed.) (1988). *Handbook of research on educational adiministration.* New York: Longman.

Burke, C. (1992). Devolution of Responsibility to Queensland Schools: Clarifying the Rhetoric Critiquing the Reality. *Journal of Educational Administration, 30*(4), 33–52.

Murphy, J. (1991). *Restructuring Schools: Capturing and Assessing the Phenomena.* New York: Teachers College Press.

Parsons, T. (1960). *Structure and process in modern societies.* Glencoe, IL: Free Press.

Sarason, S. (1990). *The Predictable Failure of School Reform.* San Francisco: Jossey-Bass.

Tompkins, A. (1895). *School Management.* Boston: Ginn.

Tyack, D. (1993). School Governance in the United States: Historical Puzzles and Anomalies. In J. Hannaway & M. Carnoy (Eds.), *Decentralization and School Improvement* (pp. 1–32). San Francisco: Jossey-Bass.

CHAPTER 1

A Brief History of Scholarship on Educational Administration

Donald J. Willower and Patrick B. Forsyth

The history of a field of study is a recital of its landmark events, including the problems emphasized, the lines of inquiry pursued, and the issues contested. Such recitals are necessarily selective, relying on available information and ideas that serve to make sense of and interpret that information. We believe our interpretations illuminate rather than distort, but we recognize that better interpretations, more solidly grounded in logic and evidence, might be proposed.

The chapter is divided into three main sections. Each section represents a thematic domain that has unfolded and developed throughout the history of scholarship on educational administration. The first concerns the interplay of unity and diversity. This deals with the factors that have brought the field together and those that have made for diversity and sometimes fragmentation. The second is the search for meaning. Here we examine the field in terms of both the search for knowledge and understanding and the search for appropriate moral frameworks and values. The third is the pursuit of relevance. It deals with the efforts made over time to blend theory and practice as well as develop realistic yet educative preparation for those who will serve in educational administration.

These three domains are significant because they represent strands of ongoing activity over the history of the field as an area of study. We opted for this approach to history rather than proposing a typology of periods or eras. The latter emphasis is often simplistic, typically using a rubric that covers a few main points or trends, but by its very nature misses or dismisses the diversity of a particular time span. To be sure, labeling a time interval can capture an important feature of the period in question. To do so, however, can be misleading unless sufficient attention is given to how widespread the feature was, its unintended conse-

quences, the dissension it created, and any evidence of counter trends that may have occurred. Longevity is also a consideration, especially when something is assumed to be a virtually homogenous feature of a particular period and setting, but is historically short-lived.

Our treatment of the history of educational administration is more focused on the period from the 1950s to the present than on earlier times. In the 1950s, the study of educational administration began to flower and diversify as concepts and theories from the social sciences were used more extensively in research and writing, particularly in the more visible sources of the times. Scholarship has flourished since then in a variety of forms, including disagreements over the nature and appropriateness of different kinds of inquiry. Hence, it seemed quite reasonable to emphasize the past 45 or so years and treat earlier work with a lighter touch, especially since the latter has already been closely examined (for example, Campbell, Fleming, Newell, & Bennion, 1987; Culbertson, 1988).

The chapter deals essentially with scholarship about educational administration as reflected in the usual outlets. Our charge—to provide a *brief* history—imposed a major limitation. Most topics deserve far more extensive treatment than they receive. Nevertheless, if the chapter captures the diversity and changing tides that have characterized thought and research in this broad and complex academic field, it will have served its purpose.

Unity and Diversity

Plato, among other philosophers, explored the problem of the one and the many. Just as Socrates, in the Platonic dialogues, saw that something could be one in a particular category and many in another, so it has been in educational administration. It has been relatively unified in some respects, divided in others.

The divisions are many. As in the social sciences, humanities, and derivative fields, they appear to have increased and widened in recent decades. Three unifying elements are discussed, followed by a number of diversifying ones.

Unifying Elements

The three unifying elements discussed are first, an ongoing line of scholarship on democratic, participative, and open administration and institutions, reflecting melioristic intentions and commitments; second, a continuing reliance on logic and evidence in research even among those who are critical of objectivity; and third, a number of associations, rituals, and symbolic activities that have served to affirm common goals.

Participation and Openness

The emphasis on open, participative, democratic organization, attitudes, and conduct as well as an array of concepts of a similar kind has been an important part of educational administration since World War II, although there were many earlier writings (such as Dewey, 1916). Indeed, one could argue a cultural connection illustrated by the founding ideals of the American Republic, which stressed democracy and citizen participation, and the fact that much of the relevant literature was produced in the United States.

The emphasis on open concepts in scholarship and research had, from its origins, melioristic intentions, that is, concern for reform and more desirable forms of leadership and organizational life. This helps to explain the longevity of that emphasis because school improvement is virtually a *sine qua non* of educational administration as a profession. Open, participative practices and structures are also widely seen as desirable in themselves and appear to have some advantages in terms of outcomes.

Although this emphasis in educational administration has had a unifying effect, it has been anything but unitary. That is, a wide array of concepts has been used to describe participative and open practices. Among them are democratic administration, participative management, human relations, organizational development, shared decision making, open climates, and empowerment. In addition, such concepts vary in their particulars and contexts despite their general similarity. For example, democratic administration stressed philosophical values, while human relations was more concerned about interpersonal relations and problem solving (Campbell, et al., 1987). Open climates, as well as concepts of participative and humane styles of leadership, appear in conjunction and contrast with their opposites, closed climates and authoritarian styles. The

contemporary concept of empowerment, when applied to teachers, is often tied to processes aimed at restructuring decision making at the school building level. Regardless of these kinds of variations, however, such concepts share a general orientation to participation, openness, cooperation, inclusiveness, and respect for individuals.

The widespread commitment to such ideals, especially in the Western democracies, and the influence of political figures, social philosophers, and activists who saw such ideals as imperfectly achieved goals to be more fully implemented, reinforced receptivity to them in smaller arenas like educational administration. Campbell *et al.* (1987) have documented the popularity in the 1930s and 1940s of democratic administration among professors and professional associations, such as the National Education Association and the American Association of School Administrators, which issued a variety of supportive publications. These authors also emphasized the receptivity of professors of school administration to "human relations" ideas as developed in scholarship outside of education.

Three works, all published in 1939, were especially noteworthy. One was the study of autocratic, democratic, and laissez-faire leadership of children's groups by Lewin, Lippett, and White (1939). The second was the Western Electric studies of Elton Mayo and his colleagues that resulted in Roethlisberger and Dickson's (1939) *Management and the Worker,* and the third was Lynd's (1939) *Knowledge for What?* Lewin and his associates found that democratic leadership elicited superior productivity and attitudinal and social outcomes, while the Western Electric studies suggested the importance of interpersonal interactions and relationships to such outcomes. Lynd's monograph, famous in sociology, was perhaps less known than the other two among educational administration professors. It was, as its title suggests, a call for science that serves human purposes and a criticism of the separation of knowledge and its uses. These works, though later criticized, were symptomatic of social science that fits the melioristic drive for organizational improvement in applied fields like educational administration and, in the case of education, the kinds of societal values the schools taught, even if they didn't always exhibit them.

The emphasis on "human relations," which became important in the social sciences, was part of this melioristic press. Because it not only emphasized participation and cooperative processes but claimed empirical support for their efficacy, it added a dimension of legitimacy to an already ideologically attractive approach. Moreover, the human relations literature was often practice-oriented, which increased its appeal for many educational administration professors.

An example of a work that stressed the connections of human relations inquiry with practice was sociologist Robert Dubin's (1951) *Human Relations in Administration,* which consisted of major pieces on human relations scholarship, along with a variety of case studies. In educational administration, Wilbur Yauch's (1949) *Improving Human Relations in School Administration* was an important bridge between democratic administration and human relations (Campbell, *et al.*, 1987). Griffiths' (1956) popular *Human Relations in School Administration* was strongly oriented to social science theory and research. Like Dubin's book in general administration, it also contained a substantial number of cases.

The link to practice was a feature of much human relations activity. The National Training Laboratory at Bethel, Maine, with its emphasis on T-groups and group dynamics, is often cited in this connection. The organizational development (OD) movement is an example of a well-developed, training-oriented effort to improve organizations and the lives of participants largely through cooperative and participative procedures.

Fullan, Miles, and Taylor (1980) noted that OD, used earlier in business settings, has been applied in schools since the mid-1960s. While they pointed to the variety of definitions given OD, these reviewers listed key defining words (pp. 125–126). They included communication, collaboration, participation, and trust. Miles (1993) more recently noted that successful OD in schools leads to organizational health.

The concept of organizational health is, of course, not limited to OD, as Hoy, Tarter, and Kottkamp's book *Open Schools, Healthy Schools* (1991) illustrates. Those authors emphasized organization climate as a central variable and provided updated measures of openness and health that can be used by practitioners seeking school improvement. Indeed, the voluminous literature on organizational climate and leadership has been an important part of the open, participative, and melioristic orientation that we see as a unifying force in educational administration.

The legitimation for such an orientation was, as we suggested, philosophical and cultural but was also sustained by numerous scholars of note. For example, McGregor (1960), Likert (1961), and Argyris (1964) all advocated collaborative leadership. Maslow (1965) presented a style of leadership and a kind of organization based on his earlier theories of personal and organizational fulfillment and renewal, and Burns (1978) advanced a kind of transformational leadership grounded in humanitarian ideals.

Blake and Mouton's (1964) managerial grid, which in its high-high category stressed concern for both people and tasks, illustrated a blending of those dimensions in leadership. This was similar to the consideration-initiating structure measure developed at Ohio State University that was widely used in research in educational administration (Halpin, 1959), although Yukl (1989) contended the Ohio State measure's categories, but not the grid's, were merely additive. Be that as it may, both instruments were very

popular, and the high-high category was widely regarded to be the most desirable one.

Similarly, open organizational climates were deemed better than closed ones. In educational administration, numerous studies were done using the measure of climate devised by Halpin and Croft (1963) and updated by Hoy and his associates. (See Hoy & Miskel, 1996, pp. 143–150.)

Restructuring has been one of the more recent reform efforts. Although it is susceptible to varied definitions (Tyack, 1990), school restructuring usually refers to site-based management using shared or participatory processes. In his review of the topic, Foster (1992) made a clear connection between that reform and valued purposes. Writing of school restructuring, he said, "By empowering teachers and students, it hopes to teach democracy through example, and . . . develop capable, thinking, and effective citizens" (p. 1113).

Systemic reform, or reform on a broad or national scale, is another recent movement. In a report for the National Policy Board for Educational Administration, Crow and Slater (1996) discussed systemic reform and leadership and explicitly associated them with democracy. Again, meliorism and widely-shared values were emphasized. Miles (1993) noted that other countries have fewer constraints than the United States on such reforms, a well-taken point, as indicated in a number of sources on reform in various parts of the world. See, for example, special issues of the *Journal of Educational Administration* (1991) and *Educational Administration Quarterly* (1997).

In contending that commitment to openness and democratic administration and organization is a unifying factor in educational administration, we make no broad claims for the efficacy of such processes, although research has often indicated their worth. We recognize, with Immegart (1988), that approaches to leadership and change that are essentially untested are sometimes moved directly to training where they can be packaged and commercialized, becoming popular but short-lived fads.

The unifying emphasis described did not exist independently of other forces. Sometimes it reacted against them, such as scientific management and over-bureaucratization. At the same time, an emphasis can co-exist with other quite different ones, for example, participation and efficiency. This is the kind of thing that can be overlooked when eras are stressed.

Finally, democratic and participatory leadership and organization have been relatively immune to the field's philosophical debates. They appear to be embraced, in one form or another, by the various contenders. Even those who raise questions about the limitations of participatory processes are concerned with such issues as the organizational conditions under which they are most and least appropriate, or with their relationship to outcomes. One looks in vain for outright attacks on democratic and participative procedures as such.

Reliance on Logic and Evidence

Since the mid-1970s, educational administration has witnessed numerous attacks on science and its methods (such as Greenfield, 1986). These attacks were essentially derivative, having been made earlier in various disciplines in the social sciences and humanities (on sociology, see Smelser, 1988). Such attacks were abetted by the resurgence of subjectivist and neo-Marxist thought and the spread of postmodernist and poststructuralist views in the academy, along with the rise of work on gender and race/ethnicity. These perspectives tended to stress advocacy and political agendas and either downplayed or rejected scientific inquiry. Much of the writing from such sources tended to be prose arguments rather than empirical research.

Yet when those advocating views antithetical to science did empirical work, they faced the problem of legitimating their efforts and adopted the usual standards employed in inquiry. For example, Smelser (1988) noted for sociology that when "phenomenological and Marxist critics" conduct empirical research themselves, they adopt the methods of traditional science. He further stated that "attacks on sociological empiricism have not been very successful; the vast majority of those engaged in sociological research . . . still adhere to a kind of theoretically eclectic empiricist perspective" (p. 11). Culbertson (1988) made the same point for educational administration, explaining that "scholars of educational administration still look to science . . . as a legitimizing cloak, facilitator of inquiry, and a tool to be used in the continuing quest for knowledge" (p. 24).

Scholars whose predilections are antiscience but who do empirical work are often drawn to high interpretation-low evidence kinds of research. One example is critical ethnography (Anderson, 1989). Yet the studies done in that style that are well regarded, such as Willis' (1977) of a group of English working-class boys, attend to empirical grounding and are explicit about author ideology. Put differently, in those basic respects, they are hardly distinguishable from traditional studies.

Even at the broader levels of argument, those who oppose science are caught in the logic of argument. That is, although they may wish to put advocacy or intuition ahead of reasoned debate and logic, they cannot escape what philosophers call the logocentric predicament: one cannot criticize logic without using logic. So we find that those holding philosophical views of every stripe advance their views through reasoning and logical argument. Indeed, philosophical literature is largely made up of that kind of subject matter.

Logical argument is also at the heart of scientific interpretation and explanation. A coherent explanation enhances credibility. This dimension of science is a subjective and creative activity, but logic provides a crucial criterion of its efficacy. In the realm of empirical research, if one casts aside the norms and standards of science, the work appears flawed to other researchers. It is attention to these norms and standards, growing human creations though they be, that confers legitimacy in matters of inquiry. A commitment to logic and evidence remains the touchstone of quality scholarship in educational administration despite debates about philosophy and science. We contend that this commitment, despite its ritual de-emphasis in some quarters, remains a unifying factor for scholars in educational administration.

Associations, Rituals, Symbolic Activities

Professors of educational administration are in effect both university teachers and researchers, and contributors to the profession of educational administration. The former is their occupation, but improving professional practice and, ultimately, education as a social institution remains an overarching goal.

Parsons (1949) contrasted business and the professions, noting that although the former was grounded in economic considerations, professions were thought to be based on service to humankind. However, he also saw that a desire for success and honors, as well as concrete contexts of personalities and cliques, were found across fields. This underscored the importance of the integration of personal self-fulfillment and the attainment of normatively defined goals of the profession. Well-articulated recognition symbols could abet such integration, Parsons contended.

For educational administration professors, both their associations and their universities are sources of such symbols. University tenure and promotion rituals are one example. Recognition of contributions to their field of study is conferred when candidates meet the criteria defined by their institutions. Even if the specifics vary across different types of institutions, a standard of excellence presumably governs the process. In addition, most universities give an array of awards for teaching, advising, research, mentoring, community service, and other contributions, all of which have the potential to integrate the personal and professional purposes of both the recipients and their colleagues.

The associations in which many professors participate also provide a great many forms of recognition. Such organizations as the National Conference (now Council) of Professors of Educational Administration, the University Council for Educational Administration, the American Association of School Administrators, and the American Educational Research Association, among others, give awards that range from best dissertation through efforts as a junior professor to honors for career achievements. There are also prizes for best book or article, research project, contribution to practice, teaching innovation, and so on. Those receiving awards are usually recognized in a public forum, often at a meeting of the conferring association or organization, but our emphasis is, of course, on audience effects, not on the awardees.

Such awards and their attendant ceremonies furnish illustrations of what are thought to be excellent performances within the profession or occupation. These types of rituals serve a socializing function, as they call attention to both excellence and the kinds of superordinate goals to which the recognized achievements contribute. Individuals who serve as elected officials of the various associations also gain recognition as a result and provide additional models of occupational success, as do persons who hold editorships, serve as members of commissions or study groups, or in other similar capacities.

As befits an occupational group, such as the educational administration professorship, that is characterized by multiple roles and specializations, there is a wide variety of different forms of public recognition. Because award ceremonies ordinarily connect the activities of the person being recognized to one or another of the basic purposes of the professorship, or to the superordinate goals of the profession, a form of reinforcement and legitimation occurs in which valued and normatively approved activities and goals are highlighted and presented as models for emulation.

Professional socialization and integration are also promoted by general participation in conferences and related activities, independent of more formal ceremonies. Such participation is more common than symbolic recognition ceremonies, and is, in itself, a kind of ritual professional identification abetted by the colleagueship usually displayed at such gatherings.

Although we recognize that such ceremonies and professional meetings are sometimes viewed with cynicism, we argue that they serve to unify by furnishing instances of worthwhile activities that advance common purposes. Thus they add something to what Hughes (1928) long ago called professional attitudes, a professional conscience, and solidarity. The downside of such attitudes is captured in what Thorstein Veblen called trained incapacity and John Dewey labeled occupational psychosis. However, given the many different kinds of professors and multiple tasks of educational administration departments, that kind of malady seems somewhat less likely to be uniform there than in some other fields.

Diversifying Elements

The first diversifying element examined is the variety of roles and specializations that are found in educational administration, a field devoted to both scholarship and its applications to practice. The second is variously referred to as differences in philosophy, world views, ideology, or politics. These two broad categories encompass an array of diversifying dimensions, many of which cut across one another.

Roles and Specializations
The field's roles and specializations reflect its multiple and complex activities. These include the many kinds of edu-

cational organizations and positions studied, the impact of different levels of community and governance on schools, the importance of teaching subject matter with attention to practical usage, the need to maintain symbiotic relationships with schools and school administrators, as well as with scholarly communities and associations, and the interrelated significance of philosophic ideals and theoretical and empirical knowledge in school improvement.

Much of the specialization in the field has come since the 1950s. Earlier scholars tended to be broad gauged. Two of the earliest blended scholarship with careers as administrators. W. T. Harris was superintendent of schools in St. Louis and long-time United States Commissioner of Education. William H. Payne, credited by Culbertson (1988) with publishing the first book on school administration in 1875,[1] served for a decade as a school superintendent in Michigan and then chaired the education department at the University of Michigan, before heading the University of Nashville and the Peabody Normal School in Tennessee. Both men wrote extensively and held important editorial posts. Harris founded and edited for many years *The Journal of Speculative Philosophy*, developing a reputation as a Hegelian scholar. Both men also served on influential national committees and appeared to believe in the importance of ideals and of science, as they construed it, and sought to develop principles or generalizations that could serve as guides to practice (Culbertson, 1988).

However, neither man is easy to categorize. For instance, the Hegelian scholar Harris was also a practical empiricist. Travers (1983) reported that Harris believed that facts and statistics were vital to school improvement and that he "loved compilations of statistics" (p. 36). Indeed, numbers had a special utility for politically vulnerable organizations such as public schools, where they could be used to make a case for efficiency, as chronicled by Callahan (1962).

Ellwood P. Cubberley and George D. Strayer, described by Campbell and Newell (1973) as "the progenitors of the academic field" (p. 1) of educational administration, received their doctorates from Teachers College, Columbia, in the first decade of the 20th century, the same decade in which Harris and Payne died. Cubberley enjoyed a long career at Stanford, as did Strayer at Teachers College. Both were interested in the larger issues of education and science but were also concerned with the specifics of educational administration. Each produced popular texts and was prominent in promoting and conducting school surveys, in which substantial amounts of data were gathered to serve as a basis for improving policy and practice. Such surveys became well established and accepted between 1910 and 1930 and were, in many cases, quite comprehensive studies of school systems (Campbell *et al.*, 1987). They are still done in various formats, often applied to only one or a few problems.

Although not stinting ideals and the broad concerns of education and society, Cubberley and Strayer were also involved in the world of school administrators, as for example in the particularistic and practical research of the school survey. The next generation of scholars shared their concerns for both the broadly theoretical and the practical (Culbertson, 1988). However, they were critical of much of the research in education and sought to make research and relations with schools more systematic.

Paul Mort of Columbia University's Teachers College can be taken as an exemplar. He produced a significant text in which he attempted to develop principles of administration, but more important he devoted much of his career to the study of school finance, an interest of his mentor Strayer. A noteworthy contribution was Mort's work with the concept of the foundation plan, which featured mandated minimum expenditure levels per pupil. Mort also established the Metropolitan School Study Council (Culbertson, 1988), an effort to institutionalize the dissemination of research and best practices to schools. In addition, he did substantial work on the adoption of innovations (Mort, 1964).

The scholars considered so far were all concerned with ideals, ideas, and practical applications. To varying degrees, all of them were also concerned about the relationship of schools and society and with using the empirical methods of their day to study and improve education.

The roles they played included social commentator and critic, consultant, participant, often leader in professional associations, teacher, data-gatherer, writer of articles and scholarly treatises, and mentor to school administrators among others. They were far less specialized than today's scholars, with the most recent group, Mort's, being the most specialized.

Genuine specialization was to come with the development and professionalization of educational administration as a field of study, which became more serious after World War II. Critically important was the National Conference of Professors of Educational Administration (NCPEA), which held its founding meeting in 1947. Although Walter D. Cocking, longtime editor of the *School Executive*, was described as the "father" of NCPEA in the brief history of its first decade (Flesher & Knobloch, 1957), most professors who taught educational administration, including virtually all of the most respected ones, participated in or were influenced by the NCPEA. This organization, with its interest groups, spurred the development of specializations and also helped to advance the interdisciplinary study of educational administration. A political scientist and a sociologist addressed its 1949 meeting, and social scientists and philosophers were frequently invited to participate in subsequent NCPEA annual conferences.

The Cooperative Program in Educational Administration, with the backing of the Kellogg Foundation, which was generous in its support of the field, established university centers for the study of educational administration and

was another important influence. Later, the University Council for Educational Administration was established. These organizations and others stressed the improvement of scholarship and practice in educational administration, especially through the use of concepts, theories, and methods from the social sciences. Specialization occurred as scholars selected specific areas of inquiry for study, and specializations often reflected social science fields, as politics of education, for example, mirrored political science (Willower, 1988).

At the same time because of the multiple expectations faced by educational administration departments, another kind of specialization occurred, less in terms of subject interests, but rather in terms of the kinds of activities undertaken. Griffiths (1964b) adapted and expanded Burton Clark's typology to describe six professorial types. These included the researcher and the teacher. Additional types were the consultant, who has a national reputation, may write textbooks, and serves on numerous professional committees; the demonstrator, who may supervise internships, conduct field trips, and convey his or her "on the job" experiences; the conductor, who may be in charge of workshops and conferences and, as a teacher, tends to bring in a succession of visiting lecturers or simply moderate exchanges of student views; and the entrepreneur, who performs services such as surveys or other "studies" for schools and other agencies, and in many ways operates a business with the university as a base.

Such typologies suggest dimensions of activity that are variable for given individuals. Because specialization of tasks is common in multipurpose units, it is not surprising that some educational administration professors would be, for example, mainly researchers while others would be mainly involved with schools and practitioners. That dichotomy is a standard one in professional fields.

In educational administration, the theory-practice division goes beyond differentiated roles. Glass (1986), in his study of 100 general textbooks in educational administration in the 1955–1985 period, found a definite move "to a quest for theory and theory application" (p. 94). However, he stated that some writers only grudgingly acquiesced and that differences along theory-practice lines led to a "devisive factionalism" in many university programs. Halpin and Hayes (1977) contended that the influence of the social sciences in educational administration was short-lived, declining in the 1960s because of the resistance of practice-oriented professors. Although Halpin and Hayes probably overstated the case, especially with regard to research universities, this division will presumably always be found in varying degrees, despite the ongoing pursuit of relevance discussed in section three.

Scholarly specialization increased after World War II, particularly with the influence of the social sciences on thought and research in educational administration. To give just one example, courses and scholarship on school community relations gradually gave way to the politics of education. The latter soon became more specialized with emphases on different levels of governance and community, leading to a focus on policy, a concept that remains hazy, but very popular. The area eventually developed its own literature and journals (such as *Educational Evaluation and Policy Analysis*), and in 1996 spun off from the American Educational Research Association's division on administration to form a division of its own.

This kind of subject matter specialization, which has occurred in most areas of educational administration, has led to new research and the flowering of new ideas, but too often at the expense of narrowness of the kind captured by the concept of trained incapacity. Such narrowness can move the field away from more holistic and integrative perspectives (Willower, 1988). At the same time, the shared commitment in educational administration to school improvement, reflected in the attention given to democratic and participative processes and purposes, already discussed, raises the question of desirable policy in that area of specialization, as it does of the good organization, and the just allocation of resources in others.

Allegiances and Commitments

Within and across specializations are divisions that stem from allegiances to schools of thought or theories, as well as to styles of research. An instance of the latter is the resurrection in the social sciences and education of the richness versus rigor debates that characterized sociology in the 1930s (e.g., Waller, 1934), although field research has been part of educational administration since at least the 1950s (see Boyan, 1951).

Still another division has been based on philosophical views. In educational administration, subjectivistic, critical theory/neo-Marxist and naturalistic/pragmatist positions have been debated, and postmodernism has begun to enter the lists.

Another kind of fragmentation stems from concerns with gender, race/ethnicity, and social class. This work has sometimes been oriented to identity politics or advocacy on behalf of a particular group, ordinarily seen as lacking a fair share of societal resources, or even as oppressed. Special areas of study, for example, women's studies or black studies, have developed as part of this focus. The differing allegiances noted will be examined more substantively in the section on the search for meaning, where their divisive roles will also be discussed.

Unity and Diversity: Crosscurrents and Contradictions

By declining to use an approach emphasizing eras in this brief history, labeling a particular time as if it were a period of uniformity of thought and activity is avoided. Crosscurrents and even contradictions are highlighted next.

The commitment to democratic and participative administration and its coupling with school improvement was ongoing, but not without critics. However, the target commonly was the relevant empirical work. An excellent illustration is Conway's (1984) aptly titled, "The Myth, Mystery, and Mastery of Participative Decision Making in Education." Its author argued that the faith put in such approaches was not supported by the research, yet he recognized their "logically defensible intent" (p. 34), calling for better research rather than their rejection.

The very associations that draw professors together can also set them apart. The new policy and politics division in the American Educational Research Association has already been mentioned. Both NCPEA and the University Council for Educational Administration (UCEA) serve the professoriate, yet UCEA is limited to institutional membership, to date of North American doctoral level universities, while NCPEA is open to individual professors without regard to institutional type. However much NCPEA and UCEA share and emphasize similar purposes, an underlying exclusivity issue remains.

There are also counter trends with regard to the broad orientations and specialization discussed. Campbell and Newell (1973) reported that only about half of the professors they surveyed were full-time in educational administration. Further, around two-fifths of their respondents either cut across or did not fit their three main categories of cosmopolitans (researchers), locals (teachers, student advisors) and practice-oriented professors.

In a later survey, McCarthy, Kuh, Newell, and Iacona (1988) indicated greater specialization and somewhat more research activity. However, preparation programs had proliferated beyond the research universities and had fewer faculty per program (half had four or fewer), creating a press for generalists rather than specialists and perhaps portending a reduction in scholarship, even though the research universities had larger departments. The most recent survey (McCarthy & Kuh, 1997) shows that overall the number of institutions and faculty have remained fairly stable, but faculty numbers are closer across university types. Substantial movement toward gender, but not racial, diversity has occurred. Compared with the 1988 report, faculty are more oriented to teaching, practice, and field activities. Thus the professorial roles discussed are somewhat fluid, and there are counter pressures to specialization.

In regard to philosophical and ideological differences, it is well to keep in mind that schools of thought are made up of individuals who are often not in agreement with one another. Some of the most contested issues may be within a particular philosophy or ideology. An example was the reproduction-resistance debates within critical theory/neo-Marxism on whether an emphasis on societal reproduction of the status quo ignored the capacity for resistance on the part of underprivileged classes (see Giroux, 1983). Labels are sometimes misleading and scholars may develop views that draw from and mix a number of perspectives in novel ways. Thus Davies (1995) noted that some critical theorists attempted to blend their perspective with elements of postmodernism and identity politics. Today, as in the past, philosophical "isms" and labels can deceive when individuals or clusters of thinkers dissent on particular points.

The Search for Meaning

We have already taken note of early scholars of educational administration. We now turn to the search for meaning as represented in two major thrusts. The first sought to increase knowledge and understanding through the use of a variety of concepts, theories, and methods. The second brought philosophical analysis to bear on both questions of epistemology, that is, the nature of knowing and knowledge, and of ethics, the realm of values and moral choice.

Theory and Empirical Studies

A number of writings influenced the greater use, from the 1950s on, of social science theories and methods in educational administration. Getzels (1952) published an early version of his theory, which was to become quite popular, and led to a variety of studies, especially at the University of Chicago. Many of these studies appeared in the *Administrators Notebook*, published by Chicago's Midwest Administration Center from 1952 to 1995. Walton (1955) decried the lack of substantive theory in the field, while in the same year Coladarci and Getzels' (1955) pamphlet examined the uses of theory with educational administration specifically in mind. The NCPEA-sponsored book on administrative behavior, edited by Campbell and Gregg (1957), and Griffiths' (1959) monograph on administrative theory were more general influences in the same direction, as was the collection edited by Halpin (1958) that contained the papers presented at the first UCEA seminar, sponsored jointly with the University of Chicago.

In the 1960s and into the 1970s, the influence of the social sciences grew. A number of books, such as the work of Downey and Enns (1963), used formats that featured social scientists commenting on the potential uses of their disciplines in educational administration, paired with educational administration professors who canvassed the same topic. The 1964 Yearbook of the National Society for the Study of Education was titled *Behavioral Science and Educational Administration* and was edited by Griffiths (1964a), an early champion of the value of the social sciences for the field. The *Review of Educational Research* began publication in 1931 and covered a variety of topics, often in three year cycles. Reviews in the educational administration issues with the titles of "Administrative Role and Behavior," "Ad-

ministrative Behavior: Theory and Research," and "The Science of Administration" appeared respectively in 1955, 1961, and 1964. In 1970, this journal dropped cyclic reviews and the new *Review of Research in Education* took on a review function, but in a limited and unsystematic way. Textbooks also incorporated more social science-oriented scholarship. Glass (1986) cited the 1968 work by J. W. Getzels, J. M. Lipham, and R. F. Campbell as a text that was primarily devoted to theory and research and W. K. Hoy and C. G. Miskel's 1978 textbook as "perhaps the best integration of research findings and administrative theory" (p. 111).

As the social sciences gained acceptance in educational administration, research more and more reflected their theories and methods. Halpin (1970) selected five substantive research contributions to educational administration prior to 1964, two of them his own. He chose the work of J. W. Getzels, Richard Carlson's research on superintendent succession, the Hemphill, Griffiths, Frederiksen study of administrative performance in the principalship, and his own studies of leadership and climate that respectively used the Leadership Behavior Description Questionnaire and the Organizational Climate Description Questionnaire. Griffiths (1983) writing of the same period chose the same studies, except that, instead of Carlson's work, he selected the research of Neal Gross and his colleagues, Mason and McEachern, that used role theory to examine the school superintendency.

After pointing out that the larger scale, well-funded studies of an earlier time have given way to professors probing lines of research with their students and colleagues, Griffiths selected four examples of the best work of the latter kind, mostly from the 1970s. They were Edwin Bridges' research on teacher absenteeism, Neal Gross and colleagues' field studies of innovation, C. G. Miskel's work on motivation, work, and job satisfaction, and the investigations of educator pupil control attitudes and behavior conducted by Willower and his students.

Boyan's (1982) comprehensive review on administration in the *Encyclopedia of Educational Research* considered five approaches he called within the "traditional paradigm." These were social system and role, bureaucratization, decision making, leadership, and motivation and satisfaction. Much of the 1970s scholarship noted here was examined by Boyan, but he cited a great many additional works of importance including Bidwell's chapter in the 1965 *Handbook of Organizations*, Iannaconne's descriptive research on informal organization, Cusick's portrayal of student subculture, and Lortie's treatment of teacher life and socialization. Boyan then considered what he called four major challenges to the traditional paradigm. These were contingency theory, organized anarchy and garbage can approaches, loose coupling, and institutional theory. He also briefly mentioned the phenomenological and Marxist critiques, and cited in passing a number of other frameworks including incentive systems, natural selection, political economy, and negotiated order. Finally, he discussed studies of work activities in the Mintzberg style, and ethnographic inquiries such as Wolcott's observations of a school principal.

The comparable review to Boyan's in the next edition of the *Encyclopedia* (Willower, 1992) considered neo-Marxist critical theory and subjectivism more extensively. It then more briefly discussed work in institutional theory; public choice theory; politics; anarchies, garbage cans, and coupling; administrative life; and organizational culture. This review dealt essentially with newer conceptual approaches, specifically those that gained visibility since Boyan's piece.

The World Yearbook of Education, titled *The Management of Schools* (Hoyle & McMahon, 1986), and the first *Handbook of Research on Educational Administration* (Boyan, 1988) appeared between these two reviews, and the second *International Encyclopedia of Education* (Husen & Postlethwaite, 1994) was published slightly later, a first edition having appeared in 1985. A more recent work was the *International Handbook of Educational Leadership and Administration* (Leithwood, *et al.*, 1996), but as its title suggests, this source did not include a number of administration's special fields, although rich in the areas covered. The *Handbook of Research* and the second *International Encyclopedia* were the most noteworthy of these reviews.

The *Handbook* consisted of 32 chapters with multiple entries on administrative behavior and effects, organizational concerns, politics and policy, economics and finance, and methodological themes. Three chapters were devoted to gender, race/ethnicity, and equity issues, and the rest were specialized single entries. The *Encyclopedias of Educational Research* and the *International Encyclopedias* address virtually all aspects of education. In educational administration, the 1992 edition of the former included a state of the art piece and 15–20 specialized reviews, depending on what counts within that field. The 1994 edition of the latter listed about 70 such entries, but many were more relevant to other areas.

A general trend suggested by these broad reviews is toward a greater variety of divergent perspectives of both theoretical and philosophical kinds. Theory and empirical work are becoming more oriented to complexity and various ways of attempting to comprehend it better. Philosophical writing, which has dealt mainly with epistemology and ethics, has reflected disputes over the nature of knowledge, while concerns about ethics have been more diffuse.

Turning first to theory and research, such concepts as organized anarchy, garbage cans, and loose coupling, which attend to fluidity and fluctuation, have provided vivid metaphors that capture certain realities of organizational life, but they have not resulted in serious, cumulative research on schools or in sociology (Aldrich & Marsden, 1988). Institutional theory has grown in both conception and in its place in the literature but has not been "institutionalized" because it still exhibits little consensus on the definition of key concepts, measures, and methods and because of its lack of attention to the processes of institutionalization (Tolbert & Zucker, 1996). Meyer and Rowan's seminal work in the late 1970s stressed the symbolic and normative influences of environment on organizations, and the "new institutionalism" (Powell & DiMaggio, 1991) acknowledged its indebtedness to such writers as Philip Selznick and Talcott Parsons and fashioned concepts that drew upon earlier work, but gave it a new twist. For example, concepts like scripts and routines replaced norms, and goals were seen as ambiguous rather than displaced. One of institutional theory's key ideas, the impact of environment on organization, has been central to much scholarship on public school organizations at least from Waller's (1932) time. However, institutional theory might well displace older forms of social system theory in educational administration. The reasons are straightforward: institutional theory is "up-to-date," doesn't carry the baggage of some versions of social system theory, and can be used for similar purposes as it offers many parallel concepts.

To be sure, institutional theory provides its special veneer. Just as role theory's concept of expectations is quite similar to the social system notion of norms, though more position-specific, the meaning of script is similar to both of those terms, but, in Goffmanesque fashion, it emphasizes the actor who interprets and plays out the socially defined script. This suggests a reality check on diverse theories. They all need to deal with commonplace human arrangements and activities, which gives them similar casts, albeit with different shades of emphasis. A general appraisal suggests that institutional theory is conceptually underdeveloped but could eventually become much more salient. Further, like the briefly popular micropolitics, it has cross-disciplinary appeal to students of organizational and/or political phenomena.

Two other perspectives that attend to fluidity and fluctuation are chaos theory and cognitive studies. The former has generated more enthusiasm than substance in education according to Griffiths, Hart, and Blair (1991). They note that the concepts of chaos theory do not easily translate into meaningful social research and that the need for precise measures limits applications to educational administration. In contrast, cognitive studies are well established in psychology and have been applied to administration by Herbert Simon and his colleagues in a long term program of research into the intricacies of decision making. In educational administration, Leithwood and his students have undertaken a series of interrelated studies (Leithwood & Steinbach, 1995) that are a current exemplar of the kind of 1970s work Griffiths (1983) described as the best of the efforts of a single professor and his or her students.

We turn next to philosophical issues in the search for meaning in educational administration, but before doing so we want to emphasize that empirical studies and lines of research in the field go far beyond what we were able to note above. Examples include areas such as school finance, law, human resource management, and labor studies, all of which are concerned with equity issues, and studies on a host of special topics such as positions, the principalship or superintendency, effective schools, succession and socialization, non-public schools, and evaluation to name a few. The various encyclopedias and handbooks mentioned, as well as other chapters in the present volume, provide a more complete picture of the scope of research on educational administration.

Philosophical Issues

Philosophical concerns in educational administration over the past 20 years or so have been centered chiefly on knowledge and ethics. From a historical perspective, debates on knowledge and ethics have reflected the social and political events of the times. During the 1960s and early 1970s, concerns about such issues as the possibility of nuclear war, environmental deterioration, and economic and social injustices conjoined with the struggles of various groups to attain equity and influence, fueled a powerful social activism. Students and academics, particularly those in the social sciences and humanities, were among the most engaged. Neo-Marxism and subjectivism, both of which had long been part of the intellectual scene, fit these times and gained renewed influence. Another, much newer perspective, postmodernism, and its French version poststructuralism, also benefited.

Historically, critical theory came out of the Institute for Social Research, which was founded in 1923 in Frankfurt, shut down by the Nazis in 1933 to reappear at Columbia University in 1939, and returned to Frankfurt in 1950. The Institute's project was to revamp Marxism to fit changing times. Early leaders were Horkheimer, Adorno (of F-Scale fame), and Marcuse, with Habermas as the major later figure. For histories, see Jay (1973) and Held (1980).

Subjectivism is used here as a broad term to refer to perspectives that look inward to the mind rather than outward to experience and that connect to philosophical idealism and, more recently, often to phenomenology or existentialism. Like Marxism, phenomenology had a single founder, Edmund Husserl, while Sartre and Heidegger were leading existentialists, although the latter rejected that label. Postmodernism began to flower in the 1960s and 1970s, with its major figures including Derrida, Foucault, and Lyotard.

Various forms of subjectivism have long been influential in the social sciences (and the humanities). For example, in the 1960s, books and articles on phenomenological and existential sociology began being published. Although such writing often had only vague connections to the named philosophies, it did attend to individual and microsociological concerns (Smelser, 1988). Neo-Marxism, including critical theory, and postmodernism both did more than focus attention on their special areas of concern; they had political agendas as part of their programs. These agendas reflected the kind of values promoted by adherents, although much more explicitly in the case of neo-Marxists/critical theorists. All three views challenged, each in its own way, what was perceived to be the domination of a "positivistic" theory of knowledge.

Connections run from the spirit of the times to philosophic perspectives, to reflections of the philosophies in social science and other disciplines, and to fields like educational administration that draw from those disciplines. To be sure, some alterations and adaptations occur at each juncture, but the end products are usually quite recognizable as to their general origins. Subjectivism did not get serious attention in educational administration until the middle to late 1970s, followed by neo-Marxism/critical theory in the early 1980s. Postmodernism is now widely mentioned and occasionally written about but has not yet become an influential point of view in educational administration.

Although Hartley (1970) had earlier extolled humanistic existentialism as an appropriate philosophy for educational administration, it was Greenfield's attacks from a subjectivistic perspective on what he saw as the field's controlling view that made Greenfield the chief advocate of that perspective from 1975 until his death in 1992. For a collection of his writings, see Greenfield and Ribbins (1993). A major feature of his view was that scholarship on educational administration should deal with such issues as right and wrong, will, intention, and compulsion. He argued that such issues were vital but ignored by writers in educational administration. He was critical of science, which he believed was dominated by positivism, and of quantitative research, which he saw as irrelevant to the realities and personal travails of administrative life. Although Greenfield's position points to the importance of a subjectivist or idealist conception of values, and of the desirability of qualitative over quantitative research styles, he did not deal substantively with ethics or with field research, focusing instead on the shortcomings of positivistic science and what he saw as its dehumanizing effects on scholarship and administrative practice.

Neo-Marxism/critical theory was initially represented in educational administration by Foster and by Bates. Both published noteworthy journal articles in 1980. Bates (1980), influenced by work in the new sociology of education in Great Britain, argued that knowledge is defined and shaped by social and economic forces that exert power in ways that benefit the privileged at the expense of the less fortunate. In addition, he faulted school administrators because they failed to become advocates for those who were disfavored by the way knowledge is organized and transmitted. Foster (1980, 1986) presented a broader set of arguments, sometimes drawing on the ideas of Habermas. Foster rejected scientific approaches as exemplified in the writings and research of Herbert Simon (also a favorite target for Greenfield) in favor of normatively informed stances geared toward the attainment of greater equity and social justice.

The same social forces that led to the renewal of subjectivism and various forms of neo-Marxism also spawned scholarship on gender, race/ethnicity, and class. The literatures (Richards, 1988) that eventually developed in educational administration were mixtures of descriptive studies that documented inequities, and advocacy in behalf of a greater share of societal influence and benefits for particular groups. In many fields, including educational administration, women and minorities got the most attention, while the traditional Marxist conception of class received less emphasis, even from critical theorists who began to incorporate gender and race in what they saw as a more inclusive theory of domination, resistance, and equity (Davies, 1995).

Postmodernists were also concerned with oppression and the part played by language in fostering it. The deconstruction of texts, for example, was used to illustrate the oppressive character of words, as well as the omission of certain voices in discourse. Although postmodernism has not become a major force in educational administration, some of its ideas have been adopted by critical theorists, and especially in identity politics where they have been invoked by academics who become advocates for groups that they see as silenced and oppressed.

Historically, Marxism, subjectivism, and postmodernism have been philosophical enemies. Habermas, for instance, has been highly critical of postmodernism, and so have any number of subjectivistic scholars, even though Marxist-oriented approaches and subjectivism have entirely different traditions and emphases. However, in spite of this history, contemporary writers, who might identify with one or another of these views, have begun to agree on a variety of topics. For example, all three associate science with positivism and reject theories of knowledge that are inquiry-oriented. Critical theorists, postmodernists, and those involved with identity politics subscribe to a theory of the imposition of subtle forms of oppression by the socially privileged, with the less privileged defined as victims. Contemporary philosophical debates are increasingly less clearly tied to comprehensive philosophical positions, especially in derivative fields like educational administration, where scholars often have limited training in philosophy and are, in any case, more concerned about specific social and educational issues than broader philosophic questions. This is especially so in the case of critical theory, postmodern ideas, and identity politics. Subjectivism has stronger ties to a philosophic tradition.

This is also the case with the inquiry-oriented, science-friendly perspectives that take issue with the approaches just discussed. There the ties are to philosophical naturalism and pragmatism. Such positions were elaborated in educational administration by Evers and Lakomski (1991, and previous work cited there) and Willower (1994, and his earlier writings cited therein). Both were critical of the association of science with positivism, an easy target, but long dead in philosophy. Willower (1996) reviewed major sources of the mid-1950s through the 1970s in educational administration and reported that philosophical positivism was barely discussed during the time critics claimed it was overwhelmingly influential. He also found this to be true of sociological functionalism, often described today as both conservative and virtually dominant over the same earlier timeframe.

Evers and Lakomski were critical of naive empiricism, presenting a conception of science that they called coherentism. This view contends that knowledge claims should be assessed on the basis of their testability, simplicity, consistency, comprehensiveness, fecundity, familiarity of principle, and explanatory power. Such concepts were familiar because they had long been accepted as part of scientific methods as criteria for adequate theories or sometimes adequate hypotheses. Evers and Lakomski blended coherentism with an emphasis on physicalism that favors reduction, "in principle." Willower (1994) depicted science, or inquiry, as a very human activity, having a crucial subjective side geared to the creation of explanations that furnish plausible accounts of empirical phenomena. He emphasized the fallibility of science, but also its self-corrective character, contending that, despite its limitations, its methods have been more successful than others in generating knowledge and resolving problems.

Both Evers and Lakomski and Willower faulted subjectivism and postmodernism for their relativism arguing that while no theories can be seen as certain, the superiority of some over others can be demonstrated using the methods of logic and science. Neo-Marxism, in its various forms, has been widely criticized for holding beliefs as part of an ideological canon rather than treating them as hypotheses to be tested publicly, and for its notion of the dominance of a unitary and oppressive ruling class, despite political theory and research in the pluralist tradition that shows a multiplicity of interest groups and diverse sources of power and influence in modern society. Such flaws also are found in elements of postmodernism and identity politics.

Naturalistic and pragmatist critics reject what they see as the essentially ideological, relativistic, and politically driven stances of subjectivism, critical theory, and postmodernism, while also rejecting positivism and naive empiricism as narrow and uninformed science. Their touchstones are variously called scientific methods, inquiry, or reflective methods. Put simply, they rely on logic and evidence, consistent with such definitions of truth as Dewey's (1938) warranted assertibility.

In an earlier section, we noted that reliance on logic and evidence continued to set the standards by which research is judged. Of course, such standards are not uncontested, despite their legitimacy among those who do empirical work. One argument is that different paradigms are incompatible with one another and should be judged on their own terms. Thus Clegg and Hardy (1996) indicated that the widely cited work by Burrell and Morgan (1979) had broader purposes than the classification of strands of thought about organizations into four categories: radical humanism, radical structuralism, interpretive, and functionalist. Clegg and Hardy, who are supportive of Burrell and Morgan, explained that the latter wanted "to carve out a protective niche where 'alternative' researchers could do their thing, protected from the criticisms of functionalists, free from the necessity to explain their work to them" (p. 5). Burrell and Morgan have been criticized for the simplistic nature of their scheme and for their indiscriminate, all-inclusive use of the term functionalism (Willower, 1988), but that aside, the point here is their desire to divide scholars into independent and presumably noncommunicating camps, at least as far as criticism goes. Although this might reduce the burden of criticism for some, it appears to be antithetical to the norms for open communication and critical discourse that touch the heart of scholarly and university life.

In any event, there are now a variety of allegiances and alternative views in most social and humanistic fields, including educational administration. Most of the writing along these lines has been on philosophical issues of the kind under discussion, but there also appears to be more publication of personal narratives and social criticism with little attention to philosophy. Still, it is unclear how much impact the latter work will have, especially when it is subjected to critical analysis.

We have remarked how the spirit of the times seems to be related to the rise and fall of particular perspectives. Merton and Wolf (1995) made a related point; they described an association between increased societal dissensus and disciplinary fragmentation in sociology. That there should be a concomitant fragmentation in a derivative field like educational administration is no cause for surprise.

How far such fragmentation will go is uncertain. It seems unlikely to us that the incommensurability type argument of Burrell and Morgan will be very widely accepted, in part because openness to new ideas is a value for most scholars, including those who may oppose alternative views. Also, there are already forums in place for dissident groups in the forms of publishing outlets that favor a particular perspective and focus, and sessions at scholarly meetings where such groups have had numerous opportunities to present and persuade. Beyond that, many schol-

arly organizations have attempted to provide special opportunities for underrepresented members using race and gender as criteria. However, uniform support for the Burrell-Morgan thesis seems unlikely even among those advocating positions outside of the mainstream. Naturalistic philosophers argue that judgments of better and worse can be made about competing perspectives and theories, but so would many of those Burrell and Morgan wish to protect. It's just that the latter judgments would be based on a special standard consistent with the perspective in question. However, standards that ignore logic and evidence will continue to have credibility problems.

Meanwhile, it is important to recognize that the debates over epistemology, fundamental though they may be from a philosophic standpoint, have not altered in a major way most of the ongoing research in educational administration. That work cuts across such viewpoints and aims at gaining an increased understanding of how to improve school organizational arrangements and achieve better outcomes for students.

Ethics and Values

Work on ethics and values, the other main thrust of philosophical work on educational administration, has recently entered what seems to be a period of increased activity. For example, the Universities of Toronto and Virginia established a Center for the Study of Leadership and Ethics, which sponsored its first international conference in 1996, and attention to this area of inquiry appears to be reflected in growing publication in both scholarly sources and in textbooks.

Historically, writing on values in educational administration has been far less given to formal philosophical treatments and far more concerned with broad issues and directions, such as the purposes of education and how to enhance the learning and growth of each individual pupil. Thus for example, Mason (1986) contended that books on educational administration in the 1800s and early 1900s were influenced by a "universal humanism" that led to the belief that all children were perfectible, and Carver (1986) described the overriding importance given in such books in the 1946–1955 period to democratic administration and the concept of community.

Work on values after 1955 included, for example, Graff and Street's (1957) lengthy discourse on that topic in the landmark theory-oriented book edited by Campbell and Gregg, Willower's (1964) treatment of situations of concrete moral choice, and the book edited by Ohm and Monahan (1965) that included papers presented at a UCEA seminar on philosophy and educational administration. The analysis of cases was also used to explore value decisions and several books of the kind; for example, Sargent and Belisle

(1955) and Culbertson, Jacobson, and Reller (1960) were especially popular.

More recent writing on values has consisted of both relatively systematic philosophical treatments of the topic and policy- or issue-oriented commentaries of various kinds. We emphasize the former because views on the nature of principles and moral choice, with clear connections to more general philosophical positions, are critical to ethical theory. In doing so, we omit work that is devoted mainly to descriptions of morally good schools or ideal educational situations. Two of the most philosophically grounded perspectives were those of Hodgkinson and Willower. Hodgkinson (1991, and writings cited there) has for over 20 years worked on a hierarchical theory of values. Three value types were distinguished. From lowest to highest, these were subrational, matters of preference and affectivity; rational, matters of consequences and consensus; and transrational, matters of right principle that have metaphysical grounding. Such principles, labeled type one values by Hodgkinson, are "unverifiable by . . . science and cannot be justified by merely logical argument" (p. 99), but have "a quality of absoluteness" (p. 103). In this hierarchical theory, transrational values are superior to rational values that are superior to subrational ones. A related view is that there are objective and fundamental principles of right and wrong. This approach stems from the philosophical work of Alasdair MacIntyre, among others, and writing in educational administration by Mark Holmes. It is currently being advanced by Campbell (1994) who has combined that philosophical orientation with studies of moral choices made by school personnel. Criticisms of such approaches include questions about the source and justification of absolute (or objective) principles and the point that such principles can come into conflict with one another in actual situations.

Willower, like Hodgkinson, a long time student of the topic, situated values in the context of the inquiry-based epistemology described earlier. He contended that, to apply values in concrete situations, a process of valuation was essential (Willower & Licata, 1997, and sources cited there). That process consisted of a clarification of the competing values involved in particular moral choices and an assessment of the desirable and undesirable consequences that seemed likely to accompany the main alternatives. Also stressed were the utility of explanatory theories in exploring consequences and the mitigation of the negative consequences that often resulted from moral choices. Principles were defined in Deweyan terms as derived from experience and cumulative moral inquiry. That there is reasonably good agreement on general principles, that is, on general goods or evils, across various ethical approaches was seen as a sign of cumulative inquiry. However, the thorny issues of which principles apply and how they are to guide choice in concrete situations, were taken as signs of the necessity of valuation. A further point was the importance of scanning for possible desirable futures and the use of valuative processes in making choices about them, as well as in the resolution of the everyday problems that are thrust upon administrators and others. Criticisms of this type of view include the charge that it lacks standards for good and evil because absolute principles are rejected, and that processes are given precedence over principles.

Another ethical position, in this case related to the emergence of feminist studies, stresses the concept of caring. Stemming in education from the more general work of Nel Noddings, it has been elaborated in educational administration by Beck (1994). Caring is widely regarded in education circles to be a desirable quality. The usual criticisms of this approach are that, while caring may even be a necessary condition to doing good, it is not a sufficient one, and that, for school personnel, caring is not the problem so much as is translating good intentions into tangible outcomes for students.

The various Marxist-related views tend to stress political ideology and programs rather than more abstract philosophical analyses. Although equity is a key value, it is not a distinctive one because it is also a value in many other perspectives across the political spectrum. Emancipatory ethics is perhaps a more relevant designator, more in line with the critical stance that depicts society as dominated by a ruling class to the detriment of the less privileged who are seen as oppressed, and especially so in the cases of women and minorities.

The concept of oppression provides one among a number of the intersections between Marxist-related critical theory and postmodernism (Alvesson & Deetz, 1996). Such a focus leads to an analysis of social institutions and arrangements that channel or divert attention from political consciousness. Commerce and consumerism, entertainment, work place organization, mass media, language, science, and education, among others, have been subjected to critical examination with special attention to subtle mechanisms of repression and control. Most work of this kind has been in the form of social criticism and demands for reform rather than in the form of empirical studies (Alvesson & Deetz, 1996). An example in education was Giroux and McLaren's (1987) call for radicalized teachers who could work in the interest of an emancipatory vision to expose entrenched power in schools reflected in texts, curricula, and an array of other practices and policies. Typical criticisms of Marxist-related views include those cited earlier, the uncritical treatment of political ideology as doctrine, and the assumptions made about a unitary ruling class, along with the attribution by radical scholars of their own views to various underprivileged groups (Davies, 1995). Postmodernism, harder to pin down, is usually criticized for its relativism and nihilism.

Much of the discussion of policy options in education is essentially an exploration of competing values. This kind of discussion ordinarily deals with matters directly related to educational goals and issues rather than with a more abstract analysis of values. In their review, Boyd and Crowson (1981) suggested that the work on educational policy would be well served by research that was concerned with outcomes rather than processes and by interdisciplinary approaches to policy issues. An example of a current policy issue that features competing values is the allocation of limited and increasingly scarce resources among worthy programs, for instance, special education needs versus the curricular needs of a larger number of students (Monk, 1996).

Another example of a policy-oriented value is found in the frequent advocacy of more democratic, participative administrative and organizational arrangements in schools. As discussed in an earlier section, this kind of value has served a unifying function in educational administration, but so also has a commitment to school improvement, a concern reflected in research on the effects of schooling, usually measured in terms of student results (for example, Bidwell & Friedkin, 1988). Commonly held values, however, do not guarantee continuing harmony. It seems inevitable that there will be less commonality when it comes to the specifics of implementation.

The general picture in educational administration with regard to the search for meaning in the area of ethics and values could be described as kaleidoscopic. A number of philosophy based perspectives have been advanced. They probe basic value concerns and provide frameworks that stem from general philosophical positions. However, policy issues and current problems continue to be the main arenas for debates on goals, directions, and activities. Reformism and advocacy on behalf of various groups and causes cuts across both areas.

Philosophy, policy, and advocacy are not necessarily tightly coupled. For instance, a philosophic perspective usually features a social philosophy, or theory of the good society and government, within the framework of its particular ethical scheme, but it might be vague about a currently contested reform. In contrast, advocates might be wholly committed to a particular social change but be vague about the philosophical context and arguments that are relevant.

Further, as discussed earlier, there are multiple mixes and crosscurrents. Some accept part or most but not all of a general philosophy, and writers differ about the implications of a philosophy for a particular policy or reform. Sometimes advocates favor a policy, but only if certain changes are made. Some reformers want major alterations in society and its institutions, others smaller or more focused ones. Advocates for a special group can, and do, have conflicting opinions about what is best for that particular group. In matters of social action, issues of the ends justifying the means, a classic ethical concern, also arise.

Finally, although general philosophies and support for particular reforms and policies often match up in at least a rough way, there are many exceptions. For instance, some might favor radical reform to gain benefits for a particular group but be otherwise conservative or, as an example of another combination, some who accept a generally Marxian view might also be committed to scientific methods and reject those parts of Marxism at odds with or not supported by evidence. In the literature, this is the strand of thought called analytic Marxism (e.g., Roemer, 1986).

It remains to be pointed out that, in general philosophies, theories about values and knowledge are usually relatively consistent. For instance, naturalistic philosophies accept scientific methods as sources of knowledge and as relevant to moral choice. More interpretivist types of philosophies are likely to de-emphasize scientific methods, both in ethics and epistemology, in favor of a kind of humane reason or intuition. Although orthodox Marxism was grounded in the philosophy of dialectical materialism, the diverse Marxist and Marxist-related views of today are more eclectic. An example cited earlier is the critical theorists' incorporation of themes from postmodernism and identity politics (Davies, 1995). Alvesson and Deetz (1996), who are sympathetic to critical theory and postmodernism, see similarities between the two and contend that deliberate blending strengthens both.

Hence, if a comparison is made of three very broad philosophical camps, naturalist-pragmatist, interpretivist-humanist-subjectivist, and Marxist-Marxist related-critical theory, the latter category is probably more fluid than the others, as ideology continues to evolve. Meanwhile, although postmodernism has been a recognizable part of the philosophical landscape since the 1960s, its influence in educational administration has been limited, even though some of its concepts and ideas have been used by critical theorists and by advocates for particular groups. Examples are the examination of language as a vehicle for misleading or silencing, and of the use of power for the control of social institutions to maintain privilege and disadvantage others.

Work on racial/ethnic and gender issues is a related area. Identity politics have led to an important strand of scholarship and the categories of race/ethnicity and gender have tended to eclipse the standard measure of previous studies, social class. Although the concepts of domination and oppression play a larger part in Marxist-related views, like critical theory, and in postmodernism than in most other philosophies, advocates for particular groups run the philosophical gamut and many, as is the case for a large number of scholars and researchers, are not interested in systematic philosophy or find it irrelevant to their main concerns. Furthermore, in a field such as educational administration, which deals with individual growth and learning and is dedicated to the improvement of the lot of students, the notions of equality and of fairness are non-controversial because they are almost universally valued. Debates center more on means and the pros and cons of particular programs, rather than on values and ideals. An example of a debated issue is whether equal opportunity or compensatory advantage should be a preferred goal. A more methodologically-oriented debate is over the legitimacy of scholarship designed to demonstrate a particular injustice to make a political statement, often the case in critical ethnography. Scholars and activists on all sides of such issues typically see their positions as advancing justice and the welfare of students. This is likely not surprising to anyone who studies human behavior but is worthwhile to keep in mind when proposals and policies are contested.

The Longer View

The history of scholarship in educational administration reflects the influence of the social sciences, which in turn reflect broad social and political contexts. An additional factor for educational administration is its scholarly responsibility to speak to the problems and issues that are central to education.

Empirical and theoretical work in educational administration often is relevant to such problems and issues, but its deliberate use to guide practice is probably quite limited. The same can be said for philosophical views. Critical theory and postmodernism appear to suffer additional handicaps. The former is grounded on a radical critique of society that demands political action and is often seen as utopian and overly critical of practitioners. The latter is more obscure in presentation than most philosophies and is imbued with pessimism and nihilism. Neither is likely to have much of an appeal for educators seeking to cope with daily school concerns. Although interpretivist-subjectivist and naturalistic-pragmatist approaches may seem more readily understandable and perhaps more oriented to common sense, the extent to which practitioners will choose to expend the reflective effort required to bring either of these perspectives to bear on their problems is problematical.

As far as theories of knowledge are concerned, as a practical matter, reason and evidence continue to ground the general standards by which scholarship is judged by the community of scholars. Whatever the criticisms made of such standards, more compelling alternatives and associated norms are lacking. Relativism abandons standards, and political ideology usually claims its notion of justice as a form of grounding. However, in the end, even political ideologies are widely judged by their cogency as ideas and ideals and by how well they played out when used in real situations.

In the case of values, there is considerable agreement about principles and ideals. However, this agreement is about abstractions. It is in the interplay of conflict between principles and in the application and implementation of ideals that difficulties and disagreements arise.

The practical and real life nature of the professional field of educational administration shapes the impact and utility of knowledge and ethics in a major way. This can make some scholarship in educational administration academic in both senses of that word. Nevertheless, regardless of how infrequently or imperfectly knowledge and values currently are employed to guide practice, it is genuinely possible for their use to be more widely internalized by reflective individuals and institutionalized in educational organizations. These considerations set the stage for our third and final section on the pursuit of relevance.

The Pursuit of Relevance

In the present context, the pursuit of relevance is concerned with the ideas and concepts that speak to the problems of practice, along with the methods that facilitate their use in real situations. Philosophers have long been concerned with that pursuit, as seen in the emphasis of early Greek philosophers on praxis or thoughtful, deliberate practice, including Aristotle's exploration of what he called practical intellect, to John Dewey's (1922) condemnation of the separation of reflection and practice and his powerfully argued contention that the methods of inquiry are as relevant to everyday problems as they are to scientific ones.

Practice ordinarily has been discussed in terms of problem solving and decision making. In the present century and especially in more recent years, these phenomena have been the object of considerable empirical study by psychologists and others, using a variety of methods and theoretical frameworks (Sternberg & Davidson, 1992). Work in administration, including some in educational administration, has explored how executives confront problems and make choices. This work often attends to the organizational context within which administrators function.

In a professional field like educational administration, relevance is also a matter of preparing future administrators with knowledge and skills that will enable them to become successful practitioners. Consequently, a great deal of activity and writing has been devoted to relevant preparation programs. Some of the scholarship on problem solving and decision making will be examined, but the main focus will be on preparation programs.

The question of what knowledge should constitute the subject matter of preparation is another crucial issue. Knowledge and explanation can play a critical part in thoughtful action. They are reflected in the various compilations of theory and research and in the course content of preparation programs. Although the published work on theory, research, and philosophy in a field can materially influence the substance of the courses taught in preparation programs, organized efforts aimed at securing agreement on the specifics of a knowledge base tend to mirror the various schools of thought, philosophies, and ideologies found in that field. Hoy's (1994) summary of the work of one such effort in educational administration suggests how difficult it is for diverse groups of scholars to reach a consensus, predetermined to a degree by the custom of including representatives of virtually every persuasion in such projects in the name of fairness.

Understanding Problem Solving

The empirical study of thinking, problem solving, and decision making has been long-standing. Some illustrations include C. H. Judd's research on transfer in the early 1900s, E. L. Thorndike's on mental associations and problem solving, the laboratory studies of J. B. Watson and other behaviorists, the efforts of Gestalt psychologists to explain insight, and the more recent research in cognitive science. The latter term, cognitive science, is ordinarily used in a broad sense to include work over a range from the neurophysiology of the brain to artificial intelligence and computer simulations of problem solving to the way experts confront complex problems and resolve them. A noteworthy point is that the various approaches encompassed by the cognitive science rubric tend to recognize the complexity of problem solving to a greater degree than did some of the narrower perspectives that preceded it, such as behaviorism.

Research on problem solving distinguishes between domain-general processes and domain-specific knowledge (Sternberg & Davidson, 1992). The former are general procedures that cut across various domains, while the latter represent information relevant to the solution of problems in a particular area of subject matter.

In their review of research on problem solving, Sternberg and Davidson discuss six domain-general processes: Identifying the problem, forming a mental map of the problem's elements and relationships, retrieving information relevant to those features, planning how to proceed, selecting an implementation strategy, and monitoring how the solution plays out. The similarity of these steps to those in normative decision models is remarkable. Such models commonly include problem formulation, devising alternative solutions, canvassing the consequences of each alternative, and choosing and implementing a solution. The general resemblance of these procedures to those of scientific method are also worth noting.

The work on domain-specific knowledge (such as Chase & Simon, 1973; Simon, 1993) shows that a major difference between expert and novice decision makers is knowledge. Studies of different subject matter indicate the importance of knowledge to experts. The main exception occurs when there is a fundamental change in task structure (Sternberg & Davidson, 1992), in other words, in new situations where domain-specific knowledge is less relevant.

In educational administration, Leithwood and his students (Leithwood & Steinbach, 1995) have produced an ongoing body of research employing a cognitive science framework. To cite just one major result, expert school administrators appear to be more concerned with planning and thinking ahead than their novice counterparts. Interestingly, an earlier study by Hemphill, Griffiths, and Frederiksen (1962) reported similar findings. Using the work done as a springboard, Leithwood set an agenda for future research (Leithwood & Steinbach, 1995, pp. 314–315). It included more empirical work on the nature of expertise in educational administration, the nature of the problems to be solved, and the domain-specific knowledge that abets their solution.

Preparation Programs

According to Miklos (1992), the formal preparation of school administrators in university programs has largely been limited to the 20th century and largely to the United States until the 1950s. Since then, formal programs have emerged in many parts of the world, beginning in other English-speaking countries.

The early programs emphasized practical subjects such as business principles, accounting, efficient management, and some philosophy, yet during the 1930s, 1940s, and 1950s the foundations shifted towards education and democratic administration, mixed with financial and practical subjects (Culbertson, 1988; Miklos, 1992).

As more states required graduate study for administrator licensure (19 in 1939, 41 by the mid-1950s, McCarthy, et al., 1988), more university programs became available and professors of educational administration began to form their own associations, which not surprisingly, often devoted much energy to preparation. One of the committees reporting at the first NCPEA meeting in 1947 had as its topic "The Preparation of the School Administrator" (Flesher & Knobloch, 1957). This group called for a broad general education for administrators and for professional experiences geared to learning, school, and society, developing a consistent philosophy, correctly interpreting research, and developing the ability to administer all phases of the educational program. The 1948 sessions quickly turned to recruitment and selection, courses and problems, surveys, internships, social science knowledge, and the principles that would integrate such experiences in a program. These kinds of concerns heralded a preoccupation with preparation programs that continues to the present day.

Such concerns were not limited to higher education but were taken up by the profession's practitioners as well. One of the milestones of improved preparation was the Cooperative Program in Educational Administration (CPEA), which was funded by the W. K. Kellogg Foundation. This resulted in grants beginning in 1950 to eight university centers to study the whole field of educational administration with its improvement as the primary goal. As Moore (1957) made clear, the CPEA resulted from initiatives begun in 1947 by the American Association of School Administrators. The advisory council to Kellogg for the project was a development committee appointed by AASA's executive board. That advisory group served until it was succeeded by the Committee for the Advancement of School Administration in 1955, another AASA body. A large number of studies was done through the CPEA initiative; Moore (1957) listed more than 300 publications, many on preparation programs.

The 1960 AASA Yearbook included a sometimes critical examination of preparation programs and the presentation of a fictional high-quality one. Major components included a rigorously selected core group of students exposed to a mix of practical and theoretical studies. Such a program was seen as realistic because many of its elements were drawn from existing programs at Oregon, Stanford, Harvard, Maryland, Columbia, Buffalo, and Texas.

AASA studies of school superintendents' appraisals of their own preparation usually found high levels of satisfaction. Generally, high marks were given to both theoretical and practical work in educational administration, while some social science fields, and especially courses in teaching methods and curriculum, were judged to be of lesser importance (e.g., Knezevich, 1971; Cunningham & Hentges, 1982).

Cooperation between practitioners and professors of educational administration has always been a hallmark of the field and it continues to the present day. The 1960s and 1970s, however, appear to have been the high point of university influence in organizations like AASA. For example, the AASA Commission on the Preparation of Professional School Administrators, whose 1971 report was just cited, was composed of four professors, two education deans, two urban school superintendents, and one state superintendent, the kind of numbers rarely seen in later years.

In university preparation programs, the transfer of training has been an assumed, if often unstated, theme underlying problem-based learning, practicums, and internships. The governing principle is that transfer is more likely to take place when learning and use occur in similar situations. The importance of the school survey, which in this context is research on a school system or one of its problems, to some early professors has already been noted. It remains to add that some preparation programs incorporated the study of school systems into their curriculums as core experiences. The use of cases in the 1950s and 1960s was also cited earlier and this too continues today.

In the 1960s new instructional materials were developed with UCEA taking a leadership role. This organization, founded in 1956, was heavily oriented to the improvement of administrator preparation. It produced cases and simulations with the earliest ones stemming from the development of materials on the Whitman School of the Jefferson Township School System. These materials, first made available in 1959, were adapted from the project on administrator performance reported in Hemphill and his associates (Hemphill, *et al.*, 1962). As the Jefferson materials appeared to become obsolete, UCEA developed the Madison School System simulation in 1967 and the Monroe City simulation based on the whole gamut of urban school problems in 1970–1971 (Wynn, 1972). Over the years, a variety of specialized simulations for collective bargaining, special education administrators, rural principals, school psychologists, and others were devised. Most were quite extensive; for example, the Adams School System simulation from the 1980s listed a page and a half of available training materials.

Other initiatives included games, especially in the areas of collective bargaining and politics, individualized learning systems, best lecture cassettes, and films (Wynn, 1972). During the 1960s, UCEA also published more general works on an array of preparation issues (e.g., Culbertson & Hencley, 1962), including common and specialized learning for the various administrative positions in education (Leu & Rudman, 1963). In the latter 1970s, instructional modules to be used in the preparation of women administrators were tried out at conferences at 22 university sites and made available in 1981.

Through the development of instructional materials, conferences, workshops, and numerous publications, UCEA became an important force for reform and improved preparation. At one time well supported by a variety of grants, it adapted to harder times in the 1980s by reducing staff and delegating many of its activities to its member universities. The *UCEA Newsletter*, renamed the *UCEA Review* in 1974, and the history of UCEA by Jack Culbertson (1995), its executive director from 1959–1981, are valuable sources for information on that organization's activities.

The internship in administration, stressed in many AASA publications as a vital component of preparation, has been the object of considerable attention for many years. For instance, in Hencley (1963) and in Milstein, Bobroff, and Restine (1991), a host of issues were explored, from the relation of university and onsite mentors to the length and content of intern experiences.

A concern with values has been another focus of reform. As noted earlier, this topic is increasingly a source of debate with regard to which values should be stressed and how they should be presented, but there is virtually universal agreement on the importance of the topic. Beck and Murphy (1994) reported that in a sample of more than 40 universities, cases, formal courses, issues courses, and other approaches to values and ethics were used, but there was no dominant approach and some institutions indicated that values were taught in the various courses examining alternative choices and futures.

Related to values is the place of humanities in preparation. Two examples of work in that area are Farquhar's (1970) treatment of the use of humanities in preparation and Popper's (1994) classics-oriented book, first published in 1985 and now in its fourth, revised edition. Novels, plays, poetry, art, music, and film have all been used in preparation programs, although not widely, and usually as a result of the interests of selected professors.

Given the trend toward research that deals with people in real-life settings (Willower, 1988), courses in qualitative research are becoming much more common in educational administration programs. With many of the specialized fields of education incorporating such work in their own offerings on the grounds of their subject matter's singular nature, proliferation has occurred. This has fed discussion of how generic such courses should be and what qualifications their instructors should have. Such issues will often be settled with local contingencies in mind, as seems to have been the case with the study of values and with many other perennial problems such as internships.

Recent reform efforts have been sparked by the report of the National Commission on Excellence in Educational Administration (NCEEA, 1987).[2] Sponsored by UCEA and supported by a variety of funding agencies, this body consisted of 27 people from universities (from professors to presidents), NCPEA, and all the major practitioner and school board organizations, as well as state education officials, school superintendents, and individuals from politics, business, and labor. The Commission recommended that preparation programs be designed around the study of administration, the technical core and skills, the application of research findings and methods to problems, and supervised practice leading to demonstrated competence (p.19). Furthermore, it proposed more stringent selection and retention processes, cohort student groups, and special efforts to recruit promising candidates, especially from underrepresented groups. Partnerships and collaboration with practitioners and school districts in all aspects of reform were strongly recommended.

In addition, the NCEEA report made a variety of suggestions to universities including their administrators and professors, State and Federal education policymakers, and the private sector. These included fewer and better preparation programs, more stringent licensing that would be portable along with such items as pension benefits, and the formation of a National Policy Board on Educational Administration (NPBEA).

Such a national board was subsequently established. It was made up of representatives of the various groups and associations likely to be interested in the preparation of school administrators. This body issued an agenda for reform (NPBEA, 1989) that included many of the recommendations of the NCEEA, but it also proposed professional Ed.D. programs requiring one year of study and one year of field residency, as well as standards for universities aimed at quality.

Another recent development has been the creation of an interest group on teaching administration within the educational administration division of the American Educational Research Association. This group has sponsored a number of seminars, including descriptions of some fledgling efforts to develop materials that approximate virtual reality, such as those of J.G. Claudet and his colleagues at Texas Tech.

Program reform has been going forward at a number of universities, often along lines that are consistent with NCEEA recommendations. One set of such reforms has been funded in part by the Danforth Foundation, also one of the financial supporters of the NCEEA. Murphy (1993) recently edited a collection of reports from nine universities that described the specifics of their program reforms. Some reform features may be adopted more readily than others. For instance, core or cohort groups, already in place in some institutions, seem to have spread, judging from the narratives in the Murphy book, and a survey by Scott Norton reported in the Fall 1995 *UCEA Review* indicating their use by 70 percent of 43 responding universities. UCEA's Information Environment for School Leaders Preparation project and the University of Alberta's Project Decide, both devoted to advanced computer-based simulations (see Maynes, McIntosh, & Mappin, 1996), represent more complex creations and probably, slower adoptions.

Research

Most of the scholarly writing on preparation programs consists of broad treatments that connect reforms to issues in education and society or analyses of particular reforms, often critical of the status quo and supportive of specific changes, seen as improvements. Such discussions are essential precursors of thoughtful change and are an important phase of program reform.

Also important are empirical studies that assess how well adopted reforms have worked, but they are rare. In his extensive review, Miklos (1992) stated that research on the effectiveness of preparation programs is "fragmented, few questions are pursued in depth, and patterns in results are difficult to discern" (p.27). He noted that most studies were assessments of particular programs, usually based on reported student satisfaction, or surveys of practicing administrators' opinions of the adequacy of their preparation. Miklos cited only one "exploratory" investigation of the effects of training on participants.

Although the latter type of inquiry is scarce, it should be kept in mind that the general grounding of much reform can be found in transfer theory and the work in cognitive science noted earlier, even when program reformers might not be entirely explicit about such grounding. At the same time, there is a danger, warned against by Leithwood and Steinbach (1995), of applications outrunning theory and research. This danger exists whenever the desire or need for action outweighs available information, a topic returned to below.

The Broader Context: Practice and Its Problems

The earliest scholars of educational administration were practitioners. For example, Harris, Payne, and Cubberley had all been school superintendents. The first formal programs under the guidance of Cubberley and Strayer stressed field surveys and practical concerns, as well as philosophy and the science of that time (Culbertson, 1988). During Paul Mort's reign at Columbia, field studies continued to be done, and the study council movement, a way of bridging the gap between universities and school systems to work on practical problems, began to develop and grow. Practice and practitioner organizations have had a major influence on preparation programs from the beginning.

The first comprehensive organization for individuals teaching educational administration was conceived at the March, 1947 conference of AASA at Atlantic City, where the initial meeting of what was to become NCPEA was planned for later that year, a meeting where preparation was to be a featured topic. The genesis of UCEA, formed nine years later, appears to have stemmed from the CPEA, which was a creature of AASA, with support from Kellogg, as noted earlier.

Another indicator of the crosscurrents of influence can be seen in the marked similarity of a number of the recommendations of the UCEA-sponsored NCEEA and those found in the 1960 AASA Yearbook (AASA, 1960).[3] Both recommended, for instance, stringent selection rather than mere admission, fewer part-time students, student cohort or core groups, field studies, internships and an array of realism-oriented teaching methods, attention to administrative skills and to knowledge based on a variety of good theories, the inclusion of practicing administrators in program planning, greater financial support for programs in educational administration, and fewer but higher-quality programs.

In addition to preservice university preparation, many other initiatives also contribute to administrator preparation. Miklos (1992) discussed a variety of them including AASA's National Academy and numerous state and regional activities sponsored by associations, study councils, and governmental agencies, aimed at professional development. Another effort, initially spearheaded in education by the National Association of Secondary School Principals, was assessment programs and centers designed to profile likely administrator behavior for both self-development and possible employer use. Whether programs of this general type, now sponsored by various groups, have more than palliative effects is not clear. For instance, based on a review of the literature and their own research, Sirotnik and Durden (1996) indicated that assessment programs appear to have low levels of predictive validity and should be used very cautiously, especially in light of their high cost and time- and labor-intensive nature.

The complexities and difficulties of school administration create pressures for timely solutions to current problems. These problems are ubiquitous: the current ones include special needs students, state and Federal mandates, various special interest and community pressure groups, diversity issues, technological change, drugs, violence, dysfunctional families, and economic constraints, to name a few. Some of them are essentially societal problems, and some lie beyond administrator control. The difficulties of the work of educators helps to explain the recurring fads and panaceas that have characterized education for so long. Independently of whether they work, they provide at least an impression of action directed toward problem solution. Preparation programs, as well as in-service ones, often incorporate elements of the latest fads, usually some of the more useful elements, in the names of relevance and timeliness.

It seems clear that the pursuit of relevance reflects the issues and trends of the times. Nevertheless, it also appears that the kinds of analyses and reports done over the years concerning ideal preparation have been remarkably consistent, as in the 1960 AASA report and the NCEEA one almost 30 years later. The barriers to progress have also been quite consistent including lack of financial support, program proliferation, unselected students, a fairly weak research base accompanied in recent decades by contested knowledge and philosophical debates, and part time and intermittent patterns of study by those seeking to enter the profession. An obvious feature of the pursuit of relevance has been the variety of players involved in efforts to improve preparation programs in educational administration. Practitioners and their associations and university personnel and groups have been the main ones, but other interests have also been represented. This reflects the importance of education to many segments of the population and to society as a whole.

Concluding Comments

Our depiction of scholarship in educational administration in terms of strands, counterstrands, and crosscurrents of activities, we believe, is a more realistic one than chopping time into eras in which one or a few strands dominate all else. It is easier and more attention-getting to put labels on time spans, but the cost can be high: the neglect of the relevant diverse and multiple forces at work in human affairs. However, our approach also has its limitations. An illustration can be found in our contention that certain symbols and rituals that recognize high quality performance are a force for unity. We based this on social theory and provided some early citations to influential scholars, but we are not sure just how this plays out in the educational administration professoriate, given the field's multiple subject matters and many varieties of tasks and commitments. Still, this interpretation seemed quite reasonable, though less concrete than the other unifying elements—a melioristic commitment to the improvement of education, as reflected in substantial amounts of scholarship over time on democratic and participative administration and organization, and a continuing reliance on logic and evidence to assess scholarly work, even during a period rife with relativistic criticisms of standards of many kinds.

The unifying elements deserve greater attention than they have received. It appears to be far more popular to stress only fragmentation and disarray. Even when unity is acknowledged, it has often been portrayed as undesirable or even malevolent, as of bland conformity or of oppressive dominance, arranged to serve the interests of privileged elites.

The popularity of disarray may be related to the rhetoric of crisis that has been endemic to educational administration and to education generally over the years. Perceptions and talk of crisis have been buttressed, especially since the 1940s and the growth of technology and mass media, by predictions of exponential and even overwhelming change. The political vulnerability of schools as societal institutions is an additional factor, as illustrated by the reaction in Western nations to the 1957 Soviet launch of Sputnik, and by the periodic reports on the dire state of education from various commissions and other sources, of which the 1983 publication *A Nation at Risk* can be thought of as a paradigmatic prophecy of educational catastrophe in American education. Although such reports are frequently guilty of overstatement, the schools and their administrators do face undeniably daunting problems. The litany of specifics need not be repeated.

Scholarship in educational administration appears to have been influenced by the sense of urgency that stems from a rhetoric of crisis. The search for more effective and more appropriate modes of organization and leadership to improve schools is an obvious example. The emphasis on democratic and participative arrangements was, after all, an effort to confront problems by bringing all of the stakeholders, including members of the community, more directly into decision processes. Although the philosophical debates in the field of the past several decades mirror work in philosophy and the social sciences, when applied to ed-

ucational administration, they also can be seen as attempts to furnish an intellectual grounding for more desirable futures, albeit from conflicting perspectives. Concern for underprivileged and at risk individuals and groups, and the study of their problems along with efforts aimed at improvement, cut across all areas of education, including administration.

However, a critical feature of the attempt to understand and improve schools (as well as society) is that it is a battle that is never finally won. When a particular reform or change is successfully implemented, a small victory is achieved, but the battle is ongoing and there are almost always reverses and defeats to come. This is one reason that reform efforts often seem so familiar as they re-emerge in slightly different guises over time. It is also another reason why the field is so prone to fads. One large lesson that history teaches is that educational change and reform, like inquiry and science, are never finished. The work is always in progress. The rhetoric of crisis, perceptions of exponential change, and the ongoing nature of educational improvement represent continuing conditions that have influenced scholarship in educational administration. At the same time, there is now a substantial body of knowledge about schools that provides a variety of frameworks for addressing educational problems. However, whether it will be used widely or wisely remains problematic.

NOTES

1. Mason (1986) cites two works in educational administration by Samuel R. Hall published in 1829 and 1832, well before Payne's 1875 book. However, there is room for argument as to what constitutes a book on school administration; whether Payne wrote the first or just an early work on the topic, his contributions to the field were substantial.

2. A larger document, in book form, reprints the report of the Commission and adds a large number of papers, many reprinted from their original sources, some prepared for the book. These papers speak to a variety of issues and include the range of perspectives in educational administration, often perspectives not represented on the Commission. See Griffiths, Stout, and Forsyth (1988).

3. It can be noted that Daniel E. Griffiths, who chaired the National Commission on Excellence in Educational Administration, was also a member of the yearbook commission for that 1960 AASA publication.

REFERENCES

Aldrich, H. E. & Marsden, P. V. (1988). Environments and organizations. In N. J. Smelser (Ed.), *Handbook of sociology* (pp. 361–392). Newbury Park, CA: Sage.

Alvesson, M. & Deetz, S. (1996). Critical theory and postmodernism approaches to organizational studies. In S. R. Clegg, C. Hardy & W. R. Nord (Eds.). *Handbook of organizational studies* (pp. 191–217). London: Sage.

American Association of School Administrators. (1960). *Professional administrators for America's schools*. (38th Yearbook). Washington, DC: The Association.

Anderson, G. L. (1989). Critical ethnography in education. *Review of Educational Research*, 59, 249–270.

Argyris, C. (1964). *Integrating the individual and the organization*. New York: Wiley.

Bates, R. J. (1980). Educational administration, the sociology of science and the management of knowledge. *Educational Administration Quarterly*, 16, 1–20.

Beck, L. G. (1994). *Reclaiming educational administration as a caring profession*. New York: Teachers College Press.

Beck, L. G. & Murphy, J. (1994). *Ethics in educational leadership programs*. Thousand Oaks, CA: Corwin.

Bidwell, C. E. & Friedkin, N. E. (1988). The sociology of education. In N. J. Smelser (Ed.), *Handbook of sociology* (pp. 449–471). Newbury Park, CA: Sage.

Blake, R. R. & Mouton, J. S. (1964). *The managerial grid*. Houston, TX: Gulf.

Boyan, N. J. (1951). *A study of the formal and informal organization of a school faculty*. Unpublished doctoral dissertation, Harvard University, Cambridge, MA.

Boyan, N. J. (1982). Administration of educational institutions. In H. E. Mitzel (Ed.), *Encyclopedia of Educational Research* (5th ed., pp. 22–49). New York: Macmillan.

Boyan, N. J. (Ed.). (1988). *Handbook of research on educational administration*. New York: Longman.

Boyd, W. L. & Crowson, R. L. (1981). The changing concept and practice of public school administration. *Review of Research in Education*, 9, 311–373.

Burns, J. M. (1978). *Leadership*. New York: Harper and Row.

Burrell, G. & Morgan, G. (1979). *Sociological paradigms and organizational analysis*. London: Heinemann.

Callahan, R. E. (1962). *Education and the cult of efficiency*. Chicago: University of Chicago Press.

Campbell, C. E. (1994). Personal morals and organizational ethics: A synopsis. *Canadian Administrator*, 34, 1–10.

Campbell, R. F. & Gregg, R. T. (Eds.). (1957). *Administrative behavior in education*. New York: Harper.

Campbell, R. F. & Newell, L. J. (1973). *A study of professors of educational administration*. Columbus, OH: University Council for Educational Administration.

Campbell, R. F., Fleming, T., Newell, L. J. & Bennion, J. W. (1987). *A history of thought and practice in educational administration*. New York: Teachers College Press.

Carver, F. D. (1986). A return to rhetoric: School administration texts 1946–1955. In T. E. Glass (Ed.). *An analysis of texts on school administration 1820–1985* (pp. 75–91). Danville, IL: Interstate.

Chase, W. G. & Simon, H. A. (1973). The mind's eye in chess. In W. G. Chase (Ed.). *Visual information processing* (pp. 215–281). New York: Academic Press.

Clegg, S. R. & Hardy, C. (1996). Introduction: Organizations, organization and organizing. In S. R. Clegg, C. Hardy & W. R. Nord (Eds.). *Handbook of organizational studies* (pp. 1–28). London: Sage.

Coladarci, A. P. & Getzels, J. W. (1955). *The use of theory in educational administration*. Stanford, CA: Stanford University Press, Educational Administration Monograph No. 5.

Conway, J. A. (1984). The myth, mystery, and mastery of participative decision making in education. *Educational Administration Quarterly*, 20, 11–40.

Crow, G. M. & Slater, R. O. (1996). *Educating democracy: The role of systemic leadership*. Fairfax, VA: National Policy Board for Educational Administration.

Culbertson, J. A. (1988). A century's quest for a knowledge base. In N. J. Boyan (Ed.), *Handbook of research on educational administration* (pp. 3–126). New York: Longman.

Culbertson, J. A. (1995). *Building bridges: UCEA's first two decades*. University Park, PA: University Council for Educational Administration.

Culbertson, J. A. & Hencley, S. P. (1962). *Preparing administrators: New perspectives*. Columbus, OH: University Council for Educational Administration.

Culbertson, J. A., Jacobson, P. B. & Reller, T. L. (1960). *Administrative relationships: A case book*. Englewood Cliffs, NJ: Prentice-Hall.

Cunningham, L. L. & Hentges, J. T. (1982). *The American school superintendency, 1982*. Arlington, VA: American Association of School Administrators.

Davies, S. (1995). Leaps of faith: Shifting currents in critical sociology of education. *American Journal of Sociology*, 100, 1448–1478.

Dewey, J. (1916). *Democracy and education*. New York: Macmillan.

Dewey, J. (1922). *Human nature and conduct*. New York: Henry Holt.

Dewey, J. (1938). *Logic: The theory of inquiry*. New York: Henry Holt.

Downey, L. W. & Enns, F. (Eds.). (1963). *The social sciences and educational administration*. Edmonton, Alberta: University of Alberta and University Council for Educational Administration.

Dubin, R. (1951). *Human relations in administration*. Englewood Cliffs, NJ: Prentice-Hall.

Educational Administration Quarterly. (1997). Special issue on British educational reform, 33, 136–251.

Evers, C. W. & Lakomski, G. (1991). *Knowing educational administration*. Oxford: Pergamon.

Farquhar, R. H. (1970). *The humanities in preparing educational administrators*. Eugene, OR: ERIC Clearinghouse on Educational Administration.

Flesher, W. R. & Knobloch, A. L. (1957). *A decade of development in educational leadership: The first ten years of NCPEA*. National Conference of Professors of Educational Administration.

Foster, W. (1980). Administration and the crisis in legitimacy. *Harvard Educational Review*, 50, 496–505.

Foster, W. (1986). *Paradigms and promises*. Buffalo, NY: Prometheus.

Foster, W. (1992). Restructuring schools. In M. C. Alkin (Ed.), *Encyclopedia of educational research* (6th ed., pp. 1108–1114). New York: Macmillan.

Fullan, M., Miles, M. B. & Taylor, G. (1980). Organizational development in schools: The state of the art. *Review of Educational Research*, 50, 121–183.

Getzels, J. W. (1952). A psycho-sociological framework for the study of educational administration. *Harvard Educational Review*, 22, 235–246.

Giroux, H. A. (1983). Theories of reproduction and resistance in the new sociology of education. *Harvard Educational Review*, 53, 257–293.

Giroux, H. A. & McLaren, P. (1987). Teacher education as a counter-public sphere: Radical pedagogy as a form of cultural politics. *Philosophy and Social Criticism*, 1, 51–69.

Glass, T. E. (1986). Factualism to theory, art to science: School administration texts 1955–1985. In T. E. Glass (Ed.), *An analysis of texts on school administration 1820–1985* (pp. 93–114). Danville, IL: Interstate.

Graff, O. B. & Street, C. M. (1957). Developing a value framework for educational administration. In R. F. Campbell & R. T. Gregg, *Administrative behavior in education* (pp. 120–152). New York: Harper.

Greenfield, T. B. (1986). The decline and fall of science in educational administration. *Interchange*, 17, 57–80.

Greenfield, T. B. & Ribbins, P. (1993). *Greenfield on educational administration: Towards a humane science*. London: Routledge.

Griffiths, D. E. (1956). *Human relations in school administration*. New York: Appleton-Century-Crofts.

Griffiths, D. E. (1959). *Administrative theory*. New York: Appleton-Century-Crofts.

Griffiths, D. E. (Ed.). (1964a). *Behavioral science and educational administration*. Chicago: University of Chicago Press.

Griffiths, D. E. (1964b). The professorship in educational administration: Environment. In D. J. Willower & J. A. Culbertson (Eds.), *The professorship in educational administration* (pp. 29–46). Columbus, OH and University Park, PA: University Council for Educational Administration and The Pennsylvania State University.

Griffiths, D. E. (1983). Evolution in research and theory: A study of prominent researchers. *Educational Administration Quarterly*, 19, 201–221.

Griffiths, D. E., Hart, A. W. & Blair, B. G. (1991). Still another approach to administration: Chaos theory. *Educational Administration Quarterly*, 27, 430–451.

Griffiths, D. E., Stout, R. T. & Forsyth, P. B. (1988). *Leaders for America's schools: The report and papers of the NCEEA*. Berkeley, CA: McCutchan.

Halpin, A. W. (Ed.). (1958). *Administrative theory in education*. Chicago: Midwest Administration Center.

Halpin, A. W. (1959). *The leadership behavior of school superintendents.* Chicago: Midwest Administration Center, University of Chicago.

Halpin, A. W. (1970). Administrative theory: The fumbled torch. In A. M. Kroll (Ed.), *Issues in American education* (pp. 156–183). New York: Oxford University Press.

Halpin, A. W. & Croft, D. B. (1963). *The organizational climate of schools.* Chicago: Midwest Administration Center, University of Chicago.

Halpin, A. W. & Hayes, A. E. (1977). The broken ikon or whatever happened to theory? In L. L. Cuningham, W. G. Hack & R. D. Nystrand (Eds.). *Educational administration: The developing decades* (pp. 261–295). Berkeley, CA: McCutchan.

Hartley, H. J. (1970). Humanistic existentialism and the school administrator. In F. W. Lutz (Ed.), *Toward improved urban education* (pp. 7–22). Worthington, OH: Charles H. Jones.

Held, D. (1980). *Introduction to critical theory: Horkheimer to Habermas.* Berkeley & Los Angeles: University of California Press.

Hemphill, J. K., Griffiths, D. E. & Frederiksen, N. (1962). *Administrative performance and personality.* New York: Teachers College Press.

Hencley, S. P. (Ed.). (1963). *The internship in administrative preparation.* Columbus, OH and Washington, DC: University Council for Educational Administration and The Committee for the Advancement of School Administration.

Hodgkinson, C. (1991). *Educational leadership: The moral art.* Albany, NY: SUNY Press.

Hoy, W. K. (1994). Foundations of educational administration: Traditional and emerging perspectives. *Educational Administration Quarterly,* 30, 178–198.

Hoy, W. K. & Miskel, C. G. (1996). *Educational administration: Theory, research and practice,* (5th ed.). New York: McGraw Hill.

Hoy, W. K., Tartar, C. J. & Kottkamp, R. (1991). *Open schools, healthy schools.* Newbury Park, CA: Sage.

Hoyle, E. & McMahon, A. (Eds.). (1986). *The management of schools.* London: Kogan Page.

Hughes, E. C. (1928). Personality types and the division of labor. *American Journal of Sociology,* 33, 754–768.

Husen, T. & Postlethwaite, T. N. (Eds.). (1994). *International encyclopedia of education* (2nd ed.). Oxford: Pergamon.

Immegart, G. L. (1988). Leadership and leader behavior. In N. J. Boyan (Ed.), *Handbook of research on educational administration* (pp. 259–277). New York: Longman.

Jay, M. (1973). *The dialectical imagination: A history of the Frankfurt School and the Institute for Social Research, 1923–1950.* Boston: Little, Brown.

Journal of Educational Administration. (1991). Special issue on the restructuring of educational systems, 29, 5–83.

Knezevich, S. J. (Ed.). (1971). *The American school superintendent.* Washington, DC: American Association of School Administrators.

Leithwood, K., Chapman, J., Corson, D., Hallinger, P. & Hart, A. W. (Eds.). (1996). *International handbook of educational leadership and administration.* Norwell, MA and Dordrecht, Netherlands: Kluwer.

Leithwood, K. & Steinbach, R. (1995). *Expert problem solving.* Albany, NY: SUNY Press.

Leu, D. J. & Rudman, H. C. (1963). *Preparation programs for school administrators.* East Lansing, MI: Michigan State University.

Lewin, K., Lippitt, R. & White, R. K. (1939). Patterns of aggressive behavior in experimentally-created social climates. *Journal of Social Psychology,* 10, 271–301.

Likert, R. (1961). *New patterns of management.* New York: McGraw-Hill.

Lynd, R. S. (1939). *Knowledge for what?* Princeton, NJ: Princeton University Press.

McCarthy, M. M. & Kuh, G. D. (1997). *Continuity and change: The educational leadership professoriate.* Columbia, MO: University Council for Educational Administration.

McCarthy, M. M., Kuh, G. D., Newell, L. J. & Iacona, C. M. (1988). *Under scrutiny: The educational administration professoriate.* Tempe, AZ: University Council for Educational Administration.

McGregor, D. (1960). *The human side of enterprise.* New York: McGraw-Hill.

Maslow, A. (1965). *Eupsychian management.* Homewood, IL: Irwin.

Mason, R. (1986). From idea to ideology: School administration texts 1820–1914. In T. E. Glass (Ed.), *An analysis of texts of school administration 1820–1985* (pp. 1–21). Danville, IL: Interstate.

Maynes, B., McIntosh, G. & Mappin, D. (1996). Computer-based simulations of the school principalship: Preparation for professional practice. *Educational Administration Quarterly,* 32, 579–594.

Merton, R. K. & Wolf, A. (1995). The cultural and social incorporation of sociological knowledge. *The American Sociologist,* 26, 15–39.

Miklos, E. (1992). Administrator preparation, educational. In M. C. Alkin (Ed.), *Encyclopedia of Educational Research* (6th ed., pp. 22–29). New York: Macmillan.

Miles, M. B. (1993). 40 years of change in schools: Some personal reflections. *Educational Administration Quarterly,* 29, 213–248.

Milstein, M. M., Bobroff, B. M. & Restine, L. N. (1991). *Internship programs in educational administration.* New York: Teachers College Press.

Monk, D. (1996). Resource allocation for education. *Journal of School Leadership,* 6, 216–242.

Moore, H. (1957). *Studies in school administration.* Washington, DC: American Association of School Administrators.

Mort, P. R. (1964). Studies in educational innovation from the Institute of Administrative Research: An overview. In M. B. Miles (Ed.), *Innovation in education* (pp. 317–328). New York: Teachers College, Columbia University.

Murphy, J. (Ed.). (1993). *Preparing tomorrow's school leaders: Alternative designs.* University Park, PA: University Council for Educational Administration.

National Commission on Excellence in Educational Administration. (1987). *Leaders for America's schools.* Tempe, AZ: University Council for Educational Administration.

National Policy Board for Educational Administration. (1989). *Improving the preparation of school administrators: An agenda for reform.* Charlottesville, VA: The Board and the University of Virginia Curry School of Education.

Ohm, R. E. & Monahan, W. G. (Eds.). (1965). *Educational administration: Philosophy in action.* Norman, OK: University of Oklahoma.

Parsons, T. (1949). The professions and social structure. In *Essays in sociological theory: Pure and applied* (pp. 185–199). Glencoe, IL: Free Press.

Popper, S. H. (1994). *Pathways to the humanities in administrative leadership* (4th ed.). Columbia, MO: University Council for Educational Administration.

Powell, W. W. & DiMaggio, P. J. (Eds.). (1991). *The new institutionalism in organizational analysis.* Chicago: University of Chicago Press.

Richards, C. (1988). The search for equity in educational administration: A commentary. In N. J. Boyan (Ed.). *Handbook of research on educational administration* (pp. 159–168). New York: Longman.

Roemer, J. E. (Ed.). (1986). *Analytic Marxism.* Cambridge, England: Cambridge University Press.

Roethlisberger, F. J. & Dickson, W. J. (1939). *Management and the worker.* Cambridge, MA: Harvard University Press.

Sargent, C. G. & Belisle, E. L. (1955). *Educational administration: Cases and concepts.* New York: Houghton-Mifflin.

Simon, H. A. (1993). Decision making: Rational, non-rational, and irrational. *Educational Administration Quarterly,* 29, 392–411. Other articles on cognitive studies also appear in this themed issue.

Sirotnik, K. A. & Durden, P. C. (1996). The validity of administrator performance assessment systems: The ADI as a case-in-point. *Educational Administration Quarterly,* 32, 539–564.

Smelser, N. J. (1988). Introduction. In N. J. Smelser (Ed.), *Handbook of sociology* (pp. 9–19). Newbury Park, CA: Sage.

Sternberg, R. J. & Davidson, J. E. (1992). Problem solving. In M. C. Alkin (Ed.), *Encyclopedia of Educational Research* (6th ed., pp. 1037–1045). New York: Macmillan.

Tolbert, P. S. & Zucker, L. G. (1996). The institutionalization of institutional theory. In S. R. Clegg, C. Hardy & W. R. Nord (Eds.), *Handbook of organizational studies* (pp. 175–190). London: Sage.

Travers, R. M. W. (1983). *How research has changed American schools: A history from 1840 to the present.* Kalamazoo, MI: Mythos Press.

Tyack, D. (1990). Restructuring in historical perspective: Tinkering toward Utopia. *Teachers College Record*, 92, 170–191.

Waller, W. (1932). *The sociology of teaching*. New York: Wiley.

Waller, W. (1934). Insight and scientific method. *American Journal of Sociology*, 40, 285–297.

Walton, J. (1955). The theoretical study of educational administration. *Harvard Educational Review*, 25, 169–178.

Willis, P. (1977). *Learning to labor*. Lexington, MA: Heath.

Willower, D. J. (1964). The professorship in educational administration: A rationale. In D. J. Willower & J. A. Culbertson (Eds.), *The professorship in educational administration* (pp. 87–105). Columbus, OH and University Park, PA: University Council for Educational Administration and The Pennsylvania State University.

Willower, D. J. (1988). Synthesis and projection. In N. J. Boyan (Ed.), *Handbook of research on educational administration* (pp. 729–747). New York: Longman.

Willower, D. J. (1992). Educational Administration: Intellectual trends. In M. C. Alkin (Ed.), *Encyclopedia of Educational Research* (6th ed., pp. 364–375). New York: Macmillan.

Willower, D. J. (1994). *Educational administration: Inquiry, values, practice* (rev. ed.). Lancaster, PA and Basel, Switzerland: Technomic.

Willower, D. J. (1996). Inquiry in educational administration and the spirit of the times. *Educational Administration Quarterly*, 32, 344–365.

Willower, D. J. & Licata, J. W. (1997). *Values and valuation in the practice of educational administration*. Thousand Oaks, CA: Corwin.

Wynn, R. (1972). *Unconventional methods and materials for preparing educational administrators*. Danville, IL: Interstate.

Yauch, W. A. (1949). *Improving human relations in school administration*. New York: Harper.

Yukl, G. A. (1989). *Leadership in organizations*. Englewood Cliffs, NJ: Prentice-Hall.

CHAPTER 2

The Continuing Quest for a Knowledge Base: 1976–1998

Robert Donmoyer

The first chapter in The American Educational Research Association's first *Handbook of Research on Educational Administration* (Boyan, 1988) was titled, "A Century's Quest for a Knowledge Base." Its author, Jack A. Culbertson, began the chapter by juxtaposing two seminal publications, one from 1875, the other from 1975. The 1875 work was school superintendent William Harold Payne's book on school administration, the first such book ever published. Culbertson said of Payne and his work:

> In outlining his hopes for an educational science, Payne expressed aspirations that were to persist in the thoughts and actions of educational leaders and scholars for at least a century (p. 3).

Most of the remainder of Culbertson's chapter, in fact, chronicles—in baroque-like detail—how various individuals and groups tried to create a science of educational administration and, in the process, professionalize the emerging field.

Before Culbertson does this, however, he jumps ahead one hundred years and discusses a 1975 paper by Thomas Greenfield in which Greenfield critiques research and theory in the educational administration field. Greenfield's critique, as Culbertson notes, often focused on research methodology; he championed the use of qualitative methods and criticized the field's past reliance on quantitative procedures. Yet, as Parsons (1937, p. 481) long ago observed, methodological disputes are seldom about methodology alone, and Culbertson, in fact, notes that undergirding Greenfield's endorsement of qualitative research methods is a very different view of educational organizations than the one held by those who sought to construct a science of educational administration:

"[Greenfield] argued that educational organizations are not 'objective' phenomena regulated by general laws," Culbertson writes; "rather, they are mental constructs that reflect the perceptions and interpretations of the members" (p.3).

Culbertson also implies that Greenfield's conception of organizations challenges the field's traditional—and largely unquestioned—search for a science of education. This implication is stated more explicitly when Greenfield re-enters the picture at the end of Culbertson's chronological account in the role of chief critic of the movement within the field to create scientific theories of educational administration:

> While most professors in the 1970s adjusted in incremental ways to criticism [of the theory movement], Greenfield argued for a more radical reorientation . . . He fired a shot at the theory movement that was heard around the world . . . Striking hard at the presuppositions of the theory movement, he precipitated controversy which has not yet ended (Culbertson, 1988, p. 20).

In short, Greenfield and an intellectual sidekick, Australian critical theorist Richard Bates (1982), are the principal antagonists in Culbertson's epic tale of "a century's quest for a knowledge base." The phenomenological/cultural views Greenfield advanced suggested that both a science of educational administration in particular and a science of human behavior in general are impossible to create because human behavior is constructed, not caused.

While Greenfield's views raised questions of feasibility, Bates' perspective explicitly raised questions about the desirability of trying to create a scientific knowledge base. The focus of Bates' critical theory was on power relationships in general and the political nature of scientific knowledge in particular. In essence, Bates argued that even if social scientists succeeded in constructing a science of causal relationships that make it possible for educational administrators to predict and control events, their findings would reflect and, in the process, help legitimate culturally constructed social relationships, rather than a natural and inevitable reality. Because both material and symbolic resources in hierarchically organized societies are unequally distributed, anything that makes the status quo seem natural, inevitable, and legitimate, in effect, would aid and abet the privileged class and further disadvantage those at the bottom of the social ladder, according to Bates.

Thus the net effect of the Greenfield and Bates critiques, when seen in tandem, is essentially to call into question the legitimacy and appropriateness of the previous century's quest for a scientific knowledge base and the professional status such a knowledge base confers. Unfortunately, however, Greenfield and Bates arrive on the scene too late to play a very significant role in the story Culbertson tells about the field's first 100 years. Except for its final few pages and Culbertson's use of Greenfield at the beginning of his story to foreshadow the contents of these pages, Culbertson's story is an epic tale of a group of people struggling valiantly to generate scientific knowledge and, in the process, to secure for themselves and their academic colleagues (as well as for the practitioners they and their colleagues educated) the sort of professional status specialized knowledge tends to confer (Lagemann, 1997).

To be sure, the people in Culbertson's epic did not always agree about what the term *scientific knowledge* meant and the procedures they proposed using to generate such knowledge varied. Until Greenfield and Bates appear near the end of Culbertson's story, however, the general, interrelated goals of creating a scientific knowledge base and using it to professionalize the educational administration field go largely unchallenged in Culbertson's work.

The task here is to update Culbertson's saga. Have Greenfield and Bates' attempts to radically reorient the academic wing of the field been successful during the 20-plus years after Culbertson's story ends? Or has the search for a scientific knowledge base for educational administration continued and possibly even netted some definitive results? These are the questions to be addressed in this installment of a continuing saga.[1]

Exposition:
The Changing Intellectual Landscape

Any story requires exposition. Here exposition takes the form of a discussion of work by selected scholars from outside the field of educational administration who challenged traditional ideas about science and knowledge, influenced thinking beyond the disciplines or fields of study in which

they worked, and consequently helped shape the general intellectual landscape in which educational administration scholars worked during 1976 to 1998.[2]

The Changing Intellectual Landscape Within Education

In Culbertson's story, Greenfield and Bates play the role of "voices crying in the wilderness" in a field characterized by considerable consensus about how scholars in the field should do their work. Even in the 1970s, however, Greenfield and Bates had articulate and increasingly influential intellectual allies in the fields of curriculum, educational evaluation, and even educational psychology.

Within the field of curriculum, for example, Michael Apple (1979, 1982) and Henry Giroux (1981) were making virtually the same argument about the political nature of scientific knowledge that Bates was making in the educational administration field, and William Pinar (1975) was attempting to reconceptualize the curriculum field in a manner consistent with Greenfield's thinking. Also in the curriculum field, Elliot Eisner (1975, 1979, 1988) discussed the limitations of quantitative research procedures and called for the increased use of qualitative methods, much as Greenfield had done.

The case for qualitative methods also was increasingly being made in the evaluation field (Stake, 1975; Patton 1975, 1980; Parlett and Hamilton, 1977). Guba and Lincoln (1981) were particularly influential advocates for the use of qualitative procedures in educational evaluations. In addition, they shared Greenfield's view that organizations were not objective entities governed by laws but rather ideational entities held together by humanly constructed and intersubjectively shared meanings. They, like Greenfield, also believed that meanings were never static but rather were constantly being reconstructed in the course of human interaction; consequently, meanings could not simply function as a stand-in for causes or even be cast in the role of intervening variables in the traditional cause-effect explanatory framework.

Even the renowned educational psychologist and quantitative methodologist, Lee Cronbach (1975), was beginning to question the utility of quantitative procedures and argue for research approaches that are "historical more than scientific" (p. 125) during the period when Greenfield first attached the theory movement within the educational administration field. Cronbach cited Geertz (1973) (see the discussion of Geertz below) and invoked Geertz's notion of "thick description" in arguing that a researcher's "first task is to describe and interpret the effect [he or she is investigating] anew in each locale, perhaps taking into account factors unique to that locale" (p. 125). Later, Cronbach would challenge in even more significant ways the logic and assumptions that undergirded most of the work done in the field of educational psychology up to that point, including the work he, himself, did during the first part of his distinguished career.

Cronbach's story, in fact, mirrors the changes in thinking at the individual level that were occurring in much of the educational research community as a whole. The Cronbach story begins in the mid-1950s. Cronbach had been given an award for achievement in the area of educational psychology by the American Psychological Association. In an address to the annual meeting of the association after receiving his award, Cronbach acknowledged that the field of educational psychology had, up to that point, failed to deliver on promises made. It had not, in short, produced the sort of definitive generalizations that psychologists like E. L. Thorndike (1910) had promised would make us "masters of our own souls as we are now masters of heat and light" (p. 6).

Cronbach (1957) then went on to tell the American Psychological Association that the complexity of human phenomena required an alteration in the traditional research game plan. Rather than searching for laws that were universal and context free, Cronbach argued that researchers should attempt to identify cause-effect relationships between certain educational treatments on the one hand and certain types of individuals (in Cronbach's terms, individuals with certain aptitudes) on the other. In colloquial terms, he was making a kind of learning styles argument, although Cronbach's aptitudes category encompassed a broader array of variables—everything from ethnicity to IQ to personality type—than is normally encompassed by the learning styles construct.

In the mid-1970s, however, after nearly 20 years of searching for "aptitude × treatment interactions" and nearly 20 years of frustration brought on by "inconsistent findings coming from roughly similar inquiries," Cronbach (1975) told the American Psychological Association:

> Once we attend to interactions, we enter a hall of mirrors that extends to infinity. However far we carry our analysis to third order or fifth order or any other, untested interactions of still higher order can be envisioned (p. 119).

Compounding the problem of complexity, according to Cronbach, was the problem of culture. Cronbach cited Bronfenbrenner's (1958) historical look at child rearing practices of middle- and lower-class parents to demonstrate the significance of this variable: Class differences documented in the 1950s were often just the reverse of practices that had been observed in the 1930s. Cronbach concluded:

> The trouble, as I see it, is that we cannot store up generalizations and constructs for ultimate assembly into a network. It is as if we needed a gross of dry cells to power an engine and could only make one a month. The energy would leak out of the first cells before we had half the battery completed. So it is with the potency of our generalizations" (p. 123).

In his 1975 article, Cronbach emphasized that the social world was no less lawful than the physical world. The problem was that social laws were too complex and the social world too changeable to identify laws in the social domain. By the early 1980s, however, Cronbach had rejected even the notion of social laws. He began suggesting that the entire cause-effect way of thinking that undergirded traditional views of social science was an inappropriate way to characterize social phenomena. In a 1982 paper, for example, Cronbach declared that human action is constructed not caused; those who expect research to produce the sort of definitive cause-effect generalizations that can be translated into prescriptions for practice or even general theories that can simply inform practice are, in Cronbach's words, "waiting for Godot."

By the 1980s, in other words, Cronbach—arguably the most influential scholar in the areas of educational psychology and quantitative research methodology—had arrived at a view of human action and organizational life that was remarkably similar to the view being propounded by Greenfield in the educational administration field. The view that social action was constructed and not caused also lent credence to Bates position that the regularities observed in the social world were humanly created artifacts, rather than a reflection of natural laws.

The Changing Intellectual Landscape Outside of Education

Ideas consistent with the thinking of Greenfield and Bates could also be found outside the education field. Indeed, changes in the intellectual landscape probably were even more pronounced in the social sciences and the humanities. A chorus of sociologists, anthropologists, philosophers, and organizational theorists, for example, endorsed the phenomenological and cultural view of organizational life that Greenfield advanced within the educational administration community.

Examples of Support for Greenfield's Thinking

Herbert Blumer, the father of the symbolic interactionist school of sociology, for instance, argued in 1969 that human beings' behavior toward things is based on the meanings that things have for them and that meanings are generated through social interaction. Blumer also argued that meanings are not static but must constantly be constructed and reconstructed by actors during social interaction. Thus even if meanings and reasons are allowed to substitute for causes in a cause-effect explanatory framework—if we treat them, in other words, as independent or possibly intervening variables—Blumer would not be satisfied. According to Blumer, the cause-effect explanatory framework itself sends an inaccurate message regardless of its substantive content. The social world, according to Blumer, is not a deterministic one and, hence, any attempt to discover cause and effect relationships or to build theory grounded in testable propositions about such relationships is doomed to failure.

Clifford Geertz, in the field of cultural anthropology, also indicated that humanly constructed meanings were what held social organizations together. Geertz also emphasized the importance of attending to variation across social organizations. Rather than focusing on universal theories that ignored and obscured cultural variation, Geertz argued for the importance of what he called "local knowledge" (Geertz, 1983) and the need for "thick description" of particular idiosyncratic contexts (Geertz, 1973).

Similar ideas were also being advanced in the field of philosophy. The importance of attending to contextual idiosyncrasy, for instance, was a theme in the influential book by philosopher Peter Winch (1958, c1990) entitled *The Idea of a Social Science and Its Relation to Philosophy*. In the book, Winch, much like Greenfield, Blumer, and Geertz, argued that meaning was the defining characteristic of organizational life, that meaning was socially constructed, and that different social groups constructed radically different meanings. For all of the above reasons, Winch argued that social science, at least as it has been traditionally defined, was not a viable concept.

The problems with traditional notions of social science were also being emphasized in more application-oriented fields. Organizational theorist, Donald Schön (1983), for example, talked about a contextually-oriented, problem-centered epistemology of practice that was radically different from and virtually incommensurable with the theory-oriented conceptions of knowledge that undergirded work in the academy.

Examples of Support for Bates' Ideas

Bates' idea that no knowledge is objective and that all knowledge, including scientific knowledge, is inevitably political was also supported in one way or another by a growing cadre of scholars from a variety of fields and theoretical orientations outside of education, including the philosophy and history of science (Kuhn, 1962, c1970; Feyerabend, 1970; Toulmin, 1983, 1972), the sociology of knowledge (Berger and Luckmann, 1967; Young, 1971; Garfinkel, 1967; Gusfield, 1976), critical theory (Williams, 1963; Habermas, 1984–87, 1978), feminist theory (Harding, 1991, 1986; Haraway, 1989, 1988), postmodernist and poststructuralist thought (Foucault, 1972; Lyotard, 1988; Cherryholmes, 1988; Marcus and Clifford, 1986), and Black studies (Stanfield, 1985 and Gordon, Miller, and Rollock, 1990).

Thomas Kuhn, for example, challenged the notion that scientific knowledge, even in the physical sciences, was objective and uncontaminated by human subjectivity. He indicated that scientists, at least in reasonably mature scientific disciplines, employed what he called paradigms to simplify the complexity of the empirical world. These paradigms were not primarily determined by the data; rather, they determined what the relevant data were.

Kuhn, in fact, used imagery from gestalt psychology along with important caveats to explain what happens when a field of study shifts from one paradigm to another. Such a shift is like "a change in visual gestalt," according to Kuhn. "The marks on paper that were first seen as a bird are now seen as an antelope, or vice versa." He also added that this comparison can be a bit misleading:

> Scientists do not see something as something else; instead, they simply see it . . . . In addition, the scientist does not preserve the gestalt subject's freedom to switch back and forth between ways of seeing. Nevertheless, the switch of gestalt, particularly because it is today so familiar, is a useful elementary prototype for what occurs in a full-scale paradigm shift (Kuhn, 1970, p. 85).

Kuhn's paradigms were not synonymous with Bates' hegemonic cultural beliefs, of course, but the difference had more to do with the very different problems and phenomena Kuhn and Bates were focusing on than with the general view of knowledge and knowing which undergirded each scholar's thinking. Kuhn was trying to account for conceptual change in the physical sciences, while Bates and his fellow critical theorists within and outside of education were trying to account for inequities in the larger culture.

The psychological and social mechanisms identified in both accounts and the resulting epistemologies, however, were quite similar. Kuhn's account of paradigm revolutions in the physical sciences, for instance, suggested that organizations (in his account, academic disciplines) were held together by ideas and beliefs, that these ideas and beliefs were more constructed than discovered, that some organization members have a vested interest in maintaining existing ideas and beliefs, and consequently that changing ideas, beliefs, and, by implication, organizational life is inevitably a political process. Bates and his fellow critical theorists, of course, told a similar tale about stability and change in the world beyond academia.

Contemporary linguists' discussions of the nature of language help clarify and also provide additional support for Bates' views about the political nature of social life in general and science, in particular, by suggesting how one very important cultural artifact, language, can function as a political weapon. Linguists do this by emphasizing the constructive nature of language. Their argument, in essence, is that the process of perceiving and the formulation of perceptions into language are not discrete, sequential activities. Language does not simply point to pre-existing things and ideas or even pre-existing perceptions of things and ideas; rather, language helps construct the world we see and know. Linguists demonstrate the constructive nature of language by pointing to differences in language across cultures: "If words stood for pre-existing concepts," Saussure (1974) wrote, "they would all have exact equivalents in meaning from one language to the next, but this is not true" (p. 116).

The cross-cultural linguistic differences Saussure and like-minded linguists alluded to are most apparent when we look at cultures that are radically different from our own. The anthropologist, Conklin (1955), for example, reported that the Hanunoo people of the Philippines have only four terms to describe color and that these terms also simultaneously describe the texture of objects. But even among cultures that are quite similar, there are often subtle but significant linguistic differences that impact what we say and ultimately what we see and know. Belsey (1992), for instance, noted that even contemporary languages often divide the color spectrum differently.

> In Welsh, the color glas (blue), like the Latin glaucus, includes elements that English would identify as green or grey. The boundaries are placed differently in the two languages and the Welsh equivalent of English grey might be glas or llwyd (brown) (Belsey, 1992, p. 39).

Belsey added:

> Nor is this process of differentiation confined to objects of the senses. The distinction in French between *science* and *connaissance* does not correspond to the English *science* and *knowledge*: indeed each term can be translated from one language to the other only approximately and by what seems a very circumlocutory process, because the words have the effect of limiting each other's range of meaning within the interdependent whole which constitutes each language (Belsey, 1992, p. 40).

But what, one might ask, do these insights from linguists about the constructive nature of language have to do with politics and with what Bates claims about the political nature of science? In commonsense parlance, at least, the term politics implies a process for allocating scarce resources, for legitimating certain values rather than others, and ultimately for determining who wins and who loses.

A relatively simple example can demonstrate how language and other cultural artifacts can function politically: For years, researchers characterized lower-class and minority students as *culturally disadvantaged* rather than using a less judgmental and somewhat more neutral label such as *culturally different*. To the extent that the culturally disadvantaged label was uncritically accepted, its use promoted uncritical acceptance of the "fact" that the disproportionately high failure rate for poor minority students resulted from inadequacies in the children, their families, and their cultures. It also directed attention away from inadequacies within the mainstream culture and its schools. The label, in short, aided and abetted those who were engaged in "blaming the victim." Researchers' uncritical acceptance of the label and their use of it in framing their "scientific" work

helped legitimate the label and the inequities such a label obscured and, in effect, sanctioned.

This simple example demonstrates three things. First, it demonstrates quite clearly that aspects of everyday life, including everyday language, do indeed produce winners and losers. Therefore, the sort of politics Bates and his intellectual allies talk about is not totally incompatible with our commonsense notion of politics.

Second, the example demonstrates that, although the sort of politics being talked about by Bates and others who see knowledge as inevitably political is not totally incompatible with commonsense notions of politics, it also differs from our traditional Machiavellian conception of politics in at least one significant respect. A Machiavellian view assumes that individuals see the world in the same way but have different, often mutually exclusive interests that they consciously attempt to maximize through the use of power. The sort of politics being talked about by Bates and other critical, postmodern, and like-minded scholars is a politics of differing perceptions; "a fascism in our heads" is what postmodern scholars call it. It is also, contemporary linguists remind us, a politics that plays itself out in our language as well as in the routines and standard operating procedures of organizational life. Hence, although language as well as perceptions and procedures can certainly be consciously manipulated to serve Machiavellian purposes (consider, for example, television commercials and photo opportunities in political campaigns), no Machiavellian intent is required for perceptual/procedural politics to allocate resources, legitimate values, and determine winners and losers. This characteristic makes this version of politics more subtle, more difficult to recognize, and therefore potentially more insidious than Machiavellian politics.

A final and, for this discussion, crucial implication can be drawn from the example presented above: Empirical research cannot free us from the spell of perceptual and procedural politics. Indeed, in the example presented above, empirical research helped legitimate the disadvantaged label that, after all, was not determined by the data but, to a large extent, determined what the data were and what they meant. Therefore, Bates and his allies inside and outside of education can legitimately claim a professionalism that is grounded in a knowledge of empirical research is not an alternative to political control; rather it is simply a different kind of political control.

The Changing Educational Landscape Beyond the Academy

The big ideas discussed above have not only been a prominent part of the academic landscape during the 20-plus years since Culbertson's story ended; many of these ideas also began to "trickle down" to more colloquial and common sense ways of thinking and talking during this period.

(One might also argue for a trickle-up effect, of course.) For instance, consider the following speech by Trudy the Bag Lady, a central character in Jane Wagner's (1988) popular play, *The Search for Signs of Intelligent Life in the Universe*:

> I refuse to be intimidated by reality anymore. After all, what is reality anyway? Nothin' but a collective hunch . . . a primitive method of crowd control that got out of hand (p. 18).

Bates and Greenfield said much the same thing, although not as succinctly or as humorously.

Also, during the 1980s and '90s, school and business leaders and even a U.S. President appropriated Kuhn's language about paradigms to discuss their work; leaders within and outside of the field of education began to increasingly think and talk of organizations in cultural terms, rather than in terms of bureaucratic rules, regulations, and organizational charts (Peters and Waterman, 1982; Deal and Kennedy, 1982; Sergiovanni and Corbally, 1984; Sarason, 1996, 1971, c1982); and the media began to portray social science research in increasingly skeptical terms (Washington Post, 1994). In addition, critical theorists concerns about class, race, and gender became central concerns in real-world public policy debates, as well and, even in an era dominated by conservative Republicans and new Democrats, these issues still frame much of the policy debate.

The Storyline: Building Big Tents

The thinking described in the previous section created an intellectual environment during the period from 1976 to 1998 that was very different from the intellectual environment during the preceding 100 years. Consequently, an account of the 1976–1998 period requires a very different sort of storyline than the kind employed by Culbertson. The story for this period cannot be an epic tale of a field striving valiantly to produce scientific knowledge and, as a consequence, to guarantee professional status for its members. Nor, for that matter, can it be a simple reversal of the Culbertson tale; in short, it is not a story of Greenfield and Bates' ideas triumphing and of the field being recreated in the images of organizations and knowledge they provided. Rather, the storyline here must be more akin to the storyline of many contemporary short stories that are nonlinear, essentially plotless, somewhat disjointed, and riddled with ruptures, contradictions, and inconsistencies.

Formalizing and Institutionalizing the Quest for a Knowledge Base

The complexity of the situation may not immediately be apparent because it is indeed the case that, during the pe-

riod of time being discussed in this chapter, the search for a knowledge base for educational administration not only continued, it also was formalized and institutionalized. In its 1989 report, "Improving the Preparation of School Administrators: An Agenda for Reform," the National Policy Board for Educational Administration, a consortium of 10 national school administration-related organizations, recommended that the field rethink and clearly articulate its knowledge base. The board even suggested seven general categories of knowledge that could be used to frame the discussion: (1) societal and cultural influences on schooling; (2) teaching and learning processes and school improvement; (3) organizational theory; (4) methodologies of organizational studies and policy analysis; (5) leadership and management processes and functions; (6) policy studies and politics of education; and (7) moral and ethical dimensions of schooling.

Subsequently, the University Council for Educational Administration (UCEA), one of the National Policy Board's member organizations, took up the challenge and began a 10-year effort "to identify the knowledge essential for school leaders to solve critical contemporary problems of practice" (UCEA 1992, 13). The first phase of the UCEA project was completed in 1993 and the products of that first phase were published by McGraw-Hill in 1994 in the form of a set of documents called PRIMIS (Hoy, 1994b). PRIMIS is organized around the categories proposed by the National Policy Board. Each of the seven sections of PRIMIS includes an overview essay about the category, a case study, an annotated bibliography of representative readings, and a number of illustrative papers.

Patrick Forsyth (1994), the executive director of UCEA, indicated that the second phase of the 10-year project would be built around seven additional objectives: (1) to review the completeness of the seven domain structure, making adjustments and additions where necessary; (2) to expand the knowledge in each domain; (3) to analyze each knowledge domain for adequacy; (4) to modify the content of each domain; (5) to articulate the knowledge of each domain; (6) to identify appropriate media for communication to multiple audiences; and (7) to search for ways to integrate knowledge across domains.

These goals display little or no sensitivity to the critiques of knowledge put forth by Bates and Greenfield in the administration field and their intellectual allies elsewhere. Forsyth's comments suggest that articulating a knowledge base is a technical problem that may be difficult but certainly not logically impossible to accomplish. One gets no sense in Forsyth's talk of completeness and adequacy, for example, of Bates' notion that knowledge will inevitably serve the interests of some at the expense of others or Greenfield's notion that social life is always in the process of being constructed and reconstructed. Indeed, the very metaphor of a knowledge base seems totally out of sync with Greenfield's constructivist view of organizational life, but Forsyth's comments suggest he is either unaware of or unconcerned about such inconsistencies.

Expanding the Definition of Knowledge

The developers of PRIMIS, however, could not totally ignore the thinking of individuals like Bates and Greenfield. As the first part of this chapter indicates, their thinking began to be mirrored throughout the academy and even beyond during the 20-plus years following the conclusion of Culbertson's tale. Furthermore, even within the educational administration field, there was an ever-growing and increasingly vocal cadre of scholars who could in some sense be considered Greenfield and Bates' intellectual descendants. This group included a growing cadre of feminist scholars. To be sure, some feminist scholars used relatively traditional methods to demonstrate that gender bias was endemic both to educational administration practice (Shakeshaft, 1989; Pounder, 1988; Eagly, Karau and Johnson, 1992) and the way traditional research methods were employed in the field (Epp, Sackney, and Kustaski, 1994; Shakeshaft and Hanson, 1986). There were also those, however, who used feminist critiques to develop and enact different—sometimes radically different—approaches to inquiry (e.g. Dillard, 1995; Capper, 1992; Glazer, 1991; Marshall, Patterson, Rogers, and Steele, 1996).

The cadre of less-than-traditional scholars also included: advocates of qualitative research such as Lincoln and Guba (1985), as well as Catherine Marshall and Gretchen Rossman (1989); scholars of color such as Kofi Lomotey and Cynthia Dillard (1995) who argued that traditional methods of doing research were laced with ethnocentric biases and who sometimes made the case for and used alternative methodologies that they believed were more consistent with and could better represent their particular life experiences; critical theorists such as William Foster (1986) whose book *Paradigms and Promises: New Approaches to Educational Administration* was increasingly being used in administrator preparation programs throughout the country; critical ethnographers such as Gary Anderson (1989); scholars like Stephen Ball (1991, 1989, 1987) and Joseph Blase (1988, 1989) whose work on micropolitics represents a Greenfield-like take on the study of politics of school life; postmodernists like Spencer Maxcy (1994, 1995) and James Scheurich (1994, 1997); and proponents of the use of queer theory to make sense of educational organizations and administrative issues such as Wanda Pillow (1996). Even Daniel Griffiths, a virtual patron saint of the scientific theory movement Greenfield railed against, discovered chaos *theory* (Griffiths, Hart, and Blair, 1991) and began to argue for theoretical pluralism (Griffiths, 1995b). From a

practical and political standpoint, if a document base was to be created for the field, the thinking of at least some these individuals would have to be included.

But how could such scholars and their work be incorporated into the field's now institutionalized quest for a knowledge base without displacing the thinking of those who were already at the center of things and whose ideas many of this new cadre of scholars were challenging? A motion to develop an eighth knowledge category for emergent, nontraditional knowledge was defeated at a UCEA plenary session. Instead, the developers of PRIMIS chose a more subtle solution, a solution which is well known to political operatives who practice what some call "big tent politics."

In the political world, big tent politics involves individuals and organizations (political parties, for example) supporting proposals with contradictory goals in an effort to garner broad-based support and build winning coalitions. Legislators, for example, have been known to vote both for price supports to keep tobacco farmers in business and for funding for advertising campaigns to discourage smoking.

In the case of PRIMIS, big tent politics took the form of expanding the definition of knowledge to include nontraditional along with more traditional work. PRIMIS editor, Wayne Hoy, in fact, confirms in his introduction to the document base, that he and the other developers "were charged with the responsibility of (among other things) incorporating multicultural, emergent, feminist, and traditional perspectives" (Hoy, 1994a, p.7), and the big tent strategy is quite apparent in many of the products produced. Consider, for example, the products produced and collected by the team that constructed the Organization Studies section of PRIMIS. The team's overview essay discusses functionalist, neo-Marxist, feminist, postmodern, and pragmatism-based theories of organizations, and it seems to endorse eclecticism as a strategy for making sense of organizational life and for acting intelligently in organizational contexts. In at least one other section of PRIMIS, the Societal and Cultural Influences on Schooling section, nontraditional perspectives are at the center of the documents on display. One would be hard pressed to find in the Societal and Cultural Influences on Schooling section, for instance, examples of Parsonian-type functionalist thinking.

Indeed, the very fact that Societal and Cultural Influences on Schooling, historically an underdiscussed topic in the educational administration literature (Cambron-McCabe, 1993), was elevated to one of the seven categories of knowledge in PRIMIS could be considered a victory of sorts for Bates and his fellow critical theorists. A similar case might be made about the impact of Greenfield's work on the decision to make moral and ethical dimensions of schooling a discrete knowledge category. Ethics, after all, was a topic that positivism (the intellectual tradition historically associated with the theory movement[3]) regarded as subjective, incapable of being studied scientifically, and, consequently, unworthy of academic attention (Hanfling, 1981). At the very least, its prominent place in the University Council for Educational Administration's document base combined with the growing literature on this topic elsewhere (Beck and Murphy, 1994; Starratt, 1991; Heslep, 1997; Enomoto, 1997; Greenfield, Jr., 1985; Marshall, Patterson, Rogers, and Steele, 1996; Evers, 1985; Strike, Haller, and Soltis, 1988; Husman, 1990) is further evidence that the tent under which educational administration scholars gather has been enlarged.

Other Examples of Big Tent Politics in the Field

There are many other indicators that an academic version of big tent politics has become a virtual standard operating procedure within the educational administration field. Here I will focus on two of the most prominent examples, beginning with the fields most prominent academic journal, *Educational Administration Quarterly*.

A Journal as a Big Tent

When one is discussing the *Educational Administration Quarterly*, in fact, one need not rely on metaphorical talk about big tents to make the point about the field expanding to accommodate the thinking of Greenfield, Bates, and their intellectual descendents in the field. Rather, one can simply point out that, during the time period being discussed in this chapter, this "quarterly" quite literally went from publishing three to four and eventually five issues per year and that much of the additional space has been taken up by the sort of work that Bates and Greenfield would undoubtedly endorse. During the 20-plus years since Culbertson's story ended, in fact, *Educational Administration Quarterly* has published articles by both Greenfield (1978, 1980) and Bates (1980, 1987, 1989); generally sympathetic articles about Greenfield's body of work (Harris, 1996; Samier, 1996)[4] and Bates' critical theory (Robinson, 1994); special issues on nontraditional theory and research (Griffiths, 1991) and the implications of post-positivist views of science (Evers and Lakomski, 1996), as well as a number of articles about the sort of qualitative methods Greenfield championed (Owens, 1982; Wolcott, 1985).

There may be an even better indicator of impact: The journal has not just published work about qualitative methods; since the early 1980s, it also has published numerous studies that employed qualitative research procedures. Indeed, one can find a fairly wide array of different kinds of qualitative methods on display on the pages of *Educational Administration Quarterly* throughout the 1980s and '90s, including: speech acts analysis borrowed from the field of linguistics (Levine, Donnellon, Gioia, and Sims, 1984); ethnographic semantics techniques adapted from cognitive anthropology (Donmoyer, 1985); more or less

traditional case study work (Brieschke, 1983); qualitative work inspired by an ingenious blend of functionalism and critical theory (Reyes and Capper, 1991); Geertzian-inspired "thick description" (Reitzug and Reeves, 1992); evaluation methods that focused as much on the values implicit in the conceptualizations that framed data collection as on the data themselves (Donmoyer, 1991); and an analysis strategy that compares and contrasts the storylines that emerge when different theoretical perspectives (including the perspectives championed by Bates and Greenfield) are layered onto the data (Scheurich and Imber, 1991).

In addition to the methodological diversity found on the pages of *Educational Administration Quarterly*, one can also point to more substantive indicators of the impact of Greenfield's and Bates' thinking on the journal's pages. One example is a special 1992 issue edited by Ann Weaver Hart and Diana Pounder that featured research-based articles on leadership produced by two research centers funded by the very mainstream Office of Educational Research and Improvement of the United States Department of Education. In his introductory essay to the special issue, Thomas Sergiovanni both echoes Greenfield's meaning-based conception of organizational life and certifies that Greenfield's conception of organizational life is now prominently displayed on the pages of *Educational Administration Quarterly*. "The invited articles in this special issue," Sergiovanni writes,

> affirm that educational administration is moving in a new direction and that's good news. In recent years, educational administration bashing has become somewhat of a sport with much of the criticism deserved. We gave too much emphasis to studying and writing about schools as if they were organizations and events in schools as if they were manifestations of organizational behavior. With the organization frame in mind, we sought to identify generic characteristics of schools thought to be important, to validate competencies needed for effective behavior, and to search for steps and procedures thought to be the most true. The language we used tended to be abstract with images of schools and schooling, and teachers and principals plugged in almost as an afterthought. Research designs, theoretical speculations, and practice prescriptions were largely grounded in social science and management constructs. The articles in this issue take a different stance by legitimizing the subjective realities of practice, emphasizing meaning, acknowledging the moral as a source of authority for what happens in schools, focusing on the context and substance of schooling, and viewing human nature as encompassing the ability of individuals to sacrifice self-interest for ideals held (pp. 304–5).

On the other hand, traditional thinking and traditional forms of research have not disappeared from the pages of the journal. In the Fall of 1987, for example, the journal devoted an entire issue to the notion of culture (Cusick, 1987). This sort of attention to the cultural dimensions of organizations might be taken as a victory of sorts for the Greenfield camp; even Richard Bates (1987) was one of the invited contributors. Several of the other contributors, however, tended to treat culture as a kind of intervening variable that leaders could manipulate to produce desired effects, a decidedly unGreenfield-like idea. Quite different conceptions of culture, in other words, were allowed to coexist—without comment and apparent conflict—on the pages of the journal.

Here is another example of peaceful coexistence: The lead article for the special issue on research methodology in which Wolcott's (1985) article on qualitative methods appears is Sirotnik and Borstein's (1985) "Measurement and Statistical Issues in Multilevel Research on Schooling." The concluding article, authored by Crehan (1985) is "An Exploration of the Usefulness of Meta-Analysis in Educational Administration." Greenfield and Wolcott's conception of organizations as ideational entities held together by meanings that are constructed (and constantly being reconstructed) by an organization's members is nowhere in evidence—even as a foil—in either the Crehan article or the article by Sirotnik and Borstein.

Nor can Greenfield's influence be seen in the introduction written by the special issue's guest editors, Haller and Knapp. In this introduction, the two editors first indicate that they do not wish to be mere dust bowl empiricists. Consequently, they tell us, a conception of what research in educational administration should be guided decision making about what to include in their special issue on research methodology for the field. And what is their conception of school administration as a field of inquiry? "It is suggested here," they write,

> that it can be usefully conceived as the study of the patterned relationships among the five commonplaces of subject matter, learners, teachers, milieus, and administrators with particular attention to the effects of those relationships on the transmission of subject matter to learners (Haller and Knapp, p. 161).

For the guest editors, in other words, research in educational administration revolved around the search for cause-effect relationships. Given this definition, one wonders how an ethnographer such as Wolcott got invited to contribute. The field's commitment to playing big tent politics is the likely explanation.

The same sort of mixture of antithetical perspectives can be seen in more recent issues of the journal. The February 1992 issue, for example, contains both an article by Colleen Capper (1992) that employs a critique strategy rooted in feminist and poststructural theory and an examination of the relationship between gender and leadership style which uses the very traditional methodological lens of meta-analysis (Eagly, Karau, and Johnson, 1992). Meta-analysis techniques, of course, treat as unproblematic the very assumptions feminist poststructuralists problematize.

Similarly, we find in the 1996 volume of the journal, not only the special issue on post-positivist conceptions of science (Evers and Lakomski, 1996) and Harris' (1996) sympathetic discussion of Greenfield's aesthetics, but also Hallinger and Heck's (1996) review of empirical research on the principal's role in school effectiveness. The review focuses on such things as sample size ("Smaller samples became problematic when seeking to determine effects on student achievement" [Hallinger and Heck, 1996, p. 35]), the number of dependent variables used, the analytic techniques used to make sense of quantitative data (mere description, correlational analysis, T-tests, ANOVA/MANOVA, regression, and structural/path modeling), whether statistically significant effects of principal leadership behavior were found, and the a priori theories employed to conceptualize hypotheses to be tested and make sense of relationships found ("The review reinforces the importance of beginning with theoretically informed models of leadership and how it influences school performance" [Hallinger and Heck, 1996, p. 34].).

The authors, in fact, acknowledge that the criteria they used for selecting studies to review "weighed heavily toward quantitative studies" and state their belief that "quantitative methods are essential for assessing the extent to which administrative effects are present in schools" (Hallinger and Heck, 1996, p. 14). They do not dismiss qualitative research entirely, however. In fact, they say that "the dearth of mixed-method studies is disappointing." "The use of qualitative approaches is essential," they write, "if we are to understand the more complex processes that underlie cause and effect relationships" (Hallinger and Heck, 1996, p. 14). This use of qualitative methods to ferret out difficult to discern intervening variables would hardly have placated Greenfield, of course. Even Evers and Lakomski, the editors of *Educational Administration Quarterly*'s special issue on post-positivist conceptions of science, would undoubtedly argue that Hallinger and Heck overestimated the potential for empirical data (whether qualitative or quantitative) to provide definitive answers to the sort of questions they pose. No mention is made of these disagreements, however; there is room in the journal's spacious tent for everyone.

Do not mistake my point here. I am not attempting to criticize the *Educational Administration Quarterly* articles I have referenced or even at this point to critique the journal's big tent practices. (In fact, I have selected the articles to discuss because I believe them to be truly excellent examples of work within the scholarly traditions they represent; consequently, they reflect well on the journal that published them.) My purpose at this point is merely descriptive; I want to demonstrate (1) that a diverse array of scholarly traditions and orientations are indeed represented on the pages of the *Educational Administration Quarterly*; and (2) that those who work within a particular orientation seldom engage with the thinking of those who hold a different orientation. There are a handful of exceptions to this second generalization (see, for example, the Evers and Lakomski [1996] rejoinder to Scheurich and Griffiths' [1995] review of the collected works of his old nemesis, Thomas Greenfield). For most of the 20-plus years since Culbertson's saga ended, however, contributors to *Educational Administration Quarterly* have treated those with whom they disagree with benign neglect. Instead of discussing and debating, our field has diversified its document bases and expanded the pages in its journals. Metphorically speaking, it has enlarged its tents and welcomed very diverse people inside. Those who enter find a comfortable and polite, but also a very balkanized environment.

An Introductory Text as a Big Tent

The other example of big tent politics I want to focus on appears in a most unlikely place: Hoy and Miskel's 1996 edition of *Educational Administration: Theory, Research, and Practice*. This book, arguably the field's most influential introductory text, is nothing if not an updated, somewhat more sophisticated version of theory movement thinking, the sort of thinking, in other words, that Greenfield and Bates challenged. The authors, for example, endorse Fred N. Kerlinger's (1986) traditional definitions of both theory ("A theory is a set of interrelated constructs [concepts], definitions, and propositions that present a systematic view of phenomena by specifying relations among variables with the purpose of explaining and predicting phenomena" [p. 9]) and research ("Scientific research is systematic, controlled, empirical, and critical investigation of hypothetical prepositions about the presumed relations among natural phenomena" [p. 10]); limit their criticisms of the theory movement to acknowledging relatively modest and clearly correctable flaws (such as its neglect of gender issues, its failure to examine schools in the larger social context in which schools exist, its tendency to seek universal rather than context-specific theories); and endorse Willower's 1987 conclusion "that theoretical explanation linked to careful empirical work is central to the whole enterprise of educational administration" (Hoy and Miskel, 1996, p. 22). "Although problems in the development of theory in educational administration remain," Hoy and Miskel contend, "that does not mean that the effort should be abandoned" (Hoy and Miskel, 1996, p. 22).

Yet despite this obvious affinity for the theory movement, Hoy and Miskel also devote a section of their book to what they label "emergent nontraditional perspectives" in which they discuss in exceedingly positive terms critical theory, postmodern, poststructural, and feminist theory approaches to inquiry. "The perspectives supply a countervailing set of forces to traditional organizational science," they write. They add:

These alternative views focus attention on important, contemporary organization issues: the irrational, the unique, the repressed, the borderline, the rejected, the marginal, the silenced, the decentered, and the powerless (Hoy and Miskel, 1996, p. 17).

In short, even in a book that touts the virtues of traditional conceptions of social science, the authors have kind words for perspectives that they acknowledge "often repudiate the claims of objectivity, causality, rationality, materialistic reality, and the universal rules of inquiry used by the scientific social sciences" (Hoy and Miskel, 1996, p. 17).

Summary

Educational administration academics during the 20-plus years since Culbertson's 100-year saga ended have not ignored the changes in the larger intellectual landscape outlined in the first part of this chapter, but neither have they redefined research and inquiry in the field in the direction scholars like Greenfield and Bates proposed. The field instead built a bigger tent (or, to use a less metaphorical example, expanded the number of issues of *Educational Administration Quarterly* published every year) and invited the intellectual descendants of Greenfield and Bates inside.

Critiques of the Big Tent Strategy

Tokenism, Inappropriate Framing, and the Problems with Eclecticism

This big tent strategy is not without its critics, of course. There have been charges of tokenism, for example. The discussion of emergent nontraditional perspectives in the Hoy and Miskel text discussed above, for instance, takes up only three and a half pages in a book of nearly 500 pages. Indeed, the authors admit at the outset of their brief discussion of nontraditional perspectives that their treatment of organizational thought in the rest of their book is "conventional and orthodox" and "emphasizes mainline theory and research, which is anchored in the traditions of the social sciences" (p. 17).

Even when nontraditional work is given relatively equal time, however, the big tent strategy can generate a barrage of criticism. PRIMIS is a prime example. James Scheurich, for instance, has criticized the UCEA document base on the grounds that the seven general categories of knowledge proposed by the National Policy Board for Educational Administration and utilized by the University Council of Educational Administration in developing PRIMIS frame the knowledge base discussion in very traditional ways. He compares attempts to fit new perspectives into these traditional categories to pouring wine into old bottles. "While it is certainly possible, in a practical sense, to pour new wine in old bottles by redefining each subject area to fit an interpretivist or critical theory frame," Scheurich (1995) writes,

> the old functionalist list of seven areas would not be the list that critical theorists would derive from their frame of reference. For instance, from a critical theory position, moral and ethical dimensions, one of the seven subject areas, would not be categorically separated from the other areas; these dimensions would be redefined as emancipatory interests and would be infused throughout all categories. Also, 'leadership and management processes and functions,' another of the subject areas, is according to critical theorists, historically related to hierarchy-oriented, authoritarian control of subordinates . Although a critical theorist might be able to survive within the Board's seven areas, it would be neither an honest survival nor a comfortable one (pp. 21–22).

Scheurich also notes that many of the paradigms represented in the UCEA knowledge base are inherently contradictory. PRIMIS, in other words, does not so much provide the field with a knowledge base; rather, it represents at best a collection of very different and even at times incommensurable knowledge bases. It does not, in other words, provide the sort of definitive answers anticipated by most characters in Culbertson's 100-year chronicle. Rather, the best that scholars can do under their big tent is to lay out a smorgasbord of possibilities and encourage decision makers to sample it eclectically.

Significant problems are associated with this sort of eclecticism, however:

> [A]lthough the eclectic response does a good job of exposing future professionals to alternative possibilities, it says little or nothing about how to choose among these alternatives. Even greater problems come into view when we focus on the expectation that the knowledge base we articulate will help legitimate professionals. Quite simply, a knowledge base which simply articulates an array of alternative, often contradictory paradigms and perspectives inspires little confidence because it provides little assurance that professionals will know what to do; indeed Broudy (1981) has argued that the presence of conflicting educational paradigms is the source of professional educator's credibility problem. It is not surprising, therefore, that NCATE, the national accrediting organization, does not consider eclecticism an adequate response to its standard that education programs be based on a clearly defined knowledge base (Donmoyer, 1995, pp. 18–19).

Even More Fundamental Critiques

Other critics have challenged the very idea that any sort of academic knowledge, whether traditional or nontraditional, can ground a profession such as educational administration. Littrell and Foster (1995), for example, have argued that the notion of a knowledge base is simply a myth concocted and perpetuated by professors of educational administration to justify their own privileged posi-

tions. In the process of developing their argument, Littrell and Foster invoke philosopher Allistair MacIntyre's (1984) version of Cronbach's unpredictability-of-human-phenomena argument reviewed above and conclude:

> If a social science cannot approach the avenues of law-like generalization demanded of other sciences, then its status as a science is considerably undermined, and "the salient fact about those [social] sciences is the absence of the discovery of any law-like generalization whatsoever" (MacIntyre 1984, 89). This means, in essence, that the overlay that management and administrative theorists put on their theory, that it indeed can provide meaningful and predictive generalizations about human behavior in organization, consists of a basically false assumption, one that only shores up the power and status of university professors, highly paid consultants, and other so-called "imagers" of managerial expertise (p.35).

Littrell and Foster also reference critiques by postmodern and poststructuralist thinking (they use the terms synonymously) to argue against the notion of value-free knowledge. "Poststructionalist, or postmodernist, thought," they write,

> reflects an analysis of language and society that accepts their dependence, acknowledges the fact that power relates to language use, and . . . asserts that the many divisions a society accepts between classes, races, genders, and so on are related to the ways in which the power elite dominates the signifiers in a language (p. 36).

What is the upshot of all of this according to Littrell and Foster? They write:

> Postmodern thought, combined with an analysis of modern social science, thus suggests that there is no foundation or ultimate position for theories of management or administration. Indeed, such theories in management science represent attempts to solidify the power base of those presenting them. Such theories represent the methods used to initiate the student into the mystifications of management science or administrative behavior. And such theories reflect a more basic preoccupation with how economics drives the social sciences. Such a pessimistic view of administrative science is not meant to impugn the many people who work in this area; rather, it is to suggest that they perhaps labor under conditions of false consciousness, although they do in fact believe in the power of social science (p. 36).

Michael Imber (1995) reaches a conclusion which is, in many respects, strikingly similar to the conclusion reached by Littrell and Foster, albeit by a somewhat different route. Consider, for instance, one of the reasons Imber gives for professors of educational administration continuing to generate and teach knowledge that evidence suggests is neither used nor usable.

> At most research universities, educational administration must engage in a continual process of self-justification. One way to

succeed in this process is to appear to be as similar to the high-status disciplines, especially the hard sciences, as possible. A theoretical knowledge base is a key element in maintaining this appearance, however irrelevant the knowledge base may be to practitioners of the field (p. 122).

Imber does suggest that there is a kind of practical knowledge about what works and how to make things work, a kind of knowledge Imber dubs "technical knowledge," which would be useful to administrators. Like organizational theorist Donald Schön, however, Imber argues that professors in universities have little interest in or ability to generate such knowledge.

Some authors, in fact, have even suggested that theoretical and practical knowledge are encoded in fundamentally different ways. Whereas theoretical knowledge normally takes the form of testable propositions, practical knowledge normally is encoded in narrative form (Holland, 1992). Anderson and Page (1995), for example, have explicitly linked discussions of narrative with the larger debate about the knowledge base within the educational administration field:

> Discussions should not be concerned so much with how we structure our programs or content for a knowledge base, but rather with how we choose the processes we use to engage with practitioners around the knowledge base that they already possess. Only by taking the narrativity of experience seriously can we produce dialogue and critical reflection in our programs, and model the process necessary to promote empowered practitioners and democratic educational institutions (pp. 132–133).

A fundamental question, of course, is whether practitioner knowledge—in whatever form it takes—can be incorporated in whatever knowledge base the field generates. On this point there is, once again, considerable disagreement within the field.

Representing the positive view is Joseph Murphy (1995, 1993). Murphy sees the breach between theory and practice as a historical artifact, a product of two earlier eras that were, in one case, overly concerned with providing prescriptions for practitioners and, in the other, obsessed with generating theoretical knowledge without engaging in dialog with practitioners. Murphy characterizes the current era a dialectic one and cites a number of initiatives being undertaken during this era that are designed to link the worlds of theory and practice both for purposes of knowledge generation and for purposes of administrative preparation.

Muth (1995), by contrast, is much less optimistic. He cites a number of real-world constraints, including many that hark back to the critiques of both Imber and Littrell and Foster, which almost inevitably will inhibit the inclusion of practitioners' craft knowledge within the field's knowledge base.

Thus the field's position on whether practitioners' knowledge will get incorporated into the knowledge base sanctioned by academics is like its position on most issues surrounding the knowledge base question: it is confused and, at the aggregate level at least, contradictory.

A Story in Search of an Ending

Contemporary short stories seldom have neat and tidy, much less happy, endings. Nevertheless, it may be worth our while to try to envision a different ending than the ones suggested by this installment of our field's quest for a knowledge base. Neither perpetuating our big tent way of operating or dismissing the whole knowledge base concept because it is a myth put forth by self-serving academics represent very satisfying conclusions to the tale that has been told here. If we accept the Imber/Littrell and Foster conclusion that the knowledge base notion is nothing more than a self-serving myth, for example, we are in effect taken back in time to a period when brute power was the only way to resolve educational disputes. Even if we concede that the Imber/Littrell and Foster analysis has some merit, in other words, we should remember that the century's quest for a knowledge base that Culbertson wrote about was not exclusively prompted by academics' self-interest. Rather, there was a sincere desire among scholars and practitioners alike to take the schools out of politics by basing educational decision on knowledge and expertise rather than on political considerations (Tyack, 1974; Callahan, 1964; Rice, 1896).

On the other hand, we can hardly ignore the conclusion of Greenfield and others that research is incapable of providing the definitive answers to educational questions that earlier members of our field hoped for. Nor can we cavalierly dismiss the claims of Bates and like-minded scholars about the inevitable political dimensions of knowledge. The way we frame our research questions and the designs we use to construct our studies do indeed reinforce certain values rather than others and consequently serve the interests of some while also disadvantaging some.

Yet the big tent reaction to all this also seems less than satisfactory. The complex and contradictory conceptualizations assembled under the big tents we construct to accommodate our differences are more likely to confuse than enlighten administrators and policy makers who look to the academy for an alternative to brute politics as a way to make decisions. Indeed, when we recommend contradictory things, we almost guarantee that research will be used selectively as a political weapon instead of as a tool to help resolve educational disputes intellectually rather than through the use of brute power.

Thus it seems appropriate to search for a different sort of ending to the story that has just been told, an ending that might encourage us to confront our differences and to try to resolve them intellectually before we turn to brute power as the only source of a solution. We need an ending, in other words, which will encourage us to try to find the best solution rather than simply the most politically expedient one.

A Possible Better Ending

I believe the gist of an alternative ending to the tale that has been told here can be found in a most unlikely place: Hoy and Miskel's most recent edition of *Educational Administration: Theory, Research, and Practice*. The location is unlikely because Hoy and Miskel's goal is not to map out an alternative to the "big tent" strategy; on the contrary, as noted above, they actually employ this strategy in the course of trying to make theory movement thinking palatable in a world influenced by Greenfield and Bates' thinking. In the process of giving theory movement thinking a makeover, however, Hoy and Miskel also inadvertently suggest an alternative ending to the "big tent" story that has been told here.

In essence, Hoy and Miskel's defense of social science research and theory involves scaling down claims about what social science can do. In and of itself, this strategy is hardly novel. It has been employed by a number of theory movement apologists who responded to Greenfield's initial broadsides against the movement's assumptions. In 1984, for instance, Knezevich wrote:

> Educational administration may never attain the tightly structured theories characteristic of the "hard" sciences such as physics; human behavior may be clouded by emotions and is influenced by far more antecedents and stimuli than the behavior of electrons or other inanimate objects. Nonetheless, it is possible to establish on at least a probabilistic basis a set of functional relations between antecedents and consequences in human behavior in organizations or elsewhere. This approach enables a reduction in, even if it does not eliminate, the margin of error in administrative decisions (p. 135).

The problem with Knezevish's reduction-in-the-margin of error argument is that it is only viable if variations across cultural contexts and individual variations within particular contexts are not too great; in short, if there is sufficient regularity across contexts to net statistically significant probabilistic findings. Furthermore, even the utility of statistically significant probabilistic generalizations has not gone unchallenged. Consider the commentary made by a team of leading scholars reviewing the findings produced by ABT Associates' (1977) evaluation of the various approaches to early childhood education experimented with in the government's large-scale planned variation study. The team took note of the probabilistic nature of the findings and pointed out that probabilistic findings meant that approaches to early childhood education, which aggregate data suggested were most effective, were not effective in all places and that approaches that probabilistic data certified as relatively ineffective were, in certain settings, among the most effective of all the strategies studied. The team concluded:

> [T]his aspect of the results . . . should be honored widely and serve as a basis of educational policy. Local schools do seem to make a difference. The peculiarities of individual teachers, schools, neighborhoods, and homes influence pupils' achievement far more than whatever is captured by labels such as basic skills or affective education (House, Glass, McLean, and Walker, 1978, p. 462).

Hoy and Miskel, by contrast, sidestep the whole question of whether or not social science can mirror reality (even incompletely) and instead focus on the heuristic value of social science research and theory. Hoy and Miskel, in fact, go so far as to acknowledge that "the models, theories, and configurations used to describe organizations in [their] book are mere words and pictures on pages, not reality itself," that "actual organizations are much more complex than these representations," and that "they distort reality," as a consequence (p. 3).

Rather than focusing on reality claims, they make a utilitarian case. They argue that research and theory-building activity can serve as useful models for practitioners to emulate as they engage in real-world problem solving. "The scientific approach provides a way of thinking about events for both theorists and practitioners alike" (p. 8), Hoy and Miskel write.

Furthermore, even when the discussion shifts from the research process to the products produced by research activity, Hoy and Miskel promise no easy answers or formulas for practice, not even probabilistic ones. Rather, just as in sociologist Carol Weiss' (1981) empirical studies of knowledge use, the emphasis is on theory and research as aids in problem formulation—in other words, as a source of concepts to help define what the problem is—rather than on problem solving. "Theory forms a frame of reference for the practitioner" (p. 7), Hoy and Miskel tell us.

In short, Hoy and Miskel's case for social science theory is a utilitarian one and is based more on arguments about social science's heuristic value than on claims about its capability to adequately represent reality. As a consequence, Hoy and Miskel's reformulated rationale makes theory and traditional forms of research immune to much of the criticism Greenfield and others leveled against the theory movement.

One is reminded of the response of philosophers to Peter Winch's "Idea of Social Science," which was discussed briefly in the first part of this chapter. Peter Cohen (1968), for instance, responded to Winch's Greenfield-like view that organizational life was constructed rather than caused as follows: "One would agree that the use of the term 'causation' does not have as precise a reference in the social world as it does in the natural world," Cohen wrote.

> But if one is to use such criteria one wonders what is to be offered in place of 'causation.' In fact, one begins to wonder how social policy would be possible without some idea of causation (Cohen, 1968, p. 416).

Other Examples of a Possible Better Ending

The Hoy and Miskel text is not the only place where one can observe a utilitarian justification strategy being employed. The utilitarian orientation, for example, is at the center of Robinson's (1994, 1998) problem based methodology, a methodology that involves researchers deliberating with practitioners and policymakers about how local problems should be defined to help insure that researchers' work will be relevant and, ultimately, used.

One can also see utilitarian arguments undergirding Evers and Lakomski's (1996) defense of what they call a "coherentist" view of science, if one can get past the sense of certainty projected by their rhetoric. Indeed, after accepting the notion "that foundational patterns of justification are mistaken and that empirical evidence is never sufficient for rational theory choice" (p. 381), one wonders what recourse Evers and Lakomski have other than to use some variation of a utilitarian argument to make their case. How else, in other words, could they justify their "additional, superempirical" criteria—consistency, simplicity, comprehensiveness, unity of explanation, learnability, and fecundity—which they propose using to justify a theory's worth. Indeed, even Evers and Lakomski's allegiance to the physical sciences' conception of theory is predicated on claims about accomplishments in physical science fields. In short, once one adopts an anti-foundational stance, it makes sense to make the sort of instrumental claims Evers and Lakomski make, claims such as the following:

> [We] claim that . . . coherentism is a rather more inclusive approach to administrative theory than current alternatives. Because the most *useful* knowledge, from any perspective, is often hard won, there is a premium on being inclusive. (Evers and Lakomski, 1996, p. 398, emphasis added.)

Making Cases, Not Merely Claims

Of course, utilitarian claims, in and of themselves, are not convincing to anyone other than true believers. Claims must be supported and a case must be made to justify what is being asserted. On this point, the authors discussed above have some work to do. It is not self-evident, for ex-

ample, that Hoy and Miskel's claim about social scientists' thinking being a good model for practitioners' problem solving is, in fact, defensible. As noted above, Schön and others would argue it is not.

Furthermore, to make a truly convincing case, a scholar will undoubtedly have to focus on the comparative utility of particular theories, research methods, and conceptualizations. It is not enough to argue that traditional approaches to theory construction generate frames that practitioners can put to use in making sense of and responding to real-world problems. That is too easy a task; almost anything might pass that test. The real question is what is the added value of traditional research procedures. Why are frames emerging from social science theory building better than images and concepts emerging from single case qualitative research or even literature and the arts (Donmoyer, 1995; Brieschke, 1990), and why should limited resources be used to support this sort of work rather than other initiatives?

Finally, the criteria employed to make a convincing utility-based case cannot be merely technical; the values implicit in criteria must also be assessed. The question is never merely, what works? That question must always be followed by a series of other questions: For whom does it work? What and whose values are implicit in the criteria we use to assess utility? Are these values defensible? Are they more defensible than the competing values implicit in alternative ways of doing the business of administrative research and practice?

It would not be sufficient, in other words, for Hoy and Miskel to make the case for causal as opposed to contructivist views of organizations solely on technical grounds. They must also attend to questions about who will benefit if different conceptions of organizations get employed. Whether we think of human action as being caused or constructed, for example, can have a significant impact on whether we believe that school governance should be lodged mainly at the local level or whether we believe it is possible and/or desirable to have more distant bodies, such as state legislatures, choreograph what happens in schools. Such considerations must be part of debates about utility.

Similarly, it is interesting that Evers and Lakomski's utility-based defense of using the physical sciences as a model for theorizing in the educational administration field makes no mention of the physical sciences contributions to making weapons of mass destruction or to environmental contamination. This is, I believe, a rather glaring omission; a utilitarian case, if it is to be truly convincing, must articulate and defend the criteria employed to make utility claims (Cherryholmes, 1988; Donmoyer, 1996).

In addition to the three general issues raised above, there also will always be a host of case-specific questions that anyone who makes a utilitarian case must answer. Robinson's case, for instance, invites questions of feasibility

(Donmoyer, 1998) and concern about whether the "what works" concerns of practitioners might result in value questions being relegated to a secondary status when Robinson's methodology gets implemented. With respect to Evers and Lakomski, one might ask whether it is really possible to construct a single, unified grand theory of educational administration—at least one that meets Evers and Lakomski's criterion of simplicity—and also accommodate the multiple values and concerns that legitimately should come into play in administrative decision making. Should we really use the natural sciences as our model for inquiry as Evers and Lakomski propose doing, or is ours more a public policy field than an academic discipline, and do public policy fields inevitably require the balancing of a variety of different, even contradictory theories (both formal and informal) and the different values they serve (Toulmin, 1972; Donmoyer, 1996)? To state this issue another way: Does the concept of coherence really represent an appropriate and, dare I say, useful grounding for our field?

Hard Questions/No Easy Answers

Questions like the ones posed above cannot be answered easily. Consequently, the utilitarian strategy being advocated here provides no quick and efficient exit from the big tents we have constructed to house our differences. Indeed, I fully expect reviewers of this handbook to chide me for my apparent naiveté in raising the utilitarian justification strategy as a potentially helpful way out of the less than satisfying situation in which we find ourselves. Utilitarianism does not avoid the epistemological difficulties associated with attempts to talk across paradigms and perspectives, the critics will undoubtedly say, and, at least at some abstract, theoretical level, they will be right. The alternative ending I have proposed is what I refer to as a Kris Kristofferson type of solution, i.e. a "help-me-make-it-through-the-night" kind of response to a problem.

Furthermore, before we can answer even technical sorts of utility questions, our perceptions will have to be similar enough for us to agree on the indicators and evidence we will employ. Such agreements will be especially difficult if our goal is to compare the relative utility of different perspectives. Even more fundamental difficulties are associated with reaching some sort of agreement about the values that undergird the criteria we use to answer technical questions. To further complicate matters, technical and value questions are always linked. Our values help to determine what we see and what we see, in turn, reinforces our values.

Despite these very real impediments to cross-perspective communication, however, I suspect we have a better chance of understanding each other and even of finding some sort of appropriate balance among competing perspectives and values if we talk in instrumental rather than

epistemological terms. The latter sort of talk is not only exceedingly abstract; more often than not it also assumes that different perspectives are incommensurable (Lincoln and Guba, 1985). This latter assumption can stop a conversation before it has begun, just as abstraction almost guarantees that people will define language differently and, as a consequence, end up talking past each other.

By contrast, when scholars such as Hoy and Miskel commit to justifying their positions on more utilitarian grounds, they direct our attention away from ephemeral, abstract concepts and toward more tangible outcomes. To be sure, we may still observe things differently and, even if our observations are relatively in synch, we may attach different value to what we see. Having a relatively concrete referent, however, even if we see and value it somewhat differently, should still help ground talk about the different ways we perceive and the different values we hold.

Such talk still will not be easy to engage in, of course. Our forums are not designed to promote it. As I write this, I am in the last year of a three-year term as the editor of the American Educational Research Association journal, *Educational Researcher*. I had hoped to use my tenure as editor to encourage the sort of cross-perspective interaction I am talking about here but found this difficult to do. Responses arrived long after articles appeared; policies required they be sent out for review; reviewers did not always respond in a timely fashion; rejoinders also required review. The whole process was elongated, exceedingly formal and more than a little artificial.

The Internet seems to provide a less mediated, more naturally interactive (although no less disembodied[5]) forum, but even in such a forum the way we talk with each other is as important as the fact that talk occurs. Unfortunately, the scripts our field's history provides for scholarly discourse—including the writings of Greenfield and Bates—are needlessly adversarial and consequently can easily generate more heat than light. For our conversations to be productive, I suspect we must learn to talk with each other in fundamentally different ways. Elbow's (1986) notion of "embracing contraries" captures some of what I have in mind, as do comments by philosopher Richard Bernstein. We must, according to Bernstein,

assume the responsibility to listen carefully, to use our linguistic, emotional, and cognitive imagination to grasp what is being expressed and said in alien traditions. We must do this in a way where we resist the dual temptations of either facilely assimilating what others are saying in our own categories and language without doing justice to what is genuinely different and may be incommensurable or simply dismissing what the other is saying as incoherent nonsense . . . [T]he plurality of rival incommensurable traditions imposes a universal responsibility that should not be confused with an indifferent superficial tolerance where no effort is made to understand and engage with the incommensurable otherness of 'the Other' (Bernstein, 1993, pp. 65–66).

Oddly enough, one of the best enactments of Bernstein's advice in the educational administration field can be found in Daniel Griffith's review of *Greenfield on Educational Administration: Toward a Humane Science*, (Greenfield and Ribbins, 1993), a collection of the papers of Thomas Greenfield. In his review, published in 1995, Griffiths demonstrates a sincere desire to understand what his old nemesis (see, for example, Griffiths, 1979) was trying to do in his program of scholarship. "Seeing the papers together," Griffiths writes, "made me see Greenfield in a new way and answered a question I asked myself whenever I read one of his papers or heard him speak, What is he trying to do?" (Griffiths, 1995a, p. 151). Griffiths' review demonstrates that a commitment to understand does not have to translate into the tyranny of politeness; even though he may now have a better understanding of Greenfield and his scholarly agenda, he still does not agree with some of what Greenfield is about and, to his credit, he does not hesitate to make his disagreements known. Unfortunately, Griffiths also demonstrates on occasion how difficult it is for us to understand those whose thinking is radically different from our own, such as when he chides Greenfield for not liking to do empirical work.

Conclusion

Will academics be willing and able to do what Bernstein asks them to do? I must admit, I do not know. And even if they follow Bernstein's lead, will practitioners, who Imber argues are concerned primarily with technical questions about what works, tolerate talk that does not exclusively define utility in technical terms? Once again, I do not know the answer to the question I have posed. The alternate ending I have fashioned from the utilitarian strategy evident in the Hoy and Miskel text, as well as in the articles by Robinson (1994) and Evers and Lakomski (1996), is intentionally more prescriptive than predictive, more focused on what I believe ought to happen than on what I believe is likely to occur.

Indeed, if I were a betting man, I would bet that most members of the field would be quite reluctant to abandon the comfort and civility of their "big tents" in order to talk (even in utilitarian terms) about seemingly intractable problems with those who think and talk differently than they do. Furthermore, even if members of our field are willing to engage in discussion and debate, it will be hard for them not to re-enact the sort of adversarial scripts employed in the past, despite the fact that such scripts did little to promote understanding of a rival's position and functioned primarily to reassure each debater and his (or, in a few instances, her) supporters of the correctness of their a priori point of view.[6]

Ultimately, of course, time is required to answer questions about what *will* happen. It should be interesting 20 or so years from now to open the third edition of the *Handbook of Research on Educational Administration* and read the next installment of our field's continuing quest for a knowledge base.

NOTES

1. The focus on this chapter is on activity and discourses within the United States. The work of scholars from outside the United States is discussed only to the extent that it made its way into the discourses on educational administration knowledge in this country. I readily acknowledge the problems associated with such ethnocentrism and the benefits that accrue from more comparative work. Space limitations, however, dictated that this chapter's focus be narrowed.

2. I acknowledge that the list of scholars discussed is not an exhaustive one. Sampling of literature is always required in a review of this sort and sampling is also always a bit problematic. The authors discussed in this section certainly meet the selection criteria outlined in the text. I believe most of the "big ideas" that were part of the intellectual landscape from 1976 to 1997 are represented in the discussion, though, of course, subtle but potentially significant differences among those who advanced these "big ideas" are not. I readily acknowledge, however, that the work of many other scholars could have been discussed and that, in the end, the literature selected in a chapter of this sort always reflects, to some extent, the personal reading habits of the chapter's author.

3. For an alternative perspective on the relationship between positivism and the theory movement, see Willower, 1996.

4. See also the generally positive review of *Greenfield on Educational Administration: Toward a Humane Science* [Greenfield and Ribbins, 1993] by Greenfield's intellectual adversary, Daniel Griffiths, in the February 1995 issue of the *Educational Administration Quarterly*.

5. For an interesting discussion that juxtaposes recent literature on the body and embodied knowledge and knowing with the literature on educational technology, see McWilliam and Taylor (1998).

6. See, for example, the rhetorical tactics employed in the recent exchange between Scheurich (1994) and Evers and Lakomski (1996a).

REFERENCES

ABT Associates. (1977). *Education as experimentation: A planned variation model* (Vol. IV A–D). Boston: ABT Associates.

Anderson, G. (1989). Critical ethnography in education: Origins, current status, and new directions. *Review of Educational Research 59* (3), 249–270.

Anderson, G. & Page, B. (1995). Narrative knowledge and educational administration: The stories that guide our practice. In R. Donmoyer, M. Imber & J. Scheurich (Eds.), *The knowledge base in educational administration: Multiple perspectives* (pp. 124–138). Albany: State University of New York Press.

Apple, M. (1979). *Ideology and curriculum.* London: Routledge & Kegan Paul.

Apple, M. (1982). *Education and power.* Boston: Routledge & Kegan Paul.

Ball, S. (1987). *The micropolitics of the school: Towards a theory of school organization.* London: Methuen.

Ball, S. (1989). The micropolitics of the school: The everyday political perspective of teachers toward open school principals. *Educational Administration Quarterly 25* (4), 377–407.

Ball, S. (1991). *The politics of life in schools: power, conflict, and cooperation.* Newbury Park, CA: Sage.

Bates, R. (1980). Educational administration, the sociology of science, and the management of knowledge. *Educational Administration Quarterly 16* (2), 1–20.

Bates, R. (1982). Toward a critical practice of educational administration. Paper presented at the annual meeting of the American Educational Research Association, New York.

Bates, R. (1987). Corporate culture, schooling, and educational administration. *Educational Administration Quarterly 23* (4), 79–115.

Bates, R. (1989). Educational administration, the sociology of science, and the management of knowledge. *Educational Administration Quarterly 16* (2), 1–20.

Beck, L. & Murphy, J. (1994). *Ethics in educational leadership programs: An expanding role.* Thousand Oaks, CA: Corwin Press.

Belsey, C. (1992). *Critical Practice.* London: Routledge.

Berger, P. & Luckmann, T. (1967). *The social construction of reality.* New York: Anchor Books.

Bernstein, R. (1993). *The New Constellation: The Ethical Political Horizons of Modernity.* Cambridge, MA: Harvard University Press.

Blase, J. (1988). The politics of favoritism: A qualitative analysis of the teachers' perspective. *Educational Administration Quarterly 24* (2), 152–177.

Blase, J. (1989) The micropolitics of the school: The everyday political orientation of teachers toward open school principals. *Educational Administration Quarterly 25* (4), 377–407.

Blumer, H. (1969). *Symbolic interactionism: Perspective and method.* Englewood Cliffs, N. J. : Prentice-Hall.

Boyan, N. (1988). *Handbook of research on Educational Administration* (first addition). New York: Longman.

Brieschke, P. (1983). A case study of teacher role enactment in an urban elementary school. *Educational Administration Quarterly 19* (4), 59–84.

Brieschke, P. (1990). The administrator in fiction: Using the novel to teach educational adminstration. *Educational Administration Quarterly 26* (4), 376–393.

Bronfenbrenner, U. (1958). Socialization and social class through time and space. In E. E. Maccoby, T. M. Newcomb & E. L. Hartley (Eds.), *Readings in social psychology* (third edition) (pp. 400–425). New York: Holt Rinehart & Winston.

Callahan, R. E. (1964). *The cult of efficiency: A study of the social forces that have shaped the administration of public schools.* Chicago: University of Chicago Press.

Cambron-McCabe, N. (1993). Leadership for democratic authority. In J. Murphy (Ed.), *Preparing tomorrow's school leaders: Alternative designs* (157–175). University Park, PA: University Council for Educational Administration.

Capper, C. (1992). A feminist poststructuralist analysis of nontraditional approaches in educational administration. *Educational Administration Quarterly 28* (1), 103–124.

Cherryholmes, C. (1988). *Power and criticism: Poststructural investigation in education.* New York: Teachers College Press.

Cohen, P. (1968). The very idea of a social science. In I. Lakatos & A. Musgrave (Eds.), *Problems in the philosophy of science* (pp. 407–432). Amsterdam: North-Holland Publishing Company.

Conklin, H. (1955). Hanunoo color categories. *Southwestern Journal of Anthropology, 11,* 339–344.

Crehan, P. (1985). An exploration of the usefulness of meta-analysis in educational administration. *Educational Administration Quarterly 21* (3), 263–281.

Cronbach, L. (1957). The two disciplines of scientific psychology. *American Psychologist, 12,* 671–684.

Cronbach, L. (1975). Beyond the two disciplines of scientific psychology. *American Psychologist, 30,* 116–127.

Cronbach, L. (1982). Prudent aspirations of social inquiry. In W. Kruskal (Ed.), *The social sciences: Their nature and lines* (pp. 42–54). Chicago: University of Chicago Press.

Culbertson, J. A. (1988). A century's quest for a knowledge base. In N. J. Boyan (Ed.), *Handbook of research on Educational Administration* (pp. 3–26). New York: Longman.

Cusick, P. (Ed.). (1987). *Special issue:* Organizational culture and schools. *Educational Administration Quarterly 23* (4).

Deal, T. & Kennedy, A. (1982). *Corporate Culture: The rites and rituals of corporate life.* Reading, MA: Addison-Wesley Publishing Co.

Dillard, C. (1995). Leading with her life: An African American feminist (re)interpretation of leadership from an urban high school principal. *Educational Administration Quarterly 31,* (4) 539–563.

Donmoyer, R. (1985). Cognitive anthropology and research on effective principals. *Educational Administration Quarterly 21* (2), 31–58.

Donmoyer, R. (1991). Post-positivist evaluation: Give me a for instance. *Educational Administration Quarterly 27* (3), 265–296.

Donmoyer, R. (1995) A knowledge base for educational administration: Notes from the field. In R. Donmoyer, M. Imber & J. Scheurich (Eds.), *The knowledge base in educational administration: Multiple perspectives* (pp. 74–95). Albany: State University of New York Press.

Donmoyer, R. (1996). The concept of a knowledge base. In F. Murray (Ed.), *The teacher educator's handbook: Building a knowledge base for the preparation of teachers* (92–119). San Francisco: Jossey-Bass Publishers.

Donmoyer, R. (1998). Talking power to "truth." *Educational Researcher 27* (1), 4, 27, 4.

Eagly, F., Karau, S. & Johnson, B. (1992). Gender and leadership style among school principals: A meta-analysis. *Educational Administration Quarterly 28* (1), 43–75.

Eisner, E. (1975). *The perceptive eye: Toward the reformation of educational evaluation.* Address to the American Educational Research Association, Division B, Washington, D. C.

Eisner, E. (1979). *The Educational imagination.* New York: Macmillan.

Eisner, E. (1988). The primacy of experience and the politics of method. *Educational Researcher, 7*(5), 15–20.

Elbow, P. (1986). *Embracing contraries: Explorations in learning and teaching.* New York: Oxford University Press.

Enomoto, E. (1997). Negotiation the ethics of care and justice. *Educational Administration Quarterly 33* (3), 351–370.

Epp, J., Sackney, L. & Kustaski, J. (1994). Reassessing Levels of Androcentric Bias in *Educational Administration Quarterly. Educational Administration Quarterly 30* (4), 451–471.

Evers, C. (1985). Hodgkinson on ethics and the philosophy of administration. *Educational Administration Quarterly 21* (4), 27–50.

Evers, C. & Lakomski, G. (1996a). Science in educational adminstration: A post-positivist conception. *Educational Administration Quarterly 32* (3), 379–402.

Evers, C. & Lakomski, G. (Eds). (1996b). *Special Issue:* Post-positivist Conceptions of Science in Educational Administration. *Educational Administration Quarterly 32,* 3.

Feyerabend, P. (1970). Against method: Outline of an anarchistic theory of knowledge. In M. Rodner & S. Winokur (Eds.), *Analyses of theories and methods of physics and psychology.* Minneapolis: University of Minnesota Press.

Forsyth, P. (1994). Forward. *Primis.* New York: McGraw-Hill.

Foster, W. (1986). *Paradigms and promises: New approaches to educational administration.* Prometreus: Buffalo, N. Y.

Foucault, M. (1972). *The archaeology of knowledge* (A. M. Sheridan Smith, Trans.). New York: Pantheon Books.

Garfinkel, H. (1967). *Studies in ethnomethodology.* Englewood Cliffs, NJ: Prentice-Hall.

Geertz, C. (1973). *The interpretation of culture.* New York: Basic Books.

Geertz, C. (1983). *Local Knowledge.* New York: Basic Books.

Giroux, H. (1981). *Ideology, culture and the process of schooling.* Philadelphia: Temple University Press.

Glazer, J. (1991). Feminism and professionalism in teaching and educational administration. *Educational Administration Quarterly 27* (3), 321–342.

Gordon, E. W., Miller, F. & Rollock, D. (1990). Coping with communicentric bias in knowledge production in the social sciences. *Educational Researcher, 19*(3), 14–19.

Greenfield, T. (1975). *Theory about organization: A new perspective and its implications for schools.* In M. Hughes (Ed), *Administering education: International challenge.* London: Athlone.

Greenfield, T. (1978). Reflections on organizational theory and the truths of irreconcilable realities. *Educational Administration Quarterly 14* (2), 1–23.

Greenfield, T. (1980). The man who comes back through the door in the wall: Discovering truth, discovering self, discovering organizations. *Educational Administration Quarterly 16* (3), 26–59.

Greenfield, T. & Ribbins, P. (Eds.) (1993). *Greenfield on Educational Administration: Towards a Humane Science.* London: Routledge.

Greenfield, W., Jr. (1985). The moral socialization of school administrators: Informal role learning outcomes. *Educational Administration Quarterly 21* (4), 99–120.

Griffiths, D. (1979). Intellectual turmoil in educational administration. *Educational Adminstration Quarterly 13* (3), 43–65.

Griffiths, D. (Ed) (1991). Special issue: Nontraditional theory and research. *Educational Administration Quarterly 27* (3).

Griffiths, D. (1995a). Review of Greenfield on Educational Administration: Towards a Humane Science. *Educational Administration Quarterly 31*(1), 151–165.

Griffiths, D. (1995b). Theoretical pluralism in educational administration. In R. Donmoyer, M. Imber & J. Scheurich (Eds.), *The knowledge base in educational administration: Multiple perspectives* (pp. 300–309). Albany, NY: State University of New York Press.

Griffiths, D., Hart, A. & Blair, B. (1991). Still another approach to administration: Chaos theory. *Educational Administration Quarterly 21* (2), 430–451.

Guba, E. & Lincoln, Y. (1981). *Effective evaluation*. San Francisco: Jossey-Bass Publishers.

Gusfield, J. (1976). The literary rhetoric of science. *American Sociologist, 41*, 11–33.

Habermas, J. (1978). *Knowledge and human interests* (J. Shapiro, trans.). London: Heinemann.

Habermas, J. (1984–87). *The theory of communicative action* (Vols. 1–2, T. McCarthy, Trans.). Boston: Beacon.

Haller, E. & Knapp, T. (1985). Problems and methodology in educational administration. *Educational Administration Quarterly 21* (3), 157–168.

Hallinger, P. & Heck, R. (1996). Reassessing the principal's role in school effectiveness: A review of empirical research, 1980–1995. *Educational Administration Quarterly 32* (1), 5–44.

Hanfling, O. (1981). *Logical Positivism*. Oxford: Basil Blackwell.

Haraway, D. (1988). Situated knowledge: The science question in feminism and the privilege of partial perspective. *Feminist Studies, 14*(3), 575–99.

Haraway, D. (1989). *Primate visions: Gender, race, and nature in the world of modern science*. New York: Routledge.

Harding, S. (1986). *The science question in feminism*. Ithaca, NY: Cornell University Press.

Harding, S. (1991). *Whose science? Whose knowledge?* Ithaca, NY: Cornell University Press.

Harris, C. (1996). The aesthetic of Thomas B. Greenfield: An exploration of practices that leave no mark. *Educational Administration Quarterly 32* (4), 487–511.

Hart, A. & Pounder, D. (Eds.) (1992) Special Issue: Leadership. *Educational Administration Quarterly 28*, 3.

Heslep, R. (1997) The practical value of philosophical thought for the ethical dimension of educational leadership. *Educational Administration Quarterly 33* (1), 67–85.

Holland, P. (1992). Recovering the story: Understanding practice through interpretation of educational narratives. In N. Haggerson & A. Bowman (Eds.) *Informing educational policy and practice through interpretive inquiry* (199–215). Lancaster, PA: Technomic Pub.

House, E., Glass, G., McLean, D. & Walker, D. (1978). No simple answer: Critique of the follow-through evaluation. *Educational Leadership, 35*, 462–464.

Hoy, W. (1994a). Introduction: Essential Knowledge for school leaders. *Primis*. New York: McGraw-Hill Inc.

Hoy, W. (Ed.) (1994b). *PRIMIS: The University Council of Educational Administration Document Base*. New York: McGraw Hill.

Hoy, W. & C. Miskel (1996). Educational Administration: Theory, Research, and Practice. New York: Random House.

Husman, C. (1990). Teaching ethics (Comment on Giarelli, *EAQ*, August, 1989). *Educational Administration Quarterly 26* (2), 183–184.

Imber, M. (1995). Organizational Counterproductivism in educational administration. In R. Donmoyer, M. Imber & J. Scheurich (Eds.), *The knowledge base in educational administration: Multiple Perspectives* (pp. 113–123). Albany: State University of New York Press.

Kerlinger, F. (1986). *Foundations of behavioral research* (Third edition). New York: Holt, Rinehardt, and Winston.

Knezevich, S. (1984). *Administration of public education: A sourcebook for the leadership and management institutions*. New York: Harper and Row.

Kuhn, T. (1962, c1970). *The structure of scientific revolutions*. Chicago: The University of Chicago Press.

Lagemann, E. (1997). Contested Terrain: A history of educational research in the United States: 1980–1990. *Educational Researcher, 26*, 9, 5–17.

Levine, V., Donnellon, A., Gioia, D. & Sims, H. Jr. (1984). Scripts and speech acts in administrative behavior: The interplay of necessity, chance, and free will. *Educational Administration Quarterly 20* (1), 93–110.

Lincoln, Y. & Guba, E. (1985) *Naturalistic Inquiry*. Beverly Hills, CA: Sage Publications.

Littrell, J. & Foster, W. (1995). The myth of a knowledge base in educational administration. In R. Donmoyer, M. Imber & J. Scheurich (Eds.), *The knowledge base in educational adminstration: Multiple perspectives* (pp. 32–46). Albany: State University of New York Press.

Lomotey, K. (1995). Social and cultural influences on schooling: A commentary on the UCEA Knowledge Base Project, I, *Educational Administration Quarterly 31 (2)*, 294–303.

Lyotard, J. (1988). *The differend: Phrases in dispute*. Minneapolis: University of Minnesota Press.

MacIntyre, A. (1984). *After Virtue* (Second edition). Notre Dame, IN: university of Notre Dame Press.

McWilliam, E. & Taylor, P. (1998) Teacher Immaterial: Challenging the New Pedagogies of Instructional Design. *Educational Researcher 27*(8).

Marcus, G. & Clifford, J. (1986). *Writing culture: The politics and poetics of ethnography*. Berkely: the University of California Press.

Marshall, C. & Rossman, G. (1989). *Designing qualitative research*. Newbury, CA: Sage Publications.

Marshall, C., Patterson, J., Rogers, D. & Steele, J. (1996). Caring as career: An alternative perspective for educational administration. *Educational Administration Quarterly 32* (2), 271–294.

Maxcy, S. (Ed.) (1994). *Postmodern school leadership*. Westport, CT: Prager.

Maxcy, S. (1995). Beyond leadership frameworks. *Educational Administration Quarterly 31* (1), 473–483.

Murphy, J. (Ed.) (1993). *Preparing tomorrow's school leaders: Alternative designs*. University Park, PA: University Council for Educational Administration.

Murphy, J. (1995). The knowledge base in school administration: Historical footings and emerging trends. In R. Donmoyer, M. Imber & J. Scheurich (Eds.), *The knowledge base in educational administration: Multiple perspectives* (pp. 62–69). Albany: State University of New York Press.

Muth, R. (1995). Craft knowledge and institutional constraints. In R. Donmoyer, M. Imber & J. Scheurich (Eds.), *The knowledge base in educational administration: Multiple perspectives* (pp. 96–112), Albany: State University of New York Press.

National Policy Board for Educational Administration. (1989). *Improving the preparation of school administrators: An agenda for reform*. Charlottesville, VA: National Policy Board for Educational Administration.

Owens, R. (1982). Methodological rigor in naturalistic inquiry: Some issues and answers. *Educational Administration Quarterly, 18* (2), 1–21.

Parlett, M. & Hamilton, D. (1977). Evaluation as illumination: A new approach to the study of innovatory programs. In D. Hamilton, B. MacDonald, C. King, D. Jenkins & M. Parlett (Eds.), *Beyond the numbers game* (pp. 6–22). Berkeley, CA: McCutcheon.

Parsons, T. (1937). *The structure of social action*. New York: McGraw Hill.

Patton, M. (1975). *Alternative evaluation research paradigm*. Grand Forks, North Dakota: Study Group on Evaluation, University of North Dakota.

Patton, M. (1980, c 1990). *Qualitative Evaluation Methods*. Beverly Hills: Sage Publications.

Payne, W. H. (1875). *Chapters on school supervision*. New York: Wilson, Hinkle.

Peters, T. & Waterman, R. (1982). *In search of excellence*. New York: Harper and Row.

Pillow, W. (1996, November). *Practices within and against: Ironic intervention and Pissed Criticism*. Paper presented at the Annual Meeting of the American Studies Association, Montreal, Canada.

Pinar, W. (1975). *Curriculum Theorizing: The Reconceptualists*. Berkeley: McCutchan.

Pounder, D. (1988). The male/female salary differential for school administrators: Implications for career patterns and placement of women. *Educational Administration Quarterly 24* (1), 5–19.

Reitzug, U. & Reeves, J. (1992). Miss Lincoln doesn't teach here: A descriptive narrative and conceptual analysis of a principal's symbolic leadership behavior. *Educational Administrative Quarterly 28* (2), 185–219.

Reyes, P. & Capper, C. (1991). Urban principals: A critical perspective on the context of minority student dropout. *Educational Administration Quarterly 27* (4), 530–557.

Rice, J. (1896). Obstacles to rational educational reform. *The Forum*, 22. 385–395.

Rivlin, A. (1971). *Systematic thinking in social action*. Washington, DC: Brookings Institute.

Robinson, V. (1994). The practical promise of critical research in educational administration. *Educational Adminstration Quarterly 30* (1), 56–76.

Robinson, V. (1998). Methodolgy and the research practice gap. *Educational researcher 27* (1), 17–26.

Samier, E. (1996). The Weberian Legacy of Thom Greenfield. *Educational Administration Quarterly, 32* (supplemental), 686–704.

Sarason, S. (1971, c1982). *The culture of the school and the problem of change*. Boston: Allyn and Bacon.

Sarason, S. (1996). *Revisiting The culture of school and the problem of change*. New York: Teachers College Press.

Saussure, F. (1974). *Course in general linguistics* (Wade Baskin, Trans.). London: Fontana.

Scheurich, J. (1994). Social relativism: A postmodernist epistemology for educational administration. In S. Maxcy (Ed.), *Postmodern school leadership: Meeting the crisis in educational administration* (pp. 17–46). Westport: Praegar.

Scheurich, J. (1995). Knowledge Base in Education Administration: Postpostivist Reflections. In R. Donmoyer, M. Imber & J. Scheurich (Eds.), *The Knowledge Base in Educational Administration: Multiple Perspectives* (pp. 17–31). Albany: State University of New York Press.

Scheurich, J. (1997). *Research method in the postmodern*. Washington, DC: Falmer Press.

Scheurich, J. & Imber, M. (1991). Educational reforms can reproduce societal inequities: A case study. *Educational Administration Quarterly, 27*, (3) 297–320.

Schön, D. (1983). *The reflective practitioner: How professionals think in action*. New York: Basic Books.

Sergiovanni, T. Reflections on administrative theory and practice in schools. *Educational administration quarterly 28* (6), 304–313.

Sergiovanni, T. (1992). Reflections on administrative theory and practice in schools. *Educational administration quarterly, 28* (3) 304–313.

Sergiovanni, T. & Corbally, J. (1984). Leadership and organizational culture. *New perspectives on administrative theory and practice*. Urbana: University of Illinois Press.

Shakeshaft, C. (1989). *Women in educational administration*. Newbury Park, CA: Sage.

Shakeshaft, C. & Hanson, M. (1986). Andocentric bias in the *Educational Administration Quarterly 22* (1), 68–92.

Sirotnik, K. & Borstein, L. (1985). Measurement and Statistical Issues in Multilevel Research on Schooling. *Educational Administration Quarterly*, 21(1), 169–187.

Stake, R. (1975). *Evaluating the arts in education: A responsive approach*. Columbus, OH: Charles Merrill.

Stanfield, J. H. (1985). The ethnocentric bias of social science knowledge production. *Review of Research in Education*, 12, 387–415.

Starratt, R. (1991). Building an ethical school: A theory for practice in educational administration. *Educational Administration Quarterly*, 27 (2), 185–202

Strike, K., Haller, E. & Soltis, J. (1988). *The ethics of school administration*. New York: Teachers College Press.

Thorndike, E. L. (1910). The contribution of psychology to education. *The Journal of Educational Psychology*, 1, 5–12.

Toulmin, S. (1972). *Human understanding*. Princeton, NJ: Princeton University Press.

Toulmin, S. (1983). The construal of reality: Criticism in modern and postmodern science. In W. J. T. Mitchel (Ed.), *The politics of interpretation*. Chicago: University of Chicago Press.

Tyack, D. (1974). *The one best system*. Cambridge, MA: Harvard University Press.

University Council for Educational Administration. (1992). *Essential knowledge for school leaders: A proposal to map the knowledge base of educational administration*. Unpublished proposal.

Wagner, J. (1986). *The search for signs of intelligent life in the universe*. New York: Harper and Row.

The Washington Post (July 14, 1994). Editorial.

Weiss, C. (1981). Policy research in the context of diffuse decision making. *Journal of Higher Education 53*, 619–639.

Williams, R. (1963). *Culture and society 1790–1950*. London: Penguin.

Willower, D. (1996). Inquiry in educational administration and the spirit of the times. *Educational Administration Quarterly 32* (3), 344–365.

Winch, P. (1958, c1990). *The idea of a social science and its relationship to philosophy*. New York: Humanities Press.

Wolcott, H. (1985). On ethnographic intent. *Educational Administration Quarterly 21* (3), 187–204.

Young, M. (Ed.). (1971). *Knowledge and control: New directions for the sociology of education*. London: Collier-Macmillan.

CHAPTER 3

A Century's Quest to Understand School Leadership

Kenneth Leithwood and Daniel L. Duke

Educational administration scholars have devoted considerable time over this century trying to understand school leadership and leaders. They have done so for several reasons. Some assumed that a concept of leadership would be of assistance to them in describing the behavior of individuals in the roles of leaders. Others apparently were prompted to conceptualize leadership in ways that could help explain school outcomes or effects. Still others seemed intent on developing concepts of leadership for such prescriptive purposes as guiding the preparation of future administrators or the further education of incumbent administrators.

This chapter explores two major sources of insight about school leadership. Concepts of leadership found in the educational literature are the first source of insight. In order to facilitate the empirical study of schools as organizations, school leaders, and school effects, a number of scholars have tried either to conceptualize leadership in general and school leadership in particular or they have endorsed an already existing concept of leadership. To appreciate work of this kind, the next section of this chapter describes the results of a review of all articles dealing with leadership in four major educational administration journals over approximately the past decade. These results suggest that six major categories of leadership dominate contemporary writing about school leadership.

A second major source of insight about school leadership, explored in the third section of this chapter, is the historical and theoretical sources to which alternative conceptions of school leadership appeal for their authority. These sources—tradition, religion, and fields of inquiry such

as psychology, sociology, social psychology, and philosophy—help to explain why each leadership concept at some point during the century has had a dominant influence on both the understanding and practice of school leaders. They also explain why that dominance eventually was overshadowed by an alternative. Educational leaders have both changed and expanded the number of such sources as the century unfolded in response to changing social forces impinging on schools.

It is important to be clear at the outset that what has been learned about leadership in schools over the century has not depended on any clear, agreed-upon definition of the concept, as essential as this would seem at first glance. Indeed, Yukl argues that:

> It is neither feasible nor desirable at this point in the development of the discipline to attempt to resolve the controversies over the appropriate definition of leadership. Like all constructs in social sciences, the definition of leadership is arbitrary and very subjective. Some definitions are more useful than others, but there is no correct definition (1994, p. 4–5).

This observation, echoed by other respected students of leadership (Bennis, 1959; Burns, 1978; Bass, 1981), might be viewed as casting a pall over the central purpose of this chapter. Clark and Clark, for example, argue that you cannot talk about leaders with anyone until you agree on what you are talking about. That requires a definition of leadership and a criterion for leadership acts that can be agreed on (1990, p. 20). In the same vein, Rost begins his analysis of leadership and leadership literature in non-school organizations by arguing that lack of attention to definition has been one of the main impediments to progress in the field. Indeed, he notes that over 60 percent of the authors who have written on leadership since about 1910 did not define leadership in their works (1991, p. 6).

One wonders how so many smart people could have overlooked such an obvious issue. Or did they? More likely, we think, they were at least in implicit agreement with Lofti Zadeh, the father of fuzzy logic, who framed the Law of Incompatibility: As complexity rises, precise statements lose meaning and meaningful statements lose precision (McNeil & Frieberger, 1993, p. 43). As these authors go on to point out, the Law of Incompatibility captures a feature common to most complex disciplines, that is, they teem with complex concepts. Responding to worries over the lack of precision in defining the meaning of strategic management, for example, Thomas and Pruett (1993) ask: "how much more precise are economists when they discuss 'innovation' or 'regulation,' or psychologists when they talk about 'intelligence'?" Whereas simple concepts are typically open to crisp definition, complex concepts are usually defined vaguely. Persevering on the development of a precise definition of a complex concept like leadership is likely to be counterproductive, following this line of reasoning.

Although Yukl pointed to lack of consensus about the precise meaning of leadership, he did discern a core of agreement across definitions very similar to what Bass (1981) detected a decade earlier. "Most definitions of leadership," Yukl claimed, "reflect the assumption that it involves a social influence process whereby intentional influence is exerted by one person [or group] over other people [or groups] to structure the activities and relationships in a group or organization" (1994, p 3). Influence then seems to be a necessary part of most conceptions of leadership. It suggests, as Yukl does, that most of the variation in leadership concepts, types, or models might be accounted for by differences in who exerts influence, how influence is exerted, the purpose for the exercise of influence, and its outcomes. In the conclusion to this chapter, we begin to develop a relational conception leadership by identifying the "elements" potentially interacting to generate influence and the different types of influence that may be generated.

Models of Contemporary Leadership Practice

Six distinctly different models or approaches to leadership are described in this section. These models were identified through analyses of a representative sample of contemporary literature concerning leadership in schools, a sample intended to reflect the result of this century's quest. The sample consisted of all feature length articles concerned with leadership published in four representative English-language educational administration journals. These journals were reviewed at least as far back as 1988, the year in which the *Handbook of Research in Educational Administration* (Boyan, 1988) was published. The chapter in that text by Immegart entitled "Leadership and Leader Behavior" provided a point of departure for the present chapter.

Two of the four journals selected for review in this section, *Educational Administration Quarterly* (EAQ), and the *Journal of School Leadership* (JSL), publish work largely from North America. Papers in the *Journal of Educational Administration* (JEA) reflect perspectives from Australia, New Zealand, and other countries, as well as North America. *Educational Management and Administration* (EMA) primarily reflects contemporary thought on leadership in the United Kingdom, but some other countries as well. Because of the reputations of each of these journals and the relatively broad theoretical perspectives they reflect collectively, it seems likely that most significant contemporary conceptions of leadership would find some expression in their contents.

Table 3.1 notes the total number of volumes reviewed in the case of each of the four journals and the total number of articles included in each volume. Approximately eight volumes were reviewed for each journal, several less in the case of JSL because it was not established until 1991, and several more in the case of EMA so as to balance the almost exclusively North American perspectives reflected in EAQ and JSL.

Table 3.1 also shows how many articles were concerned directly or indirectly with leadership and were therefore used as the basis for helping answer the questions of interest in this section of the chapter. These articles, totaling 121, were of several types, including descriptions of leadership theories, reviews of literature, empirical reports, and critical analyses.

Table 3.2 lists 20 different leadership models or concepts explicitly mentioned in the 121 articles (the category label "participative" was not explicitly mentioned). We applied it as a category label to include "group," "shared," and "teacher," leadership). Noted, as well, are the number of articles from each journal, and the total number of articles from all four journals mentioning each concept. Based on Table 3.2, the three most frequently mentioned conceptions (versus categories) of leadership over the past decade were instructional leadership (13 mentions), transformational leadership (11), and contingent/leadership styles (9). Instructional leadership appeared almost exclusively in the North American journals or in papers written by North Americans published in the non-North American journals. Although most often mentioned in North American journals, all four journals also contained papers about transformational leadership. Mention of leadership styles was distributed across the journals. The next most frequently mentioned leadership concepts were moral leadership (8),

Table 3.1
Leadership Articles in Four Journals

Year	EAQ[1]		JSL[2]		JEA[3]		EMA[4]	
	Total Articles	Ldrship Articles	Total Articles	Ldrship Articles	Total Articles	Ldrship Articles	Total Articles	Ldrship Articles
1985	—	—	—	—	—	—	38	2
1986	—	—	—	—	—	—	25	3
1987	—	—	—	—	—	—	24	3
1988	30	1	—	—	14	3	21	5
1989	28	1	—	—	14	3	6+ (2 issues missing)	—
1990	12	2	—	—	18	3	missing	—
1991	21	1	33	6	17	5	32	2
1992	22	8	33	6	25	9	28	5
1993	19	4	50	7	20	1	28	6
1994	20	4	38	4	24	4	25	5
1995	22	7	28	8	27	2	26	1
Totals	174	28	182	31	159	30	201	32

[1] Educational Administration Quarterly

[2] Journal of School Leadership

[3] Journal of Educational Administration

[4] Educational Management and Administration

managerial leadership (8), and cultural leadership (6). The remaining 14 leadership concepts were found in five or fewer articles. Some articles explicitly discussed as many as three or four such concepts (such as Cusack, 1993; Walker, 1989; and Gronn, 1996). This is why the number of mentions of leadership concepts exceeds the total number of articles reviewed.

In the case of 54 articles, the focus was on leadership but no attempt was made to label leadership or to conceptualize it as a particular form of leadership. Some of these articles supported multiple perspectives on leadership, while others treated leadership as a generally understood phenomenon without specific discussion of its meaning. There were also many instances in which an implicit leadership concept was evident, such as Hayes' (1995) study of collaborative relationships (or "shared leadership") in a British primary school, and Goldring's (1990) examination of principals' boundary spanning activities (or "organizational leadership").

Finally, as is also evident in Table 3.2, each of the 20 separate leadership concepts has been assigned to one of six broad categories. These categories cluster together leadership concepts sharing the same primary focus and key assumptions. The remainder of this section describes the central focus and assumptions of each of these categories and summarizes what the review articles had to say about each. Where one was available, a relatively well-developed exemplar of each leadership category also is described as a means of further clarifying the features of each leadership category. The sources of these exemplars are not confined to articles included in the four journals.

Instructional Leadership

This concept of leadership was mentioned in 13 of the 121 articles selected for review. Instructional leadership, a single, separate category, typically focuses *on the behaviors of teachers as they engage in activities directly affecting the growth of students*. Many versions of this form of leadership focus additionally on other organizational variables (such as school culture) that are believed to have important consequences for such teacher behavior. This has led Sheppard (1996) to distinguish between "narrow" and "broad" views of instructional leadership. Most conceptions of instructional leadership allocate authority and influence to formal administrative roles (usually the principal), assuming as well considerable influence through expert knowledge on the part of those occupying such roles.

Lack of explicit descriptions of instructional leadership (Foster, 1986) makes it difficult to assess the extent to which such leadership means the same thing to all those writing about it. Geltner and Shelton (1991) modified the term, referring to "strategic instructional leadership," but offering no notion of what non-strategic instructional leadership might mean. Stallhammar (1994) used the term "pedagogical

Table 3.2
Categories and Concepts of Educational Leadership Mentioned in Four Journals

Leadership Category and Concept[1] J O U R N A L S					
	EAQ	JSL	JEA	EML	Total
1. Instructional	4	7	—	2	13
2. Transformational	3	4	2	2	11
charismatic	—	—	—	1	1
visionary	—	1	1	2	4
cultural	2	1	—	3	6
empowering	—	1	1	—	2
3. Moral	3	2	1	2	8
democratic	—	1	—	—	1
normative-instrumental	1	—	—	—	1
symbolic	3	—	1	—	4
political	—	—	—	2	2
4. Participative	—	—	—	—	0
group	—	1	—	—	1
shared	—	2	2	1	5
teacher	3	—	1	—	4
5. Managerial/Strategic	1	—	1	6	8
organizational	2	—	—	—	2
6. Contingency/Styles	5	—	2	2	9
problem solving	3	1	—	—	4
craft/reflective	—	—	3	2	5
No Explicit Concept	6	13	19	16	54

[1]The number of articles listed for each "category" (such as transformational or moral) refers to the number of articles that explicitly used the category label. Subcategory citations are independent. For example, charismatic leadership was the explicit focus of one article (in EML) and this is in addition to the 11 articles explicitly concerned with transformational leadership, the superordinate leadership concept.

leadership." Kleine-Kracht (1993) differentiated between "direct" and "indirect" instructional leadership, noting that principals alone cannot fulfill all of a school's need for instructional leadership. Others argued that original beliefs concerning the principal as the primary or most important instructional leader required rethinking. Davidson (1992), for example, argued for the value of teachers serving as instructional leaders, while Floden *et al.* (1988) focused on district-level instructional leadership. Achilles (1992) challenged the idea that instructional leadership (or any form of leadership for that matter) was necessarily a substitute for capable management.

Examples of extensively elaborated contemporary models of instructional leadership include Duke (1987), Smith & Andrews (1989), and Hallinger and his colleagues. In each case, this orientation to leadership is described along multiple dimensions, each of which incorporates a number of functions or behaviors, and evidence is reviewed concerning the effects of these practices on important outcomes. The most fully tested of these models, the one developed by Hallinger and his associates (Hallinger & Murphy, 1985; Hallinger & McCary, 1990, for example),

consists of three broad categories of leadership practice: defining the school mission, managing the instructional program, and promoting school climate. Associated with these broad categories of practice are a total of 21 more specific functions (such as supervising instruction). Using a teacher survey developed by Hallinger (1992), considerable empirical evidence has accumulated in support of the contribution these leadership practices and functions add to student achievement as well as other types of outcomes (see Sheppard, 1996, for a review of this evidence).

Transformational Leadership

In addition to writing that refers explicitly to transformational leadership (11 articles), included as part of this leadership category are writings about charismatic, visionary, cultural, and empowering concepts of leadership. Mentioned in a total of 24 articles, the focus of this category of leadership is on *the commitments and capacities of organizational members*. Higher levels of personal commitment to organizational goals and greater capacities for accomplishing those goals are assumed to result in extra effort and greater productivity. Authority and influence are not necessarily allocated to those occupying formal administrative positions, although much of the literature adopts their perspective. Rather, power is attributed by organization members to whomever is able to inspire their commitments to collective aspirations, and the desire for personal and collective mastery over the capacities needed to accomplish such aspirations.

In the literature reviewed for this study, the concept of transformational leadership was subject to varying interpretations. Kowalski and Oates (1993), for instance, accepted Burns' (1978) original claim that transformational leadership represents the transcendence of self-interest by both leader and led. Dillard (1995, p. 560) preferred Bennis' modified notion of "transformative leadership—the ability of a person to 'reach the souls of others in a fashion which raises human consciousness, builds meanings, and inspires human intent that is the source of power.'" Leithwood (1994) used another modification of Burns, this one based on Bass' (1985) two-factor theory in which transactional and transformational leadership represent opposite ends of the leadership continuum. Bass maintained that the two actually can be complementary. Leithwood identified seven factors that make up transformational (and transactional) leadership. Hipp and Bredeson (1995), however, reduced the factors to five in their analysis of the relationship between leadership behaviors and teacher efficacy. Gronn (1996) noted the close relationship, in much current writing, between views of transformational and charismatic leadership, as well as the explicit omission of charisma from some current conceptions of transformational leadership.

The most fully developed model of transformational leadership in schools has been provided by Leithwood and his colleagues. This model conceptualizes such leadership along seven dimensions: building school vision, establishing school goals, providing intellectual stimulation, offering individualized support, modeling best practices and important organizational values, demonstrating high performance expectations, creating a productive school culture, and developing structures to foster participation in school decisions (Leithwood, 1994). Each dimension is associated with more specific leadership practices and the problem-solving processes used by transformational leaders has also been described (Leithwood, Steinbach, & Raun, 1993).

A recent review of empirical research on transformational school leadership offers modest amounts of evidence for the contributions of such leadership to student participation in school with a variety of psychological teacher states mediating student learning (such as professional commitment, job satisfaction), as well as organization-level effects such as organizational learning, and the development of productive school climate (Leithwood, Tomlinson & Genge, 1996).

Downton's (1973) study of rebel leadership is often cited as the forerunner of systematic inquiry about transformational leadership in non-school organizations. However, charisma, often considered an integral part of transformational leadership, has substantially more distant origins, typically attributed to Max Weber's (1947) efforts almost five decades ago. James McGregor Burns' (1978) prize-winning book first drew widespread attention to the concept of transformational leadership. Based on a sweeping historical analysis, Burns argued that most understandings of leadership not only overemphasized the role of power but held a faulty view of power, as well. There were, he claimed, two essential aspects of power—motives or purposes and resources—each possessed not only by those exercising leadership but also by those experiencing it. The essence of leadership is to be found in relationships between motives, resources, leaders, and followers: "the most powerful influences consist of deeply human relationships in which two or more persons engage with one another" (p. 11). Burns' distinction between transactional and transformational types of leadership hinges on this appreciation of power-as-relationships.

In contrast to transformational leadership, transactional leadership occurs when one person takes initiative in making contact with others for the purpose of exchanging valued things (economic, political, or psychological "things," for example). Each person in the exchange understands that she or he brings related motives to the bargaining process and that these motives can be advanced by maintaining that process. But because of the nature of the motives at issue, those involved are not bound together in any continuing, mutual pursuit of higher purposes. With this form of leadership, motives or purposes may well be met using the existing resources of those involved in the exchange. Neither purposes nor resources are changed, however.

Transformational leadership entails not only a change in the purposes and resources of those involved in the leader-follower relationship, but an elevation of both—a change "for the better." With respect to motives or purposes: "transforming leadership ultimately becomes moral in that it raises the level of human conduct and ethical aspiration of both leader and led, and thus has a transforming effect on both" (Burns, 1978, p. 20). This form of leadership, according to Burns' view, also aims to enhance the resources of both leader and led by raising their levels of commitment to mutual purposes and by further developing their capacities for achieving those purposes.

Burns' seminal work provided a solid conceptional footing on which to build the distinction between transactional and transformational types of leadership, and it also illustrated the meaning of these forms of leadership in many different contexts. Not to be found in this work, however, was a testable model of leadership practices or any empirical evidence of their effects. The prodigious efforts of Bass and his associates have responded to these limitations. Bass' (1985) book *Leadership and Performance Beyond Expectations* provided an impressive compendium of survey research evidence about the effects of one model of transformational leadership. Among the most important features of this model are the dimensions of leadership practice it includes and the proposed relationships among these dimensions.

Referred to in more recent publications as the four I's (Bass and Avolio, 1993, 1994), Bass and his colleagues consider transformational leadership to include idealized influence or charisma, inspirational motivation, intellectual stimulation, and individualized consideration. In addition to these dimensions of transformational leadership, three dimensions define the meaning of transactional leadership: contingent reward, management-by-exception, and a laissez-faire or a "hands off" form of leadership.

Whereas Burns considered transformational and transactional practices as opposite ends of the leadership continuum (essentially more and less effective forms of leadership), Bass offers a quite different conception, a "two-factor theory" of leadership; transactional and transformational forms of leadership, in his view, build on one another (Avolio & Bass, 1988; Waldman, Bass & Yammarino, 1990; Bass & Avolio, 1993; Howell & Avolio, 1991). Transactional practices foster ongoing work by attending to the basic needs of organizational members. Such practices do little to bring about changes in the organization, however. For this to occur, members must also experience transformational practices. Enhanced commitment and the extra effort usually required for change, it is claimed, are consequences of this experience.

Transactional practices were the traditional focus of attention for leadership theorists until the early 1980s. Disillusionment with the outcomes of that focus, however, gave rise to a number of alternative approaches, among them transformational leadership. These approaches are referred to collectively by Bryman (1992), Sims and Lorenzi (1992), and others as the "new leadership paradigm." Empirical studies of transformational leadership, reflecting this pessimism with transactional practices, often give them minimum attention. This is the case with Podsakoff, MacKenzie, Moorman, and Fetter (1990), for example. Although Podsakoff and his associates adopted a quite limited conception of transactional leadership for their research, they offered arguably the most comprehensive set of transformational leadership dimensions available to that point, dimensions based on a synthesis of seven prior perspectives on transformational leadership.

Moral Leadership

As a category, moral leadership includes those normative, political/democratic, and symbolic concepts of leadership mentioned in a total of 16 articles included in the review.

During the 1990s, the normative dimension of leadership has been one of the fastest growing areas of leadership study (Duke, 1996). Those writing about moral leadership argue that values are a central part of all leadership and administrative practice (Bates, 1993; Evers & Lakomski, 1991; Greenfield, 1991). Indeed, Hodgkinson, one of the best known proponents of this orientation to leadership, claims that "values constitute the essential problem of leadership . . . If there are no value conflicts then there is no need for leadership" (1991, p. 11). The focus of moral leadership is on *the values and ethics of the leader*, so authority and influence are to be derived from defensible conceptions of what is right or good. Nevertheless, much of the writing about moral leadership, as in the case of transformational leadership, adopts the perspective of those in formal administrative roles.

Many of those writing about moral leadership over the past decade take, as their point of departure, Herbert Simon's claim that values have no place in administrative decision making as well as positivistic conceptions of knowledge assumed by the "Theory movement" in educational administration. Attempts to cast the study of administration in purely rational terms unconcerned with values are seen as dangerously misguided because, as Hodgkinson points out, "The intrusion of values into the decision-making process is not merely inevitable, it is the very substance of decision" (1978, p. 59).

The papers reviewed from the four journals illustrate quite different approaches to moral leadership. For example, Duignan and MacPherson (1993, p. 10), in discussing their concept of "educative leadership," contended that leadership should be concerned with right and wrong, not attitudes, styles, or behaviors. William Greenfield (1995) maintained that leadership entails five "role demands" or "situational imperatives," including the moral, instructional, political, managerial, and social/interpersonal. Reitzug and Reeves (1992) argued that cultural leadership involves defining, strengthening, and articulating values but warned that leaders may manipulate culture to further their own ends. Reitzug (1994) argued further that leadership is moral, but only under certain conditions. Lees (1995, p. 225) argued that leadership in a democratic society entails a moral imperative to "promote democracy, empowerment, and social justice."

Among the issues of greatest concern to those exploring moral perspectives on leadership is the nature of the values used by leaders in their decision making and how conflicts among values can be resolved. A brief synopsis of the well-developed positions of Hodgkinson, Evers and Lakomski, and Slater help illustrate the range of views on these issues evident in contemporary literature.

At the heart of Hodgkinson's position on the nature of administrative values is an "analytic model of the value concept" (Hodgkinson, 1978, 1991). This model includes three categories of values, distinguished from one another by their adequacy in justifying administrative choices. In general, the model recommends that leaders choose higher over lower level values when confronted with value conflicts. Related to this general position, however, are refinements allowing for difficult cases to be addressed in authentic and morally responsible ways.

The least adequate set of values are "subrational" and encompass the leader's self-justifying preferences, manifestations of feeling and emotion. More defensible are a set of "rational" values. Leaders using this set of values justify their choices based on either consensus among those effected, or an appeal to some future consequences of choice held to be desirable. The most defensible set of values on which to base decision making, according to this model, are "transrational." No particular set of values is associated with this category. Rather, Hodgkinson refers to such values as having a metaphysical grounding: they are principles that "take the form of ethical codes, injunctions, or commandments . . . their common feature is that they are unverifiable by the techniques of science and cannot be justified by merely logical argument" (1991, p. 99).

Evers and Lakomski (1991) offer a thoughtful analysis of Hodkinson's position on moral leadership and go on to develop their own. A fully adequate description of their position is beyond the bounds of this chapter. Central to their position, however, is the claim (after the importance Dewey attributed to the virtues of problem solving as a means of improving the human condition) that "the basic normative framework for educational administrators is provided by the general requirement that decision and action should be, in the long term, educative; that the growth of knowledge be promoted" (1991, p. 186). Because administrative structures are not morally neutral, Evers and Lakomski advocate forms of educational leadership that enhance organizational learning. In these respects, the views of Evers and Lakomski are essentially similar to those of Willower (1994).

A third position on leaders' values and how value conflicts are to be resolved is political in its origin. In addition to a concern for specific sets of values, this aspect of moral leadership focuses on *the nature of the relationships among those within the organization and the distribution of power between stakeholders both inside and outside the organization*. This form of leadership assumes that even though the formal organization may clearly specify power relationships, lines of communication, and procedures for carrying out the organization's work, the informal organization may be quite different, as well as providing a more authentic explanation for organizational activity.

Forms of leadership referred to as "symbolic," "democratic," or "political" can equally well be placed in either moral or participative categories of leadership because the central argument for participation is justified by democratic theory. Slater (1994) illustrates this orientation to moral leadership. Because democracies value freedom, he argues, they are opposed to traditional sources of authority and encourage "fresh examination and scrutiny" (p. 98) of almost everything. But for reasons related to lack of time, energy, or capacity, this examination does not often happen and there is a tendency for majority opinion to prevail and for the meaningfulness of community values eventually to be eroded. Under such conditions the purpose of leadership is to correct the tendency to rely only on majority opinion "which in very large groups tends to be lowest common denominator" (p. 98). Leadership should also "help restore meaning and common purpose to daily life" (p. 99). School leaders, from this perspective, should be committed to the democratic ideal and work toward replicating that ideal in the life experiences of students in school organizations.

As Slater makes clear, political and symbolic versions of moral leadership value wide participation as a reflection of the society in which we live. Public institutions, such as schools, cannot be governed or administered in ways that violate democratic principles no matter how cumbersome some might think those forms of governance and administration to be.

Participative Leadership

The term "participative leadership" was adopted from Yukl's (1994) description to encompass a total of 10 articles concerned with "group," "shared," and "teacher" leadership. Participative leadership stresses *the decision-making processes of the group*. One school of thought within this category of leadership argues for such participation on the grounds that it will enhance organizational effectiveness. A second school rests its case for participation on democratic principles, such as those discussed above in relation to moral leadership. Additional reasons for participation emerge in the context of site-based management approaches to participatory leadership. In the case of this form of leadership, authority and influence are available potentially to any legitimate stakeholder in the school based on their expert knowledge, their democratic right to choose, and/or their critical role in implementing decisions.

A majority of the 10 articles associated participative leadership with enhanced organizational effectiveness. For example, evidence from Hayes' (1995) study in a single primary school demonstrated that the head's success in managing the government-driven change agenda depended on forging mutually beneficial relations with all significant groups of internal and external stakeholders. Johnston and Pickersgill (1992) as well as Vandenberghe (1992) argued that the substantially increased demands placed on school leaders by changing contexts and expectations could best (or only) be met by moving toward forms of shared or team leadership. Citing such changes as increased complexity, uncertainty, ambiguity, workload, and expectations for innovation, Murphy and Hallinger (1992) and Hallinger (1992) conclude that school leaders will need to adopt more participatory forms of leadership, forms of leadership that are more consultative, open, and democratic and that involve teachers and parents much more in school decision making.

Savery, Soutar, and Dyson (1992) illustrate approaches to participatory leadership driven largely by arguments for democratic processes. The framework for this study included seven categories of decision making (such as school policy and student discipline), each of which incorporated from two to five more specific decision categories. Teachers were asked to indicate their preferences for five different types of participation in each decision category ranging from the principal making the decision herself to staff deciding themselves. This study began to illustrate what would be required to develop a fully specified model of participatory leadership in a school, viewed from a democratic perspective.

The centerpiece in a majority of the past decade's school restructuring initiatives, site-based management (SBM) is arguably the most fully developed and widely advocated conception of participatory leadership available. Murphy and Beck (1995) suggest that SBM usually takes one of three forms; administrative-controlled SBM, professional-controlled SBM, and community-controlled SBM. Much less in evidence but still visible is a fourth type of SBM in which power is exercised equally by school professionals, parents, and other community members.

Administrative-controlled SBM is aimed at increasing accountability to the central district or board office for the efficient expenditure of resources on the assumption that such efficiencies will eventually pay off for students. These efficiencies are to be realized by giving local school administrators greater authority and influence over such key decision areas as budget, personnel, and curriculum. Advocates of this form of SBM reason that such authority, in combination with the incentive to make the best use of resources, ought to get more of the resources of the school into the direct service of students. To assist in accomplishing that objective, the principal may consult informally with teachers, parents, students, or community representatives. Site councils are typically established to advise the principal.

When teacher-controlled SBM is advocated, the goal is to make better use of their knowledge in such key decision areas as budget, curriculum, and (occasionally) personnel. Basic to this form of SBM is the assumption that professionals closest to the student have the most relevant knowledge for making such decisions (Hess, 1991) and that full participation in the decision-making process will increase their commitment to implementing whatever decisions are made. Participatory democracy, allowing employees greater decision-making power, is also presumed to lead to greater efficiency, effectiveness, and better outcomes (Clune & White, 1988; David, 1989; Mojkowski & Fleming, 1988).

Site councils associated with this form of SBM typically have decision making power and although many groups (parents, students, administration) are often represented, teachers have the largest proportion of members.

Increased accountability to parents and the community at large along with "consumer satisfaction" are the central purposes for establishing community-control forms of SBM (Lee, *et al.*, 1993; Malen, Ogawa & Kranz, 1990; Wohlstetter, 1990; Wohlstetter & McCurdy, 1991; Wohlstetter & Mohrman, 1993). The basic assumption giving rise to this form of SBM is that the curriculum of the school ought to directly reflect the values and preferences of parents and the local community (Ornstein, 1983; Wohlstetter & Odden, 1992). School professionals, it is claimed, typically are not as responsive to such local values and preferences as they ought to be. Their responsiveness is greatly increased, however, when the authority to make decisions about curriculum, budget, and personnel is in the hands of the parent and other community constituents of the school. School councils in which parent and other community constituents have a majority of the membership are the primary instruments for the exercise of such authority.

Community-control SBM aims to increase the authority and influence of parents and community members. There is, however, another focus of community control in which parents are given a choice of schools, the most direct form of accountability by schools to the community. Although analysis of such choice is beyond the boundaries of this chapter, it is part of some forms of community control found, for example, in England. It has been suggested that, as SBM evolves and schools become unique, choice will eventually be an integral part of the SBM approach to participatory leadership.

Finally equal participation forms of SBM attempt to accomplish the purposes of both community control and professional control forms: making better use of teachers' knowledge for key decisions in the school and being more accountable to parents and the local community. Unlike the pure community-control version of SBM, the equal control versions assume that professionals are willing to be quite responsive to the values and preferences of parents and the local community under conditions in which parents are in a position to act as partners with schools in the education of their children. Both parents and teachers, it is assumed, have important knowledge to bring to bear on key decisions about curriculum, budget, and personnel. Site councils associated with this form of SBM have decision-making power and their membership is balanced between school staff and parent/community members.

Managerial Leadership

In addition to explicit concepts of management, this leadership category subsumes a form of leadership referred to as organizational in a total of 10 articles. Managerial leadership focuses on *the functions, tasks, or behaviors of the leader* and assumes that if these functions are carried out competently the work of others in the organization will be facilitated. Most approaches to managerial leadership also assume that organizational members behave rationally. Authority and influence are allocated to formal positions in proportion to the status of those positions in the organizational hierarchy. The terms "management" and "manager" frequently appear, especially in papers originating in the U.K., but without explicit attempts to conceptualize their meaning.

Several studies included in the review characterized management as a form of leadership to be replaced or supplemented in the face of present organizational challenges and the need for change (Cusack, 1993; Hallinger, 1992). Lesourd, Tracz, and Grady (1992) contrasted "managerial leadership" with "visionary leadership," for example. Others assumed the utility of managerial tasks and inquired about how they had been intensified by recent changes (Dunning, 1993) or how they affected the quality of teachers' work lives (Rossmiller, 1992). Other articles continued the long-standing debate over the relationship between the concepts of leadership and management. The majority of these articles (Achilles, 1992; Atkinson & Wilmore, 1993; Bolman & Deal, 1992; Bolman & Deal, 1994; Reilly, 1993; Whitaker *et al.*, 1991) treated leadership and management as distinct and, to some extent, as competing concepts. But two articles (Leithwood, 1994; Reitzug & Reeves, 1992) regarded leadership and management as complimentary concepts that should not be considered separately.

The distinction between leadership and management found outside these papers usually entails allocating management the responsibilities for policy implementation, maintaining organizational stability, and ensuring that routine organizational tasks are "done right." Classical management theory (March & Simon, 1958; Massie, 1965) assumes that these purposes are likely to be accomplished through such functions as planning, organizing, supervising, coordinating, budgeting, and staffing. Leadership, in contrast, is assigned the challenges of policy making, organizational change, and making sure "the right things get done" (Zaleznick, 1970; Bennis & Nanus, 1985; Hodgkinson, 1991).

The exchange relationship between leaders and followers, which Bass' conception of transactional leadership is based on, points to one of the central psychological mechanisms through which this view of managerial practices provides the organizational stability on which transformational leadership builds. "Transactional leadership," according to Bass, "is contingent reinforcement. The leader and follower agree on what the follower needs to do to be rewarded or to avoid punishment. If the follower does as agreed, the leader arranges to reward the follower" (1985, p. 121).

In school contexts at least, justifying a conceptual distinction between management and leadership is difficult. For example, Duke's (1995) historical analysis of one school's struggle for survival over a 63-year period provides vivid evidence that maintaining organizational stability in a turbulent environment requires the same types of responses on the part of organizational leaders as does organizational change. Furthermore, close analysis of the actual activities of formal school leaders (Kmetz & Willower, 1982; Harvey, 1986; Davies, 1987) indicates that whatever influence they exercise in their schools takes place through their responses to a host of often seemingly mundane tasks that they face from day to day. As a minimum, school leaders need to adopt a "bifocal" perspective (Deal and Peterson, 1994) in carrying out their tasks.

To what does management refer, however, when it is treated as a unique form of school leadership in its own right? Those studies explicitly responding to this question illustrate a range of possibilities. For example, Rossmiller identified two broad functions: buffering the technical core (curriculum and instruction) of the school from excessive distractions and interruptions, and smoothing "input or output transitions [such as organizing support groups for students experiencing stress]" (1992, p. 143). This study also described a number of subdimensions, specific ways in which principals carried out each of the two broad functions. In a second example with private sector origins, managerial functions in Myers and Murphy's (1995) study included six "organizational control" mechanisms: supervision, input controls (such as teacher transfers), behavior controls (such as job descriptions), output controls (student testing), selection/socialization, and environmental controls (community responsiveness). Goldring (1990) inquired about the "boundary spanning" function of school principals. Caldwell (1992) argued that leaders of self-managing schools should engage in a cyclical process "of goal-setting, needs identification, priority-setting, planning, budgeting, implementing, and evaluating in a manner which provides for the appropriate involvement of staff, and community" (1992, p. 16–17).

Duke and Leithwood's (1994) review of five different types of leadership literature identifies a relatively comprehensive set of school management dimensions. Two of the five sets of literatures addressed managerial issues most directly; these included 21 original studies of principal leadership specifically in the context of school restructuring and an additional 19 studies describing principals' practices and effects across varied contexts. These studies provided evidence of many aspects of leadership encompassed in other categories. As well, there were 10 sets of managerial tasks or functions described in these 40 studies as a whole:

• Providing adequate financial and material resources;
• Distributing financial and material resources so they are most useful;

- Anticipating predictable problems and developing effective and efficient means for responding to them;
- Managing the school facility;
- Managing the student body;
- Maintaining effective communication patterns with staff, students, community members, and district office staff;
- Accommodating policies and initiatives undertaken by district office in ways that assist with school improvement goals;
- Buffering staff so as to reduce disruptions to the instruction program;
- Mediating conflict and differences in expectations;
- Attending to the political demands of school functioning.

These 10 functions summarize most of the explicit as well as implicit conceptions of managerial functions in schools as they have been portrayed in writing over the past decade, separated from those leadership dimensions associated with other models. As Rost (1991) suggests, there is evidence of considerable support in the literature and among practicing leaders for managerial approaches to leadership, but this support and the meaning of such leadership often has to be inferred. As a whole, these functions convey an orientation to leadership similar to the orientation found in the classical management literature. This is quite different from the relatively entrepreneurial, creative, and change-oriented view of leadership referred to as "strategic management" in the non-school literature (Thomas & Pruett, 1993; Spencer, 1993). Those writing about educational leadership in the past decade appear to have incorporated such orientations in other, non-managerial models.

Contingent Leadership/Leadership Styles

Included as part of this category are leadership "styles" and "problem-solving" concepts referred to in a total of 18 articles (including "reflective" and "craft" views of leadership). The focus of this approach is on *how leaders respond to the unique organizational circumstances or problems that they face* as a consequence, for example, of the nature and preferences of coworkers, conditions of work, and tasks to be undertaken. This approach to leadership assumes that there are wide variations in the contexts for leadership and that to be effective these contexts require different leadership responses. Also assumed by this approach to leadership is that individuals providing leadership, typically those in formal positions of authority, are capable of mastering a large repertoire of leadership practices. Their influence depends, in large measure, on such mastery.

While sharing the same focus and assumptions, the "styles" and "problem-solving" orientations to contingent leadership are otherwise quite distinct. Leadership styles have been the stimulus for extensive empirical investigation in both school and non-school organizations. Examples of earlier research include the Ohio State studies, which led to the widely used Leadership Behavior Description Questionnaire and subsequent work by investigators such as Blake and Mouton (1964) and Hersey and Blanchard (1977). Nine studies included in this review made explicit reference to leadership style. Dimensions of leadership style investigated in these nine studies varied considerably: task versus relationships (Heller, Clay & Perkins, 1993), managerial versus visionary (Lesourd, Tracz & Grady, 1992), initiating structure versus consideration, autocratic versus facilitative (Cheng, 1991; Fenech, 1994; Hoy & Brown, 1988; Johnston, 1986; Uwazurike, 1991), and male versus female (Coleman, 1996). Bredeson (1993) inquires about the relationship between an individual's leadership style and the role strains resulting from restructuring efforts in schools.

The literature on leadership styles focuses on overt leadership practice, attempting to define a relatively small number of coherent, effective patterns of such practice. In contrast, the literature on problem solving focuses on the internal cognitive and affective processes engaged in by leaders as they ponder the challenges facing them and decide how best to act. From this perspective, there is a virtually unlimited universe of leadership practices. Leaders choose or invent those patterns of practice that appear to make most sense to them in response to the challenges they are addressing. What leaders do depends on what they think.

Problem-solving orientations to leadership, reflected in nine studies included in the review, are of two types. Those describing leadership as a reflective or craft-like enterprise stress the importance of leaders' internal processes without attempting to explicitly model such processes. For example, Sergiovanni (1989), Battersby (1987), and Clark (1988) use Schön's (1983) concept of reflective practice, or knowing-in-action, to explore the limited utility to practicing leaders of formal, scientific theory. Bredeson (1988) advocates the use of metaphors as stimulants for administrators' thinking and problem solving, whereas Willower (1994) invokes Dewey's method of inquiry as a frame to use in developing habits of reflection on the part of school leaders.

Also focused on leaders' thinking were four articles explicitly framed by contemporary cognitive science models of such processes. Three of these studies appeared in a special issue of EAQ entitled *Cognitive Perspectives On Educational Administration* (see also Hallinger, Leithwood and Murphy, 1993). Leithwood and Hallinger (1993) and Leithwood (1995) argued for the usefulness of cognitive perspectives on leadership and outlined what inquiries guided by such an orientation would entail. Allison and Allison (1993) invoke schema theory in their comparison of the domain-specific knowledge structures of novice and experienced school principals. Elsewhere, Allison (1996) reviews the literature on cognitive processes associated with problem interpretation and its application to the thinking of school leaders. Leithwood, Steinbach, and Raun (1993) describe the problem-solving processes of superintendents within a framework that attends to those cognitive processes entailed in problem interpretation, goal setting, anticipating constraints, the use of personal values and principles (see also Moorhead & Nediger, 1991), solution processes, and the mood or affect. Based on this framework, Leithwood and Steinbach (1995) offer the most comprehensive set of research results to date, exploring the nature of expert school leaders' problem-solving processes and their consequences for leadership practice.

Summary

What have been the results of a century's quest for a conception of school leadership? The six different categories of leadership described in this section is one answer to this question. These approaches include instructional, transformational, moral, participative, managerial, and contingent forms of school leadership. Although they have been presented as distinctly different leadership models, they are by no means pure types. The six approaches are most distinct with respect to their basic foci and the key assumptions on which they are premised. Significant differences also exist with respect to the nature and locus of leadership power.

But there are many aspects of these approaches that are quite similar, depending on whose version of an approach one adopts. For example, although moral leadership was the approach most visibly concerned with leadership ethics and values, there is a value position at least implicit in all six approaches. And transformational and participative approaches are quite explicit about the centrality of specific types of values to leadership. Additionally, whereas transformational approaches are arguably most explicit in their concern for organizational culture, many forms of instructional and moral leadership show evidence of a similar concern.

In sum, then, approaches to conceptualizing school leadership in contemporary literature offer eclectic and overlapping perspective on what should be the focus of leaders' attention and how leadership manifests itself in practice. Five of the six approaches (instructional leadership excepted) have well developed counterparts in the non-school literature and this literature figures prominently in how school leadership is conceptualized. This is probably both good and bad, good because there is an extensive academic and popular leadership literature that in our view has too often been ignored when it could have enriched thinking about leadership in schools, and bad because most of the literature included in our review that relied on a concept of leadership developed outside school contexts failed to address sufficiently the significance of that context for how leadership ought to be conceptualized.

Historical and Theoretical Sources of School Leadership Authority

Described in this section are the sources of authority that those writing about leadership in schools have appealed to over the century. One purpose of the section is to show how those sources have evolved and multiplied. A second purpose is to explore the extent to which contemporary models of leadership, summarized in the previous section, depend on one or more of these sources including tradition, religion, psychology, sociology, and a combination of social psychology, philosophy, and critical theory.

After *Webster's Third New International Dictionary* (1967), authority is defined as "the power to influence." Herbert Simon (1965) defined authority as the power to make decisions that guide the actions of others. Extending Simon's definition to focus more clearly on the consequences of decision making, Daniel Griffiths, in his theory of administration-as-decision making, argued for an understanding of authority as:

> the willingness of some to accept the power of another. That is, members of the organization acknowledge the legitimacy of the decisions made by some to control the decisions of others (1959, p. 88).

Conceived of in this way, the meaning of authority is essentially the same as Weber's concept of domination, "the probability that a command will be obeyed" (Roth & Wittich, 1968, p. 53).

Although status in the organizational hierarchy is the source for authority most readily evoked by Weber's definition, he argued that there were actually three "pure types of (or grounds for) legitimate domination," in addition to any other "less pure" grounds, such as habit, persuasion, and the like. These included rational or legal grounds (essentially the commonly evoked grounds mentioned above), traditional grounds (rooted in widely shared beliefs of the sort that allowed males to be the taken-for-granted heads of the households in many Western cultures until quite recently, for example), and charismatic grounds (the authority that flows from the perception that a person possesses exceptional or exemplary characteristics).

The meaning associated with the term "authority" as it is explored in this section includes but is not limited to the control-oriented views of authority offered by Simon, Griffiths, and Weber. Also included is, for example, the authority or power that a person or group is awarded as a consequence of special or highly valued knowledge (about the nature of human learning, for example), expert levels of skill in the execution of a task or performance considered important by others (such as the facilitation of group problem solving), and exceptional capacities for appreciation (such as understanding the hostile behavior of a student at school). Kenneth Benne's concept of anthropological authority, "a teaching authority who seeks to both mother and wean the young relative to the wider life in a community" (cited in Maxey, 1991, p. 9) is relevant as well. This section demonstrates that the historical sources for understanding the authority that contemporary leadership models rest on include but extend considerably beyond Weber's "pure types."

This section also demonstrates that the history of educational leadership and administration in North America, as it has been told in the most frequently cited and widely respected sources (Tyack, 1976; Tyack & Cummings, 1977; Tyack & Hansot, 1982; Callahan, 1962; Campbell, 1972; Campbell *et al.*, 1987; Culbertson, 1981, 1988; Griffiths, 1959), does not fully reflect the variety of grounds that have been appealed to historically as sources of authority by practicing school leaders. Rather, with the notable exception of Beck and Murphy's (1993) recent text, the story captured in these scholarly sources appears to have been influenced, to a fault, by efforts to establish and maintain a distinctive discipline of educational administration within the university.

Tradition

Tradition, one of Max Weber's three "pure types of legitimate domination" (Roth & Wittich, 1968, p. 215), is defined by Weber as "belief in the everyday routine as an inviolable norm of conduct . . . (and as) piety for what actually, allegedly, or presumably has always existed." He further argued that:

> Patriarchalism is by far the most important type of domination the legitimacy of which rests upon tradition. Patriarchalism means the authority of the father, the husband, the senior of the house, the sib elder over the members of the household and sib; the rule of the master and patron over bondsmen, serfs, freed men . . . of the patrimonial lord and sovereign prince over the subjects (Gerth & Mills, 1946, p. 296).

The system of norms associated with traditionalism is typically considered sacred and there is an element of arbitrariness associated with enforcing these norms on the part of the leader who judges primarily in terms of personal as distinct from functional criteria. Traditional authority is in this sense irrational (Gerth & Mills, 1946).

Traditional authority is, of course, an important instrument for cultural transmission and the preservation of community. As Slater points out, in the absence of tradition "old attachments to family, neighborhood, and community, attachments upon which and out of which one's sense

of self developed, lose their vitality" (1994, pp. 98–99). Evidence available concerning the effects of using tradition as a source of leadership authority in schools suggests that those effects have been largely negative, however.

Traditionalism based on patriarchy has manifested itself in prejudicial hiring practices applied to women in favor of an "old boys network" (Miklos, 1988), widely shared, male-dominated, leadership stereotypes that result in perceptions that women lack critical leadership skills and dispositions (Riehl & Lee, 1996) and ostracism from informal leadership networks (Shakeshaft, 1987). Factors such as these help explain the continuing disproportionate number of males occupying formal, especially senior, leadership positions. Tallerico and Burstyn (1996) cite evidence indicating that between 1928 and 1993 the percent of all U.S. superintendents of K–12 school districts who were women changed from 1.6 percent to only 5.6 percent. Cummings (Appended to Tyack, 1976) reported that 99.4% of American superintendents were male in 1952; typically, they also have been overwhelmingly Protestant, white, middle-aged, and from a rural background with no experience in a job outside of education (Tyack, 1976). In 1993, Montenegro reported that in the U.S., 71% of all K–12 teachers were female, whereas only 7.3% of superintendents, 24% of assistant superintendents, and 34% of principals were female. In addition to gender biases, tradition also has introduced bias into the ecology of school leadership based on culture, language, and race (Anderson, 1996; Mitchell, Ortiz, & Mitchell, 1987).

The influences of tradition on the development of contemporary leadership models appears to have been neither direct nor clear.

Religion

Protestant religious values were the source of authority appealed to by pre-1900 public school leaders, especially in the United States. These were men, not infrequently ministers, who preached both the value of public schooling and aims for such schooling based on their interpretation of the virtues required to lead a "good" life. These values were considered both absolute and equally appropriate for all students, even though a very high proportion of such students were not of the Protestant faith.

In these early years, religious values served as the base for determining the more exalted aims of education, but they were considered values that school leaders should themselves live by and model as well. Based on a reading of superintendents' own writings from that era, Tyack suggested that:
"superintendents in the nineteenth century conceived of their task in part as an evangelical enterprise, a search for organizational means to realize the goal of creating a 'redeemer nation'" (1976, p. 258).

Certification of superintendents, Tyack also concluded, was based not so much on possession of some body of professional knowledge as by their church membership and a shared earnestness. Superintendents in homogeneous small communities personified and enforced the official morality of the village. Tyack refers to the image that many superintendents of this period had of themselves, which was as "aristocrats of character" (1976, p. 258) who helped create an ideal of heroic leadership.

That school leaders of this period should look to religion as the basis for their legitimacy is not surprising. Many Victorian Americans believed that their country had been chosen as the preeminent Christian nation and that good citizens acted in accord with Christian values. The public school was viewed by these people as a key instrument for institutionalizing their beliefs and so they were among the most vigorous in the development of such schools (Smith, 1967; Tyack, 1970).

The influence of religious values as a source of public school leadership authority persisted well into the 1920s (Beck & Murphy, 1993) during which time it was invoked alongside "scientific management." But as the Protestant church and its values gradually relinquished its hold on the public school, the leadership of those schools turned to other sources of authority. By the 1930s, religion was rarely seen as a source of authority among public school leaders. During the 1990s, public schools have been reintroduced to the political power of religious values as a source of leadership authority. This has occurred as the "religious right" has challenged the leadership provided by local trustees and senior administrators to set outcomes for student learning that appear to usurp domains of children's development traditionally assumed to be the responsibility of families and the church (Spady, 1994). In many instances, these challenges have been successful with majority representatives from the religious right elected to local school boards.

Throughout the twentieth century, religion consistently has been a critical source of leadership authority in a significant proportion of North American schools established with the express purpose of transmitting the values of specific religions. Catholic schools are the most conspicuous examples, attracting 5.4% of the student population in the U.S. (Bryk, Lee, & Holland, 1993). Although Catholic school leaders are the largest single group of North American educational leaders continuing to use religion as a significant source of their authority, many in North America were established to transmit the values of some other religion. It is safe to infer that religion remains a strong basis for the authority of leaders in these schools as well.

Contemporary approaches to moral leadership, as described in the previous section, rarely consider religion a source of values, preferring instead to draw on democratic traditions and values. Nonetheless, in making the case that leadership authority should be based on concepts of what

is right and good, religion provided one of the earliest roots of today's concept of moral leadership.

Psychology

The contributions of psychology, both positive and negative, typically are underestimated in the most frequently cited accounts of the evolution of sources of school leadership authority. However, developments in psychological theory and research begun in the 1880s have informed and helped legitimate the decision making of school leaders about both students and teachers throughout the twentieth century. These developments also have assisted in the understanding of school leadership practices directly.

Students

As Campbell *et al.* (1987) argue, "science" as a source of leadership authority was founded originally on the early work of Cattell, James, Thorndike (in particular), and others who extended and applied the ideas of these pioneers beginning in the 1880s:

> Thorndike's work, perhaps more than any other single factor, imbued the scientific movement in education with its psychological and statistical character . . . In 1902, Thorndike offered a course in the application of 'psychological and statistical methods to education' . . . [this course] outlined what would be the emphasis and content of educational research for at least the next three decades (Campbell *et al.*, 1987, p. 30).

As tools for the measurement of intelligence, aptitude, and achievement were further developed, school leaders were provided with a basis for managing students: grouping, sorting, and advancing students, as well as screening them for subsequent levels of schooling. The birth of quantitative student testing arising from this early work in psychology persists with many refinements and modifications as a major influence on decision making in schools to this day. Debates also continue to rage about issues such as the validity of information collected through standardized achievement tests for decision making (Worthen, 1993), the meaning of "intelligence" and its educational role (Sternberg & Wagner, 1986), and the effectiveness and equity of tracking decisions based on pupil achievement and aptitude tests (Oakes, 1985).

During the 1940s the emphasis in psychology began to move from its interest in human traits and their measurement toward the development of formal behaviorial theories of human functioning. Due in no small measure to the seminal work of B. F. Skinner (1938), educators found themselves being admonished to approach curriculum, instruction, and student discipline using theories of contingent reinforcement.

These contributions by psychology to student testing practices, along with the implications for instruction flowing from behaviorism, were perceived to establish a highly "scientific" basis for managing the technical core of schooling. In combination with those methods of job analysis initially developed outside schools and associated with the scientific management movement, these developments in psychology provided considerable impetus for managerial approaches to leadership.

During the past 20 years, developments in psychology with clear relevance to education have rejected behaviorism in favor of attempting to better understand mental processes (Anderson, Reder, & Simon, 1997). Cognitive psychology has made considerable progress in developing constructivist (Bereiter & Scardamalia, 1996), connectionist (Rumelhart, 1989), and social cognitive (Vygotsky, 1978) understandings of the nature of student learning. These more recent understandings have resulted quite directly in the development of such student-related educational innovations in North America as discipline-based curricular frameworks (Robitaille, et al., 1993) and curriculum guidelines, as well as content and performance standards (National Council for Teachers of Mathematics, 1989) developed by many states and provinces.

Such developments demand high levels of professional expertise and judgment on the part of teachers to implement. So, while a potential source of leadership authority, they do not justify highly control-oriented approaches to such leadership. Depending on the amount of discretion left to school leaders in implementing such changes and the extent to which further local development of these changes is required for actual use, these sources of power nourish a view of school leaders as either middle managers or instructional leaders.

Teachers

At least four lines of psychological research and development have been especially influential as sources of authority for school leadership. One line of research was the extension of tools for student testing, initially developed in the early 1900s, to the evaluation of teachers. This practice became especially pronounced in North America in the context of the behaviorally-guided "process-product" era of research on teacher effectiveness (Brophy & Good, 1986). Research with this focus produced lists of discrete teacher behaviors that correlated positively and significantly with student achievement. These behaviors, in turn, became the basis for summative evaluation instruments, often checklists, used by administrators while observing classroom teaching (Popham, 1987). These contributions of relatively behavioristic forms of psychology to the supervision of teaching have been widely criticized, for example, as assuming a labor- or craft-like view of an activity and role better conceived of as a profession or an art (Darling-Hammond & Wise, 1985) and providing no information

to assist in the explanation for observed practices (Stiggins & Duke, 1988).

Widespread use of these approaches to the evaluation of instruction was fostered by the parallel work of Madeline Hunter (Hunter, 1976) and her associates, along with the calls for a simple, managerial, and control-oriented form of instructional leadership emanating from the effective schools research of the 1970s and early 1980s.

Results of psychological research describing the career stages of teachers is a second source of leadership authority with respect to teachers (Fuller, 1969; Huberman, 1989). Evidence from this research indicates that teachers pass through a relatively predictable set of stages over the course of their careers. These career stages intersect in crucial ways with broader life stages and cannot be separated from them. Furthermore, early career stages are formative and administrative decisions concerning teaching assignments and the like make an enormous difference to long-term career success and satisfaction. This evidence also suggests that, during the middle stages of a career, teachers are highly motivated to experiment with change initiatives. Most teachers become especially interested in their own classrooms as distinct from the school or district as a whole during the later stages of their careers.

This research is a rich source of understanding about the motivational predispositions of teachers, helping to match expectations for improvement efforts in the school, with the interests of individual staff members (Leithwood, 1989). As a source of authority most consistent with transformational approaches to leadership, it also offers useful guidelines to educational leaders for the continuous professional development of teachers (Oja, 1979).

As a third source of leadership power with respect to teachers, psychology has provided theoretical tools for better understanding forms of leadership that are appropriate in influencing a host of teacher variables considered to be critical mediators standing between leaders' practices and the effects of these practices on students. Throughout the century, research about school leadership has inquired about forms of leadership that influence, for example, teacher job satisfaction (Conley, Bacharach, & Bauer, 1989), teachers' commitment to change (Leithwood & Menzies, in press), and willingness to participate in school decisions (Kushman, 1992). For the most part, this line of research is a source of power for participative and transformational approaches to school leadership.

A fourth and final line of psychological research serving as a source of leadership authority with respect to teachers is to be found in applications of cognitive psychology to a better understanding of the nature of teachers' thinking and decision making (Clark & Peterson, 1986). Although the results of this research had a considerable impact on some teacher preparation programs, there is little evidence of their application as sources of leadership authority. This is in spite of their considerable potential to help those providing transformational leadership to develop a better understanding of the thinking of their teacher colleagues and to inform them about how to exercise influence with their teacher colleagues in ways productive to them both.

Expert Leadership

Research on teacher thinking, however, did provide a well-developed set of theories and methods to help guide parallel research on the nature of school leaders' thinking and decision making (Leithwood & Steinbach,1995; Hallinger, Leithwood & Murphy, 1993; Allison, 1996). This quite recent research, a source of authority for contingent approaches to leadership, offers insights concerning the nature of leaders' expertise (Leithwood and Steinbach, 1995) as well as experiences useful in the development of such expertise (Bridges & Hallinger, 1992).

In addition to the work on teacher thinking and decision making, current research on expert leadership thinking can be traced back to a much earlier preoccupation with administrative problems and decision making. Allison (1996) dates the beginning of this line of work to Strayer's 1925 volume *Problems in Educational Administration* and describes an ongoing interest in the use of case problems in textbooks for the purpose of helping to teach conceptual material throughout the subsequent 70 years (Hoy & Tarter, 1995; Culbertson, Jacobson & Reller, 1960). Griffiths (1959) theory of administration as decision making provided the pre-cognitive framework for a substantial research effort by Hemphill, Griffiths, and Frederiksen (1962) to understand the nature of administrators' problem interpretation. Curiously, in spite of its scope, the work begun in this study does not seem to have been pursued by others between its completion and the quite recent spate of cognitively-oriented research on leadership expertise and its development.

Sociology

Two distinct lines of theory and research have been appealed to by school leaders as sources of authority for their practices during the twentieth century: theory and research about organizational change and about organizational design.

Organizational Change

One of the main sources of school leaders' power in implementing change can be traced to the seminal works of Everett Rogers (Rogers & Shoemaker, 1971) and Ronald Havelock (1971). In both cases, the primary focus of attention was on what would now be called the pre-adoption and adoption phases of the change process. During the 1960s and 1970s, this phase of change also was the object of attention by those interested in school leadership. Carlson's (1972) study of the processes used by superintendents in the adoption of innovations in school districts exemplifies this work. In this work, roots can be found leading not only to a middle manager view of school leadership but also aspects of participative, instructional, and transformational approaches to leadership.

Although knowledge about pre-adoption and adoption processes offered some useful guidance, especially to senior school leaders, it soon became apparent that adoption decisions by such leaders did not have much to do with actual uses of whatever was adopted in classrooms. Charters and Jones' widely influential paper, *On the Risk of Appraising Non-Events in Program Evaluation* (1973), made this point from the perspective of those evaluating the impact of changes on classroom practices and student achievement. John Goodlad's widely cited study, *Behind the Classroom Door* (1970), also made this case in an especially compelling way for school practitioners. His League of Cooperating Schools focused attention on implementation processes within the school as the unit of change and on the principal as a key agent of change.

The Charters and Jones and Goodlad papers were among the more visible early stimulants for a line of sociological research about implementation processes. This research acquired considerable currency as a formal source of authority for how leaders should approach change in their schools during the 1970s and 1980s. Early stages of this research entailed mostly case studies of failed change initiatives in schools. For example, Gross, Giacquinta & Bernstein (1971) described the troubled path of an elementary school staff faced with implementing an activity-based curriculum without adequate material support or consistent, supportive leadership; Smith & Keith's (1971) ethnography documented the gradual "normalization" of a much-publicized, newly constructed public school built around the ambitious and innovative open education visions of the district superintendent and the school's first principal, both of whom exhibited strong transformational and participative leadership features.

This early work contributed in turn to a line of essentially sociological research and development about educational change and school improvement processes that had become a dominant source of authority for many school leaders by the mid-1980s. This source supported a more decidedly "change agent" view of school leadership than had any other prior source. In relation to the six categories of leadership concepts outlined in the previous section, this source provided support for some elements and versions of participative, transformational, instructional, and managerial orientations to leadership.

Among the more noteworthy large scale research efforts aimed at providing a data-based set of prescriptions for practice were the Rand Change Agent studies (Berman *et al.*, 1975) and the "DESSI" study (Loucks *et al.*, 1982).

Michael Fullan had begun his career-long effort to synthesize research on educational change and to make it accessible to educational practitioners (Fullan & Pomfret, 1977; Fullan, 1982; Fullan & Steiglebauer,1991).

Also by the mid-1980s, Gene Hall and his associates had fully developed their Concerns-Based Adoption Model (CBAM). Used widely in the U.S., as well as in parts of Canada, the Netherlands, Belgium, Australia, and elsewhere, CBAM provided school leaders with tangible tools for diagnosing key aspects of their organization and specific strategies for implementing innovations (Loucks, Newlove & Hall, undated). Although clearly one of the best researched and disseminated, CBAM was but one example of a genre of R&D products, school improvement procedures, of which there were many others. Indeed, one outgrowth of the effective schools movement was a set of models specifically designed to implement the correlates of effective schools.

Common among all these products was an attempt to simplify the complex processes of school change and make them more manageable for school leaders. Usually this meant conceptualizing the change process as a series of temporally sequenced stages, each focused on a key set of functions or tasks such as diagnosing readiness for change, developing goals for change, choosing programs to achieve the goals, and the like. School improvement models served as the basis for considerable in-service training of school leaders and became for a while the official approach to change not only in many school districts (Stoll & Fink, 1994) but in whole states and provinces as well. (Matthew Miles [1993], a seminal figure throughout this 40-year period of research and development, provides a much more extensive and reflective analysis of the evolution of approaches to change).

Approaches to change described to this point, emerging largely from sociological inquiry and serving as major sources of power for several different approaches to school leadership, evolved through three stages. The first stage documented failure and drew general implications or guidelines for success; this stage assumed that the seeds of success are evident in failure, a risky assumption. The second stage found examples of successful practice and recommended they be used by others; this gives little weight to the importance of the context for change, also a risky approach. At a third stage are efforts to prescribe a set of sequenced tasks to be carried out in order to manage the change process in an orderly fashion; the obvious flaw in this approach is the assumption that an invariant set of tasks is useful for all changes and for all points of departure.

These shortcomings, among others, gave rise to school restructuring, an elastic concept often including many components of change (Murphy, 1991) but usually including at least some form of school-based management (Murphy & Beck, 1995). School-based management brings together

sources of school leadership authority based on knowledge of change processes and knowledge about organizational design, largely in support of participative and transformational models of leadership.

Organizational Design

Throughout the twentieth century, organizational design theory has provided another, primarily sociological, source of authority for educational leadership. The story of how this source of authority evolved in schools begins with Frederick Taylor and the scientific management movement, transforms itself into a preoccupation with bureaucracy, and then moves on to an interest in open systems theory. The atheoretical correlates of effective schools' research then supplants formal open systems theory, although the correlates themselves contain an open systems perspective. During the past 10 years, a resurgence of interest has occurred in a more complex, open systems theory that has yet to be synthesized into a formal theory. This more complex design characterizes the school as a learning organization or a learning community.

Managerial leadership has its genesis most directly in scientific management. This approach to organizational design emerged as a significant source of leadership authority in the second decade of the twentieth century (Tyack, 1976; Campbell et al., 1987; Callahan, 1962). At the core of this form of organizational design was the time and motion study, a procedure to be used by supervisors to find the best way for carrying out a task and then telling the workers responsible for the task how to do it. The initial attractiveness of scientific management was as a response to two problems. First, traditional forms of control, authority, and communication, as well as existing methods to measure productivity, had proven ineffective in dealing with modern industrial problems. Second, industry was marked by intense labor unrest stemming from substantial changes in the nature of the work; there was an absence of effective supervisory procedures and uniform production standards required in a modern industrial organization.

Within education, scientific management offered itself as a solution, particularly for superintendents of large city school districts, to managing rapid growth in facilities, school staffs, and increasingly diverse student populations. The immense growth in school systems during this time also prompted growing concerns among the public about the costs of education and the need for greater financial accountability. These were problems scientific management seemed to have the potential to solve. Callahan (1962) argues as well that the high social status of business leaders who were promoting efficiency through the use of scientific management in their own organizations, in combination with the low status and public vulnerability of school leaders, made it inevitable that such practices would be adopted in schools for purposes of self-preservation, whether or not they had any effect on the quality of education. Pajak (1993) claims, however, that although scientific management was the focus of considerable writing in education, it had very little influence on the actual practices of educational leaders at the school level.

Although explicit interest in Tayloristic versions of scientific management (Taylor, 1947) had dissipated by 1930, it continued less explicitly as a part of the classical approach to administrative study into the 1940s that was reflected, for example, in the work of Fayol, Gulick, Urwick, and Mooney (Campbell *et al.*, 1987). It also was reflected in analytic approaches to administration, part of the Theory Movement in educational administration during the '50s and '60s.

As originally conceived by Weber, bureaucracy provides the organizational basis for one of his three pure types of authority (rational grounds) and another key source of power for managerial approaches to leadership. According to Weber, this source of authority rests on a belief in the legality of enacted rules and the right of those elevated to authority under such rules to issue commands (Roth & Wittich, 1968, p. 215). Conceived of as an especially enlightened form of organization, Weber described it in terms of rule-governed systems of relationships defined by a hierarchy of roles and duties (Gerth & Mills, 1946, p. 196).

The translation of Max Weber's work into English (Gerth & Mills, 1946) prompted considerable attention outside of education to the study of bureaucracy between the mid-1940s and mid-1970s. Particularly influential were the extensions and critiques of this work by the influential sociologists C. Wright Mills, Talcott Parsons, and Amatai Etzioni. Bureaucracy became a popular focus of study within education especially after 1960 "when students of educational management began to work within the framework of general administration and began to employ behavioral science approaches to organizational study" (Campbell *et al.*, 1987). Its attractiveness can be partly explained by its following on the heels of the Human Relations movement in school leadership, which gave no attention to structure and organization.

At the same time, post-war expansion of the educational system created levels of administrative complexity that added to the hierarchical character of school systems; in the U.S., for example, the number of school districts went from 100,000 (Campbell, *et al.*, 1987, p.86, originally reported by the National Commission on School District Reorganization) to 16,000 between 1948 and 1980.

Bureaucracy is rarely viewed today as the enlightened form of organizational design conceived by Weber. Nevertheless, the work of Eliot Jaques (1989), a scholar and consultant to governments and private enterprise, continues as a powerful justification for hierarchy in organizations. This work is presently an important and growing source of leadership authority outside education and may be instrumental in fostering renewed interest in bureaucracy

in school organizations (see Gronn, 1996). Other aspects of Weber's work also served as important elements in the attack led by Greenfield (Greenfield & Ribbins, 1993) on positivistic and rational approaches to educational administration and, ironically, managerial approaches to school leadership.

From the late '50s to the mid-'80s, considerable effort was made by organizational theorists inside and outside education to formulate a clearer conception of the place of the wider environment in the functioning of schools and other types of organizations. Interest in the development of open systems theory was stimulated in part by growth in skepticism on the part of the public concerning all social institutions, changing social values, and a general questioning and reexamination of the traditions and cultures of North American society. Considerable efforts were made to rid social institutions of racism, for example, including school desegregation, the Civil Rights Act of 1964, and the Voting Rights Act of 1965. Also evidence of the emergence of a newly dominant set of values was the youth revolt against the Vietnam war, rise of a new individualism, and the women's movement.

These social forces created a substantially changed milieu within which educational leaders had to work. Changing the context of leaders' work even more directly was a loss of consensus about the purposes of education in the U.S. (Ravitch, 1983). Collective bargaining for teachers was widespread by the mid-1960s and there emerged a strong trend at this time toward federal intervention into education: PL 94–142 (education of students with special needs) and PL 92–318 (end of sex discrimination in schools and colleges) are just two examples of such intervention.

During this period, schools also experienced a rise in the number of special interest groups trying to influence their programs. Educational administrators now had to work not only with parents and trustees, but the wider community as well. Increased demand for parental choice helped create alternative schools (Raywid, 1985) and gave rise to experimentation with voucher systems (Hertling, 1985).

Many of these pressures on schools to envision themselves as more integrally connected with their wider environments continue to evolve unabated to the present. Rooted directly in these earlier pressures are current efforts, such as altering the governance of schools to give greater control to the local community (Malen, *et al.*, 1990) to develop "full service schools" and to redesign secondary education so that it is more sensitive to the needs and demands of business and wider public interests (Hogan, 1992).

Open Systems theory stresses the complexity and variability of component parts of the system (both individual and subgroups) and the looseness of the connections between them. The interdependence of the organization and its environment shifts attention away from structure and purely managerial orientations to leadership, as in the case of bureaucracy, to process in organizations (Campbell *et al.*, 1987). Outside of education, the theory is illustrated in Talcott Parsons' (1960) concept of formal organizations including three levels, systems, or functions, the technical, managerial, and institutional or community systems. According to this conception, no organization is wholly independent, especially in the relationships between the managerial and institutional systems. Three types of institutional control stand over the managerial system—generalized norms, interstitial organization (trustees, for example), and governmental structure to oversee the interstitial and managerial levels (such as state education agencies).

Another example of Open Systems theory, one providing sources of power for political versions of participatory leadership, can be found in the work of David Easton (1965). Schools are viewed as political subsystems, the larger social environment providing input to the subsystem. The idea of systems, including schools, operating in a "loosely coupled" fashion (Weick, 1976) is also part of the Open Systems' rationale that has received considerable attention in the literature aimed at school leaders (Deal & Kennedy, 1982). Conceiving of schools as learning organizations (Watkins & Marsick, 1993) or professional learning communities (Louis, Marks & Kruse, 1996) can be considered a continuation of the interest in Open Systems' theory. Knowledge generated from research about this design is a source of power for transformational approaches to school leadership.

The so-called correlates of effective schools were and in many places continue to be unprecedented in the extent of their use as sources of authority for instructional approaches to school leadership created by the academic community. Research to discover these correlates was initiated more or less in parallel in U.K. secondary schools (Rutter *et al.*, 1979) and in U.S. inner city elementary schools (Edmonds, 1979). By 1980, the original empirical work from this perspective had accumulated to a corpus of at least a dozen studies. Reviews and critical analyses of these studies were being widely published and explicit efforts were underway to bring results of this research to the attention of school leaders (Duckett, *et al.*, 1980).

For academics conducting the original effective schools research, controversial evidence presented by James Coleman (1966) concerning the small proportion of variation in student achievement accounted for by schools, as compared with other factors, was the main stimulus for their inquiry. They viewed schools as a primary instrument for the achievement of social and economic equity and were alarmed that Coleman's findings would be used by policy makers as a reason to allocate fewer resources to public education. Thus it was crucial from their point of view to find evidence to dispute Coleman's claim and to embark on efforts to recreate as many schools as possible in conformity with this evidence.

For school leaders, the attractiveness of effective schools research as a source of authority could be accounted for by its accessibility and the straightforward, "implementable" nature of its findings. Creating a safe and orderly environment, providing strong leadership, monitoring student progress, and engaging in active instruction, while not simple tasks to carry out in schools, were at least on the surface clear and familiar. Furthermore, the inner-city, economically-disadvantaged context in which much of the research had been carried out was the same context in which many school leaders were experiencing their greatest challenges.

Diffusion of effective school research also was speeded up considerably by the unusually well-targeted communication channels used for disseminating the research results; the emergence of a widespread perception that education was in crisis; and the fact that effective school research does not require fundamental revisions in the way schools are run, which rather works on improving existing practices; and the amount of effort devoted by districts, states, and professional associations to creating in-service programs for school leaders built around effective schools correlates (such as the Harvard principal center, and so on).

By the time Louis and Miles were ready to undertake their study of effective secondary schools in the U.S. (1990), they were able to select their sample from a population of schools claiming to be implementing effective school research results, estimated to be approximately 279.

Philosophy, Social Psychology, and Critical Theory

These three sources are discussed together because, although independent in their genesis, they combine in giving rise to and sustaining interest in participative and democratic forms of school leadership. These forms of school leadership came to prominence first in the early 1930s, and interest in them in their original form was sustained into the 1960s, especially in the teacher supervision literature (Pajak, 1993; Lindsay & Schwarcz, 1960). Support for these forms of leadership initially arose in response to the dehumanizing aspects of scientific management, greater community involvement in schools because schools were increasingly situated in suburban areas and in closer proximity to parents, and a trend toward administrative decentralization.

During the early development of participative and democratic concepts of leadership, "educational" philosophy was an important source of authority. In this context, educational philosophy refers to a position initially developed by Dewey (1916, 1929, 1946) concerning democracy and scientific inquiry. In Dewey's view, the challenge to democracy lay in extending the spirit of participation at the heart of the American political system to the economic world of men and women at work. The long standing goal of political and social equity was to be reflected in participatory forms of organizational governance, allowing the benefits of production and decisions about work to be shared by all. These decisions would be arrived at through consciously reasoned, cooperative problem solving (reflective inquiry).

This position was further developed by others in education and promoted as an ideal form of school organization and leadership. As Kilpatrick explained, "education will not contribute to the reconstruction of the social process until it seriously experiments with the reconstruction of its own procedures" (1933, p. 210). Although somewhat dormant for several decades, this basic position has been resuscitated more recently by critical theory, as we explain below.

Although democratically-oriented educational philosophy promoted participatory forms of leadership on essentially moral grounds, parallel developments in social psychology provided evidence that such participation was an effective means of achieving organizational goals. The Hawthorne Studies carried out by Mayo, Lewin, and others (Mayo, 1933) are typically cited as the genesis of this work. The ideas of Mary Parker Follett (Metcalf & Urwick, 1940) concerning the nature of power and decision making were almost identical to those expressed in the current literature on educational restructuring and teacher empowerment (Dunlap & Goldman, 1991). Reflecting these ideas, the 1943 ASCD Yearbook portrayed leadership in schools as an educative force. Its aim, according to the authors, was to expand the horizons of the group by encouraging group members to think beyond the level of existing opinion and practice. This perspective is remarkably similar to Argyris and Schön's (1978) concept of "double loop" learning.

Although early interest in participatory and democratic forms of leadership were promoted by Dewian philosophy and social psychology, the emergence of critical theory, along with post-positive orientations to the philosophy of science, has resulted in them being attributed renewed relevance in response to contemporary problems. Evers and Lakomski (1991) characterize critical theory approaches to administration as complex and covering ethical, political, social, linguistic, and personal dimensions. This analysis is limited to features of both post-positivism and critical theory stimulated in response to three features of the theory movement in educational administration: a positivist orientation toward knowledge, a structural-functionalist conception of organizations, and a control-oriented, managerial, view of leadership. Critical theory, arising in objection to these features, among others, is defined for our purposes by the positions it has developed as alternatives.

Structural-functional assumptions about the nature of school organizations are rejected by critical theory. Such "systems-based functionalism" in Foster's terms (1986, p. 3) includes assumptions about a high level of consensus in respect to existing school goals, the appropriateness of such goals for all stakeholders, and the non-political nature of defensible processes for arriving at an agreement about such goals. These assumptions also treat as unproblematic contemporary developments in science and technology, as well as the hierarchical nature of relationships traditionally found within the school organization. According to Maddock (1995), the task of critical theory is to subject such contemporary developments and relationships to continual scrutiny on their own terms and to demonstrate the contradictions and limitations of these ideas and practices.

Critical theory also offers a more decisively normative, socio-cultural analysis of schools. This analysis points out how structural-functional assumptions have encouraged schools to establish structures of authority and control, both mirroring and reproducing systematic inequalities in the wider society. These inequalities arise from differences among groups of people in race, class, religion, gender, and geography. Cultural analysis, explains Bates:

> insists that the culture of a society cannot be understood unless the nature and organization of the relationships and struggles between dominant and subordinate cultures are taken into account. Indeed, it is the struggle among such cultures that constitutes the major dynamic of cultural change (1987, p. 90).

Structural-functional views of the school organization remove the possibilities of schools serving as agents of democracy and social justice.

This basic objection to how school organizations have been conceptualized in the context of the theory movement in educational administration has given rise to a view of leadership that, although somewhat distinct in its emancipatory emphasis, supports at least three of the leadership models described in earlier sections of this chapter. Critical theorists argue that a managerial conception of leadership has dominated the field over the past several decades (Smyth, 1989; Bates, 1993; Foster, 1986). This conception of leadership assumes dominance or control over organizational members and separates educational from administrative concerns, privileging the latter (Ortiz & Marshall, 1988; Bates, 1993). The genesis of critical theorists' orientation to leadership is its responsibility to develop educational organizations whose fundamental purposes are to nurture not only equity among organizational stakeholders but also the freedom and autonomy of individual members. A control orientation to leadership and administration flies in the face of these emancipatory intentions. Foster (1989), as a consequence, argues that leadership must be critical, transformational, educative, and ethical.

Critical leadership assumes that because existing conditions of social life have been constructed by people (rather than simply received), they can be reconstructed to be more equitable, democratic, and just if they are found wanting in these respects. One of the key responsibilities of leaders is to engage colleagues in self-reflection on and analyses of existing social and organizational conditions, along with the social cultures of both the school and the local community.

When these analyses reveal room for improvement in social and organizational conditions, leadership also entails assisting colleagues to envision more suitable social and organizational conditions appropriate to the social culture. Foster (1986) refers to this visioning process as "educative leadership," a process that enables colleagues to consider alternative ways of ordering their lives and raising their level of consciousness about social conditions.

Leadership also entails ethical commitments. Building on Burns' (1978) conception of how transformational leadership functions, such commitments are the elevation of colleagues' moral consciousness about the social conditions in which they find themselves. As part of their ethical commitments, leaders should be advocates for principles of democracy, respect for others, social justice, and equality. According to Foster (1989) and Bates (1987), leaders always have a moral agenda.

Given a vision of a more desirable set of social and organizational conditions, transformative leadership entails assisting colleagues in making judgments about suitable courses of action to achieve these conditions (Bates, 1987; Foster, 1986) and implementing these actions. Judgments about suitable courses of action require:

> a balancing of theory and empirical understanding, of political and ethical factors, and of traditions and customs. It is in this way that administrators approaches go beyond the scientific without becoming arbitrarily subjective (Maddock, 1995, p. 66).

The contributions of critical theory to conceptualizing leadership have been quite significant. As the exercise of critical theory matures, its potential contributions promise to be far greater, not least because of the balance it provides to the neo-conservative philosophy presently raging through most Western political systems and posing unprecedented threats to equity and social justice as goals of education systems.

We are much less positive, however, about the contemporary contributions of philosophy in educational administration to the development of concepts of leadership. Clearly this is a contrarian view, one that flies in the face of judgments by many presently writing in the field. We refer here to the extensive literature in educational administration devoted to post-positive or post-empiricist conceptions of epistemology and the role of science in informing leadership practice. Greenfield is generally acknowledged as having initiated (Greenfield, 1975) and nourished this literature along (Greenfield & Ribbins, 1993), in concert with scholars who joined him in debate (Griffiths, 1979; Willower, 1985). And Evers

and Lakomski (1991) have offered cogent overviews, analyses, and extensions of their own.

What this line of theorizing in educational administration adds up to, stripped of its often obtuse references and dense, abstract language, appears to be as follows:

- Agreement with and understanding of knowledge as personally constructed;
- Claims that organizational behavior is often not especially rational, not only because people lack information but also because organizational members pursue their own goals and values;
- Most decisions faced by administrators are value-laden;
- Human systems are by definition less predictable than physical systems;
- What passes for "scientifically objective knowledge" in human organizations is more adequately characterized as "socially shared" knowledge;
- The meaning people give to events is shaped by their goals, values, feelings, existing knowledge, and past experiences.

Perhaps there is more to it than this, but not much. And what it adds up to is a series of "blinding flashes of the obvious"—obvious in terms of existing understandings from other scholarly sources, not to mention the common understandings of most school leaders. At least for the purposes of this chapter, it is remarkable that, whatever current writings in educational administration philosophy might have contributed, a more sophisticated conception of educational leadership is not one of them.

Summary

This section of the chapter identified, as historical and theoretical sources of leadership authority, tradition, religion, psychology, sociology, and a combination of philosophy, social psychology, and critical theory. Knowledge developed through psychological and sociological inquiry have been especially influential in justifying the exercise of leadership, but most contemporary approaches to leadership in schools have significant roots in at least several different sources of power and authority. Further, each source of power, while capable of nourishing several different leadership offspring, is relatively hostile to others. Finally, this section also has shown that all the sources of leadership authority, save postpositivism and critical theory, are quite mature. To the extent that these sources are central to concepts of leadership, as we have argued, contemporary leadership approaches are best characterized as evolutionary in nature.

Conclusion

Few attempts have been made to look broadly at the quest for an adequate conception of leadership in schools as it has unfolded over the twentieth century. Beck and Murphy's (1993) work is likely the most recent among these efforts. Having attempted the task ourselves, we are especially aware of the many different ways in which any single description of the quest could be viewed as missing essential understandings critical in someone's view. In this concluding section, we briefly reflect on the nature of the quest itself, offer a synthesis of results to the mid-1990s, and identify some priorities for future theory and research.

Nature of the Quest

Viewed up close or at one point in time, it would be easy to conclude that efforts to conceptualize leadership in schools over the past century have been going in circles. From an up-close perspective, it is especially difficult to understand several issues with which this chapter has been centrally preoccupied: the genesis of different concepts of leadership; why a leadership concept falls into favor at one point in time only to fall out of favor eventually, overshadowed by a different concept; and whether the multiple leadership concepts encountered in the literature are truly competing with one another or, rather, reflecting different elements of some, as yet to be described, more sophisticated conception of leadership in schools. Chaos or complexity?

Although chaos seems to be the fashionable answer among most of those who have written about development in the field of school leadership, the inquiry described in this chapter arrived at a moderately more optimistic conclusion. Unquestionably, conceptual development related to educational leadership over the century has not occurred through any widely agreed on, explicit game plan (more like the flight of the bumble bee than a bullet, to use Phil Jackson's metaphor). But then what social science concept has? Rather, the developmental process seems to be well captured by Hutchin's (1995) view of organizational learning as a process of mutual adaptation manifest in the actions of individual members of the leadership community as they reacted to, criticized, and built on one another's ideas. It is neither necessary nor likely that many individual members of the leadership community have understood the pattern of actions represented in the community as a whole. So justifying the claim that the concept of school leadership has developed through some defensible process does not also require justifying the claim that those in the midst of the process intentionally designed it that way.

From the perspective of our own analysis, the mutually adaptive process through which concepts of school leadership have developed over this century has consisted of conceptual differentiation, recalibration, and elaboration. This seems to be the case for all leadership concepts. Some version of each category of leadership concept, if not the specific models that each subsumes, was evident by the middle of the century. Differentiation is evident, for example, in the gradual increase in number of sources of power and authority used by scholars to justify the exercise of leadership and in the further clarification of implications of each of these sources for leadership practice. Recalibration is visible in the adaptation or updating of the meaning and expression of enduring leadership concepts in acknowledgment of changing problems and contexts. Elaboration is illustrated in efforts to deepen understandings of those sources of leadership legitimization as well as to extend knowledge of the practices associated with each different approach to leadership. The outcomes of this process, although not synthesized well to date, are conceptions of leadership in schools that are increasingly complex (a good thing), multi-dimensional, ecologically valid, defensible, and user-friendly.

A Relational Conception of Leadership

A type of synthesis of contemporary leadership literature has been accomplished through the six-fold classification of leadership concepts that subsumes an initial, more specific set of 20 (refer to Table 3.2). These categories, however, are not directly comparable. They do not provide alternative solutions to the same problem. Rather, these concepts focus attention on different aspects of the organization. For instance, managerial leadership awards considerable importance to organizational policies and procedures, whereas instructional leadership focuses on the organization's core technology. The six leadership categories also attend to different pieces of the leadership puzzle. Contingency approaches, for example, focus on leaders' problem-solving processes whereas moral leadership attends to leaders' values. Finally, the six sets of leadership concepts also concern themselves with different aspects of those designated as followers. Transformational leadership emphasizes the importance of followers' commitments whereas participative leadership concerns itself largely with followers' roles in decision making, as an illustration.

Thus these six approaches to leadership do not explicitly represent a set of discrete dimensions that, taken together, provide a comprehensive account of what is entailed in leadership. They still place excessive emphasis on the practices or internal processes of an individual person designated as "leader," for example.

In this concluding section of the chapter, we explore and illustrate the possibility of developing a more comprehensive account of leadership based on relationships. After Wheatley (1994) and others, such a conception views leadership as a more or less complex set of relationships cohering around a core of common intentions. The ways in which existing leadership concepts differ from one another suggest three of the four sets of elements likely to be interacting in such relationships: the leader, the follower, and the organization. The fourth element is the environment within which the organization and its individual members find themselves.

Leaders and Followers

For purposes of developing a more comprehensive account of leadership, these elements of both leader and follower that interact might be conceptualized as capacities (knowledge and skills), attitudes, values, and goals (elements of motivation), and practices (more or less overt behaviors). School leadership literature is replete with treatments of leadership defined by the relationships between one or more of these elements of leaders and followers; for example, the relationship between a principal's vision (goals) and a teacher's classroom practices (as in instructional leadership), or a principal's practices and a teacher's motivations (as in transformational leadership).

Organizations

Organizational theory offers several ways to conceptualize relevant elements of an organization. By way of illustration, we have found significant relationships in some of our own work (Leithwood, Jantzi, & Steinbach, 1995) between leadership and a set of six organizational elements derived from such a theory (Daft, 1988; Banner & Gagné, 1995; Galbraith, 1977; Bolman & Deal, 1991). These elements include mission and vision, culture, structure, information collection and decision-making processes, programs and instruction, strategies for change, and policies and resources. The literature on school leadership also provides many examples of leadership defined in terms of the relationships between some of these elements of the organization and one or more of the other sets of variables included in this conception. Symbolic leadership, for example, describes relationships between the values both implicit and explicit in a leader's practices and the culture of the school. Participative leadership focuses attention on, among other things, the relationships among teachers' practices, principals' practices, and organizational structures.

Environment

A fourth element interacting in a relational conception of leadership is the environment within which the organization functions (in other words, whatever is defined as outside the "boundaries" of the organization). Although given considerable attention in organizational theory, this element is not well represented in most existing categories of leadership concepts: the subcategory of moral leadership referred to as "political" in Table 3.2 is the primary exception, sometimes focusing on the relationship between the interests of those inside and outside of the organization. Our review of the historical and theoretical roots of these concepts suggests that this is an unfortunate shortcoming. The perceived value of a leadership concept at any point in time, as well as its eventual fall from favor, seem largely to be explained by events in the larger environment within which the organization finds itself.

As with organizations, critical elements of the environment in which schools find themselves can be defined in a variety of ways. Daft (1988) offers a set of elements with demonstrable relevance to schools:

- The pool of human resources which employees are drawn from (such as the extent to which talented college graduates choose to enter or not enter teaching);
- The market for services provided by the organization (the challenge to public schools' quasi-monopoly on students provided by the recent charter schools movement);
- The availability of financing for the organization's initiatives (erosion of support for school funding by increased public demand for health care and other social services);
- New technologies in the environment that may threaten the need for the services provided by the organization (the extent to which computer-based technologies provide access to educational services and information outside the bounds of formal educational institutions);
- Economic conditions that influence the volume of business (the impact on support for school bond issues of recessionary business cycles);
- Governments and the nature of their policies and regulations (the extent to which many current western governments are embarked on major educational restructuring initiatives);
- Sociocultural conditions such as social value systems and demographics (generational shifts in the size of the school age population and the effects this has on support for education of youth).

These elements making up the wider environment of schools and other organizations offer leadership some of its greatest challenges, as just the handful of examples provided here demonstrates. Some recent leadership inquiries have begun to take them explicitly into account. For example, an interest in the relationship between leader practices, teacher practices, and government restructuring initiatives is evident in recent research on leadership in the context of school-based management (Murphy & Beck, 1995). Goldring and Rallis (1993) explore the meaning of school leadership through the relationship between leaders' practices and most of the elements of the environment identified by Daft (1988). But the importance of most environmental elements has not been well reflected in efforts to conceptualize school leadership to date.

Relationships

Although it is necessary to specify at least illustrative elements of each of the constructs interacting in a relational conception of leadership, the most complex and important aspects of leadership are to be found in the nature of the relationships themselves. How can such relationships adequately be conceptualized? The generic definition, with which the chapter began, of leadership as an influence process concerning the choice of goals and the development and implementation of the means for their achievement, is one starting point for answering this question. Additionally, these relationships can be viewed from both descriptive and normative perspectives. With purely descriptive purposes in mind, variation in influence processes can be explored within such dimensions as strength, direction (one way, reciprocal), and type, for example. Normative interests in the relationships defining a leadership act require exploration of additional dimensions of influence. For example, transformational theorists argue that such influence ought to elevate the motives of both leaders and followers (Burns, 1978). Critical theorists argue that influence exercised through leadership ought to stimulate analysis and reflection about collective intentions and the means of their achievement, as well as be empowering (Foster, 1986). Warwick and Kelman (1976) provide an illustration of the different forms that influence can take and how these forms vary in the autonomy and freedom they offer individuals affected by them, an essential condition of empowerment. At the least empowering end of their continuum of influence types is coercion, "[a situation in which] one person or group forces another person or group to act or refrain from acting under the threat of severe deprivation" (1976, p. 484). Facilitation, the most empowering form of influence according to this view, is "designed to make it easier for an individual to implement his own choice or to satisfy his own desires" (1976, p. 491). Between these two extremes is persuasion (the use of argument and reason to influence a person to change), and manipulation (altering factors that influence a person's choices without their knowledge).

The distinction between management and leadership contributes little or nothing to an understanding of leadership conceived of as a set of relationships. Relationships simply vary in their complexity. At the least complex extreme, such relationships entail a relatively small number of transparent interactions. Someone in a formal leadership role, for example, tells a willing member of the organization to undertake a non-trivial task, understood by leader and follower in the same way, in order to accomplish a goal of the organization that both leader and follower value. Although this interaction might be considered a prime candidate for classification as "management," it still conforms to the basic properties of leadership conceptualized from a relational perspective.

Given this conception of leadership, such simple forms of leadership are probably in the minority, however. The potential complexity arising from varying forms of relations among leaders, followers, organization, and environment helps explain the difficulties leadership theorists have experienced in developing a widely agreed-upon understanding of leadership. Stimulated by complexity theory (Waldrop, 1992), it is reasonable to represent the relationships constituting many individual leadership interactions as forming a system. Although each such system may include some relationships that are linear, many are likely to be dynamic, reciprocal, and, therefore, highly unpredictable. Potential followers, for example, may develop quite different interpretations of the same influence initiative, interpretations sufficiently varied as to make the same initiative both facilitative and coercive, depending upon who is doing the interpreting. What distinguishes a relationship defined as leadership from some other type of dynamic, non-linear, social interaction is its intentionality.

Implications for Future Research and Theory

It is possible to imagine a large number of promising directions for future theory and research about school leadership in light of our relational conception of leadership. Two directions stand out as deserving special attention. First, rather than devoting exclusive energy to the development of new leadership concepts, there is much to be learned from further development of existing concepts such as the six categories of leadership summarized in this chapter. In particular, it would be useful to pursue such questions as: What are the similarities and differences among these leadership categories in terms of key relationships? What is the nature of the influence evident in these relationships? and What are the consequences of these key relationships for followers and the organization as a whole?

The second promising direction for future theory and research would be to extend the small body of recent research examining, in particular, the relationships between leadership practices, capacities, and motives, and selected elements of the environment in which schools are located. An especially neglected aspect of that environment is social values. Although such values appear to be of increasing salience in a rapidly globalizing world (Hallinger & Heck, 1996; Wong & Cheng, 1996), all six conceptions of leadership reviewed in this chapter reflect western values and have been developed within a framework of western assumptions, problems, and evidence. "Which cultural values have different conceptions of leader capacities, motives, and practices most adequate?" is a question that needs to be pursued as part of the agenda for future research and theory concerning school leadership. Part of the inquiry required by this question includes the identification of additional leadership concepts, those with their genesis in non-western cultures.

NOTE

1. Because of space restrictions, references are made in the text only to examples of articles in each category. A complete bibliography is available from the first author on request.

REFERENCES

Achilles, C. M. (1992). The leadership enigma is more than semantics. *Journal of School Leadership*, 1(1), 59–65.

Allison, D. J. (1996). Problem finding, classification and interpretation: In search of a theory of administrative problem processing. In K. Leithwood *et al.* (Ed.), *The international handbook of educational leadership and administration* (pp. 477–549). The Netherlands: Kluwer Academic Press.

Allison, D. J. & Allison, P. A. (1993). Both ends of a telescope: Experience and expertise in principal problem solving. *Educational Administration Quarterly*, 29(3), 302–322.

Anderson, G. L. (1996). The cultural politics of schools: Implications for leadership. In K. Leithwood, *et al.* (Ed.), *The international handbook of educational leadership and administration* (pp. 947–966). The Netherlands: Kluwer Academic Publishers.

Anderson, J. R., Reder, L. M. & Simon, H. (1997). Situative versus cognitive perspectives: Form versus substance. *Educational Researcher*, 26(1), 18–21.

Argyris, C. & Schön, D. A. (1978). *Organizational learning: A theory of action perspective*. Reading, MA: Addison-Wesley.

Atkinson, N. J. & Wilmore, B. E. (1993). The management profile: Identification of the management and leadership skills of school administrators. *Journal of School Leadership*, 3(5), 566–578.

Avolio, B. J. & Bass, B. M. (1988). Transformational leadership, charisma, and beyond. In J. G. Hunt, B. R. Baliga, H. P. Dachler & C. A. Schriesheim (Eds.), *Emerging leadership vistas* (11–28). Lexington, MA: Lexington Books.

Banner, D. K. & Gagné, T. E. (1995). *Designing effective organizations: Traditional and transformational views*. Thousand Oaks, CA: Sage.

Bass, B. M. (1981). *Stogdill's handbook of leadership*, Chapter 4: Leadership traits, 1904–1947 (pp. 43–72). New York: Free Press.

Bass, B. M. (1985). *Leadership and performance beyond expectations*. New York: The Free Press.

Bass, B. M. & Avolio, B. J. (1993). *Transformational leadership: A response to critiques*. Leadership theory and research: Perspectives and directions (49–80).

Bass, B. M. & Avolio, B. J. (1994). *Improving organizational effectiveness through transformational leadership*. Thousand Oaks, CA: Sage.

Bates, R. (1987). Corporate culture, schooling, and educational administration. *Educational Administration Quarterly*, 23(4), 79–115.

Bates, R. (1993). On knowing: Cultural and critical approaches to educational administration. *Educational Management and Administration*, 21(3), 171–176.

Battersby, D. (1987). Is there a place for "craft theory" in educational administration? *Educational Management and Administration*, 15, 63–66.

Beck, L. G. & Murphy, J. (1993). *Understanding the principalship: Metaphorical themes 1920s–1990s*. New York: Teachers College Press.

Bennis, W. (1959). Leadership theory and administrative behavior: The problem of authority. *Administrative Science Quarterly*, 4, 259–260.

Bennis, W. & Nanus, B. (1985). Leaders: *The strategies for taking charge*. New York: Harper & Row.

Bereiter, C. & Scardamalia, M. (1996). Rethinking learning. In D. R. Olson & N. Torrance (Eds.), *Handbook of education and human development: New Models of learning, teaching, and schooling* (pp. 485–513). Cambridge, MA: Basil Blackwell.

Berman, P., Greenwood, P. W., McLaughlin, M. W. & Pincus, J. (1975). *Federal programs supporting educational change, volume V: Executive summary*. Washington, DC: U. S. Office of Education.

Blake, R. R. & Mouton, J. S. (1964). *The managerial grid*. Houston, TX: Gulf.

Bolman, L. G. & Deal, T. E. (1991). *Reframing organizations: Artistry, choice, and leadership*. San Francisco: Jossey-Bass.

Bolman, L. G. & Deal, T. E. (1992). Leading and managing: Effects of context, culture, and gender. *Educational Administration Quarterly*, 28(3), 314–329.

Bolman, L. G. & Deal, T. E. (1994). Looking for leadership: Another search party's report. *Educational Administration Quarterly*, 30(1), 77–96.

Boyan, N. J. (Ed.) (1988). *Handbook of research on educational administration*. New York: Longman.

Bredeson, P. V. (1988). Perspectives on schools: Metaphors and management in education. *Journal of Educational Administration*, 26(3), 293–310.

Bredeson, P. V. (1993). Letting go of outlived professional identities: A study of role strain for principals in restructured schools. *Educational Administration Quarterly*, 29(1), 34–68.

Bridges, E. & Hallinger, P. (1992). *Problem based learning for administrators*. Eugene, OR: ERIC Clearinghouse on Educational Management.

Brophy, J. E. & Good, T. L. (1986). Teacher behavior and student achievement. In M. C. Wittrock (Ed.), *Handbook of research on teaching* (pp. 328–375). New York, NY: Macmillan.

Bryk, A. S., Lee, V. E. & Holland, P. B. (1993). *Catholic schools and the common good*. Cambridge, MA: Harvard University Press.

Bryman, A. (1992). *Charisma and leadership in organizations*. Newbury Park, CA: Sage.

Burns, J. (1978). *Leadership*. New York: Harper & Row.

Caldwell, B. J. (1992). The principal as leader of the self-managing school in Australia. *Journal of Educational Administration*, 30(3), 6–19.

Callahan, R. E. (1962). *Education and the cult of efficiency*. Chicago, IL: University of Chicago Press.

Campbell, R. F. (1972). Educational administration: A twenty-five year perspective. *Educational Administration Quarterly*, 8(2), 1–15.

Campbell, R. F., Fleming, T., Newell, L. J. & Bennion, J. W. (1987). *A history of thought and practice in educational administration*. New York: Teachers College Press.

Carlson, R. O. (1972). *School superintendents: Careers and performance*. Columbus, OH: Charles E. Merrill.

Charters, W. W. & Jones, J. E. (1973). On the risk of appraising non-events in program evaluation,. *Educational Researcher*, 2, 5–7.

Cheng, Y. C. (1991). Leadership style of principals and organizational process in secondary schools. *Journal of Educational Administration*, 29(2), 25–37.

Clark, C. M. (1988). Is there a place for "craft theory" in educational administration? Yes, but not in the way Battersby suggests. *Educational Management and Administration*, 16, 65–68.

Clark, C. M. & Peterson, P. L. (1986). Teachers' thought processes. In M. C. Wittrock (Ed.), *Handbook of research on teaching* (pp. 255–296). New York, NY: Macmillan.

Clark, K. E. & Clark, M. B. (Eds.) (1990). *Measures of leadership*. West Orange, NJ: Leadership Library of America, Inc.

Clune, W. H. & White, P. A. (1988). *School-based management: Institutional variation, implementation, and issues for further research*. New Brunswick, NJ: Eagleton Institute of Politics, Center for Policy Research in Education.

Coleman, J. S., *et al.* (1966). *Equality of educational opportunity*. Washington, DC: U. S. Government Printing Office.

Conley, S. C., Bacharach, S. B. & Bauer, S. (1989). The school work environment and teacher career dissatisfaction. *Educational Administration Quarterly*, 25(1), 58–81.

Culbertson, J. (1981). Perspective: Antecedents of the theory movement. *Educational Administration Quarterly*, 17(1), 25–47.

Culbertson, J. (1988). A century's quest for a knowledge base. In N. Boyan (Ed.), *Handbook of research on educational administration* (pp 3–26). New York: Longman.

Culbertson, J., Jacobson, P. & Reller, T. (1960). *Administrative relations: A case book*. Englewood Cliffs, NJ: Prentice-Hall.

Cusack, B. O. (1993). Political engagement in the restructured school: The New Zealand experience. *Educational Management and Administration*, 21(2), 107–114.

Daft, R. L. (1988). *Organization theory and design (third edition)*. St. Paul, MN: West Publishing Co.

Darling-Hammond, L. & Wise, A. E. (1985). Beyond standardization: State standards and school improvement. *Elementary School Journal*, 85, 315–336.

David, J. L. (1989). Synthesis of research on school-based management. *Educational Leadership*, 46(8), 45–53.

Davidson, G. (1992). Beyond direct instruction: Educational leadership in the elementary school classroom. *Journal of School Leadership*, 2(3), 280–288.

Davies, L. (1987). The role of the primary school head. *Educational Management and Administration*, 15, 43–47.

Deal, T. E. & Kennedy, A. (1982). *Corporate cultures*. Reading, MA: Addison-Wesley.

Deal, T. E. & Peterson, K. D. (1994). *The leadership paradox: Balancing logic and artistry in schools*. San Francisco: Jossey-Bass.

Dewey, J. (1916, 1929, 1946)

Dillard, C. B. (1995). Leading with her life: An African-American feminist (re)interpretation of leadership for an urban high school principal. *Educational Administration Quarterly*, 31(4), 539–563.

Downton, J. V., Jr. (1973). *Rebel leadership*. New York: Free Press.

Duckett, W. R., *et al.* (1980). *Why do some urban schools succeed?* Bloomington, IN: Phi Delta Kappa.

Duignan, P. A. & MacPherson, R. J. S. (1993). Educative leadership: A practical theory. *Educational Administration Quarterly*, 29(1), 8–33.

Duke, D. L. (1987). *School leadership and instructional improvement*. New York: Random House.

Duke, D. L. (1995). *The school that refused to die: Continuity and change at Thomas Jefferson High School*. Albany, NY: SUNY Press.

Duke, D. L. (1996). Perception, prescription and the future of school leadership. In K. Leithwood *et al.* (Ed.), *The international handbook of educational leadership and administration* (pp. 841–872). The Netherlands: Kluwer Academic Publishers.

Duke, D. L. & Leithwood, K. (1994). *Management and leadership: A comprehensive view of principals' functions*. Toronto: OISE, mimeo.

Dunlap, D. M. & Goldman, P. (1991). Rethinking power in schools. *Educational Administration Quarterly*, 27(1), 5–29.

Dunning, G. (1993). Managing the small primary school: The problem role of the teaching head. *Educational Management and Administration*, 21(2), 79–89.

Easton, D. (1965). *A systems analysis of political life*. New York: Wiley.

Edmonds, R. R. (1979). Effective schools for the urban poor. *Educational Leadership*, 37(1). 15–27.

Evers, C. W. & Lakomski, G. (1991). *Knowing educational administration*. Oxford: Pergamon Press.

Fenech, J. M. (1994). Managing schools in a centralized system: Head-teachers at work. *Educational Management and Administration*, 22(2), 131–140.

Floden, R. E., Porter, A. C., Alford, L. E., Freeman, D. J., Irwin, S., Schmidt, W. & Schwille, J. R. (1988). Instructional leadership at the district level: A closer look at autonomy and control. *Educational Administration Quarterly*, 24(2), 96–124.

Foster, W. (1986). *The reconstruction of leadership*. Victoria, Australia: Deakin University Press.

Foster, W. (1989). Toward a critical practice of leadership. In J. Smyth (Ed.), *Critical perspectives on educational leadership* (pp. 39–62). London: The Falmer Press.

Fullan, M. (1982). *The meaning of educational change*. Toronto: OISE Press.

Fullan, M. & Pomfret, A. (1977). Research on curriculum and instruction implementation. *Review of Educational Research*, 47(1), 337–397.

Fullan, M. & Steiglebauer, S. (1991). *The new meaning of educational change*. New York, NY: Teachers College Press.

Fuller, F. (1969). Concerns of teachers: A developmental conceptualization. *American Educational Research Journal*, 6(2), 207–226.

Galbraith, J. R. (1977). *Organization design*. Reading, MA: Addison-Wesley.

Geltner, B. B. & Shelton, M. M. (1991). Expanded notions of strategic instructional leadership: The principal's role with student support personnel. *Journal of School Leadership*, 1(4), 338–350.

Gerth, H. & Mills, C. (Eds.) (1946). *From Max Weber: Essays in sociology*. New York: Oxford University Press.

Goldring, E. B (1990). Elementary school principals as boundary spanners: Their engagement with parents. *Journal of Educational Administration*, 28(1), 53–62.

Goldring, E. B. & Rallis, S. F. (1993). *Principals of dynamic schools*. Newbury Park, CA: Corwin Press.

Goodlad, J. I. & Klein, M. F. (1970). *Behind the classroom door*. Worthington, OH: Charles Jones Publishing Co.

Greenfield, T. (1975). Theory about organization: A new perspective and its implications for schools. In M. Hughes (Ed.), *Administering education: International challenges* (pp. 71–99). London: Athlone Press.

Greenfield, T. (1991). Re-forming and re-valuing educational administration: Whence and when cometh the phoenix? *Educational Management and Administration*, 19(4), 200–217.

Greenfield, T. & Ribbins, P. (Eds.) (1993). *Greenfield on educational administration: Towards a humane science*. London: Routledge.

Greenfield, W. D. (1995). Toward a theory of school administration: The centrality of leadership. *Educational Administration Quarterly*, 31(1), 61–85.

Griffiths, D. E. (1959). *Administrative theory*. New York: Appleton-Century-Crofts Inc.

Griffiths, D. E. (1979). Intellectual turmoil in educational administration. *Educational Administration Quarterly*, 15(3), 43–65.

Gronn, P. (1996). From transactions to transformations: A new world order in the study of leadership. *Educational Management and Administration*, 24(1), 7–30.

Gross, N., Giacquinta, J. B. & Bernstein, M. (1971). *Implementing organizational innovations*. New York, NY: Basic Books.

Hallinger, P. (1992). The evolving role of American principals: From managerial to instructional to transformational leaders. *Journal of Educational Administration*, 30(3), 35–48.

Hallinger, P. & Heck, R. (1996). The principal's role in school effectiveness: An assessment of methodological progress, 1980–1985. In K. Leithwood, *et al.* (Ed.), *The international handbook of educational leadership and administration* (pp. 723–783). The Netherlands: Kluwer Academic Press.

Hallinger, P. & McCary, C. (1990). Developing the strategic thinking of instructional leaders. *Elementary School Journal*, 91(2), 89–107.

Hallinger, P. & Murphy, J. (1985). Assessing the instructional management behavior of principals. *Elementary School Journal*, 86(2), 217–247.

Hallinger, P., Leithwood, K. & Murphy, J. (Eds.) (1993). *Cognitive perspectives on educational leadership*. New York: Teachers College Press.

Harvey, C. W. (1986). How primary heads spend their time. *Educational Management and Administration*, 14, 60–68.

Havelock, R. G. (1971). *Planning for innovation through dissemination and utilization of knowledge*. Ann Arbor, MI: Institute for Social Research, University of Michigan.

Hayes, D. (1995). The primary head's tale: Collaborative relationships in a timer of rapid change. *Educational Management and Administration*, 23(4), 233–244.

Heller, H., Clay, R. & Perkins, C. (1993). The relationship between teacher job satisfaction and principal leadership style. *Journal of School Leadership*, 3(1), 74–86.

Hemphill, J., Griffiths, D. & Frederiksen, N. (1962). *Administrative performance and personality: A study of the principal in a simulated elementary school*. New York: Teachers College, Columbia University.

Hersey, P. & Blanchard, K. H. (1977). *Management of organizational behavior (3rd edition)*. Englewood Cliffs, NJ: Prentice-Hall.

Hertling, J. (1985). E. D. voucher bill in shift, offers parents choices. *Education Week, November 13*, 1–13.

Hess, G. A., Jr. (1991). *School restructuring Chicago style*. Newbury Park, CA: Corwin.

Hipp, K. A. & Bredeson, P. V. (1995). Exploring connections between teacher efficacy and principals' leadership behaviors. *Journal of School Leadership*, 5(2), 136–150.

Hodgkinson, C. (1978). *Towards a philosophy of administration*. Oxford: Basil Blackwell.

Hodgkinson, C. (1991). *Educational leadership: The moral art.* Albany, NY: SUNY Press.

Hogan, D. (1992). ". . . the silent compulsions of economic relations": Markets and the demand for education. *Educational Policy,* 6(2), 180–205.

Howell, J. M. & Avolio, B. J. (1991). *Predicting consolidated unit performance: Leadership ratings, locus of control and support for innovation.* Paper presented at the 51st annual meeting of the Academy of Management, Miami, Florida.

Hoy, W. K. & Brown, B. L. (1988). Leadership behavior of principals and the zone of acceptance of elementary teachers. *Journal of Educational Administration,* 26(1), 23–38.

Hoy, W. K. & Tarter, C. (1995). *Administrators solving the problems of practice: Decision-making concepts, cases and consequences.* Boston: Allyn & Bacon.

Huberman, M. (1989). The professional life cycle of teachers. *Teachers College Record,* 91(1), 31–57.

Hunter, M. (1976). Teacher competency: Problem, theory, and practice. *Theory into Practice,* 15(2), 162–171.

Hutchins, E. (1995). *Cognition in the wild.* Cambridge, MA: The MIT Press.

Jaques, E. (1989). *Requisite organization.* Arlington, VA: Cason Hall and Co.

Johnston, J. (1986). Gender differences in teachers' preferences for primary school leadership. *Educational Management and Administration,* 14, 219–226.

Johnston, J. & Pickersgill, S. (1992). Personal and interpersonal aspects of effective team-oriented headship in the primary school. *Educational Management and Administration,* 20(4), 239–248.

Kilpatrick, W. H. (1933). *The educational frontier.* New York: Century.

Kleine-Kracht, P. (1993). Indirect instructional leadership: An administrator's choice. *Educational Administration Quarterly,* 29(2), 187–212.

Kmetz, J. T. & Willower, D. J. (1982). Elementary school principals' work behavior. *Educational Administration Quarterly,* 18(4), 1–29.

Kowalski, J. & Oates, A. (1993). The evolving role of superintendents in school-based management. *Journal of School Leadership,* 3(4), 380–390.

Kushman, J. W. (1992). The organizational dynamics of teacher workplace commitment: A study of urban elementary and middle schools. *Educational Administration Quarterly,* 28(1), 5–42.

Lee, V. E., Bryk, A. S. & Smith, J. B. (1993). The organization of effective secondary schools. In L. Darling-Hammond (Ed.), *Review of research in education, volume 19* (pp. 171–267). Washington, DC: American Educational Research Association.

Lees, K. A. (1995). Advancing democratic leadership through critical theory. *Journal of School Leadership,* 5(3), 220–230.

Leithwood, K. (1989). *The principal's role in teacher development: 1990 ASCD Yearbook.* Alexandria, VA: ASCD.

Leithwood, K. (1994). Leadership for school restructuring. *Educational Administration Quarterly,* 30(4), 498–518.

Leithwood, K. (1995). Cognitive perspectives on school leadership. *Journal of School Leadership,* 5(2), 115–135.

Leithwood, K. & Hallinger, P. (1993). Cognitive perspectives on educational administration: An introduction. *Educational Administration Quarterly,* 29(3), 296–301.

Leithwood, K., Jantzi, D. & Steinbach, R. (1995). An organizational learning perspective in school responses to central policy initiatives. *School Organization,* 15(3), 229–252.

Leithwood, K. & Menzies, T. (in press). A review of research concerning the implementation of site-based management. *Educational Policy.*

Leithwood, K. & Steinbach, R. (1995). *Expert problem solving.* Albany, NY: SUNY Press.

Leithwood, K., Steinbach, R. & Raun, T. (1993). Superintendents' group problem-solving processes. *Educational Administration Quarterly,* 29(3), 364–391.

Leithwood, K., Tomlinson, D. & Genge, M. (1996). Transformational school leadership. In K. Leithwood *et al.* (Ed.), *The international handbook of educational leadership and administration* (pp. 785–840). The Netherlands: Kluwer Academic Publishers.

Lesourd, S., Tracz, S. & Grady, M. L. (1992). Attitude toward visionary leadership. *Journal of School Leadership,* 2(1), 34–44.

Lindsay, M. & Schwarcz, E. (1960). Imperative demands upon educational leaders. In *Leadership for improving instruction: The 1960 ASCD yearbook* (pp. 5–24). Alexandria, VA: ASCD.

Loucks, S. F., Bauchner, J. E., Crandall, D., Schmidt, W. & Eiseman, J. (1982). *Setting the stage for a study of school improvement.* Andover, MA: The Network, Inc.

Loucks, S. F., Newlove, B. & Hall, G. (n. d.). *Measuring levels of use of the innovation: A manual for trainers, interviewers, and raters.* Austin, TX: University of Texas at Austin, Research and Development Center for Teacher Education.

Louis, K. S. & Miles, M. B. (1990). *Improving the urban high school.* New York: Teachers College Press.

Louis, K. S., Marks, H. & Kruse, S. (1996). Teachers' professional community in restructuring schools. *American Educational Research Journal,* 33(4), 757–798.

McNeil, D. & Frieberger, P. (1993). *Fuzzy logic: The discovery of revolutionary computer technology and how it is changing our world.* New York: Simon & Schuster.

Maddock, T. H. (1995). Science, critique and administration: The debate between critical theorists and the materialist pragmatists. *Educational Management and Administration,* 23(1), 58–67.

Malen, B., Ogawa, R. T. & Kranz, J. (1990). What do we know about school-based management? A case study of the literature—a call for research. In W. H. Clune & J. F. Witte (Eds.), *Choice and control in American education, volume 2: The practice of choice, decentralization, and school restructuring* (pp. 289–342). London: Falmer.

March, J. & Simon, H. (1958). *Organizations.* New York: John Wiley & Sons.

Massie, J. (1965). Management theory. In J. March (Ed.), *Handbook of organizations* (pp. 387–422). Chicago: Rand McNally.

Maxey, S. J. (1991). *Educational leadership: A critical pragmatic perspective.* New York: Bergin & Garvey.

Mayo, E. (1933). *The human problems of an industrial civilization.* Boston, MA: Harvard Business School.

Metcalf, H. C. & Urwick, L. (Eds.) (1940). *Dynamic administration: The collected papers of Mary Parker Follett.* New York: Harper & Bros.

Miklos, E. (1988). *Administrator selection, career patterns, succession, and socialization.* In N. J. Boyan (Ed.). Handbook of Research on Educational Administrations (pp. 53–76). New York: Longman.

Miles, M. B. (1993). Forty years of change in schools: Some personal reflections. *Educational Administration Quarterly,* 29(2), 213–248.

Mitchell, D., Ortiz, F. & Mitchell, T. (1987). *Work orientation and job performance: The cultural basis of teaching rewards and incentives.* Albany, NY: SUNY Press.

Mojkowski, C. & Fleming, D. (1988). *School-site management: Concepts and approaches.* Andover, MA: Regional Laboratory for the Educational Improvement of the Northeast and Islands.

Montenegro, X. (1993). *Women and racial minority representation in school administration.* American Association of School Administrators.

Moorhead, R. & Nediger, W. (1991). The impact of values on a principal's daily activities. *Journal of Educational Administration,* 29(2), 5–24.

Murphy, J. (1991). *Restructuring schools: Capturing and assessing the phenomena.* New York: Teachers College Press.

Murphy, J. & Beck, L. G. (1995). *School-based management as school reform.* Thousand Oaks, CA: Corwin Press.

Murphy, J. & Hallinger, P. (1992). The principalship in an era of transformation. *Journal of Educational Administration,* 30(3), 77–88.

Myers, E. & Murphy, J. (1995). Suburban secondary school principals' perceptions of administrative control in schools. *Journal of Educational Administration,* 33(3), 14–37.

National Council for Teachers of Mathematics (1989). *Curriculum and evaluation standards for school mathematics.* Reston, VA: Author.

Oakes, J. (1985). *Keeping track: How schools structure inequality.* New Haven: Yale University Press.

Oja, S. (1979). *A cognitive-structural approach to adult ego, moral and conceptual development through in-service education.* Paper based on presentations at the annual meeting of the American Educational Research Association, San Francisco.

Ornstein, A. C. (1983). Administrative decentralization and community policy: Review and outlook. *Urban Review, 15*(1), 3–10.

Ortiz, F. I. & Marshall, C. (1988). Women in educational administration. In N. Boyan (Ed.), *Handbook of research in educational administration* (pp. 123–142). New York: Longman.

Pajak, E. (1993). Change and continuity in supervision and leadership. In G. Cawelti (Ed.), *Challenges and achievements: The 1993 ASCD yearbook* (pp. 158–186). Alexandria, VA: ASCD.

Parsons, T. (1960). *Structure and process in modern societies*. Glencoe, IL: Free Press.

Podsakoff, P., MacKenzie, S. B., Moorman, R. H. & Fetter, R. (1990). Transformational leadership behaviors and their effects on followers' trust in leader, satisfaction and organizational citizenship behaviors. *Leadership Quarterly, 1*(2), 107–142.

Popham, W. J. (1987). The shortcomings of Champagne teacher evaluations. *Journal of Personnel Evaluation in Education, 1*, 25–28.

Ravitch, D. (1983). *The troubled crusade*. New York: Basic Books.

Raywid, M. A. (1985). Family choice arrangements in public schools: A review of the literature. *Review of Educational Research, 55*, 435–467.

Reilly, D. H. (1993). Educational leadership: A new vision and a new role within an international context. *Journal of School Leadership, 3*(1), 9–20.

Reitzug, U. C. (1994). Diversity, power and influence: Multiple perspectives on the ethics of school leadership. *Journal of School Leadership, 4*(2), 197–222.

Reitzug, U. C. & Reeves, J. E. (1992). Miss Lincoln doesn't teach here: A descriptive narrative and conceptual analysis of a principal's symbolic leadership behavior. *Educational Administration Quarterly, 28*(2), 185–219.

Riehl, C. & Lee, V. E. (1996). Gender, organizations, and leadership. In K. Leithwood *et al.* (Eds.), *The international handbook of educational leadership and administration*. The Netherlands: Kluwer Academic Publishers

Robitaille, D. F., *et al.* (1993). *Curriculum frameworks for mathematics and science*. Vancouver, BC: Pacific Educational Press.

Rogers, E. M. & Shoemaker, F. F. (1971). *Communication of innovations: A cross-cultural approach*. New York: The Free Press.

Rossmiller, R. A. (1992). The secondary school principal and teachers' quality of work life. *Educational Management and Administration, 20*(3), 132–146.

Rost, J. C. (1991). *Leadership for the 21st century*. New York: Praeger.

Roth, G. & Wittich, C. (1968). *Economy and society; an outline of interpretive sociology*. New York: Bedminster Press.

Rumelhart, D. E. (1989). The architecture of mind: A connectionist approach. In M. I. Posner (Ed.), *Foundations of cognitive science* (pp. 133–159). Cambridge, MA: MIT Press.

Rutter, M., Maughan, B., Mortimore, P. & Ouston, J. (1979). *Fifteen thousand hours: Secondary schools and their effects on children*. Cambridge, MA: Harvard University Press.

Savery, L. K., Soutar, G. N. & Dyson, J. D. (1992). Ideal decision-making styles indicated by deputy principals. *Journal of Educational Administration, 30*(2), 18–25.

Schön, D. (1983). *The reflective practitioner*. San Francisco: Jossey-Bass.

Sergiovanni, T. J. (1989). Mystics, neats and scruffies: Informing professional practice in educational administration. *Journal of Educational Administration, 27*(2), 7–21.

Shakeshaft, C. (1987). *Women in educational administration*. Newbury Park, CA: Sage.

Sheppard, B. (1996). Exploring the transformational nature of instructional leadership. *Alberta Journal of Educational Research, XLII*(4), 325–344.

Simon, H. (1965). *Administrative behavior, second edition*. New York: The Free Press.

Sims, H. P., Jr. & Lorenzi, P. (1992). *The new leadership paradigm*. Newbury Park, CA: Sage.

Skinner, B. F. (1938). *The behavior of organisms: An experimental analysis*. New York: Appleton-Century-Crofts.

Slater, R. O. (1994). Symbolic educational leadership and democracy in America. *Educational Administration Quarterly, 30*(1), 97–101.

Smith, L. M. (1967). Protestant schooling and American nationality, 1800–1850. *Journal of American History, 53*, 679–695.

Smith, L. M. & Keith, P. M. (1971). *Anatomy of educational innovation: An organizational analysis of an elementary school*. New York: John Wiley.

Smith, W. F. & Andrews, R. L. (1989). *Instructional leadership: How principals make a difference*. Alexandria, VA: Association for Supervision and Curriculum Development.

Smyth, J. (1989). A "pedagogical" and "educative" view of leadership. In J. Smyth (Ed.), *Critical perspectives on educational leadership* (pp. 179–204). London: The Falmer Press.

Spady, W. G. (1994). Choosing outcomes of significance. *Educational Leadership, 51*(6), 18–22.

Spencer, J. C. (1993). Some frontier activities around strategy theorizing. *Journal of Management Studies, 30*(1), 11–30.

Stallhammar, B. (1994). Goal-oriented leadership in Swedish schools. *Educational Management and Administration, 22*(1), 14–25.

Sternberg, R. J. & Wagner, R. K. (Eds.) (1986). *Practical intelligence: Nature and origins of competence in the everyday world*. Cambridge, UK: Cambridge University Press.

Stiggins, R. J. & Duke, D. (1988). *The case for commitment to teacher growth: Research on teacher evaluation*. Albany, NY: SUNY Press.

Stoll, L. & Fink, D. (1994). *School effectiveness and school improvement: Voices from the field*. School Effectiveness and School Improvement, 5(2), 149–177.

Tallerico, M. & Burstyn, J. (1996). Retaining women in the superintendency: The location matters. *Educational Administration Quarterly, 32* (supplemental), 642–664.

Taylor, F. W. (1947). *Scientific management*. New York: Harper and Row.

Thomas, H. & Pruett, M. (1993). Introduction to the special issue: Perspectives on theory building in strategic management. *Journal of Management Studies, 30*(1), 3–10.

Tyack, D. B. (1970). Onward Christian soldiers: Religion in the American common school. In P. Nash (Ed.), *History and education: The educational uses of the past* (pp. 212–255). New York.

Tyack, D. B. (1976). Pilgrim's progress: Toward a social history of the school superintendency, 1860–1960. *History of Education Quarterly, 16*(3), 257–300.

Tyack, D. B. & Cummings, R. (1977). Leadership in American public schools before 1954: Historical configurations and conjectures. In L. L. Cunningham *et al.* (Eds.), *Educational administration: The developing decades*. Berkeley, CA: McCutchan.

Tyack, D. B. & Hansot, E. (1982). *Managers of virtue: Public school leadership in America, 1820–1980*. New York: Basic Books.

Uwazurike, C. N. (1991). Theories of educational leadership: Implications for Nigerian educational leaders. *Educational Management and Administration, 19*(4), 259–263.

Vandenberghe, R. (1992). The changing roles of principals in primary and secondary schools in Belgium. *Journal of Educational Administration, 30*(3), 20–34.

Vygotsky, L. (1978). *Mind in society*. Cambridge, MA: Harvard University Press.

Waldman, D. A., Bass, B. M. & Yammarino, F. J. (1990). Adding to contingent reward behavior: The augmenting effect of charismatic leadership. *Group and Organizational Studies, 15*(4), 381–394.

Waldrop, M. M. (1992). *Complexity: The emerging science at the edge of order and chaos*. New York: Touchstone.

Walker, W. G. (1989). Leadership in an age of ambiguity and risk. *Journal of Educational Administration, 27*(1), 7–17.

Ward, J. G. (1994). Reconciling educational administration and democracy. In N. Prestine & P. Thurston (Eds.), *Advances in educational administration* (pp. 1–27). Middlesex, UK: JAI Press Ltd.

Warwick, D. & Kelman. H. (1976). Ethical issues in social intervention. In W. G. Bennis, K. D. Benne, L. Chin & K. Corey (Eds.), *The planning of change, third edition* (pp. 470–496). New York: Holt, Rinehart & Winston.

Watkins, K. E. & Marsick, V. J. (1993). *Sculpting the learning organization.* San Francisco: Jossey-Bass.

Weber, M. (1947). *The theory of social and economic organization* (A. M. Henderson & T. Parsons, translators). T. Parsons (Ed.). New York: Free Press.

Webster's Third New International Dictionary (1967). Toronto: Thomas Allen & Sons.

Weick, K. E. (1976). Educational organizations as loosely coupled systems. *Administrative Science Quarterly, 21,* 1–19.

Wheatley, M. J. (1994). *Leadership and the new science.* San Francisco: Berrett-Koehler.

Whitaker, K. S., McGrevin, C. & Granier, A. (1991). Know thyself: A prerequisite for educational leaders. *Journal of School Leadership, 1*(2), 168–175.

Willower, D. J. (1985). Philosophy and the study of educational administration. *Journal of Educational Administration, 23*(1), 5–22.

Willower, D. J. (1994). *Educational administration: Inquiry, values, practice.* Lancaster, PA: Technomic.

Wohlstetter, P. (1990). *Experimenting with decentralization: The politics of change.* University of Oregon: Eric Document Reproduction Service No. ED337861

Wohlstetter, P. & McCurdy, K. (1991). The link between school decentralization and school politics. *Urban Education, 25*(4), 391–414.

Wohlstetter, P. & Mohrman, S. A. (1993). *School-based management: Strategies for success.* New Brunswick, NJ: Rutgers University.

Wohlstetter, P. & Odden, A. (1992). Rethinking school-based management policy and research. *Educational Administration Quarterly, 28*(4), 529–549.

Wong, K. & Cheng, K. (1995). *Educational leadership and change: An international perspective.* Hong Kong: Hong Kong University Press.

Worthen, B. R. (1993). Critical issues that will determine the future of alternative assessment. *Phi Delta Kappan, February,* 444–453.

Yukl, G. (1994). *Leadership in organizations: Third edition.* Englewood Cliffs, NJ: Prentice-Hall.

Zaleznick, A. (1970). Power and politics in organizational life. *Harvard Business Review, 55*(5), 67–78.

CHAPTER 4

Internationalization in Educational Administration: Policy and Practice, Theory and Research

Judith D. Chapman, Larry E. Sackney, and David N. Aspin

In this chapter we shall examine the impact of forces of internationalization and globalization in the field of educational administration. Implications will be drawn for policy, practice, theory, and research. We begin the chapter with a discussion of the ways in which the term "internationalization" is being used currently in educational discourse. We identify two main senses in which the term is used: one relates to "internationality" and the flow of ideas, actions, initiatives, and programs between countries, agencies, and institutions; the other relates to the effect of international forces and initiatives, some of them deliberately directed and some of them spontaneous and self-generating, which combine to make education transnational in scope, remit, and effect.

We look at the way in which internationalization in both these senses is impacting upon educational policy and practice. In particular, we analyze the ways in which global trends in economy and society contain within them a set of implicative conclusions that highlight the need to adopt a lifelong approach to learning. An examination is made of the attention being given to the nature, aims, and purposes of lifelong learning by policy-making bodies in the international domain. The implications of adopting a lifelong learning approach, particularly for the restructuring of education, are considered. Efforts at restructuring education in specific countries are described; convergences and divergences among countries' policies and practices are also noted. Factors influencing policy borrowing and cross-national exchanges are examined as well. We conclude this part of the chapter with some suggestions for further internationalizing scholarly undertakings, research enterprises, and substantive policy initiatives in the domain of educational administration.

We go on to consider the ways in which internationalizing influences have impacted upon theory and research in the field of educational administration. We identify internationalizing forces in academia and delineate some of the ways in which advances in scholarship in the philosophy of science and the social sciences emanating from around the world, particularly from Europe, have shaped and framed the principle perspectives in educational administration.

We note the part played by the dominant orthodoxy of positivism in theory and research in educational administration, which characterized much work in the U.S. until the late 1970s and early 1980s, and we point to the ways in which scholars of educational administration, particularly from Canada, the United Kingdom, and Australia, challenged this dominance. We note that the field of educational administration is now very much an international one in which a plurality of versions of theory and research proliferates. We applaud this plurality but point to its dangers; these, we suggest, might be avoided by adopting a piecemeal problem-solving approach that exposes itself to criticism and potential refutation from every corner of the "open society" that we now see as constituting the field.

Internationalization

The international setting in which educational institutions, organizations, and agencies operate exhibits all the manifestations of substantial change as we move towards the beginning of the twenty-first century. The reasons for the emergence of a new international perspective in education are manifold. In the past, "internationalization" in education tended to be a term associated with specific international programs and student exchanges. Today the term means far more than this.

There are at least two senses in which the term "internationalization" is currently being used in educational discourse. One is that associated with the conception of "internationality." This arises from the already massive and almost exponentially increasing rate at which exchanges are increasingly "flowing"—occurring or being brought about—between individuals, groups, countries and regions in the world. These "flows" of exchange are not only of products, finance, and information, but also of communication generally: ideas, knowledge, technology, media, sporting activities, economic developments, culture and cultural preferences, religious movements and political ideologies, and, of course, educational undertakings and initiatives. The ways in which these flows act upon occurrences and movements elsewhere, influencing and shaping the growth, development, and direction of similar entitites, indicate one sense applied to the term "internationalization" (see Appaduria, 1990; Waters, 1995).

In the field of educational administration, what is being discussed and studied by international-minded scholars, researchers, policymakers, and administrators are the ways in which the actions, initiatives, and programs of different educational systems, agencies, and institutions across the world have relevance for the work of the "home" country and its policies, education systems, and institutions. An example of this is the way in which some policy-making bodies in "home" countries study the advances in educational policy and administration being made in other countries with a view to "borrowing" or in some other way benefiting from the experiences of other countries and applying their policies and practices in their own setting. Another example is the study of international developments in educational policy and administration undertaken by certain academic institutions and academic researchers: from the point of academic interest pure and simple, as a means of comparability or comparative study, or as a means of enlarging the understanding of the context in which policies or institutions at home and around the world are working.

The second sense in which the term "internationalization" is increasingly being used is that in which there is an emphasis upon the international agencies, instrumentalities, and forces that act and react in and upon different countries' educational systems, institutions, and organizations. The effect of the working of such forces is increasingly to involve countries widely across the international arena in interactions or overt cooperations with similar institutions in other countries, thus making the overall enterprise one that can be regarded as "inter-" and transnational in scope, remit, and effect. Here there is much more of an active, conscious, and deliberate overtone to the use of the term of any institution's interests in or activities of "internationalization." Moves here can be the result of deliberate decisions of policy on the part of such bodies or they can generate their own momentum, having a life of their own developed in response to the various globalizing forces and factors that are playing on them.

This sense is well summed up by Professor K. Ebuchi of Japan. Speaking at a Meeting of Experts and Officials associated with the OECD/CERI Study, *Education in a New International Setting* (OECD, 1994e, p. 7), he suggests

> Internationalization is a process by which the education provision . . . becomes more sophisticated, enriched and broadly applicable to students from all backgrounds and countries. Emphasis is placed on the development of programs which are internationally and cross culturally compatible, with a view towards providing all students with experiences and training necessary to develop skills for life in a world characterized by increasing international exchange.

Internationalizing forces understood in this second sense are now in operation in education generally. They impact on conceptualizations of the aims and purposes of education; opinions and policies for the curriculum, content, and methods of programs of study; proposals for change in the structure and administration of educational institutions and systems; and initiatives in the assessment and accreditation of programs of study across the international arena.

As economies move from a concentration upon national to international markets, policymakers, system administators, and school-based educators are being driven to consider the needs of graduates entering the global economy of the twenty-first century (OECD, 1995). This has been characterized as the "knowledge economy and learning society." Changes in the economy and in employment demand a supply of workers whose education and training require them to be in possession of different knowledge and skills commensurate with the move towards the global knowledge-based economy. Such knowledge and skills these days need to be international and intercultural; among other kinds of mastery and areas of understanding, they include a range of broad-based and transferable competences, especially those in foreign languages; the understanding of different cultures, business practices, and social conventions; and a sensitivity to different values and standards of moral conduct and interpersonal behavior. It is becoming increasingly clear that educators must be aware of international trends at work in economics, society, and in their design and the delivery of education, curriculum, and learning opportunities to ensure that young people are being properly prepared for the exigencies of life in the twenty-first century.

An effect of internationalization and globalization, facilitated by advances in technology, has been the development of linkages crossing traditional boundaries between schools, Technical and Further Education institutions (TAFEs), and universities in different nations. This development has brought to the forefront the need and opportunity for providing a more international emphasis in educational arrangements. Internationalization offers many opportunities for the development of cross-institutional alliances, staff and student exchanges, and new multinational educational consortia. The need to maintain enrollments and attract full-fee paying students has meant that some schools and school systems have engaged in enrollment drives to attract foreign students; in some instances, schools have set up campuses in overseas locations. Already we see the emergence of private schools, with their main campuses in Australia, establishing school sites in other overseas countries, such as Thailand and Indonesia. The emergence of multisite educational consortia, partnership arrangements, and split-site schemes for educational provision, which operate both within and between different educational institutions and cross traditional boundaries of geography, space, and time, are new trends in the provision of educational opportunities. These developments have clear implications for the structure and administration of educational institutions.

In this context, it will be necessary to consider institutional strategies for internationalizing the school. Consideration will need to be given to the sorts of principles that will guide the management of schools in developing international study programs and cross-cultural curricula. The financing of such provision, the legal and industrial dimensions of employment arrangements for staff, housing for staff and students, counseling and support services for staff and students, and evaluation and accreditation procedures to ensure international comparability are just some of the issues for study and review. This holds a *fortiori* for other forms of educational institution and organization, particularly those beyond the period of formal or compulsory attendance.

Increased possibilities and opportunities for internationalizing schools often result in schools being established in very different cultural, political, and economic conditions to those in the context within which the "home" institution operates. International links with schools and groups in Eastern Europe and Asia, for example, often pose problems and obstacles for educators from a predominantly Western European or North American background of culture and tradition. This has important implications for the training of administrators. The preparation of leaders for such schools calls for the consideration of the ways in which leaders and administrators in such surroundings can be provided with new competences and skills in areas such as funding mechanisms and finance options generally, issues to do with control and management, and matters to do with increasing and promoting intercultural understanding and sensitivity.

Novel and groundbreaking developments in communication technology and the rapid advance and spread of telecommunications have been among the most crucial factors in the process of internationalization, along with increased opportunities for rapid, cheap, and flexible international travel. Increasing interest and activity in developing and offering collaborative programs in distance and offshore education have the benefit of providing a wide range of options available to students in quality teaching and learning across borders. Educational policymakers and administrators need to be fully conversant with such developments and must be able to work with those institutions and agencies offering such opportunities in modern modes of communication and telecommunication in order to benefit from the possibilities they provide (OECD, 1994a).

In the move towards internationalization, the growth of initiatives aimed at increasing the flow of foreign students is a matter of particular interest and concern. Programs such as "Erasmus" have already been established to facilitate such increased flow in the higher education sector; the increasing flow of students willing to cross national boundaries at a secondary level calls for a similar systematic approach. Considerations of such matters must form part of the main agenda of discussions among policymakers and administrators in the international and national arenas to ensure that policies are in place that reflect the importance of understanding and sharing aims, goals, and objectives in these arenas.

Many of the implications of growing international interdependence in all economic and social activity now need to be worked out. The call for a more international approach to education requires that the diversity of views and approaches be addressed. This diversity reflects national policy priorities in areas not only associated with education but also with economic and defense concerns. The diversity also reflects the concerns of stakeholders in the private sector, the interests of schools and school systems, the needs of students, and the expectations of multinational employers (OECD, 1994c).

With the increasing globalization of economic productivity and development, the increasing mobility of workers with high levels of skills and competences, and the increased portability and applicability of high level employment-related knowledge, the time is right for serious attention to be paid to the need for coordinated and interconnected programs of further education and training across the international arena. This constitutes one of the major challenges for policy makers, scholars, researchers, and practitioners in the field of educational administration in the future.

Educational Policy and Practice: Globalization and Education

The increasing globalization of all aspects of production and exchange—products, personnel, processes, and raw materials—is recognized as a factor exercising a growing influence on national economies and international cooperation and development. The international investment boom at the end of the 1980s increased the importance of the roles played by foreign affiliates and the great multinational corporations in most economies. International collaboration among firms increased, especially in manufacturing, Research and Development (R&D)–intensive and assembly industries. Although the emerging global economy is characterized by increased flows of information and financial capital between corporations, institutions, and agencies of all kinds, these tend to decrease the traditional hold of national governments over specific policy domains, including that of education (Chapman & Aspin, 1997).

The implications of these aspects of economic globalization for education are wide-ranging. These factors in economic development, and the effects and phenomena resulting from it, portend the need for a very extensive range of education and training programs to be made available for individuals across their lifespans. It also forecasts that these educational programs should be available across countries yet operate on an integrated, properly coordinated, and interconnected basis in which not only most of the courses offered have similar aims, content, and applicability but that many of the examination credits and terminal qualifications must have portability, interchangeability, and acceptance.

In this section of the chapter, we analyze the impact of globalization on educational policy and practice. It will be argued that global trends in economy and society contain within them a set of implicative conclusions that highlight the need to adopt a lifelong approach to learning. An examination will be made of the attention being given to the nature, aims, and purposes of lifelong learning by policy bodies in the international domain. The implications of adopting a lifelong approach to learning will be discussed with particular emphasis on implications for the restructuring of education and the management of schooling. Convergence and divergence among countries in the educational policies and administrative arrangements emerging to meet these global challenges will be identified and the factors influencing policy "borrowing" and the cross-national exchange of administrative strategies and "solutions" will be examined.

The Knowledge Economy and Learning Society

The demand for people to acquire further and different knowledge, master general competences, and learn new skills has always played an important role in society and economy (Chapman & Aspin, 1997). Today, however, the mode of production and the distribution of knowledge has changed so radically that it is considered

> legitimate to speak of a new historical era—the knowledge based economy or the information society—where the economy is

more strongly and more directly rooted in the production, distribution and use of knowledge than ever before (Foray & Lundvall, 1996, p. 12).

Although the provision of widespread access to opportunities to increase knowledge, skills, and competencies is now seen by many governments as a key element in economic growth, one of the striking facts about the knowledge-based economy is its impact on the structure of employment, unemployment, and social cohesion (Fittoussi & Luna, 1996, p. 327).

High unemployment creates insecurity and resistance to organizational and technological change. The rise in youth unemployment means that many young people are losing or never even gaining appropriate job-related skills and competencies, and hence are failing to secure for themselves the goal of employability. Groups in society that have never before faced unemployment, such as mid- and late-career white collar workers, are losing jobs with all the personal and societal costs that occasions and implies. Long-term unemployment lowers self-esteem and has the potential to impact adversely on health, interpersonal relationships, and social and community structures, leading at its most extreme to an increase in the occurrence of such individually and socially dysfunctional phenomena as crime, substance abuse, domestic violence, and suicide (OECD, 1994a, p. 41).

The impact of unemployment upon the nature, direction, and chances of success of educational programs is now receiving the most serious attention and consideration from governments around the world. It is not too much to say, as has been claimed, that the provision of lifelong learning to respond to all this is the key international issue across the whole educational arena for the next decade.

The work of the UNESCO International Commission on Education in the twenty-first century, for instance, called for a lifelong approach to learning after taking as its starting point a consideration of the needs of education in a context of worldwide interdependence and globalization. In this context, according to the Commissioners (UNESCO, 1996, p. 47), developing countries are feeling:

> an uneasiness engendered by the indecipherable nature of the future . . . combined with ever-sharpening awareness of the huge disparities existing in the world.

The OECD has also called for a lifelong approach to education. On the completion of Ministerial Meeting held in January 1996 to consider the agenda for work in education to be undertaken by OECD in the next five years, the Chair of the OECD Meeting of Ministers stated (OECD Press Release, Paris, 17 January 1996):

> We are all convinced of the crucial importance of learning throughout life for enriching personal lives, fostering economic growth, and maintaining social cohesion and we have agreed on strategies to implement it. OECD societies have made great

strides during the 1990s, but we need to find more effective ways of offering every one of our citizens such an opportunity. The target may be ambitious but we cannot afford not to work towards it.

Internationally speaking, young people in every country need an education that will befit them for employment on leaving school and for a number of job changes across their working lives. The long-term unemployed need opportunities to upgrade and/or change the employable and job-related skills and competences they possess. However, they also need access to lifelong education programs of other kinds that will offer them access to a range of interesting and life-enhancing activities and that will in turn assist or enable them to reconstruct satisfying and potentially enriching patterns of new-life choices for themselves in case the availability of employment opportunities remains restricted.

The implications for education and training of the working and effects of these trends and differentiating processes are obvious and manifold. Programs of compulsory and post-compulsory education must reflect and seek to address the requirements flowing from and generated by these realities, particularly insofar as they impact upon people's life chances and their preparation for frequent job changes, periods of unemployment, increased longevity, and non-work discretionary time. For the unskilled, the implications of these trends will be especially acute.

All this highlights the need for a multifaceted approach to policy development, incorporating serious and detailed appraisal and considerations of the relationship between economic policy, education, and social welfare services. The policy challenge for governments around the world is to provide for economic advance in a competitive global economy at the same time as ensuring that all citizens are able both to participate in that process and to take benefit from it; for without contributions from all its citizens—from all its potential pool of talent—the chances of a country's being able to achieve economic stability and social cohesion is likely to be significantly impaired. As we approach the twenty-first century, many governments are addressing this challenge through the development, articulation, and implementation of policies associated with the realization of lifelong learning for all. This challenge and these policies will clearly emerge as matters for sustained and serious study in the field of educational policy and administration in countries across the world in years to come.

The International Concern for Lifelong Learning

The topic of lifelong learning has thus assumed immense importance in the discourse and policies of a number of bod-

ies and agencies across the international arena. An increasing number of countries has concluded that a lifelong approach to learning should be deployed as one of the main lines of attack on some of the major problems needing to be addressed as we approach the turn of the twentieth century. The deliberations of OECD (1996), UNESCO (1996), the European Parliament (1995), the Asia-Pacific Economic Cooperation (APEC) Forum (Hatton, 1997), and the Nordic Council of Ministers (1995), for example, all reveal a commitment to policies of learning across the lifespan. In the policy documents emanating from such bodies, we see a commitment to lifelong education as an investment in the future, a precondition for economic advance, democracy, social cohesion, and personal growth (Chapman & Aspin, 1997).

Consideration of the deliberations of major international agencies and policymaking bodies reveals a number of common themes: the emergence of an awareness of the importance of the notions of the knowledge economy and the learning society; an acceptance of the need for a new philosophy of education and training, with institutions of all kinds—formal and informal, traditional and alternative, public and private—having new roles and responsibilities for learning; the necessity of ensuring that the foundations for lifelong learning are set in place for all citizens during the compulsory years of schooling; the need to promote a multiple and coherent set of links, pathways, and articulations between schooling, work, further education, and other agencies offering opportunities for learning across the lifespan; the importance of governments providing incentives for individuals, employers, and a range of social partners with a commitment to invest in lifelong learning; and the need to ensure that emphasis upon lifelong learning does not reinforce existing patterns of privilege and widen the existing gap between the advantaged and the disadvantaged simply on the basis of their differential access to education.

Across the world it is clear that there is widespread agreement about the need for the institution, continuation, or confirmation of policies of lifelong learning for all. As a reading of policy documents will intimate, however, whilst there is on the part of many governments and government authorities a perceived need to respond to common global economic and social pressures and a sincere commitment to the ideal of "lifelong learning," there is much less clarity and uniformity about the ways in which schools and school systems should be organized and administered to bring about the realization of the ideal of lifelong learning for all.

Reconsidering the Provision of Education

The central elements in what has been described (Chapman & Aspin, 1997) as the triadic emphasis of lifelong learning (for economic progress and development, for personal development and fulfillment, and for social inclusiveness and democratic understanding and activity) are now widely seen as fundamental to bringing about a more democratic polity and set of institutions in which the principles of social inclusiveness, justice, and equality are practiced and promoted; an economy that is strong, adaptable, and competitive; and a richer range of provision of those activities on which individual members of society are able to choose to spend their time for the personal rewards and satisfaction they confer. To bring this about, a substantial reappraisal of the provion of education is required.

In such countries as Australia, Norway, Denmark, Finland, and France, public education systems have traditionally been based on the assumption that the public interest is best served when public goods such as education are provided by agencies under public control. In these countries, education has been considered a "public good," one of the most important foundations of a more just and equitable society (Aspin & Chapman, 1994).

In countries such as England, Wales, and New Zealand, an alternative view has emerged over the last decade that rests on the assumption that education is to be conceived of less as a "public good" and much more as a "commodity," dependent upon personal and individual choice and provision and the norms of the market place. This solution to the provision of education is alleged to offer the "consumers" of education—parents and members of the community—better "goods," products and services, wider choice, and greater autonomy regarding expenditure on education. Such proposals reflect broader changes in economic policy with an emphasis on forces such as "liberalization" and "deregulation" and mirror changes in public sector management more broadly.

It is important to recognize that in many countries reservations have been expressed regarding the implications of the "more market" approach for the full range of values vested and embodied in public education systems. It has been argued that one of the results of the market approach may be the undermining of the vital importance of a shared commitment on the part of all constituencies in the public realm to funding education as something necessary not only to provide for and promote the democratic ideal of an informed society of knowledgeable citizens but as a precondition of economic growth.

Critics of the market approach (Grace, 1994; McLaughlin, 1994) argue that these commitments are functions of people's deepest moral and political preconceptions and these can only develop and be articulated if people generally and equally have the ability, the means, and the will to do so. Such preconditions are vital to the exercise of subsequent choices, but the acquisition of the means to exercise such powers can only be gained, maintained, and safeguarded if developing people's cognitive capacities for appraising alternatives and rationally choosing between them is made an indispensable feature of preparation for life in a liberal democracy. This must mean an education that will, at least in part, be provided and supported by the public exchequer as a "public good" available to all.

The point to be emphasized in analyzing this debate and in seeking to understand these developments from a perspective of "internationalization" is that government policies, and the administrative decisions emanating from them, concentrate upon the commitments people have to a set of fundamental beliefs regarding the nature of human beings and the ways they can best arrange and institutionalize their relationships for the various purposes—individual, social, and communal—they value, have in mind, and want to achieve.

Although there has been much discussion in the international arena regarding the onset, desirability, or adoption of a more market-oriented approach to educational provision, it would be erroneous to assume that this has been a worldwide trend accepted and implemented by all governments operating on the international stage. The development of public policy in a field such as education is far more complex than this, reflecting as it does a multifaceted relationship between influential factors and variables, including values and ethical concerns, political ideology, national goals, worldwide economic forces, public pressures, and personal and community forces operating to bring about social change.

The Restructuring of Schools and School Systems

As governments, policymakers, system administrators, and school-based educators consider the operational and implementation matters associated with the realization of lifelong learning for all, it is essential that they reconsider the organization and management of initial education to ensure that young people get the "right start" to their lifelong learning experiences (Ball, 1993, 1994).

Debate about the form that the organization of formal schooling should take has been one of the dominant themes of educational change and reform in recent years. Most countries seem to be agreed that the educational exigencies they face call for nothing less than a restructuring of their schools and school systems. The call for the restructuring of schools has been heard in most countries around the world, but "there is no consensus as to how this restructuring should take place" (Sackney & Dibski, 1994, p. 104). Some argue for increased autonomy for schools; some call for privatization and schools of choice; others call for increased quality control, evaluation, and testing, contending that schools should be held more accountable for their results.

In countries as distant and diverse as the United States of America, Canada, the United Kingdom, The Netherlands, Australia, New Zealand, Indonesia, Thailand, and Hong Kong, academics, policymakers, system, and school-based administrators are engaged in debates over decentralization and school-based management (SBM), privatization and school choice, and assessment and accountability.

Decentralization and School-Based Management

Considerations of the ways in which schools and school systems might decentralize are hardly new. According to Malen, Ogawa, and Kranz (1989), moves to delegate decision making to individual school sites "have been enacted, rescinded, and reenacted for decades" (1989, p. 6).

Lauglo (1996, p. 22), in an analysis of forms of decentralization, identifies three main values invoked in rationales for decentralization: a politically legitimate dispersal of authority; quality of services rendered; and efficient use of resources. Countries differ in the forms of decentralization they adopt, depending upon which of these values they are primarily concerned with. For example arguments concerning political legitimacy, whether explicitly formulated as theories or ideologies or implicit in a country's political traditions, are concerned with addressing the value question of who has a legitimate right (or duty) to decide or take part in decisions of different kinds. Political rationales for decentralization find expression in forms of decentralization characterized by liberalism, federalism, populist localism, and participatory democracy. Concerns for quality or efficiency find expression in decentralizing trends characterized by pedagogic professionalism, management by objectives, the market, and deconcentration.

Lauglo argues (1996, p. 43) that countries are:

> likely to evince a mix of traits in the way that education is governed with founding conditions having an especially enduring effect and the system gradually being modified by a succession of different influences.

Such influences include political expediency and practical considerations. To speak of the trend towards the "decentralization" characterizing changed organizational structures and administrative relationships in school systems around the world is to overlook the differences in the schools of thought and values underpinning different forms of decentralization and the different political expediencies and practical pressures that influence trends in specific settings.

School-based management, a term applied to an approach to educational management usually associated with decentralization, also manifests itself in a variety of ways and forms in different settings (Hannaway, 1992). In fact, there is no standard version or model of site-based management (Sackney & Dibski, 1994). Models used in England and Wales differ from those used in Canada and the U.S.A., and these differ from those in Australia, The Netherlands, Denmark, Finland, Sweden, and Italy.

In the Danish context, for example, the move towards school-based management has been based on the view that innovation and quality are best created through decentralization of competence and responsibility. Given the essentially "democratic" orientation towards school-based management, in Denmark deliberate steps were taken by Danish authorities to avoid those aspects of school-based management that might promote competition among institutions (Chapman & Aspin, 1993).

The democratic principle has also been an important aspect of reforms to give more autonomy to schools in Italy. It is important to note, however, that in Italy the concern has been expressed that giving schools greater autonomy might have the effect of causing disequilibrium across the system. It has been argued that schools with a greater degree of autonomy might make it difficult to achieve the highest priority in education in Italy—that educational access must be the same for all citizens.

In North America, Murphy and Beck (1995) contend, school-based management has two central tenets: school-level autonomy and participant decision making. Murphy and Beck (1995) view the decentralization movement in North America as having a focus on empowerment, autonomy, decision involvement, voice, rights, ownership, and professionalism. It is believed that people who have influence over decisions will be more satisfied with those decisions and that there will be more efficient use of human resources (Sackney & Dibski, 1994). Further, Murphy and Beck (1995) contend that the downward shift of power to local communities will decrease feelings of alienation between the school and the community. As well, Malen, Ogawa, and Kranz (1989) argue that under school-based management the role of the teacher in the classroom will be strengthened and school improvement efforts will flourish and prosper.

The early results of school-based management in North America, however, have not been promising. Research shows that participants experience limited shift in power (Malen & Ogawa, 1988). School-based management often leads to involvement but not to empowerment, and the role of stakeholders tends to become one of ratifying decisions made at another level. Furthermore, Murphy and Beck (1995) note that the involvement of minority and poor parents is virtually nonexistent. Although teacher participation has increased, it has come at the expense of time from teaching, involves a small cadre of teachers, and participation often becomes disconnected from influence. The evidence of teacher professionalism is spotty and thin (Malen, Ogawa & Kranz, 1989). School councils pay little attention to teaching, learning (Malen & Ogawa, 1988), and curriculum (Wohlstetter & Odden, 1992). The research indicates no evidence supporting improved learning on the part of students (Wohlstetter & Odden, 1992; Sackney & Dibski, 1994; Summer & Johnson, 1995). It may well be that the real impact of school-based management is more symbolic than substantive.

Murphy and Beck (1995) suggest a number of reasons for the mixed results of school-based management in North America: (1) there may be a lack of district board and central office support and commitment; (2) school-based management places new demands on teachers and administrators, which means less time for the instructional role; and (3) school-based management can create role conflict and confusion.

In countries such as New Zealand, England, and Wales, the educational debate is also pervaded by discourse that employs the language of decentralization, school-based management, and local management of schools. In observing this phenomenon, some might believe that they can discern at least superficially a straightforward connection with the democratic principles that have guided the move towards school-based management in other countries (Chapman & Aspin, 1993). But closer examination reveals fundamental differences in ideology and patterns of control where school-based management rests just as much if not more on the application to education of the values of the market—diversity, competition and choice.

In England and Wales, school-based management, parental choice, accountability, and the application of market principles and forces for the efficient, effective, and economic use of public resources were the key themes of the 1988 *Education Reform Act*. Hardikes (1988) argued that, in order to operate successfully in the new educational market place, schools in the United Kingdom were seen as needing to change "from a predominant focus on teaching and administration, to one of strategic planning, policy formulation, and implementation" (1988, p. 17). According to Giles (1994), unfortunately, many schools displayed little understanding of marketing and strategic planning processes.

Under the 1988 Education Reform Act, the United Kingdom witnessed two seemingly contradictory trends: increased central government intervention in curriculum and assessment accompanied by the delegation of budgetary control to schools themselves. This is in line with developments in some other countries, such as Scandinavia, which has not adopted the market philosophy yet nevertheless has undertaken reforms that show an increased assignment of financial responsibility and resource decision making to schools being offset by a simultaneous and parallel increase in the arrogation of other major functions of decision-making power and influence, particularly as they relate to purpose and accountability, to the center.

It is clear that education authorities in many countries have been undertaking reforms that have direct implications for the redistribution of administrative power among various levels in the education system. Although many of these reforms have been undertaken under the overt agendum of "decentralization" and "school-based management," a closer examination of trends within and between countries suggests that any elucidation of the redistribution of power and authority in the administration of schools and school systems will result in an analysis far more complex than any account based on a one-dimensional conception of changed arrangements along the centralization —decentralization continuum. All-encompassing terms such as "decentralization" and "school-based management" are, in the current context, really too limited to be of any real use in giving a complete account of what are far more complex, varied and heterogeneous concerns, developments, problems, and issues within countries and among countries in the international domain.

Privatization and Choice

In the last decade a central concern in many countries has been the issue of how governments might respect the rights of particular parents and parent groups to provide the education they want for their children while at the same time meeting the wider obligation of governments to ensure that all children receive the best possible education in an equitable arrangement for educational provision.

The possibility of the existence of segregated systems of public and private education, in which private educational institutions receive public funds, has been considered in many countries, especially in Europe, to run counter to the interests of a just and cohesive society. Similarly, until recent years, the idea of the "common school" in the United States (Boyd, 1993) was seen as an institution for the promotion of democracy and an equitable society. According to this ideology, it was thought that American children from all social classes and all cultural backgrounds should have the unifying experience of attending an undifferentiated, state-supported, and state-operated school.

But private sector growth and government subsidies to private schools appear often to go hand in hand. Experiences in countries such as Australia suggest that enrollments in private schools are closely related to "the private price of private schooling." Thus it is interesting to note that, in current reform efforts in New Zealand, an increase in government funding to private schools is seen as an inherent part of providing "choice" and at the same time of reducing the amount of government funds expended on the provision of education and educational services.

In Australia, where private schools are subsidized by public funds, more than one-quarter of students now attend private schools. Although under the funding arrangements in Australia, higher levels of aid are given to schools with lower private resource levels, critics of government funding point to continuing problems, such as the "creaming off" process that functions so as to drain off from government schools a large proportion of academically able, middle-class students. The "creaming off" process explains in part the comparatively high degree of success of private school pupils in public examinations. Critics of government subsidies to private schools argue that poorer and less affluent students must get first priority in the allocation of government funds for education. It is only when schools in less affluent areas become "good schools" that, it is argued, "choice" will cease to have class overtones and will become a value available to all (Aspin & Chapman, 1994).

In the United States, "magnet" schools, alternative schools, charter schools, open enrollment, back-to-basics schools, technology academies, and minority schools are just some examples of the ways in which, it is held, "choice" has been made available to parents during the past decade. Advocates of "choice" schools say that greater variety among schools will increase the likelihood that parents will find the type of school that reflects their educational values and their child's learning needs (Nathan, 1996). Banks, Huston, Murphy, and Muth (1996) reported that by April of 1996 some 21 states of the U.S. have adopted a form of charter school legislation as a way of facilitating "choice" and more than 200 schools had undergone some change along the lines of charter and choice.

In Canada, to date, only the Province of Alberta has passed charter school legislation. In the majority of cases in North America, charter schools remain public schools. Banks *et al.* reported that the reasons charter schools emerged included the desire to experiment with specific modes of instruction, to advance innovation, to serve a special segment of the population, and to offer more choice.

In a recent issue of *Educational Leadership*, Nathan (1996) contends that charter schools promise two-way accountability. They must declare what they do for students and they must demonstrate to parents that they are doing what they promised. For Molnar (1996), this obligation is not enough. He argues that the idea of the charter school and the way in which some have implemented it is undermining the education profession. Worse, such a notion allows the public to avoid the ultimate accountability of providing high quality education for all students, especially children who live in poor areas.

The increase in the number of "choice" programs has raised some fundamental questions in North America. What type of schools should the state permit? Will parents be able to make informed decisions? Will choice help or hinder equity? Will choice improve the quality of education? How will the new options affect traditional notions of public education for the common good? Will choice exacerbate the racial and ethnic differences in society?

In England, Wales, and New Zealand, wider choice has been regarded as a crucial means of helping raise standards and improve quality. In England and Wales, one way of fa-

cilitating choice is claimed to have been provided by means of the policy of open enrollments; another has been via the mechanism of "grant maintained schools" whereby schools are able to opt out of local financial provision and receive funds directly from the U.K. Department of Education and Science. This has created three types of schools available to the education "consumer": LMS schools that have remained within the local authority, GMS schools receiving direct grants, and private schools with "assisted places." Publication of examination results and league tables, "open days," and extensive public relations campaigns by individual schools will, it is believed, enable parents better to discriminate among schools and exercise their right to "choice" in the education of their children.

Boyd, in writing about reforms in both England and the Unites States, notes: "the market model is obvious in policies in both countries to promote parental choice of schools" (Boyd, 1992, p. 516). The survival of schools operated according to the market model depends upon customer satisfaction. The end result, according to Sackney and Dibski (1994, pp. 108–9), is that:

> Schools that gain pupils gain revenues and the ability to buy more teachers and more equipment, thus becoming bigger and better. Schools that lose pupils lose money, becoming smaller, less efficient, less prestigious, and less able to compete for and attract students. As in the market system, the rich get richer and the poor get poorer unless there is some centralist intervention on the part of the governing authorities to provide adequately for the educational welfare of all pupils . . . it is in everyone's interest that all children regardless of where they live or what their circumstances have access to equal educational opportunity.

Evaluation and Accountability

Evaluation and accountability are critical parts of the whole process of reform and renewal, especially where there is an emphasis upon improving efficiency and effectiveness in a time of budgetary constraint.

At the present time, it is possible to identify at least three main orientations towards evaluation and accountability. To begin with, there are those countries in which it is argued that centrally determined quality control is the most powerful means of ensuring the effectiveness of a school and school system; secondly, there are those countries that attempt to combine school-based evaluation strategies with centralized accountability mechanisms; and thirdly, there are those who maintain that, in the interests of equity and quality, a high degree of professional school-based autonomy is required. On the latter view, it is the individual teacher who sees most directly the diversity and individual differences that exist among and between their students at the level of the classroom and the school site (Aspin & Chapman, 1994). In some states of Australia, for instance, a long-term commitment to enhancing quality has been in evidence, and the strategies to achieve it have been set in operation based upon the desideratum of the enhancement of the personnels' capabilities at the school site. In such states, there has been very little centralized quality control.

This approach is under challenge elsewhere in Australia, reflecting developments in other countries, where recent reforms have incorporated, as an essential component, the establishment of central bodies to monitor quality and performance. In New Zealand, procedures for reviewing and assessing the outcomes and effects of stated goals in the Charter are required by institutions themselves and their communities every three years, but in addition outcomes are also assessed by external national examinations, nationally moderated internal assessment, and the Educational Review Office, a newly created Crown agency formed as part of the recent reforms and whose task is to assess the educational effectiveness of schools and to ensure that public funds for education are being used effectively and efficiently. The New Zealand Qualifications Authority has also been established to coordinate and rationalize national secondary, vocational, and advanced academic qualifications.

In Spain, the National Institute of Quality Evaluation has been established and it is designed to measure the effectiveness of Spain's schools with some rigor, not only from the point of view of pupils' results but from a broader perspective of the concept of school effectiveness, which takes into account school and social circumstances.

In Scotland, the range and quality of the outcomes attained by students and exhibited by them on their leaving schools, the style and quality of teaching and learning activities and encounters, the range and quality of resources, the quality of school management, pupil support, and school ethos—all of these are measured against criteria drawn up by the Schools Inspectorate in the light of their experience and taking account of the views of regional authorities, schools, teachers, and others. It is a responsibility of inspectors to ensure full debate of educational issues by publishing consultative papers, by maintaining close liaison with education authorities, and by discussing them as often as possible with teachers in schools.

It is significant to point out that a new understanding of and approach towards the issue of educational and administrative "control" can be discerned in recent developments in the field of evaluation and accountability. In many Scandinavian countries, for example, there has been a movement away from regulating control towards management by objectives. This is particularly evident in the reforms in Norway where there is a shift in the field of public administration from working according to set rules, to working towards set goals. This shift in the broader field of public sector management is seen as relevant to schools also. Consequently demands have been made for develop-

ing systems for follow-up procedures and evaluation to ensure that goals have been met.

In Denmark also, where in the past Parliament and the government set goals, defined content, and left it to the local powers to see to it that the tasks were carried through, the authorities have now reached a point where they are showing great interest in developing at both national and local levels a base of documentation that proves goals are being reached. Similarly in Finland, where decentralization of administration and delegation of decisions stress results rather than the methods by which they are achieved, measures have been taken to improve the efficiency of both central and local administration by means of management by results.

One interesting indication of future directions in evaluation and accountability can perhaps be seen in the developments in France. The development of evaluation and accountability mechanisms in that country is based on an increasing use of the computer and data processing equipment. Associated with this development will be the establishment of statistical and analytical databases that can be accessed by those in charge of the education system at the various levels—central government, academy, department, and, for schools, local level—and the processing of information that is being obtained in increasing quantities as a by-product of management data files, which will also be welded into a coherent whole.

In France, as well as in many other European countries, there is an eye to the development of closer international cooperation so as to permit objective comparisons of standardized data on a bilateral or multilateral basis, the exchange of experience, and joint or convergent action. It is with this principle in mind that France is participating in the EURYDICE project for a database on education systems in the EC countries. And it is this same objective of closer international cooperation that motivates the work that is being done within the OECD on a common set of indicators for evaluating national education systems (Aspin & Chapman, 1994).

Internationalizing Influences: Convergence and Divergence in Policy and Practice

A number of attempts have been made to identify common elements and similarities in educational policy and administration in recent years.

Guthrie (1993, pp. 239–246) has identified the following as common trends in the "industrialized world": the extension of publicly funded schooling to lower age groups (preschool), central government curriculum influence, intensified instructional emphasis upon scientific and technological subject areas, expanded use of standardized examinations and centralized evaluation procedures, expanded central reporting and monitoring, and the devolution of operating authority to schools. In the "Western bloc" nations in particular, he identified the following elements that he held were shared: the attempt to introduce into schooling some of the features of the marketplace, enhanced teacher professionalization, and identification of policies to deal with underparticipating youth (1993, pp. 248–252).

Fowler, *et al.* (1993) suggest that in The Netherlands, Portugal, Spain, and France there have also been common elements in reform efforts. They suggested these include the adoption of a wide range of assessment programs to measure student performance, the introduction of restructured teacher training programs, an extension of educational provision in an attempt to raise the educational level of all people, and reform of the curricula with an emphasis on technology.

Fowler, Boyd, and Plank (1993) claim that such similarities and common elements exist, especially in the English-speaking countries of North America, the United Kingdom, Australia, and New Zealand, largely because in these countries the reform efforts were driven and justified by the claim that a better-educated workforce was needed to enhance economic competitiveness.

Cibulka (1996, p. 124) elaborates on this explanation for convergence:

> various nations face increasingly common problems such as low student achievement, teacher training needs, inadequate vocational and school to work transitions programs, and inadequate money to fund refoms . . . Stated more academically there are structural problems underlying national developments which push policy in converging directions and these properties are linked to globalization of national economies.

Cibulka points out that this structural perspective offers insight into one dimension of policy convergence, but he adds another dimension to the analysis of policy convergence by pointing to the political process in democratic political systems that may serve to push policies in different countries in certain directions. A third explanation for policy convergence emerges from the concept of "policy borrowing."

There are a number of reasons offered for policy borrowing. Raffe and Rumberger (1993) suggest that policy borrowing can arise from a heightened awareness of the domestic system generated by comparative analysis and the recognition of functional equivalence in different systems. Robertson and Waltman (1993, p. 23) suggest that policy borrowing is most likely to occur when an organization is perceived to be performing poorly and when no past or present internal solution can rectify the problem. Under these circumstances policy borrowing provides an opportunity for policymakers to solve complex problems. They add that

policy borrowing tends to result in more far-reaching changes in a particular policy direction when the process is dominated by "ideological and political partisans" (1993, p. 25).

Finegold, McFarland and Richardson (1993, p. 4) suggest:

> the process of transnational borrowing is likely to become more common in the years ahead. This is a comment . . . on the general internationalization of the world's academic and policy communities. As the cost of sending people and information between countries has fallen, it has become more practical to include another country's experiences in the domestic policy equation. And with growing interdependence between industrialized economies, the pressures are likely to increase on those nations trailing in the competitive race to emulate their more successful rivals.

Policy communities exchange information about new ideas and policies regularly and sytematically (Robertson & Waltman, 1993, p. 31). National policy networks, private think-tanks such as the Brookings Institution, international organizations such as OECD and UNESCO, conferences on themes of policy importance conducted by government agencies, international organizations, and academic institutions are all ways in which ideas can be disseminated and cross-national exchange promoted.

Vickers, in an analysis of the impact of OECD on recent educational policy in Australia, argues that the major role that information and knowledge from an international agency such as the OECD play in the Australian policy-making process is a political one. Politicians, she argues, selectively use knowledge from cross-national exchange in international policy arenas, such as the OECD, to legitimize what they want to do and to consolidate support. She argues (Vickers, 1995, p. 119):

> When pursuing an unpopular course of action, it strengthens a politician's case considerably if he or she can demonstrate that governments in several other counties have found it necessary to follow the same difficult path.

Green (1993) also supports the view that one of the major purposes of cross-national exchange and borrowing is political. He demonstrates how the idea of "magnet schools" caught on, lost energy, and had all but disappeared three years after Kenneth Baker, U.K. Secretary of State for Education, returned from the U.S. recommending magnet schools as a promising way forward in educational reform. Nevertheless, Green argues (1993, p. 228):

> the concept did its work in that it initially helped deflect opposition to, and provide a clear articulation for, elements of Conservative policy. It contributed to the politics of deconstructing commitment to "system thinking" lodged in the social democratic ideology of entitlement and public service. By the same token it legitimized "individual thinking" in both personal and institutional terms, and promised the systematic benefits of competition. . . .

Thus although there was no widespread implementation of the idea of "magnet schools" in the U.K., Green argues that the history of magnet schooling in the U.K. is significant in its role in political discourse and its legitimating of other related policies.

Even if policy makers do successfully import and apply a policy, it does not necessarily follow that it will solve the targeted problem successfully. Prospective borrowers must adapt programs developed in one context to their own unique socio-economic, political, and cultural circumstances. As Robertson and Waltman (1993, p. 39) argue, the process of policy borrowing is especially difficult, messy, and uncertain in democratic polities:

> Seldom will every political interest view a policy import in the same light and struggles will ensue to alter the distributions of its costs and benefits. Furthermore, even if policy is adopted in a semblance of its original form, it may produce suprising and unintended results when torn from its native habitat of institutional structure and political culture. In the uncertain world of public policy a solution that works anywhere has much to recommend it. But even a policy that fails or yields ambiguous results provides a valuable lesson on which counterparts abroad may draw. For that reason, a judicious seeking and tracking down of other nations policies is part of the essence of political wisdom. Thus one should not conclude that a policy maker should "neither a borrower or a lender be". One must be a politically cautious policy borrower who is cognizant of the prerequisites of innovation, the political benefits and liabilities of a foreign model and the opportunity and risks of importing policy solutions.

The most intensive analyses of the factors associated with policy convergence and divergence have been offered in analyses of the reform efforts of the Thatcher and Major governments in the U.K. and the Reagan and Bush governments in the U.S.

Boyd argues (Boyd, 1996, p. 75) that some of the similarities in educational reform between the U.S. and the U.K. come from the conscious transatlantic borrowing of policies. This often resulted when a government minister or team of experts paid a short visit across the Atlantic. This occurred, for example, when Kenneth Baker made his whirlwind visit to the U.S. in 1987 and saw some examples of "magnet" schools. Similarly some of the market-oriented aspects of the British Education Reform Act (ERA) were strongly echoed in "America 2000," but Boyd points out (1996, p. 77) that:

> Despite all the parallels and common language, some of the key words and concepts in market oriented education reform do not mean quite the same thing to "Brits" and "Yanks." We are as Winston Churchill liked to say "divided by a common language."

Boyd identifies the major overarching factors that shape reform and explain variations among nations: the historical social context, political culture, ideology and paradigms, and governance structures. These factors, he argues, contribute to a situation in which words such as "choice" and "market," though both used as general terms to describe reforming trends in the U.K. and U.S., connote different meanings and have different administrative implications in the two different countries.

These case studies of the international exchange of ideas and of policy borrowing highlight the difficulty of making broad generalizations about policy trends from one country or one setting to another. This has implications, not only for our analysis of international trends in educational policy and administration, but also for research in the area of internationalization. With respect to policy borrowing, for instance, Robinson and Waltman (1993, p. 34) comment:

> policy may be borrowed intact or may be borrowed in a transformed version. Even if conscious borrowing does not occur, separate national policies may converge in a common policy direction and settle upon nearly identical programs. Among the next logical steps in diffusion research are "tracer" studies that focus on the generation and spread of specific policies addressing related problems. There is also a critical need for rich contextual analysis of the process of borrowing by particular polities. . . .

This comment illustrates our general point that movements and influences of policies from one environment to another carry not only substantive policy implications, requiring the application of a range of caveats in respect of particular national interests and concerns, but also bear a number of concerns regarding the quality, range, and diversity of the issues needing analysis, research, and development in the field. It is our awareness of such concerns that, we believe, helps generate and set some of the agenda for a future research program for those studying, researching, and working in the field of the internationalization in educational administration.

A Possible Agenda for Considering Internationalization in Policy and Practice

At the present time, internationalization in education generally is occurring at two levels: (a) goals and strategies at the national level and (b) the level of individual institutions. Policymakers and administrators need to consider the interface and the interaction between the two levels of decision making and action (see OECD, 1994e).

Informed by the OECD work on *Education in a New International Setting* (OECD, 1994e), we tentatively offer the following list of items that we suggest might usefully be placed among the issues for consideration for policy, practice, and research over the next decade:

- Consideration of the impact of internationalization on educational policy and the interface of education and other policy areas such as international relations, defense, and economic policy.
- Consideration of the education of the global knowledge workforce. This imperative has wide-ranging implications for curriculum, cross-crediting, modularization, and international collaboration in the conception, delivery, and assessment of educational programs of all kinds. Indeed, the time may have come for consideration of areas of common interest and activity in education curricula, credit, and qualifications across national borders.
- Consideration of the international dimensions of teaching, learning, and educational delivery in the context of internationalization. What should students learn in order to be better equipped for the new global economy? How can the content of curricula be changed in line with the need for internationally relevant knowledge and abilities? How can delivery be improved by use of modern technology, modularized courses, and so on?
- Consideration of the ways in which more extensive cross border use of distance learning in the schooling sector as well as in higher education can be promoted. There is also a need to consider how developments in distance education and telecommunications can be locally and nationally sensitive.
- Consideration of the interface between schooling and higher education. The internationalization of higher education has implications for the content and structure of upper secondary education, especially in view of the increasing interest in the International Baccalaureate.
- Consideration of the boundary between pecuniary interest and educational provision. At the moment, government schools as well as private schools are moving into internationalization, especially in the attracting of foreign students. There is a need to consider the ethical as well as the administrative dimensions of this trend. What sorts of sanctions can be imposed for bad practice? How can arrogance, development frenzy, or exploitation be avoided?
- Consideration of the costs and benefits, the options, and priorities for internationalization. How are the mechanisms for setting international priorities in education to be decided and put into operation? How are these to be defined? In what international arena? Who should be involved? How can interagency cooperation in the context of increasing interdependency be promoted? How can accountability be ensured? How can coherence be achieved in the formulation and development of policies and practices relevant to the fostering of appropriate international roles, dimensions, and initiatives?
- Consideration of the context within which learning takes place to respond to a student population that is internationally diverse. This has implications not only for the socialization of foreign students but also for domestic students who need to be sensitized to different cultural beliefs and values. We need to identify innovative approaches for curriculum design, teaching and learning, and the culture of the learning environment, in support of a more international approach.

As part of our consideration of internationalization, we also need to take into account the barriers that particular nations or groups build up against the rest of the world. We shall need to consider issues such as competition and tribalism, regionalism and coherence, and integration and diversity in internationalizing trends. Although there may be much to be lauded about pluralism and the desire on the part of some governments for independence and autonomy of national education policies and initiatives, it is worthwhile noting that increasing globalization may result in the distancing and marginalization of particular countries and their education systems from all the benefits and advantages that internationalization will undoubtedly confer.

At the same time, however, it is important to acknowledge that increasing globalization and internationalization carries with it the danger of a new type of imperialism. In the present context, it cannot be ruled out that the most powerful countries of the world with their potential for control over economic development, modern modes of communication, and cultural hegemony may begin to exert a dominance over other countries and cultures that risks stifling independent initiatives and iconoclastic experiments in autonomous policy development. Such initiatives might well prove to be of considerable interest and advantage to other, larger countries, as well as to the country in which they are originally essayed. The dangers of the role played by the centripetal forces operating as a result of increasing internationalization are too great to be ignored and need to be guarded against if countries and thought-systems are to maintain a real autonomy in a world in which governments and peoples everywhere are increasingly concerned about the preservation and expansion of democracy and an "open" society internationally.

In the section which follows, we suggest that the same dangers associated with internationalization obtain in respect to the development of thinking in matters of theory and research in the field of educational administration. Notwithstanding the immense benefits that accrue from the cross-national exchange of ideas, there are also risks of which not only policymakers and administrators must be aware, but against which it also behoves those working in theory and research in the field to be particularly on their guard if they value independence in their thinking, access to a broad range of intellectual traditions, and genuine reciprocity in exchange and multiple points of growth in the cross-fertilization of ideas. For these are, after all, among the prime presuppositions of and preconditions for valid and effective theory and research.

Theory and Research in Educational Administration

Until the 1970s, the main limits to the field of educational administration had largely been set by scholars and researchers in the U.S. whose work exhibited a strong adherence to positivist principles and methods. It was not until the late 1970s, and largely from the work of scholars living outside the U.S., that objections began to be mounted to the dominant (positivist) orthodoxy in such a way and to such an extent that alternative paradigms began to be advanced and put into place. Through and from the intellectual turmoil of the 1980s emerged powerfully held alternative approaches: some that resulted from and embodied subjectivist and interpretivist standpoints, illustrated by the work of scholars such as Greenfield in Canada; some from neo-Marxist and "critical" theories, illustrated by the work of Bates (1980) and others of the Deakin School in Australia; and some from the work of post-modernists, especially in Europe, Australia, and New Zealand.

In the 1990s, such approaches have themselves been subject to critical scrutiny by the powerful epistemological arguments advanced by a number of international scholars, perhaps best exemplified in the activity of two Australian scholars, Evers and Lakomski. Their work has offered a new approach to science and theory in educational administration, based on post-empiricist lines and going beyond such distinctions as those of fact and value, theory and practice, objectivism and relativism.

Internationalizing Forces in Academe

The "Theory" movement in the academic field of educational administration developed in the U.S. in the mid-1950s. In 1959, the University Council for Educational Administration (UCEA) was created, which allowed for scholarly interaction among academics and researchers in the North American context. The UCEA also founded the *Educational Administration Quarterly* (EAQ) and the Educational Administration Abstracts; these journals were distributed to researchers, policymakers, and practitioners in countries around the world (Culbertson, 1969).

Until that time there was little if any serious scholarly work or research in the field of educational administration outside of North America. In 1963, however, at the University of New England in Australia, William Walker (1991), a graduate of the University of Illinois, was the first to blaze the trail of scholarship in the field in Australia and,

as part of his commitment to extending academic activity in it, established the *Journal of Educational Administration* (*JEA*). This journal declared that educational administration "will best be served through an international approach to the field" (Hughes 1988, p. 655). The editorial board of the *JEA* included members from Australia, Canada, New Zealand, Great Britain, and the U.S.

The first International Intervisitation Program (IIP) in educational administration took place in the fall of 1966 at various universities in the U.S. and Canada. Supported in part by the Kellogg Foundation, the program was developed by the UCEA (Culbertson, 1969). The objectives of the UCEA were to advance research and development in educational administration through inter-university cooperation and communication. In large part, the UCEA and the Commonwealth Council of Educational Administration (CCEA), who collaboratively sponsored the IIPs from 1974 onwards, fostered the international dissemination of the major ideas associated with the Theory movement and encouraged the development of comparative efforts in theorizing, research, and teaching. Hughes (1988) claimed "the Program challenged North American scholars to look outward, while stimulating the academics and practitioners from the United Kingdom, Australia, and New Zealand, who also attended to learn and profit from the insights developed in the United States and Canada" (1988, p. 660).

This claim is indicative of the spirit that animated many academics working outside of North America in those earlier days; the suggestion is plainly that there was little if anything that might be called academic programs in serious scholarly study of and thoroughgoing research in educational administration outside institutions in the U.S. and North America more generally.

To an extent, this sentence expresses a truth: the only attention paid to thought about achieving success in educational administration in the United Kingdom resided largely in historical studies of "great" men in education and "great" schools, or in comparative studies of schools and school systems in other countries. In the Federal Republic of Germany, there was in those times little that united the professional concerns of teachers operating in the Teacher Training institutions (Pädagogische Hochschulen) and the academic interests and activities of professors and lecturers in universities. In Commonwealth countries, such as Australia, there were no formal programs in educational administration until the 1960s when William Walker established the Educational Administration program at the University of New England. Programs in other Australian universities were not established until the 1970s and 1980s.

The dominance of North American thinking began to change in the 1970s with the increasing number of academics returning home from study in North America and instituting or becoming part of degree programs and research projects in their own countries. For them the IIP and its initiatives was a source of further encouragement and increasing international connectedness. Culbertson, who was for many years executive director of the UCEA (1969), indicated that the IIP had three purposes: (1) to open channels of communication among leaders interested in the study and practice of educational administration; (2) to provide opportunities to share and examine ideas within an international perspective; and (3) to provide opportunities to explore potential follow-up endeavors in the areas of research, development, and dissemination for those interested in the study and practice of educational administration.

One of the prime sources of further growth in internationalization can be found in the major outcome of the 1970 IIP held in Australia: the establishment of the Commonwealth Council for Educational Administration (CCEA). The mission of CCEA was to encourage teaching and research in educational administration in Commonwealth countries and to work internationally with the UCEA (Hughes, 1988, p. 661). Links with the CCEA have also been fostered through national educational administration organizations such as the British Educational Management and Administration Society (BEMAS), the Canadian Society for the Study of Educational Administration (CASEA), and the Australian Council of Educational Administration (ACEA). These networks also overlap and cooperate with the European Forum for Educational Administration, which includes the national associations of France, Germany, and other European countries (Hughes, 1988). Other linkages have been developed with commonwealth countries such as Barbados, Malaysia, Nigeria, and Kenya.

Since these times, it would be not too much to say that, although the outreach movement and the growth of ideas and networks was initially from North America, the movement is now quite as much the other way. The evolution of journals such as *Educational Management and Administration*, published by BEMAS, *The Canadian Administrator*, published by the University of Alberta Department of Educational Administration, and *The International Journal of School Improvement and School Effectiveness* have all contributed to the growth and extension of an international perspective in the field. One only needs to examine *The Journal of School Effectiveness and School Improvement* (ICSEI) to appreciate the diversity of board members representing the U.S., Israel, Australia, Hong Kong, Germany, Canada, the United Kingdom, Hungary, The Netherlands, New Zealand, and Switzerland. At a recent meeting of ICSEI, over 40 countries were represented. Similarly the programs of Division A at the annual meetings of the AERA now have presentations given by scholars from around the world. Such professional interaction results in joint presentations, publications and research endeavor, institutional links programs, schemes of inter-institutional

collaboration and review, staff visitation and student exchange, and constant communication on the Internet and by other means. International communication, connectedness, and further outreach is now becoming truly global in its scope, range, and proliferation.

Despite the growth of these international activities and networks, however, the field's communication network has remained strongly dominated by academics working in the English language. The major journals continue to be located, with only one or two exceptions, in North America, Britain, and Australia and the bulk of internationally circulated writing is in English. It is perhaps for this reason that the significance and value of some of the international influences in the field of educational administration theory, especially those in the philosophy of science and the social sciences emanating from non-English speaking countries, particularly from Europe (West and East), have been so little recognized. Any analysis of major theoretical developments in the twentieth century must take account of the signal importance of thought experiments and theoretical advances proposed by scholars working in other linguistic and cultural milieux than the ones that have been likely to secure publication in the journals that have hitherto dominated scholarship in educational administration.

Positivism—the Dormant Orthodoxy in Educational Administration Until the 1970s

Perhaps at this stage then something needs to be said about the background and contexts of the different traditions of thinking in which theory and research in the field of educational administration has developed, so that the truly international character of the influences upon it can be recognized (see Aspin, 1996, 1997).

In the development of philosophy in the Anglo-American analytic tradition, two main schools of thought emerged. One was known as "Rationalism." According to rationalist thinking, human reason has pride of place over all other human endowments and can offer the human being a safe guide in the pursuit of knowledge and truth. Rationalists such as Plato, Descartes, and Kant hold that the human mind can attain to true knowledge independently of any assistance from the senses. Such thinkers operate on the premise that there is either a rational structure in the mind that apprehends and cognises external reality in such a way as to give it an order and definite structure; or, as other rationalists hold, that there is a cosmos of law and order in external reality itself and this is somehow reflected in the inner workings of the mind that is brought to bear upon it and that can cognise its cosmic regularity by applying a similar sort of structure to it. Such theories entail a view of knowledge as objective, absolutely "true" and reified, with a status that is independent of other conditions in the beings who possess that knowledge. On this premise, knowledge is timeless, objective, and owes nothing to the particular times or circumstances of the different periods in human history and the societies, cultures, and communities in which human beings have lived.

Set against such views is the other tradition of thinking, that has come to be described as "empiricism." Empiricist thinkers maintain that knowledge of the world can only be derived from the evidence coming to us from the world via the sense organs with which we are all equipped. Though the works of Aristotle, Aquinas, and Sir Francis Bacon were in some sense precursors of this view, its fundamental tenets are most clearly expressed in the philosophy of John Locke, who is generally regarded as the founder of modern empiricism. For Locke and his followers, the principal claim is that no knowledge comes into the mind except through the gates of the senses. Such knowledge as the mind gains can be acquired only through experience. For empiricists, there is no source of knowledge other than that provided by the senses; empiricists deny the validity of any other claims to knowledge than those which derive ultimately from sense perception, experience.

This view was embraced and carried forward in the early part of this century by a group of philosophers who gathered in Vienna and came to be known as the "Vienna Circle." It is from their influence that the version of philosophy known as "logical empiricism" or "logical positivism" derived. From these, in turn, there developed "positivism"—the view that any approach to any investigation in the field of the sciences or the social sciences that was to be considered academically acceptable must be derived from, rest on, and incorporate empiricist postulates.

The world view that members of the Vienna Circle and subsequent logical empiricists/positivists were concerned to propound had the aim of confirming that all knowledge of the world derives ultimately from sense experience and observation; that science and the "scientific method," with mathematics as its handmaiden, is not only the best but the only way of bringing about knowledge; and that all the different branches of science could be integrated and unified and so provide that comprehensive picture of the sensible universe for which metaphysical philosophers had so long striven and in which, in the view of the Vienna Circle, they had so clearly failed.

Logical positivists, perhaps best illustrated by the English philosopher Ayer (1946), assumed the validity of a number of dichotomies that were laid down as normative for all valid philosophical (and scientific) investigation by members of the Vienna Circle and its adherents: the dis-

tinctions between science and metaphysics; facts and theories; facts and values; logical and factual truths; verifiable and non-verifiable, corrigible and incorrigible propositions; that which can be said, and that which can only be shown. Fundamental to the force of these distinctions was the view that experience is the only way in which human beings acquire their knowledge of the world and that empirical observation, together with certain dispositions or tendencies, is responsible for the totality of the contents of our minds and thinking.

Sense data were thus held to be prime items in providing the basic and incontestable foundations of all subsequent knowledge and thought. Sense data were regarded as absolutely objective, in that they were held to be uncontaminated by any hint of theory or value; indeed, it was on their value- and theory-free character that their claim to objectivity was claimed to rest. Between the world of "facts," as observed, established, and recorded by empirical science, and the realm of "values" (insofar as "values" had any meaning at all) lay an absolute divide— a technical scientific gap between theory-free and theory-full, between impartial and partial, between objective and subjective, between the hard, probabilistic pronouncements of science and the "soft" idiosyncratic sentiments that (where they were not totally meaningless) passed for wisdom in such other realms as ethics, aesthetics, and religion.

These views and developments of them dominated the field of educational administration in the U.S. until the late 1970s and early 1980s and can indeed still be seen at work in many areas of enquiry and discourse in educational administration today. The point being made above is that, even in the earliest stages of the "Theory" movement in educational administration with its emphasis upon positivism, the underpinning vitalizing forces and theoretical constructs came to it as an outgrowth of work completed or being carried on elsewhere (principally in Europe). The effects of the work of previous thinkers in philosophy and the social sciences are testimony to the international influence in the development of thinking in educational administration at that time.

The Challenge to the Dominant Orthodoxy

Modern philosophers and philosophers of science argue that the logical empiricist/positivist approach is replete with problems of both a methodological and conceptual kind. The principal problem of empiricism is that, as Dewey showed, it incorporates a major fallacy:

> The fallacy of orthodox logical empiricism is . . . [that] it supposes that there can be "givens," sensations, percepts, etc., prior

to and independent of thought or ideas, and that thought or ideas may be had by some kind of compounding or separating of the givens. But it is the very nature of sensation of perception . . . already to be, in and of itself, something which is so internally fractionalized or perplexed as to suggest and to require an idea, a meaning [Dewey, 1907, p. 309].

This is a point that had been tellingly summarized by Kant in the well-known aphorism of "No percepts without concepts." Perception is not "theory-free"; our observations are not free from our past preconceptions, prejudices, and expectations. This is a point that emerges strongly from and is powerfully developed in the work of the German philosopher Gadamer (1976, 1979a, and 1979b), a representative of the German "hermeneutic" tradition that originated in the work of Schleiermacher (1984) and Dilthey (1976). The Austrian Wittgenstein, also something of a linguistic phenomenologist (see Roche, 1973), put it more forcefully in his later works (1953, 1968). For him, all human perception, appraisal, judgment, and action is not neutral: the processes that human beings undergo, the actions they perform, the main operations, interests, and concerns of their existence qua human beings are embedded in, made manifest, and given sense and significance in the particular "form of life" into which they are born, have to operate, and conduct themselves: "What has to be accepted, the given, is—so one could say—*forms of life*" (1953, pp. 174, 221, 226 [italics in original]).

What Dewey called a fallacy was attacked as one of the two "dogmas" of empiricism exposed to telling refutation by W. V. Quine (1951); Quine's refutation was adopted and ably redirected towards the rebuttal of some key theories of educational policy and administration by the Australian scholars Evers and Lakomski (1991). One of the basic tenets of that dogma, according to Quine, is the positing of an absolute divide between what are held to be the "neutral," factual, and "value-free" statements, regarded as distinctive of mathematics and the natural sciences, which are thus paradigms of "objectivity," and those of other such realms of discourse as ethics and politics that are held to be non-factual, value-laden, and irredeemably subjective.

Recent work in the epistemology and methodology of the natural and social sciences has moved decisively away from the positivist emphasis upon measurement and so-called "value-neutral" description. Nowadays many modern theorists in the field of educational administration are moving much more towards an approach based on advances in epistemology and methodology, that have rejected positivism, and that take their inspiration from post-empiricist work in the philosophy of science and the social sciences, such as that of Dewey (1938a), Quine (1953, 1974), and Davidson (1980) in the U.S., and Popper (1949, 1960, 1972), Lakatos (1976, 1978), and Winch (1958, 1973) from the continent of Europe and the United Kingdom.

Other powerful influences on the development of thinking in the social sciences, and in turn in educational administration, were generally exercised by the work of Rorty (1980), Kuhn (1973), and Feyerabend (1975) in America, and Giddens (1990) and Foucault (1977, 1983, 1988) in Europe. As a consequence, a strong turn towards subjectivist and relativist interpretations of social phenomena became evident in much writing in educational administration by the 1980s. The influence of subjectivists and ethnomethodologists of various kinds was perhaps most noticeable in the work of those following the lead of and working in the tradition of Mead, Schutz, Garfinkel and their like; among these perhaps the most influential for educational administration was the powerful alternative voice uttered by the Canadian scholar, T. B. Greenfield.

Those views, though still held in sway in various quarters in the field of educational administration, would probably no longer constitute the major alternative to the previous orthodoxy. The work of more modern epistemologists in educational administration, such as Evers and Lakomski, have enabled those working in this field to move beyond positivist, relativist and subjectivist views and to begin to articulate accounts, develop analyses, and produce tentative conclusions that are quite as complex, heterogenous, and multiform as the corpus of material upon which they are based and towards the elucidation of which they may be applied.

With the application to the field of educational administration of internationally-influenced advances of thinking in epistemology and the philosophy of science and language more generally, there is now an increasing acceptance of the need to bring together areas of enquiry and forms of discourse that were previously thought to be mutually opposed and exclusive. There is now recognized to be a need in educational enquiry to fuse description-evaluation, fact-value, quantitative-qualitative methods in new forms of enquiry that are valuable both for the researcher and the policymaker. Such an approach will involve both groups in a common enterprise, what Lakatos (1976, 1978) called a "progressive research program," of understanding and policy generation.

For Quine, Popper, Winch, Evers, Lakomski, and many others, all language and all inquiries are inescapably and *ab initio* theory-laden, far from value-free, and a mixture of both descriptive and normative elements. Indeed, says the Hungarian-Australian scholar Kovesi (1967), in all discourse and enquiry, there is an unbroken continuum, at one end of which lies "fact" and at the other end lies "value." Description, for such thinkers, is a way of evaluating reality; evaluation is a way of describing states of affairs.

These arguments have been used by a number of thinkers to develop a new approach to the elucidation of problems in educational policy and administration. In this view, all discourse on these matters can be conceived of as being in itself a "theory," embodying a complex "web of belief" (see Quine & Ullian, 1970), shot through differentially with descriptive and evaluative elements, according to the contexts and purposes of which our theories of education, policy, and administration are brought to bear and applied in our world.

Research in Educational Administration

In light of the development of these different theoretical traditions, we may now attempt to give some account of the ways in which research has developed in the field of educational administration over recent times and the extent to which these developments have been in response to, or influenced by, international developments in the philosophy of science and the social sciences, and international developments in "theory" in educational administration.

Earlier approaches to research in the social sciences were rooted in logical empiricism, and its derivative positivism, of which the principal scientific objective was the description of perceptual data, the clarification of understanding in respect of those data, the explanation of anomalies arising in and from those data, and the verification of hypotheses put forward to account for them. This approach was permeated by an empiricist model of science that privileged observation, hypothesis testing, and the induction of probabilities. The verification principle took its normative force from the acceptance in the 1920s and 1930s by members of the Vienna Circle of the primacy of the natural sciences and their typical methods of enquiry over all other academic activities. Regard for the "scientific method" as setting up such an exemplar can be found in the work of Sir Francis Bacon. It was he who gave impetus and authority to the formula of direct sense experience, observation, the accumulation and classification of data acquired thus, experimentation, the induction of probabilistic conclusions, the elimination of incorrect hypotheses, and the establishment of probable causations as being *the* method par excellence of natural philosophy (see Sir Francis Bacon; editions McClure, 1928 and Stephens, 1975).

The social sciences were heavily influenced by this method and attempted to apply the criteria and procedures of the natural sciences to the study of human affairs. Empirical observation and a reasoning based upon and rooted firmly in what was held to be the theory-free and value-neutral sense perception of human and social phenomena were regarded as the only valid sources and foundations of human knowledge. Central to this position was the idea that there are states of affairs and "facts" that are "out there" in the natural and social worlds and that these exist "objectively" outside and independent of human consciousness.

This standpoint was adopted by researchers in educational administration, particularly in the U.S. in the 1950s and was reflected in the dominant emphasis on quantitative methods in earlier research in educational administration. The aim of research in educational administration undertaken from this perspective was to seek to understand the relationships subsisting between these objective states of affairs and natural or social facts *and* the responses, reactions, and behavior of organizations, institutions, and human beings to them, and to construct explanations of these interactions and a coherent social system theory that could then be applied to and guide the organization and management of schools and school systems.

The positivist approach to research may therefore be characterized as being concerned with the use of a particular inductivist version of what was called the scientific method (Aspin, 1996). On this model, science consists of a small number of primary functions: (1) the observation of phenomena in the natural and social worlds; (2) the development of theories capable of being inferred from such observations or descriptions; and (3) the testing and verification of substantive hypotheses that may then be employed in the verification of the theories derived from the observation of data. This has been the approach that, until the late 1970s, dominated work in educational administration.

The traditional empiricist paradigm embraced a number of quantitative research techniques, strongly associated with logical-positivist views of "knowing" and "understanding" social and organizational phenomena and resting upon and incorporating empiricist postulates. For quantitative researchers, science seeks to generalize and predict, and it is dependent upon the assumption of the existence of some form or degree of order in the physical and social world under study. The notion of order is closely related to the concept of a "natural universe." Thus as some scholars have maintained, we can, by using the paradigm scientific method—that of the natural sciences—empirically advance valid and reliable accounts, analyses and explanations of objects, events, occurrences, states of affairs, and relationships in the administrative domain, and thus further the ends of administrative science.

Quantitative methods were introduced to the field of educational administration early with the advent of the school survey (Tatsuoka & Silver, 1988, p. 677). With the increasing use of computers, large-sample surveys became common in the 1960s. What Tatsuoka and Silver call the "heyday" of quantitative research was in the 1950s, 1960s, and early 1970s. An examination of the research literature of that period shows the predominance of statistical methods as a research tool. Examples of the type of research done during this period include the LBDQ studies of leadership and the Halpin and Croft (1963) studies of school climate in the U.S., which were replicated in thousands of similar studies, not only in America but also in other countries such as Australia; the studies on bureaucracy based on Hall's (1963) work (Isherwood & Hoy, 1973; Moeller, 1964; Kolesar, 1967; Mansfield, 1967); and the Aston studies on bureaucracy (Child, 1972; Hinnings *et al.*, 1967; Holdaway *et al.*, 1975; Pugh *et al.*, 1968). An examination of published research during this period clearly reveals the dominance of quantitative methods in these studies. Research instruments developed in the U.S. were readily available and applied, often without modification, in countries such as Australia.

Tatsuoka and Silver (1988), in reviewing the methods for treating quantitative data, identified modes of enquiry that could be divided broadly into four types: (1) survey-descriptive methods, in which data are reported in terms of central tendencies, frequency distributions, and simple tests of differences between groups; (2) analysis of variance methods, in which the extent of variation among groups is compared; (3) correlational methods, in which relationships are compared; and (4) causal methods, such as experiments, regression analysis, and path methods (1988, pp. 678–699). In reviewing the research reported in the *Education Administration Quarterly* from 1965 to 1983, Tatsuoka and Silver noted that in 167 studies, numerical data served as the primary research method. This is considerably different in the 1990s, when an examination of the *EAQ* for the years 1994–1996 produced only two studies of this kind.

In the 1970s and 1980s, faculties, schools, and departments of education in institutions around the world began to witness the emergence of more interpretivist accounts of phenomena in the social and organizational worlds. These accounts were led in educational administration by the work of the Canadian scholar Thomas Greenfield (1975, 1979, 1986). The work of Greenfield (see Greenfield & Ribbins, 1993) ushered in a period of intellectual ferment in the field of educational administration. This saw the growth and application of a range of diverse standpoints and methods to the problems, topics, and issues in the field. If it was not a case of "let a hundred flowers bloom, a hundred schools of thought contend," there certainly emerged a plethora of approaches from among which researchers in educational administration could choose their preferred perspective and their place "on which to stand."

The approach of Greenfield and of those working subsequently within this tradition is based upon and embodies subjectivist views of knowing and understanding, heavily influenced by and emanating from the work of phenomenologists in Europe such as Husserl, Heidegger, and Schutz in the early part of the twentieth century. This alternative view attempts to understand human beings as creators and bearers of intersubjective "meanings," that give their communications, actions, and relationships their intelligibility and significance. Thus what must be studied is

human interaction and meaning in context, which for students of educational administration is the administrative milieu. Traditions as diverse as ethnography, hermeneutics, phenomenology, and various versions of postmodernism have been located within this particular conception of social science, were developed and brought to bear, and are still at work in the field of educational administration. From this perspective, ethnographic research has become very popular in educational administration with a focus on participant-observation and interviewing techniques. It should be noted however that despite the proliferation of this research, Wolcott (1988) contends that much of what passes for ethnographic research is poorly done.

It should be noted that Europe, the United Kingdom, and Australia have had a longer tradition of research involving hermeneutic, phenomenological, symbolic interactionst and interpretivist methods and methodologies than has North America. More recently, the work of a number of European existentialists, Marxists, and postmodernists has exerted considerable influence upon the extension and increasing sophistication in the development of such standpoints. These have been adopted and applied in the field of educational administration. Among the range of thinkers adopting such alternative views, the work of critical theorists was particularly dominant in educational administration theory and research in Australia and New Zealand in the 1980s and has been strongly associated with the work of Bates and his associates at Deakin University and found expressions in a number of "action research" projects (see Carr & Kemmis, 1986).

The regeneration of action research began in Europe, inspired by epistemic and value commitments, and originally found expression in the work of critical sociologists of the "Frankfurt" School (such as Adorno, Horkheimer, and Marcuse), and became more sharply focused in the work of Habermas, perhaps that school's best known descendent (see Bernstein, 1972 and 1976; Carr & Kemmis, 1986). Parallel influence was also being exercised by French Marxists, such as Althusser, Bourdieu, and Bachelard, the latter two pointing their work especially towards education, as also did the Italian Marxist, Gramsci. The work of such thinkers was of enormous importance and had great influence upon the development of later thinking in education elsewhere in Europe, particularly in the United Kingdom, and also in North America.

The education research approach that built upon these footings and began to be applied was particularly influential in the United Kingdom in the late 1960s in the development of the conception of education as a species of resistance to technical theories of curriculum and teaching that had by then become increasingly separated from practice. This emphasis on action research has flourished not only in Australia and the United Kingdom, but also in North America. Perhaps this is partly because of the focus on teachers as reflective practitioners (Schön, 1983), rather than passive implementers of "expert" knowledge.

Action research is a method of inquiry that brings together academics and practitioners, such that practitioners move in a cyclical manner between understanding, action, and the assessment of alternative practices. This method is held to "empower" practitioners because it enables those who make decisions to base those decisions on critical reflection (see Habermas, 1972, 1984, and 1987). To ensure that academics do not try to control practitioners, Elliott (1991) argues for a form of action research wherein the goal is autonomous reflective practice.

Reason (1994) identifies three approaches to action research and participative inquiry: cooperative inquiry, participatory action research (PAR), and action inquiry. Although PAR is more politically oriented, Reason feels that there is complementarity in the three approaches. Others (such as Stringer, 1996) view action research as empowerment, democracy, equity, liberation, freedom from oppression, and life enhancement. The dilemma for action researchers is, according to Gitlin and Thompson (1995, p. 131):

> [w]hether to impose a political agenda on those conducting action research projects and thus violate a basic tenet of this research methodology, or leave the adoption of a political agenda optional, thereby running the risk that the action research project will neither examine nor act on schools' role in reproducing social inequities.

Another "critical" perspective to research in educational administration has come from feminist scholarship. The impetus for such studies and their driving concerns has been well expressed by the Australian feminist scholar Ann Curthoys (1991):

> Most academics in the humanities and social sciences, and so far as I am aware, in the physical and natural sciences as well, now reject positivist concepts of knowledge, the notion that one can objectively know the facts. The processes of knowing, and the production of an object that is known, are seen as intertwined. Many take this even further, and argue that knowledge is entirely an effect of power, that we can no longer have any concept of truth at all.

This impulse has been powerfully articulated in the work of feminist researchers in educational administration. The work of scholars such as Shakeshaft and Hanson (1986), Shakeshaft (1989), and Lather (1991) has added an important element of critique to work in the field of educational administration. Feminist research in educational administration has been particularly influential in North America over the last decade and has been increasingly taken up in Australia, New Zealand, and the United Kingdom. Feminist researchers draw attention to what they see as the dangers of some past research in educational administration in which they see a hierarchical research relationship, one that is potentially exploitative (Lather, 1991). As Munro comments:

> Rather, both the researcher and the researched are active participants in the research relationship and knowledge is viewed as socially and intersubjectively constructed (Munro, 1991, p. 7).

The goal of feminist research is seen as being emancipatory or empowering (see Habermas, 1972, 1984, and 1987). Lather, for example, integrates feminism and postmodernism into a critical education theory for emancipatory theory and practice. This approach to research design envisions a democratized process of inquiry, characterized by negotiation and reciprocity. Researchers become cultural workers whose duty is to allow subjects to speak on their own behalf and to respond to their wishes and needs by focusing on how they understand their own condition (Munro, 1991, p. xvii).

This approach reflects another powerful influence upon the conception and elaboration of much recent research in educational administration. The work of Foucault (Foucault, 1977, 1983, 1988) has strongly influenced the thinking of scholars and researchers such as Stephen Ball (1990, 1995) in the United Kingdom and Marshall and Peters (1994, pp. 4639–4642; Peters, 1995) in New Zealand. The outcome has been an increase in the number of those proposing postmodernist and poststructuralist theories.

Postmodernists working within the field of educational administration have been strongly influenced by the work of French and European forbears, not only Kierkegaard, Husserl, Heidegger, Nietzsche, and Merleau-Ponty but also Foucault, Lyotard, and Baudrillard, and deconstructionists such as Derrida, Ricoeur, and Lacan. Such researchers are concerned with the place, meaning, and value to be gained from and given to "voice" and "alternative voices" (but see Best & Kellner, 1991; and Norris, 1990). Consequently, we now see an increase in the number of research projects that use the narrative approach and even attempts to count fictional work as educational research, as highlighted in the debates at the 1996 meeting of AERA on what counts as a Ph.D. in education: could a novel be submitted as a Ph.D. thesis in this field? (Donmoyer, 1996b).

The narrative inquiry approach is increasingly being used in studies of educational experience (Connelly & Clandinin, 1990). Methods include interviews, storytelling, letter writing, and autobiographical and biographical writing. The narrative approach has been relatively slow to be accepted in American research. In contrast, Josselson and Lieblich (1993) noted that Europeans, who had not taken the intellectual turn toward American behaviorism and had instead "a rich heritage of phenomenological philosophy, were somewhat ahead of the Americans in pursuit of narrative study" (1993, p. xi).

Most recently, the work of positivists, subjectivists, critical theorists, and postmodernists of various persuasions has come under attack, and their intellectual limits have been exposed. New accounts of knowledge, understanding, and "theory" have been articulated and promulgated by a number of scholars. Among these, mention must be made of Australian scholars such as Evers and Lakomski (1996). Their accounts draw upon advances in the philosophy of science emanating from North America and from Europe, and which are strongly influenced by the work of Dewey (Dewey, 1938b, 1966), Popper, and Quine and, in the case of Evers and Lakomski, by pragmatists and by other materialists such as Paul M. Churchland (1988), Patricia Smith Churchland (1986), and Stich (1983).

In the approach to research developed from the work of such scholars (see Aspin & Chapman, 1994), researchers do not attempt to reduce everything to some absolute foundations of "fact" and "value," "theory" and "practice," or "policy" and "implementation" in the (vain) attempt to educe some "analyses" of concepts and theories that can be completely "correct" or "true"; or to produce some fundamental matters of indisputable research "findings" about the objectivity and existence of which there can be no dispute. Researchers working from this perspective share the Quinean view that what is important in research is not to establish which analyses are "true" (in some sort of "correspondence" sense) or which facts are "correct" (in some sort of "positivist" sense), but rather, in our endeavor to improve education

1. To query which of our values and beliefs we should be least willing to give up
2. To grasp the theories determining and predicting advance
3. Then by critical theory appraisal and comparison, to show which of them is better and for what purpose

International Developments in Theory and Research in Educational Administration: Past, Present, and Future

During the past two decades, there has been a methodological revolution in the field of educational administration, reflecting broader international developments in epistemology and the social sciences.

Until the 1970s, it was largely structural-functionalist and positivist orthodoxy that dominated educational administration thinking and research in the U.S. and elsewhere; this in turn led to an emphasis in research on quantitative methods. In the late 1970s and 1980s, there emerged a number of different and competing theoretical and research paradigms: subjectivist, radical functionalist, humanist, and radical humanist (Burrell & Morgan, 1979). These all challenged the theoretical orthodoxy and

brought on a period of exploration in research methods. This was followed by a period in the 1990s in which a number of more heterogeneous modes of investigation, analysis, and interpretation emerged, such as culturalism, feminism, postmodernism, poststructuralism, and these were variously explored, developed, and applied. Such different meta-theories, methodologies, and approaches have had considerable impact and influence on the field of educational administration at the present time and are likely to sustain that influence in the future.

Much of modern research in educational administration draws upon different European traditions and tendencies in the philosophy and sociology of knowledge, hermeneutics, and Marxism. The resulting debates have brought into question some of the basic assumptions by which people have engaged in inquiry. Many of the basic assumptions around which quantitative research centers, such as "objectivity" and "verification", have been challenged (Popkewitz, 1984).

Until the late 1960s, structural-functionalism and statistical paradigms shaped the research agenda. The shift from quantitative to qualitative approaches in the study of educational administration represents a change in basic philosophy. In part, the shift from structural functionalism and statistical inferences to interpretive paradigms (such as phenomenology, culturalism, social interactionism, critical theory, feminism, postmodernism, and poststructuralism) has resulted in the popularity of qualitative methods. The result has been the usage of various labels: ethnography, participant observation, fieldwork, qualitative methods, case studies, and naturalistic inquiry; these approaches are all attempts to understand educational processes *in situ*.

Intersections of gender, race, and class now serve as important analytical categories in fields of study. These intersections, made viable through the interdisciplinary fields such as women's studies, embody strong political and social concerns, moving theory and research away from previous and now discredited intellectualist conceptions of an "ivory-tower" separation between theory and practice, directly into the world of practice.

In the introduction to the *Handbook of Qualitative Research*, Denzin and Lincoln (1994) comment: "A blurring of the disciplinary boundaries has occurred. The social sciences and humanities have drawn closer together in mutual focus on an interpretive, qualitative approach to research and theory" (1994, p. ix). Where previously experimental and quasi-experimental designs and survey research methods were the norm, particularly in research emanating from the U.S., currently researchers around the world are using ethnography, action research, unstructured interviewing, textual analysis, historical analysis, and narrative approaches. Denzin and Lincoln comment:

[S]cholars are now experimenting with the boundaries of interpretation, linking research to social change, delving into characteristics of race, ethnicity, gender, age, and culture to understand more fully the relationship of the researcher to the research. In various disciplines in various guises, this implicit critique of the traditional world view of science and quantitative methods is taking place. All of these trends have fallen under the rubric of "qualitative research" [loc. cit.].

Denzin and Lincoln review the history of qualitative research as consisting of a number of phases: the traditional (1900–1950), the modernist (1950–1970), blurred genres (1970–1986), the crisis of representation (1986–1990), and the postmodern (1990 to the present). In their view, qualitative research includes case study, personal experience, introspective life story, interview, observational, historical, interactional, and visual texts "that describe routine and problematic moments and meanings in individuals' lives. Accordingly, qualitative researchers deploy a wide range of interconnected methods, hoping always to get a better fix on the subject matter at hand" (1994, p. 2).

In qualitative research, the issue of the logical value to be assigned to and the part to be played by concepts such as "truth" have been subject to major reappraisal. In quantitative research, the concept of validity, operative in empiricist epistemologies, assumes an absolute, fixed truth value that can be measured, validated, and verified (Wolcott, 1988). By contrast, in the accounts offered by various alterative approaches employing qualitative methods, the concept of truth is forced "to stand up to examination against other facts, standards, experiences, and perspectives" (Munro, 1991, p. 1). Munro suggests that, in doing fieldwork on the life histories of women, for instance, the concept of validity has little to do with "truth" but rather with understanding how the research process can serve to "illuminate" women's way of knowing. As a result, we see much nontraditional scholarship arising in this field.

There are dangers in this approach, however. Silverman (1993, p. 211) contends that:

> The worst thing that contemporary qualitative research can imply is that, in this post-modern age, anything goes. The trick is to produce intelligent disciplined work on the very edge of the abyss.

In all likelihood, researchers in the field of educational a dministration are now entering a phase where "messy, uncertain multivoiced texts, cultural criticism, and new experimental works will become more common, as will more reflexive forms of fieldwork, analysis, and intertextual representation" (Denzin & Lincoln, 1994, p. 583).

Robert Donmoyer, recently appointed editor of the *Educational Researcher*, has commented on the current state of educational research: "[O]urs is a field characterized by paradigmatic proliferation and, consequently, the sort of field in which there is little consensus about what research and

scholarship are and what research reporting and scholarly discourse should look like" (1996a, p. 19; see also 1996c). He argues that many of the issues discussed (such as the significance of discourse style, the inadequacy of the qualitative/quantitative distinction, the problems of what he calls "balkanization" responses) and the principles articulated (paradigmatic incommensurability, for instance) are all concerns that journal editors have to deal with. Unfortunately, even with peer reviews, contradictory advice is given. Ultimately, he intimates, the editors of journals decide what to publish, and this may in consequence act so as to define and even dictate what is acceptable research in the field.

This seems to suggest that what is really going on in international scholarship at the present time is an example of the kind of scholarly anarchy and theory competition for which Feyerabend argued so powerfully in his classic *Against Method* (1975). But in such competitions and theoretic free-for-alls lie the dangers of the drive to power and dominance which he also adumbrated and which many, interested in internationalization and plurality but observing the globalizing imperatives in the economy for uniformity and control by the great multinational corporations, will say is one of the strongest forces and impulses towards uniformity, conformity, and "the end of history" (Fukuyama, 1992).

The possibilities and dangers of this kind of coercion must be obvious to all those with a concern for the insights available through plural insights on academic activities and interests, curiosity-driven research, creativity and iconoclasm in problem solving, and theory and research in this field. It is a danger that scholars internationally must guard against and seek to eliminate if research and theory in this field is not to become suborned by the imperatives of a new form of "imperialist" mentality. The best guard and bulwark against that danger is that scholars working in educational administration embrace and adopt the kind of piecemeal problem-solving approach apotheosized by Popper (1943) as the only way in which societies of any sort committed to "openness" and growth can hope to survive and flourish.

Commitment to the "open society," we contend, is a way forward in the internationalization of policy, practice, theory, and research in the field of educational administration in the future.

REFERENCES

Appaduria, A. (1990). Disjuncture and Difference in the Global Political Economy. In M. Featherstone (Ed.), *Global Culture: Nationalism, Globalisation and Modernity* London: Sage pp. 295–310.

Aspin, D. N. (1996). Logical Empiricism and Post-Empiricism. In P. Higgs (Ed.), *Meta-Theories in Philosophy of Education.* London and Durban: Heinemann.

Aspin, D. N. (Ed.) (1997). *Logical Empiricism and Post-Empiricism in Educational Discourse.* London and Durban: Heinemann.

Aspin, D. N. & Chapman, J. D., with Wilkinson, V. R. (1994). *Quality Schooling: A Pragmatic Approach to Some Current Problems, Topics, and Issues.* London: Cassell.

Ayer, A. J. (1946). *Language, Truth, and Logic*. Harmondsworth: Penguin Press (2nd Ed).

Bacon, F. (1928). *Magna Instauratio*. In M. T. McClure, *Bacon: Selections* London: Scribner.

Bacon, F. (1975). *Novum Organon*. See J. Stephens, *Francis Bacon and the Style of Science*. Chicago: University of Chicago Press.

Ball, C. (1993). *Lifelong Learning and the School Curriculum*. Paris: OECD/CERI.

Ball, C. (1994). Summation of the Conference at the Conclusion of the *First Global Conference on Lifelong Learning*. Rome.

Ball, S. J. (1990). *Politics and Policy-making in Education*. London: Routledge

Ball, S. J. (1995). *Education Reform: A Critical and Poststructuralist Perspective*. Buckingham: Open University Press.

Banks, D., Huston, P., Murphy, M. & Muth, R. (1996). Charter Schools: Let The Games Begin. A paper presented at the annual Conference of the *American Educational Research Association*, New York.

Bates, R. (1980). Educational Administration, the Sociology of Science and the Management of Knowledge. *Educational Administration Quarterly*, 16 (2), 1–20.

Bernstein, R. J. (1972). *Praxis and Action*. London: Duckworth.

Bernstein, R. J. (1976). *The Restructuring of Social and Political Theory*. London: Methuen.

Bernstein, R. J. (1983). *Beyond Objectivism and Relativism*. Oxford: Blackwell.

Best, S. & Kellner, D. (1991). *Postmodern Theory: Critical Interrogations*. Basingstoke: Macmillan.

Boyd, W. L. (1992). The Power of Paradigms: Reconceptualizing Educational Policy and Management. *Educational Administration Quarterly*, 28, 504–528.

Boyd, W. L. (1993). Choice and Market Forces in American Education: A Revolution or a Non-event? In D. Finegold, L. McFarland & W. Richardson (Eds.), *Something Borrowed, Something Learned? The Transatlantic Market in Education and Training Reform*. Washington, DC: The Brookings Institution.

Boyd, W. L. (1996). The Politics of Choice and Market-oriented School Reform in Britain and the United States: Explaining the Difference. In J. D. Chapman, W. L. Boyd, R. Lander & D. Reynolds (Eds.), *The Reconstruction of Education*. London: Cassell.

Bridges, D. & McLaughlin, T. H. (Eds.) (1994). *Education and the Market Place*. London: Falmer Press.

Burrell, G. & Morgan, G. (1979). *Sociological Paradigms and Organizational Analysis*. London: Gower.

Carr, W. & Kemmis, S. (1986). *Becoming Critical: Education, Knowledge and Action Research*. London: Falmer.

Chapman, J. D. (1990). School-based decision making and management: Implications for school personnel. In J. Chapman (Ed.), *School-based Decision making and Management* (pp. 221–244). London: Falmer.

Chapman, J. D. (1994). *Devolution: Where to next?* A Key Note Address presented at a conference held by the Australian Council of Educational Administration at the Graduate School of Education, University of Western Australia.

Chapman, J. D. & Aspin D. N. (1993). *Securing the Future*. Paris: OECD.

Chapman, J. D. & Aspin D. N. (1995). *Learning: Realizing a Lifelong Approach for All: A Review of OECD Work 1990–95*. Paris: OECD.

Chapman, J. D. & Aspin, D. N. (1997). *The School, the Community and Lifelong Learning*. London: Cassell.

Child, J. (1972). Organization Structures and Strategies of Control: A Replication of the Aston Study. *Administrative Science Quarterly*, 16, 163–177.

Churchland, P. M. (1988). *Matter and Consciousness*. Cambridge, Mass: MIT Press.

Churchland, P. S. (1986). *Neurophilosophy*. Cambridge, Mass: MIT Press.

Cibulka, J. G. (1996). The Evolution of Education Reform in Great Britain and the United States: Implementation Convergence of Two Macro-policy Approaches. In J. D. Chapman, W. L. Boyd, R. Lander & D. Reynolds (Eds.), *The Reconstruction of Education*. London: Cassell.

Connelly, F. M. & Clandinin, D. J. (1990). Stories of Experience and Narrative Inquiry. *Educational Researcher*, 19 (5), 2–14.

Culbertson, J. (1969). A New Initiative in Educational Administration. In G. Baron, D. Cooper & W. Walker (Eds.), *Educational administration: International perspectives* (pp. 1–8). Chicago: Rand McNally and Co.

Curthoys, A. (1991). Unlocking the Academies: Responses and Strategies in Meanjin 50, 2/3, p. 391 ff. (quoted in Windschuttle, K. (1994), *The Killing of History*. Sydney: Macleay Press.)

Davidson, D. (1980). *Essays on Actions and Events*. Oxford: Clarendon Press.

Delors, J. (Ed.) (1996). *Learning: The Treasure Within*. Paris: UNESCO.

Denzin, N. K. & Lincoln, Y. S. (Eds.) (1994). *Handbook of Qualitative Research*. Thousand Oaks, CA: Sage.

Dewey, J. (1907). The Control of Ideas by Facts. *Journal of Philosophy*, 4 (12), p. 111.

Dewey, J. (1938a). *Logic: The Theory of Enquiry*. New York: Holt, Rinehart and Winston.

Dewey, J. (1938b). *Experience and Education*. New York: Macmillan.

Dewey, J. (1966). *Democracy and Education*. New York: Free Press.

Dilthey, W. (1976). *Selected Writings* (edited, translated and introduced by Rickman, H. P.). Cambridge: Cambridge University Press.

Donmoyer, R. (1996a). Educational Research in an Era of Paradigm Proliferation: What's a Journal Editor to Do? *Educational Researcher*, Vol. 25, No. 2, pp. 19–25.

Donmoyer, R. (1996b & c). "Yes, but Is It Research? The Conversation Continues: Should A Novel Count as a Dissertation in Education?" and "Can We Talk? Attempted Conversation Across Research Paradigms, Purposes and Perspectives." Discussion sessions moderated at the *Annual Conference of the American Educational Research Association*. AERA: New York.

Elliott, J. (1991). *Action Research for Educational Change*. Milton Keyes: Open University Press.

European Parliament-Commission of the European Communities (1995). Amended Proposal for a European Parliament and Council Decision establishing a European Year of Lifelong Learning–Brussels: European Parliament.

Evers, C. & Chapman, J. (1995). *Educational Administration: An Australian Perspective*. Allen and Unwin: St. Leonards.

Evers, C. & Lakomski, G. (1991). *Knowing Educational Administration*. Oxford: Pergamon Press.

Evers, C. & Lakomski, G. (1996). Post-positivist conceptions in educational administration: An introduction. *Educational Administration Quarterly*, 32 (3), 341–344.

Feyerabend, P. (1975). *Against Method: Outline of an Anarchistic Theory of Knowledge*. London: New Left Books.

Finegold, D. (1993). The Changing International Economy and Its Impact on Education and Training. In D. Finegold, L. McFarland & W. Richardson (Eds.), *Something Borrowed, Something Learned?* Washington, DC: Brookings.

Finegold, D., McFarland, L. & Richardson, W. (1993). Introduction. In D. Finegold, L. McFarland & W. Richardson (1993), *Something Borrowed, Something Learned?* Washington, DC: Brookings.

Fittoussi, J. & Luna, F. (1996). Wage Distribution, Social Cohesion and the Knowledge-based Economy. *Employment and Growth in the Knowledge-based Economy*. Paris: OECD.

Foray, D. & Lundvall, B. (1996). The Knowledge-based Economy: From the Economics of Knowledge to the Learning Economy. *Employment and Growth in the Knowledge-based Economy*. Paris: OECD.

Foucault, M. (1977). *Discipline and Punish: The Birth of the Prison*. London: Allen Lane.

Foucault, M. (1983). *The Archaeology of Knowledge* (translated by Sheridan Smith, A. M.). New York: Pantheon Books.

Foucault, M. (1988). *Madness and Civilization: A History of Insanity in the Age of Reason*. New York: Vintage Books.

Fowler, F., Boyd, W. & Plank, D. (1993). International School Reform: Political Considerations. In S. Jacobson & R. Berne (Eds.), *Reforming Education: The Emerging Systemic Approach* (pp. 153–167). Thousand Oaks, CA: Corwin Press.

Fukuyama, F. (1992). *The End of History and the Last Man*. London: Hamish Hamilton.

Gadamer, H. G. (1976). The Historicity of Understanding. In P. Connerton (Ed.), *Critical Sociology*. Harmondsworth: Penguin.

Gadamer, H. G. (1979a). *Truth and Method* (translated by W. Glen Doepel). London: Sheed and Ward.

Gadamer, H. G. (1979b). The Problem of Historical Consciousness. In P. Rabinow & W. M. Sullivan (Eds.), *Interpretive Social Science—A Reader*. Berkeley, Los Angeles: University of California Press.

Garmston, R. (1993). Reflections on Cognitive Coaching. *Educational Leadership*, 51(2), 57–61.

Giddens, A. (1990). *The Consequences of Modernity*. Cambridge: Polity Press.

Giles, C. (1994). *Marketing, Parental Choice and Strategic Planning: An Opportunity or Dilemma for UK Schools?* A paper presented to the International Intervisitation Program Conference in Buffalo, USA, May.

Gitlin, A. & Thompson, A. (1993). Foregrounding Politics in Action Research. *McGill Journal of Education*, 30 (20), 131–147.

Grace, G. R. (1994). Education is a Public Good: On the Need to Resist the Domination of Economic Science. In D. Bridges & T. H. McLaughlin (Eds.), *Education and the Market Place*. London: Falmer.

Green, A. C. (1993). Magnet Schools, Choice and the Politics of Policy Borrowing. In D. Finegold, L. McFarland & W. Richardson (Eds.), *Something Borrowed, Something Learned*? Washington, DC: Brookings.

Greenfield, T. (1975). Theory about Organizations: A New Perspective and its Implications for Schools. In M. Hughes (Ed.), *Administering Education: International Challenge* (pp. 71–79). London: Athlone.

Greenfield, T. (1979). Ideas vs. Data: How Can the Data Speak for Themselves? In G. L. Immegart & W. L. Boyd (Eds.), *Problem-Finding in Educational Administration: Trends in Research and Theory* (pp. 167–190). Lexington, MA: Lexington.

Greenfield, T. (1986). The Decline and Fall of Science in Educational Administration. *Interchange*, 17 (2), 57–80.

Greenfield, T. B. & Ribbins, P. (Eds.) (1993). *Greenfield on Educational Administration*. London: Routledge.

Guthrie, J. W. (1993). School Reform and the "New World Order." In S. Jacobson & R. Berne (Eds.), *Reforming Education: The Emerging Systemic Approach* (pp. 231–255). Thousand Oaks, CA: Corwin Press.

Habermas, J. (1972). *Knowledge and Human Interests* (translated by Shapiro, J. J.). London: Heinemann.

Habermas, J. (1984, 1987). *Theory of Communicative Action*, Vols. 1 and 2. Boston: Beacon Press.

Hall, R. (1963). The Concept of Bureaucracy: An Empirical Assessment. *American Journal of Sociology*, 63, 32–48.

Halpin, A. & Croft, D. (1963). *The Organizational Climate of Schools*. Chicago: University of Chicago Press.

Hannaway, J. (1992). *Decentralization in Education: Technical Demands as a Critical Ingredient*. ERIC Document (ED 345 362).

Hardikes, T. (1988). Marketing the School. *Educational Change and Development*, 9 (l), 16–19.

Hatton, M. (Ed.) (1997). *Lifelong Learning: Policies, Practices and Programs*. Toronto: APEC-HURDIT Network.

Hinnings, C., Pugh, D., Hickson, D. & Turner, C. (1967). An Approach to the Study of Bureaucracy. *Sociology*, l, 61–72.

Holdaway, E., Newberry, J., Hickson, D. & Heron, R. (1975). Dimensions of Organizations in Complex Societies: The Educational Sector. *Administrative Science Quarterly*, 20, 37–58.

Hughes, M. (1988). Comparative Educational Administration. In N. Boyan (Ed.), *Handbook of Research on Educational Administration* (pp. 655–675). New York: Longman.

Isherwood, G. & Hoy, W. (l973). Bureaucracy, Powerlessness and Teacher Work Values. *The Journal of Educational Administration*, ll, 124–137.

Josselson, R. & Lieblich, A. (Eds.) (1993). *The Narrative Study of Lives*. London: Sage.

Kolesar, H. (1967). *An Empirical Study of Client Alienation in the Bureaucratic Organization*. Unpublished doctoral dissertation, University of Alberta, Edmonton.

Kovesi, J. (1967). *Moral Notions*. London: Routledge & Kegan Paul.

Kuhn, T. S. (1973). *The Structure of Scientific Revolutions*. Chicago: Chicago University Press.

Lakatos I. (1976). Falsification and the Methodology of Scientific Research Programs. In I. Lakatos & A. W. Musgrave, *Criticism and the Growth of Knowledge*. Cambridge: Cambridge University Press.

Lakatos, I. (1978). *The Methodology of Scientific Research Programmes*. Cambridge: Cambridge University Press.

Lather, P. (1991). *Getting Smart: Feminist Research and Pedagogy within the Postmodern*. London: Routledge.

Lauglo, J. (1996). Forms of Decentralisation and their Implications for Education. In J. D. Chapman, W. L. Boyd, R. Lander & D. Reynolds (Eds.), *The Reconstruction of Education: Quality, Equality and Control*. London: Cassell.

Lyotard, J. F. (1984). *The Postmodern Condition*. Minneapolis: University of Minneapolis Press.

McLaughlin, T. H. (1994). Politics, Markets and Schools: The Central Issues. In D. Bridges & T. H. McLaughlin (Eds.), *Education and the Market Place*. London: Falmer Press.

Malen, B. & Ogawa, R. (1988). Professional-Patron Influence on Site-based Governance Councils: A Confounding Case Study. *Educational Evaluation and Policy Analysis*, 10(4), 251–270.

Malen, B., Ogawa, R. & Kranz, J. (1989). What Do We Know About School-based Management? A Case Study of the Literature—A Call for Research. Paper presented at the Conference on Choice and Control in American Education. Madison: University of Wisconsin-Madison.

Mansfield, E. (1967). *Administrative Communication and the Organizational Structure of the School*. Unpublished doctoral dissertation, University of Alberta, Edmonton.

Marshall, J. D. & Peters, M. (1994). Post-modernism and Education. In T. Husen & T. H. Postlethwaite (Eds.), *The International Encyclopaedia of Education* (2nd Ed). Oxford: Pergaman.

Moeller, G. (1964). Bureaucracy and Teachers' Sense of Power. *School Review*, 9, 137–157.

Molnar, A. (1996). Charter Schools: The Smiling Face of Disinvestment. *Educational Leadership*, 54 (2), 9–15.

Morris, L. (1994). *Dangerous Classes: The Underclass and Social Citizenship*. London: Routledge.

Munro, P. (1991). Multiple "I's": Dilemmas of Life History Research. Paper presented at the annual conference of the *American Educational Research Association*, Chicago.

Murphy, J. & Beck, L. (1995). *School-based Management as School Reform: Taking Stock*. Newbury Park, CA: Corwin Press.

Nathan, J. (1996). Early Lessons of the Charter School Movement. *Educational Leadership*, 54 (2), 16–22.

Nordic Council of Ministers, The (1995). *The Golden Riches in the Grass—Lifelong Learning for All*. Copenhagen: Nordic Council of Ministers.

Norris, C. (1990). *What's Wrong with Post-modernism: Critical Theory and the Ends of Philosophy*. Hemel Hempstead: Harvester Press.

OECD (1994a). *Jobs Study: Facts, Analysis, Strategies*. Paris: OECD.

OECD (1994b). *OECD Societies in Transition: the Future of Work and Leisure*. Paris: OECD.

OECD (1994c). The Views and Activities of Stakeholders in the Internationalization of Higher Education. Paper presented at the International Conference on *Learning Beyond Schooling*. OECD/CERI. Part of the CERI Study *Education in the New International Setting*. Paris: OECD. December 1994.

OECD (1994d). *Distance Education and the Internationalization of Higher Education*. Paris: OECD. December.

OECD (1994e). *Education in the New International Setting*. Paris: OECD/CERI.

OECD (1995). *Literacy, Economy, and Society*. Paris: OECD.

OECD (1996). *Making Lifelong Learning a Reality for All*. Paris: OECD.

Peters, M. (Ed.) (1995). *Education and the Postmodern Condition*. New York: Bergin and Garvey.

Popkewitz, T. (1984). *Paradigm and Ideology in Educational Research*. London: Falmer Press.

Popper, K. R. (1943). *The Open Society and its Enemies*, Vol. I, Plato, Vol. II: Hegel and Marx. London: Routledge & Kegan Paul.

Popper, K. R. (1949). *The Logic of Scientific Discovery*. London: Hutchinson.

Popper, K. R. (1960). *The Poverty of Historicism*. London: Routledge & Kegan Paul (2nd Ed).

Popper, K. R. (1972). *Objective Knowledge*. Oxford: Clarendon Press.

Pugh, D., Hickson, D., Hinnings, C. & Turner, C. (1968). Dimensions of Organizational Structure. *Administrative Science Quarterly*, 13, 65–105.

Quine, W. V. (1951). Two Dogmas of Empiricism. In *Philosophical Review*, Vol. 60, pp. 20–45.

Quine, W. V. (1953). *From a Logical Point of View*. Cambridge: Harvard University Press.

Quine, W. V. (1974). *The Roots of Reference*. LaSalle: Open Court.

Quine, W. V. & Ullian, J. S. (1970). *The Web of Belief*. New York: Random House.

Raffe, D. & Rumberger, R. W. (1993). Education and Training for 16–18 Year Olds in the UK and USA. In D. Finegold, L. McFarland & W. Richardson, *Something Borrowed, Something Learned* ? Washington, DC: The Brookings Institution.

Reason, P. (1994). Three Approaches to Participative Inquiry. In N. K. Denzin & Y. S. Lincoln (Eds.), *Handbook of Qualitative Research* (pp. 324–339). Thousand Island, CA: Sage.

Richardson, W. (1993). Employers as an Instrument of School Reform? Education-Business "Compacts" in Britain and America. In D. Finegold, L. McFarland & W. Richardson (Eds.), *Something Borrowed, Something Learned?* Washington, DC: Brookings.

Robertson, D. B. & Waltman, J. L. (1993). The Politics of Policy Borrowing. In D. Finegold, L. McFarland & W. Richardson (Eds.), *Something Borrowed, Something Learned* ? Washington, DC: Brookings.

Roche, M. (1973). *Phenomenology, Language, and the Social Sciences*. London: Routledge and Kegan Paul.

Rorty, R. (1980). *Philosophy and the Mirror of Nature*. London: Allen & Unwin.

Sackney, L. & Dibski, D. (1994). School-based Management: A Critical Perspective. *Educational Management and Administration*, 22 (2), 104–112.

Schleiermacher, F. E. D. (1984). *Philosophische Schriften*, edited and introduced by Jan Rachold. Berlin: Union.

Schön, D. (1983). *The Reflective Practitioner*. New York: Basic Books.

Schutz, A. (1967). *The Phenomenology of the Social World* (translated by Walsh & Lehnert). London: Heinemann.

Shakeshaft, C. (1989). *Women in Educational Administration* (updated Ed). Newbury Park, CA: Sage.

Shakeshaft, C. & Hanson, M. (1986). Androcentric Bias in the *Educational Administration Quarterly*. Educational Administration Quarterly, 22 (l), 68–92.

Silverman, D. (1993). *Interpreting Qualitative Data*. Thousand Oaks, CA: Sage.

Stich, S. P. (1983). *From Folk Psychology to Cognitive Science*. Cambridge, Mass: MIT Press.

Stringer, E. T. (1996). *Action Research: A Handbook for Practitioners*. Thousand Oaks, CA: Sage.

Summer, A. & Johnson, A. (1995). Doubts about Decentralized Decisions. *School Administrator, 52*(3), 24–26, 28, 30, 32.

Tatsuoka, M. & Silver, P. (1988). Quantitative Research Methods in Educational Administration. In N. Boyan (Ed.), *Handbook of Research on Educational Administration* (pp. 677–702). New York: Longman.

Tuijnman, A. & Van Der Kamp, M. (1992). Learning for Life: New ideas, New Significance. In A. Tuijnman & M. Van Der Kamp (Eds.), *Learning Across the Lifespan: Theories, Research, Policies*. Oxford: Pergamon Press.

UNESCO (1996). *Learning: The Treasure Within*. Paris: UNESCO.

Vickers, M. (1995). Cross National Exchange and Australian Education Policy. In C. W. Evers & J. D. Chapman (Eds.), *Educational Administration: Australian Perspectives*. St. Leonards, NSW: Allen and Unwin.

Walker, W. G. (1991). "Tight ship to tight flotilla: the first century of scholarship in educational administration. " Invited address, Division A, *American Educational Research Association Annual Conference*, Chicago.

Waters, M. (1995). *Globalisation*. London: Routledge.

Willower, D. (1979). Contemporary issues in theory in educational administration. *Educational Administration Quarterly*, 16 (3), 1–25.

Willower, D. (1996). Inquiry in Educational Administration and the spirit of the times. *Educational Administration Quarterly*, 32 (2), 344–365.

Winch, P. G. (1958). *The Idea of a Social Science and its Relation to Philosophy*. London: Routledge and Kegan Paul.

Winch, P. G. (1973). *Ethics and Action*. London: Routledge and Kegan Paul.

Wittgenstein, L. (1953). *Philosophical Investigations* (translated by G. E. M. Anscombe). Oxford: Basil Blackwell.

Wittgenstein, L. (1968). *Preliminary Studies for the Philosophical Investigations* (also known as *The Blue and Brown Books*). Oxford: Blackwell.

Wohlstetter, P. & Odden, A. (1992). Rethinking School-based Management Policy and Research. *Educational Administration Quarterly*, 28, 529–549.

Wolcott, H. F. (1988). A Case Study Using an Ethnographic Approach. In R. Jaeger (Ed.), *Complementary Methods: For Research in Education*. Washington, DC: American Educational Research Association.

CHAPTER 5

The Struggle to Create a More Gender-Inclusive Profession[1]

Charol Shakeshaft

This chapter examines the representation of women in school administration and the struggle to expand the profession both through increased numbers of women and through conceptualizing administration in ways that are inclusive of gendered experience and perception.

If one piece of evidence of inclusion is numbers, then tracing the changes in the profession means examining the numerical representation of women administrators in administration. If we add professors who teach administration to the pool that we label the profession, then we have an additional way to think about inclusion. Compared to men, women have always been the minority of professionals holding formal administrative positions in schools. However, understanding exactly what the percentages of men and women in school administration have been and are currently is difficult to determine, both for the United States and for other countries of the world.

In the United States, we lack a reliable, uniform, nationwide database that lets us know just how many women are school administrators and at what levels. The last national data on school staff was collected for 1993–94 (U.S. Department of Education, 1996). Although states collect data, these data are often not comparable because of methods and definitions and, therefore, while we might understand what is happening in one state, it is very difficult to compare those statistics to staff in another state. Sometimes the membership breakdowns of professional organizations for administrators are used as proxies for all administrators; these reports may not be accurate because they report only members, not all administrators.

In addition to the limitations of the sampling unit, national, state, and organization data rarely provide breakdowns for sex and race together. Thus although we might be able to approximate the percentage of women administrators or the percentage of administrators of African descent, we are rarely able to understand the representation of women of African descent in the profession.[2] Even more difficult is to document the number of Asian American, Native American, Mexican American and Latina women school administrators. There have been no studies that report nationwide numbers for these women.

Tyack and Hansot (1982) point out that the absence of such a database is no mistake and has historical precedent:

> Amid proliferation of other kinds of statistical reporting in an age enamored of numbers—reports so detailed that one could give the precise salary of staff in every community across the country and exact information on all sorts of other variables—data by sex became strangely inaccessible. A conspiracy of silence could hardly have been unintentional (p. 13).

This "conspiracy of silence" has ramifications for inclusion. If we don't have annual comparisons by sex[3] and race[4], it is difficult to know in what ways the makeup of the profession might be changing. Determining inclusion and equality of representation of women can be examined from two perspectives.

The first places women in the context of their proportion in the population and in relationship to men. "Are women and men represented in administrative roles in the same proportions as they exist in the population?" If we examine our most recent national public school data, the answer is clearly no. Although women constitute 51% of the population and 51% of school children, the most recent national statistics on their representation in the school population indicate that women are 65% of the teachers (83% of elementary and 54% of secondary teachers), 43% of the principals (52% of elementary and 26% of secondary principals) and 7% of the superintendents.[5] Thus women are overrepresented in teaching and may be in the elementary principalship in relation to their proportions in the population as a whole (65% of teachers, 52% of elementary principals versus 51% of the population) and underrepresented in the secondary principalship and the superintendency (26% of secondary principals and 7% of superintendents versus 51% of the population).

If we examine equality based upon the proportions in the profession, the question is "Are women represented in administration in equal proportions to their representation in teaching?" The answer here is clearly no: 52 versus 83% in elementary schools; 26 versus 54% in secondary schools; and 7 versus 65% at the superintendent level. Females are overrepresented in teaching and underrepresented in administration.

Although 15.9% of the U.S. population is Hispanic, non-white, or of African descent, 28% of students, 10.9% of public school teachers, 12.3% of public school principals, and 2.8% of superintendents are of African descent, non-Hispanic, or Hispanic (1990 U.S. Census Data; U.S. Department of Education, July, 1996). The percentage of Asian and Pacific Islander principals is 1.5 and Native American principals are not plentiful enough to even warrant a report. None of these figures are available by both race and sex.

Although there are no comparable nationwide statistics that report both administrative representation by race and sex, a recent study by the District Superintendents Committee on Women and Minority Administrators in New York (1997) documents an increase in women and members of minority groups in all administrative positions. For women, these increases still do not bring women into administration in proportion in any of the positions to their numbers in teaching (see Table 5.1).

Although minority elementary principals are roughly proportional to the percentage of minority elementary teachers, the percentages of minority secondary principals and superintendents are less than the proportion of teachers in New York school districts. However, administrative certification in New York State was acquired largely by women and members of minority groups. Women earned about two-thirds of all administrator certification and members of minority groups earned about a third. This might mean that a growing number of women and minority members are gearing up to become school administrators. It might also mean that most majority males who are interested in becoming administrators already have certification. It certainly means that women and minority candidates are certified in much larger numbers than they are chosen for administrative positions.

With only 2.6% of New York State superintendents from minority groups, it is hard to understand much trend data. However, male and female minority school superintendents are evenly divided; as of June 1997, there were nine female and nine male minority superintendents in New York State. The New York data provide no support for the stereotype that minority women have it made and are a shoo-in for administrative positions (see Table 5.2).

Trying to document the number of women in school administration worldwide is even more difficult; administrative titles and jobs are not comparable across countries and few countries keep accurate records by sex of administrative office holders. Thus there is no one study that gives a global snapshot of the number of women in school administration. Nevertheless, there are individual country-by-country accounts that attempt to document the underrepresentation of women in school management and that offer a reliable understanding of international practice. Table 5.3 brings these reports together and, although they give an idea of the disproportionate representation of women in school administration, the data are not precisely comparable, having been collected at different times and using differing methods.

For instance, a study of women in educational management in 10 European countries indicates that the majority of school managers are men, while the majority of teachers are women (Ruijs, 1990). This study highlights the disparity between the number of male and female school administrators:

> There is a large gap between the percentages of male teachers and principals . . . In the average European country (with the exception of Greece) the percentage of female principals should be almost doubled to reflect the percentage of female teachers. This is true for primary as well as secondary education (Ruijs, 1990, pp. 1–2).

Women in third world countries fare no better, according to Davies' (1990) study of women in educational management in third world countries. She reports that in the countries she studied:

> Teaching is by no means a "feminine" profession internationally. At the primary level, 46 of the 71 countries . . . have fewer than 50% women teachers; at the secondary level, 50 out of 60 countries have fewer than 50% women.

The proportions of female head teachers, inspectors, or senior Ministry personnel bear no relation to their proportions in the teaching force as a whole. Women are seriously underrepresented in power positions across the world, even in countries where education is seen as the prerogative of the female (Davies, 1990, p. 2).

The figures from these studies are summarized in Table 5.3 and illustrate that women are underrepresented in positions in school management worldwide.

Table 5.1

Representation by Women and Members of Racial and Ethnic Minorities in Teaching and Administration in New York State, 1996–1997

	Percent Female	Percent Minority
Elementary Teachers	88.0	16.1
Elementary Principals	46.0	16.5
Secondary Teachers	56.0	12.4
Secondary Principals	23.0	7.9
Superintendents	14.4	2.6
Issued Administrative Certification	65.8	30.3

Source: New York State Department of Education, June 1997. Preliminary Report of the District Superintendents Committee on Women and Minority Administrators, June 1997.

Table 5.2

Ethnicity and Gender of New York State Superintendents, 1997

	Percent Female	Percent Male	Total Percent
Percent Minority	1.3	1.3	2.6
Percent Majority	13.1	84.3	97.4
Total	14.4	85.6	100.0

Source: New York State Department of Education, June 1997. Preliminary Report of the District Superintendents Committee on Women and Minority Administrators, June 1997.

Table 5.3

Women's Representation in Educational Management

Country	Percent Elementary Teachers	Percent Elementary Principals	Percent Secondary Teachers	Percent Secondary Principals
Belgium	75	32	55	33
Botswana	*	11	*	9
Brunei	66	2	49	27
China	*	*	29	11
Denmark	57	1	*	7
Greece	49	41	48	43.5
France	71	45	50	23
Ireland	76	47	*	35
Italy	*	34	*	27.5
Netherlands	65	12	27	4
Philippines	77	22	57	12
Portugal	*	90	*	34
Spain	*	*	*	19.5
United Kingdom	78	44	50	16
United States	88	46	56	23
Zimbabwe	40	1	32	10

Note: Years when data collected may not be the same.

Sources: Davies, 1990; Ruijs, 1990; National Center for Education Statistics, 1993.

* Data not available.

In addition to indicating that proportionately fewer women than men are school administrators, Tables 5.1, 5.2, and 5.3 also make clear that the older the child and the higher the grade, the fewer women teachers and administrators. Thus when women become school administrators, it is more likely to be in the primary or elementary grades.

The history of school administration documents consistent male dominance in all positions except during a small span of time in which women were the slight majority of elementary principals in urban settings.

Opening the Profession to Women

The history of women in school administration is intertwined with the history of women in teaching. To understand the former, one must know the latter. Although teaching has been identified in the twentieth century as a female profession, teachers have not always been women. Records indicate that until the late eighteenth century, all teaching was done by men. As Woody points out, the in-

junction of St. Paul, "I permit not a woman to teach" was enforced until there was a shortage of men for such positions (Woody, 1966/1929, p. 129). However, by the close of the Colonial period, the practice of utilizing women to train boys and girls, ages 4–7, developed. The teacher-housewife would assemble the local children in her home where she taught the little ones their letters. These women became known as school dames and later their establishments were known as dame schools. Such women were at the bottom of the educational career chain. They were often married to the local minister and taught because the family needed additional income. During this time, women teachers were paid 1/5 of what schoolmasters were paid and were permitted to teach only the very young and only in the summer. Because they had received no formal education for teaching, they were not considered as qualified or as important as men teachers, yet often they did the same work (Stern, 1973, p. 47).

Between 1820 and 1830, growth in industry and business generated more jobs, and many men who might have become teachers moved into the private sector. At the same time, the country was growing and the increase in immigrants added to the school-age population but not the tax base. Then, as now, local councils (or school boards) were looking for cheaper ways to do the work of schooling. The combination of increased need and a shortage of men available to teach were pivotal events in the inclusion of women in the profession of teaching and later managing.

School boards searching for male teachers found few candidates, particularly in the middle class. Although there were men from what we might think of today as working and non-propertied classes, at the time school boards were not interested in any but middle class applicants. School boards wanted literate, middle class men, men for whom there were no other opportunities at much higher pay and status.

The few middle class men who were available tended to be young men who dabbled in teaching, using it as a stepping stone to another career. They were men with short-term commitments who were satisfied with the minimal pay as it required little personal or professional effort (Galludet, 1838). At the same time, school teaching provided visibility to men who sought careers in law, commerce, or the ministry. Young men, working for money to attend college, often taught for a short time as did men beginning as farmers who used the winter as a time to earn extra money. Many of our agrarian school attendance schedules were influenced not only by student availability to school, but also the schoolmaster's schedule as a farmer-teacher. Teaching asked very little of these men; in rural areas, minimal preparation was required, and it only took a few months out of the year to accomplish the duties of a teacher.

Interestingly, as teaching became more professional, demanding certification and longer terms (but no more money), even these men dropped out because what they had to put into the job was more than they could take away from it. Between 1840 and 1860, the percentage of male teachers in Massachusetts dropped from 60% to 14% and school boards were faced with a labor shortage (Reich, 1974).

As the following passage from an 1838 issue of *The Connecticut Common School Journal* indicates, women were chosen to meet this labor shortage:

> How shall we get good teachers for our district schools, and enough of them? While we should encourage our young men to enter upon this patriotic, and I had almost said, missionary field of duty, and present much higher inducements to engage them to do so, I believe . . . that there is but little hope of attaining the full supply . . . from that sex. This will always be difficult, so long as there are so many other avenues open in our country to the accumulation of property, and the attaining of distinction. We must . . . look more to the other sex for aid in this emergency (Galludet, 1838, p. 10).

Although women were first sought for teaching because men were unavailable, womens' entrance into teaching had been promoted and rationalized already by the work of such leaders as Catharine Beecher and Emma Willard.

These women had set the stage for women to become teachers by popularizing the concept of womens' true sphere. Professing that teaching was a proper sphere for a woman and that it prepared her for the work of marriage and motherhood, these women, along with other crusaders, offered a socially acceptable rationale for hiring women, at the same time that jobs were going unfilled by men.

Women were portrayed as the civilizers of society and the transmitters of middle class values. They were educated and trained in the East to act as missionary teachers in the West and South, serving to provide both knowledge and reproduction of middle class values. In recruiting women for this endeavor and in raising money to support this work, Beecher employed three distinct tactics. The first was to secure the support of leading community women, the second was to enjoin the cooperation of religious organizations and the third was to have a man deliver her speeches.

The latter tactic illuminated her position and the one acceptable by mainstream society at the time on women's proper sphere. Like Emma Williard, Beecher believed that women and men belonged in different worlds. In addition to marriage, she advocated only three fields of work for women: domestic service, nursing, and education. Beecher crusaded fervently against the employment of women in mills and factories, believing that men were "designed by God" for this type of work and that women did not belong in these spheres. On the other hand, teaching was woman's "natural profession" and women were described as the solitary possessors of the nurturing, receptive qualities necessary to be both a teacher and a mother (Sklar, 1973).

Thus women were seen as natural teachers—using their nurturing "maternal" abilities in an extension from home to schoolroom and back again. Women were also cheap. In 1838 in Connecticut, for example, men earned $14.50 per month whereas women were paid $5.75. In that same year in Massachusetts, men took home $23.10 a month whereas women had to make do on $6.49 (Melder, 1972, p. 22). From the beginning, women teachers were treated less favorably than were men teachers, whether it was measured by pay or by status. In common schools, men were the masters or principals whereas women were the assistant teachers; in high schools, males were called "Professor" and females were addressed as "Miss." Women were identified by their sex, whereas men were acknowledged for the roles they played.

Despite low pay and status, women flocked to teaching. During the pre-Civil War era in Massachusetts, when the average woman teacher earned but one-fourth of what her male counterpart was earning, 20% of all women became teachers at some point in their lives (Bernard & Vinovskis, 1977). A number of reasons have been offered to explain why women would engage in a profession that wasn't very kind to them. The most compelling reason that women chose to teach seems to be that it was better than the alternative of complete dependence on their families. Solomon (1985) points out that demographic and social changes in the country resulted in more unmarried women than available men. Teaching made it possible for women to support themselves, thus reducing the financial burden on their parents and providing a measure of self-sufficiency, control, and safety. The economic need for women to work combined with Beecher's rationale that teaching was not only woman's natural profession but also a benefit to society coalesced to make it both possible and desirable for women to become educational professionals. Taking a school [job] offered a respectable and sometimes pleasant alternative to young women who needed to work and found few alternatives except textile mills or domestic service. Teaching permitted educated women, who found most professional roles closed to them, an outlet for their skills (Melder, 1972, p. 25).

Most of the foregoing discussion has centered on white women teachers. We know little of early minority women teachers and what we do know tends to be about women of African descent. Collier-Thomas points out that "black women had no real status in the teaching profession until the late nineteenth century" (1982, p. 175). However, this does not mean that women teachers of African descent were not educators early on. Despite the odds, they taught.

Slave owners usually forbade education for slaves as they feared uprising and rebellion. In addition to strong unwritten rules in the South against teaching people of African descent to read and write, formal laws were passed that made it a crime. South Carolina, for instance, passed a law in 1740 that punished those who taught slaves to read. Similar laws were passed up to the beginning of the Civil War throughout other southern states (Weinberg, 1977).

When people of African descent did receive an education, research suggests that free men were more likely than free women to be taught to read and write (Vinovskis & Bernard, 1978), but there is little information on the literacy rates of female and male slaves. We do know that prior to the Civil War, despite the threat of punishment and death, some women slaves learned to read and write, becoming teachers and passing these skills on to others. For instance, Milia Granson, a woman slave in Natchez, Louisiana, held school between midnight and 2:00 a.m. for seven years and taught many pupils of African descent (Lerner, 1972).

In Georgia, slave Susie King Taylor wrote about the secret school she attended in which the teacher was a free woman of African descent:

> I was born under the slave law in Georgia in 1848 ... My brother and I being the two eldest, we were sent to a friend of my grandmother, a Mrs. Woodhouse, a widow, to learn to read and write. She was a free woman and lived ... about half a mile from my house.
>
> We went every day with our books wrapped in paper to prevent the police or white persons from seeing them. We went in,

one at a time, through the gate into the yard to the kitchen, which was the school room. She had 25 or 30 children whom she taught, assisted by her daughter, Mary Jane. The neighbors would see us going in some time, but they supposed we were there learning trades, as it was the custom to give children a trade of some kind. After school we left the same way we entered, one by one and we would go to a square about a block from the school and wait for each other (cited in Lerner, 1972, pp. 27–28).

Teaching and learning were also dangerous activities for women of African descent in the North. In Connecticut in 1833, Prudence Crandall, a white Quaker teacher, was arrested for opening a school for girls of African descent that would train them to be teachers. Crandall's problems had begun in 1832 when she admitted a woman who "wanted to get a little more learning, enough if possible to teach colored children" (Fuller, 1971, p. 16). In response, the parents of the white students removed their daughters from school. Those white students who had not already withdrawn were asked to do so by Crandall to make room for 19 women of African descent to be trained as teachers. This caused the townspeople to pass a law making it illegal to teach students of African descent from other states. This law was used as the basis for Crandall's arrest. Further, local residents attempted to burn down the school as well as to physically harm Crandall and her pupils (Fuller, 1971).

A similar problem was encountered by Myrtilla Miner in 1851 when she tried to open a school for students of African descent in Washington, D.C. Mobs attacked the school several times, setting it on fire and threatening the students and Miner. Nevertheless, Miner's school endured for 10 years and was successful enough to be accused of "educating colored children beyond their station in life" (Green, 1967, p. 51; O'Connor & Miner, 1885/1969).

Not all teachers-to-be faced such overt hostility. For instance, Charlotte Forten was sent by her parents from segregated Philadelphia to nonsegregated Salem, Massachusetts, to live with an abolitionist family and get an education. In 1855, she entered a teacher training school and in 1856, upon graduation, was offered a teaching position in Salem:

> Amazing, wonderful news I have heard today. It has completely astounded me ... I have received the offer of a situation as teacher in one of the public schools of this city of this conservative, aristocratic old city of Salem!!! Wonderful indeed it is! ... Again and again I ask myself—Can it be true? It seems impossible. I shall commence tomorrow (Billington, 1953/1981, p. 82).

Education became more accessible to women of African descent after the Civil War when schooling for freed slaves in the South was attempted by the federal government and northern philanthropic agencies. This need for teachers provided opportunities for women of African descent as over 9,000 teachers, more than half of them women and many of them women of African descent, journeyed to the South during Reconstruction to teach people of African descent (Jones, 1979). Charlotte Forten was among these who moved from Salem, Massachusetts, to the Georgia Sea Islands to teach in a newly formed school. Although Forten was protected from hostile crowds of white people by Union troops who helped her succeed in her mission to teach people of African descent, other such women teachers were less fortunate. Julia Hayden, 17 years old, was murdered in Tennessee for teaching people of African descent. Not only teachers, but people who boarded teachers from the North were killed. For instance, in Mississippi, a black man, Charles Caldwell, was murdered by a mob for harboring a white woman who had come South to teach. She stayed, rearing Caldwell's daughter, and many of her pupils went on to become teachers themselves (Kerber, 1983).

Despite the hostilities facing women teachers of African descent in all parts of the United States, their numbers continued to grow throughout the nineteenth century. An article published in 1904 (Hunton), claimed that more than 25,000 women teachers of African descent had been educated, whereas another writer (Jones, 1905) pointed out that over 4,000 black women had graduated from normal schools and universities by 1905. After 1890, women teachers of African descent outnumbered men teachers of African descent, and by 1910 two-thirds of black teachers were women (Collier-Thomas, 1982, p. 175).

In the period from 1830 through 1900, women of both European and African descent became more identified with teaching, so that by 1880, 57.2% of the teachers in the United States were women and by 1900, 70.1% were women (Woody, 1929/1966, p. 499).

Women Move into Administration: The Early Years

Although women were seen as appropriate candidates for teaching positions, administrative positions during this time were usually given to men. Between 1820 and 1900, a handful of women held administrative positions. Some of these women managed public schools, but the majority founded their own schools and served as the chief administrator (Giddings, 1984; Solomon, 1985). Some states resisted allowing women to move into administration. Beliefs about women's place sometimes found their way into laws restricting women in school administration. Until 1858 in New Hampshire, men and women needed different qualifications to become school administrators. As late as 1875, the circuit court in Iowa ruled that Elizabeth Cook could not be Warren County superintendent despite the fact that she was elected by the citizens of the county (Beale, 1936, p. 495).

In the first decade of the twentieth century, a larger number of women began to win positions in school administration so that by 1909, when Ella Flagg Young made her optimistic predictions for women in school administration, she had reasons to believe them.

> Women are destined to rule the schools of every city. I look for a majority of big cities to follow the lead of Chicago in choosing a woman for superintendent. In the near future we will have more women than men in executive charge of the vast educational system. It is woman's natural field, and she is no longer satisfied to do the greatest part of the work and yet be denied leadership (*The Western Journal of Education*, 1909).

The years leading up to Young's superintendency of Chicago, the first big city superintendency ever held by a woman, were ones in which women had begun to make an impact through political activism and social reform designed to bring women into school administration. As a result, the years 1900–1930 are sometimes referred to as a golden age for women in school administration (Hansot & Tyack, 1981). But even during this period, women achieved only modest success, arriving "in numbers only in the lower strata of the upper crust" (Connolly, 1919, p. 841).

Between 1900 and 1930, women primarily occupied elementary principalships and county and state superintendencies. By 1928, women held 55% of the elementary principalships, 25% of the county superintendencies, nearly 8% of the secondary school principalships, and 1.6% of the district superintendencies. These advances are not as significant as they might seem. Unlike the higher status and higher paying secondary principalships and district superintendencies held by men, elementary principalships and county and state superintendencies were low-paying, low-status, low-power positions.

In the beginning, county superintendencies oversaw a number of localities. As the populations of these towns grew, the school districts hired their own superintendents, usually replacing a female county superintendent with a male district superintendent who entered with more power and almost always with more pay. County superintendencies were seldom stepping stones to positions with higher power, and elementary principals seldom moved up the hierarchy. Similarly, by 1928, women were only 8.4% of university or college presidents and 14.3% of heads of departments of education in higher education institutions (*Educational News and Editorial Comment*, 1928, p. 327).

Understanding the movement of African-American women into school administration up to 1930 is more difficult because not as much information that documents or compiles these experiences is available; the history of members of other minority groups is even more scarce. By the mid-1800s, some women of African descent had begun their own schools and, thus, served as both the teacher and the administrator (Giddings, 1984; Green, 1967; Jones, 1980). In Georgia, for instance, Lucy Craft Laney graduated from Atlanta University in 1873 and began the Haines Normal and Industrial Institute, which offered a full liberal arts program. Some of the teachers who worked in Laney's school went on to found their own schools and become administrators in their own right; for instance, Janie Porter Barrett started a vocational school for girls in Virginia and Mary McLeod Bethune founded Bethune-Cookman College in Florida (Giddings, 1984; Kerber, 1983). These schools continued into the twentieth century and both employed and trained many women teachers and administrators.

An important vehicle for minority women to achieve positions of formal leadership was the Jeanes Supervisory Program begun in 1907 with a million dollar endowment from a Philadelphia Quaker, Anna T. Jeanes, for the

> maintenance and assistance of rural, community and country schools for the Southern Negroes and not for the use or benefit at large institutions, but for the purpose of rudimentary education . . . and to promote peace in the land (Williams *et al.*, 1979, p. 97).

This endowment became the core of the Southern Education Foundation and supported Jeanes' supervisors, mostly women of African descent, who began working at "improving educational programs in segregated schools" (Williams *et al.*, 1979, p. 15). The Jeanes supervisors were a force that helped increase the number of women in school leadership by providing "unprecedented professional leadership . . . for black teachers and principals" (1979, p. 59).

Gains made by women in administration during the first three decades of this century were not sustained after 1930. The number of female elementary principals and county and state superintendents began to decrease and the major power position in the school—the district superintendency was still almost always held by a man. In 1932, there were "still 25 states with no woman serving as a superintendent" (Hansot & Tyack, 1981, p. 15).

Cuban (1976) reports that between 1870 and 1970 in the 25 largest cities, only six women served as superintendents. The majority of the most prominent women superintendents of urban or large city schools systems served prior to 1915: in Los Angeles, C. B. Jones was superintendent from 1880 to 1881, in Portland, Ella Sabin served from 1888 to 1891, in Seattle, Julia Kennedy was the superintendent between 1888 and 1889; Ella Flagg Young was Chicago's superintendent between 1909 and 1915; Julia Richman was a New York City district superintendent from 1903 to 1912. Susan Dorsey served in Los Angeles from 1922 to 1929. Mildred Doyle was superintendent of Knoxville, Tennessee, from 1946 to 1976 and Ira Jarrell was superintendent of Atlanta from 1944 to 1966.

Blount's (1998) reconstruction of the number of women superintendents in big city schools between 1930 and 1970 documents one woman in 1930, one in 1950, and one in

1970 serving in a district of more than 100,000. For districts with a population between 25,001 and 100,000, Blount found one woman superintendent in 1930, three in 1950, and three in 1970.

Women primarily held positions in the lower strata of school administration: supervisors of art, home economy, hygiene, kindergartens, music; staff positions as opposed to line positions; and the elementary principalship. A piece written in 1919 predicted the limits for women in administration:

> A place, usually in the supervisorship of primary work, domestic work, or welfare work is set apart for some women, and the woman is selected by a board of men (Connolly, 1919, p. 843).

Several factors worked against women and resulted in their decline in administrative positions after 1930, primary among them was the Great Depression. Refining earlier work that had begun to document the historical trends of women in school administration (Shakeshaft, 1987; 1989; Tyack & Hansot, 1982), Blount (1998) compared the number of women in the superintendency from 1910 to 1990 and found that overall the representation of women in the 1930s had not yet been equaled. More recent data shows that in the past five years, women have surpassed their representation in the superintendency in the 1930s, but not by much. Certainly, this isn't the kind of proportional increase that was expected by the women then or is acceptable by women candidates now. The gains have been slow and uneven and Blount documents the difficulties in trying to understand the trends and patterns of women in school administration (see Table 5.4).

Many of the barriers to women in the mid-twentieth century were indistinguishable from those of prior years. Century-old patterns of male dominance had solidified a number of beliefs about women that both men and women accepted and that limited women's access to school administration. Negative attitudes toward women continued to be a major barrier. Women were thought to be constitutionally incapable of discipline and order, primarily because of their size and supposed lack of strength.

Table 5.4

Comparison of Women in Administration 1910 to 1990

Year	Percent Women in State Superintendencies	Percent Women in Intermediate Superintendencies	Percent Women in Local District Superintendencies	Percent Women Overall
1910	4.0	14.1	6.2	8.9
1930	8.0	27.4	1.7	11.0
1950	10.0	23.2	1.5	9.1
1970	2.0	14.3	0.7	3.4
1990	12.0	23.1	3.9	4.9

Source: Blount, 1998, p. 181.

Where administrators were not elected by popular vote, women seeking administrative positions still had to confront the ever present bias of local school board members, most of whom were men. Then, as now, schoolmen tended to hire those most like themselves, white, middle-aged, Protestant males. Not surprisingly, they chose those with whom they felt most comfortable, and most members of school boards did not feel at ease with women. In a textbook for school administrators written by Elwood Cubberley in 1929, "businessmen" were listed as the best candidates for school boards. Those to be kept off boards included inexperienced young men, unsuccessful men, retired men, politicians, uneducated or ignorant men, saloon keepers, and all women (1929, p. 212).

Further, school boards claimed they didn't want to invest time and money in workers with short-term commitments, a description often given to women who were expected to leave teaching for marriage. Typically, men didn't stay in teaching much longer than did women, but curiously the undependable label was applied only to women, thus limiting their opportunities for administrative posts. Men moved in and out of teaching, but they usually left for positions that offered higher pay or status or both; thus, they were seen as professionals, even if transitory. Women, on the other hand, usually left for marriage. They were branded unprofessional, despite laws in many communities that forbade married women, but not married men, from continuing to teach.

Women's marital choices were directly related to their employment opportunities in education. In 1900, 90% of female teachers were unmarried (Hansot & Tyack, 1981, p. 23). The married women who taught or administered did so for the survival of the family. Laws were passed that kept the teaching force composed of single women. In 1903, the New York Board of Education adopted a bylaw barring married women from teaching:

> No woman principal, woman head of department, or woman member of the teaching or supervising staff shall marry while in the service. It shall be the duty of a District Superintendent to bring to the notice of the Board of Superintendents the marriage of any such person in his district, and such fact shall be reported to the Board of Education, which may direct charges to be preferred against such teacher by reason of such marriage (Woody, 1929/1966, p. 509).

However, there were exceptions for some married women:

> No married woman shall be appointed to any teaching or supervising position in the New York Public Schools unless her husband is mentally or physically incapacitated to earn a living or has deserted her for a period of not less than one year (Woody, 1929/1966, p. 509).

The position of the board was challenged and subjected to ridicule and in 1920 the regulation was repealed—however, not before it had kept many married women from teaching as well as serving as a rationale and model for school districts in other parts of the country to adopt similar regulations.

In 1928, 60% of urban districts still prohibited the hiring of married teachers, and only half of those systems permitted teachers who married after becoming teachers to continue in their jobs (Peters, 1934). By 1942, a nationwide survey of school districts reported that 58% of school systems would not employ married women teachers (NEA, 1942).

These policies had a wide-ranging effect on the sex structuring of education, and in 1936, Helen Davis observed that education, "will be occupied on the whole by two kinds of women, those who refuse marriage except on their own terms and those who have not been able to find husbands, while the general run of able and so-called 'normal' women will be excluded because they prefer marriage" (Hansot & Tyack, 1981, pp. 23–24). Thus communities often made injustice legal by forcing women from teaching if they desired marriage and children.

Besides having to continue to fight public prejudice against them, women continued to have to deal with exclusionary practices. Men had the advantage of being able to interact with other men who held power and who were often in positions to hire. Clubs such as the Rotary were (and often still are) limited to male members. Even school organizations kept women out; the NEA at first admitted only men and was more an administrative association than a teacher-oriented one, and until the 1970s Phi Delta Kappa was an all-male organization. Although the NEA had women presidents beginning with Ella Flagg Young in 1910, she describes her first meeting in 1867 as one in which women were only "permitted to sit in the gallery and listen to discussions carried on by the men" (Tyack & Hansot, 1982, p. 64).

Another bias that continued to work against women was the belief that males had a special gift for dealing with community issues and problems. The mores and beliefs at the time tended to separate women from men; thus, hiring a female administrator who would have daily interactions with local businessmen was often unthinkable to hiring committees.

Women in School Administration in the Twentieth Century

The history of women in school administration in the United States documents disproportionate representation and resistance to women in positions of leadership and authority. Historically, a number of factors coalesced to shape the movement of women into positions in educational administration in the twentieth century. The struggle for inclusion can be understood by examining events and periods that shaped the ebb and flow of women into school administration:

1. The bureaucratization of schools that promoted men into management in schools and limited the opportunities for women.
2. The early suffrage movement in the United States that increased the number of women in school administration.
3. The movement for equal pay and the economic depression of the 1930s that decreased the number of women administrators.
4. The advent of World War II that opened up jobs for women as men fought the war; and the post-war period that prepared male teachers on the G.I. Bill, moving them into school administration.
5. The Cold War, which spiraled the country into a panic about the lack of preparation of students in math and science and increased the number of men teachers and administrators.
6. Societal Expectations for women which cast females into roles at odds with leadership and administration.
7. The most recent women's movement expanded career options for women and drew women away from education. In addition to opening doors for women, there was subtle and sometimes not-so-subtle pressure on women to reject teaching as a career. During this time, bright women particularly have been discouraged from entering the profession of teaching, while at the same time women and feminists have also fought to increase the number of women in school administration.

Bureaucratization of Schools

In the early days of public schooling in the United States, the teacher did everything including administration. However, as schooling became more complex and as bureaucratization was imposed upon schools, the functions of administrator and teacher became more distinct.

In 1890 in "Middletown," the superintendent was "the only person in the system who did not teach," but by 1929 there was between the teacher and the superintendent "a galaxy of principals, assistant principals, supervisors of special subjects, directors of vocational education and home economics, deans, attendance officers, and clerks, who do no teaching but are concerned in one way or another with keeping the system going" (Lynd & Lynd, 1929, p. 210). By 1918, teaching and administration were two separate professions; special requirements to become an administrator had been instituted in several states, and departments of educational administration were begun in universities (Callahan, 1962). Separation of work in schools into administration

and teaching categories had serious implications for women. Cubberley (1929) notes that the subject of school administration did not begin to attract attention until 1875. At that time there were only 29 school superintendents.

> With the still more rapid growth of cities since 1880, and the still more rapid expansion of our city school systems since 1900, even further specialization of functions and delegations of authority has become a necessity (Cubberley, 1929, p. 161).

As schools were reorganized from one-room centers of teaching to cost-efficient models of business, it was no longer thought appropriate for teachers to carry out all duties. Instead, a hierarchy of roles was to be instituted so that the work of schooling could be done more efficiently. Typical was the reorganization of the Quincy Grammar School in 1870 to a graded school that followed the principles of scientific management; a manager oversaw a number of teachers who instructed several hundred students. For schools to be transformed from fairly autonomous organizations with loosely coupled classes headed by strong school women and men into bureaucracies under the role of one administrator, superordinates and subordinates had to be manufactured. Male teachers were put in charge and women were looked to as the ideal subordinate:

> Their minds are less withdrawn from their employment, by the active scenes of life; and they are less intent on scheming for future honors or emoluments. As a class, they never look forward, as young men almost invariably do, to a period of legal emancipation from parental control, when they are to break away from the domestic circle and go abroad into the world, to build up a fortune for themselves (Mann, 1841, p. 45).

Supporters of bureaucratization argued that "women should be teachers while men should be retained as principals and superintendents" (Tyack & Strober, 1981, p. 141), and the graded school became the vehicle that carried out this two-tiered system, as the Quincy School Committee noted in the 1870s:

> One man could be placed in charge of an entire graded school of 500 students. Under his direction could be placed a number of female assistants. Females "are not only adapted, but carefully trained, to fill such positions as well as or better than men, excepting the master's place, which sometimes requires a man's force; and the competition is so great, that their services command less than half the wages of male teachers" (cited in Katz, 1973, p. 73).

Scientific management and, specifically, bureaucratization then helped keep women out of administrative roles because of the belief in male dominance that made it easier for both males and females to view women as natural followers and men as their leaders.

> Hierarchical organization of schools and the male chauvinism of the larger society fit as hand to glove. The system required subordination; women were generally subordinate to men. The

employment of women as teachers thus augmented the authority of the largely male administrative leadership (Tyack, 1974, p. 60).

In addition to patriarchal views, a female style of administration, taught and fostered by such organizations as the national Congress of Mothers (now known as the Parent Teachers' Association) was seen as inconsistent with the efficient functioning of schools. Women in these organizations had learned, both formally in classes and informally through experience, leadership skills that promoted democratic and egalitarian styles of decision making. These styles of administration were at odds with the authoritarian approaches to school leadership in vogue in the first third of the twentieth century, comfortable styles for males with backgrounds in both business and the military (Burstyn, 1980).

Bureaucratization and the emphasis on business-like procedures chipped away at the autonomy of teachers, most of whom were women, and often interfered with the educational goals of schools (Callahan, 1962). The demand for a division of labor resulting in an assembly line approach, which forced unquestioning acceptance by teachers, most of whom were women, was resented. Teachers, and particularly women teachers, began to fight back. Ella Flagg Young, Chicago's first woman superintendent noted:

> There has been a tendency toward factory-evolution and factory-management, and the teachers, like children who stand at machines, are told just what to do. The teachers, instead of being the great moving force, educating and developing the powers of the human mind in such a way that they shall contribute to the power and the efficiency of this democracy, tend to become mere workers at the treadmill, but they are doing all thru [sic] this country that which shows that it is difficult to crush the human mind and the love of freedom in the hearts and lives of people who are qualified to teach school. As a result they are organizing federations to get together and discuss those questions which are vital in the life of the children and in the life of the teachers (Young, 1916, p. 357).

Despite resistance, bureaucracy reigned and with it male dominance of administrative positions.

Suffrage Movement

Many women, both in and out of education, were part of a larger feminist movement that sought female power and leadership in many spheres, but particularly in that of the school. Margaret Gribskov (1980) writes of women reformers who saw school administration as an extension of women's natural sphere. In the beginning of this feminist movement, suffrage was but one of the goals of these female reformers. For instance, at the Seneca Falls, New York, convention of 1848, one of the resolutions unanimously adopted stated that women should have "equal participation with men in the various trades, professions,

and commerce" (Anthony, Stanton, & Harper, 1881/1922, p. 73). Promoting women into spheres where men had always been then became a central part of the feminist movement.

Because doors were tightly shut in most professions, education was thought to be a good place to begin the assault as women were already a large part of the professional work force. Thus it was that women hoping to become school administrators had the backing of a diverse group of women—feminists, temperance activists, members of women's clubs—who could put pressure both on local decision makers as well as cast their votes for women in school administration. Gribskov (1980) points out that the General Federation of Women's Clubs was one of the most influential forces in promoting equality for women and for supporting women professionals, including women in school administration. Not concerned just with suffrage (the Federation of Women's Clubs endorsed suffrage only in 1914), they worked hard to increase women's participation in management. These associations of women backed women candidates for school administration because they believed, as had Catharine Beecher 75 years earlier, that women would clean up the system, injecting a purity of purpose and a morality that men failed to possess.

In addition to the direct impact they had on increasing women in school administration, these groups helped swell the numbers of women in administration through indirect methods as well. For instance, they encouraged the increase in the number of women who attended college. More women in college meant more women trained to be teachers and, subsequently, to aspire to and achieve administrative positions.

Together with these strong women's groups outside of education, women candidates for administrative positions often had the support of female teacher organizations. Originally established to improve the working conditions for teachers, these organizations were begun in New York, Chicago, Atlanta, and Pittsburgh at the turn of the century. The associations battled centralization, which shifted power and autonomy from female teachers to newly appointed male administrators. From the beginning, these organizations were clearly identified with improving the condition of women and were seen by many as run by militant feminists. Grace Strachan headed the Interborough Association of Women Teachers in New York and worked to equalize male and female pay. Margaret Haley, an architect of the Chicago Teachers Federation, was called a "fiend in petticoats" (Tyack & Hansot, 1982, p. 186) because of her efforts to keep the NEA from becoming an organization of elite schoolmen who would forget the needs of the women teachers who supported it. In working both to organize women teachers and to promote women into administration, the Chicago Teachers Federation helped Ella Flagg Young win her superintendency in Chicago (Reid, 1982).

The impact of both the feminist movement and the teacher associations was strengthened in states where school directorships and county and state superintendencies were elected by popular vote. In these areas, schools were small and remote, and districts were managed by a head teacher or principal. The elected county superintendents oversaw these "middle managers" by traveling to all the districts in her county, often over rough and hazardous roads and sometimes even by boat. Difficult as it was for the county superintendent to reach these schools, it was often more difficult to "supervise" the head teacher or principal once there. A great deal of personal power and skill was needed to manage such scattered personnel, and the county superintendency often proved to be an effective training ground for developing the political, social, and oratorical skills women needed to win state superintendency elections.

Although women's suffrage was not won until 1920, by 1910 women could vote in school elections in 24 states. In these states, primarily in the West and Midwest, the right to vote provided the support for women that women-teacher associations provided in cities. Permitted to vote in school elections, members of women's groups and teacher organizations formed coalitions to ensure that women candidates would receive sufficient votes to win school elections. These women devoted considerable time and energy to electing women candidates and attending to local politics (Gribskov, 1980).

As a result, in states where women could vote, women won school elections. By 1922, women had been elected as state superintendents in nine states and 857 women held county superintendencies, up from 276 in 1900 (Lathrop, 1922). Six years later, 900 county superintendents were female and, in states where women could vote, two-thirds of the county superintendents were women (*Educational News and Editorial Comment*, 1928). Edith Lathrop pointed out in a 1922 article that opportunities for women in administration were rich in the West, where county and state superintendents were elected, not appointed:

> There are more women state superintendents at the present time than ever before in the history of the country . . . It is interesting to note, in this connection, that in these states this officer is elected by direct vote of the people . . . The advancement of women in administrative positions is nowhere more evident, with the exception of grade school principalships, than in the county superintendency . . . A large majority . . . of women county superintendents are found in the states west of the Mississippi River . . . selected by a direct vote of the people . . . The college girl who is ambitious for educational leadership, won by way of political competition, may well take Horace Greeley's advice to young men anxious for opportunity and a career: "Go West, young man, go West!" (Lathrop, 1922, pp. 418–419)

Although it is true that the primary reason women won elections was the support of women's political and social groups, it must also be pointed out that these were low-pay, low-status positions that few men sought. Like their teacher counterparts, women administrators sometimes attained their positions by default—either because no men were available or because women were a bargain as they were paid less than men. For instance, a 1905 study of 467 city school systems found that the average male elementary principal was paid $1,542 whereas the average female elementary principal earned $970 (NEA, 1905, p. 23). Lathrop reported that in 1922, women still earned three-quarters of what men earned for the same work. Just as women teachers had been hired because they came cheaper than men teachers, so too were economic considerations paramount in the appointment of some women administrators.

In addition to the barriers that kept women out of administration from the beginning, the 1930s brought additional obstacles to the movement of women into school administration. Gribskov (1980) points out that after women were granted the right to vote, many of the strong women's organizations that had rallied around women administrative candidates were disbanded. For instance, after women's suffrage was achieved, many women switched from the Federation of Women's Clubs, an organization with feminist goals, to the League of Women Voters, a group that was not identified with women's issues. Thus a strong force of support for women in administration vanished.

At about the time that suffrage was won, the growth of the teachers unions began to slow, a decline that lasted approximately 40 years. Bureaucratization, against which early teacher leaders had organized, was fully implemented by 1920, and the other issues that the organizations were working to rectify—equal pay and tenure—also lost support as the economic depression spread.

Equal Pay for Women and Men and the Depression

Achieving equal pay for men and women educators has also affected the number of women school administrators. San Francisco passed the first equal pay law in 1894, after a fight led by a woman elementary school principal. By 1930, 10 states had equal pay laws; unfortunately, these were not always enforced and during the Economic Depression they were often ignored (Kerber, 1983). Equal pay laws were just as likely to be used to hurt women educators as to help them. If the laws weren't being ignored, they were being used to justify hiring males over females. Schmuck (1979) points out that given a choice of a male or a female for the same pay, the woman lost the edge she once held when she was paid less. Many school boards believed, erroneously, that men had more financial obligations than did women (Davis & Samuelson, 1950) and thus used this as a rationale for hiring men. Several decades earlier, Grace Strachen had attacked the notion of paying a man more because he had a family to support: "Salary is for service and should be measured by the service rendered" (1910, p. 118). Kalvelage (1978), in an analysis of hiring patterns, supports the argument that equal pay affected the number of women hired in school administration and points out that because state equal pay laws were instituted, more males have been hired as elementary teachers and administrators.

The Depression caused another set of conditions that led school boards and communities to cut back on the number of women teachers and administrators. In many localities, additional laws were passed that barred married women teachers and administrators from working, citing the financial needs of men, married or unmarried, for the jobs that women had previously held. Single women were also discriminated against in promotions. School boards legitimized their actions by arguing that men had families to support, whereas single women supported only themselves. The economic reality was, of course, quite different. Single women were more often than not responsible for parents and siblings, and these responsibilities were most often equal to or greater than the obligations of their male counterparts (Gribskov, 1980).

World War II and Its Aftermath

After 1930, the number of women in administration progressively decreased except for during World War II, when male educators began serving in the armed forces. Ironically, communities reversed discriminatory hiring policies during World War II, and married women were welcomed into schools to teach and administer schools. Some systems even provided day care, yet the opportunities provided were brief. Women who served their country during World War II by taking on school jobs were rewarded by being dismissed when the men returned. Men who served their country in the armed forces were rewarded with the G.I. Bill, which provided funds for their education—education that trained them to be teachers and administrators.

At the conclusion of World War II, employment patterns returned to prewar conditions. Many men who returned to school on the G.I. Bill used their formal education as men had done before them, becoming teachers in an effort to move across social class lines. Once again, social class differences between males and females surfaced in schools as lower socio-economic class men became teachers, joining the middle and upper-middle class women already there. Some of the tension between men and women at this time was due to social class difference. With the increase in the number of men receiving a college education, which prepared them to be teachers and administrators,

women's role in educational administration declined after World War II. Fewer women than in previous years were trained as educators, and males appeared in surplus. In some communities, prohibitions against married female teachers were reinstated. The NEA reported that in 1948, the salaries of male elementary principals were substantially higher than those of women.

The 1950s saw a move to consolidate several small school systems into one large one. This practice almost always resulted in women administrators from small districts losing their positions to men in the new structure. Consolidation of racially segregated schools in the late 1950s and 1960s hurt minority administrators. School districts, which had formerly employed both an administrator of African descent and an administrator of primarily European descent to head segregated units, when forced to consolidate, almost always kept the supervisor of European descent and eliminated the administrator of African descent (Williams *et al.*, 1979).

The 1950s were discouraging years for women educators; men were encouraged to become teachers and administrators, while women were encouraged to remain at home. The 1950 yearbook of the American Association of School Administrators urged superintendents to recruit men so that "more competent" staffs would exist in public schools.

Societal Proscriptions for Women's Proper Role

The domestic script that had been used by Beecher and Willard in the nineteenth century to place women appropriately within the context of the teaching profession was used in the twentieth century to both rationalize the movement of women into administration and provide arguments for why administrative careers were inappropriate. Initially, women had been urged to enter teaching because it prepared them for marriage and motherhood; during the 1950s, teaching was presented as a good job for married women because it was a vocation that made it easier to work outside the home. For women who had to work outside the home, the summer vacations and the shorter in-school working day were seen as an ideal complement to a career as mother and wife.

The notion that teaching was compatible with the duties of wives and mothers had been created as a rationale for hiring married women teachers during World War II to fill the vacancies left by men who served in the military. During World War II, even maternity leaves were arranged (NEA, 1942). These leaves were not all that women might have liked because they were unpaid and usually mandatory for pregnant women, but they did signify a change in attitudes toward married women and motherhood. Unfortunately, as the mood swung toward married women beginning in the 1940s, public sentiment against single women increased.

> The attractive woman who finds it easy to marry and establish a home is the kind of woman that the schools need and cannot secure or retain under regulations against marriage . . . married women tend to have a saner view on sex, and are less likely to become "queer" (Chamberlain & Meece, 1937, p. 57).

Chamberlain and Meece's observations foreshadowed the changing view of the kind of woman appropriate to be a teacher. Where once only single women had been allowed to teach and be administrators, now they were described as deficient. In the 1940s, school boards wanted married women.

Both ideologies, as single woman or married partner, have limited women's participation in school administration by forcing them into extreme cultural stereotypes.

Woman Peril, the Cold War, and the Vietnam War

The 1950s and 1960s witnessed a revival of the prejudices against women that had hindered their advancement into administration from the colonial period onward. In the late 1950s and early 1960s, women, married or single, began to be seen once again as the problem in education, instead of the solution. Since the beginning of women's participation in teaching and administration, there had been periodic bursts of protest against the effects so many women in such influential positions would have on society. Given the latent prejudices that American society held against professional women, it was inevitable that the increase in the number of women educators would be viewed with alarm. And indeed, the first outcries against "woman peril" sounded in the late nineteenth century, almost immediately after women began to predominate numerically. In 1908, G. Stanley Hall blamed many of the nation's troubles on female educators: "I think it is impossible not to connect a certain wildness of boys with the feminization of the schools" (Hall, 1908, p. 10239). A few years later, Robert Rogers, a professor at MIT, asserted:

> For a half-century now, the largest part of our young people have been trained exclusively by women teachers . . . Fifty years of this has produced a people incompetent to think politically and philosophically . . . Our American thinking is feminine thinking, inculcated by women teachers, highly competent in detail, immediate in its applications, rigidly idealistic regardless of the working facts, and weak on critical examination (Rogers, 1929, p. 24).

Probably the most influential expression of this myth of woman peril during the 1960s and 1970s was Patricia Cayo Sexton's polemic entitled "Schools Are Emasculating Our Boys" (1973). Sexton charged that the preponderance of women in the school system has caused it to become "too much of a woman's world" (1973, pp. 138–139) with untold deleterious effect on generations of male students. According to Sexton, women teachers and administrators not only underrated "Johnny's" talents but they emasculated him. Under women, only girls could achieve in school because the successful student value system was feminine. Female teachers and administrators were suspect because they extended mother's protective role and utilized teaching methods correspondent only with feminine (frilly) values.

The onset of the Cold War intensified concurrently the importance of education and America's insecurity vis-a-vis the Soviet Union. Although women's influence in education had existed since the mid-1800s and had obviously produced generations of well-educated Americans, suddenly there arose the inordinate fear that America was ill prepared to meet the challenge of the Communists. In the Cold War era, the school was zealously focused on as the instrument for social change. It was idealized as the means by which the American warrior state could ready itself for the oncoming ideological and perhaps military conflict.

In response to the deep chord rung anew by Sexton and in the context of the Cold War, many educators and the general public joined the chorus of voices raised in opposition to the woman teacher and administrator. All chimed in with support for the proposition that more men were needed to enter teaching and administration to overcome the handicap that boys suffered as a result of being taught by females. It was widely believed that a man could take charge more quickly and efficiently than a woman, that he could establish better contact with the children—particularly the boys—and that he specifically could be relied upon to maintain discipline.

Everyone welcomed carte blanche the avalanche of males eager to avoid the Vietnam war by entering teaching, a draft-proof profession. The historical circumstances of the 1960s dovetailed neatly with the supposed psychological prerequisites of male teachers and administrators as role models, disciplinarians, and strong academicians. Carol Poll (1979), in a study of why males and females choose elementary education, found that many males entered teaching to avoid the draft during the 1960s and, not surprisingly, that their commitment to education was minimal. Typifying these men is Bob, who said, "I decided to go into teaching to stay out of the Army. My last year at (college) I took six credits of ed each semester, which was enough at that time to get a sub [substitute] license" (Poll, 1979, p. 6).

This push for males into school, first as teachers, had an enormous impact upon the administrative structure. Most of the men stayed in teaching for only short periods. Some left education for other fields, a handful taught a few years in impoverished school systems and then made their careers writing books criticizing schools, but most moved quickly into administration. These young men provided the bulk of administrators as school systems expanded and the call for administrators was greatest. This movement of men into administration in the 1960s served to keep the number of women administrators to a minimum through the 1980s.

The Modern Feminist Movement, the Civil Rights Movement, and Affirmative Action

Although the Women's Liberation Movement, beginning in the late 1960s, drew attention to the underrepresentation of women in traditional positions of leadership in the schools, very little change occurred for women in school administration during the 1960s and 1970s. The percentage of women in school administration in the 1980s was less than the percentage of women in 1905.

However, during the late 1970s, a number of activist approaches encouraging women to enter school administration began and are continuing today. Efforts toward adding women to school administration have come through women's caucuses in professional organizations and separate women's administration organizations. Courses and workshops for women on how to succeed are common, as are recruitment efforts. Although women are still not represented in proportion to their numbers in teaching in the late 1990s, the majority of students gaining certification in school administration are women, a trend that some believe will insure women's equitable representation (Pounder, 1994).

As career options have expanded for women, there has also been a subtle and sometimes not-so-subtle movement to discourage all women, and especially very academically-able women, from entering teaching. Within this set of interactions is a notion that teaching is not an appropriate career for a high-achieving female, a pattern which follows the advice given to most males. Thus there has been speculation that the profession of teaching and, relatedly, school administration will face a crisis as the more able teachers retire, while not being replaced with equally able candidates. Although this has yet to be fully documented, professors of education continue to report that education students are in the lower academic strata of all university students.

There is anecdotal evidence that some women who were counseled away from teaching in the late 1980s and 1990s and who entered business and legal careers are returning to schools of education to prepare to be teachers, careers they had originally desired, but from which they had been discouraged.

Women professors of educational administration may help encourage and support women in school administra-

tion. Since 1972, when women were only 2% of professors of educational administration, the numbers of women in academic positions has increased to 20% by 1994 (McCarthy & Kuh, 1997). The effects of these increases on the field are unclear beyond adding women to the mix. Whether or not an increase of women in the professorate will change the nature of the field is yet to be determined. There is evidence that affirmative action policies in universities have helped to increase the number of women professors who teach in departments of educational administration.

Although there have not been many studies that directly connect the Civil Rights movement or affirmative action policies to the increase of women in school administration, the numbers in reports by women link the two. Women report that affirmative action pressure helped because such policies forced an opportunity for the women to be interviewed. Sometimes that was all that was necessary. In addition, as affirmative action questions were raised in communities, the pressure to hire from unrepresented groups increased (Edson, 1995). However, studies reflect the risk to women in school administration for becoming advocates for women and for being seen as speaking affirmatively for women (Bell, 1995; Schmuck, 1995; Schmuck & Schubert, 1995).

The relationship between affirmative action and women's participation in administration is complex, with affirmative action being a factor that might have encouraged women to apply or encouraged committees to interview women they might not otherwise have heard from. However, there is little evidence that women have been hired because they are women; rather the evidence indicates they are hired despite being women.

Inclusion in the Knowledge Base

In addition to efforts to bring more women into school administration, there has been an increase in the research on women school administrators as well as on administration itself, which has focused attention on a female perspective or experience. Most of this research has at its foundation a feminist perspective. Most of the inquiry on women and gender has come as a response to the androcentric nature of research in the field of educational administration. Thus researchers have begun to document the experiences of women and the influence of gender on leadership and organizations. Since the mid-1970s, hundreds of dissertations and studies have been completed that can be used to assess the experience of women.

This research can be examined from a developmental perspective. Research on women and gender in educational administration has progressed through six stages essential in the evolution of a paradigmatic shift, stages similar to those involved in curriculum change reported by Schuster and Van Dyne (1984). Table 5.5 presents these stages and the research questions they represent in the literature on women, gender, and school administration.

Each of these stages follows from the previous stage. The answers to the questions posed in an earlier stage lead to the questions in later stages. Much research spans two or more stages. For instance, in Stage 1 we have documented how many women are in school administration. Once the answer to that question is determined, the obvious follow-up questions (Stage 2 and 3) are "Who are these women?" and "Why are there so few?" Conceptually these stages build on each other, although we never completely answer the questions at earlier stages and these stages overlap.

Documenting the Number of Women in School Administration

The first stage documents the lack of women in positions of administration, providing the reader with information about where women are and aren't in the school hierarchy. This stage is guided by such questions as "How many women are in school administration?" and "What kinds of positions do they hold?" This research tended to be done in the 1970s and the early 1980s. We have very little current reporting on where women can be found. Since there is no national data base that helps us understand women's employment in school administration, there is still a need to continue to document women's career paths and the strength in numbers of women in various positions. Blount (1994), in her historical analysis of women in the superintendency, completed detailed and painstaking documentation of the number of women superintendents from 1910 to 1990. Her work is very helpful in making sense of the past and serves as a way to understand what is currently happening with women in school administration.

An analysis of the changing career paths for women examined the ever-more prevalent position of administrative assistant and the meaning of this position for women. Goldberg documented a higher number of women than men who were hired as administrative assistants with lower salaries than comparable positions. However, those positions did serve as entry-level positions for the women as they moved into principalships and central office positions (Goldberg, 1991).

Table 5.5

Stages of Research on Women and Gender

Stage	Questions	Approach	Outcome
Stage 1 Absence of women documented	How many women are in school administration? What positions do they hold?	Surveys that count	Documentation of numbers by administrative position
Stage 2 Search for women who have been or are administrators	What are the characteristics of women who are in school administration? What is the history of women in school administration?	Surveys of women administrators. Historical research that uncovers "great" women.	Demographic and attitudinal descriptions of women administrators. Stories of former administrators.
Stage 3 Women as disadvantaged or subordinate	Why so few women leaders in schools?	Surveys of attitudes toward and of women. Surveys of experiences of women. Experimental and quasi-experimental studies of discrimination.	Identification of barriers to advancement of women in administration
Stage 4 Women studied on their own terms	How do women describe their experiences and lives?	Survey, interview, observational studies of women	A view of the world from a female perspective
Stage 5 Women as challenge to theory	How must theory change to include women's experience? What effects does gender have on behavior and effectiveness in organizations?	Analysis of theories/methods as appropriate for women	Reality that theories don't always work for women
Stage 6 Transformation of Theory	What are theories of human behavior in organizations?	Surveys, analysis of theories, action, research, observational and interview studies	Reconceptualization of theory to include experiences of women

There is still ample room for historical approaches for understanding women in administration. In addition, there still needs to be continued reporting at this first stage so that women's participation in administration is clearly documented. Currently, the next national data collection is scheduled to be done by the National Center for Education Statistics (NCES) in their School Staff Survey scheduled for 1999–2000. Although there is pressure on NCES to expand the data collection to include central office staffing, including the superintendency, there is no current plan to do so. The American Association of School Administrators, in partnership with Superintendents Prepared, has scheduled a survey of superintendents during 1998.

Great Women in School Leadership

The second stage identifies famous or exceptional women in the history of school administration, adding to the existing data in the conventional paradigm. The work here answers in the affirmative the question, "Is there a history of great women in school leadership?" It examines whether women have done the same things that men have done and if women's achievements meet male standards. We have very little work in the knowledge base that tells us about outstanding women in school administration. Surprisingly, even accounts of Ella Flagg Young (Smith, 1979) or Grace Strachen (1910) are few. There are scores of great women whose stories lie buried in school histories, in local historical societies, and in the archives of national organizations. Learning more of their lives may help to shape and understand the knowledge base; at the very least, such research will provide a fuller explanation of the legacy of their early courage and sacrifice.

Barriers to Women in Administration

Stage 3 scholarship investigates women's place in schools from the framework of women as disadvantaged or subordinate, and the question asked is, "Why are there so few women leaders?" Extensive and continued work on the reasons that women are not in school administration in greater numbers has aided both understanding and prompted action.

In the 1970s and 1980s, understanding the barriers constituted the bulk of the research on women in administration. Although internal motivation and lack of preparation accounted for some of the explanation, the major reason that women weren't hired in school administration came from stereotypic attitudes toward women and beliefs that women weren't as competent as men. In other words, women weren't hired because of sex discrimination (Shakeshaft, 1987/89).

More recently, scholarship has focused on the reasons why women who might be hired in positions of school ad-

ministration aren't interested in pursing these opportunities. Beekley (1996), Brunner (1997), Grogan (1996), Riehl & Byrd (1997), and Tallerico (1998) are among the researchers who have been investigating the tradeoffs for women in administration, and which of the costs for women might be more than the value of the position itself. This research indicates that balance between the personal and family on the one side and career on the other is central to women, and that women are less likely than men to give up one for the other.

Continued race and sex discrimination is the focus of studies that are looking at the secondary or peripheral gatekeepers such as professors of educational administration and search consultants. Alston (1998), Brunner (1998), Jackson (1995), and Ortiz (1998) extend the analysis of the conventional selection process and describe the race and ethnic discriminators embedded in this process. They examine how women of African descent, Latina women, and European-American women engage the superintendency. The attitudes of school board members in relation to their role in hiring superintendents continues to be charted (Grogan & Henry, 1995). This work indicates that there have been attitude changes as school board members have slowly become more accepting of women candidates. The research further documents that women school board members are, as a group, more favorable toward women candidates than are men school board members (Fairbairn, 1989).

Kamler and Shakeshaft (1998) document the role of the search consultant as gatekeeper for women and the interaction between search consultants and boards of education. Crane (1992) examined the cost of advanced work in educational administration at the university and the payoff for graduates. This work explores the criticism that universities are admitting women students but are doing very little to place female graduates.

The impact on women of being a younger candidate (Harrington, 1991) or coming from an early childhood or early elementary background (Galin, 1995) extends the understanding of the ways in which women candidates are dismissed or devalued. Johnson and Douglas (1985) document that decisions about hiring made upon observable evidence of administrative ability are more likely to advantage women.

The impact of mentoring, both by university faculty and senior administrators, represents a strand of research that attempts to document effective strategies for overcoming the barriers to women in administration (Acker, 1995; Daws, 1995; Edson, 1995; Epp, 1995; Hart, 1995; Pence, 1995; and Romero & Storrs, 1995). The effects of mentoring, as opposed to sponsorship, are detailed with the latter more likely to result in a job offer for the mentee.

Overall, Stage 3 research is plentiful, continuing the search for ways to overcome the barriers to women in administration first by describing the barriers and then by examining the effectiveness of responses. We currently know more about the barriers than we do about effective responses, and research which evaluates outcomes is much needed.

Small but Brilliant Lives of Women Administrators

At Stage 4, women are finally studied on their own terms and female perspectives are identified and described. It is at this stage where research in the past decade has blossomed. From dissertations to books, there are numerous qualitative accounts of women school administrators. Everyday women, if there is such a thing, are brought to life as researchers hear their stories and share them with readers. A major concern of these studies is to better understand how women construct their gender as one of a few women in a male-dominated profession. Bell (1990) led the way with her study of women superintendents and their experiences with board members.

Much of this literature builds the case that women bring practices to administration that haven't existed before and that are necessary for reform. This literature, almost all qualitative in nature, portrays women administrators as more democratic, caring, and reform-minded than their male counterparts (Beck, 1994; Chase, 1995; Grogan, 1996; Myers & Hajnal, 1995; Randall, 1993; Regan & Brooks, 1995; Rusch & Marshall, 1995; Sernak, 1995). Unlike studies in the 1970s and 1980s, few of these more recent studies provide comparable data from males. If it is true that women approach the job of administration in ways that differ from men, the reason why is less clear. Are these approaches representative of token or new entrants to the field? Are they related to female socialization? Are they related to what actions women are allowed within a social organizational context to achieve success? The answers are not yet available.

Challenging Existing Theories

Interestingly there isn't much available that directly challenges existing theory in the social sciences, not because it might not be possible to do so, but because many of the researchers in the field of gender and schools are less interested in the academic theoretical discussions than in the practical application of the research. Many of the researchers communicate a message of the irrelevance of the traditional literature in educational administration. The work that is currently being done is considered so rich, new, and exciting that it almost seems that time spent on countering the traditional literature is time wasted. Although these arguments are not stated, the complete absence of any connection to the traditional literature in

management and school administration by those who study women may imply that the traditional literature isn't worth engaging. Among others, Corson (1992) and Capper (1993) have asked "How must theory change to include women's experience?" and have responded with more expanded theoretical conceptions.

Feminist Praxis

One contribution of the literature in Stage 4 is that it provides a rich and descriptive storehouse of human female administrative behavior upon which to make sense of organizational, political, and individual behavior. This often challenges conventional notions of decision making in schools or theories that explain actions through benefit analysis. As a whole, this work is building the field's understanding of the nature of gender in organizations and gender theory is what is being constructed. Researchers in England, Australia, and Canada have focused more on these theoretical connections than have researchers in the United States. Blackmore (1993, 1995, 1998), Capper (1993), and Kenway (1993) have consistently pushed the thinking about the meaning of gender in organizations, in politics, in policy making, and in perceptions and impacts of leadership.

Stage 6 transforms theory so that we can understand women's and men's experiences together. At this level, we will hopefully be able to produce an inclusive vision of human experience based on differences and diversity, rather than on sameness and generalizations.

In the 1990s, much work has centered around trying to understand the experiences of women administrators and making meaning of those experiences within the organizational context. Researchers have questioned the usefulness of both theory and conceptions of organizations for explaining women's participation (Blackmore, 1995; Chase, 1995; Cooper, 1995; Grogan, 1996; Limerick & Lingard, 1995; Rusch & Marshall, 1995; Regan & Brooks, 1995; Reynolds & Young, 1995; Scherr, 1995).

Summary

This chapter was intended to trace how the profession of educational administration has become more gender inclusive. While full inclusion of women in the profession has still not occurred, the numbers are changing as is the research. While one school of thought responds optimistically and codes the evidence as an example of social change and the way it occurs, another school of thought believes that women are only being allowed into a profession that has declined in power and influence. Additionally, many question whether or not the entrance of women into administration has any meaning other than changing the way the administrator looks.

Much of the research and discussion in the late 1990s has centered upon whether there is a woman's way of leading. These questions take us full circle and require an analysis of the meaning of inclusion. If it means more women in administration and leadership in education, then the field has become more inclusive, although not in proportion with women's numbers. If it means thinking about administration and schools differently by taking in a female or other perspective, then again, there has been some change as researchers and practitioners have come to try and understand how women experience administration and schools. And if inclusion means that the purposes and processes of schooling have changed because of women's influence, the answers are less clear. We don't yet know what the impact of more women administrators will have upon teaching and learning in schools.

NOTES

1. Parts of this chapter have been previously published in *Women in Educational Administration*, Sage, 1987 and Corwin Press, 1989.
2. I have chosen, in this chapter, to use the term "of African descent" to describe people often referred to as Black or African-American. I am still struggling with the most useful, accurate, and respectful way to talk about the artificial divisions of race that have all too real historical roots and social policy outcomes.
3. I use the term sex to refer to demographic categories. I do this because when people fill out surveys, they do so based upon their biological identification. Sex is a biological identifier. Gender is a cultural term and the one I use to describe the ways people behave, think about themselves or others, and are treated based upon their biological category.
4. We use racial and ethnic categories in most surveys to divide people into one group or another. However, there is very little evidence that these categories are based upon genetic foundations. These are historical and social categories, ones we use for many reasons. However we may use them, I believe they are artificial, though sometimes useful. I use them in this paper because they identify groups that have been treated in different ways as groups, even though there is wide variance in individual experience.
5. The most recent national compilation of the education workforce by gender is *Schools and Staffing in the United States: A Statistical Profile, 1993–94*, published by the National Center for Education Statistics. This survey provides information on teachers and principals but not on superintendents. The next Schools and Staffing survey will be undertaken in 1999–2000. The most recent report of AASA (1997) membership indicates that 15.2% of the superintendents that belong to AASA are female. Educational Research Service conducted a 1990 survey of school superintendents and found that 8.2% were female.
6. The title comes from C. Brunner.

REFERENCES

Acker, S. (1995). The head teacher as career broker: Stories from an English primary school. In D. M. Dunlap & P. A. Schmuck (Eds.), *Women Leading in Education*. Albany: State University of New York Press.

Alston, J. A. (1998). *Climbing hills and mountains: Black females making it to the superintendency*. Paper presented at the annual meeting of the American Educational Research Association, San Diego, CA.

Anthony, S. B., Stanton, C. E. & Harper, I. H. (1922). *The history of woman suffrage*. (Vol. 1). New York: Fowler & Wells (original work published 1881).

Beale, H. K. (1936). *Are American teachers free? An analysis of restraints in American schools*. New York: Scribner.

Beck, L. G. (1994) *Reclaiming educational administration as a caring profession*. New York: Teachers College Press.

Beekley, C. X. (1996). *Gender, expectations and job satisfaction: Why women exit the public school superintendency*. Paper presented at the annual meeting of the American Educational Research Association, New York, NY.

Bell, C. S. (1990). *Gender and the meaning of professional relationships for women in the superintendency*. Paper presented at the annual meeting of the AERA SIG: Research on Women in Education, Milwaukee.

Bell, C. S. (1995). "If I weren't involved with schools, I might be radical": Gender consciousness in context. In D. M. Dunlap & P. A. Schmuck (Eds.), *Women Leading in Education*. Albany: State University of New York Press.

Bell, C. S. & Chase, S. E. (1995) Gender in the theory and practice of educational leadership. *Journal for a Just and Caring Education*, 1(2), 200–222.

Bernard, R. M. & Vinovskis, M. A. (1977). The female school teacher in ante-bellum Massachusetts. *Journal of Social History*, 10(3), 332–345.

Billington, R. A. (Ed.). (1981). *The Journal of Charlotte Forten: A free Negro in the slave era*. New York: W. W. Norton. (Original work published 1953).

Blackmore, J. (1993). "In the shadow of men": The historical construction of administration as Masculinist Enterprise. In J. Blackmore, J. & J. Kenway (Eds.), *Gender Matters in Educational Administration and Policy*. London: The Falmer Press.

Blackmore, J. & Kenway, J. (1993). *Gender Matters in Educational Administration and Policy*. London: The Falmer Press.

Blount, J. M. (1994). One postmodern feminist perspective on educational leadership: and ain't I a leader? In S. J. Maxcy (Ed.), *Postmodern School Leadership*. Westport, CT: Praeger, 47–60.

Blount, J. M. (1998). *Destined to Rule the Schools. Women and the Superintendency, 1873–1995*. Albany, New York: State University of New York Press.

Brunner, C. C. (1997). Working through the "riddle of the heart": Perspectives of women superintendents. *Journal of School Leadership*, 7, March, 138–164.

Brunner, C. C. (1998). *Power, gender, and superintendent selection*. Paper presented at the annual meeting of the American Educational Research Association, San Diego, CA.

Burstyn, L. N. (1980). Historical perspectives on women in educational leadership. In S. K. Biklen & M. B. Brannigan (Eds.), *Women and educational leadership*, pp. 65–75. Lexington, MA: D. C. Heath.

Callahan, R. E. (1962). *Education and the cult of efficiency*. Chicago: University of Chicago Press.

Capper, C. A. (1992). *An "otherist" post-structural perspective of educational administration: a case in point: The proposed knowledge base in educational administration*. Unpublished paper. University Council for Educational Administration, Minneapolis, MN.

Capper, C. A. (1993). *Educational Administration in a Pluralistic Society*. Albany, NY: SUNY Press.

Capper, C. A. (1995, October). *Discourse of dysfunction: Being silenced and silencing*. Unpublished paper. University Council for Educational Administration.

Chamberlain, L. M. & Meece, L. E. (1937, March). Women and men in the teaching profession. *Bulletin of the Bureau of SchoolService*, University of Kentucky, 9(3).

Chase, S. (1995). *Ambiguous Empowerment*. Amherst: The University of Massachusetts Press.

Collier-Thomas, B. (1982). The impact of black women in education: An historical overview. *Journal of Negro Education*, 51(3),173–180.

Connolly, L. (1919, March 8). Is there room at the top for women educators? *The Woman Citizen*, 3 (41), 840–841.

Cooper, J. E. (1995). Administrative women and their writing: Reproduction and resistance in bureaucracies. In D. M. Dunlap & P. A. Schmuck (Eds.), *Women Leading in Education*. Albany: State University of New York Press.

Corson, D. J. (1992). Language, gender and education: A critical review linking social justice and power. *Gender and Education*, 4(3), 229–254.

Corson, D. J. (1995). *Discourse and Power in Educational Organizations*. Cresskill, NJ: Hampton Press, Inc.

Craig, R. P. & Gulley, I. T. (1997). Five Hispanic women in positions of leadership: An ethnographic approach. *Record.* 16 (1–2) and 17(1–2), 15–22.

Crane, E. (1992). *A study of the relationship between level of education, career paths, and earnings for graduates of advanced programs in educational administration.* Doctoral dissertation, Hofstra University.

Cuban, L. (1976). *Urban school chiefs under fire.* Chicago: University of Chicago Press.

Cubberley, E. P. (1929). *Public school administration.* Boston: Houghton Mifflin Co.

Davies, L. (1990) *Women and educational management in the Third World.* Paper presented at the Equal Advances in Education Management Conference. Council of Europe: Vienna, Austria.

Davis, H. (1936). *Women's professional problems in the field of education: A map of needed research* (Pi Lambda Theta Study). Unpublished manuscript.

Davis, H. & Samuelson, A. (1950). Women in education. *Journal of Social Issues* 6(3), 25–37.

Daws, L. (1995). To fields of tall poppies: The mentored pathway. In B. Limerick & B. Lingard (Eds.), *Gender and Changing Educational Management.* 2nd Yearbook of the Australian Council for Educational Administration. Australia: Hoder Education.

District Superintendents Committee on Women and Minority Administrators (June, 1997). *Preliminary Report and Recommendations.* C. Fowler, The University of the State of New York, New York State Education Department.

Driver, K. (December, 1990). *United Kingdom: Quality matters, an initiative in developing school leadership from the secondary heads association.* Paper presented at the Equal Advances in Education Management Conference. Council of Europe: Vienna, Austria.

Dunlap, D. M. & Schmuck, P. A. (Eds.) (1995). *Women Leading in Education.* Albany: SUNY Press.

Edson, S. K. (1995). Ten years later: Too little, too late? In D. M. Dunlap & P. A. Schmuck (Eds.), *Women Leading in Education.* Albany: SUNY Press.

Educational news and editorial comment: Women in educational administration. (1928). *School Review,* 36(5), 326–327.

Epp, J. R. (1995). Insidious deterrents: When educational administration students are women. In C. Reynolds & B. Young (Eds.), *Women and Leadership in Canadian Education.* Calgary: Detselig Enterprises Ltd.

Fairbairn, L. (1989). *A survey of board of education/superintendent relationships: Does sex of the superintendent make a difference.* Doctoral dissertation. Hofstra University.

Fuller, E. (1971). *Prudence Crandall: An incident in racism in nineteenth century Connecticut.* Middletown, CT: Wesleyan University Press.

Galin, M. (1995). *Principals' perceptions of grade level teaching experience on evaluations of administrative applicants.* Doctoral dissertation. Hofstra University.

Galludet, T. H. (1838). Female teachers of common schools. *Connecticut Common School Journal,* 1(2), 9–1 0.

Giddings, P. (1984). *When and where I enter: The impact of black women on race and sex in America.* New York: William Morrow.

Goldberg, C. (1991). *A study of the career paths of administrators in central office positions in New York State public school districts.* Doctoral dissertation. Hofstra University.

Gougeon, T. (1995). Teacher perceptions of male and female principals. In C. Reynolds & B. Young (Eds.), *Women and Leadership in Canadian Education.* Calgary: Detselig Enterprises Ltd.

Green, C. M. (1967). *The secret city: A history of race relations in the nation's capital.* Princeton, NJ: Princeton University Press.

Gribskov, M. (1980). Feminism and the woman school administrator. In S. K. Biklen & M. B. Brannigan (Eds.), *Women and educational leadership,* pp. 77–91. Lexington, MA: D. C. Heath.

Grogan, M. (1996). *Voices of Women Aspiring to the Superintendency.* Albany: SUNY Press.

Grogan, M. & Henry, M. E. (1995). *Women candidate for the superintendency: Board perspective.* Paper presented at the annual meeting of the American Educational Research Association, San Francisco, CA.

Hall, G. S. (1908, May). Feminization in school and home. *The World's Work,* 10237–10243.

Hall, V. (1996). *Dancing on the Ceiling: A Study of Women Managers in Education.* London: Paul Chapman Publishing Ltd.

Hansot, E. & Tyack, D. (1981). *The dream deferred: A golden age for women school administrators* (Policy Paper No. 81–C2). Stanford, CA: Stanford University, Institute for Research on Educational Finance and Government.

Harrington, P. (1991). *The young school principal: A qualitative study.* Doctoral dissertation. Hofstra University.

Hart, A. W. (1995). Women ascending to leadership: The organizational socialization of principals. In D. M. Dunlap & P. A. Schmuck (Eds.), *Women Leading in Education.* Albany: SUNY Press.

Hunton, A. (1904) Negro womanhood defended. *Voice of the Negro,* 1(7), 280–282.

Jackson, B. L. (1995). *The voices of African American women public school superintendents: A preliminary report.* Seminar: National Alliance of Black School Educators Annual Conference, Dallas, TX.

Johnson, M. C. & Douglas, J. R. (1985). Assessment centers: What impact have they had on career opportunities for women? *NASSP Bulletin,* 69(484), 105–111.

Jones, A. H. (1905). A century's progress for the American colored woman. *Voice of the Negro,* 2(9), 631–633.

Jones, J. (1979). Women who were more than men: Sex and status in freedmen's teaching. *History of Education Quarterly* 19(l), 47–59.

Jones, J. (1980). *Soldiers of light and love: Northern teachers and Georgia blacks,* 1865–1873. Chapel Hill: University of North Carolina Press.

Kalvelage, J. (1978). *The decline in female principals since 1928: Riddles and clues.* (ERIC Document Reproduction Service No. ED 163 594). Eugene, Oregon: Sex Equity in Educational Leadership Project.

Kamler, E. & Shakeshaft, C. (1998). *The role of search consultants in the career paths of women superintendents.* Paper presented at the annual meeting of the American Educational Research Association, San Diego, CA.

Katz, M. (1973). The new departure in Quincy, 1873–81: The nature of 19th century educational reform. In M. Katz (Ed.), *Education in American history,* pp. 68–84. New York: Prague.

Kenway, J. (1993). Nontraditional pathways: Are they the way to the future? In J. Blackmore & J. Kenway (Eds.), *Gender Matters in Educational Administration and Policy.* London: The Falmer Press.

Kerber, L. A. (1983). *The impact of women on American education.* Newton, MA: Women's Educational Equity Act Publishing Center, U. S. Department of Education.

Lathrop, E. A. (1922). Teaching as a vocation for college women. *The Arrow,* 38(3), 415–425.

Lerner, G. (1972). *Black women in white America.* New York: Pantheon.

Limerick, B. & Lingard, B. (Eds.) (1995). *Gender and Changing Educational Management.* 2nd Yearbook of the Australian Council for Educational Administration. Australia: Hoder Education.

Lynd, R. S. & Lynd, H. M. (1929). *Middletown: A study in American culture.* NY: Harcourt, Brace & Jovanovich.

McCarthy, M. & Kuh, G. (1997). *Continuity and change: The educational leadership professoriate.* Columbia, MO: University Council for Educational Administration.

Mann, H. (1841). *Fourth annual report to the board of education together with the Fourth annual report of the secretary of the board.* Boston: Dutton and Wentworth.

Melder, K. E. (1972, Fall). Woman's high calling: The teaching profession in America, 1830–60. *American Studies,* pp. 19–32.

Myers, F. & Hajnal, R. (1995). Reflections on the leadership styles of women in Saskatchewan Adult Education Institutions. In C. Reynolds & Young (Eds.), *Women and Leadership in Canadian Education.* Calgary: Detselig Enterprises Ltd.

National Education Association. (1905). *Report of the Committee on Salaries, Tenure, and Pensions of Public School Teachers in the United States to the National Council of Education.* Winona, MN: Author.

National Education Association. (1942) Marriage as related to eligibility. *NEA Research Bulletin,* 20(2), 60–62.

New York State Education Department, BEDS Data, 1995–1996; 1997.

Noddings, N. (1984). *Caring.* Berkeley: University of California Press.

O'Connor, E. M. & Miner, M. (1969). *Myrtilla Miner: A memoir.* New York: Arno. (Original work Published 1884/5)

Ortiz, F. I. (1998). *Seeking and selecting Hispanic female superintendents.* Paper presented at the annual meeting of the American Educational Research Association, San Diego, CA.

Pence, L. J. (1995). Learning leadership through mentorships. In D. M. Dunlap & P. A. Schmuck (Eds.), *Women Leading in Education.* Albany: SUNY Press.

Peters, D. W. (1934). *The status of the married woman teacher.* New York: Teachers College, Columbia University Press.

Poll, C. (1979, August). *It's a good job for a woman (and a man): Why males and females choose to be elementary school teachers.* Paper presented at the annual meeting of the American Sociological Association, Boston, MA.

Pounder, D. (1994). Educational and demographic trends: Implications for women's representation in school administration. In P. Thurston & N. Presetine (Eds.), *Advances in Educational Administration,* Vol. III, pp. 135–149. Greenwich, CT: JAI Press.

Randall, P. (1993). *Weaving a tapestry: Stories women tell.* Doctoral dissertation. Hofstra University.

Regan, H. B. & Brooks, G. H. (1995). *Out of Women's Experience, Creating Relational Leadership.* Thousand Oaks, CA: Corwyn Press.

Reich, A. (1974). Teaching is a good profession . . . for a woman. In J. Stacey, S. Bereaud & J. Daniels (Eds.), *And Jill came tumbling after: Sexism in American education,* pp. 337–343. New York: Dell.

Reid, R. L. (Ed.). (1982). *Battleground: The autobiography of Margaret A. Haley.* Urbana, IL: University of Illinois Press.

Reynolds, C. & Young, B. (1995). *Women and Leadership in Canadian Education.* Calgary: Detselig Enterprises Ltd.

Riehl, C. & Byrd, M. A. (1997). Gender differences among new recruits to school administration: Cautionary footnotes to an optimistic tale. *Educational Evaluation and Policy Analysis,* 19(1), 45–64.

Rogers, R. (1929). Is woman ruining the country? *Literary Digest,* 102(13), 24.

Romero, M. & Storrs, D. (1995). Is that sociology?: The accounts of women of color graduate students in Ph. D. programs. In D. M. Dunlap & P. A. Schmuck (Eds.), *Women Leading in Education.* Albany: SUNY Press.

Ruijs, A. (November, 1990). *Women in educational management in European countries: The statistical picture.* Paper presented at the Equal Advances in Education Management Conference. Council of Europe: Vienna, Austria.

Rusch, E. & Marshall, C. (1995). *Gender filters at work in the administrative culture.* A paper presented at the annual meeting of the 1995 American Educational Research Association. San Francisco.

Scherr, M. W. (1995). The glass ceiling reconsidered: Views from below. In D. M. Dunlap & P. A. Schmuck (Eds.), *Women Leading in Education.* Albany: State University of New York Press.

Schmuck, P. (1979). *Sex equity in educational leadership: The Oregon story.* Eugene: University of Oregon, Center for Educational Policy and Management.

Schmuck, P. (1995). Advocacy organizations for women school administrators, 1977–1993. In D. M. Dunlap & P. A. Schmuck (Eds.), *Women Leading in Education.* Albany: State University of New York Press.

Schmuck, P. A. & Schubert, J. (1995). Women principals views on sex equity: Exploring issues of integration and information. In D. M. Dunlap & P. A. Schmuck (Eds.), *Women Leading in Education.* Albany: State University of New York Press.

Schuster, M. & Van Dyne, S. (1984). Placing women in the liberal arts: Stages of curriculum transformation. *Harvard Educational Review,* 54(4), 413–428.

Sernak, K. S. (1995). *Conceptualizing an ethic of caring within bureaucracy: A study of leadership.* Paper presented at the annual meeting of the American Educational Research Association, San Francisco.

Sexton, P. C. (1973). The feminized male. In C. S. Stoll (Ed.), *Sexism: Scientific debates.* Reading, MA: Addison-Wesley.

Shakeshaft, C. (1989). *Women in educational administration.* Newbury Park, CA: Sage; update, Corwyn (1989).

Shakeshaft, C., Nowell, I. & Perry, A. (1991). Gender and supervision. *Theory into Practice.* 30(2), 134–139.

Sklar, K. (1973). *Catharine Beecher: A study in domesticity.* New Haven, CT: Yale University Press.

Skria, L. E. (1998). *The social construction of gender in the superintendency.* Paper presented at the annual meeting of the American Educational Research Association. San Diego, CA.

Smith, J. K. (1979). *Ella Flagg Young: Portrait of a leader.* Ames: Educational Studies Press and Iowa State University Research Foundation.

Solomon, B. M. (1985). *In the company of educated women: A history of women and higher education in America.* New Haven, CT: Yale University Press.

Stern, M. (1973). An insider's view of the teacher's union and women's rights. *Urban Review,* 6(5–6), 46–49.

Strachan, G. C. (1910). *Equal pay for equal work.* New York: B. F. Buck.

Tallerico, M. (1998). *Crawling through the window of a dream.* Paper presented at the annual meeting of the American Educational Research Association, San Diego, CA.

Tyack, D. (1974). *The one best system: A history of American urban education.* Cambridge, MA: Harvard University Press.

Tyack, D. & Hansot, E. (1982). *Managers of virtue: Public school leadership in America, 1820–1980.* New York: Basic Books.

Tyack, D. B. & Strober, M. H. (1981).) Jobs and gender: A history of the structuring of educational employment by sex. In P. A. Schmuck, W. W. Charters, Jr. & R. O. Carlson (Eds.), *Educational policy and management, sex differentials,* pp. 131–152. New York: Academic Press.

U. S. Department of Education. National Center for Education Statistics. (1996). *Schools and Staffing in the United States: A Statistical Profile, 1993–94.* NCES 96–124, by Robin R. Henke, Susan P. Choy, Sonya Geis & Stephen P. Broughman. Washington, DC.

Vinovskis, M. A. & Bernard, R. M. (1978). Beyond Catharine Beecher: Female education in the ante-bellum period. *Signs: A Journal of Women in Culture and Society,* 3(4), 856–869.

Weinberg, M. (1977). *A chance to learn: The history of race and education in the United States.* New York: Cambridge University Press.

Western Journal of Education, The highest salaried woman in the world. (1906). 14(10), 515–516.

Williams, M., Jackson, K., Kincy, M., Wheelter, S., Davis, R., Crawford, R., Forte, M. & Bell, E. (1979). *The Jeanes story: A chapter in the history of American education 1908–1968.* Atlanta, GA: Southern Education Foundation.

Woody, T. (1966/1929). *A history of women's education in the United States.* New York: Octagon Books. (Original work published 1929).

Young, E. F. (1916, July 1–8). A reply. *Addresses and Proceedings of the National Education Association, 356–359.*

CHAPTER 6

The Evolution of Educational Leadership Preparation Programs

Martha M. McCarthy

Compared with many arts and sciences disciplines, educational leadership graduate programs have a relatively brief history. The first school management course was offered at the University of Michigan in 1881, but formal university preparation programs were not organized until several decades later (Culbertson, 1988). By the mid-twentieth century about 125 universities were offering graduate programs in K–12 educational administration/leadership (Silver, 1982). During the next two decades, the number of programs almost tripled (Peterson & Finn, l985), in part due to burgeoning public school enrollments creating a demand for more school administrators.

This chapter reviews and analyzes the literature pertaining to the evolution of educational leadership preparation programs. The first section addresses external factors, beyond the control of any single university, that have influenced preparation programs, such as governmental regulations and initiatives of professional associations. The next section highlights evidence of stability as well as modifications over time regarding the structure of educational leadership units and degree offerings; the focus and content of the curriculum; pedagogical approaches; university connections with the field; characteristics, activities, and attitudes of faculty members; and characteristics, recruitment, and assessment of students. More attention is given to developments since the mid-1980s, as earlier periods have already received substantial attention in the literature (see Boyan, 1988; Griffiths, 1988; McCarthy, Kuh, Newell, & Iacona, 1988). The final section highlights gaps in our knowledge about leadership preparation programs and identifies selected topics that warrant additional research. Throughout this chapter, the term "educational leadership"

is used to refer to school administration, school leadership, educational administration, and educational leadership units, programs, faculty, and students.

In an effort to identify all relevant materials, the ERIC database, Dissertation Abstracts, and journals targeting educational leadership were systematically reviewed. The reference lists from articles and books thus located were also examined to identify any additional materials that had not surfaced in the primary search. Furthermore, annual convention programs of the American Educational Research Association, the National Council of Professors of Educational Administration, and the University Council for Educational Administration were reviewed for the past decade to identify pertinent unpublished studies and documents. Materials pertaining to the preparation of school leaders also were gathered from the National Policy Board for Educational Administration, the Danforth Foundation, and the major professional organizations focusing on school administrators and educational leadership faculty.

External Influences on Leadership Preparation Programs

To fully understand the evolution of university programs that prepare school leaders, it is necessary to explore the external forces that have helped to shape them, such as the interests and activities of professional organizations and state and federal governments, economic cycles, and other societal developments. Some conditions that have influenced American higher education in general have had an impact on educational leadership units as well. For example, the dramatic faculty growth across academe from 1950 until about 1970 was accompanied by increased availability of federal funds for research and graduate assistantships. Moreover, rapid technological advances since the 1980s have revolutionized access to information and altered concepts of what education is and where it takes place. Increased calls for faculty accountability in the 1990s, especially in connection with teaching loads, have focused substantial attention on the improvement of teaching throughout higher education (Schuster, 1990; Zimbler, 1994).

In addition, some developments pertaining to K–12 education have had an impact on most programs in schools and colleges of education. For example, the plethora of reports criticizing American education in the 1980s and the involvement of coalitions of business leaders (such as Business Roundtable) in fashioning school reforms have catapulted education to a position of prominence on political agendas ("Education Ranks as Major Issue in Elections," 1996). Changing school demographics, especially in cities, and the introduction of competition and consumer choice into the educational enterprise through voucher plans, charter schools, and private management (Buechler, 1996; Chubb & Moe, 1990) have presented new challenges in the preparation of teachers and administrators. Also, changes in public school governance, such as site-based management and interagency collaborative arrangements, are influencing how and where education decisions are made. And the national focus on standards and assessments for elementary and secondary students has nurtured similar efforts targeting teachers and administrators (see Council of Chief State School Officers, 1996).

Although these and other developments affecting academe and the field of education in general have had an impact on educational leadership units, some external groups have focused attention specifically on the preparation of school leaders. Several of the more important initiatives are briefly discussed below.

Government Initiatives

The most profound government influence on leadership preparation programs is through state licensure mandates. Indeed, the initial growth of university programs was precipitated by such licensure requirements. State governments generally have preferred to monitor individuals through issuing licenses, which in turn influences the content of preparation programs, rather than by imposing mandates directly on universities. By the mid-1950s, 41 states required K–12 administrators to have completed some graduate work to be licensed, and 26 states required a master's degree for an administrative license. In 1993, 45 states required at least a master's degree (or equivalent courses) for a principal's license (Tryneski, 1993). The majority of leadership preparation programs continue to mirror licensure standards in their respective states.

Although pre-service programs for school leaders remain primarily the responsibility of universities, several federal and state government initiatives have been designed to improve the quality of practicing school leaders without necessarily involving universities. Disillusioned with university offerings, some state and federal policymakers have sought other venues for the professional development of school leaders (Logan & Pounder, 1989). At the federal government level, for example, heightened concern over the quality of school leaders and their preparation inspired passage of the Leadership Development Act (LEAD), which was funded from 1986 until 1992. Under this program, technical support centers to develop and disseminate exemplary school leadership practices and provide in-service education for practitioners were established in each state and the District of Columbia. Most centers were not directed by or housed in universities, although universities were involved in consortia arrangements to implement several LEAD projects. Some of these projects stimulated cooperation among professional associations, state departments, and universities; however, less than one-third of the LEAD projects contained any provisions for research activities (Wildman, 1988).

Over the past two decades, state governments increasingly have supported leadership academies or equivalent programs to provide in-service sessions for new and veteran administrators (Crews & Weakley, 1995). Donaldson (1987) reported that principals often view activities sponsored by such academies as more valuable than their university coursework. Most of these academies are run by state education departments or state professional associations, but some are operated by consortia that include universities. Academies with no formal university connections often hire faculty members as consultants. This perhaps explains in part why faculty have not asserted more opposition to the reduced role of universities in orchestrating these in-service activities (Logan & Pounder, 1989); faculty members often benefit financially when external groups offer the programs.

In addition to providing professional development activities for school leaders, some states have enacted policies that target pre-service preparation. For example, a few state legislatures are considering alternatives to traditional licensure for school administrators, which would not necessarily be tied to graduate courses in educational leadership. In addition, several states, such as Indiana, Kentucky, and North Carolina, have established professional standards boards to develop standards for administrative licensure and, in some instances, to implement assessment programs as a prerequisite to receiving a license.

A few states have directly addressed the quality of educational leadership preparation programs by reviewing existing programs and eliminating some of them. For example, the Ohio Board of Regents in 1995 charged a national panel with evaluating the quality of educational administration doctoral programs at state-assisted universities and recommending curricular and structural changes to improve the quality of these programs (Ohio Board of Regents, 1996). As a result of this process, the Board of Regents placed a moratorium on admitting students to some educational leadership doctoral programs and restructured other programs in various ways (for example, it recommended that an urban university focus on school leadership in urban settings). Mississippi also is involved in a comprehensive review of all leadership preparation programs in the state, based in part on performance assessments of program graduates (Murphy, Shipman, & Pearlman, 1997).

North Carolina has demonstrated its commitment to improve the quality of school leaders in the state and bring administrator supply and demand into better balance by allocating substantial funds to a multifaceted effort. A 1993 law funded an educational leadership master's degree program (leading to principal licensure) in which outstanding teachers are identified to participate (Clark, 1997). The fellows, selected by a statewide commission, receive $20,000 annually for a year of academic study and a year of field-based study (Educational Leadership Task Force, 1993). One goal of the legislation was to reduce the number of educational leadership preparation programs offered by state universities; through a competitive process, eight universities were selected from 12 to offer the master's degree.

In Hawaii, the State Department of Education and the University of Hawaii have jointly implemented a program in which up to 50 interns (usually teachers with at least five years of teaching experience) participate annually in a blend of clinical and academic work leading to administrative licensure and a master's degree in educational administration (Araki, 1993). Both the North Carolina and Hawaii programs rely heavily on cooperative arrangements between the universities and public schools in recruiting graduate students and in delivering the field-based components of leadership preparation.

Practitioner-Oriented Organizations

Various practitioner-oriented professional organizations, particularly the American Association of School Administrators (AASA) and the National Association of Secondary School Principals (NASSP) have exhibited a long-standing commitment to the improvement of leadership preparation. For example, starting in the 1970s, NASSP championed competency-based and then performance-based preparation for school administrators. A 1985 NASSP report called for universities to develop personalized perfor-

mance-based programs for principals based on a diagnosis of generic and task-specific skill needs (NASSP Consortium, 1985). The report also urged universities to evaluate their programs, analyze reasons for common practices (tradition, market, preferences of professors), and eliminate outmoded or unjustified practices.

In 1978, NASSP launched its assessment center initiative (Collet, 1989). The project was designed to identify individuals likely to succeed in the principalship by analyzing their skills in 12 key areas through simulated exercises and a structured interview. Although the process was intended for use in selecting principals, some preparation programs have incorporated all or part of the assessment center concept in screening candidates for educational leadership graduate programs (Collet, 1989; Milstein & Krueger, 1993). The substantial costs associated with the process (Wildman, 1988), however, have deterred its widespread use in university admissions.

More recently, NASSP in conjunction with the National Association of Elementary School Principals established the National Commission for the Principalship, led by Scott Thomson, to explore development of a national certification process and to influence the preparation and licensing of principals. The Commission asserted that university preparation programs were outdated, that most principal licensing requirements were irrelevant to current job demands, and that preparation should reflect the realities of operating schools (National Commission for the Principalship, 1990). The Commission identified 21 functional domains, and subsequently, the National Policy Board for Educational Administration assigned working teams to delineate the knowledge and skill base for principals in each of these domains (Thomson, 1993).

AASA also has been involved over time in the provision of in-service programs for administrators (for example, the National Academy for School Executives) and in efforts to improve pre-service preparation by establishing performance goals and guidelines for the preparation of administrators (see Hoyle, English, & Steffy, 1985, 1990). In 1989, AASA introduced a five-year project for the professional development of school leaders (National Executive Development Center) designed to diagnose administrators' needs, assist in developing professional growth plans, and monitor implementation of the plans. A few years later, AASA developed a superintendent assessment program for Kentucky, which has since been adopted by several other states. In 1993, AASA distributed eight professional standards for superintendents pertaining to leadership and district culture, policy and governance, communications and community relations, organizational management, curriculum planning and development, instructional management, human resources management, and values and ethics (Hoyle & AASA Commission, 1993). AASA has urged universities to focus on these standards in pre-service preparation and has launched a project, Leadership Institute for School Administrators (LISA), to provide professional development based on these standards that can lead to national certification for superintendents (LISA Update, 1996).

Professor-Oriented Organizations

The National Council of Professors of Educational Administration (NCPEA) and the University Council for Educational Administration (UCEA) are the two professor-oriented organizations that concentrate primarily on the improvement of school leadership preparation through collective efforts. NCPEA, created in 1947, provided the first vehicle to link educational leadership faculty across universities. UCEA, a consortium of about 50 universities in the United States and Canada with doctoral programs in educational administration, was established in 1956. From the 1950s until the 1970s, both of these organizations influenced leadership preparation programs through publications, seminars, and other activities that drew heavily on the social sciences to better understand administrative behavior (Campbell, Fleming, Newell, & Bennion, 1987).

Following a decade of inconsequential activity in the educational leadership professoriate, UCEA reasserted its leadership role by sponsoring the National Commission on Excellence in Educational Administration (NCEEA). The Commission was directed by Daniel Griffiths from 1985 until 1987. Among recommendations in its final report, *Leaders for America's Schools*, NCEEA (1987) suggested that at least 300 of the 500 institutions offering courses in educational administration should eliminate such offerings because their programs were inadequate. The NCEEA further recommended that the remaining preparation programs should adhere to a professional school model, like law and medicine, incorporating additional clinical experiences and enlisting the involvement of outstanding practitioners. The Commission suggested that a national policy board, with representation from the primary professional associations having a stake in improving school leadership, be established to monitor implementation of the NCEEA's recommendations and provide policy leadership to the field.

Since 1987, UCEA has held an annual convention, and these gatherings, along with NCPEA annual meetings, have become forums for the discussion of preparation program issues. Also, a special interest group on teaching in educational administration was created in the American Educational Research Association in 1993, and this group focuses additional attention on curriculum and pedagogy in educational leadership units. These initiatives have given program reform efforts more national visibility, credibility, and status and have generated professional publications focusing on pedagogical and curricular innovations (Milstein

et al., 1993; Mulkeen, Cambron-McCabe, & Anderson, 1994; Murphy, 1993a).

The National Policy Board for Educational Administration and Related Initiatives

As recommended by the NCEEA, the National Policy Board for Educational Administration (NPBEA) was established in 1988 with David Clark as its first executive secretary. The creation of this Board was a milestone event because it brought together the major professional associations[1] interested in improving school leadership after they had drifted apart for more than two decades. The NPBEA's (1989) reform agenda, *Improving the Preparation of School Administrators: An Agenda for Reform*, advocated a reduction in the number of educational leadership programs, greater differentiation between Ed.D. and Ph.D. degrees, and an emphasis on doctoral-level coursework to prepare educational leaders. The NPBEA further recommended that all preparation programs maintain at least five full-time faculty members and a student-faculty ratio comparable to the ratio in other professional graduate programs. The NPBEA also began disseminating occasional papers and hosting national seminars on various aspects of educational leadership.

The Board's 1993 revised mission statement focuses on the improvement of educational leadership licensure and preparation, recruitment and selection of administrators, and development of models of integrated leadership emphasizing student outcomes. In 1994, the NPBEA, under the leadership of Scott Thomson, appointed a working group to develop contemporary and unified curriculum guidelines for educational leadership programs to be accredited by the National Council for the Accreditation of Teacher Education (NCATE). These guidelines were approved by NCATE in 1996 for use in educational leadership program reviews starting in 1997.

In a second major project, which received support from the Pew Charitable Trust, the NPBEA in conjunction with the Council of Chief State School Officers (CCSSO) launched a consortium in 1994 to establish national licensure standards for administrators, based on the belief that standards provide "an especially appropriate and particularly powerful leverage point for reform" (CCSSO, 1996, p. 7). The Interstate School Leaders Licensure Consortium (ISLLC), chaired by Joseph Murphy, developed six standards that were adopted in 1996 by the 24 states in the consortium. The standards, intended to upgrade the quality of the profession, are compatible with the NCATE Curriculum Guidelines and the 1993 AASA standards. Each ISLLC standard is framed in terms of "an educational leader who promotes the success of all students," explicitly underscoring the centrality of student learning in assessing the effectiveness of school leaders (CCSSO, 1996, pp. 10–20). The standards focus on the role of school leaders in developing and sustaining a shared vision of learning within the school community; nurturing a school culture and instructional program conducive to learning and staff development; ensuring a safe, efficient, and effective learning environment; collaborating with families and community members in mobilizing community resources; acting fairly and ethically; and understanding and responding to the larger political, social, economic, legal, and cultural context of schools. Five of the states in the ISLLC Consortium have joined the Educational Testing Service to develop a performance-based assessment instrument based on these standards that will be used in conjunction with other measures for licensing and relicensing administrators.

The NPBEA is attempting to ensure that these projects to establish standards and assessments for school administrators are compatible with one another and influence leadership preparation programs in appropriate ways. These initiatives may have significant implications for educational leadership units. Not only must units comply with the NCATE Guidelines for their programs to be accredited, but also they will likely modify the content of their programs to ensure that candidates are prepared to meet the AASA and ISLLC standards. If administrator candidates from particular universities consistently perform poorly on assessments based on these standards, prospective students may choose graduate programs at other institutions. States might even tie their accreditation of leadership preparation programs to student performance assessments as has been done in some states with teacher education programs and graduates' scores on the National Teacher Examination.

Foundation-Supported Initiatives

A number of foundation-supported projects have affected selected educational leadership programs and individual faculty members. In fact, most major initiatives in the field since the mid-twentieth century have received some support from Carnegie, Danforth, Ford, Kellogg, Pew, or other philanthropic organizations. Although most of these projects have been associated primarily with the recipient institutions or organizations, a few projects with broad impact on the field nationally have been identified with specific foundations rather than with the agencies receiving the funds.

For example, the Kellogg Foundation in 1950 supported the Cooperative Program in Educational Administration (CPEA) at five universities recognized as national leaders; three additional CPEA centers were added in 1951. The central purpose of CPEA was to initiate changes in leadership preparation (Murphy, 1993b), and this consortium influenced preparation programs by encouraging a multidisciplinary approach in analyzing administration (Gregg, 1969). Reports sponsored by CPEA in the 1950s brought new substance to the field, replacing descriptive

analyses with deductive theory and the behavioral sciences. These ideas dominated preparation programs for more than 30 years (National Commission for the Principalship, 1990).

The Danforth Foundation has supported a variety of initiatives in the field since the 1970s. Two recent projects in particular have significantly influenced leadership preparation programs. These projects, focusing on preparing principals and revitalizing the professoriate, have targeted attention on preparation program reform through collaboration across universities. Moreover, these projects have nurtured a professional culture encouraging "reconstruction rather than simply reshaping existing programs" (Cambron-McCabe, 1993, p. 170).

The Danforth principalship preparation program was offered by 22 universities selected in five cycles from 1987 until 1991. A basic assumption of the field-based program was that effective leadership depends on the recruitment of talented people, and one of its goals was to increase minority and female representation among school leaders (Playko & Daresh, 1992). Candidates for the program were classroom teachers identified by their school districts as having the potential to be outstanding school leaders. At most of the participating universities, the principalship preparation program entailed certain common features, such as the use of student cohort groups, heavy emphasis on clinical experiences and field mentors, extensive collaboration with school districts, and a coordinated curriculum across courses (Milstein *et al.*, 1993).

The Danforth program for professors was designed to create opportunities for faculty to share ideas with colleagues from other universities and to engage in comprehensive program development with the assistance of outside consultants. Teams from 21 universities participated in cycles over a six-year period from 1987 until 1993. In 1991, this program issued a platform for preparing school administrators, declaring that leadership is an intellectual, moral, and craft practice and emphasizing hands-on experiences and clinical inquiry regarding practical problems (Cambron-McCabe, Mulkeen, & Wright, 1991). As discussed in the next section, most of the educational leadership units that have recently been involved in substantial preparation program reforms have participated in one of the two Danforth programs.

Stability and Change in Educational Leadership Units

Episodic investigations of educational leadership units, programs, faculty, and students have been conducted during the past several decades. Some characteristics have reflected remarkable continuity over time, whereas others have changed substantially. This section explores features that have remained stable or changed incrementally as well as recent transformations in a few educational leadership programs.[2]

Structure of Units and Degree Offerings

From the 1970s until the mid-1990s, there has been stability in the number of institutions offering graduate degrees in educational administration/leadership; 375 universities in 1976, 372 in 1986, and 371 in 1994 (Culbertson & Silver, 1978; McCarthy, *et al.*, 1988; McCarthy & Kuh, 1997). These figures do not include more than 100 institutions that offer licensure courses only (Lilley, 1995; NCEEA, 1987). The titles attached to most of these units or program areas are "school administration," "educational leadership," or some variation of these terms, and there has been recent movement to substitute "leadership" in place of "administration." Although some educational leadership units stand alone, most are combined with other program areas in larger departments. Since the early 1980s there has been a trend toward consolidating program areas; most often educational leadership faculty are housed with higher education and foundations faculty (McCarthy & Kuh, 1997; McCarthy, *et al.*, 1988; Norton, 1994).

The mean number of faculty in educational leadership units has fluctuated somewhat over the past two decades from a high of 6.5 faculty members in 1976 (Davis, 1978) to a low of 5.0 in 1986 (McCarthy, *et al.*, 1988). Many educational leadership units in the mid-1980s did not appear to have sufficient personnel to offer adequate, much less high quality or innovative, programs. By the mid-1990s, average faculty size increased to 5.6 (McCarthy & Kuh, 1997). Although the mean number of faculty per unit increased only slightly between 1986 and 1994, the modal number jumped from two to five faculty members. This increase in faculty was concentrated in universities that do not emphasize doctoral programs (comprehensive institutions)[3] and those not affiliated with UCEA. In fact, faculty size declined slightly from the mid-1980s until the mid–1990s in UCEA programs and in those at research universities.

For the past two decades, more than half of the educational leadership units have been housed at comprehensive institutions, which employ almost half of all educational leadership faculty members and enroll more than two-fifths of the students in graduate degree programs (McCarthy *et al.*, 1988; McCarthy & Kuh, 1997). When institutions that offer only licensure courses are also considered, the proportion of school leaders prepared by institutions with limited or no doctoral offerings increases significantly.

The nearly universal "one best model" of leadership preparation is "state controlled, closed to nonteachers, credit-driven, and certification-bound" (Cooper & Boyd,

1988, p. 251). Despite recommendations of the NCEEA (1987) and the NPBEA (1989) to restrict preparation of school leaders to the doctoral level, master's programs have not been eliminated. Indeed, the master's remains the most popular educational leadership graduate degree, and the percentage of units offering master's degrees (between 90% and 92% of all units with educational leadership graduate degrees) has fluctuated very little during the past two decades. It is understandable that institutions are hesitant to eliminate master's degrees and licensure programs because of the revenue they generate. Although the proportion of units offering doctoral degrees has remained relatively stable for more than a decade, fewer units offered the Education Specialist (Ed.S.) degree in 1994 than in 1986. The number of Ed.S. degree programs expanded dramatically from 1960 until the mid-1980s, when 52% of the educational leadership units offering graduate degrees had Ed.S. programs (McCarthy *et al.*, 1988), but only about two-fifths of the units offered this degree by 1994 (McCarthy & Kuh, 1997).

Within degree programs, structural components have reflected considerable continuity over time. For example, since the 1970s most educational leadership doctoral programs have included a specified number of required courses in educational administration/leadership, written and oral qualifying exams, a dissertation, possibly an internship, and often a campus residency requirement (Hackmann & Price, 1995; Silver & Spuck, 1978; Farquhar, 1977). McLaughlin and Moore (1990) reported that the 17 new educational leadership Ed.D. programs initiated during the 1980s were very much like their predecessors in that they followed traditional patterns in curriculum, structure, admissions, and course delivery. In many units, doctoral degrees are simply placed on top of master's degrees. The two degrees often are indistinguishable in terms of methods of instruction and types of learning activities, and they differ only in a few additional course requirements, the dissertation, and perhaps a residency requirement for the doctorate (Davis & Spuck, 1978; Pitner, 1988).

Several studies have documented that educational leadership units are reluctant to engage in substantial programmatic transformations. In a major study of educational leadership preparation programs conducted in 1975–76, Silver and Spuck (1978) found little evidence of "radical departures from the norm" in program components from the 1960s to the mid-1970s (p. 193), nor did they find signs of any dramatic changes on the horizon. More recent studies have similarly characterized changes in educational leadership programs as incremental. Murphy (1991) reported that the education reform activities of the 1980s had little effect on leadership preparation programs by the end of the decade, falling far short of calls for "comprehensive and radical reform" (p. 52). Pohland and Carlson (1993) subsequently found incremental changes in educational leadership programs but little evidence of dramatic departures from traditional program components or delivery systems. Despite the sincere efforts of various reformers, some commentators contend that most leadership preparation programs remain in the 1990s much as they were a decade or even longer ago (Duke, 1992; Thomson, 1993).

Focus and Content of the Curriculum

Mirroring the continuity in degree offerings and components of preparation programs, the array of courses offered by most educational leadership units has been relatively stable for several decades. Yet there are recent signs that some units are beginning to incorporate content grounded in new perspectives on leadership and that these changes may eventually influence the curriculum of programs nationally.

Reliance on the Social Sciences

In the 1950s, substantial criticism was directed toward the practice of recruiting educational administration professors from the ranks of practitioners who, drawing on their experience, taught predominantly by "personal success stories and lively anecdotes" (Marland, 1960, p. 25) and who had little interest in research or theory building (Hills, 1965). Those trying to reform leadership preparation shifted their attention to expanding the knowledge base in the field, drawing heavily on the social sciences (Getzels, 1977; Griffiths, 1964). This effort was part of a larger movement to infuse the social sciences into the curriculum throughout schools and colleges of education.

The quest for a science of school administration stimulated a decade (1947–1957) of great ferment in the field (Culbertson, 1965; Murphy, 1993b). Even though most activity during the height of the so-called theory movement was concentrated at a few universities and involved a small circle of researchers, the movement's focus on the social sciences eventually affected the curriculum and faculty hiring practices of many administrative preparation programs. In 1977, Farquhar asserted that this incorporation of content grounded in the social sciences was the most significant improvement in preparation programs during the preceding quarter century (see also Greenfield, 1975). Educational leadership faculty members' regard for the value of theory, emphasis on theory in coursework, and support for hiring discipline-based scholars (rather than practitioners) as faculty colleagues crested in the early 1980s (Miklos, 1983; Newell & Morgan, 1980; Nagle & Nagle, 1978). In 1983, Miklos observed that "the relevance of the social sciences to the preparation of administrators is generally acknowledged by those who conceive of the practice of administration as something more than the execution of technical tasks" (p. 159).

During the past decade, however, there has been a sharp decline in faculty support for the utility of theory

(McCarthy & Kuh, 1997). Murphy (1990) observed that a major force contributing to calls for reform in educational leadership units has been increasing disillusionment with the usefulness of the theory movement and the social sciences frameworks, particularly an "overemphasis on the hypothetico-deductive approach and the concomitant failure to stress inductive approaches and to use qualitative lenses to examine organizational phenomena" (p. 284).

Another central criticism of preparation programs grounded in the social sciences has been that course content gives insufficient attention to curriculum, instruction, and learning and to linkages between preparation and practice (what administrators do on the job). Griffiths (1988) opined that theory and research borrowed from the social sciences "never evolved into a unique knowledge base informing the practice of school administration" and that "the attempt by professional educators to develop a pseudo-arts and science degree has been met with scorn in most universities" (pp. 18–19). Among other criticisms of preparation programs during the last decade have been assertions that courses are not rigorous enough, that the content is boring and outdated, and that courses lack cohesion and grounding in principles of cognition or leadership (Murphy, 1993b; National Governors Association, 1990; Van Berkum, Richardson, & Lane, 1994).

Similarities in Course Offerings Since the 1960s

Despite the increasing disillusionment with the social sciences framework to guide leadership preparation, patterns are difficult to change. Educational leadership course titles, and in many instances the topical areas addressed within courses, have remained essentially the same for several decades. Griffiths (1966) noted in the mid-1960s that doctoral programs followed the traditional structure of a core of basic courses in educational organization and administration, curriculum, supervision, school finance, school law, research, educational psychology, history and philosophy of education, school plant, and personnel. This description still applies to many programs in the 1990s. Pohland and Carlson (1993) reported that the most popular topical emphases in graduate programs noted by Davis and Spuck (1978) in 1976 (administrative theory, leadership, educational law, decision making, school district administration, business finance/budgeting, organizational development, and school-community relations) were consistent with the content areas most commonly covered in educational leadership programs in 1993.

Studies also have found little distinction in course offerings between Ed.D. and Ph.D. degrees in educational leadership (Davis & Spuck, 1978; Pitner, 1988). Norton (1992) reported that the most prevalent courses in Ph.D. programs were school law, education policy, education finance, personnel administration, and administrative theory. This list was quite similar for Ed.D. students, except that policy courses were not among the five most popular, while leadership courses were.

The NPBEA (1989) recommended that the curriculum of leadership preparation programs focus on societal and cultural influences on schooling, teaching and learning processes and school improvement, organizational theory, methodologies of organizational studies and policy analysis, leadership and management processes and functions, policy studies and politics of education, and the moral and ethical dimensions of schooling. However, only two of these content areas—leadership and organizational theory—were among the seven most frequently reported content specializations of faculty members in 1994 (McCarthy & Kuh, 1997). Faculty most often listed leadership, law, organizational theory, the principalship, economics and finance, and supervision of instruction as their primary areas of specialization (see also Flanigan & Richardson, 1992).

In general, faculty teach what they know; thus, faculty specializations influence program emphases. Content specializations of faculty members in the 1990s for the most part mirror traditional course areas included in leadership preparation programs (McCarthy & Kuh, 1997; Norton, 1992; Pohland & Carlson, 1993). Faculty often are hired to cover courses in particular areas; therefore, they may resist dramatic programmatic changes that would cause them to lose their instructional niche.

The continuity in course offerings also can be explained in part by the strong influence that state licensure requirements exert on what is emphasized in the educational leadership curriculum. Courses in specified areas are required for individuals to be licensed as school administrators, and securing exemptions from such requirements for graduates of particular programs often is a cumbersome process. Licensure requirements for school administrators have remained strikingly similar across states and have helped to keep the "one best model" of leadership preparation entrenched (Cooper & Boyd, 1988).

Of course, the similarity over time in course titles, topics emphasized, and areas of faculty expertise does not mean that the content of individual courses has remained the same. Content has likely been updated, and there may have been changes in the emphasis placed on particular topics. Also, it is possible that the similarities in course titles mask more substantive content changes. Because getting new courses approved by university graduate schools often is a time-consuming process, one way to circumvent the process is to offer new content under old course names.

Curriculum Revisions in the 1990s
Although the majority of educational leadership programs have remained relatively unchanged, a few units (primarily those involved in one of the two Danforth Foundation initiatives) have radically redesigned the content of their preparation programs based on a concept of leadership that shifts the focus from plant manager to educational leader. In the managerial paradigm, which was prevalent across educational leadership preparation programs until the mid–1980s and is still dominant in many units, administrators are trained "not to challenge the status quo, but to maintain it, not to reconceptualize schools but to reproduce them" (Cambron-McCabe, et al., 1991, p. 4). Accordingly, preparation programs have been grounded in "empiricism, predictability, and scientific certainty" (Cooper & Boyd, 1988, P. 252). New roles and responsibilities of school administrators have in part provided the impetus for moving away from the managerial paradigm. With decentralization of many school districts, more authority has shifted to school sites. School-based management, shared governance, team leadership, and other reforms call for school leaders to become facilitators, mentors, and coaches (Danforth Foundation, 1987). These new roles require preparation that emphasizes curriculum and instruction, teaching and learning, the social context of education, school culture, and values (Case, Lanier, & Miskel, 1986; Murphy, 1993c; Shibles, 1988; Schmuck, 1992). According to Crews and Weakley (1995), leadership preparation, in contrast to management training, emphasizes "decision making, problem solving, team building, goal setting, encouraging innovation, self-assessment, delegating, and conflict resolution—all aimed at developing leaders who motivate people to bring about improvements in the organization" (p.7). The new view of leadership focuses on the centrality of student learning (Cambron-McCabe, 1993; Wilson, 1993).

In 1994, heads of educational leadership units were asked to identify topics that were receiving more attention in the curriculum as compared with a decade earlier. About one-fifth of the respondents listed new concepts of leadership, and the only other item that received as many notations was the use of technology (McCarthy & Kuh, 1997). A study of the 22 educational leadership units involved in the Danforth Foundation's principal preparation program revealed that 90% of the program facilitators rated "leadership" as the most important content area in their programs (Cordeiro et al., 1993). However, a new concept of leadership, distinct from school management, may not be as clearly delineated or as widely endorsed in preparation programs as the rhetoric suggests.

Often mentioned as essential in redesigning the curriculum is a common vision of what constitutes desirable leadership preparation and a sense of community among faculty and students who are striving toward common objectives (Bennis & Nanus, 1985; Geltner & Ditzhazy, 1994; Milstein et al., 1993; Reitzug, 1989; Murphy, 1993c). For example, educational leadership faculty members at Northern Colorado University agreed on seven nonnegotiable core values to guide curriculum development when they undertook a major revision of their leadership preparation program (Daresh & Barnett, 1993). Identification of a core set of values to guide reform efforts also has been considered a prerequisite to major curricular transformations at other institutions such as East Tennessee State University, Hofstra University, Miami University, the University of Michigan, and the University of Washington (Cambron-McCabe, 1993; Geltner & Ditzhazy, 1994; Gresso, Burkett, & Smith, 1993; Shakeshaft, 1993; Sirotnik & Mueller, 1993). In several of these units, faculty also are asking graduate students to explore their own visions of schooling and leadership by developing and continually refining personal platforms (Barnett, 1992).

There has been considerable debate during the past decade regarding the nature of the core knowledge base on which the curriculum is built. Two major projects in the 1990s sponsored by the NPBEA and UCEA attempted to articulate the knowledge and skill base for school leaders (see Hoy, 1994; Thomson, 1993). The preface of the NPBEA compendium covering 21 domains asserts that "the knowledge and skill base of a profession should provide a platform for practice" and "must address core professional responsibilities so that persons qualifying for practice can fulfill the essential tasks of the profession in various contexts" (Thomson, 1993, p. ix). Some scholars have debated the orientation of these projects and whether they give sufficient attention to diverse perspectives, and a few have even questioned the wisdom of attempting to explicate the knowledge base at all (Bartell, 1994; Donmoyer, 1995; Gosetti & Rusch, 1994; Scheurich & Laible, 1995). Wilson (1993) has asserted that since "the learner must construct knowledge for him- or herself" and be actively engaged in the process, efforts to articulate a knowledge base using old frameworks are misguided (p. 223).

A few units have shifted the focus of the curriculum from a positivist to a constructivist paradigm, emphasizing multiple perspectives to address complex school issues that include some traditionally excluded perspectives (such as feminist views) (Achilles, 1994; Cambron-McCabe & Foster, 1994; Milstein et al., 1993; Murphy, 1993c). The professor is no longer viewed as the one with expertise and the dispenser of knowledge to students. An asserted advantage of this shift is that the constructivist paradigm empowers the learner by changing the focus from teaching to learning and from consuming knowledge to creating it (Schmuck, 1992; Wilson, 1993). Also, students are being encouraged to pursue a variety of approaches in conducting research. Qualitative research strategies have steadily gained popularity since the 1980s, so findings from qualitative studies have been given more prominence throughout the curriculum in educational leadership programs (McCarthy & Kuh, 1997).

Many of the redesigned programs give greater emphasis to the foundations of education in their core experiences than do traditional programs, and they give far less atten-

tion to technical topics such as management of school facilities (Cambron-McCabe, 1993; McCarthy & Kuh, 1997; Shakeshaft, 1993). As Cambron-McCabe (1993) has observed, the positivist/functionalist paradigm deflected attention away "from moral questions related to purpose and values," whereas the new paradigm moves the "social and cultural context of schools to center stage" (p. 161). Reconstructed programs also usually give more attention to cultural diversity and social activism (Maniloff & Clark, 1993; Murphy, 1993c).

An emphasis on ethics is particularly noteworthy across programs reporting major curricular redesigns; most of these programs include seminars or courses on ethics in the core experiences for students. And the interest in ethics extends beyond programs that have undergone a significant transformation. In contrast to Farquhar's (1981) findings that little attention was being given to ethical issues in UCEA leadership preparation programs in the late 1970s, by the 1990s most UCEA programs were addressing ethics to some extent through incorporation in traditional courses or the creation of special seminars, units, or courses focusing on ethical concerns (Beck & Murphy, 1994; Murphy, 1993b). Indeed, increased emphasis on ethics received widespread support among educational leadership faculty surveyed in 1994, and unit heads reported that the expansion of ethics instruction was a major curricular change in their programs within the preceding decade (McCarthy & Kuh, 1997).

In most of the redesigned programs, the traditional potpourri of disconnected courses has been replaced with a more coherent curriculum that the faculty members have jointly planned (Daresh, 1994). In these programs, all students generally take an identified substantive core of courses in cohort groups (Milstein et al., 1993; Murphy, 1993c).

Pedagogy

As noted previously, anecdote and prescription dominated educational leadership preparation until the 1960s. Although the content emphasis began to shift to the social sciences, no significant attention was given to pedagogy throughout the 1970s and early 1980s. There were a few exceptions, such as the Center for Advancing Principalship Excellence at the University of Illinois that experimented with case studies and "learning-in-action," thereby incorporating opportunities for administrators to learn as they reflected on their own actions (Silver, 1987). Also during this period, some individual faculty members used in-basket exercises and simulations, but the lecture method remained dominant (Murphy, 1992).

Consistent with a recent national trend across academe (Barr & Tagg, 1995), some educational leadership faculty members are urging a pedagogical shift from faculty-centered to student-centered approaches that actively involve students in the learning process, eliminate student anonymity, and personalize instruction. They are encouraging the use of inductive, problem-based strategies that are grounded in adult learning theory and the reality of schools (Bridges, 1992; Collet, 1989; Hallinger & McCary, 1991; Mulford, 1985; Murphy, 1992; Shibles, 1988). As noted in the previous section, this shift affects the substance of the curriculum as well as the pedagogy. In several redesigned programs, faculty members involve graduate students in defining problems and designing strategies for solutions, and they provide opportunities for students to engage in collaborative research (Milstein *et al.*, 1993; Murphy, 1993a; Schmuck, 1992; Shibles, 1988). Also common in redesigned programs are reflective seminars in which students explore values that guide decisions and apply multiple perspectives to assess the complexities of various courses of action (in other words, reflection in action, Schön, 1987). A few units are shifting away from traditional three-credit courses to modules and seminars, but university bureaucracies often pose barriers to such changes in course structure and faculty loads (Sirotnik & Mueller, 1993).

Several of the most prevalent recent changes in educational leadership programs, while structural in nature, reflect more fundamental shifts in program orientation. For example, many units admit students to degree programs in cohort groups. Cohorts provide support systems and foster a sense of community among students and faculty; in the K—12 context, such community building has become an important part of a school leader's role (Yerkes, Basom, Norris, & Barnett, 1995). Norris and Barnett (1994) have asserted that the cohort structure by itself is not a major innovation unless used as a laboratory "in which collaborative leadership can be examined and refined" (p. 2). After studying 51 students who were involved in cohort groups at four universities, they concluded that cohort groups assist individuals in understanding the benefits of dynamic interactions in a community of learners; as the group is strengthened, the individual's development is also enhanced. In 1995, the Center for the Study of Preparation Programs reported that half of the UCEA units used cohorts at the master's level and 80% used them at the doctoral level (Norton, 1995). In a study that included non-UCEA as well as UCEA programs, McCarthy and Kuh (1997) reported that half of the educational leadership Ed.D. students and one-fourth of the Ph.D. and master's students were enrolled in cohort groups in 1994.

A few units have implemented team approaches to instruction (Shakeshaft, 1993). As with cohorts, this might be viewed as a structural change, but it also reflects a willingness to engage in collaborative activities. It often provides a model of team leadership, which is considered increasingly important in K—12 settings. Daresh and Barnett (1993) have asserted that leaders in schools are more likely to emulate co-operation and collegiality if preparation programs emphasize these values. Others have observed that faculty should be learners along with their students and model "a learning organization" (Gresso, Burkett, & Smith, 1993, p. 119).

Some recent pedagogical changes have been prompted by economic and market conditions. For example, distance learning is being used in an increasing number of graduate programs. In 1994, educational leadership unit heads listed "technology" more than any other item as the most significant pedagogical change in their units within the preceding decade (McCarthy & Kuh, 1997). Also, to accommodate students who hold full-time jobs, some educational leadership units are adopting alternative course formats (such as weekend programs) in lieu of traditional residency on campus (Hackmann & Price, 1995).

Field Connections

Because educational leadership has always been an applied area of graduate study, connections with the field traditionally have been important. However, the nature of these connections has changed over time. Until the 1960s, faculty members preparing school leaders generally felt more allegiance toward practitioners and practitioner organizations than to academe and knowledge production. As a result, many educational leadership students who moved into the professorial ranks had been socialized to be practitioners, not academics.

In the 1960s and 1970s, with the focus on the social sciences and hiring discipline-based faculty, interest in promoting practical experiences for students declined. Fewer than 12% of faculty members surveyed in the mid-1970s anticipated an increased emphasis on clinical experiences (Silver & Spuck, 1978). But, as noted previously, by the mid-1980s, serious concerns were being raised about the relevance of educational leadership preparation to the real world of schools, the large number of faculty without experience as school administrators, and the lack of opportunities for prospective administrators to apply theoretical knowledge to practice (Foster, 1988; Greenfield, 1988).

At one level, it may appear that educational leadership units have come full circle with the renewed emphasis on connections with the field, but this is not actually the case. Field connections recommended in the 1990s differ significantly from practices in the 1950s, when theory and research were downplayed (Sergiovanni, 1991). The NPBEA, professional associations, and champions of preparation program reform are pressing for field-based instruction that applies research to problems faced on the job and brings practitioners and researchers together to seek solutions. They propose that multiple perspectives be used to address problems of practice and that clinical experiences (internships, practica, field-based research) be interwoven throughout leadership preparation, not delayed until course work is completed as in traditional programs. The current interest in strengthening field connections in educational leadership units parallels efforts in teacher education programs to tighten university connections with schools (Goodlad, 1994; Sizer, 1988, 1991).

Calls for an expansion of field connections have been heeded in some educational leadership units; program heads as well as individual faculty members in 1994 noted the increase in the number and types of connections with the field among the most significant recent developments in their units. Renewed commitment in this regard also is reflected in faculty hiring patterns. Whereas about one-third of all educational leadership faculty members in 1994 had been school administrators, almost half of those hired within the prior five years had such experience. Also, as a group, newly hired faculty with administrative experience indicated greater interest in problems of practice than did their peers without such experience. Whereas faculty in 1972 considered "a more extensive knowledge base" the most critical need in the profession, and 1986 respondents ranked "curriculum reform" first, the largest proportion of the 1994 cohort felt that "more attention to problems of practice" was the most pressing need. Also, more than four-fifths of the faculty respondents in 1994 indicated that service to school districts and the state should be valued more highly by universities (McCarthy & Kuh, 1997).

University norms, however, are difficult to change. "Academe has always valued discovery more than application of knowledge;" research universities especially "have not given high status to applied research and have relegated field-based and other outreach activities to a distant third tier in the reward system" (McCarthy & Kuh, 1997, p. 253). Clark (1989) observed that with every passing decade universities have become more committed to rewarding academics on the basis of research and published scholarship. Educational leadership faculty members often feel a tension in that they are urged to become more connected with the field, but there is little evidence that institutions of higher education are embracing an expanded definition of research to recognize field-based projects, as proposed by Ernest Boyer (1990). Junior faculty members who heed advice to engage in outreach activities and applied research may be at risk of not surviving in academe.

Characteristics, Activities, and Attitudes of Faculty Members

Several studies have tracked the characteristics, activities, and attitudes of educational leadership faculty members since the mid-1960s. Hills (1965) surveyed 150 NCPEA members in 1964 and concluded that most faculty members were not involved in research or interdisciplinary ac-

tivity. He found that the majority of educational leadership faculty members were generalists, 90% had been practitioners prior to joining academe, and their heavy emphasis on teaching and service activities precluded meaningful involvement in research.

Campbell and Newell (1973) subsequently surveyed the educational leadership professoriate in the United States and Canada and found that faculty members in 1972 were overwhelmingly male, Caucasian, Protestant, and of rural origin. In general, they were very satisfied with their roles and complacent about problems in preparation programs or the field. Most had received their doctorates from about 20 prestigious universities, and a higher proportion was involved in research than had been the case in the mid-1960s. In a follow-up study, Newell and Morgan (1980) surveyed a sample of faculty and documented an increase between 1972 and 1980 in faculty members' respect for theory, commitment to research, and belief that discipline-based scholars make the best educational leadership faculty members.

The educational leadership professoriate during the 1970s and early 1980s became increasing specialized; faculty identified with subfields, such as law, finance, and politics (Boyan, 1981). Moreover, new faculty hires were less likely to have served as school administrators than in the 1950s and 1960s. The small group of knowledge producers with a common heritage and shared perspectives no longer dominated the educational leadership professoriate (McCarthy & Kuh, 1997). Professors had traditionally participated in AASA, but this organization became more practitioner-oriented and raised dues above what many professors were amenable to pay (Achilles, 1994). Perhaps this in part stimulated the growth of specialized professional organizations, such as the American Education Finance Association, the Education Law Association (formerly the National Organization on Legal Problems of Education), and the Politics of Education Association, which increasingly provided reference groups for educational leadership professors (McCarthy & Kuh, 1997). Murphy (1993b) observed that by the early 1980s, the typical educational leadership faculty member was "concerned primarily with the professorial (if not scholarly) aspects of the profession" (p. 7).

A 1986 study, replicating in part the Campbell and Newell study, reported a decrease in the number of full-time faculty in many educational leadership programs since the mid-1970s and predicted substantial turnover in the educational leadership professoriate by the year 2000 (McCarthy *et al.*, 1988). About three-fifths of the units offering educational administration graduate degrees were located at universities with limited or no doctoral programs. As in earlier studies, faculty members in 1986 generally were satisfied with their positions and complacent about problems in preparation programs and the field. The professoriate was top heavy with tenured full professors, and faculty no longer had received their doctorates from a handful of research universities.

The most recent large-scale study of the educational leadership professoriate was conducted in 1994 (McCarthy & Kuh, 1997). Educational leadership units did not differ as significantly by type of institution and UCEA affiliation as had been the case in 1986 in terms of unit size, faculty commitment to research, and other characteristics. Also, the educational leadership professoriate was grayer in the mid-1990s than previously; the mean age increased from 48 in 1972 to 54 in 1994. New faculty in 1994 (those hired within the preceding five years) were older upon entering the professoriate and more likely to have been school administrators compared with their senior colleagues.

The most significant shift in the educational leadership professoriate since the early 1970s has been the change in gender composition. Between 1972 and 1994 the percentage of women increased tenfold, from 2% to 20% (Campbell & Newell, 1973; McCarthy & Kuh, 1997). In 1994, women constituted almost two-fifths (39%) of the faculty members hired within the preceding five years (new hires), but the gender distribution of educational leadership faculties was not uniform across types of institutions. Indeed, in 1994, more than half of the new hires at research and UCEA programs were women.[4] It is possible that female professors soon will dominate educational leadership units at these institutions and "will become the primary knowledge producers and set the inquiry agenda for the educational leadership profession as males did in earlier decades" (McCarthy & Kuh, 1997, p. 256).

Until the 1990s, educational units appeared inhospitable toward women. For example, in 1986, women were not paid as well and were less satisfied with their jobs, compared with their male counterparts (McCarthy et al., 1988). But by 1994 this had changed; women were more satisfied with their roles and the quality of their preparation programs than they had been in the mid-1980s. Also, there were no significant differences between men and women as to job satisfaction in 1994, and gender-based salary differentials had disappeared. McCarthy and Kuh (1997) observed that in recent years

> women have assumed leadership roles in their institutions, which puts them in positions to influence faculty hires, components of the curriculum, teaching loads, program reform, student recruitment, and so forth. Women also are exerting leadership at the national level. Since the late 1980s, women have been well represented among the leaders of UCEA, NCPEA, Division A of the American Educational Research Association, and specialized organizations that focus on law, finance, and politics of education (p. 255).

Given the gender-based differences in faculty members' activities and attitudes documented in the mid-1980s (McCarthy et al., 1988), it was expected that the presence of more women faculty by the mid-1990s would result in overall changes in the culture of the educational leadership professoriate. In short, the higher levels of satisfaction among female faculty members in the 1990s would be attributed to changes in the environment. However, this prediction has not materialized. Between 1986 and 1994, gender-based content specializations were reduced, and the attitudes of women and men toward the field and toward problems in the profession converged, with women's attitudes becoming more closely aligned with those of men. Instead of women changing the overall culture, it appears that they have adopted the dominant values and beliefs (McCarthy & Kuh, 1997). Moreover, gender-based attitude differences were less pronounced in the 1994 new faculty group than they had been in the 1986 new faculty cohort. This is somewhat disheartening for those who had expected new faculty, who are disproportionately women, to bring fresh perspectives to teaching and research in the field.

Whereas in 1972 female representation and minority representation among faculty members in educational leadership units were similarly dismal (2% and 3% respectively), the recent dramatic gains made by women in the professoriate unfortunately have not been realized for people of color. In 1994, only 11% of the educational leadership faculty members were people of color. Unlike the steady increase in hiring women, in 1994, minority representation was lower among faculty hired in the preceding five years (10%) than among faculty hired six to 10 years earlier (15%). This finding is troublesome because racial diversity is essential among school leaders and those preparing them to effectively meet the challenges of the changing demographics in our nation's schools (McCarthy & Kuh, 1997).

In recent years, educational leadership units have experienced substantial faculty turnover, as faculty hired during the 1960s (when programs across academe were expanding at a phenomenal rate) have reached retirement age. Program heads in 1986 reported that 57% of the faculty members across units had been hired within the past decade (McCarthy et al., 1988), and heads in 1994 reported that 63% of the faculty had been hired in the preceding 10 years (McCarthy & Kuh, 1997). However, some of the faculty members hired during these periods were not new to academe in that they were previously employed at other universities. To illustrate, whereas two-fifths of the educational leadership faculty members in 1994 indicated that they had joined the professoriate within the preceding decade, program heads reported that more than three-fifths of the faculty had been employed in their units less than 10 years.

Given the mean age of faculty members and their anticipated retirement dates, continued faculty turnover can be expected into the twenty-first century. But an adequate supply of new faculty members to replenish professorial ranks is not assured. Since the 1970s, there has been a steady decline in the number of educational leadership units that place an emphasis on preparing individuals for the professorship (McCarthy & Kuh, 1997), and it is increasingly difficult to motivate doctoral students to consider careers in academe when they can earn substantially more in entry-level administrative roles at the K–12 level.

Salaries of educational leadership faculty members compared favorably with those of faculty members in other academic units in the mid-1980s, but this was not the case by the mid-1990s. According to the National Survey of Postsecondary Faculty (1993), faculty across disciplines made $7,000 more than educational leadership faculty members in 1993. However, as noted previously, gender-based salary discrepancies documented in the 1980s (McCarthy et al., 1988; Pounder, 1989) had been eliminated by 1994 (McCarthy & Kuh, 1997).

Many faculty attitudes about the field and professoriate were similar across the 1972, 1986, and 1994 studies; indeed, during the past quarter century demographic characteristics of educational leadership faculty have changed more than have their attitudes and job satisfaction (Campbell & Newell, 1973; McCarthy et al., 1988; McCarthy & Kuh, 1997). In all three cohorts, respondents indicated that the most enjoyable aspect of the professorial role was teaching graduate students, and faculty devoted the largest proportion of their time to teaching and advising graduate students. The most widely read periodical remained the *Kappan*, a practitioner-oriented journal. The percentage of faculty involved in research steadily increased from 71% in 1972 to 85% in 1994. Data were gathered on faculty members' most important professional associations in 1986 and 1994, and in both studies, the first choice of the largest percentage of faculty was the American Educational Research Association (AERA).

Although in 1994, faculty continued to rate very few items as serious problems in their profession, at least half of this cohort felt that the small number of minorities in the profession and the lack of financial support for graduate students were rather or very serious problems. Other noteworthy changes since 1980 have been a steady and significant increase in faculty interest in qualitative research methods and a decrease in support for the statement that more of the literature should be theory-based. Also, faculty in 1994 were less likely than colleagues in the 1986 cohort to specialize in organizational theory. As discussed previously, between the mid-1980s and mid-1990s faculty became more interested in strengthening connections with practitioners and adding field-based components to leadership preparation (McCarthy & Kuh, 1997).

Characteristics, Recruitment, and Assessment of Students

Educational leadership graduate students have not been studied as frequently or as systematically as faculty members. A few national studies in the 1970s focused on selected student characteristics, but recent data on educational leadership students have not been collected across units.

Davis and Spuck (1978) reported that in 1976 more than two-fifths of educational leadership master's students were enrolled at the same institutions where they received their undergraduate degrees, and about three out of 10 doctoral students were enrolled at their undergraduate institutions. The majority of master's students and more than two-fifths of doctoral students lived within 25 miles of the university they were attending. Minority students comprised 18% of master's, 23% of Ed.D., and 16% of Ph.D. students, whereas women comprised 31% of master's, 24% of Ed.D., and 23% of Ph.D. students. These percentages may in part reflect the availability in the early 1970s of considerable federal support for fellowships to increase diversity among graduate students (Scribner, 1973).

In a 1978 study of educational administration doctoral students enrolled in 62 universities in the United States and Canada, the mean age of the students was 37, 80% were married, and 29% were women (McCarthy, Kuh, & Beckman, 1979). The doctoral students' most frequently reported undergraduate majors were secondary or elementary education; about one-fourth had degrees in one of these two areas, and 45% had some type of education undergraduate degrees. One-third had master's degrees in educational administration, and almost four-fifths had master's degrees in education-related fields. Eighty-five percent had been classroom teachers, and four-fifths aspired to administrative roles upon degree completion. The doctoral students were most likely to read practitioner-oriented journals (*Kappan, NASSP Bulletin, Educational Leadership*). Female students exhibited greater appreciation of and interest in inquiry than did males (Kuh & McCarthy, 1980). Also, students were more interested in research if they held research assistantships, read more journals, had less administrative experience, or had conducted original research other than the dissertation. However, students' affinity for research was not associated with whether their doctoral institution was a research university. This unexpected finding can probably be attributed to the fact that educational leadership students select their graduate programs primarily for geographic accessibility, not for the program's reputation in knowledge production.

Although many individual units maintain records on the characteristics of their own educational leadership graduate students, such data have not been gathered across institutions as they have for faculty members. The few units that have published descriptions of their preparation program reforms in the 1990s, however, consistently have noted that at least half of their master's and doctoral students are women and at least one-fifth are racial minorities (Milstein et al., 1993; Murphy, 1993a). Indeed, case studies of five of the educational leadership units offering the Danforth Foundation principal preparation program documented that females far outnumbered males in the student cohorts; between 63% and 85% of the students in these five programs were women. Minorities represented between 21% and 33% of the students (Milstein *et al.*, 1993). Furthermore, women and people of color have been well represented among students participating in recent doctoral student seminars at the AERA and UCEA annual meetings. Thus although not confirmed by national studies, it seems clear that there has been a dramatic increase in female representation among educational leadership students since the 1970s. The increase has not been as significant for people of color, but minority representation among educational leadership graduate students appears to be far higher than minority representation among faculty. Units that have redesigned their preparation programs have given more attention to marketing strategies to increase student diversity, but still less than 30 percent of the educational leadership doctoral programs have specific procedures to recruit students from underrepresented groups (Hackmann & Price, 1995).

The number of units requiring students to complete a period of residency on campus has remained quite stable for the past two decades. In 1978, 83% of the educational leadership doctoral students were required to complete some type of residency on campus (McCarthy, Kuh, & Beckman, 1979), and in 1994, 84% of the Ph.D. programs and 78% of the Ed.D. programs had residency requirements (McCarthy & Kuh, 1997). In 1994, about one-fifth of the master's degree programs, where the majority of school leaders are prepared, had residency requirements. These data must be interpreted with caution because the definition of "residency" and the experiences students are expected to have during their residency period vary across educational leadership units, as do restrictions on whether students must be full-time students or can complete their residency while continuing to work off campus. There appears to be a trend toward cohort group involvement in a cohesive graduate program that provides many of the benefits of intensive study, even though participants continue to work full time (Clark, 1997).

The NPBEA's (1989) recommendation that students engage in full-time graduate study appears to have been unrealistic. Without specific state appropriations to support graduate students in educational leadership programs, a limited number of graduate assistantships are available and the level of financial remuneration associated with such appointments is inadequate to support mid-career students with families and other financial obligations. Therefore, most graduate students across educational leadership degree programs continue to be commuters who pursue their degrees on a part-time basis (Davis & Spuck, 1978; Flanigan & Richardson, 1992; McCarthy & Kuh, 1997). Evening and summer classes have remained the dominant delivery structure (Hackmann & Price, 1995).

In a 1994 study of educational leadership doctoral programs, Hackmann and Price (1995) reported that the typical doctoral program admitted 18 students annually and generally required Graduate Record Examination (GRE) scores totaling 1000 on the verbal and quantitative subtests. Other common admission requirements entailed a 3.00 undergraduate grade point average (GPA) and a 3.25 graduate GPA, a personal interview, and a writing sample including a personal statement of goals. The majority of programs used the GRE (58%), although one-third used instead the Miller's Analogies Test. More than half of the units (52%) required applicants to have prior teaching experience, but only 27% required prior administrative experience.

Although calls for reform in leadership preparation consistently emphasize the need for more rigorous admission standards, recruitment of highly talented students has been a persistent problem (Achilles, 1984; Gerritz, Koppich, & Guthrie, 1984; Murphy, 1990; Shibles, 1988). Murphy (1993c) has chronicled the widespread perception that "professors and programs trade off academic integrity and rigor for student enrollment and compliant behavior" (p. 227). Rejection rates remain low at all educational leadership degree levels (Murphy, 1990), and Jacobson (1990) has lamented that "for too many administrator preparation programs, any body is better than no body" (p. 35).

Graduate students majoring in educational administration/leadership score poorly on the GRE in comparison with students majoring in other areas. In the mid-1980s, students marking educational administration as their intended major ranked fourth from the bottom in GRE scores among the 94 majors listed in the *Graduate Record Examinations: 1985–86 Guide to the Use of Scores* (see Griffiths, 1988). The situation has not improved since then. In the *1996–97 Guide*, school administration students again were close to the bottom. They ranked above only home economics compared with 40 other majors outside education. Compared to nine other education majors, school administration students ranked above only early childhood education.

Some units, however, have recently altered their admission practices in an attempt to be more selective. For example, some have experimented with variations of the NASSP assessment center process in admitting students to educational leadership graduate programs (Collet, 1989; Milstein & Krueger, 1993). Others that have implemented innovative degree programs have pursued cooperative arrangements in which school districts nominate exemplary teachers with leadership potential (Bridges, 1993; Ogawa & Pounder, 1993). Candidate interviews and personal statements also are important considerations during the screening process in most units with redesigned preparation programs (Murphy, 1993a).

Educational leadership units have been criticized not only for their nonselective admission criteria, but also for their failure to monitor adequately student progress (Hawley, 1988). Perhaps the lack of rigor in selection and assessment practices should not be surprising given that educational leadership faculty members consistently have voiced little concern about admission or graduation standards or the caliber of their students. Indeed, the percentage of faculty members indicating that competency standards for students was a very or rather serious problem dropped from one-third of the faculty in 1972 (Campbell & Newell, 1973) to less than one-fifth of the faculty in 1994 (McCarthy & Kuh, 1997). Also, faculty were more likely to be satisfied with the caliber of their students in the mid-1990s than in the mid-1980s.

Along with their efforts to strengthen selection criteria, some units are using alternative assessment strategies in an attempt to make student assessment more meaningful. The use of portfolios to evaluate student performance has been gaining popularity in the 1990s (Barnett, 1995; Gresso *et al.*, 1993). These portfolios include materials documenting what an individual has learned over a period of time. They may contain performance assessments of the individual's ability to apply concepts in completing complex tasks, personal reflections, testimonials from instructors and fellow students, and other artifacts that reflect an individual's knowledge and skills. Several units that have significantly redesigned their preparation programs now place more emphasis on student self-assessment and personal reflection (Murphy, 1993c). Of course, recent efforts to establish a national performance-based licensure examination could have an impact on student assessment practices in educational leadership programs. If performance assessments become the norm as a prerequisite to licensure, they are likely to be incorporated in preparation programs as well.

Filling in the Gaps

A number of gaps are apparent in the information available on educational leadership units and preparation programs. Most significantly, there is insufficient research documenting the merits of program components in relation to administrator performance. Do preparation programs actually achieve their asserted purpose of producing effective leaders who create school environments that enhance student learning? Unlike most other nations, the completion of post-baccalaureate coursework is a prerequisite to administrative licensure in the United States. Are American school administrators better leaders because of their graduate programs? Hopefully so, because "graduate training in educational administration is expensive—to individuals, to universities and to society" (Haller, Brent, McNamara, & Rufus, 1994, p. 22). Adequate justification has not been provided for mandatory graduate preparation for one to lead a public school in our nation, even though similar preparation is not required for individuals to lead other

large organizations, agencies, and corporations. Data are needed either to justify the expense of such education or suggest that resources be directed elsewhere.

Various strategies are available to assess the effectiveness of educational leadership preparation programs (such as participant perception studies, analyses of how program graduates apply what they have learned, assessments of relationships between school outcomes and leader preparation). The simplest and most widely used strategy is to gather data from program graduates regarding their perceptions of elements of their programs. Similar perception data can be gathered from faculty members. Educational leadership graduates traditionally have been less positive about their preparation programs than faculty have been (Heller, Conway, & Jacobson, 1988; House, Sommerville, & Zimmer, 1990). However, some recent case studies of redesigned programs have included favorable faculty and student assessments of certain program features, such as student cohort groups, field mentors, problem-based learning, field-based research, and policy-oriented alternatives to traditional dissertations (Clark, 1997; Milstein *et al.*, 1993; Murphy, 1993a; Pounder, 1995; Sirotnik & Mueller, 1993). Such perception studies are useful in determining the level of satisfaction among those directly involved in preparation programs, but testimonials are not sufficient to conclude that particular preparation program features have merit.

A more complicated and less used strategy to evaluate preparation programs involves developing measures of leader effectiveness and relating effectiveness scores to the amount and type of graduate preparation. For example, using a national database (1987–88 School And Staffing Survey [SASS]), Fowler (1991) created a measure of perceived principal effectiveness (PPE) based on teachers' perceptions, and then he related PPE scores to principals' level of education. Disturbingly, he found that principals with only bachelor's degrees had higher effectiveness scores than did their colleagues with master's and doctoral degrees. Fowler cautioned, however, that while the PPE scale had strong internal validity, replication studies with larger samples of teacher respondents from individual schools were needed to substantiate its external validity. Haller and associates (1994) used the same database and developed five indices of school effectiveness from teachers' perceptions. They assessed the amount of graduate education as well as the type of graduate degree (educational administration, other education field, or discipline outside education) and found that graduate preparation in educational administration had little impact on leader effectiveness. Using the 1993–94 SASS database, Zheng (1996) subsequently conducted a multivariate analysis of contextual influences on principals' instructional leadership and found no relationship between the amount of graduate preparation or major and perceived effectiveness of principals as instructional leaders. A few other studies also have failed to find positive correlations between amount of graduate education and administrators' perceived effectiveness (Bauck, 1987; Gross & Herriot, 1965), but these studies have not dealt with the impact of specific elements of the preparation received.

Only recently are evaluation studies beginning to appear in the literature that isolates particular components of preparation programs. For example, Leithwood, Jantzi, Coffin, and Wilson (1996) gathered data from principals, who graduated from nine institutions involved in the Danforth Foundation principalship preparation program, and from teacher colleagues of these graduates. The program graduates were asked about their perceptions of the value of various features of their university preparation in developing effective school administrators, and their colleagues were asked whether the graduates were perceived to be effective leaders. Graduates highly valued their participation in group learning activities, internships, and mentoring experiences. Colleagues agreed that the graduates used effective leadership practices, rating highest the graduates' success in "fostering staff development" and "setting school directions." The authors concluded that the innovative program features in the Danforth program for preparing principals not only were valued by graduates but also enhanced how graduates were viewed by colleagues.

Beyond studies of perceptions of graduates' effectiveness as school leaders, there is meager research relating recent curriculum and pedagogical innovations in preparation programs to administrative success or evaluating administrators' use of knowledge gained in their preparation programs. Such assessments deserve attention, given the significant costs associated with graduate education for school leaders (Haller et al., 1994). Although consensus has not been reached regarding what constitutes administrative effectiveness, there is general agreement that a school leader's impact on student learning is an important consideration. Studies are needed to evaluate the elements of redesigned preparation programs in relation to student performance in schools where the graduates are employed. The profession needs to address whether individuals prepared in redesigned programs, most of which embody common features, function differently and are ultimately more effective in enhancing student learning. Considering the complexities involved in conducting such studies, it is not surprising that the limited assessments of preparation programs to date have been confined primarily to perception data.

It would be instructive to investigate a number of other issues pertaining to pre- and in-service education for school leaders. For example, how do school leaders view professional development activities provided by professional associations, businesses, and government agencies in comparison to university preparation programs? What is the impact of these professional development activities on leader effec-

tiveness as measured by perceptions of colleagues and by student learning? How is technology being used in pre- and in-service education for school leaders, and how should it be used? What entities are likely to be major competitors with universities in providing leadership preparation in the twenty-first century?

Furthermore, it may be enlightening to study preparation programs in other professional fields (such as law or medicine). Although educational leadership units have been encouraged to adopt a professional school model for more than a decade (Griffiths, 1988; NCEEA, 1987; NPBEA, 1989; Teitel, 1996), there is little evidence of substantial movement in this direction. Perhaps systematic investigation of the professional school model would shed some light on why educational leadership units have been reluctant to embrace the concept. Other widely endorsed recommendations (for example, calls for a reduction in the number of preparation programs) that have not been implemented also warrant attention. Indeed, educational leadership reform proposals, including reports of the NCEEA (1987) and the NPBEA (1989), have been surprisingly similar since the 1950s, causing Achilles (1994) to question why our field keeps proposing "refinements of a goal long since set but not yet attained" (p. 18)?

Implications of the increasing homogeneity across educational leadership units also should be studied. Between the mid-1980s and mid-1990s, differences were reduced among units by type of institution (based on the Carnegie Foundation [1994] classification scheme) and by UCEA affiliation along several measures including faculty size, teaching loads, faculty involvement in research, and attitudes toward issues in the field (McCarthy & Kuh, 1997). Is this dissipation of distinctiveness across educational leadership units a positive or negative sign for the field and for the preparation of school leaders?

Additional information is needed about students in educational leadership graduate programs, as they appear to have been routinely overlooked in most studies of units and faculty members. A database on the personal and professional characteristics of educational leadership graduate students would be instructive. What are their backgrounds, visions of schooling, and attitudes toward educational reform? Do student characteristics and beliefs differ by type of institution where enrolled? Do male and female students differ as to professional backgrounds and goals? Have student characteristics changed over time, and if so, how? Why have school leaders often voiced frustration and disappointment with their university preparation programs (see Heller, Conway, & Jacobson, 1988; House, Sommerville, & Zimmer, 1990; Peterson & Finn, 1985)? Do graduates who plan to become faculty members rate their programs more favorably than do aspiring practitioners? To date, no trend data on student characteristics and attitudes across programs are available.

Although more is known about educational leadership faculty than about students, additional studies on educational leadership faculty would also be instructive. Studies are needed to track the research productivity of faculty members and to examine the types of projects they are pursuing and the relative influence of those projects on preparation programs, leadership practices, and the improvement of learning in our nation's schools. Are recently hired faculty more or less likely to receive tenure than was the case for their veteran colleagues? McCarthy and Kuh (1997) have raised several related questions concerning recent hiring trends:

> How will the new group of faculty with practitioner backgrounds affect the structure and content of preparation programs and the nature and quality of research conducted in the field? Are these faculty members likely to embrace service activities and eschew research? Or will they bring new inquiry approaches to bear on field-based problems? What impact on the perceived status of educational leadership units will result from this influx of practice-oriented faculty members (p. 259)?

In addition, more in-depth research is warranted on the effects of the changing gender composition in educational leadership units. What are the implications of the increase in female faculty members and students on the nature of preparation programs, program reform efforts, and school reform in general? Since female educational leadership faculty members are more interested than their male colleagues in research, what impact will this have on knowledge production in the field? Do males and females differ regarding the research topics and methods they pursue, as has been documented in other fields (Bean & Kuh, 1988)?

Moreover, are new perspectives on leadership and the nature of knowledge guiding revisions in preparation programs? What effects are new and emerging schools of thought, such as postmodernism, poststructuralism, feminist theory, and critical theory, having on curriculum development and pedagogy in educational leadership units? Are the most popular texts in the field still grounded in a structural-functionalist, positivist paradigm, or has their orientation shifted to embrace alternative voices (see Gosetti & Rusch, 1994)? Are educational leadership programs at certain types of institutions or in certain locales more likely than others to incorporate multiple perspectives?

Research on educational leadership preparation programs, faculty members, and students is needed to inform deliberations about how to better prepare school leaders for the next century. Such data may provide a rationale for continuing or expanding certain practices as well as for eliminating program features that have outlived their usefulness. Given the criticism of the licensure-driven, social sciences model of leadership preparation that has been dominant from the mid-twentieth century through the

1980s, before replacing this with a different "one best model," data are needed that relate program features to enhanced school leadership.

Conclusion

"We should believe the past as well as doubt it" (Weick, 1996, p. 302).

Since the late 1980s there have been calls for reform in nearly every aspect of the preparation of school leaders and admonitions that universities may be replaced in this regard unless their programs are substantially transformed (Achilles, 1994; Griffiths, 1988; Murphy, 1993b). Although the reform rhetoric has been much stronger than actual changes in practices, there is recent evidence that some university units are redesigning their preparation programs. Champions of transforming leadership preparation are becoming more visible and numerous, and program reform efforts have attained greater legitimacy across the field. Nonetheless, units engaged in significant programmatic changes, while increasing in number, still must be viewed as outliers. They are receiving considerable attention at professional meetings and in professional publications, but their impact to date on the majority of educational leadership programs has been only modest.

When changed circumstances call for new ways of behaving and looking at the world, individuals often cannot make the transition; they continue to hold on to traditional ideas and behaviors because these patterns are familiar and at times entwined with their professional identity. While transformations are essential, responding to the future and adapting to changed conditions does not mean that everything from the past must be discarded. As Weick (1996) has observed, it is important to connect the past with the present, "accept mutation," and "modernize remembered values" (p. 302).

In the few educational leadership units where dramatic changes have taken place in leadership preparation, it is too soon to know whether these innovations will spread to other units and reshape the culture of educational leadership preparation programs nationally. Also, it is not possible yet to determine whether such changes have actually improved leadership preparation, made it more responsive to the needs of the field, and, most importantly, had a positive impact on students in American schools.

Perhaps historians will look back on the 1990s as the beginning of a transformation in educational leadership preparation akin to how we view the shift to the social sciences almost half a century ago. Or they may conclude that this period of ferment in the field generated considerable rhetoric but little change in preparation programs or that changes adopted had little impact on K–12 schools. With increasing public interest in staffing schools with high quality leaders, university preparation programs will surely face mounting scrutiny and additional competition from other service providers in the twenty-first century.

NOTES

1. Institutional members of the National Policy Board for Educational Administration are the American Association of Colleges for Teacher Education, American Association of School Administrators, Association for Supervision and Curriculum Development, Council of Chief State School Officers, National Association of Elementary School Principals, National Association of Secondary School Principals, National Council of Professors of Educational Administration, National School Boards Association, and University Council for Educational Administration. The Association of School Business Officials was an original member but subsequently dropped off the Board.
2. Some subdivisions of this section build in part on *Continuity and Change: The Educational Leadership Professoriate* by Martha McCarthy and George Kuh (1997).
3. Educational leadership units are housed at research, doctoral, or comprehensive universities according to the Carnegie Foundation (1994) classification of institutions of higher education. Research universities award 50 or more doctoral degrees each year and receive annually at least $15.5 million in federal support. Doctoral universities award at least 10 doctoral degrees in three or more disciplines or 20 doctoral degrees in one or more disciplines. Comprehensive universities award at least 20 master's degrees annually in one or more disciplines.
4. Similarities are to be expected between UCEA programs and those at research universities because about 85% of the UCEA programs are housed at research universities.

REFERENCES

Achilles, C. M. (1984). Forecast: Stormy weather ahead in educational administration. *Issues in Education*, 2(2), 127–135.

Achilles, C. M. (1994). Searching for the golden fleece: The epic struggle continues. *Educational Administration Quarterly*, 30, 6–26.

Araki, C. T. (1993). The impact of training on management style and interpersonal competence. *NASSP Bulletin*, 77(553), 102–106.

Barnett, B. G. (1992). Using alternative assessment measures in educational leadership preparation programs: Educational platforms and portfolios. *Journal of Personnel Evaluation in Education*, 6, 141–151.

Barnett, B. G. (1995). Portfolio use in educational leadership preparation programs: From theory to practice. *Innovative Higher Education*, 19, 197–206.

Barr, R. B. & Tagg, J. (1995, November/December). From teaching to learning —A new paradigm for undergraduate education. *Change*, 13–25.

Bartell, C. A. (1994, April). *Preparing future administrators: Stakeholder perceptions*. Paper presented at the annual meeting of the American Educational Research Association, New Orleans.

Bauck, J. M. (1987). Characteristics of the effective middle school principal. *NASSP Bulletin*, 71(500), 90–92.

Bean, J. & Kuh, G. (1988). The relationship between author gender and the methods and topics used in the study of college students. *Research in Higher Education*, 28, 130– 144.

Beck, L. & Murphy, J. (1994). *Ethics in educational leadership programs: An expanding role*. Newbury Park, CA: Corwin.

Bennis, W. & Nanus, B. (1985). *Leaders: The strategies for taking charge*. New York: Harper & Row.

Boyan, N. (1981). Follow the leader: Commentary on research in educational administration. *Educational Researcher*, 10(2), 6–13.

Boyan, N. (Ed.) (1988). *Handbook of research on educational administration: A project of the American Educational Research Association*. New York: Longman.

Boyer, E. L. (1990). *Scholarship reconsidered: Priorities of the professoriate*. Princeton, NJ: Princeton University Press.

Bridges, E. M. (1992). *Problem-based learning for administrators*. Eugene, OR: ERIC Clearinghouse on Educational Management.

Bridges, E. M. (1993). The prospective principals' program at Stanford University. In J. Murphy (Ed.), *Preparing tomorrow's school leaders: Alternative designs* (pp. 39–55). University Park, PA: University Council for Educational Administration.

Buechler, M. (1996). Out on their own. *Technos*, 5(3), 30–32.

Cambron-McCabe, N. (1993). Leadership for democratic authority. In J. Murphy (Ed.), *Preparing tomorrow's school leaders: Alternative designs* (pp. 157–176). University Park, PA: University Council for Educational Administration.

Cambron-McCabe, N. & Foster, W. (1994). A paradigm shift: Implications for the preparation of school leaders. In T. Mulkeen, N. Cambron-McCabe & B. Anderson (Eds.), *Democratic Leadership: The changing context of administrative preparation* (pp. 49–60). Norwood, NJ: Ablex.

Cambron-McCabe, N., Mulkeen, T. & Wright, G. (1991). *A new platform for preparing school administrators*. St. Louis: The Danforth Foundation.

Campbell, R. F., Fleming, T., Newell, L. J. & Bennion, J. W. (1987). *A history of thought and practice in educational administration*. New York: Teachers College Press.

Campbell, R. F. & Newell, L. J. (1973). *A study of professors of educational administration*. Columbus, OH: University Council for Educational Administration.

Carnegie Foundation for the Advancement of Teaching. (1994). *A classification of institutions of higher education*. Princeton, NJ: Carnegie Foundation for the Advancement of Teaching.

Case, C. W., Lanier, J. E. & Miskel, C. G. (1986). The Holmes Group report: Impetus for gaining professional status for teachers. *Journal of Teacher Education*, 37(4), 36–43.

Chubb, J. E. & Moe, T. M. (1990). *Politics, markets, and America's schools*. Washington, DC: Brookings Institute.

Clark, D. (1997, March). *The search for authentic educational leadership: In the universities and in the schools*. Division A invited address presented at the annual meeting of the American Educational Research Association, Chicago.

Clark, R. R. (1989). The academic life: Small worlds, different worlds. *Educational Researcher*, 18(5), 4–8.

Collet, L. S. (1989, October). *Improving faculty and dissertation research through problem-centered instruction*. Paper presented at the annual convention of the University Council for Educational Administration, Scottsdale, AZ.

Cooper, B. & Boyd, W. L. (1988). The evolution of training for school administrators. In D. Griffiths, R. Stout & P. Forsyth (Eds.), *Leaders for America's schools* (pp. 251–272). Berkeley: McCutchan.

Cordeiro, P. A., Krueger, J. A., Parks, D., Restine, N. & Wilson, P. (1993). Taking stock: Learnings gleaned from universities participating in the Danforth program. In M. Milstein & Associates (Eds.), *Changing the way we prepare educational leaders* (pp. 17–38). Newbury Park, CA: Corwin.

Council of Chief State School Officers (CCSSO). (1996). *Interstate school leaders licensure consortium: Standards for school leaders*. Washington, DC: CCSSO.

Crews, A. C. & Weakley, S. (1995). *Hungry for leadership: Educational leadership programs in the Southern Regional Education Board (SREB) states*. Atlanta: SREB.

Culbertson, J. A. (1965). Trends and issues in the development of a science of administration. Center for the Advanced Study of Educational Administration, *Perspectives on educational administration and the behavioral sciences* (pp. 3–22). Eugene: University of Oregon, Center for the Advanced Study of Educational Administration.

Culbertson, J. A. (1988, August). *Tomorrow's challenges to today's professors of educational administration*. W. D. Cocking Lecture presented at the annual meeting of the National Council of Professors of Educational Administration, Kalamazoo.

Culbertson, J. A. & Silver, P. (1978). Purposes and structure of the study. In P. Silver & D. Spuck (Eds.), *Preparatory programs for educational administrators in the United States* (pp. 52–82). Columbus, OH: University Council for Educational Administration.

Danforth Foundation (1987, September). *The Danforth program for professors of school administration.* St. Louis: Danforth Foundation.

Daresh, J. C. (1994). Restructuring educational leadership preparation: Identifying needed conditions. *Journal of School Leadership, 4,* 28–38.

Daresh, J. C. & Barnett, B. G. (1993). Restructuring leadership development in Colorado. In J. Murphy (Ed.), *Preparing tomorrow's school leaders: Alternative designs* (pp. 129–156). University Park, PA: University Council for Educational Administration.

Davis, W. J. (1978). Departments of educational administration. In P. Silver & D. Spuck (Eds.), *Preparatory programs for educational administrators in the United States* (pp. 23–51). Columbus, OH: University Council for Educational Administration.

Davis, W. J. & Spuck, D. (1978). A comparative analysis of masters, certification, specialist, and doctoral programs. In P. Silver & D. Spuck (Eds.), *Preparatory programs for educational administrators in the United States* (pp. 150–177). Columbus, OH: University Council for Educational Administration.

Donaldson, G. A. (1987). The Maine approach to improving principal leadership. *Educational Leadership, 45* (1), 43–45.

Donmoyer, R. R. (1995, April). *The very idea of a knowledge base.* Paper presented at the annual meeting of the American Educational Research Association, San Francisco.

Duke, D. L. (1992). The rhetoric and the reality of reform in educational administration. *Phi Delta Kappan, 73,* 764–770.

Education ranks as major issue in elections. (1996). *The College Board News, 25*(1), 2.

Educational Leadership Task Force. (1993, February). *Leaders for schools: The preparation and advancement of educational administrators.* Report to the Joint Legislative Education Oversight Committee of the 1993 General Assembly of North Carolina.

Farquhar, R. (1977). Preparatory programs in educational administration, 1954–1974. In L. Cunningham, W. Hack & R. Nystrand (Eds.), *Educational administration: The developing decades* (pp. 329–357). Berkeley: McCutchan.

Farquhar, R. (1981). Preparing educational administrators for ethical practice. *Alberta Journal of Educational Research, 27,* 192–204.

Flanigan, J. L. & Richardson, M. D. (1992, April). *Analysis of educational administration programs in doctoral granting institutions.* Paper presented at the annual meeting of the Society of Professors of Education, San Francisco.

Foster, W. (1988). Educational administration: A critical appraisal. In D. Griffiths, R. Stout & P. Forsyth (Eds.), *Leaders for America's schools* (pp. 68–81). Berkeley: McCutchan.

Fowler, W. J. (1991, April). *What are the characteristics of principals identified as effective teachers?* Paper presented at the annual meeting of the American Educational Research Association, Chicago.

Geltner, B. B. & Ditzhazy, H. E. (1994, October). *Shaping departmental community: Engaging individualism and collegiality in pursuit of shared purpose.* Paper presented at the annual convention of the University Council for Educational Administration, Philadelphia.

Gerritz, W., Koppich, J. & Guthrie, J. (1984, November). *Preparing California school leaders: An analysis of supply, demand, and training.* Berkeley: Policy Analysis for California Education.

Getzels, J. W. (1977). Educational administration twenty years later, 1954–1974. In L. L. Cunningham, W. G. Hack & R. O. Nystrand (Eds.), *Educational Administration: The developing decades* (pp. 3–24). Berkeley: McCutchan.

Goodlad, J. (1994). *Educational renewal: Better teachers, better schools.* San Francisco: Jossey Bass.

Gosetti, P. P. & Rusch, E. A. (1994, April). *Diversity and equity in educational administration: Missing in theory and in action.* Paper presented at the annual meeting of the American Educational Research Association, New Orleans.

Graduate Record Examinations: 1985–86 guide to the use of scores. (1985). Princeton, NJ: Educational Testing Service.

Graduate Record Examinations: 1996–97 guide to the use of scores. (1996). Princeton, NJ: Educational Testing Service.

Greenfield, T. (1988). The decline and fall of the science in educational administration. In D. Griffiths, R. Stout & P. Forsyth (Eds.), *Leaders for America's schools* (pp. 131– 159). Berkeley: McCutchan.

Greenfield, W. D. (1975). *Organizational socialization and the preparation of educational administrators.* Paper presented at the annual meeting of the American Educational Research Association, Washington, DC.

Gregg, R. T. (1969). Preparation of administrators. In R. L. Ebel (Ed.), *Encyclopedia of educational research* (4th ed., pp. 993–1004). London: MacMillan.

Gresso, D. W., Burkett, C. W. & Smith, P. L. (1993). Time is not of the essence when planning for a quality education program: East Tennessee State University. In J. Murphy (Ed.), *Preparing tomorrow's school leaders: Alternative designs* (pp. 109–127). University Park, PA: University Council for Educational Administration

Griffiths, D. E. (Ed.) (1964). *Behavioral science and educational administration.* Chicago: University of Chicago Press.

Griffiths, D. E. (1966). *The school superintendent.* New York: Center for Applied Research in Education.

Griffiths, D. E. (1988). *Educational administration: Reform PDQ or RIP* (UCEA Occasional Paper No. 8312). Tempe, AZ: University Council for Educational Administration.

Gross, N. C. & Herriott, R. E. (1965). *Staff leadership in public schools: A sociological inquiry.* New York: Wiley.

Hackmann, D. & Price, W. (1995, February). *Preparing school leaders for the 21st century: Results of a national survey of educational leadership doctoral programs.* Paper presented at the National Council of Professors of Educational Administration conference-within-a-conference at the American Association of School Administrators Annual Convention, San Francisco.

Haller, E. J., Brent, B. O., McNamara, J. F. & Rufus, C. (1994). *Does graduate training in educational administration improve America's schools? Another look at some national data.* Paper presented at the annual meeting of the American Educational Research Association, New Orleans.

Hallinger, P. & McCary, C. E. (1991). Using a problem-based approach for instructional leadership development. *Journal of Staff Development, 12*(2), 6–12.

Hawley, W. D. (1988). Universities and improvement of school management. In D. Griffiths, R. Stout & P. Forsyth (Eds.), *Leaders for America's schools* (pp. 82–88). Berkeley: McCutchan.

Heller, R., Conway, J. & Jacobson, S. (1988). Here's your blunt critique of administrator preparation. *The Executive Educator, 10* (9), 18–22.

Hills, J. (1965). Educational administration: A field in transition. *Educational Administration Quarterly, 1,* 58–66.

House, J. E., Sommerville, J. C. & Zimmer, J. W. (1990, October). *Make haste slowly: The linkage between tradition, preparation, and practice.* Paper presented at the Annual University Council for Educational Administration Convention, Pittsburgh.

Hoy, W. K. (1994). Foundation of educational administration: Traditional and emerging perspectives. *Educational Administration Quarterly, 30,* 178–198.

Hoyle, J. R. & American Association of School Administrators (AASA) Commission on Standards for the Superintendency. (1993). *Professional standards for the superintendency.* Arlington, VA: AASA.

Hoyle, J. R., English, F. W. & Steffy, B. (1985, 2nd ed., 1990). *Skills for successful school leaders.* Arlington, VA: American Association of School Administrators.

Jacobson, S. L. (1990). Reflections on the third wave of reform: Rethinking administrator preparation. In S. L. Jacobson & J. A. Conway (Eds.), *Educational leadership in an age of reform* (pp. 30–44). New York: Longman.

Kuh, G. & McCarthy, M. (1980). Research orientation of doctoral students in educational administration. *Educational Administration quarterly, 16*(2), 101–121.

Leithwood, K., Jantzi, D., Coffin, G. & Wilson, P. (1996). Preparing school leaders: What works? *Journal of School Leadership, 6,* 316–342.

Lilley, H. E. (1995). *Educational administration directory—1994–95.* Morgantown, WV: West Virginia University.

LISA (Leadership Institute for School Administrators) update. (1996, December). Arlington, VA: American Association of School Administrators.

Logan, C. S. & Pounder, D. G. (1989, October). *Limitations on change: Current conditions influencing academic intransigence in educational administration preparation programs.* Paper presented at the annual convention of the University Council for Educational Administration, Scottsdale, AZ.

McCarthy, M. & Kuh, G. (1997). *Continuity and change: The educational leadership professoriate.* Columbia, MO: University Council for Educational Administration.

McCarthy, M., Kuh, G. & Beckman, J. (1979). Characteristics and attitudes of educational administration doctoral students. *Phi Delta Kappan, 61,* 200–203.

McCarthy, M., Kuh, G., Newell, L. J. & Iacona, C. (1988). *Under scrutiny: The educational administration professoriate.* Tempe, AZ: University Council for Educational Administration.

McLaughlin, J. M. & Moore, C. E. (1990, October). *The reform movement and Ed. D. expansion.* Paper presented at the meeting of the Midwest Council for Educational Administration, St. Cloud, MN.

Maniloff, H. & Clark, D. (1993). Preparing effective leaders for schools and school systems: Graduate study at the University of North Carolina-Chapel Hill. In J. Murphy (Ed.), *Preparing tomorrow's school leaders: Alternative designs* (pp. 177–203). University Park, PA: University Council for Educational Administration.

Marland, S. P. (1960). Superintendents' concerns about research applications in educational administration. In R. F. Campbell & J. M. Lipham (Eds.), *Administrative theory as a guide to action* (pp. 21–36). Chicago: University of Chicago, Midwest Administration Center.

Miklos, E. (1983). Evolution in administrator preparation programs. *Educational Administration Quarterly, 19* (3), 153–177.

Milstein, M. & Associates (1993). *Changing the way we prepare educational leaders: The Danforth experience.* Newbury Park, CA: Corwin.

Milstein, M. & Krueger, J. A. (1993). Innovative approaches to clinical internships: The New Mexico experience. In J. Murphy (Ed.), *Preparing tomorrow's school leaders: Alternative designs* (19–38). University Park, PA: University Council for Educational Administration.

Mulford, B. (1985, August). *Assessing effectiveness in the field of professional preparation programs in educational administration.* Paper presented at international symposium, The Professional Preparation and Development of Educational Administrators in Commonwealth Developing Areas, Barbados.

Mulkeen, T., Cambron-McCabe, N. & Anderson, B. (Eds.) (1994). *Democratic Leadership: The changing context of administrative preparation.* Norwood, NJ: Ablex.

Murphy, J. (1990). The reform of school administration: Pressures and calls for change. In J. Murphy (Ed.), *The reform of American public education in the 1980s: Perspectives and cases* (pp. 277–303). Berkeley: McCutchan.

Murphy, J. (1991). The effects of the educational reform movement on departments of educational leadership. *Educational Evaluation and Policy Analysis, 13,* 49–65.

Murphy, J. (1992). *The landscape of leadership preparation: Reframing the education of school administrators.* Newbury Park, CA: Corwin.

Murphy, J. (Ed.) (1993a). *Preparing tomorrow's school leaders: Alternative designs.* University Park, PA: University Council for Educational Administration.

Murphy, J. (1993b). Ferment in school administration: Rounds 1–3. In J. Murphy (Ed.), *Preparing tomorrow's school leaders: Alternative designs* (pp. 1–38). University Park, PA: University Council for Educational Administration.

Murphy, J. (1993c). Alternative designs: New directions. In J. Murphy (Ed.), *Preparing tomorrow's school leaders: Alternative designs* (pp. 225–253). University Park, PA: University Council for Educational Administration.

Murphy, J., Shipman, N. & Pearlman, M. (1997, September). Strengthening educational leadership: The Interstate School Leaders Licensure Consortium (ISSLC) standards at work. *NAESP Streamlined Seminar,* 16(1), 1–4.

Nagle, J. & Nagle, E. (1978). Doctoral programs in educational administration. In P. Silver & D. Spuck (Eds.), *Preparatory programs for educational administrators in the United States* (pp. 114–149). Columbus, OH: University Council for Educational Administration.

National Association of Secondary School Principals (NASSP) Consortium for the Performance-Based Preparation of Principals. (1985). *Performance-based preparation of principals: A framework for improvement.* Reston, VA: NASSP.

National Commission for the Principalship. (1990). *Principals for our changing schools: Preparation and certification.* Fairfax, VA: National Policy Board for Educational Administration.

National Commission on Excellence in Educational Administration (NCEEA). (1987). *Leaders for American Schools: The report of the National Commission on Excellence in Educational Administration.* Tempe, AZ: University Council for Educational Administration.

National Governors Association (NGA). (1990). *Educating America: State strategies for achieving the national education goals.* Washington, DC: NGA.

National Policy Board for Educational Administration (NPBEA). (1989). *Improving the preparation of school administrators: An agenda for reform.* Charlottesville, VA: NPBEA.

National survey of postsecondary faculty. (1993). [CD-ROM of restricted data]. Washington, DC: National Center for Education Statistics, U. S. Department of Education.

Newell, L. J. & Morgan, D. A. (1980). [Study of professors of higher education and educational administration]. Unpublished data.

Norris, C. J. & Barnett, B. (1994, October). *Cultivating a new leadership paradigm: From cohorts to communities.* Paper presented at the annual convention of the University Council for Educational Administration, Philadelphia.

Norton, M. S. (1992). Doctoral studies of students in educational administration programs in non-member UCEA institutions. *Educational Considerations, 20,* 37–41.

Norton, M. S. (1994). *Department organization and faculty status in educational administration.* Tempe, AZ: UCEA Center for the Study of Preparation Programs.

Norton, M. S. (1995). *The status of student cohorts in educational administration preparation programs.* Tempe, AZ: UCEA Center for the Study of Preparation Programs.

Ogawa, R. & Pounder, D. (1993). Structured improvisation: The University of Utah's Ed. D. program in educational administration. In J. Murphy (Ed.), *Preparing tomorrow's school leaders: Alternative designs* (pp. 85–108). University Park, PA: University Council for Educational Administration.

Ohio Board of Regents. (1996, March 11). *Summary of recommendations regarding educational administration programs.* Columbus, OH: Ohio Board of Regents.

Peterson, K. D. & Finn, C. E. (1985). Principals, superintendents, and the administrator's art. *The Public Interest, 79,* 42–62.

Pitner, N. (1988). School administrator preparation: The state of the art. In D. Griffiths, R. Stout & P. Forsyth (Eds.), *Leaders for America's schools* (pp. 367–402). Berkeley: McCutchan.

Playko, M. A. & Daresh, J. C. (1992). *Field-based preparation programs: Reform of administrator training or leadership development?* Paper presented at the annual convention of the University Council for Educational Administration, Minneapolis.

Pohland, P. & Carlson, L. (1993, fall). Program reform in educational administration. *UCEA Review,* 4–9.

Pounder, D. (1989). The gender gap in salaries of educational administration professors. *Educational Administration Quarterly, 25,* 181–201.

Pounder, D. (1995). Theory to practice in administrator preparation: An evaluation study. *Journal of School Leadership, 5,* 151–162.

Reitzug, U. C. (1989, October). *Utilizing multiple frameworks to integrate knowledge and experience in educational administration preparation programs.* Paper presented at the annual convention of the University Council for Educational Administration, Scottsdale, AZ.

Scheurich, J. & Laible, J. (1995). The buck stops here in our preparation programs: Educational leadership for all children (no exceptions allowed). *Educational Administration Quarterly, 31*, 313–322.

Schmuck, P. (1992). Educating the new generation of superintendents. *Educational Leadership, 49* (5), 66–71.

Schön, D. (1987). *Educating the reflective practitioner.* San Francisco: Jossey-Bass.

Schuster, J. (1990). Faculty issues in the 1990s: New realities, new opportunities. In L. Jones & F. Nowotny (Eds.), *An Agenda for the new decade* (pp. 33–42) (New Directions for Higher Education, No. 70). San Francisco: Jossey-Bass.

Scribner, J. (1973, Spring). Urban educational policy and planning: Leadership development for urban careers. *UCLA Educator,* 115(2), 26–29.

Sergiovanni, T. (1991). Constructing and changing theories of practice: The key to preparing school administrators. *Urban Review,* 23, 39–49.

Shakeshaft, C. (1993). Preparing tomorrow's school leaders: The Hofstra University experience. In J. Murphy (Ed.), *Preparing tomorrow's school leaders: Alternative designs* (205–223). University Park, PA: University Council for Educational Administration.

Shibles, M. R. (1988). *School leadership preparation: A preface for action.* Washington, DC: American Association of Colleges for Teacher Education.

Silver, P. F. (1987). The Center for Advancing Principalship Excellence (APEX): An approach to professionalizing educational administration. In J. Murphy & P. Hallinger (Eds.), *Approaches to administrative training in education* (pp. 48–67). Albany, NY: State University of New York Press.

Silver, P. F. (1982). Administrator preparation. In H. E. Mitzel (Ed.), *Encyclopedia of educational research,* (5th ed., vol. 1, pp. 49–59). New York: Free Press.

Silver, P. & Spuck, D. W. (1978). *Preparatory programs for educational administrators in the United States.* Columbus, OH: University Council for Educational Administration.

Sirotnik, K. A. & Mueller, K. (1993). Challenging the wisdom of conventional principal preparation programs and getting away with it (so far). In J. Murphy (Ed.), *Preparing tomorrow's school leaders: Alternative designs* (57–83). University Park, PA: University Council for Educational Administration.

Sizer, T. R. (1988). A visit to an essential school. *School Administrator,* 45(10), 18–19.

Sizer, T. R. (1991). No pain, no gain. *Educational Leadership, 48*(8), 32–34.

Teitel, L. (1996, winter). Leadership in professional development schools: Lessons for the preparation of administrators. *UCEA Review,* 10–11, 15.

Thomson, S. D. (Ed.) (1993). *Principals for our changing schools: The knowledge and skill base.* Fairfax, VA: National Policy Board for Educational Administration.

Tryneski, J. (1993). *Requirements for certification of teachers, counselors, librarians, administrators for elementary and secondary schools 1993–94.* Chicago: University of Chicago Press.

Van Berkum, D. W., Richardson, M. D. & Lane, K. E. (1994, August). *Professional development in educational administration programs: Where does it exist?* Paper presented at the annual meeting of the National Council of Professors of Educational Administration, Indian Wells, CA.

Weick, K. E. (1996). Drop your tools: An allegory for organizational studies, *Administrative Science Quarterly,* 41, 301–303.

Wildman, L. (1988). Where will LEAD lead? *Viewpoints,* California State University—Bakersfield, EA 021 557, ED 318 078.

Willower, D. J. (1983). Evolution in the professorship: Past, philosophy, future. *Educational Administration Quarterly, 19*, 179–200.

Wilson, P. (1993). Pushing the edge. In M. Milstein & Associates (Eds.), *Changing the way we prepare educational leaders* (pp. 219–235). Newbury Park, CA: Corwin.

Yerkes, D., Basom, M., Norris, C. & Barnett, B. (1995). *Using cohorts in the development of educational leaders.* Paper presented at the annual international conference of the Association of Management, Vancouver, Canada.

Zheng, H. (1996). *School contexts, principal characteristics, and instructional leadership effectiveness: A statistical analysis.* Paper presented at the annual meeting of the American Educational Research Association, New York.

Zimbler, L. (1994*). Faculty and instructional staff: Who are they and what do they do?* Washington, DC: National Center for Education Statistics, U. S. Department of Education.

CHAPTER 7

Next Generation Methods for the Study of Leadership and School Improvement

Ronald H. Heck and Philip Hallinger

The belief that principals have an impact on schools is long-standing in the folk wisdom of educational history. Despite this belief, before the 1980s few empirical studies explored the effects of school leadership. An increasing concern for educational accountability during the 1980s, however, brought greater urgency to documenting whether and how principals make a difference in schooling (Glasman & Heck, 1992).

We recently reviewed research that focused on the principal's contribution to school effectiveness (Hallinger & Heck, 1996a, 1996b). In contrast to earlier reviews, we found a clear trend toward the accumulation of knowledge about school leadership and its effects (Bridges, 1982; Erickson, 1979). We concluded that principal leadership does have indirect effects on student outcomes via a variety of in-school processes (Hallinger & Heck, 1998). In addition, the review highlighted an increasing conceptual and methodological sophistication within this body of research on educational administration.

At the same time, we noted that important questions about how leaders achieve improvement in schools remain unanswered. An important *blank spot* concerns in-depth description of how principals and other school leaders create and sustain the in-school factors that foster successful schooling. Sustained, narrowly-focused inquiry of this type is necessary to fill blank spots in the knowledge base.

The review also identified *blind spots*, areas in which existing views of knowledge impede us from seeing other facets of the phenomenon under investigation (Wagner, 1993). By way of illustration, the preoccupation with documenting *if principals make a difference* has subtly reinforced the assumption that school leadership is synony-

mous with the principal. Scholars have, therefore, largely ignored other sources of leadership within the school such as assistant principals and senior teachers.

Another blind spot concerns how researchers conceive of effectiveness. Since 1980, scholars have most frequently studied effectiveness indicators concerned with student achievement. Consequently, they have conducted relevant empirical research from a limited epistemological perspective and with a bias toward quantitative methods.

Immersion in this set of studies revealed the need to examine the role of school leaders through more diverse lenses and methods. Other orientations toward the study of school leadership have emerged in recent years that offer potential for addressing blind spots in our picture of school leadership. These include sense-making, or the social construction of leadership; distributed leadership; micropolitics of leadership within the school; leadership as influenced by cultural norms of the society; and gender and ethnicity in leadership roles. These orientations derive from a broader range of epistemological views, raise different research questions, and lead researchers toward other methods of empirical study.

In this chapter, we explore the role of methodology in the next generation of studies of leadership and school improvement. Methodology is the description, explanation, and justification of research methods (Kaplan, 1964). It concerns underlying theories of how we construct knowledge (epistemology) and also the interpretive frameworks that guide research (Everhart, 1988; Lather, 1991). We examine the epistemological and methodological stances that underlie recent efforts to illuminate blind spots in our field of inquiry.

Our goal in this chapter is to provide an organizing structure for the study of school leadership in the future. We hope to delineate more clearly:

1. The theoretical frameworks scholars are using to explore school leadership
2. The processes of scientific inquiry they are using in empirical study

We offer concluding remarks on directions the field of school leadership research could take over the next decade.

A Framework for Viewing Research on School Leadership

The objective of science is to understand the world in terms of its regularities and to formulate explanations of our observations (Hoy, 1996; Willower, 1996). Theories are general explanations of phenomena. The test of a theory is not its truth, but its usefulness in generating accurate predictions and, therefore, useful understanding (Hoy, 1996). Theories are embedded in the cultural fabric that forms the foundation for the creation of knowledge (Kuhn, 1970). Challenges to dominant ways of thinking —paradigms—are useful because they question our assumptions, ways of knowing, and methods of investigation. During the past decade, the fields of education and management have both been in the midst of paradigm shifts. These shifts have led to the reconsideration of theoretical conceptualizations as well as research methods.

Historical traditions exert a powerful, though at times unacknowledged, influence on the way scholars think about theoretical, epistemological, and methodological issues. Logical positivism and the "Theory movement" framed the quantitatively-oriented discipline of educational administration as it matured during the 1950s, 1960s, 1970s, and 1980s. This mode of scientific inquiry was the foundation from which professors forged their quest to establish departments of educational administration within the academy. It came to define accepted norms of research.

To illustrate this point, only a decade ago, Griffiths (1988) concluded there was little diversity in the methodological approaches used in the study of educational administration. He examined proposals submitted to the Administration Division of the American Educational Research Association in 1985 and found that only three of the 230 proposals employed qualitative research methods. Moreover, authors of all but 10 submissions framed their studies within a "functionalist" view of organizational life (Burrell & Morgan, 1979). Functionalism emphasizes systems and contingency theory, rational models of decision making, and a positivist, or so-called "objective," view of science.

Subsequently, scholars have directed an enormous amount of criticism at traditional conceptualizations, methodologies, and constructions of knowledge (Burnstein, 1983; Denzin & Lincoln, 1994; Foster, 1986; Greenfield, 1980; Habermas, 1975; Lather, 1991). Sustained criticism has led to new ways of thinking about knowledge construction and the role of the researcher in the scientific process (Bloom & Munro, 1995; Jensen & Peshkin, 1992; Lather, 1991; Roman, 1992). These "new schools" include variants on traditional views of science (such as naturalist or phenomenological), advocacy (for example, critical theorist, neo-Marxist, feminist), and perspectives that undercut the idea of theory (such as post-structural, post-modern).

We must note at the outset of this review that proponents of these emerging schools have focused on conceptualization rather than on empirical explication (Evers & Lakomski, 1996; Willower, 1996). Thus this current review necessarily focuses on the promise of these emerging perspectives rather than on what they have accomplished to date.

Conceptualizing School Leadership Research

Historically, research on school leadership has focused predominantly on the principal's role. This resulted from beliefs about the centrality of the principal's management to the school's governance and from cultural inclinations to associate leadership with formal administrative roles (Bossert et al., 1982; Boyan, 1981, 1988). Thus in preparing this chapter, we began with the set of studies collected for our earlier review of the principal's role in school effectiveness (Hallinger & Heck, 1996a). We supplemented these studies with additional empirical reports selected specifically to illustrate alternate conceptual and methodological stances.

In Table 7.1, we locate selected studies discussed in this chapter according to their broad conceptualization of knowledge, philosophical frame, research orientation, leadership model, and method. This table highlights the increasing flexibility of perspectives and corresponding methods of investigation scholars are using to study school leadership. We emphasize that this sample is not inclusive. It is intended only to illustrate several new generation approaches to studying school leadership.

Broadly speaking, positivist, interpretive, and critical theories of knowledge have characterized social research during the 20th century (Denzin & Lincoln, 1994; Soltis, 1984). Each has spawned various theoretical approaches to investigating social phenomena (such as structural-functionalism, political conflict, constructivism, feminism, postmodernism). These three broad perspectives

Table 7.1

Framework of Approaches for Studying School Leadership

Knowledge:	Positivist		Interpretive		Critical-Contextual			
Lens	Structural-functional (Rational)		Political-Conflict	Constructivist	Critical-Constructivist	Feminist	Gender Culture	(No Lens) Postmodern Post-structural Pragmatic
Research Orientation	Nature of the Work	Administrator Effects	Sense-making in Schools		Sense-making About Social Constructions (Whose interests are served?)			
Example Studies	Peterson (1978) Kmetz & Willower (1981) Martin & Willower (1982) Chung & Miskel (1989)	Scott & Teddie (1887) Eberts & Stone (1988) Hallinger *et al.* (1989) Bamburg & Andrews (1990) Snyder & Ebmeier (1992) Brewer (1993) Hannaway & Talbert (1993) Bass & Avolio (1989) Leithwood (1994) Silins (1994)	Gronn (1984a) Ball (1987) Greenfield (1991) Blase (1993)	Varenne (1978, 1983) Wolcott (1973) Leithwood & Stager (1989) Ogawa (1991) Duke & Iwanicki (1992) Hart (1994) Murphy & Beck (1995) Anderson & Shirley (1995) Cooper & Heck (1995) Begley (1996) Walker *et al.* (1996) Lum (1997)	Lomotey (1989, 1993) Anderson (1991) Keith (1996)	Regan (1990) Chase (1992) Ortiz (1992) Dillard (1995) Benham (1997) Benham & Cooper (1998)		Blount (1993) Bloom & Munro (1995) Gronn & Ribbins (1996) Robinson (1996)
Leadership	None	Instructional Transformational	Micropolitics	Symbolic, Metaphorical Values-oriented Social Cognition	Moral-Educative (Social Responsibility)		Nontraditional Interim Informal	
Method	Descriptive	Quantitative Modeling	Ethnography, Case Study, Historical		Critical Ethnography		Biography, Narrative	

partition the domain of knowledge arbitrarily. When traced to their origins, they largely reflect discipline-related expressions of ideological commitment, rather than universally reliable truths (Macpherson, 1996). Moreover, the proliferation of paradigms has made it difficult to establish a "neat" system of categorizing these approaches (Denzin & Lincoln, 1994; Donmoyer, 1996; Evers & Lakomski, 1996; Goetz *et al.*, 1988; Hoy, 1994; Maxcy, 1995; Slater, 1995; Wolcott, 1992).

In Table 7.1, we suggest that the various theoretical perspectives cluster around different types of research questions, leadership interests, and methods of study. Researchers working within each perspective focus on answering particular questions (for example, "what are the effects of school leadership?"). There is accumulation of knowledge within a given paradigm as researchers conduct inquiry that fills the blank spots in their particular program of research.

Although theories aim at inclusiveness, no one approach is likely to yield a universal understanding of schools (Denzin & Lincoln, 1994; Eisner, 1993; Everhart, 1988; Evers & Lakomski, 1996; Hallinger & Heck, 1996b). Scholars are often unaware of what scholars interested in different questions and operating from different paradigms are investigating. The acknowledgment of blind spots in the field means that at best we have developed an incomplete and distorted view of the role of school leaders in school improvement.

Adding to our difficulty in devising a classification of the empirical work on school leadership is the realization that any given study is comprised of philosophical and theoretical underpinnings, research questions and design, and methods of data collection and analysis (Jacob, 1992). Researchers may define some facets in detail; others are vaguely acknowledged, or even remain unstated. For example, the term "qualitative" refers to various levels of the research process. Qualitative research may be interpretive at an epistemological level, open-ended in terms of data collection, or involve "grounded theory" in the analysis of data.

After noting these limitations, we now turn our attention to the research orientations and lenses used in investigating school leadership. In the next section, we review five of the lenses used in framing the study of school leadership in terms of their guiding research questions: 1) structural-functional and bureaucratic-rational theory; 2) political conflict; 3) constructivist; 4) critical constructivist, feminist and cultural; and 5) postmodern or post-structural.

Structural-Functionalism and Rational Systems Theory

Most previous research on leadership and school improvement has embraced a bureaucratic-rational and structural-functional orientation toward human organizations. Traditionally, scholars adopting this perspective viewed organizations as closed systems whose purpose was to maintain equilibrium as they strove to accomplish set goals or purposes. Given this orientation, structural-functionalism focuses on mapping interconnections between the internal subsystems of an organization. This approach emphasizes identifying the structural features that form the framework within which organizational activity takes place (Lewellen, 1992).

From structural-functional perspective, managers play an important role in coordinating and controlling the organization's work and achievement of goals. Leadership is the influence that individuals exert by virtue of a combination of personal traits and organizational position (Bossert et al., 1982). Ogawa and Bossert (1995) have referred to this broad perspective as a technical-rational system's view of leadership. They note several defining assumptions:

a. leaders function to influence organizational performance and maintain stability
b. leadership is aligned with organizational roles;
c. leaders are individuals who possess certain attributes and act in certain observable ways.

Descriptive studies of administrators conducted within a structural-functional frame were the norm from the 1960s to 1980s (Bridges, 1982; Immegart, 1988). The orientation of much of this research focused on describing the nature of administrative work and the beliefs and tasks of those who occupied these roles in schools (Chung & Miskel, 1989; Crowson & Porter-Gehrie, 1980; Gronn, 1984a; Inbar, 1977; Kmetz & Willower, 1982; Martin & Willower, 1982; Peterson, 1978; Wolcott, 1973). Another branch within this orientation studied the personal traits of administrators (experience, intelligence, training, locus of control, leadership style) to their perceptions, values, and actions (Salley et al., 1979).

This research served an important early purpose by providing grounded descriptions of the work of school administrators. However, scholars have also noted important limitations of this line of inquiry (Boyan, 1988; Bridges, 1982; Immegart, 1988). Few studies have validated administrative traits as indicators of important theoretical domains of leadership. Nor are traits reliable predictors of school outcomes (Hallinger & Heck, 1996a; Slater, 1995). Boyan (1988) and Bridges (1982) specifically highlight its atheoretical orientation and inattention to the effects of administrative leadership. As a result, no particular conceptualizations of school leadership emerged from these studies as dominant. Bridges went so far as to conclude that further inquiry via this intellectual orientation was unlikely to bear fruit.

A second structural-functional research orientation concerned the study of principal effects. Drawing upon the broader base of school effectiveness research, during the 1980s, scholars narrowed their focus to study the behavior of principals as instructional managers (Bossert et al., 1982). Researchers sought to understand the effects of administrators on school-level (as opposed to classroom) improvement (Andrews & Soder, 1987; Brewer, 1993; Eberts & Stone, 1988; Goldring & Pasternak, 1994; Heck, Larsen, & Marcoulides, 1990; Leithwood, 1994; Louis & Miles, 1991; Silins, 1994; Smylie, 1992). This research assumed, often explicitly, that administrative leadership consists of particular behaviors (Bamburg & Andrews, 1990; Hallinger et al., 1990; Heck et al., 1989). Investigators sought to link these leader behaviors to patterns of impact on school-level processes and outcomes.

Reflecting this interest in administrators' impact, Pitner (1988) detailed conceptual models for investigating the effects of administrative leadership. In analyzing the patterns of research models employed during the 1980s and 1990s by scholars in this domain, we found that three major approaches dominated: direct effects, mediated effects, and antecedent effects (Hallinger & Heck, 1996a).

Studies conducted before 1987 emphasized determining whether there were direct effects of principal leadership on school outcomes. These studies typically employed bivariate models, occasionally including control variables. Direct-effects models, however, did not produce any consistent pattern of findings.

Mediated-effect studies of leadership employed more comprehensive conceptual models. These focused on the principal's leadership as the primary independent variable, in-school processes (for example, goal orientation) as mediating variables, and school outcomes. This approach identified possible indirect, or mediated, effects of the principal's leadership on school effectiveness. These studies produced more consistent support for the belief that principal leadership is a central component in school effectiveness and improvement (Hallinger & Heck, 1996a, 1996b, 1998).

Conducted from a "closed system" orientation, however, these studies limited empirical investigation to variables within schools such as leadership, school climate, teacher expectations, or school mission (Eberts & Stone, 1988; Goldring & Pasternak, 1994). Though it is now widely accepted that schools operate as open systems, mediated-effect studies largely ignored important social, cultural and institutional forces that act on school leaders. As such, they offer an incomplete picture of how leaders respond to the contextual conditions in which they work.

Beginning in the mid-1980s, researchers also began to explore the possible relationships among environmental factors (such as socio-economic status or community type), leadership, and school improvement (Andrews & Soder, 1987; Glasman, 1984; Hallinger & Murphy, 1986b; Hannaway & Talbert, 1993; Heck *et al.*, 1990; Leithwood *et al.*, 1993; Leithwood, 1994; Pounder, Ogawa, & Adams, 1995; Rowan & Denk, 1984; Scott & Teddlie, 1987). The sum of this research suggested that school leaders implement those values endorsed by the culture of the broader community (Hallinger & Murphy, 1986a; Ogawa & Bossert, 1995). Yet we must emphasize that few studies included a full range of environmental and school contextual indicators in their analyses of school leadership. As a result, the theoretical formulation of environmental relationships between and school leadership remains thin.

Since 1980, two images of school leadership dominated the landscape within this research orientation: instructional leadership and transformational leadership. Studies from the early 1980s to early 1990s typically used the instructional leadership conceptualization drawn from the effective schools literature (Andrews & Soder, 1987; Bamburg & Andrews, 1990; Biester *et al.*, 1984; Brewer, 1993; Cheng, 1994; Goldring & Pasternak, 1994; Hallinger & Murphy, 1985; Hallinger & Murphy, 1986b; Hallinger, Bickman, & Davis, 1989; Heck *et al.*, 1990; Hoy, Tarter, & Witkoskie, 1992; Kleine-Kracht, 1993; Krug, 1986; O'Day, 1983; Scott & Teddlie, 1987; Tarter, Sabo, & Hoy, 1995). This image of leadership focused on the principal's efforts to establish school goals, align its curriculum, develop a safe school environment, and supervise classroom instruction. This image portrayed the administrator as "hip-deep" in instruction (Cuban, 1984).

In contrast, studies during the 1990s have often adopted a transformational model of leadership (Leithwood, 1994; Silins, 1994). Researchers have argued that the instructional leadership focus on the school's core technology of curriculum and instruction tended to overlook other important dimensions of leadership within the school. The instructional leadership image did not account for leadership by staff other than the principal, which was particularly salient with respect

to secondary schools, nor did it attend to important influences from outside the school.

The school restructuring agenda that emerged during the late 1980s focused more broadly on changing the school culture as a means of improving its outcomes. This was consistent with the transformational image, which posited a more overarching view of school leadership. Transformational school leaders develop conditions that support school improvement (staff development, building collaborative culture) rather than by direct intervention in curriculum and instruction. The results of studies by Leithwood and colleagues (Leithwood *et al.*, 1993; Leithwood & Jantzi, 1990; Silins, 1994) suggested promise in the transformational leadership conception, though with modifications from the corporate literature.

Other manifestations of the structural-functional approach to leadership included situational theory and contingency theory (Slater, 1995). However, these latter notions have fallen out of favor among scholars in the field.

Although scholars have recently proclaimed the need for greater flexibility (Anderson, 1990, 1991; Greenfield, 1980; Maxcy, 1995; Ogawa & Bossert, 1995), variants of structural-functionalism continue to maintain a strong grip on the field of educational administration (Hallinger & Heck, 1996a). Identifying and addressing blind spots in the field resulting from continued over-reliance on this orientation will entail the explication of different epistemological views and conceptual models of leadership.

Political-Conflict Perspective on Leadership

In the last *Handbook*, Griffiths (1988) asserted that "although paradigm diversity is catching on in many parts of the social sciences, to date there is little interest on the part of researchers in educational administration" (p. 46). Studies from a political conflict perspective provide a different view on how leaders work in schools (Anderson, 1991; Blase, 1989, 1993, Gronn,1984b; Greenfield, 1991; Jantzi & Leithwood, 1996). Scholars adopting this lens do not start with the assumption that leadership necessarily resides in the school's administrator. Nor do they see the school's formal system (goals, authority, rules, and plans) as the primary source of initiative for improvement or reform.

In general, researchers employing a political conflict perspective are less concerned with issues such as organizational goals and school effectiveness. Instead, there is greater interest in exploring how competing interest groups within the school and its community negotiate for power. In the context of school reform, for example, researchers study the nature of participation in decision making, rather than the linkages between particular principal behaviors and school outcomes. They may be interested in studying how leaders engage different constituencies in the school in order to select school goals and related programs. Scholars adopting this perspective would not, for example, simply accept the assumption that student achievement is the de facto purpose to which leaders ought to direct their efforts.

Researchers adopting this perspective begin with the assumption that schools are characterized by multiple goals, diverse instructional strategies, and relatively high degrees of teacher autonomy. They then proceed to examine how leaders function under such conditions (Bacharach & Mundell, 1993; Ball, 1987; Hoy & Miskel, 1996). They view power relations between teachers and administrators as complex and multidirectional. For example, administrators are sometimes subordinate to teachers. Teachers are the experts in their fields of instruction. Thus administrators (and other informal leaders) must negotiate their mandate to lead. In doing so, they must grant considerable autonomy to teachers as they facilitate curriculum, instruction, and learning processes at the school level (Hoy & Miskel, 1996).

The focus on political dimensions of role relationships within the school has been termed "micropolitics" (Anderson, 1990; Bacharach & Mundell, 1993; Ball, 1987; Ball & Bowe, 1991; Blase, 1993). Proponents of this approach contend that the structural-functionalist paradigm underestimates the influence of power and political relations that predominate in and around schools. In fact, they observe that studies located within the dominant rational system's paradigm generally ignore political issues. This oversight is evident in the effective schools studies, which one could read thoroughly without considering the role teacher unions play in school improvement.

Studies of the micropolitics of school leadership provide a new perspective on how control and legitimization of activities unfold at the school level (Anderson, 1990). Where the structural-functional view focuses on the beliefs and actions of formal leaders, the micropolitical perspective examines the belief systems of teachers, parents, and students as well. The political conflict approach begins with the assumption that order inside the school is negotiated among interest groups.

Indeed, political negotiation is at the heart of what such theorists term *leadership*. For example, Bacharach and Mundell (1993) posited a framework that focuses on how groups come to agree or disagree over values that underlie the policies and practices of schooling. More specifically, they identified "logics of action," or belief systems, that govern decisions about means and goals employed by subgroups within the political system of the school.

Blase's (1993) study of micropolitics examined how individuals and groups use formal and informal power to achieve their ends in schools. Blase studied how principals described by teachers as "effective" influenced the day-to-day lives of teachers. The shift from leader effects to the processes by which leaders negotiate their mandate led Blase to a closer investigation of how leadership is enacted within schools. He concluded that principals most often use normative strategies (for example, manipulate rewards such as prestige, rituals, symbols) to influence teachers to achieve agreed-upon goals.

The political conflict approach, therefore, forms a type of bridge connecting those studying the nature of the principal's work and those interested in its effects. It highlights the role of hidden relations among different groups that comprise the school and its community. It suggests that leadership is not simply a function of role but instead results from a negotiation among constituent groups. This implies the importance of looking beyond the principal in a search for sources of leadership that contribute to school improvement, however it may be defined.

In focusing on political processes within schools, over time researchers have proceeded away from a positivist view of knowledge toward an interpretive approach. As Blase (1993) acknowledged, however, there is a need for further empirical studies (see Greenfield, 1991). In sum, the contribution of this approach to understanding school leadership and improvement lies in its potential for explicating how leadership forms in a complex social-political setting. Scholars may adopt this perspective to portray more completely the multiple value perspectives that come into play as schools create and sustain a direction—school improvement. Indeed, this lens holds potential for illuminating two of the blind spots noted at the outset of this review: sources of leadership and notions of effectiveness.

Constructivist Perspectives on Leadership

Anthropologists and sociologists have maintained a long-standing focus on methods of capturing the interpretive, subjective aspects of life. This has often involved describing how participants construct knowledge used within particular social settings (Everhart, 1988; Grant & Fine, 1992; Wolcott, 1992). The constructivist, or sense-making, research orientation examines how leaders and others in the organization create shared understandings about their role and participation in school (Duke, 1986; Everhart, 1988; Slater, 1995). From this viewpoint, leaders help others create meaning and make sense of their work (Blase, 1993; Duke & Iwanicki, 1992; Everhart, 1988; Firestone, 1990; Gilmore & Murphy, 1991; Greenfield, 1991; Lambert et al., 1995; Lotto & Murphy, 1990; Lum, 1997; Ogawa, 1991; Pitner, 1986).

Wolcott (1973) pioneered the constructivist application to school leadership in his landmark ethnographic case study, *Man in the Principal's Office*. Rather than cutting leadership up into component parts, Wolcott provided a rich description of the full context in which the principal worked. This revealed how the culture or context shapes leadership. Despite the promise of his work, few have followed up to apply this method to leadership in school improvement.

Gronn's (1984a) research documented how administrative communication shaped the nature of a leader's work. Similarly, Varenne (1978, 1983) looked at the use of language in building social reality within the school. This involved analyzing the texts of conversations and memos between a principal and teachers. These early ethnographic studies often used the interpretive frame with respect to how the researcher made sense out of participants' actions, rather than how the participants themselves made sense of the actions (Everhart, 1988).

Over the past decade or so, constructivist researchers have used diverse conceptualizations: symbolic, metaphorical, aesthetic, cognitive, and values-oriented leadership (Cooper & Heck, 1995; Duke & Iwanicki, 1992; Gronn, 1984a, Hart, 1994; Leithwood & Stager, 1989; Lum, 1997; Marshall, 1995; Murphy & Beck, 1995; Ogawa, 1991). Duke and Iwanicki (1992), for example, examined the extent to which the values and skills of principals fit with the social norms and needs of their school community. Ogawa (1991) studied leadership succession within a school, examining how the school's normative structure shaped the socialization of a new principal. Lum (1997) investigated how students in a high school constructed metaphorical images of the principal's leadership. Other researchers identified norms and values related to teachers' efforts to resist school change (Anderson, 1991; Corbett, Firestone, & Rossman, 1987; Ogawa, 1991), the manner in which school principals and teachers implement change (Lambert, 1995), or differences in the ways that male and female principals lead (Marshall, 1995).

Role theory has also continued to influence scholars in the study of how teachers and administrators construct school life (see Everhart, 1988). Researchers have shown increasing concern for how organizational norms and values affect participants' construction of their roles and shape leadership behavior. They have also sought to explore how the behavior of leaders influences other school improvement processes.

For example, Hart (1994) used role theory to examine how principals and teachers coped with the implementation of teacher career ladders. In one school, teachers' role orientation changed as they undertook new activities or activities that were previously the responsibility of administrators. They engaged in supervising other teachers, organized and conducted in-service training, coordinated school-wide planning for instruction, and organized a system for student discipline. They worked as a cohesive group. In the other school, however, teachers did not talk at all about how reshaping roles would benefit students or provide increased opportunities for the teachers' professional development. Teachers continued to work in isolation from the others and to maintain their traditional roles.

Over time, teachers in the two schools developed very different "constructions" of the career ladder experience. One set of teachers concluded that career ladders resulted in a new sense of community, while the other group lamented their isolation. Using a constructivist approach and ethnographic methods, Hart's (1994) study aptly juxtaposed the competition between traditional mindsets and new possibilities within the cultures of the schools studied. It provided a concrete instance of the difficulty involved in reshaping the normative structure of the school to support proposed reforms or improvements.

Several researchers (Beck, 1993; Begley, 1996; Hodgkinson, 1983, 1991; Leithwood, Begley, & Cousins, 1992; Leithwood & Hallinger, 1993; Leithwood & Stager, 1989; Leithwood & Steinbach, 1991) investigated the relationship of social cognition and values to school leaders' problem solving and decision making. Leithwood and Stager (1989) studied the problem-solving practices of effective and typical school principals. They found that the two groups of principals differed most with respect to how they solved ill-structured problems. Effective principals expended more energy in selecting their goals, showed greater clarity of personal values, provided more detail about their solution strategies, and focused more directly on the solution (Begley, 1996; Leithwood & Stager, 1989).

Building on Leithwood and Stager's (1989) approach, Cooper and Heck (1995) studied how leaders make meaning out of the crises or problems within their professional lives. This study stemmed from two premises: 1) school administration is experienced as complex social events that hinge on experience and tacit knowledge; 2) knowledge is ordered into explanatory frameworks that can serve as a lens to comprehend experience. Life histories and narrative stories of organizational members may reveal legitimating myths that serve to smooth contradictions between espoused values and practice (Anderson, 1990; Dillard, 1995). Few examples exist, however, in the literature on the inner dialogs of school administrators (Ribbins, 1995).

Cooper and Heck (1995) identified four functions that emerged from interviews and journal entries of principals as they solved messy, ill-structured problems. These included heightened awareness of events as they are unfolding, a means of exploring possible solutions to problems, a means of examining their personal values with respect to decision making, and a record of personal growth in solving complex problems over time (a metacognitive function). The process of analyzing these constructions of leadership in practice provided a glimpse of how principals draw upon their values and commitment to influence school improvement.

The strength of the constructivist approach is in illuminating that which is little known or hidden from view. For example, Leithwood and colleagues' research on administrator thinking sought to uncover the thought processes behind behavior. Dwyer *et al.*'s (1983) study engaged successful principals in reflection on their observed behavior. These approaches reveal how leadership unfolds within school settings as a shared, constructed phenomenon. It forces us to accept that our educational organizations are constructed realities, as opposed to systems or structures that operate independently of the individuals in them.

Critical, Feminist, and Cultural Perspectives on Leadership

The constructivist approach outlined above shares some structural-functionalist assumptions, in that researchers have often investigated the school as a relatively closed system. Other researchers have extended this focus on sensemaking to the dynamics and contradictions of culture and society in the everyday lives of teachers, students, and administrators (Everhart, 1988). The critical (or emancipatory) research orientation to social analysis entails a critique of existing social relationships and advancement toward desired ones (Keith, 1996). The critical stance questions the legitimating role that school leaders play in endorsing and reinforcing existing social arrangements within society. This orientation encompasses feminism and Marxism.

Anderson (1990, 1991), for example, called attention to how the school creates its social reality. He highlighted the potential of tapping the school's most overlooked source of leadership for school improvement: students. He has argued that researchers in educational administration must find ways to study the invisible and unobtrusive forms of control exercised in schools. Otherwise, how can schools hope to improve the lives of clients who attend them?

The critical or emancipatory perspective centers on social change. Thus it provides a different lens through which to view school improvement (Slater, 1995). From the critical standpoint, schools (and their leaders) implicitly institutionalize societal inequity by reinforcing dominant social values. Proponents would not accept predominant notions of school effectiveness as appropriate criteria for assessing a leader's success. They would argue for equity-based criteria as well.

These researchers also argue that traditional images of school leadership offer incomplete explanations of the practical realities and problems of schools (Dillard, 1995; Lomotey, 1989; Marshall, 1993; Maxcy, 1995). Schools exist within a larger institutional and cultural context. Given this broader orientation toward schooling, the closed system orientation of the dominant paradigm has led researchers to ignore the relationship between leadership inside the schoolhouse and the society at large.

Complementing this view of leadership within the social context of schooling is an emerging concern with the impact of cultural context on leadership in schools. Like gender and ethnicity, culture represents a significant blind spot in our field of scholarship. Predominant models and theories in educational administration and leadership of the 20th century have been informed by a Western cultural perspective. It has been assumed that such theories apply in other societies. Although this assumption lacks both conceptual and empirical support, scholars are only beginning to address this blind spot (Cheng, 1995, 1996, in press; Cheng & Wong, 1996; Hallinger, 1995; Hallinger & Leithwood, 1996, in press; Heck, 1996, in press; Leithwood & Duke, in press; Ribbins, 1995; Walker, Bridges & Chan, 1996; Wong, in press).

Gender, Ethnicity, and Leadership

Prior to the 1980s, scholars paid little attention to women and ethnic minority leaders (Lomotey, 1989; Marshall, 1995; Ortiz, 1982; Shakeshaft, 1989; Valverde & Brown, 1988). In part, this lack of attention resulted from the scarcity of women and ethnic minorities occupying administrative positions in schools and research roles in universities. Consequently, there was little academic interest in exploring related issues (Benham, 1997; Cheng and Wong, 1996, in press; Hallinger, 1995). To illustrate this oversight, Epp and colleagues (1994) concluded that between 1980 and 1990 studies in *Educational Administration Quarterly* tended not to report the gender of subjects. They gave even less attention to discussing gender differences among subjects (such as administrators or teachers).

Scholars operating within this line of inquiry evidence a concern for addressing blind spots in studying school leadership that result from societal and cultural inequities in power and social relations. Members of previously marginalized groups are beginning to gain presence in leadership roles in schools and universities (Bloom & Munro, 1995; Benham & Cooper, 1998; Lomotey, 1993). This has resulted in a new expression of voice for those who have not been heard in the past (Benham & Cooper, Bloom & Munro, 1995; 1998; Dillard, 1995).

Scholars have begun to describe how marginalized educational backgrounds have shaped the views of minority school leaders (Benham, 1997, in press; Lomotey, 1993). Findings within this frame highlight the broader goals of education such leaders endorse and the varied demands they face in negotiating dominant cultural and institutional norms (Benham & Cooper, 1998; Bloom & Munro; 1995; Lomotey, 1989; 1993). As summarized in Table 7.1, there is an emerging empirical literature investigating how ethnicity and gender frame the lives of school leaders (Bell & Chase, 1993; Benham, 1997; Benham & Cooper, 1998; Chase, 1992; Dillard, 1995; Goldring & Chen, 1993; Ortiz, 1992; Regan, 1990). A variety of personal experience methods (narrative, biography, life history) and critical ethnography have been used in these investigations.

In one feminist study, Dillard (1995) explored how a school leader's actions were grounded in her personal values, background, and experience. This case study focused on the principal's determined and deliberate student-centered acts on behalf of African-Americans and others. Through her actions, "she gains the authority and credibility needed to shape a more responsive ethos of leadership in and through the multicultural contexts of schools today" (p. 561). This principal focused on building collaborative relationships with staff, students, and parents, and on promoting social justice in the education of all children.

Dillard's study of an African-American female principal provides a vivid contrast to Wolcott's (1973) classic study of principal Ed Bell. Wolcott captured the essence of the school principalship in the 1950s—a closed system dominated by white, male administrators. Wolcott's study did not view the principal's role as inducing change; rather, he concluded that school principals "serve their institutions and society as monitors for continuity" (p. 321). Dillard's case study, in turn, revealed the complexity of leadership in an urban high school of the 1990s. These two case studies provide metaphorical bookends to changing school contexts, leaders' values, and resulting actions. Although both Wolcott and Dillard employed ethnographic methods, they adopted different philosophical stances and asked very different questions.

Researchers using a critical perspective ask explicit questions about existing social relationships and the role of administration in defining and changing them. For example, Benham (in press) studied the cultural and professional stories of three ethnic minority women school leaders. Through an eclectic research process (interviews, writing of narratives, interacting with the women to rewrite the texts, reading of other narratives), she identified several recurring themes in these women's stories. The first theme focused on the leaders' development of strong self-identity in order to recast negative stereotypes. The second described their efforts to redefine the work of their schools in light of their own educational marginalization. The third theme highlighted their strong commitment to educating all children.

This line of inquiry is not without its critics. When viewed from the dominant paradigm, this orientation can appear highly subjective, ideologically-driven, and nonsystematic. This is the nature of cross-paradigm discourse, as differences in the content and process of research derive from varying epistemological foundations. In the next section of the paper, we will comment further on methodological issues.

Here we would simply note that the importance of this approach lies in giving voice to those on the margins of schooling. There is no denying the bias toward the dominant paradigm that has characterized educational administration since the 1950s. Dillard (1995) and Benham (1997, in press) both focused on the leaders whom researchers would have ignored without ideologically-based concern with exploring the social context of schooling. As its proponents argue, this approach can help scholars and practitioners see leadership in more expansive and diverse ways (Benham & Cooper, 1998; Dillard, 1995; Regan, 1990).

Societal Culture and Leadership

Another line of inquiry that emphasizes the social construction of meaning is the cross-cultural study of school leadership. Early ethnographic studies in anthropology sometimes mentioned the cultural transmission of knowledge in primitive societies. Yet these applications of anthropology were infrequent, thin, and rarely consisted of focused empirical study in educational settings (Everhart, 1988). Similarly, over time there has been surprisingly little research on school leadership that is either cross-cultural or that employs indigenous conceptions of leadership in non-Western cultures (Bajunid, 1996).

A cultural lens, like those offered by feminist and critical theorists, reveals different blind spots in the study and practice of school leadership and improvement (Hallinger & Leithwood, 1996). The culture construct has the potential for expanding our field of vision in understanding school leadership. As Hallinger and Leithwood (1996) noted:

> On the practical front, an explicit consideration of culture in administrative practice may illuminate new possibilities for attacking persisting problems (Hallinger, 1995). Morally, the globalization of the world economy and society brings with it demands for a new intellectual honesty. This requires recognition that for a variety of historical reasons the twentieth century witnessed an implicit international collusion that resulted in an hegemony of Western ideas . . . it is time to enrich theory and practice in education by seeking out the diversity of ideas and practices that have existed largely hidden in the shadows of the dominant Western paradigms that have guided the field (p. 100).

Beginning with the work of Getzels *et al.* (1968), administrative theorists sought to develop comprehensive conceptualizations of educational leadership (Hallinger & Leithwood, 1996). In their work, Getzels and his colleagues located the school administrator within a social-cultural context. They discussed the impact that cultural values could exert on the thinking and behavior of leaders and others in the school (Hallinger & Leithwood, 1996). Nonetheless, researchers have subsequently selected pieces of this model for study, ignoring the impact of culture. Only recently have researchers even noticed the dearth of theoretical or empirical research on cultural foundations of leadership (Bajunid, 1996; Cheng & Wong, 1996, in press; Chung & Miskel, 1989; Hallinger, 1995; Walker, Bridges, & Chan, 1996; Wong, in press).

As with other frames noted in this section, the cultural lens can illuminate previously unnoticed aspects of school improvement. For example, there is considerable variation across societies concerning the desired outcomes of education. Canadians place considerably less emphasis on student achievement as a primary outcome of education than do their close neighbors in the United States. Southeast Asian nations view social and cultural transmission as more important than academic purposes of education. These differences are rooted in cultural values and carry through to conceptions of what it means for a school (or administrator) to be effective.

Cultural foundations also have implications when considering methodology. Heck (1996), for example, conducted a secondary analysis of data on school leadership and school effects. His analysis uncovered many methodological issues that researchers encounter in treating the concepts of effectiveness and improvement cross-culturally. It is not nearly as clean as the popular cross-national comparisons of educational progress might suggest.

Culture may also prove to be a powerful lens by highlighting the manner by which societal norms shape and support the practice of school leaders. For example, Cheng and Wong (1996) concluded that many practices noted in Western studies of school effectiveness were readily observable in very typical Chinese schools; they were the norm. Safe, orderly environment, high expectations for all children, rewards and recognition, and clear mission appeared to exist as normative practices that arise out of the societal culture. They concluded that social culture exerts a strong influence on how school administrators conceive of and enact their roles.

Bajunid (1996) has drawn attention to the importance of uncovering indigenous leadership practices within different cultures. He has, for example, explored in-depth the derivation of Malaysian school leadership norms in Muslim religion and Malay culture. At the same time, Bajunid also asserted that there is an important place in Malaysian school administration for global (Western) methods of leadership. These must, however, be adapted to the norms of the particular society.

Hallinger, Taraseina, and Miller (1994) drew a similar conclusion in a study of secondary school instructional leaders in Thailand. Interestingly, their American instrumentation yielded reliable data, yet it failed to capture facets of the school leadership role as constructed by Thai secondary school principals. For example, the American instrument ignored the principal s role in linking the school and its instructional program to community institutions such as the Buddhist temple. This highlights, as Heck's (1996) study, the importance and difficulty of establishing validity in cross-cultural work.

This study also supports the notion that conceptions of effectiveness differ across cultures. The authors noted that the Thai principals' conceptualization of their instructional leadership role was not oriented toward school improvement in any discernible way. Rather, they defined their role as meeting institutional bureaucratic mandates (curriculum) and fostering staff and community cohesion.

These observations suggest that predominant notions of leadership vary across cultures. Nonetheless, both differences and similarities represent grist for the mill of scholars in years to come. For example, Wong (in press) examined the construct of moral leadership as conceptualized by Sergiovanni (1992) and others in the West. He observed that this construct has a history of cultivation within Confucian-influenced Chinese cultures (China, Taiwan, Hong Kong, Singapore). Wong concludes that scholars from Eastern and Western societies can learn by sharing ideas about this construction of the leader's role. These analyses suggest the potential of cross-cultural study for revealing and filling blind spots in school leadership research within and between cultures.

Postmodernism

Other recently developed perspectives toward the study of school leadership include postmoderism and poststructuralism (Bloom & Munro, 1995; Blount, 1993; Maxcy, 1995). Postmodern and poststructural approaches deconstruct the scientific knowledge base of traditional theory. Rather than focusing on a particular lens for understanding phenomena, these schools imply that there is no clear window into the inner life of subjects. From this perspective, attempts to understand a research subject's motivations and behavior are always filtered through lenses of gender, class, and ethnicity. These lenses affect the researcher's construction of the study's text. Consequently, proponents assert that no single method can capture all the variations in human experience (Denzin & Lincoln, 1994).

The postmodern perspective has led scholars to examine the research process, in particular the role of the researcher. Ultimately, this opens up a discussion of how practitioners will apply the results of research studies. There are, however, few empirical examples of this type of work on school leadership.

In one study, Robinson (1996) used problem-based methodology (PBM) to analyze the practices that several schools used to solve educational problems. PBM assumes that research is an interactive process that involves the researcher and the study's subjects. The social relations of inquiry incorporated into PBM are called "critical dialog."

Robinson sought to explain practices in use by identifying the contextual constraints of the situation. Unlike structural-functional approaches, PBM de-emphasizes individual roles (the principal, for example). In this regard, postmodern and poststructural approaches view leadership from nontraditional standpoints. They shift attention away from leadership bound to hierarchical position and are open to leadership that may be more informal and often interim. Moreover, by explicitly focusing on contextual constraints, this lens turns away from great man or hero-oriented stereotypes of leadership.

Methodological Issues in Studying School Leadership

The process of research involves not only philosophical and conceptual foundations, but also methodology. Two general approaches to methodology have emerged from academic debate conducted over the past 20 years. The dominant approach remains the positivist pursuit of a structural interpretation of social processes (in other words, looking for regularities in social data). Researchers working within this framework tend to use quantitative methods of analysis.

Interpretivist and critical theorists expound a contrasting approach that seeks to describe how participants construct their social lives. It attends more specifically to the contextual, evolutionary, and political nature of knowledge construction (Dobbert & Kurth-Schai, 1992). These approaches draw heavily on qualitative methodologies. Some excellent reviews of the application of qualitative and quantitative methods and techniques in educational administration were provided in the previous *Handbook* (Everhart, 1988; Griffiths, 1988; Pitner, 1988; Tatsuoka & Silver, 1988).

In this section, we discuss quantitative and qualitative methodological concerns that emerged from our study of this empirical literature on school leadership (summarized in Table 7.1). In particular, we focus on: (1) trends in quantitative methods of studying school leadership, (2) emerging empirical work in personal experience methods and textual concerns in presenting research.

Trends in the Use of Quantitative Methods for Studying School Leadership

We have reviewed quantitative research within this domain extensively elsewhere (Hallinger & Heck, 1996a, 1996b). Here we outline our major findings. Almost all the quantitative studies reviewed used some form of cross-sectional, correlational design. These often employed surveys or interviews to collect data. Studies of this type fall under the broad design of nonexperimental research (Pedhazur & Schmelkin, 1991).

Conceptualizing and Operationalizing Variables

In contrast to experimental or quasi-experimental designs, nonexperimental research does not seek to manipulate the independent variables. Because of this, the relationships explicated in the conceptual model play an important role in interpreting the results. Attempts are made to account for a dependent variable such as school outcomes or improvement by "uncovering" relevant independent variables. Model specification must include all relevant independent variables. Empirical research grounded in overly simplistic conceptualizations of leadership is unlikely to yield results that are useful, practically or theoretically.

Differences in how theoretical models of school leadership are conceptualized and operationalized have important implications for the ways in which they are tested. This, in turn, has an impact on the conclusions that we can draw about the nature of leadership and its effects. The complexity of relationships among environmental influences, leadership, school processes, and school outcomes has often overmatched the conceptual models and methodological tools being used by researchers.

When we inquire into the effects of school leadership, a wide range of dependent variables is available for study. The dependent variables may be broadly grouped into school and environmental variables (parent satisfaction, community participation, perceptions of school functioning), intra-organizational processes (leadership, staff morale, curricular organization, instructional effectiveness), and student effects (student achievement, attitudes, attendance). The priority assigned to these variables varies widely, both within and across countries, and is implicitly value-laden.

During the 1980s, policymakers cast the question of principal impact in terms of its effects on a single variable —student achievement. Research adopting this perspective began to appear in 1984 (Biester *et al.*, 1984; Glasman, 1984; O'Day, 1984; Rowan & Denk, 1984). Although research that examines principal impact on school outcomes is highly attractive from a policy perspective, it has been fraught with conceptual and methodological problems. A salient strength of this research—its reliance on standardized test scores—has become its greatest limitation. Internationally, educators now believe that an effective education is comprised of a wider range of cognitive and affective variables than achievement on standardized tests (Leithwood *et al.*, 1990). Continued reliance on narrow standardized measures for assessing the impact of school leadership distorts the meaning of the question, "Does school leadership make a difference?"

As restructuring gathered steam during the 1990s, we have noted a corresponding shift in thinking toward broader views of school leadership effects. Researchers have now turned their attention to leadership aimed at "second order changes" (Heck & Brandon, 1995; Leithwood *et al.*, 1993; Leithwood, 1994; Louis & Miles, 1991; Murphy & Louis, 1994; Silins, 1994). Consequently, they have begun to study how principals influence in-school variables as well as outcomes (teacher perceptions of change implementation; teacher perceptions of program, school, and student outcomes; student persistence; grades; attendance). Researchers should continue this trend toward broadening the conceptualization and measurement of leader effects.

Scholars have also sought to understand how the school context influences expectations for leadership and the leader's subsequent responses. Though our understanding of contextual influences on school leadership has increased, scholars have only begun to scratch the surface. A few variables (such as socio-economic status and school level) have received more attention than others (district structures, community political conditions, rural/urban, cultural distinctions). The theoretical conceptualizations underlying the investigation of school context variables are in sore need of further development.

Similarly, outside of earlier trait studies on administrators, personal variables (experience, educational backgrounds, gender, professional socialization) have received little sustained consideration in studies of leadership effects. This state is particularly surprising because empirical studies consistently support the finding of gender differences in leadership effects at the elementary school level. From our perspective, future research should incorporate socialization processes and gender into models that explore the effects of leaders on school improvement.

Finally, as a group, these studies have identified promising mediating variables between school leadership and school effectiveness. Some mediating variables ripe for study include goal development, decision-making participation, teacher commitment and expertise, monitoring of change implementation, staff development, and changes in teacher classroom practices (see Hallinger & Heck, 1998 for a comprehensive discussion). These are among the key blank spots we referred to earlier.

Methods of Analyzing Data

Analytical techniques also affect substantive conclusions that can be drawn concerning school leadership (Hallinger & Heck, 1996b; Tatsuoka & Silver, 1988). Analyses using multivariate approaches, such as structural equation modeling, may uncover relationships in the data that more simplistic analyses do not reveal. However, they will lead to fewer findings of substance (Pedhazur & Schmelkin, 1991). More complex analyses control the effects of extraneous predictor variables in a single multivariate test. This is highly preferable to conducting several single predictor tests (t-tests or bivariate correlations) on a dependent variable.

It is not just the sophistication of analytic method that determines whether and to what extent a study verifies a particular set of theoretical relations. Rather, it is the manner in which the study is conceptualized, designed, and conducted that matters (Tatsuoka & Silver, 1988). Ultimately, this affects the confidence that we can place in the interpretation of an investigation's findings.

The pattern of findings in previous research on school leadership effects illustrates this point. Researchers investigating direct principal effects on school outcomes tend to use descriptive statistics, correlational analysis, and tests of differences between groups of principals. These approaches do not allow for testing complex models. Multiple regression is also used in several studies, but even this test cannot fully detect the indirect effects of leadership on school outcomes.

As conceptualizations of administrative effects shifted from direct effects on outcomes to indirect effects, researchers sought other more powerful analytic methods. Structural equation modeling (SEM) are one of these methods. SEM can examine a variety of theoretical models including those with latent (unobserved) variables, direct and indirect effects (Hallinger et al., 1990; Heck et al., 1990; Leithwood, 1994; Scott & Teddlie, 1987; Silins, 1994; van de Grift, 1990), reciprocal effects, data collected at several points in time, and data that are hierarchical in nature. SEM techniques, when combined with a comprehensive conceptualization of leadership, have produced consistent findings across several countries. The approach is likely to become widely used in educational administration over the next decade.

Another useful quantitative modeling technique that is likely to gain popularity in studies of leadership effects (Rowan, Raudenbush, & Kang, 1991) is multilevel (or hierarchical) modeling. Such studies focus on the effects of variables across levels of the organization. In education, these distinctions are readily apparent but have been difficult to investigate empirically. Students bring individual abilities to their classrooms; teachers shape the children's classroom environment; principals monitor teachers within their schools; superintendents develop improvement plans for their districts.

Scholars also refer to this as a nested data structure (Bossert et al., 1982). In the study of principal effects, this structural feature of educational organizations takes on particular importance. Principals are likely to influence the school level of the organization more directly than the classroom or student levels. Decisions about whether to use disaggregated (individual) data or aggregated (school) data raise the unit of analysis problem. This issue has limited the accurate investigation of leadership effects, as relatively few researchers have taken advantage of this method of analysis.

The approach can illuminate many research situations. It allows the researcher to decompose the variability in important dependent variables (outcomes or leadership) across different levels of the school. After determining the proportions of variance that exist within schools or classrooms within schools, multilevel regression models can analyze the within-unit and between-unit variance (Rowan et al., 1991). Thus school data can account for within-school differences in staff composition and student background variables, making comparisons between schools more meaningful.

Although we found evidence of indirect administrative effects across several studies conducted in a variety of settings, major design limitations also continue to be evident: sampling, data collection design, over-reliance on elementary settings, and inconsistency in the choice of variables included for study. These limitations make it difficult to account for causal relationships within individual studies. Flaws in design and sampling among individual studies limit the ability to generalize results. This raises the importance of replication of results across a variety of settings and research conditions.

Trends in the Use of Qualitative Methods in Studying School Leadership

In recent years, some scholars have changed their assumptions about the role of leadership in school improvement by asking different questions. Rather than seeing leadership as part of a production function—the epitome of structural-functionalist inquiry—they have asked questions about how leaders create meaning within social systems, or they have inquired into leadership exercised by others in the school community than the principal. Or they have asked how school leaders shape and are shaped by their experiences within the social-political context in which they have lived and in which they work.

As interest in alternate orientations toward school leadership has increased over the past decade, there has been a concomitant increase in the use of qualitative methods of study. These include traditional ethnography, naturalistic inquiry, case study, and several personal experience approaches (Begley, 1996; Benham, 1997; Benham & Cooper, 1998; Bloom & Munro, 1995; Blount, 1993; Cooper & Heck, 1995; Keith, 1996; Lomotey, 1989, 1993; Ortiz, 1992; Ribbins, 1996; Robinson, 1996). Qualitative approaches offer a useful avenue for understanding how leadership is defined and implemented, how leaders are shaped by their backgrounds and beliefs (gender, ethnicity, culture, educational experiences), and how they think about and resolve educational problems. These are characteristics of leadership that are difficult to uncover through surveys and quantitative inquiry. As such, qualitative inquiry has a role to play in filling blank spots and also blind spots.

Ethnography and Fieldwork
Ethnography is the starting point for any discussion of qualitative methods. It involves immersion over a substantial period in a single setting. Its goal is to reveal the shared cultural norms and values that guide people's behavior within the school. As Everhart (1988) noted, Wolcott (1973), Varenne

(1978, 1983), and Gronn (1984a) provided early examples of the use of ethnography to help construct understandings of leadership in schools. These studies show how the constructivist orientation departed from observation research that simply described the work of administrators (Martin & Willower, 1982; Peterson, 1978).

Wolcott (1973) used participant-observation to conduct an intensive ethnographic case study with one principal. He relied on various sources of information to generate a rich description of the principal in his school context. In addition, Wolcott attempted to "provide his reader with something of his personal biases and with an account of the context in which he has conducted his fieldwork and translated it into an ethnographic statement" (p. 18). Thus Wolcott began to focus on the effect of the researcher on the research process and the constructing of the research narrative.

In the previous *Handbook*, Everhart (1988) provided a rationale and description of how one might conduct fieldwork on leadership from a constructivist perspective. Because of their focus on process over structural regularities, interpretive approaches such as constructivism have relied largely on fieldwork and ethnographic methods as preferred methods for studying school phenomena. Beginning in the mid-1970s, researchers began to address the limitations associated with the structural approach (positivism) with respect to issues of subjectivity and the social construction of knowledge (Erickson, 1973; Everhart, 1988; Wolcott, 1975). Ethnographic studies reveal the context and social reality existing for the participants in a study. With this goal, the role of the researcher in the investigation, understanding, interpretation, and writing of the research text became an important focus (Everhart, 1988).

With its roots in anthropology, ethnographic methods have the longest track record of the qualitative methods in use today. Consequently, researchers have had more time to craft the tools of ethnographic observation and interviews into a cohesive and articulate methodology. Thus unlike the other qualitative methods we discuss, there is a more fully-developed shared technology for conducting ethnographic inquiry and for assessing its results.

Ethnography is highly appropriate for investigating certain blank spots that we have discussed. For example, ethnography might reveal much about the mediating variables linked to leadership. It could also illuminate the personal motivations and contextual forces that shape a leader's behavior in context.

Ethnographic analysis is also capable of addressing blind spots in this field of study. As an anthropological method, it is aptly designed to describe how leaders help others make meaning from their work. Similarly, it can be used to describe how people construct the social relations that we call leadership and followership. A related approach, critical ethnography, carries a social concern for power inequities into the field setting. This agenda enters into the construction of text about the social relationships studied and highlights the further responsibility of the researcher, after identifying and studying inequities, to promote social justice.

Ethnography is highly appropriate to studying leadership across cultures. Indeed, the starting point for programmatic cross-cultural research on school leadership is to uncover indigenous conceptions of school leadership. Ethnography is the preferred method for this purpose. In light of this endorsement, it is surprising that researchers have so seldom used it in the field. It is, of course, an intensive, time-consuming methodology and requires intensive training that goes beyond the capacities of most doctoral programs.

Case Study

Case studies encompass a related set of qualitative techniques. Although case study research can employ a quantitative approach, it is a preferred method for qualitative inquiry. As such, it is a broad category and could include anything from ethnography, narrative, biography, reflective interviews, and historical analysis to time and motion analysis.

In general, case study designs are limited in terms of the extent to which we can transfer the findings to other settings. They provide rich description, but of only a small number of individuals (principals or teachers) or schools. Researchers often argue that generalizability is not a main goal of case analyses; however, in the field's overall construction of knowledge about educational processes, researchers must be conscious of potential limitations of their research settings. Although some researchers are cautious in interpreting findings from very limited settings, others readily extend their conclusions over the full population.

We also suggest the need for researchers to give attention to the quality of the data collection that goes into the construction of the research text. In reviewing studies, for example, we found great differences in the amounts of time researchers spent in the field. At one end of this spectrum, researchers interviewed subjects for an hour or so. In other cases, they spent a few days, a week, or up to a year at a site.

We also noted considerable variation across the studies in the extent to which researchers provided a rationale for their methods of fieldwork. Especially in interpretivist and critical-contextual approaches, it is essential for researchers to delineate how they treated the data, the intellectual processes used to arrive at conclusions, and the level of credibility warranted in the findings. Although fieldwork researchers typically suggest that they are using "thick" description, there is often little "evidence" included in the text. Consequently, the reader is forced to trust the researcher's interpretations of the data without sufficient sense as to the boundaries of their application.

We do not suggest specific rules covering the length of time in the field or the description of method. We do, however, urge scholars to attend more carefully to such methodological issues as the quality of their data collection procedures, the presentation of sufficient data within the research text, and the description of their analytic and interpretative processes. Elsewhere, we and others have subjected researchers' uses of quantitative designs and analysis to hard-nosed critique. We believe that advocates of new generation approaches must similarly demonstrate the rigor of their methods within the text of their reports.

Narrative and Personal History

Narrative inquiry is situated within qualitative research methodology. It has evolved out of ethnographic concerns with presenting subjects' constructions of their worlds. It also expands somewhat on the examination of the researcher's role in investigating and interpreting phenomena.

Narrative is philosophically aligned with work in experiential philosophy, critical theory, and anthropology (Eisner, 1988). It includes closely related modes of inquiry such as studies of "the personal" and the use of "voice" in feminist studies (Elbaz, 1988). Narrative functions as both phenomenon and method (Connelly & Clandinin, 1990; Cortazzi, 1993). Commonly, the phenomenon is referred to as story and the inquiry as narrative.

Several researchers (Benham, 1997; in press; Benham & Cooper, 1998; Bloom & Munro, 1995; Dillard, 1995; Ortiz, 1992; Regan, 1990) have used narrative and life history to show how values and background (gender, ethnicity, cultural experiences) shape the professional practice of minority and women school leaders. They seek to reveal cognitive and affective connections that undergird subjects' leadership (philosophy, educational experience, lineage, family, motherhood, community).

These studies typically focus on a small number of subjects, ranging from one to several leaders. As we have suggested, this limits generalizability, although this is not the primary concern. Some researchers, however, have used multiple case studies to present a more complete (or contrasting) view. In one example study, Benham and Cooper (1998) examined the shared narratives (text constructed by both researchers and subjects working together) of nine minority women school leaders. Their constructed narratives function as metaphors for the women's conceptions of school leadership. They provide a rich picture of how leadership evolves among minority women educators. The particular form of leadership the women conceived of and enacted was embedded in their personal experience. It was also intimately linked to the surrounding social, historical, and cultural institutions in which they lived and worked (Benham & Cooper, 1998). As one principal said:

It's taken me years to get that [diminished expectations] out of their minds. They don't see it as a problem. One of the counselors I work with refers to the children as "those" kids [African-American, inner city high school students]. Her words were, "Those kids don't need arts and culture classes." Let's face it. This is divisive behavior! (p. 92–93).

Finally, their experiences made them seek a type of leadership that focused on connecting with people and increasing their participation in decision making processes. As one woman explained:

I don't see myself as being central to other individuals' lives. I mean, I might be a piece, but I am not central . . . I understand my responsibility to [the school] and what goes with it. It is a very collaborative, mutual vision and effort. It is dynamic and not static. I know that's a very different way to look at it. It's the Anglo world view that you can freeze-frame life (p. 29).

The benefit of the narrative approach in these studies is that they are rich in detail derived from human relationships in the school and the personal context of the leader (Benham, 1997). Allowing leaders to give voice to their experiences challenges the traditional view of scientific neutrality. However, by studying events as they unfold through those who live them, we gain new insight into what administrators know and how this is altered through experience.

Cooper and Heck (1995) provided an initial framework for using narrative in studying school administration. They followed with an exploratory study of four school administrators' problem-solving practices through the use of narrative and a critique of the approach as a method of analysis. Narrative is not designed to be a method for objectively observing and understanding phenomena (Benham, 1997; Bloom & Munro, 1995; Clandinin & Connelly, 1994).

Narrative may also be useful in understanding decision-making or problem-solving practices of school leaders. It provides a deeper look into what is primarily an internal process that is difficult to measure through survey techniques. Cooper and Heck (1995) used journals as one data source to provide insight into how administrators make sense out of and cope with various messy problems. The data were helpful in defining how the personal values of school administrators interact with political and organizational issues to create personal action to solve day-to-day school problems. They found, however, that principals differed in their uses of the journal. Moreover, what was entered as data varied widely across individuals.

This approach has merit for development of principals through sharing narratives from mentors to novice. Experienced principals draw on a rich store of knowledge about solving problems. Readers of narratives need to be prepared to see possible meanings in the story and to see possibilities

for telling their own stories (Clandinin & Connelly, 1994; Cooper, 1995; Ortiz, 1992).

Narrative presents numerous difficulties in terms of construction and presentation. Much needs to be learned, for example, about the range of purposes and variants of this method. Thus we suggest several cautions. Subjects differ in their understanding of the method and in their ability to use sources for data collection (such as personal journals or written accounts of experience). Recollections or attributions concerning how one's personal leadership has developed are by definition highly subjective (Cooper & Heck, 1995). The developmental stage and personal style of the subject can influence the trustworthiness of the narrative. Processing subjects' accounts therefore becomes an important consideration.

The central capacity of narrative to describe life experiences in relevant and meaningful ways can deceive as easily as it can inform. One common pitfall is for subjects to smooth the narrative by leaving out details that may be controversial or overly revealing. Because stories that serve as data are "created" by the teller, researchers must use care in moving from individual cases or stories to comparisons (or generalizations) across several narratives.

Finally, in such forms as oral history, there are few norms on how to analyze or interpret the data (Grant & Fine, 1992). Some researchers do not analyze the stories, arguing that this would impose their own biases on the narrative (Bloom & Munro, 1995). Others attempt to find emergent categories across several narratives (using the comparative method). The diversity of approaches to analyzing narrative data suggests the need for the development of guidelines to assess these research efforts.

Textual Issues

Critical and post-structural approaches to the construction of scientific knowledge have called attention to the use of language in the research process (Gee *et al.*, 1992; Grant & Fine, 1992; Jensen & Peshkin, 1992; Wolcott, 1994; Woods, 1992). This concern for language emerged as scholars gave greater attention to how subjects construct meaning in social relationships and activities (Grant & Fine, 1992; Roman, 1992; Wolcott, 1994). This placed the researcher at the center of how research is conducted and text written.

Issues concerning language are salient to data collection, analysis, and interpretation (Erickson, 1992; Gee *et al.*, 1992; Grant & Fine, 1992; Jensen & Peskin, 1992; Ortiz, 1992; Wolcott, 1994; Woods, 1992). Concern with the dialog of subjects stems from ethnographic attempts to reveal ordinary life in schools through the routine actions and sense-making of individuals (students, teachers, administrators). These issues emerge, for example, as researchers attempt to make use of new research techniques such as narrative, biography, or critical ethnography.

The intellectual roots of this work are the analysis of verbal and nonverbal behavior, communication within and across cultural groups, conversational analysis, and discourse analysis (Erickson, 1992; Gee *et al.*, 1992; Psathas, 1995). For example, discourse analysis focuses on the structure of language and features of texts. It also delves into how texts relate to social, cognitive, political, and cultural constructions. The interpretation of texts, therefore, is influenced by the text's structure and the social circumstances surrounding its production (Gee *et al.*, 1992).

How readers read and interpret the research text is at the core of textual concerns. Readers' own backgrounds may differ from those of the researchers. This in turn can influence their interpretations of the text.

The subject's language may also differ from the researcher's (Gee *et al.*, 1992). As critics have noted, researchers often speak as experts, using language that other researchers understand. This can evolve into the language of social elites (Grant & Fine, 1992; Jensen & Peshkin, 1992). Research, therefore, is always a construction because the researcher puts himself or herself into the process in collecting, analyzing, and interpreting the data. This is the case regardless of the extent to which the researcher has or has not participated in what is being studied (Woods, 1992).

The relationship between researcher and subject certainly has some impact on what is seen and how it is translated into text. As Everhart (1988) noted, early efforts to construct social meaning in work on school leadership focused on the researcher's attempts to make sense of the data. Gradually, this attention shifted to the participants' constructions of social reality. Researchers are still left with an unresolved dilemma. They may intentionally acknowledge (or unintentionally overlook) how the researcher-subject relationship impacts the research. As we have noted, one attempted solution has been to present the participants' texts with little or no analysis from the researcher or to allow the participants to construct and interpret their own texts.

This can be especially problematic in doing life history, as subjects' thoughts and accounts are of unknown scope even to themselves. As Woods (1992) argues, the experiences subjects recall are reconstructed over time. How they perceive the researcher may interact with how they interpret the data collection process (counseling, spying). Currently, there are few disciplinary norms for editing subjects' stories or for presenting such oral histories (narrative, biography) as research.

Concerns with textual issues have led some doing research on school leadership to examine more closely the construction of their research texts. These concerns include how to present the researcher-subject relationship, how to write up field notes, and how to present holistic accounts of experience or administrators in schools (Benham, 1997; Bloom & Munro, 1995; Dillard, 1995; Ortiz, 1992;

Regan, 1990). Although some could argue that any attempt to explain subjects' accounts results in a researcher's "grand narrative," most researchers focusing on narrative reject the notion that presenting and explaining the experiences of marginalized subjects results in a biased, and privileged, narrative (Grant & Fine, 1992; Roman, 1992).

In this set of studies, researchers handled the construction of texts and their analysis in different manners. Bloom and Munro (1995) used life history (narrative) to study the construction of gender and self-identity among four women school administrators. The stories focused on the women's transitions from teachers to administrators. The study described their experiences facing contradictory expectations arising from their positions of authority and their identities as women.

In presenting the stories, Bloom and Munro (1995) drew on both feminism and postmodernism to make sense of the administrator's life histories. Rather than focusing on their own construction of emergent themes running across the stories, in the article's discussion section, they opened a dialog about what they learned about interpretive research in the process of writing the narratives. As Bloom and Munro concluded, the process of doing the research generates questions (as opposed to answers) about what it means to do interpretive work about social and cultural constructions.

Benham, (1997), addressed the text construction issue somewhat differently. They included the subject of the study as an author in the research article; the text's construction became a joint effort. The examination of the school leader's experiences also presented an opportunity for self-reflection on the part of the researcher.

Dillard's (1995) study of school leadership represented another attempt to explore the relationship between researcher and subject. In her case study, Dillard argued that the researcher's interests originated primarily in her own personal background and life circumstances. As she reflected:

> As an African-American woman researcher, I am particularly interested in the inclusion of African- American women's realities in the shaping of policy and literature surrounding effective schools and schooling . . . throughout these narratives the reader will find my own interpretations of the meaning of these narratives in relation to the body of knowledge surrounding the effective school principal (p.543).

The blending of researcher and subject suggest ways in which both engage in the process of interpreting their lives and work. Thus the method used in narrative studies (Benham & Cooper, 1998; Bloom & Munro, 1995; Dillard, 1995) provides a sharp contrast to the traditional objective stance of the researcher in most of the school leadership studies we reviewed previously. Regan's (1990) account of her experiences as a feminist administrator is another attempt to challenge the dominant view of school administration and the construction of the research text. Keith's (1996) study of teachers and school reform, and Marshall *et al.*'s (1996) examination of the ethic of care among school assistant principals draw on similar methods.

Postmodern studies also raise textual issues about how research is conducted, analyzed, written, and presented to practitioners. This has led to experiments intended to enlarge the range of possibilities available for expressing "voice" in the research text (Bloom & Munro, 1995; Blount, 1993; Lincoln, 1996). Personal experience methods such as narrative and biography uncover subjects' beliefs and perceptions and articulate them directly to readers. The intent of postmodern scholars is to reduce the intrusion of their own biases by letting subjects construct their own stories of experience.

Empirical studies that illustrate these newer approaches are often not fully refined. In some cases (narrative, for example), there are few guidelines governing the methodology. We believe that there is value in this type of experimentation. The researchers raise questions about such issues as the relationship between researcher and subject-practitioner, and the construction of research texts. They also highlight substantive concerns such as cultural norms governing the selection and socialization of school leaders.

The Future Study of Leadership and School Improvement

In the first *Handbook*, Griffiths (1988) pointed out that despite the dominant hold of the positivist paradigm, several new theoretical schools were beginning to emerge within the field. This included negotiation (political conflict), metaphor and culture (which we view as sense-making), and Marxist, critical, and feminist theory. We found this trend of diversity in conceptual and methodological approaches to research has developed further over the ensuing decade. In this last section, we comment on where school leadership research stands today and where it may head over the next decade.

This review suggests that researchers have adopted considerable flexibility in their approaches to the structure of knowledge (positivist, interpretive, critical) and corresponding theoretical lenses (structural-functional, constructivist, feminist, postmodern). These approaches have produced several identifiable research strands of varying depth in the investigation of school leadership. These include studies of the nature of the leader's work, leadership effects, the social construction of leadership, the leadership's contribution to wider issues of social justice, and leadership across cultures.

As theorists have argued (Evers & Lakomski, 1996; Griffiths, 1988; Maxcy, 1995), researchers in educational administration do not start with well-developed theories. Instead, as Willower suggested in 1975, the use of conceptual frameworks has been a sufficient orientation to accommodate the interpretation of empirical data in educational administration. Despite the impressive progress made by those working within the functionalist paradigm over the past 20 years, it is clear that more informal approaches to theory are being used (Griffiths, 1988). These alternate frameworks illuminate important blind spots. They force us to question the meaning of effectiveness and improvement. Whether operating from a feminist or cultural framework, clearly the definition (meaning) and form of leadership is itself subject to subjective interpretation.

The social science paradigm that guided educational administration's development since the 1950s has been critiqued by scholars around the world (Evers & Lakomski, 1996; Greenfield, 1980; Maxcy, 1995; Murphy, 1992; Murphy & Hallinger, 1992). Permeating these critiques is the growing recognition of important intellectual blind spots in the discipline 's field of vision (Hallinger & Leithwood, 1996). The influences of broader theories of knowledge, human cognition, research methodology, and relationship of theory to practice have markedly influenced the field (Evers & Lakomski, 1996).

One challenge concerns how researchers integrate findings from studies conducted using different philosophical perspectives and methodologies. Our capacity to make sense of this patchwork of findings is severely limited. While we can summarize the approaches researchers are using to study school leadership, it is not possible to reconcile them. At one end of the spectrum, the positivist tradition has delineated conditions that must be present in order for a study to be accepted as research. At the other end, there are no common foundations for creating knowledge. How can we draw conclusions or organize findings across studies (Maxcy, 1995)?

Criticisms of positivist approaches imply empirical inadequacies in supporting proposed theories (Evers & Lakomski, 1996; Willower, 1996). Yet these criticisms leave problematical the questions of why some theories or models are useful in answering questions or solving problems. Our analysis of school leadership effects suggested consistency in the finding of indirect effects in a line of research conducted over a 15-year period and in a variety of different settings.

We have only begun to learn about school leadership via alternative conceptualizations and methodologies. We detailed several issues dealing with the description, analysis, interpretation, and writing of research texts. These issues go to the core of how we construct knowledge in the research community. We believe this should draw the attention of researchers (and editorial boards) in the future.

Although we cannot synthesize the contribution of the new generation studies, we will summarize salient points that emerged from the review. The studies highlight the benefits of exploring leadership in school improvement from multiple perspectives. For example, the political conflict perspective revealed the gross failure of a major body of research on leadership effects to address the role of political processes. This includes the role of unions as well as the messy, sometimes unpleasant, process by which a school selects its goals. This lens also led researchers to explore how the leader negotiates support from the school community and gains its commitment to change.

The political, critical, and cultural lenses illuminated the narrow focus evident in functionalist research on leadership effects. In an instant, they reveal the implicit functionalist assumption that student achievement ought to represent the dominant criterion for assessing leader effectiveness. This raises a host of issues concerning the goals for school improvement: what they should be and who should define them.

Feminist, critical, and cultural lenses have focused new attention on the personal dimensions of school leadership. Again, this is an area in which the functionalist orientation has had little success. Through the study of nontraditional subjects (using nontraditional methods) researchers have begun to reveal different conceptions of leadership that seem related to personal background. These have potential for deepening our understanding of school leadership.

In particular, these studies call attention to the impact of the context in which leaders work. Bridges (1982) earlier noted the inclination to ignore contextual constraints when considering school leadership and its effects. We noted that functionalist methods have been singularly ineffective at attacking this issue. Until we better understand the relationship between leader and school context, it will be difficult to alter our belief that leaders provide the critical impetus for school improvement.

Here the critical line of inquiry could be particularly illuminating. Recall that this orientation seeks to understand leadership and schooling from the perspective of those who have been previously led or marginalized. This could be teachers, students, or parents. This and other alternate orientations toward the study of schooling offer the possibility of resolving persistent problems in the study of leadership by radically altering our perspective.

Another salient issue emerging from this review concerns the cultural context of school leadership. There is a dearth of solid comparative research in educational administration. One limitation is that the bulk of the studies were conducted in contexts where Western systems of education predominate. The serious consideration of non-Western conceptions of leadership can open our eyes to theoretical treatments derived from very different intellectual traditions (Confucian, Muslim, Buddhist). Future research in this subdomain should view school leadership as located within a cultural context (Hallinger & Leithwood, 1996). Such research will need to account not only for potentially different conceptualizations of leadership, but also different views on the desired outcomes of leadership across cultures.

The study of school leadership across cultures also has methodological implications. There is a long tradition of using qualitative and quantitative techniques in cross-cultural studies (Lewellen, 1992). We can best gain culturally appropriate definitions of leadership through qualitative methods. Subsequently, quantitative study will allow researchers to compare definitions of leadership (and its effects) across settings. This will raise a variety of challenging quantitative research issues (Heck, 1996). This again highlights the fact that theory and method play a mutually reinforcing nature in the creation of new knowledge.

This coming decade is likely to see greater flexibility, experimentation, and eclecticism in terms of philosophical stances and methodologies used to study educational phenomena (Donmoyer, 1996; Jermier, 1985). The new generation orientations and methodologies described in this review will require considerable testing, demonstration, exposition, and further discussion among scholars and practitioners. We believe that these approaches have a role to play in scholarly inquiry, but the extent and nature of that role in the creation of knowledge remains unclear at this time.

We suggest that interested scholars proceed on two fronts. Thus far, these new approaches have illuminated blind spots—previously unnoticed or undervalued facets of leadership in school improvement. Critique and exposition of relevant philosophical frameworks have served a useful purpose to date, but this will not suffice in the future. More scholars operating in these lines of inquiry must conduct empirical studies with the same systematic and sustained effort that has characterized the functionalist school over the past 15 years. Only in this way will they fill the blank spots in these alternate epistemological frames.

Second, there is a need to continue conversations about philosophical foundations, relevant leadership constructs, and empirical methods in academic and practitioner forums. Proponents of the alternate orientations have a responsibility to make their case in a means that is accessible to both audiences. Only in this way can their peers make informed judgments. If the field proceeds on both of these fronts, reviewers of this research a decade hence will be in a far better position to form substantive judgments. They will be able to determine the substantive contribution of these new generation approaches to understanding the role of leaders in school improvement. We look forward to that development as it will also indicate a further maturation of this domain as a field of study.

REFERENCES

Anderson, G. (1990). Toward a critical constructivist approach to school administration: Invisibility, legitimation, and the study of nonevents. *Educational Administration Quarterly, 26*(1) 38–59.

Anderson, G. (1991). Cognitive politics in principals and teachers: Ideological control in an elementary school. In J. Blase (Ed.) *The politics of life in schools: Power, conflict, and cooperation.* Newbury Park, CA: Sage, 120–138.

Anderson, L. & Shirley, R. (1995). High school principals and school reform: Lessons learned from a statewide study of project Re: Learning. *Educational Administration Quarterly, 31*(3), 405–423.

Andrews, R. & Soder, R. (1987). Principal instructional leadership and school achievement. *Educational Leadership, 44,* 9–11.

Bacharach, S. & Mundell, B. (1993). Organizational politics in schools: Micro, macro, and logics of action. *Educational Administration Quarterly, 29*(4), 423–452.

Bajunid, I. (1996). Preliminary explorations of indigenous perspectives of educational management: the evolving Malaysian experience. *Journal of Educational Administration, 34*(5), 50–73.

Ball, S. (1987). *The micropolitics of the school: Toward a theory of school organization.* New York: Methuen.

Ball, S. & Bowe, R. (1991). Micropolitics of radical change: Budgets, management, and control in British schools. In J. Blaise (Ed.) *The politics of life in schools: Power, conflict, and cooperation.* Newbury Park, CA: Sage, 19–45.

Bamburg, J. & Andrews, R. (1990). School goals, principals and achievement. *School Effectiveness and School Improvement, 2*(3), pp. 175–191.

Bass, B. & Avolio, B. (1989). Potential biases in leadership measures: How prototypes, lenience, and general satisfaction relate to ratings and rankings of transformational and transactional leadership construct. *Educational and Psychological Measurement.* 49(3), 509–527.

Beck, C. (1993). *Learning to live the good life.* Toronto: Ontario Institute for Studies in Education.

Begley, P. (1996). Cognitive perspectives on values in administration: A quest for coherence and relevance. *Educational Administration Quarterly, 32*(3), 403–426.

Bell, C. & Chase, S. (1993). The underrepresentation of women in school leadership. In C. Marshall (Ed.), *The new politics of race and gender.* Washington, DC: Falmer Press, 141–154.

Benham, M. (1997). The story of an African-American teacher-scholar: A woman's narrative. *Qualitative Studies in Education, 10*(1), 63–83.

Benham, M. (In press). Silences and serenades, The journeys of three ethnic minority women school leaders. *Anthropology and Education Quarterly.*

Benham, M. & Cooper, J. (1998). *Let my spirit soar! Narratives of diverse women in school leadership.* Newbury Park, CA: Corwin Press.

Biester, T., Kruse, J., Beyer, F. & Heller, B. (1984, April). *Effects of administrative leadership on student achievement.* Paper presented at the annual meeting of the American Educational Research Association, New Orleans.

Blase, J. (1989). The micropolitics of the school. The everyday political orientations of teachers toward open school principals. *Educational Administration Quarterly, 25,* 377–407.

Blase, J. (1993). The micropolitics of effective school-based leadership: Teachers perspectives. *Educational Administration Quarterly, 29*(2), 142–163.

Bloom, L. & Munro, P. (1995). Conflicts of selves: Nonunitary subjectivity in women administrators life history narratives. In J. Hatch & R. Wisniewski (Eds.) *Life history and narrative.* Washington, DC: Falmer Press (99–112).

Blount, J. (1993). One postmodern perspective on educational leadership: And ain' t I a leader? In S. Maxcy (Ed.) *Postmodern school leadership.* Westport, CT: Praeger (47–59).

Bossert, S., Dwyer, D., Rowan, B. & Lee, G. (1982). The instructional management role of the principal. *Educational Administration Quarterly, 18*(3), 34–64.

Boyan, N. (1981). Follow the leader: A commentary on research in educational administration. *Educational Researcher, 10*(2), 6–13,21.

Boyan, N. (1988). Describing and explaining administrative behavior. In N. Boyan (Ed.), *Handbook of research in educational administration.* New York: Longman, 77–98.

Brewer, (1993). Principals and student outcomes: Evidence from U.S. high schools. *Economics of Education Review, 12*(4), 281–292.

Bridges, E. (1982). Research on the school administrator: The state-of-the-art, 1967–1980. *Educational Administration Quarterly, 18*(3), 12–33.

Burnstein, R. (1983). *Beyond objectivism and relativism: Science, hermeneutics, and praxis.* Philadelphia: University of Pennsylvania Press.

Burrell, G. & Morgan, G. (1979). *Sociological paradigms and organizational analysis.* London: Heinemann.

Chase, S. (1992). Narrative practices: Understanding power and subjection and women's work narratives. Paper presented at the qualitative analysis conference. Carleton University, Ottawa.

Cheng, K. (1995). The neglected dimension: Cultural comparison in educational administration. In K. C. Wong & K. M. Cheng (Eds.) *Educational leadership and change: An international perspective.* Hong Kong: Hong Kong University Press, 87–104.

Cheng, K. (In press). Can education values be borrowed? Looking into cultural differences. *Peabody Journal of Education.*

Cheng, K. & Wong, K. (1996). School effectiveness in East Asia: Concepts, origins and implications. *Journal of Educational Administration, 34*(5), 32–49.

Cheng, Y. (1994). Principal's leadership as a critical factor for school performance: Evidence from multi-levels of primary schools. *School Effectiveness and School Improvement, 5* (3), 299–317.

Chung, K. & Miskel, C. (1989). A comparative study of principals administrative behavior. *Journal of Educational Administration, 27,* 45–57.

Clandnin, D. J. & Connelly, M. (1994). Personal experience methods. In N. Denzin & Y. Lincoln (Eds.) *Handbook of qualitative research.* Newbury Park, CA: Sage. 413–427.

Connelly, F. & Clandnin, D. (1990). Stories of experience and narrative inquiry. *Educational Researcher, 19*(5), 2–14.

Cooper, J. (1995). The role of narrative and dialogue in constructivist leadership. In D. Lambert *et al.* (Eds.), *The constructivist leader.* New York: Teachers College Press (p. 121–133).

Cooper, J. & Heck, R. (1995). Using narrative in the study of school administration. *Qualitative Studies in Education, 8*(2), 195–210.

Corbett, H., Firestone, W. & Rossman, G. (1987). Resistance to planned change and the sacred in school cultures. *Educational Administration Quarterly, 23*(4), 36–59.

Cortazzi, M. (1993). *Narrative analysis.* London: Falmer Press.

Crowson, R. & Porter-GehRie, C. (1980). The discretionary behavior of principals in large city schools. *Educational Administration Quarterly, 16*(1), 45–69.

Cuban, L. (1984). Transforming the frog into a prince: Effective schools research, policy, and practice at the district level. *Harvard Educational Review, 54*(2), 129–151.

Denzin, N. & Lincoln, Y. (1994). Introduction: Entering the field of qualitative research. In N. Denzin & Y. Lincoln (Eds.) *Handbook of qualitative research.* Newbury Park, CA: Sage, 1–18.

Dillard, C. (1995). Leading with her life: An African American feminist (re)interpretation of leadership for an urban high school principal. *Educational Administration Quarterly, 31*(4), 539–563.

Dobbert, M. & Kurth-Schai, R. (1992). Systematic ethnography: Toward an evolutionary science of education and culture. In M. LeCompte, W. Millroy & J. Preissle (Eds.) *The handbook of qualitative research in education.* San Diego: Academic Press, Inc. (p. 93–160).

Donmoyer, R. (1996). Editorial: Educational research in an era of paradigm proliferation: What's a journal editor to do? *Educational Researcher, 25*(2), 19–25.

Duke, D. (1986). The aesthetics of leadership. *Educational Administration Quarterly, 22*(1), 7–27.

Duke, D. & Iwanicki, E. (1992). Principal assessment and the notion of fit. *Peabody Journal of Education, 68*(1), 25–36.

Dwyer, D., Lee, G., Rowan, B. & Bossert, S. (1983). *Five principals in action: Perspectives on instructional management.* San Francisco: Far West Laboratory for Educational Research and Development.

Eberts, R. & Stone, J. (1988). Student achievement in public schools: Do principals make a difference? *Economics of Education Review, 7*(3), pp. 291–299.

Eisner, E. (1988). The primacy of experience and the politics of method. *Educational Researcher, 20*, 15–20.

Eisner, E. (1993). Forms of understanding and the future of educational research. *Educational Researcher, 22*(7), 5–11.

Elbaz, F. (1988). *Knowledge and discourse: The evolution of research on teacher thinking.* Paper presented at the Conference of the International Study Association on Teacher Thinking, University of Nottingham, September.

Epp, J., Sackney, L. & Kustaski, J. (1994). Reassessing levels of androcentric bias in *Educational Administration Quarterly. Educational Administration Quarterly, 30*(4), 451–471.

Erickson, D. (1979). Research on educational administration: The state of the art. *Educational Researcher, 8*, 9–14.

Erickson, F. (1973). What makes school ethnography "ethnographic"? *Council on Anthropology and Education Newsletter, 4*(2), 10–19.

Erickson, F. (1992). Ethnographic microanalysis of interaction. In M. LeCompte, W. Millroy & J. Preissle (Eds.) *The handbook of qualitative research in education.* San Diego: Academic Press, Inc. (p. 201–226).

Everhart, R. (1988). Fieldwork methodology in educational administration. In N. Boyan (Ed.) *The handbook of research on educational administration.* NY: Longman, 703–727.

Evers, C. & Lakomski, G. (1996). Science in educational administration: A postpositivist conception. *Educational Administration Quarterly, 32*(3), 379–402.

Firestone, W. (1990). Succession and bureaucracy: Gouldner revisited. *Educational Administration Quarterly, 26*, 345–375.

Foster, W. (1986). *Paradigms and promises: New approaches to educational administration.* Buffalo, NY: Prometheus.

Gee, J., Michaels, S. & O'Conner, M. (1992). Discourse analysis. In M. LeCompte, W. Millroy & J. Preissle (Eds.) *The handbook of qualitative research in education.* San Diego: Academic Press, Inc. (p. 227–292).

Getzels, J., Lipham, J. & Campbell, R. (1968). *Educational administration as a social process.* New York: Harper & Row.

Gilmore, M. & Murphy, J. (1991). Understanding classroom environments: An organizational sense-making approach. *Educational Administration Quarterly, 27*(3), 392–429.

Glasman, N. (1984). Student achievement and the school principal. *Educational Evaluation and Policy Analysis, 6*(3), 283–296.

Glasman, N. & Heck, R. (1992). The changing leadership role of the principal: Implications for principal assessment. *Peabody Journal of Education, 68*(1), 5–24.

Goetz, J., LeCompte, M. & Ausherman, M. (1988). *Toward an ethnology of student life in classrooms.* Paper presented at the American Anthropological Association meeting, Phoenix, AZ.

Goldring, E. & Pasternak, R. (1994). Principals coordinating strategies and school effectiveness. *School Effectiveness and School Improvement, 5* (3), 239–253.

Goldring, E. & Chen, M. (1993). The feminization of the principalship in Israel: The tradeoff between political power and cooperative leadership. In C. Marshall (Ed.) *The new politics of race and gender.* Washington, DC: Falmer Press, 175–182.

Goldring, E. & Pasternak, R. (1994). Principals' coordinating strategies and school effectiveness. *School Effectiveness and School Improvement, 5*(3), 239–253.

Grant, L. & Fine, G. (1992). Sociology unleashed: Creative directions in classical ethnography. In M. LeCompte, W. Millroy & J. Preissle (Eds.) *The handbook of qualitative research in education.* San Diego: Academic Press, Inc, 405–446.

Greenfield, T. (1980). The man who comes back through the door in the wall: Discovering truth, discovering self, discovering organizations. *Educational Administration Quarterly, 16*(3), 25–59.

Greenfield, W. (1991). The micropolitics of leadership in an urban elementary school. In J. Blase (Ed.) *The politics of life in schools: Power conflict, and cooperation.* Newbury Park, CA: Sage, 161–184.

Greenfield, W. (1995). Toward a theory of school administration: The centrality of leadership. *Educational Administration Quarterly, 31*(1), 61–85.

Greenfield, W., Licata, J. & Johnson, B. (1992). Towards measurement of school vision. *Journal of Educational Administration, 30*(2), 65–76.

Griffiths, D. (1988). Administrative theory. In N. Boyan (Ed.) *The Handbook of Research on Educational Administration.* New York: Longman, 27–52.

Gronn, P. (1984a). On studying administrators at work. *Educational Administration Quarterly, 20*(1), 115–129.

Gronn, P. (1984b). I have a solution . . . : Administrative power in a school meeting. *Educational Administration Quarterly, 20*(2), 65–92.

Gronn, P. & Ribbins, P. (1996). Leaders in context: Postpositivist approaches to understanding educational leadership. *Educational Administration Quarterly, 32*(3), 452–473.

Habermas, J. (1975). *Legitimation crisis.* Boston: Beacon Press.

Hallinger, P. (1992). Changing norms of principal leadership in the United States. *Journal of Educational Administration, 30*(3), 35–48.

Hallinger, P. (1995). Culture and leadership: Developing an international perspective in educational administration. *UCEA Review, 36*(1), 3–7.

Hallinger, P. & Heck, R. (1996a). Reassessing the principal's role in school effectiveness: A review of empirical research, 1980–1995. *Educational Administration Quarterly, 32*(1), 5–44.

Hallinger, P. & Heck, R. (1996b). The principal's role in school effectiveness: An assessment of methodological progress, 1980–1995. In K. Leithwood *et al.* (Eds.), *International handbook of research in educational leadership and administration.* New York: Kluwer Press.

Hallinger, P. & Heck, R. (1998). Exploring the principal's contribution to school effectiveness. *School Effectiveness and School Improvement.* 9(2) 157–191.

Hallinger, P. & Leithwood, K. (1996). Culture and educational administration: A case of finding out what you don't know. *Journal of Educational Administration, 34*(1), 98–116.

Hallinger, P. & Leithwood, K. (In press). Unseen forces: The impact of social culture on leadership. *Peabody Journal of Education.*

Hallinger, P. & Murphy, J. (1985). Assessing the instructional management behavior of principals. *Elementary School Journal, 86*(2), 217–247.

Hallinger, P. & Murphy, J. (1986a). Instructional leadership in school contexts. In W. Greenfield (Ed.), *Instructional leadership: Concepts, issues and controversies.* Lexington, MA: Allyn & Bacon.

Hallinger, P. & Murphy, J. (1986b). The social context of effective schools. *American Journal of Education, 94*(3), pp. 328–355.

Hallinger, P., Bickman, L. & Davis, K. (1989). *What makes a difference? School context, principal leadership and student achievement.* Paper presented at the annual meeting of the American Educational Research Association, San Francisco.

Hallinger, P., Bickman, L. & Davis, K. (1996). School context, principal leadership and student achievement. *Elementary School Journal, 96*(5).

Hallinger, P., Taraseina, P. & Miller, J. (1994). Assessing the instructional leadership of secondary school principals in Thailand. *School Effectiveness and School Improvement, 5* (4), 321–348.

Hannaway, J. & Talbert, J. (1993). Bringing context into effective schools research: Urban-suburban differences. *Educational Administration Quarterly, 29*(2), 164–186.

Hart, A. (1994). Creating teacher leadership roles. *Educational Administration Quarterly, 30*(4), 472–497.

Heck, R. (1991). Towards the future: Rethinking the leadership role of the principal as philosopher-king. *Journal of Educational Administration, 29*(3), 67–79.

Heck, R. (1993). School context, principal leadership, and achievement: The case of secondary schools in Singapore. *The Urban Review, 25*(2), 151–166.

Heck, R. (1996). Leadership and culture: Conceptual and methodological issues in comparing models across cultural settings. *Journal of Educational Administration, 34*(5), 74–97.

Heck, R. (In press). Conceptual and methodological issues in investigating principal leadership across cultures. *Peabody Journal of Education.*

Heck, R. & Brandon, P. (1995). Teacher empowerment and the implementation of school-based reform. *Empowerment in Organizations: An International Journal, 3*(4), 10–19.

Heck, R., Larsen, T. & Marcoulides, G. (1990). Principal instructional leadership and school achievement: Validation of a causal model. *Educational Administration Quarterly, 26*, 94–125.

Hodgkinson (1983). *The philosophy of leadership.* Oxford: Basil Blackwell.
Hodgkinson, (1991). *Educational leadership: The moral art.* Albany, NY: SUNY Press.

Hoy, W. (1994). Foundations of educational administration: Traditional and emerging perspectives. *Educational Administration Quarterly, 30*(2), 178–198.

Hoy, W. (1996). Science and theory in the practice of educational administration. A pragmatic perspective. *Educational Administration Quarterly, 32*(3), 366–378.

Hoy, W. & Miskel, C. (1996). *Educational administration: Theory, research and practice, Fifth Edition.* New York: Random House.

Hoy, W., Tarter, C. & Witkoskie, L. (1992). *Faculty trust in colleagues: Linking the principal with school effectiveness.* Journal of Research and Development in Education, 26(1), 38–45, Fall.

Immegart, G. (1988). Leadership and leader behavior. In N. Boyan (Ed.), *Handbook of research in educational administration.* New York: Longman, 259–278.

Inbar, D. (1977). Perceived authority and responsibility of elementary school principals in Israel. *Journal of Educational Administration, 15*(1), 80–91.

Jacob, E. (1992). Culture, content, and cognition. In M. LeCompte, W. Millroy & J. Preissle (Eds.) *The handbook of qualitative research in education.* San Diego: Academic Press, Inc, 293–335.

Jantzi, D. & Leithwood, K. (1996). Toward an explanation of variation in teachers perceptions of transformational school leadership. *Educational Administration Quarterly, 32*(4), 512–538.

Jensen, G. & Peshkin, A. (1992). Subjectivity in qualitative research. In M. LeCompte, W. Millroy & J. Preissle (Eds.) *The handbook of qualitative research in education.* San Diego: Academic Press, Inc, 681–726.

Jermier, J. (1985). When the sleeper wakes : A short story extending themes in radical organization theory. *Journal of Management, 2*, 67–80.

Kaplan, A. (1964). *The conduct of inquiry: Methodology for behavioral science.* San Francisco: Chandler.

Keith, N. (1996). A critical perspective on teacher participation in urban schools. *Educational Administration Quarterly, 32*(1), 45–79.

Kleine-Kracht, P. (1993). Indirect instructional leadership. An administrator's choice. *Educational Administration Quarterly, 29*(2), 187–212.

Kmetz, J. & Willower, D. (1982). Elementary school principals work behavior. *Educational Administration Quarterly, 18*(4), 62–78.

Krug, F. (1986). *The relationship between the instructional management behavior of elementary school principals and student achievement.* Unpublished doctoral dissertation, U. of San Francisco, San Francisco, CA.

Kuhn, T. (1970). *The structure of scientific revolutions.* (2nd Edition) Chicago: University of Chicago Press.

Lambert, L. (1995). Constructing school change. In L. Lambert *et al.* (Eds.). *The constructivist leader.* New York: Teachers College Press. (52–82).

Lather, P. (1991). Critical frames in educational research: Feminist and post-structural perspectives. *Theory into Practice, 31*(2), 87–99.

Leithwood, K. (1994). Leadership for school restructuring. *Educational Administration Quarterly, 30*(4), 498–518.

Leithwood, K. & Duke, D. (In press). Mapping the conceptual terrain of leadership: A critical point of departure for cross-cultural studies. *Peabody Journal of Education.*

Leithwood, K. & Hallinger, P. (1993). Cognitive perspectives on educational administration: An introduction. *Educational Administration Quarterly, 24*(3), 296–301.

Leithwood, K. & Jantzi, D. (1990). Transformational leadership: How principals can help reform school cultures. *School Effectiveness and School Improvement, 1*(1), 249–280.

Leithwood, K. & Stager, (1989). Expertise in principals problems solving. *Educational Administration Quarterly, 25* (2), 126–161.

Leithwood, K. & Steinbach, R. (1991). Indicators of transformations leadership in the everyday problem solving of school administrators. *Journal of Personnel Evaluation in Education, 7*(4), 221–244.

Leithwood, K., Begley, P. & Cousins, B. (1990). The nature, causes and consequences of principals practices: A agenda for future research. *Journal of Educational Administration, 28*(4), 5–31.

Leithwood, K., Begley, P. & Cousins, B. (1992). Developing expert leaders for future schools. Bristol, PA: Falmer Press.

Leithwood, K., Jantzi, D., Silins, H. & Dart, B., (1993). Using the appraisal of school leaders as an instrument for school restructuring. *Peabody Journal of Education, 68*(1), 85–109.

Lewellen, T. (1992). *Political anthropology: An introduction* (2nd edition). Westport, CT: Bergin & Garvey.

Lincoln, Y. (1996). *Performance scripts beyond race and gender: Reframing the grand narratives of higher education.* Paper presented at the annual meeting of the American Educational Research Association, New York, April.

Lomotey, K. (1989). *African-American principals: School leadership and success.* Westport, CN: Greenwood Press.

Lomotey, K. (1993). African-American principals: Bureaucrat/administrators and ethno-humanists. *Urban Education, 27*(4), 395–412.

Lotto, L. & Murphy, J. (1990). Making sense of schools as organizations: Cognition and sense-making in schools. In P. Thurston & L. Lotto (Eds.) *Advances in educational administration: Changing perspectives on the schools.* Greenwich, CT: JAI Press, 201–240.

Louis, K. & Miles, M. (1991). Managing reform: Lessons from urban high schools. *School Effectiveness and School Improvement, 2*(2), 75–96.

Lum, J. (1997). Student mentality: Intentionalist perspectives about the principal. *Journal of Educational Administration, 35*(3), 210–233.

Macpherson, R. (1996). Educative accountability policy research: Methodology and epistemology. *Educational Administration Quarterly, 32*(1), 80–106.

Marshall, C. (1993). Politics of denial: Gender and race issues in administration. In C. Marshall (Ed.) *The new politics of race and gender,* Washington, DC: Falmer Press, 168–174.

Marshall, C. (1995). Imagining leadership. *Educational Administration Quarterly, 31*(3), 484–492.

Marshall, C., Patterson, J., Rogers, D. & Steele, J. (1996). Caring as career: An alternative perspective for educational administration. *Educational Administration Quarterly, 32*(2), 271–294.

Martin, W. & Willower, D. (1982). The managerial behavior of high school principals. *Educational Administration Quarterly, 17*, 69–90.

Maxcy, S. (1995). Responses to commentary: Beyond leadership frameworks. *Educational Administration Quarterly, 31*(3), 473–483.

Murphy, J. (1992). *The landscape of leadership development.* Newbury Park, CA: Corwin Press.

Murphy, J. & Beck, L. (1995). *School-based management as school reform: Taking stock.* Newbury Park, CA: Corwin.

Murphy, J. & Hallinger, P. (1992). The principalship in an era of transformation. *Journal of Educational Administration, 30*(3), 77–88.

Murphy, J. & Louis, K. (1994). *Reshaping the principalship: Insights from transformational reform efforts.* Newbury Park, CA: Corwin.

Murphy, J., Hallinger, P. & Mitman, A. (1983). Research on educational leadership: Issues to be addressed. *Educational Evaluation and Policy Analysis, 5*(3), 297–305.

O'Day, K. (1983). *The relationship between principal and teacher perceptions of principal instructional management behavior and student achievement.* Unpublished doctoral dissertation, Northern Illinois University, Normal, Illinois.

Ogawa, R. (1991). Enchantment, disenchantment, and accommodation: How a faculty made sense of the succession of its principal. *Educational Administration Quarterly, 27*(1), 30–60.

Ogawa, R. & Bossert, S. (1995). Leadership as an organizational quality. *Educational Administration Quarterly, 31*(2), 224–243.

Ortiz, F. (1982). *Career patterns in educational administration: Women, men, and minorities in educational administration.* New York: Praeger.

Ortiz, F. (1992). *Women's ways of becoming leaders: Personal stories.* Paper presented at the annual meeting of the American Educational Research Association, San Francisco, April.

Pedhazur, E. & Schmelkin, L. (1991). *Measurement, design, and analysis: An integrated approach.* Hillsdale, NJ: Lawrence Erlbaum Associates.

Peterson, K. (1978). The principal's tasks. *Administrator's Notebook, 26,* 1–4.

Pitner, N. (1986). Substitutes for principal leadership behavior: An exploratory study. *Educational Administration Quarterly, 21*(2), 23–42.

Pitner, N. (1988). The study of administrator effects and effectiveness. In N. Boyan (Ed.), *Handbook of research in educational administration.* New York: Longman, 99–122.

Pounder, D., Ogawa, R. & Adams, E. (1995). Leadership as an organization wide phenomenon: Its impact on school performance. *Educational Administration Quarterly, 31*(4), 564–588.

Psathas, G. (1995). *Conversation analysis: The study of talk-in-action.* Newbury Park, CA: Sage.

Regan, H. (1990). Not for women only: School administration as a feminist activity. *Teachers College Record, 91*(4), 565–577.

Ribbins, P. (1995). Principals and principalship: Towards a context based approach to the study of school leadership. *Journal of Pengurusan Pendidikan, 2*(4), 88–105.

Robinson, V. (1996). Problem-based methodology and administrative practice. *Educational Administration Quarterly, 32*(3), 427–451.

Roman, L. (1992). The political significance of other ways of narrating ethnography: A feminist materials approach. In M. LeCompte, W. Millroy & J. Preissle (Eds.) *The handbook of qualitative research in education.* San Diego: Academic Press, Inc., 555–594.

Rowan, B. & Denk, C. (1984). Management succession, school socioeconomic context and basic skills achievement. *American Educational Research Journal, 21*(3), 17–537.

Rowan, B., Raudenbush, S. & Kang, S. (1991). Organizational design in high schools: A multilevel analysis. *American Journal of Education, 99*(2), 238–266.

Salley, C., McPherson, R. & Baehr, M. (1979). *A national occupational analysis of the school principalship.* Chicago: Industrial Relations Center, University of Chicago.

Scott, C. & Teddlie, C. (1987, April). *Student, teacher, and principal academic expectations and attributed responsibility as predictors of student achievement: A causal modeling approach.* Paper presented at the annual meeting of the American Educational Research Association, Washington D.C.

Sergiovanni, T. (1992). *Moral leadership: Getting to the heart of school reform.* San Francisco, Jossey Bass.

Shakeshaft, C. (1989). *Women in educational administration.* Newbury Park, CA: Sage.

Silins, H. (1994). The relationship between transformational and transactional leadership and school improvement outcomes. *School Effectiveness and School Improvement, 5* (3) 272–298.

Slater, R. (1995). The sociology of leadership and educational administration. *Educational Administration Quarterly, 31*(3), 449–472.

Smylie, M. (1992). Teacher participation in school decision making: Assessing willingness to participate. *Educational Evaluation and Policy Analysis, 14*(1), 53–67.

Snyder, J. & Ebmeier, H. (1992). Empirical linkages among principal behaviors and intermediate outcomes: Implications for principal evaluation. *Peabody Journal of Education, 68*(1), 75–107.

Soltis, J. (1984). On the nature of educational research. *Educational Researcher, 13*(10), 5–10.

Tarter, C., Sabo, D. & Hoy, W. (1995). Middle school climate, faculty trust, and effectiveness: A path analysis. *Journal of Research and Development in Education, 29*(1), 41–49.

Tatsuoka, M. & Silver, P. (1988). Quantitative research methods in educational administration. In N. Boyan (Ed.) *The handbook of research on educational administration.* NY: Longman, 677–701.

Valverde, L. & Brown, F. (1988). Influences on leadership development among racial and ethnic minorities. In N. Boyan (Ed.) *The handbook of research on educational administration.* NY: Longman 143–158.

Van de Grift, W. (1990). Educational leadership and academic achievement in elementary education. *School Effectiveness and School Improvement, 1*(3), 26–40.

Varenne, H. (1978). Culture as rhetoric: Patterning in the verbal interpretation of interaction in an American high school. *American Ethnologist, 5*(4), 635–650.

Varenne, H. (1983). *American school language.* New York: Irvington.

Wagner, J. (1993). Ignorance in educational research: Or, how can you not know that? *Educational Researcher, 22*(5), 15–23.

Walker, A., Bridges, E. & Chan, B. (1996). Wisdom gained, wisdom given: Instituting PBL in a Chinese culture. *Journal of Educational Administration, 34*(5), 12–31.

Willower, D. (1975). Theory in educational administration. *Journal of Educational Administration, 13*(1), 77–91.

Willower, D. (1996). Inquiry in educational administration and the spirit of the times. *Educational Administration Quarterly, 32*(3), 344–365.

Wolcott, H. (1973). *The man in the principal's office: An ethnography.* New York: Holt, Rinehart & Winston, Inc.

Wolcott, H. (1975). Criteria for an ethnographic approach to research in schools. *Human Organization, 34*(2), 111–128.

Wolcott, H. (1992). Posturing in qualitative research. In M. LeCompte, W. Millroy & J. Preissle (Eds.) *The handbook of qualitative research in education.* San Diego: Academic Press. (p. 3–52).

Wolcott, H. (1994). *Transforming qualitative data: Description, Analysis, and Interpretation.* Newbury Park, CA: Sage.

Wong, K. (in press). Culture and moral leadership in education. *Peabody Journal of Education.*

Woods, P. (1992). Symbolic interactionism: Theory and method. In M. LeCompte, W. Millroy & J. Preissle (Eds.) *The handbook of qualitative research in education.* San Diego: Academic Press. (p. 337–404).

The authors wish to thank Maenette Benham, Joanne Cooper, Valerie Lee, and C. J. Tarter for reading and commenting on earlier versions of this chapter.

CHAPTER 8

Ideological Lenses for Interpreting Political and Economic Changes Affecting Schooling

James G. Cibulka

American society, like all other post-industrial societies, has experienced many political and economic "changes" in recent decades.[1] Examples are not hard to find. Declining public faith in governmental authorities and institutions has manifested itself. The shift to a global economy carries enormous consequences. These and other trends seem obvious enough.

I argue in this chapter, however, that political and economic phenomena are interpreted inevitably through competing ideological prisms. Although change certainly can be measured, any analysis that undertakes to capture changing political and economic phenomena cannot escape the fact that there is sharp disagreement over what change means and which changes should be considered significant. If the nature of the changes themselves are open to disputed interpretations, it follows that the interpretation of what these changes mean for the administration and governance of elementary and secondary education cannot enjoy consensus either.

Stated differently, my first aim in this chapter is to illustrate the contested nature of economic and political changes in our society, as well as their inconclusive implications for the enterprise of schooling. A second aim is to examine the implications of these competing political ideologies for the development of the knowledge base in educational administration as well as preparation programs in it.

I begin with some caveats. My purpose in this chapter is primarily conceptual. For a survey of the broad context of the political economy and the forces shaping it, the reader is referred to the chapter in this volume by Reyes, Wagstaff, and Fusarelli. Not only do I try not to chronicle all the political and economic changes that might have implications

for education, but I make no attempt to include in this chapter broader social changes with educational implications. For instance, one could focus at length on the implications of the nation's changing demography. These could be treated as economic and political inputs to the educational system or new challenges to workforce preparation, as well as new sources of political attitudes, beliefs, and interest group mobilization. These issues will receive some attention in these pages, but less than systematically and working from a somewhat narrower aim. In short, unless one's purpose is to lay out a broad political economy of schooling, which is beyond my purpose here, it is difficult to draw the lines so that all noteworthy topics receive equal attention.

In this chapter, my more modest aim is to show how ideology frames the interpretation of political and economic changes affecting schooling. I will give heavier emphasis to political dimensions. The reader is referred elsewhere for broad overviews of economics of education research (Cohn & Geske, 1990; Monk, 1990) or for reviews on specific aspects of the economics of education, such as education production research (Hanushek, 1986), benefits of education (Haveman and Wolfe, 1984), or education and the labor market (Hinchliffe, 1987; Levin, 1987).

As a practical matter dictated by limited space, my attention centers on public schools. Consideration of private schools will be addressed here only insofar as I address questions of school choice. Also, this chapter examines political and economic changes affecting elementary and secondary education; post-secondary education would require a chapter in itself.

A final qualification: Because of space limitations, I draw mainly on the American context for examples of how ideologies play in educational policy discussions. To do justice to a international approach to understanding ideological influences is beyond what is manageable here. Nevertheless, it is hoped that the essential arguments I make about the role of ideology in interpreting political and economic changes will be applicable in other national settings.

Several Ideological Frames for Understanding Political and Economic Changes

I will use the term "political ideology" here to cover belief systems about what is and what ought to be in defining how government relates to civil society and to the economy (the role of the state). As they pertain to civil society, ideologies express beliefs about political rights of individuals, the scope of governmental involvement in shaping the value orientations and life chances of individuals, the appropriate regulation of private actions, and related matters. In the economic sphere, political ideologies express preferences for how much the government can and should regulate economic growth, the accumulation of private capital, the distribution of economic benefits, and the nature and extent of taxation of wealth and income.[2]

There are many ways of cutting up the ideological landscape as it pertains to economic and political phenomena.[3] The approach here is straightforward. I will present several ideological frames that begin to capture the dominant perceptions of political life—liberal, radical, and conservative. Within each there are many strains.

Each of these three frames, when they are applied to elementary and secondary education, can lead to distinct assumptions. In this chapter, for illustrative purposes, I look at how each ideology interprets a small number of political and economic trends and changes and how this interpretation, in turn, carries over into interpretations of how to improve schools. This is, of course, only a small piece of the way each ideology treats schools in its analyses.

These three frames are not coterminous with political parties or specific political alignments. In the American context, for example, the two major political parties embrace within their ranks divergent political alignments and ideologies. Also, although ideologies generally provide orientations to action, they are not necessarily codified to provide an interpretation of concrete problems, issues, or events with which political parties must wrestle.

Ideologies rarely achieve logical consistency. Indeed, it may be impossible to define ideologies rigorously (Strike, 1982). Ideologies frequently embrace tensions among key values and beliefs, and these contradictions may be an inherent feature of the belief system itself. This helps explain

why ideologies evolve over time, both in their key concepts and in the way these concepts are formulated, or why their application by different individuals can yield different conclusions. We are persuaded by Edelman's (1985) observation that "there is not one 'real' perception (of events) . . . but a cognitive structure with alternative facets, possibilities, and combinations appearing as the observer encounters new situations." Indeed, although ideologies help us make sense of our world, they are at best imperfect guides to interpreting all phenomena. This loose fit between the way policy problems present themselves and the assumptions of the ideology is one reason why individuals and groups working from the same ideological assumptions may come to different conclusions about what a policy development means or how it should be addressed. Because particular individuals may articulate the belief system in different ways, the most that can be done here is to present the central features of the belief system, treating it as a Weberian ideal type, and recognizing that its application in the real world may vary from the "ideal."

A complication also arises in moving from a total ideology, which is an ideal type (a composite of more partial versions of the ideology) to its application by particular groups. Ideologies as systems of thought exist independent of the individuals and groups who articulate aspects of those ideologies.[4] The policy agendas groups employ may draw on more than one ideological frame. The fact that one may recognize more than one ideology in a policy proposal, or in the coalition that embraces it, is not inherently problematic. Different groups can see different ways to attach their interests to each perspective (Kingdon, 1995), and particular policy issues and problems encourage different configurations of ideologies and interests. Under these circumstances, it should not be surprising that some individuals and groups do not see themselves represented perfectly by any one ideology because the positions they take may reflect more than one ideology, depending on the issue. Also, I attempt to articulate here only the dominant belief systems.

In this paper, I will make rather limited use of these frames. I shall not, for example, address how ideological frames shape behavior, influence social structure, or perpetuate social inequality. Because my purpose is to use these ideal types to interpret the meaning of economic and political trends and changes affecting the enterprise of schooling, I shall not attempt to cover everything that might said about each ideology. Entire books have been written on each tradition alone.

The three frames that are outlined below are, I would argue, the main ones in use in the American political culture at this time. For sake of simplicity and comparability, each ideology is highlighted very briefly within two broad categories: first, the assumptions the ideology makes about human nature and the character of civil society, and second, the resulting nature and role of the state. Implications for education will be addressed in a later section where specific political and economic changes in American society are examined.

Liberal Ideology: Human Nature and the Character of Civil Society

"The liberal tradition" is at the core of American politics (Hartz, 1955; Lowi, 1995). Liberalism has been defined as "faith in the right and strength of the individual, tempered by doubt in the perfection of things human . . . The moral element of liberal thought is the conviction that it is the individual who matters, and the defense of his inviolability, of the unfolding of his potential, of his life chances . . . follows from this conviction" (Dahrendorf, 1979: 97–98). Society must be organized as an instrument for individual expression; hence, groups and institutions are not ends unto themselves.

Although the individual is central to liberal thought, liberal ideology rejects the premise that any one person, group, or set of ideas has a claim to being right. Humans are fallible, given to selfishness and error of judgment. Hence, society must protect individuals from dominance by others, including the orthodoxy of an established belief or religion. The autonomous individual, while bound to obey society's limits on her freedom, must be free as much as possible. In Jefferson's famous words from the Declaration of Independence, individuals are "created equal" and endowed by their Creator with "inalienable rights" such as "life, liberty, and the pursuit of happiness." Liberalism requires growth of three kinds: the development of autonomy, rationality, and self-respect; the development of the capacity to be a good citizen; and, finally, the ability to choose and pursue one's own conception of the good (Strike, 1989: 48).

Liberalism also is committed to equalizing social opportunities for individuals. They should be free to fulfill their potential and to exercise their freedom of choice across a range of human endeavors.

The Nature and Role of the State

The state is a key actor in defining what the liberal vision of equal opportunity actually means for individuals. Liberal thought proceeds from the faith that both individuals and society are capable of improvement and that government is an instrument of that improvement. There is an optimism that social and economic problems can be solved, or at least ameliorated, with government's help. Problems may be complex but are not intractable. They are not fixed by limitations of human nature, human will, or intelligence, or by

immutable social laws. The malleability of individuals and society is at the heart of the liberal world view. Also, liberal ideology takes a pragmatic approach to addressing social problems; policy problems can be addressed sequentially or even incrementally as new problems evolve or as old problems (such as poverty and illiteracy) take on new forms.

Liberal ideology supports the idea that government must be actively committed to protecting individuals. The favored approach to equality is for government to guarantee fair competition. Another manifestation of this is reflected in a commitment to helping individuals fulfill their rights to political equality as citizens. Political equality means not only political protection from infringements on one's freedom by other individuals, groups, and organizations but, perhaps more important, protection against the abuses of governments. Governments are necessarily circumscribed by constitutional provisions such as the Bill of Rights, which protect the political rights of individuals. This has meant expanding the right to vote and broadening access to political participation for all individuals, including groups such as African-Americans who were systematically excluded from voting in the South until the 1960s.

Fear of a strong political sovereign animated the thinking of the American founding fathers. Political power must be divided, both as a protection against ambition and the "mischief of faction" and to permit progress to occur because no one has a corner on truth.[5] Division of powers among branches of government and separation of church and state are two examples of the liberal approach to dispersal of government power.

The modern liberal tradition rejects the limited state that was long associated with classical liberalism—a view that confined the state's role to that of a night-watchman concerned largely with safety for individuals (Hayek, 1944). Government should promote "positive freedom" toward desired social ends, not merely "negative freedom" to protect individuals from harm. Liberal philosophy undergirds the programs that have come to be known as "the welfare state." These programs aim to provide a wide variety of protections for including old-age pensions, support for dependent children and populations, unemployment insurance, health care, and so on. The rationales for these programs have varied but normally involve helping worthy individuals to attain (or maintain) self-sufficiency in time of need—circumstances that are beyond their control such as becoming unemployed, sick, old, or mentally incompetent.

Liberal ideology can operate comfortably with private property and capitalist economic systems, even though capitalism is not democratic (Heilbroner, 1995). Competition among individuals and firms is compatible with defining society as a collection of individuals who pursue their self-interest in producing and consuming goods and services. The task of government, working from this logic, is to regulate the economy in a variety of ways to protect individual consumers from economic disaster, to assure they will play "fair," not be exploited, and so on. An extension of that same liberal philosophy is that particular firms and industries promote the national interest and deserve special consideration.

Precisely how activist government should be in protecting and promoting individual rights in the name of the public interest is a matter of debate within the liberal tradition. Although government can and should regulate the economy, how far should this intervention reach and for precisely what purposes? How much should government seek to guarantee not only "life" but also "liberty" and "the pursuit of happiness?"[6]

Liberal ideology embraces quite another rationale for state activism. Variously called capacity building or patronage (Lowi, 1995: 8–9), this rationale is built on the idea that government should provide benefits to individuals and groups. As the Republic has evolved, the avenues through which patronage is provided also have expanded. The logic of "functional federalism" (Peterson, 1995) takes many forms besides paying for roads, prisons, and other obvious "pork." Government, for example, promotes opportunities and offering incentives in the form of grants and special provisions in the tax code. In short, in its embrace of the activist state, modern liberal ideology has expanded both patronage and regulatory conceptions of the public interest.

Finally, the role of experts is indispensable in the liberal activist state, which relies on scientific rationality to expand and protect individual opportunities and choices. Experts classify, measure, and analyze problems and policies. They manage public institutions such as education. The role of experts is, of course, circumscribed by efforts to assure that the mass citizenry plays some role in shaping policy, whether through electoral channels, bureaucratic implementation, or legal redress.

In sum, liberal ideology has enjoyed enormous political power in the United States, where it was the dominant philosophy after the New Deal, even among so-called conservatives (Lowi, 1995). Since the 1980s, however, liberal ideology has been under attack, both in the United States and in many other countries. This attack has transcended particular political parties. Perhaps the main organized challenge to liberalism has come from the right.

Conservative Political Ideology[7]

Human Nature and the Character of Civil Society

Conservative thought is rooted in a pessimistic view of human nature; one need not paint as bleak a picture as the seventeenth century English philosopher Thomas Hobbes, who portrayed human instinct as "nasty" and "brutish,"

but certainly conservatives are skeptical about our capacity to change the darker side of human nature through education, positive legislation, and other attempts to alter people's environments. Humans are ruled more by emotion than by reason. These moral frailties and selfish appetites must be curbed through social conventions and institutional constraints, not by social engineering.

Conservatives believe that all persons are morally equal, but that in other respects they are sharply different. They vary in intellectual capacity and other talents, as well as in their ambitions and tastes. Consequently, even equal opportunity to succeed will result in a gradation of social and economic benefits accruing to individuals. Although luck may play a factor in creating unequal life chances for individuals, conservatives believe that little can be done to erase these differences. Moreover, those with greater talent and ambition should play a greater leadership role in society and are entitled to enjoy disproportionate benefits and social positions. Inequality, far from being an abnormal state of affairs, is both an inevitable and desirable feature of social life. It is desirable because society benefits when the most able and ambitious are able and obligated to contribute their talents to the social good.

Social class inequality is one manifestation of these inevitable inequalities among individuals. The interests underlying these inequalities are, moreover, relatively fixed and do not fluctuate from issue to issue; consequently, social and political conflicts have a predictable quality because they are rooted in these immutable differences.

Conservatives believe that "divine intent rules society as well as conscience, forging an eternal chain of right and duty" (Kirk, 1953: 7). Religion serves to curb the selfish passions of human nature. In that way, it serves not merely to reclaim lost souls, but to shape the social order in positive ways.

Conservatism defends the role of tradition in public life and the place of families and local communities in preserving tradition. Tradition, in turn, is associated with certain core values that social conservatives believe are necessary to building character and the well-being and preservation of the social fabric, such as respect for authority, obedience to God and to the scriptures, commitment to the sanctity of marriage, and defense of hard work as a virtue. Patriotism is another of these traditional virtues.

Conservatives believe resolutely in the capitalist system and defend the right to acquire property and other forms of wealth. The right to acquire and maintain wealth is viewed as reward for effort, even when it is inherited.

The Nature and Role of the State

Given human nature and the character of civil society, conservatives tend to distrust government. Activist governments destroy the fabric of civil society (Murray, 1997). The underlying differences of interests between individuals and social classes are so fundamental that government should do little to try to alter their effects. Therefore, the state rarely solves problems without creating a host of new ones. Conservatives are particularly suspicious of a strong *central* government, and they favor limited government in many respects.

Government action can be justified in limited circumstances. One area is the preservation of economic liberty. Capitalism should be allowed to flourish unfettered to the maximum extent possible.[8] Conservatives believe that the state should do as little as possible to interfere with economic exchanges among individuals and groups, except to promote fair competition.

A second area where government action is justified, according to some versions of conservative political ideology, is regulation of morality and ethics. These government actions require some efforts to define and protect "positive freedoms" (Rossiter, 1962). Conservatives believe that this formal separation should not be construed to make the state hostile to religion, as liberals allegedly have done through an activist judiciary. Efforts to restore traditional values require removing "secular humanist" values that social conservatives associate with atheism, communism, and other alien belief systems and replacing them with the virtues and traditions they hold as sacred (Martin, 1996). This populist, libertarian strain in American conservative thought expresses itself as hostility to large institutions, such as the federal government, and to professional "elites" and "modernist" forces, who often seek to impose their will through government authority. Individuals should have the freedom to protect themselves from public authorities who seek to destroy their values. Privacy, then, is a tool to enforce traditional values.

Because of the skepticism of conservatives concerning human nature, and their conception of the social order as inevitably hierarchical and stubbornly resistant to fundamental reconstruction, there is limited faith that information and expertise can improve the social order. Modern conservatism, to be sure, appreciates the role of expertise, particularly as it applies to the analysis of markets, and when it can be used to bolster conservative interests. But unlike liberalism, conservative thought is far less enthusiastic that positive policies of the state are either philosophically appropriate or likely to be effective.

Radical Political Ideology[9]

Human Nature and the Character of Civil Society

If conservatism emphasizes the inherent limits of individual character and ability, which are reflected in societal institutions, radical political thought begins from the opposite point of view. Society has failed the individual—at least those who have been exploited through current economic, social, and political arrangements. Consequently rearranging the social order will eliminate many problems that mistakenly are attributed to individuals as defects of character or evidence of their limited ability.

Radical ideology focuses on the injustice of social inequality. According to radical theorists, these forms of social inequality are rooted in a hierarchy of power that permits some individuals and groups to exploit other groups. This exploitation results in fewer privileges, opportunities, and rights for the exploited. Hierarchies are inherently inequitable because they are the result not of the achieved status of individuals but reflect the social reproduction of inequality. Although social class is the most often cited source of inequality, such inequalities can be rooted in race, gender, ethnicity, age, sexual identity, disability, or other classifications that relegate an individual's possessing those traits to inferior status. One's unequal status in the social order is to a degree preordained to the extent that one inherits (or as the case may be, develops) these traits.

According to Marxist versions of this ideology, economic exploitation persists through a process of social reproduction. Marx believed that the material conditions of society, specifically its mode of production, shape not only economic life but, more broadly, social, political, and intellectual life. In the present historical period, according to Marx, the bourgeoisie (the capitalist class) exploits labor by its control of these institutions.

Although the concept of social reproduction also plays a role in liberal and conservative ideology, it plays a special role in radical analysis. This process explains why class inequality extends beyond the life of any individual and is perpetuated from generation to generation. Social reproduction lends predictability to social cleavages.

Power is a central mechanism creating and maintaining inequality. Power manifests itself in both macro and micro contexts. Everyday settings and events are venues for discovering how cultural symbols, norms, and beliefs structure inequality. In fact, power is everywhere, waiting to be made manifest. It is often hidden and oriented toward preventing conflict (Lukes, 1974). In critical analysis, all phenomena are political.

The forms of power and the processes through which it works are a preoccupation of radical social analysis, particularly study of which social actors maintain their dominant positions and the mechanisms by which this oppression is accomplished. There are many positions within radical ideology on these questions. Although Marxists begin from common assumptions about the material origins of class, for example, they have developed differing explanations of how the economic base relates to other superstructures (Carnoy, 1984). Social organization, structures, cultures, or subcultures can be a means of maintaining inequality. Structure is defined broadly. For example, Popkewitz (1991:

22) defines it as patterns that impose on social life certain regularities, boundaries, and frames. He distinguishes between structures as objects of analysis and structures as institutional relations. The processes of social reproduction are part of these "deep structures of society," the taken-for-granted institutional norms, routines, habits, and histories of organizations.

Cultural Marxists focus on consciousness as a component of social reproduction (Apple, 1995), giving greater attention to the social relations of production growing out of other institutions besides the economic base. Accordingly, gender, race, and sexual identity become important categories for analyzing power. On the micro level, this perspective also tries to expose how individuals and groups may get labeled, marginalized, or "pathologized" in order to protect the legitimacy of established institutions and the entrenched interests of these institutions (Marshall & Anderson, 1995).[10]

The shaping of attitudes and beliefs can be accomplished by the regulation of language and by development of knowledge. Radical ideology characterizes knowledge as an economic commodity constitutive of relations of ruling as well as of knowing (Bordieu & Passeron, 1977; Foucault, 1980). Many post-structural theorists have criticized the "metanarratives" that dominate the study of academic disciplines, including education (Cherryholmes, 1988.) They see power manifesting itself in myriad changing ways that must continuously be rediscovered.

This reproduction of inequality can occur because it is legitimate. Although coercion may be a factor, such as was certainly the case in the racial caste system of the American South, power works most effectively when subordinated individuals and groups acquiesce willingly in their inferior status, as an inevitable or even rightful station. Marxian ideology assumes that power operates to create a "false consciousness" that conceals from subordinated individuals and groups their true interests.

The Nature and Role of the State

As has been implied above, the state can be an instrument of the ruling class used to exploit labor and maintain oppression. However, Marxism and other radical ideologies have provided different answers as to how the state exercises its power. In some versions, the bourgeoisie directly controls the state (Althusser, 1971), while in other versions the state acts autonomously even though it favors the interests of the ruling class. In the American context, some radical analyses portray the struggle for social equality as a contest over the scope of government actions and policies designed to protect the working class. The so-called welfare state that emerged out of the economic depression of the 1930s was a class compromise. Thus the state is an arena

for class struggle, not a mere instrument of oppression. To maintain its legitimacy the state must accommodate demands from both the capitalist class and workers, and it does so more or less autonomously from control by either group (Carnoy, 1984).

Professionals often lend their expert knowledge to legitimate the power of the state. What passes for "reform" may be no more than a new tool of oppression. Hence, the radical critique is suspicious of the rules and standards of science associated with the professionalization of knowledge. Professionals and experts do not possess "factual" knowledge free of values or interests. Because all knowledge serves particular interests, technocratic power cannot be apolitical; it is in fact a deeply seated challenge to democracy and its political form of decision making (Fischer, 1990: 24) Indeed, radical perspectives see professionalization as a way to conceal power inequalities and also to create new kinds of inequality (Popkewitz, 1991: 230). Professionals have privileged knowledge and cloak this. They use the politics of expertise in the play of power. For example, the science of management is but another means of asserting control over employees (Ball, 1990). The challenge then is to remove these cloaks of specialized privilege.

Radical analysis does not entirely ignore the question of how actions of subordinated individuals and groups can improve their social condition. Although the state is an instrument of oppression, its power can liberate as well. The concept of resistance involves the study of how power is sustained, bestowed, and challenged (Popkewitz, 1991: 235). Resistance is exemplified by the oppositional strategies of the dominated against those who dominate. In radical social analysis, conflict is a potentially positive force in promoting social change; oppressive forces can be resisted and transformed, (Alinsky, 1971). Some theorists focus on how to free one's mind and to raise one's consciousness about one's potential (Freire, 1990) as a component of political struggle against state-sanctioned oppression. Radical feminists, for example, seek to help women discover their own knowledge (Hollingsworth, 1997). From this perspective, the Civil Rights movement, protests against the war in Vietnam, and other broad social movements may be required to upset the balance of power in favor of a new more equitable power constellation.

Interpreting Political and Economic "Changes" and Their Implications for Education

There are many political and economic changes that arguably are sufficiently important to warrant our attention here because of their implications for public schooling.

Space does not permit, nor does logical coherence require, a survey of the entire political and economic landscape for a comprehensive list of these changes.

Two Political Changes

In my view, however, two overarching shifts, from the perspective of several decades, have changed the politics of education remarkably. The first is declining public support for government, and within that trend, declining public support for public schools. This signals an erosion of legitimacy for public schools. Second, there has been an increase in mobilization of interest groups, which has reduced the autonomy of educational professionals to run schools. Each is discussed below.

Declining Public Support and Erosion of Legitimacy

Luttbeg and Gant (1995: 131) describe the situation well when they observe that "political scientists have seen a shift in American attitudes from benign affection for government during the 1950s and early 1960s to apparent distrust, lack of confidence, and alienation during the 1970s and early 1980s." Declining public trust in government threatens a democratic political system because it signals political alienation.

When Americans were asked whether the government is run by a "few big interests" or for the benefit of all people, the percentage indicating that it is run for the benefit of all declined from 64 percent in 1964 to 20 percent in 1992, while those believing it is run for a few big interests rose from 29 percent to 74 percent in that same period. It is not entirely clear, however, whether this signals primarily a loss of faith in political leaders or our institutions more broadly. It is at least partly institutional. Support for the U.S. Congress, for example, declined between 1973 and 1996, from 58 percent to 20 percent. Public schools are part of this same trend. Figure 8.1 indicates that support for public schools has declined since the early 1970s, when 58 percent expressed high levels of confidence in the institution, to only 38 percent today.

This poor rating comports with Gallup polls conducted annually asking Americans to grade their public schools quality. In 1996, only eight percent gave schools in the local community an A and even fewer (1 percent) rated the nation's schools as favorably. Furthermore, the total percent giving A or B grades to the nation's schools has declined since the publication of *A Nation at Risk* (1983). In 1984, 25 percent gave one of these two grades (23 percent A's and 2 percent B's). In 1996, the percent had declined to 21 percent (1 percent A's and 20 percent B's).

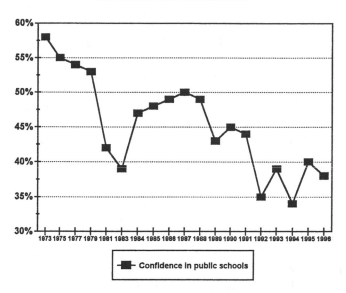

Figure 8.1

Confidence in Public Schools.

Note: The data are from *The Gallup Monthly*, June, 1996.

Interest Group Mobilization

This loss of public support has been accompanied by rising evidence of organized interest group activity and opposition to school authorities and their policies. This growth of organized interests has occurred throughout our political system. Policy arenas such as agriculture, energy, and health have experienced the growth of organized interests (Cigler, 1991: 121–22). Policy making is more open, more conflictual, and less stable.

School officials, in the United States at least, long have complained about being vulnerable to political pressures from special interests. There has never been actual evidence that school politics is any more beset by organized political pressures than other policy areas, however (Peterson, 1974). In fact, there is some evidence to the contrary that professional control of schools has reduced the influence of school boards, parents, and other members of the public, compared with non-school, general purpose municipalities. (Zeigler, Kehoe, and Reisman, 1985). In the past, the perception of school officials that they were subject to political pressures of special interests was more a reflection of the ideology of school administration, which proposed that schools be apolitical, than it was an accurate empirical description of the state of school politics.

Whatever actual autonomy did exist, though, does appear to have been reduced in recent decades. (See the chapter in this volume by Reyes, Wagstaff, and Fusarelli for a fuller description.) Symptomatic evidence of those larger changes at work in the politics of education can be seen in the rapid turnover of school superintendents, particularly in large cities (Jackson and Cibulka, 1992.) Involuntary turnover on boards of education in urban districts has also increased (Twentieth Century Fund, 1992). Although less systematic data are available for school districts in other jurisdictions, this trend seems to be nationwide (Danzberger, Kirst, and Usdan, 1992). This turnover often occurs when one-issue candidates mount a protest campaign with strong support from narrowly-based constituencies.

One of the major sources of interest-group mobilization in school affairs occurred as a result of the Civil Rights movement in the 1960s and 1970s. Racial protests were intermingled with legal battles over desegregation of public schools. School systems often were subject to court decrees mandating the eradication of one or another form of segregation by race. Thus public school administration and politics not only became more conflictual; school administration became more dependent on external actors, such as judges and court monitors, and on state legislatures responding to public demands for reform.

Building on the legacy of the early Civil Rights movement's victories, in the 1970s, a host of other special groups mobilized at all levels of the political system to extend privileges to previously underrepresented or under-served groups—children with special education needs, limited English-speaking pupils, the gifted, and others. Sometimes these groups won special representation within school administration as a result of federal and state laws designed to serve these groups. National networks of specialists emerged whose expertise, career ambitions, and loyalties contributed to fractionation of policy-making in local school districts. One of the biggest changes is greater representation of these diverse groups and points of view on boards of education, although not necessarily in proportion to their numbers in the population. Not surprisingly, greater compositional diversity on boards often leads to challenges in the distribution of values and interests by school authorities. Particularistic benefits such as jobs, contracts, and budget priorities are bargained. Universalistic claims also become matters of dispute, often overlapping with the above, on such matters as affirmative action, school busing for racial balance, and adopting curricula that represent alternatives to European and Western cultural "hegemony."

All these changes made less probable and even obsolete the traditional ideology of school administration as an autonomous, apolitical, professional, technically neutral enterprise. Indeed, the greater demographic diversity of the country has merely reinforced the trend toward more overt "politicization" of school affairs. Although public schools in some communities have long been a battleground for racial and ethnic struggles over curricula and jobs, particularly in our cities where racial and ethnic diversity has been most apparent, this dimension of school politics is likely to grow as more communities become multi-ethnic and multi-racial.

Business activism is another kind of interest group mobilization that has occurred in school politics. Although businesses have always been active in school affairs, particularly at the local level, this activism has reasserted itself after a period of relative quiescence in the 1970s and early 1980s. Business groups have mobilized at all levels of the political system to reassert influence on school boards; to win support for specific school policies, programs, and curricula; to restructure and downsize educational bureaucracies; and to influence the level and kinds of school system spending (Jones and Otterbourg, 1998). Statewide business coalitions have supported gubernatorial and state legislative pushes for educational reforms. At the national level, groups such as the Business Roundtable, the Committee on Economic Development, and the National Alliance of Business have been active in pushing their version of education reform. They have issued reports urging more reforms, sometimes in conjunction with major foundations. These leading business groups have collaborated with national political leaders at two Education Summits. Business leaders have lobbied Congress to support specific education reforms, and they have even set up special structures such as the New American Schools Development Corporation (NASDC) to advance their ideas about the kinds of reforms that they believe are necessary. At the local level, business groups in many cities such as Chicago, Milwaukee, New York, and elsewhere have been one of the key interest groups urging significant reforms or even overhaul of urban school systems at a time when the perceived quality of urban schools perhaps has reached an all-time low.

The growth of the religious right in school affairs is further evidence of the mobilization of interest groups in school politics. Although religious right groups began to mobilize against public schools in the 1950s and 1960s (Martin, 1996), their tactics have become increasingly sophisticated and reflect the skills and resources available to national conservative groups (Boyd, Lugg, and Zahorchak, 1996; McCarthy, 1996). These groups have employed many of the direct action protest tactics first used effectively by the Civil Rights movement. They are well financed, have strong grassroots support, can mobilize pressure on public officials quickly, and have strong organizational and informational networks reaching across states and indeed the entire country. As a result of these organizing resources, they have had a major impact on school politics in many localities and at the state level. They have elected supporters to school boards. They seek to influence curricular issues such as teaching of religion, advocacy of family values, and teaching of phonics in reading. They have resisted state testing programs whose features they find too intrusive and whose values they interpret to be hostile. Religious conservatives also have been active in calling for a ban on library books that they consider objectionable. In many communities, they have pressed for prayer in schools. They have actively resisted federal policies, which they see as attempts to dictate a national curriculum and introduce other programs they regard as potentially undermining family values, such as school-to-work programs.

Elected public officials also have become more active in demanding school reforms. Since the 1980s, governors across the country have spearheaded education reforms (Odden, 1995), often over the objections of chief state school officers and their allies. Indeed, from the perspective of traditional school groups such as teachers unions, administrator groups, and school board associations, this new activism by governors often was perceived as a threat and was treated as another example of outside political pressures on schools. In many states, this gubernatorial activism has changed the state-level politics of education by introducing new issues and new coalitions of actors.

Mayors in a number of cities such as Chicago and New York have demanded changes in their city's school system and thereby introduced another source of political pressure that school leaders traditionally resisted as not in the best interests of children. In many cases, mayors have advocated not only dramatic reforms but also sought to expand their own authority over these school systems. For example, they have sought greater control over selection of school board members and greater tax and budgetary control of school system resources in cities where schools have been fiscally-independent. They have sought to influence personnel appointments such as the superintendent of schools and to overhaul educational bureaucracies. Some mayors have sought the right to operate charter schools, while others have requested authority to close failing schools (Cibulka, 1997; Bloomfield and Cooper, 1997).

Several factors motivate heightened interest in school politics by mayors. First, as public concerns over the quality of public schools have increased, mayors have sought to respond to those public concerns. Second, mayors are influenced by business and civic group pressures to improve schools. Many accept the economic development argument that improving school quality is a key to retaining or attracting middle-class residents, and rebuilding the economic infrastructure of the city. Third, because public education is such a large tax expenditure in local communities, generally at least 40 percent in cities and 60 percent or higher in other communities, mayors seek to leverage their influence as best they can.

Economic Changes

Arguably the major economic change affecting educational policy in recent decades has been the transformation of the American economy. The economy has undergone two closely related changes: a more or less dramatic process of "de-industrialization alongside globalization of the world's economies" (Giddens, 1994: 80–81). In abbreviated terms,

the American economy, formerly sustained by rather localized or regionalized agricultural and industrial developments, is now highly susceptible to national and global forces and heavily dependent upon developments in the informational and service sectors of society. (For further analyses see Thurow, 1992, 1996.)

This shift from an industrial to an information society has had effects on particular individuals through, for example, the structure of employment opportunities, on groups of individuals who are impacted in certain ways, such as blacks, the poorly educated, and women, as well as on particular locales, such as urban centers whose economies formerly were dependent on manufacturing. These impacts on individuals, groups, and locales have feedback effects on one another. For example, individuals and groups living and working in jurisdictions disproportionately impacted by de-industrialization, such as African-Americans living in "rust-belt" cities, may feel a heavier negative impact through loss of employment opportunities than those individuals and groups living elsewhere. These multilevel effects are complex and still being documented and debated. For example, an analysis by Sawhill and Mc-Murrer (1998) argues that distribution of incomes alone is not the way to understand the effects of the new economy on upward mobility. They show that inherited advantages of class appear to be playing a smaller role in shaping success than in the past due to slower economic growth and greater social openness. However, the new economy has altered the distribution of wage gains in favor of women and college-educated men over high school graduates. Poorly educated men now have sharply decreased incomes compared to 25 years ago.

Other analyses emphasize that recent economic changes have resulted in overall declines in living standards for most of the middle class, a reduced middle class and corresponding expansion of the economically poor, and widening disparities in the gap between rich and poor. For example, a major characteristic of the U.S. economy is stark, stubborn inequities in distribution of wealth. In the U.S., the wealthiest one percent of the population holds 36 percent of the country's wealth—a higher proportion than any other industrialized country (Ginsberg, Lowi, and Weir, 1995). Although the figures fluctuate somewhat, the gap between rich and poor is, by most indicators, growing. The share of total income of the top quintile (20 percent) of households has been rising, while the bottom quintile has shrunk; in the 1980s, this gap rose by a third. By 1993, the top quintile of income earners was making 13.4 times as much as earners in the lowest quintile. In the 1980s, all the gains in male earnings went to the top 20 percent of the workforce and 64 percent to the top one percent. The average CEO of a fortune 500 company earns 35 to 157 times that of the average production worker (Thurow, 1996: 21–22). Whether the measure is the extent to which a small percentage of persons control large percentages of the wealth or the percentage of persons in various income brackets, the economic distance between the haves and have-nots appears to be increasing.

Once these broad political and economic trends are outlined, however, consensus tends to erode on what these phenomena mean: what is causing them, how they relate to past developments, and which public policies, if any, are appropriate responses to the changes. Obviously, the implications for schooling are central features of these contested ideological interpretations, and the discussion below will focus heavily on how each ideological perspective moves from the political and economic phenomena to issues of schooling. I will spend less time on other aspects of these respective ideologies. For example, although the merits of a free trade policy are approached differently by those who work from different ideological positions, it is not central to our focus in this chapter and is therefore ignored.

In order to facilitate comparisons among the three ideologies, the discussion below proceeds first by outlining conservative perspectives. This is because conservative ideology has in many respects driven the debates about how schools should respond to the political and economic changes in question. Following this, radical perspectives are summarized, followed by liberal points of view.

Conservative Interpretations

Conservative ideology has shaped educational policy debates since the 1970s, and therefore it is useful to begin with this perspective. The decade of the 1970s began a partial retreat from the Civil Rights advances of the 1960s, which continues to the present day. Rather than equality of educational opportunity, other values representing a more conservative point of view began to win prominence.

According to conservative ideology, the nation's political and economic problems can be traced to the failures of government, including our public schools. Schools have failed to transmit the traditional values necessary for responsible citizenship and the skills needed to function in the new global economy. Some conservative analyses focus mainly on the need to restore these traditional values, while others emphasize the need for greater productivity. In either case, the problems of American society are linked inextricably to the performance of public schools. For example, Hanushek (1994) rejects the argument that changes in the broader society, such as family life and the socio-economic environment surrounding schools, are primarily responsible for declining student achievement. The problem is one of declining institutional performance.

Traditionalist conservative ideology, which focuses on the importance of restoring religious and cultural values, argues that liberal interests now dominate public schools, and that conservative groups need to restore a balance by asserting their own values. Conservative political action groups such as the Christian Coalition (Reed, 1993) argue that the public, in particular "people of faith" and "pro-family voters," have become dissatisfied with schools because they no longer reflect the values of average Americans but instead the "elitist" agenda of educators that has replaced family values with "modernist" ideas (Lind, 1996). Since the 1960s, Christian conservatives have argued that public schools should not teach sex education because it represents modern values, which run contrary to their traditional family values. Also, they seek to prohibit the teaching of evolution ("atheism") in school and promote instead the teaching of "creation science" in science classes. Christian conservatives believe that many textbooks denigrate traditional family roles that do not portray women remaining at home to raise children or that are tolerant of "extreme" lifestyles such as homosexuality.

A major thrust of this cultural critique is a diagnosis of why an underclass has emerged that rejects core American values such as hard work. Murray (1984), for example, places the blame for increased poverty squarely on the dependency-producing effects of our social welfare policies. His answer to the key question of why so many basic trends in the quality of life for the poor take a turn for the worse in the 1960s and beyond is that "we tried to provide more for the poor and produced more poor instead" (1984:9). His recommended remedy is to eliminate the "perverse incentives" that prompted the poor to behave in ways that weakened the social as well as the economic fabric of families and communities; to reverse differential treatment according to race (1984: 223), and to use entrance tests as mechanisms for screening students' access to courses and programs.

Traditional conservative ideology also emphasizes the need for higher educational standards by restoring traditional pedagogy and curricular content. For example, Hirsch (1996) argues that public schools fail to inculcate "cultural literacy"; they are in the grip of faulty progressive theories of education, which Hirsch decries as the "Thoughtworld." Hirsch wishes to replace the intellectual monopoly controlled by educational professionals.

According to conservative ideology, schools also must keep pace with changes in the economy, thereby preparing students for productive economic roles in society. Under these conditions, schools will help individuals improve their life chances and protect the nation's economic well-being. If schools fail to adapt to new economic realities, however, they place both individuals and society at risk. In recent decades, the failure of schools to respond effectively to economic changes has reduced educational achievement and has contributed to the nation's economic problems by reducing its capability to compete in a global economy.

Conservatives argue that schools have become too bureaucratic. The growth of interest groups in school politics has crippled the performance of public schools. Chubb and

Moe (1990), for example, argue that public schools, to maintain their monopolistic status, must be responsive to a variety of special interests, who obtain concessions through political pressures they bring to bear on school officials. One of these special interests is professional educators, who run public schools for their own benefit and inculcate their own value biases. In particular, teachers unions have inordinate influence. Murray (1988: 208–231) attacks the idea that higher pay, more professionalization of the working environment, and certification will help attract and keep better teachers. He cites efforts by teachers unions to block or water down minimum competency tests and merit pay systems. Nor will certification reform work, he speculates, because unions will fight demanding tests as being invalid. Creating increased teacher autonomy runs the risk of reducing the principal's power to deal with poor teachers. Moreover, he argues, "if salaries are increased without any other changes in doing business, the wrong people are likely to end up in control." Murray believes that it is the intrinsic rewards of teaching that are key and that many teachers cannot enjoy teaching in schools as they now are organized.

Another manifestation of bureaucratization is inefficient patterns of school expenditure. Conservative ideology holds that spending more money on schools is not a guarantee that quality will improve. Spending increases often reflect demands of powerful groups such as teachers unions, who lobby for salary raises or class size reductions. Hanushek (1986) spawned this debate, as mentioned earlier, about whether "money matters." Although school spending has jumped enormously in recent decades, performance has not increased. After an extensive round of debates with Hedges, Laine, and Greenwald (1994) (also see Hanushek, 1994), Hanushek did not rule out money as a factor in improving schools. Instead, he argued, consistent with conservative philosophy, that the key to improving public school performance is to create incentives for teachers, administrators, and students to improve their performance. Incentives can create risk-taking behavior and adoption of cost-effective innovations.

Markets are the way, it is said, to break the deadlock of institutional control. Firms are accountable to their customers and compete for their allegiance. Also, markets offer an institutional alternative to direct democratic control (Chubb and Moe, 1990: 167). Effective school organization requires development of clear objectives and high academic expectations that can only be produced where there is "substantial school autonomy from direct external control" (p. 183). This, in turn, is needed to attract and retain qualified teachers and principals and to motivate parents to be involved and supportive of their children's schooling. The "dynamism of the market," according to this argument, is that it creates rewards for success and penalties for poor performance (Gerstner, Semerad, Doyle, and Johnston, 1994: 20).

Conservative supporters of school choice believe that it will alter the balance of power between professionals and parents. Parents should have the right to choose a school according to their values and educational philosophy.

Advocates of choice also point out that middle-class Americans have choice already, while poor Americans lack the financial means to self-select into affluent neighborhoods and/or school districts with good schools. Thus they seek to frame their defense of markets in terms of equity and liberty, as well as productivity and efficiency.

In conclusion, conservative ideology sees the institutional performance of schools as a central cause of the nation's political and economic problems. Schools are failing to convey traditional values, provide rigorous instruction in core subjects, or prepare students to function in the new economy.

Radical Interpretations

Radical interpretations of the political and economic problems confronting our society are, as we might expect, fundamentally different than those promulgated by conservative ideology. Hence, although radical ideology has tended to be critical of the performance of schools in meeting societal needs, this critique of institutional performance has little in common with its conservative counterpart. Indeed, radical perspectives view the loss of confidence in public schools as largely contrived. The entire education reform movement is viewed as a systematic campaign launched by conservatives to mislead the public and to delegitimize public schools. Business interests are behind this attack on public school performance, using their influence on foundation boards and their financial support of conservative think-tanks to generate reports, research, and policy proposals that constantly keep public schools on the defensive. Radical analyses see education reform issues as serving economic power and "the policy needs of the government," rather than the "individual desires or requirements of [a] democratic citizenry" (Spring, 1989: vii-viii).

Thus education reforms rarely target the real problems, let alone transform either the education system or the broader society. Rather, they "reinforce the underlying values, power relationships, and learning experiences embedded within the conventional ways of educating children" (Goodman, 1995: 3). The results of current and recurrent reform initiatives are captured in what Roemer terms "change without difference" (1991: 447). Neither the power relations in educational institutions nor the power constellations in the broader society are disturbed. Rather, they are reinforced, as the various reform movements consciously or unwittingly mask the inequities rooted in matters of race, class, and gender and mute the calls for more radical educational and societal reforms (Cuban, 1990).

Radical ideology rejects the diagnosis that school politics reflect the influence of too many special interests. The capitalist class still controls schools. The so-called special interests are minorities, teachers, parents, and other often excluded groups whose voices need to be heard more in school policy making. Hence, often what passes for reform really is an attempt to maintain bureaucratic modes of governance rather than expand participation by subordinated groups in the workplace or society more broadly (Fischer, 1990).

Some radical analyses see school reform proposals as a reflection of the crisis of the state in advanced capitalist countries. The state is attempting to deal more effectively with its internal and external needs (Apple, 1995: 113). One such strategy of the political right is to reduce the scope and legitimacy of government, thereby cutting back on socially redistributive policies that favor the poor and minorities and providing tax cuts or benefits to the middle-class or wealthy.

The schools are an instrument for carrying out a new form of social regulation represented by this conservative new right agenda (Popkewitz, 1991), which is an alternative to overt controls exercised over individuals in the past. This agenda was adopted first by private firms through various schemes to devolve more discretion and responsibility to workers and now has been transposed to legitimate a new and reduced role for government.

School choice, according to radical ideology, is a prime example of this new form of social regulation. Although it is held out by conservatives as a way to restore public confidence in schools and to overcome the grip of special interests, choice really has different aims and would have different effects than those trumpeted by its supporters. It is impossible, according to a radical critique, to separate the merits of choice from the political agenda of the "new right" (Apple, 1995; Whitty, 1997). Markets, in the name of expanding individual choice, will in fact exacerbate inequalities in educational opportunity and social condition. Since schools have become an important vehicle for moderating the most flagrant inequalities created by the capitalist economic system, choice is a way to reverse the gains of minorities and other subordinate groups without raising the need for overt struggle and subordination.

Working with the assumptions of Marxist analysis, where economic interests of the capitalist class are viewed as dominant, choice is a tool to reduce tax burdens for the rich while simultaneously increasing their educational benefits. It is also a way to expand the reach of business into the schools (Molnar, 1996). Markets are essentially by-products of private property relations (Katz, 1997). Indeed, choice can be expected to exhibit all the negative consequences attributable to market systems generally—insecurity, inequality, alienation, and so on (Polanyi, 1957).

As explained in an earlier section, some radical analyses see power as entailing the ability to shape ideas. The hidden curriculum is a way of shaping beliefs and socializing children, as well as a means for differentiating knowledge that becomes available to students of different groups. However, the curriculum is not only a tool for social control; it also is a means of social regulation. Pedagogy links the administrative concerns of the state with the self-governance of individual students (Popkewitz, 1991: 14). (For related analyses, see Apple, 1995.) School administrators also play a legitimization role, through the mobilization and management of meaning (Anderson, 1990; Ball, 1987; Bates, 1980).

Expanding the role of markets in education should be seen as away of extending these regulatory processes. If markets became the dominant metaphor for organizing schools, they would undermine the concept of citizenship and the collective obligations that role entails (Gewirtz, Ball, and Bowe, 1995). Markets reduce education to a private consumption act. The ability to choose one's school allegedly offers only symbolic benefits and, similar to decentralization policies in general, has little to do with what actually happens in schools (Carnoy and Hannaway, 1993). Choice would deflect criticism from the state and instead place responsibility on individuals for their success or failure, blurring the structural sources of inequality rooted in social class and race.

Radical analyses of economic changes cast doubt on a variety of the premises and conclusions animating conservative analyses of recent economic transformations. Viewed from more radical perspectives, scholars suggest that economic forces have historically had undue influence on educational institutions, particularly public schools. Traditional Marxian analysis views schooling as a process of social reproduction; schools produce a class-based labor market and economy. They are a sorting mechanism for children of different social classes (Robinson, 1994: 57). (Also see Bowles and Gintis, 1976; Bourdieu and Passeron, 1977). It is important from this perspective to understand the underlying continuity in materialist historical processes.

It comes as no surprise, therefore, that economic developments are continuing to have a significant influence on education reform. Both signs that the U.S. economy was not in an advantageous, competitive position as well as signs that the economy was undergoing a "transformation" have fueled the fires of education reform (Shea, 1989). A conservative attack on public school performance was achieved by defining the economic crises of the 1980s as a labor and education problem (Goertz, 1990; Berliner and Biddle, 1995).

These analysts offer conflicting portraits of the labor market, and relatedly, conflicting prescriptions of the particular skills individuals will need in order to effectively compete for decent paying jobs. Carnoy (1994) also offers a radical analysis of economic changes sharply critical of the "individual responsibility" thesis he attributes to liberal reformers. First, he dismisses the de-industrialization argument (Bluestone and Harrison, 1982). He also rejects the argument that improved schooling and attendant improvements in achievement of young blacks will lead to economic gains for them: "Our data suggests that the business cycle and relative unemployment rates also appear to have a greater impact on relative wages than longer-term increases in test scores" (p. 79). Racial discrimination, not employment opportunities and school achievement, are a principal cause of economic inequality. Although Carnoy does not reject the need to improve schooling investments, he places greater focus on the need for economic and social policies external to the school.

Changes in job opportunities and income gaps due to de-industrialization and economic restructuring suggest that the problem is in the capitalist economy, not in schools. The gradual white-collarization of manufacturing has had a significantly different impact on minorities than on whites, with the latter moving into the expanded ranks of managers and professionals while the former found their unskilled and semiskilled blue collar jobs replaced with clerical ones (Carnoy, 1994: 97–98). Schools have continued to produce worker schooling levels that exceed the skills required by their jobs (1994: 108). The declining demand for high school graduates in middle-level jobs is due to the fact that employers have raised the educational requirements for these positions; college graduates now fill jobs for which high school graduates once were considered qualified. These negative effects of the new economy are not inevitable, however. Carnoy argues that adverse changes in government policies between the 1960s and 70s and the 1980s explain much of the problem.

Liberal Interpretations

Since conservative ideology has set the terms of educational policy debates in recent decades, liberal ideology has been in a reactive posture. The discussion below emphasizes how this perspective interprets and addresses the political and economic changes to which we have been giving attention.

For the most part, liberal analyses of the political and economic challenges facing schools now accept the reality that public schools have to improve their performance. The assumption has been that low public confidence in public schools, while to some degree shaped by conservative attacks and media-bashing of schools, is fundamentally valid in its perception that school quality needs to improve.

Liberal ideology has evolved a wide variety of strategies to improve quality of the existing institution, some of which are programmatic, some pedagogical, some curricular, some monetary, and others in the realm of governance. I shall focus primarily on the last of these because these proposed reforms address most directly the issues of how to restore public support.

Liberal ideology, as was pointed out initially, approaches policy problems as capable of amelioration through pragmatic and incremental strategies. Incremental strategies are those that emphasize *reform* of existing structures and power relationships rather than *radical* surgery. Working within these meliorist assumptions, liberal analyses have endorsed several approaches to reforming educational governance: decentralization, policy coherence, and accountability. These strategies are at best loosely connected and some would argue are contradictory.

Decentralization strategists argue, following the logic of reforms to private firms in the marketplace, that more discretion should be given to schools and to teachers. Site-based management has been advocated for over a decade, although the concept has never been clearly articulated; who is in charge—the principal, teachers, parents? What functions and responsibilities are devolved to the school level and what powers remain in the hands of central administrators and boards of education? Many approaches to site-based management, for example, provide no budgetary or personnel authority to schools. (For a discussion see Brown, 1991.) Collective-bargaining agreements, for instance, remain centrally determined. Other versions of the model, such as was adopted in Chicago, emphasized actual *political* decentralization, rather than mere administrative delegation (Hess, 1991).

Many problems attend the implementation of this reform (Malen and Ogawa, 1988; Malen, Ogawa, and Kranz, 1988). These ambiguities tend to be inherent in decentralization strategies. Although their ostensible purpose is to increase discretion of "street-level bureaucrats" such as teachers (Lipsky, 1980) in order to make them more effective, such reforms also serve the tacit purpose of deflecting political pressure and demands from the top of the educational system to the bottom.

Much of the literature on teacher professionalization falls within the decentralization strategy. According to this line of analysis, it is not administrators or parents who require more discretionary authority, but teachers. The report of the National Commission on Teaching and America's Future (1996) takes this tack but does recommend a variety of other strategies besides decentralization for improving the recruitment, preparation, and retention of good teachers.

A second liberal reform strategy focuses on policy coherence. According to this analysis (Smith and O'Day, 1991), the American system of public education is characterized by a lack of coherent policies extending from the federal level down to the local school, and extending later-ally to other institutions such as employers. At the state level, for example, there seldom are policies that attempt to align policies pertaining to the curriculum, student assess-ment, teacher certification and professional development, and finance. What is needed, in other words, is "systemic reform" so that policies and practices are more tightly coupled. In order for true reform to occur, it is necessary for these policies to penetrate to the "core technology" of schools—"how teachers understand the nature of knowl-edge and the student's role in learning" and "how these ideas about knowledge and learning are manifested in teaching and classwork" (Elmore, 1996: 2094–295). Educational standards are the newest thrust in the systemic reform strat-egy. These standards serve as guides to the development of curricula and assessments.

Standards also lay the foundation for a third strategy that liberal ideology has gradually and somewhat reluc-tantly embraced: accountability. For students, the conse-quence for failing to perform well on assessments might be not graduating from high school. Administrators or teach-ers who are not performing adequately might be trans-ferred or even dismissed. Under an accountability strategy, there also can be negative consequences to organizational units that are performing below expectations. Thus schools can be declared in "decline" or "crisis" and become eligible for "reconstitution" or take-over by state or district authori-ties; and districts can be taken over for a range of indicators of unacceptable performance. Liberal ideology also em-braces the appropriateness of providing some rewards to organizational units for high performance (Mohrman, Wohlstetter, and Associates, 1994; Odden, 1996).

Although liberal analyses accept the view that public schools need to be restructured, they also resist some solu-tions advocated by conservative critics of the public schools. For example, despite growing public support for some kind of school choice/voucher system, there have been many lib-eral critiques of these plans.[11]

Although liberal ideology seeks to reverse the loss of public confidence in schools by these governance strategies, it has no overall strategy for dealing with the mobilization of special interests in school politics. Many liberal analyses focus on the dangers posed by the growing strength of the political right. However, groups on the political left also seek to purge the curriculum of white Eurocentrism. The mobi-lization of a variety of interest groups on both the political left and right poses a serious challenge to liberal ideology.

Liberal analyses of the changes in our economy tend to accept these changes as an inexorable fact and a natural progression of capitalism and the global economic system (Reich, 1988; Thurow, 1996). The task of public policy is to respond to those changes intelligently so as to preserve the American quality of life and equality of economic op-portunity. Business has a legitimate role to play in shaping

public policies and has become concerned about and in-volved in public schools for civic as well as economic rea-sons (McGuire, 1990). Liberals differ from conservatives, however, in favoring greater intervention in the market-place to encourage economic productivity. Also, schools are seen as only one of the institutions that must be restruc-tured to meet the demands of the new economy.

Reich (1992: 208–19) argues that there has been a changing demand for different kinds of labor. Because most Black Americans finish only high school and attend schools of relatively poor quality, they have been least well prepared to handle a shift to the rising demand for "sym-bolic analysts." Schools must be retooled so that they no longer mirror the old organization of production. The new economic system will require workers who take responsi-bility for their education, collaborate with one another, think critically, and continually learn on the basis of new data and experience (Reich, 1988: 17–21).

Murnane and Levy (1996) argue that the key to pros-perity resides in correcting the "mismatch" between the skills these jobs require and the skills that students procure in the public schools. Schools have not kept pace with what the economy requires. They argue that the economy is likely to generate a significant, if not altogether sufficient, number of "good jobs." Ensuring that all students secure the "new basic skills" is the primary prescription for equal access to economic opportunity.

The economic transformation in major cities, along with other factors such as suburbanization and out-migration, have eroded the economic base of major cities (Rury, 1993; Peterson, 1993) and contributed to the creation of an urban "underclass," comprised primarily of minority pop-ulations and subject to the cumulative, deadening effects of "unstable employment, restricted opportunities and low wages" (Wilson, 1987: 148). Wilson (1987: 39) draws on multiple case studies of urban areas to conclude that "the transformation of major northern metropolises from cen-ters of good processing to centers of information processing has been accompanied by a major shift in the educational requirements for employment." Job losses in these cities have been greatest in industries with lower educational re-quirements, while job growth has been concentrated in in-dustries that require higher levels of education.

Wilson (1996: 220) argues that U.S. social policies have not adjusted to these problems of joblessness and so-cial dislocation in the inner city. Public schools are one of the major institutions in need of restructuring:

> The strengths of some of the approaches in other countries are apparent. For example, in Japan and Germany most high school and college graduates leave school with skills in keeping with the demands of the highly technological marketplace in the global economy. In the United states, by contrast, only college graduates and those few with extra-specialized post-high school training acquire such skills. Those with only high school diplomas do not.

Wilson calls for a variety of strategies to reinvest in and restructure urban schools. He also argues for a host of other broadly targeted policies to create public employment opportunities for low-skilled workers, universal health care, day care, and so on. Wilson's makes clear his disapproval of many simplistic efforts to dismantle the so-called welfare state.

Levine and Zipp (1993) document the economic changes that have occurred in Milwaukee, notably the shift from a predominantly manufacturing, blue-collar trade employment structure to a service economy. They identify the implications of that shift for the wage structure and for the educational requirements that may be viewed as the appropriate credentials for employment. These changes have decreased the prospects of minorities securing higher-paying positions. The authors call for a "substantial commitment by the federal government to a renewal in urban education" (p. 67). They warn, however, that schooling alone will not prevent cities like Milwaukee from remaining at risk and call for "energetic, coordinated actions in other areas of economic and social policy" (p.68).

Levin and Kelley (1994) argue that education cannot be the sole or even primary solution to improving productivity without complementary inputs such as new investment and capital formation, management approaches that utilize new methods of work organization which take advantage of the greater productive capacity of educated workers, as well as more integrated approaches to research, training, product development, marketing, production, and finance. Liberal economists, in other words, favor expanding policies in private firms and in government that support the conditions for a more productive workforce, of which education is one only piece. Some, such as Levin and Kelley, worry that placing too much emphasis on schools as the key to economic competitiveness flies in the face of much contrary research evidence.

In sum, each of these ideologies offers a different interpretive frame for why public support for public schools has declined, what role special interests have played in that process, and how to respond to the demands of the new economy. Conservatives see the performance decline in public schools as the predictable result of liberal philosophies and dominance by liberal special interests ("elites"). Liberal analyses accept that there is a legitimate basis for public concern and seek programs and policies to restore confidence, while at the same time seeking to protect the institution against the mobilization of the political right (but not necessarily business interests). Radical interpretations, by contrast, stress that the performance problems of public schools are rooted in the structural inequities of the larger social and economic order. Schools both reflect these inequities and are an arena of struggle for subordinate groups to maintain their limited gains. "Reforms" such as school choice are tools to maintain the dominance of cap-

italist economic interests. These three ideologies then, underscore the fundamentally contested nature of how to interpret important political and economic developments and their implications for educational policy making.

Conclusion

I have argued that the debates over economic and political changes in our society and their implications for the enterprise of schooling are rooted in competing ideological frameworks rather than mere differences of factual interpretation. Facts are important, to be sure, but they are unlikely to be determinative because facts can carry different meanings. It is worth underscoring once again that my intent in this chapter has been conceptual and illustrative. I have not tried to cover exhaustively, much less interpret, the changes in our political and economic system and their implications for public schools.

In this concluding section, I will turn to the implications of the analytical methodology employed here. The knowledge base in educational administration has been in dispute for a long time. Arguments over the so-called Theory movement in educational administration (Griffiths, 1964) are one example. It is now widely noted that the study of educational administration no longer reflects one dominant theoretical perspective or paradigm (Cibulka and Mawhinney, 1995; Griffiths, 1995). Murphy (1995) describes three eras of research in the field of educational administration. In the prescriptive era (1900–1946) and the behavioral science era (1947–1985), societal context was not emphasized in a central way. Murphy argues that in the current "dialectic era," social context of schooling issues are emerging as more central. This is the case, he asserts, due to an increased focus on equity and diversity.

In this post-positivist period, competing ideological and theoretical views have legitimacy. The challenge now is to develop scholarship that draws upon these differences of ideological and theoretical perspective as a positive force.

The Value of Multiple Perspectives in Intellectual Inquiry

It is possible for a knowledge base to build within the context of contested ideologies and theoretical eclecticism.

The three ideological frames used in this chapter are one approach to the use of multiple perspectives in understanding education policy phenomena. Multiple perspective approaches have been employed for some time: Allison, 1971; Cibulka, 1991; Cuban, 1990; Peterson, 1976; Malen and Knapp, 1997, to name only some of the contributors. Griffiths (1995) argues for a multiple theoretical perspective in studying educational administration; the applied nature of the field should be problem-focused rather than theory-focused. I have tried to show in this chapter how a specifically ideological approach to framing political and economic problems can be useful.

If one accepts the premise that actual administrative or policy problems should guide the use and development of theory in the field of educational administration, there are at least four ways that this can occur. It is not always clear at the start, however, where the multiple perspectives approach will lead and, therefore, which of the following uses of multiple perspectives will have the most payoff for a particular problem.

One approach views the use of multiple perspectives as a way of illustrating irreconcilable truths. With regard to certain educational problems, conservative and liberal ideology, for example, may provide fundamentally different points of view. Those who believe firmly in the impermeable boundaries dividing academic paradigms might well take this approach to multiple perspectives. Often, however, the advocates of these paradigms sit at separate tables and are unwilling to dine together.

A second approach for using multiple perspectives is to find a best fit. This approach is less pertinent to competing ideologies than it is to different theories. Some kinds of problems lend themselves to a fuller understanding through one kind of theory than another. Griffiths (1995) uses the example of a census study of how many children are eligible for admission to public schools. Traditional empirical methods used by demographers may be the best analytical framework to use, whereas the interpretation of these phenomena lends itself to a variety of theoretical approaches, including versions of critical theory. From this perspective, no one theory is best for all problems.

A different approach is to view multiple perspectives as a way of illuminating partial truths. The key is to define the problem's components with sufficient breadth and richness to encourage use of different perspectives for capturing different pieces of the problem. The composite snapshot that emerges as a result of this approach may show that each approach provides only a piece of understanding the problem and therefore only a partial solution. No one approach provides the full answer, which can be derived only by juxtaposing, pyramiding, or scaffolding the partial truths found in any one perspective. The nearest thing we have to this in traditional scholarship is literature reviews of a body of knowledge or in a quantitative mode, meta-analysis of research findings.

Conceivably an approach that reveals partial truths will lead to still a more advanced critiquing of the perspectives themselves. A good example of this is Strike's (1989) analysis of the conflicting research programs of liberalism and Marxism. In a particularly insightful section of the analysis, while he defends liberalism, he demonstrates what each perspective misses, to which the other perspective gives central attention. Marxism attends little to the issue of rights. Strike asks: "Is it possible to have an adequate conception of human life in society without some conception of rights?" Concerning liberalism he poses this question: "Do the rights generated by liberal theories of justice in fact promote human flourishing, or do they ultimately generate practices and institutions that prevent the full development of human character?" Rights protecting individual growth mean little if they are undermined by lack of social opportunities. Following Strike's lead, an analysis of each perspective with respect to particular policy problems might lead to diagnoses and solutions that reach beyond each perspective and seek to account for their shortcomings. Whether it is possible to achieve a new synthesis that operates on a more comprehensive plane remains an open question, but as an epistemology this route has potential.

Problem-Framing as a Means of Preparing Practitioners

In an applied field such as educational administration, an important, although not exclusive, goal of scholarship must be to improve the capacity of leaders to act intelligently. One of the most important skills a leader can learn is how to frame problems clearly. However, we inhabit a policy universe, in education particularly, where practitioners as well as policy makers jump for ready and new solutions.

This approach has implications for teaching as well. Administrative preparation programs should help students understand administrative and policy problems as contested domains of action. Similarly, the institutional enterprise of schooling within which policy is formulated and implemented by administrators reflects values and interests. Because this value approach to problem-framing requires coming to terms with ideological differences embedded in the world of administration, it should also help would-be administrators to reflect on the tentative nature of their own actions. Administrators should be prepared to test the fit between the facts of the particular problem and the assumptions of alternative ideological frames. This requires seeing the strengths as well as the limitations of each ideological frame, which can vary according to the problem at hand. Administrative preparation needs to play out the implications of leadership enactment under conditions of value conflict and uncertainty. Once one assumes that the achievement of a consensus and the regulation of others' behavior is not the central aim of administration, only one available means toward some larger ends, a whole range of new options for conceptualizing the knowledge required for effective administrative leadership begins to become evident.

There is, of course, a long history of attempts in pedagogy to help students understand real-world problems, as distinct from teaching that is bereft of the context of action. Case-study methods and internships come to mind, yet too often these approaches immerse the student in the world of action without providing the intellectual tools to understand the broader societal context of administrative action. Rather, actions are reflected upon, if reflection is encouraged at all, in relation to theories of management. (For an exception, see Robinson, 1993.)

We could not do better for our students today than Mannheim (1936: 81) stated it: "The task of a study of ideology, which tries to be free from value-judgements, is to understand the narrowness of each individual point of view and the interplay between these distinctive attitudes in the total social process."

NOTES

1. Although she declined to be a co-author, I am indebted to Betty Malen, who helped me conceptualize and develop the arguments in this chapter. The author is indebted to the editors and to Gary Crow and Henry Levin for helpful comments on an earlier draft of this chapter.

2. This does not exhaust every matter to which political ideologies attend. For example, there are ideologies on gender roles, on race, and on poverty that intersect with broad political ideological perspectives covered here. This level of ideological specificity need not concern us here.

3. Alford and Friedland (1985), for example, distinguish between the pluralist, managerial, and class perspectives. In their study of approaches to the study of organizations, Burrell and Morgan (1979) distinguish among the functionalist paradigm, interpretive models of inquiry, radical humanism, and radical structuralism. Foster (1986) examines three frameworks for conceptualizing administrative activity—the functionalist, phenomenological, and critical approaches.

4. In his classic study of ideology, Mannheim (1936) distinguishes between particular (or, individually held) and general-total conceptions of ideology. Particular conceptions of ideology are normative; they grow out of individual's ideas as they experience their social milieu and try to make sense of it. By contrast, the attempt to understand a total ideology is non-evaluative. Although many of the ideas we express as individuals have their roots in ideologies, this does not mean that we embrace the total ideology or are even aware of it as a cognitive orientation that helps us comprehend particular events. Thus systems of thought we call ideologies are constructs that may be only partially perceived by these individuals or may not be claimed at all by those who articulate them.

5. Madison's Federalist Paper #51 is an excellent statement of this thesis.

6. Critics of liberalism's perceived excesses, such as Lowi (1995) and Spragens (1981), argue that this inherent problem in the liberal tradition has created a crisis of legitimacy today as government regulations become more coercive in an effort to achieve liberal ideals for the individual.

7. Conservative ideology, at least as it exists in the United States, is an amalgamation of two distinct strains, classical liberalism, which is libertarian, and orthodox conservatism, which is traditional (Meyer, 1964). Each has different philosophical roots. The former is a wing of liberalism, while the latter is rooted in the philosophy of the eighteenth century philosopher and statesman Edmund Burke (Stanlis, 1963) and other European conservatives who rejected the tenets of the French Revolution and Enlightenment thought. The resulting ideology is not always logically consistent, but in this respect conservatism is not unique.

8. Conservative ideology embraces a range of opinions about the degree to which state regulation of free markets is appropriate, both for the well-being of individuals and the management of the economy (Lowi, 1995).

9. Radical ideology, as employed here, is really a loose collection of many perspectives. Because it is an ideology that is not represented in the mainstream of American political thought, its articulation has been mainly through theorists, particularly academicians. It encompasses Marxist theory (in all its variations), critical theory, many feminist perspectives, such as Ferguson's (1984) critique of bureaucracy as well as Marshall's (1997) feminist critical policy analysis, and post-modern/post-structuralist theories. The gradations of viewpoint amongst these ideological strands can

be significant, such as the rejection by post-structuralists of "isms" such as Marxism. Thus our label is not meant to imply uniformity here any more than it does when we describe liberalism or conservatism, nor can we capture all the nuances in the space available. Also, it is important to reemphasize our earlier discussion of ideology; not all who have contributed to development of this perspective through one or another of their insights would identify themselves with the label "radical theorist."

10. This perspective has been criticized as "one-sided" and offering too much of an elite focus, even by its proponents (for example, Reese, 1986; Harvey, 1989).

11. Liberal ideology shares certain arguments with radical rebuttals of choice discussed earlier. For a useful summary of these arguments, see Bierlin, 1993, 105–120. Liberal analyses sometimes qualify their criticism by saying that the results of choice arrangements depend on the specifics of the choice plan (Fuller, Elmore, and Orfield, 1996: 199–200).

REFERENCES

Alford, R. A. & Friedland, R. (1985). *Powers of theory: Capitalism, the state, and democracy*. London: Cambridge University Press.

Alinsky, S. (1971). *Rules for radicals: A practical primer for realistic radicals*. New York: Vintage.

Allison, G. (1971). *Essence of decision*. Boston: Little-Brown.

Almond, G. A. (1990). *A discipline divided: Schools and sects in political science*. Newbury Park, CA: Sage.

Althusser, L. (1971). *Lenin and philosophy and other essays*. New York: Monthly Review Press.

Anderson, G. (1990). Toward a critical constructivist approach in educational administration. *Educational Adminstration Quarterly 26*, 38–59.

Apple, M. W. (1995) *Education and power* (2nd ed.). New York: Routledge.

Ball, S. J. (1987). *The micro-politics of the school: Towards a theory of school organization*. London: Methuen.

Ball, S. J. (1990). Management as moral technology: A Luddite analysis. In S. J. Ball (Eds.), *Foucault and education: Disciplines and knowledge* (pp. 153–166). London: Routledge.

Bates, R. J. (1980). Educational administration, the sociology of science and the management of knowledge. *Educational Administration Quarterly, 16*(2), 1–20.

Berliner, D. C. & Biddle, B. J. (1995). *The manufactured crisis: Myth, fraud, and the attack on America's public schools*. Reading, MA: Addison-Wesley.

Bierlin, L. A. (1993). *Critical issues in educational policy*. Newbury Park, CA: Sage Press.

Bloomfield, D. C. & Cooper, B. S. (1997, October). *Recentralization or strategic management?* Paper presented at the annual meeting of the University Council for Educational Administration, Orlando, FL.

Bluestone, B. & Harrison, B. (1982). *The de-industrialization of America*. New York: Basic Books.

Bordieu, P. & Passeron, J. (1977). *Reproduction in education, society, and culture*. New York: Basic Books.

Bowles, S. & Gintis, H. (1976). *Schooling in capitalist America*. New York: Basic Books.

Boyd, W. L. (1988). Policy analysis, educational policy, and management: Through a glass darkly? In N. J. Boyan (Ed.), *Handbook of research on educational administration* (pp. 501–524). New York: Longman.

Boyd, W. L., Lugg, C. A. & Zahorchak, G. L. (1996). Social traditionalists, religious conservatives, and the politics of outcome-based education. *Education and Urban Society, 28*, (3), 347–365.

Bracey, G. W. (1996, October). The sixth Bracey report on the condition of public education, *Phi Delta Kappan, 78*(2), 127–138.

Brown, D. J. (1991). *Decentralization: The administrator's guidebook to school district change*. Newbury Park, CA: Corwin Press.

Burrell, G. & Morgan, G. (1979). *Sociological paradigms and organization analysis*. Exeter, NH: Heinemann.

Carnoy, M. (1984). *The state and political theory*. Princeton, NJ: Princeton University Press.

Carnoy, M. (1994). *Faded dreams: The politics and economics of race in America*. New York: Cambridge University Press.

Carnoy, M. & Hannaway, J. (Eds.) (1993). *Decentralization and school improvement: Can we fulfill the promise?* San Francisco: Jossey-Bass.

Cherryholmes, C. H. (1988). *Power and criticism.* New York: Teachers College Press.

Chubb, J. E. & Moe, T. M. (1990). *Politics, markets, and America's schools.* Washington, DC: Brookings.

Cibulka, J. G. (1991). Educational accountability reforms: performance information and political power. In S. Fuhrman & B Malen (Eds.), *The politics of curriculum and testing* (pp. 181–201). London: Falmer Press.

Cibulka J. G. (1995). Policy analysis and the study of the politics of education. In J. D. Scribner & D. H. Layton (Eds.), *The study of educational politics* (pp. 105–126). New York: Falmer Press.

Cibulka, J. G. (1995). The institutionalization of public schools: The decline of legitimating myths and the politics of organizational instability. In R. T. Ogawa (Ed.), *Advances in research and theories of school management and school policy. Vol. 3,* (pp. 182–157). Greenwich, CT: JAI Press, Inc.

Cibulka, J. G. (1997). Two eras of urban schooling: The decline of the old order and the emergence of new organizational forms. *Education and Urban Society 29,* (3), 317–341.

Cibulka, J. G. & Mawhinney, H. (1995). Administrative leadership and the crisis in the study of educational administration: Technical rationality and its aftermath. In P. W. Cookson, Jr. & B. L. Schneider (Eds.), *Transforming schools* (pp. 489–532). New York: Garland Press.

Cigler, A. J. (1991). Interest groups: A subfield in search of an identity. In W. Grotty (Ed.), *Political science: Looking to the future, Volume 4: American institutions* (pp. 99–136). Evanston, IL: Northwestern University Press.

Clune, W. H. (1994). The shift from equity to adequacy in school finance. *Educational Policy, 8*(4), 376–394.

Cohn, E. & Geske, T. G. (1990). *Economics of education* (3rd ed.). New York: Pergamon Press.

Coons, J. E. & Sugarman, S. D. (1978). *Education by choice: The case for family control.* Berkeley, CA: University of California Press.

Cooper, B. S., Sarrel, R., Darvas, P., Alfano, F., Meier, E., Samuels, J. & Heinbach, S. (1994). Making money matter in education: A micro-financial model for determining school-level allocations, efficiency, and productivity. *Journal of Education Finance, 20* (Summer), 66–87.

Cuban, L. (1990). Reforming again, again, and again. *Educational Researcher, 19,* (1), 3–13.

Dahrendorf, R. (1979). *Life chances: Approaches to social and political theory.* Chicago: University of Chicago Press.

Danzberger, J. P., Kirst, M. W. & Usdan, M. D. (1992). *Governing public schools: New times, new requirements.* Washington, DC: Institute for Educational Leadership, Inc.

Dreeben, R. (1968). *On what is learned in school.* Reading, MA: Addison Wesley.

Easton, D. (1965). *A systems analysis of political life.* New York: Wiley.

Edelman, M. (1985). *Politics as symbolic action: Mass arousal and quiescence.* Chicago: Markham.

Elam S. M., Rose, L. C. & Gallup, A. M. (1994, September). The 26th annual Phi Delta Kappa/Gallup poll of the public's attitudes toward the public schools. *Phi Delta Kappan, 76* (1), 41–56.

Elam S. M., Rose, L. C. & Gallup, A. M. (1996, September). The 28th annual Phi Delta Kappa/Gallup poll of the public's attitudes toward the public schools. *Phi Delta Kappan, 78* (1), 41–59.

Elmore, R. F. (1996). Getting to scale with successful educational practices. In S. H. Fuhrman & J. A. O'Day (Eds.), *Rewards and reform: Creating educational incentives that work* (pp. 294–329). San Francisco: Jossey-Bass.

Ferguson, K. E. (1984). *The feminist case against bureaucracy.* Philadelphia: Temple University Press.

Fischer, F. (1990). *Technocracy and the politics of expertise.* Newbury Park, CA: Sage.

Foster, W. (1986). *Paradigms and promises: New approaches to educational administration.* Buffalo, NY: Prometheus Books.

Foucault, M. (1980). *Power/knowledge.* New York: Pantheon.

Fowler, F. C. (1995). The neoliberal shift and its implications for federal education policy under Clinton. *Educational Administration Quarterly, 31*(1), 38–60.

Freire, P. (1985). *The politics of education culture, power and liberation.* South Hadley, MA: Bergin & Garvey Publishers, Inc.

Freire, P. (1990). *Pedagogy of the oppressed.* New York: Continuum.

Fuhrman, S. & Elmore, R. (1990). Understanding local control in the wake of state education reform. *Educational Evaluation and Policy Analysis, 12*(1), 82–96.

Fuller, B., Elmore, R. F. & Orfield, G. (Eds.). (1996). *Who chooses? Who loses?: Culture, institutions, and the unequal effects of school choice.* New York: Teachers College Press.

Gerstner, L. V., Semerad, R. D., Doyle, D. P. & Johnston, W. B. (1994). *Reinventing education: Entrepreneurship in America's public schools.* New York: Dutton (Penguin Books USA).

Gerzon, M. (1996). *A house divided.* New York: Putman's Sons.

Gewirtz, S., Ball, S. J. & Bowe, R. (1995). *Markets, choice, and equity.* Buckingham, England: Open University Press.

Giddens, A. (1994). *Beyond left and right: The future of radical politics.* Cambridge, England: Polity Press.

Ginsberg, B., Lowi, T. & Weir, M. (1995). *We the people.* New York: W. W. Norton & Co.

Goertz, M. E. (1990). Education politics for the new century: Introduction and overview, in D. E. Mitchell & M. E. Goertz (Eds.), *Education Politics for the New Century,* pp. 1–10). New York: Falmer Press.

Goodman, J. (1995). Change without difference: School restructuring in historical perspective. *Harvard Educational Review, 65* (1), 1–29.

Griffiths, D. E. (1964). *Behavioral science and educational administration.* 63rd Yearbook of the National Society for the Study of Education. Chicago: University of Chicago Press.

Griffiths, D. E. (1995). Theoretical pluralism in educational administration. In R. Donmoyer, M. Imber & J. J. Schuerich (Eds.), *The knowledge base in educational administration: Multiple perspectives* (pp. 302–311). Albany, New York: State University of New York Press.

Guthrie, J. W., Garms, W. I. & Pierce, L. C. (1988). *School finance and education policy: Enhancing educational efficiency, equality, and choice.* (2nd ed.). Englewood Cliffs, NJ: Prentice-Hall.

Hannaway, J. & Carnoy, M. (Eds.). (1993). *Decentralization and school improvement: Can we fulfill the promise?* San Francisco: Jossey-Bass.

Hanushek, E. A. (1986). The economics of schooling: Production and efficiency in public schools. *Journal of Economic Literature 24* (September), 1141–77.

Hanushek, E. A. (1994). Money might matter somewhere: A response to Hedges, Laine & Greenwald. *Educational Researcher 23* (May), 5–8.

Hanushek, E. A., *et al.* (1994). *Making schools work: Improving performance and controlling costs.* Washington, DC: The Brookings Institution.

Hartz, L. (1955). *The liberal tradition in America: An interpretation of American political thought since the revolution.* New York: Harcourt Brace.

Harvey, D. (1989). *The urban experience.* Baltimore: Johns Hopkins University Press.

Haveman, R. H. & Wolfe, B. I. (1984) Schooling and economic well-being: the role of nonmarket effects. *Journal of Human Resources 19,* 377–407.

Hayek, F. A. von (1944). *The road to serfdom.* London: G. Routledge and Son.

Hedges, L. V., Laine, R. D. & Greenwald, R. (1994). Does money matter? A meta-analysis of studies of the effects of differential school inputs on student outcomes. *Educational Researcher 23* (April): 5–14.

Heilbroner, R. (1995). *Visions of the future: The distant past, yesterday, today, and tomorrow.* New York: Oxford University Press.

Hess, G. A., Jr. (1991). *School restructuring, Chicago style.* Newbury Park, CA: Corwin Press.

Hinchliffe, K. (1987). Education and the labor market. In G. Psacharopoulos (Ed.), *Economics of education research and studies* (pp. 141–146). New York: Pergamon Press.

Hirsch, E. O., Jr. (1996). *The schools we need: Why we don't have them.* New York: Doubleday.

Hollingsworh, S. (1977). Feminist praxis as the basis for teacher education: A critical challenge. In C. Marshall (Ed.), *Feminist critical policy analysis I: A perspective from primary and secondary schooling,* (pp. 165–182). Washington, DC: Falmer Press.

Jackson, B. L. & Cibulka, J. G. (1992). Leadership turnover and business mobilization: The changing political ecology of urban school systems.

In J. G. Cibulka, R. J. Reed & Ken K. Hong (Eds.), *The politics of urban education in the United States* (pp. 71–86). London: Falmer Press.

Jones, B. A. & Otterbourg, S. (In press). Education-business partnerships: The context and issues for evaluation. *Teachers College Record.*

Katz, C. J. (1997). Private property versus markets: democratic and communitarian critiques of capitalism. *American Political Science Review 91* (2), 277–289.

Kingdon, J. W. (1995). *Agendas, alternatives, and public policies.* New York: HyperCollins College Publishers.

Kirk, R. (1953). *The conservative mind.* Revised edition. Chicago: Gateway.

Levin, H. M. (1987). Work and education. In G. Psacharopoulos (Ed.), *Economics of education research and studies* (pp. 146–157). New York: Pergamon Press.

Levin, H. M. & Kelley, C. (1994). Can education do it alone? *Economics of Education Review 13* (2), 97–108.

Levine, M. V. & Zipp, J. F. (1993). A city at risk: The changing social and economic context of public schooling in Milwaukee. In J. L. Rury & F. A. Cassell (Eds.), *Seeds of crisis: Public schooling in Milwaukee since 1920,* (pp. 42–72). Madison, WI: The University of Wisconsin Press.

Lind, M. (1996). *Up from conservatism: Why the right is wrong for America.* New York: The Free Press.

Lipsky, M. (1980). *Street-level bureaucracy: Dilemmas of the individual in public service.* New York: Russell Sage.

Lockard, D. (1971). *The perverted priorities of American politics.* New York: Macmillan Company.

Lowi, T. J. (1995). *The end of the republican era.* Norman, OK: University of Oklahoma Press.

Lukes, S. (1974). *Power: A radical view.* London: Macmillan.

Luttbeg, N. H. & Gant, M. N. (1995). *American electoral behavior 1952–1992.* Itasca, IL: E. E. Peacock Publishers.

McCarthy, M. M. (1996). People of faith as political activists in public schools. *Education and Urban Society, 28,* (3), 308–326.

McGuire, K. (1990). Business involvement in the 1990s. In D. E. Mitchell & M. E. Goertz (Eds.), *Education politics for the new century* (pp. 107–118). New York: Falmer.

Malen, B. (1995). The micropolitics of education: Mapping the multiple dimensions of power relations in school polities. In D. H. Layton & J. D. Scribner (Eds.), *The Study of Educational Politics* (pp. 147–168). New York: Falmer.

Malen, B. & Knapp, M. (1997). Rethinking the multiple perspectives approach to education policy analysis: implications for policy-practice connections. *Journal of Education Policy 12* (5), 419–445.

Malen, B. & Ogawa, R. T. (1988). Professional-patron influence on site-based governance councils: A confounding case study. *Educational Evaluation and Policy Analysis, 10,* 251–279.

Malen, B., Ogawa, R. T. & Kranz, J. (1990). What do we know about school-based management? A case study of the literature-A call for research. In W. H. Clune & J. F. Witte (Eds.), *Choice and control in American Education, Volume 2: The practice of choice, decentralization and school restructuring* (pp. 289–342). New York: Falmer Press.

Mannheim, K. (1936). *Ideology and utopia: An introduction to the sociology of knowledge.* New York: Harcourt, Brace, and World.

Marshall, C. (1997). *Feminist critical policy analysis.* London: Falmer Press.

Marshall, C. & Anderson, G. L. (1995). Rethinking the private and public spheres: Feminist and cultural studies perspectives on the politics of education. In J. D. Scribner & D. H. Layton (Eds.), *The study of educational politics* (pp. 169–184). New York: Falmer Press.

Martin, W. (1996). *With God on our side: The rise of the religious right in America.* New York: Broadway Books.

Meyer, F. S. (1964). *What is conservatism?* New York: Holt, Rinehart, and Vinston.

Mickelson. R. A. & Wadsworth, A. L. (1996). NASDC's odyssey in Dallas (NC): Women, class and school reform. *Educational Policy, 10,* 315–344.

Mohrman, S. A., Wohlstetter, P. A. & Associates (1994). *School-based management: Organizing for high performance.* San Francisco: Jossey-Bass Publishers.

Molnar, A. (1996). *Giving kids the business: The commercialization of America's schools.* Boulder, CO: Westview Press.

Monk, D. H. (1990). *Education finance: An economic approach.* New York: McGraw Hill.

Murnane, R. J. & Levy, F. (1996). *Teaching the new basic skills: Principles for educating children in a changing economy.* New York: The Free Press.

Murphy, J. (1995). The knowledge base in school administration: Historical footings and emerging trends. In *The knowledge base in educational administration: Multiple perspectives* (pp. 62–73). Albany, New York: State University of New York Press.

Murray, C. (1984). *Losing ground: American social policy 1950–1980.* New York: Basic Books, Inc.

Murray, C. (1988). *In pursuit of happiness and good government.* New York: Simon and Schuster.

Murray, C. (1997). *What it means to be a libertarian: A personal interpretation.* New York: Broadway Books.

National Commission on Teaching and America's Future (1996). *What matters most: Teaching for America's future.* New York: Teachers college, Columbia University.

Odden, A. R. (Ed.) (1992). *Rethinking school finance: An agenda for the 1990s.* San Francisco: Jossey-Bass.

Odden, A. R. (1995). *Education leadership for America's schools.* New York: McGraw Hill.

Odden, A. R. (1996). Incentives, school organization, and teacher compensation. In S. H. Fuhrman & J. A. O'Day (Eds.) *Rewards and reform: Creating educational incentives that work* (pp. 226–256). San Francisco: Jossey-Bass Publishers.

Peterson, P. E. (1974). The politics of American education. In F. Kerlinger & J. Carroll (Eds.), *Review of research in education Vol. 2* (pp. 348–389). Itasca, IL: Peacock.

Peterson, P. E. (1976). *School politics: Chicago style.* Chicago: University of Chicago Press.

Peterson, P. E. (1993). Are big city schools holding their own? In J. L. Rury & F. A. Cassell (Eds.), *Seeds of crises: Public schooling in Milwaukee since 1920,* 269–301. Madison, WI: The University of Wisconsin Press.

Peterson, P. E. (1995). *The price of federalism.* Washington, DC: Brookings.

Polanyi, K. (1957). *The great transformation.* Boston: Beacon Press.

Popkewitz, T. S. (1991). *A political sociology of educational reform: Power/knowledge in teaching, teacher education, and research.* New York: Teachers College Press.

Pressman, J. & Wildavsky, A. (1973). *Implementation.* Berkeley, CA: University of California Press.

Reed, R. (1993). The agenda of the Religious Right: The Christian Coalition. *The School Administrator, 50* (9), 17–18.

Reese, W. J. (1986). *Power and the promise of school reform: Grassroots movements during the Progressive era.* Boston: Routledge & Kegan Paul.

Reich, R. (1988) *Education and the next economy.* Washington, DC: National Education Association.

Reich, R. (1992). *The work of nations.* New York: Vintage Books.

Rich, W. C. (1996). *Black mayors and school politics: The failure of reform in Detroit, Gary and Newark.* New York: Garland Publishing, Inc.

Robinson, V. M. J. (1993). *Problem-based methodology: Research for the improvement of practice.* London: Pergamon Press.

Robinson, V. M. J. (1994). The practical promise of critical research in educational administration. *Educational Administration Quarterly, 30* (1), 65–76.

Roemer, M. (1991). What we talk about when we talk about school reform. *Harvard Educational Review, 61,* 434–448.

Rossiter, C. (1962). *Conservatism in America: The thankless persuasion.* New York: Vintage Books.

Rury, J. L. (1993). The changing social context of urban education. In J. L. Rury & F. A. Cassell (Eds.), *Seeds of crisis: Public schooling in Milwaukee since 1920,* 10–41. Madison, WI: The University of Wisconsin Press.

Sawhill, I. V. & McMurrer, D. P. (1998). *Getting ahead: Economic and social mobility in America.* Washington, DC: Urban Institute Press.

Shea, C. M. (1989). Pentagon vs. multinational capitalism: The political economy of the 1980s school reform movement. In C. M. Shea, E. Kahane &

P. Sola (Eds.), *The new servants of power: A critique of the 1980s school reform movement* (pp. 3–38). New York: Praeger.

Smith, M. S. & O'Day, J. (1991). Systemic school reform. In S. H. Fuhrman & B. Malen (Eds.), *The politics of curriculum and testing*, pp. 233–268. London: Falmer Press.

Spraegens, T. A., Jr. (1981). *The irony of liberal reason.* Chicago: University of Chicago Press.

Spring, J. (1989). *The sorting machine revisited: National educational policy since 1945.* New York: Longman.

Stanlis, P. J. (1963). *Edmund Burke: Selected writings and speeches.* Garden City, NY: Doubleday and Company, Inc.

Strike, K. A. (1982). *Education policy and the just society.* Chicago: University of Illinois Press.

Strike, K. A. (1989). *Liberal justice and the Marxist critique of education: A study of conflicting research programs.* New York: Routledge.

Swanson, A. D. (1989). Restructuring educational governance: A challenge for the 1990s. *Educational Administration Quarterly* 25 (3), 260–293.

Thurow, L. C. (1992). *Head to head: The coming economic battle among Japan, Europe, and America.* New York: William Morrow and Company, Inc.

Thurow, L. C. (1996). *The Future of capitalism: How today's economic forces shape tomorrow's world.* New York: William Morrow and Company, Inc.

Twentieth Century Fund (1992). *Facing the challenge: the report of the Twentieth Century Fund Task Force on School Governance.* New York: The Twentieth Century Fund Press.

Whitty, G. (1997). Creating quasi-markets in education: A review of recent research on parental choice and school autonomy in three countries. In M. W. Apple (Ed.) *Review of research in education: Vol. 22.* Washington, DC: American Educational Research Association.

Wilson, W. J. (1987). *The truly disadvantaged: The inner city the underclass and public policy.* Chicago: The University of Chicago Press.

Wilson, W. J. (1996). *When work disappears.* New York: Knopf.

Wong, K. K. (1994). Linking governance reform to schooling opportunities for the disadvantaged. *Educational Administration Quarterly, 30,* (2), 153–177.

Wong, K. K. (1995). The politics of education: From political science to interdisciplinary inquiry. In D. H. Layton & J. D. Scribner (Eds.), *The study of educational politics* (pp. 21–38). New York: Falmer.

Zeigler, H., Kehoe, E. & Reisman, J. (1985). *City managers and school superintendents.* New York: Praeger.

CHAPTER 9

Delta Forces: The Changing Fabric of American Society and Education

Pedro Reyes, Lonnie H. Wagstaff, and Lance D. Fusarelli

Probably no other idea has seemed more typically American than the belief that schooling could cure society's ills (Ravitch, 1983, p. xii).

Americans have always turned to public schools both to improve and preserve society. At various times in our history, we have expected public schools to help eliminate poverty, reduce crime, lower unemployment, ease the assimilation of diverse ethnic groups, build moral character, advance scientific progress, and preserve democracy (Ravitch, 1983). In short, schools have been expected to compensate for the shortcomings of our society (Drachler, 1977). Yet policymakers and educators have failed to examine how these social ills themselves impact and shape public schools. All of society's ills, which public schools are expected to ameliorate, are simultaneously reshaping and reconstructing the schools themselves.

We examine the changing forces that have shaped primary and secondary education in the United States in the last half century, evaluating the impact these changes have had on American education, particularly as they have shaped the context of school reform. Schattschneider (1960) argues that the definition of alternatives "is the supreme instrument of power" (p. 66). It is our contention that numerous outside forces, which we call "delta forces," play a determinant role in shaping the structure of education, particularly with respect to various efforts at school reform.

We argue that much of the impetus for change in education has originated not from professional educators themselves, but from policy entrepreneurs largely outside the educational establishment who were able to take advantage of changes in the external environment. As Wong

(1992) observes, "increasingly, external political and economic forces are found to shape school finance, leadership succession, the student population, racial desegregation, and issues related to the education of the disadvantaged" (p. 3). Through the policy windows created by changes in the external environment (Kingdon, 1984), a multitude of policy actors helped shape the nature and context of education in America.

Despite the diversity of policy entrepreneurs, we argue that various policy initiatives, particularly recent initiatives, may be traced to and have their origins in what we call a neo-corporatist model of schooling based on "the idea of bringing school decision making closer to the 'customer' (parents and students)" (Miron, 1996, p. 69).[1] This model assumes that the answer to social problems lies outside of government (public schools) to accomplish excellence (Miron, 1996, p. 70). Virtually without exception, all the waves of school reform from the 1980s through the present share this fundamental premise. Since this model emphasizes competitive, hierarchical achievement, punitive discipline, and segregation of diverse populations, the implication of current reforms is that they will reproduce rather than transcend societal inequities and stratifications (Bastian, et al., 1985). This is particularly problematic given the acceleration of several demographic trends discussed.

We highlight in this chapter significant events (with emphasis on the post-World War II era) that opened these policy windows and thus shaped the fundamental structure of education in America. Because of the vast scope of the period being covered, we selected only those events that we believe have had a significant effect on shaping education policy. The focus of the chapter is, almost exclusively, macro-level forces that have shaped policy change in education. This is not to minimize the micro-level forces that exerted substantial influence on policy change, particularly policy implementation. However, given the extraordinary degree to which similar reforms are being implemented in state after state (see, for example, Fowler, 1994; Fuhrman, 1989; Mazzoni, 1993), and the macro-level forces shaping those changes, we argue that a macro-level lens is most appropriate for this analysis. The chapter concludes with a projection of the nature of education in the twenty-first century and discusses the implications of these changes for educational administration as we prepare education leaders for the coming millennium.

The Great Depression, the Cold War, and *Brown*: The 1940s and 1950s[2]

During the 1940s, the total student enrollment in public schools was approximately 25 million children; at the end of the 50s, the total number had increased to 35 million children (NCES, 1995). No statistics exist concerning the social characteristics of such students. Nonetheless, Margo (1994) estimated that at least in the South 61% of black males (age five to 20) attended public schools, while 62% of black females enrolled in school. Among the white student population, Margo estimated that 72% or more attended school in the South. During these decades, federal investment in education increased from $39,810,000 to $486,480,000 (NCES, 1995).

Three events significantly impacted education policy during the 1940s and 1950s: the Great Depression, the Cold War, and the *Brown V. Board of Education* decision. Up until the Great Depression, federal involvement in domestic affairs was limited by the dominant laissez-faire ideology of the era. This philosophy significantly constrained the power of the federal government and reserved much of the responsibility for domestic affairs to the states. Several scholars refer to this as the period of dual federalism (Patterson, 1996). Aside from a few limited federal initiatives in education[3], the federal government was little more than an interested observer whose "explicit role in education continued to be limited" (Tyack and Hansot, 1982, p. 243). The severity of the Great Depression, coupled with Franklin Roosevelt's policy responses to it, initiated a paradigm shift from the dominant laissez-faire ideology of dual federalism to the more active, interventionist philosophy of cooperative federalism (Frantzich and Percy, 1994). This led to a number of new federal initiatives in education, including the National School Lunch and Milk programs (1946) that provided grants and commodity donations for public and private schools; it also led to the Federal Impacted Areas Aid program (1950) that authorized federal funds for "federally impacted" areas of the nation (Dye, 1992, p. 171). Consequently, the power of the federal government expanded dramatically and it became a much more active participant in domestic affairs, particularly in education.

The increased power of the national government, coupled with the emphasis on sorting and classifying personnel in the Army and the abuse and misuse of IQ testing during the war, significantly impacted education in the post-war years. The educational emphasis throughout the 1940s was on life adjustment education, popularized by Charles Prosser, a leading vocational educator of the period (Prosser, 1939). Life adjustment education emphasized the importance of functional education, including the development of such skills as citizenship, health, home and family life, and occupational adjustment (Ravitch, 1983). Educators and others considered occupational adjustment education as weak policy; they feared that the country would slide back into a depression after the war. This concern resulted in an increased emphasis on practical subjects such as business math as opposed to advanced math, and standard or business English as opposed to poetry (Ravitch, 1983). This shift in educational philosophy fit perfectly the social norms and needs of the post-war period.

If the emphasis on life adjustment education fit the perceived needs of society in the 1940s and early 1950s, these priorities suddenly changed with the Soviet Union's successful launch of Sputnik in 1957. Sputnik sent shock waves among federal policymakers by giving the appearance that the Soviet Union was ahead of the United States in the areas of science and technology. Given the presence of the Cold War, in which the United States and the Soviet Union were locked in an ideological battle for superiority in all areas including education, Sputnik was taken as definitive proof that the United States was lagging behind the Soviets in the areas of science, technology, and education. Almost overnight, the public education system (which had long been criticized by professional educators such as Robert Maynard Hutchins at Chicago for its neglect of higher education standards) came under sharp attack by the public and congressional leaders.

As a result, Congress created the National Defense Education Act of 1958 that authorized federal aid to states and schools to improve instruction in science, mathematics, and foreign languages. The federal government began to finance training programs for teachers, established research centers, and purchased equipment (Rippa, 1992). What had heretofore been almost solely a state responsibility now became a significant federal concern. Federal assistance to education became a matter of national security.

The Cold War served to enhance further the role of the federal government in shaping education policy at the state and local levels and significantly shaped many of the state and local reform initiatives of the period. Many of these initiatives, particularly the emphasis on building more classrooms and training large numbers of new teachers, were designed to meet the need to educate the unprecedented numbers of students produced during the post-war baby boom. The student population attending all levels of primary and secondary education increased dramatically throughout the 1940s and 1950s (Ravitch, 1983; Office of Education, 1963).

The third major national event shaping education policy was the *Brown* decision in 1954. As Diane Ravitch (1983) notes, it was a "historic affirmation of the egalitarian ideals of American society" (p. 127). More significantly, the decision had major ramifications for the structure of society and affected school children throughout the country. According to Ravitch (1983)

> Never before had the Supreme Court reached so deeply into the lives, laws, and mores of so many people; nearly half the states of the nation were living according to laws that the Court had ruled unconstitutional. Approximately 40 percent of the public school pupils in the nation were enrolled in segregated systems (p. 127).

The *Brown* decision is significant not so much for its immediate effect but as the trigger event that helped spawn the Civil Rights movement. To be sure, President Truman's integration of the armed forces in 1946 and the Democratic Party's gradual acceptance of civil rights planks into the party's platform were significant events. However, the *Brown* decision clearly affirmed the irrelevance of color to the rights of American citizens (Clark, 1965). As Lowe and Kantor (1995) argue, there followed an accelerating, many faceted struggle for equality of which school desegregation was a modest part (p. 188). A year after *Brown*, Rosa Parks refused to give up her seat to an Anglo male, and shortly thereafter sit-ins were organized at segregated restaurants, hotels, theaters, and numerous other places of segregation (Ravitch, 1983). As Lowe and Kantor assert, from the Montgomery Bus Boycott to the lunch counter sit-ins and freedom rides, from the Albany and Birmingham movements to the Selma march for voting rights, a mobilized black population dramatized injustice and prompted passage of the Civil Rights Act of 1964 and the Voting Rights Act of 1965 (p. 188). Thus the *Brown* decision, delayed in implementation as it was, is significant for the principles it espoused and the impetus it gave to the growth of the Civil Rights movement. Although no Supreme Court decision since *Brown* has had such a monumental impact on education policy[4], state courts have become increasingly active participants in the battle over equitable school finance.

Thus it is clear that the courts, as policymaking institutions, will continue to shape education policy in the coming century.

Turbulence Amid the Struggle for Equity: The 1960s

Although the '40s and '50s brought increased activity in education, the 1960s was a period of immense change in American society, particularly in the cities. From 1940 to 1966, nearly four million African-Americans migrated from the South and settled into largely urban areas in the North (Margo, 1994; Ravitch, 1983). According to Ravitch (1983), the African-American population in cities nearly doubled, from 6.5 million to 12.1 million people, a rate of growth from 43% to 56% of the total African-American population. Meanwhile, the percentage of Anglos living in the cities declined noticeably, particularly in many northern cities (Wong, 1992). Jobs appear to have followed them out of the central cities. The migration of many businesses out of the central cities into the suburbs closed off large sectors of the job market to minorities in the cities.

These trends, begun in the post-war era, continued throughout the decade and well into the 1970s and 1980s (Wong, 1992; Ravitch, 1983). For example, in the late 1980s, "over 60% of blacks and over 70% of Hispanics enrolled in predominately minority schools" (Wong, 1992, p. 16). Residential segregation produced a marked increase in school segregation throughout the nation. Residential segregation was facilitated by numerous programs and policy initiatives undertaken by the federal government. In fact, any analysis of residential segregation in the post-war period must recognize the degree of federal complicity in fostering its onset and wide-ranging development. In reaction to widespread housing foreclosures during the Depression, in the 1940s the federal government began underwriting mortgages through the Federal Housing Authority (FHA) "in an effort to enable citizens to become homeowners" (Wilson, 1997, p. 46, Tyack, 1974). This included low-interest mortgages for veterans, mortgage-interest tax exemptions, and the cheap production of massive amounts of tract housing (Wilson, 1997).

However, as Wilson (1997) observes, these programs were selectively administered by the FHA. Mitchell (1985) argues that the Depression created "a virtuous class of poor people"—the "deserving" poor who were temporarily unemployed and down on their luck (p. 7). This group, of which nearly all were white and many were veterans, pushed for federal action in the area of housing. However, loan applications from urban neighborhoods considered poor risks were systematically redlined and excluded from this process. This widespread practice excluded virtually all neighborhoods with high concentrations of African-Americans. "By manipulating market incentives, the federal government drew middle-class whites to the suburbs and, in effect, trapped blacks in the inner cities" (Wilson, 1997, p. 46). This blatantly discriminatory practice continued until 1968, when the Civil Rights Act of 1968 "expressly established equal opportunity in housing as an official U.S. policy by prohibiting all actors in the housing market from discriminating on the basis of race, color, creed, or national origin" (Mitchell, 1985, pp. 11–12). Although the FHA subsequently discontinued its racial restrictions on mortgages (Wilson, 1997), a report by the U.S. Commission on Civil Rights (1979) concluded that Title VIII of the Act failed to provide effective enforcement mechanisms for ensuring fair housing and that fully 10 years after the passage of the Act the Departments of Housing and Urban Development and Justice had failed to devise satisfactory strategies for combating racial discrimination in housing.

Thus this policy change did nothing to reduce white flight from the cities, which had been "underwritten in part by federal mortgage insurance" (Mitchell, 1985, p. 13). In fact, the unwillingness of the federal government to enact policies to counteract decades of racial discrimination in housing, coupled with efforts of suburban communities to draw "tighter boundaries through the manipulation of zoning laws and discriminatory land-use controls and site-selection practices," has effectively denied inner-city minorities access to these suburban enclaves (Wilson, 1997, p. 47).[5]

Other federal policy initiatives encouraged white flight from the urban core. The suburbanization of the white middle class was facilitated by federal transportation policies, principally the development of massive freeway networks through the heart of central cities (Wilson, 1997, Tyack, 1974). These policies destroyed many viable low-income communities[6], displaced thousands of urban poor, and effectively walled in minority neighborhoods with high concentrations of urban poverty (Wilson, 1997). The cumulative effect of numerous federal policies in creating urban ghettos is undeniable. Whether intentional or not, federal policies in the areas of housing and transportation policy have contributed significantly to economic and racial segregation in the United States.

Kozol (1991) was shocked by the extent to which racial segregation has intensified and, worse still, is now largely uncontested. Orfield (1994) found that segregation in the South as well as segregation of African-Americans and Hispanics has increased. This is particularly problematic when one considers that both African-Americans and Hispanic students are more likely than their Anglo counterparts to attend schools in areas of concentrated poverty (Orfield, 1994).

These significant, often rapid, changes posed enormous challenges to urban schools, in part, for the inability of schools to handle the developing urban crisis (Ravitch, 1983; Drachler, 1977). As Drachler (1977) observes, "efforts such as open enrollment, the Princeton Plan, magnet schools, and educational parks failed with the flight of the white families from the cities" (p. 209). As a further result of these demographic changes, cities were unable to collect adequate tax revenue from residents. The declining tax base, coupled with significant increases in unemployment, crime, and housing problems, forced many urban districts to do more with less money (Drachler, 1977). As Cibulka (1992) notes, spending in urban school districts is far below suburban districts with fewer pupil needs. During this decade, the student population rose from 36 million to 45 million pupils. Similarly federal spending in education rose from $651,639,000 to almost three billion dollars (NCES, 1995).

The 1960s may be characterized as a period in which the value of equity was emphasized as a goal of society, particularly in the area of education. The politics of the 1960s brought to life a serious federal commitment to improve the quality of life among the disenfranchised. The election of John F. Kennedy brought an activist president sympathetic to the struggle for civil rights. His subsequent assassination did little to stop and in fact may have fueled the movement toward de jure equality. In 1963, nearly a quarter of a million people marched on Washington to demand civil rights and jobs programs (Ravitch, 1983). The passage of the Civil Rights Act of 1964 and the Voting Rights Act of 1965 served to reaffirm, at least as codified in law, the commitment to equity. Title VI of the Civil Rights Act is particularly important because it provided for the "termination of financial assistance if states and communities receiving federal funds refused to comply with federal desegregation orders" (Dye, 1992, p. 55). The *Brown* decision was never popular in the South. In the decade following *Brown*, only about 2% of African-American school children in the South were attending integrated schools (Dye, 1992). As Lowe and Kantor (1995) observed, "the pace of school desegregation was glacial" (p. 188). The threatened cut-off of federal funds effectively encouraged rapid desegregation in the South.

During the 1960s, the nation "discovered" poverty and the significant achievement gaps between ethnic groups were cause for concern (Passow, 1995). Continuing the trend of cooperative federalism begun three decades earlier, Congress passed the Elementary and Secondary Education Act of 1965 (ESEA), which established the single largest federal program to aid education (Dye, 1992). ESEA was originally intended to improve the educational opportunities of poor children (Ravitch, 1983). However, when implemented, ESEA provided financial assistance to nearly every school district in the country (Peters, 1986). Approximately $10 billion was "invested in compensatory programs designed to improve the educational achievement of the disadvantaged" (Rippa, 1992, p. 354). ESEA provided "poverty-impacted" schools with federal aid, instructional materials, educational research, and training (Dye, 1992, p. 171). Three years later, Congress passed the Bilingual Education Act of 1968 to provide funds to districts to meet the needs of children with limited English-speaking ability (Ravitch, 1983). The creation of these federal programs, together with other federal initiatives designed to assist low-income children, "made solid gains in preschool education (Head Start), compensatory reading (Chapter 1) and precollege preparation (Upward Bound), while sharply cutting the rates of infant death and child malnutrition" (Kozol, 1990/1994 , p. 76).

The federal commitment to research led to sponsorship of the now famous Coleman Report. The Coleman Report found that a student's family background and the background of classmates had a significant effect on student learning (Coleman, 1966). In 1967, the U. S. Commission on Civil Rights used the findings of the report to press for an end to segregation in public schools (Dye, 1992). The Commission recommended an end to neighborhood schools and the busing of students to create racially balanced schools (Dye, 1992). Perhaps no other educational issue of the decade was as controversial as school busing. Virulent opposition arose in many affluent neighborhoods and contributed to white flight (Coleman, et al., 1975; Orfield, 1994). Despite this opposition, by the late 1960s, the U. S. Supreme Court was in no mood to allow various freedom-of-choice plans to delay the duty to comply with *Brown* (Ravitch, 1983). Consequently, beginning in 1968, the U.S. Supreme Court issued a series of rulings that struck down various plans that did not produce measurable desegregation.

For example, in *Green v. County School Board of New Kent County* (1968), the Supreme Court struck down choice plans that did not produce measurable desegregation. In *Swann v. Charlotte-Mecklenburg* (1971), the Supreme Court upheld the reassignment of students by race and approved the use of busing to end segregation (Orfield, 1978). In *Keyes v. School District No. 1, Denver, Colorado* (1973), which "extended desegregation to the North and included Chicanos as well as African-Americans in desegregation plans," (pp. 192–193), the Supreme Court ruled that a system of de facto segregation was unconstitutional. As a result of these decisions and others by lower courts, by 1972 over 91% of all African-American students in the South attended school with Anglos (Ravitch, 1983). This high level of involvement of the federal courts in educational issues is consistent with the activist courts of the period. In the post-war period, the federal courts became increasingly involved in educational matters. For example, from 1946 to 1956, federal courts rendered 112 decisions affecting education; from 1956 to 1966, the total reached 729; from 1966 to 1970, the courts issued over 1200 decisions on educational issues as diverse as classroom discipline/due process to black English and/or black idiom (Ravitch, 1983).

An oft overlooked, but critically important, source of power during the 1960s was the media, particularly television. The 1960 presidential debates between Richard Nixon and John F. Kennedy were the first televised debates in the nation's history. For the first time in history, the national media, particularly television, was able to bring the brutality of the struggle for civil rights into the homes of large numbers of citizens (Ravitch, 1983). Television brought to life the first lunar landings as well as graphic pictures of the Vietnam War. It affected how Americans felt about their society and the world around them. This is nowhere more true than in depressed urban areas. Rippa (1992) argues that

> Perhaps the deepest impressions of the mass media were made on people in the inner-city ghettos and in rural poverty areas where television, for the first time, offered a glimpse of the sharp contrasts in daily existence. Stories, programs, and advertisements instantly showed an affluent way of life beyond easy reach. For the rural and the urban disadvantaged, for children growing up in the culture of poverty, hopelessness and apathy slowly turned to frustration and rage (p. 327).

It did not take long for this rage to spill out into protests, riots, and violence. The subsequent social upheaval, fueled by antiwar protests and protests against the establishment in general, brought a raucous end to a decade that began with the hope of creating a more equitable society.

Disappointment and Drift: The 1970s

While the '60s brought excitement to education, the 1970s was a period of disappointment and drift. The student population declined from 45 million in the early '70s to 41 million in the late '70s. Of these students 76% were white, 16% black, 6% Hispanic, and the rest belonged to other minority groups (NCES, 1995). The federal investment in public education ranged from four billion in the early seventies to 8.5 billion at the end of the decade (NCES, 1995). This decade also witnessed the narrowing of the gap between the rich and the poor. Peters (1986) indicates that the income gap narrowed during the '60s and '70s as a result of Johnson's war on poverty and increased expenditures for programs such as social security.

Despite increased federal aid to education, student achievement test scores declined (Dye, 1992). Busing turned violent in many communities and did not substantially end the racial imbalances in most schools. When busing was implemented, it did not produce the expected gains in student achievement among minority students (Dye, 1992; Orfield, 1994).

The two areas in which the federal government did have a significant influence was (1) the increasing proportion of students served in federal programs for the learning disabled and (2) aid to handicapped children. The late 1970s brought about a significant increase in the proportion of students identified as learning disabled. In 1976, approximately 8% of the total student population was categorized as learning disabled; by 1992, it had risen to 12% of all students enrolled in public primary and secondary education (National Center for Education Statistics, 1995c). Although substantial debate exists as to whether this move benefited these children, its impact on the educational system is undeniable. The second area in which the federal government took great interest was in the education of the handicapped. In 1975, Congress passed PL 94–142, entitled the "Education for All Handicapped Children Act" (Ravitch, 1983). This law required districts to provide appropriate educational services to all handicapped children, including an individualized education program (IEP) in "the least restrictive environment" (Cummins, 1986; Ravitch, 1983). Although the law required assessment procedures that are nonculturally discriminatory, the dramatic overrepresentation of minorities identified as learning disabled has led many to question the overall benefits of the law (Cummins, 1986, Ortiz and Yates, 1983).

The resultant disappointment in the school reform efforts of the 1970s mirrored the general malaise prevalent in the country throughout the decade. Trust in public institutions, weakened by the prolongation of the Vietnam War, declined further during the Watergate scandal and subsequent resignation of President Nixon. The economic outlook was similarly grim. Inflation rose and stagflation worked its way into the lexicon. The OPEC oil embargo and subsequent gasoline shortages made Americans aware of how vulnerable the country was to outside forces.

Cities deteriorated with a rapid loss of middle-class families and jobs to suburbia. The national super highway system designed to serve communities also helped to tear them down by making out migration from them convenient. From 1970 to 1980, the number of poor people living in the poorest neighborhoods (census tracts with at least 40% of residents with poverty-level incomes) increased nearly 30% to an estimated 2.45 million (National Research Council, 1993). The result was substantial growth in underclass neighborhoods (National Research Council, 1993).

The decade concluded with a lengthy hostage crisis that emasculated the presidency of Jimmy Carter. Even the music and fashion styles of the period were considered by many as best forgotten. From politics to the economy, from domestic problems to foreign misadventures, from education to music and fashion, the decade was one of disappointment and drift. The new society that many in the 1960s thought could be produced did not come about and they were left looking for strong leadership and direction. The leadership never arrived and the direction was mainly drift.

Retrenchment and Reform in the 1980s and 1990s

During these decades, student enrollment declined in the early '80s and increased in the '90s. In 1980, the student population was 41.7 million, which dropped to 40.5 million in 1990; by 1994, the student population increased to 43.5 million. Table 9.1 shows the distribution of students by ethnic category.

At the same time, income inequality widened during these decades. The gains made during the '60s and '70s almost disappeared (see Figure 9.1). Kiefer and Phillips

Table 9.1
Distribution of Students by Ethnicity

	1980	1986	1994
Anglo	73%	70%	66%
African/Am.	16%	16%	17%
Hispanic	8%	10%	13%
Asian/Pac. Islander	2%	3%	4%
Am. Indian/Als. Nat.	1%	1%	1%

Source: National Center for Education Statistics, 1996.

Figure 9.1
Income Inequality in the United States, 1974–94

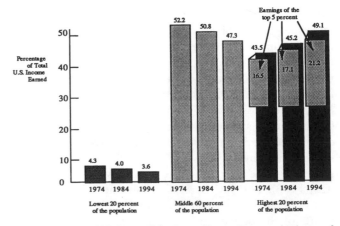

Source: U.S. Bureau of the Census, "Income, Poverty, and Valuation of Noncash Benefits: 1994," *Current Population Reports*, Series P60-189 (Washington, D.C.: Government Printing Office, 1996), p. xii.

(1988) attribute the widening gap between the rich and the poor to the policies of the Reagan Administration, from antitrust enforcement to (lack of) deregulation policies. This period is characterized as the triumph of upper-class America via glorification of capitalism, finance, and free markets. The truly wealthy (upper one percent) flourished under President Reagan. A Brookings Institution study indicated that the share of national income going to the wealthiest one percent of the population rose from 8.1% to 14.7% in 1986 (cited in Kiefer and Phillips, 1988). Under the Reagan Administration, the top personal tax bracket dropped from 70% to 28%.

The decade of the 1980s witnessed a resurgence of conservatism throughout the country. With an almost religious fervor, President Reagan used the bully pulpit to press for an end to what he viewed as the liberal excesses of a previous era and a scaling back of federal authority. The first groups to benefit from this philosophy were large corporations and the uppermost income segments of society. Under President Reagan, corporate taxes were cut in half and "the income tax on the wealthiest citizens . . . was the lowest of any industrialized nation in the world" (Spring, 1992). This posed particular difficulties for urban schools because the corporate share of local property tax revenues declined from 45% in 1957 to 16% in 1987 (Reich, 1991).

The conservatism of the 1980s and early 1990s is at least attributable to significant changes in the structure of the economy during this period. Singh (1991/1994) observes that "global competition, technological changes, and product substitutions have forced accelerated economic restructuring in several mature industrial regions" of the United States (p. 63). Plant and factory closings were common, particularly in the industrial Northeast and Midwest. The savings and loan crisis forced the closing of numerous banks. The economy became more polarized between high and low-wage occupations (Wilson, 1987) and there were fewer jobs available in the middle range (Ward, 1993). As a result of the bifurcated economy, a large and growing segment of the school population was excluded from high-wage occupations and relegated to low-paying positions in the expanding service industries. Despite an economic recovery, the restructured economy remains effectively closed off to these students. There is little evidence that the economic recovery benefited in any significant way those living in the inner city or in many of the older industrial towns (Singh, 1991/1994). The declining number of blue-collar positions in the restructured economy has significantly decreased the life chances of those students for whom higher education is not practicable.

Although the complexity of governing a modern republic has made a return to dual federalism impracticable, the federal government did push more of the governing responsibility for domestic programs back to the states. This period, which continues through the present, is character-ized as competitive or new federalism (Frantzich and Percy, 1994). Due to persistent budget deficits and a burgeoning national debt, the federal government is scaling back its commitment to several domestic programs and transferring responsibility back to the states by way of block grants. The Welfare Reform bill signed by President Clinton in 1995 is evidence of the continuing trend toward competitive federalism. As with welfare, several programs in education have been consolidated into block grants. The Education Consolidation and Improvement Act of 1981 "consolidated ESEA and other federal educational grant programs into single 'block' grants for states and communities" (Dye, 1992, p. 171).

Although the federal government attempted to shift the financial burden and responsibility for education back to the states, it was by no means indifferent to the effect of education on the economic health of the nation. This reflects the fact that in an interdependent and interconnected world, nations are increasingly affected by national and global forces. Increased international economic competition has shifted the focus of the policy debate over school effectiveness from the local and state arenas to the international arena (see *A Nation at Risk*). This report explicitly linked education with economic productivity. Asserting that standards were low and schools ineffective, policy makers became obsessed with international comparisons of student performance. Invariably, these reports found U.S. students lagging far behind their peers in other industrialized countries (Del Valle, 1991). In response to these conditions, business leaders assumed leading roles in the education reform movement. David Kearns, former chairman of Xerox, became Undersecretary of Education under President Bush.

Larry Cuban (1992) comments upon the increased role played by business in education policy:

> Beginning in the early 1980s, groups of corporate executives, concerned about the lack of workplace skills of high school graduates, formed business roundtables to lobby local, state, and national policy makers for school improvement. In addition, national commissions chaired by chief executives of the country's leading firms and national business groups began issuing reports (more than 300 had appeared by 1990) expressing the corporate view of what should be done to improve the public schools (p. 157).

The increased involvement of business leaders in education during the 1980s was in response to concerns over changes in national and international economic conditions, particularly the perceived decline of worker productivity and competitiveness in world markets (Mazzoni, 1993; McGuire, 1990). Business leaders view education not simply as a social concern, but as a key component of economic growth (Cuban, 1992). The widespread belief that education reform is pivotal to economic development and success in the global marketplace permeates state education policy systems (Mazzoni, 1993).

Looking back upon the education platforms of the Democrat and Republican presidential candidates since 1980 (including then President Carter and challenger Ronald Reagan), Doyle (1992) sees a great deal of commonality and continuity among the candidates. He attributes this to the recognition of the limits of federal activity in education and the tradition of local control over education. The federal government has traditionally accounted between six to eight percent of total educational expenditures (Sroufe, 1995; Del Valle, 1991). It has never exceeded 10 percent (Dye, 1992).

However, expenditures on education understate the influence of the federal government on shaping education. The role is more than symbolic. The influence of the federal government on state education is real in that it represents a set of expectations and aspirations—an ideology for education that the states are encouraged to adopt (Mazzoni, 1993). This is particularly true when there is substantial agreement on federal education policy among successive presidential administrations. For example, the broad policy statements and education bills of Presidents Bush and Clinton (America 2000 and Goals 2000 respectively) are remarkably similar (see Bush, 1992; Clinton, 1992). Cuban (1992) notes that recommendations from top corporate leaders, the National Governors' Association, and key officials in present and past Administrations all echo similar themes, though the specifics vary slightly. These policy entrepreneurs, whether Republican or Democrat, share a neo-corporatist ideology based largely on the forces and values of free market competition.

The decade of the 1980s also witnessed an expansion of the power of the media as a significant player in shaping education policy (Feir, 1995). Kaplan and Usdan (1992) note that national, state, and local media coverage of America 2000 and Goals 2000 was voluminous and generally supportive. This is not altogether surprising given that the media in the U.S., unlike in other countries, is almost without exception privately owned and espouse the neo-corporatist ideology of other major powerbrokers. Media reports lent credibility to the various policy networks and brought preferred policy options to public attention. This is not altogether surprising given that the primary sources of news for most people are television, newspapers, and radio (Frantzich and Percy, 1994). The vast resources of the media, particularly ready access to the public, served to generate a critical mass of support for reform efforts (Dede, 1992). Downs (1972) termed this phenomenon the "issue-attention cycle."

The context that state-level policymaking occurs within has changed. Weaver and Geske (1996) assert that "the political context for state educational policymaking has changed dramatically during the past 50 years. During the 1950s and 1960s, a state's educational establishment, including its chief state school officer, state education agency officials, and major education interest group leaders, was a dominant force in shaping educational policy for the public schools" (p. 1). However, unlike previous reform movements, the school reform movement of the 1980s was largely dominated by a group of actors who had previously played only a minor role in education. These included business executives, governors, key state and federal legislators, and the media (Feir, 1995; Mazzoni, 1993, 1995; Odden, 1991; Weaver and Geske, 1996). James (1991) notes that the capacity for governors to exert leadership in the education reform movement was enhanced by several organizations including the National Governors Association and the Education Commission of the States. Unlike the 1960s, traditional education interest groups played minor roles in the reform movement. Feir (1995) concludes that

the expansion of the conflict over education reform to include business, political, and media leaders, coupled with the substantial neutralization of education interest groups, provided opportunities for new actors to set the agenda (p. 29).

These factors, coupled with the influence of national and global economic pressures, have changed the context within which education reform occurs (Mazzoni, 1993). Mazzoni (1993) argues that the education policy system "has steadily become more pluralistic, politicized, and bureaucratized since 1971" (p. 372). This has shifted the context for education reform from a local-state axis to a state-federal axis (Ravitch, 1983). This turnabout has left educational establishment actors, especially principals and superintendents, with the limited roles of program implementation and accountability for reform outcomes.

Few important policy initiatives are offered in education without the support of these new policy networks, particularly those composed of members of the business community such as the Business Roundtable, the National Alliance for Business, and the Business Coalition for Education (Borman, Castenell, and Gallagher, 1993; Kaplan and Usdan, 1992). America (now Goals) 2000 is an example of a national network where reformers gather to exchange ideas and coordinate reform efforts. Examples of effective policy networks are those promoting national standards and examinations, increased school graduation requirements, and teacher accountability (Feir, 1995; Kaplan and Usdan, 1992). These reforms reflect the prevalence of the neo-corporatist ideology in educational thought.

Many of these networks, such as the National Governors' Association, have significant credibility among policymakers and the public. These networks are able to influence what gets on the public's agenda. According to Kaplan and Usdan (1992), we are being conditioned in large part by these networks toward a reform agenda featuring readiness for school and work, testing, standards, choice, and the push for international competitiveness. The policy networks serve to define and limit the parameters within which discourse on education reform occurs. If Schattschneider (1960) is correct in his assertion that the definition of alternatives "is the supreme instrument of power" (p. 66), then the battle over educational reform is already over, and proponents of the neo-corporatist ideology have won.

These policy networks play an important role in shaping and coordinating reform efforts throughout the nation. Feir (1995) notes that "the national commission reports opened the policy window, established a sense of crisis, and generated potential solutions and these policy issue networks served to create relatively uniform responses in 50 different states" (p. 28). It is no accident that reform movements in states look so alike (Mazzoni, 1993; Fowler, 1994). Fuhrman (1989) observes that the variation from state to state that has so characterized state policy making in the past is dwarfed by the similarities among state reform efforts. What was unique about these policy networks is the relatively small role played by traditional education interest groups in influencing the shape and direction of reform efforts (Feir, 1995; Mazzoni, 1993).

In addition to the growing influence of these policy networks, individual policy entrepreneurs were able to exert substantial influence on education reform in many states (Mazzoni, 1993). Feir (1995) argues that "the expansion of the conflict over education reform to include business, political, and media leaders, coupled with the substantial neutralization of education interest groups, provided opportunities for new actors to set the agenda" (p. 29). Several studies of the school reform movements at the state level note the emerging influence of individual governors in shaping and promoting reform (Weaver and Geske, 1996; Mazzoni, 1993; James, 1991). James (1991) notes that "governors are taking the lead in nationwide policy formulation for educational systems" (p. 197).

In response to repeated criticisms of public education (National Commission on Excellence in Education, 1983), the decade of the 1980s brought about an unprecedented wave of school reform efforts (Fuhrman, 1989; Murphy, 1990; Timar and Kirp, 1989). A major national survey by the U.S. Department of Education found that the education reform movement was sweeping the nation (U.S. Department of Education, 1986). Boyd (1988) argues that "since 1983, American public schools have been experiencing the most sustained and far-reaching reform effort in modern times" (p. 299). During this period, every state engaged in some type of reform (Feir, 1995). These reforms included but were not limited to increased school graduation requirements, teacher accountability, student testing, teacher preparation, teacher compensation, principal prepa-

ration, and shared decision-making (Feir, 1995; Hill and Bonan, 1991; Wagstaff and Reyes, 1992).

Despite changes in the context of education reform, it is unclear whether any of the reforms introduced during the 1980s will actually improve public schools. Several studies suggest they may not (Malen and Ogawa, 1988; Sarason, 1990; Scribner, 1990). Boyd (1988) observes that "changing schools is like punching a pillow. They absorb innovative thrusts and soon resume their original shape" (p. 299). This is due to the fact that these periodic reforms represent temporary accommodations in the conflict over competing values (Cuban, 1988). Ellis (1993) shows that political conflict "has been and continues to be animated by fundamentally different visions of the good life" (p. 151). Therefore, the issue in these disputes "is not merely the best means to an agreed upon end but competing conceptions of the ends worth pursuing" (Ellis, 1993, p. 151). Thus conceived, school reforms constitute the "tactical moves to ease political tensions over the role of schools in meeting two competing values (excellence and equity)" (Cuban, 1988, p. 333). Since these conflicts are "struck and restruck over time" (Cuban, 1988, p. 329), the process of school reform is unending (Scribner, Reyes, and Fusarelli, 1995).

However, as critics of these neo-corporatist reforms have noted, the reforms have introduced these changes "without addressing the underlying circumstances that lead to failure" for many students (Maeroff, 1988/1994). The debate over school reform "has had virtually nothing to say about problems of racial and economic isolation" that directly affect the quality of education children receive (Orfield, 1994, p. 6). This is attributable, in large part, to the fact that the neo-corporatist ideology does not seek to address problems of racial and economic isolation and equity. These problems do not fit within the policy parameters delineated by the ideological paradigm.

Education and Society in the Twenty-First Century

It seems to be an American trait to see our own history as a history of individual events and not a product of long-term social trends which affect our economy, our politics and our daily lives. Yet, it is demographic forces and population trends that we scarcely recognize and little understand which have a profound impact on our lives (Ward, 1993, p. 7).

Demographic Trends

Over the past three decades, significant changes have occurred in the student population; these changes are expected to continue well into the next century. The traditional nuclear family has been supplanted by the more diverse families of today. From 1960 to 1990, the percentage of children living apart from their biological fathers has nearly doubled (Popenoe, 1996). By 2000, nearly half of all children are projected to be living without their fathers with much of the increase attributable to out-of-wedlock births and divorce (Popenoe, 1996). Although the effect of this trend is a source of considerable dispute, some attribute the absence of fathers to the increased incidence of teenage sexual intercourse, teen suicide, and even declining scores on SAT tests (Popenoe, 1996). The number of children from single-parent homes as well as from homes in which both parents work is accelerating (Huelskamp, 1993). As a consequence, teachers and school administrators are encountering students from backgrounds much different than those of the 1940s and 1950s.

The youth population has steadily risen since 1985 (NCES, 1995b), a trend expected to continue well into the next century. After a period of nearly steady decline from 1970 to the mid-1980s, public school enrollment has risen throughout the 1990s (NCES, 1995a). Enrollment in public schools fell 15% from 1970 to 1984 but rose 13% from 1984 to 1994 (NCES, 1995a). Public school enrollment is projected to increase another 10% from 1995 to 2005 (NCES, June 1995a). Enrollment in grades K–8 is projected to increase 5% from 1994 to 2006, while enrollment in grades 9–12 is projected to increase 21% for the same period (NCES, 1996). According to Pallas, Natriello, and McDill (1989), "the 0 to 17 population is expected to increase by about 17%" from 1982 to 2020 (p. 18). Part of this increase is attributable to the extraordinarily high rates of immigration in the 1980s and 1990s. Immigration was higher in the 1980s than in any other decade this century except the first (Huelskamp, 1993). Much of the increase in enrollment between 1994 and 2006 will be in the West (21%) and South (10%) (NCES, 1996). In conjunction with this increase, the number of classroom teachers is projected to increase by 11–20% from 1994 to 2006 (NCES, 1996).[7]

This increase in enrollment is not limited to primary and secondary education. Enrollment in preprimary education has grown dramatically in the past two decades. According to data from the National Center for Education Statistics (NCES, 1995b), "between 1970 and 1980, preprimary enrollment of three- to five-year-olds rose by 19%; between 1980 and 1993, it increased an additional 35%" (p. 43). Unfortunately, significant differences exist in the rate of participation by family income and by race/ethnicity. In 1973, a difference of 20% existed between low income and high income families; by 1993, the gap had widened to 28% (NCES, 1995a). In 1973, enrollment rates of African-Americans and Anglos were similar, with the gap between these groups and Hispanics being less than 5% (NCES, 1995a). However, by 1993, the gap in enrollment rates between African-Americans and Anglos had

widened to 8%, while the gap between Anglos and Hispanics had widened to 22% (NCES, 1995a). Given the importance of such programs for preparing children for formal schooling, the widening gap along class and ethnic lines may result in growing numbers of students who are ill-prepared to function at the expectation levels of public schools.[8]

In addition to the projected increase in the youth population, the ethnic composition of the student population is changing as well. According to Pallas, Natriello, and McDill (1989), "the number of white non-Hispanic youngsters is expected to decline about 13% from 1982 to 2020" (p. 18). In 1982, whites/Anglos constituted approximately 73% of the U.S. population in the age category 0 to 17 years; 15% were classified as African-American, 9% Hispanic, and approximately 3% were classified as "Other" (usually Asian or Pacific Islander) (Pallas, Natriello, and McDill, 1989). By 2010, the Asian immigrant population is expected to double (Rippa, 1992).

Hispanics are one of the nation's fastest growing ethnic groups. In 1972, Hispanics constituted 6% of public school enrollment; by 1993, they made up 12% (NCES, 1995a). From 1982 to 2020, the number of Hispanic children is expected to more than triple (Pallas, Natriello, and McDill, 1989). According to Pallas, Natriello, and McDill (1989), "by 2020, the Hispanic proportion of the youth population is expected to be 25.3%" (p. 19). In 1982, nearly three of four children were white; in 2020, only one in two will be classified as white (Pallas, Natriello, and McDill, 1989). The proportion of Hispanic children changes from one in 10 in 1982 to one in four in 2020 (Pallas, Natriello, and McDill, 1989). This constitutes a "remarkable transformation of the American youth population" (Pallas, Natriello, and McDill, 1989, p. 19).

Not only is the student population becoming more diverse, it is also becoming more impoverished (Wagstaff and Gallagher, 1990). In 1984, one in five children lived below the poverty line (Pallas, Natriello, and McDill, 1989). In 1990, one in four children under the age of six, nearly five million children, were in families living beneath the poverty line (Rippa, 1992). Approximately 16% of white/Anglo children lived in poverty (Pallas, Natriello, and McDill, 1989). The rates were even higher for African-Americans and Hispanics. In 1984, 46% of African-American children lived in poverty and 39% of Hispanic children lived under similar conditions (Pallas, Natriello, and McDill, 1989). These rates remained stable from 1984 to 1992.

Although African-Americans and Hispanics "made up one-quarter of the 0- to 17-year-old population in 1984, they represented more than one half of the children in poverty" (Pallas, Natriello, and McDill, 1989, p. 17). Poverty is most common in households headed by a female (Dye, 1992). Female heads-of-households and their children "comprise over two-thirds of all the persons living in poverty in the United States" (Dye, 1992, p. 118). The percentage of female heads-of-households is expected to increase into the next century. The burdens of poverty tend to fall on these groups. Currently, 22% of all children live in poverty (NCES, 1995a). This is particularly problematic for schools in urban districts. As Maeroff (1988/1994) observes, the flight of middle-class African-Americans from the cities has contributed to the increase in poverty in urban areas. As the suburbs have steadily grown over the past five decades, urban areas have become more poor and desolate (Jackson, 1985).

The outlook for the future is even more bleak. Despite some progress in the 1960s and 1970s, the gap between rich and poor in the United States is widening and is wider now than at any time since 1940 (Kozol, 1990/1994; Rizvi, 1993). The richest 20% received nearly half (44%) of total national family income, while the poorest 20% received only 4.6% (Kozol, 1990/1994). According to Pallas, Natriello, and McDill (1989), "the number of children in poverty is expected to rise [from 1984 to 2020] from 14.7 million to 20.1 million children, an increase of 37%" (p. 19). This leads Pallas, Natriello, and McDill (1989) to conclude that "the single most important factor in the school-age population of the future is the expected increase in both the number and proportion of traditionally disadvantaged young people" (p. 18).

These trends are particularly ominous because achievement gaps in student achievement continue to persist among subgroups in the student population. Based upon 1992 scores on the National Assessment of Educational Progress (NAEP), average reading proficiency scores of African-American 17-year-olds were 36 points below their Anglo counterparts; the gap between Anglos and Hispanics was more than 25 points (NCES, 1995a). Similar differences were observed in science and mathematics, although the differences were smaller in mathematics (NCES, 1995a). Of grave concern is the observation that "despite a narrowing in the white-minority gap in achievement during the 1980s, particularly in mathematics, recent data raise the possibility that the gap is no longer closing" (NCES, 1995a, p. v). 1994 NAEP data "suggest that minority groups have lost some of the earlier gains they had made relative to whites" (NCES, 1995a, p. v).[9] The closing of the gap seemed to have stopped between 1988 and 1990, and the gap is now widening at most grade levels and in most subjects. For example, African-Americans in 1973 scored 40 points below Whites/Anglos on the 12th grade National Assessment of Educational Progress (NAEP) mathematics examination. By 1990, the gap had closed to 21 points. But four years later the gap had grown to 27 points. By the same token, in 1973 the gap between 13-year old Hispanics and Whites/Anglos on the NAEP mathematics examination was 35 points, then it narrowed

to 19 points in 1986. But in 1994, the gap had grown to 25 points. The trend is similar in reading (Council for the Great City Schools, *Urban Educator*, p. 2). Race and poverty appear to continue to be variables with which schools have great difficulty.

Further, persistent gaps continue to exist in the dropout rates among various ethnic groups. Although the overall dropout rate among 16–24-year-olds has fallen during 1970 to 1994 and differences in dropout rates among ethnic groups has narrowed (NCES, 1995c), persistent gaps remain. For example, based on 1994 data, the Anglo dropout rate is 8%, compared with 13% for African-Americans and 30% for Hispanics (NCES, 1995c). Although African-Americans have experienced the greatest decline in the number of students of color dropping out of school from 1970 to 1994, the gap between African-American and Anglo students remains.

Of more concern from a policy standpoint is the persistence of an extraordinarily high dropout rate for Hispanic youth. By age 25, only 60% of Hispanics will have completed high school (Huelskamp, 1993). Approximately 37% of Hispanics aged 14–34 are high school dropouts (NCES, 1993). From 1970 to 1994, the dropout rate of Hispanic youth declined only 5%, the same decline found among Anglos (NCES, 1995c). The dropout rate among African-American students, however, declined by 15% during this same period (NCES, 1995c). Thus although the overall dropout rate is declining and the gap between African-American and Anglo students is narrowing, not all ethnic groups are benefiting equally from the decline in dropout rates.

Trends in the Workplace

In conjunction with the rapidly changing student population, significant changes are expected in the composition and structure of the workplace in the twenty-first century. Upon reviewing the "futurist" literature, several trends in the workplace emerge.

First, because of the rapid pace of the high-tech revolution, it is estimated that workers will be displaced every five to 10 years and will need frequent retraining (Cetron, 1985). Long-term job security, even in nations such as Japan that have traditionally guaranteed "lifetime employment" for most workers in larger companies, is becoming an anachronism (Watanabe and Holley, 1996, p. D4).

Second, the majority of jobs created in the twenty-first century will be in the service and information industries, not in industrial production (TEA, 1994). Fewer unskilled factory jobs are available, although many positions require a broad repertoire of skills. According to Pallas, Natriello, and McDill (1995), "school dropouts and high school graduates who do not pursue post-secondary education are at particular risk of finding themselves in dead-end jobs or on the outside of the labor market looking in" (p. 34). The information economy in particular will produce an extraordinary number of well-paying jobs. Naisbitt and Aburdene (1990) estimate that more than 70% of new job growth will be in occupations currently averaging more than $20,000 annually. In many places, this shift is already well underway. Between 1985 and 1987, Massachusetts lost 75,000 jobs in manufacturing, yet median income rose 41% during this period (Naisbitt and Aburdene, 1990). Most of this increase was attributable to an increase in the number of white collar positions available in the service industry, particularly the financial industry. Currently, more than two million new managerial, administrative, and technical positions are being created annually (Naisbitt, 1982; Cetron, 1985; Naisbitt and Aburdene, 1990; Marshall and Tucker, 1992). Innovations in telecommunications technology are expected to allow more people to work at home. This will transform the work/home place into an electronic cottage (Toffler's "Third Wave"). The impact of this change on work and social relations has yet to be determined (Toffler, 1980; 1990).

Meeting These Challenges: What Schools Need to Do

Given the enormity of these trends, what must schools do to effectively educate a rapidly changing student population for an increasingly complex post-industrial society? Pallas, Natriello, and McDill (1989) assert that considerable additional public resources must be devoted to education. This will entail mobilizing public support for increased expenditures. Clearly such an investment is necessary to effectively meet this educational challenge. According to the National Center for Education Statistics (1996), expenditures for public education increased 43% in constant dollars between 1980 and 1992. Given the projected increase in enrollment through 2006, expenditures on public education are projected to increase 41% from 1992 to 2006 (NCES, 1996).[10]

Despite the obvious need for such expenditures, it should not be assumed that such increases are certain. Although the youth population is growing, American society is also aging. According to Ward (1993), "in the 1990s and beyond, the age cohorts over 35 years of age will grow faster than the younger cohorts. Education of children will be less important to the nation, as fewer adults have children in schools, and this older generation will be more interested in financial and personal security, recreation and cultural activities, and health care" (p. 8). Given the strong positive correlation between age and rate of participation via voting, the elderly will continue to exert a disproportionate influence on the political system. To the extent that their spending priorities differ from the youth population, the expected increases in spending on public education may be less than projected.

Given the struggle for adequate funding of public education likely to result from these demographic changes, schools of the future will stress the importance of obtaining a fundamentally sound, basic education. Higher-level academic courses will still of course be offered, but wide varieties of electives may become a thing of the past (Powell, Farrar, and Cohen, 1985). This is attributable in part to the growing unwillingness of an increasingly aging population to support bond issues to finance schools. Wong (1992) notes that "the aging of the city's taxpaying population has placed public education in competition with transportation, hospital and community development over local tax revenues" (p. 10). This raises the spectre of what sociologists term "generational warfare" erupting between an older, largely Anglo, propertied class without children in school being asked to support tax increases for "other people's children".[11] In some districts, this generational warfare has already begun. For example, many schools have been forced to curtail extracurricular activities or require parents to pay equipment and related costs. Likewise, tight budgets may make it more difficult for schools to finance courses that are not directly related to the tested curriculum.

This budgetary constraint, coupled with the rapidly changing job market, may have a significant impact on areas such as vocational education. According to Ted Sizer, in a rapidly changing job market, the most important vocational training is general education, which equips students with the skills necessary to adapt to a rapidly changing environment (Brandt, 1988). Calls for this type of education have been echoed by the Committee on Economic Development and other business groups the past few years (Brandt, 1988).

This emphasis on basic education does not imply a narrow, non-thinking curriculum (Finn, 1991). Rather, the curriculum will focus upon what students most need to know and be able to do to be successful in twenty-first century society. The ever-increasing pace of technological innovation requires students who are well grounded in the basics (Cetron, 1985). Senge (1990) observes that "perhaps for the first time in history, humankind has the capacity to create far more information than anyone can absorb, to foster far greater interdependency than anyone can manage, and to accelerate change far faster than anyone's ability to keep pace" (p. 69). To provide a quality education to meet this need, Cetron (1985) asserts that schools must place emphasis on the basics (the three Rs in particular). Since individuals will need to be retrained several times throughout the course of their working lives, industry will need workers who have a firm grasp of the basics and who are committed to lifelong learning (Naisbitt, 1982). This recommendation follows the logic that technical retraining is expensive enough without having the additional burden of offering remedial courses in the basics.[12]

In addition to the three Rs, students will have to leave school being computer literate. Currently, 75% of all jobs involve computers in some way (Naisbitt, 1982) . Unfortunately, access to these jobs requires advanced skills and training. As young adults strive in search of the "good life," a significant barrier toward upward mobility is the lack of opportunities available for those with little post-secondary education or advanced technical training. Since the early 1970s, real wages of young adults with a GED or high school diploma have declined, while the proportion receiving AFDC or other forms of public assistance has risen (NCES, 1995a). Those who do not possess the skills needed by a rapidly changing society are at a competitive disadvantage. As Naisbitt (1982) asserted, the two required languages for future workers will be English and computer terminology.

Given the rapidly changing business climate, employers will need people who can think critically, plan strategically, and adapt well to change (Naisbitt, 1982). The coming changes in the workplace will force workers to seek repeated retraining throughout their professional lives. In such an economy, much more emphasis will be placed on lifelong education. Accordingly, schools will need to educate generalists who can effectively adapt to a rapidly changing, turbulent environment, rather than specialists whose skills are soon obsolete (Naisbitt, 1982; Naisbitt and Aburdene, 1990).

These then are the skills and traits that schools will need to foster in students such that they may be adequately prepared to function in their role as workers in the twenty-first century. However, there are other roles for which students need to be prepared as well, including students as consumers and as citizens.

The rapidly changing workplace has brought about a corresponding change in the social and cultural environment (and options) available to consumers (Naisbitt and Aburdene, 1990). Given rapid technological advances, consumers are constantly being introduced with a sometimes bewildering array of new products and services. The rapid expansion of such communication tools as the Internet, e-mail, and fax modems into the home has changed the modes by which people communicate. The further expansion of consumer-oriented advances, such as virtual reality and interactive television, has the potential to fundamentally alter how we entertain ourselves.

To make intelligent choices in this consumer-oriented society, students will need the knowledge and the skills to select wisely among alternatives. This requires the development of some of the same skills needed by industry, including critical thinking skills, computer literacy, and the ability to adapt well to a rapidly changing social, cultural, and consumer environment (Naisbitt and Aburdene, 1990).

The other role for which students need be prepared is for the role of citizen. The noted sociologist Emile Durkheim suggested that every society sets up a certain ideal of "man," of what he or she should be (Durkheim, 1922/1972). It is this ideal that is the focus of education. He concluded that education is "the means by which society prepares, in its children, the essential conditions of its own existence" (Durkheim, 1922/1972 , pp. 203–204). It follows that one of the purposes of education is to prepare children for citizenship. According to Wood (1992), the most fundamental purpose of public education is the development of the habits of heart and mind that make democratic life possible.

No less an educator than James Conant (1953) has suggested that the basic tenets of American democracy should be taught in schools along with history, economics, language, natural science, mathematics, and the arts. Wood (1992) picks up this theme when he argues that the basics of democratic citizenship should be taught in schools. These include the development of traits such as a commitment to community and a desire to participate; values such as a sense of justice, equality and liberty; skills of interpretation, debate, and compromise; habits of reflection and study; and the ability to examine issues from multiple perspectives (Wood, 1992). It is this foundation upon which democracy is built.

Unfortunately, these traits, which will be needed by students to fulfill their responsibilities as citizens, are in decline or have atrophied. For example, voter turnout among America's youth ages 18–30 is lower than any other group (Patterson, 1996; Bennett and Bennett, 1990). Of particular concern is the finding that this group has little sense of *civitas* (political obligation or responsibility) (Bennett and Bennett, 1990). Several researchers have concluded that such responsibility (via participation in the political system) is necessary for the preservation of a democratic state (Barber, 1984; Etzioni, 1993; Strike, 1991). These are some of the traits schools of the future need to instill in students to better prepare them for their role as citizens in the twenty-first century.

Reconstituting Schools

As currently constituted, schools are frequently impersonal places that offer limited contact between students and teachers and other school personnel. Although these conditions are most commonly found in high schools, increasingly middle and even some elementary schools have become depersonalized. Though rare, some kindergarten classes have become specialized. Considering that schools have used the organizing principles of the factory model of efficiency, we should not be surprised that the result is they do not provide time for the development of quality interpersonal relationships between students and adult school personnel. Given an increasing proportion of students frequently lacking such relationships at home, it is essential that schools be places that foster and nurture quality interpersonal relationships, thereby promoting a culture of care (Beck, 1994; Noddings, 1988).

Other than mandates and exhortations to decentralize, organizational perspectives and principles have not been salient features of the reform movement. True, the concept of restructuring has been front and center in much of what has been written and said about reform, but the specifics of size, design, and relationships have been largely omitted, with Sizer (1992) and Sergiovanni (1994) being notable exceptions. The general tendency for organizational principles seems to be a swap of the factory model of efficiency for the market economy model of competition with choice for those dissatisfied with their school. Under the factory model, schools perpetuated rather than transcended the social stratifications of our society. Schools were often characterized as being microcosms of the larger society. Emphasis on competitive achievement, punitive discipline, and segregation of diverse populations all work to reproduce rather than transcend societal inequalities and stratifications (Bastian, *et al.*, 1985). The effects of the market model remain to be seen.

Schools of the future will need to be structured in a manner that recognizes the human needs of students—inclusion, control, affection (Schutz, 1960). Of course, these are not just the needs of students but also of teachers and all others who comprise the workforce of the school. Designing school structures and processes capable of meeting these needs is the challenge of school leadership and administration. If students are to develop the ability to think critically, act deliberately, acquire the competence to function well in a democratic community, demonstrate the literacy to be successful in a technological society, and refine the empathy to hear and respond to others (Barber, 1992), then the school must be their incubator where appropriate knowledge is acquired and requisite skills are learned, practiced, and honed. The school must align itself with their needs. Collins (1996) reminds us that "the first task for leaders is to create environments and processes that enable people to safely identify and eliminate misalignments."

Whole schools and parts of schools through school-within-a-school arrangements are reconstituting themselves to eliminate these misalignments. Sizer's Essential Schools movement emphasizes the necessity for schools to be small and to do fewer things so that quality relationships between students and teachers can be developed and sustained. Smaller steps are being taken by other schools such as block scheduling, team teaching, and providing opportunities for collaborative learning (A+ Coalition, 1992; Texas I.E.F., 1990; Brandt, 1988). Some schools are organizing courses around thematic units (A+ Coalition, 1992; Stepien, Gallagher, and Workman, no date). This reflects that students

learn most when facts are located within a context that provides meaning, not presented as disembodied data that they are expected to regurgitate (Brandt, 1988). This integrated curriculum approach requires teachers who are more than mere specialists within a field. Many will need to be competent in related disciplines as well (Brandt, 1988). These changes and many others are already underway; however, more will be needed.

The Changing Role of Technology in Schools

Technology is playing an increasingly prominent role in education (NAESP, 1990). The development and refinement of multimedia technology will have a significant impact on schools in the coming century (personal communication, 1995; Picciano, 1994; Dede, 1992). Cutting-edge classroom computers are finally beginning to deliver on their promise.[13] Used in conjunction with CD-ROMs and other new technologies, they are breaking the mold of traditional teaching (Toch, 1991). Software companies, together with teachers and textbook publishers, are joining forces to develop interactive multimedia learning software (Levin, 1993). "Electronic field trips," in which students use two-way audio and video to speak to others in distant countries, are now in use in some schools. Through the National Geographic Kids' Network, for example, science students use telecommunications equipment to participate in an acid rain research study that includes schools in 48 states and 18 foreign countries (Toch, 1991). The potential seems limitless, but teachers must play a critical role in bringing productive technology into the classroom (Papert, 1993; Lockard, Abrams, and Many, 1990).

One advantage of these technological innovations is that they will allow schools that cannot otherwise afford courses in advanced subjects access to enriched learning material. These distance learning networks are a boon to many rural communities, supplying teachers with information that would otherwise be unavailable to students (Toch, 1991). This is particularly important given the increased financial constraints schools will operate under. Distance learning is a strategy to exploit scarce resources, to save cost and time, and to equalize educational opportunities (Mecklenburger, 1990).

Some of this technology is already being applied today. In rural Kentucky, for example, technology is being used to bring French and physics to schools throughout the state (Lawson, 1991). The cost is significantly less expensive than hiring a teacher for each class (Lawson, 1991). Currently, 78 schools in Kentucky are utilizing this method of instruction; 120 schools in 17 other states are also taking part in the project (Lawson, 1991). Plans are underway to install these electronic courses in all of Kentucky's public schools (Lawson, 1991). New courses to be offered include statistics, German, Latin, pre-calculus, and college-level mathematics (Lawson, 1991). This technology offers a means of obtaining educational equity (Bruder, 1990).

Appropriate use of new technologies will also enable students and parents to access information relating to class assignments, schedules, and homework through a system of networked, open-systems workstations. Teachers will utilize this technology to monitor electronic portfolios of student work and manage information and record systems (A+ Coalition, 1992). This technology will also provide opportunities for self-paced learning and advancement based upon demonstrated competence (Toch, 1991; Texas IEF, 1990). Technology can customize instruction to accommodate individual student needs and progress (Mecklenburger, 1990).

It will also enable teachers to give struggling students more individual attention. Several teachers have commented that it helps them pick up a lot of the borderline students who might otherwise fall through the cracks (Toch, 1991). There is a general consensus that the appropriate assignment of new technologies within effectively organized schools could make a big difference in academic performance if teachers are given the appropriate staff development training to use these technologies (Orwig, 1994; Toch, 1991).

School Restructuring Through Accountability

Restructuring through accountability is the one topic that has recently dominated and will continue to dominate discussion of schools of the future. Schools of the future will emphasize accountability to a much greater extent than they do now. Although education has historically been under local control, that control has slowly eroded over time as the nation has modernized (Tyack, 1990). States and the national government are increasingly important actors in determining the nature, shape, and outcomes of education (Sroufe, 1995; Mazzoni, 1995; 1993). Under the banner of school restructuring, particularly in response to outside economic threats such as global competition and concerns over worker productivity, the business community will also be a major player in shaping schools of the future (Kaplan and Usdan, 1992).

Individual states and a variety of national commissions and organizations are already well on their way to establishing clear national goals and standards (Parker, 1994; Cuban, 1992; G.T.E., 1992; Finn, 1991). Examinations based upon these standards are currently in development (Parker, 1994). Given the similarity across states of these exams, they could be looked upon as a form of a national examination system. Indeed, President Clinton has proposed national examinations. Periodic report cards will be issued to keep parents and taxpayers informed of student and school performance (Cuban, 1992; Finn, 1991). A form of a "Dow Jones Index" may be implemented as a standard by which to measure the state of U.S. education (Guthrie, 1993).

It is becoming more commonplace for rewards and punishments to be distributed in accordance with how well these performance goals are met (Harvey, Frase, and Larick, 1992; Dougherty, no date). Many teachers and administrators work under systems of merit pay rather than the traditional scale wage system (Graves, 1995; Cetron and Gayle, 1990). The emphasis on accountability at all costs, coupled with the willingness of state education agencies to waive regulations if performance can be demonstrated, should encourage innovation in schools. High-risk, high-gain strategies aimed at enhancing educational effectiveness may become the norm (Dede, 1992). Many of these are included in the reform strategies of several states, including Texas. These include charter schools, vouchers, and privatization plans. The number and effectiveness of business-education partnerships to reduce remediation costs and to develop technical skills will increase (Cetron and Gayle, 1991). Some districts, such as the Baltimore public school system, had turned over school administrative functions to private corporations in an effort to obtain better performance at a lower cost, although it is unclear to what extent such reforms are effective (McLaughlin, 1994). The Baltimore school system has, in fact, suspended this arrangement. Interestingly, implementation of these numerous schooling alternatives may erode the traditional pattern of schooling and create an even more fragmented educational system than is in place now (Cetron and Gayle, 1990).

Interagency Partnerships

Since an ever-increasing proportion of students falls under the category disadvantaged[14], and since this trend is expected to continue through the year 2020, there will be an expansion of interagency partnerships designed to provide coordinated social services to children and their families (Wang, Haertel, and Walberg, 1995).[15] Many authors have noted that the gap between the haves and have nots is widening (Payzant, 1992). To compensate, some schools have created day-care centers for infants and toddlers and offer services for latchkey children. Research suggests that early interventions targeted at the whole family system are more effective than those that focus solely upon the individual student (Payzant, 1992). Thus there will be an intensified effort by communities, schools, and social service agencies to mobilize to meet these needs (Kaplan and Usdan, 1992).

The momentum for the creation of these partnerships stems from a recognition of the needs of the child (Banerji and Malone, 1993). These include not only basic academic education but also attention to meeting the child's social, physical, psychological, and economic needs as well (Constable, 1992; Texas I.E.F., 1990). There is a precedent for such programs. In the 1960s, the federal government recognized that children could learn better when they had adequate nutrition and were in good health. This recognition led to the establishment of programs offering free and reduced lunches. They have since been expanded in several states to include breakfast as well.

The movement toward providing more comprehensive and coordinated services is an extension of this philosophy. Schools based on the Comer model are a prime example of this philosophy in action (Comer, 1993). It reflects a recognition that current practices are insufficient to meet the serious needs of youth and their families (Melaville and Blank, 1991). It also reflects the belief held by reformers of municipal government that the current system of provision of social services to families is fragmented, uncoordinated, inconsistent, and often wasteful (Payzant, 1992). Dryfoos (1994) refers to schools that coordinate these services as full-service schools and describes how the concept is developing in schools and communities across the nation. Thus it is part of a growing effort to make government more responsive to the needs of constituents (Thompson and Harris, 1995).

Several attempts to create such partnerships are underway now, such as the "New Beginnings" project in San Diego (Payzant, 1992). This project is part of a long-term strategy for systemic change in the way services are provided to youth and their families. It involves a variety of city and county agencies, as well as local hospitals and community colleges. Schools of the future will have a one-step coordinated services center located at or near the school site. Due to the traditional local control of schools, and the political sensitivity of locating these centers in schools, research suggests that a school-governed integrated services program would not be wise (Payzant, 1992). Thus these centers will likely be located near schools and not in them.

The advantages of such a system is that it could cut bureaucratic red tape, reduce program duplication and fragmentation, standardize application procedures, and offer direct, easily accessible support to children and their families in one central location (Hobbs, 1994; Kahne and Kelley, 1993). The current system is so fragmented that families often have to travel to several different locations to obtain comprehensive services (Soler and Shauffer, 1993). Preliminary results of these efforts are promising (Hobbs, 1994; Banerji and Malone, 1993; Soler and Shauffer, 1993; Payzant, 1992). Given demographic trends, these programs will multiply throughout the education system in the coming century.

Summary

Numerous forces have had a significant impact on shaping education policy in the past half-century. These forces, as well as others, will shape education policy in the coming millennium. Despite the diversity of policy entrepreneurs, we conclude that they all share the basic assumptions of the neo-corporatist model of schooling. Virtually without exception, all the waves of school reform from the 1980s through the present share this fundamental premise. Since this model emphasizes competitive, hierarchical achievement, punitive discipline, and segregation of diverse populations, the fundamental implication of current reforms is that they will largely reproduce rather than transcend societal inequalities and stratifications (Bastian, *et al.*, 1985). This is particularly problematic given the acceleration of several demographic trends discussed in this chapter. Given projected demographic trends, the changing nature of society, and the needed workforce, it is clear that the tasks facing future education leaders are more complex than ever. In light of changing demographics, changing societal expectations, and changing fiscal conditions, education leaders must be vigilant to ensure that the value of *equity* is not lost in the rush toward *quality* and *excellence*. Recent history suggests that in an increasingly competitive environment, the value of equity is often the first disposed of and easiest to ignore. Given past experience, present conditions, and future demographic trends, this would be a costly error.

We believe that equity and excellence can be simultaneously achieved in schools. Policymakers and school leaders need only incorporate what we know about teaching and learning as substance and process in crafting educational policy and creating educational environments for children and youth. A brief glance down the corridors of history reveals to us the cost in broken and unfulfilled lives if such is not done. Teaching and learning for everyone's children in environments that liberate their thinking and develop their potential should be the force that shapes the educational policy for our schools as we approach and the twenty-first century.

NOTES

1. Miron (1996) refers to this as an entrepreneurial coalition, although we believe the term neo-corporatism is more accurate.
2. The impact of the Second World War was omitted from the analysis due to much dispute among academics as to its lasting effect on education policy. In a well-respected early analysis, Kandel (1948) argued that the effects of World War II included recognition of the importance of education, societal illiteracy, a lack of quality child care, provision of extended school services for children, cooperation between social services agencies, teacher shortages, educational inequalities, and an emphasis

on vocational education. Recent research by Cohen (1992), however, disputes the actual, lasting impact of the war on education policy. Cohen (1992) asserts that the lasting impact was confined to a greater post-war emphasis on vocational education and training.

3. Notable initiatives were the Northwest Ordinance (1787), the Morrill Land Grant Act (1862), and the Smith-Hughes Act (1917).

4. Since the focus of this chapter is on primary and secondary education, Court decisions involving higher education such as *Bakke* and *Hopwood* are excluded from the analysis.

5. Massey and Denton (1988) note that in 1980, 86% of suburban whites lived in census tracts with less than 1% African-American residents.

6. Kozol (1995) eloquently makes the point that minority communities in urban areas were not always urban ghettos as depicted in the popular press.

7. These variations in this data reflect the range of low, middle, and high alternatives.

8. It should be noted that African-American and Hispanic children were more likely to be enrolled in kindergarten programs than their Anglo counterparts enrolled in preprimary education programs (NCES, 1995a). According to the NCES (1995a), "as a result, a similar percentage of blacks and whites were enrolled in some type of school program at age 3–4 in 1993. Hispanic school enrollment rates were still substantially lower that year" (p. 4).

9. We paint too dim a picture of the outlook for public education as it enters the coming century; it should be noted that not all the data on minority group achievement are unpropitious. The dropout rate for Hispanics has dropped from 19% in 1982 to 12% in 1992, although the Anglo dropout rate for the same period was cut in half (NCES, 1995). Also, the gap between African-Americans and Anglos who complete high school declined from 23 points in 1971 to only 7 points in 1994 (NCES, 1995). Clearly, progress has been made in some areas, although given recent trends the continuity of such progress is in question.

10. Based on the middle range alternative.

11. This term is borrowed from Delpit (1995).

12. Currently, industry spends millions of dollars each year in remedial instruction (primarily in reading, writing, and basic mathematical computation) for employees (Naisbitt, 1982; Cetron, 1985). Over 300 of the nation's largest companies offer remedial courses in English and basic math for entry-level workers (recent high school graduates) (Naisbitt, 1982).

13. Until recently, computers in the classroom have served more as expensive flashcards than as knowledge machines (Papert, 1993).

14. This includes children living in poverty, coming from single parent homes, whose parents have low levels of educational attainment, and whose primary language is not English.

15. It is commonly assumed that interagency partnerships are new phenomenon. However, during the Second World War, the Wartime Commission of the U.S. Office of Education approved recommendations for the coordination of federal activities dealing with the care of children of working mothers (Kandel, 1948, p. 47).

REFERENCES

A+ Coalition (1992). *Building a comprehensive learning community: An America 2000 proposal to design a new generation of American schools.* Austin: A+ Coalition Design Team.

Banerji, M. & Malone, P. (Fall 1993). Effects of a multi-agency intervention program on at-risk middle school students. *ERS Spectrum,* 3–12.

Barber, B. R. (1984). *Strong democracy: Participatory politics for a new age.* Los Angeles: University of California Press.

Barber, R. (1992). *An Aristocracy of Everyone: The Politics of Education and the Future of America.* New York: Ballantine Books.

Bastian, A., *et al.* (1985) *Choosing Equality: The Case for Democratic Schooling.* New York: The New World Foundation.

Beck, L. G. (1994). Cultivating a caring school community: One principal's story. In J. Murphy & K. S. Louis (Eds.). *Reframing the principalship: Insights from transformational reform efforts.* Thousand Oaks, CA: Corwin Press.

Bennett, L. M. & Bennett, S. E. (1990). *Living with leviathan: Americans coming to terms with big government.* Lawrence, KS: University of Kansas Press.

Borman, K., Castenell, L. & Gallagher, K. (1993). Business involvement in school reform: The rise of the Business Roundtable. In C. Marshall (Ed.). *The new politics of race and gender,* pp. 69–83. London: Falmer Press.

Boyd, W. L. (1988). How to reform schools without half trying: Secrets of the Reagan administration. *Educational Administration Quarterly, 24*(3), 299–309.

Brandt, R. (1988). On changing secondary schools: A conversation with Ted Sizer. *Educational Leadership, 45*(5), 30–36.

Brown v. Board of Education, 347 U. S. 483 (1954).

Bruder, I. (Dec. 10, 1990). Restructuring through technology. *Business Week.*

Bush, G. W. (1992). A revolution to achieve excellence in education. *Phi Delta Kappan, 74*(2), 130, 132–133.

Cetron, M. J. (1985). *Schools of the future.* New York: McGraw-Hill.

Cetron, M. J. & Gayle, M. E. (Sept.–Oct. 1990). Educational renaissance: 43 trends for U. S. schools. *The Futurist,* 33–40.

Cetron, M. J. & Gayle, M. E. (1991). *Educational renaissance: Our schools at the turn of the century.* New York: St. Martin's Press.

Cibulka, J. G. (1992). Demographic diversity in urban schools. In J. G. Ward & P. Anthony (Eds.), *Who pays for student diversity?: Population changes and educational policy.* Newbury Park, CA: Corwin Press.

Clark, K. B. (1965). *Dark ghetto.* New York: Harper & Row.

Clinton, B. (1992). The Clinton plan for excellence in education. *Phi Delta Kappan, 74*(2), 131, 134–138.

Cohen, R. D. (1992). Schooling Uncle Sam's Children: Education in the USA, 1941–1945. In R. Lowe (Ed.), *Education and the second world war: Studies in schooling and social change,* pp. 46–58. London: Falmer Press.

Coleman, J. S. (1966). *Equality of educational opportunity.* Washington, DC: U. S. Government Printing Office.

Coleman, J. S., Kelly, S. D. & Moore, J. A. (1975). *Trends in school desegregation 1968–1973.* Washington, DC: Urban Institute.

Collins, J. (1996) Aligning Action and Values. *Leader to Leader. (Premier Issue).* San Francisco: Jossey-Bass Publishers.

Comer, J. P. (1993). *School power: Implications of an intervention project.* New York: The Free Press.

Conant, J. B. (1953). *Education and liberty: The role of the schools in a modern democracy.* New York: Vintage Books.

Constable, R. (1992). The new school reform and the school social worker. *Social Work in Education, 14*(2), 106–113.

Cuban, L. (1988). Why do some reforms persist? *Educational Administration Quarterly, 24*(3), 329–335.

Cuban, L. (1992). The corporate myth of reforming public schools. *Phi Delta Kappan, 74*(2), 157–159.

Cummins, J. (1986). Empowering minority students: A framework for intervention. *Harvard Educational Review, 56*(1), 18–36.

Dede, C. J. (1992). Education in the twenty-first century. *The Annals of The American Academy of Political and Social Science, 522,* 104–115.

Del Valle, C. (Oct. 25, 1991). Readin', writin', and reform. *Business Week,* 140–142.

Delpit, L. (1995). *Other people's children: Cultural conflict in the classroom.* New York: The New Press.

Dougherty, C. (no date). *Standards, information, and consequences in an accountability system.* Unpublished manuscript. Austin: The University of Texas at Austin.

Downs, A. (1972). Up and down with ecology—"the issue attention cycle." *Public Interest, 32,* 38–50.

Doyle, D. P. (1992). The white house and the school house. *Phi Delta Kappan, 74*(2), 129.

Drachler, N. (1977). Education and politics in large cities, 1950–1970. In J. D. Scribner (Ed.), *The politics of education,* pp. 188–217. Chicago: University of Chicago Press.

Dryfoos, J. G. (1994). *Full Service Schools.* San Francisco: Jossey-Bass Publishers.

Durkheim, E. (1972). Education and sociology. In A. Giddens (Ed. and Trans.), *Emile Durkheim: Selected writings,* pp. 203–205. Cambridge: Cambridge University Press. (Original work published 1922).

Dye, T. R. (1992). *Understanding public policy, Seventh ed.* Englewood Cliffs, NJ: Prentice Hall.

Ellis, R. J. (1993). *American political cultures.* New York: Oxford University Press.

Etzioni, A. (1993). *The spirit of community: The reinvention of American society.* New York: Simon & Schuster.

Feir, R. E. (1995). *Political and social roots of education reform: A look at the states in the mid-1980s.* Paper presented at the Annual Meeting of the American Educational Research Association. San Francisco, CA.

Finn, C. E., Jr. (1991). *We must take charge: Our schools and our future.* New York: The Free Press.

Fowler, F. C. (1994). Education reform comes to Ohio. *Educational Evaluation and Policy Analysis, 16*(3), 335–350.

Frantzich, S. E. & Percy, S. L. (1994). *American government: The political game.* Madison, WI: Brown & Benchmark.

Fuhrman, S. H. (1989). State politics and education reform. In J. Hannaway and R. Crowson (Eds.). *The politics of reforming school administration*, pp. 61–75. New York: Falmer Press.

G. T. E. Southwest Inc. (1992). *High performance learning communities.* G. T. E. Southwest Inc.

Graves, B. (Feb. 1995). Putting pay on the line. *The School Administrator.*

Green v. County School Board of New Kent County, 391 U. S. 430 (1968).

Guthrie, J. W. (1993). Do America's schools need a "Dow Jones Index"? *Phi Delta Kappan, 74*(7), 523–529.

Harvey, T. R., Frase, L. E. & Larick, K. T. (1992). 8 tasks for superintendents of the '90s. *The Education Digest, 58*(3), 9–13.

Hill, P. T. & Bonan, J. (1991). *Decentralization and accountability in public education.* Santa Monica, CA: Rand.

Hobbs, B. B. (Summer 1994). Collaboration between schools and community agencies in rural settings. *ERS Spectrum*, 25–33.

Huelskamp, R. M. (1993). Perspectives on education in America. *Phi Delta Kappan, 74*(9), 718–721.

Jackson, K. (1985). *Crabgrass frontier: The suburbanization of the United States.* New York: Oxford University Press.

James, T. (1991). State authority and the politics of educational change. *Review of Research in Education, 17*, 169–224.

Kahne, J. & Kelley, C. (1993). Assessing the coordination of children's services: Dilemmas facing program administrators, evaluators, and policy analysts. *Education and Urban Society, 25*(2), 187–200.

Kandel, I. L. (1948). *The impact of the war upon American education.* Chapel Hill: University of North Carolina Press.

Kaplan, G. R. & Usdan, M. D. (1992). The changing look of education's policy networks. *Phi Delta Kappan, 73*(9), 664–672.

Keifer, D. & Phillips, P. (1988) Doubts regarding the Human Capital Theory of recial equality. *Industrial Relations* 27 (Spring): 251–262.

Keyes v. School District No. 1, Denver, Colorado, 413 U. S. 189 (1973).

Kingdon, J. W. (1984). *Agendas, alternatives, and public policies.* Boston: Little, Brown and Company.

Kozol, J. (1991). *Savage inequalities: Children in America's schools.* New York: Crown Publishers, Inc.

Kozol, J. (1994). The new untouchables. In J. Kretovics & E. J. Nussel (Eds.), *Transforming urban education*, pp. 75–78. Boston: Allyn and Bacon. (Reprinted from *Newsweek*, 48–53).

Kozol, J. (1995). *Amazing grace: The lives of children and the conscience of a nation.* New York: Crown Publishers.

Lawson, G. (1991). Education by satellite. *Technology Review, 94*(5), 18–19.

Levin, C. (1993). Multimedia tools for teaching. *PC Magazine, 12*(16), 32.

Lockard, J., Abrams, P. D. & Many, W. A. (1990). *Microcomputers for educators* (2nd ed.). New York: Harper Collins.

Lowe, R. & Kantor, H. (1995) Creating educational opportunity for African Americans without upsetting the status quo. In E. Flaxman and A. H. Passow (Eds.), *Changing populations, changing schools*, pp. 186–208. 94th Yearbook of the National Society for the Study of Education. Chicago: University of Chicago Press.

McGuire, K. (1990). Business involvement in education in the 1990s. In D. Mitchell & M. Goertz, (Eds.). *Education politics for the new century*, pp. 107–117. New York: Falmer Press.

McLaughlin, J. M. (1994). The private management of public schools. *Principal, 73*(4), 16–19.

Maeroff, G. I. (1994). Withered hopes, stillborn dreams: The dismal panorama of urban schools. In J. Kretovics & E. J. Nussel (Eds.), *Transforming urban education*, pp. 32–42. Boston: Allyn and Bacon. (Reprinted from *Phi Delta Kappan, 69*, pp. 632–638).

Malen, B. & Ogawa, R. (1988). Professional-patron influence on site-based governance councils: A confounding case study. *Educational Evaluation and Policy Analysis, 10*(4), 251–270.

Margo, R. A. (1994). Race and Schooling in the South, 1880–1950: An economic history. Chicago, Ill: The University of Chicago Press.

Marshall, R. & Tucker, M. (1992). *Thinking for a living.* New York: Basic Books.

Massey, D. & Denton, N. (1988). Suburbanization and segregation in U. S. metropolitan areas. *American Journal of Sociology, 94*(3), 592–626.

Mazzoni, T. L. (1993). The changing politics of state education policy making: A 20-year Minnesota perspective. *Educational Evaluation and Policy Analysis, 15*(4), 357–379.

Mazzoni, T. L. (1995). State policymaking and school reform: Influences and influentials. In J. D. Scribner & D. H. Layton (Eds.). *The study of educational politics*, pp. 53–73. London: The Falmer Press.

Mecklenburger, J. A. (Dec. 10, 1990). The new revolution. *Business Week.*

Melaville, A. I. & Blank, M. J. (1991). *What it takes: Structuring interagency partnerships to connect children and their families with comprehensive services.* Washington, DC: Human Services Consortium.

Miron, L. F. (1996). *The social construction of urban schooling: Situating the crisis.* Cresskill, NJ: Hampton Press.

Mitchell, J. P. (1985). The historical context for housing policy. In J. P. Mitchell (Ed.) *Federal housing policy and programs: Past and present*, 3–17. New Brunswick, NJ: Center for Urban Policy Research.

Murphy, J. (Ed.). (1990). *The educational reform movement of the 1980s.* Berkeley: McCutchan Publishing.

Naisbitt, J. (1982). *Megatrends.* New York: Warner Books.

Naisbitt, J. & Aburdene, P. (1990). *Megatrends 2000.* New York: William Morrow & Co.

National Association of Elementary School Principals (1990). *Principals for 21st century schools.* Alexandria, VA: N. A. E. S. P.

National Center for Education Statistics (1993). *Digest of education statistics 1993.* U. S. Department of Education. Washington, DC: U. S. Government Printing Office.

National Center for Education Statistics (1995c). *Mini-digest of education statistics 1995.* U. S. Department of Education. Washington, DC: U. S. Government Printing Office.

National Center for Education Statistics (June, 1995a). *The condition of education 1995.* U. S. Department of Education. Washington, DC: U. S. Government Printing Office.

National Center for Education Statistics (October, 1995b). *Digest of education statistics 1995.* U. S. Department of Education. Washington, DC: U. S. Government Printing Office.

National Center for Education Statistics (March, 1996). *Projections of education statistics to 2006* (25th ed.). U. S. Department of Education. Washington, DC: U. S. Government Printing Office.

National Commission on Excellence in Education (1983). *A nation at risk: The imperative for educational reform.* Washington, DC: U. S. Government Printing Office.

National Research Council (1993). *Losing generations: Adolescents in high-risk settings.* Washington, DC: National Academy Press.

Noddings, N. (1988). An ethic of caring and its implications for instructional arrangements. *American Journal of Education, 96*(2), 215–231.

Odden, A. R. (Ed.). (1991). *Education policy implementation.* New York: State University of New York Press.

Office of Education (1963). *Digest of education statistics 1963.* U. S. Department of Health, Education, and Welfare. Washington, DC: U. S. Government Printing Office.

Orfield, G. (1978). *Must we bus? Segregated schools and national policy.* Washington, DC: Brookings.

Orfield, G. (with Schley, S., Glass, D. & Reardon, S.) (1994). The growth of segregation in American schools: Changing patterns of separation and poverty since 1968. *Equity & Excellence in Education, 27*(1), 5–8.

Ortiz, A. A. & Yates, J. R. (1983). Incidence of exceptionality among Hispanics: Implications for manpower planning. *NABE Journal*, 7, 41–54.

Orwig, A. H. (Sept. 1994). Begin with teachers and watch students benefit. *Technology & Learning, 15*(1), 74–76.

Pallas, A. M., Natriello, G. & McDill, E. L. (1989). The changing nature of the disadvantaged population: Current dimensions and future trends. *Educational Researcher, 18*(5), 16–22.

Pallas, A. M., Natriello, G. & McDill, E. L. (1995). Changing students/changing needs. In E. Flaxman and A. H. Passow (Eds.), *Changing populations, changing schools*, pp. 30–58. 94th Yearbook of the National Society for the Study of Education. Chicago: University of Chicago Press.

Papert, S. (1993). *The children's machine: Rethinking school in the age of computers*. New York: Basic Books.

Parker, W. C. (1994). The standards are coming. *Educational Leadership, 51*(5), 84–85.

Passow, A. H. (1995). Nurturing potential talent in a diverse population. In E. Flaxman and A. H. Passow (Eds.), *Changing populations, changing schools*, pp. 59–80. 94th Yearbook of the National Society for the Study of Education. Chicago: University of Chicago Press.

Patterson, T. E. (1996). *The American democracy*. Third Ed. New York: McGraw-Hill.

Payzant, T. W. (1992). New beginnings in San Diego: Developing a strategy for interagency collaboration. *Phi Delta Kappan, 74*(2), 139–146.

Personal communication (1995). With Orbry Holden, Director of the Educational Productivity Council. The University of Texas at Austin.

Peters, B. G. (1986). *American public policy: Promise and performance*. Second Ed. London: Macmillan Education Ltd.

Picciano, A. G. (1994). *Computers in the schools: A guide to planning and administration*. New York: Merrill.

Popenoe, D. (1996). *Life without father*. New York: The Free Press.

Powell, A. G., Farrar, E. & Cohen, D. K. (1985). *The shopping mall high school*. Boston: Houghton Mifflin.

Prosser, C. A. (1939). *Secondary education and life*. Cambridge: Harvard University Press.

Ravitch, D. (1983). *The troubled crusade: American education, 1945–1980*. New York: Basic Books.

Reich, R. (1991). *The work of nations: Preparing ourselves for 21st-century capitalism*. New York: Alfred A. Knopf.

Rippa, S. A. (1992). *Education in a free society: An American history*. Seventh Ed. New York: Longman.

Rizvi, F. (1993). Race, gender and the cultural assumptions of schooling. In C. Marshall (Ed.). *The new politics of race and gender*, pp. 203–217. Washington, DC: Falmer Press.

Sarason, S. B. (1990). *The predictable failure of educational reform*. San Francisco: Jossey-Bass.

Schattschneider, E. E. (1960). *The semi-sovereign people: A realist's view of democracy in America*. Hinsdale, IL: Dryden Press.

Schutz, W. C. (1960). *FIRO: A Three Dimension Theory of Interpersonal Behavior*, p. 15. New York: Holt, Rinehart and Winston, Inc.

Scribner, J. D. (1990). *Liberating educational administration from hedgehog thinking: A planning proposal for the new millennium*. U. C. E. A. presidential address, 1990. Presented at the Annual Conference of the University Council for Educational Administration. Pittsburgh, PA.

Scribner, J. D., Reyes, P. & Fusarelli, L. D. (1995). Educational politics and policy: And the game goes on. In J. D. Scribner and D. H. Layton (Eds.). *The study of educational politics*, pp. 201–212. London: Falmer Press.

Senge, P. M. (1990). *The fifth discipline: The art and practice of the learning organization*. New York: Doubleday.

Sergiovanni, T. (1994) *Building Community in Schools*. San Francisco: Jossey-Bass Publishers.

Singh, V. P. (1994). The underclass in the United States: Some correlates of economic change. In J. Kretovics & E. J. Nussel (Eds.), *Transforming urban education*, pp. 57–72. Boston: Allyn and Bacon. (Reprinted from *Sociological Inquiry*, 61(4)).

Sizer, T. R. (1992). *Horace's school: Redesigning the American high school*. Boston, MA: Houghlfin Mifflin Co.

Soler, M. & Shauffer, C. (1993). Fighting fragmentation: Coordination of services for children and families. *Education and Urban Society, 25*(2), 129–140.

Spring, J. (1992). Knowledge and power in research into the politics of urban education. In J. G. Cibulka, R. J. Reed & K. K. Wong (Eds.), *The politics of urban education in the United States*, pp. 45–55. Washington, DC: Falmer Press.

Sroufe, G. E. (1995). Politics of education at the federal level. In J. D. Scribner & D. H. Layton (Eds.). *The study of educational politics*, pp. 75–88. London: The Falmer Press.

Stepien, W. J., Gallagher, S. A. & Workman, D. (no date). *Problem-based learning for traditional and interdisciplinary classrooms*. Aurora, IL: Illinois Mathematics and Science Academy.

Strike, K. A. (1991). The moral role of schooling in a liberal democratic society. *Review of Research in Education, 17*, 413–483.

Swann v. Charlotte-Mecklenburg, 402 U. S. 1 (1971).

Texas Education Agency (August, 1994). *Raising expectations to meet real world needs*. Report of the State Panel on Student Skills and Knowledge to the State Board of Education. Austin, TX.

Texas Interfaith Education Fund (1990). *The Texas I. A. F. vision for public schools: Communities of learners*. Austin: Texas Interfaith Education Fund.

Thompson, S. & Harris, E. (1995). Knowledge and skill base for interagency coordinations. *Design for Leadership, 5*(3), 1–5.

Timar, T. B. & Kirp, D. L. (1989). Education reform in the 1980s: Lessons from the states. *Phi Delta Kappan, 70*(7), 504–511.

Toch, T. (1991). Wired for learning: Does computer technology have the power to revolutionize schooling? *U. S. News and World Report, 111*(18).

Toffler, A. (1980). *The third wave*. New York: Bantam Books.

Toffler, A. (1990). *Powershift*. New York: Bantam Books.

Tyack, D. B. (1974). *The one best system: A history of American urban education*. Cambridge: Harvard University Press.

Tyack, D. B. (1990). "Restructuring" in historical perspective: Tinkering toward utopia. *Teachers College Record, 92*, 170–191.

Tyack, D. B. & Hansot, E. (1982). *Managers of virtue: Public school leadership in America, 1820–1980*. USA: Basic Books.

U. S. Commission on Civil Rights (1979). *The federal fair housing enforcement effort*. Washington, DC: U. S. Government Printing Office.

U. S. Department of Education. (1986). *What works: Schools that work: Educating disadvantaged children*. Washington, DC: U. S. Government Printing Office.

Urban Educator (Jan./Feb. 1997) Council for the Great City Schools. Washington, D. C.

Wagstaff, L. & Gallagher, K. S. (1990). Schools, Families, and Communities: Idealized Images and New Realities. In *Educational Leadership and Changing Contexts of Families, Communities, and Schools*, Part II, pp. 91–117. 89th Yearbook of the National Society for the Study of Education. Chicago: University of Chicago Press.

Wagstaff, L. & Reyes, P. (1992). *Report on school site-based management*. Presented to the State of Texas Educational Economic Policy Center. Austin: The University of Texas at Austin.

Wang, M. C., Haertel, G. D. & Walberg, H. J. (1995). The effectiveness of collaborative school-linked services. In E. Flaxman and A. H. Passow (Eds.). *Changing populations changing schools*. Chicago: University of Chicago Press.

Ward, J. G. (1993). Demographic politics and American schools: Struggles for power and justice. In C. Marshall (Ed.). *The new politics of race and gender*, pp. 7–18. Washington, DC: Falmer Press.

Watanabe, T. & Holley, D. (1996, August 31). Brutal shakeout forcing change on Japan's workers. *Austin American-Statesman*, pp. D1, D4.

Weaver, S. W. & Geske, T. G. (1996). *Educational policymaking in the state legislature: Legislator as policy expert*. Paper presented at the Annual Meeting of the American Educational Research Association. New York, NY.

Wilson, W. J. (1987). *The truly disadvantaged: The inner city, the underclass and public policy*. Chicago: University of Chicago Press.

Wilson, W. J. (1997). *When work disappears: The world of the new urban poor*. New York: Alfred A. Knopf.

Wong, K. K. (1992). The politics of urban education as a field of study: An interpretive analysis. In J. G. Cibulka, R. J. Reed & K. K. Wong (Eds.), *The politics of urban education in the United States*, pp. 3–26. Washington, DC: Falmer Press.

Wood, G. H. (1992). *Schools that work: America's most innovative public education programs*. New York: Dutton.

CHAPTER 10

Social Constructivist Views of Learning

Richard S. Prawat and Penelope L. Peterson

The decade-long effort to reform education, while focused on teachers, has not ignored administrators. Educational administrators are being asked to change how they define and approach their work in fundamental ways. The premise here is straightforward: Schools that evidence a commitment to student learning are headed up by school leaders that have a profound knowledge of teaching and learning. Thus what is being asked of administrators—a shift from a management mentality to one that stresses the importance of guiding and improving the quality of teaching and learning in school—promises to be every bit as wrenching as what is being asked of teachers.

Some of the most helpful substantive guidance for teachers has come from the burgeoning curriculum standards movement spearheaded by professional organizations like the National Council of Teachers of Mathematics (NCTM, 1989). This group has produced an influential document aimed at changing the nature of what teachers do in mathematics in most K–12 classrooms. It calls for a more conceptually-oriented approach to teaching—one that emphasizes mathematical thinking and reasoning in students as opposed to the more common focus on correct answers and procedures. Given the positive response that followed this and similar curriculum standards documents, it is understandable why other professional organizations would want to follow suit.

The standards effort most germane to the present chapter was collaboratively developed by the Interstate School Leaders Licensure Consortium, an organization that involves no fewer than 11 professional associations concerned about the quality of school administration in this country. In keeping with its avowed aim to reorient the field of educational administration, the School Leaders Consortium assigns highest priority to the following two standards: "Facilitating the development, articulation, implementation, and stewardship of a vision of learning that is shared and supported by the school community" and "Advocating, nurturing, and sustaining a school culture and instructional program conducive to student learning and staff professional growth," which falls second on the overall list. Both of these standards, we will argue, point toward a particular view of learning termed "social constructivism."

Social constructivism represents more than an addition to the traditional, individualistic perspective that has dominated research on learning for most of this century. It represents, in other words, more than a broadening of the typical purview—a social add-on, as it were, to the existing paradigm. Social constructivism represents a dramatically different approach to learning, requiring fundamental changes in how psychologists and educators think about the process. Social constructivism is implicated, we will argue, in an ongoing, often heated debate about the nature of knowledge itself. Wright (1971) and Mahajan (1992), among others, argue that this debate has given rise to two research traditions in social science. The first, based on the so-called "positivist" tradition in science—especially the natural sciences—has been around a long time. The second, "post-positivist" approach, challenges this tradition, calling for a rethinking of many time-honored assumptions about the creation and nature of knowledge. Because it is so tightly linked to social constructivism, we examine this perspective in the next section.

Social Constructivism as a New Science

According to the positivist tradition, the role of the scientist is to seek causal explanations for phenomena, be they social or physical. To achieve this aim, the scientist needs to maintain his or her objectivity, to keep the world at a distance, so to speak. Facts, which exist independently of the observer, are the building blocks of valid scientific analysis. The aim of this analysis, as indicated, is to sort through the facts in a way that point to causal laws, which can then be verified through a process of controlled experimentation. It is exactly at this point that social constructivists, who support an alternative "interpretive" or "narrative-descriptive" view of social science, part company with the positivists.

There is no such thing as brute or unconstrued facts, the post-positivist social constructivists argue. Events are always construed—and it is this construction that one seeks to verify. Facts do not force themselves upon us but are constructed in the process of developing and testing out concepts or ideas. Concepts, scientific or otherwise, "are the possession of communities" (p. 20), according to Thomas Kuhn (1970). They are "embedded in the culture to which current practitioners are initiated by training" (p. 22) and play an indispensable role—in a sense providing the "spectacles" that members of a science community use to describe and explain their world.

As these quotes suggest, Kuhn problematized the relationship between observation and knowledge, and in so doing legitimated use of the dreaded "I" word in discourse about science. Scientists, like other lay people, Kuhn argued, interpret facts in light of the concepts or ideas they share with other members of the community. These concepts, though more powerful than those commonly entertained by lay people, are nevertheless social in origin and thus are influenced by social factors like habit and bias. Kuhn's notions have profoundly altered the way many scientists view their work—especially social scientists. If interpretation plays an important role in the natural sciences, it stands to reason it is doubly important in the human sciences where the objects of study act in intentional ways. Because human action is meaningful, the effort to understand that action is itself an act of sense-making. Like the reader of a text, the researcher both *assigns* and *extracts* meaning in trying to understand human events; the result is an interpretive product that represents a complex interplay between both interpreter and participant.

Narration, according to Bruner (1986; 1990), may be the best vehicle for capturing human intentionality. Unlike the logico-scientific mode of analysis, which seeks to categorize and quantify human action, the narrative-descriptive mode is aimed at telling a convincing story about what has transpired. Actually, this "qualitative" approach to research assumes that there are two stories in each event—two "landscapes" to be addressed using Bruner's language. The first is the landscape of real-world action, where things are done in a specific context that result in a particular outcome. The second, the concurrent landscape, occurs within the consciousness of the participants, their understanding—or lack of understanding—of why they did what they did.

Narrative-descriptive accounts of human behavior of the sort employed by historians and anthropologists attempt to describe both landscapes, and do so in ways that practitioners and other researchers will find persuasive. A persuasive case in interpretive research hinges on what Mishler (1990) terms its "trustworthiness," defined as the extent to which the process of data collection and distillation is open to interrogation by fair-minded colleagues who may or may not agree with the findings. It also turns on its plausibility and intelligibility; Interpretive research, Shweder (in press) writes, "aims to represent 'otherness' in such a way that 'we,' who are outside the relevant situation, can imagine what it is like to be in it."

One thing that becomes evident when one examines social constructivism, which is consistent with post-positivist thinking, is the extent to which its development is marked by a fair amount of accident and contingency. An example of the role of accident or contingency, in fact, serves as the starting point in our discussion: a decision on the part of two main actors in the story, Bronfenbrenner and Cole, to travel to Russia. These scholars gained exposure to Vygotskian theory just at the time when their colleagues in the U.S. were casting about for a more "ecologically valid" approach to learning and development. As will become evident, this cultural or historical factor plays a key role in the theory's development, exactly as one would predict on the basis of interpretive social constructivist theory.

A Short History of Social Constructivism

As will become evident, constructivism, the forerunner of social constructivism, is a loosely defined theory of learning. Many scholars over the years have contributed bits and pieces to constructivist theory, but one name stands out above all others as being the chief proponent of this approach—the Swiss psychologist and epistemologist, Jean Piaget. It was Piaget who first introduced U.S. educators to the novel notion that learning involves far more than the taking in and processing of knowledge provided by the environment—both social and physical. Real learning, Piaget argued, is a process of invention. The common assumption in the "taking in and processing" model of learning is that mental structure is somehow distilled from outside input.

Piaget challenged the inductionist approach favored by U.S. psychologists, offering a unique "inside-out" alternative that came to be called "constructivism." Echoing earlier rationalists like Kant and even Descartes, Piaget argued that the mind imposes its own logical structure on sense experience. The test of whether or not the learner has constructed a new and viable way of representing reality is internal—there for the mind's eye to see: "Rightness," advocates of Piagetian constructivism aver, "must be seen as the fit with an order one has established oneself" (von Glasersfeld, 1987, p. 329). Internal coherence, not external correspondence, is the test of truth according to constructivists. One can assess the elegance of the model one creates, but the model affords no direct insight into the nature of the world.

Eventually most learning theorists in the U.S. would embrace the most general aspect of Piagetian constructivism, the notion of the learner as theory builder. The learner, according to this view, develops theoretical stances about everything; though often wrong-headed from a disciplinary perspective, these views represent the novice learner's best efforts to impose order or bring coherence to a mishmash of informally acquired experience. Far less controversial for traditional learning theorists was the priority Piaget assigned to the individual. The individual, Piaget believed, represents the collective. Society, he argued, is equivalent to one person learning throughout history (Piaget, 1971). Piaget's individualistic approach fit with mainstream thinking in the U.S. and in Europe. It did not go unchallenged, however.

Lev Vygotsky was a Russian psychologist. Born the same year as Piaget, Vygotsky first became aware of Piaget's work in the late twenties. He immediately questioned the validity of Piaget's focus on the individual. In his book *Thought and Language*, which was written in 1934 and translated into English in 1962, Vygotsky presented data that refuted Piaget's portrayal of the young child as an egocentric language user. The fact that preschool children frequently engage in side-by-side or monologic talk ought not to be taken as evidence of a failure to communicate. Turning Piaget's argument on its head, Vygotsky viewed monologic speech as evidence that the young child is intensely social rather than individualistic. Monologic speech—speech for oneself—represents a cultural tool acquired from others and used to regulate one's activity, Vygotsky argued. Talking out loud, particularly in problematic situations, is evidence of overt self-regulation—a socially acquired strategy or technique that eventually goes underground, becoming inner speech.

Piaget's views prevailed in the first round of this debate with Vygotsky.[1] Introduced into the U.S. in the early 1960s by John Flavell, a young developmental psychologist, Piaget's brand of constructivism fit a need. It provided the scientific backing for yet another effort to create child-centered classrooms on the part of the educational reformers. Silberman (1970), for example, in a widely read and influential critique of traditional education, drew heavily on Piaget's work to support his premise that the "child learns through doing" (p. 215). Like Dewey before him,

Piaget's theory was used by reformers to promote a child-friendly, activity-oriented approach to education, seen as one answer to what was viewed as the glaring weakness of U.S. education in light of Soviet scientific success (such as Sputnik, for example). Perhaps due to its prominent role in the 1960s reform discourse, Piaget's theory came under intense scrutiny by learning theorists.

As a result of this scrutiny, many tenets of Piaget's theory were found wanting; the notion that "society is equivalent to one person learning throughout history" was the first to be questioned. Thus the universal, logical structures he posited turn out to be much more tied to specific contents than the theory allows—and their development varies more across individuals and cultures than Piaget thought (Brainerd, 1978). Furthermore, subtle variations in the ways logical tasks are presented to children resulted in different test outcomes.

The Push for a More Ecologically Valid Approach

Limitations associated with Piaget's approach to learning and development forced many learning theorists in the 1970s to re-examine dominant approaches to human cognition. As Ingleby (1986) points out, this led to a re-examination of both the *content* of theory and the *mode* of investigation. On the content side, it was obvious that Piaget's individual-abstracted-from-society view of learning and development was in need of revision. Society, increasingly, was viewed as a driving force behind individual learning and development. "Developing human beings change not only in respect to what they know how to do," Harre (1986) wrote, "but also and more importantly with respect to what their society permits them to do" (p. 294). Bronfenbrenner (1979), among others, called for a radical change in the way psychologists study learning and development. "Much of developmental psychology as it now exists," he complained, "is the science of the strange behavior of children in strange situations with strange adults for the briefest possible periods of time" (p. 19).

By the early 1980s, many aspects of Piaget's theory had been called into question. What remains as a relatively enduring legacy is the constructivist notion that children are active participants in their own learning and development. This idea, if anything, was reinforced as researchers began more and more to heed Bronfenbrenner's (1979) call to study the learning and development process in an "ecologically valid" way. Bronfenbrenner was calling for a dramatic reorientation of thinking on the part of learning theorists and developmentalists. Several psychologists and anthropologists heeded this call, moving out into settings—homes and tailor shops, for example—that had not previously been viewed as sites for human learning and development. What this research revealed was surprising, to say the least.

The learning that occurs in real-world problem solving settings frequently surpasses classroom learning. A classic study by Scribner and Fahrmeirer (1982), for example, showed that dairy workers with sixth grade educations were capable of doing arithmetic typical of eighth or ninth graders in the course of filling complex dairy orders. Another study by Carraher (1986) contrasted the performance of two groups on a series of scale conversion problems: students and construction foremen. Both groups used the same procedure to calculate the target dimensions on a blueprint. It was the students in this study who more often made errors of the nonsensical variety—placing decimals in the wrong place, for instance, which resulted in wildly inflated answers. None of the foremen made these sorts of mistakes. Their real-world experience with this kind of task insulated them against these kinds of errors.

Two findings began to emerge from the sort of ecologically valid research described above: First, context matters.[2] When learning is embedded or situated in a real-world setting, it is enriched in ways that go far beyond what one finds in the typical classroom. As Brown *et al.* (1989) put it, situated knowledge or skill is recast "in a new, more densely textured form" (p. 33). Second, real-world learning almost always occurs in a rich social context. In apprenticeship situations, for example, novices often learn as much from one another as they do from the master craftsman. Collaborative learning is the norm rather than the exception. In other words, knowledge and skill in real-world settings is socially constructed.

Collins, Brown, and Newman (1989), in a widely disseminated paper, used these ideas to analyze schooling. The problem with most school tasks, they argued, is that they are presented in a way that invites a formulaic or procedural response. Schoenfeld (1991) presents a vivid example of this, citing a study in which three-quarters of the second graders interviewed by a researcher "solved" the following problem by simply adding the numbers 26 and 10: "There are 26 sheep and 10 goats on a ship. How old is the captain?" Missing from most school tasks are the exact elements that make out-of-school apprenticeship learning so powerful and robust. The focus on *tools and techniques* is one such element; the focus on *activity* is another.

It is the expert's responsibility in apprenticeship programs to ensure that novice learners master the tools and techniques necessary to participate successfully in a given practice or activity. This goal is accomplished through a process of guided practice. The novice works alongside one or more skilled practitioners, receiving guidance that is carefully calibrated to his or her level of skill and knowledge. Each separate skill is acquired in a meaningful context—one that allows the novice to see how it fits in the larger scheme of things. When one participates in culturally relevant, real-world activity like tailoring or carpentry, this "big picture" knowledge is acquired automatically as part of the process of talking through the task with others.

Activity as the Unit of Analysis

Use of the term "activity" in descriptions of authentic learning is viewed as important because it allows researchers to bound or put limits around the phenomena they wish to study. In the past, the individual or the environmental enclosure (classroom or laboratory) had defined the unit of analysis. Activity is a more inclusive construct, allowing the researcher to examine the phenomenon of interest from several different perspectives as well. As Rogoff (1995) explains,

> The use of "activity" or "event" as the unit of analysis—with active and dynamic contributions from individuals, their social partners, and historical traditions and materials and their transformation—allows a reformulation of the relation between the individual and the social and cultural environments in which each is inherently involved in the other's definition. None exists separately (p. 140).

Rogoff goes on to demonstrate what an activity focus can do from an analytic perspective. She argues that such a focus involves taking into account several "planes of focus," each of which is implicated in the other. "Without an understanding of such mutually constituting processes," Rogoff writes, "a sociocultural approach is at times assimilated to other approaches that examine only part of the package" (p. 141). An example of this problem is a tendency on the part of researchers to single out dyadic interaction as the site for learning and development while brushing aside the cultural activity in which this interaction is embedded. The three planes of focus—or analytic lenses—discussed by Rogoff are *apprenticeship learning, guided participation*, and *participatory appropriation*.

The first plane of focus, apprenticeship learning, views activity from a societal standpoint. As has already been demonstrated, this analytic lens highlights qualities associated with culturally sanctioned activities. It thus provides an entree for researchers interested in "ecologically valid" learning. Apprenticeship learning, Rogoff explains, typically involves a "small group in a community with specialization of roles oriented toward the accomplishment of goals that relate the group to others outside the group" (1995, p. 143). Contained in this brief statement are a number of attributes that distinguish apprenticeship-like activity from non-apprenticeship-like activity.

First and foremost, it seems to us, is the notion that whatever the group is doing, it is contained within and connected to the larger cultural surround. Apprenticeship activity, in other words, has achieved a certain status within the larger community; it is seen as making a valued contribution to the larger culture. This attribute probably relates to the fact that apprenticeship-like activity is highly focused. Even outsiders know exactly what the group is trying to achieve—its goals are transparent in that sense. Tailoring, as an example, is an apprenticeship activity that has one major goal in mind, that of producing garments that meet the needs of the clients being served. Carpentry is a second example.

As the Rogoff quote suggests, apprenticeship-like activity involves a small number of individuals who often wind up playing "specialized roles." Not surprisingly given the goal-oriented and instrumental nature of the activity, the basis for assigning people to roles is typically their level of expertise. The fact that less experienced, less skilled "newcomers" are included in the activity along with more masterful "old-timers" is both a blessing and a curse. It is the basis for the healthy (and sometimes unhealthy) tension Lave and Wenger (1991) refer to as the "double bind."

Because the larger community has a stake in outcomes associated with apprenticeship-like activity, newcomers are expected to adhere to tried and true processes. On the other hand, the community itself is undergoing change. This typically creates new expectations for societal work groups. Results that were considered acceptable at one point (stiff formal attire in tailoring) may not be viewed this way at a later time. Groups responsible for meeting societal needs are thus expected to push existing techniques and tools—an expectation that usually falls on the shoulders of newcomers as opposed to old-timers. Lave and Wenger elaborate on the tension between *re*productivity and *pro*ductivity that is at the heart of the double bind:

> Newcomers are caught in a dilemma. On the one hand, they need to engage in the existing practice, which has developed over time; to understand it, to participate in it, and to become full members of the community in which it exists. On the other hand, they have a stake in its development as they begin to establish their own identity in its future (1991, p. 119).

Seeking ways to improve upon process and product, then, is one way newcomers evidence personal investment and ownership in the activity.

Despite the fact that they are a bit uncomfortable with the newcomers' role, it is the unique responsibility of old-timers to bring newcomers into the fold. They accomplish this through the process of "guided participation," the second plane of focus singled out by Rogoff. (Lave and Wenger, however, prefer the term "legitimate peripheral participation" to that of guided participation.) Brought to the fore with this analytic lens are the dynamics through which old-timers gradually grant more and more responsibility to newcomers as they evidence the ability to handle that responsibility.

Vygotsky, who had developed a sophisticated theory to account for apprenticeship learning, had also coined an expression that was helpful in accounting for how responsibility is delegated to newcomers. Vygotsky (1978), focusing on the young child's development, argued that adults can best facilitate growth in their charges if they pay attention to what he called the "zone of proximal development." By this, Vygotsky meant the naturally occurring gap that all learners evidence between what they are capable of doing on their own and what they can accomplish with the help of more capable others.

This notion, that old-timers help newcomers by guiding them through a kind of "zone of proximal development," seemed to capture exactly what was going on in apprenticeship-like learning situations as studied by Rogoff and others. Master tailors, for example, start their apprentices out on the simpler processes involved in the final stages of garment production: attaching buttons, hemming cuffs, and so on. Gradually they introduce novices to more complicated processes like cutting out and piecing together the main parts of the final product (cf., Lave, in Lave & Wenger, 1991). The strategy of getting novices to work on the final product first, albeit in fairly low-level ways, helps them focus throughout their apprenticeship on the end goal. To reiterate, the presence of an easily understood instrumental goal is at the heart of the educational advantage supposedly enjoyed by apprenticeship-like informal learning situations.

The third and final plane of focus used by Rogoff highlights the process of learning as viewed from the newcomers perspective. Rogoff uses the term "participatory appropriation" to describe this process, arguing that it calls attention to the dramatic nature of the change that learners undergo as they participate in apprenticeship-like activity. Typically learning is defined as a process of taking in or storing knowledge, Rogoff argues, which misses the mark by a wide margin: "Instead of studying individuals' possession or acquisition of a capacity or a bit of knowledge," Rogoff writes, "the focus is on the active changes involved in an unfolding event or activity in which people participate" (1995, p. 151). In many cases of "participatory appropriation," people are literally transformed as they become more integral players in the overall collective.

As they learn to function in new ways, newcomers in apprenticeship activity take on a new persona as well. Lave (1996) is a firm believer in what might be termed a more expansive "enculturation" view of what happens during apprenticeship learning. Moving from novice to master status is akin to the process of socialization, she argues. People come more and more to talk and behave in ways that are consistent with the cultural norms associated with a particular type of "sociocultural" activity. Individuals involved in this sort of activity, Lave argues, are doing more than learning a trade; they are developing a new social identity: "Crafting identities in practice becomes the fundamental project subjects engage in; crafting identities is a *social* process, and becoming more knowledgeably skilled is an aspect of social participation" (1996, p. 157).

This tendency, early on, to cast apprenticeship-like activity and learning in the broadest possible terms received support from an unlikely source—a theory of human development formulated in the 1920s and '30s by Lev Vygotsky, a contemporary of Piaget's who, unlike the latter, died young (38), succumbing to tuberculosis in 1934. Although known in Western circles for his criticism of Piaget (see above), Vygotsky's work had been all but ignored in the U.S. until the late 1970s, a situation that changed dramatically thanks to several factors.

Vygotsky and the Role of Practical Activity

By the late 1970s, as we pointed out above, many U.S. psychologists were beginning to express doubts about the generalizability of laboratory research as it relates to human learning and human development. Urie Bronfenbrenner was one of the first to challenge the dominant paradigm, both for its failure to consider setting and for its preoccupation with the individual as opposed to social and cultural factors. Michael Cole, who wrote the preface to Bronfenbrenner's influential book criticizing mainstream psychology, *The Ecology of Human Development* (1979), related this critique to the social and political forces at work at that time in the U.S.:

> Coming on the heels of a decade of social and scientific activism in the 1960s (in which he took an active part) Urie Bronfenbrenner's work represents the continuation of efforts by this small, heterogeneous, but significant group of psychologists to overcome the "crisis" in psychology by constructing a discipline that is *both* experimental *and* descriptive of our lives as we know them (p. ix).

Bronfenbrenner's sensitivity to these issues had also been heightened by his work in the 1960s with Soviet psychologists. This is an important point to keep in mind as we talk about the pivotal role that Vygotsky's theory played in the development of the social constructivist perspective in this country. Bronfenbrenner was not the only American to work with Russian psychologists in the 1960s. Michael Cole spent a year studying in Moscow and it is he who deserves much of the credit for introducing American psychologists to Vygotskian theory, and for continuing to cultivate that interest.

Cole, by his own admission, was slow to see how Vygotsky's theory related to the concerns being raised by U.S. psychologists. He was apprenticing under Alexander Luria, a Soviet neuropsychologist who had happened to be Vygotsky's student and early colleague. He found Luria's interest in Vygotsky's work incomprehensible, Cole writes. He was polite when Luria pushed Vygotsky but found the latter's prose impenetrable: "Both Vygotsky's prose and the style of his thought defeated my attempts to understand Luria's admiration for him," he writes (1979, p. 194). It took a full 16 years for Cole and others to develop an appreciation of Vygotsky's theory.

In 1978, four scholars, Michael Cole, Vera John-Steiner, Sylvia Scribner, and Ellen Souberman, edited an English translation of Vygotsky's essays, *Mind in Society*. In a preface to that book, they endorsed Vygotsky's approach, arguing

that the Russian demonstrated how individual development can be rooted in society and culture. It was during this time, that Cole was getting his Laboratory for Comparative Human Cognition underway at Rockfeller University in New York City. The laboratory, which relocated to the University of California at San Diego in 1979, pioneered multidisciplinary approaches to psychological research, integrating ideas from diverse fields such as anthropology, ecological psychology, systems theory, and cognitive science. It also produced a widely disseminated newsletter that played an important educative role vis-à-vis Vygotsky's main ideas. For these reasons, Newman and Holzman conclude that, "Cole, more than any other individual, is responsible for making Soviet psychology scientifically legitimate in the West" (1993, p. 20).

Vygotsky's approach, not surprisingly given its Marxist origins, represents an outside-in view of human development. Imbued with the revolutionary ideals that motivated many intellectuals in the early years following the rise of the Soviet state, Vygotsky's research interests—like all Soviet psychologists—were firmly located in the workaday world. Vygotsky took his lead in this regard from Marx, who rejected any non-materialistic explanation of human behavior. Sounding very much like an "activity-oriented" psychologist, Marx wrote,

> The mode of production of material life determines the social, political and spiritual processes of life. It is not the consciousness of men that determines their being; on the contrary, it is their social being that determines their consciousness (in Payne, 1968, p. 19).

This quote captures well the approach to human development adopted by Vygotsky. It is "outside-in" in the sense that participation in social activity, in particular, *instrumental* social activity, is seen as the source of the psychological effects associated with individual development. Internal mental activities emerge from practical activity developed in human society on the basis of labor, one of Vygotsky's colleagues concludes (Leont'ev, 1978, p. 59).

The notion of instrumental social activity is a broad one in Vygotskian theory. Nardi (1996), in her interesting recent comparison of activity theory and the situated learning approach, points to the priority assigned to the instrumental factor as being the prime difference between these two perspectives. Attention to the shaping force of instrumental goals is critical in activity theory. It is the starting point of all analyses done from this perspective. Advocates of situated cognition, according to Nardi, sometimes downplay instrumental goals in their analyses, focusing instead on individuals' often serendipitous responses to changing conditions.[3] Although this work represents a healthy tonic to the psychologists' tendency to view problem solving as cut and dry, Nardi adds, it also departs a bit from the middle ground perspective advanced by activity theorists, who are especially interested in more durable situations where goals remain constant even while actions or operations change.

Activity theorists argue that a wide range of activity fits the criterion mentioned above, that of flexible actions aimed at achieving well-defined, longer-term instrumental goals. Mothers and toddlers trying to solve the toilet training problem meet this criterion, as do master tailors and their apprentices trying to solve the problem of how to construct a new and different kind of garment. In both cases, participants master tools and artifacts as part of the process of coming to terms with the problem. These tools and artifacts exert an external influence, changing objects and events associated with the activity; they also exert an internal influence, leading to psychological changes in the those participating in the activity. The important point to keep in mind in Vygotskian theory is that this internal influence represents a kind of incidental though serendipitous outcome, a *result of* participating in the external activity, rather than a *prerequisite for* doing so.

Vygotsky cited a number of examples in his work with children illustrating how the availability of a new artifact or tool can change the way people think during an activity. In one study, Vygotsky demonstrated how children's use of dice to select between two equally attractive actions transformed the psychological nature of the process of choosing, apparently by lessening the tendency to respond impulsively (cf., van der Veer & Valsiner, 1991, pp. 239–240). Vygotsky distinguished between cultural artifacts like dice, which he refers to as "technical tools," and a second set of tools or artifacts that has a much greater potential for influencing mental functioning. This second set, unlike the first, is aimed at influencing others, including oneself, rather than reality. Vygotsky termed this set of tools "psychological tools."

Like technical tools, psychological tools (signs and words) are used to mediate activity. In the case of technical tools, the mediational role is defined as being a two-way role: On the one hand, mediational tools amplify or improve on what individuals are able to do to affect changes in situations. The hammer, compared to the rock, allowed people to strike small objects with much greater force and precision than was the case hitherto. It thus facilitated an existing function. On the other hand, mediational tools opened the door for new functions to emerge in a kind of chicken and egg way. Hammers allowed for the possibility of nailing boards together, a new function that had profound implications for how builders went about their work.

Psychological tools play an analogous sort of mediational role, Vygotsky argued. "The psychological tool alters the entire flow and structure of mental functions. It does this by determining the structure of a new instrumental act, just as a technical tool alters the process of a natural adaptation by determining the form of labor operations" (1981, p. 137). As in the case of technical tools, the alteration of function at the individual level is directly related to the group's effort to enhance its own functioning. Changes in the individual are a by-product of group problem solving. Vygotsky thus avoided the circularity

evident in explanations that attribute the development of mental function to individual choice and need.

It is up to different cultural groups with well-defined histories and missions to define what intellectual and physical tools are needed to carry out their social practices. It is also up these groups to ensure that newcomers are enculturated into these social practices. This approach challenges the standard assumption that individuals develop psychological tools in the course of pursuing their own developmental agendas, a position consistent with Piagetian constructivism. Vygotsky argued that psychological tools are picked up or appropriated by individuals as they work with others to achieve a culturally relevant and socially shared goal. As Wertsch *et al.* (1993) explain, the Vygotskian approach "challenges an assumption often held by psychologists that the mechanisms that mediate human mental functioning somehow exist solely for that purpose."

> In our view, the psychological tools that mediate thinking, memory, and the other mental functions are typically shaped strongly by forces distinct from the dictates of mental functioning and for this reason import "foreign" structures and processes into this functioning (p. 353).

The notion that the individual "imports foreign structures" in the normal course of working with others to achieve an instrumental goal is worth emphasizing. It helps explain why educators who resonate to Vygotskian theory are so adamant about the need to embed or "situate" learning in real-world "authentic activity."

According to Brown, Duguid, and Collins (1989), it is up to practitioners in certain well-defined communities to determine the authenticity of activity engaged in by non-practitioners, particularly non-practitioners in the school setting. Some school activities, such as solving word problems in a mathematics textbook, are clearly non-authentic from the standpoint of those who belong to the mathematics community. In fact, Brown *et al.* (1989) argue that most classroom activity fails the disciplinary community test: "School activity too often tends to be hybrid, implicitly framed by one culture (the school) but explicitly attributed to another (disciplinary cultures or communities)" (p. 34). The problem with this mixed approach, Brown *et al.* insist, is that educators who go this route fail to capitalize on one of the powerful "sociocultural" learning mechanisms highlighted by Vygotsky: Acquiring, through a kind of emersion process, the sign systems associated with disciplinary activity.

As will become evident in the next section, the importance of sign systems in human thinking was, toward the end of Vygotsky's life, becoming a highly contentious issue. It is worth exploring this controversy because it gives rise to the continuing divide in Soviet psychology between those who wish to build on Vygotsky's final work, which emphasizes language, and those who wish to highlight the role of practical activity with language cast as a supporting player. In this view, language, along with other tools, helps define the nature of the work. Vladimir Zinchenko (1995), the son of a key player in this dispute, goes so far as to characterize the two traditions emerging after Vygotsky's death as two separate "paradigms." His description of the two strands of research is a good advance organizer for the brief discussion that follows:

> The main difference is that for cultural-historical psychology, the central problem was and remains the mediation of mind and consciousness. For the psychological theory of activity, the central problem was object-orientedness, in both external and internal mental activity. Of course, in the psychological theory of activity the issue of mediation also emerged, but while for Vygotsky consciousness was mediated by culture, for Leont'ev mind and consciousness were mediated by tools and objects (p. 41).

As we will show in later sections of the chapter, this subtle distinction—language first versus activity first—underlies much of the research and rhetoric on social constructivist theory.

Vygotsky and the Authorities

As suggested, Vygotsky, by emphasizing the role that psychological tools play in mediating all forms of human activity, soon ran afoul of the authorities in Stalinist Russia. The distinction he drew between psychological and technical tools, with the former exerting more influence on human mental functioning than the latter, was the major bone of contention. It smacked of bourgeois "idealism" and thus became a target of the hard-core materialists under Stalin. As Ingleby (1986) points out, Vygotsky hoped to avoid this charge by emphasizing the objective and therefore materialistic side of the language process. Sign systems, like physical artifacts, exist in the social world. They structure human interaction and thus have an observable influence on human beings. Despite his attempts to objectify the language process, Vygotsky's work was considered to be more and more politically incorrect.

Petr Zinchenko's denunciation of Vygotsky was typical of the criticisms being raised in the mid-1930s, many by Vygotsky's own students as he lay on his deathbed. Vygotsky's fundamental error, Zinchenko senior argued shortly after Vygotsky's death, was in assuming that practical activity exerts its influence on mental functioning indirectly, through language. "Vygotsky understood the Marxist perspective idealistically," Zinchenko wrote (1939/1984, p. 67). "The source of mental development was thought to be the interaction of the subject's mind with a cultural, ideal reality, rather than his actual relationship to reality."

According to the revisionist version of Vygotskian theory, which his disciples were forced to introduce as a way literally to avoid death, activity, or, rather, the actions associated with activity, exert their own direct influence on intellectual development. As Kozulin explains, this version of Vygotskian theory pushed practical actions to the forefront while at the same time ignoring the role of language as a mediator of human activity. Non-materialistic concepts like meaning and value lost out in this emphasis on practical activity. This problem was eventually solved, however, according to Bakhurst. Toward the end of the Stalinist era, Bakhurst (1995) writes, the revisionists were able to find a place for meaning in their theory. They simply moved it out of the head and onto physical artifacts in the environment. "What distinguishes an artifact from a brutely physical object?" Bakhurst asks. "The artifact bears a certain *significance* which it possesses, not in virtue of its physical nature, but because it has been produced for a certain use and incorporated into a system of human ends and purposes. The object thus confronts us," Bakhurst continues, "as an embodiment of meaning, placed and sustained in it by 'aim-oriented' activity" (p. 164). Meaning, in a less extreme version of this view, is distributed between the heads of participants in shared activity and the artifacts that play a crucial mediating role in that activity.

The dispute that started in Soviet Russia in 1930 between Vygotsky and the revisionists continued right through the collapse of Communism. In fact, Joravsky (1989) argues that the seeds of a practical activity versus symbolic activity dispute were planted by no less a Communist ideologue than Lenin himself. Lenin, according to Joravsky, vacillated as to how best to achieve his revolutionary goals in Russia, first embracing Bogdanov's notion of trying to win the minds and hearts of the peasants (consciousness raising) but ultimately settling on a more instrumental approach. The latter strategy eschewed symbolic action in favor of an imposed direct action solution, brought to fruition by a small cadre of hard-core activists.

Because the dispute that Vygotsky found himself embroiled in predated the revolution, it is not surprising that it lasted as long as Communist ideology itself. Thus as late as the mid-1980s, those who had rallied to the revisionist banner after Vygotsky's death, proudly declaring themselves "activity theorists," refused to have anything to do with scholars like Luria who wanted to return to Vygotsky's original "mixed" model (one that allowed for the symbolic mediation of practical activity). They accused the Vygotskians of being "signocentric" in their orientation and excluded them from the First Activity Congress in Berlin in 1986. Since that time, Cole (1995) reports, there has been an easing of tensions and a gradual rapprochement between members of the two camps, activity theorists and sign-mediationalists.

Vygotsky's Final Work: The Role of Language Revisited

Activity theorists may be coming to terms with Vygotsky's early emphasis on sign mediation in practical activity. His final work is another matter. This research is so far out on the symbolic end of the continuum as to constitute a different way of thinking about human development. In fact, as we will argue shortly, Vygotsky's last work, dictated in the spring of 1934 just before his death, was "discovered" by Western psychologists a full 20 years after his more widely-known views on tool-mediated practical activity. Several things happened in the meantime to pave the way for a fresh look at the language phase of Vygotsky's research. One was a re-examination of many of the ideas presented in his 1962 landmark book, *Thought and Language.*

In the early 1980s, Vygotskian scholars like James Wertsch and Rom Harre, influenced by developments in philosophy, looked at Vygotsky's writings on language with new eyes. Wertsch (1979) speculated that inaccuracies in the original translation of Vygotsky's book may have caused psychologists to underestimate the range of his thought about language. In fact, Wertsch argued, Vygotsky's interest in the issue of how language systems are used in human social interaction is as broad as those expounded by the famous philosopher, Ludwig Wittgenstein. Harre (1986) nicely summarized the effect on psychologists of Wittgenstein's controversial view that all human meaning resides in language:

> Wittgenstein's philosophy of language has prompted, directly or indirectly, the daring suggestion . . . that much, perhaps all of the *fine grain* of human psychological functioning is a product of the language that a person has acquired. For that reason psychology must from now on must be thought of as much a collective as an individual phenomenon (p. 288).

Wittgenstein's views about language have had an equally profound effect on philosophers. He, along with other postmodern philosophers like Richard Rorty, turn away from the search for truth. "Truth is a property of linguistic entities, of sentences," Rorty is fond of saying (1989, p. 7). There is nothing outside of language that individuals can refer to in order to validate the truthfulness of the language a particular community has chosen to use. Truth, in the strictest sense, is a successful move in the "language game," an expression first coined by Wittgenstein. It is a statement that others in the community allow one to get away with saying.

The important point to keep in mind in telling the story of social constructivism is the remarkable way in which Vygotsky's later work on language has caught on, albeit only recently, among a second group of social constructivists, those that focus on language and the discourse community, rather than practical activity and instrumental problem solving. There are very few examples of one man's work being taken up by two different groups of theorists in the way Vygotsky's has. Vygotsky himself could not have predicted how a deceptively simple shift in his focus toward the end of his life toward meaning and away from practical activity would later serve as the basis for an important split in the ranks of social constructivists. This, however, is exactly what has happened.[4] Before elaborating further on this split, it is necessary to provide a brief description of Vygotsky's important research on language.

Davydov and Radzikhovskii (1985), two well-known Russian commentators on Vygotsky, described the about-face he made in the final stage of his career: "In Vygotsky's last works," they wrote, "the problem of meaning acquired an independent character, while the idea of determination through activity (even if indirectly) was not represented as logically necessary" (p. 58). Vygotsky, while continuing his interest in the role of psychological tools in mediating human to nature interaction, was clearly taking it to a new level. Concept formation, he reasoned, would be a good site for studying human-to-human mediation.

Vygotsky (1986) approached the issue of the role of language in concept formation with his typical down-to-earth orientation, asking a straightforward question: "The main question about the process of concept formation or about any goal-directed activity is the question of the means by which the operation is accomplished" (p. 102). Vygotsky thought that was true of work and of the so-called higher forms of behavior as well. In both cases, the researcher must uncover the means individuals use to organize and direct their behavior.

From what has been said so far, it should be obvious where Vygotsky was heading with this question. Language is the *means* for concept formation. In fact, Vygotsky soon decided, language is the basis for all human thought. "Human thought development is determined by language, by the linguistic tools of thought," Vygotsky wrote, in one of the strongest statements of what later came to be known as the "linguistic hypothesis" (1986, p. 94). Because word meaning changes and develops in the child, thought changes and develops as well. The two are thus bound together as part of a dynamic relationship: "The relation between thought and word is a living process," Vygotsky insisted (1986, p. 255). This is best illustrated in Vygotsky's work on concept formation.

Concepts are formed in two different language contexts. The first is an informal, everyday context—in Vygotsky's parlance, a spontaneous context. As with the more formal context, the language used by adults in this situation points to objects and events in the real world. This activity is not a central part of the conversational agenda, however; there is no explicit attempt to teach the child about the objects and events. As a result, the child attends to these entities in a hit and miss way.

In the second language context, which Vygotsky associated with school, the conversational agenda *is* focused on getting children to form new concepts. In this context, adults are much more precise in their language use. The intent here, in this more scientific or formal context, is to orient students to just those attributes of objects or events that, from a disciplinary perspective, are most worth attending to. The advantage in this more definitional approach is that the child is made aware of how the concept connects with other concepts in an overall system. In this way, the child gains a sense of the order of things. It is important to understand, however, that formal instruction complements rather than supplants informal instruction. The understandings about objects and events gained from formal and informal conversations represent two perspectives on the same thing. "One concept (the formal) reaches the level it has attained while having undergone a certain portion of its development from above. The other (the informal) reaches this level having completed the lower portion of its developmental path" (1987, p. 219).

According to Vygotsky, language, whether encountered in a formal, school context, or in informal, everyday context, plays a key orienting role for individuals: "By means of words, children single out separate elements, thereby overcoming the natural structure of the sensory field and forming new (artificially introduced and dynamic) structural centers" (1978, p. 32). Language, as a key psychological tool, is ideally suited to play this role. Unlike visual perception, language requires sequential processing. The elements or attributes singled out by language are dealt with separately at first, thus facilitating analysis, an important process in the development of spontaneous and scientific concepts.

As this last statement suggests, the psychological tools that enable the child to form concepts get internalized in the same way as those that mediate other activities. These tools replicate, at the *intra*mental level, the role they previously played at the *inter*mental level. Children, then, as a result of this internalization, are able to use the words used by others to control the concept formation process from within: to get themselves to focus attention, to select distinctive features, to analyze and synthesize those features, to do all of those things internally that once were under the external control of others. Individuals instruct themselves the way others have instructed them.

Teleological versus Symbolic Action in Social Construction

As we have tried to point out, Vygotsky's theory has played a key role in the two modern day versions of social constructivism: that associated with practical activity, best exemplified by the work of Rogoff and Lave and others on apprenticeship learning, and the version that focuses on the role of language. Wertsch *et al.* (1995) present a useful analytic scheme that highlights the differences between these two versions of social constructivism. Consistent with the argument presented above, they argue that one version highlights instrumental or teleological action, while the other focuses on symbolic action. The concept of teleological action dates back to Aristotle, if not before. This form of action is results-oriented. The focus is on executing a series of actions to achieve a well-defined goal. The efficiency or effectiveness of the process in teleological action is thus easily measured: Was the goal attained with a minimal expenditure of time, cost, and effort?

This second, symbolic action approach to social constructivism is harder to characterize, perhaps because it has

just emerged. It has strong support from several different quarters, including the recent discovery of Vygotsky's theorizing about the centrality of language in human affairs. As indicated, several scholars see connections between Vygotsky's idea that mental functions originate in language relationships and ideas propounded by influential philosophers like Wittgenstein and Rorty. Wittgenstein was one of the first to argue for a *non*-representational view of thought and language. In other words, he was one of the first to *refute* the idea that language expresses some inner reality in the individual and that this inner reality, in its most trustworthy state, simply mirrors objective reality.

Wittgenstein, and postmodern philosophers like Rorty, questioned the representation notion by going after the weakest link, the notion of "mind as mirror." The rejection of this premise shakes traditional philosophy and psychology to the core. As Rorty so aptly puts it, "Without the notion of mind as mirror, the notion of knowledge as accuracy of representation would not have suggested itself" (1980, p. 12). Trying to discover the grounds for accurate mental representations, in turn, has been a virtual cottage industry in philosophy and psychology for 200 years.

Vygotsky and the postmodernists opened the door to a novel possibility: Knowledge and meaning reside in language or, rather, in the conversations made possible by language. Shotter (1993) captures this newfound understanding well:

> In shifting to a focus upon our conversational talk among ourselves, we direct our attention to different factors in our human existence. Instead of to events within the inner dynamics of the individual psyche . . . or to events within the already determined characteristics of the external world . . . the two polarities in terms of which we have thought about ourselves in recent times . . . in social constructionism, we attend to events within the contingent flow of continuous communicative interaction between human beings (p. 7).

This, essentially, was Wittgenstein's message. It also maps nicely onto Vygotsky's later work and to the thinking of a host of scholars who now reject the dualist assumption built into the mental representation view of knowledge, the assumption that mind is somehow separate from world. Symbolic or language-oriented social constructivism eliminates this gap, either by locating mind *in* language and thus *in* the world, the more radical position advocated by theorists like Rorty and Gergen, or at least assuming that language is the mechanism for bringing world *to* mind. The second, less radical view is what Vygotsky and Wittgenstein believed about language.

According to this second view, one looks to the structure of language rather than individual understanding for the organizing principles of thought. As Bloor (1983) explains, even this second, less radical view flies in the face of the traditional notion that a theory of knowledge must begin with the individual and, so to speak, work outwards.

"Wittgenstein took the opposite approach," he adds, and one can include others here as well. "Instead of approaching public knowledge via individual experiences, he approached the intimacies of the self via the public categories with which they must be grasped" (p. 50). Knowledge about objects, events, and even self is socially constructed according to this second view.

Other Differences: Scene versus Agency, Agreement versus Dialog

Vygotsky's theorizing, then, points to two distinctly different ways of thinking about social process, each with its own complex views about what it means to construct knowledge in a social setting. To further sharpen the differences between the teleological and symbolic action perspectives, Wertsch *et al.* (1995) draw on Burke (1969) and his classic analysis of the five elements of drama. Of these five elements, an *act*, an *agent*, a *scene*, the employment of a means or *agency*, and an overall *purpose*, the instrumental or teleological action-orientation to social constructivism is said to elevate the role of scene or setting above all else. In authentic situations, the scene or setting, following Burke, "pulls" the act and the agent along. Knowledge of settings, in a sense, serves as a constraint on act and agent.

The figure-ground relationship in Burke's scheme changes when symbolic action is the focus. Now agency comes to the fore, a concept that is profoundly altered because of the role that language plays. Agency is no longer bound to the individual according to Vygotskian theory. It is tied to the kind of language being used, which is a group rather than an individual decision. Communities hit on certain ways of talking about things. According to Rorty, judgments about the worth of the language are iffy at best. Language is not like a tool, he emphasizes: "The person who designs a new tool can usually explain what it will be used for, why she wants it, in advance." Rorty contrasts this with language. The creation of new language, he argues, "will have its utility explained only retrospectively" (1989, p. 55). The best the community can do by way of addressing the agency issue, according to Rorty, is to wait and see if something good comes out of it.

Resolution of the agency question is not a problem after the fact, according to Rorty. Once a group figures out how to use its new "vocabulary," it is able to tell a story of progress, "showing how the literalization of certain metaphors served the purpose of making possible all the good things that have recently happened" (p. 55). The problem is predicting ahead of time how all of this will work out. Individuals who wish to introduce new ways of talking have to work hard to have their voices heard. Even great developers of new vocabulary like Darwin are not above putting a rhetorical spin on their ideas. Ghiselin (1969) argues that Darwin only pretended to arrive at his theory inductively because that was how science was done in the nineteenth century.

It should be pointed out that not all social constructivists buy into Rorty's notion. Those who subscribe to Dewey's version of symbolic social constructivism argue that he believed that individuals could tell immediately whether or not a new *idea*—Dewey used this construct rather than language—had merit. The test of an idea's agency lies in its "cash value." Dewey took great pains to explain what he meant by that. General notions "cash in" to the extent that they are "translatable into verifiable specific things" (1916/1980, p. 367). Although ideas are developed through a social process, it is up to the individual to determine if the idea yields the sort of payoff Dewey had in mind. Take, for example, the idea of photosynthesis, the notion that plants, among all living things, are the sole food producers. Students who acquire this idea and carry it out of the classroom, one would hope, would look at green leafy plants with new eyes as it were—that this idea would translate into new, verifiable, specific things.

Dewey's statements about the "agentic" value of ideas are important; we will return to them shortly. For now, we want to consider one other important factor that distinguishes between the two mainstream approaches to social constructivism. In addition to the teleological versus symbolic action difference, and the setting versus agency difference, advocates for the two approaches have a different stance toward discourse. Those who focus on teleological action and setting argue that it is important that participants in joint action reach agreement about goals—that they arrive at a mutual understanding about what they are doing and why they are doing it. Groups that function are those that have a shared sense of purpose, characterized by harmonious discourse, smooth turn taking, and the like. As Wertsch *et al.* (1993), point out, disagreements, misunderstandings, and conflicts are regarded as impediments to efficient functioning in the teleological action model. The newcomer in an apprenticeship situation, for example, is not expected to rock the boat; oldtimers know it is in their interest to bring newcomers along. The mutual desire to get on with the task at hand, then, often leads to a muting of difference and a highlighting of shared perspective.

The productive coordination of dispute or disagreement, on the other hand, fits well with the symbolic action approach to social constructivism. The kind of discourse that turns up new ideas or new ways of talking about things has its ups and downs, its centrifugal as well as its centripetal aspects. Centrifugal forces, as Billig (1987) explains, are those that disperse language into difference; centripetal forces—also present in discourse—are those that work toward agreement. Dialog, which is at the heart of the symbolic action process, is a "continuing carnival of difference," to quote Billig (p. 18). In fact, Billig goes so far as to say that what is highly prized in instrumentally oriented groups is not so kindly viewed from the symbolic action perspective. "The goal of communication is not accord, as if all voices should seek to be similar, and, being similar, can then stay happy. The image is one of chatter and discussion," he insists (p. 17).

If apprenticeship activity is the model for the teleological approach to social constructivism, then the disciplinary learning community is the model for the second mainstream view of teaching and learning. Clearly these two views, while originating to a great extent in one man's mind, represent different approaches to the social construction of knowledge. The first approach assumes that participation in goal-directed action is what binds the group together and provides the impetus for group "social construction." The latter, incidentally, mostly takes the form of shared instrumental problem solving. The second approach assumes that creating meaning is what the group is all about—the development and testing out of new ways of looking at the world. In the next section of the chapter, school administration is used as a site for examining these differences. In this context, we will explore the strengths and weaknesses of both approaches and illustrate how each might be used by administrators interested in drawing on the rich theory and practice associated with the two social constructivisms. First, however, a little more needs to be said about the Deweyan version of symbolic action as it compares to what the modern day followers of Vygotsky and Wittgenstein have in mind.

Rules versus Ideas in Symbolic Action

Kegan and Lahey (1984) present an anecdote that nicely summarizes the Vygotskian/Wittgensteinian position on symbolic action. Three umpires, they report, were discussing their work. "Some are balls and some are strikes," the first umpire stated, "and I call them like I see them." The second agreed with the first part of what his colleague had said but disagreed with the second part: "I call them," he stated emphatically, "like they *are*." The third, having studied post-modern philosophy, demurred: "Well, some are balls all right," he said, "and some are strikes. But until I call them, they are *nothing*." It is language that confers status on reality, not reality on language, according to the post-modernists. The rules that govern discourse communities like baseball, a post-modernist would point out, assign to certain of its members the right to name the events that fall under their purview.

The analogy between the rules of baseball and the rules that govern most other language games in our culture is misleading in one sense: The rules of baseball have been formally codified. The rules governing language games are harder to pin down. Proof of their existence lies in the fact that people constantly make judgments about language behavior based on common knowledge about what constitutes more or less permissible moves in the various language games they play. Wittgenstein, in fact, regards these culturally mediated "agreements in judgment" as the key to understanding how language works (Bloor, 1983). Not

surprisingly, Wittgenstein has firm, if vague, beliefs about how individuals in a language community come to share these agreements. "It is our acting," Wittgenstein writes, "which lies at the bottom of the language game" (1969, paragraph 204). He has little doubt about the fact that language is rule-governed, but he believes these rules are "caught" rather than "taught." That is, they are acquired during the process of language use. There is no learning to swim before entering the water, Brockmeier (1996) explains. "How to follow a rule can only be learned by participating in social and discursive practices themselves" (p. 292).

Language rules, for Wittgenstein and Vygotsky, represent shared norms. As such, they constitute predispositions to respond in certain ways rather than natural science-like causes that compel people to behave. If the latter were true, language rules would always be followed, enabling researchers to explain and predict human behavior. Clearly, that is not the case. People are flexible in their use of language rules. As Harre (1993) puts it, "People use rules, rules do not use people" (p. 182). It is the creative side of rule use, Newman and Holzman (1993) argue, and not the constraining side, that Vygotsky most resonated to as a revolutionary Marxist. They maintain that Vygotsky, along with Wittgenstein, was one of the few to explore the complex role that language rules play, both as an enabler and as a constrainer of human action in the symbolic domain.

Newman and Holzman (1993) worry that scholars have misconstrued Vygotsky's interest in language rules to mean that he emphasized rule following at the expense of the creative or revolutionary aspect of language activity. Rule following focuses on the *use* of language as a tool, a societal product used to achieve certain goals. What is missing in this account is the way children and adults bend rules when necessary. There is nothing a priori about language rules for the child, in particular. "The historical child uses what she or he can obtain from society. But her or his activity is not determined by what there is to use" (Newman & Holzman, p. 129). When uncertain or stymied, the language user invents new ways to achieve language goals in much the same way that newcomers improve on the techniques being taught by old-timers in apprenticeship activity. Unfortunately, neither Newman or Holzman, or Vygotsky himself, are very explicit about how the pro-cess of language invention proceeds. Neither is Wittgenstein, for that matter: He argues that people "decide spontaneously" on new language games (in Bloor, 1983, p. 191).

Bloor (1983) discusses the issue of language invention in Wittgenstein's theory. The best Wittgenstein comes up with by way of explanation, Bloor complains, is to argue that language inventions are intended to satisfy certain needs that are not being satisfied within the context of existing language games. This is as far as Wittgenstein goes in dealing with this subject, however, an omission that Bloor regards as "scandalous." "Search as we may, the references to needs are never properly explained," he writes. "Wittgenstein indicates a subject that is clearly central to his theory, and then does not bother to explore it" (1983, pp. 47–48).

Rorty, the modern day patron saint of the rule-oriented language approach, is equally vague about how the process of language invention works.[5] New ways of talking about things, if not the rules that permit these new usages, are introduced into language through metaphor. The problem with this mechanism, however, is that new ways of talking about things are always, at least initially, understood in terms of existing ways of talking about things. At best, Rorty (1989) argues, new metaphors signal the fact that someone is proposing a new move in the language game. He says this about the process of language invention:

> For all we know, or should care, Aristotle's metaphorical use of *ousia*, Saint Paul's metaphorical use of *agape*, and Newton's metaphorical use of *gravitas*, were the results of cosmic rays scrambling the fine structure of some crucial neurons in their respective brains. Or, more plausibly, they were the result of some odd episodes in infancy, some obessional kinks left in these brains by idiosyncratic traumata. It hardly matters how the trick was done (Rorty, 1989, p. 17).

Rorty or Vygotsky not withstanding, it does matter "how the trick was done," especially if you are a teacher intent on using the symbolic action version of social constructivism to change the way students view the world. Before elaborating on what all of this means from an educational perspective, we want to briefly present an alternative view of symbolic action, one that is based on the work of the early pragmatists, particularly Charles Sanders Peirce, the person who coined the term "pragmatism," and John Dewey, who was Peirce's student at Johns Hopkins. The advantage in this approach to symbolic action is that is does address the issue of invention or creativity. It also deals with a second vexing issue that tends to be shortchanged in current rule-oriented approaches to symbolic action, that of how local discourse communities relate to society as a whole or, at least, to larger communities within society.

As we indicated in the previous section, ideas play a key role in the approach to symbolic action developed by Dewey and his colleagues, James and Peirce. First, however, it should be pointed out that Dewey's use of the term "idea" has resulted in a number of misunderstandings, usually because it was grafted on to more traditional ways of thinking about knowledge. Thus one critic wrote, "There is no word which is apt to give more trouble to Professor Dewey's readers than the word 'idea'" (1977a, p. 317). This is especially true because this word is often combined with the word "action," as in the following: "Action is at the heart of ideas" (Dewey, 1929/1988, p. 134). Dewey explains what he means by this pairing in several of his writings, however. The word "action" is used in a formal sense, he writes, and when coupled with ideas is meant to get at the part they play in directing observation and "colligating" (grouping together) data (1908/1977c).

As the above suggests, ideas have a number of special qualities that make them ideal instruments of knowledge. For one, they are "skin traversable," to borrow the terminology used by one of Dewey's co-authors (Bentley, 1941/1954, pp. 195–198). They can travel out into the world and engage with objects and events, thus overcoming the limitations of the "skin impounded" approaches favored by traditional philosophers (the rationalists and empiricists). Ideas have a second unique quality; they represent an interesting mix of the social and the individual. Though they are socially authored, according to Dewey, it is the up to the individual to validate them. "The individual qua individual is the organ or instrument of truth," writes Dewey, "but not its author" (in Diggins, 1994, p. 140).

In a footnote that elaborates on the process of authoring and validating ideas, Dewey answers critics who argue that he sees it as an entirely individualistic undertaking. This is their assumption, he writes, but not his. "As I see it, the individual is within, not without, the act, and within it as only one of its factors" (1909/1977d, p. 153). Being *within* the act of idea construction allows the individual to be heavily influenced by social factors during the origination of ideas and during the later stages of locating ideas within networks of other ideas, while still allowing for an all important one-on-one reality check. Stated another way, it is the responsibility of individuals to test out ideas, but to do so as agents of a community.[6] It might be helpful to present an example of what Dewey means at this point.

Assume that a fifth grade teacher is trying to get students to understand the concept of photosynthesis, the idea that plants, alone among all living things on our planet, are food producers, not food users. To grasp this process we have to go back a few years before Dewey to the writings of Charles Sanders Peirce, Dewey's predecessor as a pragmatist. Peirce developed a theory about how groups of individuals constructed ideas. (These individuals can be physically located in a classroom, as in our example, or dispersed across a number of universities but networked through journals and conferences as in the academic disciplines.)

According to Peirce (1934, Vol. 5), the process of idea construction proceeds in three stages. Ideas originate as rich, metaphorical images. Our fifth grade teacher, drawing upon his or her disciplinary knowledge, might begin the lesson on photosynthesis with a simple yet elegant impression: A leaf as "food factory." In this way, the teacher is able to build from the known, something that members of a group understand, and use that as a kind of springboard to new understanding. (Scientists who develop new ideas rely on metaphors as well; Darwin, for example, is said to have used the practice of animal breeding, selecting individuals with certain characteristics to form a new species, as a metaphor for his powerful notion that "nature selects" [Ghiselin, 1969].)

Metaphors, though richly evocative, are helpful in some ways, misleading in others. The second stage in the social construction of ideas, according to Peirce, takes this "two-sidedness" into account. This is the "indexical" stage of idea development. Here, to continue the example, our fifth grade teacher would help students distill what is most useful about the metaphor while discarding incidental or irrelevant aspects (for example, that real factories have doors and roofs). Real factories and leaf factories do convert raw materials into useful products, discharging by-products in the process; real factories and leaf factories warehouse those products somewhere, and so forth. The third and final stage of the idea construction process according to Peirce is the so-called symbolic stage. Here language, as opposed to images or indexes, is used to situate the new idea vis-a-vis other ideas. The group talks or shares its writing about the idea in an effort to situate or locate it in a network of related ideas: What, for example, does the notion of photosynthesis, the fact that humans have a "parasitic" relationship with plants, say about our overall relationship to green leafy things? About our need to preserve the environment?

Ideas, like the one under discussion, are socially constructed. An idea can be viewed, Dewey writes, as a set of "shared anticipations," a set of possibilities members of the group need to carry forward into the world, as it were, to test out. Our hypothetical fifth grader, for example, if he "gets" the idea of photosynthesis, might expect to see plants in a new light. "An idea is a draft drawn upon existing things, an intention to act so as to arrange them in a certain way," Dewey writes (1908/1977b, p. 102). From this, he continues, "it follows that if the draft is honored or if existences, following upon the actions, rearrange or readjust themselves in the way the idea intends, the idea is true." Individuals, in testing the validity of their ideas, must remain open to the possibility of changing both idea and fact. Too rigid an adherence to either expectation or brute fact is counterproductive according to Dewey:

> The more stubbornly one maintains the *full* reality of either his facts or his ideas, just as they stand, the more accidental is the discovery of relevantly significant facts and of valid ideas, the more accidental, the less rational, is the issue of the knowledge situation. Due progress is reasonably probable in just the degree to which the meaning, categorical in its existing imperativeness, and the fact, equally categorical in its brute coerciveness, are assigned only a provisional and tentative nature with reference to control of the situation (1907/1977a, p. 86).

"Idea-based social constructivism," as this approach has been termed (Prawat, 1995; 1996a; 1996b), enjoys certain advantages over the linguistic version favored by the modern day followers of Vygotsky and Wittgenstein. For one, as indicated, it explicitly deals with the issue of invention or creativity in symbolic action. Although Peirce's views have not been subject to specific empirical tests, there is a growing body of evidence to support the general outlines of his approach. Gibbs' (1994) research on the metaphoric basis of thought may be the most prominent example of this line of work.

A second advantage enjoyed by the idea-based approach relates to the issue of how individual discourse communities connect to a larger set of societal institutions. This was an issue that Vygotsky did not adequately handle in his initial forays into the symbolic action domain. As Wertsch (1985) points out, Vygotsky understood that his work with small groups was just a starting point in his efforts to understand symbolic action—that a larger set of "social institutional processes" were implicated in the process and that their influence had to be studied as well. Unfortunately, Wertsch *et al.* (1993) add, Vygotsky died before he could explore this relationship. His work on concept development was a move in this direction, however. "It was a move toward recognizing that an account of the social origins of intramental functioning cannot stop with the intermental plane"—that forms of intermental functioning "must themselves be recognized as being socioculturally situated" (p. 344).

Dewey and Peirce do a much better job of explaining how symbolic action in discourse communities is shaped by social forces that lie outside the confines of those communities, at least in the domain of ideas. Their approach makes sense, in our opinion. Ideas are not all equal, Dewey believed. Some ideas, those developed within the disciplines, are more powerful than others. This is true in two ways according to Dewey: They are more powerful because they do a better job of illuminating specific experience, and they are more powerful because they place that specific experience in a much wider and more significant context.

The first criterion is analytic in nature; the second is synthetic. At issue in the second criterion is whether or not the idea has "legs," whether or not it can shed light on objects or events beyond those that are of immediate concern. Dewey argued that the two aspects of ideation, the analytic and the synthetic, typically complement one another. Analysis should lead to synthesis, Dewey wrote (1933/1986), while synthesis ought to perfect analysis. They are correlative. "As analysis is *emphasis*," he argued, "so synthesis is placing; the one causes the emphasized fact to stand out as significant; the other puts what is selected in its *context*, its connection with what is signified" (p. 218).

Analysis gets at depth, synthesis at breadth. Powerful ideas developed within the disciplines have both qualities. Local learning communities, intent on understanding phenomena that fall within a particular discipline's purview, would do well to consult with representatives of the discipline. In school, responsibility for maintaining ties to the disciplinary community typically falls on teachers. It is part and parcel of a larger responsibility teachers share with curriculum developers to carefully attend to the quality of the ideas that are brought into the classroom. Having a powerful idea to work with is half the battle: "A central idea moves of its own accord to application; it seeks opportunities for operation in use to bring other facts into line" (1933/1986, p. 337). Educators do not fully appreciate this notion, according to Dewey. "There is no mistake more common in schools than ignoring the self-propelling power of an idea," Dewey writes. "Once aroused, an alert mind fairly races along with it. Of itself, it carries the student into new fields; it branches out into new ideas as a plant sends forth new shoots" (p. 335). Teachers should constantly keep one eye on the disciplinary horizon, as Ball effectively argues (1993).

In addition to dealing with the issue of how the classroom learning community ought to relate to one set of societal institutions, the disciplines, idea-based social constructivism enjoys another advantage. Unlike the language based approach, it assigns a prominent role to objects and events in the *real world*. For this reason, Dewey and the other early pragmatists have been, correctly we think, characterized as "transactional realists" (Sleeper, 1986). Ideas in Dewey's theory are "rigorously controlled by the nature of objects" (Boisvert, 1988, p. 206).

The world not only exists for Dewey, it "talks back" loudly and clearly in the process of verifying ideas. This represents a real strength in the Deweyan approach and points to a corresponding weakness in the language-based version of constructivism. (Vygotsky, by the way, is not considered the current major proponent of this view; that honor probably belongs to Kenneth Gergen [1994].) By locating all meaning in language, theorists and researchers who embrace this approach appear to shut out the real world. They are subject to what Caputo, a well-known philosophical critic of the language view, terms a kind of "linguistic house arrest" (1983, p. 672). The result, he states, "is a mirror play of words in which words lead to more words but never to the matter itself" (p. 669)—a criticism that has been leveled at Gergen (1994), among others.

We have attempted, in this section, to present the two most prominent options being considered by learning theorists in the symbolic action domain. The option that we prefer is based on the work of Dewey, Peirce, and James, and thus is part of a rich tradition in American philosophy and psychology. The groundwork for a resurgence in interest in pragmatic or idea-based social constructivism was laid by two Europeans—Vygotsky, a Russian, and Ludwig Wittgenstein, an Austrian. Vygotsky, of course, was equally instrumental in heightening interest in the second major line of work discussed in this chapter, that dealing with the social organization of practical or teleological action (apprenticeship-like arrangements). These two, idea-oriented symbolic action and apprenticeship-like practical action, constitute two powerful frames for thinking about the social organization of learning and teaching. It is our intent in the next major section of this paper to examine how these two social constructivisms can inform and, indeed, advance practice at the classroom and school level. The discussion thus develops in two parts: First, we will elaborate on how the two approaches can be applied to *instruction*; we then build on these ideas to indicate how the two approaches can inform and, indeed, transform, *school administration*.

Social Constructivism and Educational Administration

Apprenticeship Learning in the Classroom

Thus far, we have argued, people come together to share knowledge and expertise in two quite different ways. The first, best described as a process of joint problem solving, is ubiquitous in all cultures. As a type of social practice, joint problem solving is characterized by a number of easily recognized criteria or attributes. First and foremost, participants in the practice are pursuing a well-defined, culturally valued instrumental goal. This goal serves as a beacon for members of the group; it is their reason for being. Apprenticeship activity, still common in developing countries, is a prototypic example of this sort of social arrangement.

Apprenticeships of the sort one associates with traditional crafts like weaving, carpentry, and tailoring predate formal schooling; more to the point, as examples of situated, on-job-training, they enjoy certain advantages over traditional classroom instruction. The goals that drive apprenticeship activity are made concrete, so much so that they become, in the process, functionally equivalent to the products that need to be produced; this conforms to one of the main requirements of Vygotskian activity theorists like Leont'ev (1978). Operationalizing goals in terms of concrete products allows the novice to simultaneously take account of the big picture, the end result the group is trying to achieve, and the procedural detail that goes into producing this end result. Too often in school, according to critics of traditional education, learners remain mired in detail and never do get a chance to see how the pieces of what they are learning fit together. (This is particularly true of lower-achieving children. Their reading group experience, for example, may consist entirely of learning to master isolated skills; their higher achieving peers, on the other hand, by being encouraged to read for meaning, do develop some sense of what the enterprise is all about [Eisenhart & Curtis-Dougherty, 1991].)

The quality of the products produced in apprenticeship activity matters greatly to the group; their livelihood depends upon their ability to maintain and enhance this quality. This fact, more than any other, accounts for the social dynamics at work in this arrangement. It explains why the experts who have primary responsibility for the product carefully calibrate the amount of responsibility they turn over to the novices. The latter carefully attend to processes modeled by the experts; they then demonstrate what they have learned with help and guidance (or coaching) from their mentors, typically tackling the easiest subskills first, gradually taking on more and more complex pieces of the whole.

Novices, newcomers, are thus expected to maintain the quality of the products produced by experts. However, they also have an important role to play in getting the collective to enhance the quality of the products that are produced. Healthy apprenticeships thus contain an optimal mix of newcomers and old-timers. The task of the newcomers is to interrogate the practices modeled by the old-timers; they must be constantly on the alert for promising new approaches whether coming from without, from others who have successfully dealt with similar problems, or from within, as creative reworkings of tried and true techniques or strategies.

It is fair to say that apprenticeship learning, despite a few misgivings (cf., Marshall, 1972), is now viewed as the most popular version of Vygotskian social constructivism. A growing army of educational reformers has attempted to adapt this arrangement for use in schools (cf., Collins, Brown, & Newman, 1989). Resnick paints a picture of what apprenticeship-like learning looks like in the classroom:

> Children work to produce a product that will be used by others (e.g., they produce a book on a history topic that is then used to teach others, or they collect data that are used to produce a scientific report); they work collaboratively, but under conditions in which individuals are held responsible for their work; they use tools and apparatus appropriate to the problem; they read and critique each other's writing; they are called upon to elaborate and defend their own work until it reaches a community standard (1990, p. 183).

It is not surprisingly, given his description, that educators like Howard Gardner (1991) see a parallel between Vygotsky's teleological approach to learning and the activity- or project-based instruction advocated by the earlier generation of progressives.

There is one problem with Resnick's learner-centered depiction of apprenticeship learning that must be addressed. It is unclear in her example how the expert-novice mentoring role is accommodated. In other, specific illustrations of apprenticeship learning, this is made explicit. In one widely-cited example of apprenticeship learning—the approach referred to as "reciprocal teaching" (cf., Palincsar & Brown, 1984)—it is clear that the teacher is the one who models the process that students are to emulate. In this approach, the teacher works with small groups of students, gradually shifting responsibility as dialog leader to one or more students until such time as they are able to function as surrogate teachers. The expert-novice, old-timer-newcomer issue is one we will return to shortly. First, however, more needs to be said about classroom applications of the symbolic action approach.

Disciplinary Learning Communities in the Classroom

If craft apprenticeship is the model for the teleological action approach, then the disciplinary learning community is the model for the symbolic approach. Our views about how disciplinary communities operate have undergone considerable change in recent years. Philosophers of science now emphasize the extent to which all knowledge is the product of a social process. One implication of this notion is that we have to abandon the old pecking order, which had the so-called hard sciences at the top and softer disciplines (history and the humanities) at the bottom. New ideas in all disciplines have to contend for a hearing.

The acceptance or rejection of new ideas in a disciplinary community is in part determined by what McEwan and Bull (1990) term their "pedagogical power" ("Ideas are intrinsically pedagogical," they write. "To understand a new idea . . . is to grasp hold of its heuristic power—its power to teach" [p. 332].) It is also determined by a set of social and rhetorical factors that we are just now beginning to appreciate. This is just as true in physics as it is in anthropology. As Latour and Woolgar (1989) explain, somewhat pejoratively, "Scientific activity is not 'about nature,' it is a fierce fight to *construct* reality" (p. 243). Ideas do not speak entirely for themselves; they need advocates within the community, which is the final arbiter of the truth-value of all knowledge claims. Thus as we argued earlier, ideas must pass both an individual and a social test.

At this point, it might be helpful to consider an example of idea construction at the classroom level. The situation we have in mind involves a gifted mathematics teacher and researcher, Magdalene Lampert (1989), who, in the process of using various examples of money to teach about decimals, suddenly had been confronted with a startling revelation on the part of her students. Several of her fifth graders, near the end of a lesson, blurted out that the addition of another zero in front of what appeared to be nearly 9 cents ($.089) had dramatically tipped the balance, converting the number from positive to negative.

The lesson ended with Lampert puzzling about this strange turn of events. She quickly realized, however, that students had incorrectly grabbed hold of a powerful idea, symmetry, which had been used successfully on an earlier occasion to explain the distribution of positive and negative numbers along the number line. Although the notion of zero as a point of symmetry on the number line makes sense, it does not work in the same way for decimals. That is, it does not mark the divide between positive and negative numbers in the decimal system; it simply serves as a placeholder between the decimal point and the non-zero digits in the decimal number. It was up to Lampert, in this situation, to get the community to negotiate a second meaning for the symmetry metaphor. Namely, that the line of symmetry separating whole numbers and decimal numbers runs through the decimal point. Students, then, had seized upon a powerful idea (zero as a point of symmetry), which had illuminated one phenomenon (the number line) and attempted to apply it to a second, equally important phenomenon (decimal numbers). Lampert was able to intercede in a helpful way with her students, pointing out how a variant of the original notion could be applied to decimals.

As with all powerful ideas, the notion of symmetry in mathematics opens up new ways of viewing the world for students, in this case, the world of numbers. Communities often resist new ideas, at least initially, preferring to see objects and events through the lenses of existing ideas, even though they may not bring things into as sharp relief. Elbow (1986) addresses this issue in ways that are relevant for teachers and school administrators intent on building on the idea-based approach to social constructivism.

Elbow uses the expression "methodological doubt" to describe the process a community goes through when it subjects new ideas to a kind of analytic "trial by fire." Methodological doubt predominates at all educational levels, Elbow argues. Educators often assume that it is their primary responsibility to encourage members of a community to hold ideas at bay, to adopt a wait and see attitude as regards all ideas. This underestimates the power of a community to test ideas and compounds a problem associated with methodological doubt: that of submitting ideas to a fair test. Thus educators, Elbow writes, underestimate the problems involved in getting individuals to entertain ideas, especially to "*experience* or *feel the force*" of new ideas (1986, p. 285). A vibrant learning community is hungry for new ideas; it eagerly embraces them and quickly seeks to determine how deeply and widely they illuminate things about which the community cares.

Arguing against ideas can contribute to understanding, Elbow believes, but not as effectively as an alternative process, which he terms "methodological belief." This route to understanding, which involves opening oneself up to new perceptions or formulations, plays a much more central role in examining knowledge claims than is generally recognized. To engage in the "believing game," people have to momentarily set aside their doubts and allow themselves to experience the full force of an unfamiliar or threatening idea.

> Methodological belief, strictly speaking, may not look like practice in having ideas, just practice in trying to believe the misguided ideas of the other fellow. But it is a powerful aid to heuristic. It's like brainstorming, but here the listeners don't just shut up, they help you find the fruitful implications in your suggestion. Such practice in looking at things differently in a supportive setting helps us learn to produce more and better ideas. Also, when trying to explore an idea, there is a peculiar fertility that comes from moving back and forth between doubting it and believing it (1986, p. 288).

As the last sentence above indicates, Elbow assigns an important role to methodological doubt; his objection to current practice is that this process has come to dominate educational discourse.

Playing the believing game in the classroom is a community-wide responsibility, a point that requires some discussion. The believing game, Elbow (1986) points out, is often played in a "downward" direction, that is, from the teacher to the student. Recognition of the need to take student utterances seriously, saying, "Wait a minute. There is something sensible here: how can I see the validity in it?" (Elbow, p. 271) is now commonly accepted as a defining feature of a constructivist approach to teaching and learning. What is missing in many classrooms, however, is a commitment on the part of students to play the believing game in a "lateral" direction, extending to peers the same right to be heard on ideas that they deem important that they grant to the teacher, as an authority figure.

What does all this mean for school administration? Like classroom teachers, school administrators who embrace a social constructivist philosophy also have two robust frames they can rely on: The apprenticeship model and the disciplinary community model.

Apprenticeship Learning and School Administration

An administrator who opts for the apprenticeship approach might function like an entrepreneur who is intent on establishing a number of thriving craft guilds. First, he or she would need to identify a group of individuals who might be interested in working together, making sure even at the initial stages that the group consists of a healthy blend of old-timers, known for their expert practice, and novices or newcomers. The administrator as entrepreneur would then work with members of the group to make sure that there is general agreement about the kinds of products or outcomes they intend to produce. The more concrete the group can become in this regard, the better. This contention is supported by both theory and research.

In a series of case studies of reform-minded schools developed by Elmore, Peterson, and McCarthey (1996), goal clarity emerges as an important variable in successful teacher teaming. One of the teachers who played a leadership role in a team of four primary teachers intent on promoting a more constructivist pedagogy is quite explicit about the importance of this variable. Teachers need to have shared goals if they are to succeed as a team, this informant insists. Talking about goals was one of the first things her team did when it was formed: "What are your expectations for the children? Are they going to come in and sit at desks in rows? I think that's something you work out as a team, and I think you have to come to somewhat of an agreement there," she added.

Teaming absent investment in the hard work needed to forge a consensus among team members about where the team is headed, social constructivist theory and research suggests, is counterproductive. It is not enough simply to encourage greater teacher collaboration, as Little (1990) explains: "The assumed link between increased collegial contact and improvement-oriented change does not seem to be warranted," she warns. "Closely bound groups are instruments both for promoting change and for conserving the present" (p. 509).

A commitment to collective improvement on the part of teachers must be connected to a coherent goal if it is to be effective; otherwise, teachers will feel overloaded, their efforts fragmented (Grossman, 1992). School administrators who wish to encourage teacher change in groups of teachers must be prepared to function, as intermediaries, to facilitate deliberation that results in the establishment of a common goal or outcome. This requires a set of skills, such as active listening and the ability to find common ground, that are not typically associated with effective school administration.

In addition to a common goal, the success of apprenticeship-type learning also depends upon the quality of the interaction taking place between more experienced and less experienced participants (between old-timers and newcomers). Although the research on teacher mentoring is scant, what little there is suggests that it can be a powerful force for change—given the right structural arrangement. Fullan and Stiegelbauer (1991) suggest that making teacher mentoring a generalized responsibility of "teacher leaders" at the school level is not effective; they cite research indicating that although teacher leaders see their main role as that of helping other teachers, they actually wind up spending most of their time on quasi-administrative tasks. Context matters, as a careful examination of mentoring programs in Los Angeles and Albuquerque, reveals: In Albuquerque, unlike Los Angeles, mentors are much more closely involved with small groups of teachers, functioning, according to the authors of the study, as "educational companions" with their colleagues (Feiman-Nemser & Parker, 1992). The data suggest that Albuquerque represents a better model.

Stein, Silver, and Smith (1994) describe a mentoring project in mathematics that is explicitly based on an apprenticeship model. Selected teachers in the middle school involved in this project were released from their normal duties to serve as mentors, a resource that became increasingly important to those who were recipients of this help as the project proceeded. Through in-depth interviews, researchers monitoring the project were able to single out a number of additional factors that were instrumental to the project's success. The first, being part of an identifiable group, bound together by a well-articulated goal, fits with the apprenticeship model, as does the second factor, having time for daily, informal interactions around important issues in addition to the more formal set-aside times. One variable that emerged as being particularly important was the way project designers were able to provide a staged entry for newcomers as they joined the project. The fact that newcomers were never asked to teach a course that was not simultaneously being taught by an old-timer contributed to the staging process; old-timers were also careful in the way they gave advice to newcomers, always qualifying their suggestions "as something that worked for them, not as prescriptions" (p. 26).

In addition to thoughtful work like the Stein *et al.* study, compelling evidence in support of the practice of teacher apprenticeship-like mentoring comes from abroad, specifically, from China and Japan. In both countries, as Fullan (1993) explains, mentoring within teams is an integral part of the teacher preparation program. In Japan, Stevenson and Stigler (1992) report, learning from one another is more than an expectation; Japanese law mandates a minimum of 20 days of master-teacher mentoring for first year teachers. Teachers in Japan are also expected to participate in study groups with other teachers. Stevenson and Stigler tell about a conversation they had with a teacher about this form of mentoring:

> She and her colleagues spend a good deal of time together working on lesson plans. After they finish a plan, one teacher from the group teaches the lesson to her students while the other teachers look on. Afterward, the group meets again to evaluate the teacher's performance and to make suggestions for improvement (p. 160).

It is not surprising, given this description, why Stevenson and Stigler (1992) characterize the Japanese approach to mentoring as the prototypic apprenticeship-like arrangement.

School administrators who wish to ground their leadership in social constructivist learning theory can build on the apprenticeship learning framework established by Vygotsky and fleshed out by a host of researchers who have worked to understand its unique strengths and weaknesses and its extraordinary durability in a myriad of guises around the world. As we have argued, the social constructivist framework that we equate with disciplinary learning communities is equally robust. It also can function as a model for those intent on reforming education. The central resource for this model, building on the theorizing of Peirce and Dewey, is powerful ideas.

Disciplinary Learning Communities and School Administration

Powerful ideas, developed within the disciplines, have the capability to open up aspects of the world that otherwise would remain closed off to us. Teachers who understand, in a deep and profound way, a powerful idea behind much of the current discourse on learning and teaching—the notion that children literally *construct* their own knowledge, drawing on whatever resources, past or present, are available—not only think differently about student learning, they also view teaching and even disciplinary knowledge in a new light (Prawat, 1992). Thus several studies show that teachers who attend to students' ideas and explanations during instruction, perhaps the best indicant of constructivist thinking, tend to have a dynamic view of subject matter, seeing it as continually undergoing change and revision (Thompson, 1984; Pope & Gilbert, 1983); they also tend to teach in ways that promote student efforts after understanding, capitalizing on student remarks, and making sure that students get the point of the various representations used to elucidate key ideas during instruction (Roth, 1989).

Studies like those mentioned above indicate why the focus in educational reform is shifting away from attempts to alter school structure as a top priority in favor of efforts to change the way teachers think about or view their work. As Elmore, Peterson, and McCarthey's study (1996) shows, changes in school structure can help promote teachers' knowledge and belief by providing opportunities for teachers to learn, but structural change alone does not accomplish this goal. Fullan (1993) argues that the converse does occur. That is, changes in teachers beliefs about teaching and learning, which he equates with school "reculturing," can lead to changes in the way teachers' work is organized or structured: "To restructure is not to reculture," Fullan insists, "but to reculture is to restructure" (p. 131). It is not surprising, then, that in schools that define reform largely in restructuring terms there is often a dearth of new ideas about pedagogy and curriculum (Murphy, Evertson, & Radnofsky, 1991; Hallinger, Murphy, & Hausman, 1992). The most important structures in educational reform, arguably, are those that determine how teachers think about their work and their students (i.e., ideas).

Cohen and Hill (1997, March), in a paper recently given at the American Educational Research Association annual meeting, present data from over 700 respondents that support the contention that situating ideas in teachers' current practice influences that practice. Specifically, Cohen and Hill used surveys to examine the relationship between teacher reports of involvement in professional development activity, either generic or curriculum-related, and their responses to a classroom practice questionnaire. They found that participation in mathematics-related workshops, particularly those dealing with specific topics in the curriculum, was more related to innovative practice in mathematics than participation in what were considered general or peripheral type workshops (those dealing with issues like cooperative learning or the use of math manipulatives).

The relationship described above held even when teacher familiarity with reform themes in mathematics was included in the regression equation. It was thought that familiarity with reform themes might influence results in two ways: Familiarity with the reform effort might encourage teachers to seek out mathematics-related workshops; more importantly, it might bias respondents against reporting—as opposed to engaging in—traditional, drill, and skill practice. The fact that the "opportunity to learn"/reform practice relationship was obtained even when the familiarity variable was included in the regression supports the researchers' contention that focused teacher professional development makes a difference. Consistent with this notion, teachers who reported devoting more *time* to specific mathematics-related professional activity also reported engaging in more innovative mathematics practice, further

evidence of the importance of the "opportunity to learn" effect.

Finally, an effort was made in the Cohen and Hill study to examine the relationship between teacher reports of professional development activity and performance on CLAS (California Learning Assessment System), an ambitious effort to assess conceptual level mathematics learning in students. Because CLAS student scores were available only at the school level, the researchers had to work with school averages on the teacher self-report surveys. Despite this limitation and the resulting reduction in sample size (161), a significant relationship was obtained between participation in mathematics curriculum workshops and school average mathematics scores (at the fourth grade). This held even taking into account student SES and school variables like condition of facilities and amount of parental support. The Cohen and Hill study is important because it is one the few that directly connects involvement with reform ideas, teacher practice, and student learning.

As the above study shows, focused teacher learning is a key factor in efforts to reform schools. From a social constructivist perspective, this process involves, first and foremost, providing opportunities for teachers to construct and test out ideas that illuminate aspects of their world. The role of the school administrator intent on promoting teacher learning, in this context, is to be the honest broker of these ideas. As such, the administrator is fully part of the process. His or her relationship to the group differs then from that described above for apprenticeship learning. The administrator in the apprenticeship approach plays the role of initiator and facilitator, helping identify groups of teachers that might profitably work together, and aiding those groups in their efforts to reach consensus on a set of shared outcomes or goals. Otherwise, the school administrator remains outside the process of teacher mentoring. This is not the case in idea-based social constructivism. Here the school administrator plays a key role as an active participant in the process.

Consistent with the process of idea construction as outlined earlier, there are two main aspects to the administrator's role: The first is to ensure that all members of the community, including the administrator, are provided with ample opportunity to try out or verify the ideas being considered. Powerful ideas can function as epistemological tools, opening up important new aspects of the environment. In a fully functioning learning community, each and every member of the community is willing to assess the cash value of a potentially helpful idea. "What do we gain by viewing the subjects we teach as dynamic entities—as bodies of knowledge that grow and change as opposed to a cut and dried set of facts and procedures?" the learning community might ask itself, picking up on a big idea that many philosophers find useful and exciting. It is counterproductive for administrators to be anything other than fully engaged in this discussion.

Administrators have a responsibility at least as great as the teaching staff to examine phenomena that need understanding through the lens of promising new ideas. Administrators thus should be expected to weigh in with their own views about the cash value of ideas. Ultimately, however, it is up to the community to decide which ideas are worth keeping and which ought to be discarded. Administrators, we submit, have a special responsibility to oversee the process of social negotiation that results in these decisions. The social negotiation process, based on one or two intriguing studies, appears to require special attention on the part of participants. McDonald (1986), for example, describes the history of a teacher study group in terms of three distinct stages. The first two phases of the group's development, McDonald reports, were primarily political in nature: Teachers had to learn to voice their opinions, and to do so in a way that advanced their collective, professional agenda. Once teachers had found their voice, attention shifted to the epistemological agenda of analyzing experience in the light of theory and ideas. As McDonald's analysis suggests, anyone who assumes a leadership role in a learning community must be extremely sensitive to political issues, like who gets the floor, whose arguments prevail and why, and who is silenced (cf., Prawat, 1991).

Just as ideas travel freely between individual minds and the world, so, too, do they travel between communities. School learning communities, are most likely to get powerful ideas about learning, teaching, students, curriculum, and assessment from the disciplines. It is the responsibility of members of the community to try out these ideas, perhaps emphasizing methodological belief before turning to doubt (see above). Those worth keeping will evidence analytic depth *and* synthetic breadth; they will illuminate specific aspects of the school environment but also connect up in generative ways with other important ideas. Analytic depth alone is not enough, we argue.

Many ideas that have gained currency among teachers, such as the notion of "learning style," or "right-brain/left-brain" have a kind of analytic depth. That is, they help teachers understand a phenomenon that is of great concern to them: why similar kinds of students respond so differently to instruction. Advocates of the learning styles notion attribute this outcome to modality differences. Some children, they argue, based on scanty research evidence (cf., Barbe & Milone, 1981), function best as learners in the auditory modality; others are visual or kinesthetic learners. The problem with this idea, as a learning community playing the doubting game would soon find out, is that it lacks legs. It has some cash value in helping teachers account for a specific kind of individual difference. Because that difference is perceived as hard and fast, however, because it is perceived as being a difference that does not make a difference in terms of anything that a teacher might do, other than accommodate to it, it calls for greater scrutiny. Our hypothetical school learning community, then, might do well to emulate teach-

ers in other countries, like Japan and Korea, who reject the notion of fixed individual differences on empirical grounds, and the grounds that it does not yield any really useful information about students (cf., Resnick, 1981).

The real issue faced by a school learning community then does not appear to be a lack of new ideas. Education is like business in this regard; both are under constant assault from those who are pushing new quick fix ideas and theories, often with the best of intentions. Micklethwait and Wooldridge (1996), in their book *The Witch Doctors*, argue that the life cycle of new ideas in business management has shrunk from a decade to less than a year. "Humble businessmen trying to keep up with the latest fashion often find that by the time they have implemented the new craze, it looks outdated" (p. 15). Similar claims have been made about education.

The authors of *The Witch Doctors* suggest some commonsense remedies to deal with the idea-overload problem. One thing that consumers of management theories can do is to consult with those in the know—those in business schools or those who write for the business press. Their second proposed remedy is classically rationalist in orientation: Look for contradictory ideas and use that information to more intensely scrutinize the value of each idea. Micklethwait and Wooldridge use the example, not uncommon in recent years, of calls for greater organizational flexibility, which often means firing people, coupled with concerted efforts to develop more trust. Managers in companies that undertake such contradictory fad surfing, they conclude, are not tending to the quality of the ideas that enter their organizations. The third remedy, like the other two, is also worth heeding in education: Be selective, Micklethwait and Wooldridge urge. "Nothing is more witch-doctorish than the suggestion that one magic potion will cure all ills" (1996, p. 324). More needs to be said about this remedy.

The first criterion that any powerful idea must meet is that of shedding light on specific phenomena. Ideas that do not do this, despite our best efforts, are vague and ought to be rejected. (Power or generalizability builds from specificity, according to Peirce, and in this way differs from vagueness. A vague idea is indeterminate to begin with; it does not inform either a specific or a general set of objects or events [1905/1934, Vol. 5].) Vague ideas, like the notion of hands-on learning, plague education.[7] It is the responsibility of teachers and administrators, functioning as school-wide learning communities, to discard ideas that are vague or contradictory, or that command little support from those within the disciplinary communities. Ideas that survive this double, methodological belief-methodological doubt test, ought to be the focus of the community's deliberations.

The tone of the discussion in the last few pages has been speculative. The process of idea verification that we have proposed is derived from theory. Although not directly tested, the successful enactment of this process, or a close approximation to it, is singled out as being essential to the progress made by faculty in one of the schools studied by Elmore *et al.* (1996). The staff in this school, the most advanced of the three being studied from a reform perspective, was able to develop a school-wide learning community that wrestled with cutting edge issues in efforts to teach for understanding, like how to reconcile the students' need to control their own learning with the teachers' responsibility to structure and guide that process. Elmore *et al.* (1996) argue that the school was quite distinctive in this regard:

> Teachers talked regularly to each other about students and about the problems they were facing in getting students to engage in learning. They met regularly, at least weekly, in loosely structured meetings focused alternatively on administrative business or on teaching and learning issues—in the latter case often focused on specific students and their work (p. 224).

This in-school structure was supplemented by informal out-of-school contacts with other teachers in the district and in various professional organizations.

In an important new study, Louis, Marks, and Kruse (1996) looked at factors contributing to the development of a sense of community among teachers like that evident in the school described above. (Sense of community was measured by items on a questionnaire that got at issues like shared sense of purpose, a collective focus on student learning coupled with reflective dialog, "deprivatized" practice, and so forth.) Not surprisingly, they pinpoint two key variables in their large sample of restructuring schools that relate to teacher community: Having regularly scheduled opportunities to talk and plan together, and being able to use that time to good effect—which is to say, being able to influence decision making at the school level.

Quantitative and qualitative data gathered in the sample of 24 schools, which was evenly divided across the three levels of elementary, middle, and high school, belies the notion that large staff size works against the formation of community. Problems associated with size can be addressed by administrators, the researchers conclude, through the use of "specific targeted efforts and supportive leadership that create denser patterns of interaction within the school" (p. 781). Although generally the sense of community was lower in secondary schools, largely because departments and specializations work against developing a common framework or lens for viewing teaching and learning, Louis *et al.* found exceptions, typically headed up by administrators who worked hard to create a common language of reform (p. 783).

Conclusion

Micklethwait and Wooldridge (1996) identify two conflicting views of leadership. The first, the scientific view, focuses heavily on the technology of effective leadership while the second attends to the role of social factors in the organization. The role of the manager in the first view is akin to that of the engineer. He or she must design a system that operates efficiently and effectively, one that uses a well-defined method or technique to produce a constant product or outcome. It is the manager's responsibility to determine the most efficient way to get things done, and then to see that people follow through with this plan. This view prevailed until the Second World War.

The second, humanist view, first surfaced by accident, as a result of the famous Hawthorne Studies conducted in the 1930s. In these studies, intangible attitudinal factors emerged as being important in accounting for worker productivity. The humanist orientation to management came into its own in the 1950s and 1960s, reaching its apex when a host of studies pointed to the importance of designing environments that satisfied workers needs, especially their so-called higher order needs. Other philosophies of management and administration have come and gone, including the recently popular re-engineering craze.

Social constructivist learning theory points away from the notion of administrator as a person who smoothes the way, who helps ensure that the organization operates efficiently. It does not denigrate that role, but neither does it elevate it. Instead it points in another direction toward the importance of encouraging members of an organization to learn and develop, realizing that that goal is apt to be met when members of the organization work together to make it happen. Administrators cannot remain neutral or on the sidelines if the learning and development goal is to be achieved. Minimally, administrators share responsibility with others within the organization who are committed to ensuring that learning and development happens; optimally, they play a key role in establishing and nurturing the organizational arrangements that enable learning to occur.

In this chapter, we have examined two social arrangements, apprenticeship learning and idea-based social constructivism, which current theory and research suggests are ideally suited for fostering a collective commitment to learning and development. These social arrangements have proven effective in this regard at the classroom level and there is every reason to think that this effectiveness transfers to the school and district level. It is our hope that the ideas presented here will be subjected to the process of individual and social verification outlined earlier by all current and future school administrators and that this will lead to an increase in the number of schools where teachers and administrators are actively engaged in the process of socially constructing knowledge about teaching and learning.

AUTHOR NOTES

In addition to the excellent feedback received by our two assigned readers, Hermine Marshall and Willis Hawley, the authors would like to thank Joseph Murphy and Barbara Rogoff for their very helpful additional suggestions for improving the manuscript.

NOTES

1. Actually, as van der Veer (1991) makes clear, Piaget avoided engaging Vygotsky in a debate until 1962 despite the fact that he was aware of the latter's challenge to his theory as early as 1929. Van der Veer attributes Piaget's reticence to take on Vygotsky's views to personal style. Piaget deliberately ignored developmental work being done by others, contending that it was the inherent logic of his own research plan that dictated the pace and direction of his research. As indicated, Piaget finally broke his silence in 1962, when he formally responded to Vygotsky in a preface to the English translation of the latter's book. Vygotsky's ideas were beginning to find an audience at that point, mostly psycholinguists, even though their originator had died in 1934.

2. In discovering that "context matters," psychologists figured out what anthropologists had known for some time. Shweder (1990) describes the origination of this new orientation in psychology, which he and others label "cultural psychology."

3. Here Nardi cites Lave's (1988) classic example of the weight watcher who solved a "mathematics" problem, the need to take three-quarters of a two-thirds cup of cottage cheese, in a situated way, dumping the full amount onto a cutting board, shaping it into a circle, marking it with a cross, and then scooping away one quadrant. Lave's descriptions of situated problem solving in the grocery store is another prominent example of what Nardi terms "a one-time solution to a one-time problem," which characterizes an important part of the work on situated cognition (1996, p. 72).

   Greeno's (1997) elaboration of an alternative approach, which he terms "situativity theory," represents an effort to broaden situated cognition and activity theory by arguing that all learning represents "social practice." This latter notion, Greeno argues, is extremely broad, encompassing non-instrumental as well as instrumental undertakings (students playfully interacting on a computer), and even the activities of individuals if they are under the influence of prior social arrangements, like those embodied in a textbook. The advantage Greeno sees in the adoption of the social practices notion is that it forces educators to attend less to individuals and more to the activities that surround and structure their learning (cf., Anderson, Reder, & Simon, 1997). In response, we wish to note that social constructivist approaches of the sort considered here, of necessity, carefully attend to this variable.

4. In hitherto unpublished notes, there is evidence that Vygotsky did grasp the import of the shift he had made. "In older works we ignored that the sign has meaning," Vygotsky lamented (1997, p. 130). Yaroshevsky and Gurgenidze, in a commentary on these notes, argue that Vygotsky was fully aware of how much his new thesis that meanings, as opposed to acts or signs, constitute the real "tissue of consciousness" represented a break with his past thinking (1997, p. 352).

5. One can recognize in Rorty's statements shades of the traditional position assumed by philosophers, which is to ignore the messy process of discovery in science and other fields in favor of the more rational process of justifying knowledge claims. Popper (1959) expressed this view well when he wrote, "The question of how it happens that a new idea occurs to a man . . . may be of great interest to empirical psychology; but it is irrelevant to the logical analysis of scientific knowledge" (p. 133). Only the process of justification is amenable to logical analysis of the sort engaged in by philosophers.

6. Peirce, Dewey's predecessor, was the first to formulate this argument. He also broadened the notion of what it means to know or understand something so that it encompasses an interaction between mind, which is heavily social, and the independent objects and events that mind seeks to understand. ("Just as we say that a body is in motion, and not that motion is in a body, we ought to say that we are in thought and not that thoughts are in us" [Vol. 5, p. 289].) Almeder captures this complex interactivity well when he writes, "The real [for Peirce] is dependent for its being known (or knowable) upon the minds of the community. This latter determination, however, is not such as to constitute the *being* of the objects known" (1980, p. 153). There is room, then, in the activity of idea development and verification for both individual and social processes.

7. Dewey argues that the hands-on approach represents a "things-to-thought" view of learning. "The notion that we have only to put physical objects before the senses in order to impress ideas upon the mind amounts almost to a superstition," he complains (1929/1988, p. 134).

REFERENCES

Almeder, R. (1980). *The philosophy of Charles S. Peirce: A critical introduction.* Oxford: Basil Blackwell.

Anderson, J. R., Reder, L. M. & Simon, H. A. (1997). Situative versus cognitive perspectives: Form versus substance. *Educational Researcher, 26* (1), 18–21.

Bakhurst, D. (1995). On the social constitution of mind: Bruner, Ilyenkov, and the defense of cultural psychology. *Mind, culture, and activity, 2* (3), 158-171.

Ball, D. L. (1993). With an eye on the mathematical horizon: Dilemmas of teaching elementary school mathematics. *Elementary School Journal, 93,* 373–397.

Barbe, W. B. & Milone, N. M. (1981). Modality strengths: A reply to Dunn and Carbo. *Educational Leadership, 38,* 489.

Bentley, A. F. (1954). The human skin: Philosophy's last line of defense. In S. Ratner (Ed.), *Inquiry into inquiries. Essays in social theory by Arthur F. Bentley* (pp. 195-211). Boston, MA: Beacon Press. (Original work published 1941)

Billig, M. (1987). *Arguing and thinking. A rhetorical approach to social psychology.* Cambridge, UK: Cambridge University Press.

Bloor, D. (1983). *Wittgenstein: A social theory of knowledge.* New York: Columbia University Press.

Boisvert, R. D. (1988). *Dewey's metaphysics.* New York: Fordham University Press.

Brainerd, C. J. (1978). The stage question in cognitive-developmental theory. *Behavioral and Brain Sciences, 2,* 327–352.

Brockmeier, J. (1996). Explaining the interpretive mind. *Human Development, 39,* 287–294.

Bronfenbrenner, U. (1979). *The ecology of human development.* Cambridge, MA: Harvard University Press.

Brown, J. S., Collins, A. & Duguid, P. (1989). Situated cognition and the culture of learning. *Educational Researcher, 18* (1), 32-42.

Bruner, J. (1986). *Actual minds, possible worlds.* Cambridge, MA: Harvard University Press.

Bruner, J. (1990). *Acts of meaning.* Cambridge, MA: Harvard University Press.

Burke, K. (1969). *A grammar of motives.* Berkeley, CA: University of California Press.

Caputo, J. D. (1983). The thought of being and the conversation of mankind: The case of Heidegger and Rorty. *Review of Metaphysics, 36,* 661-685.

Carraher, T. N. (1986). From drawings to buildings: Working with mathematical scales. *International Journal of Behavioral Development, 9,* 527–544.

Cohen, D. K. & Hill, H. (1997, March). *Policy, practice and performance: The effects of policy on teaching and learning.* Paper presented at the annual meeting of the American Educational Research Association, Chicago.

Cole, M. (1979). Epilogue: a portrait of Luria. In A. R. Luria, *The making of mind: a personal account of Soviet psychology* (pp. 189–225). Cambridge, MA: Harvard University Press.

Cole, M. (1995). Socio-cultural-historical psychology: some general remarks and a proposal for a new kind of cultural-genetic methodololology. In J. V. Wertsch, P. del Rio & A. Alvarez (Eds.), *Sociocultural studies of mind* (pp. 1-36). London: Cambridge University Press.

Collins, A., Brown, J. S. & Newman, S. E. (1989). Cognitive apprenticeship: Teaching the crafts of reading, writing, and mathematics. In L. B. Resnick (Ed.), *Knowing, learning, and instruction. Essays in honor of Robert Glaser.* Hillsdale, NJ: Lawrence Erlbaum Associates.

Davydov, V. V. & Radzikhovskii, L. A. (1985). Vygotsky's theory and the activity-oriented approach in psychology. In J. V. Wertsch (Ed.), *Culture, communication, and cognition: Vygotskian perspectives* (p. 58). New York: Cambridge University Press.

Dewey, J. (1916). *Democracy and education.* New York: Macmillan.

Dewey, J. (1977a). Appendix 3. In J. A. Boydston (Ed.), *John Dewey: The middle works, 1907–1909, Vol. 4* (pp. 317–327). Carbondale: Southern University Press.

Dewey, J. (1977b). Logical character of ideas. In J. A. Boydston (Ed.), *John Dewey: The middle works, 1907–1909, Vol. 4* (pp. 91–97). Carbondale: Southern University Press. (Original work published 1908).

Dewey, J. (1977c). The control of ideas by facts. In J. A. Boydston (Ed.), *John Dewey: The middle works, 1907–1909, Vol. 4* (pp. 78–90). Carbondale: Southern University Press. (Original work published 1907).

Dewey, J. (1977d). What pragmatism means by practical. In J. A. Boydston (Ed.), *John Dewey: The middle works, 1907–1909, Vol. 4* (pp. 98–115). Carbondale: Southern University Press. (Original work published 1908).

Dewey, J. (1986). Logic. In J. A. Boydston (Ed.), *John Dewey: The later works, 1925-1953, Vol. 8*. Carbondale: Southern University Press. (Original work published 1933).

Dewey, J. (1988). The quest for certainty. In J. A. Boydston (Ed.), *John Dewey: The later works, 1925-1953, Vol. 4* . Carbondale: Southern Illinois University Press. (Original work published 1929).

Diggins, J. P. (1994). *The promise of pragmatism*. Chicago: University of Chicago Press.

Eisenhardt, M. A. & Curtis-Dougherty, K. (1991). Social and cultural constraints on students' access to school knowledge. In E. H. Hiebert (Ed.)., *Literacy for a diverse society: Perspectives, practices, and policies*. New York: Teachers College Press.

Elbow, P. (1986). *Embracing contraries. Explorations in learning and teaching*. Oxford, UK: Oxford University Press.

Elmore, R. F., Peterson, P. L. & McCarthey, S. J. (1996). *Restructuring in the classroom*. San Francisco, CA: Jossey-Bass Publishers.

Feiman-Nemser, S. & Parker, M. (1992). *Mentoring in context: A comparison of two U. S. programs for beginning teachers*. East Lansing, MI: National Center for Research on Teaching.

Fullan, M. (1993). *Change forces. Probing the depths of educational reform*. London: Falmer Press.

Fullan, M. & Steiglebauer, S. (1991). *The new meaning of educational change*. New York: Teachers College Press.

Gardner, H. (1991). *The unschooled mind*. New York: Basic Books.

Gergen K. J. (1994). *Realities and relationships. Soundings in social constructionism*. Cambridge, MA: Harvard University Press.

Ghiselin, M. T. (1969). *The triumph of the Darwinian method*. Berkeley, CA: University of California Press.

Gibbs, R. W., Jr. (1994). *The poetics of mind*. Cambridge, UK: Cambridge University Press.

Glasersfeld, E., von (1987). *The construction of knowledge: Contributions to conceptual semantics*. Seaside, CA: Intersystems.

Greeno, J. G. (1997). Response: On claims that answer the wrong question. *Educational Researcher, 26* (1), 5–17).

Grossman, P. (1992). In pursuit of a dual agenda: Creating a middle level professional development school. In L. Darling-Hammond (Ed.), *Professional development schools: Schools for developing a profession*. New York: Teachers College Press.

Hallinger, P., Murphy, J. & Hausman, C. (1992). Restructuring schools: Principals perceptions of fundamental reform. *Educational Administration Quarterly, 28* (3), 330–349).

Harre, R. (1986). The step to social constructionism. In M. Richards & P. Light (Eds.), *Children of social worlds* (pp. 287–296). Cambridge, MA: Harvard University Press.

Harre, R. (1993). *Personal being: A theory for individual psychology* (2nd ed.). Oxford: Blackwell.

Ingleby, D. (1986). Development in social contexts. In M. Richards & P. Light (Eds.), *Children of social worlds* (pp. 297–317). Cambridge, MA: Harvard University Press.

Joravsky, D. (1989). *Russian psychology: A critical history*. New York: Basil Blackwell.

Kitchener, R. F. (1996). The nature of the social for Piaget and Vygotsky. *Human Development, 39*, 243–249.

Kuhn, T. (1970). The natural and the human sciences. In D. R. Hiley, J. F. Bohman & R. Shusterman (Eds.), *The interpretive turn. Philosophy, science, culture* (pp. 17–24). Ithaca, NY: Cornell University Press.

Lampert, M. (1989). Choosing and using mathematical tools in classroom discourse. In J. Brophy (Ed.), *Advances in research on teaching* (Vol. 1, pp. 223-264). Greenwich, CT: JAI Press.

Latour, B. & Woolgar, S. (1986). *Laboratory life. The construction of scientific facts*. Princeton, NJ: Princeton University Press.

Lave, J. (1988). *Cognition in practice: Mind, mathematics, and culture in everyday life*. Cambridge, MA: Cambridge University Press.

Lave, J. (1996). Teaching, as learning, in practice. *Mind, Culture, and Activity. An International Journal, 3* (3), 149–164.

Lave, J. & Wenger, E. (1991). *Situated learning. Legitimate peripheral participation*. Cambridge, UK: Cambridge University Press.

Leont'ev, N. R. (1978). *Activity, consciousness, and personality*. Englewood Cliffs, NJ: Prentice Hall.

Little, J. W. (1990). The persistence of privacy: Autonomy and initiative in teachers' professional lives. *Teachers College Record, 91*, 509–536.

Louis, K. S., Marks, H. M. & Kruse, S. (1996). Teachers professional community in restructuring schools. *American Educational Research Journal, 33*, 757–798.

McDonald, J. (1986). Raising the teachers voice and the ironic role of theory. *Harvard Educational Review, 56*, 355–378.

McEwan, H. & Bull, B. (1991). The pedagogic nature of subject matter knowledge. *American Educational Research Journal, 28*, 316–334.

Mahajan, G. (1992). *Explanation and understanding in the human sciences*. New York: Oxford University Press.

Marshall, H. (1972). Structural constraints on learning: Butcher's apprentices. In B. Geer (Ed.)., *Learning to work* (pp. 39–48). Beverly Hills, CA: Sage Publications.

Micklethwhait, J. & Wooldridge, A. (1996). *The witch doctors. Making sense of the management gurus*. New York: Times Books.

Mishler, E. G. (1990). Validation in inquiry-guided research: The role of exemplars in narrative studies. *Harvard Educational Review, 60*, 415–442.

Murphy, J., Evertson, C. & Radnofsky, M. (1991). Restructuring schools: Fourteen elementary and secondary teachers proposals for reform. *Elementary School Journal, 92* (2), 135–148.

Nardi, B. A. (1996). Activity theory and human-computer interaction. In B. A. Nardi (Ed), *Context and consciousness. Activity theory and human-computer interaction* (pp. 7-16). Cambridge, MA: MIT Press.

National Council of Teachers of Mathematics (NCTM). (1989). *Curriculum and evaluation standards for school mathematics*. Reston, VA: NCTM.

Newman, F. & Holzman, L. (1993). *Lev Vygotsky. Revolutionary scientist*. New York: Routledge.

Palincsar, A. S. & Brown, A. L. (1984). Reciprocal teaching of comprehension-fostering and comprehension-monitoring activities. *Cognition and Instruction, 1*, 117–175.

Payne, T. R. (1968). *S. L. Rubenstein and the philosophical foundations of Soviet psychology*. New York: Humanities Press.

Peirce, C. S. (1931–1935). In C. Hartshorne & P. Weiss (Eds.), *Collected papers of Charles Sanders Peirce* (Vols. 1–6). Cambridge: Harvard University Press.

Piaget, J. (1971). *Biology and knowledge*. Edinburgh: Edinburgh University Press.

Pope, M. L. & Gilbert, J. K. (1983). Personal experience and the construction of knowledge in science. *Science Education, 67*, 193–204.

Popper, K. (1959). *The logic of scientific discovery*. New York: Harper & Row.

Prawat, R. S. (1991). Conversations with self and settings: A framework for thinking about teacher empowerment. *American Educational Research Journal, 28*, 737–757.

Prawat, R. S. (1992). Teachers beliefs about teaching and learning: A constructivist perspective. *American Journal of Education, 100*, 354–395.

Prawat, R. S. (1995). Misreading Dewey: Reform, projects, and the language game. *Educational Researcher, 24* (7), 13–22.

Prawat, R. S. (1996a). Constructivisms, modern and postmodern. *Educational Psychologist, 31*, 215–225.

Prawat, R. S. (1996b). Ideas and their objects: A reply to Garrison. *Educational Researcher, 25* (6), 23–24.

Resnick, L. B. (1981). Social assumptions as a context for science: Some reflections on psychology and education. *Educational Psychologist, 16*, 1–10.

Rogoff, B. (1995). Observing sociocultural activity on three planes: participatory appropriation, guided participation, and apprenticeship. In J. V. Wertsch, P. Del Rio & A. Alvarez (Eds.), *Sociocultural studies of mind* (pp. 215–248). New York: Cambridge University Press.

Rorty, R. (1980). *Philosophy and the mirror of nature.* London: Allen & Unwin.

Rorty, R. (1989). *Contingency, irony, and solidarity.* Cambridge, MA: Cambridge University Press.

Roth, K. J. (1989). *Subject matter knowledge for teaching science, or How long does it take oxygen to get to the cells?* Paper presented at the annual meeting of the American Educational Research Association, San Francisco.

Schoenfeld, A. (1991). On mathematics as sense-making: An informal attack on the unfortunate divorce of formal and informal mathematics. In D. W. Perkins & G. J. Voss (Eds.), *Informal reasoning and education.* Hillsdale, NJ: Erlbaum.

Scribner, S. & Fahrmeirer, E. (1982). *Practical and theoretical arithmetic: Some preliminary findings* (Industrial-literacy project, Working Paper No. 3). New York: Graduate Center, City University of New York.

Shotter, J. (1993). *Conversational realities. Conducting life through language.* London: Sage Publications.

Shweder, R. (1990). Cultural psychology: What is it?. In N. R. Goldberger & J. B. Veroff (Eds.), *The cultural and psychology reader* (pp. 41–86). New York: University Press.

Shweder, R. A. (in press). True ethnography. In R. Jessor, A. Colby & R. A. Shweder (eds.), *Ethnography and human development: Context and meaning in social inquiry.* Chicago, IL: University of Chicago Press.

Silberman, C. E. (1970). *Crisis in the classroom.* New York: Random House.

Sleeper, R. W. (1986). *The necessity of pragmatism. John Dewey's conception of philosophy.* New Haven: Yale University Press.

Stein, M. K., Silver, E. A. & Smith, M. S. (1994). *Mathematics reform and teacher development: A community of practice perspective.* Pittsburgh: Learning Research and Development Center, University of Pittsburgh.

Stevenson, H. W. & Stigler, J. W. (1992). *The learning gap.* New York: Summit Books.

Thompson, A. G. (1984). The relationship of teachers conceptions of mathematics and mathematics teaching to instructional practice. *Educational Studies in Mathematics, 15,* 105–127.

van der Veer, R. & Valsiner, J. (1991). *Understanding Vygotsky: A quest for synthesis.* Oxford, UK: Blackwell.

Vygotsky, L. (1962). *Thought and language.* Cambridge, MA: MIT Press.

Vygotsky, L. (1966). Development of the higher mental functions. In A. N. Leontiev, A. R. Luria & A. Smirnov (Eds.), *Psychological research in the USSR.* Moscow: Progress Publishers.

Vygotsky, L. (1978). *Mind in society: The development of higher psychological processes.* Cambridge, MA: Harvard University Press.

Vygotsky, L. (1981). The instrumental method in psychology. In J. V. Wertsch (Ed.), *The concept of activity in Soviet psychology* (pp. 134-143). Armonk, NY: Sharpe.

Vygotsky, L. (1986). *Thought and language.* Translation newly revised by Alex Kozulin. Cambridge, MA: MIT Press.

Vygotsky, L. (1987). In R. W. Rieber & S. Carton (Ed. and Trans.), *The collected works of L. S. Vygotsky: Problems of general psychology.* New York: Plenum Press.

Vygotsky, L. (1997). The problem of consciousness. In R. W. Rieber & J. Wollock. (Eds.), *The collected works of L. S. Vygotsky: Vol. 3. Problems of the theory and history of psychology* (pp. 129–138). New York: Plenum Press.

Wertsch, J. V. (1979). From social interaction to higher psychological processes: A clarification and application of Vygotsky's theory. *Human Development, 22,* 1–22.

Wertsch, J. V. (1985). *Vygotsky and the social formation of mind.* Cambridge, MA: Harvard University Press.

Wertsch, J. V., del Rio, P. & Alvarez, A. (1995). Sociocultural studies: history, action, and mediation. In J. V. Wertsch, P. del Rio & A. Alvarez (Eds.), *Sociocultural studies of mind* (pp. 1–34). New York: Cambridge University Press.

Wertsch, J. V., Tulviste, P. & Hagstrom, F. (1993). A sociocultural approach to agency. In E. A. Forman, N. Minick & C. A. Stone (Eds.), *Contexts for learning: Sociocultural dynamics in children's development* (pp. 336–356). Oxford, UK: Oxford University Press.

Wittgenstein, L. (1969). *On certainty.* (D. Paul & G. Anscombe, Trans.). Oxford: Blackwell.

Wright, G. H., von (1971). *Explanation and understanding.* Ithaca, NY: Cornell University Press.

Yaroshevsky, M. G. & Gurgenidze, G. S. (1997). Epilogue. In R. W. Rieber & J. Wollock. (Eds.), *The collected works of L. S. Vygotsky: Vol. 3. Problems of the theory and history of psychology* (pp. 345–369). New York: Plenum Press.

Zinchenko, P. (1984). The problem of involuntary memory. *Soviet Psychology, 22* (2), 55–111. (Original work published 1939)

Zinchenko, V. (1995). Cultural-historical psychology and the psychological theory of activity: retrospect and prospect. In J. V. Wertsch, P. del Rio & A. Alvarez (Eds.), *Sociocultural studies of mind* (pp. 37–55). New York: Cambridge University Press.

CHAPTER 11

The "New Professionalism" in Education: An Appraisal

Gary Sykes

Professionalism stands as one among the core values that organize the educational enterprise in our society. It is a term with a long history, functioning sometimes as an honorific to denote a set of valued qualities and dispositions ("a very professional job"), other times as an indication of a certain kind of occupation that may be distinguished from other kinds ("the professional-managerial class"). As in other fields, educational workers seek the attributes and benefits of the designation, so that teachers, school administrators, school social workers, and guidance counselors all desire to be regarded as "professional."

At the same time, however, the history of professionalism as an effort on the part of certain favored occupations to gain special status and standing has come under serious criticism, so that professionals in our society today are regarded with some mixture of respect and suspicion (Sullivan, 1995).

The so-called true professions rose to prominence in our society during the Progressive Era that spanned the decades from the close of the last century into the first quarter of the present century. These were buoyant times in the modern era, when the miracles of science, the rise of industry, and the continuing growth of the nation gave promise of substantial human progress. In the post-modern world, however, many of the certainties that surrounded the rise of the professions are no longer with us. The present age is more skeptical and less certain about most of the ideologies that organize post-modern life, and this cultural circumstance influences professionalism along with the other "isms" that shape our collective lives (Hargreaves, 1994).

Any account of the "new professionalism" in education must recognize this social and historical context. To consti-

tute a professionalism that suits the mood and spirit of our times will require invention rather than reliance on a well-established, serviceable tradition. The essence of professionalism has always been a social compact between a particular occupational group and those it serves, at the heart of which is trust. In exchange for certain privileges, such as autonomy, service providers pledge to do what is in the best interest of their clients or patients, who must depend both on the conscience and the expertise of the professional. But trust is precisely what has eroded in the post-modern era in nearly all the central institutions in our society, including the institution of professionalism. Consequently, the ideal of professionalism must be reclaimed even as important social and cultural supports have weakened substantially. The overarching question that this review poses, then, concerns the bases and strategies that educators might employ to renew a public-professional compact in education in the post-modern era.

A second framing issue concerns the implications of professionalism for educational administration. Sociologists (for example, Abbott, 1988) have noted that occupational fields are structured increasingly via interaction among professionalized groups seeking jurisdiction over contested territory. This is true of administrative and practicing professionals in such fields as medicine, engineering, management, and education, where modern work increasingly takes place in corporate organizations that feature a division of expert labor between front-line workers and those who manage them (Benveniste, 1987; Friedson, 1986; Raelin, 1986). The older system of freestanding, fee-for-service professionals has gone the way of the horse and buggy in all fields, replaced by bureaucratically organized workplaces. In the new contexts of professional work, conflict over jurisdiction is commonplace (for one treatment of this phenomenon in education, see Shedd & Bacharach, 1991). Under site-based management, for example, how shall school decision-making be allocated among central office and school administrators and schoolteachers? If peer review is to replace or augment traditional models of administrator evaluation, then what is the new role for administrators in teacher evaluation? These and other tensions complicate administrator-teacher relations today, but they are of a piece with similar tensions in other fields where multiple professional claims vie for scope. All the educating occupations seek to professionalize and tend to mimic one another in the strategies they employ. If, for example, teachers establish a board to set professional standards, then administrators will do the same, and other occupations as well. Mimesis not only structures institutional fields in modern life (DiMaggio & Powell, 1983), but also serves as a tactic in jurisdictional disputes among professions.

Although this chapter concentrates on teacher professionalism, the parallel efforts of administrators to professionalize must be kept in mind, together with the question of how relationships between teachers and administrators are evolving. Conflicts of authority and jurisdiction among occupations are not necessarily zero-sum games in which one player's gain is another's loss; efforts to "empower" teachers might increase administrative authority as well, but it depends on how the players conceive and enact their roles and relationships. The new professionalism in teaching, then, creates a range of strategic choices for administrators that likely will lead to a range of responses from resistance to cooperation.

A final framing issue takes note of teacher unionism as a competing strategy for the collective advancement of teaching. While occupations such as medicine and law evolved a distinctive professional model in our society that other occupations sought to emulate, in teaching the decisive turn came in the late 1950s with the resort to labor unionism as the collective strategy of choice. In the ensuing half-century, labor management relations structured around state collective bargaining laws and locally negotiated contracts have defined the education field more sharply than professionalizing moves. As the 20th century draws to a close, however, organized teachers are reconsidering the forms of collective action they will pursue, and in many quarters aspects of the professional ideal are under review, prompting questions about the evolution of labor unionism toward a hybrid model that has been identified as the "professional union" (Kerchner & Mitchell, 1988; Kerchner & Koppich, 1993; Kerchner, Koppich, & Weeres, 1997). New practices such as peer evaluation of teachers, educational trust agreements, district-community-union partnerships, and others are changing the face of labor relations in education, as elements of the professional model are adapted to a traditional labor union context. Labor relations will be one important arena in which "the new professionalism" will be forged, and developments there may well influence if not determine the trend, as the educating professions seek to define their place in 21st century America.

Organization of the Chapter

What follows is a selective review of research and related literature on professionalism, that is bounded chiefly with reference to this handbook's focus on educational administration. The reader is referred to a large, general literature on professionalism (a sampling of useful references includes Friedson, op cit.; Bledstein, 1976; Kimball, 1992; Larson, 1977; Metzger, 1987; Starr, 1982; Vollmer & Mills, 1966; Wiebe, 1967; Wilensky, 1964), a subfield of which concerns teacher professionalism (see, for example, Bull, 1990; Cohn & Kottkamp, 1993; Darling-Hammond, 1990; Lortie, 1975; Sykes, 1990; Talbert & McLaughlin, 1994). Rather than reviewing this literature yet again, this chapter selects a small set of topics that bear directly on theory and practice in the field of educational administration, constituting, in effect, a modest primer on professionalism for an administrative and policy audience.

The chapter begins with an orienting overview of the topic, introducing some of the classic tensions and issues in the effort to "professionalize" education. Scholarly commentary has divided occupations into two classes, distinguishing "true" professions from others designated as semi, partial, lesser, or truncated professions (see, for example, Etzioni, 1969). Teaching falls into this latter class, raising questions about its status, about the bases for professional claims, and about prospects for the future. Next, the chapter considers the policy framework for professionalism in education, where the arena is public policy and collective action by various organizations that represent the profession. A third section shifts the locus to the school as work organization, exploring how professionalism is locally constructed out of the interactions among teachers, administrators, and parents. A central question here asks, how are professionalized workers to be managed? A fourth section introduces a number of trends that together are predicted to shape professionalism into the next century, alerting readers to topics that will require continued attention from scholars, policy analysts, and practitioners alike. The chapter concludes with a brief section that draws out some implications of the foregoing for the field of educational administration, then outlines a research agenda for the coming decade.

A note on terminology. The root word, "profession," denotes an occupational class distinguished according to certain characteristics, situated in place and time (for example, the clergy, historically regarded as one of the "true professions," has declined in significance in a more secular age). Related terms include "professional" and "professionalism," indicating a set of traits, attributes, or dispositions associated with those occupations, and two others, "professionalize" and "professionalization," which refer to historical processes through which occupations seek to become—or to be regarded as—professions. Considerable scholarly commentary and argument surrounds the definition and use of these terms, treatment of which extends beyond the bounds of this chapter (for a good, brief review on the rhetoric of professionalism, see Chapter 1 of Kimball, op. cit.). Rather than entering this terminological thicket at the outset, the chapter will selectively consider the meaning of these terms in the context of their use here.

Teaching as a Profession?

To begin, it is useful to identify two perspectives from which to view the complex historical phenomenon known as "professionalism." One perspective is collective in analyzing broad characteristics of occupations that influence their claim to the term. The other is individual in analyzing what it might mean for a teacher or a group of teachers to enact a "professional" conception of their role. These two perspectives are related. As Lortie (op. cit.), following Waller (1932) and Elsbree (1939), has explicated, both occupational processes and conditions of work shape modal tendencies in the formation of personal/professional identity. As a backdrop against which to assess emerging developments, the historical legacy is worth reviewing.

Occupational Processes and the Historical Legacy

The occupational claim to the term "profession" rests on several central tenets: that practitioners possess specialized, codified, expert knowledge, acquired through years of training, guided practice, and induction; that they place the welfare of those they serve above other considerations; and that the occupation assumes collective responsibility for the definition, transmittal, and enforcement of standards of practice and norms of conduct. Considerable authority is granted to experts over many important matters in our society, based on these twin claims—that they know better and that they protect the best interests of those they serve. In its simplest form, this is the professional model, along with its accompanying ideology favoring scientific knowledge as the warrant for practice, considerable autonomy, fiduciary responsibility, and the professional guild as primary reference group.

To enact this model, occupations with professional aspirations sought to restrict entry through selective admissions to professional schools coupled with prolonged, rigorous training and demanding licensure examinations. In the early decades of the century, the tradition of apprenticeship as the primary route into the professions gave way to university-based education followed by attendance at a professional school. Accompanying this crucial shift was the rise of science and the evident progress made in such fields as engineering and medicine. As the true professions appropriated the values of science and service, they gained great cultural authority and substantial autonomy. Other occupations naturally sought to establish a scientific basis for practice, to create university-based professional schools, to elevate entry requirements, and to enlist the support of the state in creating licensure and accreditation standards. These movements came to define the professional project in the early to mid-decades of the century and to influence the education field along with many others.

The teaching occupation, however, possesses certain attributes that hindered the professionalization effort. Chief among these have been its sheer size, its gender-related complexion, its public control, and its cultural status as ordinary work. The teaching occupation was never allowed to insist either on high standards for entry or on prolonged rigorous training because a burgeoning American school system simply required too many teachers. Although the so-called "true professions" could afford elite status, teaching became a mass "profession," in which painful tradeoffs were necessary between standard-setting and the generation of sufficient supply. These tensions persist to this day as witnessed by continuing recourse to emergency credentials, teaching out of area, and alternative certification as a means of speeding recruits into the classroom without much prior training (see Darling-Hammond, 1992).

Equally critical, women became the chief source of supply in the teacher labor market; at the elementary level, roughly two-thirds of U.S. teachers are women, one-half at the secondary level. As in other feminized occupations, women have constituted a relatively cheap, available, and pliable source of labor, and the recruitment inducements for women have been substantial—working hours that are compatible with family life and child rearing, summers off, and a calling that draws on the "feminine" virtues of care, compassion, and love of children. While teaching became women's work, however, administration became a male pursuit, so that teachers were subordinated to administrators not only organizationally but culturally, buttressed by long-standing traditions of patriarchy. Under these cultural circumstances, the feminized occupations of nursing, social work, teaching, and others never gained the authority and public regard accorded to the male-dominated professions.

Teacher salaries, too, have rarely reflected professional status and in the competition for talent in the college-educated labor pool, teaching has always ranked toward the bottom in salary inducements. This is partly a function of large demand for teachers and partly a result of the direct connection between teacher salaries and taxation. Teachers depend on citizens and their representatives to vote for salary increases, which require tax increases. Unlike health care, there is no third-party system of finance; teaching is a public profession that subsists on tax dollars and the on-going political effort to balance state and local budgets. Consequently, teaching has always struggled to maintain wage levels commensurate with professional aspirations that would attract the best and brightest to the occupation. The evidence, based on various measures of academic ability, however, suggests that teaching has been only modestly successful in this quest (see, for example, Murnane, *et al.*, 1991; Schlechty & Vance, 1983; Vance & Schlechty, 1982).

Teaching is a public profession in another sense as well. Teachers operate under the delegated control of local school boards and their agents, school administrators. The authority system they work within provides some modest support for professional controls but includes a much heavier reliance on democratic and bureaucratic forms of authority. As Kimball (1988) argues, if a central tenet of professionalism is guild-control of the work, then teaching has never enjoyed this attribute. Even if teachers develop professional standards and codes of conduct, they may not be able to implement these in cases of conflict with public policies and decisions.

Finally, the professional claim in teaching is suspect on knowledge grounds as well. Although the past several decades arguably have witnessed promising growth in technical knowledge underlying teaching and learning, popular conceptions continue to regard teaching as relatively easy, accessible work. Teaching, after all, is ubiquitous; it occurs in homes, on playgrounds, in summer camps, churches, community gatherings, and on television. Teaching appears not to require much specialized, expert knowledge. The old formula—knowledge of subject matter plus love of kids—still captures the popular view of teaching. Pedagogy as a specialized body of knowledge within a larger domain of professional knowledge is not widely credited in the public mind, and thus one of the central tenets of professionalism enjoys meager and equivocal public support. Efforts by vanguard teaching groups to promote professional standards, expert knowledge, and rigorous, prolonged training contend with long-standing cultural stereotypes (Cohen, 1988).

The Ethos of Teaching as Historical Legacy

These cultural and structural attributes of the teaching occupation constitute historical barriers to professionalization efforts in teaching. They also influence the personal/professional identity of individual teachers. The sociological commentary on teachers' basic orientations and dispositions emphasizes a number of characteristics that generally are deemed antithetical to professionalism, originating in occupational processes and conditions of work. For this chapter's purposes, four characteristics are worth mentioning: the "apprenticeship of observation" as formative socialization experience, occupational commitment and the pattern of teaching careers, individualism and isolation in the classroom, and craft-oriented conceptions of teaching work.

Lortie (op. cit.) first introduced the "apprenticeship of observation" to describe how prospective teachers develop powerful, hard-to-change images of what it means to teach based on watching their teachers over many years as students. This form of pre-socialization to the role is distinctive to the teaching occupation (the average individual does not grow up spending thousands of hours watching accountants, lawyers, or engineers at work); it is hypothesized to exert formative influence that a slender amount of professional education cannot fully offset. The effect is conservative in perpetuating traditional conceptions of teaching and in creating resistance to reform ideas that cannot overturn deeply held images of what it means to teach and to learn. Whereas professional education in many fields constitutes an ordeal that remakes the individual, molding him or her to conceptions of the role and the work that are sanctioned by the profession, this process occurs imperfectly in teaching. Formal training and socialization, then, fails in significant ways to create professional orientations and dispositions, at least as defined by teacher educators.

Equally crucial has been the historical pattern that has institutionalized teaching as temporary work that may be entered, exited, and reentered as convenient. Professions such as architecture and law exact high entry costs in terms of selective admission, long years of rigorous training, deferred work, heavy tuition payments, and demanding examinations staged over time. Such early demands engender occupational commitment and strong identification with the profession. As well, this professional bargain also relies on handsome lifetime earnings together with considerable social status and a fair measure of autonomy. In teaching, however, recruitment has featured a different set of inducements and a different bargain: relatively easy entry, training of limited rigor in a large set of geographically and academically accessible institutions, and the opportunity to leave, then return, to teaching at any time (due to child rearing, for example) in exchange for modest salaries, middling social status, and constrained control over work. Teaching careers then allow for various levels of occupational commitment and identification, ranging from highly dedicated career teachers to those who regard teaching as "easy work" that is compatible with other aspects of their lives.

A third, widely noted characteristic of teaching is the isolating condition of teachers' work. Teachers spend their time in individual classrooms with little feedback, little opportunity to interact with other adults during the workday, and with maximum responsibility to control often unruly groups of children. This structural circumstance—one teacher working alone who confronts students in batches of 20 to 30—over time induces an individualistic orientation to work (see Lortie, op cit.; Little, 1990; Huberman, 1993; and Hargreaves, 1993). Whereas the professional ideology emphasizes the guild or collegium as the critical point of reference for practice, teachers learn to rely on themselves to solve the fundamental problems of their craft. In the process, they develop powerful beliefs that learning from personal experience is best, that what works for one teacher may or may not work for another, and that success in the classroom depends on personal style and manner, rather than on professionally sanctioned technical knowledge and standards of good practice. Low levels of collegiality and interdependence then foster attitudes and beliefs that outside observers frequently have characterized pejoratively as anti-professional, anti-scientific, or even anti-rational.

The experience of teaching under modal conditions persuades many teachers that their success depends on the chemistry of particular classes and other fickle factors. Rather than viewing teaching as an endeavor susceptible to rational planning and analysis and the application of technical knowledge, they tend to see it as ineffable. In describing teaching's "endemic uncertainties," Lortie (op. cit.) writes, "The teacher's craft, then, is marked by the absence of concrete models for emulation, unclear lines of influence, multiple and controversial criteria, ambiguity about assessment timing, and instability in the product" (p. 136). He goes on,

> The fact that some teachers explain good days . . . in terms of subtle, changeful moods is provocative. The explanatory theories they are relying upon do not, in such instances, emphasize rational choice. Strategy counts for less than chance when mood is king. Such a view underlines the transitory, uncertain course of teaching; it also magnifies psychological processes which are usually thought to be beyond intentional control. One suspects that most people think of mood as something that happens to them, not as something they select. To link teaching effectiveness and rewards to mood is to make them contingent rather than manipulable . . . it connotes caprice rather than craft. Those who hold such a view telegraph uncertainty rather than sure control; good days—and their benefits—are not something one orders up at will (p. 174).

The uncertainties of teaching and the personal-practical warrant for teaching style and method contribute another orientation as well, often identified as "egalitarian." The experience of teaching convinces many teachers that objective standards for evaluating the work are highly suspect and cannot account for the subtle differences from class to class, teacher to teacher. As a result, teachers shy away from evaluative judgments of one another (except on moral rather than technical grounds) and tend to regard a wide range of approaches as acceptable. Lacking traditions of close scrutiny to teaching and of external standards for judging the work, teachers resist evaluative judgments in favor of the leveling assumption that all teachers succeed with some students and few (or none) succeed with all students. Again, the structural circumstances of teaching work, including isolation in the classroom, lack of a staged progression in the career, and the absence of peer review of teaching work, support such egalitarian beliefs while denying that common standards could provide a meaningful basis for evaluative judgments.

Finally, the term "craft" is sometimes contrasted with the term "profession" to denote kinds of work that are rationalized according to different principles. Whereas the professional model came to emphasize technical knowledge with a theoretical base and a scientific warrant, craft work emphasizes knowledge and skill that is more tacit, less codified, conveyed via apprenticeship, and acquired through trial and error processes, rather than through formal, academic training. (In fact, these labels do not clearly distinguish among "professions" because nearly all forms of complex work feature a mix of craft know-how and technical knowledge.) In challenging the professional model, some contemporary accounts of teaching stress its craft-like characteristics (see, for example, Huberman, op. cit.). Teachers are portrayed as gradually building up a repertoire of materials and methods through informal trial and error, consultations with colleagues, and examination of new practices that come their way. Teacher development appears as a personally controlled process featuring strong idiosyncratic elements; teachers pick and choose what to implement and what to ignore, adapt rather than adopt new practices, and experiment singly or in small groups. The process resembles tinkering rather than the progressive incorporation of scientifically validated knowledge or technology. The standard applied to new knowledge is not its scientific warrant within a professional community but what has been termed the "practicality ethic:" does it work for me in my classroom (Doyle & Ponder, 1978).

This abbreviated account that compares teaching to the classic professional model generally finds teaching to be lacking in one or more attributes of professionalism. Structural characteristics of teaching as occupation and work, deeply rooted in history and culture, have shaped the ethos of the occupation as evidenced in the modal beliefs and orientations of teachers. In his history of efforts to reform teaching, for example, Cuban (1993) concludes that the "situational constraints" faced by teachers have made change unusually difficult to sustain and to spread. In turn, this portrayal has prompted two kinds of responses: a revisionist critique of the argument itself and a family of reforms that seeks to address one or more of teaching's perceived shortcomings in the name of greater professionalism. The revisionists challenge the professional model as the appropriate standard (see Soder, 1990). Feminist scholars argue that professional conceptions of careers implicitly refer to men (see Biklen, 1995; Noddings, 1990); others have challenged the knowledge claims of science as the proper standard for teaching work (see Schön, 1983) and still others have argued that classic professionalism ill serves a field such as education, where status-equalizing partnerships between teachers and parents are desirable, rather than the creation of social distance that accompanies professional-client relations (see Burbules & Densmore, 1991). These critiques all make important points, and they all contribute to the post-modern climate of skepticism surrounding professional claims. A full review of the anti-professional critique is beyond the bounds of this chapter, but the reader should be aware that one strain of contemporary scholarship seeks not to increase professionalism in teaching but to challenge and redefine it in fundamental ways.

The reform response to perceived shortcomings in teaching has sought through policy, management, and improvements in teaching practice to enhance professionalism by altering some of the long-standing structural features of the occupation, by restructuring the teacher's workplace, and by initiating new policies that support teachers' professional knowledge and skill. The chief points of intervention in the family of reforms that may be labeled "professional" are state policy and local school management, topics addressed in the following sections of the chapter. In effect, the professional reforms of teaching seek to overcome one or more of the anti-professional attributes of teaching, just reviewed, that compose the historical legacy.

The Policy Framework for Professionalism

One arena that reformers pursuing the professional theme have operated in has been policy at national, state, and district levels. Historically, occupations seeking professional status became allies with states to create a framework of standards that regulated entry to practice together with practice itself. The policy instruments in use have been state license regulations and program accreditation standards. Medicine represents the most fully developed case, where the standards for entry include academically demanding pre-medical coursework (such as organic chemistry), competitive entrance examinations, a three-part staged license examination, formal training in accredited medical schools and in hospital-based internships that also are accredited, and continuing professional education in the form of specialty training within accredited residencies, advanced specialty examinations, and general requirements to maintain the physician's license.

Several features of this elaborate set of standards are noteworthy. The medical profession succeeded in gaining a substantial measure of control over these standards, as delegated by state legislatures (see Ludmerer, 1985; Starr, 1982). In the early decades of the century, the profession established the National Board of Medical Examiners (NBME), which developed the licensure examination that all states subsequently adopted. The NBME together with other standard-setting bodies, including the medical specialty boards and the National Council for Medical Education, exercises considerable authority over standards for entry and training. Equally important, the medical school became established on a unitary model following the 1910 Flexner report and the total number of medical schools fell from 160 to 85. All of these standard-setting moves helped to institutionalize medicine as a high status profession featuring stringent requirements for entry and licensing.

Teaching has employed a similar, professionalizing strategy, but the social characteristics of the occupation have created difficulties. If considerable authority over educational decision-making is to be delegated to teachers, then the professional compact requires that they be highly qualified and demonstrably so. Processes of recruitment, selection, training, induction, and continuing education are the critical targets of policy intervention, and the development of standards serves as the basis for asserting professional authority. States have developed complex teacher licensing laws in the post-war era, complete with approved program requirements, examinations, and, increasingly, mentoring experiences as part of induction. At the same time, however, states also have maintained a variety of loopholes within the standards in order to generate sufficient supply, particularly in such hard to staff areas as the inner city and in rurally isolated communities. Emergency credentials, teaching outside one's area of certification, adjusting examination cut scores, and so-called alternate route programs are long-standing expedients. In their recent report (*What Matters Most*, 1996), the National Commission on Teaching and America's Future compiled state-by-state statistics on indicators of teacher quality that reveal the continuing extent of the standards problem. On measures of unqualified hires, out-of-field teaching, and others (see Appendix F of *What Matters Most*), all states exhibit some quality-depressing policies and many states reveal substantial problems. For example, in 1996, 53% of new hires are unlicensed in the District of Columbia, compared with 23% in Louisiana, 14% in South Carolina, 8% in Illinois, and 0% in Ohio. Unreported in this document is variation across communities within states, which is likely to be just as great, with rural and urban areas facing the greatest difficulty in attracting and retaining highly qualified teachers.

As a state and district policy choice, professionalization relies on two broad strategies that have been characterized as screens and magnets (Sykes, 1983). The first utilizes standards to screen recruits to teaching at various points along the career; the second employs rewards and incentives to draw in and retain teaching recruits, increasing the occupation's "magnetic" attraction in the competition for college-educated talent.

Standard-Setting in Teaching

Developing standards of various kinds to produce a highly qualified teacher workforce is a top priority in the movement to professionalize teaching. Standards have a two-fold significance: they "stand for" or represent the knowledge and skill underlying the claim to expertise, and they serve to screen out the unqualified. Beginning in the 1980s, movement on three fronts propelled the prospects for standard-setting in teaching. These included the establishment of the National Board for Professional Teaching Standards (NBPTS), the creation of the Interstate New Teacher Assessment and Support Consortium (INTASC) under the auspices of the Council of Chief State School Officers (CCSSO), and the revision of program accreditation standards for teacher education by the National Council for the Accreditation of Teacher Education (NCATE).

First, following the report of the Carnegie Forum on Education and the Economy (*A Nation Prepared*, 1986), a number of educational groups, including the National Education Association and the American Federation of Teachers, established a new organization in the field—the National Board for Professional Teaching Standards (NBPTS). Modeled loosely on the specialty boards in medicine, the NBPTS has been working for 10 years to develop an assessment process for the voluntary certification of teachers to a high standard of excellence (see The National Board for Professional Teaching Standards, 1994). Teacher certification is intended to signal advanced standing in teaching based on measurable, demonstrable excellence as codified in a set of standards and an assessment process that supplies objective evidence of teaching excellence. The National Board has developed standards in an initial set of certification areas together with a complex assessment system. To date, several hundred teachers have been certified with the full system projected to come on-line over the coming years.

National Board certification represents the potential of professionalism in a number of respects. First, the architects of the system intend that the process of preparing for certification will serve as a form of high-quality teacher development that will enhance the knowledge and skill of those who undertake what is an extensive and rigorous process. Second, the growing numbers of board-certified teachers in the school system constitute a leadership cadre in the field that can be utilized in a variety of ways that might include mentoring of new teachers, school improve-

ment, curriculum development, peer evaluation, and others. Third, the introduction of this new status in the teaching field supplies a basis for merit-based salary increases to enhance the career earnings of senior teachers. And fourth, the standards and assessments may come to exercise influence in defining excellence in teaching, as represented in teacher education, evaluation, and continuing education. The standards and the assessments may serve as instruments for progressively rationalizing preparation for and judgments about teaching.

In addition, board certification and the existence of objective, verifiable standards in teaching serve a less tangible but no less significant purpose for professional prospects. They may come to exercise influence on public perceptions about teaching, serving to modify if not replace widespread views that teaching is relatively easy, non-specialized work akin to parenting that does not require the trappings of professionalism. If the claim to expert knowledge and skill may be represented in standards and assessments that gain credibility and legitimacy in the public mind, then teaching's equivocal status may be elevated in the process, with attendant benefits to teacher morale, commitment, and the respect accorded them by students, parents, and others.

A second development followed from the first. Although standards for advanced certification are voluntary, are under the control of the profession, and possess no legal status, the essential mechanism for controlling occupational entry is the standard for initial licensing that possesses the power of state law. Professionalization advocates have long bemoaned the relatively weak, dilatory standards for entry into teaching. As already indicated, teacher licensing has served neither to represent expert knowledge in teaching nor to screen out the unqualified. Instead, license examinations in most states have been little more than tests of basic skills, and even these are routinely waived in the face of teacher shortages. Consequently, a top priority for professional reformers is to create a stronger, more unified set of licensure standards together with a staged process of entry to the field that gradually builds up the competence of new teachers.

In the 1980s, a number of states began to reform their licensing systems together with other requirements for entry into teaching. Among the most long-standing problems for entry have been the weak support for new teachers, resulting in high rates of attrition from teaching in the early years (see Murnane, *et al.*, op cit.). The short period of practice teaching during initial training, the lack of induction programs in schools, and the prevalence of assigning new teachers to the most difficult classes and schedules have all contributed to early attrition; "sink or swim" is the phrase that has been used most commonly to describe entry. At the same time that license requirements have failed to support entry, they also have failed to screen out the unqualified, both as a function of the standards themselves and of the waiver policies that disarm them. In response, vanguard states such as Connecticut, California, Georgia and others began to reform the system. Early efforts included requirements for mentored induction and the development of new assessment instruments. The Educational Testing Service contributed as well by substantially revising its National Teacher Examination, producing a new set of assessments known as PRAXIS, which a number of states adopted.

Cognizant of these efforts, another project also emerged in this period that aimed to produce license standards and performance assessments that were compatible with the standards established by the NBPTS. The INTASC project seeks to create a continuum of standards from initial to advanced that draws on a common conception of teaching, that employs similar approaches to assessment, and that contributes a unified set of professional standards. Meeting license standards early in the career would thus establish a platform for subsequent engagement in the NBPTS standards for advanced certification. And, under the auspices of the CCSSO, the intent of the project is to propagate these standards across states through a confederated effort, much as medical standards have been diffused through public-professional alliances at state and national levels. INTASC already has issued a set of basic standards (see Interstate New Teacher Assessment and Support Consortium, 1992) and is at work developing assessments together with subject-specific standards that states may use in the future.

Finally, a third policy strand aims to develop standards for the accreditation of teacher education programs. The university-based professional school is a crucial resource in developing new knowledge and in preparing practitioners. Educators all know the story of the Flexner report in medicine that hastened the demise of many weak medical schools, while establishing the model of the modern medical school with its blend of research and teaching. Program standards, then, constitute the "third leg of the stool" together with licensure and certification standards, and efforts are underway to strengthen and renew accreditation for teacher education.

Individual states have the authority to approve programs of teacher education, and most states have program standards, but these tend to vary from state to state, are weakly enforced, and enjoy little credibility within the profession. The alternative to state program approval is the National Council for the Accreditation of Teacher Education (NCATE), which offers voluntary accreditation based on standards developed by the educating professions. NCATE seeks to establish uniform, national standards for all programs that prepare educators and for the professional schools in which such programs are located. Over the past decade, NCATE has strengthened and refined its standards, has increased its denial rate for accreditation, and has made headway in securing cooperation from states that have adopted NCATE standards. At the same time, however, many states still do not recognize NCATE and many institutions do not participate in the process of voluntary accreditation.

Rewards and Incentives in Teaching

Standards may constitute the primary resource in the drive to professionalize teaching, but most observers recognize that efforts to elevate standards, and so raise the quality of practitioners, require a parallel investment in the rewards and incentives in teaching. It little profits the profession, for example, if stringent licensure requirements simply induce a shortage of teachers. Standards, though, are not necessarily the enemy of teacher supply for the historical record reveals that during periods when entry standards were increased, the profession also became more attractive (see Sedlak & Schlossman, 1986).

However, teaching also suffers a number of widely noted and long-standing problems associated with its incentive structure. These include a front-loaded earnings profile, a relatively unstaged career, and an absence of merit or productivity-based rewards. Coupled with the heavy attrition in the early years of teaching, these incentive-related structural characteristics call into question the nature of professional commitment to teaching and the capacity of incentives or rewards to direct the nature of teaching work. Beginning in the 1940s, teacher salary schedules were standardized around years of experience and continuing education, so that all teachers progressed through a stepped schedule that provided modest additional increments, with most teachers reaching the top of the salary scale 15 to 20 years into the profession. Thereafter, earnings flatten out, involving little more than cost of living adjustments.

At the same time, the teaching ranks are relatively undifferentiated. The 20-year veteran occupies the same position and carries out the same duties as the first-year novice. As already noted, these features of the occupation make teaching easy to enter, leave, and re-enter, which is a common pattern, particularly for women interested in integrating their career with child-raising. From the perspective of managing and motivating the profession, however, teaching's incentive and reward profile is deeply problematic. In school districts filled with a veteran, aging staff, administrators may have few financial incentives available to motivate and direct the efforts of teachers who already are at the top of the salary scale and who must move out of teaching into administration if they seek greater responsibility or increased salary.

Interventions to alter rewards and incentives in teaching have featured a mix of managerial and professional approaches, blending reforms drawn from business and industry with others that are more compatible with the professional model. Efforts to introduce career stages in teaching, for example, are based not on predecents in other professions but on business firms, although the line is not hard and fast (engineering, for example, enjoys professional attributes and in large firms may be organized either according to teams or hierarchies). In contrast, proposals to introduce performance-based pay based on national board certification or related processes appear more closely aligned with professional orientations. So, while reward and incentive policies do not derive strictly from professional conceptions of work, they have entered the mix of approaches aimed at restructuring fundamental features of the teaching occupation.

Beginning in the 1980s, many states and localities experimented with a variety of merit pay and career ladder plans, allocating rewards in some cases to individual teachers, in others to schools based on group results. These policy reforms often revived plans that had been tried in the past, particularly those that allocated merit-based pay. A large literature emerged that evaluated and assessed the results of these state- and district-based efforts, review of which lies beyond the bounds of this chapter (see Brandt, 1990; Firestone & Bader, 1992; Murnane & Cohen, 1986; Smylie, 1994; Southern Regional Education Board, 1994), and several summary comments must suffice.

By and large, these incentive-based reforms were tried, found wanting, and then abandoned. Merit pay and career ladder plans each suffered serious defects. Studies of individual merit pay revealed that the plans typically devolved into extra pay for extra work (rather than rewarding merit), distributed the additional monies to all teachers on some rotating basis, and produced low participation from teachers who regarded the modest awards relative to the trouble of applying as not worth the effort. Most plans have died out. With career ladders, the problems stemmed from the creation of additional, bureaucratic positions within districts that failed to produce useful new roles for teachers in terms of instructional improvements. Again, career ladder schemes elevated a few teachers into new positions, enhancing their salaries, but did not introduce efficacious new roles into school work settings.

Historians (such as Tyack & Cuban, 1995) have argued that schools have changed reforms more often than the other way around, and this appears to be the case with both merit pay and career ladders. Fundamental aspects of teaching's ethos, including its egalitarian, leveling tendency and its pursuit as relatively isolated, individualistic work, have frustrated efforts to introduce instrumental status differences into schools or to reward teaching quality on objective criteria that are widely accepted by teachers themselves. Certain delimited new roles, such as mentor-teacher or peer-evaluator, have gained footholds in some

districts and states, and the allocation of incentive pay according to school-wide rather than individual achievement also has met with some success; but the widespread reforms envisioned by those seeking to reengineer teaching work have not materialized.

In summarizing policy approaches to professionalism, several generalizations appear warranted. Standards-based reforms have made notable headway, particularly through the pioneering work of the NBPTS and the companion INTASC project. However, these initiatives have yet to gain widespread recognition among educators or to have broad effects. They are promising reforms in progress, about which an historical judgment concerning their import must be deferred. In contrast, the incentives and rewards-based reforms now appear less promising than they did a decade ago; their transformative potential has dimmed considerably. States and localities have enjoyed a measure of success utilizing traditional measures such as raising starting salaries across the board or creating scholarship, fellowship, and loan forgiveness programs as a means of recruiting new candidates to teaching, particularly as such initiatives may be targeted both to underserved areas (such as urban schools) and to underrepresented minority groups in the teaching occupation (see Darling-Hammond & Berry, 1988). Future experiments with incentives, however, may continue, particularly around efforts to restructure compensation systems according to performance-based criteria and procedures (see, for example, Conley & Odden, 1995; Odden & Conley, 1992), but it is too early to tell how robust such approaches will be within state or district policy.

The School as Locus for Professionalism

As the foregoing illustrates, the professional ideal has served as a powerful stimulus for a line of policymaking and reform that seeks to alter teaching's occupational characteristics together with its ethos. If teaching falls short on one or more of the fundamental features of professionalism, then well-planned efforts must be mounted to introduce those features into the occupation. Gradually, then, teaching may undergo "professionalization" as a conscious, concerted policy choice (Sykes, 1991). Such developments, however, tend to operate at a high level of aggregation, unfold slowly over time, and are relatively remote from the quotidian realities of teachers and schools. Consequently, the professional ideal also has been associated with a set of reform ideas that are more closely reflected in the everyday work of schools.

Taking schools as the locus of professionalism, the analytic strategy is to explore differences among schools on characteristics associated with professionalism, and then seek to diffuse those attributes more broadly across schools.

Rather than concentrating on broad generalizations about the teaching occupation as a whole, this strategy capitalizes on naturally occurring variation in schools, identifying how the organization and management of schools can promote professional orientations among faculty. The construct synthesizing such attributes is "professional community" (see, for example, Lieberman, 1990; Louis, *et al.*, 1995; Weick & McDaniel, op. cit.).

Professional Community Within Schools

Several programs of research launched in the early 1990s identified professional community within schools as an important mediating construct in shaping teachers' beliefs and practices, student learning, and overall school effectiveness. This line of work posits that professional characteristics are not only fashioned by broad occupational processes, they are socially constructed within particular work settings. In this view, although such occupation-wide processes as strong professional socialization are weak, there is significant variation across settings in the professional orientations of teachers. The recent research then explores how a variety of contextual factors shapes professional dispositions and how the presence of professional community mediates teacher beliefs and practices as well as influencing student learning. This social constructivist approach posits a conceptual model that explores connections among four sets of factors: (1) cultural and structural characteristics of schools; (2) characteristics of professional community; (3) dispositions and beliefs among teachers identified normatively as professional; and (4) student learning as measured in a variety of ways.

Two programs of research in particular have contributed to this model, together with related literature (see, for example, Bryk, Lee, & Holland, 1993; Sergiovanni, 1994). The multi-school study completed by the Center for Research on the Context of Secondary Teaching (CRC) at Stanford University, concentrated on identifying the contextual factors associated with secondary teachers' professional dispositions (for reports of this work see McLaughlin, *et al.* 1990; McLaughlin & Talbert, 1993; Talbert & McLaughlin, op. cit.). A second, converging program of research also has been completed recently by the Center on Organization and Restructuring of Schools (CORS) at the University of Wisconsin (for general reports of this work, see Newmann & Associates, 1996; for treatment of professional community in particular, see Louis, Marks, & Kruse, 1996, and Louis, Kruse, & Associates, 1995). This center conducted a series of investigations including a multi-site field study on a sample of schools reputed to be engaged in substantial restructuring. While the CRC study explored relationships between measures of professional community and teacher beliefs and dispositions

(factors two and three above), the CORS study included attention to all four factors.

The CRC study identified professional community in terms of three characteristics. *Technical culture* referred to the presence of shared standards for curriculum, subject matter instruction, relations with students, and school goals. *Service ethic* combined two measures—a sense of responsibility and caring for all students as individuals and expectations for student academic success. *Professional commitment* included devotion or allegiance to teaching, subject matter, and continued professional growth. (A fourth characteristic, *collegial controls* over teachers' performance evaluations and careers, was not included because "None of the schools in the sample has established formal sanctioning authority for teachers" [Talbert & McLaughlin, op. cit., p. 131].)

The dependent variable, teacher professionalism, was conceived as an index combining several dimensions that included the extent of collaboration or collegiality among teachers, teacher opportunities to learn, and encouragement to experiment or innovate (for related work exploring these aspects of professionalism, see Little, 1982; and Rosenholtz, 1989). The study reported substantial relationships between the index of professional community and the professional dispositions of teachers. Furthermore, context effects emerged at multiple, embedded levels of the department, school, district, sector (public-private), and even state (McLaughlin & Talbert, op. cit.). "Teacher professionalism," the study concluded, "depends to a significant degree on the extent and character of local teacher community . . . teachers who participate in strong professional communities within their subject area departments or other teacher networks have higher levels of professionalism, as measured in this study, than do teachers in less collegial settings" (Talbert & McLaughlin, op. cit., p. 142–43).

Within the CORS study, "school-wide professional community" is a normative construct generally directed at staff members taking collective responsibility for achieving a shared educational purpose for the school as a whole and collaborating with one another to attain it (Newmann & Associates, op. cit.). Five elements make up this construct. *Shared norms and values* is most fundamental and refers to the extent of consensus among teachers in the school around a core of values and norms related in particular to student welfare and learning. *Reflective dialog* refers to regular discussions among teachers about curriculum, instruction, and student learning that is both supportive and critical or evaluative. The *deprivatization of practice* is a related characteristic referring to open scrutiny of individual teachers' practices through dialog, observation and feedback, examination of student work, and other means. A *school-wide focus on student learning* reflects an emphasis not simply on students but on the quality of their learning as a regular and shared feature of teacher engagements and activities. Finally, *collaboration* is a natural outgrowth of dialog and openness about practice. Teachers work together to produce materials, co-teach, supply feedback to one another, study new practices, and try out new ideas.

The CORS study associates the presence of these school-wide communal elements with a number of cultural and structural factors. Cultural attributes include a climate of inquiry that encourages teacher engagement in regular study of and reflection on teaching and learning; support for risk-taking around innovations and experiments with teaching, curriculum, assessment, and other core matters; and a style of leadership that relies on delegated authority, shared decision-making, and effective management of conflict. Structural conditions supporting the school-wide professional community include small school size and a reduction in the number of specialized programs that require differential staffing (Title I, special education, and so on). Other structural conditions include school autonomy to create instructional programs, select staff, and organize staff development around local needs, schedules and workspaces that encourage teacher planning and dialog, and professional development that connects teacher learning to shared purposes.

Associated in the CORS study with the presence of strong professional community is a set of carefully measured teaching and learning outcomes. The study defined both "authentic pedagogy" and "authentic student achievement" in terms of a set of standards that were then used to evaluate observed samples of teaching and of student work. Focusing on student learning in mathematics and social studies, the CORS study found significant relationships among the professional teacher community, authentic pedagogy, and authentic student achievement.

Several points are worth noting about these descriptions of teachers' professional community as socially constructed within particular school settings. First, the identified factors and their causal relationships are unclear. A case in point is the concept of collaboration or collegiality among teachers. Little (1990), for example, notes that a wide array of teacher exchanges may be subsumed under such terms as collegiality or collaboration. She distinguishes strong from weak ties, arraying these along a continuum from independence to interdependence. Under the modal condition of substantial independence, teachers engage in the quick exchange of stories with colleagues and the opportunistic search for ideas and practices they may borrow and integrate into their individual classroom routines. Yet greater forms of collegiality involve occasional aid and assistance, supported by teacher induction and mentoring programs and the like, together with the routine sharing of materials and ideas. Strong ties, however, require the interdependence of joint work in which teachers engage with one another on a regular basis on the core tasks of teaching—

instruction, assessment, and curriculum planning. Little (ibid.) frames this continuum in the following terms: "At one extreme, teachers conduct their work as fully independent entrepreneurs. In this conception, individual discretion takes precedence and teachers' initiative on matters of practice is constrained by norms of noninterference and equal status. At the other, teachers as members of an occupational community exert reciprocal influence on one another and on the school as an organization in the interests of a student clientele for whom they accept joint responsibility" (p. 523).

Other concepts as well require fuller elaboration. "Shared norms and values" is a general construct that does not specify the content of either norms or values, while "focus on student learning" also leaves much to interpretation (but see Louis, Kruse, & Associates, op. cit., for greater elaboration). Furthermore, while the CRC study treats collaboration as a professional disposition correlated with characteristics of professional community, the CORS study treats it as a characteristic of professional community. Most likely, the two usages are related. When teachers value and are inclined to collaborate, then a higher incidence of collaboration may actually occur within a worksetting; the causal relation may be circular, not linear. It appears, then, that the model of professional community incorporating its antecedents and consequences is conceptually underdeveloped and causally ambiguous.

An ambiguity of another sort concerns the scope of teachers' professional community. Although the CORS study clearly focused on the whole school as a community, identifying school cultural and structural factors as important supports for community, other scholars describe "communities of practice" as networks linking teachers within or across schools around common interests (for a case study comparing differences between two teacher's professional communities, see McCarthey & Peterson, 1993). Within this usage, professional community may even vary within a teacher. Another study (Spillane, 1995), for example, describes an elementary teacher creating a rich community around her efforts to improve literacy instruction but with a much thinner set of supports around her mathematics teaching, even as she professes the desire to improve in both content areas. This work, along with related studies (see Stodolsky & Grossman, 1995; Siskin, 1994; Siskin & Little, 1995) suggests that subject matter is a significant influence on teachers' professional communities. Teachers then participate in creating communities for themselves that operate within schools, between schools, or as an integral element of a whole school.

The topic of teachers' professional community also raises the problem of teacher authority. Teachers are free to construct professional communities for themselves within the traditional zone of their authority in schools. That domain has been associated primarily with the classroom and with decisions pertaining to the core of instruction rather than with school functioning in a broad sense (Conley, 1991). Professional organization, however, implies increased authority and expanded teacher participation in school-wide decisions. Although the emergence of informal communities of practice among teachers may not disturb the traditional zoning of decisions between teachers and administrators (even accepting that these zones overlap and are contested), the press to implicate the whole school has more profound consequences for power and authority relationships within schools.

The construct of teacher empowerment has been proposed as an element of professionalism, as it refers to increases in teacher decision-making authority and accountability at the school level. Often associated with governance reforms that devolve authority to the school site, the idea is attractive yet elusive. "Does empowerment simply affirm teachers' long-standing classroom autonomy," write Marks and Louis (1997, p. 245), "or does it newly recognize the potential of teachers as professionals to reform education from the ground up? Is teacher empowerment best understood (and evaluated) broadly as a global phenomenon, or is it inherently domain-specific?" Participatory decision-making, advocates believe, can enhance teachers' commitment, expertise, and effectiveness, but much depends on its enactment. Nominal forms may initially entice but subsequently alienate teachers; authentic forms, though, may produce genuine benefits in terms of worker morale and effectiveness. Yet, as analysts have noted, participatory decision-making may actually reduce individual autonomy even as it increases collective efficacy.

Early approaches to empowerment stressed coordination and commitment-building among teachers as an aspect of sound administrative practice but did not establish connections to instructional improvement. Contemporary work, however, explores the relationships among teacher empowerment, school organization, teaching, and learning (see Newmann & associates, op. cit.; Marks & Louis, op. cit.). The most recent studies posit that teacher empowerment is a necessary but insufficient condition for improving student academic performance on complex and higher-order learning objectives. However, this work introduces a crucial distinction in describing empowerment processes that disrupt the traditional, individualistic ethos of teaching in favor of greater collective authority for teachers in schools. Mere freedom from bureaucratic constraints may do little to reduce privatized practice or to direct teachers attention to matters that improve student learning. Empowerment improves instruction only as it works through those school-wide organizational attributes, identified above, that make up professional community and collective responsibility for student learning and welfare.

More particularly, studies using the CORS sample have found significant relationships between teacher empower-ment, participation in the professional community, and collective responsibility for student learning (Marks & Louis, op. cit.). Four domains of decision-making combine to influence overall empowerment: school operations and management (budgeting, scheduling, hiring), students' school experiences (student discipline and behavior codes), teachers' worklife (decisions that directly affect staff), and classroom instruction (selecting instructional materials and teaching methods). Teachers who actually exercise influence in these domains benefit most from empowerment, which results in greater school-wide attention to instruction and to student learning. Although this study's results found no direct effects of empowerment on authentic pedagogy, the various measures of professional community and of collective responsibility for student learning were related strongly to indicators of teaching and learning, leading the researchers to conclude that empowerment exercises indirect effects on the nature of teaching through school organizational factors characterized as professional community.

Based on this research, several conclusions seem warranted. First, when schools combine efforts to empower teachers with a school-wide press to improve the learning environment, then instruction will benefit. Where governance changes proceed with little connection to the core of teaching and learning, they will have little impact. Furthermore, in the domain of the individual classroom, teachers already exercise considerable autonomy, so it is not the most salient decision-making context. What has been termed "collective professionalization" (Marks & Louis, op. cit., p. 265) is more important: decisions affecting mid-level policies regarding school functioning that are broader than single classrooms but still directly related to instructional improvement. Finally, expanded teacher engagement in school-wide decisions will avoid the danger of over-commitment and burnout only if full-school faculties are involved so that additional work can be spread around.

Finally, interest in teachers' professional community raises questions about the scope of community and the nature of school change. One line of work suggests that teachers' efforts to construct professional community in local contexts is a productive means for improving teaching and learning (see, for example, Talbert & McLaughlin, op. cit.). The contours of teachers' professional community may extend across school lines to connect collectivities of like-minded teachers around reform ideas, stimulated by professional associations, school networks, and other means. Another line of argument, however, judges that organizational change at the school level is a necessary precondition for the school-based professional community (see Cuban, 1988). Yet some research indicates that interventions at the level of school structure and governance typically fail to penetrate to the instructional level, so that starting with school restructuring may not yield benefits to instructional improvements (see, for example, Elmore,

Peterson, & McCarthey, 1996). Can the professional community flourish within nonprofessional work organizations? Does the formation of community among reform-minded teachers impel changes in their work organization?

These questions raise the problem of change. Most schools do not resemble professional organizations or feature a strong professional community among teachers. If organizing and organization are needed to support new approaches to teaching and learning, then it would be useful to know more about the dynamics of change around these themes. Guidance for school administrators interested in leading a community of professionals is relatively scarce, and the complexities of transforming bureaucratically organized schools into professional communities must be reckoned with care.

Trends Affecting Professionalism

This review has been largely retrospective to this point in describing professionalism as an historical phenomenon that has taken uncertain root in the teaching occupation. What follows is prospective and speculative in reflecting on the future of professionalism as an advancement strategy. A number of broad trends in American education currently vying for influence may shape the future of professionalism and it is to a sample of these that the chapter turns. First, though, a reminder about American education will set the stage. In U.S. society, education appears at once to be unchanging and in a state of constant change. Fundamental features of schools—the age-graded classroom, one teacher facing a batch of 25 or so students, the Carnegie unit definition of the high school curriculum, the textbook as primary technology, a largely feminized workforce, and others —seem impervious to widespread change, even as local experiments may interrupt such elements here and there for periods of time. Predictions about the impact of trends on such features may well provoke skepticism, for they have proven remarkably resistant to change. From another perspective, however, American education is remarkably open to reform ideas issuing from many sources. Schools are constantly adopting new practices, exploring innovations, revising their curricula, and so on. And, many interests in the U.S. are engaged in the school reform game, seeking to exert influence from points in the system as various as the U.S. Congress, the media, or the local school board (Cusick, 1992).

The notion then that some particular set of trends is likely to exert decisive influence in shaping the future of American education is difficult to sustain. A more likely prediction is that any trend in policy or practice may have influence in some locales, but not others, and may be absorbed into the resilient system of education without af-

fecting any grand transformations. Nevertheless, certain developments today are prominent and have attracted a following. A selection of such trends is somewhat arbitrary and many others might be added to the list below. In particular, enthusiasts might argue that the sun is rising on a new technological era that will transform teaching and learning in our society, and not only in the schools. If teachers, students, and parents can gain access to and can master the new technologies, then a great educational leap forward may be possible that provides the basis for a new professionalism among teachers. However, although advanced uses of new technologies may indeed transform teaching and learning, they may not overcome the institutionalized context of the school system, and so their transformative potential may be blunted at the schoolhouse door. The schools may not change even as it becomes theoretically possible to dramatically enhance learning through the application of technology.

These same arguments may be applied with equal force to the trends selected for review. Each arguably may serve as a basis for change, but each may be thwarted ultimately by opposing forces and by the inertia of institutions. With these caveats in mind, four developments appear noteworthy at the dawn of the 21st century. They include (1) the movement to establish standards and assessments of various kinds as a basis for accountability; (2) the "new unionism" that may redefine the nature of labor-management relations in U.S. education; (3) the effort to decentralize important functions to the school site; and (4) the introduction of school choice into the system of schools.

The Educational Standards Movement

One basis for reckoning the importance of standards comes from cross-national comparisons. Various studies and reports (see, for example, Eckstein & Noah, 1993; Stevenson & Stigler, 1992) portray high-achieving nations such as Germany, Japan, and other Asian countries as possessing a common set of standards that define the content of the school curriculum, the knowledge and skill that students are to master, and definite levels of proficiency or attainment for that knowledge. Such standards are conveyed to educators and to the public through such policy instruments as curriculum frameworks, instructional materials, and national examinations. Teacher education and professional development also are linked to the school curriculum and to the standards for student learning so that a systematic approach to teaching and learning can be fashioned out of the constituent elements of curriculum, instruction, assessment, and teacher education.

By contrast, critics have portrayed the U.S. education system as fractured by multiple competing sources of ambiguous guidance about instruction and as unstable in the face of constantly changing signals and priorities. What undercuts the prospects for greater professionalism in teaching, according to this analysis, is the lack of agreement on what American students should know and be able to do as the basis on which to construct a stable conception of practice. A case in point of this general argument may be located in the Third International Mathematics and Science Study (TIMSS), which characterized the U.S. mathematics and science curriculum as "a mile wide and an inch deep" (see Schmidt, McKnight, & Raizen, 1997). Curriculum guidance in these fields requires teachers to cover too many topics and learning objectives in the limited time available for instruction, forcing superficial treatment of knowledge and skill that is reinforced through textbooks, tests, and instructional practice. Other systemic difficulties include the practice of social promotion, by which students are advanced through the grades without much accountability for what they have learned (see American Federation of Teachers, 1997), and the absence of visible connection between school success and occupational access. Motivating students to engage in academics has proven difficult in the face of widespread beliefs that success in school is weakly related to obtaining a good job or gaining access to advanced education and training (see Steinberg, 1996; Bishop, 1995).

Problems of this order will continue to hamper teacher professionalization, for these are issues that lie beyond the control of individual teachers yet decisively influence the prospects for teaching effectiveness. The system within which teachers work, this analysis proposes, fails to support academic engagement; the remedy lies in creating a strong, uniform set of standards to guide instructional decision-making and to motivate student effort.

Learning standards are important to professionalization for another reason as well: they serve to anchor teaching standards. The vanguard efforts of the NBPTS and the companion INTASC project require validation in terms of student learning. What ultimately justifies claims about teaching standards is their relationship to student learning, even as this connection is difficult to establish empirically. What reformers envision, though, are efforts to use coordinated teaching and learning standards to direct the efforts of teachers. Such standards come together in teacher education and professional development that is oriented around the student curriculum. Teachers situate their professional learning within the context of what students are to learn (see Cohen & Hill, in press). One powerful image of this development process comes from Asian classrooms, where teachers progressively refine their practice around common, well-taught lessons. The phrase for such practice, "polishing the stone," intimates how Asian teachers build up shared conceptions of teaching over time, honing the technical aspects of their profession (for accounts, see Stigler & Stevenson, 1995; and Stigler & Hiebert, 1997).

Educational standard-setting then holds a potential key to the improvement of teaching effectiveness, providing a basis on which to develop and refine practice, to organize teacher learning, and to evaluate teaching. Efforts to set standards for learning are unfolding across the country today at every level of the system. States and districts are engaged in this work together with professional associations and even the federal government as it develops voluntary national tests in reading and mathematics. Questions, though, perplex these efforts, particularly related to governance. Who shall be in charge of standards? Through what process will they be developed and implemented? What kinds of federal-state-local partnerships are best suited to standard-setting in a federal system? How shall public and professional interests be reconciled in determining the content of the school curriculum and the appropriate standards for learning? Although the problem of educational standards is now recognized across the political spectrum, the effort to remedy the problem has produced as much contention as consensus. Some states such as Kentucky have made progress in standard-setting, but others, including California, have experienced turbulence and turmoil in the process, as first one faction then another gains influence over policymaking. So while standards arguably constitute a necessary element to professionalization and considerable activity is underway across the country, the outcome for the educational system as a whole is unclear. Continued attention to standard-setting at all levels of governance is likely, but the outcome of this activity remains in doubt.

The New Unionism

As mentioned at the chapter's outset, the turn to unionism in the 1950s has created a distinctive context for professionalism in education. Over the past 40 years, 34 states have enacted collective bargaining laws, teaching has become the most unionized occupation in the United States, and local contracts now create a complex system of rules that regulate labor-management relations. Teachers have gained much from unionism that at times has been quite militant in resorting to strikes and job actions at the local level together with aggressive lobbying at the state level. In most states today, teacher unions are a powerful political force. Unionization clearly has brought benefits to the teacher workforce in terms of salaries, benefits, working conditions, and protection of basic rights.

But times are changing, and many union leaders today seek to move beyond an industrial-style mode of operating. A new paradigm has not emerged fully, but innovative developments are occurring across the country that signal a shift underway. At the national level, leadership in both the National Education Association and the American Federation of Teachers has begun to call for change and to champion educational reforms of various kinds. At the local level, vanguard unions in a number of districts are beginning to transform labor-management relations. "Labor scholars describe two modes of bargaining, distributive and integrative," write Kerchner and Koppich (in press, p. 7). "In distributive negotiations, the parties see the bargaining table as laden with items each side wants to claim, or preserve, for itself. Bargaining is about dividing up the spoils—money, rights, power—and carrying them away. Integrative bargaining focuses on union and management seeking common roads for mutual benefit. The parties treat each other as professionals and consciously consider those issues which are important to both and the tradeoffs with which each side can live."

Three developments—joint union-management committees, educational policy trust agreements, and contract waivers—illustrate the possibilities of integrative bargaining. Pittsburgh, Pennsylvania has established a joint committee to oversee the district's school-based management reform; in Cincinnati, Ohio, the union and the district removed class size disputes from the contract grievance procedure and placed it in the hands of a joint committee; and, under Glenview, Illinois' unique labor-management constitution, much of the district's instructional decision-making takes place in joint committee. A second innovation, the educational policy trust agreement, is a legally binding bilateral accord that sits outside the collectively bargained contract and is designed to deal with educational issues that lie beyond the scope of the contract. A four-year-long experiment involving 12 California districts has explored the use of this new instrument (for accounts, see Koppich & Kerchner, 1990). Yet a third approach allows individual schools to apply for contract waivers as a means of encouraging experimentation. Waivers provide room for school-level flexibility to accommodate reforms that might be impeded by particular provisions in a union contract, such as class size requirements.

In general, the move toward "professional unions" is associated with greater school-site autonomy, expanded decision-making for teachers, and new forms of accountability in which teachers share certain responsibilities in exchange for increased professional control. The lightening rod for these trends is peer evaluation. A central tenet of professionalism is guild control over standards, while under industrial unionism, management evaluates work and the workers. Beginning in Toledo, Ohio in the early 1980s, local unions have developed peer evaluation procedures that involve teachers in setting and enforcing standards for entry and continuing employment. Some 20 districts across the country, including Cincinnati and Columbus, Ohio; Rochester, New York; and Seattle, Washington, for example, have experimented with forms of peer evaluation, concentrating on beginning teachers but in some cases including interventions around teachers in difficulty.

To date, innovative forms of cooperation between labor and management have unfolded in relatively few districts,

leaving open the question whether these experiments will continue indefinitely as isolated instances or will point the way to a gradual transformation in the nature of labor-management relations. Many teacher unionists today continue to operate within the industrial union model that institutionalizes adversarial relations between labor and management. Vanguard unionists, however, now argue that new forms of cooperation between labor and management are necessary and that teacher unions must engage more pro-actively in efforts to reform and improve education, not as a subsidiary to the main business of seeking wage increases and job protections, but as a central goal of organization that is intertwined with the traditional interest in wages, job security, and due process protections. There is no single blueprint for professional unionism; instead, it appears that local innovations will lead the way, based on good faith negotiations among parties in particular locales where the circumstances are ripe for experimentation.

School-Based Management

A popular reform complementing teacher professionalism is the movement to decentralize decision-making to the school site. If teachers' professional community as a school-wide attribute requires a fair measure of autonomy from bureaucratic constraints imposed from outside the school, then school-based decision-making may be a sine qua non of professionalism at the local level. Further supporting this reform is the call to increase the involvement of parents and other community members in the schools, so that shared governance at the school level among parents, teachers, and administrators is an attractive idea.

Many countries today are experimenting with a variety of decentralization plans and the United States is no exception. Many urban districts in particular have devolved authority to the school level. Notable instances include Chicago, Miami-Dade County, Salt Lake City, San Diego, Santa Fe, Jefferson County (Colorado), Hammond (Indiana), Memphis, and many districts in Kentucky under the statewide reforms there. Although this idea has achieved widespread popularity, the research generally reveals (1) that school-based management has not demonstrated strong effects on school effectiveness or student achievement; and (2) that it comes in many varieties and is often ambiguous in both its implementation and effects (see Malen, *et al.*, 1996; Hannaway & Carnoy, 1993; and Mohrman, *et al.*, 1994).

Accounts of school-based management emphasize the devolution of control over three domains—budget, personnel, and instructional programs. Programs vary in the extent to which power in each of these areas is delegated to the school site and in the governance arrangements that organize decision-making. Other dimensions of devolution, however, include information, rewards, knowledge and skill, and extent of participation. In some districts, all schools participate, while in others, involvement is voluntary or restricted to a subset of schools. A broad continuum of arrangements then stretches across the country, creating new opportunities for teacher empowerment and involvement.

Do teachers want to become involved in school management, though? The evidence indicates that relatively few teachers choose to participate. The time commitment can be great, the skills of negotiation and conflict management underdeveloped, and the pull away from the rewards of the classroom can be frustrating (see Smylie, op. cit., and Weiss, Cambone, & Wyeth, 1992). As well, many teachers have experience with nominal forms of involvement in which their ideas are ignored and their input overlooked. Despite these problems, though, school-based management in some form appears to be a powerful idea that will continue to influence governance and practice. Furthermore, teacher professionalism itself calls on teachers to exercise greater influence over educational decisions, so that these twin ideas are compatible and mutually reinforcing together with the reforms of labor-management relations that further underscore teachers' organized engagement in school reform. What remains to be worked out more systematically is the connection among these governance and structural reforms and the improvement of instruction, which is the direction for future research and development.

School Choice

A final trend that also is exerting real influence in the educational system today is the introduction of various plans to increase parental choice of schools and to stimulate the invention of new schools. As with decentralization, the theme of school choice now encompasses a broad range of plans, the most prominent of which includes interdistrict choice, post-secondary options, magnet schools, alternative schools, charter schools, and voucher programs that may or may not include access to private schools (for review of the issues associated with school choice, see Carnegie Foundation for the Advancement of Teaching, 1992; Cookson, 1994; Henig, 1994; Nathan, 1996; and Wells, 1993).

School choice is a controversial topic in American education today, particularly regarding voucher plans, charter schools, and related proposals. Evidence on the effects of choice is still relatively limited (but see Fuller & Elmore, 1996, and Rasell & Rothstein, 1993) and the literature tends to be polarized between advocates and critics who typically find little common ground. Advocates stress the potential of choice arrangements to enhance professionalism, while opponents perceive various risks in choice. It is too early to tell which predictions may bear out, particularly as it depends on the design of choice plans. The varieties of choice and their impact on American education is a large,

complex issue in its own right; here, a few observations in relation to the topic of professionalism serve as the focus.

Choice advocates have appropriated the value of professionalism, arguing that it will more likely flourish in schools of choice. Chubb and Moe (1990, pp. 86–91), for example, define teacher professionalism as a composite of traits that include sense of personal efficacy, extent of influence over school decision-making, and low absenteeism as an indicator of commitment. Their data indicate that high performance schools feature high levels of professionalism within a school organization that emphasizes teams of teachers, rather than bureaucratic hierarchy. They go on to argue that schools of choice, under voucher or charter school plans, will feature less bureaucratic oversight from the district level and fewer entanglements from district-bargained contracts. Consequently, there will be greater scope for professional community to form in schools of choice than in schools operating within the traditional public system.

In addition to greater freedom from bureaucratic constraints, schools of choice also offer teachers the benefits of small scale, focused mission, and values match between school faculty, parents, and community. Because schools of choice must be responsive to parents, teacher professionalism may be more tightly related to parental involvement, rather than emphasizing distance between parents and teachers. Finally, school choice plans create new opportunities for entrepreneurial teachers to participate in the creation of new schools and so exercise leadership in the field. Again, the teacher as autonomous professional is counterposed to the image of teacher as a bureaucratic functionary in a top-heavy, over-constrained system.

Critics of choice respond in several ways. They argue that choice already exists within the public school system and may be further enhanced through such plans as constrained public choice where districts establish all schools as choice options that are jointly developed by teachers, administrators, and the community. Such plans have proven successful in such communities as Montclair, New Jersey, and Cambridge, Massachusetts where they have been conceived within the context of desegregation policy (see Carnegie Foundation for the Advancement of Teaching, op. cit.). Whereas unconstrained choice options tend to increase social stratification and produce schools that are winners and losers in the unequal competition for students, controlled choice preserves the benefits of professional community without sacrificing education's broader civic purposes.

At this stage in the development of school choice policy, several conclusions may be warranted. First, it appears that school choice is here to stay as a policy theme, although the form it will take is open to question and continuing experimentation. Second, school choice does hold potential to enhance teacher professionalism at the local level by creating conditions where strong professional communities may take shape, but such developments are not automatic. Schools of choice also open the prospect for communities of value to form around parental preferences that may be antithetical to professional ideals, where teacher judgments and standards of best practice are subordinated to the interests of particular communities. This uncertainty about the impact of choice leads to a third conclusion that the details of choice plans will matter together with the overarching accountability framework that is put into place from the state level to regulate all schools receiving public monies. Around this question of accountability, tensions will arise between those who favor relatively few regulatory constraints and those who call for more extensive regulation. In particular, the professionalization strategy relies on state-sanctioned standards for teacher licensing and the accreditation of teacher education programs, while the choice strategy might well dispense with such regulations in favor of allowing schools to hire whatever faculty meets the approval of parents and community. Consequently, at the level of state policy, choice and professionalization advocates are likely to disagree over necessary accountability arrangements, even as they may agree on the value of professional community within individual schools.

Implications for Educational Administration . . .

The ultimate goals of the new professionalism are deceptively simple: to place a fully qualified teacher in every classroom in the nation and to support such teachers' best efforts to promote all children's learning. In pursuit of this goal, a linked set of reforms makes up the professional agenda within the spheres of policy, organization, management, and instruction. Standards occupy a prominent place in this agenda. Standards for student learning are important in directing the efforts of teachers to instructional content and objectives. Equally important are best practice standards of teaching. The future of the new professionalism then depends to some significant degree on the propagation and use of professional standards for teaching, with the National Board for Professional Teaching Standards and the Interstate New Teacher Assessment and Support Consortium leading the way.

State policy is a particularly important arena within which to establish standards for the profession. Within this century, states have made strides in developing license standards, but the task remains to be completed. Recourse to quality-depressing expedients, such as emergency credentials, continues in many states when shortages emerge, so that doubts about the qualifications of the teacher work-

force plague professionalization efforts. Accompanying the development of standards for teaching must be compatible standards for teacher education programs to carefully regulate the production of teachers. In the face of recurrent dissatisfaction with teacher education, the best pathway to systematic improvements appears to be the reform of accreditation policy under the leadership of NCATE.

A combined state and district role is also imperative to alter the systematic features of education that limit teachers' effectiveness. The Third International Mathematics and Science Study is but the latest critique of the American school curriculum as overcrowded, redundant, and fixated on basic skills at the expense of more ambitious learning goals (see also Porter, 1989). Problems of this order are not amenable to "professional" solutions alone; they require public actions by a variety of governmental agencies including state boards of education, departments of education, legislatures, and governor's offices. At the same time, curriculum reform also requires teacher input because teachers are the ones who must implement any changes in curriculum.

England offers the most recent cautionary tale in this regard. There, a new national curriculum was mandated and developed together with new assessments. Initially, the government agency overseeing the process failed to consult with teachers and the results were disastrous. The curricular guidance was overly detailed and prescriptive, covered too many topics and subjects in each of 10 curricular areas, and imposed a heavy paperwork burden on teachers. The upshot? Teachers effectively boycotted the system and refused to implement the new curriculum, prompting its revision (for a concise account of English school reform, see Stearns, 1996). Policy and administrative leaders then must continue the process of reforming instructional guidance but with the cooperation of teachers, for such work lies at the intersection of public and professional concerns.

Along with state and district policy reforms must be improvements in personnel management. School systems are responsible for recruiting, selecting, hiring, placing, and inducting new teachers. Particularly in large, urban districts, these processes can be inefficient and depersonalizing. The early years of teaching are vitally important in launching careers in the classroom, yet the record indicates that in many districts, new teachers are given the most difficult assignments (abetted by seniority provisions in teacher contracts) and are not provided with adequate support. Mentor and induction programs are an especially important area of policy and managerial practice for the future. Although the teaching profession can lead the process of developing standards of good practice, support for highly qualified teachers depends on administrative practices around such functions as recruitment and selection, regular evaluation, staff and professional development, and teacher involvement in decision-making.

The theme of professional community also has emerged in multiple programs of research as an important construct to guide administrative practice. Associated with this idea are structural, cultural, and governance attributes of schools, and each constitutes a potential target for administrative attention. The elusive aspect of this construct, however, concerns the orchestration of these elements so that they bear directly on instructional improvement and, ultimately, student learning. School reformers can begin with any of these starting points, expend considerable energy in making change, yet fail to have impact on the academic core of schooling. One clear precept from the literature on such changes is to begin with ideas about teaching and learning that are rich, elaborated, and open to continuous development. Around such ideas then can school-wide changes be constructed that support the shared or communal vision at the heart of the educational enterprise. Equally important, administrative and other leaders must create multiple, ongoing opportunities for dialog, collaboration, and critique in schools, grounded in close observation of teaching and learning. By increasing opportunities for interaction and for learning, an instrumentally focused community may emerge.

An additional theoretical orientation provides further leads to professional community in schools. Various analysts (Kerr, 1977; Kerr & Jermier, 1978; Weick & McDaniel, op. cit) have identified "substitutes for leadership" as central to professional organization. These are individual, task, and organizational characteristics that neutralize the capability of hierarchical superordinates to influence subordinate behavior. Individual substitutes, for example, include ability, experience, training, knowledge, need for independence, and indifference to organizational rewards. Task characteristics include activities with built-in feedback or high intrinsic satisfaction. Organizational characteristics include cohesive workgroups, rewards not under the control of leaders, spatial distance between superiors and subordinates, and others. Substitutes work in two ways: "They decrease hierarchical influence so that changes can be made at lower levels, where decisions are made. Second, they require subordinates to act in a more professional, self-determining manner" (Weick & McDaniel, op. cit., p. 344). The more substitutes that are present, the more an organization approximates the professional form.

From this theoretical perspective, administrative leadership involves actively creating as many substitutes as possible in order to obviate direct supervision and control. Leading a professional community means building up a rich set of substitutes so that the staff of the organization has the capacity, the resources, and the autonomy to optimally fulfill the organization's mission. This approach to administrative leadership appears to be the antithesis of classic bureaucratic management that operates through hierarchical, command and control structures and processes around the routinization of work. However, as organizational theorists have long recognized, schools have a mixed character: "both the looseness of system structures and the nature of the teaching task seem to press for a professional mode of school system organization, while the demands for uniformity of product and the long time span over which cohorts of students are trained press for rationalization of activities and thus for a bureaucratic basis of organization" (Bidwell, 1965, p. 988).

School management is likely to require some blend of commitment and control strategies (Rowan, 1992) that empowers and enables leadership and initiative on the part of teachers yet also creates accountability frameworks that attend both to public and professional expectations. "A major problem that emerges in professional organizations," write Weick and McDaniel (op. cit., p. 342), "is the problem of control: how to get unity of effort and subordination of individual, idiosyncratic behavior when the interpretation and decision-making functions are in the hands of those responsible for doing the work." The traditional ethos of teaching that favors personal autonomy unconstrained by collective norms and expectations must be replaced with some form of collective professionalism. Striking the right balance, however, has proven deceptively difficult. One evident response has been to increase external accountability over schools via testing mandates, manipulation of incentives such as school-based pay, and others. Some research now indicates that policy measures of this type have not been productive in creating good schools (see Darling-Hammond, 1997; Jones & Whitford, 1997; and Newmann, King, & Rigdon, 1997) and that what has been termed "internal accountability" is critical. Members of a school community must develop ownership in the local processes through which they evaluate their work and its results in student learning. As one administrator in a high performance school put it, "I defy anyone anywhere to come in and say that the state could do a better job of setting standards . . . What people are doing are setting national standards in a vacuum; they are . . . better than nothing, but it's certainly not better than the enacted standard-setting practices that we have here" (quoted in Newmann, King, and Rigdon, op. cit., p. 59).

Finally, administrators are implicated in the growing efforts to improve schools through reforms that are negotiated at the local level, often in the context of school-site management plans, school choice arrangements, and the new unionism. Taken singly and together, these initiatives establish the starting point for change processes that lead to productive collaboration between teachers and administrators. Recent studies comparing school and district deployment of human resources reveal considerable variation in the midst of which are some successful arrangements (see Darling-Hammond, 1997; Miles, 1995; Murnane & Levy, 1996). This is both good and bad news. Many school systems are using human resources ineffectively, while some are achieving success. So the answer to the much-debated question, do additional resources make a difference, is a qualified "yes," depending on how individual schools allocate those resources. Although there is no single best system for using resources productively, some uses do make a difference, and these are best worked out at the local level through planning that involves the community, administrative leadership, and school staffs. Such collaborations may be nurtured through new labor-management relationships, school-based management, and, under the right conditions, school choice arrangements. Professionalism then is likely to flourish when school and community leaders work with teachers in joint efforts to improve schools.

. . . And a Research Agenda

Fueled by state and national developments together with government and private support, research on the new professionalism will flourish in the coming decade.[1] Seven lines of research appear most promising and these may be outlined briefly.

Uses and Effects of Standards

Reformers adopted standard-setting as a prominent improvement strategy in the 1990s, including those stimulated both by professional and public groups. Standards have been developed for curricular content, for student performance, for teacher and teaching competence, and for schools. Many questions surround these standards. On what basis are they to be validated? How do educators use the new standards in their work? How are various standards related one to another? What impact do standards have in regulating the teacher workforce? In influencing teaching effectiveness? In contributing to educational accountability? Standards occupy a central position in the theory of professionalism, but how they may actually work to improve teaching and learning is largely an unanswered question. While the past decade has witnessed an explosion of standard-setting as reform (Sykes & Plastrik, 1995), the next decade requires careful attention to the effects of professional standards and of public standards established by states and districts.

Teachers' Professional Development Opportunities

Awareness is also growing among policymakers and administrators that teachers require richer and better focused opportunities to learn, particularly in the context of new standards. What might distinguish the meaning of professionalism in teaching is the commitment to continue learning as central to the work of teaching. At the same time, conventional approaches to in-service education are widely decried as inadequate, stimulating the search for alternatives. Under this rubric, a number of concerns likely will shape inquiry. One is the relationship between teacher and student learning. Studies in future must seek explicit connections here. Teacher learning will also be a critical issue in future studies of policy implementation, particularly policies that aim to influence curriculum and instruction. And a third focus will be on supports for teacher learning as a fundamental aspect of both school and district organization. Local capacity will be reconceptualized in teacher learning terms, based on the centrality of this factor to reform. Subject matter is likely to play a critical role in this work, given the pronounced differences across subject areas in what teachers bring and in the supports they require for continued learning. Finally, in light of the growing gap between the composition of the teacher workforce (white, middle class) and of the school age population (increasingly diverse), studies also will be needed to explore not only how teachers acquire subject matter and pedagogical content knowledge but also how they learn about students who are different from themselves in many respects. Professional learning then must embrace as touchstones policy, subject matter, and students.

Managing the Teacher Workforce

A third important topic concentrates on how school systems manage such personnel functions as teacher recruitment, selection, assignment, induction, evaluation, and continuing development. Better understanding of effective administrative practices at district and school levels around these responsibilities is needed, which concentrates not only on description of exemplary practices, but on how personnel management fits with and supports the creation of effective schools more generally. In particular, indications are that many districts mismanage support for new teachers in the early years of their careers, contributing to heavy attrition. In the context of the new unionism, these functions may be shared increasingly with teachers themselves, who will participate more actively in mentoring, peer evaluation, teacher selection and assignment, and school-based professional development. Understanding how shared responsibility for these functions influences organizational capacity and effectiveness is an important topic for future studies. Likewise, understanding the impact of state policy on personnel management at the local level is a topic of related importance.

Impact of Resources on Teaching and Learning

Inquiries related to resources may begin with work to conceptualize more fully the nature of resources that contribute to productivity in teaching and learning. Resource studies typically examine the allocation of funds, but more complete accounts of resources may include attention to organizational support, cognitive and interpersonal elements, political stability, and others. Provocative work on resource use has uncovered wide variation in patterns of resource use, together with indications of systematic misallocation (see references cited above). Future studies should explore the impact of alternative patterns of resource use on teaching and learning within the political economy of education at the local level, including attention to organizational and political as well as fiscal patterns of use and impact. The focal question concerns how effective schools and districts are organized to make use of resource inputs to enhance teaching and learning.

Effects of School Reform on Teaching and Learning

The context for efforts to introduce professional community into schools is often whole-school reform. In light of the policy interest in "scaling up" reform (see Elmore, 1996), educators are exploring the spread of schooling models through various mechanisms such as voluntary networks, educational contracting, schools of choice, and others. Across the country, a wide range of experiments are underway to create new schools or to transform existing schools according to new models. Examples include New American Schools, the Edison Project, the Coalition of Essential Schools, the Success for All program, the Accelerated Schools network, and many others. Studies are needed that test the impact of these interventions on teaching and learning and that compare their characteristics and their success. Teachers' roles in such schools are important to understand, together with the relationship between schoolwide characteristics and the nature of teaching and learning that unfolds in such schools.

Interorganizational Collaboration as a Reform Context

Teachers' professional relationships also constitute an important topic for future research. Another prominent development across the country is the creation of extended networks, partnerships of various kinds, and collaborations among institutions aimed at instructional improvement. Schools, universities, professional associations, intermediate education agencies, reform networks, and other entities create a rich set of opportunities for schools and teachers to make connections to outside resources and to enhance organizational and individual effectiveness. Understanding how these entities support teacher learning, student engagement, and school effectiveness is critically important. More particularly, initiatives of various kinds may foster interprofessional collaboration between educators and other

providers of services to youth, school-business partnerships as contexts for reform efforts, and school-university alliances around such entities as Professional Development Schools and such functions as teacher education. Studies are needed to evaluate how such collaborations work and their impact on school effectiveness, teaching, and learning.

Federal, State, and District Policy as a Context for Teaching and Learning

Finally, as this review has indicated, policymaking is a central stimulus for the new professionalism. The policy research agenda includes the study of various kinds of policies' effects on teachers and teaching, the implementation of instructional policy as a function of teacher-learning opportunities, and the impact of multiple policies on teaching and learning where the accretion of policy over time can produce reinforcing or conflicting effects. The process of policymaking is also an important topic for investigation, exploring in particular how public and professional interests are represented and given voice.

NOTE

1. A broad coalition of advocates and analysts has organized a number of initiatives in pursuit of the new professionalism, and this section of the chapter draws explicitly on the work that is being launched. The National Commission on Teaching and America's Future (NCTAF) continues to support R & D activity together with policy activism at state and national levels. Compatible with its agenda, two new R & D efforts also are underway, supported by the U.S. Education Department. The National Partnership on Excellence and Accountability in Teaching (NPEAT) connects the major stakeholders in teaching to a broad R & D agenda that will unfold between 1998 and 2003. The Center for the Study of Teaching and Policy (CTP) will carry out a set of related studies at the core of the new professionalism. The reader should be aware, then, that a network of investigators across the country is actively shaping the agenda for inquiry on this topic.

REFERENCES

Abbott, A. (1988). *The system of professions. An essay on the division of expert labor.* Chicago, IL: University of Chicago Press.

American Federation of Teachers. (1997). *Passing on failure.* Washington, DC: Author.

Benveniste, G. (1987). *Professionalizing the organization. Reducing bureaucracy to enhance effectiveness.* San Franciso, CA: Jossey-Bass.

Bidwell, C. (1965). The school as a formal organization. In J. March (Ed.), *Handbook of organizations* (pp. 927–1022). Chicago, IL: Rand McNally.

Biklen, S. (1995). *School work: Gender and the cultural construction of teaching.* New York, NY: Teachers College Press.

Bishop, J. (1995). The impact of curriculum-based external examinations on school priorities and student learning. *International Journal of Educational Research, 23* (8).

Bledstein, B. (1976). *The culture of professionalism.* New York, NY: W. W. Norton & Co.

Brandt, R. (1990). *Incentive pay and career ladders for today's teachers.* Albany, NY: State University of New York Press.

Bryk, A., Lee, V. & Holland, P. (1993). *Catholic schools and the common good.* Cambridge, MA: Harvard University Press.

Bull, B. (1990). The limits of teacher professionalization. In J. Goodlad, R. Soder & K. Sirotnik (Eds.), *The moral dimensions of teaching* (pp. 87–129). San Francisco, CA: Jossey-Bass.

Burbules, N. & Densmore, K. (1991). The limits of making teaching a profession. *Educational Policy, 5*, pp. 44–63.

Carnegie Forum on Education and the Economy. (1986). *A nation prepared: Teachers for the 21st century*. Washington, DC: Author.

Carnegie Foundation for the Advancement of Teaching. (1992). *School choice*. Princeton, NJ: Author.

Chubb, J. & Moe, T. (1990). *Politics, markets, and America's schools*. Washington, DC: The Brookings Institution.

Cohen, D. (1988). Teaching practice: Plus que ca change . . . In P. Jackson, (Ed.), *Contributing to educational change: Perspectives on research and practice* (pp. 27–84). Berkeley, CA: McCutchan.

Cohen, D. (1996). Standards-based school reform: Policy, practice, and performance. In H. Ladd (Ed.), *Holding schools accountable. Performance-based reform in education* (pp. 99–127). Washington, DC: The Brookings Institution.

Cohen, D. & Hill, H. (1997, April). *Teaching and learning mathematics in California*. Paper presented at the annual meeting of the American Educational Research Association, Chicago, IL.

Cohn, M. & Kottkamp, R. (1993). *Teachers. The missing voice in education*. Albany, NY: State University of New York Press.

Conley, S. (1991). Review of research on teacher participation in school decision-making. In G. Grant (Ed.), *Review of research in education* (Vol. 17, pp. 225–265). Washington, DC: American Educational Research Association.

Conley, S. & Odden, A. (1995). Linking teacher compensation to teacher career development. *Educational Evaluation and Policy Analysis, 17*, pp. 219–237.

Cookson, P. (1994). *School choice. The struggle for the soul of American education*. New Haven, CT: Yale University Press.

Cuban, L. (1988). A fundamental puzzle of school reform. *Phi Delta Kappan, 70*, pp. 341–344.

Cuban, L. (1993). *How teachers taught. Constancy and change in American classrooms, 1880–1990*. (2nd Edition). New York, NY: Teachers College Press.

Cusick, P. (1992). *The educational system: Its nature and logic*. New York: McGraw-Hill.

Darling-Hammond, L. (1990). Teacher professionalism: Why and how. In A. Lieberman (Ed.), *Schools as collaborative cultures: Creating the future now* (pp. 267–290). Bristol, PA: Falmer Press.

Darling-Hammond, L. (1992). Teaching and knowledge: Policy issues posed by alternate certification for teachers. *Peabody Journal of Education, 67*, pp. 123–154.

Darling-Hammond, L. (1997). *The right to learn: A blueprint for creating schools that work*. San Francisco, CA: Jossey-Bass.

Darling-Hammond, L. & Berry, B. (1988). *The evolution of teacher policy*. Santa Monica, CA: The Rand Corporation.

Darling-Hammond, L., Wise, A. & Klein, S. (1995). *A license to teach. Building a profession for 21st century schools*. Boulder, CO: Westview Press.

DiMaggio, P. & Powell, W. (1983). The iron cage revisited: Institutional isomorphism and collective rationality in organizational fields. *American Sociological Review, 48*, pp. 147–160.

Doyle, W. & Ponder, G. (1978). The practicality ethic in teacher decision-making. *Interchange, 8*, pp. 1–12.

Eckstein, M. & Noah, H. (1993). *Secondary school examinations. International perspectives on policies and practices*. New Haven, CT: Yale University Press.

Elmore, R. (1996). Getting to scale with successful educational practices. In S. Fuhrman & J. O Day (Eds.), *Rewards and reform. Creating educational incentives that work* (pp. 294–329). San Francisco: Jossey-Bass.

Elmore, R., Peterson, P. & McCarthey, S. (1996). *Restructuring in the classroom. Teaching, learning, and school organization*. San Francisco, CA: Jossey-Bass.

Elsbree, W. (1939). *The American teacher*. New York, NY: American Book Co.

Etzioni, A. (Ed.) (1969). *The semi-professions*. New York, NY: Free Press.

Firestone, W. & Bader, B. (1992). *Redesigning teaching. Professionalism or bureaucracy?* Albany, NY: State University of New York Press.

Friedson, E. (1986). *Professional powers*. Chicago, IL: University of Chicago Press.

Fuller, B. & Elmore, R., with Orfield, G. (Eds.) (1996). *Who chooses? Who loses?Culture, institutions, and the unequal effects of school choice*. New York, NY: Teachers College Press.

Hannaway, J. & Carnoy, M. (Eds.) (1993). *Decentralization and school improvement*. San Francisco, CA: Jossey-Bass.

Hargreaves, A. (1993). Individualism and individuality: Reinterpreting the teacher culture. In J. Little & M. McLaughlin (Eds.), *Teachers' work: Individuals, colleagues, and contexts* (pp. 51–76). New York, NY: Teachers College Press.

Hargreaves, A. (1994). *Changing teachers, changing times. Teachers work and culture in the post-modern age*. New York, NY: Teachers College Press.

Henig, J. (1994). *Rethinking school choice*. Princeton, NJ: Princeton University Press.

Huberman, M. (1993). The model of the independent artisan in teachers professional relations. In J. Little & M. McLaughlin (Eds.), *Teachers work: Individuals, colleagues, and contexts* (pp. 11–50). New York, NY: Teachers College Press.

Interstate New Teacher Assessment and Support Consortium. (1992). *Model standards for beginning teacher licensing and development: A resource for state dialogue*. Washington, DC: Council of Chief State School Officers.

Jones, K. & Whitford, B. L. (1997). Kentucky's conflicting reform principles: High stakes school accountability and student performance assessment. *Phi Delta Kappan, 79*, pp. 276–281.

Kerchner, C. & Koppich, J. (Eds.) (1993). *A union of professionals. Labor relations and educational reform*. New York, NY: Teachers College Press.

Kerchner, C. & Koppich, J. (in press). Organizing the other half of teaching. In L. Darling-Hammond & G. Sykes (Eds.), *The heart of the matter: Teaching as the learning profession*. San Francisco, CA: Jossey-Bass.

Kerchner, C. & Mitchell, D. (1988). *The changing idea of a teacher's union*. New York, NY: Falmer Press.

Kerchner, C., Koppich, J. & Weeres, J. (1997). *United mind workers: Unions and teaching in the knowledge society*. San Francisco, CA: Jossey-Bass.

Kerr, S. (1977). Substitutes for leadership: Some implications for organizational design. *Organization and Administrative Sciences, 8*, pp. 135–146.

Kerr, S. & Jermier, J. (1978). Substitutes for leadership: Their meaning and measurement. *Organizational Behavior and Human Performance, 22*, pp. 375–403. Kimball, B. (1989). The problem of teachers' authority in light of the structural analysis of professions. *Educational Theory, 38*, pp. 1–9.

Kimball, B. (1988). The problems of teachers' authority in light of the structural analysis of professions. *Educational Theory, 38*(1), 1–9.

Kimball, B. (1992). The *"True Professional Ideal" in America. A history*. Cambridge, MA: Blackwell.

Koppich, J. & Kerchner, C. (1990). *Educational policy trust agreements: Connecting labor relations and school reform, annual report*. Berkeley, CA: Policy Analysis for California Education.

Larson, M. L. (1977). *The rise of professionalism*. Berkeley, CA: University of California Press.

Lieberman, A. (Ed.) (1990). *Schools as collaborative cultures: Creating the future now*. New York, NY: Teachers College Press.

Little, J. (1982). Norms of collegiality and experimentation: Workplace conditions of school success. *American Educational Research Journal, 19*, pp. 325–340.

Little, J. (1990). The persistence of privacy: Autonomy and initiative in teachers professional relations. *Teachers College Record, 91*, pp. 509–536.

Lortie, D. (1975). *Schoolteacher*. Chicago, IL: University of Chicago Press.

Louis, K. S., Kruse, S. & Associates. (1995). *Professionalism and community: Perspectives on reforming urban schools*. Thousand Oaks, CA: Corwin.

Louis, K. S., Marks, H. & Kruse, S. D. (1996). Teachers professional community in restructured schools. *American Educational Research Journal, 33*, pp. 757–798.

Ludmerer, K. (1985). *Learning to heal*. New York, NY: Basic Books.

McCarthey, S. & Peterson, P. (1993), Creating classroom practice within the context of a restructured professional development school. In D. Cohen,

M. McLaughlin & J. Talbert (Eds.), *Teaching for understanding. Challenges for policy and practice* (pp. 130–166). San Francisco, CA: Jossey-Bass.

McLaughlin, M. & Talbert, J. (1993). *Contexts that matter for teaching and learning.* Stanford, CA: Stanford University, Center for Research on the Context of Secondary School Teaching.

McLaughlin, M., Talbert, J. & Bascia, N. (Eds.) (1990). *The contexts of teaching in secondary schools.* New York, NY: Teachers College Press.

Malen, B., Ogawa, R. & Kranz, S. (1996). What do we know about school-based management? A case study of the literature—a call for research. In W. Clune & J. Witte (Eds.), *Choice and control in American education, Vol. 2. The practice of choice, decentralization and school restructuring* (pp. 289–342). London: Falmer Press.

Marks, H. & Louis, K. S. (1997). Does teacher empowerment affect the classroom? The implications of teacher empowerment for instructional practice and student academic performance. *Educational Evaluation and Policy Analysis, 19,* pp. 245–275.

Metzger, W. (1987). A spectre haunts American scholars: The spectre of "professionism." *Educational Researcher, 16,* pp. 10–19.

Miles, K. H. (1995). Freeing resources for improving schools: A case study of teacher allocation in Boston Public Schools. *Educational Evaluation and Policy Analysis, 17,* pp. 476–493.

Mohrman, S., Wohlstetter, P. & Associates. (1994). *School-based management. Organizing for high performance.* San Francisco, CA: Jossey-Bass.

Murnane, R. & Cohen, D. (1986). Merit pay and the evaluation problem: Why most merit pay plans fail and a few survive. *Harvard Educational Review, 56* (1), pp. 1–17.

Murnane, R. & Levy, F. (1996). *Teaching the new basic skills.* New York: Free Press.

Murnane, R., Singer, J., Willett, J., Kemple, J. & Olsen, R. (1991). *Who will teach? Policies that matter.* Cambridge, MA: Harvard University Press.

Nathan, J. (1996). *Charter schools: Creating hope and opportunity for American education.* San Francisco, CA: Jossey-Bass.

The National Board for Professional Teaching Standards. (1994). *What teachers should know and be able to do.* Southfield, MI: Author.

National Commission on Teaching and America's Future. (1996). *What matters most: Teaching for America's future.* New York, NY: Teachers College, Columbia University.

Newmann, F. & Associates. (1996). *Authentic achievement. Restructuring schools for intellectual quality.* San Francisco, CA: Jossey-Bass.

Newmann, F., King, B. & Rigdon, M. (1997). Accountability and school performance: Implications from restructuring schools. *Harvard Educational Review, 67,* pp. 41–74.

Noddings, N. (1990). Feminist critiques in the professions. In C. Cazden (Ed.), *Review of research in education* (Vol. 16, pp. 393–424). Washington, DC: American Educational Research Association.

Odden, A. & Conley, S. (1992). Restructuring teacher compensation systems. In A. Odden (Ed.), *Rethinking school finance: An agenda for the 1990s* (pp. 41–96). San Francisco, CA: Jossey-Bass.

Porter, A. (1989). A curriculum out of balance. The case of elementary school mathematics. *Educational Researcher, 18,* pp. 9–15.

Raelin, J. (1986). *The clash of cultures. Managers and professionals.* Boston, MA: Harvard Business School Press.

Rasell, E. & Rothstein, R. (Eds.) (1993). *School choice: Examining the evidence.* Washington, DC: Economic Policy Institute.

Rosenholtz, S. (1989). *Teachers' workplace: The social organization of schools.* New York, NY: Longman.

Rowan, B. (1992). Commitment and control: Alternative strategies for the organizational design of schools. In C. Cazden (Ed.), *Review of research in education* (Vol. 16, pp. 353–369). Washington, DC: American Educational Research Association.

Schlechty, P. & Vance, V. (1983). Recruitment, selection, and retention: The shape of the teaching force. *Elementary School Journal, 83,* pp. 469–487.

Schmidt, W., McKnight, C. & Raizen, S. (1997). *A splintered vision.* Boston, MA: Kluwer Academic Publishers.

Schön, D. (1983). *The reflective practitioner.* New York, NY: Basic Books.

Sedlak, M. & Schlossman, S. (1986). *Who will teach? Historical perspectives on the changing appeal of teaching as a profession.* Santa Monica, CA: The Rand Corporation.

Sergiovanni, T. (1994). *Building community in schools.* San Francisco, CA: Jossey-Bass.

Siskin, L. (1994). *Realms of knowledge: Academic departments in secondary schools.* London: Falmer.

Siskin, L. & Little, J. (Eds.) (1995). *The subjects in question. Departmental organization and the high school.* New York, NY: Teachers College Press.

Shedd, J. & Bacharach, S. (1991). *Tangled hierarchies. Teachers as professionals and the management of schools.* San Francisco, CA: Jossey-Bass.

Smylie, M. (1994). Redesigning teachers work: Connections to the classroom. In L. Darling-Hammond (Ed.), *Review of research in education* (Vol. 20, pp. 129–177). Washington, DC: American Educational Research Association.

Soder, R. (1990). The rhetoric of teacher professionalization. In J. Goodlad, R. Soder, K. Sirotnik (Eds.), *The moral dimensions of teaching* (pp. 35–86). San Francisco, CA: Jossey-Bass.

Southern Regional Education Board (1994). *Reflecting on ten years of incentive programs. The 1993 SREB career ladder clearinghouse survey.* Atlanta, GA: Author.

Spillane, J. (1995, April). Constructing an ambitious pedagogy in fifth grade: The mathematics and literacy divide in instructional reform. Paper presented at the annual meeting of the American Educational Research Association, San Francisco, CA.

Starr, P. (1982). *The social transformation of American medicine.* New York, NY: Basic Books.

Stearns, K. (1996). *School reform. Lessons from England.* Princeton, NJ: The Carnegie Foundation for the Advancement of Teaching.

Steinberg, L. (1996). *Beyond the classroom. Why school reform has failed and what parents need to do.* New York, NY: Simon & Schuster.

Stevenson, H. & Stigler, J. (1992). *The learning gap: Why our schools are failing and what we can learn from Japanese and Chinese education.* New York, NY: Summit Books.

Stigler, J. & Hiebert, J. (1997). Understanding and improving classroom mathematics instruction: An overview of the TIMSS video study. *Phi Delta Kappan, 79,* pp. 14–21.

Stigler, J. & Stevenson, H. (1991). How Asian teachers polish each lesson to perfection. *American Educator, 15,* pp. 12–20, 43–47.

Stodolsky, S. & Grossman, P. (1995). The impact of subject matter on curricular activity: An analysis of five academic subjects. *American Educational Research Journal, 32,* pp. 227–250.

Sullivan, W. (1995). *Work and integrity. The crisis and promise of professionalism in America.* New York, NY: HarperCollins Publishers.

Sykes, G. (1983). Public policy and the problem of teacher quality: The need for screens and magnets. In L. Shulman & G. Sykes (Eds.), *Handbook of teaching and policy* (pp. 97–125). New York, NY: Longman.

Sykes, G. (1990). Fostering teacher professionalism in schools. In R. Elmore (Ed.), *Restructuring schools* (pp. 59–96). San Francisco, CA: Jossey-Bass.

Sykes, G. (1991). In defense of teacher professionalism as a policy choice. *Educational Policy, 5,* pp. 137–149.

Sykes, G. & Plastrik, P. (1993). *Standard-setting as reform* (Trends and Issues Paper No. 8). Washington, DC: ERIC Clearinghouse on Teacher Education, American Association for Colleges of Teacher Education.

Talbert, J. & McLaughlin, M. (1994). Teacher professionalism in local school contexts. *American Journal of Education, 102,* pp. 123–153.

Tyack, D. & Cuban, L. (1995). *Tinkering toward utopia. A century of public school reform.* Cambridge, MA: Harvard University Press.

Vance, V. & Schlechty, P. (1982). The distribution of academic ability in the teaching force: Policy implications. *Phi Delta Kappan, 64*, pp. 22–27.

Vollmer, H. & Mills, D. (Eds.) (1966). *Professionalization.* Englewood Cliffs, NJ: Prentice-Hall.

Waller, W. (1932). *The sociology of teaching.* New York, NY: Wiley.

Weick, K. & McDaniel, R. (1989). How professional organizations work: Implications for school organization and management. In T. Sergiovanni & J. Moore (Eds.), *Schooling for tomorrow: Directing reform to issues that count* (pp. 330–355). Boston, MA: Allyn & Bacon.

Weiss, C., Cambone, J. & Wyeth, A. (1992). Trouble in paradise: Teacher conflicts in shared decision-making. *Educational Administration Quarterly, 28*, pp. 350–367.

Wells, A. (1993). *Time to choose: America at the crossroads of school choice policy.* New York: Hill & Wang.

Wiebe, R. (1967). *The search for order: 1877–1920.* New York, NY: Hill & Wang.

Wilensky, H. (1964). The professionalization of everyone? *American Journal of Sociology, 70*, 136–158.

CHAPTER 12

Rethinking School Improvement[1]

Karen Seashore Louis, James Toole, and Andy Hargreaves

Will Rogers once suggested that the way to end World War I was to drain the Atlantic Ocean and there would not be any more German submarine threat. When asked how he was going to do it, he is reported to have answered, "Well, that is a detail. I am not a detail man."

Rogers' comment still amuses us after three quarters of a century because we recognize the temptation to proclaim grand truths (national standards, professional community, or every child can learn) while understanding the complex context into which these ideas must fit.

In the area of school improvement, the details have proven so perplexing that the domain has become one of the most researched in educational administration. This chapter therefore needed both to recognize the value and depth of the existing literature and the need to articulate and provoke fresh perspectives on change, practice, and policy.

Ten years ago the first edition of this handbook (Boyan, 1988) contained an excellent review by Firestone & Corbett (1988). The earlier and subsequent comprehensive reviews by Fullan (1982) and Fullan & Stiegelbauer (1991) acted as important references for the field. School improvement has received serious attention by scholars who have engaged in efforts to redefine the field, vigorously mining related areas of organizational theory, public management, and business administration. New theoretical paradigms like postmodernism and organizational learning have generated debates at professional conferences and in print. Most importantly, a new *International Handbook of Educational Change* (Hargreaves, Lieberman, Fullan, & Hopkins, 1998) covers virtually every imaginable topic. It would be hubris for us to synthesize this opus in a few pages, and we do not seek to do so.

Our goals for this chapter are, thus, to briskly review some highlights of what is known and then make the issue of school improvement problematic (to explore why it is so challenging). We introduce a set of frames that, we argue, help to sort the most current research into useful analytic categories. We finally focus on possible future research and leadership perspectives on school change. In each section we seek to provoke new reactions rather than reaffirm current wisdom that is well supported elsewhere.

The scholarly language in the research domain that we review is imprecise. The terms "change," "improvement," "implementation," and "reform" are, along with others, often used interchangeably. We acknowledge that there are significant differences, but we do not compensate for the lack of agreement among scholars whose work has contributed to our thinking. Change (defined as doing something differently) may occur without any improvement (defined as a progress toward some desired end). Change is also different than implementation, which is commonly viewed as accomplishing a set of pre-determined goals, which is, when the goals are broad, categorized as reform. In this paper we will use these terms interchangeably in order to focus on deeper issues and leave it to other authors to propose a definitive lexicon. In general, when we use any of these terms, we mean altering the behavior of school employees or the performance of the school on any set of pre- or post-determined indicators as within the bounds of our review.

Lastly, we want to acknowledge before we enter this territory that the large research base on school improvement has moved us a remarkable distance over the past 30 years. There is a wealth of information to help those seeking to improve schools. At the same time, as we will discuss later, the nature of our educational problems, our proposed solutions, change itself, and the environment in which change happens, ensure that anyone interested in healthy intellectual and emotional challenges can choose this field as an area of study for many years to come.

Research Traditions

Early Research

Empirical research on change in American education originated in the over 200 studies of school adaptiveness conducted at Teachers College between the 1930s and the 1950s (Mort, 1963). This research examined the diffusion of innovations within the educational system and, while criticized for its narrow focus (Firestone & Corbett, 1988), it produced enduring observations about educational and social change. Among the most important findings were that:

- The time between the introduction of a new idea and its spread throughout the entire educational system takes decades, although there is often a "burst of action" during which a new practice is adopted in many schools at the same time.
- Schools vary systematically in their willingness/capability to consider and adopt new practices.
- The various interest groups in the schools and community are critical determinants of the adoption process and its outcomes.
- Innovation diffusion in education is typically an organizational change process, rather than one of individual decision-making.

Strategies of Change

During the '60s, the study of change expanded rapidly. Research began to emphasize goal-directed strategies, identifying "organizational health" or generally improved school functioning as a preferred end state (Miles, 1965). Havelock, Guskin, Frohman, Havelock, Hill & Huber's (1969) comprehensive review of the '60s literature on planned change located three streams of research. The *Social Interaction Perspective* focused on the adoption of specific new practices by individuals, examining the effects of adopter characteristics and social networks on behavior (Rogers, 1983; Carlson, 1965). The *RDDU Perspective* (Research, Development, Diffusion, and Utilization) research model emphasized the flow of research-based information from universities to schools (Guba, 1968). Finally, the *Problem Solver Perspective*, based on the work of Kurt Lewin and the group dynamics research conducted at the Institute for Social Research at the University of Michigan, focused on the process of individual or group change, and identified distinctive stages in the change process (Lippitt, Watson & Westley, 1958).[2]

Empirical studies throughout the 1970s continued to reflect the influence of these research traditions, including the development of the Concerns Based Adoption Model at the University of Texas (Hall & Hord, 1987), studies of educational dissemination (Louis & Sieber, 1979; Goodlad, 1975), and research about successful technical assistance and organizational development (Miles, Fullan & Taylor, 1980), as well as unsuccessful interventions (Gross, Guacquinta and Bernstein, 1971). The major emphasis of these studies was on:

- Illuminating the importance of interactions between external "change agents" and school innovators;
- Examining the impact of external agents on the school at various stages in the change process;
- Identifying mechanisms for overcoming barriers to cooperation between schools, school personnel, and other educational agencies with new ideas or developed programs; and
- Describing organizational or individual characteristics that promote the development of "temporary problem-solving systems."

Innovative Organizations

The new organizational change research model emerging in the mid-1970s, however, shifted temporarily away from finding better organizational intervention strategies and toward an elaboration of Mort's finding that schools vary in their adoption of new practices. This shift was part of a broader change in organizational studies, in which an emphasis on studying coherence in organizational behavior gave way to a fascination with the ways in which organizations exhibit regular, but non-rational behavior. Many studies attempted to locate statistical correlates of change in schools, rather than studying decision-making and intentionality (Deal, Meyer & Scott, 1975; Berman, McLaughlin, *et al.*, 1977; Daft & Becker, 1979; Rosenblum & Louis, 1981). The factors most frequently examined in these were:

- Structural features of the organization, such as size, complexity, formalization, or centralization;
- Characteristics of school "technology" (degree of individualization, pedagogical differences or curriculum focus);
- Organizational climate, including staff morale or past innovativeness; and
- Aggregate personnel characteristics (such as experience or professionalism), student characteristics, (racial or

socio-economic mix), and environmental characteristics (region or political context).

The "RAND Change Agent Study" (Berman, McLaughlin, *et al.*, 1977; McLaughlin, 1990) identified the organizational consequences of federal grant programs designed to stimulate improvement. It was influential in shifting the emphasis away from adoption of innovations and toward implementation. Among the study's most frequently noted findings were that many innovations are abandoned quite quickly and that the organizational characteristics of schools and their settings help to account for this discontinuation. In addition, even implemented programs are often radically changed during implementation through "mutual adaptation," typically making them less potent.

Other studies of federal programs promoting educational change also suggested limited success for the large-scale improvement efforts designed around change models developed in the 1960s (Louis & Sieber, 1979, Herriott & Gross, 1979). Emergent organizational theories, such as those of March & Olsen (1976) and Weick (1976) pointed to the way in which events and structures limit the influence of "change management." The decade of the 70s thus ended with a sense of disillusionment about the possibility of easily engineered improvement in school organizations.

Models of Successful Change and Improvement

During the 1980s, research on organizational change in education began to develop two divergent themes. The first examined policy and practice levers that could explain why change happens in some contexts but not in others; the second focused on the development of better information about the nature of effective schools.

Successful Change Processes

In the 1980s, attention returned to studies of the relationship between education and environment. Meyer & Rowan (1977) emphasized that reform in education is usually imposed from the outside, through changes in social consensus about what schools "should look like," rather than generated from within, through organizational decision processes (Meyer, 1987). This line of research has prompted some policy researchers to argue that external pressures for change can be more effective than the capacity-building or grant-based inducements strategies generally advocated in the 1960s and 1970s (McDonnell & Elmore, 1987).

At the same time, there was a retreat from the large-scale quantitative studies of change conducted in the 70s (induced by declining federal funding for educational research), and an increase in research that attended to issues of leadership and design in the change (Huberman & Miles, 1984; Firestone & Wilson, 1985). In particular, role structures, values, and interactions and collaboration in schools were found to be related to the success or failure of change efforts (Little, 1982; Rossman, Corbett & Firestone, 1985). The capability of these smaller-scale studies to locate factors that seemed to influence the outcomes of change encouraged an interest in revisiting the question of "strategies of change," focusing on how to better manage a change process that inevitably takes place in rather chaotic, unpredictable, and often non-rational contexts (Louis & Miles, 1990).

Effective Schools

Influenced by the results of early studies of high performing schools (Brookover, 1979; Rutter, 1982), the "effective schools movement" moved into higher gear in the 1980s and 1990s. While the initial studies focused on factors that contributed to the success of students who typically did less well in schools, the more recent trend has been to look for characteristics of schools and classrooms that add to the performance of all students. There is a great deal of evidence that change programs that emphasize school effectiveness/teaching effectiveness practices can be successful, even in urban high schools (Louis & Miles, 1990; Stringfield & Teddlie, 1991; Mortimer, Sammons, Stoll, Lewis & Ecob, 1988). Stringfield (1995) has advocated more attention to school-based interventions that use effective schools' research, arguing that "high reliability" (vigilance in maintaining the organizational features that obtain successful achievement outcomes) outweighs other considerations in school improvement.

There are almost as many lists of effectiveness factors as there are research studies. Nevertheless, there are consistent themes that emerge from this line of research that suggest important areas for school-wide intervention. These have been summarized by Creemers (1994) and Scheerens (1992). Most of these authors call for a synthesis of school effectiveness research with school improvement research (Reynolds, Bollen, Creemers, Hopkins, Stoll, & Lagerweij, 1996).

The recent school effectiveness models are subject to several lines of criticism. Many critical and constructivist theorists object to the idea that one can identify specific aspects of the school's culture and/or instructional practices that will improve student learning, particularly if one is concerned with achievement beyond standardized test results. The predictive power of school effectiveness models —even when they include variables that are not amenable to practical interventions—suggest that we know a lot, but not enough to guarantee school success. Finally, the effective schools research is largely silent on the issue of "how to get there"—the process by which less effective schools may become more effective.

The Problem of Change

Our brief review demonstrates that school improvement has been well studied over the past decades, but our knowledge base is never sufficient to keep pace with current demands. That change is a recurring, festering problem reflected by titles like Sarason's (1990) "The Predictable Failure of Educational Reform," and Cuban's (1990) "Reforming Again, Again, and Again." Research has taught us that the problem of change is much deeper than the *adoption* of new innovations. It also includes *implementation* (was the innovation ever really implemented?); *fidelity* (once implemented, did the innovation maintain its integrity and purpose?); *impact* (have students been positively and significantly affected?); *institutionalization* (did the innovation become integrated into the school's mission and organization?); *maintenance* (did successful programs continue to exist?); and *replication* (was it possible to transfer the innovation from one school context to another?).

Out of all these dimensions, one of the most perplexing continues to be how to make changes in the "substantive core of teaching and learning"—what it is that teachers actually do in their classrooms (Tyack & Cuban, 1995; Elmore, 1995; Fullan, 1997). There is a great deal of "school improvement" activity that is ultimately unconnected to any improvement in student learning. As Newmann & associates (1996) point out, it is easy for instructional techniques that are potentially intellectually stimulating, like cooperative learning or student portfolios, to be implemented in ways that promote only lower-level thinking. In exploring why change has been and continues to be perceived as an unsteady course for school organizations, we examine in this section seven core problems related to school improvement that have important implications both for research and practice.

Problem #1: How We Evaluate the Success of School Improvement Efforts

All is flux, nothing is stationary. — Heraclitus.

It is demonstrable that many of the obstacles for change which have been attributed to human nature are in fact due to the inertia of institutions.—John Dewey (1938).

Public discussions about school improvement often focus on a single question: are things getting better or worse? As with most questions that assume a dichotomous answer, the data are mixed. On the one hand, evidence of relatively systematic change and improvement abounds. Over the past

50 years, the rate of students completing a high school education and obtaining some post-secondary experience has expanded enormously. Between 1950 and 1980, for example, the high school graduation rate for the United States rose from approximately 65% to nearly 80%, and it has continued to increase (Fitzpatrick & Yoels, 1992). The same trends are apparent in all other developed countries (OECD, 1998). At the other end of the spectrum, preschool and kindergarten attendance also increased. During this time, the equity education landscape also changed significantly. However controversial, laws governing the education of handicapped children changed opportunities for students who would previously have been consigned to limited roles in society, although it is an incomplete revolution in most countries (Sarason, 1996). The performance of some minority groups—notably African-Americans in the U.S.—on standardized tests has risen, although the gaps between their scores and those of white students have not been eliminated. In recent years, research has resulted in a host of new school-wide improvement efforts that appear to have evidence of success in increasing the reading achievement of disadvantaged students in multiple settings, such as Robert Slavin's "Success for All" and the "Reading Recovery" program (which originated in New Zealand). The positive side of the school improvement story in the U.S. has been documented by Berliner & Biddle (1995) and the annual "Bracey Reports" (for example, Bracey, 1997) that appear in *Phi Delta Kappan*.

On the other hand, there is ample evidence of stability. In spite of generations of work on the part of educators to introduce new teaching methods into American schools, knowledgeable scholars such as Goodlad, Cuban, and Sarason continue to argue that there has been little change in the culture of schools and classrooms. High school teachers who read Willard Waller's (1965) dyspeptic descriptions from the 1930s of the struggles between rigid community values, adolescent subcultures, and powerless teachers believe that they have stumbled on to descriptions of their own school. In spite of massive social efforts to desegregate our schools, minority "graduates" of Head Start programs still enroll in settings that are not well-funded and are less supportive than programs for middle-class students (Lee & Loeb, 1995). There is little empirical evidence that supports the contention that an increased focus on complex student learning (as measured by the National Assessment of Education Progress) has led to improved student achievement. The annual U.S. surveys conducted by the National Opinion Research Center indicate that anomie—an indicator of low social and civic cohesion—is increasing among youth.

The mixed evidence makes it impossible for scholars to give a single answer to the progress of past school improvement efforts. However, we argue that this is not an especially fruitful line of inquiry for the future. Studies that attempt to force a dichotomous answer are often methodologically flawed; others are rear-guard actions that are intended to rebut an over-ambitious conclusion. It is therefore important to view school improvement from multiple perspectives and to expand the questions that have been asked in previous research.

Problem #2: Identifying the Ends of School Improvement

The highest result of education is tolerance. — Helen Keller, (1903).

Education is a wonderful thing. If you couldn't sign your name, you'd have to pay cash. —Rita May Brown (1988).

When school districts battle over innovations such as authentic assessment, site-based management, or a new math textbook, the real disagreements are often not only about whether the program will produce the intended outcomes. Hidden in many educational debates is a deeper question about the legitimacy and desirability of the innovation; critical theorists follow Pablo Freire in asserting that educational practice is a demonstration of assumptions about the nature of humankind and society. The two quotations at the start of this section illustrate the divergence of perspectives that are uncovered in any conversation about the ends of improvement.

We assume that research on school improvement must be attentive to the multiple goals of education (Labaree, 1997). Surveys consistently reveal that educators and the public in all countries expect a great deal from schools, just as they do from other major institutions (Townsend, 1997). Students of organizational effectiveness in the private sector have long cautioned against measuring any sector's productivity against a single standard (Goodman, Pennings & Associates, 1977). However, current wisdom (and the available large-scale databases) in education tend to focus attention on easily measurable cognitive achievement (Maehr & Maehr, 1996). School improvement can become reduced to an "Educational Olympics" or "League Tables" where newspapers publicly report and rank the scores of individual schools on a single test of student achievement. In a few cases, longitudinal data have permitted scholars to examine cognitive growth over a multi-year period. However, other themes that are equally important to both participants in the system and those who receive its graduates have snared little attention in recent improvement research.

Kliebard (1995) and Brouillette (1996) identify four broad categories of educational goals: *humanist* (an emphasis on traditional, rigorous academics; a classical liberal education to pass on the culture's heritage); *developmental* (emphasis on the whole child; instruction focused more on the process than product of learning); *social efficiency* (emphasis on vocation and employability skills to produce a vibrant economy); and *social meliorist* (emphasis on social justice, giving equal opportunity and outcomes to all students; education as an agent of social change). Any improvement agenda may make appeals to one or more of these categories. The four rationales are continually updated to address emerging social and political trends (for example, a current social efficiency argument is to prepare youth for the "knowledge age" with a "high literacy" curriculum) (Resnick, 1987). Clearly there are also other goals that individuals and groups might have for their own children.[3]

Problem #3: Choosing the Means of School Improvement

But to manipulate men, to propel them toward goals that you— the social reformer—see, but they may not, is to deny their human essence, to treat them as objects without wills of their own.—Sir Isaiah Berlin (1958).

Just as we have different ideas about what should happen when schools change, we also disagree about how we can effect improvement. In most countries today there are a variety of common policy levers that are simultaneously expected to foster educational reform (McDonnell & Elmore, 1987). These levers are based on very different assumptions about where and how improvement might be initiated.

School improvement research has typically assumed that the source of change was the "educational establishment," variously defined as teachers, educational administrators, and teacher preparation programs. In other words, change in schools was largely a function of the preferences of those who benefit from the status quo. In reality, however, this assumption is historically and currently at odds with the quotidian nature of educational reform: the impetus for change comes from multiple sources and pursues multiple inconsistent purposes. In most countries, increasing influence over school change activities is applied from disparate sources, ranging from unions to political groups. Yet most studies of school improvement still tend to limit their inquiries to what is happening within the system itself and focus on creating the conditions in which all (or most) members assent to the ends and means in question.

Studies of school improvement have, thus, typically acknowledged only the most local and immediate policy environment of schools: *this* classroom, *this* program, *this* year, *this* district, or occasionally *this* state/province. Often little attention is paid to the oral and actual history of the school and locality, although these may have a significant impact on how and what is happening at the present.

Although the work of Tyack and Cuban (1995) has focused attention on the historical dimensions of school improvement, less attention is paid to the dominant national and international policy streams that create the setting for change efforts than is warranted. At the end of the 1990s, these are largely subsumed under the headings of systemic reform, decentralization and school-based management, and parental choice. Although these are the broad public debates over the means to improve schools that affect current policy initiatives within individual districts and schools, they will inevitably shift over the next decade. What we are calling for is not studies of how particular pieces of legislation are implemented (or not), but for research that takes a historical and policy perspective in studying school change at the local level.

Problem #4: The Wicked Nature of School Improvement Problems

Disorder is the condition of the mind's fertility . . . since its fertility depends upon the unexpected, it depends rather on what we do not know . . . than what we know.—Paul Valéry, contribution, Southern Review *(Winter, 1940; tr. Jackson Mathews).*

Approaching the problem of change, we argue that school improvement is not just complicated but inherently chaotic and unpredictable in the short term. In our increasingly complex world, problems are becoming correspondingly more complex.[4] The new classes of social problems are "wicked" instead of "tame" (Mason & Mitroff, 1981), which means that they are not amenable to solution through traditional linear planning and management initiated activities. What are the characteristics of "wickedness" as they can be viewed in education?

- *Lack of a definitive formulation.* The "problem of school improvement" is defined in so many ways that it is not possible to arrive at a single, agreed upon definition even within a group of like-minded individuals.
- *Problem interconnectedness.* Discussions of school improvement inevitably drift toward other identified social problems. We cannot discuss improving education without running squarely into issues such as school financing, poverty and its increasing concentrations in inner-city areas, the "new immigrants" and issues related to bilingual education, and higher education's role in preparing teachers and administrators.
- *Multiple explanations for every aspect of the problem.* Is the low performance of minorities due to racial and cultural issues, or to poverty? Would focusing the curriculum induce higher cognitive development, or do we need to address "multiple intelligences?" Is the problem with bilingual education that it should be improved or eliminated?
- *Separation of direct links between cause and effect.* In complex systems, causal connections are often indeterminate

and distant in time. Improving schools in such non-linear feedback systems (Stacey, 1992) increases the level of conceptual and practical difficulty.

- *Depending on the diagnosis, the solution may be different.* If the problem is racial and cultural, Afrocentric schools might provide a key; if the problem is poverty and economic segregation, then other solutions are more appropriate.
- *No simple ways of choosing between solutions.* If we could experiment, we might find an answer to some dimensions of the problem. However, the most significant issues, such as race versus poverty, are not amenable to valid and ethical experimentation.
- *Many leverage points.* Because the problems are multidimensional, experimentally manipulating one dimension is rarely possible. From a practical perspective, every school is involved with multiple and overlapping improvement programs, even if they are not formally identified as such.
- *Lack of closure.* School improvement is not a solvable but an open-ended problem. Many problems, even when successfully addressed, never go away. They need constant tending and new refinements for "success" to continue.

As teachers work to improve their schools, they are both energized and exhausted by the challenge of facing wicked problems. As Evans (1996) comments on today's schools, "Never have so many teachers and administrators worked so hard or so long and felt less rewarded or more alone" (p. iii). Although Evans doesn't mention it, the investment of great effort, coupled with limited progress, is a sign that teachers are struggling with wicked problems.

Problem #5: Schools Are a Dynamic and Uncertain Environment for Change

The art of progress is to preserve order amid change and to preserve change amid order.—Alfred North Whitehead (Forbes, *December 1, 1957).*

School improvement is more difficult because educators must try to solve wicked problems in what might be called an equally wicked environment (i. e., one that is dynamic and uncertain). A favorite teacher cliché for many years has been that school improvement was like changing a tire while going down the freeway at 90 miles per hour. It has been educators' way of saying that the organizational conditions in which they work are hostile to the thoughtfulness and time-intensive nature of improvement efforts.

It is not hard to locate examples of "change-unfriendly" environmental conditions that exist in schools. The tenure of superintendents who provide at least one source of pressure and support for local school improvement is increasingly brief. No one can predict what will happen with the multiple lawsuits that challenge current school financing and governance, or legislative efforts to introduce vouchers. The schools that most need to institute compelling change are often burdened by high staff turnover. Experiments in high stakes accountability are introduced in most states, in spite of the limited evidence that society is willing to pay for a reliable accountability system (Linn, 1998).

This instability of school environments must be integrated into any powerful conceptualization of productive change. Our concepts of change are critical because they invisibly dictate the types of strategies, expectations, and research questions that we pursue. The traditional assumptions about change have been built on the seventeenth century Newtonian view that postulated a world crafted like a fine clock set in motion by God (Stoll & Fink, 1994). If the educational world worked in this manner, then vision statements, top-down leadership, strategic plans, and good social engineering would be rewarded by measured, predictable outcomes (Morgan, 1997; Caine & Caine, 1997). Fullan (1993) talks about this as making the world better by brute sanity.

There is an alternative view that illuminates unplanned change and the interactions between order and chaos in organizations. It applies the emerging insights from biology, quantum physics, and chemistry to organizational life (Wheatley, 1992; Stacey, 1992; Morgan, 1997; Caine & Caine, 1997). The seminal metaphor for this competing perspective is that we live in a world where "a butterfly stirring the air today in Beijing can transform storm systems next month in New York" (Gleick, 1988). The butterfly does not "cause" distant storms. Rather, insignificant disturbances in one part of a system can have a substantial impact because they trigger a small change that triggers another and, by chance, eventually moves a system (Morgan, 1997). Examples of "butterflies" that might affect school improvement could be that the outbreak of a war in Somalia had great impact on the enrollment, staffing, culture, and programs of the Minneapolis school system months later. In another example, a collapse in the Asian financial markets may send strong ripples through the economy, and indirectly the schools, in the Pacific Northwest for several years.

At the same time, it is important to note that not all the chaos, complexity, and uncertainty in the educational world can be accounted for by transposing the principles of chaos theory over rational science (Hargreaves, 1993). Indeed, it may be politically evasive to rationalize all apparent educational chaos and complexity in this way. In many weaker educational systems, policy research has exposed how much of the chaos in education is actually *manufactured chaos*. The "butterflies" are governments whose policies may have reduced confidence in public education, while at the same time demanding untested reform at an increased pace and intensity.

Problem #6: Developing Wicked Solutions to Meet Wicked Problems

For every complex problem there is a simple solution that is wrong. —U.S. aphorism.

As we move into the next century, public pressure for reforms in education has become much more complex than higher performance in the three Rs of reading, 'riting and 'rithmatic. We have gone, at the beginning of the 1980s, from calls for a longer school day and more rigorous coursework to demands for nothing less than a transformation of the schools and rigorous standards and accountability for student achievement. Innovations and focused improvement programs have been replaced with systemwide reform programs not only in the U.S. but a number of other countries as well. All developed countries are being challenged to revitalize education and meet the demands of the emerging national and global economies (for a highly-skilled workforce), of persistent social problems (for competent and active citizens), of under-served groups (for equity and opportunity in education), and, in some cases, of positive youth development (for healthy people and communities).

While we label the problems and environment of change as wicked, the proposed solutions themselves often embody some of the same elements of wickedness (such as solution interconnectedness). This should not be surprising. The same features that make problems wicked make school improvement models challenging to formulate and implement. Proposed innovations, like fostering a professional learning community among teachers or designing authentic learning in the classroom, simultaneously involve technical, social, political, interpersonal, historical, personal identity, structural, and leadership dimensions of the school.

Organizational change research will inevitably follow the efforts that are made to alter structures, role definitions, and expectations of school systems. Whether or not these reforms are successful, the research questions that will be used to examine them will be increasingly complex. In preparation for developing better research questions, it is useful to review theoretical frames in the rest of this chapter that may be used to generate such questions, some of which have been applied in only limited ways.

Problem #7: The Need to Reconfigure School Improvement Research Knowledge

From our earlier discussion of the research traditions, we can see that our past thinking has been dominated by a number of critical assumptions that are necessary but insufficient for successful change:

- The school is the unit of change;
- The emphasis is on a systematic (planned) approach within the school;

- Internal capacities, including planning skills, leadership, and appropriate school cultures are prerequisite for change; and
- External support is needed from authoritative or professional agencies and networks.

Looking over the first six problems cited in this section, it is not surprising that we hear increasing criticism from many quarters of the assumption that change can be "managed" by focusing resources around these four assumptions. Planned change approaches are criticized for their confidence in a linear improvement process and the "manageability" of organizations (Louis, 1994). Mintzberg (1994) described *The Rise and the Fall of Strategic Planning*; Beer, Eisenstat & Spector (1990) formulated the problem as "Why Change Programs Don't Produce Change." Morgan (1997) asserted, based on his research, that an individual's direct leverage over work results, and by extension a school's capability to influence a change process and outcomes, is very limited. Along the same theme, one popular "solution" to increased organizational productivity—Total Quality Management—was shown to fail for 70% of those who implemented it (Beer, *et al.*, op. cit.), and some excellent companies identified by Peters & Waterman (1982) appeared to be in trouble after a three-year follow-up (Easterby-Smith, 1990). Thus the problems cited in this section—the wicked nature of the problems, environments, and solutions involved in school improvement—are asking for new and more generative conceptualizations of both the "change problem" and of school improvement paradigms.

Although recognition of the problems involved in school improvement fosters humility, it should not amend the intensity of our efforts to meet the current pressing needs of youth and schools. The challenge facing research and practice in school improvement is to work within the "wicked problem" assumptions noted above. Two of the authors of this review regularly show a short film on river rafting to staff development audiences and ask teachers if they see any analogies to their lives in school. Teachers laugh in recognition. But as one insightful teacher who was an experienced outdoor enthusiast recently observed, if you go into the whitewater pointing the right direction, you are much more likely to come out whole. So it becomes critical for organizations to learn what is the right direction to head into the educational whitewater.

"The reform movement" in the U.S. and other countries is now more than a decade old. There are increasing numbers of journalistic and more systematic reports that demonstrate that it is possible to find exciting public schools where administrators, teachers, and parents collaborate to produce higher achievement for more students. Nevertheless, the spread of restructuring is limited: most schools (and districts) do not have the ideas or the internal resources to grapple with the basic challenge being posed. We often see districts that have restructured by proclamation, but in which schools are engaged in activities that maintain the status quo. More often than not this is due to a mix of good will with an inability to envision other ways to organize and practice.

School Improvement and Change, or School Development?

To advance research and practice in the area of school change, the concept of school development (Voogt, Lagerweij, and Louis, in press) provides an expanded and alternative paradigm from school improvement. School development is the result of three influences, and therefore integrates under-researched components of the change process:

- *Planned efforts* (from within and from outside) to bring about educational and organizational changes;
- *Autonomous developmental* processes (organizational life cycles) that cover natural processes such as the aging and replacement of staff, cultural changes in response to internal and external evolution, and changes in technology or other core components of organizational functioning; and
- *Major anomalies, and minor unanticipated events*, both positive and negative, that must be factored into the organizational learning process. These might include unanticipated deaths or departures of key people, radical changes in environmental characteristics or policies over a short period of time, or newsworthy events such as fires.

The three incorporate both the small proportion of improvement outcomes that can be directly affected by deliberate efforts to improve and the much larger proportion that is not directly subject to planned intervention. This leads to the following definition: School development is a process that occurs as a result of the interacting influences of three sources of change—that which is deliberately planned, that which is naturally occurring in the life cycle of organizations, and that which is unforeseen or unknowable in advance.

What is surprising in studies of school improvement is the lack of powerful empirical evidence for the unplanned components of the development process. Too often analyses of organizational change examine planned or strategic efforts, while noting only in passing that unplanned change is also important (Daft & Huber, 1987). More unplanned organizational learning is also increasingly considered as an additional "tool" to create more effective organizations (see, for example, Smylie, Lazarus & Brownlee-Conyers, 1996), although we know little about when or how unplanned but productive change occurs. Less attention than is desirable is paid to the indirect effects of "normal crises" on school functioning, although there are many case studies that testify to its impacts on learning and development (see, for example,

Rollow & Bryk, 1995; Louis & Miles, 1990). Even less research emphasis is placed the developmental life cycles of school (see Sarason, 1972, on new organizations, and Tichy, 1981, on the relationship between autonomous development cycles and planned change.)

We report one example of the complementary and real-life effects of the three streams of change implementation in a case of service learning in a K–8 school (Toole, forthcoming). In this school, the vice-principal's initial *planned strategy* was to send two respected teaches to a national conference to become knowledgeable and hopefully inspired about the concept. The potential support for service learning might have been predictably limited because of what was happening in the *autonomous stream* of school change (an aging staff, many of whom had increasing family obligations), and cultural changes caused by *unanticipated events* (political demands for higher student achievement and a recent expansion from 20% to over 50% of students qualifying for free and reduced lunch). These naturally occurring and unpredictable changes in the school environment had created more "whitewater" in teachers' days and left less enthusiasm about new programs.

In this case, however, the stream of *unanticipated events* also worked in favor of school change. Returning from the national conference, the two teachers announced an after-school meeting for anyone who wanted to hear about service learning. When they showed up, the two were shocked to find virtually the entire staff in attendance. When one of the convening teachers expressed her astonishment, the audience burst out laughing and revealed that they had come to surprise her on her 40th birthday. In return, the birthday person laughed and told them that they all had to learn about service learning before one piece of cake was cut. An hour later, the cake was cut and a major school-wide commitment and implementation of service learning had begun that would last several years.

Frames for Understanding Improvement

Frame analysis complements the emerging notions of school development because it is particularly well adapted to the understanding of "wicked problems." In the classic tale, five blind men describe the same elephant differently because each touches a different part. What is intriguing and timeless about the tale is that the men are accurate in what they describe, but each individual's perspective is limited to one dimension of "elephantness" (Toole, forthcoming). In a similar fashion, educational thinkers today are increasingly aware that complex organizations must be described and understood systemically, not from any one position. The perspectives chosen by organizational researchers to study and manage the organizational elephant have been variously called frames (Bolman & Deal, 1997; Carlson, 1996; Har-

greaves, Shaw, & Fink, 1997; Telford, 1996), metaphors (Wincek, 1995; Morgan, 1997), paradigms (Barker, 1992), mental models (Senge, 1990), images (Firestone, 1980), and dimensions (Eisner, 1992). Goffman's sociological theory of *Frame Analysis* (1975) was an early precursor for these works.[5] What these authors have in common is their advocacy for using multiple perspectives to study the same element of a system, such as leadership or change. Just as compelling as the multiple perspectives are the interrelationships and interdependence between frames—like a mobile, it is hard to touch one frame without setting off a reaction in all the others.

There is no incontrovertible number of frames. Their value—for researchers and school practitioners alike—is heuristic insofar as they point to neglected or hidden questions about school improvement and educational change, as well as helping to put more common questions in a new context. We use Hargreaves, Shaw & Fink's (1997) explication of seven frames—the purpose, cultural, structural, political, leadership, learning, and emotional—as pertinent for understanding and discussing the wicked problem of school improvement.[6]

Much previous work on frame analysis has been directed towards educating leaders how to manage organizations (Bolman and Deal, 1997; Telford, 1996), but this chapter will begin by applying frames to research on school improvement and change.[7] We have added metaphors for each frame (Toole, forthcoming), borrowing sometimes from the authors above and sometimes substituting our own notions of what best captures the relationship between the frame and change. Our choices of metaphors are important both because they reflect our beliefs and because they shape how we see (Wincek, 1995). In addition, recent research indicates that metaphors can be very useful in working with administrators and teachers to change their approach to leadership and school improvement (Dana and Pitts, 1993; Hargreaves, Earl, and Ryan, 1996).

While the use of the frames is relatively common in the organizational literature, the application of frame analysis to the problem of school improvement in empirical research is less so.[8] However, we see considerable potential for frame analysis to illuminate the empirical questions and issues related to "wicked problems." One recent example is Hatch's (1998) analysis of the difficulties faced in the early development of the ATLAS project, one of several "New American Schools Development Corporation" designs. The ATLAS project deliberately brought together four "innovation entrepreneurs" who had a solid national track record in developing both the theory and practice of educational reform. The four, and their associated teams, came together because they shared the belief that the wicked problem of creating effective schools required their combined talents. Yet each group brought to the joint project the "elephant issue" in their deeply espoused theory of actions, which led them to identify different problems, change strategies, participants, and resources as "most critical." Differences in assumptions made the ATLAS development process extremely difficult, in spite of high levels of personal and institutional commitment. This single case illustrates the assumption that although many educators have a passing familiarity with the concept of frames, their application of the theory to problems of change is still limited. With a "frame intervention," differences in assumptions would not be eliminated but clearly acknowledged in the design process.

1. The Purpose Frame: Organizations as a Compass

Scratch a good teacher and you will find a moral purpose. — Michael Fullan (1993, p 10).

Greatness is a road leading toward the unknown.—Charles De Gaulle quoted in Esquire *(Dec. 1991).*

Purpose is at the heart of organizational life.[9] As March and Sutton (1997) write, "Organizations are commonly defined as instruments of purpose" (p. 698). Purpose involves directing an organization's energies towards changing the world into a better place (Kofman and Senge, 1995). It is more significant than a goal, which is about getting things done (Louis and Miles, 1990) and is often guided by the larger ends of education that we have discussed previously. The purpose frame is crucial for the professional fields, like education, since they, by definition, involve moral as well as a technical endeavors (Durkheim, 1956; Hargreaves & Fullan, 1998; Sergiovanni, 1994). The language spoken in this frame includes vision, direction, ownership, consensus, transparency, embeddedness, authenticity, coherence, values, outcomes, passion, and impacts—terms that are frequently found in current empirical research on school reform.

The central question of this frame is: *what is the purpose of school improvement?* This is, as we noted above, a question that is not always adequately addressed in school improvement research. Ideally, the purpose should provide guidance in determining how the innovation will enhance the schools' pursuit of high quality learning (Newmann & associates, 1995). As a metaphor, purpose acts as a strategic and moral *compass* for the implementation process.

But purpose does not just happen to a school. Many mission statements hang on the walls of district offices, having no impact on teaching and learning. Schools may pursue grants to address critical needs—or merely to bring in extra dollars (McLaughlin, 1990). The frequent misapplication of new technologies in schools is a prime example of this (Levin & Riffell, 1997). Just as Hargreaves

(1995) warns about contrived collegiality, purposes are sometimes little more than a public posture. Developing a genuine, animating, and practical rationale for education has been identified in many studies as central to school change in a today's society (Goodlad, 1990; Conley, Dunlap and Goldman, 1992; Daloz, Keen, Keen, & Parks, 1996; Labaree, 1997).

The compass metaphor has multiple meanings, however. In a rational world, we would develop a strategic plan and use our institutional tools to map our route towards a predetermined, fixed outcome. Through procedures of school-based planning and the like, this is a familiar school improvement approach. But the compass will need to play a different role if the routes and destinations are less clear. Wheatley (1992) states that "There are no pre-fixed, definitely describable destinations" (p. x). Purpose doesn't necessarily precede practical action and even schools that are well long on the school improvement path will spend some time lost in the woods (Louis & Miles, 1990; Fullan & Hargreaves, 1991). The compass will help schools remember where they are and permit a choice among alternative paths, but it will not help them to locate the precise destination, which is unknowable in advance.

The theme of purpose and vision is embedded in many recent school improvement studies. Leithwood and Jantzi (1997) use survey data to demonstrate that an administrator's "transformational" influence is affected by teachers' perceptions of leadership in providing a vision. Qualitative interviews (Conley, Dunlap, and Goldman, 1992) indicate that when teachers and principals are motivated by common purpose, they can use it to bring about significant change. Louis and Miles (1990) found that working on a common vision helped urban schools positively face huge challenges, and claimed that "few really excellent schools lack (visions)" (p. 219). In the difficult work of implementing instructional innovations, clearly and jointly held purposes help give teachers and administrators an increased sense of certainty, security, energy, coherence, direction, and accountability (Rosenholtz, 1989; Conley, Dunlap, and Goldman, 1992). Hargreaves, Earl, and Ryan (1996) note that this must be a "moving mission" that constantly adapts to changing circumstances and children.

Yet although the importance of purpose is attested to in virtually every recent school change *study*, many change *programs* assume it rather than enabling it. For example, only a few of the New American Schools Projects provide a structured process whereby communities can come together both to form and implement new directions for their schools (Stringfield, Ross & Smith, 1996). Qualitative studies of school restructuring suggest that schools that work hard to establish common purpose still find it very difficult to do so (Newmann & Associates, 1997).

2. The Structural Frame: Organizations as Architecture

A schedule defends from chaos and whim . . . It is scaffolding on which a worker can stand and labor with both hands at sections of time. A schedule is a mock-up of reason and order — willed, faked and so brought into being. — Dillard (1989).

Streams have more than one response to rocks; otherwise, there'd be no Grand Canyon. Or else, Grand Canyons everywhere.— Wheatley (1992, p. 16).

The central question in the structural frame is: *How does the school need to be restructured to support the purposes and processes of improvement?* Time and space, roles and responsibilities, policies and resources are the focus of this question (Bolman & Deal, 1997). Structural decisions help determine everyday patterns of school life like class schedules, student groupings, teacher assignments, budgets, building layouts, divisions of subject matter, teaching materials, and even teaching content. Curriculum frameworks, for instance, if well-developed, can offer content structure that can give schools "raw material for visions, inspire hope, and add coherence to dispersed, segmented programs" (Louis & Miles, 1990, p. 247).

A commonly used metaphor for this frame is that organizations have typically been assembled like factories or machines (Morgan, 1997). If the school is adequately engineered, then its components will function smoothly. In this metaphor, employees become production-line workers who transform raw material (students) into finished products (predetermined outcomes) (Cubberley, 1916 in Wincek, 1995). Bolman and Deal (1997) point out that "the structural perspective is not inherently as machinelike or inflexible as many often believe" (p. 39). Ideally structure is emergent, flexible, and functional (Wheatley, 1992). In her best team experiences, Wheatley (1992) points out that people were so focused on getting things done that "our roles and tasks moved with such speed that the lines between structure and task blurred to nothing" (p. 22).

However, in most schools this image of constant flux would appear overwhelming, so we would propose organizations as *architecture* as a more suitable metaphor. Organizations have a geometry of their own as they divide time, space, and job responsibilities by length, width, density, shape, and ratios. If we accept architecture as a metaphor for school structure, it is with the understanding that there will be constant remodeling going on throughout the life of vibrant organizations.

Many advocates of school reform have defined the structure of schools as a central problem (Murphy, 1992). Large-scale studies in the U.S. suggest that emerging constructivist models of teaching and learning don't fit into the traditional structures (Newmann & associates 1997; Cohen, McLaughlin, & Talbert, 1993). The conflict is buffered by what Tyack and Cuban (1995) call a histori-

cally rooted "grammar of schooling" composed of subjects, specialized subjects, grades, individual teachers in their classrooms and paper and pencil assignments—a grammar that has, for many people, become synonymous with schooling itself. The combination of these characteristics can balkanize schools into isolated units that only sporadically communicate across boundaries (Hargreaves, 1994).

The belief that educational *systems* may be designed to operate like the efficient office buildings of modern businesses is also questionable. Decisions made in the corner offices on the top floors (state or provincial boards) may have little impact on the "real work" of managers on the next floor (superintendents), much less in the mail delivery room (teachers and students). Spillane's (1998) examination of district and school responses to a state-initiated reading policy showed both within and between-district variation, some of which was explainable by structures. He located two kinds of structural segmentation. First, as noted in earlier studies, the state-district-school floors are not well connected. In addition, the architecture on each floor is complex: the responsibility for organizational implementation is segmented and given to a variety of individuals, each of whom has little interaction with the others.[10]

Recent empirical research, on the other hand, suggests that "tinkering" with existing structures *in schools* can make a difference for students and adults. Lee & Smith (1997) use data from the National Educational Longitudinal Study to show that high school students learn the most in schools of moderate size (600–1200 students), while Freeman, Maruyama, Frederickson & Walkowiak (1997) examine block scheduling and find positive effects for students and teachers under some conditions. Other kinds of structural changes, such as school-based decision-making (involving teachers and parents in policy decisions) may be related to school effectiveness (Marks & Louis, 1997) and the adoption of new educational ideas (Evans & Hopkins, 1998). Reducing teacher isolation (Little, 1990) and student tracking (Oakes, 1994) are other structural changes that suggest demonstrable effects in some empirical research.

In the reform literature, structure is seen as a necessary but not sufficient ingredient for change at the school level (Fullan & Hargreaves, 1991; Louis & Kruse, 1995; Elmore, 1995). Elmore points out that many structural innovations have not affected real changes in the core of teaching and learning. Structural change will never be successful until there is accompanying changes in the norms governing behaviors (Fullan, 1991; Louis and Kruse, 1995).

Cuban (1988) distinguishes between first-order change (doing what we have always done better; not disturbing existing structures) and second-order change (doing things differently; or making fundamental changes in goals and roles). Since first-order changes are considerably easier and more common, transformative models (second-order change) are often downsized and implemented as first-order changes. Instead of altering the core of teaching and learning, for instance, structural changes are often "bolted" onto the surfaces of schools as an enrichment (Southworth, 1996). Prestine and McGrael's (1997) examination of how "authentic assessment" practices were implemented in several schools illustrates how potentially fundamental changes may be reduced to more acceptable but less penetrating shifts in practice. The implementation of computers in isolated and inaccessible computer laboratories staffed by parent volunteers is another common example.

3. The Political Frame: Organizations as Legislatures

All politics is local. — Tip O'Neill, U.S. Senator.

Every thinking individual puts some portion of an apparently stable world in peril.—John Dewey (1929).

The central question in this frame has two parts: *How does the school create the internal and external support to change current practices? And how does it simultaneously manage the internal and external challenges to improvement?* Implementation requires both power to get something done and skill to manage the political issues provoked by change (Huberman & Miles, 1984). Political issues are "provoked" because implementation efforts affect "not only roles and skills but also power relationships and status" (Evans, 1996, p. 36).

Both Morgan (1997) and Bolman and Deal (1997) see organizations through this frame as metaphorical jungles. In jungles we are surrounded by a wide variety of species (diversity), the survival of the fittest (conflict), and foraging for food (scarcity). The jungle metaphor gives a picture of a dangerous organizational ecosystem in which acquiring and applying resources is central to survival. An alternative metaphor, more consistent with many people's daily experience of organizational life, is that of a legislature or parliament—a place where one might not be eaten, but where there is a constant struggle for power and influence. The language of educational change is full of political terms: agenda setting, stakeholders, coalitions, political will, arenas, conflict resolution, resource allocation, political pressures, and constituencies.

While teachers don't typically think of themselves as political, they use substitute terms that identify the political activity that surrounds them every day at work: "schmoozing," "stepping on people's toes," "getting your voice heard," "competing agendas," "playing hardball," and "he killed the project" (Toole, forthcoming). All of these point to what academics call "micropolitics" (Ball, 1987; Blase, 1991; Blase and Anderson, 1995) or the person on the street might call "office politics," and they deeply affect

teachers' experience of schools and the potential success of change efforts (Oakes, Wells, Yonuzawa & Rey, 1997).[11]

In legislatures, it is also important to remember that effective politicians survive as much by cooperation as by competition. We can practice "politics over" (getting compliance) or "politics with" others (working together to get something done) (Blase, 1988; Oakes, 1993). "The choice," notes Carlson (1996) "is not whether politics should occur in organizations but rather what kind of politics should prevail" (p. 51). Positive politics is central to the work of implementation, notes Cusick (1997) in his case studies of the Coalition of Essential Schools, because political ambiguity may leave participants unconvinced and reluctant (Dimmock, 1995) and lead to failures in change (Mirel, 1994).

In the United States, schooling has a distinctly political tone because we have framed many of the greatest twentieth century social debates as educational questions. Cremin (1988) observes dryly that other countries stage revolutions, but the U.S. writes curriculum. Educational policies have become the arena for national battles over religious beliefs (the Scopes Trials), race relations (the desegregation of Little Rock's schools), morality (sex education), the value of community (the closing of small rural schools), and, more recently, service-learning, which has been the subject of three high-profile legal cases where the larger issue was the relationship between the government and the private citizen. Ultimately, these battles were over the cast of a national soul, not just what students should know, how they should be taught, or where they should attend school (Cremin, 1988).

Teachers are often poor political participants. They are typically better at explaining the world to their students than at explaining what they do to the world. In contrast, Louis & Murphy (1994) note that effective principals in restructuring schools are avowedly political—perhaps compensating for the limited political skills within their staff. Wohlstetter & McCurdy's (1991) comparison of several efforts to decentralize decision-making in large districts found that the more local-level policy-making that was encouraged, the more successful the improvement programs. Leithwood, Steinbach & Jantzi (1995) support this finding, showing that in-school conditions, including the presence of transformational leadership, are more important in determining teachers' commitment to change than the external political environment. In the case of school improvement, educational professionals need positive political skills to build and sustain support among administrators, connect to parents, obtain external funds to attend a national conference to improve their practice, or get permission for innovative activities.

These studies do not address, however, another fundamental issue: school improvement options are constrained by lack of support for transformational change among influential actors (Labaree, 1997). To the degree that education is viewed as a "private good," it is likely to be controlled by those who currently benefit from it (higher income citizens); to the degree that it is viewed as a "public good," it may be dominated by the "educational establishment." In addition, debates about educational policy intersect with other social policies in increasingly apparent ways. For example, studies of out-of-school learning opportunities point to the availability of resources in the community (like neighborhood youth organizations) to supplement formal education (Heath and McLaughlin, 1993), but these rarely mesh with schools. Data on the decline of employment opportunities in urban centers, however, suggest that the most dedicated schools will not be able to provide their students with images of success through formal education alone (Wilson, 1997).

Thus the political frame must also ask who is involved in school improvement programs and for what purpose. School improvement is often a process that is confined to professionals, with parents and the community only involved later, if at all. Students are also marginalized in school improvement efforts, with their view controlled by adults rather than through direct and open-ended discussions about matters such as what schools do that helps or interferes with their learning (Rudduck *et al.*, 1997).

Finally, one of the unexplored issues within this frame is how educators engage productively with the unpredictable policies that challenge everyday school and classroom realities. Hargreaves and Fullan (1998) assert that collective union protest against government actions is one legitimate way to do this, but much less is known about how unions and other educational professional associations shape positive politics at the state level (Kerchner, Koppich & Weeres, 1997). Even less research has been conducted during the last decade about the role of professional associations at the local level. How professionals communicate their practice in ways that affect policy is a practical dilemma and empirically puzzling.

4. The Learning Frame: Organizations as Brains

Is it possible to design "learning organizations" that have the capacity to be as flexible, resilient, and inventive as the functioning of the brain? Is it possible to distribute capacities for intelligence and control throughout an enterprise so that the system as a whole can self-organize and evolve along with emerging challenges? — Gareth Morgan (1997, p. 74).

In the beginner's mind there are many possibilities; in the expert's mind there are few. —Shunryu Suzuki (1970, p. 21).

People in the learning frame are thinkers, reflective practitioners, risk-takers, learners, knowledge dissemina-

tors, inquirers, and experimenters. The central question they face is: *How do teachers and administrators in schools collectively learn to use innovations to change their practices, solve problems, and enhance teaching, learning, and caring?* It is a crucial question. Joyce and Showers (1995) note that "the key to student growth is educator growth" (p. xv). The language of the frame includes professional development, mental models, systems thinking, organizational learning, double-loop learning, continuous improvement, and reflection.

The metaphor for the learning frame—brains—is open to multiple interpretations (Carlson, 1996, Morgan, 1997).[12] Brains are commonly viewed as information processing systems—complex computers, libraries, chemical reactions, or mysterious black boxes. The old joke about "Where are the brains of this outfit?" assumes that the source of thinking and expertise is centralized in some specially gifted part of the organization. This view of "brains" suggests that the problem of learning converges on acquiring the correct information and the skills to use it.

Hall & Hord (1987) capture an older paradigm as "simply delivering the innovation 'box' to the classroom door" (p. 7). Implicit in this tiny metaphor is a view that mirrors a generation of documented implementation failures. However, of all the seven frames, our approaches to and understanding of the learning frame have changed most dramatically over the past 20 years, with new emphasis being given to forms of learning that are more consistent with current psychological research (Senge, 1990; Sparks & Hirsh, 1997; Caine & Caine, 1997). Brains in today's organizations need to reflect newer images from neuroscience: decentralization, not centralization; parallel, not linear processing; the encoding of the whole in all of the parts, not in some exclusive center; and the brain's role in both emotional and cognitive processing.

Still, investigations of organizational learning in schools have emerged slowly. One example (Huberman, 1993) involved looking at successful collaborations between university researchers and school practitioners, where the importance of sustained interaction and mutual influence were critical to finding positive improvement effects. Leithwood and Steinbach's (1995) analyses suggest that it is not specific knowledge and skills, but problem-solving behaviors and strategies that distinguish effective principals from less effective ones. The image that these, and other authors, invoke is the brain as a set of malleable circuits and networks. More often, however, the image of organizational learning has been driven by the notion that externally provided information reporting on indicators of accountability or success would guarantee improvement through the provision of negative or positive incentives, an assumption that has not proven to be warranted in education (Ruscoe & Miller, 1991).

The new understanding of professional learning and school change emphasizes the importance of individual development models, but it also pays attention to organizational learning (Fullan, 1993). Louis & Kruse (1995; in press), Schön (1984), Hopkins (1993), and Toole (forthcoming) see a de-emphasis on teachers as consumers of innovations to teachers as generators of professional knowledge. Prepackaged innovations have given way to serious redesigning of innovations to fit specific school cultures and contexts (McLaughlin, 1990); training educators in new behaviors has been largely replaced by an emphasis on changing mental models (Senge, 1990; Caine & Caine, 1997; Dana & Pitts, 1993); and ongoing, job-embedded staff development has been substituted for one-shot professional development events (Hall & Hord, 1987; Sparks & Hirsh, 1997). In theory, at least, single-loop, linear learning that monitors whether a system is reaching its goals is out, while double-loop learning where systems are able to revisit whether those goals are still appropriate is in (Argyris, 1990).

Changing schools to adapt to new metaphors of the brain faces resistance both at the individual and school level. A key stumbling block to individual learning involves changing the mental models that teachers and administrators hold for education (Caine & Caine, 1997). Education is the only profession where socialization begins at age five and lasts for 13 years (Eisner, 1992). Emerging approaches to learning require deep changes in educator's beliefs and practices (Cohen, McLaughlin, & Talbert, 1993; Newmann & associates, 1995). Even when generously supported, such learning can be personally painful for both teachers (Ball & Rundquist, 1993) and administrators (Murphy & Louis, 1994). Many proposed instructional reforms require replacing exclusively traditional views of cognition and school social relations with more constructivist ones (Brooks & Brooks, 1993).

As yet, there are few institutional incentives to overcome personal anxiety about such fundamental changes in assumptions. In addition, there may be root issues related to habituated behavior. The recent Third International Math and Science Study (TIMMS) noted that teachers in the U.S. report only about one hour per week of self-initiated professional reading or other professional development. Although this may be attributable to the relatively heavy workload of U.S. teachers, it also suggests that a personal commitment to "lifelong learning" outside of the classroom is not currently a common practice in the educational profession. In addition, critiques of schools of education have frequently pointed out that few programs prepare teachers or administrators to be reflective practitioners.[13]

At the organizational level, Morgan (1997) asks whether organizations can learn how to learn. But the concept of learning organization requires strong bridges between the learning, identity, and cultural frames (Kofman & Senge, 1995). The learning literature has, particularly in the writing directed at managers, been imbued with an emphasis on the rational, calculative, and strategic nature of learning—that is, we learn to solve problems. The obverse is also found in cognitive theory, however: we find new problems *because* we have learned.

However, current organizational settings rarely foster learning. Teachers and administrators are not able and willing to examine their own practice publicly in organizational cultures that are too competitive (Kofman & Senge, 1995) or too filled with uncertainty (Rosenholtz, 1989). Organizational learning can be difficult to achieve when educators' roles are overly prescribed or where professional communities are lacking (Louis and Kruse, 1995). In addition, learning, like all organizational change, is subject to evolutionary and anomalous influences, which are rarely taken into consideration in efforts to make schools into learning organizations. Improvement efforts are counterproductive to learning when, in the name of continuous improvement, teachers and others begin to feel that they are on a treadmill of ceaseless innovation or that they are unable to perfect one achievement before they turn to another (Hargreaves, in press). Demands for incessant learning of the new, coupled with little time for reflection and rest, actually create organizational learning disabilities (Louis, 1994).

On the other hand, research also suggests that school structures and cultures may foster learning. Leithwood (1994) and Leithwood and Jantzi (in press) use several data sets to show that teachers are more likely to pursue their collective and individual learning when there are supportive conditions in the school—such as particularly effective leadership. Similar results are found in a cross-sectional study of all Chicago elementary schools (Bryk, Camburn and Louis, 1995). In particular, schools where teachers are able to come together to study issues that are related to their school improvement efforts are more likely to be able to take advantage of internally and externally generated information (Murphy, 1992; Louis and Kruse, in press). The latter qualitative studies support quantitative findings about the importance of the principal's role in stimulating an environment in which new information and practices are eagerly incorporated. Finally, studies of knowledge utilization in schools (Huberman, 1993) suggest that teachers can become eager consumers of research information if they are embedded in a setting where they have sustained interaction with researchers in an egalitarian context.

How we can intervene in schools to create propitious settings for learning is not documented. Leithwood and Louis (in press) present case studies related to intervention strategies, ranging from participatory evaluation to cognitive mapping exercises. However, the data on how to create learning schools is at a very early stage.

5. The Personal Identity and Emotions Frame: Organizations as Fire[14]

How can the teacher's selfhood become a legitimate topic in education and in our public dialogues on educational reform? — Palmer (1998, p. 3).

You can't teach anything to others that you haven't become yourself.—Mother Teresa.

The central question in this frame is: *How does educational change affect and build on the personal identity and emotions of those who are centrally involved?* Of the multiple possible approaches to this question, we will focus here on what Palmer (1998) calls the "inner landscape" composed of the intellectual, emotional, and spiritual dimensions of an educator's self.[15]

The metaphor for the personal identity and emotions frame is *fire*, which represents spirit, light, and illumination. As one ESL teacher from Oregon stated: "There is no growth without fire" (Leighton, 1996, p. 21). Our fires burn bright when we engage in meaningful work, and when we tether ourselves to something higher (Daloz, Keen, Keen, and Parks, 1996). Although school effectiveness research has not been able to identify specific, personal traits of outstanding teachers or principals, qualitative studies suggest that strong presence and character (identity and personal commitment) is important (Fullan, 1993, 1997). Furthermore, research on thinking and personal development that accompanies changes in practice suggests that incorporating a personal identity theme into studies of school improvement would be valuable (Firestone, 1996; Fink, forthcoming).

One aspect of this integration is to examine the way in which organizations have the power to help form or deform us, connecting this frame firmly to the political frame (Hargreaves, in press). Shakespeare captured this in Sonnet 111: "My nature is subdued/To what it works in, like the dyer's hand." Current research in educational administration, insofar as it attends to the individual needs of adults, has focused on the molding character of schools as workplaces. The school's culture and structure (Rosenholtz, 1989; Firestone & Louis, this volume) heavily influence teachers' identity in the workplace and the technologies of work also shape identity in other work contexts (Kilduff, Funk, & Mehra, 1997). Prestine and McGreal (1997) use case data from four secondary schools to show how adverse (but typical) organizational conditions undermined efforts by resilient teachers to do what they individually believed was right (implement more authentic assessments). Levine (1993) extends the concept of "self-managing" or

semi-autonomous schools to argue that teachers, as individuals, must become self-managers of their own professional objectives within the school context.

The power of organizational influence, however, should not eclipse the reciprocal impact of personal identity *on* the school. Even in schools with strong normative cultures, educators maintain an element of self-identity that gives texture and honesty to their particular practice (Palmer, 1998; Beck, 1994; Kruse, 1995). Every member of an executive study group studied by Kofman & Senge (1995) cited personal stories that helped explain their strong interest in systemic thinking and organizational learning. The authors concluded that differences in personal identity predispose people to different kinds of work, or different approaches to the same job. Beck's (1995) study of a single "caring" principal's efforts to create a more effective school exemplifies the potential for research on the intersection between identity and emotions with organizational change.

The research base in educational administration on practitioners' personal identity is rather limited, but research on variables that might be associated with personal identity reveals some important reasons for focusing on the individual teacher and administrator. Ross (1995), for example, found that teachers who believe that they are more effective are more likely to challenge their students, set high goals for themselves, and to take more personal responsibility for student learning. Dimmock and Hattie (1996), make a similar argument with regard to principals. Skillfulness and expertise increase individual identity and self-efficacy, which suggests that a professional development strategy can have payoffs for both individual and school (Stein and Wang, 1988; Hord and Boyd, 1995).

One of the primary change tasks in this frame is to find ways to authentically connect identity and emotions with the intended and evolving development of the school. This fits with Deming's statement that nothing significant happens without "personal transformation" (quoted in Kofman and Senge, 1995). Self-revelation is often thought to be part of this process. Hargreaves (1994) points out how important this can be: "Studies of teaching showed how teachers had to struggle hard to define and defend worthwhile selves . . . to preserve and express the people that they were, and to protect and promote the moral purposes which gave meaning to their work." (p. 30). The same can also be said for school administrators, who often find it necessary to reaffirm their own moral purpose within the muddy terrain associated with "gardening for change." This frame makes the assumption that school improvement strategies should unleash positive emotions and inner resources among educators who might make reform work, rather than negative emotions of guilt, fear, or frustration that some recent reform systems, such as "high stakes accountability," apparently engender (Hargreaves, in press).

Issues of personal identity are thus tied to increased school effectiveness. Many recent change efforts have special salience as a tool for educators' self-expression because they focus on significant social goals, such as improving achievement for disadvantaged students. Idealists are more likely to enter education than any other profession (National Education Association, NEA, 1972, 1982, 1987)[16] but are also more likely to leave. After controlling for a host of alternative explanations, Miech and Elder (1996) found that the central reason that idealistic teachers leave the profession in greater numbers is what Lortie (1975) identified as the "endemic uncertainty" built into modern schools. The same idealism that attracts people to education becomes a form of discouragement because the structure of education offers few ways to assess one's contribution to society. An important role for effective principals is to reinforce idealism, and to connect change goals and school actions with a sense of individual purpose and idealism (Louis and Murphy, 1994).

6. The Cultural Frame: Organizations as Tribes

Everything participates in the creation and evolution of its neighbors. — Wheatley and Kellner-Rogers (1996, p. 14).

It's hard to eat something that you've had a relationship with. —Hargreaves & Fullan (1998).

Although the classic image of ethnographers evokes foreign sites for research, all human groups form cultures. Colloquially, culture is "how we do things around here;" more formally, it is "the acquired knowledge people use to interpret experience and generate behavior" (Spradley, 1980, p.6). The central question of this frame for change research is: *How do differing school cultures affect a school's capability to create change and make use of autonomous and anomalous changes in positive ways?*

We use the metaphor of *tribes* for the cultural frame because, even in contemporary school systems, there is a clear distinction between people who belong in the group, and those who do not. Teachers and administrators are officially employees of school districts and not schools, but most spend a large proportion of their career in a single building and view colleagues in other schools as part of different tribes. Even more significantly, they often view people who are not professional educators with recent experience as "outside the tribe."[17] Rituals, symbols, myths, shared meanings, ceremonies, and theater still guide and inform patterns of behavior, and new members need to learn these if they are to "join the group."

The early effective schools literature, in its search to identify critical characteristics for success, virtually ignored teachers' relationships as an aspect of school culture or climate (see Edmonds, 1979). As Barth (1990) pointed out, "(Collegiality) is recognized neither as part of the problem nor as part of the solution" (p. 30). That is no longer true. Little and McLaughlin (1993) note that there is now a "virtual campaign to break the bounds of privacy in teaching" (p. 1). Collaborative teacher workplaces have now been prescribed as a near "cure-all" for teacher development, internally generated school improvement, effective implementation of instructional changes, and general organizational health (D. Hargreaves, 1995; Heck and Marcoulides, 1996).

Sarason (1996) warned in 1966 that we would waste "billions of dollars" over the next decade trying to implement school reforms because we would not understand the culture of schools. Because his insight has received considerable reinforcement in the school change literature, an entire chapter in this handbook focuses on school culture (Firestone and Louis, this volume). However, as their review suggests, little of the work on school culture, outside of that summarized by Sarason, focuses directly on change. The authors indicate that there are strong national culture effects on patterns of school change and improvement, but much of the research is focused on the way in which leadership can promote changes in school culture (Stoll and Fink, 1994; Short, *et al.*, 1994), rather than on the way in which school culture shapes change over the long run (Hord and Boyd, 1995; Hallinger and Leithwood, 1994).

Recent work on professional communities in schools suggests new directions for inquiry. The two strands in this work focus on cultures that promote organizational tribalism (school-based professional community) and those that transcend organizational tribalism (professional networks). The first, exemplified by the work of Little (1982, 1993), Rosenholtz (1989), Louis & Kruse (1995) and Louis, Kruse & Marks (1996), looks at school cultures as either fostering or impeding the kind of intense collaboration and sharing that supports the school's focus on other frames (purpose, learning, and leadership). The second, equally strong tradition emphasizes the need for teachers to be cosmopolitan in their orientations, connected to professional groups that stimulate and bring new ideas into the schools, and reinforce professional knowledge as sources of teacher identification and community (McLaughlin & Talbert, 1993; Lieberman, 1996; Lieberman & Grolnick, 1997). These authors see professional culture as connected to the search for personal identify and learning. We believe that these perspectives on educational cultures are compatible.

The overarching rationale for focusing on professional community is that it might provide the organizational conditions to facilitate significant and lasting school changes

(McLaughlin & Talbert, 1993; Louis & Kruse, 1995; Toole, forthcoming). Barth (1990) follows this logic when he argues that:

> the relationships among adults in schools are the basis, the precondition, the sine qua non that allow, energize, and sustain all other attempts at school improvement. Unless adults talk with one another, observe one another, and help one another, very little will change (p. 32).

7. The Leadership Frame: Organizations as Gardens

. . . the great leader is seen as servant first, and that simple fact is the key to his greatness. — Robert Greenleaf (1977, p. 7).

How do we build leadership plazas rather than leadership pyramids? —Suzanne Morse (1997).

The previous frames have all alluded to the important role of principals in change. It has become a maxim that their role, along with district leaders, is critical to the success of any improvement effort (Leighton, 1996). As McLaughlin (1990) reports, the classic RAND Study of Educational Change found that teachers rarely muster the will and motivation for significant changes without support from the school administrators or district officials, a finding that has been widely replicated.

However, the leadership frame views the issue somewhat differently. Rather than including leadership as one of many variables that may explain improvement, it is the central question in this frame: *What is the source and role of leadership in initiating and sustaining transformational change?* The language of leadership includes source, distribution, density, nature, depth, formal versus informal, direct versus indirect, and transactional versus transformational.

It is challenging to identify a single metaphor for leadership. It is tempting to instead use a Swiss Army Knife of multiple metaphors that can be pulled out to meet diverse leadership tasks. Murphy and Beck (1994), for example, suggest six metaphors for educational leadership. In searching for a single image, we have traditionally used metaphors like the captain of the ship or commander-in-chief that emphasize hierarchy and control.

We chose instead the much humbler organizational metaphor of a *gardener*. If organizations are seen as gardens, then leaders cannot command them to grow. They must contend with the unpredictability, environmental influences, teamwork, and risk factors that characterize trying to help anything develop. Leaders can only promote growth by "rearranging the conditions and structures" (Barth, 1990, p. 59) or "contexts" (Morgan, 1997). For gardens, those conditions are sun, moisture, soil, nutrients, and temperature; for schools, they are time, space, materials, money, training, collegiality, respect, trust, and personnel.

The conditions that have reshaped the learning frame have had the same effect on the leadership frame. In traditional organizations, people like Henry Ford or Tom Watson (IBM) did the thinking for all (Senge, 1990), just as the district superintendent was supposed to be in charge of all significant improvement efforts. A key leadership skill now is how to unleash intelligence, creativity, insight, and self-initiated activity throughout the organization (Murphy, 1994) and to focus school improvement efforts on purposes such as "authentic instruction" (Newmann & associates, 1997) and "learning for its own sake" (Maehr and Parker, 1993). Louis and Murphy (1994) found that four chapters from their edited volume "emphasize the principal's role in restructuring is intimately tied to the cultivation of human resources, supportive cultures, and goals—and not necessarily to their personal development of a change plan" (p. 269). Their use of the agricultural metaphor *"cultivation"* fits well with gardening as a metaphor for leadership. To cultivate is to be a teacher, enabler, steward, servant, model, friend, supporter, advocate, and planner (Murphy & Beck, 1994; Murphy, 1994; Louis & Murphy, 1994).

Recent quantitative (Leithwood, 1994; Evans and Teddlie, 1995; Goldring & Pasternak, 1994) and qualitative studies (Heller and Firestone, 1995; Goldman, Dunlap and Conley, 1993) provide data from multiple sites and countries to support the importance of principal leadership. However, the studies are less robust when it comes to the question of whether there is "one best way" or alternative modes of leadership for fostering change. Leithwood (1994) and Goldman, Dunlap & Conley's (1993) research, for example, suggest that there is a preferred model for creating change. Leithwood argues that "transformational leadership" that focuses on the role of the principal as setting vision, organizing resources, and creating positive pressures for change is important; Goldman, Dunlap & Conley (1993) find that "facilitative leadership" involves diffuse roles, with both administrators and teachers providing more indirect support for improvement.

Other researchers emphasize the contextually embedded nature of leadership and improvement. Goldring and Shapira (1996), for example, find that principal leadership relating to parental involvement results from the specific circumstances in each school; Evans and Teddlie (1995) found that effective principal leadership styles vary depending on the socio-economic status of the school population; Heller and Firestone (1995) identify a core set of leadership functions (such as sustaining vision, encouraging staff, and mentoring progress) but show that they are variously performed by individuals in a variety of roles, and not just by formal administrators. Similarly equivocal results have emerged from recent efforts to determine whether administrative leadership has an impact on one of the prominent ends of improvement: student achievement. Some conclude that there is little relationship (Leitner, 1994), while others argue that there is evidence of a modest but indirect relationship (Pounder, 1995; Brewer, 1993; Zigarelli, 1996; Heck and Marcoulides, 1993) largely through the varying influence that principals have on staffing and school culture.

Supporting Improvement

You take people as far as they will go, not as far as you would like them to go. — *Jeanette Rankin, quoted in Josephson (1974).*

The single greatest power in the world today is the power to change . . . the most recklessly irresponsible thing we could do in the future is to go on the way we have been for the past 10 or 20 years. — *Karl Deutch (1977).*

In America, citizens confront a country whose national seal proclaims "The New Order of the Ages" but where many school staff lounges sport a worn, photocopied picture of Clint Eastwood pointing a pistol at the reader saying "Just try to change one more thing." Clint's popularity gives testimony that educators too often conceive of change as something that is done to them, not that they initiate (Fullan, 1993). It is important to remember that when Clint points his gun, it is not at change itself, but at the way that change has been conceived and implemented in many school settings.

Our conceptions of school improvement need to move closer to the paradigms like school development that incorporate diverse streams of change. The fact that problems are "wicked" and control over change elusive does not imply that we should give up, or that leadership is unimportant. It is just that change happens differently than we have often thought. Wheatley and Kellner-Rogers (1996) capture the flavor of much real-world progress: "Life uses messes to get to well-ordered solutions. Life doesn't seem to share our desires for efficiency or neatness. It uses redundancy, fuzziness, dense webs of relationships, and unending trials and errors to find what works" (p. 13).

If this is the case, we need leaders more than ever, but leaders who are willing to face unpredictability and ambiguity head on and find *positive* ways to use instability (Stacey, 1992). While our traditional mind might want to categorize unanticipated events as obstacles, the birthday party case cited earlier illustrates how unpredictability (in the form of serendipity or synchronicity) can make large contributions to school improvement. In a similar instance, an elementary school that learned in the winter that it would receive a large influx of Cambodian children in the following autumn quickly organized a rich, interdisciplinary, school-wide unit where everyone learned about their new classmates. In this case, the school correctly positioned

its raft into the whitewater, which then became a source of organizational energy and progress.

The focus of central research and practice issues is, however, different than if one assumes that one is dealing with a manageable whole. As Hatch (1998) notes in his analysis of the collaboration of the Coalition of Essential Schools (Brown University), the Educational Development Center, Project Zero (Harvard), and the School Development Project (Yale University), "trying to come to an agreement of a single theory of education or a single answer to the dilemmas that are likely to be faced in reform efforts may be both impossible and unwise (p. 25)." We need to begin somewhere—both in research and practice—but be adept at shifting our focus as the situation warrants.

We will briefly summarize what we see as the critical theoretical domains for the next decade and spend somewhat more time discussing the implications of our perspective for applied research and practice.

Key Research Domains—A Practical Agenda

The implications of the discussion of frames for school improvement suggests that some are comparatively well researched, while others are less so. The frames can highlight central questions that need more attention:

- *What is the purpose of school improvement?* Within this frame we have shown that the importance of purpose is well established, but that we know little about how purpose is created, how it is embedded in the everyday fabric of the organization, and how it can be directed toward the multiple ends of educational improvement. Furthermore, a large number of questions remain related to the hierarchy and competition between different purposes or visions, and the way that these are affected by the less anticipated components of change.

- *How does the school need to be restructured to support the purposes and processes of improvement?* Restructuring is consequential, but not sufficient in school improvement. We are just beginning to understand which components of structure are most important to change and how to change in the desired directions. Even descriptive information about how these structures vary systematically between various countries and provinces is largely unexplored. More attention to the effects of school structures on the professional learning community, classroom practice, and student achievement is clearly warranted, as well as the way in which structures affect the response of schools to external pressures for change.

- *How does the school create the internal and external support, and control the internal and external challenges, in order to change current practices and improve?* The political aspects of school improvement are ripe for investigation. Until recently, most policy research focused on legislative and executive actions at the state and national level. As attention turns toward the district and school as units embedded in the larger environment (including the importance of micropolitics for school improvement), the integration of policy and organizational research should become increasingly productive.

- *How do teachers and administrators in schools collectively learn to use innovations to change their practices, solve problems, and enhance teaching, learning, and caring?* The emphasis on school-based accountability and management has increased in virtually all countries over the past decade. There is little evidence that central governments are prepared to resume responsibility for educational productivity. However, our knowledge about how schools manage to change from traditional modes of equilibrium based on lesson plans, curriculum coverage, and norm-referenced tests to collective responsibility for complex student learning outcomes is debated, but only recently examined in exploratory studies. This may be, at least for the next few years, the paramount issue in school improvement.

- *How does educational change affect and build on the personal identity and emotions of those who are centrally involved?* The role of individual identity, emotions, and the development of members of the school community has been virtually ignored in educational administration research, although it has been featured in studies of change in instruction. In recent years, the educational administration community has focused almost exclusively on sociological models of school organization. It is, we believe, time to bring the individual back into the picture and to link the development of groups to the development of professional practice in the classroom. While we focus on changing teachers' behavior, values, or mental models, we must not forget that the most profound and lasting educational change involves changes in teacher's personal identity.

- *How do differing school cultures affect a school's capability to create change and to make use of autonomous and anomalous changes in positive ways?* Cultural perspectives are increasingly popular in educational administration research and build on a long tradition of related studies of "school climate" or "organizational health" (Hoy, Tartar, and Kottkamp, 1992). However, as noted above, the theories that attach culture to improvement are still skeletal, and published empirical data tend towards isolated case studies. In particular, we need to add studies of student and community culture as factors in school improvement.

- *What is the source and role of leadership in initiating and sustaining transformational change?* We are well along in our discussions about school-based management and teacher empowerment. However, the number of high quality empirical studies of how shared leadership oper-

ates in well-functioning settings needs to be augmented, as well as studies of how "good leadership" fails. The literature on problem-solving in leadership settings is promising but needs to be expanded to include studies of leadership teams and diffuse decision-making settings. Less attention has been paid to the role of leadership from ancillary sources in and near the school—community, unions, and other actors—and most of these studies are of a single site or community.

These seven questions are familiar and straightforward —not very different from those posed by the earlier scholars reviewed at the beginning of this chapter. However, in no case do we believe that there is a compelling accumulation of empirical findings that take into account the contextual quandaries that are central to the study of change in contemporary settings. Thus our recommendation is not to put old wine in new bottles (a favorite activity of social scientists in search of a new concept), but to reuse the old bottles (questions) and fill them with new wine.

Additional Challenges to the Problem of School Improvement

As we noted earlier in this review, a number of principles have guided school improvement research for the past decade or more. However, the frame analysis suggests that some of these assumptions need to be either tweaked or challenged.

Assumption #1: The School Is the Unit of Change

The "school is the unit of change" was developed as a mantra to counter policymakers' ill-founded belief that "top-down" policies would suffice, and the equally misplaced assumption that individual professionalism among teachers would produce excellent schools. At this juncture, however, the most recent literature suggests that we need to modify the assertion to reassert that the school is a critical focus, but that without stable policy environments and resources outside the school, the chances of enduring change are limited. Similarly, research suggests that unless improvement efforts penetrate the classroom and affect the individual teacher directly we will continue to find far more variance within and between schools. We are not suggesting that we abandon the idea that the school is the primary unit of *intervention,* only that we expand this to include the need for simultaneous changes, and interventions, in contexts and classrooms.

Assumption #2: The Emphasis Should Be on Planned Change within the School

We identified the problematic features of change as lack of agreement among reasonable people on both the ends and means of change, the "wickedness" of educational problems, the simultaneous needs to appear to be improving while meeting demands for stability, lack of attention to the autonomous organizational life cycle, and the interruptions of equilibrium with unanticipated "normal crises." Although we are not the first to have described these as real barriers to research on and practice of school improvement, we assert that there is a need for more empirical work that builds these features into the design. A focus on the non-planned aspects, which includes greater attention to the less well-researched frames that focus on learning, politics, individual development, and evolutionary culture is important to furthering our understanding.

Assumption #3: Internal Capacities Are the Primary Prerequisite for Change

There is little in our review of the frames that causes us to contest this assertion. Nevertheless, we believe that in recent research the nature of internal capacities and resources has been overestimated in comparison to external resources. The political frame and the learning frame, in particular, emphasize the importance of outside supports for school improvement that come not from the educational professionals, but from the community and other resources.

Assumption #4: External Support from Authoritative or Professional Agencies and Networks Is Needed to Support Effective Change

The study of external assistance agencies is undergoing a resurgence of attention due to the new wave of school and system-wide interventions, ranging (in the U.S.) from the New American Schools models to the advent of externally developed national or state standards. New research agendas in this area clearly need to attend not only to today's contexts, but also to the body of research on knowledge utilization in schools that has been dormant for some time. We suggest that the organizational learning, the personal identity, and the cultural framework will need to be applied simultaneously if progress is made on this agenda.

Implications for Administrative Practice

Rather than castigating laggard schools for their inattention to research or their lack of energy, it is useful to examine some of the conditions that ensure that most schools lack the basic resources to engage in improvement in a context of "wicked problems." Today's schools rarely have a schedule that permits teachers to meet and work together for sustained periods of time. School budgets have been under increasing pressure in most countries for at least a decade, and there is typically little "fat" remaining. Teachers work has, at the same time, frequently become more demanding as many teachers notice that students are coming to school less well socialized, less prepared to deal with the material, and more frequently from family settings that are not ide-

ally supportive. The teaching and administrative forces, in many countries, are aging and often demoralized from cuts in staffing and financial support. In many countries there is a sense that education used to be an excellent occupation but is now a "dead end job," except for those who are teaching at the upper levels of university preparatory secondary schools. Teachers in virtually every country complain about the increasing levels of bureaucratization, and the rapid and frequent demands for change that come from central authorities—even in those countries that have policies to promote devolution or decentralization.

In sum, the forces listed above cause stress in schools and in teachers that is antithetical to the types of internal changes that we are asking them to make. In the name of school improvement, we sometimes treat teachers and administrators as pawns or machine parts. In intensifying the everyday tasks in schools, we implicitly devalue teachers' and administrators' relationships with each other, but for teachers to thrive in the personal identity and the learning frames, they require some balance of action and reflection, stress and repose, stretching and consolidation. In the United States, we think many people have decoupled making schools better places for students from making them better places also for the adults who work in them. We think that concepts like professional learning community can serve as a vantage point from which we can improve the lots of teachers and students simultaneously.

Nevertheless, as Weick (1989) points out, there is reason for optimism. Twenty years of research has included at least some attention to the way in which the elements of change that are not manageable intersect with those that are. Weick likens this process to jazz improvisation, which is structured, subject to certain expectations, but also to unexpected local invention by colleagues/collaborators. In order to be a improvisational master, the jazz musician needs to know where he and the particular piece that is playing have been—historically, as well as in the particular set—and needs to adjust the future to where he and others are likely to be headed. In the more common language of school reform, we need to attend to both backward and forward mapping.

The Backward Mapping Principle

We begin with a simple proposition: to be effective a support system for change within a school or district must be designed to be consistent with what we know about how to best foster school improvement, about the strains and pressures on schools outlined above, and about the need for multiple frames in order to begin to think about "wicked problems." Elmore (1992) has recently refreshed his classic concept of "backward mapping," arguing that, in the U.S., the gap between what is known about "best practice" in teaching and "ordinary practice" is widening as the research knowledge base grows, rather than narrowing. He attributes this dismal observation to the fact that major U.S. policies—particularly many of those associated with the current restructuring movement—are unconnected with the details of teaching and learning in schools and are distracting attention from the teachers' improvement of craft.

In the development of designs and strategies for changing schools, we often fall prey to the same problems, in part because what exists and "what we know" from current research guides our thinking about design and strategies. We less frequently stop and consider what support needs look like from the classroom up. Without backward mapping we run the risk of choosing strategies that do not match what practitioners want or are able to do—and research suggests that if they don't feel a pressing need for what we have to offer, they may politely accept it, but it will not affect practice.

The Need for Forward Mapping

The problem with the recommendation that change efforts should be backward designed around the research base is the following: just as the "knowledge base" available to society is growing at unprecedented rates, so is our knowledge about school effectiveness and school improvement. What we know today is different, not just more, than what we knew five years ago, and different still from what we will know in another five years. In addition, if new scholars attend to our recommendations in this chapter, our knowledge about the anomalous and autonomous change processes may increase even more rapidly in the next few years. In thinking about design and macro-strategies, we risk being caught between two unattractive poles: On the one hand, we can develop support systems that are stable but irrelevant; on the other, we may have systems that are responsive and adaptive, but confusing and uncoordinated.

Forward mapping is not the same as older models of strategic planning, although it is clearly integral to research on the components of change that can be directly influenced by an administrator. However, forward mapping also interacts with the anomalous and evolutionary components of change. First, it assumes that the future of the organization and its context is only modestly predictable. Second, it assumes that the organization cannot, by itself, choose precisely where it will go. As Louis & Miles (1990) note, there are no blueprints for change in uncertain environments. Instead, forward mapping is like an semi-planned trip: you know where you are starting from and have some ideas about possible destinations, but choose your route and your pace of travel to accommodate weather, unexpected events, and opportunities that may not have been anticipated. Finally, it is premised on the belief that all plans must be subject to continuous scrutiny that helps them adjust not only to the preferred destinations, but also to the immediate strengths and developing capacities of the school.

The Braid of School Improvement: Combining Rational and Nonrational Change

Forward and backward mapping should not occur as separate streams of action and thought. Insights into the school and its context from the seven frames (or another set of frames if a school prefers them) need to be woven into the forward and backward mapping process, tying them together in a continuing story that is neither the mission nor the culture of the organization, but contributes to both.

NOTES

1. In addition to the editorial board review, this chapter benefited from the insightful and honest criticisms of earlier drafts by James Detert, William Firestone, Kenneth Leithwood, and Gary Sykes. They bear, of course, no responsibility for the final result—none of them would have organized this chapter in the way that we have chosen to.

2. Havelock, *et al.* (1969) also proposed a *Linkage Model* that incorporated elements from each of the above and included an emphasis on the need for a "linking agent" who would deliver technical assistance and facilitate decision-making in the school. This model failed, however, to capture the imagination of many scholars of organizational change.

3. Hargreaves and Fullan (1998) argue that four basic purposes of schooling should be: to love and care—learning how to build relationships, care for others, develop emotional intelligence, and so on in classrooms, staff rooms, and communities; to serve—to connect to needs and causes beyond oneself, to develop and become an active member of one's community, to offer dedicated and authentic service to classmates, colleagues and the wider community; to empower—to develop student skills and strategies that will empower students beyond school, to empower students and give them more voice in the classroom in assessments, in educational processes, and in change itself, and to empower their parents as well; and to learn—in sophisticated ways among students, as a teacher to devise systematic ways to *learn from* students, parents, and colleagues.

4. It may, of course, be argued that social problems have always been complex, but that they were not recognized as such. However, there is a strong argument to suggest that factors such as the global economy, the mass media, and the growth of national social services have created inter-institutional relationships that are more complex than in previous periods.

5. Goffman writes: "it is obvious that in most 'situations' many different things are happening simultaneously—things that are likely to have begun at different moments and may terminate dissynchronously. To ask the question "What is it that's going on here?" biases matters in the direction of unitary exposition and simplicity" (p. 9).

6. How many frames are there? There are probably innumerable, so the task becomes to construct a manageable number that is most salient to understanding the problem of school improvement. The major educational authors and their frames include: Bolman and Deal (1991, 1997)—Structural, Human Resource. Political, and Symbolic; Robert Carlson (1996)—Cultural, Theatrical, Brain, and Political; Gareth Morgan (1997)—Factories, Organisms, Brains, Cultures, Political systems, Psychic prisons, Flux and transformation, and Instruments of domination; Andy Hargreaves (1997)—Political, Purpose, Leadership, Learning, Structural, Emotional, and Cultural. For the purposes of our analysis, we have expanded the emotional frame to include the related concept of personal identity.

7. Frame analysis makes a series of assumptions: We "frame problems" through the assumptions we bring (Goffman, 1974). Each perspective can create insights but also will be "incomplete, biased and potentially misleading" (Morgan, 1997, p. 5). Frames are useful in studying implementation because the process is multidimensional (Lippitt, *et al.*, 1958). Frames will give us "complementary and competing insights" (Morgan, 1997, p. 9). Frames are interdependent and react upon each other; they

are part of a larger system (Sarason, 1990). Artistry is important to allow "emotion, subtlety, and ambiguity" to appear in the various frames (Bolman & Deal, 1997, p. xiii). Metaphors are useful to name or augment frames (Wincek, 1995, Morgan, 1997), as evidenced by the widespread use of the "garbage can" metaphor for decision-making coined by March and Olsen (1986).

8. Many proponents of frame analysis appear to use it primarily as a device for increasing creativity in thinking about and solving problems in organizations rather than as a research tool. We suggest, on the other hand, that its utility for systematic research has been underexplored.

9. Most organizational theorists would argue that it is central, but not unique. Organizations are driven by survival instincts, tradition, and other factors that will be elaborated in other perspectives.

10. Spillane also emphasizes that school organizations are not windowless, doorless buildings. Instead they are open to all sorts of influences from the outside, some of which may be random, but some of which are associated with other related organizations such as professional associations.

11. Oakes', et al., (1997) study of untracking at 10 racially mixed schools found that implementation became difficult because it threatened the perceived interests and sense of entitlement of the parents of gifted students. The politics of race and privilege, something typically ignored in the school change literature, competed with educational research for what would happen with the innovation. Entitlement is not a pedagogical term. Such issues are inherently difficult for schools, which need parents' political support both for funding and credibility (Oakes, et al., 1997).

12. We acknowledge that in using the brain metaphor we are not addressing the full range of "intelligences" that have been identified in the literature. For example, we would place "emotional intelligence" in the personal identity frame. However, we assert that the organizational learning literature goes far beyond traditional "left brain" logical functioning to take into account a variety of other cognitive approaches that may increase productivity.

13. It is beyond the scope of this review to discuss the issues of teacher and administrator preparation. However, in the view of the authors the "problem" of inadequate preparation lies with both the university, the hiring institutions, and the larger political structures that continue to view education as a non-profession.

14. We use both the terms "personal identity" and "emotions" because we have found reactions to these terms are occasionally gender related. Men are more likely to find the personal identity theme evocative, while women are more likely to be excited about the inclusion of emotions in the discussion of change. In both cases, however, we are focused on the notion that non-cognitive issues related to "self" are critical to understanding change in behavior and practice.

15. Palmer (1998) defines identity as "an evolving nexus where all the forces that constitute my life converge in the mystery of self: my genetic makeup, the nature of the man and woman who gave me life, the culture in which I was raised, people who have sustained me and people who have done me harm, the good and ill I have done to others and to myself, the experience of love and suffering—and much, much more" (p. 13).

16. For many people, that idealism arises from their personal identity tied to some deep religious or secular beliefs. Although it is rarely acknowledged, Lortie (1975) points out that Christians see Jesus as "The Great Teacher," Roman Catholics have always highly valued teaching, and Jewish religious tradition exalts the importance of learning.

17. People who work in professional development activities in other professions, and in business, rarely encounter the suspicious attitudes of teachers and administrators toward "experts" who are not "one of us." We believe that this may be due to the relatively low esteem that teachers attribute to their own professional knowledge.

REFERENCES

Argyris, C. (1990). *Overcoming organizational defenses.* Boston, MA: Allyn and Bacon.

Ball, D. L. & Rundquist, S. S. (1993). Collaboration as a context for joining teacher learning with learning about teaching. In D. K. Cohen, M. W. McLaughlin & J. E. Talbert (Eds.), *Teaching for understanding: Challenges for policy and practice* (pp. 14–27). San Francisco: Jossey-Bass.

Ball, S. (1987). *The micro-politics of the school: Towards a theory of school organization.* New York: Methuen.

Barker, J. A. (1992). *Paradigms: The business of discovering the future.* New York: Harper-Business.

Barth, R. (1990). *Improving schools from within.* San Francisco: Jossey-Bass.

Beck, L. G. (1994). *Reclaiming educational administration as a caring profession.* New York: Teachers College Press.

Beck, L. G. (1995). Cultivating a caring school community: One principal's story. In J. Murphy & K. S. Louis (Eds.), *Reshaping the principalship: Insights from transformational reform efforts* (pp. 177–202). Thousand Oaks, CA: Corwin Press.

Beer, M., Eisenstat, R. & Spector, B. (1990). Why change programs don't produce change. *Harvard Business Review, 68* (6), 158–159.

Bender-Sebring, P. B., Bryk, A. S. & Easton, J. Q. (1995). *Charting reform: Chicago teachers take stock.* Chicago: Consortium on Chicago School Research.

Berliner, D. & Biddle, B. (1995). *The manufactured crisis.* New York: Addison Wesley.

Berman, P., Mclaughlin, M. W., Bass-Golod, G. V., Pauly, E. & Zellman, G. (1977). *Federal programs supporting educational change: Vol. VII, Factors affecting implementation and continuation.* Santa Monica: RAND Corporation.

Blase, J. (1988). The politics of favoritism: A qualitative analysis of the teachers' perspective. *Educational Administration Quarterly, 24* (2), 152–177.

Blase, J. (1991). *The politics of life in schools: Power, conflict, and cooperation.* Newbury Park, CA: SAGE Publications.

Blase J. & Anderson, G. (1995). *The micropolitics of educational leadership: From control to empowerment.* New York: Teachers College Press.

Bolman, L. G. & Deal, T. E. (1991). *Reframing organizations: Artistry, choice, and leadership,* 1st Ed. San Francisco: Jossey-Bass.

Bolman, L. G. & Deal, T. E. (1997). *Reframing organizations: Artistry, choice and leadership (2nd ed.).* San Francisco: Jossey-Bass.

Boyan, N. (Ed.). (1988). *Handbook of research in educational administration.* New York: Longman.

Bracey, G. (1997). On the difficulty of knowing much of anything about how schools reform over time. *Phi Delta Kappan, 79* (1), 86–88.

Brewer, D. J. (1993). Principals and student outcomes: Evidence from U. S. high schools. *Economics of Education Review, 12* (4), 281–292.

Brookover, W. (1979). *School social systems and student achievement: Schools can make a difference.* New York: Praeger.

Brooks, J. G. & Brooks, M. G. (1993). *In search of understanding: The case for constructivist classrooms.* Alexandria, VA: Association for Supervision and Curriculum Development.

Brouillette, L. (1996). *The geology of school reform.* Albany: SUNY Press.

Brown, R. M. (1988). *Starting from scratch: A different kind of writers' manual.* New York: Bantam.

Bryk, A., Camburn, E. & Louis, K. S. (1996). *Promoting school improvement through professional communities: An analysis of Chicago elementary schools.* Paper presented at the annual meeting of the American Educational Research Association, New York.

Caine, R. N. & Caine, G. (1997). *Education on the Edge of Possibility.* Alexandria, VA: Association for Supervision and Curriculum Development.

Canady, R. L. & Rettig, M. D., (1993). Unlocking the lockstep high school schedule. *Phi Delta Kappan, 75* (4), 310–314.

Carlson, R. V. (1965). *Adoption of educational innovations.* Eugene: University of Oregon Press.

Carlson, R. V. (1996). *Reframing and reform: Perspectives on organization, leadership, and school change.* White Plains, NY: Longman Publishers.

Cohen, D. K., McLaughlin, M. W. & Talbert, J. E. (Eds.). (1993). *Teaching for understanding: Challenges for policy and practice.* San Francisco: Jossey-Bass.

Conley, D., Dunlap, D. & Goldman, P. (1992). The "vision thing" and school restructuring. *OSSC Report, 32* (2), 1–8.

Creemers, B. (1994). *The effective classroom.* London: Cassell.

Cremin, L. A. (1988). *American education: The metropolitan experience 1876–1980.* New York: Harper & Row.

Cuban, L. (1988). A fundamental puzzle of school reform. *Phi Delta Kappan, 70* (5), 341–344.

Cuban, L. (1990). Reforming again, again, and again. *Educational Researcher, 19* (1), 3–13.

Cusick, P. A. (1997). The Coalition goes to school. *American Journal of Education, 105* (2), 211–221.

Daft, R. & Becker, S. (1979). *The innovative organization.* New York: Elsevier.

Daft, R. & Huber, G. (1987). How organizations learn. In N. DiTomaso & S. Bacharach (Eds.), *Research in the sociology of organizations, Vol. 5.* Greenwich, CN: JAI.

Daloz, L. A. P., Keen, C. H., Keen, J. & Parks, S. D. (1996). *Common fire: Leading lives of commitment in a complex world.* Boston: Beacon Press.

Dana, N. F. & Pitts, J. H., Jr. (1993). The use of metaphor and reflective coaching in the exploration of principal thinking: A case study of principal change. *Educational Administration Quarterly, 29* (3), 323–338.

Deal, T., Meyer, J. & Scott, R. (1975). Organizational influences on educational innovations. In J. Baldridge & T. Deal (Eds.), *Managing change in educational organizations.* Berkeley: McCutcheon.

Delpit, L. (1995). *Other people's children: Cultural conflict in the classroom.* New York: The New Press.

Deutch, K. (1977). *Ecosocial systems and ecopolitics: A reader on human and social implications of environmental management in developing countries.* Paris: Unesco.

Dewey, J. (1938). *Logic: The theory of inquiry.* New York: Henry Holt.

Dillard, A. (1989). *The writing life.* New York: Harper & Row.

Dimmock, C. (1995). Reconceptualizing restructuring for school effectiveness and school improvement. *International Journal of Educational Reform, 4* (3), 285–300.

Dimmock, C. & Hattie, J. (1996). School principals' self-efficacy and its measurement in a context of restructuring. *School Effectiveness and School Improvement, 7* (1), 62–75.

Durkheim, E. (1956). *Education and sociology* (translation). New York: Free Press.

Easterby-Smith, M. (1990). Creating a learning organization. *Personnel Review, 19* (5), 24–28.

Edmonds, R. (1979). Effective schools for the urban poor. *Educational Leadership, 37* (1), 15–24.

Eisner, E. (1992). Educational reform and the ecology of schooling. *Teachers College Record, 93* (4), 611–627.

Elmore, R. F. (1992). Why restructuring alone won't improve teaching. *Educational Leadership, 49* (7), 44–48.

Elmore, R. F. (1995). Structural reform and educational practice. *Educational Researcher, 24* (9), 23–26.

Elmore, R. F. & McLaughlin, M. (1988). *Steady work. Policy, practice, and the reform of American education.* Santa Monica, CA: RAND Corp.

Evans, L. & Teddlie, C. (1995). Facilitating change in schools: Is there one best style? *School Effectiveness and School Improvement, 6* (1), 1–22.

Evans, M. & Hopkins, D. (1988). School climate and the psychological state of the individual teacher as factors affecting the utilisation of educational ideas following an in-service course. *British Educational Research Journal, 14* (3), 211–230.

Evans, R. (1996). *The human side of school change: Reform, resistance, and the real-life problems of innovations.* San Francisco: Jossey-Bass.

Fink, D. (forthcoming). The attrition of change: A study of change and continuity. *School Effectiveness and School Improvement.*

Firestone, W. A. (1980). Images of schools and patterns of organizational change. *American Journal of Education, 88,* 459–487.

Firestone, W. A. (1996). Images of teaching and proposals for reform: A comparison of ideas from cognitive and organizational research. *Educational Administration Quarterly, 32* (2), 209–235.

Firestone, W. A. & Corbett, H. (1988). Planned organizational change. In N. Boyan (Eds.). *Handbook of research on educational administration* (pp. 321–340). New York: Longman.

Firestone, W. A. & Louis, K. S. (this volume).

Firestone, W. A. & Wilson, B. (1985). Using bureaucratic and cultural linkages to improve instruction. *Educational Administration Quarterly, 21,* 7–30.

Fitzpatrick, K. M. & Yoels, W. C. (1992). Policy, school structure, and sociodemographic effects on statewide high school dropout rates. *Sociology of Education, 65* (1), 76–93.

Freeman, C., Maruyama, G., Frederickson, J. & Walkowiak, G. (1997). Block scheduling: A structural change that matters. Paper presented at AERA annual meeting in Chicago on March 26, 1997.

Fullan, M. G. (1982). *The meaning of educational change.* New York: Teachers College Press.

Fullan, M. G. (1992). Visions that blind. *Educational Leadership, 49* (5), 19–22.

Fullan, M. G. (1993). *Change forces: Probing the depths of educational reform.* London: Falmer Press.

Fullan, M. G. (1997). Emotion and hope: Constructive concepts for complex times. In A. Hargreaves (Ed.), *Rethinking educational change with heart and mind: The 1997 ASCD yearbook* (pp. 216–233). Alexandria, VA: Association for Supervision and Curriculum Development.

Fullan, M. G. & Hargreaves, A. (1991). *What's worth fighting for? Working together for your school.* Andover, MA: The Regional Laboratory for Educational Improvement of the Northeast and Islands.

Fullan, M. G. & Stiegelbauer, S. (1991). *The new meaning of educational change.* New York: Teachers College Press.

Gleick, J. (1988). *Chaos: The making of a new science.* New York: Penguin Books.

Goffman, E. (1974). *Frame analysis: An essay on the organization of experience.* Cambridge, MA: Harvard University Press.

Goldman, P., Dunlap, D. & Conley, D. (1993). Facilitative power and nonstandardized solutions to school site restructuring. *Educational Administration Quarterly, 29* (1), 69–92.

Goldring, E. B. & Pasternack, R. (1994). Principals' coordinating strategies and school effectiveness. *School Effectiveness and School Improvement, 5* (3), 239–253.

Goldring, E. B. & Shapira, R. (1996). Principals' survival with parental involvement. *School Effectiveness and School Improvement, 7* (4), 342–360.

Goodlad, J. (1975). *Dynamics of educational change.* New York: McGraw-Hill.

Goodlad, J. (1990). Studying the education of educators: From conception to findings. *Phi Delta Kappan, 71* (9), 698–701.

Goodman, P. S., Pennings, J. M. & Associates. (1977). *New perspectives on organizational effectiveness.* San Francisco: Jossey Bass.

Greenleaf, R. K. (1977). *Servant leadership: A journey into the nature of legitimate power and greatness.* New York: Paulist Press.

Gross, N. Guacquinta, J. B. & Bernstein, M. (1971). *Implementing organizational innovations.* New York: Basic Books.

Guba, E. (1968). Development, diffusion and education. In T. Eidell & J. Kitchell (Eds.), *Knowledge production and utilization in educational administration* (pp. 37–63). Eugene: Center for the Advanced Study of Educational Administration, University of Oregon.

Hall, G. E. & Hord, S. M. (1987). *Change in schools: Facilitating the process.* Albany, NY: State University of New York Press.

Hallinger, P. & Leithwood, K. (1994). Introduction: Exploring the impact of principal leadership. *School Effectiveness and School Improvement, 5* (3), 206–218.

Hargreaves, A. (1993). Individualism and individuality: Reinterpreting the teacher culture. In J. W. Little & M. W. McLaughlin (Ed.), *Teachers' work: Individuals, colleagues and contexts.* New York: Teachers College Press.

Hargreaves, A. (1994). *Changing teachers, changing times: Teachers' work and culture in the postmodern age.* New York: Teachers College Press.

Hargreaves, A. (1997). *Rethinking educational change with heart and mind: 1997 ASCD yearbook.* Alexandria, VA: Association for Supervision and Curriculum Development.

Hargreaves, A. (in press). The emotional politics of teaching and teacher development: With implications for educational leadership. International Journal of Leadership in Education.

Hargreaves, A. & Fullan, M. (1998). *What's worth fighting for out there?* Toronto: OISE, New York: Teachers College Press.

Hargreaves, A., Earl, L. & Ryan, J. (1996). *Schooling for change: Reinventing education for early adolescents.* Philadelphia: Falmer Press.

Hargreaves, A., Lieberman, A., Fullan, M. & Hopkins, D. (1998). *International handbook of educational change (Vol. 5)*. London: Kluwer.

Hargreaves, A., Shaw, P. & Fink, D. (1997). *Research questions for the seven frames*. Toronto: Authors.

Hargreaves, D. H. (1995). School culture, school effectiveness, and school improvement. *School Effectiveness and School Improvement, 6* (1), 23–46.

Hatch, T. (1988). The differences in theory that matter in the practice of school improvement. *American Educational Research Journal, 35* (1), 3–31.

Havelock, R., Guskin, A., Frohman, M., Havelock, M., Hill, M. & Huber, J. (1969). *Planning for innovation through dissemination and utilization of knowledge*. Ann Arbor, MI: Institute for Social Research.

Heath, S. B. & McLaughlin, M. W. (1993). *Identity and inner-city youth: Beyond ethnicity and gender*. New York: Teachers College Press.

Heck, R. H. & Marcoulides, G. A. (1993). Principal leadership behaviors and school achievement. *NASSP Bulletin, 77* (553), 20–28.

Heck, R. H. & Marcoulides, G. A. (1996). School culture and performance: Testing the invariance of an organizational model. *School Effectiveness and School Improvement, 7* (1), 76–95.

Heller, M. F. & Firestone, W. A. (1995). Who's in charge here? Sources of leadership for change in eight schools. *Elementary School Journal, 96* (1), 65–86.

Herriott, R. & Gross, N. (1979). *The dynamics of planned educational change: Case studies and analyses*. Berkeley: McCutchan.

Hopkins, D. (1993). *A teacher's guide to classroom research* (2nd ed.). Philadelphia: Open University Press.

Hord, S. M. & Boyd, V. (1995). Professional development fuels a culture of continuous improvement. *Journal of Staff Development, 16* (1), 10–15.

Hoy, W., Tartar, J. & Kottkamp, R. (1991). *Open schools, healthy schools*. Thousand Oaks, CA: Sage.

Huberman, M. (1993). Linking the practitioner and researcher communities for school improvement. *School Effectiveness and School Improvement, 4* (1), 1–16.

Huberman, M. & Miles, M. B. (1984). *Innovation up close: How school improvement works*. New York: Plenum Press.

Josephson, H. G. (1974). *Jeanette Rankin: First lady in congress*. Indianapolis: Bobbs-Merrill.

Joyce, B. & Showers, B. (1995). *Student achievement through staff development* (2nd ed.). New York: Longman.

Keller, H. (1903). *Optimism*. New York: T. Y. Crowell & Co.

Kerchner, C., Koppich, J. & Weeres, J. (1997). *United mind workers: Unions and teaching in the knowledge society*. San Francisco: Jossey Bass.

Kilduff, M., Funk & Mehra. (1997). Engineering identity in a Japanese factory. *Organization Science, 8,* 579–592.

Kliebard, H. M. (1995). *The struggle for the American curriculum 1893–1958*, 2nd Ed. New York: Rutledge.

Kofman, F. & Senge, P. M. (1995). Communities of commitment: The heart of learning organizations. In S. Chawla & J. Renesch (Eds.), *Learning organizations: Developing cultures for tomorrow's workplace* (pp. 15–43). Portland, OR: Productivity Press.

Kruse, S. (1995). *Community as a foundation for professionalism: Case studies of middle school teachers*. Doctoral dissertation, University of Minnesota, Minneapolis.

Labaree, D. F. (1997). Public goods, private goods: The American struggle over educational goals. *American Educational Research Journal, 34* (1), 39–81.

Lee, V. E. & Loeb, S. (1995). Where do Head Start attendees end up? One reason why preschool effects fade out. *Educational Evaluation and Policy Analysis, 17,* 62–82.

Lee, V. E. & Smith, J. B. (1997). High school size: Which works best and for whom? *Educational Evaluation and Policy Analysis, 19* (3), 205–227.

Leighton, M. S. (1996, July). *The role of leadership in sustaining school reform: Voices from the field*. Washington, DC: U. S. Department of Education.

Leithwood, K. (1994). Leadership for school restructuring. *Educational Administration Quarterly, 30* (4), 498–518.

Leithwood, K. & Jantzi, D. (1997). Explaining variation in teachers' perceptions of principals leadership: A replication. *Journal of Educational Administration, 35* (3–4), 213–231.

Leithwood, K. & Louis, K. S. (Eds.). (In press). *The learning school and school improvement: Linkages and strategies*. Lisse, NL: Swets and Zeitlinger.

Leithwood, K. & Steinbach, R. (1995) *Expert problem solving: evidence of school and district leaders*. Albany, NY: SUNY press.

Leithwood, K., Jantzi, D. & Menzies, T. (1994). Earning teachers' commitment to curriculum reform. *Peabody Journal of Education, 69* (4), 38–61.

Leithwood, K., Jantzi, D. & Steinbach, R. (1995). An organisational learning perspective on school responses to central policy initiatives. *School Organisation, 15* (3), 229–252.

Leitner, D. (1994). Do principals affect student outcomes: An organizational perspective. *School Effectiveness and School Improvement, 5* (3), 219–238.

Levin, B. & Riffell, J. A. (1997). *Schools and the changing world: Struggling toward the future*. Washington, D. C. Falmer.

Levine, S. L. (1993). Developmental assessment: Accounting for adult growth in supervision and evaluation. *Journal of Personnel Evaluation in Education, 7* (3), 223–230.

Lieberman, A. (1996). Practices that support teacher development: Transforming conceptions of professional learning. In M. W. McLaughlin & I. Oberman (Eds.), *Teacher learning: New policies, new practices*. New York: Teachers College Press.

Lieberman, A. & Grolnick, M. (1997). Networks, reform, and the professional development of teachers. In A. Hargreaves (Ed.), *Rethinking educational change with heart and mind: 1997 ASCD yearbook* (pp. 192–215). Alexandria, VA: Association for Supervision and Curriculum Development.

Lieberman, A. & McLaughlin, M. W. (1992). Networks for educational change: Powerful and problematic. *Phi Delta Kappan, 73* (9), 673–677.

Linn, R. (1998). Assessments and accountability. Distinguished Contributions to Research in Education Award, Invited Address. Paper presented at the annual meetings of the American Educational Research Association, San Diego.

Lippitt, R., Watson, G. & Westley, B. (1958). *The dynamics of planned change*. New York: Harcourt Brace.

Little, J. W. (1982). Norms of collegiality and experimentation: Workplace conditions of school success. *American Educational Research Journal, 19* (3), 325–340.

Little, J. W. (1990). The persistence of privacy: Autonomy and initiative in teachers' professional relations. *Teachers College Record, 91* (4), 509–536.

Little, J. W. (1993). Teachers' professional development in a climate of educational reform. *Educational Evaluation and Policy Analysis, 15* (2), 129–151.

Little, J. W. & McLaughlin, M. W. (1993). *Teachers' work: Individuals, colleagues and contexts*. New York: Teachers College Press.

Lortie, D. C. (1975). *Schoolteacher: A sociological study*. Chicago: The University of Chicago Press.

Louis, K. S. (1994). Beyond "managed change:" Rethinking how schools improve. *School Effectiveness and School Improvement, 5,* 1–22.

Louis, K. S. & Kruse, S. (in press). Creating community in reform: Images of organizational learning in urban schools. In K. Leithwood & K. S. Louis (Eds.), *Organizational learning and school improvement: Linkages and strategies*. Lisse, NL: Swets and Zeitlinger

Louis, K. S. & Miles, M. (1990). *Improving the urban high school: What works and why*. New York: Teachers College Press.

Louis, K. S. & Murphy, J. (1994). The evolving role of the principal: Some concluding thoughts. In J. Murphy & K. S. Louis (Eds.), *Reshaping the principalship: Insights from transformational reform efforts* (pp. 265–281). Thousand Oaks, CA: Corwin Press.

Louis, K. S. & Sieber, S. (1979). *Bureaucracy and the dispersed organization: The educational extension agent experiment*. Norwood, NJ: Ablex.

Louis, K. S., Kruse, S. D. & Associates. (1995). *Professionalism and community: Perspectives on reforming urban schools*. Thousand Oaks, CA: Corwin Press.

Louis K. S., Marks, H. M. & Kruse, S. (1996). Teachers' professional community in restructuring schools. *American Educational Research Journal, 33* (4), 757–788.

McDonnell, L. & Elmore, R. (1987). Getting the job done: Alternative policy instruments. *Educational Evaluation and Policy Analysis, 9,* 133–152.

McLaughlin, M. W. (1990). The RAND change agent study revisited: Macro perspectives and micro realities. *Educational Researcher*, December, pp. 11–16.

McLaughlin, M. W. & Talbert, J. E. (1993). *Contexts that matter for teaching and learning: Strategic opportunities for meeting the nation's education goals*. Stanford, CA: Center for Research on the Context of Secondary School Teaching, Stanford University.

Maehr, M. L. & Maehr, J. M. (1996). Schools aren't as good as they used to be; they never were. *Educational Researcher, 25* (8), 21–24.

Maehr, M. L. & Parker, S. A. (1993). A tale of two schools—And the primary task of leadership. *Phi Delta Kappan, 75* (3), 233–239.

March, J. G. & Olsen, J. (1976). *Ambiguity and organizational choice*. Oslo: Universitetsforlaget.

March, J. G. & Sutton, R. I. (1997). Organizational performance as a dependent variable. *Organizational Science, 8* (6), 698–719.

Marks, H. M. & Louis, K. S. (1997). Does teacher empowerment affect the classroom? The implications of teacher empowerment for instruction practice and student academic performance. *Educational Evaluation and Policy Analysis, 19* (3), 245–275.

Mason, R. O. & Mitroff, I. I. (1981). *Challenging strategic planning assumptions: Theory, cases, and techniques*. New York: John Wiley & Sons.

Meyer, J. W. (1987). Implications of an institutional view of education. In M. T. Hallinan (Ed.), *The social organization of schools*. New York: Plenum.

Meyer, J. & Rowan, B. (1977). Institutionalized organizations: Formal structure as myth and ceremony. *American Journal of Sociology, 83*, 340–363.

Miech, R. A. & Elder, G. H. Jr., (1996). The service ethic and teaching. *Sociology of Education, 69* (3), 237–253.

Miles, M. B. (1965). Planned change and organizational health. In *Change processes in the public schools* (pp. 11–36). Eugene, OR: Center for the Study of Educational Administration, University of Oregon.

Miles, M. B., Fullan, M. & Taylor, G. (1980). Organization development in schools: The state of the art. *Review of Educational Research, 50*, 121–183.

Mintzberg, H. (1994). *The rise and the fall of strategic planning*. New York: Prentice-Hall.

Mirel, J. (1994). School reform unplugged: The Bensenville New American School Project, 1991–93. *American Educational Research Journal, 31* (3), 481–518.

Morgan, G. (1997). *Images of organization* (2nd ed.). Thousand Oaks, CA: Sage Publications.

Morgan, G. & Zohar, A. (1996). *Achieving quantum change: Incrementally!! The art of high leverage change*. Toronto: York University, Schulich School of Business Research Program. Web Version 1. 1, October. http://www. imaginiz.com/siteindex. html.

Morse, S. W. (1997). Plaza or pyramid? Metaphors for leadership. *Wingspread Journal, 19* (4), 3–4.

Mort, P. R. (1963). Studies in educational innovation from the Institute of Administrative Research: An overview. In M. B. Miles (Ed.), *Innovation in Education* (pp. 317–328). New York: Teachers College Press.

Mortimer, P., Sammons, P., Stoll, L., Lewis, D. & Ecob, R. (1988). *School matters: The junior years*. Wells: Open Books.

Murphy, C. (1992). Study groups foster schoolwide learning. *Educational Leadership, 50* (3), 71–74.

Murphy, J. & Beck, L. G. (1994). Reconstructing the principalship: Challenges and possibilities. In J. Murphy & K. S. Louis (Eds.), *Reshaping the principalship: Insights from transformational reform efforts* (pp. 3–19). Thousand Oaks, CA: Corwin Press.

Murphy, J. & Louis, K. S. (1994). *Reshaping the principalship: Insights from transformational reform efforts*. Thousand Oaks, CA: Corwin Press.

National Education Association. (1972). *Status of the American public school teacher, 1970–71*. Washington, DC: Author.

National Education Association. (1982). *Status of the American public school teacher, 1980–81*. Washington, DC: Author.

National Education Association. (1987). *Status of the American public school teacher, 1985–86*. Washington, DC: Author.

Newmann, F. M. & Associates (1996). *Authentic achievement: Restructuring schools for intellectual quality*. San Francisco: Jossey-Bass.

Oakes, J. (1993). Creating middle schools: Technical, normative, and political considerations. *Elementary School Journal, 93* (5), 461–480.

Oakes, J. (1994). More than misapplied technology: A normative and political response to Hallinan on tracking. *Sociology of Education, 67* (2), 84–89, 91.

Oakes, J., Wells, A. S., Yonezawa, S. & Rey, K. (1997). Equity lessons from detracking schools. In A. Hargreaves (Ed.), *Rethinking educational change with heart and mind* (pp. 43–72). Alexandria, VA: Association for Supervision and Curriculum Development.

Ogilvie, D. (1985). *Ogilvie on advertising*. New York: Vintage.

Organization for Economic Cooperation and Development. (1998). *Education at a glance: OECD indicators—1997*. Paris: Author.

Palmer, P. J. (1998). *The courage to teach*. San Francisco: Jossey-Bass.

Pedler, M., Burgoyne, J. & Boydell, T. (1994). *The learning company: A strategy for sustainable development* (2nd ed.). New York: McGraw-Hill.

Perrone, V. (1991). *A letter to teachers: Reflections on schooling and the art of teaching*. San Francisco: Jossey-Bass.

Peters, T. J. & Waterman, R. H. (1982). *In search of excellence: Lessons from America's best run companies*. New York: Harper & Row.

Pounder, D. G., Ogawa, R. T. & Adams, E. A. (1995). Leadership as an organization-wide phenomenon: Its impact on school performance. *Educational Administration Quarterly, 31* (4), 564–588.

Prestine, N. & McGreal, T. (1997). Fragile changes, sturdy lives: Implementing authentic assessment in schools. *Educational Administration Quarterly, 33* (3), 371–400.

Quinn, J. & Hargreaves, A. (1997, December). *Change frames creating communities of learners: Workshop handouts for the National Staff Development Conference*. Toronto: Authors.

Resnick, L. B. (1987). Learning in school and out. *Educational Researcher, 16* (9), 13–20.

Reynolds, D., Bollen, R., Creemers, B. P. M., Hopkins, D., Stoll, L. & Lagerweij, N. A. J. (1996). *Making good schools: Linking school effectiveness and school improvement*. London, New York: Routledge.

Reynolds, D., Hopkins, D. & Stoll, L. (1993). Linking school effectiveness knowledge and school improvement practice: Towards a synergy. *School Effectiveness and School Improvement, 4* (1), 37–58.

Rogers, E. (1983). *Diffusion of innovations*. New York: Free Press.

Rollow, S. & Bryk, A. (1995). Creating professional community in a school reform left behind. In K. S. Louis, S. Kruse & Associates (Eds.). *Professionalism and community. Perspectives on reforming urban schools*. Thousand Oaks, CA: Corwin.

Rosenblum, S. & Louis, K. S. (1981). *Stability and change: Innovation in an educational context*. New York: Plenum.

Rosenholtz, S. J. (1989). *Teachers' workplace: The social organization of schools*. New York: Longman.

Rosenholtz, S. J. (1991). *Teachers' workplace: The social organization of schools*. New York: Teachers College Press.

Ross, J. A. (1995). Strategies for enhancing teachers' beliefs in their effectiveness: Research on a school improvement hypothesis. *Teachers College Record, 97* (2), 227–251.

Rossman, G, Corbett, H. & Firestone, W. (1985). *A study of professional cultures in improving high schools*. Philadelphia: Research for Better Schools.

Ruddock, J., Day, J. & Wallace, G. (1997). Students' perspectives on school improvement. In A. Hargreaves (Ed.), *Rethinking Educational Change With Heart and Mind, The 1997 ASCD Yearbook*. Alexandra, VA: ASCD.

Ruscoe, G. C. & Miller, S. K. (1991). The dilemmas of change: Lessons from a school improvement effort gone awry. *Knowledge: Creation, Diffusion, Utilization, 13* (2), 170–192.

Rutter, M. (1982). *Fifteen thousand hours: Secondary schools and their effects on children*. Cambridge, MA: Harvard University Press.

Sarason, S. B. (1972). *The creation of settings and future societies*. San Francisco: Brookline Books.

Sarason, S. B. (1990). *The predictable failure of educational reform: Can we change course before it's too late?* San Francisco: Jossey-Bass.

Sarason, S. B. (1996). *Revisiting "The culture of the school and the problem of change."* New York: Teachers College Press.

Scheerens, J. (1992). *Effective schooling*. London: Cassell.

Schön, D. (1984). *The reflective practitioner: How professionals think in action*. New York: Basic Books.

Senge, P. M. (1990). *The fifth discipline*. New York: Currency Doubleday.

Sergiovanni, T. (1994). *Building community in schools*. San Francisco: Jossey-Bass.

Short, P. M., Greer, J. T. & Melvin, W. M. (1994). Creating empowered schools: Lessons in change. *Journal of Educational Administration, 32* (4), 38–52.

Slavin, R. E., Madden, N. A., Dolan, L. J. & Wasik, B. A. (1996). *Every child, every school: Success for all.* Thousand Oaks, CA: Corwin Press.

Smylie, M., Lazarus, V. & Brownlee-Conyers, J. (1996). Instructional outcomes of school-based participative decision making. *Educational Evaluation and Policy Analysis, 18* (3), 181–198.

Southworth, G. (1996). Improving primary schools: Shifting the emphasis and clarifying the focus. *School Organisation, 16* (3), 263–280.

Sparks, D. & Hirsh, S. (1997). *A new vision for staff development.* Alexandria, VA: Association for Supervision and Curriculum Development.

Spillane, J. (1998). State policy and the non-monolithic nature of the local school district: Organizational and professional considerations. *American Educational Research Journal, 35* (1), 33–63.

Spradley, J. P. (1980). *Participant observation.* Fort Worth: Harcourt Brace College Publishers.

Stacey, R. D. (1992). *Managing the unknowable: Strategic boundaries between order and chaos in organizations.* San Francisco: Jossey-Bass.

Stein, M. K. & Wang., M. C. (1988). Teacher development and school improvement: The process of teacher change. *Teaching and Teacher Education, 4* (2), 171–187.

Stoll, L. & Fink, D. (1994). School effectiveness and school improvement: Voices from the field. *School Effectiveness and School Improvement, 5* (2), 149–177.

Stringfield, S. (1995). Attempting to enhance students learning through innovative programs: The case for schools evolving into high reliability organizations. *School Effectiveness and School Improvement, 6* (1), 67–96.

Stringfield, S. & Teddlie, C. (1991). Observers as predictors of schools: Multiyear outlier status on achievement tests. *The Elementary School Journal, 91*, 358–376.

Stringfield, S., Ross S. & Smith, L. (1996). Bold plans for school restructuring: The new American schools designs. Mahwah, NJ: Lawrence Erlbaum.

Suzuki, S. (1970). *Zen mind, beginner's mind.* New York: Weatherhill.

Telford, H. (1996). *Transforming schools through collaborative leadership.* Washington, DC: Falmer Press.

Tichy, N. (1981). *Managing strategic change.* New York: Wiley.

Toole, J. (forthcoming). *Professional learning community and school reform: Case studies of service learning.* Unpublished doctoral dissertation, University of Minnesota, Minneapolis.

Townsend, T. (1997). What makes schools effective? A comparison between school communities in Australia and the USA. *School Effectiveness and School Improvement, 8* (3), 311–326.

Tyack, D. & Cuban, L. (1995). *Tinkering toward utopia: A century of public school reform.* Cambridge, MA: Harvard University Press.

Voogt, J., Lagerweij, N. & Louis, K. S. (in press). School development and organizational learning.

Waller, W. (1965). *The sociology of teaching.* New York: Wiley

Weick, K. (1976). Educational organizations as loosely coupled systems. *Administrative Science Quarterly, 21*, 1–19.

Weick, K. (1989). Organized improvisation: 20 years of organizing. *Communication Studies, 40* (4), 241–248.

Wheatley, M. J. (1992). *Leadership and the new science: Learning about organization from an orderly universe.* San Francisco: Berrett-Koehler Publishers.

Wheatley, M. J. & Kellner-Rogers, M. (1996). *a simpler way.* San Francisco: Berrett-Koehler Publishers.

Wilson, W. J. (1997). *When work disappears: The world of the new urban poor.* New York: Vintage Books.

Wincek, J. (1995). *Negotiating the maze of school reform: How metaphors shape culture in a new magnet school.* New York: Teachers College Press.

Wohlstetter, P. & McCurdy, K. (1991). The link between school decentralization and school politics. *Urban Education, 25* (4), 391–414.

Zigarelli, M. A. (1996). *An empirical test of conclusions from effective schools research. Journal of Educational Research, 90* (2), 103–110. We contend that school improvement research will not obtain the impact that we hope for until more attention is paid to the broader range of educational outcomes that the public cares about.

CHAPTER 13

Enduring Dilemmas of School Organization

Rodney T. Ogawa, Robert L. Crowson, and Ellen B. Goldring

The Sixty-fifth Yearbook (Part II) of the National Society for the Study of Education (NSSE), published in 1966, was titled *The Changing American School*. The central theme of this key volume was that "a mood of change prevails in America's schools." Although there certainly had been calls for change in earlier decades, John Goodlad, the volume's editor, noted that the schools "remained very much as they had been" (1966, p. 1). However, in the mid-1960s, others reported the schools were "changing rapidly, almost explosively, in every respect." The reason? A set of powerful societal forces were producing a "tide of change in school organization" (Heather, 1966, p. 129). Among these forces were Sputnik and the Cold War; the civil rights revolution; urban growth toward metropolitanism; the enormous scale of government, business, and labor; dynamic technological and economic changes; and the rising importance and influence of the behavioral sciences.

It is easy for us 30 years later to observe that the change of that day was not very "explosive." Indeed, major alterations in school organization highlighted in the Goodlad (1966) volume (non-grading, the end of the self-contained classroom, team teaching) were long ago relegated to the sizable "tried and failed" category of educational reform.

The Changing American School marked a vital step forward conceptually, combining the examination of organizational change in education with deep-seated alterations in American culture and society. However, we realize now how overly optimistic were predictions such as those by Francis Chase (in the final chapter of the volume) that "significant changes" are underway in elementary and secondary education and that these are a result of societal transformations "to which education must respond" (Chase, 1966, p. 271). Additionally, Chase's further speculation that the social sciences are now becoming valuable "instruments in the development of educational institutions and practices" (Chase, 1966, p. 271) serves only to add to our sense that a train, thought to be on the move in 1966, somehow lost its track.

Why does educational reform again and again seem to derail? One underexplored answer, interestingly enough, may have been implied in yet another chapter in *The Changing American School*. Ralph W. Tyler, in a brief reference to the importance of studying organizations, warned that there are many "features" of organizations that can lead in quite opposing directions. A communications system, for example, can "operate selectively to hold the organization together or to destroy its unity" (Tyler, 1966, p. 211). Despite discussions at that time of the "organization man," said Tyler, "we are only beginning to learn how organizations function" (Tyler, 1966, p. 211).

Tyler's observation regarding features that can lead in opposite directions proceeded from a rich tradition in organization theory, established by such major figures as Robert Merton and Alvin Gouldner. Yet the insight that key elements of organization can lead toward opposing tendencies (Gouldner, 1955) escaped much of the later work that used organizational analysis as a guide to changing the American school. There has been a clear-cut recognition that differing images and metaphors of organization can provide alternative understandings (Scott, 1992; Morgan, 1986; Bolman & Deal, 1991). However, the possibility that these "opposites" present us with enduring dilemmas (such as a tradeoff between centralization and decentralization), which engage us at the very heart of "tried and failed" reform in American education, has not yet reached a center stage of informed analysis.[1]

Understandably, reformers and theorists alike have conceived of organizational change as an iterative and possibly progressive improvement of schools in the face of newly discovered flaws in existing structures and processes. These "flaws" often connect well with a recognition that changing societal conditions require a reformed organization. Thus the "one best system" (Tyack, 1974) and an "efficiency movement" (Callahan, 1962) fit the progressive era's emphasis upon hierarchical structures, "business" outlooks, streamlining, professionalism, and a reduction of out-of-control localism. With perhaps less impact upon the organizational than the administrative side of schooling, a "human relations" movement (influenced by the Great Depression) tried to counter overly authoritarian tendencies with a more "consideration"-centered style of leadership (see Getzels, 1958). In our century's second half, significant new understandings of schools as organizations (for example, their permeability and vulnerability, as well as their many buffers, resource dependencies, and "politics") arose out of an open system's understanding of education's increasingly complex milieu. It was only a small step to the realization that "uncertainty" (Thompson, 1967), "loose-coupling" (Weick, 1976), and "ambiguity" (March & Olsen, 1976) may be among the defining qualities of an ongoing struggle between educational organizations and their external environments. It seemed to be only a further small step to begin to reform educational organizations toward greater responsiveness to their environments (for example, through decentralization, "markets", or even "standards"). With each "movement," a central problem of the preceding movement was hopefully to be "corrected" (such as overcoming inadequate controls, low consideration, low adaptability, or over-bureaucratization). It is possible, however, that each stage of correction or improvement merely rearranged underlying tensions, or dilemmas, that are still unresolved and may even be "fundamental" (Bidwell, 1965).

We argue that the evolution of organization theory, while a steady process of "correcting" older problems, is simultaneously a less well-recognized struggle against some very persistent dilemmas of organization. Schools and efforts toward school reform have particularly been "caught" in these dilemmas, as evidenced over the years by a host of conflicting and even contradictory organizational characteristics and conditions. It is the purpose of this chapter to identify and examine a few of the enduring dilemmas of school organization and to draw from this discussion some altered insights into practical problems of administration.

Organizational Dilemmas: Beyond Individual Choices

Enduring organizational dilemmas—what is a dilemma? Dilemmas are neither problems to be solved nor issues to be faced. Problems are presumed solvable; issues can be negotiated and thus are resolvable. As we use the term in this chapter, we assert that dilemmas reveal deeper, more fundamental dichotomies. They present situations with equally valued alternatives. As a consequence, dilemmas cannot be solved or resolved. The term dilemma, as we use it throughout this chapter, means "contradictory stance" (Elbow, 1983). It refers to the paradox of confronting conflicting positions, both of which are, or can be, "true." As Cuban (1992) points out, dilemmas occur when "competing, highly prized values cannot be fully satisfied . . . [dilemmas] are far messier, less structured and often intractable to routine solutions. They become predicaments rather than problems when constraints and uncertainty make it impossible for any prized value to triumph" (p. 6).

The very notion of a dilemma infers deep commitment to core values that are often found in conflict with one another. Precisely because the values or poles of a dilemma cannot present viable choices, the challenge in the face of a dilemma is not to choose from alternatives, but to act to create alternatives and manage the dilemma (Berlak & Berlak, 1981; Lampert; 1985). Decisions cannot be optimized in the face of a dilemma; at best, satisfying can occur.

In searching the literature for a body of scholarly writing about "organizational dilemmas," the concept usually refers to a rather problem-based, individualistic focus. Thus for example, there are discussions about moral dilemmas in the business world (Valasquez, 1996)—downsizing versus large CEO compensation, social dilemmas in decision-making—the likelihood of cooperating in groups (Chen, Au and Komorita, 1996), and human dilemmas in the workplace—alcoholism and drug abuse (Korman, 1994). A common theme is that people in organizations, whether in groups or as individuals, face problems, or dilemmas. Often the literature on dilemmas is couched in economic terms. For example, empirical studies address the question: What will person or group A decide when faced with dilemma X depending on resources from person or group B and C (Mannix, 1993)? Other writers discuss changing global market places, mergers and acquisitions, and new technologies (Korman, 1994).

Korman and associates (1994) refer to dilemmas as aspects of the changing environment and shifting work force in organizations that have significant implications for management. Specific examples include changes in family life, economic recessions, and racial, ethnic and gender issues. An example of a major dilemma from this perspective is whether executives can determine ethical behavior in a global, international context (Solomon, 1996). Chen *et al.*

(1996) use the term "social dilemma." They state, "A social dilemma may be characterized as a situation in which members of a group are faced with two choices: a cooperative choice that maximizes rewards for the group, and a noncooperative choice that maximizes rewards for the individual" (p. 37). A social dilemma, then, is a "situation in which members of a group or organization are faced with a conflict between two choices" (p. 37). This definition implies that dilemmas, like problems, must be confronted by making a clear choice.

As noted above, these descriptions are not consistent with our notion of dilemma. Dilemmas are value-laden choices that can never be resolved. Dilemmas are prevalent in organizations because multiple values are always at play. In the face of difficult choices, dilemmas still endure.

Dilemmas can occur at all levels and in various dimensions of organization. In this chapter, we confine ourselves to organization as a unit of analysis. Thus we examine dilemmas embedded in educational organizations. The organizational perspective is crucial to our discussion as we examine dilemmas that are deeply embedded in the culture and contexts of organizations and that transcend the choices made by individuals or groups within organizations. Using this perspective, organization can be viewed as "a set of people who share many beliefs, values and assumptions that encourage them to make mutually-reinforcing interpretations of their own acts and the acts of others" (Smircich & Stubbart, 1985, p. 727). Organizational members and their subjective actions and decisions are not the focal point of reference, but rather individuals are viewed as more "generic," interchangeable fillers of roles or followers of rules (Wiley, 1988; Weick, 1995). Following Schein (1996), we take a position that "such taken-for-granted, shared tacit ways of perceiving, thinking and reacting, is [was] one of the most powerful and stable forces operating in organizations" (p. 231). Thus for example, dilemmas facing organizations, such as adapting to environmental pressures versus maintaining internal certainty, are not the responsibility of a particular person's job description but touch upon all aspects of an organization.

Dilemmas, it seems, by definition are enduring; that is, they are unsolvable and irresolvable and, thus, endure. Miles (1981) suggests that organizational dilemmas are "recurrent and pervasive." As with many organizational phenomena, dilemmas can remain hidden from the view of organizational members and analysts. Although theory may illuminate dilemmas previously unrecognized by practitioners, practitioners may apprehend dilemmas for which no theories account.

Central Dilemmas of School Organization

This chapter presents a discussion of enduring dilemmas that are prominent in organizations and that have in-

formed our understanding of schools and educational administration. Our discussion focuses on seven dilemmas. Like Miles (1981) a decade and a half ago, we separate the dilemmas into two categories: internal and external. However, we depart from Miles, who identified internal dilemmas, including environmental dependence versus autonomy and environmental contact versus withdrawal, that actually concern relations with the external environment. We instead specify internal dilemmas that concern social and work relations, saving the external category for dilemmas that focus expressly on environmental relations. The internal dilemmas we identify include the following: 1) goals, 2) task structures, 3) professionalism, and 4) hierarchy. The external dilemmas involve the following: 1) persistence, 2) boundaries, and 3) compliance.

Why these dilemmas? We have chosen to focus on these dilemmas for two main reasons. First, these dilemmas serve to highlight our major premise: organizations, by definition, face dilemmas. However, a review of much of the organization theory literature suggests that theories do not often address the paradox of "contradictory stances." Instead, theories have often tried to "solve" the dilemmas by proposing alternative theories. We will discuss this point in greater detail as we review the theories related to each dilemma.

Second, these dilemmas encompass a large body of organization theory literature, having contributed to the evolution of organization theory. These dilemmas, therefore, informed the educational administration literature on school organizations. These dilemmas also pertain to the "core" aspects of all organizations: all organizations have goals, hierarchies, boundaries, and so on. Thus although the set of dilemmas presented is not exhaustive, it does represent a comprehensive analysis of organizations. The dilemmas presented in this chapter are illustrative. They illustrate key properties of organizations, which are complex, surprising, deceptive, and ambiguous (Bolman & Deal, 1991).

We treat each dilemma in two ways: 1) We explain its theoretical derivation and 2) we examine its empirical representation in the educational administration literature.

Dilemmas of Internal Relations

Our review of the literature uncovered four dilemmas involving the internal relations of organizations. They begin with the dilemma of pursuing both organizational goals and the fulfillment of individuals needs. The fundamental tension between organizational and individual levels of analysis is also reflected in a second dilemma that pits formal task structures against informal social relations. The third and fourth internal dilemmas are, in a sense, manifestations of the task structure dilemma. One entangles professionals in bureaucratic structures; the other juxtaposes centralized and participative decision-making structures.

Dilemma of Organizational Goals

An enduring and fundamental dilemma for the organization lies in the difficult relationship between organizational objectives and the motives/interests of its individual members. The dilemma, simplistically stated poses the question: How can there be a fit between organizational goals and individual needs? Indeed, this dilemma was fully recognized in the earliest, rational theories about organizations (Taylor, 1911). Thus early rational theories paid attention to structures for worker remuneration, work rules, training, supervision, and span of control. Frederick W. Taylor (1911), for example, simply assumed that employees are motivated by self-interest—that "soldiering" is an organizational problem and therefore a specially designed system of compensation must strive to bring employee contributions into alignment with organizational interests.

A much clearer recognition of the basic dilemma, but also an appealing spirit of resolution, came from Chester Barnard (1938), who reasoned that an organization must seek both effectiveness and efficiency. Effectiveness is the extent to which an organization attains its goals; efficiency is the extent to which individuals attain theirs. It was Barnard's vital insight, as Hodgkinson (1978) has observed, that effectiveness and efficiency are equally necessary; furthermore, only through a "cooperative system" can an organization develop the "capacity to maintain itself by the individual satisfactions it affords" (pp. 183–184).

A similar sense that a balancing and blending of organizational and individual interests is not only possible but necessary was fully reflected in the most frequently referenced theory to be developed in educational administration: the Getzels-Guba Model (1957).[2] Institutional role expectations (at a "nomothetic" dimension of the organization) and individual need dispositions (at an "idiographic" dimension) are in potential conflict, reasoned Getzels (1958), but they are also in dynamic interaction and can be brought toward compatibility.

This hopeful sense that there is no real dilemma here has had an enormous influence upon an additional literature in educational administration, one devoted especially to questions of work motivation. Hoy and Miskel (1996), for example, adopted Pinder's definition of work motivation as "a set of energetic forces that originate both within as well as beyond an individual's being, to initiate work-related behavior, and to determine its form, direction, intensity, and duration" (1984, p. 8). From this definition, motivation is viewed as a product of the interaction of individual and contextual, or organizational, factors. As with Barnard and Getzels, there is a sense that the interaction can lead to a productive linkage of individual and organizational goals. Bolman and Deal (1991) refer to the human resource frame as the perspective that organizations can be successful at meeting both organizational goals and individual needs.

A balancing and blending of interests, however, may be far more difficult than a Barnardian optimism of past years would lead us to believe. Other forces intervene, such as unintended consequences, social norms, and environmental controls. This complexity was seen clearly by Selznick (1957) and by Merton *et al.* (1952) who argued respectively that individuals bring much more than just themselves to their organizations and that efforts to blend goals in "intended" ways can create their own unintended consequences. Decentralizing authority for efficiency, for example, may create divisions of interest and protections of "turf," which can then hinder efficiency. Furthermore, observed March and Olsen, a "blending" of goals assumed naively that all individual participants in an organization share the same goals, "or if they do not, that conflict among them could be readily managed . . . " (1984, p. 742). That conflict and tension are as readily to be found as blending is evident in the more recent literature on efforts to reform the compensation, work, and career structure of teaching. These reforms take two basic forms. First, merit-pay plans base teacher compensation, at least in part, on job performance in order to improve the academic performance of schools, retain the best teachers, and eliminate the worst (Johnson, 1990a). Second, differentiated staffing plans vary the work of the most capable teachers, thus providing greater challenges for teachers and more human resources for schools, and compensate them for their expanded duties. The proponents of both merit-pay and differentiated staffing seek to improve the academic effectiveness of schools by enabling teachers to expand opportunities to attain personal and professional goals, bringing together the two elements of the dilemma.

Research reveals little about the impact of merit-pay on teacher and school performance, in part because teachers have resisted the adoption and implementation of merit-pay plans. Research does, however, describe three reasons for this resistance, which demonstrate the difficulty of balancing organizational goals and personal goals. First, teachers resist merit-pay because they (teachers) emphasize rewards that are intrinsic to teaching and not the financial compensation of organizationally defined "merit" (Kottkamp, Provenzo & Cohn, 1986; Mitchell & Peters, 1988). Second, teachers find fault with merit pay because it introduces competition to a profession that prizes equity (Ballou & Podgursky, 1993). This reflects the importance of social norms and relations in determining the appropriateness of compensation, suggesting that the pursuit of school organizations' goals that foster individual rewards can be out of touch with other forces in the profession. And, third, the assessment of teacher performance is unreliable (Toch, 1984). This source of teacher resistance to merit-pay highlights the slender thread of assessment and accountability that ties individual effort and attainment to the accomplishment of organizational goals. It also implies that the complexity of teaching, or uncertainty, greatly complicates the linking of individual performance and organizational effectiveness and, thus, the balancing of personal and organizational goals.

Research on the impact of differentiated staffing plans, including career ladders, is sparse and inconclusive (Hart, 1994). The findings of research on the viability of differentiated staffing, in contrast to studies of merit-pay, are mixed. Some studies indicate that differentiated staffing plans fail to redesign the formal roles and relationships of educators (Bacharach, Lipsky & Shedd, 1984). Another reveals that schools and districts absorb career ladders into existing tasks and arrangements (Malen & Hart, 1987). Firestone and Bader (1991) examined three districts that redesigned teaching with career ladders and shared governance. They found that the district that was most professional had the least differentiated hierarchy and concluded that teachers' norms of equity are in direct conflict with career ladders. Research also suggests that teachers oppose the permanence of career ladders. As with merit-pay, teachers mistrust the evaluation procedures on which placement on the ladder is based (Johnson, 1990a). However, there is evidence that teachers accept the rewarding of successful peers with traditional, quasi-administrative roles, such as the department chair, in part because such assignments are understood to be temporary, thus avoiding the sense of a permanent hierarchy and retaining the ethic of collegiality (Johnson, 1990b). These findings point again to the importance of social relations and norms in defining the appropriateness of compensation and the vital need for adequate performance evaluations to link personal rewards and organizational goals.

Whether a blending of organizational goals and individual goals is viewed with or without hope, there has been little treatment of the underlying dilemma as enduring, fundamental, and contradictory. Indeed, as mentioned earlier, the dichotomy of individual versus group has been most commonly regarded as a "social dilemma"—wherein it is thought of a "problem" that can be resolved, through a clear choice between competing options (Schroeder, 1995; Chen *et al.*, 1996). The fundamental tension between organizational and individual levels of analysis is also reflected in a second dilemma, which juxtaposes formal structures and informal social relations.

The Dilemma of Task Structure

A second enduring dilemma involves a tension between formal and informal task structures in organizations. Task structure "refers to the patterned or regularized aspects of the relationships existing among participants in an organization" (Scott, 1992, p. 16). As outlined decades ago by Roethlisberger and Dickson, formal structures comprise "the patterns of human interrelations, as defined by the systems, rules, policies, and regulations" of the organization. The concept of informal structures recognizes, however, "that there is something more to the social organization

than what has been formally recognized" (1952, p. 255). Indeed, many patterns of human interaction in organizations "have no representation in the formal organization at all" (Roethlisberger & Dickson, 1952, p. 255).

By no means should it be assumed that the informal is necessarily an oppositional structure. It can be, and often is, but it can also assist and facilitate the formal organization. In fact, Roethlisberger and Dickson suggest that without informal structures, the "formal organization would not survive for long" (1952, p. 258). And, therein lies the heart of an enduring organizational dilemma; although the informal structure may indeed be necessary for the continuation of the formal, it is usually poorly controlled by the formal, and it can just as easily serve demise and opposition.

Weber (1947), whose conceptualization of the ideal-type bureaucracy serves as a foundation of organization theory, explains that a division of labor and technical specialization undergird rationality and impersonality and, thus, lead to efficient organizational systems. Among the central characteristics of bureaucracies identified by Weber are two types of formal structure: the hierarchy of authority and written rules and regulations. Other classical theories of organization not only emphasized the functions of formal structures but also assumed that such qualities as "independence" could only be fully controlled and channeled by the formal organization (Weber, 1947).

Taylor's (1947) scientific management and its derivatives are a classic expression of organizing on the basis of technical rationality. According to the tenets of scientific management, all work, including that of managers, should be guided by formal rules and regulations stemming from the results of scientific analysis. Such analysis sought to determine the most efficient means for completing tasks.

Natural systems perspectives, generally, and the human relations movement, more specifically, broke the fixation on formal structure in organizational analysis. Reacting to the limitations of classical, rationalistic theories of organization, several observers, including Mary Parker Follett (1942) and the authors of the Hawthorne Plant experiments (Roethlisberger & Dickson, 1952), revealed that exchanges of personal resources shaped relations among organizational participants, which in turn affected work and work relations. These naturally occurring relations constitute the informal structure of organizations.

Upon recognizing that there is an informal structure with complex effects upon the organization, research into the informal domain literally "took off" in the second half of the twentieth century. Among the key topics of inquiry, in what developed into a vast literature, were studies of work groups and intergroup relations (Argyris, 1962; Blake, Shepard & Mouton, 1964; Cartwright & Zander, 1960); studies of the informality nurtured by the very formality of the organization (Blau & Scott, 1962; Gouldner, 1955); studies of power and politics in organizations (Crozier,

1964; Mechanic, 1962; Pfeffer, 1981); and studies of organizational cultures and subcultures (Deal & Kennedy, 1982; Smircich, 1983).

Although early researchers tended to conclude that organizational participants erect informal structures in order to oppose the strictures of formal structure (Roethlisberger & Dickson, 1952), later inquiry became much more sophisticated. Tichy (1973), for example, explored the forces that shape informal groupings within formal organizations. This work paralleled explorations by Etzioni (1975) into the structural conditions (including environmental conditions) under which the informal does or does not fully develop (see also, Gross & Etzioni, 1985). In some instances, formal structures facilitate the development of informal structures; in others, they hinder.

Research in education, over the years, has covered all the structure-related topics, from work groups to cultures, that comprise the larger literature on organizations. This, too, is a very sizable body of inquiry (see, for example, Corwin & Borman, 1988; Miskel, McDonald & Bloom, 1983; Miskel & Ogawa, 1988; Hart, 1990). However, surprisingly little research in schools has examined formal and informal social structures and their relationships directly and specifically. One of the earliest studies was a doctoral dissertation by Norman Boyan (1951) investigating interactions between the formal and informal organization of a school faculty. In a later review of research into administrative behavior in education, Boyan (1988) identified a number of key studies that have inquired into the informal influences of, the negotiations among, and the loyalties surrounding "subordinates" in schools (Hanson, 1972; Hoy, Newland & Blazovsky, 1977; Hoy & Rees, 1974; Barnett, 1984).

As might be expected, there has been considerable attention in educational research to that informal domain of activity labeled by Bidwell (1965) as "studentship" (see also, Cusick, 1973). Drawing heavily upon the work of Gordon (1957) and Coleman (1961), for example, Bidwell (1965) argued that the formality of organizational controls in schools, wrapped in bureaucratic rules of procedure, in standards of student accomplishment, and in professional norms, help create and "pattern" an oppositional student social structure. Such actions by the organization to "penetrate" and co-opt the social life of students, by formalizing such elements as an extra-curriculum, can have the unanticipated effects of organizationally legitimizing academic indifference and "depressing students' academic propensities" (Bidwell, 1965, p. 990). Similarly, attempts by classroom teachers to use the formal and official sanctions of grades to control student structures open teachers to the informality of a student "press for particularistic treatment, on the basis of their personal relations with teachers and their positions in the student society" (Bidwell, 1965, p. 982).

The tensions between formal and informal structures are particularly evident in studies of program and policy implementation within the arena of unanticipated effects (see particularly, Cohen, 1982; McLaughlin, 1987; James, 1991). For example, in a literature review of the relations between state policymaking toward school reform and instructional practices in schools, Cohen and Spillane concluded that the array of governmental efforts to improve instruction "rarely make broad or close contact with instruction" (1992, p. 11). Furthermore, they pointed out that "teachers' work is guided more by inherited practices and individual decisions than by any clear and common view of what is to be covered, how it is to be covered, and why" (Cohen & Spillane, 1992, p. 23).

Additionally, argued Cohen and Spillane, "efforts at tightening the links between policy and instruction by increasing central control have met with extremely limited success and produced organizational side-effects that have greatly complicated governance and administration" (1992, p. 36). Nevertheless, they continued, it is extremely interesting to note that there is evidence of the "informal" in instructional improvement, particularly in findings regarding the role of shared values and "community." The informal structures of community are emphasized in the work of Bryk and Driscoll (1988), while the importance of cooperation and collegiality is evident in the research conducted by Chubb and Moe (1990). Another expression of the tension between control vested in organizational structure and control exerted by individuals is found in organizations, such as schools, that employ large numbers of professionals.

The Dilemma of Professionalism

Shedd & Bacharach (1991) call them "tangled hierarchies." A tangled hierarchy is a snarl, an interweaving of bureaucratic management and professionalism in educational organizations that typically produces cross-pressures and compromises between key values (more discretion and more control) but no "solutions." Shedd and Bacharach (1991) observe that untangling the hierarchy will call for much more attention than educational reform has yet devoted to this topic—with attention to both what a bureaucracy is and what a professional does.

At a deeper level of explanation, Shedd and Bacharach (1991) note the importance and the organizational consequences of tensions between two, task-related demands in education: discretion and coordination. The demand for discretion lies heavily in the array of judgment calls that educators must make daily in attending to individual students, in facing the unpredictable, in being accountable to many constituencies, and in applying an imperfect body of technical knowledge. Exactly the same set of conditions, claim Shedd and Bacharach (1991), lies at the heart of the drive toward coordination. Differing and even conflicting outsiders' expectations, individual needs and abilities, the unforeseen, and day-by-day unpredictability—all form a press toward limiting discretion and "handling" environmental uncertainty. In a review of the school-as-workplace literature, Corwin and Borman identified six dilemmas, characterized as "structural incompatibilities," which are rooted heavily in organizational versus occupational role expectations (1988, p. 209). Dilemmas of control, autonomy, and "order" pit chain of command needs against the local, and uniquely professional structures that develop informally to solve local problems. Dilemmas of occupational status, of career, and of equity often pit compliance with administrative policies and procedures against professional norms. Interestingly, Corwin and Borman (1988) also discussed the filter-down effects that informally structured teacher behavior can have upon informal classroom/pupil structures.

Blau and Scott (1962) root a second, related explanation of the "tangle" in alternative rationalities. They observe that professionalism is an alternative solution to the problem of rationalizing a field of action, particularly where uncertainty and thus task complexity are high. Whereas the rationality of bureaucrats lies in their compliance with organizational rules and regulations, the rationality of professionals lies in their reliance on specialized bodies of knowledge. Indeed, Kerr claims (1981) that teacher specialization (reading specialists or specialists in teaching the gifted, the learning disabled, the limited English proficient, and so on) has grown markedly with a mushrooming of varieties of "expertise" now negotiating for professional "space" within the same organization. When specialized professionals work in large scale organizations, conflicts over the source of control can abound and there are two principle points of such conflicts. First, expertise-laden professionals operate autonomously, while organizations require compliance with rules and regulations, many of which may ask specializing professionals to collaborate. Second, professionals are constrained by the norms of their professions and thus identify with (usually like-specializing) colleagues, while organizations require participants to respond to the directives of superordinates. Thus although both bureaucracies and professions seek to rationalize work and work relations, the presence of both in organizations can present a dilemma (Blau & Scott, 1962).

Third, the dilemma has been explained as a conflict in need-dispositions. Research on work motivation in schools demonstrates the roots of conflict between the professional's need for autonomy and the organization's need for compliance with formal structures. Maslow's (1965) well-known and highly influential need hierarchy theory posits that individuals' human needs are arranged hierarchically in the following ascending order: physiological, safety and security needs, social needs, esteem needs and the need for self-actualization. Higher-level needs become activated

only when lower-level needs are satisfactorily met. Thus an individual is motivated to satisfy the need that is most important at a given point in time. Research reveals that the greatest area of deficiency and, thus, need for school administrators and teachers, alike, is autonomy (Chisolm, *et al.*, 1980).

The jury is very much out on how questions of task-definition, specialized expertise, and discretion will be sorted out organizationally as educational reform continues. In a prescient analysis decades ago, Kob (1961) warned that the contradictions of educational professionalism may be far less organizational in scope than they are contradictions between professional activities and the extra-professional environment (between school and society.) Indeed, it is probably the extra-professional environment that is currently placing the heaviest reform-minded stress upon professionalism in education.

Abbot (1992) warns, for example, that a profession is much more vulnerable than is generally understood because of "changes in the objective character of its central tasks" (p. 146). Computer professionals, for instance, are no longer experts in hardware peculiarities and in the special mysteries of programming. Similarly, the railroad professions have died. Midwifery, once lost, is re-emerging. Nursing has been attenuated into nurse-practitioner roles at a deskilled extreme and physicians' assistants at a highly-skilled end. On the horizon of change, questions are paramount as to the profession and organization effects of (a) the current information-retrieval revolution; (b) the re-definition of just what is a "public" school (chartered, contracted, vouchered, privatized, home-based, licensed for daycare?); and (c) the extent to which renewed professional regulation and credentialing in education will outlast deskilling tendencies.

Quite a different aspect of this dilemma, however, is a totally different aspect of the relationship between educator and the extra-professional environment. Increasingly, there is a press in education to extend professionalism outward from the school far into the surrounding community. Partnering with parents, building "social capital" in the community, outreach into the neighborhood with added children and family services, shared governance, a home and school network of learning environments—these are just some of the potentially profession-redefining ingredients that are embedded in new conceptualizations of school-community relationship. It has been a component of educational reform influenced heavily by the considerable respect accorded the work of such figures as James Comer (1980; 1996), James Coleman (1994), Joyce Epstein (1988; 1996), Joy Dryfoos (1994), John Goodlad (1987), and Seymour Sarason (1995).

As an exemplar, Bauch and Goldring (1997) contrast a parent empowerment mode of teacher professionalism against both a traditional or bureaucratic mode and an earlier version of "teacher professionalism." The earlier version of professionalism "casts parents into the role of 'indirect clients' of the school whereby teachers know what is best for children and parents" (Bauch & Goldring, 1997, p. 13). The emerging, parent-empowerment mode involves parents directly and actively in the work and the decision-making of the school, as indicated in a quote from Hargreaves (1994) on the identification of a "new professionalism":

> At its core the new professionalism involves a movement away from the teacher's traditional professional authority and autonomy towards new forms of relationship with colleagues, with students and with parents. These relationships are becoming closer as well as more intense and collaborative (p. 424).

Yet to be determined, acknowledge Bauch and Goldring (1997, p. 17), is whether teachers and parents can "work together effectively in a balanced power relationship" (see also, Louis & Kruse, 1995). Yet to be determined as well, adds Ogawa (1997, p. 10), is just how the new professionalism will either return to, mesh with, or counter its organizational and bureaucratic roots that incorporate an array of organizational control structures long useful in buffering the "core technology from uncertainties that parents might introduce." Carlson (1996) warns, from a critical theory perspective, of organizational controls that have long been heavily centered institutionally upon reproducing a culture full of structural inequalities and utilizing the classroom as a prime "sorting" tool, per the ideologies of the nation's dominant social system.

The Dilemma of Hierarchy

No other aspect of school reform has received close to the attention that has been devoted to a question of hierarchy. Top-down versus bottom-up has been a shorthand description of the key issue. The cry nationwide has been that local school districts, whether large or small, have become, with time, overcentralized and overbureaucratized. A full (or at least a major) reversal of the deliberative and decision-making structures of schooling has captured much attention with terms of decentralization, devolution, school-based management, and site-level autonomy emerging as the shared lexicon of educational reform.

A fourth dilemma, therefore, centers on the appropriate configuration for decision-making in organizations: centralized or decentralized. As with the dilemma of task structure, rational theories clash with human relations perspectives over what constitutes appropriate arrangements for organizational decision-making. Foreshadowed by Weber's (1947) treatment of the ideal-type bureaucracy, later management theorists, such as Gulick and Urwick (1937), stressed that organizations must coordinate work activities by adhering to key principles that placed control in the hands of superordinates arranged in a hierarchical pyramid with ultimate control resting at the apex. Early re-

search (Bavelas, 1951) on small group dynamics and communication demonstrated the relative efficacy of centralized decision-making with theorists reasoning that efficacy was a product of the formalization (Vroom, 1969) and communication efficiency (Arrow, 1974) of centralized arrangements.

Inevitably, human relations theorists, such as Lewin (1948), argued that the participation of employees (even those at the lowest levels of organizations) in decision-making would improve the overall quality of decisions and enhance employee buy-in. In contrast with earlier inquiry, new research revealed that decentralized employee networks are more efficient at completing complex or ambiguous organizational tasks (Shaw, 1964).

It has only been with time, however, that a sense of dilemma around the notion of organizational hierarchy has surfaced as something other than a choice between centralization against decentralization, or even a balance between these values. One side of the dilemma has been illustrated in explorations into the nature of the "street-level bureaucracy" (Lipsky, 1976; 1980). People in client-serving positions, at the base of the bureaucracy, typically find that an exercise of discretion is necessary amid the unpredictability and uncertainty of their very human clientele. The organization's centrality—its "orders," rules, and regulations—cannot be implemented uniformly and universally. A blending of the organization's rules and some new street- and experience-based rules (such as special simplifications and routines) are frequently needed if the street-level bureaucrat is to cope with the pressures of his or her job. The lesson is that centralized organizations produce a press toward decentralized behavior.

The other side of the dilemma is that there is also just the opposite effect—decentralization produces a press toward centralization. It was a phenomenon described clearly by Anthony Downs in *Inside Bureaucracy* (1967). Lower-level employees seek to advance themselves, to "climb," to advocate their own programs, to distort that which is reported upward in order to develop a "specialty" and control their individual outputs. All of this pulling and hauling develops organizationally, claimed Downs (1967). These processes are strongest in relation to the organization's imperative to generate hierarchy, to centralize information and task coordination networks, to structure an authority that settles disputes, indeed even to limit the opportunities for advancement-oriented individuals to "jump ship" to other organizations (Downs, 1967, p. 267).

Such is a similar situation in educational organizations. Despite a terminology suggesting considerable bottom-level autonomy (site-based management, for example), much of the experimentation in a restructuring of American public education has recognized the pressures that decentralization places upon the central and vice versa. In large measure, the wide variety of site-management approaches across the U.S.

may reflect difficult and yet unresolved struggles as to the best "mix," while some observers urge a balance of top-down and bottom-up.

For example, local school councils have been a popular decentralizing innovation, but these have differed widely in their delegation of decision-making and/or governance a uthority—ranging from merely advisory to authoritative (Ogawa & White, 1994). Interestingly, one of the most closely watched reforms is Chicago's transfer of considerable power to a parent and community-dominated council at each school-site. Very soon after these councils were implemented, the district found itself pressed to re-establish central office direction from a delegation of power that seemed to have gone a bit too far (see Crowson & Boyd, 1991; Wong & Sunderman, 1996).

Hierarchy also comes to the fore in studies of the implementation of reforms wherein decentralized self-management replaces top-down bureaucracy. Barker (1993) found a tendency (under the "concertive control" framework of self-managing teams) for organizational controls to actually tighten around norms, values, and up-from-below rules in place of the traditionally hierarchical. He concluded "a concertive system creates its own powerful set of rational rules, which resembles the traditional bureaucracy" (Barker, 1993, p. 435). It was a phenomenon discovered as well by Smylie and Denny (1990), in a case study of a single, reforming Chicago-suburban school district where teacher-leadership was found to be no less "hierarchical" than the central office-focused leadership it replaced (see also, Smylie & Brownlee-Conyers, 1992).

By no means has the press toward decentralization in American education lost its appeal. Of late, there has been a "market" (as well as a rollback-the-state) flavor to many initiatives with charter schooling, privatization, vouchers, and other forms of "choice" capturing the attention of many reformers. The tensions between decentralization and centralization are played out anew in much of this, amongst concerns in some quarters that added choice can threaten the racial, gender, ethnic, and social class balances that often tend to be monitored centrally.

Interestingly, there are also important pieces of the reform movement suggesting the need for added centralization in the form of national and state standards, but at the same time there is ongoing press toward added decentralization in allowing localities freedom to decide how to meet the standards. Simultaneously, state supreme courts are, in increasing numbers, accepting the argument that localism unchecked does not provide equality of opportunity in school finance.

With all the reform discussions, it is surprising that the centralization/decentralization question has been little attended to in great depth. Theorists studying economics of the organization have offered a "positive theory of hierarchy," arguing that individuals join organizations and accept hierarchy as a rational means of saving personal transaction costs (Barney & Ouchi, 1976; Moe, 1984; Williamson, 1975; 1991). Individual educators, from this perspective, would find themselves in far more costly professional circumstances if they had to locate their own teaching space; find, enroll, and process their own pupils; secure their own instructional materials; negotiate their own fees for service; and arrange their own academic year calendars. Instead, they accept the controls, the standardization, and even the disputes settled by fiat qualities of a hierarchy as a set of less costly or "economizing" work options.

Dilemmas of External Relations

School organizations also confront dilemmas in their relations with the external environment. These dilemmas begin with a fundamental tension between maintaining the integrity of organization, or persistence, and adapting to changes in the environment. Flowing from the dilemma of persistence are two corollary but nonetheless enduring dilemmas. One concerns the nature of organizational boundaries; the other involves conflicting forms of compliance with environmental demands.

The Dilemma of Persistence

Anyone who wishes to reform schools will discover that they are particularly "intractable" organizations, concluded Seymour Sarason (1990). It is true, add Tyack and Tobin (1994), that many of the principle structures and roles of schooling remain remarkably stable over time, despite repeated efforts to change them. A "basic grammar" of schooling has been well institutionalized with accompanying routines, procedures, and day-by-day behaviors forming a foundation of organizational persistence. Reform is more likely to be altered to "fit" existing structures and practices than it is likely to forge a grand organizational restructuring.

Nevertheless, schools have also been discovered to be rather actively adaptive systems (Ginsberg, 1995). From "new math," to the "open classroom," to criterion-referenced testing, portfolio assessment, time-on-task, whole language, and "inclusion"—elementary and secondary education have been remarkably responsive to new ideas. Similarly, innovations in organizational and administrative arrangements (site-based management, charter schools, middle schools, schools-within-schools, school-based health clinics) quite typically "go to scale" in American education with an amazing rapidity. Often criticized for more faddism than substance, this adaptiveness is nonetheless surprising and intriguing for it occurs within an organizational form widely regarded as intractable.

Cuban (1988, 1992) and others have explained this strange combination of constancy and change as a matter of first-order against second-order reforms. First-order change stays at the organizational periphery and seldom lasts; second-order change is fundamental, extensive, and deeply systemic. Reforms come and go, but not often does an innovation penetrate to the second level, to the "deep structure of schooling" (Tye, 1987).

Although instructive and sensible, this explanation fails, however, to appreciate the very existence of first- and second-order reforming as possibly the twin elements of a key dilemma of organizational behavior in education. It is a dilemma rooted in the relations of school organizations to their uncertain external environments, balancing a need for certainty against a need for adaptability (Thompson, 1967). Indeed, it may be suggested that the certainty of non-change or "persistence" depends heavily upon a capacity for adaptiveness and vice versa.

This dilemma lies at the very heart of organizing because, from the technical-rational perspective, organizing and thus organizations involve the reduction of uncertainty. In this view, organizations exist to attain specific goals, employ technologies that are effective in reaching those goals, and erect administrative structures that enhance the efficiency of those technologies. Organizations are treated as closed systems.

With the advent of open systems theory, analysts began to recognize that external environments introduce uncertainty to the internal operations of organizations. Thompson (1967) offered a solution to this problem by explaining that organizations buffer their technologies from uncertainties introduced by the environment. However, the open systems perspective led theorists to recognize that organizations also revise internal structures in order to adapt to the environment. This occurs in two ways. First, organizations change to take advantage of opportunities and overcome or avoid constraints in their environments. Second, they adapt to changes in their environments.

It was rather late in the study of organizations and environments that the realization developed; not only adaptation but persistence is very much an "environmental" activity (see Meyer & Associates, 1978; Meyer & Scott, 1983). Ritual classifications and categories, and a "logic of confidence," in American education help to maintain the legitimacy of the school as a social reality and furthermore help the organization to persist by "decoupling" the technical core from environmental uncertainty. Societal myths of teacher professionalism and teacher autonomy, for example, help to buffer the classroom and its instructional activities from the difficulties and uncertainties of "close" evaluation/inspection (Meyer & Rowan, 1978).

The rituality and "decoupledness" of it all can influence efforts to reform or restructure education in a number of ways. Research on the recent campaign to restructure American public education echoes this timeworn refrain. Murphy (1991) noted that proponents of restructuring emphasize changes in governance and management over changes in instruction and curriculum. Elmore, Peterson, and McCarthey (1996) similarly document the limited impact that restructuring has had on the instructional practices of teachers.

Although the dilemma of persistence is present throughout school organizations, it is manifest in different forms at various levels of school systems' hierarchies. On an adaptive side of persistence, the incumbents of positions at the top of school district hierarchies, namely superintendents, spend much of their time facilitating the fit of their organizations with environmental demands. Much of this has a "pattern maintenance" quality, as identified by Talcott Parsons (1960), where there are efforts to legitimate the organization's activities in the eyes of the public (see also, Boyd & Crowson, 1981).

Research suggests that superintendents play an important role in the translation of societal and community preferences in their school districts' policies and programs (Cuban, 1976; Pitner & Ogawa, 1982). In accomplishing such adaptation, superintendents tend to emphasize structural features, both literal and social, of their organizations. They take particular satisfaction in the construction of facilities, the development of new programs, and the reorganization of their administrations (Pitner & Ogawa, 1982). But on a non-adaptive side, superintendents and the central offices that surround them are also famous as a source of overly-directive management, time-consuming paperwork, "stifling" red tape, rules that match poorly with the realities of service delivery, and incentive systems that discourage lower-level initiative (Callahan, 1962; Rogers, 1968; Cronin, 1973; Peterson, 1976; Grimshaw, 1979; Morris, et al., 1984). Indeed, it has been "against" this image of the over-centralized and internally non-adaptive school district bureaucracy that much of the current reform movement in public education has been aimed.

Teachers experience the dilemma of organizational persistence quite differently. Research seems to indicate that they confront this dilemma on two levels. At the classroom level, studies of teacher knowledge demonstrate that teachers employ a measure of certainty by applying rules of practice (Elbaz, 1991) and subject matter knowledge (Grossman, Wilson & Shulman, 1989) in adapting instruction to highly variable contexts that involve complex relations between teachers, students, and content (Hollingsworth, 1989; McDonald, 1992).

On another level, teachers tend to buffer the limited certainty they carve out in their classrooms from policies, programs, and educational theories that originate in policy and academic arenas (Clandinin & Connelly, 1996). Therein lies an irony that reflects the dilemma. The governing boards and top-level administrators of school districts adopt policies and programs in adapting to claims or requirements of external stakeholders groups, including federal and state agencies, professional organizations, publishers, and university researchers. The claims and requirements made by these external stakeholders are often intended to increase the certainty and thus enhance the effectiveness of teaching. However, down at the supposedly more "adaptive" level of technically applying policy directly to practice, the policy initiatives can create back-pressures against the adaptive intent—part of that which Boyd and Crowson (1981, p. 357) have characterized as "the perverse structure of incentives in public schools."

School principals, the middle managers of public school systems, occupy a position between district administrators and classroom teachers. In this role, principals encounter the dilemma of persistence in relatively stark terms. On the one hand, principals are expected to enact policies and programs adopted by their districts' governing boards and administrators in adapting to environmental pressures. This includes overseeing the efforts of teachers to implement the policies and programs. On the other hand, teachers expect principals to buffer them from uncertainties introduced by new district initiatives (Becker, 1966; Morris, *et al.*, 1984).

Thus adaptiveness in order to persist and persistence simultaneously in the face of adaptiveness cut across each of the "levels" of the educational organization—if in somewhat different ways. "New institutional" theorizing, growing heavily out of the work of Meyer and Scott (1983) and others (Powell & DiMaggio, 1991; Scott, 1995), has produced a much renewed interest in the abilities of organizations to persist despite strong pressures to change. However, there has been surprisingly little inquiry to date that examines the means whereby school reform should be played out within, and might be better understood from, a sense of the deeply interactive nature of adaptation versus "certainty."

Research on educational organizations, for example, has not approached such topics as the Weick and Roberts (1993) study of the interactions between reliability and vulnerability in flight operations on aircraft carriers, or the Goodrick and Salancik (1996) study of what happens to the "certainties" of professional practice in hospitals as environmental uncertainty waxes and wanes. In short, a dilemma at the very heart of school reform (organizational persistence amid adaptation) has yet to receive concerted, systematic attention as a vital subject of scholarly inquiry.

The Dilemma of Organizational Boundaries
The dilemma of persistence highlights the importance of organizational boundary, and life in educational organizations, indeed, is well supplied with "boundary" language: the self-contained classroom; elementary, middle, and secondary schools; the school-community relationship; school staff members and district-level staff; in-school and out-of-school suspension; dropping out; enrolling in school; the annual open house; and graduation. All are terms convey-

ing a threshold to be crossed, a difference between something in and something out. In short, a boundary.

Unfortunately, upon close examination the distinctions between the "in" and the "out" of the organization are not all that clear. The question of where organizations end and their environments begin indicates another organizational dilemma. Because organizations are social collectivities or bounded networks of social relations (Scott, 1992), they do indeed have boundaries that set them apart from other social systems. However, the location of those boundaries is at best ambiguous.

Laumann, Marsden, and Prensky (1983) identify three features that analysts have employed to define organizational boundaries: These are people, their relations, and their activities. Many scholars look to the characteristics of people to determine organizations' boundaries. The principle characteristic on which this type of analysis focuses is membership: members lie inside organizations; non-members reside in the environment.

Admittedly, membership as a criterion assumes considerable ambiguity as one considers such categories of people as parents who volunteer in schools, specialists (psychologists, in-service consultants) who may only appear infrequently, the persons who wrote the standardized tests used twice a year, teachers-in-training at the school currently completing a practicum, their university supervisors, and even a school's parents-at-large, whose progeny are trustfully left daily in the care of other adults. As much as a sense of "we" and "they" does tend to permeate school administration (Mann, 1974), the separation of member from non-member is often blurred.

A second approach to determine an organization's boundary is to assess the network of a specific type of social relation. A common method is to determine the frequency of interactions. Those people who interact at some foundation level are considered part of the organization, while those whose interactions fall below the foundation level are not. What, however, is the foundation level of interaction in an organization known for its "self-contained" workplaces? Indeed, some teachers may interact more frequently with the parents of their children than with fellow teachers. Teachers in high school settings can sometimes have little cross-departmental interaction.

On the other hand, the concept of social relation covers much territory and it can certainly include social/professional norms, terminologies, values, and bases of knowledge. From this perspective, educators who actually interact infrequently are nevertheless "bound" together. But from this perspective as well, it is not hard to see why persons from differing professional backgrounds who are asked to "collaborate" (for example, in delivering children's services) can have difficulty in extending their own sense of boundaries to their trained-otherwise collaborators (see Crowson & Boyd, 1993).

Finally, analysts define an organization's boundary by examining activities. This approach is based on the assumption that organizations shape people's actions and interactions; thus, people act differently when they cross boundaries; in other words, "The organization ends where its discretion ends and another's begins" (Pfeffer & Salancik, 1978, p. 32). From this perspective, parent volunteers or aides in schools may lose much of their parental persona in acquiring (and indeed being socialized into) a "school" persona. Such an extension of a boundary can become an issue in situations where parental advisory councils are asked to express an "independent" voice in school decision-making and the issue can extend to the district-wide board of education, which if not fully co-opted by administrators can at least find itself frequently "cut off" from its community (Lutz & Iannaccone, 1978).

Although all these methods for determining boundaries focus on people, they conceptualize boundaries quite differently. The method that focuses simply on membership treats people as if they are either wholly inside or outside a given organization. The other two methods emphasize the partiality of membership and thus the ambiguity of boundaries. Tracing social networks reveals that actors' connectedness to a given organization varies, while analyzing activities demonstrates the relative influence that a focal organization exerts on people.

Whatever the means for boundary determination, membership by itself (in or out of an organization) does not necessarily pose a dilemma. The dilemma arises when the organizational need for internal coherence is pitted against the need to relate to and thus interface with the environment (Goldring, 1995). At that point, however defined, membership helps contribute to coherence while non-members or that portion of people that remain in the environment present uncertainty and thus threaten coherence. This dilemma is manifest in at least three tensions: between organizations' use of bridging and buffering strategies, between excluding and accommodating members' extra-organizational resources and relations, and between employees and owners.

One manifestation of the boundary dilemma is reflected in two strategies that organizations employ to manage relations with the technical environment: bridging and buffering (Thompson, 1967). Organizations bridge when they are dependent on their environments for resources to fuel their core technologies (Scott, 1992; Thompson, 1967), which is more likely under the following conditions: scarcity of resources, concentration of resources, and coordination of input sources. Organizations employ several bridging strategies, including bargaining, contracting, and co-optation.

Organizations buffer to protect their core technologies from the environment, which can undermine technical effectiveness and efficiency (Thompson, 1967). Several conditions give rise to environmental uncertainty, including heterogeneity, instability, and threat (Scott, 1992). To manage uncertainty, organizations develop many buffering strategies, including simply blocking or limiting access and coding. Coding involves the classification of inputs prior to their introduction to the technical core (such as "gifted," "at-risk," or "limited-English-proficient").

It is not unknown or unlikely for bridging and buffering to occur at the same time and particularly in a reform period such as the present, argues Mawhinney (1997), where teacher-centered professionalization is now "challenged by the proponents of parental and community involvement in schooling who want to move beyond the bake sale to have a greater role in the education of their children" (p.3).

The boundary dilemma is also reflected in the tension between excluding and accommodating the resources and relationships that members have outside the organization. From a technical-rational perspective, organizations select people for membership because of their demonstrated capacity to contribute to the attainment of organizational goals (Weber, 1947). The resources and affiliations that people have outside a given organization are viewed as potentially detrimental to its effectiveness and efficiency. Thus for example, in order to limit the impact of personal and other extramural considerations, organizations do not permit employees to engage in nepotism or to conduct personal business during the work day.

However, organizations generally do not build impermeable boundaries. As natural systems theory explains, organizations benefit substantively and symbolically from their members' extraorganizational resources and relations (Scott, 1992). Substantively, members can draw on personal resources to enhance organizational effectiveness and efficiency. For example, employees draw on avocations, such as an interest in computers, to enhance job performance. Managers call on family ties or personal friendships in order to expand business. Symbolically, organizations seek to gain legitimacy by recruiting people who bear attributes that conform to community expectations and values. For example, firms recruit graduates of highly respected, local universities.

There is relatively little research regarding boundary issues and relationships in public education (Griffiths, 1979; Hoy, 1982; Ogawa, 1994). Research does suggest, however, that public sector employees, such as teachers, principals, and welfare agency workers who face uncertainty and ambiguity respond to external client relationships with routinization, specialization, and simplification of roles and responsibilities (Hollister, 1979; Newman, 1980; Lawrence & Lorsch, 1969; Goldring & Sullivan, 1996). These employees hold strong organizational allegiances and seek distancing from their clienteles to protect their autonomy.

Scholars documented that principals often buffer their schools, sealing them off from parents and clients (Tyack &

Hansot, 1982). Hallinger and Murphy (1986) report that principals in low SES schools "acted as buffers, carefully controlling access to the school and protecting the school's program from outside influences that might dilute its effectiveness" (p. 344), whereas Goldring (1986) found that principals who work with an upper-class clientele are more likely to buffer against assertive and demanding parents. Other research suggests that principals cooperate with parents from homogeneous communities (in terms of socioeconomic backgrounds) to co-opt them, while they tended to try to socialize heterogeneous parent clienteles into acceptable and manageable styles and teach them what they can and cannot expect from the school (Goldring, 1990).

Studies of local boards of education also shed some light on the third form of the boundary dilemma: the tension between employees and owners, or governing bodies. Many early studies of the politics of education focused on local boards of education. This body of work presents two very different pictures. On the one hand, research demonstrates that school boards, while sometimes torn between conflicting factions (Agger & Goldstein, 1971; Page & McClelland, 1978), imbue schools with the dominant value of local communities (Peshkin, 1978).

On the other hand, research reveals that professional educators wield substantial influence. Studies expose the dependence of school boards on their superintendents (Kerr, 1964; Zeigler & Jennings, 1974) and highlight the influence of educational bureaucrats in large urban settings (Gittell, 1967; Rogers, 1968; Schrag, 1967). Burlingame's (1988) conclusion regarding the bipolarity of research findings starkly summarizes this form of the boundary dilemma: "One [pole] sees the board as the major force for preserving the community . . . The opposite pole sees professional educators dominating the board and the community; educational expertise rules" (p. 443).

In sum, with boundaries that are not firmly defined, and with much that produces crossover tensions in boundary-maintenance activities, it is not surprising that educational organizations wrestle constantly with such "fundamental dichotomies" (Bidwell, 1965) as the interests of management against community, buffered against responsive and "ownership" against autonomy.

The Dilemma of Compliance

The dilemma of persistence hangs on the twin organizational needs of maintaining the status quo versus adapting to the environmental press. The second horn of this dilemma, adaptability, points to yet another dilemma, one that concerns two seemingly conflicting ways in which organizations comply with environmental demands: technically versus symbolically.

Despite the vaunted localism of American education, the public schools are fully expected to "comply" with state and national initiatives. Protections of opportunity by race and gender, strictures against the misallocation of grant-in-aid dollars, an enforcement of constitutional prohibitions against school prayer, special rules to guide the education of persons with disabilities; these are just a few arenas of expected compliance with federal requirements.

At the state level, the compliance expectations may range from facilities to finances, governance, staffing, scheduling, students, curricula, and beyond. Some reform-minded efforts seek to "free" the local schools from many of the restrictions accompanying state expectations (for example, as charter schools). However, educational organizations are, will remain, and may even increasingly become expected to "comply" (particularly now with state and national standards).

But why should this be part of an enduring dilemma? Understandably, organizational compliance in public education is often far from optimal or even far from acceptable. Understandably as well, compliance is by no means a unitary construct in education's politicized environment. Schools and school districts walk a tightrope between complying with neighborhood, community, state, and federal expectations. There are religious observances, for example, in individual schools throughout the nation, no matter what the Supreme Court might say (Crowson, 1992).

These are examples of compliance problems, rather than dilemmas, similar to studies of the implementation of educational policies that address questions of capacity and will as part of the "problem" of policy compliance (McLaughlin, 1987). The compliance dilemma, by contrast, is more deeply a dilemma of having to comply simultaneously with both technical and institutional dimensions of the environment. The technical-rational model depicts organizations developing compliance structures to enhance the productivity of their core technologies (Aldrich, 1979; Thompson, 1967). In contrast, institutional theory indicates that organizations often adopt structures that mirror dominant values in order to gain societal legitimacy (Meyer, Boli & Thomas, 1987).

Kamens (1977), for example, examined the "graduation mythology" in public education. Is graduation, with all of its ceremonial trappings and symbolism (of accomplishment and transition) essentially a legitimizing event; or does graduation truly represent the product of a technical core that has successfully accomplished goals of educational preparation and development? How much of each is the greater likelihood?

From the technical-compliance perspective, the technical-rational model depicts organizations as seeking, even existing, to attain specific, predetermined goals. Organizations, from this perspective, develop formal structures in order to enhance the effectiveness and efficiency of their core technologies. In part, this involves developing structures that enable organizations to respond to important contingencies in the technical environment, including suppliers, clients, and competitors (Lawrence & Lorsch, 1967).

Thus organizations respond to the technical environment by adopting structures that exert a substantive impact on technology and goal attainment.

However, institutional theory suggests that organizations adopt structures not to enhance efficiency but to gain social legitimacy. This is accomplished by mirroring institutions that incorporate general, societal rules that take the form of cultural theories and ideologies (Meyer, Boli & Thomas, 1987). Institutions specify appropriate organizational purposes and legitimate means for pursuing them (Meyer & Rowan, 1977; Scott, 1987; Zucker, 1987). By adopting or developing structures that reflect institutions, organizations gain and maintain legitimacy with stakeholders in the environment, increasing their inclination to invest resources. Thus organizations respond to the institutional environment by adopting structures that reflect their symbolic compliance with societal values.

Research on educational administration has become increasingly interested in the impact of institutional environments upon schooling (see Crowson, Boyd & Mawhinney, 1996). Simultaneously, there appears to be less interest currently in the relations between school organizations and their technical environments. Furthermore, there has been little inquiry that examines the institutional and technical components together despite some interesting indications of a potentially rich field for inquiry.

Early research by Crain (1969) into school desegregation, for example, found that symbolic compliance (more a symbolic "gesture") tends to precede technical compliance (usually as a first, attempted substitute for technical compliance). Similarly, Moe (1990) noted that the compliance structures of organizations "are often protective devices for insulating agencies from political enemies, not for building effective organizations" (p. 229). However, Mezias (1990) discovered that a "symbol" can become powerfully institutionalized across a domain of organizations and eventually filter down to changes in the technical core.

In work close to the Mezias inquiry, the first topic on which educational researchers operating from an institutional perspective have focused, is the diffusion of organizational elements and forms. Rowan (1982) traced the adoption of administrative services by public school systems in California and concluded that school districts more readily adopted and maintained administrative services when the services had been institutionalized by balanced social control networks and, thus, served to legitimate districts. Similarly, Strang (1987) charted the spread of school district consolidation over nearly 50 years, attributing the diffusion of consolidation to conditions in the institutional environment, including the degree of control exerted by state educational agencies.

Educational reform has been a second topic of compliance to which institutional theory has been applied in the educational administration literature. Specifically, scholars have invoked institutional theory to explain how it is that various reform strategies become widely adopted despite little evidence of their effectiveness. In her case study of the Bellevue School District, Malen (1994) demonstrates that the school district gained legitimacy by enacting school-based management, which reflected social values. Ogawa (1994) adopted a more macro-styled view, revealing that school-based management was institutionalized by a combination of policy, teachers' union, and academic entrepreneurs. These actors, operating in a national network, waged a coordinated campaign to shape and promote school-based management as a means to effect educational reform.

All of this begins to raise intriguing compliance questions regarding just how symbolism interrelates with "core" —as well as far-from-answered questions regarding how well these two sides of compliance can be appreciated and understood as a dilemma of organization.

Conclusion

Since the seminal work of Charles Bidwell (1965) in which he introduced the notion of fundamental dichotomies in school organizations, and the discussion by Ralph Tyler (1966) of the opposing organizational features of schools, the field of organization studies has developed widely. In a recent reflection on 40 years of organization studies, Porter (1996) delineated some of the field's accomplishments: 1) It has evolved from a micro-dominated field (namely psychology) to a multi-disciplinary field, employing multiple paradigms and perspectives, 2) it has combined empirical and conceptual approaches, and 3) it has provided a form for serious scrutiny and analysis. Lastly, Porter notes, "If our field has proven anything over the years it is that things are not always as they seem" (p. 264). Indeed, it was the two pioneers, Bidwell and Tyler, who suggested that to fully understand the complexities of educational organization, it will be necessary to embrace the contraries in the organizational process, precisely because "things are not always as they seem" in the organizational arena.

This chapter has highlighted some examples of the "contraries" in organizations by exploring enduring dilemmas. We noted that much of the development of organizational theory has emerged in response to unanswered questions from previous empirical research and earlier conceptions. In this type of evolutionary, linear approach, however, theorists have often failed to take into account the possibility of fundamental dichotomies, opposing features, or enduring dilemmas.

Our review presents seven dilemmas: 1) goals, 2) task structures, 3) hierarchy, 4) professionalism, 5) persistence, 6) boundaries, and 7) compliance. It is interesting to note that almost all the dilemmas have their roots in the earliest conceptions of organizations as formal, rational, and hierarchically-closed systems based on the work of Weber (1947) and Taylor (1947). We cannot underestimate the extent to which these same dilemmas in school organization have been similarly influenced by these initial conceptions of organizations (see Callahan, 1962). Thus the dilemma of goals posits organizational purposes against individual needs and self-interests. The dilemma of task structures points to the interplay between the formal and informal structures of organizations. The dilemma of hierarchy turns on the tension between centralization and decentralization, while the dilemma of professionalism focuses on bureaucratic and professional controls. The dilemma of persistence presents the balancing of organizational certainty and adaptation, and the dilemma of boundaries further highlights the interplay between the integrity of organizations and the uncertainty born by environments. Lastly, the dilemma of compliance depicts the difficulty of organizations responses to technical and institutional environments.

In each case, organizational theory, empirical research, and practical application in school reform efforts seem to have fallen into the trap of trying to choose between "sides" of the dilemma, rather than aiming towards accepting and understanding the implications of embracing contraries. Thus for example, when facing the dilemma of hierarchy, the pendulum swings between centralization and decentralization with noticeable regularity (Morris, 1997). Explanations for this state of affairs also fall into the trap of "choosing" one theoretical interpretation versus another. Educational organizations do not change because they do not attend to their institutional environments and do not pay attention to the "basic grammar of schooling" (Morris, 1997; Tyack & Cuban, 1995). Or, innovation fails because there is not enough technical expertise, little relationship between means and ends, and too much uncertainty. As our discussion has suggested, both of these theoretical explanations are occurring simultaneously: the dilemma of persistence.

We conclude that the tendency to choose between alternatives, in theoretical orientation and practical application, has led to a situation where we imply that there is "one best system" if we could only find it; problems are presumed solvable; issues can be negotiated and thus are resolvable; dilemmas must be faced to make a clear choice. We assert, in contrast, that attempts to maximize do not bear fruit and attempts to solve dilemmas do not work. The dilemmas that face organizations are enduring and are part of the "grammar" of schooling.

It would be incorrect to conclude, however, that the message for school reform is: Don't try. Indeed, with enduring dilemmas of organization, it might be easy (but erroneous) to fall back upon some of the adages of long-surviving bureaucrats: "Wait 'em out, this too shall pass." Or, I remember when they tried this idea 25 years ago: "Didn't work

then, won't now." An ongoing pessimism around the pendulum swinging, and the trap of choosing, is not the central message of this chapter.

In fact, just the opposite is true. We would maintain that school reform is still a matter of active choosing, even if among equally valued alternatives and equally true but contradictory consequences. To be sure, such solutions as site-based management and decentralization may unknowingly contain the seeds of re-centralization. Similarly, market solutions and charter schooling could prove to be but the beginnings of a new regulatory spirit in public education. Or, more deeply into dilemma-effects, efforts to balance opposing values (the power of standards while simultaneously preserving local initiative and autonomy) could only serve to mask temporarily some fundamental contraries in state-local relations.

Not to choose and not to act in school reform, however, is just to swing with the pendulum. The key importance in an understanding and awareness of organizational values in conflict, and in the tendency of one of two poles to define/produce the other, is that choice implies consequence—with side effects, trade-offs, and compromises, plus problems that are re-introduced again and again. To act meaningfully in educational reform is to act with an informed sense of these phenomena.

Although reform-mindedness in education has been well laced with a language suggesting improvement, change, growth, effectiveness, and development, there has been relatively little attention to a second, key language of reform that is wrapped in some fundamental features of schools and other organizations. This is a language of dichotomy, tension, opposing forces, contraries, and that is which is ongoing or enduring. It is a language brilliantly introduced to the study of schools as formal organizations in 1965 by Charles Bidwell and has been essentially forgotten since.

NOTES

1. There is a significant and most instructive exception to this generalization. In his classic piece on "The School as a Formal Organization," Charles Bidwell (1965) discussed "fundamental dichotomies" between student and staff roles, between rationalization and structural looseness, between public regardedness and professionalism, universalism against particularism, and subordination against autonomy. While a highly regarded and much-read analysis more than three decades later, Bidwell's fundamental dichotomies became lost-to-view in much of the later attention to changed and reorganized schooling.
2. Note that David Bickimer (1968) has traced an intellectual lineage from Talcott Parsons to Barnard to Getzels.

REFERENCES

Abbot, A. (1992). Professional Work. In V. Hasenfield (Ed.), *Human Services as Complex Organizations*. Newbury Park, CA: Sage Publications, 145–162.

Abbot, M. & Caracheo, F. (1988). Power, authority, and bureaucracy. In N. Boyan (Ed.), *Handbook of research on educational administration* (pp. 239–257). New York: Longman.

Agger, R. E. & Goldstein, M. N. (1971). *Who will rule the schools*. Belmont, CA: Wadsworth

Aldrich, H. (1979). *Organizations and environments*. Englewood Cliffs, NJ: Prentice–Hall.

Argyris, C. (1962). *Interpersonal competence and organizational effectiveness*. Homewood, IL: Dorsey.

Arrow, K. (1974). *The limits of organization*. New York: W. W. Norton & Co., Inc.

Bacharach, S. B., Lipsky, D. B. & Shedd, J. B. (1984). *Merit pay and its alternatives*. Ithaca, NY: Organizational Analysis and Practice.

Ballou, D. & Podgursky, M. (1993). Teachers' attitudes toward merit pay: Examining conventional wisdom. *Industrial and Labor Relations Review, 47*, 50–61.

Barker, J. R. (1993). Tightening the Iron Cage: Conservative Control in Self-Managing Teams. *Administrative Science Quarterly, 38*, 408–437.

Barnard, C. I. (1938). *The functions of the executive*. Cambridge, MA: Harvard University Press.

Barnett, B. G. (1984). Subordinate teacher power in school organizations. *Sociology of Education, 57*, 43–55.

Barney, J. G. & Ouchi, W. G. (Eds.) (1986). *Organizational economics*. San Francisco: Jossey–Bass.

Bauch, P. A. & Goldring, E. B. (1997, forthcoming) Parent teacher participation in the context of school governance. *Peabody Journal of Education*.

Bavelas, A. (1951). Communication patterns in task–oriented groups. In D. Lerner & H. Lasswell (Eds.), *The policy sciences* (pp. 193–202). Stanford, CA: Stanford University Press.

Becker, H. S. (1966). The Teacher in the Authority System of the Public School. In A. Etzioni (Ed.), *Complex Organizations*. New York: Holt, Rinehart and Winston, 243–251.

Berlak, A. & Berlak, H. (1981). *Dilemmas of schooling*. London: Methuen.

Bickimer, D. A. (1968). *Chester I. Barnard and educational administration*. Unpublished doctoral dissertation, Department of Education, University of Chicago.

Bidwell, C. E. (1965). The school as a formal organization. In J. G. March (Ed.), *Handbook of organizations* (972–1022). Chicago: Rand McNally.

Blake, R. R., Shepard, H. A. & Mouton, J. S. (1964). *Managing intergroup conflict in industry*. Houston, TX: Gulf.

Blau, P. M. & Scott, W. R. (1962). *Formal organizations: A comparative approach*. San Francisco: Chandler.

Bolman, L. G. & Deal, T. E. (1991). *Reframing organizations: Artistry, choice, and leadership*. San Francisco: Jossey–Bass.

Boyan, N. J. (1951). *A study of the formal and informal organization of a school faculty*. Unpublished doctoral dissertation, Harvard University.

Boyan, N. J. (1988). Describing and explaining administrative behavior. In N. J. Boyan (Ed.), *Handbook of research on educational administration* (pp. 77–97). New York: Longman.

Boyd, W. L. & Crowson, R. L. (1981). The changing conception and practice of public school administration. In D. Berliner (Ed.), *Review of research in education*, Vol. 9 (pp. 311–373). Washington, DC: American Educational Research Association.

Bryk, A. & Driscoll, M. (1988). *The high school as a community: Contextual influences and consequences for students and teachers*. Madison, WI: National Center on Effective Secondary Schools.

Burlingame, M. (1988). The politics of education and educational policy: The local level. In N. J. Boyan (Ed.), *Handbook of research on educational administration* (pp. 439–454). New York: Longman.

Callahan, R. E. (1962). *Education and the cult of efficiency*. Chicago: University of Chicago Press.

Carlson, D. (1996). Teachers as political actors: From reproductive theory to the crisis of schooling. In P. Leistyna, A. Woodrum & S. A. Sherblom (Eds.), *Breaking free: The transformative power of critical pedagogy*, Reprint Series No. 27. Cambridge, MA: Harvard Educational Review.

Cartwright, D. & Zander, A. (Eds.) (1960). *Group dynamics: Research and theory*. Evanston, IL: Row, Peterson.

Chase, F. S. (1966). In J. I. Goodlad (Ed.), *The sixty-fifth yearbook of the National Society for the Study of Education: Part 2. The changing American school* (pp. 271–306). Chicago: University of Chicago Press.

Chen, X., Au, W. T. & Komorita, S. S. (1996). Sequential choice in a step–level public good dilemma: The effects of criticality and uncertainty. *Organizational Behavior and Human Decision Processes, 65*, 37–47.

Chisolm, G. B., Washington, R. & Thibodeaux, M. (1980). *Job motivation and the need fulfillment deficiencies of educators*. Paper presented at the annual meeting of the American Educational Research Association, Boston.

Chubb, J. & Moe, T. (1990). *Politics, markets, and American schools*. Washington, DC: Brookings Institute.

Clandinin, D. J. & Connelly, F. M. (1996). Teachers' professional knowledge landscapes: Teacher stories–stories of teachers–school stories. *Educational Researcher, 25*, 24–30.

Clune, W. H. & White, P. A. (1988). *School–based management: Institutional variation, implementation, and issues for further research*. New Brunswick, NJ: Rutgers University, Center for Policy Research in Education.

Cohen, D. K. (1982). Policy and organization: The impact of state and federal educational policy on school governance. *Harvard Educational Review, 52*, 474–499.

Cohen, D. K. & Spillane, J. P. (1992). Policy and practice: The relations between governance and instruction. In G. Grant (Ed.), *Review of research in education*, vol. 18 (pp. 3–49). Washington, DC: American Educational Research Association.

Coleman, J. S. (1961). *The adolescent society*. New York: Free Press.

Coleman, J. S. (1994). Parental involvement: Implications for schools. In R. J. Yinger & K. M. Borman (Eds.), *Restructuring education: Issues and strategies for communities, schools and universities* (pp. 19–31). Cresskill, NJ: Hampton Press.

Comer, J. P. (1980). *School power: Implications of an intervention project*. New York: Free Press.

Comer, J. P., Haynes, N. M., Joyner, E. T. & Ben–Avie, M. (Eds.) (1996). *Rallying the whole village: The Comer process for reforming education*. New York: Teacher College Press.

Corwin, R. G. & Borman, K. M. (1988). School as workplace: Structural constraints on administration. In N. J. Boyan (Ed.), *Handbook of research on educational administration* (pp. 209–237). New York: Longman.

Crain, R. L. (1969). *The politics of school desegregation*. Garden City, NY: Anchor Books.

Cronin, J. M. (1973). *The control of urban schools*. New York: The Free Press.

Crowson, R. L. (1992). *School-community relations, under reform*. Berkeley, CA: McCutchan.

Crowson, R. L. & Boyd, W. L. (1991). Urban schools as organizations: Political perspectives. In J. G. Cibulka, R. J. Reed & K. K. Wong (Eds.), *The politics of urban education in the United States* (pp. 87–103). Washington, DC: Falmer Press.

Crowson, R. L. & Boyd, W. L. (1993). Coordinated services for children: Designing arks for storms and seas unknown. *American Journal of Education, 101*, 140–179.

Crowson, R. L., Boyd, W. L. & Mawhinney, H. B. (Eds.) (1996). *The politics of education and the new institutionalism*. Washington, DC: Falmer Press.

Crozier, M. (1964). *The bureaucratic phenomenon*. Chicago: University of Chicago Press.

Cuban, L. (1976). *Urban school chiefs under fire*. Chicago: University of Chicago Press.

Cuban, L. (1988). Constancy and change in schools. In P. W. Jackson (Ed.), *Contributing to educational change*. Berkeley, CA: McCutchan.

Cuban, L. (1992). Managing dilemmas while building professional communities. *Educational Researcher, 21*, 4–11.

Cusick, P. A. (1973). *Inside high school: The student's world*. New York: Holt, Rinehart and Winston.

Deal, T. E. & Kennedy, A. A. (1982). *Corporate cultures*. Reading, MA: Addison–Wesley.

Downs, A. (1967). *Inside bureaucracy*. Boston: Little, Brown and Company.

Dryfoos, J. (1994). *Full-service schools*. San Francisco: Jossey–Bass.

Elbaz, F. (1991). Research on teacher's knowledge: The evolution of a discourse. *Journal of Curriculum Studies, 23*, 1–19.

Elbow, P. (1983). Embracing contraries in the teaching process. *College English, 45*, 327–339.

Elmore, R. F., Peterson, P. L. & McCarthey, S. J. (1996). *Restructuring in the classroom: Teaching, learning and school organization*. San Francisco: Jossey–Bass.

Epstein, J. (1988). *Parent involvement*. Baltimore, MD: Johns Hopkins University Center for Research on elementary and middle schools.

Epstein, J. (1996). School and family connections: Theory, research, and implications for integrating sociologies of education and family. *Marriage and Family Review, 15*, 99–126.

Etzioni, A. (1975). *A comparative analysis of complex organizations*. New York: Free Press.

Firestone, W. A. & Bader, B. D. (1991). Professionalism or bureaucracy? Redesigning teaching. *Educational evaluation and policy analysis, 13*, 67–86.

Follett, M. P. (1926). The giving of orders. In H. C. Metcalf (Ed.), *Scientific foundations of business administration*. Baltimore: Williams & Wilkins.

Follett, M. P. (1942). *Dynamic administration*. New York: Harper.

Getzels, J. W. (1958). Administration as a social process. In A. W. Halpin (Ed.). *Administrative theory in education* (pp. 150–165). Chicago: Midwest Administration Center, University of Chicago.

Getzels, J. W. & Guba, E. G. (1957). Social behavior and the administrative process. *School Review, 65*, 423–441.

Ginsberg, R. (1995). The new institutionalism, the new science, persistence and change: The power of faith in schools. In R. L. Crowson, W. L. Boyd & H. B. Mawhinney (Eds.). *The politics of education and the new institutionalism* (153–166). Washington, DC: Falmer.

Gittell, M. (1967). *Participants and participation*. New York: Praeger.

Goldring, E. (1986). The school community: Its effects on principals' perceptions of parents. *Educational Administration Quarterly, 22*, 115–132.

Goldring, E. (1990). Principals' Relationships with parents: The homogeneity versus the social class of the parent clientele. *Urban Review, 22*, 1–14.

Goldring, E. (1995). Boundary spanning and environmental management in schools. In S. Bacharach & B. Mundell (Eds.), *Images of Schools* (pp. 283–314). Thousand Oaks, CA: Corwin Press.

Goldring, E. & Sullivan, A. (1996). Beyond the Boundaries: Principals, Parents and Communities Shaping the School Environment. In K. Leithwood, J. Chapman, D. Corson, *et al.* (Eds.), *International Handbook of Educational Leadership and Administration* (pp. 195–222). London: Kluwer

Goodlad, J. I. (Ed.) (1966). *The sixty-fifth yearbook of the National Society for the Study of Education: Part 2*. The changing American school. Chicago: University of Chicago Press.

Goodlad, J. I. (Ed.) (1987). *Eighty-ninth yearbook of the National Society for the Study of Education*. The ecology of school renewal. Chicago: University of Chicago Press.

Goodrick, E. & Salancik, G. R. (1996). Organizational discretion in responding to institutional practices: Hospitals and Cesarean Births. *Administrative Science Quarterly, 41*, 1–28.

Gordon, C. W. (1957). *The social system of high school*. Glencoe, IL: Free Press.

Gouldner, A. W. (1955). *Patterns of industrial bureaucracy*. London: Routledge and Kegan Paul.

Griffiths, D. E. (1979). Intellectual turmoil in educational administration. *Educational Administration Quarterly, 15*, 43–65.

Grimshaw, W. J. (1979). *Union rule in schools: Big-city politics in transformation*. Lexington, MA: Lexington Books.

Gross, E. & Etzioni, A. (1985). *Organizations in society*. Englewood Cliffs, NJ: Prentice–Hall.

Grossman, P. L., Wilson, S. M. & Shulman, L. S. (1989). Teachers of substance: Subject matter knowledge for teaching in M. C. Reynolds (Ed.) *Knowledge base for the beginning teacher* (23–36). New York: Pergamon.

Gulick, L. & Urwick, L. (Eds.) (1937). *Paper on the science of administration*. New York: Institute of Public Administration, Columbia University.

Hallinger, P. & Murphy, J. (1986). The social context of effective schools. *American Journal of Education, 94*, 28–35.

Hanson, E. M. (1972). The emerging control structure of schools. *Administrator's Notebook, 21*, 1–4.

Hargreaves, D. H. (1994). The new professionalism: The synthesis of professional and institutional development. *Teaching and Teacher Education, 10*, 423–438.

Hart, A. W. (1990). Work redesign: A review of literature for educational reform. In S. B. Bacharach (Ed.), *Advances in research and theories of school management and educational policy*, Vol. 1 (pp. 31–60). Greenwich, CT: JAI Press.

Hart, A. W. (1994). Work feature values of today's and tomorrow's teachers: Work redesign as an incentive and school improvement policy. *Educational Evaluation and Policy Analysis, 16*, 458–473.

Heather, G. (1966). School organization: nongrading, dual progress, and team teaching. In J. I. Goodlad (Ed.), *The sixty-fifth yearbook of the National Society for the Study of Education: Part 2. The changing American school* (pp. 110–134). Chicago: University of Chicago Press.

Hill, P. T. & Bonan, J. (1991). *Decentralization and accountability in public education*. Santa Monica, CA: Rand.

Hodgkinson, C. (1978). *Towards a philosophy of administration*. New York: St. Martin's Press.

Hollingsworth, S. (1989). Prior beliefs and cognitive change in learning to teach. *American Educational Research Journal, 26*, 160–189.

Hollister, C. (1979). School bureaucratization as a response to parents' demands. *Urban Education, 14*, 221–235.

Hoy, W. K. (1982). Recent developments in theory and research in educational administration. *Educational Administration Quarterly, 18*, 1–11.

Hoy, W. K. & Miskel, C. G. (1996). *Educational administration: theory, research and practice* (5th ed.). New York: McGraw–Hill.

Hoy, W. K. & Rees, R. (1974). Subordinate loyalty to immediate superior: A neglected concept in the study of educational administration. *Sociology of Education, 47*, 268–286.

Hoy, W. K., Newland, W. & Blazovsky, R. (1977). Subordinate loyalty to superior, esprit, and aspects of bureaucratic structure. *Educational Administration Quarterly, 13*, 71–85.

James, T. (1991). State authority and the politics of educational change. In G. Grant (Ed.), *Review of research in education*, vol. 17 (pp. 169–224). Washington, DC: American Educational Research Association.

Johnson, S. M. (1990a). Redesigning teachers' work. In R. F. Elmore (Ed.), *Restructuring schools: The next generation of educational reform* (pp. 125–151). San Francisco: Jossey–Bass.

Johnson, S. M. (1990b). *Teachers at work: Achieving success in our schools*. New York: Basic Books.

Kamens, D. H. (1977). Legitimating myths and educational organization: The relationship between organizational ideology and formal structure. *American Sociological Review, 42*, 208–219.

Kerr, N. D. (1964). The school board as an agency of legitimation. *Sociology of Education, 38*, 34–59.

Kerr, S. T. (1981). Generalists versus specialists. In S. B. Bacharach (Ed.), *Organizational behavior in schools and school districts* (352–377). New York: Praeger.

Kob, J. (1961). Definitions of the teacher's role. In A. H. Halsey, J. Floud & C. A. Anderson (Eds.), *Education, economy, and society* (pp. 558–576). New York: Free Press.

Korman, A. K. & Associates, (1994). *Human dilemmas in work organizations: Strategies for resolution*. New York: Guilford Press.

Kottkamp, R. E., Provenzo, E. F., Jr. & Cohn, M. M. (1986). Stability and change in a profession: Two decades of teacher attitudes, 1964–1984. *Phi Delta Kappan, 67*, 559–567.

Lampert, M. (1985). How do teachers mnage to teach? Perspectives on problems in practice. *Harvard Educational Review, 55*, 178–194.

Laumann, E., Marsden, P. V. & Prensky, D. (1983). The boundary specification problem in network analysis. In R. S. Burt & M. J. Minor (Eds.), *Applied network analysis* (pp. 18–34). Beverly Hills, CA: Sage.

Lawrence, P. R. & Lorsch, J. W. (1967). *Organization and environment: Managing differentiation and integration*. Boston: Graduate School of Business Administration, Harvard University.

Lawrence, P. R. & Lorsch, J. W. (1969). *Developing organizations. Diagnosis and action*. Reading, MA: Addison–Wesley.

Lewin, K. (1948). *Resolving social conflicts*. New York: Harper.

Lipsky, M. (1976). Toward a theory of street–level bureaucracy. In W. D. Hawley, *et al.* (Eds.), *Theoretical perspectives in urban politics* (pp. 196–213). Englewood Cliffs, NJ: Prentice–Hall.

Lipsky, M. (1980). *Street-level bureaucracy: Dilemmas of the individual in public service*. New York: Russell Sage Foundation.

Louis, K. S. & Kruse, S. D. (Eds.) (1995). *Professionalism and community: Perspectives on reforming urban schools*. Thousand Oaks, CA: Corwin.

Lutz, F. W. & Iannaccone, L. (1978). *Public participation in local schools: The dissatisfaction theory of American democracy*. Lexington, MA: Lexington Books.

McDonald, J. P. (1992). *Teaching: Making sense of an uncertain craft*. New York: Teachers College Press.

McLaughlin, M. (1987). Learning from experience: Lessons from policy implementation. *Educational evaluation and policy analysis, 9*, 171–178.

Malen, B. (1994). *Enacting site-based management: A political utilities analysis*. Educational evaluation and policy analysis, 16, 249–267.

Malen, B. & Hart, A. W. (1987). Career ladder reform: A multi–level analysis of initial efforts. *Educational Evaluation and Policy Analysis, 9*, 9–23.

Mann, D. (1974). Political representation and urban school advisory councils. *Teachers College Record, 75*, 279–307.

Mannix, E. A. (1993). Organizations as resource dilemmas: The effects of power balance on coalition formation in small groups. *Organizational Behavior and Human Decision Processes, 55*, 1–22.

March, J. G. & Olsen, J. P. (1976). *Ambiguity and choice in organizations*. Bergen, Norway: Universitetsforlaget.

Maslow, A. H. (1965). *Eupsychian management*. Homewood, IL: Irwin.

Mawhinney, H. (1997, forthcoming). Tensions between professionalizing teaching and involving communities in schooling: School wars or school transformation. *Peabody Journal of Education*.

Mechanic, D. (1962). Sources of power of lower participants in complex organizations. *Administrative Science Quarterly, 7*, 349–364.

Merton, R. K. *et al.* (1952). *Reader in bureaucracy*. Glencoe, IL: Free Press.

Meyer, M. W. (Ed.) (1978). *Environments and organizations*. San Francisco: Jossey-Bass.

Meyer, J. W. & Rowan, B. (1977). Institutionalized organizations: Formal structure as myth and ceremony. *American Journal of Sociology, 83*, 340–363.

Meyer, J. W. & Rowan, B. (1978). The structure of educational organizations. In M. W. Meyer (Ed.), *Environments and organizations* (pp. 78–109). San Francisco: Jossey-Bass.

Meyer, J. W. & Scott, W. R. (1983). *Organizational environments: Ritual and reality*. Beverly Hills, CA: Sage.

Meyer, J. W., Boli, J. & Thomas, G. M. (1987). Ontology and rationalization in western cultural account. In G. M. Thomas, J. W. Meyer, F. O. Ramirez & J. Boli (Eds.), *Institutional structure: Constituting state, society, and the individual* (pp. 12–38). Beverly Hills, CA: Sage.

Mezias, S. J. (1990). An institutional model of organizational practice; Financial reporting at the Fortune 200. *Administrative Science Quarterly, 35*, 431–457.

Miles, M. B. (1981). Mapping the properties of schools. In R. Lehming & M. Kane (Eds.), *Improving schools: Using what we know* (pp. 42–114). Beverly Hills, CA: Sage.

Miskel, C., DeFrain, J. & Wilcox, K. (1980). A test of expectancy work motivation theory in educational organizations. *Educational Administration Quarterly, 16*, 70–92.

Miskel, C., McDonald, D. & Bloom, S. (1983). Structural and expectancy linkages within schools and organizational effectiveness. *Educational Administration Quarterly, 19*, 49–82.

Miskel, C. & Ogawa, R. T. (1988). Work motivation, job satisfaction, and climate. In N. J. Boyan (Ed.), *Handbook of research on educational administration* (pp. 279–304). New York: Longman.

Mitchell, D. E & Peters, M. J. (1988). A stronger profession through appropriate teacher incentives. *Educational Leadership, 46*, 74–78.

Moe, T. M. (1984). The new economics of organization. *American Journal of Political Science, 28*, 739–777.

Moe, T. M. (1990). Politics and the theory of organization. *The Journal of Law, Economics and Organization, 7*, 107–129.

Morgan, G. (1986). *Images of organizations*. Beverly Hills, CA: Sage.

Morris, D. R. (1997). Adrift in the sea of innovations: A response to Alexander, Murphy, and Woods. *Educational Researcher, 26*, 22–26.

Morris, V. C., Crowson, R. L., Porter-Gehrie, C. & Hurwitz, E., Jr. (1984). *Principals in action*. Columbus, OH: Charles E. Merrill.

Murphy, J. (1991). *Restructuring schools*. New York: Teachers College Press.

Murphy, J. & Hallinger, P. (1986). The social context of effective schools. *American Journal of Education, 94*, 328–355.

Newman, K. (1980). Incipience bureaucracy: Anthropological perspectives on bureaucracy. In G. M. Britan & R. Cohen (Eds.). *Hierarchy and Society: Anthropological perspectives on Bureaucracy*. (pp. 143–163). Philadelphia: Institute for Study of Social Issues.

Ogawa, R. T. (1994). The institutionalization of educational reform: The case of school-based management. *American Educational Research Journal, 31*, 519–548.

Ogawa, R. T. (1997, forthcoming). Organizing parent-teacher relations. *Peabody Journal of Education*.

Ogawa R. T. & White, P. A. (1994). School-based management: An overview. In S. A. Mohrman & P. Wohlstetter (Eds.), *School-based management: Organizing for high performance* (pp. 53–80). San Francisco: Jossey-Bass.

Page, A. L. & McClelland, D. A. (1978). The Kanawha County textbook controversy: A study of the politics of life style concern. *Social Forces, 57*, 265–281.

Parsons, T. (1960). *Structure and power in modern societies*. Glencoe, IL: Free Press.

Peshkin, A. (1978). *The imperfect union*. Chicago: University of Chicago Press.

Peterson, P. E. (1976). *School politics, Chicago style*. Chicago: University of Chicago Press.

Pfeffer, J. (1981). *Power in organizations*. Marshfield, MA: Pitman.

Pfeffer, J. & Salancik, G. R. (1978). *The external control of organizations*. New York: Harper & Row.

Pinder, C. C. (1984). *Work motivation: Theory issues, and applications*. Dallas: Scott, Foresman.

Pitner, N. J. & Ogawa, R. T. (1982). Organizational leadership. The case of the superintendent. *Educational Administration Quarterly, 17*, 45–65.

Porter, L. W. (1996). Forty years of organization studies: Reflections from a micro perspective. *Administrative Science Quarterly, 41*, 262–269.

Powell, W. W. & DiMaggio, P. J. (Eds.) (1991) *The new institutionalism in organizational analysis*. Chicago: University of Chicago Press.

Roesthlisberger, F. J. & Dickson, W. J. (1952). Formal and informal status. In R. K. Merton, A. P. Gran, B. Hockey & H. C. Selvin (Eds.). *Reader in bureaucracy* (pp. 255–264). New York: Free Press.

Rogers, D. (1968). *110 Livingston Street*. New York: Random House.

Rowan, B. (1982). Organizational structure and the institutional environment: The case of public schools. *Administrative Science Quarterly, 27*, 259–279.

Sarason, S. B. (1990). *The predictable failure of educational reform*. San Francisco: Jossey-Bass.

Sarason, S. B. (1995). *Parental involvement and the political principle: Why the existing governance structure of the schools should be abolished*. San Francisco: Jossey-Bass

Schein, E. H. (1985). *Organizational culture and leadership*. San Francisco: Jossey-Bass.

Schein, E. H. (1996). Culture: The missing concept in organizations studies. *Administrative Science Quarterly, 41*, 229–240.

Schrag, P. (1967). *Village school downtown*. Boston: Beacon.

Schroeder, D. A. (Ed.) (1995). *Social dilemmas: Perspectives on individuals and groups*. Wesport, CT: Praeger.

Scott, W. R. (1987). The adolescence of institutional theory. *Administrative Science Quarterly, 32*, 493–511.

Scott, W. R. (1992). *Organizations: Rational, natural, and open systems* (3rd ed.). Englewood Cliffs, NJ: Prentice-Hall.

Scott, W. R. (1995). *Institutions and organizations*. Thousand Oaks, CA: Sage.

Selznick, P. (1957). *Leadership in administration*. Berkeley: University of California Press.

Shaw, M. W. 1964). Some effects of problem complexity upon problem solution efficiency in various communication nets. *Journal of experimental psychology, 48*, 211–217.

Shedd, J. B. & Bacharach, S. B. (1991). *Tangled hierarchies: Teachers as professionals and the management of schools*. San Francisco: Jossey-Bass.

Shulman, L. S. (1986). Knowledge and teaching: Foundations of the new reform. *Harvard Educational Review, 57*, 1–22.

Smircich, L. (1983). Organizations as shared meanings. In L. R. Pondy, *et al.* (Eds.), *Organizational symbolism* (pp. 55–65). Greenwich, CT: JAI Press.

Smircich, L. & Stubbart, C. (1985). Strategic management in an enacted world. *Academy of Management Review, 10*, 724–736.

Smylie, M. A. & Brownlee-Conyers, J. (1992) Teacher leaders and their principals: Exploring the development of new working relationships. *Educational Administration Quarterly, 28,* 150–184.

Smylie, M. A. & Denny, J. W. (1990). Teacher leadership: Tensions and ambiguities in organizational perspective. *Educational Administration Quarterly, 26,* 235–259.

Solomon, C. M. (1996). Put your ethics to a global test. *Personnel Journal, 75,* 66–74.

Strang, D. (1987). The administrative transformation of American education: School district consolidation, 1938–1980. *Administrative Science Quarterly, 32,* 352–366.

Strauss, A. *et al.* (1966). The hospital and its negotiated order. In E. Friedson (Ed.), *The hospital in modern society* (pp. 243–251). New York: Holt, Rinehart & Winston.

Taylor, F. W. (1911). *The principles of scientific management.* New York: Harper and Row.

Taylor, F. W. (1947). *Scientific management.* New York: Harper and Brothers.

Thompson, J. D. (1967). *Organizations in action.* New York: McGraw-Hill.

Tichy, N. (1973). An analysis of clique formation and structure in organizations. *Administrative Science Quarterly, 18,* 194–208.

Toch, T. (1984). Survey indicates teacher support for merit pay. *Education Week, 2,* 1,12.

Tyack, D. (1974). *The one best system.* Cambridge, MA: Harvard University Press.

Tyack, D. & Cuban, L. (1995). *Tinkering toward utopia.* Cambridge, MA: Harvard University Press.

Tyack, D. & Hansot, E. (1982). *Managers of virtue: Public school leadership in American: 1820–1980.* New York: Basic Books.

Tyack, D. & Tobin, W. (1994). The "grammar" of schooling: Why has it been so hard to change? *American Educational Research Journal, 31,* 453–479.

Tye, B. B. (1987). The deep structure of schooling. *Phi Delta Kappan, 69,* 281–284.

Tyler, R. W. (1966). The behavioral sciences and the schools. In J. I. Goodlad (Ed.), *The sixty-fifth yearbook of the National Society for the Study of Education: Part 2. The changing American school* (pp. 200–214). Chicago: University of Chicago Press.

Valasquez, M. (1996). Why ethics matters: A defense of ethics in business organizations. *Business Ethics Quarterly, 6,* 201–222.

Vroom, V. H. (1969). Industrial social psychology. In G. Lindzey & E. Aronson (Eds.), *The handbook of social psychology* (Vol. 5) (2nd ed.) (pp. 196–268). Reading, MA: Addison-Wesley.

Weber, M. (1947). *The theory of social and economic organizations.* In T. Parsons (Ed.), A. M. Henderson & T. Parsons (Trans.). Glencoe, IL: Free Press.

Weick, K. E. (1976). Educational organizations as loosely coupled systems. *Administrative Science Quarterly, 21,* 1–19.

Weick, K. E. (1995). *Sensemaking in organizations.* Thousand Oaks, CA: Sage.

Weick, K. E. (1996). An appreciation of social context: One legacy of Gerald Salancik. *Administrative Science Quarterly, 41,* 563–573.

Weick, K. E. & Roberts, K. (1993). Collective mind in organizations: Heedful interrelating on flight decks. *Administrative Science Quarterly, 38,* 357–381.

Wiley, N. (1988). The micro-macro problem in social theory. *Sociological Theory, 6,* 254–261.

Williamson, O. E. (1975). *Markets and hierarchies.* New York: Free Press.

Williamson, O. E. (1991). Comparative economic organization: The analysis of discrete structural alternatives. *Administrative Science Quarterly, 36,* 269–296.

Wong, K. K. & Sunderman, G. L. (1996). Redesigning accountability at the system-wide level: The politics of school reform in Chicago. In K. K. Wong (Ed.), *Advances in educational policy, Vol. 2: Rethinking school reform in Chicago.* Greenwich, CT: JAI Press.

Zeigler, L. H. & Jennings, M. K. (1974). *Governing American schools.* North Scituate, MA: Duxbury.

Zucker, L. (1987). Institutional theories of organization. *Annual Review of Sociology, 13,* 443–464.

CHAPTER 14

Schools as Cultures

William A. Firestone and Karen Seashore Louis

Educational excellence has become part of the unique "feel," the inner reality, and daily routine of some American schools. *The Principal's Role in Shaping School Culture* was written to help principals make this happen in their own schools—by suggesting ideas and giving examples of the powerful but underemphasized role principals play as shapers of school culture (Deal & Peterson, 1991, p.1).

Success stories of the top corporations in this country can also be applied to the top high schools. The patterns are consistent. Writers who report on institutional success cite work culture as the distinguishing feature of excellent companies (Snyder, 1988, p. 40).

Three books from the early 1980s—*In Search of Excellence* (Peters & Waterman, 1982), *Corporate Cultures* (Deal & Kennedy, 1982), and *Theory Z* (Ouchi, 1981)—transformed organizational culture from an arcane academic concept to a staple of management thinking. The idea spread almost immediately to educational administration and has continued to suggest prescriptions for improvement, even if it inspired relatively little research.

As the upbeat quotes leading off this chapter illustrate, culture is attractive because it offers administrators ways to bring meaning and effectiveness to schools. The founders of the field—Weber, Taylor, and others—focused on organizational structures. They thought managers should rationally analyze the environment in light of the organization's purposes and design the best structures to fit those purposes (Gouldner, 1959).

This view has not helped in education. Schools have a common structure that is almost impervious to change (Tyack & Cuban, 1995). However, students learn more in schools where their peers and teachers make academics the number one priority and hold high expectations for all students, and when the climate supports adult as well as student learning (Heck & Marcoulides, 1996; Mortimore, 1991; Teddlie & Stringfield, 1991). Values are as important as structures for influencing student learning (Lee, Bryk, & Smith, 1993). Although human relations research dealt with these issues, culture seems to offer access to deeper values and more ways for administrators to influence them (Deal & Peterson, 1991; Hoy & Miskel, 1996).

Culture also offers ways to address issues of togetherness and community. Sergiovanni (1994) criticizes the dominant organizational tradition for assuming that interpersonal relationships in schools are impersonal, contractual, and self-interested. He suggests that the community metaphor encourages researchers to examine the contribution of shared values and commitments. Culture encourages the same sensitivities as his preferred metaphor community.

The optimism of culture advocates reflects the conception of culture brought to educational administration from the study of organizations.[1] Other research traditions question how well culture brings people together and the principal's capacity to influence culture. For example, anthropologists use conceptions of culture that emphasize linguistic codes, conflict, and the embeddedness of school cultural elements in distinct ethnic groups in the larger society (Erickson, 1987a, 1987b). Others note how cultures divide. Cultural elements from clothes to musical tastes to language differentiate groups. Sociologists have examined the social construction of culture, the multiplicity of cultural forms, and the role of culture in intergroup conflicts (Wuthnow & Witten, 1988; Foley, 1990).

Similarly, educational researchers treat shared values as a defining aspect of culture (Deal & Peterson, 1991; Hoy & Miskel, 1996). However, culture can be more than values. Most definitions of culture involve knowledge of various sorts (Erickson, 1987a). Wilson (1971, p. 90) defines culture as knowledge of "what is and ought to be," which includes values but considerably more. These other kinds of knowledge and their implications for life in schools deserve exploration.

Another difference between educational administration researchers and those in the disciplines is that the former analyze school cultures, while the latter look at cultures of social entities of all sizes, from villages to nation states. So where does one look for culture? And how are cultures in these various entities related to each other? Are "school cultures" really embodiments of culture centered somewhere else?

When combined with the stratification of organizations and society, the way cultures separate groups raises ethical issues. Bates (1987) argues that understanding a culture requires discerning the struggles between dominant and subordinate subcultures. Then, administrators' efforts to shape school culture, which most researchers applaud, may be a form of managerial imposition. This raises questions about how non-manipulative cultural leadership is possible (Reitzug and Reeves, 1992).

This chapter seeks to expand the understanding of culture that has dominated educational administration. We do so by asking four questions. First, what is culture? Here we provide a framework for situating different definitions of culture. Second, where is culture? We examine the aspects of culture that are situated at different levels from the nation to the classroom and look at the different cultures of adults and children. Third, what influences cultures? Here we look at out-of-school socialization and how the conflicts that surround school shape aspects of culture. Fourth, how much can administrators influence culture? Our task is to clarify the scope within which it is reasonable to expect administrators to shape culture and some of the strategies and tactics for doing so. We conclude by suggesting a research agenda for the future.

What Is Culture?

The conception of culture that influenced administrative researchers came from organizational research. An important issue in that field was how cultural analysis would be used to break with the older functionalist tradition (Greenfield, 1984). In education, researchers have stayed close to that tradition, which has had three effects on conceptions of culture that dominate the field. First, they have taken insufficient advantage of the interpretive turn in social theory generally and not attended to theories using "codes" to explain how culture works. Second, they have not adequately examined the role of culture in conflict or how culture is constructed. Finally, culture has stayed a holistic concept and researchers have not attended to the interplay of national, organizational, subgroup, and other cultures.

A useful way to explore the definitions of culture that have dominated thinking in educational administration is to begin with one of the most influential authors in organizational behavior: Edgar Schein. He defines culture as (Schein, 1992, p. 12):

> A pattern of shared basic assumptions that the group learned as it solved its problems of external adaptation and internal integration, that has worked well enough to be considered valid and, therefore to be taught to new members as the correct way to perceive, think, and feel in relation to those problems.

He further identifies three basic levels of culture, separated by how easy it is to observe them and their impact on action within the organization. These are *artifacts, espoused values,* and *basic assumptions.* Artifacts are the observable manifestations of an organization, its language, products, and artistic creations. These are easy to apprehend but difficult to interpret without knowledge of the two deeper levels. Espoused values are statements that members make about the way things are and what people are supposed to do. Although more central than artifacts, they are still subject to rational analysis and rationalization so that what is said may not be what is believed. In contrast, deeply embedded basic assumptions are difficult, if not impossible, to articulate. Taken for granted, they provide strong communal guidelines for how to act that provide continuity in rapidly shifting circumstances.

Codes and the Interpretive Turn

The idea of levels points to the deep structure and embeddedness of organizational culture. The apparent immutability of culture is often used both to differentiate the concept from the closely related idea of organizational climate and to justify the use of more ideographic methods to study culture. If the most fundamental guides to action cannot be easily articulated, they are not accessible through conventional surveys, interviews, and related methodologies. Nevertheless, the boundaries between climate and culture remain ambiguous (Denison, 1996). As researchers began using survey and experimental methods to study culture in the late 1980s (Chatman & Barsade, 1995; Hofstede, Neuijen, Ohayv, & Sanders, 1990), the distinction between these concepts became even less clear.

The idea of levels also devalues artifacts and symbols. Indeed for all their analyses of the symbolic side of organization, Schein (1992) and others (Deal & Kennedy, 1982; Deal & Peterson, 1991) view it primarily as a window on organizational values. In fact, Schein, like many others

(Denison, 1996), equates culture with values. This is clear in his treatment of his second level—espoused values—and implied in his discussion of the third level—basic assumptions—which include what he sees as real organizational values.

This emphasis on values hides much of what is interesting about culture in other research communities. Even in organizational research, other authors used ideas like artifacts and symbols to introduce an interpretive turn to their theories (Hatch, 1993; Smircich, 1983). These researchers questioned functionalist and causal paradigms and looked to culture as a way to take a more phenomenological approach to organizations. Grounded in ethnographic and symbolic interactionist approaches, they borrowed from sociology and anthropology (Barley, Meyer, & Gash, 1988; Mehan, 1992).

This interpretive turn opened up new methodological directions. Researchers adopted methodologies for decoding the symbolic side of organizations, including ethnography but also more specialized approaches like semiotics (Barley, 1983) and means for inferring grammars of action (Pentland & Rueter, 1994). These and less formalized methodologies are used to analyze the meanings made of symbols like organizational stories and rhetoric (Boje, 1991; Fine, 1996), as well as other artifacts. The new approaches highlight both the ambiguities of signs in organizational life and the processes by which sense is made of them.

The interpretive turn also opened up an alternative explanation of behavior that de-emphasized values. Values explain behavior by specifying ends to be achieved and, in conjunction with norms, clarifying "good," or at least approved, forms of interaction. They provide the motivation for action (Swidler, 1986). As a result, functionalists spend much time worrying about conformity and deviance because they are signs of the power of culture over behavior. Schein (1992) uses this approach to connect culture to action.

The problem is that the relationship between values and action is much more complex than this model suggests. Sometimes values provide a post hoc rationalization for action. Action that is not motivated is commonplace (Giddens, 1984). Swidler (1986) proposes a different explanation for how culture shapes action. In this view, culture is a "tool kit" that provides strategies for action that members of the culture can use in many different ways. The tool kit idea resembles Giddens' (1984) structuration theory. Giddens (1976) uses the analogy of language to explain how these tools work. Language provides grammar and vocabulary out of which individuals construct speech. Each speech act is unique, but it is structured and organized by rules for organizing sentences and the available vocabulary. Moreover, like much of culture, language is intangible. Although one can analyze linguistic rules, language itself is only observable through speech acts.[2]

The tool kit approach breaks with functionalist theories of how culture influences action. These latter theories emphasize how culture, especially its normative aspect, constrains action by ruling out certain kinds of behavior (Giddens, 1976). Cultural codes do allow for constraint as when a language lacks a vocabulary to express certain ideas. What an individual attends to may also be influenced by codes (Weick & Roberts, 1993). At the same time, codes allow for great playfulness and creativity as cultural elements are assembled in new and different ways. Indeed, another important aspect of this view of culture is to identify innovators who develop new cultural forms (Wuthnow & Witten, 1988). Earlier views of culture saw it as a holistic idea that helped to explain social integration by examining how things knit together in patterned ways (Benedict, 1934). This patterning was supposed to contribute to cultural conformity. The tool kit metaphor suggests that the codes that make up culture are not tightly linked to each other. There is more room for individual creativity and less likelihood that culture will inevitably bring individuals and groups together in conflict-free totalities. The idea of conformity is de-emphasized and it is easier to see ways to challenge the rules of common behavior that are not necessarily "deviant."

It is also important to recognize that codes and values may push action in divergent directions. Swidler (1995) points out that even though Americans criticize the commercial nature of the Christmas holiday, a well-developed, if implicit, semiotic code governs how the cost of gifts signal the importance of the recipient to the giver.

The tool kit idea gives more importance to the symbolic realm than the functionalist approach. If values shape action, the symbolic dimension is secondary, useful to the researcher for inferring values and to members for the same reason and perhaps for purposes of persuasion as well. On the other hand, cultural codes are part of the symbolic realm. When they are used to construct lines of action, culture shapes action through symbols, rather than simply in conjunction with them. Moreover, the tool kit idea gives more room for individual agency and cultural invention.

Culture: Uniting or Dividing?

Schein (1992) stresses the *shared* nature of organizational culture. In fact, the holistic nature of culture and the idea of deep assumptions often fit together. In organizational studies, these ideas are a functionalist holdover (Smircich, 1983). Swidler (1986) suggests that a shared culture with strong tacit assumptions requires special circumstances. She distinguishes between cultures that develop under settled and unsettled circumstances. Unsettled circumstances occur because of external pressures, internal or external cultural conflicts, or the delegitimization of social inequities (as happened in the United States during the 1960s).

During unsettled times, cultures are more explicit, taking the form of ideologies with articulated, highly organized meaning systems including both beliefs and rituals. These systems may have both political and religious aspects. They are usually more internally consistent than the commonsense culture that predominates during more settled times because they are constructed to "make sense" of turbulence. Such ideologies develop to advance the interests of particular individuals and groups and may be directly implicated in intergroup conflicts (Swidler, 1986). Still, unsettled times can place a premium on specific values that are not rated so highly during stable periods (Chatman & Jehn, 1994).

During settled times, the self-conscious development of religions and ideologies is less prevalent, and cultural improvisation happens privately as individuals and groups construct strategies for action out of available cultural elements (Swidler, 1986). Cultures are less holistic during settled times because there is little pressure for self-conscious rationalization of beliefs. Still, basic, tacit assumptions can more easily shape the lives of people during such times because they are less likely to be challenged.

The distinctions between values and codes and settled and unsettled times suggest basic dimensions that characterize researchers' assumptions about culture (see Table 14.1). The rows reflect whether the emphasis is on cultures as sources of values and norms that provide the justification for action, or cultural codes out of which action is created. Interpretive strategies are more central in to the second row. The columns reflect assumptions about how settled the conditions are for the culture being studied. Theories that attend to cultural conflict are found in the right-hand column. The boundaries between cells can be permeable. For instance, Schein views cultures as including more than values, although he does not examine codes per se. The upper left cell (emphasis on values in settled times) reflects conventional functionalist approaches to sociology and anthropology.[3]

The Location of Culture

The books that popularized the culture in organizations assumed that each organization has its own, an assumption that fits the older idea of holistic cultures. This need not be the case, however. Indeed Schein is very aware that cultural elements can be located at many organizational levels. For instances, organizations can be located in larger contexts, such as nation states (Hofstede *et al.*, 1990) with cultures that strongly shape organizations in them. Second, organizations have formal or informal subgroups including both departments and occupational groups with their subcultures (Gregory, 1983; Sackman, 1992; Anderson, Louis, & Earle, 1994; Siskin, 1991). A cultural perspective focuses on the interplay among organizational subcultures, organizational cultures, and cultural elements from outside the organization.

The next section begins our analysis of cultures in schools. We focus on the location of culture in schools, subunits, or the nation. The latter elements are particularly important because findings that seem to be school-specific may turn out to characterize schools in a larger domain. In the process, we attend to how researchers define cultures: the extent to which they analyze codes as well as values, and their assumptions about how holistic, tacit, and settled the culture is.

Where Is Culture?

It is important to understand where culture is located. Schoolwide cultures are most amenable to administrative influence. However, aspects of school culture that really reflect national cultures will be less amenable to administrative influence. Subcultures based on informal interaction or shared professional or ethnic understandings will also be difficult to affect. Culture can be located at any of three levels at least. The first two are the nation state and the school. Unity within a school is only possible to a point because schools are divided into two major subcultures: adult staff (primarily teachers) and students. These are two separate moieties, groups that are interdependent yet linked in permanent or at least potential conflict (Wolcott, 1977). Thus we treat the adult and student subcultures of the school separately.

National Cultures

Some characteristics of school culture that we tend to regard as fixed are attributable to differences in national culture and expectations, which in turn affect both school organization and the behavior of teachers, parents, and students. Most cross-national research on cultures ignores the development of codes and emphasizes differences in values, both basic cultural values that are central to most citizen's views of how school ought to work. Hodgkinson (1983) refers to this as the "transrational level" of culture. Others focus on norms about how organizations ought to be in-

Table 14.1
A Framework for Organizing Theories About Culture

Emphasis On	Assumptions About Context	
	Settled Times	*Unsettled Times*
Values		
Codes		

ternally structured and how the people who work in them ought to relate to one another. Although we cannot fully explore comparative differences and multi-country studies of school culture are not very common, some consistent themes are notable.

National Variations in Educational Values and Beliefs

Comparative analyses of educational systems often focus on governance: who has the right to make decisions about educational policy or practice. Policy trends in many developed countries put more responsibility for making decisions into the hands of teachers or schools; Sweden, Norway, Russia, Spain, the Netherlands, and France are a few where efforts to decentralize responsibility has occurred. But if we wish to understand the implicit assumptions that affect school improvement policies, a more important distinction is the degree to which schools (and the people in them) are normatively expected to be homogeneous (very similar across different units and in different parts of the country) or heterogeneous (different between schools; often coupled with the ability of parents to choose schools).

For instance, the Swiss traditionally prefer a homogeneous education, at least at the elementary level, although their system is rather decentralized (Huberman, 1990). In some cantons, identical curricula are used in each school including, in some cases, uniform texts and materials. Teachers are viewed not as employees of the school but of the cantonal educational system, and Huberman has remarked (private communication) that in some ways one could say that there is no school organization in Switzerland—just buildings where teachers work.

In sharp contrast, the Netherlands appears on the surface to be considerably more centralized than Switzerland (van den Berg & van Wijlick, 1990). There is a large national ministry and parliamentary discussion of national reforms. Yet the value system, embodied in the constitution and in educational codes, encourages diversity at the building level because of the full funding of private education and the limitations on government control over curricula and texts. Although national tests are available, few teachers use them without modification (Postlethwaite, 1986; Louis & Versloot, 1996).

Intertwined with the homogeneity versus heterogeneity issue is the question of how parental or religious values are reflected in the school's curriculum. Do parents expect the school to incorporate their own ethical or other values and, if so, do they expect to be able to make choices between schools? This question reflects the degree to which the community expects schools to respond to subcultural or local value systems. In the U.S., for example, the public tends to value heterogeneity; schools are expected to be dif-

ferent between local communities, and sometimes within communities. Parental values, however, are not expected to influence the school to any great extent. Thus the selection of community residence is given much attention, since it is only in this way that parents may choose without paying fees for private (usually religious) education.

In the Netherlands and Belgium on the other hand, parents may choose private school options at public expense, and the majority do so. Much attention, both parliamentary and otherwise, is devoted to the meaning of choice. In France, public opinion strongly supports freedom to choose private education. The public debates, however, center around the obligation of the state to protect children from poor parental choices, and the converse value of having a private choice option that prevents the development of an insensitive monopoly (Fowler, 1992). That these values are sensitive to broader political changes is clear. In Czechoslovakia, whose educational system was previously tightly controlled by the state, well over 50% of the parents who strongly value education believe that they should control the schools and are willing to pay for that privilege (Prucha & Walterova, 1992, p. 46).

Cultural Values Related to Students and Teachers

Countries vary in how much they attribute student achievement to innate individual characteristics or other factors. A classic investigation by Bronfenbrenner (1972) points out that U.S. elementary school classrooms are organized to foster individual achievement and competition between students, while Russian classrooms are organized to promote collective responsibility for learning among students. Similarly, comparative investigations of Japanese and American schools demonstrate important but deeply embedded differences. In Japan, student academic achievement is attributed to hard work and effort, while in the U.S., it is often attributed to intelligence or talent (Stevenson & Stigler, 1992). This assumption is translated into many aspects of school organization and culture; for example, the lack of special education and ability grouping in Japanese elementary schools contrasts with the prevalent use of ability groups and the increasing attention to individual differences in learning fostered through the special education system.

In countries that emphasize collective responsibility and effort, wide differences in student achievement in a school are viewed as a sign of poor functioning. These differences persist in spite of the prevalence of modernist and increasingly individualistic cultures in most developed countries. A recent investigation by Osborne (1996) highlights this difference. In inner city schools in England, teachers emphasize their responsibility to provide individualized responses to the "different" needs of poor children;

in France, on the other hand, teachers emphasize their responsibility to provide the same experiences, opportunities, and achievement that more advantaged children receive.

Hofstede's Model of Work-Related Values

Hofstede's (1980) monumental comparative study of work-related values analyzes industrial settings. Although this work has been criticized as oversimplified (examining too few values), it nevertheless has a great deal to offer in terms of thinking about how values may affect life in schools. In addition, in his more reflective and integrative review of this topic (Hofstede, 1991), he generalizes his findings to educational settings as well as providing evidence from other research studies that supports his emphasis on national values.

Hofstede examines the core workplace values of equality versus inequality, collectivism versus individualism, masculinity versus femininity, and uncertainty avoidance versus tolerance for ambiguity. In this section, we briefly review his findings and discuss their implications for school culture.

Equality and Inequality

In some countries, the power distance between students and teachers, and between teachers and administrators is great, while in others, relationships are expected to be egalitarian. Where power distances are small, all members of the workplace expect to initiate and to be consulted on change; in higher power-distance countries, both "superiors" and "subordinates" prefer to have clear relationships of authority and change initiated from above. Although most developed countries fall below the mean of preferences for inequality in Hofstede's sample of 53 countries, the range is very great. France and Belgium are well above the mean, while Denmark and Austria are at the bottom. High preferences for power distance may be associated with greater traditionalism (junior members of the faculty are less free to suggest change than those who have "been around"), and with more emphasis on status differentiation.

In developed countries, status differentiation in professional organizations rarely results in extreme "autocratic" versus "democratic" leadership patterns. Although school leaders exist in every European country (except in many primary schools in Switzerland), their roles vary enormously. In France, for example, school leaders are the sole interpreter of government regulations within the school. However, both custom and union agreements limit their ability to evaluate teachers, to make suggestions about teaching practice (functions carried out by the powerful inspectorate), or even to call staff meetings

to discuss school improvement issues (Caré, 1986). In countries that score lowest on Hofstede's power distance index, the school leader is often a "first among equals," or "head of the team." In Sweden, for example, the leader is often responsible for several buildings and therefore shares substantial responsibilities with others within the school (Stegî, 1986). In Denmark, the teacher is viewed as the central actor in school improvement and change (Anderson and Olsen, 1985). In some countries, such as Great Britain and the U.S., the principal's influence is strong enough to influence student achievement (Hallinger & Heck, 1996), while in others (the Netherlands) principal leadership does not influence student learning.

Collectivism and Individualism

This dimension refers to the relative importance of individual challenge on the job versus loyalty and support of group goals. In educational settings, this may be felt in terms of the individual's preference to "stand out" among peers versus creating group harmony. As Hofstede points out, attitudes toward education goals may vary tremendously in individualistic versus more collective nations:

> [In the individualist society] there is a basically positive attitude towards what is new. The purpose of learning is . . . to know how to learn . . . In the collectivist society there is a stress on adaptation to the skills and virtues necessary to be an acceptable group member. This leads to a premium on the products of tradition (p. 63).

Again, Hofstede's data suggest that there is a wide range among the developed countries, although most tend (in support of "modernist" interpretations of society) to be more individualistic than less developed countries. The English-speaking countries all rank at the top of the individualism scale (along with the Netherlands), while Israel, Spain, and Japan have scores around the mean for the whole sample. (All countries below the mean are developing countries.)

In Japan, teachers work together in preparing their lessons and materials and get considerable time to do so (Sato and McLaughlin, 1992); teachers' personal work spaces are often arranged in a "bull pen" setting that helps interaction (Shimahara & Sakai, 1994). In the U.S., teachers collaborate less frequently (Lortie, 1975), but more often than in France, where (secondary) teachers are viewed as autonomous professionals and, like college professors, are not required to be physically present in the school unless they are teaching a class (Louis, 1990). Thus the presence of collaborative cultures within the school varies enormously due to different countries' conceptions about appropriate models for teacher professionalism.

Gendered Cultures

Hofstede argues that his study measures the degree to which cultures value "assertiveness" versus "modesty" and this is the only dimension on which male and female respondents in his study differed consistently. But differences still appear between countries. More masculine cultures hold "tough" values (advancement, opportunity) rather than "tender" values (cooperation, opportunities to contribute). One might expect that compared to IBM salespeople, educators, for example, would score in the "tender" direction, although we have no data to this regard. Nevertheless, we might also expect cultural differences within education between the most masculine counties (Japan, Austria, and Switzerland) and the most feminine (Denmark, the Netherlands, Norway, and Sweden). There are implications for education that are clear, according to Hofstede:

> Experiences in teaching abroad and the discussions with teachers from different countries have led me to conclude that in the more feminine cultures the average student is considered the norm, while in more masculine countries like the U.S.A. the best students are the norm. (Hofstede, 1991, p. 90).

This may also have implications for how easy it is to change a school. When individualist cultures also have "tough" values, the emphasis on individual success and opportunity may detract from attention to group effectiveness and change. In Hofstede's sample, Germany, Switzerland, and Austria fall into this category and we have already remarked that these countries are characterized by educational policies that promote stability rather than change. Denmark and the Netherlands, which we have categorized as high on valuing educational change, on the other hand, are characterized as high collective/high feminine countries. Teachers expect a personal challenge in their work but expect it to be met within the group setting.

"What Is different Is dangerous"

National cultures differ, as any tourist knows, in their willingness to confront anomalies or cases that do not follow protocol. Countries where individual anxiety levels are high tend to avoid uncertainty, while those where anxiety is low (but overt conflicts including violence are high) may thrive on ambiguity. Hofstede's data suggest that among the developed countries, Belgium, Japan, and France score very high on uncertainty avoidance, while the English-speaking countries score, on the whole, very low. Of the developed countries, only Denmark ranks lower.

In terms of education, uncertainty avoidance is related to expectations about expertise. In high avoidance countries, like Germany and France, teachers are expected to have the answers. In lower uncertainty avoidance countries,

teachers may feel free to say to both students and colleagues "I don't know," and intellectual disagreement may be viewed as not only stimulating but essential for development (Hofstede, p. 120).

National Codes

There have been few international analyses of cultures as codes. However, an examination of one such code that is prevalent in the United States illustrates how general values and specific historical arrangements, including other codes, develop trans-school patterns that are very difficult to overcome in specific settings. The code in question is the bargain between teachers and high school students to reduce academic expectations (Powell, Farrar, & Cohen, 1985; Sedlak, Wheeler, Pullin, & Cusick, 1986). Such bargains are rarely made explicitly, yet they regulate the amount of time and intensity students will commit to a course. Teachers have considerable latitude in setting demands in such areas; usually demands are set rather low in exchange for positive and pleasant working relationships with students (McNeil, 1986). On occasion, demands are set very high indeed, and classes are extremely academically challenging. One understanding that regulates these bargains is the implicit agreement that the highest academic demands are set in the highest track classes that are typically for more affluent students (although not all high track classes set high demands).

Historical analysis shows how these bargains depend upon and complement a whole set of additional codes that make up the comprehensive high school. Some of these were developed by national culture-building elites. For instance, the Carnegie unit was developed at the turn of the century by the presidents of elite universities with support from the Carnegie Foundation for the Advancement of Teaching (Tyack & Cuban, 1995). The Carnegie unit was a major advancement that helped to standardize high school curricula and competition for places in institutions of higher education. However, it measured the amount of time devoted to subject areas without clearly specifying what should be taught or the knowledge or capacities that students should demonstrate at the end—as contrasted with standardization procedures in other countries that stressed either a national curriculum, national high-stakes tests, or, in some instances, both. The Carnegie unit left considerable leeway for negotiation between students and teachers.

Other codes developed more slowly. The extensive vertical differentiation of the high school curriculum into high and low track classes that made very different demands on students reflected the social efficiency movement of the World War I era. Then experts believed that testing technology could be used to humanely sort students and prepare them for different adult careers (Tyack & Cuban, 1995). By the time new scientific research suggested that tracking did more harm than good, the practice had become so ingrained in teachers' and parents' understanding of how schools operated that it was extremely difficult to change.

Similarly, the horizontal differentiation across many subject areas reflected the pressure to expand the high school's mission to not only prepare children of the elites for college but also to prepare a wide range of adolescents for adult life. This wide range of courses, each with ambiguous specifications of what should be taught, allowed teachers to negotiate the academic expectations they would set. It also let each student determine the academic demands she or he faced by choosing a course of study (Powell *et al.*, 1985). In other countries, in contrast, it is more common to have a core curriculum for all students (Scandinavia) or a tracked but more specified curriculum that differentiates between those seeking terminal vocational qualifications, further vocational education, or university degrees (Germany, the Netherlands, Switzerland).

Yet these bargains express a number of central American values. Prominent among these are the emphases on equity and individualism. The comprehensive high school appears at least to offer every child the opportunity to succeed, but the responsibility rests with the student who chooses the course of study and must continually decide whether to stick with the chosen course (Powell *et al.*, 1985). These bargains also express a national devaluation of academic knowledge (Sedlak *et al.*, 1996).

The Limits of a National Culture Perspective

Although national cultures have a significant impact on school cultures, there is also evidence suggesting that a school is a school no matter where it is located. For example, the same models of school development can work in countries as culturally dissimilar as the Netherlands, Germany, and Norway (Dalin & Rolff, 1993). More recently, Dalin's (1994) work on school improvement processes in three developing countries suggests that the same factors that have been identified in U.S. and European research apply in very different settings. Others, such as Hargreaves (1994), use comparative data sources to argue that the condition of teaching and teachers is becoming the same in all post-modern settings, while new institutionalists argue that the increasing similarities in organizational structures among countries are also forcing cultural similarities (Meyer, Boli, & Thomas, 1994). This is not an either/or argument, but these contradictory findings point out the need for more research exploring the effects of national cultures on particular schools.

School Culture: Adults

The adult culture of the school was the focus of attention among American administrative researchers bringing ideas from the business community to the study of education in the early 1980s. Because of the nature of that work, they often used a functionalist approach that assumed considerable internal unanimity and a fair amount of external stability even when they documented internal conflict and external pressures. Functionalists were aided by critical theorists who attended to external conflict over what should be taught and how students should be classified while ignoring internal processes of conflict or domination (McNeil, 1986). Research in this area has been largely qualitative, although we draw to some extent on quantitative studies using ideas from social psychology and the effective schools' research as well. They tend to view culture as consisting of shared values, although they also attend to the codes that operationalize those beliefs. What is largely missing is semiotic research that interprets rituals and practices to identify common codes or grammars of action.

Adult Culture and School Effectiveness

Analyses of adult subcultures have focused on three themes: what students are like and how to deal with them, what academics are like and how important they are, and how teachers should relate to each other. The first issue what students are like addresses the fundamental conflict of interest between adults and children in school. According to Waller (1932), the teacher-pupil relationship is a form of institutionalized domination from which the underlying hostility can never be totally removed. One root problem for all schools is to determine how to address this underlying conflict. Answers to that problem are provided through shared understandings of what students are like and appropriate ways to encourage them to participate in the legitimate life of the school.

Metz (1986) shows that these answers can differ significantly among schools. She describes teachers' orientations and interactions with students in two magnet middle schools. In Adams Avenue Middle School, teachers viewed students as serious academic learners and encouraged academic effort. Teachers focused on academic matters, cooperated with students, and treated them in a friendly manner, often using humor to get students to desist from minor distractions or to get down to work. The underlying assumption was that as people got to know each other better, they would come to like each other.

In the Horace Mann School, extensive resources were committed to maintaining order with teachers and aides spaced throughout the building to check passes. In class, teachers assumed that students would cause problems unless they were strictly regulated and closely supervised. Students were frequently sent to the office, often for minor offenses. The irony is that Horace Mann was a gifted school with students coming from more affluent, better educated homes than Adams Avenue, thus leading one to expect more cooperative students. Yet teachers denied that the Horace Mann students were truly gifted and claimed that more talented students were needed. At the same time, they occasionally insulted students and engaged in openly hostile or racist behavior.

Accounts like these illustrate how school cultures establish teachers' expectations for students. Expectations not only set standards for academic performance (Ashton & Webb, 1986; Teddlie & Stringfield, 1993), but equally important they define how much students can be expected to cooperate and what motivates them. Cultures also clarify the role teachers should play in maintaining order. This issue addresses both standards of behavior and how much teachers should be responsible for maintaining those standards in both classrooms and corridors (Rosenholtz, 1989; Rutter, Maughan, Mortimore, & Ouston, 1979). A related issue is the stance teachers take towards students. How close should they be? How much respect do students deserve (Firestone & Rosenholtz, 1988)? How caring should teachers be and should their range of interaction be circumscribed to the classroom or broader to include the halls and extracurricular activities?

The second issue concerns the place of academics in schooling. Louis and Kruse (1995) argue that an ideal school culture has a collective focus on student learning, but their case studies illustrate the variation in the extent to which schools achieve this focus. Similarly, Rossman, Corbett, and Firestone (1988) contrast one case where teaching the academic curriculum is the primary focus with another in which maintaining order had become an end in itself. Since the effective schools movement, more quantitative studies show the variation among schools in the primacy given to academics (Rosenholtz, 1989; Teddlie & Stringfield, 1993).

Some quantitative studies have linked attention to academics to improved student performance (Rutter *et al.*, 1979; Hoy, Tartar, & Bliss, 1990) and there is a tendency to see a strong focus on achievement as an unmitigated good. Schofield (1989) provides a caution to this view, however. In her study of race relations in a new, integrated middle school, she found that a faculty orientation in which academics were the first, last, and only concern became a serious impediment to dealing with separation and conflicts between students of different races (see also Metz, 1986). There are some indications that Catholic schools are better than public ones at creating a culture that gives equal, high priority to both academic and moral education (Bryk, Lee, & Holland, 1993).

School cultures may also clarify the technology and purpose of teaching. Here an element of cultural codes can be inferred from researchers' descriptions, although the authors rarely use such language directly. Rosenholtz (1989), for instance, suggests that where academics are important, teachers also share confidence that they know how to teach. Recent research by Louis, Kruse, and Marks (1995) and Louis, Marks, and Kruse (1996) show that professional school cultures seem to increase teachers' collective sense of responsibility for student achievement and common understandings of instructional processes. Metz (1978) notes two different orientations among teachers she studied. The developmental approach stresses teaching children who are viewed as active learners and building on what they know. The incorporative approach emphasizes teaching a prescribed curriculum and views children as empty vessels to be filled. These approaches combine different norms about valued educational processes with different codes for working with students. The two orientations reflect differences between progressive or constructivist and traditional pedagogies (Brooks & Brooks, 1993). The definition of academic work may be as significant as the importance given to such work in a culture, and available evidence suggests that the incorporative approach is much more common (Cuban, 1993).

The third issue addresses the interaction among educators in the school. In American schools, teaching is a private endeavor that is rarely discussed among peers; teachers even lack a language for such discussion (Lortie, 1975). More and more observers of schools are proposing that norms of collaboration be used among teachers that deprivatize practice and create opportunities for peers to learn from each other as an ideal for school cultures (Little, 1990; Louis & Kruse, 1995). The emphasis in this line of work is on encouraging sharing about teaching. There has been relatively little research on the general social life of teachers, but studies suggest that the friendships and interpersonal support that teachers give each other support collective efforts to improve practice (Bryk, Lee, & Holland, 1993).

Raywid (1995) described formal activities that were used to promote discussion of practice in one highly collaborative alternative school. These included the expert panel where senior teachers and outsiders presented on a topic of interest, a staged debate between two teachers, and an activity where teachers were asked to review and assess a number of responses to a particular questions. These formal interactions were facilitated by a normative order with high agreement on the importance of academics, a basic approach to teaching, a stance towards students, and acceptance of differences (within broad normative guidelines) among staff. The structure of the school also promoted considerable teaming, joint planning, and other collaborative work among teachers.

Sharing among teachers can progress from the more-or-less innocuous swapping of stories and complaints about students through sharing ideas to joint work (Little, 1990). Rosenholtz (1989) suggests that where teachers report a habit of collaboration, they swap stories less and share instructional materials more than in less collaborative schools, and there is an even greater difference in joint planning and instructional problem-solving. Louis, Kruse, and Marks (1995) found more intense collaboration in schools with more professional cultures. Less analyzed is the relationship between collaboration among teachers and the development of codes to construct practice in the classroom, although their data suggest that the development of more focused language to discuss common pedagogical problems was more common in the schools with stronger professional cultures.

Although we have treated these three issues of school cultures separately, they tend to coalesce in patterns that hold together in particular schools. For instance, McNeil's (1986) investigation of social studies describes a special code of incorporative or traditional instruction, which she calls "defensive teaching." Rather than dealing with current events, encouraging students to make connections between the content studied and moral issues of meaning to them, or exploring how people reach conclusions about complex evidence, the curriculum is reduced to memorizable lists to be regurgitated in tests. She argues that defensive teaching predominates when order is more important than academic learning, when teachers are under pressure to keep the lid on, and when they do not trust students to cooperate. Thus an approach to instruction reflects conceptions of what students are like and how important instruction is.

At the other extreme, in Raywid's (1995) collaborative alternative school, norms that promoted sharing among teachers coexisted with common understandings of what students were like and how they should be treated as well as a particular (constructivist) ideological approach to teaching and the curriculum. More generally, Rosenholtz (1989) and Louis, Kruse, and Marks (1996) illustrate this interlock of cultural dimensions in a different way. Both investigations supplemented quantitative analysis with interviews in 23 schools. Using both qualitative and quantitative data, some of the schools were consistently high on all dimensions, while others were consistently low.

Finally, although much of the prescriptive literature on organizational cultures has focused on how to develop ideal or healthy cultures, examples of pathological cultures are common. Here it is important to remember Schein's (1992) observation that cultures can be collective defense mechanisms to help reduce anxiety and make sense of inherently ambiguous situations, especially in unsettled times. Particularly where ambiguous situations are threatening, outsiders may find cultural explanations out of touch with the reality they see. The reason for such distortion may be that the culture was constructed to protect teachers' self-esteem in reaction to past or present threats. This seems to be the case with the Horace Mann School described above (Metz, 1986). A faculty that had worked for years with inner city children suddenly found itself staffing a gifted school with little assistance and under considerable pressure from assertive parents. The collective response was to deny responsibility and blame the school's problems on students who were not smart enough and administrators who did not create conditions for success. Firestone & Rosenholtz (1988) suggest that this culture of blaming is a common though not universal phenomenon in urban schools.

Adult Subcultures

Although school cultures are often portrayed as coherent with answers to various questions fitting together and reinforcing each other, such cultures may only apply to some groups. At the extreme are highly fractionalized schools. Metz (1978) reports on a school split between two groups, one holding a very formalized incorporative ideology of teaching and the other much more strongly and self-consciously developmental. The explanation of this split illustrates how culture can move from shared, taken-for-granted common sense to a battle over codified ideologies as people's lives become more unsettled (Swidler, 1986). Lonnquist and King (1995) report another fractionalized school where a small group of teachers with formal leadership positions shared an ideology that was opposed by nonleaders who were shut out of decision-making.

Less polarized settings have varying degrees of orthodoxy. Rossman (in Rossman et al., 1988) describes a school consisting of three concentric rings. The coterie, or inner circle organized around the principal, actively proselytized for the local orthodoxy. Most teachers shared the dominant values without actively advocating them. Finally, what the principal referred to as the lunatic fringe disagreed with the orthodox view without forming an organized opposition. Similarly, Adams Avenue School (Metz, 1986) had a clique of teachers that opposed the prevailing orthodoxy without successfully splitting the school.

Variation in adherence to a school culture may reflect differences in personal characteristics, such as teachers' family backgrounds (Metz, 1990a) or differential occupational acculturations (Hargreaves, 1986). Often, however, more or less organized subcultures develop around subunits. In a study of change in 14 elementary and secondary schools, Corbett, Dawson, and Firestone (1984) found that almost every one had at least one subunit—a grade level, a subject department, or a team—that was particularly cohesive, working closely together with members sharing a common view of their work.

Although the formation of especially cohesive subunits can happen at any level, internal segmentation that influences culture formation is especially noteworthy in high schools (and to some extent in middle schools) where departments are a recurring and institutionalized element of the formal organization. Secondary schools staffs agree less on basic educational goals, a sign of a less cohesive culture, and this weakness is attributable to their departmental organization (Wilson, Herriott, & Firestone, 1991; Louis, Marks, & Kruse, 1996).

Almost all American high schools and many middle and junior high schools share a common internal structure based on subject matter departments, which in itself has become a kind of semiotic code for organizing schools. Many departmental groupings (English, mathematics, social studies) are common to most schools, while other areas, like the placement of graphic arts in an arts or a vocational department, vary. The status order among departments is generally well understood with academic units viewed as more important than non-academic ones in most regular high schools (Grossman & Stodolsky, 1994). Although high school graduation requirements are often listed in terms of numbers of courses in particular disciplines, the departmental structure itself is not legally required of schools. However, it developed early in the 20th century as one of the reforms championed by college presidents to standardize the preparation of students for higher education. By now, this structure is part of the institutionalized grammar of school organization (Tyack & Cuban, 1995).

Two factors increase the development of departmental subcultures. The first is the amount of interaction around departments. High school teachers typically talk more to members of their own departments than other teachers in the school. They know a great deal about what is happening in their own department, both personally and professionally, and much less about what else is happening throughout the school. This is primarily because they share such problems as courses to teach and schedules to manage. Exclusive in-department interaction is facilitated by such factors as closeness of the rooms that department members use for teaching, a common office space, formal allocation of responsibilities like scheduling to the department, and strong departments chairs. Another factor that varies both among disciplines and schools is their departmental heterogeneity. For instance, social studies departments are generally more differentiated (among history, sociology, and other teachers) than are math departments (Siskin, 1991).

The other factor that helps form departmental subcultures is the disciplinary base of the department that is reinforced through common preservice training (especially at the high school level) and networks of specialists sharing common fields outside the school. Disciplines have common conceptual structures. For instance, some disciplines, like mathematics, have what Bernstein (1971) calls a collection code with strong external boundaries, a wide gap between subject and everyday knowledge, clear distinctions between topics, and few choices for students interested in them. Others, like English, have integration codes with weaker boundaries, less distance from everyday knowledge,

fuzzier distinctions between topics, and more choices for students.

Different intellectual codes or grammars bring different technical problems. The historical problem for English has been to define the core of the field, while the issues for mathematics have been who should take how much of it and how should the subject be taught. Mathematics lends itself to tracking but can handle relatively large classes with homogenous grouping. English teachers believe they can teach heterogeneous groups well but cannot teach large groups because correcting papers is an important part of the teaching process (Grossman & Stodolsky, 1994; Siskin, 1991).

Where structural factors promote interaction, departments can create strong subcultures within high schools. Rossman et al. (1988) found five perspectives on teaching in one school, including an academic view where teachers were committed to their subject matter and introducing students to more advanced aspects of it, a psychological development approach that emphasized building self-esteem, and a vocational perspective that focused on preparing students for work. These perspectives were concentrated in particular departments. Metz's (1978) incorporative and developmental perspectives were also distributed by departments. Talbert and McLaughlin (1994) found that a variety of teacher beliefs coalesced around departments and could be better predicted by knowing a teacher's department rather than his or her school. Less attention has been given to differences in codes among departments, but Siskin (1991) notes that teachers in particular departments have their own language, jokes, and ways to use space.

Student Culture

Research on adult and student cultures has progressed in parallel with very little cross-fertilization. As Bennett and LeCompte (1990) point out, the voices of students from studies of school culture have been largely absent, especially among administrative researchers. As with the studies of adults, however, research on student culture can be categorized according to whether the emphasis is on identifying commonalties or variations in student culture.

Commonalties in Student Culture

In the primary grades, the emphasis on socializing and nurturing makes it easier for students to identify with and conform to adult values (Parsons, 1959), so the distinctiveness of student culture is largely limited to the establishment of peer friendship groups in "off-task" settings such as recess. In addition, peer group relations are also mediated by adult choices because the ability groups in the classroom affect student opportunities to interact and form positive relationships (Cohen, 1986). Even in elementary schools, however, one can see a characteristic common to all student social cultures: the development of labels that clearly identify popular/higher status and unpopular/lower status children. These groups often parallel the ability groups that are prevalent in the classroom.

As students enter mid- to later adolescence, rebellion becomes an important symbol of growing up. Waller (1932) argued that distinct student cultures form in opposition to adults who try to socialize students to adult values and norms. Student culture establishes an independent social life (both inside and outside of the many events designed by adults, such as extracurricular activities), and ways to "outwit" teacher efforts to control them.

Waller's observations have been affirmed in subsequent research from the student perspective, such as Foley's (1990) decade-long ethnographic study of a small town in Texas. Many of these studies indicate that even the most conformist and popular students in high schools participate to some extent in a culture that resists adult control, and that oppositional elements even occur in the student culture of elite boarding schools where virtually all students take for granted that they are "preparing for power" to follow in their parent's footsteps (Cookson & Persell, 1985).

In a study of a desegregated secondary school, Metz (1978) argues that the "problem of order" is central to the culture of high schools and that opposition is most visible in public spaces:

> Adults and student differ over appropriate goals and means in the treatment of decorum and safety within the school, just as they differ over issues within the classroom. But in these large and open spaces, larger and more diverse aggregations must accommodate to one another without the prolonged and enforced intimacy of the classroom to motivate and assist them (p.147).

Adults try to maintain order (control) through a number of mechanisms to increase voluntary conformity. These include increasingly symbolic efforts to display coercive control, which are intended to reinforce a belief among students that the costs of some behaviors are simply too high to risk. This approach is risky since, in Metz's view, student culture in high schools is often a response to adults' definitions of school character and culture; they are responsive rather than autonomous. Where student's perceive ineffective coercion, they are even more likely to create an oppositional, disruptive culture.

Many case studies of student culture that look for uniformities draw on theories of cultural reproduction and resistance. These stress codes more than values. Such theorists as Bourdieu and Passeron (1977), Giroux (1983, 1988), and Bernstein (1975) contend that students' social class conditions their experience of school. The adult culture of schools is rooted in both middle-class values and codes of behavior.

Bernstein argues that the way that language is structured and used in middle-class and lower-class homes differs: in the former, communication uses more elaborated and generalized codes, while the latter emphasizes communication with less verbal elaboration. The linguistic codes of middle-class children are consistent with what teachers expect for "good" classroom performance, while even bright lower-class children experience frustration, failure, and, subsequently, the development of oppositional cultures that values non-academic performance and resistance to the inculcation of the adult value system in schools.

Bordieu's concept of "cultural capital" broadly defined as cultural background, knowledge, disposition, and skills also reflects this view that classes are differentiated by divergent cultural codes. All families and cultures have cultural capital, but schools favor that of upper socioeconomic groups. This gives middle-class children an initial "home advantage" (Lareau, 1989) that makes successful interactions within the adult culture schools more likely. The less successful students must either acquire middle-class cultural capital or reaffirm the values and behaviors of their own family and community. This tension leads working-class youth to prefer "profane" cultural codes that lead to manual labor, marginal brushes with the law, and self-selection into less demanding vocational tracks at school, in addition to outright defiance of adult control (Willis, 1977; McLeod, 1995; McLaren, 1994). Resistance, while creating an alternative sense of agency and success (Giroux, 1983), also reinforces low aspirations and performance, consigning the students to marginal economic futures.

Not all investigations of uniformities in student culture emphasize social class. Steinberg, Brown, and Dornbusch (1996) report that a very large proportion of U.S. students are not primarily oppositional but simply disengaged from the academic purposes of school or just going through the motions. School culture includes norms of minimal cooperation with adult preferences and expectations about purpose and effort. Like Powell and colleagues (1985), they find that student culture (and youth culture more broadly) is increasingly oriented around paid employment and consumerism, which means that school is viewed increasingly as another part-time job.

Even for those "good" students who are apparently more involved and overtly cooperative, the cultural emphasis is often more on success in the extracurriculum than the curriculum, which is a better route to maintaining "popular" status than academic performance. Many schools have accommodated to the student culture by offering programs such as the debate team, the yearbook, and the newspaper for credit, rather than as "extras" in an effort to lure more students away from non-engagement. Studies using this perspective tend to emphasize the students' agency and dominance in the bargaining culture discussed previously. The constant efforts of students, as a group, to negotiate adult expectations downward has been observed even in school settings in which adults are making major efforts to create more relevant and interesting work (Muncey & McQuillan, 1996).

Student Subcultures

Other observers of the peer organization of high schools have long been struck by the many variations that students invent to organize themselves into differentiated social groups (Hollingshead, 1949; Coleman, 1961; Cusick, 1973). In each school, these groups are known to all and have names. Foley, for example, identifies multiple gender and racial groups in a small town high school, as well as some that cross social class lines. The football players, for example, form a unique group whose solidarity persists beyond high school. Mexican students were divided into "activists" who pressed for equity and worked to succeed, and lower-achieving "vatos" who used codes of working-class opposition. High-status girls were identified by their association with high-status boys (cheerleaders and "populars"), while lower status "nobodies" and "homegirls" were largely unaffiliated with groups but reported intimate friendships.

Increasingly scholars have moved beyond the observation that each student body will invent its own version of the above groups to examine in more detail how the formation of student subcultures is affected by race and gender, as contrasted solely with class. This work provides a useful contrast to the work of critical theorists that is dominated by studies of white, working-class males. This newer research often adopts a critical perspective by disavowing any assumption that schools are equitable in their socialization and selection of students for future roles. However, the "cultural reproduction" perspective discussed above is often modified by the incorporation of other explanations for difference in culture and achievement.

Gender and Culture

Research on girl's subcultures in school is relatively recent. Earlier studies treated girls as either part of the male groups, or as "shadow groups" (like cheerleaders, who gain status through their association with football players). With the development of feminist scholarship, however, attention to "women's voices" in schools has increased, along with studies documenting differential treatment (AAUW, 1995). The earliest investigations looked at working class British girls in school environments like those studied by Willis. They observed that girls' lives were not only constrained by social class but also by strong gender expectations that labeled independent behavior negatively (McRobbie, 1978; Lees, Shaw, & Reisby, 1987).

Eder's (1995) American research on middle school girls looks at how language, informal codes, and institutional policies help construct gender inequality through con-

straints on the expression of "different" cultural beliefs. These girls focused intensely on social ranking, which was associated with both social class and conformity to prescribed codes of attractiveness (but not with race). Resistance to rankings was limited in the middle school, although prominent in the many alternative subgroups to be found in high school in the same community. At the same time, over the middle school years, boys of all classes and cliques developed a view of girls that increasingly portrayed them as sexual objects. Boys' group interactions with girls increasingly focused on attractiveness and appearance and girls, in turn, focused on appearance by ridiculing nonconformist dress and style. Thus girls began to mirror boys' aggressive sexual culture by defining themselves and others in terms of not only social ranking but also appearance and (reputed) sexual reputation.

Lesko (1988) adopts a symbolic perspective in her study of girls in an urban, Catholic high school that focuses on myths, rituals, and patterns of thought. Rather than examining the conflict between girls' development and school life, she looks at both divergence and intersections for three girls' groups at "St. Anne's." The school culture in this case emphasized two somewhat contradictory adult value systems: caring/collectivism (the "Catholic" side) and competition/individualism (the "high school" side). Each of the three groups of girls in the school developed different codes for adapting their friendship patterns to this tension in the adult culture.

The "rich and populars" group reflected the competition/individualism theme most clearly with group members emphasizing the need to be consistently active and successful in school activities, to maintain a public image of social decorum, and to minimize close relationship with boys in order to maintain status. This group also exhibited more ambivalent interpersonal relations and members acknowledged that they sometimes competed with each other. The "burn-outs" were more oppositional (although they did not necessarily get lower grades) and emphasized flouting of school rules, close association with boys as friends, and high levels of caring, interpersonal loyalty, and friendship within the group. In contrast, "mellows" had looser associations with school and exhibited stronger ties to family, friends, associates in other schools, and boyfriends.

These group identifications were, according to Lesko, largely symbolic. For example, the actual patterns of sexual experimentation, drinking, and smoking varied far less between the groups than the external appearances of dress, language, and approval of non-adult approved activities. In addition, the distinctions between the groups were blurred by the school's efforts to reinforce the symbolic "togetherness" and caring culture in a variety of schoolwide activities. The emphasis of female students in the school was also on mediation between conflicting values and distinct groups in order to preserve the school's sense of communality.

Race and Student Culture

Underachievement of ethnic minorities in the U.S. and other countries has long been of concern to scholars of school culture. Spindler and Spindler (1971), Spindler and Spindler (1987), Ogbu (1987), Gibson and Ogbu (1991), and Erickson (1987), among others, investigated the intersection between minority group and school cultures in search of an alternative to deficiency models, which argue that the traditional cultures of minority groups do not reinforce individual academic achievement. Trueba (1988) argues that the peer group is more important to minority students because they are more likely during adolescence to become alienated both from the majority culture of school and their families' culture. Other investigations emphasize that success for the minority student may require breaching peer codes against "acting white" during school and other manifestations of the "resistance culture" of peers (Delgado-Gaitan, 1988; Fordham & Ogbu, 1986). Only studies that focus on student subcultural patterns will be examined here.

Ogbu distinguishes between immigrant minorities that have chosen to come from another country in order to improve their social or economic position and involuntary minorities that consist of subjugated indigenous populations or groups who were imported as serfs or slaves to provide inexpensive labor. Those who define themselves as voluntary minorities tend to view problems of discrimination and social barriers as "more or less temporary problems, as problems they can or will overcome with the passage of time, hard work, or more education." (Ogbu, 1991, p. 11). Involuntary minorities, on the other hand, lack a comparative framework, and view their disadvantaged status as permanent and institutionalized. In a school context, all minority children experience problems of adjustment and learning that are greater than those of majority groups, but in every country some minority groups are academically successful, while others are less so. Ogbu and his colleagues argue that these differences are defined by cultural context rather than by linguistic or cultural differences that are attributable only to the minority group. For example, after initial adjustment and linguistic problems, Koreans and Sikhs perform well in U.S. schools (where they are defined as immigrant minorities) but poorly in Japan and England (where they are involuntary minorities) (Gibson & Ogbu, 1991).

One key feature that helps to explain this pattern is that immigrant minority groups tend to emphasize accommodation to the majority culture in public settings, collective responsibility for the improvement of the group's position within the mainstream culture, and coexistence between the cultural codes of the country of origin and the country of residence. This results in behavior patterns in school that emphasize conformity to the adult majority culture's expectations. Involuntary minority students, on the other hand, tend to develop codes that highlight the opposition between their family and group culture and that of the majority/adult population in school. Patterns of behavior and beliefs emerge that are legitimated because they are different from and do not accommodate mainstream expectations. Because "the system" is viewed as permanently rigged against their success, involuntary minorities doubt the value of adopting the cultural capital of the adult majority. Ogbu's involuntary minority groups thus display many of the characteristics of the "resistance" culture of working-class peer groups in England (Willis, 1977).

Ogbu's theory is a useful antidote to "cultural deprivation" theories of minority group academic performance. It does not, however, address the interaction between school culture and minority student subculture in any depth and, as Erickson (1987b) points out, it does not help to explain why some domestic minority students succeed and others do not. A few studies address this question by examining how school culture and minority student culture interact. As noted above, Foley (1990) suggests that the minority student subculture is far from uniform and that some Mexican-American students define themselves as involuntary minorities and resist the dominant culture, but that others, particularly under conditions of an active civil rights movement, make great efforts to adopt mainstream communicative codes that permit them to succeed in school. They, like the nonconforming resisters, defined their actions as rooted in resistance; they actively sought to maintain their ethnic expressive practices outside the school setting but still "beat the gringos at their own game" by publicly adopting mainstream symbols of cultural capital. Trueba's (1988) research on a drop-out program for Mexican-American students suggests that peer groups were important in helping students to manage "degradation incidents" (active experiences of failure associated with perceived or actual racism) and supporting the development of crucial dyadic relationships with caring adults/role models, which helps to mediate the "resistance culture" that justifies academic failure.

Although Metz's (1978) comparison of two desegregating schools does not focus on student culture, she emphasizes that faculty culture conditions students' response to school and vice versa. In one school, the teacher subculture was characterized by serious friction between the old guard teachers, who mourned the loss of the white, middle-class school population, and the new teachers, most of whom were "developmental" in their teaching orientation and who tended to give lower priority to subject matter distinctions. These differences reduced cohesiveness in adult expectations for students, which in turn enabled students to "get away" with various resistance behaviors in at least some settings. In the other school, a unitary faculty culture was moderate and assimilated new teachers with different experiences and perspectives. A consistent set of benign but firm expectations for students also evolved, which made open resistance difficult. The resulting order (or lack thereof) reinforced the emerging student and teacher subcultures.

Erickson (1987b) summarizes several studies that suggest that the development of resistance or oppositional cultures occurs incrementally, as students experience negative interactions with white teachers related to their linguistic differences. Where these do not occur, oppositional codes are muted. He concludes that both the macro and micro perspectives are important to understanding why resistance cultures evolve among minority students. McLeod's (1995) ethnography of black and white youth cultures in an inner city housing project also suggests that small differences in social class and family structure may account for resistance subcultures more than minority status.

In sum, schools have not one student culture, but many. National cultures, school cultures, department cultures, and the cultures of student cliques all propose values and codes that can be used to formulate and guide action. All of these sources of culture compete with administrative efforts to shape the culture in a school.

What Influences Culture?

A variety of forces affect the way cultures develop in particular schools. Here we explore two that influence the school and subunit levels: the acculturation of individuals who work in schools and organizational structures and the disputes that surround them.

Recruitment and Socialization

In part, culture comes into the school through the recruitment and socialization of participants. While we could describe the images of what school is that children get from the media, parents, and peers, we will instead focus on the acculturation of teachers through formal training or through informal socialization as students.

Future teachers are strongly influenced by the thousands of hours they spend in an apprenticeship of observation (Lortie, 1975). Because they have grown up in a school system that rewards passive obedience and presumably liked it, future teachers tend to be conformists who got ahead by figuring out what authorities wanted and delivering it, rather than creative thinkers. They often view books as authorities and knowledge as a fixed collection of facts and concepts that must be learned before they can be applied. Thus future teachers have absorbed the lesson that teaching is transmitting knowledge from adult experts to children who are supposed to be passive recipients of truth. Teachers are supposed to tell their classes what they need to know and students are supposed to listen and memorize (Feiman-Nemser & Remillard, 1996).

Preservice socialization also influences future teachers' expectations of students and how to act towards them. Generally, they emphasize the nurturing aspect of their work, rather than the intellectual one. In comparison, formal teacher education coursework especially and student teaching to a lesser extent has relatively little influence on teachers' beliefs and practices in the United States (Zeichner, & Gore, 1992), but more in smaller countries where training is more uniform (Louis & Versloot, 1996).

To this must be added the selective patterns of entry into the field. Future teachers are disproportionately white and female. They come from small towns and suburbs, go to local colleges and institutions, and are not the strongest students academically (Feiman-Nemser & Remillard, 1996). Along with these demographic characteristics comes a distinctive set of orientations to teaching. They expect their students to be much like themselves. Since for the most part, they have grown up using white, middle-class speech and conduct codes, they expect the same from their students and do not know how to interpret or relate to working-class and minority codes (Feiman-Nemser & Remillard, 1996). Thus the use of incorporative teaching approaches to manage conflicts between race and class subcultures has its roots in cultural elements that teachers bring to their work.

Although these central tendencies characterize most future teachers and many current ones, there are important differences that reflect teachers' gender, class, and race. Feiman-Nemser and Remillard (1996) attribute some of teachers' passivity to their socialization to female roles. Metz (1990a) found that teachers who associated more with middle-class adults defined their responsibility as doing a good job, while those more affiliated with the working class saw themselves as putting in time. Since she also found that teachers with more middle-class aspirations were recruited to wealthier districts and got more positive response from students, it is not clear how much their orientations reflected earlier socialization, out-of-work influences, or feedback from students.

Structure and Culture

The interplay between structure and culture is a pervasive theme in cultural studies. In this section, we will explore only a few issues: the influence of structure on school culture, the influence of modern and post-modern culture on school structure, and the tensions around structure that occur as a result of divergence between predominant cultural values and those of subcultures.

Structural Influences on Culture

Modern organizations have been viewed as consciously developed instruments or tools for accomplishing specific goals (Barnard, 1938; Thompson, 1967). This perspective emphasizes the relative efficiency of such structural features as differentiating between positions and their current occupants, formal rules, and a division of labor for accomplishing collective purposes (Weber, 1947). The field of organizational design has developed to guide managers on how to devise organizations that can best meet organizational purposes given environmental and technological contingencies (Mintzberg, 1979). To the extent that this perspective attends to culture, it is viewed as developing incrementally as a set of informal solutions and coping mechanisms to the problems created by formal structures (Blau, 1955).

Schools, of course, are formal organizations and there are numerous examples of how their common structural arrangements influence the cultures found within them. We have already suggested how subcultures form around departments in high schools. Hargreaves (1986) describes another pattern of subcultures growing up around school types in England: primary schools serving children up to the age of 11, grammar schools serving more academically talented 12- to 18-year-olds, and secondary modern schools serving older students less likely to go on to university. These cultures had their own practices for working with students and definitions of success. He attributes the failure of a middle school movement to catch on in England partly to the difficulty of getting teachers socialized within these different cultures to work together in institutions serving 8- to 13-year-olds.

Perhaps more important, some common cultural features of schools appear to stem from common structural arrangements. For instance, one of the most obvious structural characteristics of schools is that the physical arrangement of teachers' work, the placement of single teachers with classes of students, puts a premium on rewards coming from students while isolating teachers from their peers. Over 20 years ago, Lortie (1975) suggested that this isolation contributes to two common elements of school culture: values that emphasize individualism and privacy, and a diminished shared technical vocabulary of teaching. Since then a substantial body of research has suggested that collaboration among teachers can contribute greatly to improving practice (Little, 1982; Rosenholtz, 1989, Louis, Marks, & Kruse, 1996). Yet efforts to promote cooperation may lead to contrived collegiality when they simply throw teachers together without creating shared values and a common language for professional discussions (Hargreaves & Dawe, 1990). Little (1990), and Louis and Kruse (1995) suggest that effective collaboration depends on joint work, which continues to be rare because of how schools are organized.

Particularly strong and often constructive cultures develop in schools with distinctive structural arrangements or teaching practices. These include the magnet and alternative schools described by Metz (1986), Raywid (1995), and Louis, Marks, and Kruse (1996) above. In the first case, a technology of teaching that de-emphasized competition among students promoted positive relationships among students that crossed racial lines. In the second and third, frequently changing classes, teacher teaming, and other structurally interdependent roles promoted extensive cooperation among the faculty. These cases suggest that, as with the distinctive colleges in higher education (Clark, 1970), unusual school cultures are facilitated by highly divergent structural arrangements or approaches to teaching.

Although there are many examples of cultures and subcultures developing around structural arrangements, there are equally well publicized accounts of school culture undermining attempts to change school structures (as well as specific practices). Sarason's (1971) account of how the developers of the New Math of the 1950s failed to take the beliefs and codes of schools into account initiated this line of work. He describes that change effort as a clash between the cultures of schools and the universities. Later studies have documented the mismatch between school culture and a variety of innovations from program planning and budgeting systems (PPBS) (Wolcott, 1977) to minimum competency testing (Rossman et al., 1988).

The interplay between structures and cultures can be quite complex. Kirst and Jung (1982) describe how one major program, Title I, was initially forced to accommodate to the common culture of schools. Later it was given enough teeth to change the status quo, and finally it developed its own subculture among personnel teaching the disadvantaged. Thus initial resistance or cultural mismatch does not preclude the development of specialized subcultures later on. Meanwhile, the research on planned change has helped advocates diagnose cultural elements that might inhibit structural change (Fullan, 1991). Yet cultural conflict over change agendas persists. In the midst of a second effort to reform mathematics teaching, Davis (1989) has meditated on the continuing differences in the understanding of what that subject is in the cultures of mathematicians and teachers.

Modernist Culture and School Codes

More recently, the institutional perspective has questioned the assumptions that organizations are best viewed as efficient tools for meeting collective ends, and that structures and cultures are different (Powell & DiMaggio, 1991). In this view, organizations are part of a modern Western culture that emphasizes rationality, progress, and justice (Meyer, Boli, & Thomas, 1994). This larger culture is important in two ways. First, it provides the codes, categories, and forms that can be used to assemble organizations, including schools. These codes that make up the vocabulary and grammar of organizations are as fundamental as the concept of the individual or the idea of the impersonal rule of law. They also include more specific organizational features like the civil service. Second, the larger culture provides values that can be used to measure organizational adequacy. Only one of these is efficiency; for a broad range of organizations, efficiency is less important than the legitimacy that comes from adopting the appropriate forms (Meyer & Rowan, 1991). Survival for these organizations requires demonstrating that they conform to modern values. Where it is difficult to demonstrate this through an examination of organizational outputs, the key becomes adopting codes that are generally known to embody these values. The adoption of appropriate forms and codes ensures legitimacy even where performance does not meet expectations. The implications of the institutional perspective are covered in more detail in Chapter 17 (Rowan and Miskel) of this volume.

Metz (1990b) illustrates how institutionalized organization forms serve as rituals that maintain organizational legitimacy within the school as well as in public. She points out that almost all American high schools use the same codes in terms of organization charts for adults, classrooms, teacher assignments, the scope and sequence of curriculum, textbooks, and extracurricular activities. The presence of these common features demonstrates to parents and the larger public that an equal opportunity is provided to all students, not so much because they work (they don't), but because the forms themselves define what school is.

Within these common forms, however, teachers may vary in the pace they progress through the curriculum or the discipline standards they maintain, although they share images of what discipline and successful accomplishment of the curriculum should be. The reason for the persistence of these codes—Metz (1990b) argues—is that they convince the people who work there that, in spite of the setbacks they face, they are doing what they are supposed to do by accomplishing "real school." This structure is maintained even in blue-collar and urban schools where it contributes to student alienation and dropping out, thus showing limited technical efficiency.

For the most part, the institutional perspective treats such modern organizational values as rationality and progress as shared and taken for granted (Meyer *et al.*, 1994). Yet someone must advocate modern values because organizational structures are intentionally developed. Tyack and Cuban (1995) show how policy elites, including university presidents, foundations, and politicians, put the major codes of real school into place through reforms reaching back to the 1890s. They also show that once these structures were put in place, efforts by other elites to change them in a more progressive direction met with little success.

Structure-Culture Tensions

In spite of these efforts to institutionalize national codes, they become the focus of disagreement when they conflict with the preferences of subcultures. The first source of conflict occurs with rural communities that often represent more traditional values. Peshkin (1978, 1982) shows how schools in rural areas mute the mainstream emphasis on efficiency and universal achievement in favor of particularistic community-building. In small Midwestern towns, schools are a center for community activity, a means to maintain networks of relationships (including those across generations), and a way to hold children in the community. In these setting, the emphasis given to sports, fund-raising, and extracurricular activities may displace attention to the formal structures of the modern school. Rather than hiring teachers and administrators who are highly trained and best exemplify intellectual excellence, rural districts may prefer local candidates who fit in and who do not promote achievement values that might stimulate too many students to leave the community. In such instances, accommodation between universalism and particularism can be reached through subtle shifts of emphasis. More pronounced conflicts occur, however, when central authorities try to close rural schools and consolidate in the name of efficiency and intellectual excellence but at the cost of local institutions that knit small towns together.

A second source of conflict is around class and racial issues, most notably working-class and minority students who get tracked into the lower levels of the educational system or drop out entirely (Ogbu, 1991). These groups challenge the apparent egalitarianism and progressive universalism of the dominant western culture. In the larger society, stigmatized groups are separated from the middle and upper classes by distinct speech, dress, and other codes. The privileged character of middle-class codes is taken for granted and viewed as legitimate by the dominant society and to some extent by the groups that are stigmatized as well (Bourdieu & Passeron, 1977, Erickson, 1987b).

Although middle-class majority codes and values have special status in the larger society and are to some extent embedded in western culture, they still contribute to conflict among groups at both micro and macro levels. Anthropologists have attended most to the micro level. We described above how minority groups develop oppositional cultures that define conforming to the dominant codes, or "acting white," as selling out. Attention is now being devoted to developing teaching approaches that help students succeed in conventional terms, such as getting high test scores, without feeling that they have to deny their heritage (Ladson-Billings, 1995).

More macro-level conflicts have focused on what should be in the curriculum. To incorporate certain knowledge, literature, ideas, or skills in the curriculum is to give those ideas broader legitimacy in the larger society (Apple, 1990).

Although certain fields, most notably mathematics and science, disseminated rapidly throughout the world because they were so clearly linked to modernism and rationality, others that had a more particularistic focus spread more slowly (Kamens & Cha, 1992). In these areas, concerns related to class and ethnicity become more important. Goodson (1988) illustrates how as England moved from a tripartite secondary education system to the comprehensive high school, subjects that failed to sufficiently reinforce middle-class cultural capital were pushed out of the curriculum. Much of the current debate about multiculturalism, bilingual education, and history and language standards in the United States has to do with both the general portrayal and relative status of various ethnic groups. How racist should the white majority be portrayed to be, for instance?

Another challenge to the dominant modern culture in the United States comes from the religious right. There is some overlap with the issues that occur in the analysis of class. For instance, opposition from the religious right is bred in part from economic anxieties in the working class (Boyd, Lugg, & Zahorchack, 1996). However, this group questions equity-oriented curricula because it fears such curricula will provide advantages to those who are even less privileged. Religious right ideology is grounded in a distinctly anti-modern ethic based on traditional and religious authority. It seeks immediate certainty in biblical revelation rather than accepting uncertainty and slowly accumulating knowledge through enlightenment-based empiricism (Blanchard, 1994). Moreover, while the religious right may have participated in broader curricular debates, it has its own issues. These include attempts to censor library and textbooks (Adler, 1996), sex education, and more recently attacks on one of the newer control structures in American education: central (or state) assessments. The right wing launched major attacks on state assessment systems in both Pennsylvania and California because they feared that such assessments would further secular values, including toleration of homosexuality among other things (Boyd *et al.*, 1996; Honig & Alexander with Wolf, 1996).[4]

Not all threats to institutionalized structures come from clearly delineated groups. Grant (1988) depicts how a highly institutionalized culture in one urban high school disintegrated in the mid-1960s and 1970s and was partially restored in the 1980s. The major manifestation of this cultural breakdown was a near total loss of adult authority over students, punctuated by extensive student riots in the late 1960s. Grant attributes this breakdown in part to demographic change. White flight combined with desegregation policies turned a school that had been almost entirely white and middle-class to poor and black, thus generating the majority-minority conflicts described above. Yet the riots began before this demographic shift was well underway. At least as important was a change in the national

culture, a breakdown in societal support for adult authority, resulting from the social upheaval of that time both directly and through a series of court decisions limiting that authority.

The breakdown that Grant documents was more widespread than his one case can show. For instance, he puts this breakdown of authority slightly after the time when Tyack and Cuban (1995) say that elite consensus on the rightness of the real school pattern described by Metz (1990b) began to break down. Moreover, there is considerable anecdotal evidence of similar authority breakdowns in other schools around the country at about the same time.[5] Research attacking the less-work-for-compliance bargains mentioned above (Powell *et al.*, 1985) provide further evidence. The field work for these attacks was done when adult authority was at a low ebb, so such bargains were particularly favorable to students not inclined to academic activity. At the same time, these analyses were part of an elite effort to restore adult (although not always teacher) authority in the schools through what became the standards movement in the 1980s.

These macro-level culture conflicts address very different issues from those attended to inside the school. For instance, macro concerns focus more on what should be taught as a reflection of what is legitimate knowledge in the larger society. Internal concerns are more about how much attention should be given to whatever is taught as opposed to just getting through the day. Yet external concerns become linked to internal culture if only through efforts to implement new policies, structures, and practices in schools.

How Do Administrators Influence Culture?

This review has identified limits to leaders' discretion to "manage culture." National values and struggles to establish codes that guide action in schools all constrain the educational administrator. Introducing cooperative learning will demand a different approach in individualistic and collectivist cultures. Even simple tasks, like running a meeting, can demand different behaviors in different settings. The complexity of a cultural perspective on leadership is underscored by Sergiovanni's (1984) discussion of the educational administrator as a hermaneutical analyst.

Still, administrators can manage within the culture in ways that influence both adult and student cultures. Metz's (1978) study of two desegregating schools notes, for example, that the two principals were, in large measure, responsible for the very different school cultures. In the adult-controlled, orderly school, the principal maintained a "soft" but authoritative style and consistently reinforced the need for uniformity, conventionality, and incorporation of all students. In the school where teachers disagreed and order was problematic, the principal was more democratic and ambiguous. He encouraged debate but could not create consensus among the different factions within the school, which exacerbated inconsistent teacher behavior and student resistance.

Nevertheless, in spite of case study evidence of principals' effects on culture, there are still debates about how much administrators really affect the "core technology" of schools—the culture of the classroom—as contrasted with more visible public codes. Although the "effective schools" research emphasized the principal's importance in creating a culture of high expectation, orderliness, and teacher focus on student achievement (Mortimore, 1991; Rosenholz, 1989; Teddlie & Stringfield, 1993), others question the principal's "instructional leadership" in secondary schools and larger schools (see, for example, Leithwood, Jantzi, & Fernandez, 1994). Because there are enough questions about the contribution administrators can make to schoolwide culture, we address that role explicitly by examining two kinds of contribution that principals can make: transforming culture and maintaining it.

Transformational Leadership

Transformational leadership changes the school culture—often dramatically so it supports high performance. Leithwood and his colleagues (Leithwood & Jantzi, 1990; Leithwood, Jantzi, & Fernandez, 1994) have developed one of the most complete models of transformational leadership in education. According to the model, transformational leadership is conditioned by national and local culture and policies. It, in turn, affects the goals and culture of the school, which have direct ties to individual teachers' commitment to change and improvement. Data from Canadian high schools indicate that the most important transformational leadership behaviors are creating a vision, setting high expectations for performance, creating consensus around group goals, and developing an intellectually stimulating climate.

A similar model that has been proposed as transformative for school culture is "facilitative leadership" (Dunlap & Goldman, 1991; Goldman, Dunlap, & Conley, 1993; Conley & Goldman, 1994). It emphasizes tactics such as team building, coordination and feedback, conflict resolution, articulation of visions, and provision of resources—as contrasted with decision-making—as means to foster a cohesive, change-oriented school culture. This model emphasizes that the core of facilitative leadership is the creation and management of tensions that keep the school in motion, or keep the culture actively reflective. For example, "facilitative leadership requires constant development of many new leaders . . . however, the creation of new leaders and structures upsets

the existing social hierarchy" (Conley & Goldman, 1994, p. 246). Facilitation promotes, not a "feel good" culture, but one characterized by dilemmas that require constant resolution to keep the school supple.

These tensions are managed by changing structures, symbols, and standard operating practices to reflect the direction of desired cultural change (Deal & Peterson, 1994; Firestone & Wilson, 1989). As Firestone and Wilson point out, schools must balance the need for autonomy (loose linkage among classrooms, grades, departments, and so on) with that for cohesiveness and integration. Good leadership requires that principals and other administrators manipulate both the formal organization (creating new teams or interdisciplinary groups to plan curriculum and assigning leadership roles to teachers) and various symbols that express the cultural intent behind the structural changes (finding special meeting spaces for teams that belong to them and giving teacher leaders symbolic prerogatives such as some budgetary authority). Cultural and structural changes need to be interwoven in order to have the greatest impact on school culture, particularly teacher culture (Louis & Kruse, 1995).

A key element of transformational leadership, according to many authors (Louis & Miles, 1990; Deal & Peterson, 1991), is the need to manage the relationship between the internal culture of the school and an external environment that is often unpredictable, intrusive, and even hostile. The public school cannot afford to reject or isolate the external environment because it provides political as well as financial resources. In addition, like other public organizations, schools are increasingly asked to respond to the changing needs and demands and to adapt their internal culture to external cultural changes. School administrators, however, must also mediate the environment in order not to destabilize the school's culture.

Maintaining the Culture

One paradox in the principal's role is that he or she often promotes cultural change and cultural stability simultaneously. Authors who explicitly examine how the principal "manages" culture are more likely to emphasize the importance of maintaining a "strong culture" than their transformational role. Some, in particular, use behind-the-scenes strategies and the reaffirmation of symbols and practices that reinforce collective values and beliefs associated with effective school performance.

Symbolic Leadership
Deal and Peterson (1990, 1994) emphasize the symbolic roles that leaders play in managing culture, which they contrast to a more "technical" view that emphasizes specific tasks that need to be carried out. The symbolic leader's role has many aspects, including (1) a historian, who reads current

events in the school and reinterprets them for the rest of the staff (see also Louis & Miles, 1990); (2) an anthropological detective, who searches for meaning in the behavior of others; (3) a visionary, who projects hopes and dreams for the entire staff; (4) a symbol in him or herself, by making sure that important routines and ceremonies in the school's life are reliable and communicate caring (Deal & Peterson, 1994). The authors argue, based on their case studies of principals, that effective leadership work demands pay as much attention to the symbolic side as to the technical.

Several rich case studies support Deal and Peterson's emphasis on the importance of symbols in effective leadership. Kelley and Bredeson's (1991) comparison of a public and a parochial school principal show how they communicate their ideas to reinforce and interpret organizational culture. Reitzug and Reeves (1992) trace how an elementary school principal uses symbolic language, time, and the allocation of resources to enhance symbolic leadership and develop shared meanings within the staff. Beck's (1994) case study of a high school principal uses the metaphor of gardening, noting that the "caring culture" of the school occurred not only because of specific behaviors, but because of the constant reminders of personal commitment on the part of the leader.

"Stewardship" and Values

The work of Peter Block (1993) and Ronald Heifetz (1994), while not specific to educational administration, is consistent with Deal and Peterson's culture management perspective. Both authors emphasize the need for leaders to focus on values and give up "authority" associated with a hierarchical position as a means of gaining increased influence over organizational functioning. Giving up authority to gain influence has also been noted in recent studies of school administration (Louis & Murphy, 1994).

Heifetz argues that the promotion of strong, positive values oriented to socially useful results helps distinguish leadership from authority or power. In providing value-based leadership, a number of key strategic principles are effective: (1) identifying the adaptive challenges, such as the gap between the shared values that people hold and the reality of their lives, or a hidden tension and conflict in the organization; (2) moderating the distress caused by revealing adaptive challenges in order to keep people within a productive discomfort zone; (3) continuing to direct attention to the real internal issues so the hard work of adapting the culture is not avoided; and (4) giving the work back to the people.

The value basis of leadership in relation to school culture is reinforced by a number of authors. Lightfoot (1983) presents portraits of "good" high schools, including their principals. She concludes that all six appreciated students as individuals and, even when authoritative, incorporated

nurturing into their own behaviors and expected it of others. According to Beck (1994), caring is the central value in educational settings: her review of the empirical and theoretical work of a number of scholars suggests that caring cultures must be nourished through the deliberate use of appropriate metaphors for school work, storytelling to create meaning for faculty and students, interpretation of events in terms of caring and values, and symbolic celebrations of core values.

Another theme implicit in analyses of maintaining culture is the role of "followership." Too much emphasis, it is argued, has been placed on the role of the specifically designated leader when, in fact, leadership is not possible without the active engagement of many others. The more inclusive the patterns of leadership, and the more that the principal or other designated leaders have a broad cadre of dedicated supporters, the more likely it is that the culture will be strong and that leadership to mold and maintain culture will be accepted. Many studies emphasize the role of coded behavior and language to reinforce inclusion and followership. Muncey and McQuillan (1996, p. 270) state in their study of Coalition of Essential Schools participants, "Only in schools where the principal was an active and ongoing participant were the experiments of individual teachers incorporated into schoolwide change. . . . At schools that sustained their Coalition reform efforts, the principal's role involved a balancing act, one that required knowing when to be directive and assertive and when to back off and allow faculty to direct change efforts. Louis (1995) notes that organizations with cultures that focus on continuous learning exhibit leadership that is simultaneously "strong" (lots of communication from the center) and "weak" (highly decentralized with an emphasis on informal, lateral communication). She and Lightfoot (1983) both note that the successful maintainers of dynamic cultures incorporate more feminine styles of leadership into their repertoire.

Distributed Leadership

Those who study successful reform efforts consistently observe that designated leaders, usually principals, are instrumental, and as the transformative leadership models suggest, it is difficult to compensate for lack of vision and initiative "from the top." However, it is also important to emphasize the limitations of administrators in managing culture. This perspective is perhaps best expressed by March (1984) who outlines two alternatives to the strong leadership perspective. First, his own "garbage can" framework argues that organizations are organized but largely unpredictable in the short run, and that managing is rather like driving a car on an ice slick. This pessimistic perspective would, if administrators believed it, lead them to inaction. Second is an administrative competence model, which argues managers do have an effect on organizations, including their culture, but these are largely indirect. Most of what they do to support culture lies within the framework of "transactional leadership." Organizations cannot, over the long haul, rely for their success on having unusually gifted individuals to run them. Rather, it is a density of more ordinary administrative competence, coupled with rewards for leaders who are highly motivated and work hard, that accounts for successful organization culture and performance.

A number of studies suggest that teachers, rather than administrators, are the primary bearers of school culture, assuming a minimally competent principal. Rossman, Corbett, and Firestone's (1988) cultural analysis of school change makes few references to the principal. Ogawa (1991) investigates principal succession from the teachers' perspective and suggests that teacher norms and values condition how they "make sense" of a new administrator and that this process can also condition what the new principal can do.

Other authors have emphasized that leadership is an organizational property that is not easily isolated in a few positions or a role. Rather, the total amount of leadership influence available in an organization determines whether it has an effective culture and achieves its goals (Ogawa & Bossert, 1995). This proposition has been empirically tested in a sample of 60 schools (Pounder, Ogawa, & Adams, 1995), where it was found that both principal and teacher leadership accounted for the school's adult culture (as measured by organizational commitment among teachers), but that the level of parent leadership best accounts for student achievement.

Finally, it is important to emphasize that popular leaders, even charismatic leaders, do not always have a great impact on school culture. One case study of a new school, for example, found that the influence of the individual who designed and initiated the school was eclipsed by the behavior of several designated "teacher leaders" whose behavior was not consistent with the democratic empowerment principles under which the school was founded (Lonnquist & King, 1995). Nor is the impact of a popular principal on culture always positive. Rollow and Bryk (1995) describe an elementary principal in an inner city school whose need to be liked and in the center of her teachers' affection created a culture of dependence that interfered with curriculum reform.

Toward a Research Agenda

Two things strike us about the research on schools as cultures in the field of educational administration. The first is how little there is of it. The concept of culture has been alive in the management field with varying degrees of faddishness for 15 years now, and there have been several calls to conduct more research in the area. Yet the empirical ed-

ucational studies that explicitly focus on the topic remain limited. Things are somewhat better than they first seem. Some of the most relevant research is hard to find because the concept of culture is latent in the conceptualization and not part of the way the study is labeled. Still, more work is needed.

The second observation is how narrow the research in the area is. One constraint comes from the predominance of the functional paradigm that conceptualizes culture as values, focuses on placid environments, views culture as holistic, and underestimates the role of conflict. Some critical theory research has helped challenge this paradigm. However, a good deal of work in that genre takes such a strong advocacy position or adopts such a romantic view of those studied that its descriptions and conclusions are especially open to criticism. A second and not surprising constraint in educational administration comes from the instrumental interest in the role of the administrator as a potential shaper of culture combined with a failure to understand the utility of the concept if it cannot be linked to leadership.

We conclude by suggesting six leads for future research on schools as cultures. These are areas where we believe research in educational administration can complement studies of school cultures underway in other parts of the educational research community. We begin with one theoretical and one methodological arena for expansion and move to four more substantive topics.

Codes and Values

A major theme of this review has been to point to the limited theoretical integration of the cultural research traditions. Research on organizational culture has focused too exclusively on values and has paid too little attention to the linguistic and behavioral codes that provide the material for individual and group action. The latter is important for both theoretical and practical reasons. Theoretically, attention to codes will help integrate sociological and anthropological studies with organizational research. From a practical perspective, codes are generally easier for administrators and teachers to identify and name, and therefore address directly, than underlying values, which are more often tacit.

This limitation arose because more attention in educational administration research has been paid to organizational theory, rather than the emerging sociological and anthropological literature where the tool kit and structuration theories developed. As a result, with a few exceptions, attention to culture has not opened up the symbolic side of organizations as had been hoped.

Strangely enough, the closest approximation to analysis of cultural codes in education occurs in studies above and below the school level. These include institutional analyses of school structures and the analysis of conflicts over curriculum as expressions of national values on the one hand, and the more micro-oriented study of relationships between the middle-class codes of schools and the oppositional codes of various student groups on the other. An equally rich analysis of codes of school organization or the divergent codes of teachers, administrators, and national elites promoting various reforms has not developed. This could be especially fruitful because what studies we have suggest that the distinction between the tool kit perspective and research emphasizing values appears to be overdrawn at least in education. The relationship between codes and values appears to be more complex than Swidler (1986) suggests.

Methodological Eclecticism

There is an urgent need for greater methodological eclecticism. Most cultural analyses of schools rely on a limited range of qualitative approaches that feature small samples of case studies with heavy emphasis on interviewing and direct but not particularly focused observations. However, increasing emphasis on the complementarity of methodologies suggests that investing more effort in developing standardized ways of measuring culture would be useful, to supplement, not supplant current qualitative approaches.

Three directions would be most helpful supplements for this work. Perhaps the most promising, given our interest in expanding attention to symbols and codes, would be to turn to more formal semiotic analysis as developed by Manning (1987), Spradley (1979), and others. To date, these approaches have been talked about very little and used even less. A second approach would be more historical analyses of how cultural values and codes are formulated over time at various levels. Finally, there is a role for more quantitative analyses of culture as Hofstede's work has shown in the business world, and as Heck and Marcoulides (1996) and others have explored in the educational administration arena.

Here the problems are conceptual as well as methodological. The elaborate technology for measuring organizational climates (Hoy, Tartar, & Kottcamp, 1991) could well be adapted to study school cultures. Work on survey instruments to measure culture in higher education (for example, Smart & St. John, 1996) may provide a model for research in schools. Similarly, the focus of qualitative research on the use of language has not been explored at all in more quantitative studies. For that to happen, however, a better understanding about the similarities and differences between different concepts must be reached. The methodology wars have been resolved in many domains of educational research but appear to be alive and well in cultural studies.

Comparative Macro-Level Studies

Our review suggests that comparative studies of the importance of national, regional, and local cultures are needed. Most of the research reported above is conducted in single countries; cultural studies of schools that are intentionally comparative are rare. Much of the international research cited here was a result of the Organization for Economic Community Development (OECD), the International School Improvement Project (ISIP), which was minimally funded by member countries, and research that compares more than one country (of English-speaking and non-English-speaking countries is relatively rare, however). The work of Dalin and his colleagues (Dalin & Rolff, 1993; Dalin, 1994) exemplifies such broader scale studies, but most are small in scale, such as Osborne's (1996), reflecting collaboration between one or two individuals. In North America, obtaining funding for cross-national studies has been more problematic than is currently the case in Europe due to the desire of the European Union to regularize (or at least make explicit) differences in policies and perspectives among the member countries.

Integrating Cultural Research Across Levels

More research is needed that attends to the intersection of school cultures, leadership, and the outside environment. We now have an unhealthy division of labor where organizational researchers conduct case studies of a few schools to explore the effects of the local school environment, teachers' working conditions, student characteristics, or the principal on the culture of particular schools while historians, political scientists, and sociologists do broader studies of how larger social forces affect the common culture of schools. These two bodies of research are forced by their designs to speak past each other.

Several approaches could help bridge the gap between these different lines of research. One would feature comparative studies that examine the contribution of state/regional culture and local leadership to the culture of particular buildings. Another would be more historical studies of the conflicts that surround the political and social construction of school cultures and the factors that shape it. A third would be small-sample quantitative and qualitative studies that examine how external social forces and local leadership interact to influence school cultures. One subgenre of this third alternative that is reasonably well developed but that has not always sought to explain culture formation is the research on planned change.

Integrating Research on Student Cultures

An important area of research would examine the interaction of school factors, including leadership, and student cultures. Most research in educational administration has focused on the culture of adults; yet one of the principal's most important jobs is supposed to be maintaining order and otherwise influencing the student culture of the building. This work need not overlap excessively with the research of anthropologists who have a long history of examining the formation of school cultures. That work attends primarily to the effects of linguistic, economic, and other out-of-school factors that influence student cultures and subcultures. Less is known about how school policies and practices and other aspects of adult symbolic activities influence these cultures. Waller's observation about the universal tension between the interests of adults and children in school does not mean that the former cannot influence the latter. Moreover, another area of research that needs a great deal more attention is how student culture affects that of adults.

Culture and Effectiveness

More could be done to explore the relationship between culture and effectiveness. This line of work needs to be addressed from two perspectives. The most instrumentally useful and least original would be to contribute to the growing body of work on the causes and correlates of effectiveness. The research in this area is already growing, especially in the United Kingdom and the Netherlands. If learning is more than passively receiving socially certified knowledge, and teaching is not just a technical matter of delivering the curriculum, analyses of both adult and student cultures as a component of the learning environment and process have a great deal to offer. Perhaps the more useful contribution will come from a cultural analysis of the idea of effectiveness and the processes by which various definitions of the term become accepted by groups with differing levels of power in the society. For instance, reformers and the public have different ideas about what effectiveness is. Analyzing these differences could tell a great deal about the formation of national cultures related to education and their impact on schooling.

NOTES

1. Strictly speaking, this optimistic, interventionist theme came largely from practitioner-writers on organizational cultures, rather than academics in the organizational behavior world, but over time it came to characterize both communities (Barley, Meyer, & Gash, 1988).

2. Giddens, following Levi-Strauss and others, confuses things by referring to these elements of culture as "structures," a word that is generally given a different meaning by sociologists and organizational theorists (thereby providing another example of the ambiguity of symbols). We will follow Swidler's (1995) precedent and refer to this aspect of culture as codes out of which action is constructed.

3. Interestingly, even though the books that popularized the idea of organizational culture used the idea to cope with unstable markets and Japanese competition, their conceptions of culture also fit largely in the upper left cell.

4. It is interesting to note that in countries that have permitted public funding of religious schools, these conflicts are minimal. In the Netherlands, for example, fundamentalist religious schools' curricular preferences have been accommodated in both the national knowledge goals and national examinations.

5. There was a massive breakdown in order in the Philadelphia schools at about the same time with a later partial regrouping.

REFERENCES

AAUW (American Association of University Women) (1995). *How schools shortchange girls.* New York: Marlowe and Company.

Adler, L. (1996). Institutional responses: Public school curriculum and religious conservatives in California. *Education and Urban Society, 28*(3), 327–46.

Anderson, H. & Olsen, T. P. (1985). *Supporting school improvement: A Danish structure and approach.* Copenhagen: Royal Danish University for Teacher Development.

Anderson, M., Louis, K. S. & Earle, J. (1994). Disciplinary and departmental effects on observations of faculty and graduate student misconduct. *Journal of Higher Education, 65*, 3, 331–350.

Apple, M. W. (1990). *Ideology and curriculum* (2nd ed.). London: Routledge.

Ashton, P. W. & Webb, R. B. (1986). *Making a difference: Teachers sense of efficacy and student achievement.* New York: Longman.

Barley, S. R. (1983). Semiotics and the study of occupational and organizational cultures. *Administrative Science Quarterly, 28*(3), 393–414.

Barley, S. R., Meyer, G. W. & Gash, D. C. (1988). Cultures of culture: Academics, practitioners and the pragmatics of normative control. *Administrative Science Quarterly, 33*(1), 24–60.

Barnard, C. I. (1938). *The functions of the executive.* Cambridge, MA: Harvard University Press.

Bates, R. (1987). Corporate culture, schooling, and educational administration. *Educational Administration Quarterly, 23*(4), 79–115.

Beck, L. (1994). Cultivating a caring school community: One principal's story. In J. Murphy & K. Louis (Eds.) *Reshaping the principalship: Insights from transformational reform efforts* (pp. 177–202). Thousand Oaks, CA: Corwin.

Benedict, R. (1934). *Patterns of culture.* Boston: Houghton-Mifflin.

Bennett, K. & LeCompte, M. (1990). *The way schools work.* New York: Longman.

Bernstein, B. (1971). *Class codes and control,* vol. I. London: Routledge and Kegan Paul.

Bernstein, B. (1975). *Class, codes and control,* vol. II. London: Routledge and Kegan Paul.

Blanchard, D. A. (1994). *The anti-abortion movement and the rise of the religious right.* New York: Twayne.

Blau, P. M. (1955). *Dynamics of bureaucracy.* Chicago: University of Chicago Press.

Block, P. (1993). *Stewardship.* San Francisco: Berrett-Kohler.

Boje, D. M. (1991). The storytelling organization: A study of story performance in an office-supply firm. *Administrative Science Quarterly, 36*(1), 106–25.

Bourdieu, P. & Passeron, J. C. (1977). *Reproduction in education, society and culture.* London: Sage.

Bourdieu, P. & Passeron, J. C. (1990). *Reproduction in education, society, and culture* 2nd ed. Thousand Oaks, CA: Sage.

Boyd, W. L., Lugg, C. A. & Zahorchak, G. L. (1996). Social traditionalists, religious conservatives, and the politics of outcome-based education: Pennsylvania and beyond. *Education and Urban Society, 28*(3), 347–65.

Bronfenbrenner, U. (1972). *The two worlds of childhood: U. S. and USSR.* New York: Simon and Schuster.

Brooks, J. G. & Brooks, M. G. (1993). *In search of understanding: The case for constructivist classrooms.* Alexandria, VA: ASCD.

Bryk, A. S., Lee, V. E. & Holland, P. B. (1993). *Catholic schools and the common good.* Cambridge, MA: Harvard University Press.

Caré, C. (1986). France. In C. Hopes (Ed.) *The school leader and school improvement: Case studies from ten OECD countries.* Leuven: Acco.

Chatman, J. A. & Barsade, S. G. (1995). Personality, organizational culture, and cooperation: Evidence from a business simulation. *Administrative Science Quarterly, 40*(3), 423–43.

Chatman, J. A. & Jehn, K. A. (1994). Assessing the relationship between industry characteristics and organizational cultures: How different can you be? *Academy of Management Journal, 37*(3), 522–53.

Clark, B. R. (1970). *The distinctive college: Antioch, Reed & Swarthmore.* Chicago: Aldine.

Cohen, E. (1986). On the sociology of the classroom. In *The Contributions of the Social Sciences to Educational Policy and Practice* (pp. 1965–1985). McCutchen.

Coleman, J. (1961). *The adolescent society: The social life of the teenager and its impact on education.* New York: Free Press.

Conley, D. & Goldman P. (1994). Ten propositions for facilitative leadership. In J. Murphy & K. S. Louis (Eds.) *Reshaping the principalship.* (pp. 237–262). Thousand Oaks, CA: Corwin.

Cookson, P. & Persell, C. (1985). *Preparing for power: America's elite boarding schools.* New York: Basic.

Corbett, H. D., Dawson, J. A. & Firestone, W. A. (1984). *School context and school change: Implications for effective planning.* New York: Teachers College Press.

Cuban, L. (1993). *How teachers taught: Constancy and change in American classrooms, 1890–1980.* (2nd ed.) New York: Teachers College Press.

Cusick, P. (1973). *Inside high school: A student's view.* New York: Holt, Rinhart, and Winston.

Dalin, P. (1994). *How schools improve: An international report.* London: Cassell.

Dalin, P. & Rolff, H. G. (1993). *Changing the school culture.* London: Cassell.

Davis, R. B. (1989). The culture of mathematics and the culture of schools. *Journal of mathematical behavior, 8,* 1430–60.

Deal, T. E. & Kennedy, A. A. (1982). *Corporate cultures: the rites and rituals of corporate life.* Reading, MA: Addison-Wesley.

Deal, T. E. & Peterson, K. D. (1991). *The principal's role in shaping school culture.* Washington, DC: U. S. Government Printing Office.

Deal, T. & Peterson, K. D. (1994). *The leadership paradox: Balancing logic and artistry in schools.* San Francisco: Jossey-Bass.

Delgado-Gaitan, C. (1988). The value of conformity: Learning to stay in school. *Anthropology and Education Quarterly, 19,* 354–382.

Denison, D. R. (1996). What IS the difference between organizational culture and organizational climate? A native's point of view on a decade of paradigm wars. *Academy of Management Review, 21*(3), 619–54.

Dunlap, D. M. & Goldman, P. (1991). Rethinking power in schools. *Educational Administration Quarterly, 27* (1), 5–29.

Eder, D., Evans, C. & Parker, S. (1995). *School talk: Gender and adolescent culture.* New Brunswick: Rutgers University Press.

Erickson, F. (1987a). Conceptions of school culture: An overview. *Educational Administration Quarterly, 23*(4), 11–24.

Erickson, F. (1987b). Transformation and school success: The politics and culture of educational achievement. *Anthropology and Education Quarterly, 18,* 335–356.

Feiman-Nemser, S. & Remillard, J. (1996). In Murray, F. B. (Ed.) *The teacher educator's handbook* (pp. 63–91). San Francisco: Jossey-Bass.

Fine, G. A. (1996). Justifying work: Occupational rhetorics as resources in restaurant kitchens. *Administrative Science Quarterly, 41*(1), 90–115.

Firestone, W. A. & Rosenholtz, S. (1988). Building commitment in urban high schools. *Educational Evaluation and Policy Analysis, 10*(4), 285–300.

Firestone, W. A. & Wilson, B., (1989). Using bureaucratic and cultural linkages to improve instruction: The principal's contribution. In J. L. Burdin (Ed.) *School Leadership: A Contemporary Reader.* Newbury Park: Sage.

Foley, D. (1990). *Learning capitalist culture.* Philadelphia: University of Pennsylvania Press.

Fordham, S. & Ogbu, J. U. (1986). Black students school success: Coping with the burden of acting white. *The Urban Review, 18*(3), 176–206.

Fowler, F. C. (1992). American theory and French practice: A theoretical rationale for regulating school choice. *Educational Administration Quarterly, 28*(4), 452–72.

Fullan, M. G. (1991). *The new meaning of educational change.* New York: Teachers College Press.

Gibson, M. A. & Ogbu, J. U. (1991). *Minority status and schooling: A compartitive study of immigrant and involuntary minorities.* New York: Garland.

Giddens, A. (1976). *New rules of the sociological method: A positive critique of interpretative sociologies.* New York: Harper & Row.

Giddens, A. (1984). *The constitution of society: Outline of a theory of structuration.* Berkeley, CA: University of California Press.

Giroux, H. (1983). *Theory and resistance in education.* London: Heinemann.

Giroux, H. (1988). *Teachers as intellectuals: Toward a critical pedagogy of learning.* Hadley, MA: Begin and Garvey.

Goldman, P., Dunlap, D. & Conley, D. (1993). Facilitative power and non-standardized solutions to school site restructuring. *Educational Administration Quarterly, 29* (1), 69–92.

Goodson, I. F. (1988). *The making of curriculum: Collected essays.* London: Falmer Press.

Gouldner, A. (1959). Organizational analysis. In R. K. Merton, L. Broom, J. Leonard & S. Cottrell (Eds.) *Sociology today* (pp. 400–428). New York: Basic Books.

Grant, G. (1988). *The world we created at Hamilton High.* Cambridge, MA: Harvard University Press.

Greenfield, T. (1984). Leaders and schools: Willfulness and non-natural order of organizations. In T. J. Sergiovanni & J. E. Corbally (Eds.) *Leadership and organizational culture* (pp. 142–169). Urbana: University of Illinois Press.

Gregory, K. L. (1983). Native-view paradigms: Multiple cultures and culture conflicts in organizations. *Administrative Science Quarterly, 28*(3), 359–76.

Grossman, P. L. & Stodolsky, S. S. (1994). Considerations of content and the circumstances of secondary school teaching. In L. Darling-Hammond (Ed.) *Review of research in education,* v. 20. (p. 179–222). Washington, DC: American Educational Research Association.

Hallinger, P. & Heck, R. H. (1996). Reassessing the principal's role in school effectiveness: A review of empirical research, 1980–1995. *Educational Administration Quarterly, 23*(1), 5–44.

Hargreaves, A. (1986). *Two cultures of schooling: The case of middle schools.* London: Falmer Press.

Hargreaves, A. (1994). *Development and desire: A postmodern perspective.* Paper presented at the annual meeting of the American Educational Research Association, New Orleans, LA.

Hargreaves, A. & Dawe, R. (1990). Paths of professional development: Contrived collegiality, collaborative culture, and the case of peer coaching. *Teaching and Teacher Education, 6,* 227–241.

Hatch, M. J. (1993). The dynamics of organizational culture. *Academy of Management Review, 18*(4), 657–93.

Heck, R. H. & Marcoulides, G. A. (1996). School culture and performance: Testing the invariance of an organizational model. *School effectiveness and school improvement, 7*(1), 76–95.

Heifetz, R. (1994). *Leadership without easy answers.* Cambridge: Balkan.

Hodgkinson, C. (1983). *The philosophy of leadership.* Oxford: Blackwell.

Hofstede, G. (1980). *Culture's consequences.* Beverly Hills: Sage.

Hofstede, G. (1991). *Cultures and organizations: Software of the mind.* London: McGraw-Hill.

Hofstede, G., Neuijen, B., Ohayv, D. D. & Sanders, G. (1990). Measuring organizational cultures: A qualitative and quantitative study across 20 cases. *Administrative Science Quarterly, 35*(2), 286–316.

Hollingshead, A. (1949). Elmtown's youth. New York: Wiley

Honig, B. & Alexander, F. with Wolf, D. P. (1996). Rewriting the tests: Lessons from the California state assessment system. In J. B. Baron & D. P. Wolf (Eds.) *Performance-based student assessment: Challenges and possibilities* (pp. 143–65). Chicago: University of Chicago.

Hoy, W. K. & Miskel, C. G. (1996). *Educational administration: Theory, research, and practice* (5th ed.) New York: McGraw-Hill.

Hoy, W. K., Tartar, C. J. & Bliss, J. R. (1990). Organizational climate, school health, and effectiveness. *Educational Administration Quarterly, 26*(3), 260–79.

Hoy, W. K., Tartar, C. J. & Kottkamp, R. (1991). *Open schools/healthy schools: Measuring organizational climate.* Beverly Hills, CA: Sage

Huberman, M. (1990). Perspectives in external support in Switzerland. In K. S. Louis & S. Loucks-Horsley (Eds.) *Supporting school improvement: A comparative perspective.* Leuven: Acco.

Kamens, D. H. & Cha, Y. K. (1992). The formation of new subjects in mass schooling: Nineteenth century origins and twentieth century diffusion of art and physical education. In J. W. Meyer, D. H. Kamens & A. Benavot, with Y. K. Cha & S. Y. Wong (Eds.) *School knowledge for the masses: World models and national primary curricular categories in the twentieth century* (pp. 152–64). London: Falmer Press.

Kelley, B. & Bredeson, P. (1991). Measures of meaning in a public and in a parochial school: Principals as symbol managers. *Journal of Educational Administration, 29,* 6–22.

Kirst, M. W. & Jung, R. K. (1982). The utility of a longitudinal approach in assessing implementation: A thirteen-year view of Title I, ESEA. In. W. Williams (Ed.), *Studying implementation: Methodological and administrative issues* (pp. 119–48). Chatham, NJ: Chatham House.

Ladson-Billings, G. (1995). Toward a theory of culturally relevant pedagogy. *American Educational Research Journal, 32*(3), 465–91.

Lareau, A. (1989). *Home advantage: Social class and parental intervention in elementary education.* Philadelphia: Falmer.

Lee, V. E., Bryk, A. S. & Smith, J. B. (1993). The organization of effective secondary schools. In L. Darling-Hammond (Ed.) *Review of research in education, v. 19.* (pp. 171–268). Washington, DC: American Educational Research Association.

Lees, S., Shaw, J. & Reisby, K. (1987). *Aspects of school culture and the social control of girls.* Florence: European University Institute.

Leithwood, K. (1992). The move toward transformational leadership. *Educational Leadership, 49*(5), 8–12.

Leithwood, K. & Jantzi, D. (1990). Transformational leadership: How principals can help reform school cultures. *School Effectiveness and School Improvement, 1* (4) 249–280.

Leithwood, K., Jantzi, D. & Fernandez, A. (1994). Transformational leadership and teachers commitment to change. In J. Murphy & K. S. Louis (Eds.) *Reshaping the principalship* (pp. 77–98). Thousand Oaks, CA: Corwin.

Lesko, N. (1988). *Symbolizing society: Stories, rites, and structure in a Catholic high school.* New York: Falmer.

Lightfoot, S. (1983). *The Good High School.* New York: Basic.

Little, J. W. (1982). Norms of collegiality and experimentation: Workplace conditions of school success. *American Educational Research Journal, 19,* 325–40.

Little, J. W. (1990). The persistence of privacy: Autonomy and initiative in teachers professional relations. *Teachers College Record, 91*(4), 509–534.

Lonnquist, M. P. & King, J. A. (1995). Changing a tire on a moving bus: Barriers to professional community at Whitehead School. In K. S. Louis & S. D. Kruse. (Eds.) *Professionalism and community: Perspectives on reforming urban schools* (pp. 133–160). Thousand Oaks, CA: Corwin.

Lortie, D. C. (1975). *Schoolteacher: A sociological study.* Chicago: University of Chicago Press.

Louis, K. S. (1990). Social values and the quality of teacher work life. In M. McLaughlin, J. Talbert & N. Bacia (Eds.), *The context of teaching in secondary schools* (pp. 13–32). New York: Teachers College Press.

Louis, K. S. & Kruse, S. D. (1995). *Professionalism and community: Perspectives on reforming urban schools.* Thousand Oaks, CA: Corwin.

Louis, K. S. & Miles, M. B. (1990). *Improving the urban high school: What works and why.* New York: Teachers College Press.

Louis, K. S. & Murphy, J. (1994). The evolving role of the principal: Some concluding thoughts. In J. Murphy & K. S. Louis (Eds.) *Reshaping the principalship* (pp. 265–281). Thousand Oaks, CA: Corwin.

Louis, K. S. & Versloot, B. (1996). Cultural diversity and high standards: A cautionary tale of comparative research. *Educational Evaluation and Policy Analysis, 18*(3), 253–261.

Louis, K. S., Kruse, S. D. & Marks, H. M. (1995). Schoolwide professional community. In F. Newmann (Ed.) *School Restructuring and Student Achievement.* San Francisco: Jossey Bass.

Louis, K. S., Marks, H. & Kruse, S. D. (1996). Teachers professional community and school reform. *American Educational Research Journal, 33*(3), 719–52.

McLaren, P. (1994). *Life in schools: An introduction to critical pedagogy in the foundations of education.* (2nd ed.). New York: Longman.

McLeod, J. (1995). *Ain't no makin' it: Aspirations and attainment in a low income neighborhood* (2nd ed.). Boulder: Westview Press.

McNeil, L. M. (1986). *Contradictions of control: School structure and school knowledge.* London: Routledge.

McRobbie, A. (1978). Working class girls and the culture of femininity. In *Women studies group, Women Take Issue.* London: Hutchinson.

Manning, P. K. (1987). *Semiotics and fieldwork.* Newbury Park, CA: Sage.

March, J. (1984). How we talk and how we act: Administrative theory and administrative life. In T. Sergiovanni & J. Corbally (Eds.) *Leadership and organizational culture* (pp. 18–35). Urbana: University of Illinois Press.

Mehan, H. (1992). Understanding inequality in schools: The contribution of interpretive studies. *Sociology of Education, 65* (1) 1–20.

Metz, M. H. (1978). *Classrooms and corridors: The crisis of authority in desegregated secondary schools.* Berkeley: University of California Press.

Metz, M. H. (1986). *Different by design: The context and character of three magnet schools.* New York: Routledge & Kegan, Paul.

Metz, M. H. (1990a). How social class differences shape teachers work. In M. W. McLaughlin, J. E. Talbert & N. Bascia (Eds.) *The contexts of teaching in secondary schools* (pp. 40–110). New York: Teachers College Press.

Metz, M. H. (1990b). Real school: A universal drama mid disparate experiences. In D. E. Mitchell & M. E. Goertz (Eds.) *Education politics for the new century* (pp. 75–92). London: Falmer Press.

Meyer, J. W. & Rowan, B. (1991). Institutionalized organizations: Formal organization as myth and ceremony. In W. W. Powell & P. J. DiMaggio (Eds.) *The new institutionalism in organizational analysis* (pp. 41–62). Chicago: University of Chicago Press.

Meyer, J. W., Boli, J. & Thomas, G. W. (1994). Ontology and rationalization in the western cultural account. In W. R. Scott & J. W. Meyer (Eds.) *Institutional environments and organizations* (pp. 9–27). Thousand Oaks, CA: Sage Press.

Mintzberg, H. (1979). *The structure of organizations.* Englewood Cliffs, NJ: Prentice-Hall.

Mortimore, P. (1991). Effective schools from a British perspective: Research and practice. In J. R. Bliss, W. A. Firestone & C. E. Richards. *Rethinking effective schools* (pp. 76–90). Englewood-Cliffs, NJ: Prentice-Hall.

Muncey, D. & McQuillan, P. (1996). *Reform and resistance in schools and classrooms.* New Haven: Yale University Press.

Ogawa, R. (1991). Enchantment, disenchantment, and accommodation: How a faculty make sense of the succession of its principal. *Educational Administration Quarterly, 27,* 30–60.

Ogawa, R. & Bossert, S. (1995). Leadership as an organizational quality. *Educational Administration Quarterly, 31,* 224–243.

Ogbu, J. U. (1987). Variability in minority school performance: A problem in search of an explanation. *Anthropology and Education Quarterly, 18,* 312–335.

Ogbu, J. U. (1991). Immigrant and involuntary minorities in comparative perspective. In M. A. Gibson & J. U. Ogbu (Eds.) *Minority status and schooling: A comparative study of immigrant and involuntary minorities* (pp. 3–35). New York: Garland.

Olsen, T. P. (1989). Denmark: School improvement and support structure. In K. S. Louis & S. Loucks-Horsley (Eds.) *Supporting school improvement: A comparative perspective.* Leuven, Acco.

Osborne, M. (1996). *Social class, educational opportunity and equal entitlement: Dilemmas of schooling in England and France.* Paper presented at the annual meeting of the American Educational Research Association, New York.

Ouchi, W. (1981). *Theory Z: How American business can meet the Japanese challenge.* Reading, MA: Addison-Wesley.

Parsons, T. (1959). The school class as a social system. *Harvard Educational Review, 29,* 297–318.

Pentland, B. T. & Rueter, H. H. (1994). Organizational routines as grammars of action. *Administrative Science Quarterly, 39*(3), 484–509.

Peshkin, A. (1978). *Growing up American: Schooling and the survival of community.* Chicago: University of Chicago Press.

Peshkin, A. (1982). *The imperfect union: School consolidation and community conflict.* Chicago: University of Chicago.

Peters, T. J. & Waterman, R. H., Jr. (1982). *In search of excellence.* New York: Harper & Row.

Postlethwaite, T. N. (1986). *The use of standardized tests in secondary schools in four European countries.* Madison, WI: Center for Effective Secondary Schools, University of Wisconsin (xerox).

Pounder, D., Ogawa, R. & Adams, E. A. (1995). Leadership as an organization wide phenomena: Its impact on school performance. *Educational Administration Quarterly, 31,* 564–588.

Powell, A. G., Farrar, E. & Cohen, D. K. (1985). *The shopping mall high school.* Boston: Houghton-Mifflin.

Powell, W. W. & DiMaggio, P. J. (1991). *The new institutionalism in organizational analysis.* Chicago: University of Chicago.

Prucha, J. & Walterova, E. (1992). *Education in a changing society: Czechoslovakia.* Prague: Charles University.

Raywid, M. A. (1995). Professional community and its yield at Metro Academy. In K. S. Louis & S. D. Kruse (Eds.) *Professionalism and community: Perspectives on reforming urban schools* (pp. 45–75). Thousand Oaks, CA: Corwin Press.

Reitzug, U. C. (1994). A case study of empowering principal behavior. *American Educational Research Journal, 31*(2), 283–307.

Reitzug, U. C. & Reeves, J. E. (1992). Miss Lincoln doesn't teach here: A descriptive narrative and conceptual analysis of a principal's symbolic leadership behavior. *Educational Administrative Quarterly, 28*(2), 185–219.

Rollow, S. & Bryk, A. (1995). Catalyzing professional community in a school reform left behind. In K. S. Louis, S. Kruse & Associates. *Professionalism and community: Perspectives on reforming urban schools.* Thousand Oaks, CA: Corwin.

Rosenholtz, S. J. (1989). *Teachers workplace: The social organization of schools.* New York: Longman.

Rossman, G. B., Corbett, H. D. & Firestone, W. A. (1988). *Change and effectiveness in schools: A cultural perspective.* Albany: SUNY Press.

Rutter, M., Maughan, B., Mortimore, P. & Ouston, J. with Smith, A. (1979). *Fifteen thousand hours: Secondary schools and their effects on children.* London: Paul Chapman.

Sackman, S. A. (1992). Culture and subcultures: An analysis of organizational knowledge. *Administrative Science Quarterly, 37*(1), 140–60.

Sarason, S. B. (1971). *The culture of the school and the problem of change.* Boston: Allyn and Bacon.

Sato, N. & McLaughlin, M. (1992). Context matters: Teaching in Japan and the United States. *Phi Delta Kappan,* (January), 359–366.

Schein, E. H. (1992). *Organizational culture and leadership.* (2nd ed.) San Francisco: Jossey-Bass.

Schofield, J. W. (1989). *Black and white in school: Trust, tension, or tolerance?* New York: Teachers College Press.

Sedlak, M., Wheeler, C., Pullin, D. & Cusick, P. (1986). *Selling students short.* New York: Teachers College Press.

Sergiovanni, T. J. (1984). Developing a relevant theory of administration. In T. J. Sergiovanni & J. E. Corbally (Eds.) *Leadership and organizational culture* (pp. 275–291). Urbana: University of Illinois Press.

Sergiovanni, T. J. (1994). Organizations or communities? Changing the metaphor changes the theory. *Educational Administration Quarterly, 30*(2), 214–226.

Shimahara, N. K. & Sakai, A. (1994). *Learning to teach in two cultures.* New York: Garland.

Siskin, L. S. (1991). Departments as different worlds: Subject subcultures in secondary schools. *Educational Administration Quarterly, 27*(2), 134–60.

Smart, J. C. & St. John, E. P. (1996). Organizational culture and effectiveness in higher education: A test of the "culture type" and "strong culture" hypotheses. *Educational Evaluation and Policy Analysis, 18*(3), 219–41.

Smircich, L. (1983). Concepts of culture and organizational analysis, *Administrative Science Quarterly, 28*(3), 339–58.

Snyder, K. J. (1988). Managing a productive school work culture. *National Association of Secondary School Principals Journal, 72,* (510), 40–43.

Spindler, G. & Spindler, L. (1971). *Dreamers without power; the Menomini Indians.* New York: Holt, Rinehart, and Winston.

Spindler, G. & Spindler, L. (1987). Interpretive enthnography of education: at home and abroad. Hillsdale, NJ: L. Erlbaum Associates.

Spradley, J. (1979). *The ethnographic interview.* New York: Holt, Rinehart & Winston.

Stegî, N. E. Sweden In C. Hopes (Ed.) *The school leader and school improvement: Case studies from ten OECD countries.* Leuven: Acco.

Steinberg, L., Brown, B. & Dornbusch, S. (1996). *Beyond the classroom: Why school reform had failed and what parents need to do.* New York: Simon and Schuster

Stevenson, H. W. & Stigler, J. W. (1992). *The learning gap.* New York: Summit Books.

Swidler, A. (1986). Culture in action: Symbols and strategies. *American Sociological Review, 51*(2), 273–86.

Swidler, A. (1995). Cultural power and social movements. In H. Johnston & B. Klandermans (Eds.) *Social movements and culture* (pp. 25–40). Minneapolis, MN: University of Minnesota Press.

Talbert, J. & McLaughlin, M. W. (1994). Teacher professionalism in local school contexts. *American Journal of Education, 102*(2), 123–153.

Teddlie, C. & Stringfield, S. (1993). *Schools make a difference: Lessons learned from a 10-year study of school effects.* New York: Teachers College Press.

Thompson, J. D. (1967). *Organizations in action.* New York: McGraw-Hill.

Trueba, H. (1988). Peer socialization among minority students: A high school drop out prevention program. In H. Trueba & C. Delgado-Gaitan (Eds.) *School and Society: Learning Content through Culture.* pp. 201–218. New York: Praeger.

Tyack, D. & Cuban, L. (1995). *Tinkering toward Utopia: A century of public school reform.* Cambridge, MA: Harvard University Press.

van den Berg, R. & van Wijlick, W. (1991). Supporting school improvement: Strategies, structures, and policies: The Dutch case. In K. S. Louis & S. Loucks-Horsley (Eds.) *Supporting school improvement: A comparative perspective.* Leuven, Acco.

Waller, W. (1932). *The sociology of teaching.* New York: Wiley.

Weber, M. (1947). *The theory of social and economic organization.* New York: Free Press.

Weick, K. E. & Roberts, K. H. (1993). Collective mind in organizations: Heedful interrelating on flight decks. *Administrative Science Quarterly, 38*(3), 357–81.

Willis, P. (1977). *Learning to labor.* Aldershot: Gower.

Wilson, B. L., Herriott, R. E. & Firestone, W. A. (1991). Explaining differences between elementary and secondary schools: Individual, organizational, and institutional perspectives. In. P. W. Thurston & P. Zodhiates (Eds.) *Advances in Educational Administration, v. 2* (pp. 131–157). Greenwich, CT: JAI Press.

Wilson, E. K. (1971). *Sociology: Rules, roles, and relationships.* Homewood, IL: Dorsey.

Wolcott, H. F. (1977). *Teachers vs. technocrats.* Eugene, OR: Center for Educational Policy and Management.

Wuthnow, R. & Witten, M. (1988). New directions in the study of culture. In W. R. Scott & J. Blake (Eds.) *Annual review of sociology, v. 14.* (pp. 49–67). Palo Alto, CA: Annual Reviews, Inc.

Zeichner, K. M. & Gore, J. M. (1992). Teacher socialization. In W. R. Houston (Ed.) *Handbook of research on teacher education.* (pp. 329–48). New York: Macmillan.

CHAPTER 15

Schools as Polities

Robert O. Slater and William Lowe Boyd

[T]here is hope that the rhetoric of school reform will shift markedly from the narrative provided by the god of economic utility (to borrow from Neil Postman's "The End of Education") to a narrative of more promise to humankind. The core of my argument is that the public purpose of education—namely, the shaping of civility in a context of democratic social and political civitas—will not be advanced by a system of schooling geared primarily to economic ends.

—*John I. Goodlad (1997).*

John Goodlad's trenchant observation captures the essence of a mounting critique of American school reform. It contends that education reform has been hijacked by utilitarian economic interests, pushing the democratic and humanistic purposes of education almost completely off the policy agenda. While equality of opportunity and social justice continue to be debated, this discourse occurs in a truncated, marginalized way within a social milieu dominated by economic and technocratic values. Indeed, as Kahne (1994, 1996) has powerfully demonstrated, mainstream policy analysis is so technocratic that it lacks both the vocabulary and the inclination to examine important questions of democracy, community, and social justice:

Currently, policy analysts emphasize a different agenda. Assessments of educational quality focus on individual rather than group achievement and on standardized and meritocratic notions of equality. Indeed, policy analysts lack the vocabulary, the conceptual frameworks, and the technical procedures needed to consider systematically and articulate concern for these alternative ideals. Important questions regarding the relation between schooling and the promotion of democratic communities are not the subject of systematic analysis . . . Despite the respect Dewey commands among educators, those assessing educational

policy generally ignore the social concerns of democratic communitarians (Kahne, 1994, p. 246).

In this chapter, we address some of the concerns that Goodlad and Kahne share: How do American schools function as democratic institutions and communities? What is their relationship to the American polity? What is meant by polity? In what ways are schools like polities? One of the main points of this chapter is that how one answers the last question depends on definitions of polity. The meaning of polity shapes our perceptions of schools as polities.

This chapter has two main parts, each corresponding to these questions about polity. In the first part, we introduce three meanings of polity that have been prominent in the history of political thought. The discussion of schools as polities takes different turns depending on which of these definitions one adopts. In modern political science, "polity" is mainly used as a synonym for "political system." In fact, it is fair to say that in the kind of political analysis represented by the work of such scholars as David Easton (1985), political system replaced polity.

The modern notion of polity is different from the usage that prevailed in 16th-century England when the word "polity" first appeared. In this period, "polity" came very close to meaning what we today think of as "civility" and "civil society."

The third meaning of polity goes back to the Greeks who thought of a polity as a political-social organization in which the many rule in the interest of the whole, a form of governance that they always contrasted with democracy, in which the many rule not in the interest of the whole but in their own interest.

In the second part of the essay, we discuss the implications of each of these three meanings of polity for the study of schools as polities. The purpose of this part is mainly illustrative, to show how each of the three definitions of polity draws our attention to different political aspects of schooling, causing us to focus on different questions. If, for example, we look at schools as polities with the modern sense of polity in mind, our attention is drawn to issues of conflict, power, political-economy, micro-politics, rational choice theory, and the like. If, on the other hand, we consider schools as polities with questions of civility in mind, the second definition of polity, we find ourselves having to deal with recent literature on the condition of contemporary American civil society and its implications for civic education. Finally, if we look at schools from the point of view of the Greek idea of polity, we are led to the literature that critiques American schools and schooling as being undemocratic and deficient in regard to human dignity and development.

Finally, we conclude the chapter by noting that the utilitarian and technocratic nature of the discourse on school reform deflects attention from consideration of the question of whether schools should be more polity-like in the classic Greek sense of the term. We also suggest that consideration of this question might be one way to construct a bridge between more traditional analyses of school reform and educational policy and those on the left who criticize both this analysis and school reform itself.

Three Meanings of Polity

In this section, we briefly review each of the three senses of polity that have developed at various times in the history of the idea. We begin with the meaning of polity that has evolved most recently in modern political science and then introduce two other meanings, one of which evolved in 16th-century England when the actual term "polity" first appeared in the English language and one which comes from the Greeks.

Polity as Political System

In modern political science discourse, especially as it developed in the 1960s, the term "polity" is used as a synonym for "political system," the latter being much the preferred term. "Polity," for example, does not appear in the index to Dahl's (1963) *Modern Political Analysis*, nor is it central in David Easton's (1985) *A System's Analysis of Political Life*, two influential works in mainstream modern political science. In these, as well as other works, "political system" is the central concept and "polity" is simply an alternative way to refer to it.

The practice of making "polity" synonymous with "political system" has carried over into the politics of education

literature. For example, when emphasizing the importance of the concept of power in the study of the micropolitics of schooling, Malen (1994) says that "As in any polity, actors in schools manage the inherent conflict and make the distributional decisions through processes that pivot on power exercised in various ways and in various areas." Earlier references to "political systems," make it clear that by "polity," Malen means political system. Her use of the term in this way is characteristic of how other students of the politics of education tend to use it.

Polity as Civil Order

The English "polity" derives from the ancient Greek word "politea," which is usually translated as either "regime" or "constitution," though by this latter term, the Greeks never meant a written document. For the ancients, "regime" did not have the connotation that it has for us today. It was not thought of as an authoritarian form of government. It was a whole political order, authoritarian or democratic, in which they included not only politics but society as well.

By the time the English word "polity" or, as it was spelled then, "polyty," first appeared in the 16th-century, the concept still had the meaning of polity in the broad sense in which the Greeks meant it. But by this time the idea of "regime" had been replaced by "civil order."

For Englishmen at that time, polity came very close to what we think of today as polite. Our civility is the modern term that probably comes closest to what the 16th century English meant by polyty. It was typical, for example, to describe an individual as rude and without polyty, presumably a description of a member of the common folk.

Today, of course, rudeness and polity are not obviously connected and one has to dig deeply to see how they are. At bottom they can be linked through the notion of civil society, a term that has become central in recent political science discourse (Putnam, 1995; Foley & Edwards, 1986) and about which we will have more to say in due course. Civil society is the connecting point because at some level it implies civility, a characterization of the way or manner in which human beings interact and associate with one another. A civil society consists of networks of association, particularly voluntary associations (the Elks, Boy Scouts, churches). These networks of cooperation build norms of trust, tolerance, and other personal qualities needed for cooperation. These qualities are collectively referred to as social capital (Coleman, 1988; Putnam, 1995), a concept that implies civility.

An exploration of the concept of social capital with its attendant notions of trust, reciprocity, and the like suggests what was explicit in the classical point of view, namely that establishing and maintaining a polity is not simply a political problem but a moral problem as well.

The link between politics and morality was hardly unknown to the Greeks, of course. The ancients had always been concerned with the question of how to enable the good man to also be a good citizen and vice versa. And they were convinced that it was difficult, if not impossible, for people to be good in a bad regime. This is one reason why they wanted only the most virtuous to rule, fearing that with anything less, virtue could not be cultivated among the people (McIntyre, 1984).

But the link between politics and morality was so close for the Greeks that they never considered separating the two, a separation that was beginning to be apparent by the time the concept appears in the 16th century, and one that was to become routine and natural in modern thought.

It is difficult for us moderns, operating within the framework of liberal thought, a framework which wants to disconnect politics from individual morality, to imagine the implications for society of a notion of polity and civil order that dominated thinking in 17th-century England and Scotland. There was an interconnectedness that is difficult for us to comprehend, a connection that comes through clearly, for example, in McIntyre's (1987) essay on the question of what an educated public is.

Polity as Rule of the Many in the Interest of the Whole

Still a third meaning of "polity" can be found in Greek philosophy. In this instance, a polity was a particular kind of political (and social) "regime." The Greeks categorized regimes along two dimensions. First, in any particular regime rule could be exercised by the one, the few, or the many. Second, leaders could either rule in the interest of the whole or in their own interest. This categorization scheme resulted in six possibilities. A regime, for example, could be ruled by one individual who ruled in the interest of the whole. This was a monarchy, a good regime. On the other hand, if one person ruled in his own interest, it was a tyranny, a bad regime. Similarly, a regime in which the few ruled in the interest of the whole was an aristocracy, a good regime, while its bad counterpart was an oligarchy, a regime in which a few ruled in their own interest.

A polity was a regime in which the many ruled for the interest of the whole. Its counterpart was a democracy, a bad regime in which the many ruled for their own interest.

The context of this framework was, of course, a highly class-structured society in which the interests of the few were always in tension with the interests of the many. And among the "many" there were many others, such as slaves and women, who did not figure in at all.

The aim of Greek political philosophy was to ascertain the conditions and the characteristics of the best regime or polity. Many ancient Greeks thought that the polity, the regime, was supremely important because the realization of human potential and happiness were always dependent upon it. Men and women came into the world uncivilized, needy, and with little to distinguish them from other animals. They were not born complete human beings, for being human meant more than simply having a physical body, and their humanity was neither automatic nor guaranteed. In order to actualize their potential to be human, men and women needed a proper environment and the most important environment of all was the polity.

For the Greeks, the polity was not something in addition to family and social life, a separate sphere of activity somehow "outside" these more personal spheres. They did not make these distinctions. Family, society, and polity were more or less one sphere in the sense that the polity shaped the everyday lives of its citizens.

Put in more modern terms, the polity and the political values that constituted it infused every aspect of life. The polity, for example, imparted specific notions of justice and what was to be most honored and honorable. It was the environment that set the "tone" for all the other more local and individually experienced environments, such as the family and immediate community.

In What Ways Are Schools Like Polities?

The schools-as-polities problem involves both practical and theoretical questions, but these questions are shaped by how one defines "polity." If, for example, by "polity," one means "political system," then the question of how much schools are like polities leads us to consider the features of political systems and then to ask to what degree schools and school systems exhibit these features. This, then, leads to further analysis that relies on concepts central in modern political analysis, such as "power," "decision-making," "political arena," and the like.

At the same time, however, if a polity is defined as a political system, the normative question of whether schools should be more polity-like makes no sense. Why should we want to make schools more like political systems? Either they are like political systems already or they are not. There is no good reason to try to make them more so. All one can do is find out how much they are like political systems and whether their behavior can be understood in terms of political analysis. This is the main consequence of modern political analysis: it removes the normative from consideration.

On the other hand, if we define "polity" in the classic Greek sense of rule of the many in the interest of the whole, then we are confronted by very different questions. On the theoretical side, we can still ask to what extent schools look like polities, or to what degree are they examples of rule of the many in the interest of the whole? And here the theoretical question leads to a kind of literature very different in tone and content from that produced by our defining a polity as a political system, the modern meaning. It produces a literature highly critical of contemporary schooling (Apple, 1989; Bowles & Gintis, 1989; Apple & Beane, 1995). So while the modern sense of polity leads us to consider features of schools and schooling that seem to make them closely resemble political systems, when we use the old sense of polity we are led in a different direction. Moreover, when we take polity to mean "civil order," we are led in still a third direction.

In the remainder of this chapter, we simply point to the implications of three different directions in which the three meanings of polity lead us and attempt to provide a bird's-eye view of each path.

Schools as Polities/Political Systems

The study of schools as polities/political systems has a number of different dimensions to it. There are, first of all, studies that take the association literally. Schools are taken to be not simply "like" political systems, but they are political systems. They are mini-political systems with many, if not all, the features of large-scale political systems. Accordingly, in this case, theories used to understand large-scale political systems are brought to bear on schools and school systems.

Apart from these literal interpretations, are other studies that treat the association more metaphorically. If schools are not large-scale political systems writ small, they are at least highly political. They have political "aspects" to them that cannot be denied. From this perspective, one focuses on key concepts such as "power," "decision-making," and so on. The effort is to show where and how schools are political (Wimpelberg, 1997).

Finally, a third kind of study that evolves out of and is related to the consideration of schools as political systems and political entities focuses on various current issues, such as policy from a feminist perspective (Marshall & Anderson, 1994).

"Literal" Interpretations of Schools as Polities/Political Systems

A good example of the more "literal" interpretation of schools as polities, in the sense of political systems, is Wirt and Kirst's (1992) *Schools in Conflict*. The authors take David Easton's (1985) framework, originally intended to apply mainly to the political systems of nation states, and map it directly on to schools and school systems. Easton argues that political systems perform one of a society's key functions: the "authoritative allocation of values." They perform this function as part of input-throughput-output process wherein they take "demands" made and "support" given them and transform these inputs in a process that re-

sults in decisions and actions. This same input-throughput-output process, Wirt and Kirst argue, can be used to understand schools and schooling. Schools, too, allocate valued resources—revenues, programs, professionals—and values, such as honesty or timeliness. They, too, engage in a process of transforming certain inputs in the form of demands (tax cuts, accountability, religious right) made on them into particular outputs such as superintendent memos, ordinances, busing plans, and so on.

Another example of this kind of analysis is Martin Carnoy's (1994) "Political Economy of Educational Production," wherein Carnoy uses the "schools as a polity/political system" approach to critique other scholars who make a case for looking at schools as economic firms. Carnoy argues that thinking about schools as mini-political systems makes more sense than viewing them as economic organizations engaged in the production of education. Schools and school administrative districts, he argues, simply do not function like private firms. "They are part of the public sector, subject to different conditions and organizational imperatives." Moreover, unlike the managers and workers in private firms who usually have considerable control over the quality of the inputs and raw materials to the production process, principals and teachers cannot control the knowledge and skills that children bring with them to school (1994: 4562). For these and other reasons, he says, schools should be considered as political systems, albeit miniature ones.

Less Literal Interpretations: The Political Aspects of Schools and Schooling

In the two examples just given, the proposition at work is that schools "are" political systems. However, in many other studies in which the polities/political system concept is central, schools are said to be "like" political systems, but they are not taken literally to be political systems. The practical result of this more interpretive approach is that the focus is more on the political "aspects" of schooling, and the guiding question is something on the order of in what ways can schools usefully be seen as political? With this approach, the effort is not so much one of taking whole political theories and "mapping" them directly on to educational organizations—to take, as it were, the metaphor out of the metaphor—but rather one of selecting certain political concepts and then examining schools and schooling in terms of them. Key concepts, for example, would include "decision-making," political "actors," political "arenas," and "domains of influence" (Mitchell, *et al.*, 1994).

One way in which this differs from the more "literal" approach to schools as polities/political systems is that it tends to be more eclectic, often involving an effort to develop out of a number of different theories or concepts a distinctive way of looking at schools and schooling. A good example of this is the "micro-political" perspective:

Micropolitics refers to the use of formal and informal power by individuals and groups to achieve their goals in organizations. In large part, political actions result from perceived differences between individuals and groups, coupled with the motivation to use power to influence and/or protect. Although such actions are consciously motivated, any action, consciously or unconsciously motivated, may have political significance in a given situation. Both cooperative and conflictive actions and processes are part of the realm of micropolitics. Moreover, macro- and micropolitical factors frequently interact (Blase, 1991: 11).

Non-Rational Political Models: The Garbage Can Theory

Among the key political concepts used to understand education in general, and educational administration in particular, is the concept of "garbage can decision making" (March, 1976). The key idea here is that decision-making and the decision-making process are not as rational as usually assumed. Normally, we think of decision-making as involving a number of steps: 1) identifying or finding the problem, 2) proposing alternative solutions to the problem, 3) choosing a solution and implementing it, and 4) evaluating the results.

According to the garbage can model, however, things are not this straightforward and rational. In real life, solutions often precede problems, and they seldom come one at a time or in an orderly fashion. More often than not, we find ourselves confronted with streams of solutions and problems. These streams flow together and problems and solutions get mixed together like garbage in a can. Solutions often get attached to problems in a serendipitous manner.

A school or school system, for example, might invest in curricular materials or technologies that have become outdated. But, because of the costs of replacement, they are kept on despite being outmoded. They become solutions to new problems not because they are the best or most appropriate solutions but simply because they are there.

Because of its emphasis on the non-rational aspects of decision-making, the garbage can model fits well with other theories that emphasize the disorderly nature of school administration, such as the recent work on chaos and chaos theory (Maxcy, 1995).

Feminist Critical Policy Analysis

Another way in which the political is being analyzed in education is through the lens of feminist critical policy analysis (Marshall & Anderson, 1994), which begins with the assumption that gender inequity results from purposeful (if subconscious) choices to serve some in-group's ideology and purpose. Of particular interest within this sphere of research is how the political agenda in schools is automatically formulated in ways that benefit males. Feminist critical policy analysis is research that conducts analyses for women while focusing on policy and politics, and it asks of every policy or political action, how does this affect females (1994: 172)?

Schools as Polities/Civil Orders and Their Relation to the Larger Civil Order

To look at schools as polities with the second definition of polity in mind—a polity as a civil order—is to raise two kinds of considerations. One is "internal" to the school itself: In what ways may schools themselves be thought of as civil orders? The second is "external" to the school in the sense that it focuses on the relationship between the school and society: What is the role of the school in relation to the civil order of the society in which it functions? In this section, we take up both of these questions, beginning with the latter one concerning the relation of the school to the larger civil order.

The Condition of American Civil Society and Its Implications for Schools: Civic Education

The observation that schools and society are interrelated has long been commonplace; nevertheless, there has been an ongoing discussion about the nature of this connection. Granted that schools and society are linked, just how are they linked? How do schools affect society and society affect schools?

The "civil society" literature falls within the scope of this question. Generally speaking, this literature, insofar as education is concerned, involves two questions: 1) What is the condition of contemporary American civil society? and 2) What is the role of the school in relation to this condition? As for the first question, a number of empirical and theoretical studies deserve mentioning.

The Civic Culture

More than 25 years ago, Almond and Verba (1963) examined attitudes related to democracy in five nations: Britain, Germany, Italy, Mexico, and the United States. Their starting point was the proposition that values, attitudes, and skills of a subtle and complex sort, in addition to political, economic, and social performance, play an important role in the process of democratization (1963: vi). In other words, for a democracy to work, people have to think, feel, and judge or evaluate in certain ways. Put more formally, a democracy depends on and needs people with the cognitive, affective, and evaluative orientations that are supportive of a democracy. But what are these orientations?

Almond and Verba were not the first social scientists to deal with this question. Before them, Harold Lasswell, for one, had tried to come up with a defensible list of the characteristics of the democratic personality. He believed that five qualities were especially important:

(1) An open ego, by which he meant a warm and inclusive attitude toward other human beings
(2) A capacity for sharing values with others
(3) A multi-valued rather than a single-valued orientation
(4) Trust and confidence in the human environment
(5) Relative freedom from anxiety

Unlike Lasswell, however, Almond and Verba did not try to generate a list of characteristics. Instead, they argued that what was important were individual cognitive, affective, and evaluative orientations, orientations toward four things in particular: (1) the political system as a whole, (2) the political roles and the various elites that operated in this system, (3) the policies, policy-making and policy enforcement apparatus within the system, and (4) the self in relation to the polity.

If, for example, we want to know the condition of a civic culture according to Almond and Verba's approach, we must first ask how people think, feel, and evaluate their political system as a whole. What do they know about their country? Its size? The makeup of its population, its history, and so on? How do they feel about these things? How do they judge them, if they judge them at all? Similarly, we must also ask about knowledge, feelings, and judgments that pertain to political leaders.

Almond and Verba found considerable cross-national variations in people's orientations. In general, they found three types. First, there were what they called parochials, citizens who were unaware or only dimly aware of political goings-on. And even if they were aware, they were often alienated or dissatisfied with them (citizens of Italy and Mexico were good examples of this type). Second, there were subjects who were people aware of politics but passive and obedient. Finally, there were the participants, citizens who were both aware of politics and things political and actively engaged in the political process. This third type fit what they called the rationality-activist model of citizenship.

Almond and Verba concluded from their study that the rationality-activist model of a citizen was not a realistic description of the citizens surveyed in their study. What was the condition of the civil culture of these five nations? The answer, quite simply, was that it was mixed. They found the five political and civic cultures to be a mix of all three types with more parochials and subjects than citizens. This finding led them, and others after them, to speculate about the stabilizing consequences for democracy of political apathy.

Habits of the Heart
Another more recent study that looks at individual characteristics and their implications for democracy or the condition of civil society is *Habits of the Heart* by Robert Bellah and his colleagues (1985). When Alexis de Tocqueville toured America over 160 years ago and reported his obser-

vations and insights in *Democracy in America* in an effort to understand democracy and how it worked, he argued that the most important condition of democracy (polity) were certain "habits of the heart." By this phrase Tocqueville meant the sum of moral and intellectual dispositions of men in society, "their moral practices and principles, their code of right and wrong, their social values. These are the things that people use to answer questions that people in every society must answer: How ought we to live? How do we think about how to live? What is our character?" (Bellah *et al.*, 1985).

Tocqueville observed and commented on a number of what seemed to be peculiarly American habits of the heart, but he was particularly intrigued and concerned by American individualism. By individualism, Tocqueville meant "a calm and considered feeling which disposes each citizen to isolate himself from the mass of his fellows and withdraw into the circle of family and friends; with this little society formed to his taste, he gladly leaves the greater society to look after itself."

Tocqueville believed that the growth of individualism was a characteristic of democratic societies because in a democracy people had the opportunity to become self-sufficient and self-reliant, and as they became more so they needed others less and less. He was concerned that as individualism continued to grow, "Each man may be shut up in the solitude of his own heart." Concerned more and more with their own affairs, Americans would increasingly let government manage their general affairs, thus giving it increasing amounts of power. Ultimately there would come a time when power would become so concentrated that freedom itself would be lost and democracy would be replaced by tyranny and despotism.

Following up on Tocqueville's predictions, Bellah (1985) and colleagues made a study of individualism in American life. They state the purpose of their study as follows:

> The central problem of our book concerns the American individualism that Tocqueville described with a mixture of admiration and anxiety. We are concerned that this individualism may have grown cancerous, that it may be destroying those social integuments that Tocqueville saw as moderating its more destructive potentialities, that it may be threatening the survival of freedom itself.

In pursuit of this purpose, Bellah and his four co-authors interviewed over 200 persons, some of whom they talked to more than once and many of whom they observed as they participated in community activities and events. They supplemented their interviews and participant observations with data from surveys and community studies. What did they find and conclude?

What they found is that Americans suffer from radical individualism. They "suffer" because their individualism involves a kind of discourse wherein they are unable to hold a common vision of the good life. Each has his or her own view of what the good life is, but none can justify a common set of core values that would guide the behavior of all. Americans tend to think of the ultimate goals of the good life (and, by implication, the good society) as matters of personal choice.

The authors conclude that Americans today must find a way to balance individual and community, private and public. As things exist now there is a serious imbalance on the side of individualism and the private. America has developed a culture of separation, isolation, and self-orientation. Means must be found by which to combat this tendency and restore a balance between self and other.

Almond and Verba and Bellah and colleagues were mainly concerned with characteristics of individuals. What qualities do democracies need for people to have if they are to sustain and maintain themselves? Other studies, however, have looked at group characteristics, at networks of association and have been concerned to describe their condition, particularly their deteriorating condition over time. This is the aim of Robert Putnam's "Bowling Alone" (1995).

Bowling Alone

Putnam's thesis, in nutshell, is that American civil society seems to have been on the decline over the last 20 years or so. The title of his paper comes from the rather whimsical observation that while bowling is up by 10 percent, participation in league bowling has declined drastically. More people may be bowling in America, but they are bowling alone.

Probably the most visible sign of the decline of American civil society in recent decades is the low rate of political participation. The United States ranks near the bottom of 11 key developed societies in voter turnout for national elections. In the 1992 presidential election, for example, only 55 percent of the registered voters went to the polls as compared to 64 percent for Hungary in its 1990 elections, 75 percent for Japan in 1993, 90 percent for Australia in that same year, and 93 percent for East Germany in 1990. Only Switzerland ranked lower with a 46 percent turnout. Moreover, when one considers that the registered voters do not make up the entire electorate, President Clinton's 44 percent plurality translated into an endorsement of only 24 percent of the U.S. citizenry. Participation in off-year elections is even lower.

When Putnam turns to data on direct civic engagement, the statistics are no better. Weekly churchgoing dropped from 48 percent in the 1950s to 41 percent in the early 1970s. Labor union participation has fallen off from about 32 percent in 1953 to about 16 percent in 1992. Boy Scout membership is off 26 percent since 1970. Red Cross volunteering dropped 61 percent in the same period. Since 1979, membership in the Elks, Shriners, and Jaycees is off 18, 27, and 44 percent respectively. Civic engagement across the spectrum seems on the decline.

What has been responsible for the decline of civic engagement? Putnam suggests several reasons. One possibility has to do with the changing role of women in society. As American women have entered the labor force in the last three decades, they have had less time and energy to devote to such things as PTOs or PTAs, civic association in which women have traditionally been more active than men. A second factor might have to do with what Putnam calls the "re-potting" hypothesis. This is simply that Americans have been highly mobile in recent decades and when people move from one place to another it takes longer to reestablish roots and enter into new social networks. A third possibility might have to do with changing demographics such as fewer marriages and more divorces. Middle-class parents tend to be more civically engaged than others. Finally, Putnam suggests that the decline of civic engagement could be due to technology, especially the impact of technology on leisure, above all the effects of television. The point here is simply that time spent watching television (Americans watch an average of 5.2 hours per day now as opposed to 3.4 hours 25 years ago) is less time spent in face-to-face interactions with one's family, neighbors, colleagues, or friends.

Putnam has not been without his critics (Foley & Edwards, 1996). Some people, for example, have pointed to the rise of soccer leagues in America and suggested that this is one type of voluntary association that Putnam has missed. Others have observed that the link between civil society and democracy by way of association is not clear. How does association influence democracy? Presumably, it is through the social capital it builds, but again the connections between social capital and democracy, the translation from civil to political, are not clear.

Anomie

Another explanation for Putnam's findings might be found in Durkheim's (1951) work on anomie. Anomie refers to both an individual psychological state and the condition of a society, though the origin of anomie is supposedly in the society, not in the individual as such. The anomic society is an unstable society whose values and standards have broken down. Anomie is manifest at the individual level by a sense of personal unrest, alienation, and the uncertainty that comes from a lack of purpose or ideals (Orru, 1987).

Anomie, at least in U.S. survey data, has been measured in a number of ways. First, there are questions that have to do with whether citizens think that their public officials are really interested in their problems. The specific question that has been asked by the National Opinion Research Center for the last 25 years or so is "Do you agree or disagree that most public officials (people in office) are not really interested in the problems of the average man?" In 1973, 58 percent of the adult population said they agreed. By 1993, the percent of Americans in agreement had risen to 74 percent, an increase of 27 percent. In 1973, to take another example, 36 percent Americans said they believed that it was hardly fair to bring a child into the world. In 1994, 44 percent said this, a 22 percent increase. Finally, in 1973, 54 percent of Americans age 18 and over said that the condition (lot) of the average man is getting worse, not better. By 1994, the figure was 67.2 percent, a jump of 24 percent.

No matter how one measures it, anomie in the United States seems to have been on the rise in the last 20 years or so. Could this be a contributing factor for what Putnam found in his study of the decline of American civil society? This question has not yet been systematically explored.

Implications for Schools and Civic Education

What does this recent work on the condition of American civil society imply for schools and schooling, particularly civic education? Probably the most important implications are 1) life in schools should not contribute to radical individualism in America, and 2) that civic education should itself be more participatory.

As for the first point, some critics of the American curriculum and classroom instruction have long had as one of their central complaints that the structure of the typical classroom and the instruction delivered within its walls reinforces and encourages individualism. Recognition of the individualistic orientation of much of American education and its potentially counterproductive and negative effects probably lies behind the renewed interest in group and cooperative learning (Slavin, 1994), approaches that became popular in the era of progressive education but which were abandoned as that movement lost favor.

As for the second point, traditional civic education in the United States has had two prominent characteristics: it has been non-participatory and cognitive in orientation. Its aim and method has been to provide facts and information about government and the rights and responsibilities of citizens. It has not tried to provide students the experience of polity. Recently developed civic education programs that are built around the idea of community "service" are changing this tradition, but by and large civic education in America is still "classroom bound."

Perhaps one reason civic education in America has been non-participatory is that, until recently, the dominant democratic theory in political science has itself been non-participatory. Now a debate is going on in political science between two groups of democratic theorists. What has been called the "elitist" camp (Rimmerman, 1997) holds, among other things, that the low rates of participation in modern democracies are functional because if more people participated governance would become increasingly "messy" and inefficient, and it would be more difficult to

maintain order. In this view, democracies in fact work because people do not participate. These theorists argue that classical democratic theory presupposes civic virtues that citizens of modern democracies simply do not have.

"Participatory" democratic theorists, on the other hand, object to the "elitist" approach to democratic theory and argue that while the elitists claim simply to be describing democracies as they are, and not how we wish them to be, they are in fact subscribing to a normative position that reinforces the status quo. Elitists, they say, abandon the democratic aspiration.

Just how much impact has "elitist" democratic theory had on civic education in the United States? One could assume that social studies teachers would have been influenced by one of the dominant theories in their field, that in planning the civic education curriculum, in selecting textbooks, in advising publishers of textbooks, and so on, they would have been influenced by what they were taught in social studies education. One could assume, further, that the social studies curricula in teacher education programs may have been designed with the dominant paradigms in mind. But one can only speculate about these matters, as little systematic study has been done of the influence of political science theory on civic education in America.

What is clear, however, is that until recently civic education in the United States, and probably in other nations as well, has had the characteristics of the kind of civic education that is implied by the elitist paradigm. So while it cannot be shown that political theory has a significant impact on civic education in the United States, the two seem to be isomorphic.

Schools as Polities/Civil Orders

As we have already noted in the definition section of this essay, the term "polity" has sometimes been used to refer to a civil order and, as we also noted, a civil order is essentially a moral order. In what ways are schools moral orders?

Recognition of the moral life of schools goes back, in the modern literature, at least to Emile Durkheim (1961) who in *Moral Education* argues that morality does not have to be tied to a religion. In fact, morality's three key elements—a spirit of discipline, attachment to groups, and autonomy—are capable being taught without reference to religion.

Durkheim's book is one that makes a case for a certain type of moral education in the schools. More recent work, such as that by Jackson (1995), is less focused on making a case for a certain kind of moral education and more interested in describing the moral education that actually goes on in schools. They found little, if any, formal moral instruction in the classroom but a fair amount of rituals and ceremonies of a moral nature, visual displays with moral content, spontaneous interjections of moral commentary into ongoing classroom and school activities, and classroom practices and personal qualities of teachers that embody a moral outlook or stance. There is moral education, but it is usually not formal and instruction is not always explicit.

Probably the first thing that is important to remember in any discussion of civil order is that civil order is about the problem of social order, and that this problem breaks down into at least one important assumption and two important questions. The assumption is that human beings need and want a modicum of order in their lives. Without some order, daily life is impossible. The related two questions are: Granted the need for some order, how much order is necessary? How is it to be achieved?

The concept of "civil order" goes mainly to answer the second question, but it also bears on the first. A civil order is a social order that is self-directed and self-imposed. It comes from the inside-out as opposed to the outside-in. An order that derives from the outside-in is an order established and maintained through the use of strong external authorities such as a police force, surveillance, and so on. An inside-out order derives from people who voluntarily monitor their own behavior and practice self-control.

The mechanism by which a civil order is constructed and maintained is usually presumed to involve some type of "normative structure," a set of expectations about what is or is not "appropriate" behavior, and the continuous (one might even say "relentless") communication of these expectations throughout the society. These expectations may or may not be backed by some sort of collective approval or disapproval or informal sanctions. At some point in their evolution, the expectations may become codified into laws, at which time they leave the realm of civil society and enter into the realm of politics and policy.

Perhaps a good example of the above can be found in the evolution of anti-smoking norms and laws in the U.S. In the 1940s, smoking was considered to be a sign of sophistication and the prevailing norm then favored smoking. But in the 1960s and '70s, sentiments turned against it. At first the behavior was met with mild public disapproval, but this sentiment quickly grew until it became increasingly difficult to smoke in public places without being made uncomfortable. Ultimately, public disapproval became law.

From ancient times, moral education has been important to those who have taken education as a topic of interest. One can argue, in fact, that Plato's *Republic* is mainly a book about education, particularly moral education. Moral education was also an important theme for early sociologists, among others, Emile Durkheim, who even went so far as to claim that the central problem of society was moral education.

Schools as Rules by the Many in the Interest of the Whole

The third meaning of polity, rule of the many in the interest of the whole as opposed to rule of the many in their own interest, is at least implied in the critiques of American schooling made by liberals (Sizer, 1984, Levin, 1987) and those on the left (Aronowitz & Giroux, 1985; Apple, 1989; Apple & Beane, 1995; Bowles & Gintis, 1989). Neither group considers schools, as they are currently structured, to be either ruled by the many or to be ruled in the interest of the whole. But the liberal critique is more narrowly focused on schools while that of the left concerns the society as a whole. Perhaps one of the most visible components of the liberal agenda, though it has its conservative backers as well, is site-based management.

Rule of the Many: Site-Based Management

School-site management or school-based management has been one of the primary vehicles of school restructuring. With school-based management, the "many" has been mainly construed to mean teachers, parents, and community members, and these groups have been made part of the decision-making process through the invention of school-based councils. These councils operate by representation. Representatives from the teachers, parents, and community members are selected (in various ways) and given the power to make decisions.

As one might expect, there is an enormous range in the decision-making power given to those who represent parents, the community, and teachers on site-based decision councils, a range that is determined not only formally but also informally by the personalities of those involved and the general political culture of the school itself and the system within which it resides. At one extreme, as for example in Chicago, are councils whose members have power even to hire and fire principals. At the other are councils whose members do little more than sanction decisions already made by administrators.

Extreme or not, however, in most cases, school-based management does not increase students' control over their own learning. The central decisions of learning and instruction—What is to be learned? How? When? Where?—are beyond their control. Accordingly, compared to models of school reform that advocate more student control, site-based management is a conservative approach to the idea that the many should rule in the interest of the whole. The "many" generally does not include students, at least in any significant way.

Rule of the Many:
Essential and Accelerated Schools

Approaches that come closer to realizing the ideal of rule of the many in the interest of the whole are exemplified in the Essential Schools philosophy and in the assumptions behind accelerated schools (Sizer, 1984, Levin, 1987). But here, too, the critique focuses mainly on schools and does not constitute a critique of the political-economy as a whole, an approach more characteristic of the left.

One of the central propositions of the philosophy behind the Essential Schools and the Accelerated Schools programs is that students ought to have some meaningful control over their own learning. This can mean different things, but one of the key ideas is that the content of the curriculum what students learn should be determined in no small way by what students feel a need to know, and not simply by what adults say they should know. With this approach, teaching then becomes more like coaching, and the art of the craft is constructing a learning environment in which the things that students want to know are articulated with the things they need to know.

Another idea that seems central to the Essential Schools and Accelerated Schools approaches, and one that is also consistent with the third sense of polity, is the notion that learning in classrooms ought to be a process of discovering answers and solutions and learning by doing as opposed to a process of repeating what the textbooks (or teacher) says.

The Critique from the Left

The practical outcome of the leftist critique of American schooling often looks very much like the kind of schools described by both Sizer (1984) and Levin (1987). In fact, some of the schools that those on the left cite as being good examples of democratic schools are schools that have been structured in accord with the principles of the Essential Schools Coalition (Meier & Schwarz, 1995). But while sharing elements with its liberal counterpart, the critique on the left is much broader in scope. It is not simply a critique of schooling but a critique of the polity (in the modern sense of the term), the economy, and society in which the schools function. What is the jist of this critique?

Structures of Domination

A useful introduction to the left's critique of the modern American capitalist democratic society and polity can be found in Michel Foucault's (1972, 1973) metaphysical view of the fundamental nature of reality. For Foucault, reality is fundamentally disorder and chaos. Beneath the visible world, which often appears chaotic and random, he argues there is not an orderly world waiting to be discovered by way of science and scientific methods. The world is at bottom disorderly. Whatever order there is in the world is imposed on the disorder that is reality's true nature (al-

though, with this position, there is no true nature, because nature implies an order that is not there).

The implications of this proposition—that disorder, not order, is the most accurate description of reality—are many. Among the most important for present purposes is that whatever order there is in the world is imposed and arbitrary. But who imposes order on the world? It all depends, argues Foucault, but somebody does and usually, having done so, they have an interest in maintaining it.

Different orders have different sources. The order in which the modern world now finds itself is one that, in large measure, has grown out of the development of science, the historically peculiar ways of knowing associated with it, and the knowledge that has resulted from the application of these ways of knowing to politics and society. As a mode of rationality, as a way of thinking, feeling and doing, science constitutes an historically unique way of ordering the world in general and politics in particular—not only politics, but eventually economics and society as well.

Science does not exist in a vacuum but must exist and develop in some particular political, economic, and social context. Historically, the context in which modern science has developed, the Enlightenment context, was one of an increasingly capitalist economy, democratic polity, and bureaucratic society. The world we live in is an order produced and sustained by a peculiar combination of capitalism, democracy, bureaucracy, and science, a point at least implicit in Foucault and explicit in Max Weber's (1956, 1978) work.

The scientific-bureaucratic-capitalist democracy in which we live has as one of its distinguishing features the dominance of a particular form of reasoning and an unrelenting effort to apply it to all aspects of life. For Max Weber (1978), the defining element of this type of reasoning was its instrumentality. Its pervasive application produced bureaucracies or, as he described them, systems of imperative coordination. For Jacques Ellul (1964), the defining element in this type of reasoning was an excessive emphasis on technique and its application produced technological societies. For Karl Marx, it was the separation of the tools we need to do our work from the ownership of these tools, and all this separation implies, particularly for our sense of self and the meaning that our labor has for us under these conditions. For still others, the defining element was the belief that the private pursuit of gain would automatically result in the collective good. However described, though, the general point is that the peculiar form of reasoning associated with science, or at least as science has developed, is narrow in scope and only one mode of rationality of which humans are capable. Further, when carried to an extreme, the scientific mode of reasoning precludes other modes, particularly those having to do with morality and what is good.

The separation of questions of morality from questions of knowledge that is characteristic of science in scientific-bureaucratic-capitalist democracies, the familiar fact-value distinction, carries over into politics in the doctrines of liberalism wherein the state is denied any right to prioritize values and value systems, except those which are consistent with and supportive of capitalism. In the latter case, the ownership of private property and the relations of production for the formation of privately held capital are held to be sacred.

Those on the left argue further that as the (scientific-bureaucratic) capitalist democracies have developed in the late 20th century they involve a growing alliance between the state and the corporate sector. This alliance is supported by technological development in which corporations exercise complete control internally over their membership and increasing degrees of control externally. The latter occurs through their influence on government policy-making and policymakers, influence exercised directly through lobbies and lobbyists and indirectly through informal channels. Thus predatory capitalism (Chomsky, 1996) dominates polity, culture, and society.

Concomitant with the reemergence of predatory capitalism in late 20th century America (it existed as well in the latter part of the previous century, in the so-called Guilded age) has been an effort to rollback the gains made in labor and other aspects of social-welfare state in the first 60 or 70 years of the century. In education, this rollback or conservative restoration (Shor, 1992) has taken form, at least in part, in the literacy and excellence movements, the latest expressions of which are the emphasis on national standards, testing, and the privatization of education.

From the perspective of the left, one of the chief functions of schools is to reproduce work divisions and work relations (Carnoy & Levin, 1985). Two distinguishing characteristics of work in America are that it is hierarchical and fragmented. The workplace typically consists of large numbers of relatively low-paid workers at the bottom, a smaller number of middle-level managers who supervise them, and finally a few highly paid managers at the top. The work itself is fragmented. The jobs are divided up into minute and routinized functions.

Schools "reproduce" the hierarchy by the way in which they structure authority relations between teachers and students and between teachers and administrators. Those relations are "top-down." They also fragment knowledge into tiny and generally unconnected bits of information. Schools thus initiate students into the hierarchical relations of authority and fragmentation of tasks that they will encounter in the workplace. This hierarchy and fragmentation has a number of consequences, not the least of which is that the workers or students are ignorant of the larger production process and have little say about it. They also have little opportunity to gain satisfaction from having produced a whole product. The upshot of all this is that students and workers become "alienated" from their own work.

Among the major, though by no means the only, effects of "alienated labor" in classrooms are discipline problems. Discipline issues have been of increasing concern for the population in general and teachers in particular. When Americans are polled today and asked what they think are the most important issues in education, one-quarter of them cite "teaching children values and discipline" (*Education Week*, 1997: 4), the most-often cited issue. Our analysis of data from the General Social Survey, the annual survey of the American population conducted by the National Opinion Research Center (1996) indicates that concern for discipline and obedience has increased dramatically over the last three decades. In the 1970s, for example, when adult Americans were asked what they thought were the most important or among the three most important characteristics for children to have, 30.4 percent chose "being obedient." By the 1990s, 47.6 percent chose this characteristic, an increase of 56 percent. More interesting still, however, has been the change among teachers. In the 1970s, only 14.1 percent of American elementary and secondary teachers thought obedience was the most important or among the three most important qualities for children to have. By the 1990s, this figure had jumped to 36 percent, a 155 percent increase!

Most of the arguments for democratic schools start with a focus on students gaining more control over the work of learning, control that will presumably reduce their alienation and address the discipline problems that stem from it. Reports from observations of the few schools that can be identified as democratic, and in which students play a significant role in determining what they learn and how they learn it, say that they have fewer discipline problems.

Democratic Education and Critical Democracy

An oft-heard term from the left is "critical democracy" (Goodman, 1992). The critical-democracy argument is partly an argument about the nature of democracy itself and the kind of schooling required to promote and sustain a democracy broadly understood. The position taken by those who argue for "critical democracy" in education is very similar to the one taken by those who argue for participatory democracy (Rimmerman, 1997) in political science. This position is that "democracy," as it is now understood, is too narrowly construed. Democracy is more than a political arrangement. It refers also to a type of society, a living social arrangement (Dewey, 1916).

One of the major implications of the leftist critique of schooling and society, and of the critique offered by those who argue for participatory democracy, is that democratization depends upon a people's capacity to democratize, a capacity that is learned and not present at birth. Further, the attitudes, sentiments, tastes, skills, and habits of mind that democratization requires can only be learned through a critical, practical experience of democracy. Democracy has to be lived to be learned (Slater, 1994). Since most of our early lives are spent in schools, schools must become democratic places if we are to acquire the qualities that will enable us to promote and sustain a democratic society.

Summary and Conclusions: Reclaiming the Problem of Polity

Should schools be more polity-like, in the old sense of the term in which polity meant rule by the many in the interest of the whole? This question follows naturally from the questions we have explored in the preceding sections. But if our analysis suggests anything it is that this important normative question can hardly be considered in the ways in which mainstream discourse on school reform and educational administration has been structured. The problem of polity has been defined away. Dominated by economic and technocratic concerns, educational policy analysts and educational administrators usually have been unable to find ways in which they can advance the question as one worthy of serious consideration. Nor have politics of education researchers been able to help, for most have looked for their guidance to traditional political science which, by equating polity with political systems analysis, also has defined the problem away.

In the face of mounting public concern over the decline of civility in society, the increasingly obvious gap between traditional analyses of school reform and the leftist critique demands attention. Perhaps the problem of polity, especially the question of whether schools should be more polity-like, and the practical problems associated with making them so, could provide a much needed bridge between the two, not only in theory but in practice.

REFERENCES

Almond, G. & Verba, S. (1963). *The civic culture: Political attitudes and democracy in five nations.* Princeton, NJ: Princeton University Press.

Apple, M. (1989). *Teachers and Texts: A Political Economy of Class and Gender Relations in Education.* New York: Routledge.

Apple, M. & Beane, J. (Eds.) (1995). *Democratic Schools.* Alexandria, VA: ASCD.

Aronowitz, S. & Giroux, H. (1985). *Education under siege: The conservative, liberal, and radical debate over schooling.* Westport, CN: Bergen and Garvey.

Aronowitz, S. & Giroux, H. (1993). *Education still under siege.* Westport, CN: Bergen and Garvey.

Bellah, R. N., Madsen, R., Sullivan, W., Swidler, A. & Tipton, S. (1985) *Habits of the Heart: Individualism and Commitment in American Life.* New York: Harper and Row.

Blase, J. (1991). The micropolitical perspective, pp. 1–18 *The Politics of Life in Schools.* Newbury Park, CA: Sage Publications.

Borman, K. & Greenman, N. (1994). *Changing American education: Recapturing the past or inventing the future.* Albany, N. Y. Suny Press.

Bottomore, T. (1983) *Readings in Marxist Sociology.* New York: Oxford University Press.

Bowles, S. & Gintis, H. (1989). Can there be a liberal philosophy of education in a democratic society? In H. Giroux & P. McLaren, *Critical Pedagogy, the State, and Cultural Struggle.* Albany, NY: SUNY Press., pp. 24–31.

Carnoy, M. (1994). Political economy of educational production. In T. Husen & N. Postlethwaite (Eds.), *International Encyclopedia of Education.* Oxford, England: Elsevier Science, Ltd. pp. 4562–4568.

Carnoy, M. & Levin, H. (1985). *Schooling and Work in the Democratic State.* Stanford, CA: Stanford University Press.

Chomsky, N. (1996). *Class Warfare.* Monroe, Maine: Common Courage Press.

Cochran-Smith, M. (1991). Learning to teach against the grain. *Harvard Educational Review* 61:279–309.

Coleman, J. (1988). Social capital in the creation of human capital. *American Journal of Sociology.* 94: S95–S120

Cuban, L. (1990). Reforming again, again and again. *Educational Researcher* 19:39–49.

Dahl, R. (1963). *Modern political analysis.* Englewood Cliffs, NJ: Prentice Hall.

Dewey, J. (1916). *Democracy and Education.* New York: Macmillan.

Durkheim, E. (1951). *Suicide.* Glencoe, IL: Free Press.

Durkheim, E. (1961). *Moral Education.* New York: Free Press.

Easton, D. (1985). *A Systems Analysis of Political Life.* New York: Wiley.

Education Week. (1997). Oct. 12, Vol. 4.

Ellul, J. (1964). *The Technological Society.* New York: Knopf.

Foley, M. & Edwards, B. (July, 1986). The paradox of civil society. *Journal of Democracy.* Vol. 7, No. 3.

Foucault, M. (1972). *The Archeology of Knowledge.* New York: Pantheon Books.

Foucault, M. (1973). *The Order of Things: An Archeology of the Human Sciences.* New York: Vintage Books.

Foucault, M. (1978). *The History of Sexuality.* New York: Pantheon Books.

Goodlad, J. I. (1997, September 17). On shifting reform debate from utility to humanity. *Education Week*, p. 37.

Goodman, J. (1992). *Elementary Schooling for Critical Democracy.* Albany, NY: SUNY Press.

Jackson, P. (1995). *The Moral Life of Schools.* San Francisco: Jossey Bass.

Kahne, J. (1994, fall). Democratic communities, equity, and excellence: A Deweyan reframing of educational policy analysis. *Educational Evaluation and Policy Analysis*, 16, 3, 233–248.

Kahne, J. (1996). *Reframing educational policy: Democracy, community, and the individual.* New York: Teachers College Press.

Levin, H. (1987). Accelerated schools for disadvantaged students. *Educational Leadership.* 45:19–21.

MacIntyre, A. (1984). *After Virtue.* Notre Dame, IN: University of Notre Dame Press.

MacIntyre, A. (1987) The idea of an educated public. In G. Haydon (Ed.), *Education and Values: The Richard Peters Lectures.* London: University of London, pp. 15–36.

Malen, B. (1994.) The micropolitics of education: mapping the multiple dimensions of power relations in school polities. *Politics of Education Association Yearbook.* Taylor & Francis, Ltd. 147–167.

March, J. (1976). *Ambiguity and Choice in Organizations.* Bergen, Norway: Universitetsforlaget.

Marshall, C. & Anderson, G. (1994). Rethinking the public and private spheres: feminist and cultural studies perspectives on the politics of education. *Politics of Education Association Yearbook*, pp. 169–182.

Maxcy, S. (1995). *Democracy, Chaos, and the New School Order.* Thousand Oaks, CA: Corwin Press.

Meier, D. & Schwarz, P. (1995). Central Park East secondary school: The hard part is making it happen. In Michael Apple & James Beane (Eds.) *Democratic Schools.* Alexandria, VA: ASCD. pp. 26–40.

Mitchell, D., Boyd, W., Cooper, B., Malen, B. & Marshall, C. (1994). Domain V: Policy and Political Studies Taxonomy and Overview. In Wayne Hoy (Ed.) *The UCEA Document Base.* New York: McGraw-Hill.

National Opinion Research Center (1996). *General Social Surveys 1972–1996.* Chicago, IL: National Opinion Research Center.

Orru, M. (1987). *Anomie: History and Meanings*. Boston, MA: Allen and Unwin.

Putnam, R. (1995). Bowling Alone. *Journal of Democracy*. 6:65–78

Rimmerman, C. (1997). *The New Citizenship*. Boulder, CO: Westview Press.

Shor, I. (1992). *Culture Wars*. Chicago: University of Chicago Press.

Sizer, T. (1984). *Horace's Compromise: The Dilemma of the American High School*. Boston: Houghton Mifflin Company.

Slater, R. (1994). Symbolic educational leadership and democracy in America. *Educational Administration Quarterly* 30:97–101.

Slavin, R. (1994). Cooperative learning. In T. Husen & N. Postlethwaite (Eds.), *International Encyclopedia of Education*, 2nd ed. Oxford, England: Elsevier Science Ltd., pp. 1094–1099.

Tocqueville, A. (1969). *Democracy in America*. Garden City, NY: Doubleday, Anchor Books.

Weber, M. (1956). *Economy and Society*. Glencoe, IL: Free Press.

Weber, M. (1978). *Max Weber: Selections in Translation*. Edited and Translated by S. Runciman. Cambridge, England: Cambridge University Press.

Wimpelberg, R. (1997). Superintending: The undeniable politics and indefinite effects of school district leadership. *American Journal of Education* 105:319–345.

Wirt, F. (Ed.) (1975). *The polity of the school: New research in educational politics*. Lexington, MA: D. C. Heath.

Wirt, F. & Kirst, M. (1992). *Schools in Conflict*. Berkeley, CA: McCutchan Publishing Corp.

CHAPTER 16

Administration and Community: Considering Challenges, Exploring Possibilities

Lynn G. Beck and William Foster

In a thoughtful essay on alienation, Andrew Oldenquist (1991) notes that the word "'community' is . . . prone to promiscuous use" (p. 95) and calls for greater analysis of what this term means in various contexts. In his view, persons seeking to cultivate community in particular settings and those engaging in research on this phenomenon must clarify the assumptions driving their work. Others share Oldenquist's view. Frank Kirkpatrick (1986), for example, in *Community: A Trinity of Models* writes:

> Because of its extraordinarily broad application, "community" covers a number of groups, to some of which each of us probably belongs. We live in a community, perhaps work in another community, belong to a professional community, worship in still another community, and support a whole host of still more communities by virtue of our taxes, citizenship, and voluntary membership. Because of this enormous flexibility in the word "community," we often become either confused by its use or, more likely, so inured to hearing it used in a multitude of ways that it eventually collapses into a meaningless term evoked more for rhetorical or emotional reasons than for illumination or explanation. (p. 2)

Like Oldenquist, he calls upon persons using this term to clarify their interpretations of its meaning.

The words of Kirkpatrick (1986) and Oldenquist (1991) challenge us as we undertake an analysis of theoretical and empirical work on educational communities and of its implications for administrators, for their statements remind us that community is all too often a murky concept —a catch-all word used by persons attempting to describe or justify a wide range of practices and values. This reality suggests the possibility that researchers have undertaken the study of school communities operating within a number of different conceptual frameworks—something that can make any analysis of this research challenging. Further, the "promiscuous use" of the word community (Oldenquist, 1991, p. 95) has the potential to derail productive discussions of the meaning of this phenomenon in specific school settings for students, parents, teachers, administrators, and others may be talking about and even striving for community, but their varied understandings of this terms may be driving them in very different directions.

We have elected to respond to the challenge of discussing educational community and its implications for educational leaders by ordering this chapter in the following way. In the first section, we begin with an analysis of two widespread ways of understanding community. One of these, frequently labeled the "liberal" view, sees social systems as settings that ideally allow individuals maximum autonomy to determine the courses of their lives. The second of these, often called "communitarian," emphasizes, not independent individuals, but rather the primacy of communities in and for life. This way of thinking is less focused on the preservation of rights and more concerned with the fulfilling of obligations or responsibilities. (Several authors offer helpful discussions of these views including Barber, 1992; Etzioni, 1993; Feinberg, 1995; Kirkpatrick, 1986; Noddings, 1996; and Theobald & Dinkelman, 1995). In the sections devoted to this analysis, we underscore some of the assumptions underlying both views and highlight their positive and negative implications. After considering liberal and communitarian models as more of less "pure types," we conclude with a brief discussion of some authors who have expressed concerns about the extremes of both liberalism and communitarianism and discuss models of community that draw from the strengths of both perspectives.

In the second section of this paper, we turn our attention to the concept of community as it relates to educational settings. We begin this section with an overview of the history of schooling in the United States, paying special attention to beliefs about the role of schools in society and to the structures of and practices within educational settings. Our reading of history suggests that widely held notions of educational purpose have been influenced by the communitarian ideas that schools exist to support society and to meet its needs for economically productive citizens. In contrast, we contend that the bureaucratic structures of schooling have been shaped primarily by liberal/individualist concepts that stress the need to control persons through the establishment and enforcement of contracts. We suggest that policy makers, administrators, teachers, and the general public all too often have not examined the assumptions under which they are operating and that at least some of the current pathologies of schooling can be traced to unquestioning acceptance of forms and norms of schooling that may not be useful or appropriate.[1] We believe that much of the research focusing on the creation and cultivation of a spirit of community in and around educational settings has emerged as scholars have recognized that education has lost its center as it has attempted to respond to demands from many quarters. As we continue our analysis of community and educational settings, we review some of the work that is being done in this area, using a framework suggested by Merz and Furman (1997) to order our discussion. That is, we begin by considering work that has focused on the sense or spirit of community *within* schools and then turn our attention to research on efforts to establish communal links *between* schools and their larger environs.

We conclude the chapter by raising some concerns that in our view should be attended to by administrators to ensure that efforts to "create community" really move schools toward being developmentally sound places where the best impulses of liberalism and communitarianism are realized. We then offer thoughts about ways educational leaders might begin to engage in the important task of "administering community" (Starratt, 1994) in the best sense of the word.

Understanding Community: Two Influential Views

In an issue of the *Peabody Journal of Education* (1995) devoted to "Education and the Liberal Communitarian Debate," editors Paul Theobald and Dale Snauwert with contributors including Todd Dinkelman, Jeanne M. Con-

nell, Walter Feinberg, Susan F. Semel, Alan R. Sadovnik, Michael N. Johnson, and Vicky Newman analyze the "tensions between individuality and communalism" (Snauwert & Theobald, p. 1). The premise underlying the work of these authors is that there exists

> a persistent debate in the history of political and educational philosophy between the imperatives of individuality and those of community [and that] this debate reflects the fundamental tension between the needs, desires, rights, and duties of the individual qua individual and those of the individual as member of a community. (p.1)

Other scholars agree with this premise and in various ways have explored the philosophical underpinnings and practical outworkings of liberal/individualist and communitarian views. Frank Kirkpatrick, for example, discusses these two views in terms of their philosophical underpinnings and their ethical implications. He suggests that the former is essentially an "atomistic" (p. 13) view, one that posits that individuals are fundamentally independent and "self-directing [and enter] into contracts with others for self-protection" (p.17). Within this model, adherence to the terms of the contract provides the contours for ethical behavior. In contrast, the latter way of thinking sees the social system, organized hierarchically into a single "organism" (p. 64), as fundamental reality with individuals acting morally as they participate in and support this "totality" (p. 65).[2] In this section, we consider the intellectual traditions that have helped to shape two influential views.

Liberal/Individualist Perspective on Community

The conceptual underpinnings of a liberal/individualist perspective on community can be clustered under two broad themes. The first relates to the nature of persons. Theories, models, policies, laws, and organizational structures developed according to a liberal notion of human association tend to share four assumptions about human nature. Liberal/individualists tend to:

(a) believe that individuals are naturally and fundamentally independent;

(b) assume that they also are self-interested and naturally antagonistic to other self-interested persons;

(c) claim that each person has an inherent right to self-determination—that he or she deserves the opportunity to pursue things that have the potential to contribute to happiness, material prosperity, health, and the like; and

(d) expect that persons are capable of rational choice and that they are motivated to exercise this capability in order to benefit themselves.

The second set of premises linked to an individualist model relates to the nature of links among these rational, self-interested individuals. Essentially, thinkers within this vein

(a) assume that human interaction is something of a necessary evil—not pleasant but essential for individuals seeking to satisfy desires;
(b) believe that the fact that humans must interact with others necessitates a rational, overarching system to guide interactions and to ensure maximum freedom and minimal harm to persons; and
(c) see a liberal state (and its parallels in other social systems)—one that regulates persons impartially according to the dictates of laws and contracts agreed upon by those affected by them—as an ideal form of community.

In the paragraphs that follow, we provide a brief discussion of each of these and consider seminal thinkers who have articulated these assumptions.

Liberal/Individualist Assumptions Regarding Human Nature

Foundational to the liberal/individualist tradition is the assumption that the most basic unit of reality is the autonomous individual. Frank Kirkpatrick (1986) offers a helpful discussion of the history of this idea. While acknowledging that its roots can be traced as far back as the Sophists in ancient Greece, he focuses his discussion on more recent articulations of this notion. Drawing upon the writings of Otto Gierke (1934) and Dorothea Krook (1959), he argues that the clearest expression of the ideal of the autonomous individual can be found in the work of Thomas Hobbes. For Hobbes, a mathematician committed to Newtonian science, "reality was essentially composed of discrete atomic 'bits' of matter" (Kirkpatrick, p.19). Following this precept, Hobbes set out to "understand the true or essential nature of persons by examining (or imagining) it in a state of nature" (p.19). This, for him, required considering persons as single individuals before they had entered into association with others. Thus Hobbes, utilizing a geometric approach in ways consistent with his understanding of science, determined that the isolated individual represented fundamental or foundational reality.

For Hobbes, reality was "composed exclusively of discrete or mutually disconnected particular things" (Krook, 1959, p.100). This conception applied to both physical and metaphysical realms and meant, among other things, that there existed no natural connection among people. There was "no pleasure, but on the contrary a great deal of grief in keeping company" (Hobbes, 1962, p.99). This premise led quite easily to the conclusion that, in their most basic state, each individual is fundamentally and entirely self-interested and naturally antagonistic to every other being.

Hobbes believ[ed] we are so constituted by nature that we will "endeavor to destroy or subdue on another" because others will always stand ready to "dispossess and deprive" us of the fruits of our labor, as well as of our lives and liberties. From this "diffidence we feel toward each other" we seek to "master the persons of all men" till we see their power reduced enough to no longer threaten us." (Kirkpatrick, 1986, p. 20, quoting Hobbes, 1962, p. 99)

According to Hobbes, "in the state of nature . . . persons are equal" (Kirkpatrick, 1986, p,17). This is not, however, equality in terms of dignity or intrinsic value. Rather, Hobbes argued that all persons have an equal right to pursue that which they desire. "Naturally every man has a right to everything" (Hobbes, 1962, p.103). Further, he believed that persons would exercise that right to the greatest extent possible—without regard to the needs or concerns of others. The fact that persons set out to acquire material things, power, and status and to deprive others of the same was, for Hobbes, neither "sinful [n]or immoral" (Kirkpatrick, 1986, p.20). It was simply descriptive of a natural state. This view set the stage for the development of a moral code that recognized liberty as a supreme virtue. Within such a code, the ethical guidelines governing human associations had as their goal the provision of maximal levels freedom to each individual "to do what he would" (p. 103). Kirkpatrick points out that this assumption about the ideal form of human relationship "links logically with a notion of individual solitariness and defensiveness against others." He continues:

> One could define liberty with an emphasis upon the power to embrace others rather than the power to keep others at bay. But for Hobbes and those who would follow him down the path of possessive individualism, liberty is the power and right to possess whatever one can secure and hold. (p. 21)

Within a Hobbesian perspective, solitary persons desire and deserve to possess and control persons and things. They are not, however, complete slaves of their instincts and impulses. Indeed, as Theobald and Dinkelman (1995) point out, the tradition underlying a liberal notion of community views individuals as rational beings, capable of using cognition to optimize their chances of happiness and success.

Liberal/Individualist Conceptions of Structures for Human Interaction

The simple realities of life in crowded places, coupled with the fact that both self-interest and preservation require individuals to interact with one another, make association among humans necessary. Liberal/individualist thinkers believe humans cope with this necessity by acting rationally and constructing rules for living together. Indeed, most thinkers who view persons as independent, self-interested entities agree that some overarching structure must be constructed to provide a framework for reasonable interaction. Hobbes (1962) believed that such a system would need to be grand and encompassing—a leviathan—and that it could and should be established by persons voluntarily agreeing to limit their rights. He also, though, argued that these agreements needed to include provisions for "coercive power to compel men equally to the performance of their covenants by the terror of some punishment, greater than the benefit they expect by the breach of their covenant" (p. 113). Others take a more positive view of the way a liberal state functions. Adam Smith (1937), for example, suggested that a framework, such as a one provided by a market society, not only allowed persons to pursue their individual self-interests but also enabled them to act in ways that were actually beneficial to all involved parties.

Regardless of whether they perceive the larger social structure as a leviathan created to enforce human agreements or as a marketplace that provides individuals with opportunities for promoting themselves and simultaneously benefitting others, most advocates of a liberal/individualist model of interaction look to contracts, entered into by reasoning persons, as a vehicle for ordering human behavior. Selznick's (1992) discussion of the contemporary meaning of contracts is helpful in that it underscores the way these agreements assume minimal attachment and regulated involvement among consenting parties. Furthermore, Selznick's definition reminds us that contractual relationships require a moral commitment that is limited to abiding by the terms of the agreement or living with the consequences of noncompliance. He writes:

> The modern commercial contract is marked by limited commitment. Terms and conditions are specified closely, and the cost of nonperformance is calculable. Furthermore, with some exceptions, the moral or legal obligation is not necessarily to *fulfill* the agreement, but only to make good the losses that may be incurred in the case of an unjustified breach. (p.479)

Non-commercial contracts, even though they differ in some ways from those described by Selznick, are similar in that they demand little in the way of serious moral engagement. Decisions and behaviors in a contractual state are specified in laws, precepts, rules, and policies. Establishing these guidelines may require some ethical deliberation, but abiding by them, for the most part, demands a rather straightforward kind of obedience.

Communitarian Perspectives on Community

For the liberal/individualist thinker, the ontological primacy of each person provides a starting point for constructing ideas about ideal forms of human association. For this person, the social world can best be understood as a kind of "mechanic aggregate" (Tonnies, 1957, p. 35) of "free individuals contracting together" (Kirkpatrick, 1986, pp. 46–47, commenting specifically on Nozick, 1974). In contrast, the communitarian begins with a different assumption about the fundamental unit of reality. For her or him, "the organic relation between persons is more basic and ultimately more natural" (Kirkpatrick, p. 71, commenting on Tonnies, 1957) than the independent individual. From this starting point, communitarians build their ideas on a certain set of assumptions. These beliefs can be clustered under the same two themes presented in the previous discussion of liberal/individualist views. That is, communitarians hold certain assumptions about the nature of persons and, building on these, about the ideal forms of association. In regard to the former, the following ideas constitute the conceptual underpinnings of this perspective. In contrast to liberal/individualistic views, communitarians:

(a) hold that persons are, by nature, social;
(b) tend to believe that persons do possess some rights to self-determination and to the pursuit of personal happiness, material prosperity, health, and the like, but they stress that they are also responsible for protecting and pursuing the well-being of others; and
(c) believe that persons, not only are capable of "pro-social" behaviors and attitudes (altruism, generosity, cooperation), but that they also naturally exhibit these behaviors and attitudes within committed relationships.[3]

These assumptions lead quite naturally into a set of premises about the context that best supports the development of persons and the cultivation of healthy and meaningful relationships. Essentially, scholars articulating a communitarian view:

(a) assert that communities where persons "experience a sense of membership, influence members of the group, have personal needs fulfilled, and share a psychologically and personally satisfying connection with other people" (McMillan, 1976) provide ideal contexts for the flourishing of persons as individuals and within relationships;
(b) depending upon their particular theories of community, credit different factors (kinship, locale, common values, and shared history and tradition) with providing the impetus for the creation and maintenance of communities; and
(c) assume that the well-being of individuals and of their immediate relationships is linked to the health of the community; therefore, communitarians believe that persons have an obligation to pursue the health or well-being of the larger system and of its inhabitants.

Communitarian Assumptions About Human Nature

As noted above, persons embracing a liberal vision of community tend to agree that individuals are the fundamental building blocks of social reality, that human beings are capable of reason, that they possess intrinsic rights to liberty and self-determination, and that social systems should be rationally constructed to protect individual rights. However, scholars within this tradition disagree about the degree to which the pursuit of the rights of any individual clashes with the interests of others. Some (e.g., Hobbes, 1962) presume fundamental hostility among persons. Others (e.g., Smith, 1937) suggest that a benevolent system can exist that allows for the cultivation of multiple self-interests and provides for maximum autonomy for each individual. Embedded in this disagreement are a range of views about human nature. Hobbes and those who follow him assume fundamental selfishness and the possession of drives that, if unchecked, lead to "war of everyone against everyone" (p. 189). Smith, Locke, and others see individuals as more naturally amiable, able, and willing to enter into social contracts that benefit all persons. Most contemporary liberal thinkers within the western world seem to agree with the second group of scholars in that they imagine that reasonableness and a willingness to enter into social and political arrangements characterize human beings.

In a similar manner, within the communitarian tradition, agreement exists about certain fundamental ideas and a range of views about fundamental human nature. Communitarian thought is typically built on the belief that the social collectivity is the fundamental unit of reality—that in a natural state, persons are linked to one another. Communitarians differ, however, in their beliefs about the nature of those persons. Some (Hegel, 1975, 1967; Marx, 1967) posit that individual life is meaningful only as it relates to a larger social organism—that humans are parts of some larger whole and that this reality endues life with value. Others (Bellah, *et al.*, 1985; Etzioni, 1993; MacIntyre, 1981; Taylor, 1989) assert that persons are *both* autonomous, capable of reason and choice, *and* fundamentally relational. This perspective does not hold that human identity or value depends upon affiliation with others. However, it does hold that persons are drawn to relationships and that their happiness and well-being depend upon the ability to construct satisfactory connections with others. In paragraphs that follow, we consider some of the scholars who have contributed to these views of human nature.

Hegel (1975, 1967) and Marx (1967) propose the existence of a teleological impulse within human beings, driving persons toward community. In the view of these thinkers, isolation and alienation are typical, but not "normal" states. For both, full and genuine life is realized only when persons acknowledge their organic relationship to a social collectivity—to "a community that func-

tions as a fuller, more substantial embodiment than the individual" (Taylor, 1979, p. 85). To be sure, Hegel and Marx differ significantly in their vision of this organic community, and these differences are linked to their assumptions about the qualities of its members. In the first sentence of his *The Philosophy of Freedom* (1956), Hegel suggests that the ideal community is one where persons experience "the consciousness of [their inherent] freedom" (quoted in Singer, 1995, p. 340), and he argues that such a state can be attained only as a person realizes his profound spiritual connection with others. In Kirkpatrick's (1986) words, Hegel holds "the view that only as one identifies himself with a larger, more inclusive whole does he gain in [the experience of] freedom" (p. 67). For Hegel, the connections among persons that mattered are not—first and foremost—tangible, physical ones; rather, they are metaphysical and the central and defining qualities of persons are their abilities to apprehend fundamental reality about themselves and to act upon their awareness by consciously moving toward a state where they become "one with others so that there is no opposition of will" (Kirkpatrick, p. 68).

Marx, greatly influenced by Hegelian thought, agrees that individuals experience full personhood only in relationships with others. Indeed, he states, "the human essence is not abstraction inherent in each single individual. In its reality it is the ensemble of the social relations" (Marx, 1967, p. 71). He differs, however, from his mentor in that he focuses, not on a metaphysical community, but rather on one built on real, concrete social and political relationships that allow the true nature of persons to emerge and flourish. For Marx, human nature resides in "real, living, particular individuals" (Marx, 1977, p. 115). It is inextricably linked to physical and material needs of people, especially to meaningful, productive work. As Selznick (1992) points out:

> For Marx . . . people are innately active and purposeful; therefore, they cannot flourish without creative, self-fulfilling work. The good life for humans is not parasitic of self-absorbed; it requires productive participation in all aspects of social life. (p.137)

Marx's ideal community is not "a new philosophical interpretation of life but a new form of earthly existence, a new society in which the material conditions for a fulfilling human life would no longer be lacking" (Wood, 1995, p. 525). In spite of differences in their perspective, Hegel and Marx share a belief that differs dramatically from the liberal viewpoint that sees the independent individual as the basic unit of reality, for these thinkers and those influenced by them hold that functional, organic communities have a kind of ontological reality that drives, defines, and gives meaning to human life.

The idea that persons are naturally social is a starting point for contemporary communitarian thought. It does not, however, capture entirely the assumptions of everyone who falls into this camp. As Selznick (1992) reminds us, a theory that persons are predisposed to need and seek relationships is descriptive but not normative. It does not specify the ideal qualities of and conditions for interactions that promote "moral well-being" (p.120) and it, thus, implies that *human nature has no content* (p.134, emphasis in the original)—that there is no ethical dimension to life. Many contemporary communitarians disavow this neutral position and embrace a presumption that persons are agents, inherently social, but able to choose if and how to engage in relationships.

Some communitarians assert that the moral challenge facing persons is to balance an ethic of rights with one of responsibilities. They suggest that the liberal perspective which sees humans as naturally possessing rights to self-determination and to equality in the pursuit of their own interests ignores the fact that humans are also inherently responsible for protecting and even pursuing the welfare of others. Feinberg (1995), drawing upon the work of Alisdair MacIntyre (1981), discusses the differences between the liberal/individualistic perspective and communitarianism on this issue:

> Individualism, according to the communitarian, mistakenly assumes that rights somehow belong to individual people independent of their community, when in fact it is the traditions of the community itself that determine what will count as legitimate rights and obligations . . . [E]ach of us has the obligations we do because of he roles that we occupy within a communal tradition. (p. 37)

Etzioni (1993) concurs and nicely summarizes this perspective when he argues that defining humans as possessors of intrinsic rights without recognizing that they also possess intrinsic responsibilities is both "unethical and illogical" (p.9), or as he succinctly states, "rights presume responsibilities" (p.9). Thus a central tenet of much contemporary communitarian thought is that personhood brings with it inherent obligations to others and natural impulses to act in ways consonant with these obligations.

Community as the Ideal Context for Human Relationships

Communitarians insist that systems of social relationships are natural and ideal and believe that humans exist and flourish only within the context of communities. To support this argument, they often refer to the feelings of isolation and alienation and to deep and profound losses of security and self-esteem experienced by persons operating within a climate of hyper-individualism. Numerous scholars have written articulately about these losses, often using empirical evidence to support their claims. Andrew Old-

enquist (1991), for example, writes of a pervasive and destructive sense of alienation experienced by persons who do not feel that they belong within some community. Keniston (1965) concurs noting that "alienation, estrangement, disaffection, anomie, withdrawal, disengagement, separation, non-involvement, apathy, indifference, and neutralism" (p. 3) characterize the lives of persons he studied who feel disconnected from others and from society. Similar notions are proffered by Bellah, Madsen, Sullivan, Swidler, and Tipton (1985) who noted "a sense of fragmentariness" (p. 277) in a number of individuals whose lives are "in a profound sense individualistic" (p. 142).

As alluded to in the preceding section, although communitarians generally agree that social systems fostering relationships are natural and essential for life, they differ in their views about the structures of such systems and about the forces that create them. They do, however, tend to be united in the belief that social contracts are unlikely to create healthy viable communities. These voluntary agreements, in their view, are too tenuous to promote the kinds of bonds needed for healthy persons and relationships. Rather, communitarians assert that a range of factors including common traditions, proximity, shared values, and a commitment to care provide the glue that holds communities together.

As noted above, Hegel (1967) and Marx (1977) are among those who assert that participation in some social organism is driven by natural human impulses; they contend that the individual's experience of "reality is fulfilled only in and through [their identification with] the whole" (Kirkpatrick, 1987, p. 67). In contrast, Alisdair MacIntyre, in *After Virtue* (1981) and *Whose Justice? Which Rationality?* (1988), asserts that shared traditions form the basis of community and that they provide cultural and behavioral norms and the moral frameworks that sustain them. Years earlier Ferdinand Tonnies (1957) offered a similar perspective when he suggested that kinship, proximity, and similar interests form the basis of organic communities, social networks whose members are kept "together as members of a totality" by "reciprocal, binding sentiment[s]" (p. 47).

For MacIntyre (1981, 1988) and Tonnies (1957), community is, in large measure, determined by historical and geographic realities. A number of other scholars including Dokecki (1995), Kirkpatrick (1986), and Macmurray (1961) argue that true communities can be developed intentionally as persons commit to care for one another. Essentially each of these thinkers sees community as a kind of ethical imperative and asserts that the commitments of persons to act in ways that honor and support the growth, development, health, and happiness of self and others provide the foundation for "the creation and support of a *competent and caring society*" (Hobbs, Dokecki, Hoover-Dempsey, Moroney, Shane, &Weeks, 1984, p. 4). Drawing heavily upon the ideas of John Macmurray, Dokecki (1995) and

Kirkpatrick (1986) advocate a form of social interaction that fosters "other-oriented mode[s] of relationship" (Kirkpatrick, p. 186). For these scholars, only this model of community allows for a "person's full potential [to be] exercised and enjoyed" (p. 186).

Synthesizing Liberalism and Communitarianism: Alternative Conceptions of Community

Dokecki (1995), Kirkpatrick (1986), Macmurray (1961), and Noddings (1996) all argue that a vision of community that begins *either* with the assumption that the independent individual is the fundamental unit of reality *or* with the counter notion that individuals find "their fulfillment . . . their very essence, their telos, or final end . . . all spiritual reality . . . only through the state" (Kirkpatrick, p. 69, quoting Taylor, 1979, p. 86) misses several points. The first is that each human is a complete being, deserving of dignity, respect, and the full expression of the "inalienable rights" that attend personhood. The second is that persons are fundamentally relational, and the third is that the best context for their growth and development is a caring and just community. Dokecki, Kirkpatrick, Macmurray, and Noddings contend that such communities are grounded in and reflected by deep and personal caring relationships between and among persons . Kirkpatrick suggests that they both foster and are fostered by "friendship, fellowship, mutuality, and love" (p.186). Noddings, in turn, notes that "the community [relationship] is based on responsibility in the form of attentive and preservative love, and one of its beginnings can be found in the maternal relation" (p. 262). They call upon persons "to create and maintain community and friendship through practical reasoning and [to] operate according to a morality of love and friendship to achieve the community of persons in relation" (Dokecki, 1995, p. 124).

In many ways, the views of community advocated by Dokecki, (1995), Kirkpatrick (1986), and Macmurray (1961) draw from both liberal and communitarian perspectives. In framing their ideas, these scholars accept the integrity of the individual advocated by liberalism and the necessity of committed relationships and of communities that support them that is so central to communitarian views. They argue that extreme liberal and communitarians viewpoints have an inadequate view of humans, ignoring the realities that persons are simultaneously independent and related in fundamental ways. These authors also contend that persons are not merely individuals capable of reasonably seeking ways to construct functional relationships but that they are also moral agents, capable of giving and receiving love and respect.

Bellah and his colleagues (1985, 1991), Feinberg (1995), and Selznick (1992) concur that the creation of a "good society" or a "moral commonwealth," one that encourages civil interaction among "people in different communities . . . people who occupy positions in many communities . . . and those who belong to no special community," (Feinberg, p. 54) is an ethical imperative. They focus their discussions on what this means in the public sphere. Bellah and his co-authors call for consideration and appropriation of "the cultural traditions and practices that, without destroying individuality, serve to limit and restrain the destructive side of individualism and provide alternative models for how Americans might live" (1987, p. viii). In one sense, they make an argument similar to MacIntyre's by proposing that "a morally coherent [social] life" (p. vi) can occur within a "'community of memory,' one that does not forget its past" (p. 153). These authors, however, also extend MacIntyre's ideas in that they assert that "an adequate vision of the public good" (p. 250), one capable of sustaining a vital "national community" (p. 249), requires a recognition and acceptance of values that support mutual care, respect, and support. Thus they advocate remembering and celebrating particular ethical traditions that they view as foundational to a healthy sense of a public national community.

When Bellah and his colleagues (1985) call for a reappropriation of moral traditions that emphasize care, commitment, respect, and support among persons, they are not demanding a repudiation of all dimensions of liberal and individualistic thought. Rather, they "are engaged in an effort to mitigate and reverse the damage" (p. 284) created by an excessive, alienating sense of individualism. In a similar way, Feinberg (1995) and Selznick (1992) argue for a kind of "reconciliation between liberalism and communitarianism" (Feinberg, p. 54). For Feinberg, such a reconciliation involves linking the "standards of the liberal" that allow for a plurality of viewpoints with the "goals of communitarians" that include a press for mutual respect and support. Such a mingling, he suggests, would "provide the conditions in which communities can thrive" (p. 55). Selznick (1992), in great detail, discusses "a point of view [he calls] 'communitarian liberalism'" (p. xi). This perspective is one that stresses "diversity and pluralism as well as social integration" (p. xi). It also, in his view, "must embrace the idea of a common good based on objective criteria of personal and social well-being" (p. xi). Selznick suggests that a true community will be "undergirded by two norms, two sources of moral integration . . . civility and piety" (p. 387), for, he contends:

> Civility governs diversity, protects autonomy, and upholds toleration; piety expresses devotion and demands integration. The norms or civility are impersonal, rational, and inclusive, whereas piety is personal, passionate, and particularist. (p. 387)

Selznick avers that these norms, if separated, have the potential to drive culture, policies, and behaviors in very different directions, but he argues that their reconciliation can provide a powerful foundation for a public, national community. In describing such a community, Selznick "invoke[s] two old but not obsolete ideas: *covenant* and *commonwealth*" (p. 477). These words denote a type of social and political arrangement that is based upon a commitment among citizens both to certain ideals and to one another. One of the ideals driving a moral commonwealth would be a robust notion of the common good. Selznick calls upon persons to think of this phenomenon as something "profoundly systemic, not reducible to individual interests or attributes" (p. 537). This shared good would create the conditions for persons to flourish as morally competent individuals, able and willing to honor and support others and to receive care and respect.

All the authors cited above, joined by others including Dokecki (1995), Hobbs and his colleagues (1984), Kirkpatrick (1986), MacIntyre (1981, 1988), and Macmurray (1961), call for the creation of communities that are "heterocentric (not egocentric or individualistic) . . . based on the positive emotion of love (not fear), entail[ing] personal (not impersonal) social relations . . . [and seeking] the interests of the other (not exclusively the self)" (Dokecki, p. 124). In the view of these scholars, such social systems "promote human development" (Hobbs, *et al.*, p. 41). Within these communities, "there would be no fear of social catastrophe or hope of inordinate reward" (Bellah *et al.*, p. 289), and "friendship, fellowship, love, and mutuality" (Kirkpatrick, p. 186) would flourish.

Schools and the Concept of Community

At the turn of the century, John Dewey in *The School and Society* (1900/1990) argued that schools should embody the kind of community described in the preceding section. In his view, only a place that combined the best aspects of classic liberalism and communitarianism or, in Dewey's words, of "individualism and socialism" (p. 7), could prepare persons to live within and to maintain a healthy, democratic society. However, as Lagerman (1989) and Jackson (1990) point out, Dewey's vision was relatively uninfluential throughout much of the twentieth century. Indeed, a resurgence of interest in Dewey *and* his concept of community as it relates to schooling has emerged in educational circles only recently.

We begin this section by tracing views about community as they have unfolded in American education, for we contend that the current ideas about this topic need to be considered in light of historical views about the social organization of schools and about the relationships between educational institutions and the larger society. We believe that even a cursory glance at educational history reveals that schools, as communities, have in some ways been quite

consistent with the liberal vision. They have also, though, especially in regard to prevailing beliefs about education's purpose, seemed to operate within a communitarian framework. Rarely have institutions or systems sought to draw these two perspectives together to create vital, generative places of growth for students, teachers, families, and communities.

After a discussion of history, we look at some recent and current work on educational community—work that, in some ways, suggests that educational leaders are beginning to strive to create institutions where individuals and their social systems can develop a kind of powerful interdependence. As noted earlier, we organize our comments using a framework developed by Merz and Furman (1997). They suggest that recent scholarship on schools and communities tends to cluster under one of two broad categories. The first of these deals with the spirit or ethos of community as it is manifested within schools and the second with efforts to establish links between schools and their surrounding communities. We begin our review of research by considering themes that are emerging from research on schools that seem to cultivate a sense of belonging for teachers and students. Next we turn to scholarship exploring attempts to connect schools and those within them with parents, others in the community, and agencies or businesses in surrounding areas.

Historical Perspectives on Schools and Community

As noted above, with the exception of Dewey, educational scholars expressed little interest in the concept of community until the latter part of this century. In all likelihood, this was due, at least in part, to the fact that schools in the United States began as integral, even organizing, institutions within local communities (Cremin, 1988; Tyack, 1974). They typically supported local values and manifested relational patterns that were congruent with surrounding neighborhoods. Such schools were assumed to be both reflections and extensions of their communities. Because many of these neighborhoods were rural enclaves consisting of individuals bound together by shared agricultural work, family, and religion, the form of community schools in order to support and serve tended, in many ways, to resemble Tonnies' (1957) *Gemeinshaft*. In such settings, "school and community were organically related in a tightly knit group in which people met face to face and knew each other's affairs" (Tyack, 1974, p. 17).

During the middle years of the nineteenth century, the idea that schools were bound to and existed for local communities was expanded a bit as idealistic educational leaders such as Horace Mann "embarked on their most ambitious and successful social movement, the crusade to create a common school system" (Tyack & Hansot, 1982,

p. 17). Underlying this endeavor was a vision that schools existed for and in, not only local settings, but also a national community and that one of the central purposes of education was to promote "a Protestant-republican ideology [and to serve as a] source of unity in a highly decentralized nation" (Tyack & Hansot, p. 21, citing Higham, 1974). The common schools of this era were distinguished by their explicit commitment to developing citizens who could lead the U.S. toward realizing its destiny.[4] Personnel were hired and curricula adopted if they were perceived to contribute to this mission.

The assumption that a principal purpose of schools is to support the outside world by preparing citizens and workers and by modeling and promoting prevailing cultural norms and values persisted throughout the second half of the 1800s. However, during these years, this world expanded dramatically in size, scope, population, and complexity. And as the twentieth century unfolded, educational practices aimed at cultivating individuals for life within local communities were forced to change rather dramatically. Many forces combined to promote educational systems modeled after "machines and factories" (Tyack, 1974, p. 41). These included technological and industrial developments, the influx of persons into urban areas, strong national commitments to efficiency and productivity values, and faith in bureaucratically organized, scientifically managed organizations. Once again, schools not only sought to prepare persons for work in the businesses and industries that were taking over the landscape of America's cities, they also emulated the hierarchical structures and standardized processes being used in these organizations.

> Superintendents . . . from classroom to central office . . . tried to create new controls over pupils, teachers, principals, and other subordinate members of the school hierarchy. Although they often used the nonpolitical language of social engineers, they were actually trying to replace village forms in which laymen participated in decentralized decision-making with the new bureaucratic model of a closed "non-political" system in which directives flowed from the top down, reports emanated from the bottom, and each step of the educational process was carefully prescribed by professional educators. (Tyack, 1974, p. 40)

Decision-makers in central offices and on school boards and a handful of academics developed a number of structures and practices and instituted a set of roles that have shaped the face of schooling throughout the twentieth century. For instance, the development of large, comprehensive school systems governed by single administrative structures grew out of the very real pressures of trying to serve large numbers of students, but it also found support in principles of scientific management and bureaucratic control that had captured the minds and imaginations of educational policymakers and managers (Philbrick, 1885, cited in Tyack, 1974). Within these large and complex systems, teachers were subject to pressures that differed radically from those facing their predecessors in rural and common schools of the previous centuries. Conditions of employment, placement, content, teaching methods, and approaches to discipline were, for the most part, under the centralized control of district administrators, school boards, and state departments of education. Students also faced experiences that would have seemed alien to youngsters a century earlier. Instead of studying in multi-age settings, they were divided into grades (Bunker, 1916; Goodlad & Anderson, 1963; Schultz, 1973; Shearer, 1898). In addition to age, "tested proficiency" (Tyack, 1974, p. 45) was a key factor in determining student placement, a reality that promoted the development of "examinations which would test the achievement of pupils and serve as a basis for promotion" (Tyack, p. 44). In the view of reformers, the implementation of "systematic plan[s] of gradation" (p. 44) for students would enable teachers to develop and deliver "a sequential curriculum or program of studies that would [or could] be standardized" (pp. 43–44).

In the educational bureaucracies that developed in the early 1900s, roles of administrators changed dramatically. No longer were leaders viewed as transmitters and protectors of "small-town Protestant norms" (Tyack & Hansot, 1982, p. 117). Instead, the superintendency was emerging as "the central office in the school system, up to which and down from which authority, direction, and inspiration flow" (Cubberley, 1916, p. 222). Expected to "reshape schools to fit the new economic and social conditions of an urban-industrial society" (Tyack, 1974, p. 126), superintendents increasingly turned to ideas proffered by "educational scientists, often based in universities or foundations and private research bureaus" (Tyack & Hansot, 1982, p. 162) and to principles of decision-making "used by men on the board of directors of a modern business corporation" (Tyack, 1974, p. 126) to guide their work. Principals, in turn, were no longer "principal teachers" charged with performing "some minor administrative tasks" (Cooper, 1979, p. 272). Rather, they became "executives or managers" (Beck & Murphy, 1993, p. 23) responsible for organizing schools for efficient and economical processing of students through and out of the educational system (Callahan, 1962).

In an interesting way, both liberal/individualist and communitarian assumptions seem to have influenced some aspects of past educational efforts. Since the industrial revolution, for example, most schools have been organized around the assumption that individuals are solitary and self-interested. Individual students move through the system, usually complying with a set of rational rules or policies, and are ostensibly motivated by competition for rewards that cater to self-interest. On the other hand, many structural, curricular, and pedagogical decisions are made out of a belief that schools have a communitarian purpose;

they exist to prepare students to fit into, work effectively in, and serve the larger society. Ironically, in spite of the presence of liberal and communitarian tendencies in schools, most educational systems have not wrestled with ways to avoid the problems inherent in both views and, in turn, to create communities that draw upon the strengths of these two perspectives.

Most of the proponents of modern educational bureaucracies were, no doubt, well-intentioned, believing that "the very salvation of our cities depend[ed]" upon placing control of schooling "honest and competent experts" (Dutton & Snedden, 1912, p. 122). They, however, in their quest for a non-political, "modern, and rational" (Tyack, 1974, p. 143) approach to schooling managed to create something of a behemoth. Especially in recent years, people from many quarters, representing a range of ideological perspectives, have criticized efforts to consolidate educational enterprises into massive systems under the control of a small number of administrators and elected officials. For example, former Secretary of Education and frequent spokesperson for conservative perspectives, William Bennett, writing in 1988, condemned the "trend toward administrative bloat" (quoted in Hanusheck, 1994, p. 37) as being a central factor in drawing dollars away from instructional programs. Similar arguments are offered by Chubb and Moe (1990), who contend that bureaucratic systems not only drain money away from classrooms but also "inhibit initiative, creativity, and professional judgment" (Beck & Murphy, 1993). Writing from a very different position, Giroux and McLaren (1992) condemn efforts of the federal government to create and enforce national goals and standards. They are especially critical of *America 2000* put forward by then-president George Bush and Secretary of Education Lamar Alexander, arguing that even though this reform purports to debureaucratize schooling and to return power to community, it in fact simply shifts power from elected and appointed officials to "a privatized market system that enshrines individualism, self-help, management, and consumerism at the expense of those values that reflect the primacy of the ethical, social, and civic in public life" (p. 3). Others (Beare, 1989; Maccoby, 1988) taking a less ideological stand agree with the assertion of Clark and Meloy (1989) that bureaucracies are "impractical and . . . [do] not fit the psychological needs of the [modern educational] workforce" (p. 293).

In our view, some of the most penetrating criticisms of educational systems that have developed over the last century come from researchers who have focused their attention on the impact of typical structures and common practices on students. Several scholars including Feiststriser (1985) and Pallas, Natriello, and McDill (1995) contend that many of the educational structures developed during the twentieth century fail to meet the needs of a school population that is increasingly poor, non-English speaking,

and non-white for a variety of reasons. Indeed, Pallas and his colleagues argue that some structures, developed as schools have "attempt[ed] to resolve the quintessential American dilemma of creating citizens who are once individual and different on the one hand, and unified and equal on the other hand" (pp. 30–31), have actually decreased the quality of opportunities available to disadvantaged youngsters. Sedlak, Wheeler, Pullin, and Cusick (1986) in turn insist that the negative impact of practices in America's secondary schools extends to the vast majority of students who "have progressively disengaged themselves from their high school experience" (p.13; see also Powell, Farrar, & Cohen, 1985).

Each of the scholars cited in the preceding paragraph notes that the very things about schooling that are problematic for many students happened as educators sought to develop impersonal policies and rigid structures in order to respond to the challenges of preparing vast numbers of students for life in environments characterized by diversity, complexity, and fragmentation. These authors call upon persons concerned with educational reform to take seriously the challenge of crafting a viable sense of community within schools. In the next section, we offer an overview of the work of others who are attempting to understand what a generative sense of community might look like in schools.

Schools and Communities: Recent and Current Scholarship

In this section, we consider a growing body of work that is attempting to understand if and how schools might create and sustain some sense of community. For an overarching framework, we borrow from the work of Merz and Furman (1997) to help us organize our discussion. They organize their consideration of recent research by focusing first on scholarship that has attempted to understand characteristics of schools that are functioning (or striving to function) as communities for students, teachers, and administrators. Merz and Furman then concentrate upon research on efforts to establish strong and productive links between school sites and their surrounding communities.[5]

Schools as Communities

In the 1960s, University of Chicago sociologist James Coleman (1966), after engaging in an extensive analysis of factors related to academic achievement, concluded that socioeconomic status, not experience in schools, was the best predictor of student success. This idea understandably challenged educators and educational researchers, for it intimated that their work, regardless of its quality or intensity, made little difference in the lives and learning of youngsters. In an effort to respond to this finding, a set of scholars,[6] committed to the possibility that schools could have a positive impact on student achievement, set out to discover the conditions under which this might occur. Edmonds (1979, 1986), Hallinger and Murphy (1986), Lightfoot (1984), and Rutter, Maughan, Mortimore, Ouston, and Smith (1979) were among those who identified qualities or characteristics of schools that, according to a set of criteria, could be deemed effective. One of the themes emerging from this research was the notion that an "ethos . . . characterized by opportunities for collaboration among teachers, cohesion in the student culture, and positive interactions between students and teachers" (Bryk & Driscoll, 1988, p. 2) pervaded such schools.

Researchers frequently used the word "community" to describe the positive social climate in effective schools, and a number have identified specific dimensions or characteristics of schools where students and adult educators experienced a sense of belonging. Bryk and Driscoll, drawing from literature on schools as communities and from their own research on this phenomenon, suggest that "core elements . . . [or] components" of "communal school organization[s]" (p.12) can be clustered into three broad categories. First, they assert that "schools organized as communities will exhibit a system of values that are shared and commonly understood among the members of the organization" (p.12). Second, Bryk and Driscoll argue that such sites will be "characterized by a common agenda of activities that marks membership in the organization" (p.12). Finally, they contend that relationships among inhabitants of communal schools will be characterized by mutual care and support.

As researchers have delved into life within school communities, they have identified a number of values that can serve to unify students, teachers, and administrators. Early effective school research by Edmonds (1979, 1986) suggested that commitments to order, discipline, and academic achievement would pervade urban school communities that worked for low-income children. Others (Little, 1993; McLaughlin, 1993; McLaughlin, Talbert, & Phelan, 1990) suggest that when teachers are supporting one another in the quest for professional excellence—when professionalism and collegiality are valued—small pockets of community emerge. They contend that these productive and supportive teacher workgroups provide the foundation for the development of strong communal schools. Focusing on positive environments for African-American students, Ladson-Billings (1994) stresses that educators must value their students *and* their students' culture. Gerald Grant (1988), in turn, asserts that in such institutions there will exist a commitment to "intellectual and moral virtue" (p.174).

Although the researchers cited above describe different types of values that pervade communal schools, their discussions hint at the idea that there also will be certain underlying commitments in any site that is seeking community. Sara Lawrence Lightfoot's powerful description of six "good" high schools (1984) provides insights into the ways these sites are shaped both by values that are environmentally specific and by those more enduring values that seem to transcend contexts. She notes that "principles of democracy, free enterprise, and capitalism . . . [and] a belief in the fairness and rationality of 'the system'" (p. 47) provide the moral or cultural centerpiece at one Southern urban school. In contrast, at another urban site, commitments to pluralism and diversity shape the normative landscape. Other school cultures studied by Lightfoot revolved around values ranging from "educational excellence" (p. 129) to "risk taking . . . unusual openness to change, and to responsiveness to community" (p. 218) and from the development of "an inquiring spirit . . . in an environment nurtured by certainty, abundance, and respect" (p. 230) to a commitment to responding to "the individual needs of students . . . [and] the wisdom of supporting a diversity of talents" (p. 277). In her analysis of similarities and differences among her six schools, Lightfoot seems to celebrate the fact that there is no list of specific values that good institutions exhibit, for she writes with admiration of the fact that each of the sites she considered was responsive to the cultural particularities of students and their families. She also notes some values that pervaded all sites. Each school described by Lightfoot exhibited a tolerance for ambiguity and imperfection, a respect for both masculine and feminine leadership qualities, "a fearless and empathetic regard of students" (p. 342), and willingness to accommodate and support adolescent development.

A second characteristic of institutions that are consciously seeking community is the pursuit of some set of activities that fosters a sense of togetherness and belonging among participants. Virtually all the researchers cited in the preceding paragraphs, in addition to identifying specific values that permeate such schools, also describe activities that powerfully reinforce these norms and beliefs. Little (1993), for instance, describes groups of teachers becoming professional communities as they work together to solve problems. Ladson-Billings (1994) provides a rich set of descriptions of activities that demonstrate respect and care for African-American students and their culture. Grant (1988) writes that schools with a strong positive ethos create ample amounts of time to encourage dialog among and between teachers, students, and others about the ideals for which the school stands. And Lightfoot's descriptions of good schools are replete with examples of activities that create community.

Bryk and Driscoll (1988) suggest that the third characteristic of schools that are functioning as communities is a certain quality of interactions among and between administrators, teachers, and students. They suggest that the concept of caring best captures the spirit that guides and infuses relationships in communal school organizations. Beck (1994) and Noddings (1984, 1992) have written about care from a theoretical perspective. Both also offer empirical and hypothetical examples of teachers, administrators, and students giving and receiving care. Others including Kratzer (1996), Sergiovanni (1994), and Starratt (1994) describe in some detail classes and schools where teachers and students are striving to honor an ethic of care. The work of all these scholars underscores the fact that one cannot create a list of caring behaviors and it highlights the notion that care is, for the most part, driven by a commitment to respond to another's situation in ways that further her or his growth and well-being.

Schools and Communities

The researchers discussed above have concerned themselves principally with identifying characteristics of schools that are striving to be communities for those who work and study within them. A related body of work has focused less on the internal qualities of such sites and more on the ways schools have created powerful and productive bonds with students' families and with others in surrounding neighborhoods. In this section, we review some scholarship that addresses this issue.

Reflecting on the policies and programs attempting to link schools with larger communities, Cibulka (1996) notes that such efforts are part of "a broadly gauged movement with numerous strands" (p. 403). He elaborates on some of these strands noting that

> Among those who advocate coordinated service, the perceived problems usually mentioned are the declining condition of children in our society and the inadequacies of service to children and families. By contrast, for Chicago's school reformers, it has been opposition to the educational bureaucracy and the desire to replace it with greater accountability by school principals and by local school control. Choice advocates also see the problem as a lack of bureaucratic accountability, but they depart from Chicago school reformers in their effort to replace bureaucratic controls by giving families consumer power. (pp. 403–404)

Merz and Furman (1997) agree with Cibulka's assessment of motives for attempts to establish stronger linkages between schools and their communities. They point out, however, that instrumental goals represent only one set of purposes for striving to reconnect educational institutions with families and other social collectives and institutions. These authors suggest that "radical humanist critics of education have for some time called for a new mission of schools, one consonant with the ideals of a multicultural/multiracial democracy" (p. 72). Drawing upon arguments offered by Greene (1993), Giroux (1992), Lomotey (1990), and McLaren (1993), Merz and Furman suggest that this group of scholars is driven by the belief that "schools can prefigure the larger society that we want" (Lo-

motey, p. 4). This society would, in effect, be "a multicultural democracy" (Merz & Furman, p. 72).

The sheer range of motives for establishing connections between schools and communities, coupled with the great range in programs and policies attempting to do so, makes it virtually impossible to draw quick or easy conclusions about efforts that succeed in establishing strong linkages. However, such a reality does not mean that we cannot learn from the host of activities aimed at "rethink[ing] school, community, and family connections" (Cibulka, 1996, p. 404). In an effort to foster such learning, Cibulka and Kritek (1996) engaged in an impressive effort to compile research studies and analytical and theoretical work on efforts to coordinate services and to establish relationships among schools, neighborhoods, service agencies, local governments, and the like. In a similar vein, Oakes and Quartz (1995) recently produced an edited volume under the sponsorship of the National Society for the Study of Education that explores new forms of community being created both within and around schools. Much of the research contained in Cibulka and Kritek's (1996) text studies the technical and political processes involved in coordinating services among schools and other public and private agencies. The studies in Oakes and Quartz's *Creating New Educational Communities* (1995) look at this phenomenon but also at other activities aimed at engaging parents and the larger community in the life and work of schools. The reports in both volumes along with the work of Kagan, Klugman, and Zigler (1983), Danzberger, Kirst, and Usdan (1992), Merz and Furman (1997), and others reveal the complexities and tensions *and* the promises and opportunities embedded in efforts to establish new stronger school-community relationships.

As we discuss research that considers both challenges and opportunities linked to efforts to connect educational institutions and those who inhabit them with persons or groups from the "outside" world, we once again borrow Merz and Furman's (1997) framework supplementing it with work by Murphy (1996) and others. The former suggests that research on programs aimed at creating school-community connections tends to focus on one of three things: a) efforts to increase community control over schools through various forms of site-based management; b) attempts to coordinate services offered by schools and other agencies; and c) activities designed to engage parents in their children's education. They structure their discussions of promising practices and unsuccessful efforts around these three categories. Murphy adds a fourth strategy: choice opportunities to build educational communities.

Site-based management (SBM) is a "relative" (Hill & Bonan, 1991, p. 4; Wagstaff & Reyes, 1993, p. 23), "generic" (Malen, Ogawa, & Kranz, 1989, p. 7), or "umbrella" term (Conley & Bacharach, 1990, p. 540; Lawton,

1991, p. 2) that describes a wide range of strategies to decentralize school governance. Some forms of SBM simply focus on moving decision-making about personnel, curriculum, and budget (Murphy & Beck, 1995) to the principals and teachers within a local school site. However, other versions of this reform emphasize involving parents and community members in educational governance. Within this latter set, actual programs and policies vary greatly. Some, such as the reform plan in Chicago, Illinois (Bryk, 1993; Hess, 1991, 1995), mandate a radical shift in the balance of power among "local parents, community representatives, and school professionals as a strategy for improving school achievement" (Hess, 1995, p. 25). The Chicago plan dictates that Local School Councils (LSCs) are the principle decision-makers for individual schools, and it specifies that parents hold the majority of seats on this council. Thus it is "unique in that parents far outnumber school staff" (Merz & Furman, 1997, p. 84). Other plans, such as the Salt Lake City Model (Malen & Ogawa, 1988) and the Los Angeles Educational Alliance for Restructuring Now (LEARN) plan of Los Angeles, California (Beck & Murphy, 1996), insist that parents participate in school site councils but provide for different ratios among them and others. Salt Lake City's plan contains "parity provisions that 'make principals, teachers, and parents equal partners with equal power'" (Merz & Furman, p. 90, citing Malen & Ogawa, 1988, p. 253), while the Los Angeles Plan, because of provisions in teacher contracts, allows teachers to have twice as many seats on a site council as any other stakeholder group (Beck & Murphy, 1996). Regardless of the specific details of site-based management structures, most of the research (Malen, Ogawa, & Kranz, 1988; Murphy & Beck, 1995) suggests that SBM has done very little to date to strengthen broad-based links between schools and their communities. When such connections have been established within SBM schools (see Beck & Murphy, 1996; Kratzer, 1997), they appear to be related more to personal commitments of parents and/or educators than to formal changes in decision-making structures.

Merz and Furman's (1997) second category of activities aimed at linking educational institutions and outside agencies focuses on strategies to coordinate services for students and their families through (or with) schools (see Smrekar & Mawhinney, this volume). It is difficult to draw anything approaching a definite conclusion about such efforts from research for two reasons. First, many of the programs designed to coordinate services are fairly new and have not generated enough data to allow for evaluations of them. Second, the research that has been done to date is quite varied methodologically and does not lend itself to easy meta-analyses or cross-case comparisons. Still, as Merz and Furman note, "some relevant themes" (p. 96) are emerging from investigations into coordination efforts. One such theme relates to the impact of such efforts on moving

schools and service agencies away from more bureaucratic models and in the direction of more organic community institutions. The work of Crowson and Boyd (1993); Gardner, (1994); Knapp, Barnard, Brandon, Gehrke, Smith, and Teather (1994); and Melaville and Blank (1991) suggests that "school involvement in service coordination involves new professional roles . . . and the expansion of the . . . bureaucracy" (Merz & Furman, p. 96) and thus efforts to create more communal organizations paradoxically lead to an expansion and reinforcement of structured hierarchies. A second theme is that school-community ties that have been established around the coordination of services are quite fragile and that they are sustained, not by commitments among members of schools and various agencies, but rather by heavy and ongoing infusions of resources (Hord, 1986). A third theme, suggested by Smrekar's (1996) research and supported by Crowson and Boyd's (1993) analysis, is that the nature of relationships between professionals in schools and agencies and persons within communities does not become more collegial, democratic, or mutually respectful as a result of service coordination. To the contrary, school-based efforts to "connect families with the services necessary to meet basic needs" (Smrekar, p.5) have, in some instances, reinforced a sense that service providers are professionals and "givers," while persons within the community are "clients to be 'targeted' for services" (Furman & Merz, p. 97).

The third set of activities aimed at linking schools and communities as identified by Merz and Furman (1997) includes a host of efforts to engage parents in the educational experiences of their children. These authors point out that many "traditional mechanisms" for linking families and schools fall into the same trap as service coordination efforts in that they reinforce traditional power relationships in which "the school maintains control and parents continue in less influential roles (Epstein, 1995; Henry, 1996; Swap, 1993)" (p. 100). They also note, though, that some efforts, built on a "partnership model" (p. 107) stress "long-term commitments, mutual respect, widespread involvement of families and educators in many levels of activities, and sharing of planning and decision-making responsibilities" (Swap, p. 47). Epstein's work suggests that *any* effort to engage parents in their children's education is likely to enhance a youngster's academic achievement. However, she, along with Henry, Swap, and Merz and Furman, contend that genuine and powerful connections between schools and communities can be established only if educators and parents view one another as partners.

As noted above, a fourth strategy, embraced by some and fervently opposed by others, for increasing connections between schools and communities involves instituting choice opportunities so that parents and youngsters can in effect join with other like-minded people. Some scholars

(Chubb & Moe, 1990) advocating this approach to educational communities are squarely situated in the liberal-individualist tradition as articulated by Adam Smith (1937) and Milton Friedman (1955). That is, these individuals hold "that the good society and the good school, is best created and maintained through the mechanisms of the marketplace" (Friedman & Friedman, 1980, p. 86). This way of thinking has resulted in efforts to enact policies that, in a variety of ways, privatize schooling (for a through discussion of this phenomenon, see Murphy, 1996). These include provisions for intra-district "controlled choice" (Schmidt, 1991; Snider, 1990), inter-district transfer opportunities (Clune & Witte, 1990), the creation of charter public schools (Wells, 1997), and efforts to establish voucher plans (Olsen, 1990; Mazzoni & Sullivan, 1986). Others (Bryk, Lee, & Holland, 1993) disagree with the "gospel of free market choice" (Cookson, p. 92) that holds that the pursuit of "self-interest create[s] a common good because viewed collectively, self-interest is a better arbiter of human affairs than 'social engineering'" (p. 86). Their in-depth investigation of Catholic schools prompted them to speculate that "the voluntary nature of [applying for admission or employment] signifies a willingness to join the community and to accept its values" (p. 128). Researchers (Smrekar, 1996; Wells, 1997) are engaging in efforts to understand the interplay between choice and the cultivation of a sense of community. Their work to date suggests that the linkages between these two phenomenon are complex, nonlinear, and tenuous.

Challenges and Opportunities for Educational Leaders

Our analysis of historical and current attempts to create a sense of community within and around schools reinforces our belief that such efforts are vitally important as educational institutions seek to serve diverse groups of students and their families, many of whom live in worlds where little is stable, safe, or secure. We also have come to believe that community-building activities should be guided by careful reflection on the purposes of schooling and that they should be pursued in environments where open and ongoing communication among educators, students, parents, and community members is possible and encouraged.

Our support for the range of efforts to create schools where people experience a sense of connection with and commitment to others stems from our agreement with Brad Mitchell's (1990) poignant assessment of the ways that "normal" stresses and "necessary losses" (Viorst, 1986) associated with living are exacerbated by many conditions of modern life. Mitchell argues that persons, as they face "rapid and repeated episodes of loss" (p. 22), often develop a "mindset of fatalism and disempowerment" (p. 23). In his

view, this can be avoided only if individuals feel secure and purposeful. He writes:

> Loss cannot be confronted in a vacuum. It must be tied with efforts to belong and to become. We perceive loss when we feel we do not belong or something does not belong. We perceive loss when we recognize that what we wish to become is not possible. (p. 23)

Mitchell calls upon educational leaders to take seriously the challenge of creating schools where persons experience "a collective sense of belonging" (p. 39), for only in such a setting can individuals grow, develop, and "become something" (p. 40).

Mitchell (1990) also cautions that is easy "to lose sight of the delicate and intimate dimensions of human belonging" (p. 39). He suggests that efforts to build community that are not preceded by deep, honest, and unconditional regard for each person are likely to result in monolithic cultures where difference is not accepted because it somehow challenges the sanctity of the collective. In making this argument, he is echoing ideas raised by Bellah and his colleagues (1985), Dokecki (1995), Feinberg (1995), Kirkpatrick (1986), and Selznick (1992), discussed in an earlier section. Essentially all these thinkers argue that a vital and healthy community is one that combines liberalism's concern about the individual with a communitarian commitment to the creation of social systems built upon mutual acceptance, care, and respect. We argue that educational leaders who would learn from past and current efforts to develop schools that function *as* and *in* communities must embrace this way of thinking. They must balance "the competing demands of creating unified citizenry with equal rights as well as enabling each individual to achieve her or his potential" (Pallas *et al.*, 1995, p. 33), never becoming so concerned with producing workers and citizens for society's sake that they lose sight of the fact that society is composed of and exists for persons with a range of needs, wants, hopes, and desires. In the following sections, we offer ideas about ways educational administrators might meet this challenge and take advantage of the opportunities inherent in a robust school community. We begin by talking about a possible response for leaders when they are confronted with various unsatisfactory or incomplete notions of community emanating *from outside of educational arenas*. We then focus on actions and attitudes that have the potential to harness forces *within schools* so that teachers, parents, students, and others from the outside world can begin to experience and enjoy community.

Challenging Traditional Assumptions About Educational Community

As we have noted, many, if not most, models of administration look to practices of organizational management for guidance in determining both the "what" and "how" of the field. This seems to be a phenomenon inherent in the development of the modern western state and has been commented on by thinkers as diverse as Tonnies (1957), Durkheim (1933), Weber (1947), and Habermas (1984). Each of these scholars in some way suggests that a bureaucratic society advances an instrumentalist notion of being and that, further, this often leads to anomie and disenchantment. The instrumental orientation is also a contractual one, wherein the use of persons for instrumental ends is achieved through the establishment and enforcement of contracts. This reflects the type of *gesellschaft* society Tonnies wrote about, a society based in enforced obligation. He asserts that *gemeinschaft*, the social condition in which a community spirit pervades most social groupings, diminished in influence as a result of urbanization and industrialization and since that time continues to be attenuated by the ever-increasing dominance of instrumental and contractual social logic. A contemporary philosopher, MacIntyre (1981), goes so far as to suggest that the bureaucratic/ instrumentalist orientation has in fact corrupted moral language entirely. Indeed, he suggests that the "ideal" leader for our age is the bureaucratic-manager, the "character" who puts such projects as science and reason to an instrumental end: achieving the goals of the corporate state.

As we and others (Merz & Furman, 1997; Noddings, 1996; Sergiovanni, 1993) have noted, educational organizations have not been immune to the same forces shaping other institutions. Even as bureaucracy, for so many years, served as the dominant structural model for schools, business management procedures served as exemplars for the conduct of educational administration. As Callahan (1962), Tyack (1974), and Tyack and Hansot (1982) have observed, these procedures provided the ways and means for managing school systems. Such procedures, treating schools and school systems as organizations composed of people held together by goals and rules, began to dominate much of the practical, empirical, and theoretical literature in administration. This acceptance of a classic, bureaucratic model as the appropriate, if sometimes unfortunate, way to structure an educational organization contributed to the idea that schools were manageable organizations. This belief in turn helped to shape beliefs about the role of administrators and spawned a complementary set of management techniques, aphorisms, and programs to train persons to inhabit a host of hierarchical positions. In this way then, the school as an organization came (and continues) to be seen in an almost totally instrumental way: as a tool to achieve those social goals deemed important in a particular period, but almost always focusing on the development of a productive and employable citizen. This instrumental view often relegated schools to being tools of the economy and, while education itself seemed to remain universally valued as an inherent good, the school-as-organization became valued for what it could or should accomplish in relation, largely, to the economy.

As we have noted earlier, this belief that schools exist to serve society's economic needs is in some ways reflective of communitarian ideals. Interestingly, though, the actual organizational structure of schools, throughout much of this century, seems more congruent with a liberal/individualist perspective. Certainly the idea of control through social and legal contracts enforced dispassionately and objectively is consistent with liberal/individualist views. Earlier we argued that we need to develop ways of thinking about schools that reflect a mingling of the best of liberalism and communitarianism. Ironically, the blending we have gotten seems to draw upon the worst of these two traditions. All too often schools, driven by contracts, rules, and structures to enforce them, seek to serve capitalism's economic interests and loose sight of other ways to think about students, teachers, and their families as individuals *and* as persons in community.

"Administering Community" [7]: Rethinking and Reacting

In educational institutions that exist to accomplish instrumental, economic purposes, administrators are expected to control operations so that schools, in an efficient way, can produce the kind of workers society values. Administrators who set out to challenge this assumption, even in small ways, and who commit to creating environments where people and communities can flourish face something of an uphill battle. In the sections which follow, we reflect upon these challenges and offer thoughts about ways administrators and, by extension, those who prepare them might begin to construct viable and vital definitions, structures, and practices and embrace assumptions and values that support generative centers for learning. Specifically, we assert that the tasks of creating powerful communities within and around schools will require a reworking of deeply engrained administrative and organizational assumptions, not just the renaming of organizational characteristics. Leaders must rethink their understanding of education's purposes, and they must thoughtfully define or redefine their roles in accordance with their beliefs about purpose. They must confront the fact that many of the values espoused by education that relate to care and respect for persons and to the creation of powerful opportunities for their growth and development are not reflected in structures and practices and they must recommit to an ethical stance that supports generative communities. Such *rethinking* must also be accompanied by *reacting*—by a retooling of structures and practices within schools and classes in order to create conditions that promote personal and collective development and that foster "friendship, fellowship, love, and, mutuality" (Kirkpatrick, 1986, p.186). Ideals must be acted out in practices guided by critique, caring, and justice and should be reflected and shaped by changes in the way we talk about our work.

Reframing Beliefs About Education's Purposes

Thomas Sergiovanni, in an address at the 1993 meeting of the American Educational Research Association, noted that many persons viewing schools today seem to conceive of education's purpose in only instrumental terms. In his view, this tendency to think of schooling as something that exists only to serve certain externally defined ends both results from and contributes to structures and practices that ignore the possibility that learning is intrinsically related to personhood—that being fully human means always growing and developing in a host of ways. Sergiovanni issued a call to researchers and practitioners to reconsider the possibility that education is an inherently good thing and to enlarge their understanding of schools' purposes accordingly. Others concur. Andy Hargreaves, for example, in the 1997 Yearbook of the American Association of Supervision and Curriculum Development, *Rethinking Educational Change with Heart and Mind*, admonishes educators to remember that "educational change theory and practice . . . doesn't really get to the heart of what children, teachers, and parents care about and do or what moves them to do things better" (p. 2). He then insists that what is needed is a recognition that the cultivation of "openness, informality, care, attentiveness, lateral working relationships, reciprocal collaboration, candid and vibrant dialog, and the willingness to face uncertainty together" (p. 22) is a central individual and social purpose of schooling, "not merely the emotional icing that adorns" (p. 22) efforts to produce employable workers.

Administrators and others who prepare, credential, and provide ongoing support to them must rethink or reconceptualize the fundamental purposes of schooling. In Sergiovanni's (1993) terms, they must embrace metaphors of schools as communities. They must see that these institutions provide social contexts in which individuals develop morally, emotionally (Hargreaves, 1997, p. 22), intellectually, and physically and that a central and public purpose of any school is to be the kind of place that fosters the well-being of persons and their communities.

Reorienting the Administrative Role

When schools are viewed as organizations designed to achieve a set of instrumental goals, the role of administrator is rather easily defined: he or she is expected to exercise a fair measure of control over the organization to ensure that conditions, practices, and people work together to reach desired ends. In Sergiovanni's words, bureaucratic notions presume that schools

> are structured and function much like the mechanical works of a clock made of cogs and gears, wheels, drives, and pins all tightly connected in an orderly and predictable manner. The task of management [then] is to gain control or a regulate the master wheel and pin . . . Once the master wheel and pin are under control, all the other wheels and pins will move responsively and the principal's intents will be accomplished. (1993)

If and when schools function as and in communities, the administrator's role must be redefined. Such a task is a complex endeavor. The historical development of administration reflects systems of control, and the legacy of scientific management is not unimportant in attempting to understand the field. It could be claimed with some legitimacy that the field has been founded on some base assumptions of the importance of efficiency, the value of impartiality, and the dominance of individualism. Efficiency has been an end state of the administrative initiative, as Tyack (1974), Button (1966), and others have shown. This means that the role of administration, in Simon's (1945) seminal view, was not the articulation of values but their implementation in the most efficient manner: administrators put into practice what policymakers decree and they do so in a rational (some would say rationalistic) manner, where rationality is the most efficient/effective path of moving from the current state to the desired one. Those who accept this view believe leaders must always have their eyes on goals and that they must be willing, if necessary, to subvert means in order to achieve ends. This in many ways is inimical to a communal focus on articulating values and orienting the organization to them even if this means at times taking the institutions down more inefficient paths if these meanderings are seen as consistent to ethical norms and commitments.

Educational administrators, then, committed to cultivating and leading schools toward being healthy communities, must on some level be involved in careful, critical, and, ultimately, open reflection upon their own ethical commitments and those of the organizations they lead. This requires that they possess and exercise the skills of logical and critical analysis, conceptual synthesis, value analysis, and commitment and that they utilize the power of expression in language and communication, rhetoric, and, most fundamentally, the depth of understanding of human nature (Hodgkinson, 1991, p. 112). Administrators in communities must lead their colleagues in questioning the way things are (Starratt, 1994, p. 47) and in crafting humanizing and humane structures and practices.

Leaders who respond to the challenge of articulating values will find themselves in what Hodgkinson (1991) describes as an arena of "ethical excitement" (p. 164). They also, though, will be entering a world very different from the one inhabited by their colleagues who embrace an instrumental, hierarchical, and mechanistic view of schools. Hodgkinson points out that values are the ultimate subjective reality (p. 141) and that administrators who engage with them find themselves working within the non-natural order that people create and in the beliefs, attitudes, and appreciation of both self and other that shaped the formation of that order (p. 141). They will also find themselves confronting inevitable conflicts and tensions between and among different perspectives. Such administrators must possess strength (Greenleaf, 1996, p. 25), courage, and wisdom to honor the values that support communities which honor and support the comprehensive development of persons as individuals and as social beings.

Highlighting Those Values That Support Community

Above we described administrators within communities as value articulators and we noted that such leaders would honor and support those values that are consonant with honoring and supporting people and their communities. In this section, we look in more detail at the nature of such values.

Administration, as it has emerged as a discipline, has been committed to values such as efficiency and impartiality. That is, it has held that the systematic and economical movement toward goals is a good thing and that, within organizations, there are no special cases and equal justice prevails. This, as Perrow (1986) has noted, is a hallmark of bureaucratic systems and establishes the basis of systemic rewards on achievement rather than ascription. It tends to prevent, for example, nepotism and attempts to provide equal opportunities for success within large-scale systems. This, in a word, reflects an ethos of justice (Gilligan, 1982). The values of efficiency, impartiality, and equality are important in educational communities. If, however, they are the central or only guiding values, there is a risk that rules and procedures, laws, and contracts will replace personal judgments and commitments. If this occurs, the ethos of care (as presented by Gilligan and developed by Noddings, 1984) can be devalued.

As we envision an educational community that draws upon the best of liberalism and communitarianism, one that acknowledges and supports persons but that also recognizes its responsibility to and for society, we remember again the centrality of an ethic of care in such an institution. Such an ethic has the highest regard for the individual person. It, however, avoids some of the traps of classic liberalism in that it sees each individual as inevitably and, in some ways, inextricably linked to others. Such an ethic refuses to pit the well-being of any one person against the well-being of their communities. It rather insists that the pursuit of both must go hand-in-hand.

We assert that formulating an ethic of care as a guiding principle does not require administrators to abandon procedures, but rather to prioritize systems so that administrative commitment to people and values takes precedence over the universal application of rules. The normative standard of care, it could be claimed, provides a guiding framework for those communal environments that efficiently administer justice. It also provides a certain basis for a theological orientation that allows for forgiveness and redemption. To redraw administration upon *this* particular template is, however, a daunting task, given both the historical orientations of the field and the characteristics of the greater system of which it is a part. (For a discussion of this complexity, see Noddings, 1996.)

The larger system of education is one that values (beyond, perhaps, what is necessary) the concept of individualism. Individualism is expressed in educational systems, of course, in many ways: norms of achievement, reward structures, career paths, and other sociologically-dense phenomena. Individualism is not necessarily *contra* community; however, the values and norms of systems can be affected by the way the terms are nested; for the most part, in this age, the community concept tends to be nested within a more dominating notion of individualism. This is not to say that a certain tension between the "I factor" and the "we factor" in schools is a bad thing, for communities can be as domineering and disenfranchising of the person as the person can be of communities. However, the commitment to live with and manage the tension creatively must be present. For when entire systems are devoted to the advancement of the individual, there is inevitably a subsequent fragmentation of the community. On a programmatic level, the development (by which we mean the funding and implementation of particular programs, often associated, interestingly enough, with well-known individuals) of community faces certain obstacles and their success (often measured, again, by individualistic norms) can be jeopardized. On a deeper level, emotional and spiritual "poverty, bigotry, and alienation" (Purpel, 1989, p. 30) can occur, bringing tremendous loss to all involved in schooling.

Restructuring Schools as Caring Communities

It is important to note that community does not simply emerge as well-intentioned people embrace new roles and values. Indeed, in many ways, it is determined by and dependent on structures that provide enabling conditions. Administrators of communities must work diligently and strategically to create such conditions. If they do not, their best intentions can be inadequate to overcoming the structural properties of large systems. Merz and Furman make this point when they observe that

> Simply *thinking* of schools differently, as communities rather than as organizations, does not alter the deep structures of the school as organization, structures that are institutionalized and that help create the *gesellschaftlich* climate of schools. (1997, p. 86)

Indeed, the structural variable of size itself might be an overriding consideration in the establishment of community (Merz and Furman, 1997). As complex systems increase in size, organizational theorists tell us that mechanisms for both differentiation and integration are required (Burns & Stalker, 1961); these in turn can diminish the face-to-face vitality of communities by establishing hierarchies of distance and space (*central* office, *local* control) or create artificial ways of bonding and loyalty-formation (creating corporate "culture" through performance awards).

Educational administrators must participate significantly in the reformation of structure to provide conditions for the emergence of community. This requires creativity, persistence, and political acumen. A growing number of voices (Bryk, Lee, & Holland, 1993; Furman, 1997; Meier, 1987; Merz & Furman, 1997) are suggesting that the creation of smaller schools—places where students and teachers can have face-to-face, personal, sustained relationships with one another—is essential if we are to realize the promises of community. These authors describe various organizational structures and models that enable persons to experience greater contact with a smaller number of people over a sustained period of time. Some of these models stress altering the entire school's structure, limiting enrollment or breaking larger sites into "schools within a school" or family groups. Others focus on within site transformation of classes and classrooms. Restructuring classroom organization along the lines implied by a metaphor of community might mean that, for example, age-graded classrooms, originally created to facilitate bureaucratic efficiency (Goodlad, 1983), would be recast in terms of service and care. Other options, such as those explored by Meier (1991, 1992), Noddings (1992), and Purpel (1989), include keeping teachers and pupils together for several years beyond one grade level, grouping students according to criteria other than age and/or perceived academic ability, and using a curriculum determined by community standards and needs or by students' interests.

Hargreaves (1997) argues the building of powerful community means inner transformations of school sites must be accompanied by "conscious and constructive connections with the wider world" (p. 3) for moral and pragmatic reasons. In regard to the former, he writes, "Across much of the developed world, people are experiencing a crisis of community, and schools provide one of our last and greatest hopes for resolving it" (p. 5). Hargreaves insists that opportunities and problems from the outside world are increasingly invading educational settings. He suggests that educators can respond most effectively to both the negative and positive dimensions of this reality by carving out thoughtful and positive relationships with neighborhoods, citizens, political agencies, service agencies, businesses, and the like.

We contend that the establishment of structures to foster communities must be accompanied by consistent attention to what Fullan and Hargreaves (1991) call "reculturing." Administrators must "seek to identify the roots of meaning and the flow and ebb of daily life in schools" (Sergiovanni, 1994, p. 89). They must consider ways foundational norms, assumptions, and beliefs support or inhibit community, and, having done this, engage in what Selznick (1957) describes as "institution building, the

reworking of human and technological materials to fashion an organism that embodies new and enduring values" (p. 28). The transformation of schools in the direction of communities is also a political undertaking. Indeed, many classic writings on community in both liberal/individualistic and communitarian perspectives are political in nature. This requires recognizing power in all its forms and challenging people, structures, and policies that work against the healthy development of all people and their various communities, and it means that administrators must recognize and use the power inherent in education that fulfills moral purpose.

Changing the Language of Leadership

As we have pointed out, Sergiovanni (1993) proposes that thinking, language, and practice are intimately related and suggests that we adopt a metaphor of community in place of organization. His recommendation is supported by the work of Lakoff and Johnson (1980), Law and Lodge (1984), and other scholars who insist that it is metaphor that resides in the deep structures of thought and often guides our action. And while it has been claimed that the Whorfian hypothesis is overstated, it nevertheless seems to be true that in many cases action follows language. Certainly, Schön (1990) and Black (1979) are among those who believe that language has the power to generate and communicate new meanings and ideas The prototypical, public language of educational administration is replete with metaphors that value individualism, efficiency, economy, and impartiality. In hundreds of ways, we pit persons and institutions against one another as we evaluate and report on the differential ways they measure up to some set of standards that we have embraced to ensure to quality. We reassure ourselves that we are being equitable and just because we are impartially using the same assessment tools to determine the effectiveness of programs or institutions and the ability or aptitude of individuals. And we insist that, in an era of scare resources, concerns over efficiency and economics justify rewarding those who indicate their worthiness by presenting evidence of achievement. Lakoff and Johnson (1980) suggest that the figures of speech we use as we discuss our work are important, not just for what they reveal, but also for what they hide. For instance, educational language, couched in terms of impartial assessment against high standards, evokes a sense of fairness and a commitment to quality; it masks an awareness that fair tests or measures do not take into account conditions created by social upheaval, illness, poverty, and the like.

It is difficult to consistently reorganize our thinking to project different metaphors of consequence, but in our view, it is a worthwhile task for practicing educational leaders and for those in academic arenas who work with them. Perhaps we need to look to "moral, spiritual, and [traditional] educational frameworks" (Purpel, 1989, p. 156) for language. Words like compassion, forgiveness, wisdom, humility, and loyalty[8] may be worthy of consideration and use, and images of home, church, and community may provide helpful ways for us to envision schools.

Concluding Thoughts

Creating educational communities poses a host of challenges to practicing administrators and to those who work with them as professors and researchers. One of the first and most basic involves crafting a viable and vital understanding of community—one that draws upon the strengths of various perspectives and, as much as possible, avoids dangers embedded in the extremes of liberalism and communitarianism. Another challenge lies in determining the scope and focus of community-building efforts. We, however, suggest that the greatest set of challenges lies in the actual work of administering community. In our view, thoughtful educators must engage with these challenges and pursue forms of community that provide "persons . . . concrete human entities" (Selznick, 1992, p. 507) with opportunities to learn, grow, and develop in all areas of their lives. These communities will not neglect individual needs, interests, concerns, or rights and, because these persons are "embedded in social contexts" (p. 507), communal institutions will also focus on honoring and supporting relationships and environments.

We further contend that pursuing a spirit of community within and among schools is both a practical necessity and a moral imperative for educational leaders. It is a necessity because powerful fragmenting and alienating forces exist, and they are continually undermining the human and academic work of schools. The cultivation of a sense of community helps to create conditions in which the instrumental goals of schooling can be achieved. It is a moral imperative because education is, by its nature, an ethical undertaking. Hodgkinson nicely explains why this is so:

> Education . . . can be said to subserve all human values and to be prerequisite to their fulfillment. It is this all-inclusive quality which makes education so special and, at the same time, so *human*. Because of this relevance to all aspects of the human condition, education is invested from the outset with a moral character. Through it we are all inducted into the those of our particular culture. Through it we acquire our moral dimension. On it we depend for our livelihood and the quality of our life. (p. 27)

Schools and systems that function as agencies of and agents for community are those most likely to support the development of human and humane persons capable of work, love, friendship, and citizenship.

NOTES

1. In making this assertion, we do not mean to place all the blame for problems on persons and their assumptions. We certainly acknowledge that host of factors — economic, political, social, and cultural — share responsibility for struggles in educational arenas.
2. As we discuss in a subsequent section, Kirkpatrick (1986) posited three models of community. The first two, liberal/individualist and communitarian, have had a much broader influence on western thought than his third "personal" model.
3. When we use the word "committed," we are referring to relationships that involve some sense of obligation—not necessarily those that characterized by an emotional commitment.
4. Tyack and Hansot (1982) offer a nice discussion of the ways that schooling in the United States was shaped by a sense that this country was "chosen" to, in essence, be "the Kingdom of God on earth." They point out that schools and those who led them were seen as central forces in provoking the realization of this vision.
5. Merz and Furman (1997) note, and we agree, that efforts to create communities *within* schools are not necessarily separate from efforts to link communities *with* schools.
6. Coleman himself was among the group of researchers who sought to discover characteristics of schools in which low-income children (many of whom were minorities) succeeded. His research (1985) focuses especially on the ways Catholic schools served these youngsters.
7. We borrow the term "administering community" from Robert J. Starrett (1997).
8. These words are used often by Noddings (1984, 1992), Purpel (1989), Selznick (1992), Sergiovanni (1993,1994), Starratt (1997), and other writers. We have not, however, heard them with much frequency in schools and even less in districts, state departments of education, and other policymaking bodies.

REFERENCES

Barber, B. R. (1992). *An aristocracy of everyone: The politics of education and the future of America*. New York: Ballantine.

Beare, H. (1989, September). *Educational administration in the 1990s*. Paper presented at the Australian Council for Educational Administration, Armidale, New South Wales, Australia.

Beck, L. G. (1994). *Reclaiming educational administration as a caring profession*. New York: Teachers College Press.

Beck. L. G. & Murphy, J. (1993). *Understanding the principalship: Metaphorical themes 1920s–1990s*. New York: Teachers College Press.

Beck, L. G. & Murphy, J. (1996). *The four imperatives of a successful school*. Thousand Oaks, CA: Corwin.

Bellah, R. N., Madsen, R., Sullivan, W. M., Swidler, A. & Tipton, S. M. (1985). *Habits of the heart: Individualism and commitment in American life*. New York: Harper & Row.

Bellah, R. N., Madsen, R., Sullivan, W. M., Swidler, A. & Tipton, S. M. (1991). *The good society*. New York: Alfred E. Knopf.

Black, M. (1979). More about metaphor. In A. Ortoney (Ed.), *Metaphor and thought* (pp. 19–45). Cambridge: Cambridge University Press.

Bryk, A. (1993, July). *A view from the elementary schools: The state of reform in Chicago*. Chicago: Consortium on Chicago School Research.

Bryk, A. & Driscoll, M. (1988). *The high school as community: Contextual influences and consequences for students and teachers*. Madison, WI: Wisconsin Center for Educational Research, University of Wisconsin, Madison.

Bryk, A., Lee, V. & Holland, P. (1993). *Catholic schools and the common good*. Cambridge, MA: Harvard University Press.

Bunker, F. F. (1916). *Reorganization of the public school system*. Washington DC: US. Bureau of Education.

Burns, T. & Stalker, G. M. (1961). *The management of innovation*. London: Tavistock.

Button, H. W. (1966). Doctrines of administration: A brief history. *Educational Administration Quarterly, 2*(3), 216–224.

Callahan, R. (1962). *Education and the cult of efficiency*. Chicago: University of Chicago Press.

Chubb, J. E. & Moe, T. M. (1990). *Politics, markets, and America's schools*. Washington, DC: The Brookings Institute.

Cibulka, J. G. (1996). Toward an interpretation of school, family, and community connections: Policy challenges. In J. G. Cibulka & W. J. Kritek (Eds.) *Coordination among schools, families, and communities: Prospects for educational reform*. (pp. 403–435). Albany, NY: State University of New York Press.

Cibulka, J. G. & Kritek, W. J. (Eds.) (1996). *Coordination among schools, families, and communities: Prospects for educational reform*. Albany, NY: State University of New York Press.

Clark, D. & Meloy, J. M. (1989). Renouncing bureaucracy: A democratic structure for leadership in schools. In T. J. Sergiovanni & J. A. Moore (Eds.) *Schooling for tomorrow: Directing reform to issues that count* (pp. 272–294). Boston: Allyn & Bacon.

Clune, W. H. & Witte, J. F. (Eds.) (1990). *Choice and control in education* (Two vols.) Bristol, PA: Falmer.

Coleman, J. (1985). Schools and the communities they serve. *Phi Delta Kappan, 66*, 527–532.

Coleman, J. & others (1966). *Equality of educational opportunity*. Washington, DC: U. S. Department of Health, Education, and Welfare.

Conley, S. C. & Bacharach, S. B. (1990, March) From school-based management to participatory school-site management. *Phi Delta Kappan, 71*(7), 539–544.

Cookson, P. W. (1992). The ideology of consumerism and the coming deregulation of the American public school system. In P. W. Cookson (Ed.), *The choice controversy*. (pp. 83–102). Newbury Park, CA: Corwin.

Cooper, B. S. (1979). The future of middle management in education. In D. A. Erickson & T. L. Reller (Eds.), *The principal in metropolitan schools* (pp. 272–299). Berkeley, CA: McCutchan.

Cremin, L. A. (1988). *American education: The metropolitan experience*. New York: Harper & Row.

Crowson, R. L. & Boyd, W. L. (1993). Coordinated services for children: designing arks for storms and seas unknown. *American Journal of Education, 19*(2), 140–179.

Cubberley, E. P. (1916). *Public school administration*. Boston: Houghton-Mifflin.

Danzberger, J. P., Kirst, M. W. & Usdan, M. D. (1992). *Governing public schools: new times, new requirements*. Washington DC: Institute for Educational Leadership.

Dewey, J. (1990/1990). *The school and society*. Chicago: University of Chicago Press.

Dokecki, P. (1995). *The tragicomic professional: Basic considerations for ethical reflective-generative practice*. Pittsburgh, PA: Duquesne University Press.

Dunham, H. W. (1986). Commentary—The community today: Place or process. *Journal of Community Psychology, 14*(4), 399–404.

Durkheim, E. (1933). *Division of labor in society*. New York: The Free Press.

Dutton, S. T. & Snedden, D. (1912). *The administration of public education in the United States*. New York: Macmillan.

Edmonds, R. (1979). Effective schools for the urban poor. *Educational Leadership, 37*(1), 15–24.

Edmonds, R. (1986). Characteristics of effective schools. In U. Neisser (Ed.), *The school achievement of minority children: New perspectives* (pp. 93–104). Hillsdale, NJ: Lawrence Erlbaum.

Epstein, J. (1995). School/family/community partnerships: Caring for the children we share. *Educational Leadership, 76*, 701–712.

Etzioni, A. (1993). *The spirit of community*. New York: Touchstone.

Feinberg, W. (1995). The communitarian challenge to liberal social and educational theory. *Peabody Journal of Education, 70*(4), 34–55.

Feiststriser, E. E. (1985). *Cheating our children: Why we need school reform*. Washington, DC: National Center for Educational Reform.

Friedman, M. (1955). The role of government in education. In R. A. Solo (Ed.), *Economics and the public interest* (pp. 123–144). New Brunswick, NJ: Rutgers University Press.

Friedman, M. & Friedman, R. (1980). *Free to choose*, New York: Harcourt, Brace, Jovanavich.

Fullan, M. & Hargreaves, A. (1991). *What's worth fighting for in your school*. Ontario: Toronto Public School Teachers Association.

Furman, G. C. (1997, March). *Community in large schools: Contradiction or possibility?* Paper presented at the annual meeting of the American Educational Research Association, Chicago, IL.

Furman, G. C. & Merz, C. (1996). Schools and community connections: Applying a sociological framework. In J. Cibulka & W. Kritek (Eds.) *Coordination among schools, families, and communities: Prospects for educational reform* (pp. 323–347). Albany, NY: State University of New York Press.

Gardner, S. (1994). Afterword. In L. Adler & S. Gardner (Eds.), *The politics of linking schools and social services* (pp. 188–189). Washington DC: Falmer.

Gierke, O. (1934). *Natural law and the theory of society 1500 to 1800* (E. Barker, Trans.), Cambridge: The University Press.

Gilligan, C. (1982). *In a different voice*. Cambridge, MA: Harvard University Press.

Giroux, H. (1992). *Educational leadership and the crisis of democratic culture*. University Park, PA: University Council for Educational Administration.

Giroux, H. & McLaren, P. (1992). Unpublished draft of *America 2000 and the politics of erasure:* Democracy and cultural difference under siege. Submitted to the *International Journal of Education*.

Goodlad, J. I. (1983). *A study of schooling*. New York: McGraw-Hill.

Goodlad, J. I. & Anderson, R. H. (1963). *The nongraded elementary school*. New York: Harcourt, Brace, and World.

Grant. G. (1988). *The world we created at Hamilton High*. Cambridge, MA: Harvard University Press.

Greene, M. (1993). The passions of pluralism: Multiculturalism and the expanding community. *Educational Researchers, 22*(1), 13–18.

Greenleaf, R. K. (1996). *On becoming a servant leader*. San Francisco: Jossey-Bass.

Habermas, J. (1984). *The theory of communicative action: Volume I*. Boston: Thomas McCarthy.

Hallinger, P. & Murphy, J. (1986). The social context of effective schools. *American Journal of Education, 86*(2), 328–255.

Hanushek, E. (1994). *Making schools work: Improving performance and controlling costs*. Washington DC: The Brookings Institute.

Hargreaves, A. (1997). Rethinking educational change: Going deeper and wider in the quest for success. In A. Hargreaves (Ed.), *Rethinking educational change with heart and mind: 1997 ASCD Yearbook*. (pp. 1–26). Alexandria, VA: Association for Supervision and Curriculum Development.

Hegel, G. W. F. (1956). *Lectures on the philosophy of history* (J. Sibree, Trans.) New York:

Hegel, G. W. F. (1967) *Hegel's philosophy of right* (T. M. Knox, Trans.), Oxford: Oxford University Press. (Original work published 1819).

Hegel, G. W. F. (1975). *Hegel's logic* (W. Wallace, Trans.) Oxford: Clarendon Press. (Original work published 1830)

Henry, M. (1996). *Parent-school collaboration: Feminist organizational structures and school leadership*. Albany, NY: State University of New York Press.

Hess, G. A. (1991). *School restructuring, Chicago style*. Newbury Park, CA: Corwin.

Hess, G. A., (1995). *Restructuring urban schools: A Chicago Perspective*. New York: Teachers College Press.

Higham, J. (1974). Hanging together: Divergent unities in American history, *Journal of American History, 61*, 10.

Hill, P. T. & Bonan, J. (1991). *Decentralization and accountability in public education*. Santa Monica, CA: Rand.

Hobbes, T. (1962). *Leviathan, or the matter, form, and power of a commonwealth ecclesiastical and civil* (M. Oakeshott, Ed.), New York: Collier Books. (Original work published 1651)

Hobbs, N., Dokecki, P. R., Hoover-Dempsey, K. V., Moroney, R. M., Shayne, M. W. & Weeks, K. H. (1984). *Strengthening families*. San Francisco: Jossey-Bass.

Hodgkinson, C. (1991). *Educational leadership: The moral art*. Albany, NY: State University of New York Press.

Hord, S. M. (1986). A synthesis of research on organizational collaboration. *Educational Leadership, 43* (5), 22–26.

Jackson, P. (1990). Introduction. In J. Dewey, *School and society*. Chicago: University of Chicago Press.

Kagan, S. L., Klugman, E. & Zigler, E. F. (1983). Shaping child and family policies: Criteria and strategies for a new decade. In E. F. Zigler, S. L. Kagan & E. Klugman (Eds.), *Children, families, and government: perspectives on American social policy* (pp. 415–438). New York: Cambridge University Press.

Keniston, K. (1965). *The uncommitted: Alienated youth in American society*. New York: H. Wolf.

Kirkpatrick, F. G. (1986). *Community: A trinity of models*. Washington DC: Georgetown University Press.

Knapp, M. S., Barnard, K., Brandon, R. N., Gehrke, N. J., Smith, A. J. & Teather, E. C. (1994). University-based preparation for collaborative interprofessional practice. In L. Adler & S. Gardern (Eds.), *The politics of linking schools and social services* (pp. 137–151). Washington DC: Falmer.

Kratzer, C. (1997, March). *Community and diversity: Can they coexist?* Paper presented at the annual meeting of the American Educational Research Association, Chicago, IL.

Kratzer, C. (1996). *Exploring community in one urban school*. Unpublished dissertation, University of California, Los Angeles, Los Angeles, CA.

Krook, D. (1959). *Three traditions of moral thought*. Cambridge: The University Press.

Ladson-Billings, G. (1994). *The dream-keepers: Successful teachers of African-American children*. San Francisco: Jossey-Bass.

Lagerman, E. (1989). The plural worlds of educational research. *History of Education Quarterly, 29*(2), 185–214.

Lakoff, G. & Johnson, M. (1980). *Metaphors we live by*. Chicago: University of Chicago Press.

Law, D. & Lodge, P. (1984). *Science for the social scientist*. Chicago: University of Chicago Press.

Lawton, S. B. (1991, September). *Why restructure?* Revision of paper presented at the annual meeting of the American Educational Research Association, Chicago.

Lightfoot, S. L. (1984). *The good high school: Portraits of character and culture*. New York: Basic.

Little, J. W. (1993) Professional community in comprehensive high schools: The two worlds of academic and vocational teachers. In J. W. Little & M. W. McLaughlin (Eds.), *Teachers Work: Individuals, colleagues, and contexts*. New York: Teachers College Press.

Lomoty, K. (Ed.) (1990). *Going to school: The African-American experience*. Albany, NY: State University of New York Press.

MacIntyre, A. (1981). *After virtue: A study in moral theory*. Notre Dame: University of Notre Dame Press.

MacIntyre, A. (1988). *Whose justice? Which rationality?* Notre Dame: University of Notre Dame Press.

McLaren, P. (1993). Multiculturalism and the postmodern critique: Towards a pedagogy of resistance and transformation. *Cultural Studies, 7*(1), 118–146.

McLaughlin, M. W. (1993). What matters most in teachers workplace context? In J. W. Little & M. W. McLaughlin (Eds.), *Teachers Work: Individuals, colleagues, and contexts*. (pp. 79–103). New York: Teachers College Press.

McLaughlin, M. W., Talbert, J. & Phelan, P. K. (1990). 1990 CRC Report to field sites (Report No. R90–4). Stanford, CA: Center for Research on the Context of Secondary School Teaching, Stanford University.

McMillan, D. (1976). *Sense of community: An attempt at definition*. Unpublished manuscript. George Peabody College, Nashville.

Maccoby, M. (1988). A new model for leadership, *Research Technology Management, 31*(6), 53–54.

Macmurray, J. (1961). *Persons in relation*. New York: Harper and Brothers.

Malen, B. & Ogawa, R. T. (1988). Professional-patron influence on site-based governance councils: A confounding case study. *Educational Evaluation and Policy Analysis, 10*, 251–270.

Malen, B., Ogawa, R. T. & Kranz, J. (1989). *What do we know about school based management? A case study of the literature—a call for research*. Paper presented at the conference on choice and control in American education, University of Wisconsin-Madison.

Marx, K. (1967). *Capital: A critique of political economy*. New York: International.

Marx, K. (1977). *Karl Marx: Selected writings*. Oxford: Oxford University Press.

Mayeroff, M. (1971). *On caring*. New York: Harper & Row.

Mazzoni, T. & Sullivan, B. (1986). State government and educational reform in Minnesota. In V. D. Mueller & M. P. McKeon (Eds.), *The fiscal, legal, and political aspects of state reform of elementary and secondary education* (pp. 169–202). Cambridge, MA: Ballinter.

Meier, D. (1987). Success in East Harlem: How one group of teachers built a school that works. *American Educator, 11*(3), 34–49.

Meier, D. (1991). The kindergarten tradition in the high school. In K. Jervis & C. Montag (Eds.), *Progressive education for the 1990s: Transforming practice*. (pp. 135–148). New York: Teachers College Press.

Meier, D. (1992). Reinventing teaching. Teachers College Record, 93(4), 594–609.

Melaville, A. I. & Blank, M. J. (1991). *What it takes: Structuring interagency partnerships to connect children and families with comprehensive service*. Washington, DC: Education and Human Services Consortium.

Merz, C. & Furman, G. (1997). *Community: Promises and paradoxes*. New York: Teachers College Press.

Mitchell, B. (1990). Loss, belonging, and becoming: Social policy themes for children and schools. In B. Mitchell & L. L. Cunningham (Eds.) *Educational leadership and changing contexts of families, communities, and schools* (pp. 19–51). Chicago: The University of Chicago Press.

Murphy, J. (1996). *The privation of schooling: Problems and possibilities*. Thousand Oaks, CA: Corwin.

Murphy, J. & Beck, L. G. (1995). *School-based management as school reform: Taking stock*. Thousand Oaks, CA: Corwin.

Murphy, J., Weil, M., Hallinger, P. & Mitman, A. (1985). School effectiveness: A framework. *The Educational Forum, 49*, 361–374.

Nisbit, R. A. (1990). *The quest for community: A study in the ethics of order and freedom*. San Francisco: Institute for Contemporary Studies.

Noddings, N. (1984). *Caring: A feminine approach to ethics and moral education*. Berkeley, CA: University of California Press.

Noddings, N. (1992). *The challenge to care in schools*. New York: Teachers College Press.

Noddings, N. (1996). On community. *Educational Theory, 46*,3, 245–267.

Nozick, R. (1974). *Anarchy, state, and utopia*. New York: Basic Books.

Oakes, J. & Quartz, J. (Eds.) (1995). *Creating new educational communities: Ninety-fourth yearbook of the National Society for the Study of Education, Part I*. Chicago, IL: The National Society for the Study of Education.

Oldenquist, A. (1991). Community and de-alienation. In A. Oldenquist & M. Rosner (Eds.), *Alienation, community, and work*. (pp. 91–108). New York: Greenwood Press.

Olsen, L. (1990, September 12). Milwaukee's choice program enlists 391 volunteers. *Education Week, 9*, 7.

Olsen, L. (1991, February 20). Proposals for private-school choice reviving at all levels of government. *Education Week, 10*,30.

Pallas, A. M., Natriello, G. & McDill, E. L. (1995). Changing students/changing needs. In E. Flaxman & A. H. Passow (Eds.) *Changing populations: Changing schools: Ninety-fourth yearbook of the National Society for the Study of Education, Part II* (pp. 30–58). Chicago, IL: The National Society for the Study of Education.

Perrow, C. (1986). *Complex organizations: A critical essay*. New York: Random House.

Philbrick, J. (1885). *School Systems in the United States*. Washington, DC: U. S. Bureau of Education.

Powell, A. G., Farrar, E. & Cohen, D. K. (1985). *The shopping mall high school: Winners and losers in the educational marketplace*. New York: Houghton-Mifflin.

Purpel, D. (1989). *The moral and spiritual crisis in education: A curriculum for justice and compassion in education*. New York: Bergin & Garvey.

Rutter, M., Maughan, B., Mortimore, P., Ouston, J. & Smith, A. (1979). *Fifteen thousand hours: Secondary schools and their effects on children*. Cambridge, MA: Harvard University Press.

Schmidt, P. (1991, December 1). Massachusetts districts turn thumbs down on state's hastily passed choice program. *Education Week, 11*, 1,17.

Schön, D. A. (1990). *Educating the reflective practioner.* San Francisco: Jossey-Bass.

Schultz, S. (1973). *The culture factory: Boston Public Schools, 1789–1960.* New York: Oxford University Press.

Sedlak, M. W., Wheeler, C. W., Pullin, D. C., Cusick, P. A. (1986). *Selling students short: Classroom bargains and academic reform in the American high school.* New York: Teachers College Press.

Selznick, P. (1957). *Leadership and administration.* New York: Harper & Row.

Selznick, P. (1992). *The moral commonwealth.* Berkeley, CA: University of California Press.

Sergiovanni, T. J. (1993). *Organizations or communities? Changing the metaphor changes the theory.* Paper presented at the annual meeting of the American Educational Research Association, Atlanta, GA.

Sergiovanni, T. J. (1994). *Building community in schools.* San Francisco: Jossey-Bass.

Shearer, W. J. (1898). *The grading of schools.* New York: H. P. Smith.

Simon, H. A. (1945). *Administrative behavior.* New York: Macmillan.

Singer, P. S. (1995). Georg Wilhem Friedrich Hegel. In T. Honderich (Ed.), *The Oxford companion to philosophy* (pp. 339–343). New York: Oxford University Press.

Smith, A. (1937). *An inquiry into the nature and causes of wealth of nations.* New York: Modern Library.

Smrekar, C. (1996). *The impact of school choice and community: In the interest of families and schools.* Albany, NY: State University of New York Press.

Smrekar, C. (1996). The Kentucky family resource centers: The challenges of remaking family-school interactions. In J. Cibulka & W. Kritek (Eds.), *Coordination among schools, families, and communities: Prospects for educational reform* (pp. 3–25). Albany, NY: State University of New York Press.

Snauwert, D. T. & Theobald, P. (1995). Editors introduction: Education and the liberal-communitarian debate. *The Peabody Journal of Education, 70*(4), 1–4.

Snider. (1990). Voucher system for 1,000 pupils adopted in Wisconsin. *Education Week, 9,* 1,14.

Starratt, R. J. (1994). *Building an ethical school: A practical response to the moral crisis in schools.* London: Falmer.

Starratt, R. J. (1997). *Administering meaning, administering community, administering excellence: The new fundamentals of educational administration.* New York: Merrill.

Swap, S. M. (1993). *Developing home-school partnerships: From concepts to practice.* New York: Teachers College Press.

Taylor, C. (1979). *Hegel and modern society.* Cambridge: Cambridge University Press.

Taylor, C. (1989). *Sources of the self.* Cambridge, MA: Harvard University Press.

Theobald, P. & Dinkelman, T. (1995). The parameters of the liberal-communitarian debate. *Peabody Journal of Education, 70*(4), 5–18.

Theobald, P. & Snauwart, E. (Eds.) (1995). *Peabody Journal of Education, 70*(4).

Tonnies, F. (1957). *Gemeinschaft und Gesellschaft [Community and society]* (C. P. Loomis Trans.), East Lansing: Michigan State University Press. (Original work published in 1887).

Tyack, D. (1974). *The one best system: A history of American public education.* Cambridge, MA: Harvard University Press.

Tyack, D. & Hansot, E. (1982). *Managers of virtue: Public school leadership in America, 1920–1980.* New York: Basic.

Viorst, J. (1986). *Necessary losses: The loves, illusions, dependencies, and impossible expectations that all of us have to give up in order to grow.* New York: Simon and Schuster.

Wagstaff, L. H. & Reyes, P. (1993, August). *School site-based management* (Report presented to the Educational Economic Policy Center). Austin: University of Texas, College of Education.

Weber, M. (1947). *The theory of social and economic organization.* (T. Parson, Trans.) New York: Free Press.

Wells, A. S. (1997). *Understanding charter schools.* Research proposal submitted to Ford Foundation.

Wood, A. W. (1995). Karl Marx. In T. Honderich (Ed.), *Oxford Companion to Philosophy.* (pp. 523–526). New York: Oxford University Press.

CHAPTER 17

Institutional Theory and the Study of Educational Organizations

Brian Rowan and Cecil G. Miskel

In the past decade, scholars have described the emergence of a "new" institutionalism in organization theory and the core disciplines from which it draws—economics, political science, and sociology (DiMaggio and Powell, 1991; March and Olsen, 1989; Moe, 1984; Scott, 1995; Langlois, 1986; Williamson, 1995: Chapter 9). Although this movement contains diverse and sometimes inconsistent theoretical ideas, it reflects a growing tendency in the social sciences to abandon models of social and organizational action in which relatively autonomous actors are seen as operating with unbounded rationality in order to pursue their self-interests. Such models have been central to a variety of theories in the social sciences, including micro-economic theories of the firm, pluralist political theories, and closed rational systems theories of organization. In contrast, the new institutionalism sees social actors of all sorts—individuals, managers, interest groups, public agencies, and corporations—as embedded in socially-organized environments that generate rules, regulations, norms, and definitions of the situation that constrain and shape action. The goal of the new institutionalism is to study how such environments arise and to investigate their effects on social action.

Although still inchoate in form, the new institutionalism is increasingly attracting the attention of scholars in educational administration (Bacharach, Masters, and Mundell, 1995; Cibulka, 1995; Crowson, Boyd, and Mawhinney, 1996; Galvin and Barrott, 1995; House, 1996; Ogawa, 1994; Rowan, 1995). To date, however, no synthesis has been published that applies the various strands of institutional theory to the study of schooling. In this paper, we seek to address this problem. Our purpose is to describe the central elements of the new institutionalism and to explore its real and potential contributions to the study of educational organizations. In developing this analysis, we examine how the new institutionalism explains the rise of large-scale, education bureaucracies, look at what this perspective says about the structure and management of educational organizations, and explore its implications for the study of educational productivity. In developing our arguments, we will review previous research on schooling undertaken from the institutional perspective, but we also will apply institutional theory to domains of educational analysis to which it has not previously been applied. In this way, we consider both the contributions and the potential limits of this perspective to the study of education.

What Is the "New" Institutionalism?

In organization theory and in the disciplines of economics, political science, and sociology, a consensus is growing that institutional arrangements play a key role in shaping collective action. As Scott (1995: Chapter 3) shows, institutional arrangements can be found at a variety of levels in social systems—in societies (and the world system of societies), in organizational fields, in individual organizations, and in primary and small groups. Moreover, as Scott (1995) shows, institutional arrangements have regulatory, normative, and cognitive origins. Some institutions are based on formal, written codes of conduct, such as laws, constitutions, manuals of procedures, and so on, all of which are backed by the coercive power of social agencies. Other institutions exist more informally as norms and values—that is, as strongly felt obligations that have been internalized through socialization. Still others exist in the form of deeply institutionalized cognitive schemata or scripts—that is, relatively tacit, taken-for-granted, rule-like understandings of a situation. Given the diversity of institutional forms, we define an institution as "a set of more or less agreed-upon rules which carry meaning for and determine the actions of some population of actors" (Abell, 1995: 5). Furthermore, we say that an action, or sequence of actions and interactions, is institutionalized when it recurs repetitively and without overt intervention, or when a pattern of social action reproduces itself according to some orderly set of rules (cf., Jepperson, 1991).

The importance of institutions can be illustrated by briefly examining the new institutionalism as it is emerging in the various social science disciplines that contribute to organization theory and educational administration. Rather than attempting a complete review, we focus here on a small number of clearly identifiable works at the cutting edge of the movement. For an extensive review of the new institutionalism in a variety of disciplines, see Scott (1994; 1995).

The New Institutionalism in Economics

In economics, the new institutionalism responds to what many organization theorists see as unrealistic assumptions about the nature of firms (for a review, see Langlois, 1983). The orthodox view in economics regards a firm as a unitary decision-maker with an objective set of preferences acting to maximize its present value or profits. However, profit maximization can occur only in a perfectly competitive market, that is, a market with a large number of buyers and sellers, perfect information, and easily accomplished transactions. The problem with this model, of course, is that firms are seldom unitary actors and markets often fail. Principal-agent theory (Jensen and Meckling, 1976) and transaction cost economics (Williamson, 1975; 1985) address these problems. Together they constitute the core of the new institutionalism in economics.

Transaction cost economics deals with the problem of how to conduct economic transactions as efficiently as possible under conditions of market failure. Its importance to institutional theory is that it explains the emergence of *ex ante* rules governing economic exchanges, in particular, the conditions under which economic transactions come to be governed either by the pricing mechanisms of the market, the hierarchical arrangements of firms, or some hybrid form. Transaction cost economics describes how factors like uncertainty, opportunism, and asset specificity affect the potential costs of economic exchanges; and it also explains the conditions under which different governance structures (such as markets versus hierarchies) succeed in economizing on costs.

Principal-agent theory is often used to explain governance arrangements within firms. This perspective views the firm as a fictitious legal person with a set of bilateral contracting relationships with its agents. These agents, in turn, are seen as rational actors but ones who act in their own (as opposed to the firm's) best interests. Principals have a difficult time monitoring agents' activities, and agents are predisposed to engage in opportunistic behavior, to seek unreasonable growth in their budgets, and to shirk their responsibilities. As a result, under a wide range of conditions, firms produce suboptimal outcomes. Principal-agent theory describes a number of governance and control mechanisms that can be used by principals to constrain the behavior of agents and increase organizational efficiency.

Both principal-agent theory and transaction cost economics paint a much more realistic picture of the firm than does classical economic theory. Both concentrate on describing the various rules and procedures that can be used by firms to control the actions of internal and external exchange partners. However, as Williamson (1995: 211) notes, the new institutionalism in economics has a rather narrow focus, attempting to explain how economic organizations develop different governance structures under a limited set of historically-bounded economic conditions. Thus it is very different from older traditions of institutional economics that sought to describe the larger set of political, social, and legal rules that establish the basis for economic production, exchange, and distribution in societies at many different points in time. These broader questions continue to capture the interest of economists and, to some extent, sociologists, but this tradition is not usually seen as the forefront of the new institutionalism in economics.

The New Institutionalism in Political Science

Transaction cost economics, principal-agent theory, and related perspectives are also being used to develop a new institutionalism in political science. Here, however, the new institutionalism appears to be a reaction against aspects of pluralist political theory. As Bill and Hardgrave (1981) note, political science was once dominated by analyses of the formal institutions of government. However, these analyses were largely descriptive and atheoretical and by the 1960s they were pushed aside by scholars intent on examining political behavior, such as voting, party and interest group formation, the informal exercise of power and influence, and so on. One of the most important strands in the behavioralist tradition is pluralist political theory, which describes democratic politics as a fluid process in which relatively autonomous individuals and interest groups rationally pursue their self-interests in the political arena.

By the 1980s, political scientists began to reassert the importance of institutions in political life (March and

Olsen, 1984). One line of work used transaction cost economics, agency theory, and related approaches to explain why political processes are more stable than pluralist theories would predict and to show how political outcomes are affected, not only by the relatively fluid contest for power and influence among interest groups, but also by the more stable, institutionalized rules that shape legislative decision-making (Shepsle and Weingast, 1987). In related work, Moe (1984) extended this approach to the study of public bureaucracies. Moe argued that public bureaucracies take on the structures they do in order to protect political "property rights," to respond to uncertainty and change, and to control principal-agent problems inherent in the exercise of public authority (Moe, 1995). Like the new institutionalism in economics, these approaches are frequently used to explain only a small number of institutional arrangements, often those in the U.S. federal system. But a broader institutional analysis also exists in political science, one that seeks to understand how historically-grounded institutional arrangements structure interests and constrain action in different industrial sectors and nation-states around the world (Scott, 1994; Steinmo, Thelen, and Longstreth, 1992).

The New Institutionalism in Sociology

It is more difficult to pinpoint the origins of a new institutionalism in sociology. Sociology is often defined as the study of institutions, and institutional analysis (in one form or another) has characterized sociology since its inception. For convenience, we attribute the beginnings of the new institutionalism in sociology to the work of John W. Meyer, W. Richard Scott, and colleagues (Meyer and Scott, 1983). Meyer, Scott, and others are working in the tradition of organization theory and developing a form of organizational analysis that is closely allied with the open, natural systems movement in this field. Here the reaction is against closed, rational systems models that portray organizations as relatively autonomous units concerned primarily with achieving technical efficiency. In closed, rational systems models, organizational structures are typically seen to develop in response to increased needs for coordination and control that result from increases in size or technical complexity (Blau and Schoenherr, 1967; Woodward, 1965).

Beginning in the 1970s, closed, rational systems models were gradually abandoned in organization theory as open systems theorists began to look at the relations of organizations to their social environments. In the early stages of open systems theory, the emphasis was still on rational actors and the drive toward efficiency. For example, Thompson (1967) developed a form of open systems analysis in which organizations were seen as striving to be rational and efficient but constrained by the structure of exchange relationships across organizational boundaries and by various internal, technical complexities. Thompson's work was a watershed in organization theory, putting the final nail in the coffin of closed, rational systems models in organizational analysis.

The institutional theory of Meyer, Scott, and colleagues continued this tradition of open systems thinking but changed it substantially. Their emphasis was on institutional as opposed to technical sources of organization, that is, the tendency for organizations to succeed and persist as a result of conformity to institutionalized rules and procedures as opposed to technical efficiency (Meyer and Rowan, 1977; DiMaggio and Powell, 1983). As we discuss below, the conflict between pressures for efficiency and pressures for institutional conformity is a theme that dates to the earliest institutional theories of organizations (Selznick, 1957; Parsons, 1960), and one that has led Scott (1992) to view institutional analysis as a form of natural (as opposed to rational) systems theorizing.

Equally important, the institutional theory of Meyer, Scott, and colleagues changed the way institutions were thought about by organizational sociologists. In particular, the new institutionalists were influenced by phenomenological conceptions of institutions, especially Berger and Luckmann's (1967) sociology of knowledge, and by the phenomenological and symbolic interactionist conceptions of practical action developed by Schutz (1962), Garfinkel (1967), and Goffman (1967) (for a discussion, see DiMaggio and Powell, 1991: Chapter 1). In this perspective, regulatory and normative frameworks are still viewed as key components of an organization's institutional environment, but additional emphasis is placed on what Scott (1995) calls the "cognitive" conception of institutions —that is, the taken-for-granted schemata and ideological formations that define appropriate structures and lend meaning and order to practical action.

A cognitive conception of institutions allowed Meyer (1983a) and other theorists to mount a radical attack on the concepts of rationality in organizational, political, and economic analysis. In the sociological version of the new institutionalism, concepts such as rationality, self-interest, and efficiency are seen as ideological formations—that is, cultural constructions impossible to conceptualize without the creation and institutionalization of new ideologies about the nature of individuals, society, and progress and that are impossible to achieve in practical action without substantial changes in the regulatory and normative regimes of society (Dobbin, 1994; Douglas, 1995; Friedlander and Alford, 1991; Jepperson and Meyer, 1991).

Comparing the New Institutional Theories

Although the new institutionalism in sociology, political science, and economics contains diverse theoretical perspectives, some unifying themes do appear (for an attempt at a synthesis, see Scott, 1995). In each discipline, there is a rejection of models in which social actors (individuals, groups, organizations) are seen as engaging in unrestrained, rational pursuit of their interests. Instead, *all* institutional theorists see action as socially embedded and constrained by regulations, normative obligations, and/or cognitive schemata.

One way institutional approaches differ, however, is in the level of analysis at which they operate (for a discussion, see Scott, 1995: 57). In political science and economics, for example, principal-agent theory, transaction cost economics, and related perspectives pay the closest attention to the regulation of exchange relationships occurring within organizations or at their boundaries. The focus is thus on organizations or organizational subsystems, a terrain that was formerly the distinctive province of organization theorists. Sociologists are also interested in institutional analysis at these levels, but more recently they have extended organizational analysis to include attention to institutions at supra-organizational levels, such as populations of organizations, institutional sectors, and the societal and world system levels of analysis. Thus the sociological version of the new institutionalism is coming into closer alignment with current studies of industries and societies undertaken by political scientists and economists (for a discussion, see Scott, 1994).

Finally, institutional perspectives vary in the degree to which they embrace rational actor models. Principal-agent theory is built around them, but it shows how actors in rational pursuit of their own self-interests can undermine organizational goals and produce suboptimal performance at a corporate level. As a result, this version of institutional theory has some resemblance to early institutional analyses in organization theory (discussed below), which emphasize how the interactions of self-interested parties in organizations can deflect organizations from their original goals and compromise performance (Selznick, 1957). Transaction cost economics explicitly embraces a model of bounded rationality and uses this model to show how actors can design governance structures that are as efficient as possible, given a set of constraints (Williamson, 1995). In its emphasis on bounded rationality, transaction cost economics intersects with the Simon-March tradition in organization theory (Simon, 1945; March and Simon, 1958), and in its emphasis on exchange relationships at the boundary of organizations, it is working in the same terrain as the open, rational systems approach pioneered by Thompson (1967). The new institutionalism in sociology appears to be the least congruent with rational systems models of organization. It sees the rational pursuit of interests as frequently in conflict with and subordinate to the pursuit of institutional legitimacy (Meyer and Rowan, 1977; DiMaggio and Powell, 1983). In addition, it frequently sees rational action, not as a material fact, but rather as a cultural construction

in which means-end sequences and the very calculus of rational efficiency are understood as ideological constructs institutionalized in society.

Early Institutional Analyses in Organization Theory

The discussion to this point suggests that the new institutionalism provides scholars with a variety of powerful, analytic tools that help explain why large-scale, bureaucratic organizations often fail to display the technically efficient operations described in Weber's (1947) ideal model of rational bureaucracies. In this respect, however, the new institutionalism is hardly plowing new ground. Critiques of the Weberian model of organization and of the rationality of bureaucratic action were also present in an older and much revered tradition of institutional analysis that emerged at the founding of organization theory as a distinctive field of study. In this section, we discuss this older form of institutional analysis and show how, in the late 1970s, it came to be applied to the study of schools as organizations.

Early Institutional Analyses of Organizations

The most visible origins of institutional analysis in organization theory can be found in the writings of Philip Selznick and followers (for a review, see Perrow, 1986). In a series of case studies conducted in the 1950s and early 1960s, Selznick and colleagues described how organizational goals, structures, and processes developed in response to the interplay of interests among the internal and external constituents of organizations and the changing social environments in which organizations are located (Selznick, 1948, 1949, 1957; Gusfield, 1955; Clark, 1956; Perrow, 1961; Zald and Denton, 1963). In this early version of institutional theory, organizations were seen, not so much as "the structural expression of rational action," but rather as naturally evolving social systems that become institutionalized and develop stable and orderly patterns. For Selznick (1957), the gradual process of institutionalization made organizations more than rational instruments designed to meet technical ends. Instead, Selznick (1957: 17) believed that organizations are always infused with meaning and value "far beyond the technical value of the task at hand," and as a result, that organizations "never [fully] succeed in conquering the non-rational dimensions organization behavior" (Selznick, 1948: 25).

Talcott Parsons (1960) also made a major contribution to the institutional analysis of organizations. In contrast to Selznick (1949), who emphasized processes of institutionalization occurring within organizations and in their immediate environments, Parsons (1960) advanced the view that organizations are subsystems of the wider social system and gain legitimacy and resources by conforming to relevant norms, values, and technical lore institutionalized in society. As a result, Parsons (1960) believed that a key task of administrators is the alignment of an organization's aims and missions with society's norms and values. In Parsons' (1960) view, actions taken to align organizations to society's norms and values often come into conflict with actions taken to promote goal attainment. As a result, Parsons (1960) argued that organizations develop separate subsystems to attend to the potentially conflicting functional imperatives of securing legitimacy and enhancing efficiency, leading to the emergence of what he called a "qualitative break" between the institutional and technical levels of administration. In the 1960s, Parsons mode of organizational analysis was distinctive because it emphasized legitimacy (as opposed to efficiency) as a major source of organizational survival and because it emphasized organizational conformity to institutions existing at a societal (as opposed to more local) level.

The Revival of Institutional Theory

For nearly two decades, these early contributions to institutional analysis lay dormant in the field of organization theory. But in the late 1970s, they were revived and extended in an essay by Meyer and Rowan (1977) that is often cited as the beginning of the "new" institutionalism in organization theory. Building on Berger and Luckmann's (1967) sociology of knowledge, Meyer and Rowan (1977) argued that many of the elements characterizing modern, bureaucratic organization are "rationalized myths"—that is, deeply institutionalized, rule-like understandings about how best to organize to produce a given end. Following Parsons (1960), Meyer and Rowan (1977) argued that these rule-like templates are institutionalized in society and that organizations gain support and resources by conforming to them. In addition, Meyer and Rowan (1977) argued that the tendency for organizations to conform to rationalized myths explains why formal organizations look the way they do, why they adopt particular structures, include particular occupational groups in their division of labor, have particular rules and procedures, and so on. Thus in the 1970s, Meyer and Rowan (1977) rejected the view that formal organizational structures emerge in response to pressures for technical efficiency. Instead, they saw organizational structure as a reflection of rule-like assumptions about how best to organize.

In the same essay, Meyer and Rowan (1977) elaborated on Parson's (1960) ideas about the qualitative break between institutional and technical spheres of action and on Selznick's (1948) ideas about the non-rational tendencies of institutionalized organizations. In Meyer and

Rowan's (1977) view, organizations that depend for survival on conformity to institutionalized myths often engage in a process of "decoupling" that buffers work in the technical core from the consequences of institutional conformity. As part of this process, a logic of confidence and good faith develops in organizations as administrators deliberately ignore and discount information about technical activities and outcomes in order to maintain the appearance that things are working as they should be, even if they aren't. In this way, organizations continue to mobilize support and resources simply by conforming to externally-defined rules, even when such rules do not promote technical efficiency.

An Application of Institutional Analysis to the Study of Schools

In a related essay, Meyer and Rowan (1978) applied these ideas to the analysis of educational organizations. At the time, organization theorists were struggling to understand how schools could be so overtly bureaucratic in form and yet be characterized by such weak controls over teaching and learning in classrooms, a situation that led schools to be likened to "loosely coupled" systems (Bidwell, 1965; Weick, 1976). Meyer and Rowan's (1978) argument was that educational bureaucracies emerged in response to heavily rationalized, taken-for-granted theories about how best to organize education in modern society, but they also argued that this process did not lead to increased coordination and control over teaching and learning. Thus they developed an explanation for why schools existed as loosely coupled systems.

In Meyer and Rowan's (1978) argument, modern schooling in the United States developed as a way of sorting and classifying students for places in the occupational order, a societal function that required the development of a host of rationalized and standardized categories in education. For example, modern schools were staffed by standardized types of teachers assigned to teach standardized types of curriculum to standardized types of students in standardized types of schools. Such standardization created a national identity market that allowed organizations of all kinds to sort and allocate individuals to positions within the societal division of labor. Bureaucratic administration of schooling evolved to organize and manage these standardized categories and, as this occurred, the schooling enterprise gained enormous legitimacy in society and secured huge investments of resources.

However, the legitimacy of schooling as an enterprise depended crucially on maintaining the public's confidence in this highly institutionalized scheme, and this required educators (and the public) to ignore the obvious variations in classroom activities and student outcomes that occurred within standardized forms of schooling. As a consequence, schools evolved an elaborate set of administrative mechanisms like certification and accreditation, and a number of social practices (various forms of "face work") that allowed administrators to avoid inspecting technical activities while at the same time maintaining confidence in the system. In this way, an educational bureaucracy emerged that pays close attention to conformity to the institutionalized rules defining the structure of schooling, but one that gives far less attention to the actual technical activities or outcomes occurring within schools.

The Bridge from Older to Newer Forms of Institutional Theory

As the discussion above demonstrates, early institutional theorists believed that conformity to institutionalized rules could increase an organization's legitimacy and survival prospects without also increasing organizational efficiency or technical performance (Parsons, 1960; Meyer and Rowan, 1977, 1978; see also DiMaggio and Powell, 1983). This argument stands in sharp contrast to rational systems models, which hold that organizational performance (assessed in terms of efficiency) is the primary determinant of organizational survival. Thus the heavy emphasis on legitimacy as a source of organizational survival placed early institutional theory squarely in the camp of natural systems theorizing about organizations and made institutional analysis a distinctive form of theorizing in the field of organizations research.

In this section, we show how current forms of institutional analysis have modified early institutional theorists' heavy emphasis on legitimacy as a source of organizational survival, and we show how this change in emphasis has important implications, not only for understanding how newer forms of institutional theory depart from older ones, but also for understanding how newer institutional theories can be used to understand contemporary events in American education.

Tensions Between Legitimacy and Efficiency in Institutional Theory

A number of empirical studies confirm the hypothesis that increased legitimacy improves an organization's chances for survival (Baum and Oliver, 1991, 1992; Singh, Tucker, and Meinhard, 1991). However, the argument that legitimacy can enhance an organization's chances for survival without also increasing efficiency remains controversial. Perrow (1986), for example, argues that efficiency and legitimacy are closely intertwined and that inefficient organizations have a difficult time maintaining legitimacy, especially in societies that highly prize rationality and efficiency. As a re-

sult, Perrow (1986) doubts that conformity to institutionalized rules can enhance an organization's survival prospects without also improving efficiency.

By contrast, Meyer and Rowan (1977; 1978) argue that inefficient organizations are often protected by institutionalized rules and survive for long periods of time, and they cite several examples (such as Amtrack). It would be a mistake, however, to view Meyer and Rowan (1977) as primarily interested in explaining the survival of inefficient organizations. Instead, they argue that institutionalized rules often stabilize and enhance the survival prospects of organizations operating in domains characterized by high technical uncertainty where clear information about technical performance is missing or difficult to obtain.

Economists and political scientists working within the framework of the new institutionalism also argue that institutionalized rules emerge under conditions of technical uncertainty and that such rules stabilize organizational forms. What is interesting about these arguments, however, is the apparent faith placed in the rationality of institutionalized rules. In transaction cost economics and principal-agent theory, for example, institutionalized rules are typically thought to make economic transactions more efficient. Thus Williamson (1975; 1985) argues that institutionalized rules allow organizations to develop alternatives to market transactions under conditions of market failure. In his view, such rules reduce uncertainties, stabilize economic transactions, and make them more efficient. Similarly, principal-agent theory describes the various institutional rules that principals create to constrain the actions of agents, particularly when principals are unable to closely monitor performance. In this view, institutional rules prevent the kind of opportunistic behavior that undermines organizational goals and produces suboptimal performance. Thus here too, institutionalized rules are seen as enhancing organizational performance.

Technical and Institutional Environments

Clearly, these different versions of institutional theory make very different assumptions about the effects of institutionalized rules on organizational efficiency. One way to resolve these differences, however, is to turn to Meyer and Scott's (1983; 1991) distinction between technical environments that demand and reward organizational performance and institutional environments that demand and reward institutional conformity. Using this distinction, Meyer and Scott (1983; 1991) developed a typology that classifies organizations into four categories: (1) organizations that exist in weak technical but strong institutional environments (such as schools and other heavily regulated organizations with uncertain technologies); (2) organizations that exist in weak institutional but strong technical environments (many business firms in competitive markets); (3) organizations that exist in strong technical and strong institutional environments (hospitals); and (4) organizations that exist in weak technical and weak institutional environments (many personal service establishments).

This typology has a number of advantages for institutional analysis. First, it calls attention to the fact that organizations can experience differing demands for technical efficiency and institutional conformity. Second, it suggests that different versions of institutional theory can be more or less suited to the analysis of organizations operating in different kinds of environments. For example, transaction cost economics and the principal-agent theory seek to explain the emergence and functioning of institutionalized rules that materially enhance performance. Thus they seem most relevant to the analysis of social activities occurring within relatively well-defined technical environments where the ability to assess costs, measure outputs, and assign responsibility for productive outcomes allows for a direct test of the assumption that institutionalized rules enhance organizational performance (for an example, see Chubb and Moe, 1990). On the other hand, the sociological version of institutional analysis is designed to understand organizations operating in weak technical environments where information about technical productivity is difficult to obtain, uncertain, and infrequently emphasized (Meyer and Rowan, 1977, 1978; Scott and Meyer, 1991). Here one develops measures of the extent to which an organizational form is legitimate and examines the differential survival of legitimate and illegitimate forms over time in the absence of data on effectiveness (for examples, see Rowan, 1982a; Baum and Oliver, 1991, 1992; Singh, Tucker, and Meinhard, 1991).

The important point is that newer forms of institutional analysis have moved well beyond the simplistic assertion that conformity to institutionalized rules *always* conflicts with organizational efficiency. Instead, institutional theory now suggests that in some institutional environments (those with well-understood technical rules), pressures for institutional conformity can be efficiency enhancing, while in other institutional environments (those with weakly-understood technical rules), institutional conformity is best viewed as buffering organizations from technical uncertainty and decoupling demands for institutional conformity from demands for organizations to secure a weakly-specified and potentially unachievable state of technical efficiency.

Implications for the Study of Educational Organizations

There is little reason to believe that the four kinds of environments described by Scott and Meyer (1983; 1991) are fixed and immutable. Instead, the properties of technical and institutional environments probably result from the institution-building activities of interested parties in a given domain. In fact, the various versions of institutional theory just discussed suggest that under some conditions, interested parties increase demands for institutional conformity in the absence of pressures for efficiency, but under other conditions interested parties institutionalize demands for better performance. If these various demands can shift over time, it is possible for a population of organizations to exist in a weakly elaborated technical or institutional environment at one point in time, but, after concerted institution-building, to be in a strongly elaborated technical or institutional environment at a later point in time.

In fact, something like this appears to be happening in American education. Over the past 30 years, concerted institution-building by the education professions, government agencies, and private sector organizations has begun to produce a more elaborate technical environment for schooling, one that includes not only an increasingly sophisticated theory of educational productivity, but also the technical capacity to inspect instructional outcomes in schools. As a result, it appears that schools now face much stronger demands for technical performance than they did in the past, without also experiencing a decline in demands for institutional conformity.

An interesting question for educational researchers is what will happen as a result of this change. Scott and Meyer (1983: 126), following Parsons (1960), argue that organizations operating in strong technical *and* strong institutional environments experience high levels of conflict. This appears to be the case in American education, where a lack of consensus over appropriate institutional arrangements for schooling is clearly on the rise. Rowan (1982a) and Cibulka (1995) argue that this kind of dissension *destabilizes* education institutions, leading to periods of intense reform and new institution building. If this is true, it is not surprising to find that recent calls for greater accountability and productivity in education (without a corresponding decrease in demands for institutional conformity) have produced a long period of education reform in the United States. In fact, institutional theory predicts just such a trend.

Although institutional theory seems to predict the current state of conflict in American education, it says little about the likely outcomes of such a conflict. As a result, an important topic for future research is to study issues of organizational survival and institutional legitimacy in environments that demand efficiency and institutional conformity. In education, for example, historical studies are needed to better understand how increased demands for instructional accountability arose in the past and how such demands affected the institutionalization and dissemination of new instructional practices and/or patterns of regulation. Along these lines, for example, we might examine current trends in education and ask if regulatory and professional agencies are increasingly willing to endorse and disseminate only programs with "demonstrated" effectiveness, and whether the emergence of institutionalized procedures for outcome inspection gives rise to pressures for deregulation and market-based education reforms. Current events suggest that such trends exist, but more empirical studies are needed if we are to understand how increased demands for productivity arise in education and how educational organizations respond to such demands.

How Institutional Theory Explains the Structure of Educational Organizations

In the previous section, we demonstrated how recent institutional theories have modified earlier assumptions about the inherent conflict between institutional conformity and organizational efficiency. However, another central premise of early institutional theory, the idea that organizational conformity to institutionalized rules shapes the structure of organizations, has been retained as institutional theory moves forward. In this section, we examine ideas about institutional conformity and show how these ideas can be used to explain the rise of large-scale, education bureaucracies in modern societies.

The Concept of Institutional Sectors

The hypothesis that organizations conform to institutionalized rules suggests that, over time, organizations in the *same* institutional environment will come to resemble one another. DiMaggio and Powell (1983) were the first to argue that institutional environments produce homogeneity among organizational forms, a conclusion they drew by shifting the focus of institutional theory away from the study of single organizations and toward the study of what Meyer and Scott (1983; 1991) call "institutional sectors." An institutional sector can be defined as a domain of activity involving the production and distribution of a particular service or product. Such a sector is composed of the population of organizations that produce the given service or product *and* the populations of suppliers, consumers, and agencies that regularly interact with and support these organizations (DiMaggio and Powell, 1983; Meyer and Scott, 1991).

Using this definition, we can identify an education sector within American society that is composed of (1) a population of organizations providing educational services; (2) the associated organizations that supply these organizations (textbook companies, testing companies); (3) the population of people who are served by educational organizations (students, parents, businesses, and the interest groups in

they which they participate); (4) a number of groups that provide support within the sector (private foundations, independent consultants, and policy entrepreneurs); and (5) a variety of agencies of the state and the professions that regulate and give structure to the education enterprise.

As DiMaggio and Powell (1983) observe, institutional sectors originate as loose aggregations of organizations and groups. They take on a coherent structure as interactions among organizations in the sector increase, as hierarchical patterns of authority, domination, and coalition develop, and as organizations and groups in the sector exchange information and develop an awareness that they are engaged in a common enterprise (for an example, see DiMaggio and Powell, 1991). Once formed, institutional sectors can take on a variety of structural features. For example, Meyer and Scott (1983; 1991) and Scott (1994) describe how institutional sectors differ with respect to the patterns of hierarchical and lateral relationships that develop among organizations; in the kinds of rules, regulations, and prescriptions developed by institutional agencies and actors; in the levels of the social system at which institutionalized rules develop (national, regional, local); in the aspects of organizational structure and process constrained by the rules; and in the permeability of the sector to broader social forces.

Processes Leading to the Homogeneity of Organizational Forms

Once institutional sectors are well formed, various processes reduce variety and increase the homogeneity (or isomorphism) of organizational forms in the sector (DiMaggio and Powell, 1983; Scott, 1994). One such process is coercive isomorphism, in which organizations in a sector follow the formal rules and regulations laid down by the state and its agencies and thereby end up with similar structures or procedures. This, of course, is the process typically described in principal-agent theory where a principal (in this case, a state agency) uses a number of policy instruments to encourage rule-following by an agent (in this case, an organization). McDonnell and Elmore (1987) describe a number of such policy instruments in education, such as inducements, mandates, and capacity-building. Their arguments suggest that policy instruments differ in the extent to which they produce organizational homogeneity in education.

A major problem with coercive policy instruments is that they often drive up enforcement costs without producing anticipated gains in efficiency. This is especially the case in domains characterized by high technical uncertainty (see Moe, 1995). Thus a second strategy that leads to homogeneity is normative isomorphism. DiMaggio and Powell (1983) argue that this is the process by which professions commonly impose order on organizations. Here professional codes are spread to organizations by personnel who have been socialized and educated to follow professional standards. New institutional theorists in political science and economics discuss this process, for example, in describing how professional certification and accreditation can shore up markets that have failed or constrain the opportunism of agents. However, these versions of institutional theory tend to see normative constraints as an enforcement strategy, while sociologists emphasize how institutionalized norms produce homogeneous populations of organizations.

A third process that produces homogeneity of organizational forms, especially in sectors characterized by high technical uncertainty, is mimetic isomorphism. This process, which is similar to Meyer and Rowan's (1977) discussion of conformity to rationalized myths, occurs as organizations mimic successful or prestigious organizations in the field. In doing so, the less successful organizations seek to gain prestige and to assure publics that they are acting in ways that are modern and rational. In the long run, mimetic processes also lead to homogeneity as organizations in the same institutional sector adopt similar structures.

The three strategies just discussed are often criticized for portraying organizations as relatively passive actors that simply adapt to their institutional environments. However, with the growing use of rational actor models in institutional theory (such as principal-agent theory), concepts of agency have become more prominent, and institutional theorists have begun to see organizations as more pro-active with respect to their institutional environments (Oliver, 1991). In educational analysis, for example, Timar and Kirp (1988) discuss how state policy implementation is affected by local school district capacity. Their ideas correspond to the ideas of institutional theorists, who argue that the nature and timing of organizational responses to institutionalized rules can be affected by the characteristics of the conforming organization. Other researchers (Fuhrman, Elmore, and Clune, 1988; Firestone, Rosenblum, Bader, and Massell, 1991) also argue that school districts vary widely in their responses to state policy initiatives, although here an emphasis is placed on the ways in which these responses are shaped by the strategic actions of district leadership. Although this work is useful, it should be approached with caution. Studies in education often examine new education policies, not ones that are deeply institutionalized, and as many institutional theorists have shown, the effects of organizational capacity and strategic considerations on institutional conformity may be greatest in the early stages of the institutionalization process (Tolbert and Zucker, 1983). More interesting is Brint and Karabel's (1989) excellent institutional analysis of community colleges in which it is found that organizational leadership frequently plays an active role in promoting institutional change and producing institutional isomorphism.

Good demonstrations of the processes by which organizational forms in a sector become more and more alike can be found in studies tracing the diffusion of particular institutionalized forms through a population of organizations over long periods of time (Brint and Karabel, 1989; Burns and Wholey, 1993; Dobbin *et al.*, 1988; D'Aunno, Sutton, and Price, 1991; Fligstein, 1985; Mezias, 1990; Tolbert and Zucker, 1983; for a review, see Scott, 1995). These studies show that after new forms of organizing are institutionalized in the rules, norms, and regulations of powerful agencies in the institutional environment, they almost always diffuse through the population of organizations in a sector, often in the pattern predicted by theories of mimetic isomorphism. But studies also find that organizational characteristics such as size, complexity, network location and linkages, resource dependencies, and other factors affect the response and timing of an organization's response to changes in the institutional environment, especially in the early stages of the adoption process.

Organizational Isomorphism in Education

The formation of an institutional sector, the institutionalization of new rules and templates for organizing, the diffusion of these rules and templates throughout a population, and the resulting isomorphism of organizational forms appear to describe common processes in education. However, the reader interested in these developments in American education must read widely in the history of education and reinterpret the data presented in order to see such processes at work. As an example, we can trace the starting point for today's education sector to the common school movement of the 1800s. If we read various historical works, it is apparent that the education sector of the early 1800s had both a weak technical environment and a weak institutional environment. To be sure, in the first half of the 19th century, before the advent of compulsory school laws, many local communities had schools, and in many communities, school enrollments were quite high (Richardson, 1994). But there were many competing models of educational organization at this time (see Katz, 1971) and there was very little state, federal, or professional regulation (see Tyack, James, and Benevot, 1987).

Although many histories trace the development of the education sector in the United States, the work of Tyack and colleagues is especially helpful (see especially Meyer, Tyack, Nagel, and Gordon, 1979; Tyack, 1974; Tyack, James, and Benavot, 1987; Tyack and Tobin, 1994). Tyack's work is exemplary in its broad description of institution-building at the national, state, and local levels (especially in urban schools) and for its attention to the network of political, legal, and professional actors who worked together to institutionalize a rationalized, professionalized, and bureaucratized system of public schooling in the United States. Tyack describes the emergence of the "one best system" of schooling in the United States and the "grammar" of schooling associated with it, and he argues that this system and its associated grammar have enormous stability in American society. Tyack's work, therefore, is consistent with institutional theory.

Apart from general histories, other studies show how institutional environments in education create new templates for organizing and how such templates then diffuse through the population of schools. For example, Ogawa (1994) examined how various actors in the institutional environment constructed and rallied support for the innovation known as "school-based management." His study carefully described the interests of various actors in the institutional arena, in this case, policy advocates, union representatives, and academics, and showed how these actors were linked through a network of ties that allowed them to communicate with one another. It is an excellent study of the early stages of institution-building in education.

A study by Rowan (1982a) also illustrates how institutional environments are structured and how they structure educational organizations. Rowan traced the diffusion of three categories of education personnel to city school districts in California over the period 1920–1970. The creation of these personnel categories was traced to the institution-building activities of state and federal legislatures, the state education agency, professional agencies, and interest groups. The study also showed how successful institution-building was followed by the diffusion of these personnel categories to local school districts. Strang's (1987) study of school district consolidation describes a similar process. It showed that some American states exercised more centralized control over education than others, and those that did were more likely to push for school consolidation. Moreover, state-level support of consolidation created a massive process of ecological succession in which small school districts were rapidly replaced by much larger, more structurally complex, school districts. Both these studies demonstrate how, over long periods of time, new structural forms diffuse through the population of educational organizations. The studies also show how this process interacts with the characteristics of local school districts and state-level institutional environments to produce isomorphism among school districts.

Another important line of work considers these processes within the world system of societies and describes the standardization of schooling worldwide (Boli, Ramirez, and Meyer, 1985; Meyer, Kamens, and Benavot, 1992; Meyer, Ramirez, and Soysal, 1992; Ramirez and Boli, 1987). These studies trace the origins of the modern education sector to European ideologies about the state, the role of citizenship, and rights and responsibilities of individuals, all of which converge to bring about a theory of mass education for societal development. This ideology specifies the "right" to schooling, and it details the form schooling will take, in-

cluding the usual grammar of certified teachers, students, and types of schools, the age-grading of pupils, and a remarkably uniform set of curricular categories. This ideology is deeply institutionalized, first in the core societies of the world system, and later by the actions of various actors in the world education sector (the World Bank, UNESCO, professional consultants). It then spreads rapidly and universally to all states participating in the world system of societies.

A growing body of empirical work describes this process. For example, Meyer, Ramirez, and Soysal (1992) traced the expansion of mass education systems throughout the world over the period 1870–1980. They found that mass education systems appeared at a steadily increasing rate from 1870 to 1940 and expanded even more rapidly after World War II. Although a country's level of economic development, location in the world economy, and strength or weakness of the state apparatus had some effect on the adoption of a mass education system and on enrollments (see Fuller and Rubinson, 1992), the effects are surprisingly modest and are overpowered by the general trend toward state-sponsored provision of mass schooling in all societies in the world.

In another set of studies, Meyer, Kamens, and Benavot (1992) examined the national curriculum in a large sample of countries between 1920 and 1986. Here too the data indicate the presence of a standard model of schooling in the world system of societies. Virtually all countries in the world have institutionalized a core curriculum that includes attention to language, mathematics, natural science, social science, physical education, and the arts. Moreover, the number of countries in which these curricular categories are emphasized has increased through time. The study does not suggest that the curriculum in use within each of these categories is necessarily uniform (either within or across countries), and as we discuss below, it is not. Still, it is striking and consistent with institutional arguments about the standardization of organizations within a sector to find that the major categories of school curriculum are standardized worldwide.

In short, a substantial body of work on educational organizations confirms a central insight of institutional theory. Over time, in American states, in various nations of the world, and in the world system of societies, an institutional sector has emerged to define and standardize educational organization. Today virtually everywhere in the world, mass schooling is organized around a remarkably similar set of categories that defines the grammar of schooling. This grammar includes ideas about why students must attend school, the appropriate professional division of labor within educational organizations, the general categories of the school curriculum, and how all these categories of pupils, teachers, and subjects are to be organized in time and space to constitute a school. Such uniformity is not well predicted by theories that emphasize the role of local conditions (various characteristics of the local school population, the level of local economic development, and so on) in shaping schooling. Instead, the uniformity of schooling can only be accounted for by the isomorphism of schools within a well-developed institutional sector that has developed within state, national, and world systems.

Institutional Analysis and Managerial Processes Within Schools

In the previous section, we showed how the new institutionalism provides a powerful explanation for the rise of large-scale education bureaucracies in virtually all countries in the modern world. In this section, we turn to a description of how these education bureaucracies are managed. As discussed earlier, older versions of institutional theory tended to predict that organizational conformity to institutionalized rules produces "non-rational" tendencies in organizations. Selznick (1948; 1957), for example, described how responses to institutional pressures diverted organizations from their central missions, Parsons (1960) argued that institutional conformity produced a qualitative break between the technical and institutional components of organizations, and Meyer and Rowan (1977) argued that institutional conformity was often accompanied by a logic of confidence and face-saving in institutionalized organizations. Up through the 1970s, then, institutional theory tended to suggest that the isomorphism of organizations and institutional environments produces a situation in which goals are loosely coupled to technical activities, production outcomes are seldom monitored, and management turns from the problem of improving technical efficiency to the problem of maintaining institutional conformity.

In this section, we show how more recent versions of institutional analysis depart from this assumption. In fact, as we demonstrate below, the new institutionalism predicts that educational organizations, although subject to strong institutional pressures everywhere in the world, will show a variety of patterns of management depending upon the characteristics of the institutional environments in which they are embedded. The theories that lead to this prediction are the focus of discussion in this next section.

Patterns of Management Within Institutional Sectors

In newer forms of institutional theory, the patterns by which organizations are managed are seen to depend crucially on the ways in which institutional sectors are organized and on the types of controls agencies in a sector exercise over the populations of organizations within that sector. Scott and Meyer (1991) are the first to describe the structural dimensions along which institutional sectors vary. These include (1) the *complexity* of a sector (the number and types of agencies exercising controls in the sector), (2) the extent to which a clear *hierarchy* exists within a sector (the extent to which local agencies are clearly subordinate to regional agencies, which in turn are subordinate to national agencies); and (3) the amount of *horizontal coordination* among agencies and groups in the sector. Scott and Meyer (1991) also discuss different *patterns of control* that emerge in institutional sectors. For example, agencies that monitor performance and demand efficiency often create rules about and/or monitor organizational inputs, processes, and outputs; and agencies that monitor conformity often specify organizational goals, processes, and budgets.

Scott (1995) discusses a number of factors that affect the amount of complexity, hierarchy, and coordination evident in an institutional sector and the types of controls that agencies exercise over the relevant population of organizations in a sector. The factors he mentions include market conditions, political traditions, the technologies available for use in a sector, and a variety of other conditions. In our analysis of educational organizations, however, we emphasize how societal-level political traditions give rise to particular sector configurations. This emphasis is particularly appropriate, we believe, because in the modern world, education everywhere is socially constructed as a collective project of the nation-state (Fuller and Rubinson, 1992).

Jepperson and Meyer (1991) discuss the larger, political traditions within which institutional sectors emerge. They argue that the various "polities" found in modern nation-states take on a number of identifiable forms, including a liberal form (such as the United States), a corporatist form (such as Germany), and strong and weak statist forms (France is a strong form; many Latin American countries are weak forms). In order to demonstrate how larger political forces structure institutional sectors and how these, in turn, shape managerial processes, we provide some examples of the ways in which national political traditions structure the institutional environments of schooling. Our analysis concentrates on the strongest possible contrast in this process, a contrast between education sectors in liberal polities and education sectors in state-centered polities.

The Education Sector in Different Countries and Its Effects on Coordination and Control

The United States is a classic example of a liberal polity where individuals have important standing in society and are accorded many rights. Along with these rights, however, individuals are also vested with a great responsibility for carrying out society's collective projects. Thus in the United States, many important collective projects like the amelioration of poverty are thought to be handled best by the private actions of individuals. For example, in the United States today, there is much emphasis on volunteerism, on charity and philanthropy, and on corporate "responsibility" as important strategies for addressing the complex social problem of poverty. As can be seen in the current decline of social welfare programs, the state and its agencies are seen to have much less of a role to play in collective projects in a liberal polity, and state mechanisms for achieving collective ends therefore tend to be relatively weak (Jepperson and Meyer, 1991). Scott and Meyer (1991), following many others, argue that liberal polities encourage a pluralistic approach to decision-making, one that purposefully limits the powers of centralized, political agencies. As a result, institutional sectors in liberal polities are often organized as complex, multi-layered governance systems characterized by fragmented decision-making structures.

The education sector in the United States illustrates this tendency. Education is primarily a function of states within the federal system, but the federal government and local political bodies are also active in the sector as well. Indeed, all three levels contribute to decisions about program goals, operations, and/or funding. These three levels of government are not organized in a tightly coordinated way, however. Instead, authorities at multiple levels of the system are active in decisions of all kinds, creating overlapping and loosely coordinated programs that often duplicate one another and sometimes conflict. In such a situation, many agencies create programs they do not fund, fund programs over which they have little operational authority, or specify important organizational goals but leave the means and funding to be specified elsewhere in the system.

This complex and loosely coordinated system accounts for many of the peculiar characteristics of public schools and school districts in the United States. For example, Meyer (1983b) notes that public school districts in the United States are accountable to a large variety of agencies exercising control over funding and programs, and as a result, they expand their administrative components to respond to each of these agencies. This may account for the relatively higher expenditures that U.S. school systems make on administration in comparison to school systems in other nations (see, for example, OECD, 1996). In a similar way, organizational differentiation in public schools in the United States tends to mirror the diverse elements of the institutional environment, rather than being built around work flows in the technical core. Thus American public schools have many different program functionaries who respond directly to external programs (such as Title 1 teachers or special ed-

ucation teachers), but there is only one formally differentiated instructional leader: the principal.

The unique characteristics of the American education sector also account for the peculiar patterns of control found in American public school systems. In the American case, agencies that fund a program often have little or no authority over its content or operations. This is the case, for example, in many state education systems with strong traditions of local control, and, to a lesser extent, the pattern of governance found in the federal Title I program. In this situation, financial and statistical accounting tend to dominate as control mechanisms, but more substantive inspection and regulation of school processes are typically absent. Moreover, as financial and statistical controls come to dominate, American school systems develop elaborate business management operations and appoint managers of special programs, but there is correspondingly less growth of administrative components managing the technical core (cf. Rowan, 1981, 1982b). The American education system also contains cases in which program specifications originate in one agency while program funding originates in another. This accounts in part for the widespread finding that patterns of program implementation at the local level often vary widely, even though activities are conducted under the auspices of the same authorizing agency (Meyer, 1983b). The larger point is that much of the loose coupling observed in American education, the multiple and loosely coordinated programs that are present within educational organizations, the frequently loose connection of program goals to program activities, and the emphasis on statistical controls in the absence of substantive inspection are accounted for by the fragmented nature of control in the American education sector (Meyer and Rowan, 1978).

The loose coupling so characteristic of American education is unlikely to be found in the education sector of a state-centered polity, that is, a polity that tends to organize collective functions through the state. France is typically cited as an example of such a system in which "formal organizing arises in society, linked to, subordinate to, and defined in terms of state-represented actions and functions" (Jepperson and Meyer, 1991). In a state-centered polity, individuals or other social units that seek to influence collective action do so through the state. In such a system, one can expect more tightly structured and coherent institutional sectors, especially sectors organized around a collective function of society like education. In a state-centered polity, control over programs, operations, and funding would be centralized and coordinated by the state and its functionaries. All other actors in the sector (professional groups, support groups) or the field of organizations performing the function would seek influence and power by mobilizing at this central level (Jepperson and Meyer, 1991).

Such a description captures much of what is distinctive about the French education system. The system is far more centralized than the U.S. education system, with civil servants having strong powers over substantive educational matters, such as the curriculum. Moreover, there is consistent (as opposed to fragmented) control over programmatic, operational, and funding decisions. Lower levels of educational governance are subordinate to the state, and professionals in education enjoy great power by being linked to the state through graduation from state-sponsored, elite universities (for a description of the French system, see OECD, 1996). In theory, such an institutional environment should be more tightly coupled, both vertically and horizontally, than the U.S. system, and activities, once authorized or mandated, should be carried out with more fidelity than would be the case in the American setting (Scott and Meyer, 1991; Meyer, 1983b). In fact, some evidence exists to support the hypothesis that strong state control produces more straightforward and faithful implementation. For example, Stevenson and Baker's (1991) cross-national study of teaching showed that as state control over the curriculum increases, the variance in teachers' content coverage decreases, demonstrating just the effect that one would expect from a centralized and unified institutional environment.

Politics versus Markets in Institutional Sectors

The discussion has implications for current arguments about educational reform in the United States. In the 1990s, much attention has been given to the creation of coherent education policy, an approach also known as systemic reform (Fuhrman, 1994; Smith and O'Day, 1990). The main attempt here is to move away from the fragmented control system currently governing American education and to move toward closer coordination of policies about instructional goals, means, and funding. Institutional theory would predict that such a move could markedly change the way American schools are managed internally, considerably tightening the relationships between program goals, activities, and outcomes (see Meyer, 1983b). However, institutional theory also suggests that powerful forces must be overcome if such a system is to be implemented in the American polity. American states will have to work against a supremely powerful and ingrained tradition of local control in education. Moreover, systemic reform would require much more hierarchical (inter-governmental) coordination and cooperation than have been evident in the past. Such coordination would aim to link program goals and means more tightly and connect these with a more unified system of funding and monitoring. Finally, systemic reform would require much more horizontal coordination. For example, all the non-governmental groups within the education system, such as the specialized professional associations, the teacher and administrator preparatory institutions, and the textbook and test publishers, would have to closely coordinate or subordinate their activities to the state if their actions were to be brought into line in systemic reform. All of this seems to require the emergence of a more state-centered polity like France, something difficult to achieve in a liberal polity like the United States.

If moving to a strong, state-controlled educational system seems difficult to achieve in the American polity, perhaps a move toward deregulation and market controls makes more sense. In fact, this is a common theme in current efforts to reform American education, and one that is well-suited to the kinds of institutional analyses emerging in political science and economics. Market reforms have strong ideological appeal in liberal states around the world, in part because the ideological basis of liberal polities gives strong endorsement to the "private" enactment of "public" interest (Jepperson and Meyer, 1991).

An interesting empirical analysis of market controls over schooling is provided by Chubb and Moe (1990). In the classic tradition of institutional analysis, they set out to compare management practices in public and private schools in the United States, arguing that "different systems of institutional control should produce schools with quite different . . . characteristics" (Chubb and Moe, 1990: 1066). Chubb and Moe's (1990) basic argument has the familiar ring of both new and old institutional analysis. They argue that the institutional environment of public schools exerts strong pressures for conformity and brings about a "one best system," that is, a powerful pressure toward organizational uniformity. This arises, they assert, because public authority over education exists primarily to impose higher order values on schools, and its does so through bureaucratic controls such as rules and regulations, monitoring, and the creation of incentive structures that encourage conformity. Moreover, the system of public control over education is subject to capture by a wide range of special interests, many of which gain power and educational resources in the system in return for their support of politicians. As a result, the mission of public schools is deflected and made more complex.

Chubb and Moe (1990) also view public school officials as self-interested bureaucrats, interested in expanding their budgets, programs, and administrative controls, which they do by mobilizing as a political interest group that supports continued bureaucratic control over schools. Perhaps the most pernicious effect of this organizing, they argue, is the tendency for public schools to become near monopolies and to create a host of restrictions on family choice of schooling. In the American situation, parents can choose to exit the public school system by enrolling their children in private schools, but exit is difficult because private schools require tuition payments. Thus many dissatisfied clients remain in schools, attempting to exercise voice but having standing as just one of many voices that must be attended to.

By contrast, private schools in the United States are seen by Chubb and Moe (1990) as largely free of bureaucratic control, including Catholic schools (which are subject to the rules of the Catholic church). In their view, there is much autonomy in the private sector, and with this comes a number of important organizational attributes. Private schools have a greater ability to focus on a coherent as opposed to a fragmented and complex mission. Moreover, autonomy allows private schools to develop a much more participatory form of decision-making, gives schools more freedom to hire personnel that match the needs and mission of the school, and results in a higher level of employee job satisfaction and commitment. Private schools are also are free of union constraints, and, because their clients attend by choice (not constraint), private schools have better relationships with parents, higher parent involvement in schools, and a clientele that more closely monitors student work at home.

To support their arguments, Chubb and Moe (1990) present an analysis of survey data collected in 1984 from a nationally representative sample of teachers and administrators in the United States. The data show remarkable differences in the managerial features of public and private schools. As expected, private schools are less subject to external controls of all sorts, including substantive controls over instruction and curriculum practices, as well as personnel practices. Private school principals report more cooperation and support from parents. Compared to public school teachers, teachers in private schools judge their principals to be stronger instructional leaders, report having more influence on school policies of all sorts (including instructional policies), report higher levels of cooperation among teachers, and higher levels of job satisfaction and commitment. Moreover, private schools seem to be more focused on a single mission—instructional excellence—than do public schools, which tend to endorse many goals as worthy. Thus Chubb and Moe (1990) present strong evidence that differences in institutional environments affect patterns of management in schools.

Despite its appeal, Chubb and Moe's (1990) analysis is limited by its attention to the American context and by its neglect of the larger (societal) context in which American education is organized. For example, Chubb and Moe (1990) underemphasize the historical emergence of the private sector within American education, failing to show how private schooling in the United States is nested within the same fragmented, pluralistic, institutional environment in which public schools exist. In fact, private schooling in the United States results from much public institution building. For example, private schools gain their right to educate students as a result of important court rulings, and religious schools secure their freedom from institutional constraints as a consequence of the American state's reluctance to heavily regulate "private" affairs (Deavins, 1989). This stands in contrast to many other nations of the world, where the institutional environment affords choice of secular or religious schooling to students but does not afford religious or private schools the same measure of autonomy from external, institutional constraint that private schools in the United States currently enjoy (OECD, 1996).

Moreover, it would be a mistake to assume that American private schools are largely free of institutional constraint. The largest system of private education in the country, the Catholic school system, appears to have gone through much the same stages of institutional development as the public system. In the Jacksonian period, the system was "a motley collection of impoverished schools" that was increasingly brought under strong institutional control by the Roman Catholic Church (Baker, 1992: 200). By the postbellum period, the system had developed an elaborate institutional structure, complete with a unique institutional politics and a nascent professionalism. Over time, the schools in this system were deliberately constructed in reference to the public schools (Baker, 1992), bringing about what DiMaggio and Powell (1991) call "competitive isomorphism." Thus Catholic schools are in some measure a part of the "one best system" that Chubb and Moe (1990) see as composed only of public schools. Moreover, in recent years, various pressures have led the Catholic school system to begin to provide many of the special educational services that are provided in public schools (Title I) and to recruit a teaching force from the same labor pool as public schools. Thus a mix of market and other institutional pressures have structured the Catholic schools in America, and these pressures have produced substantial institutional isomorphism.

None of this is meant to deny the central point of Chubb and Moe's (1990) analysis. There *are* substantial differences in the way public and private schools in the United States are managed, and such differences result from differences in the institutional controls to which these schools are subjected. As Chubb and Moe (1990) note, however, extending the market provision of schooling in the United States to the public sector would require substantial institutional change. As in any market system, new forms of institutional regulation would be required, especially public policies designed to shore up potential market failures stemming from information problems, barriers to entry, and the various externalities that arise because education is a public good (Levin, 1989; Weimer and Vining, 1989). The point then is that even market organizations come under political and institutional control, and moving to the market provision of education in the United States would require much institution building.

Institutional Analysis and the Technical Core of Schooling

To this point, we have seen how institutional analysis accounts for the rise of large-scale education bureaucracies in modern societies and how differences in the configuration of institutional environments (within and between countries) accounts for the different patterns of management observed in different school systems. In this section, we turn to an analysis of how institutional processes affect the technical core of education.

Early institutional theories tended to ignore the effects of institutionalized rules on the technical core of schools—teaching and learning in classrooms. For example, Meyer and Rowan's (1978) analysis of loose coupling in educational organizations followed Parsons (1960) by positing a qualitative break between institutional and technical levels of management in schools and by predicting that managerial actions were most frequently devoted to buffering the technical core from institutional pressures. In retrospect, however, Meyer and Rowan's (1978) emphasis on loose coupling appears to have been a shortcoming of early institutional analysis, as various proponents of the new institutionalism have argued (Powell, 1991). In this section, we therefore develop a set of arguments about the ways in which institutional processes *do* affect the technical core of schools.

Institutional Effects on the Teachers' Instructional Work

There are a number of ways that institutional arrangements can affect technical or work activities within an organization. First, the structure of institutional sectors, and the types of rules promulgated therein, can affect the nature of work in organizations. As discussed above, complex and fragmented institutional sectors exercise only weak constraints on organizational work, but as an institutional environment becomes more unitary, as rules about work in the technical core become more specific, and as these rules get attached to outcome assessments or other inspection systems, institutional theory (like organization theory more generally) predicts stronger effects of institutionalized rules on work activities (Scott and Meyer, 1991; Meyer, 1983b).

An interesting analysis of the effects of institutionalized rules on teachers' work can be found in Cohen and Spillane's (1992) discussion of instructional guidance systems (institutionalized rules about instruction). In a test of the ideas developed there, Spillane and Jennings (1997) investigated curricular reforms in a school district that had carefully aligned its various instructional policies in support of an ambitious, new model of literacy instruction. The purpose of the study was to examine the effects of these policy changes on teachers' instructional practices. The study found that

when policies about a particular instructional practice were unambiguous and clear, the fidelity of implementation was high and variation in practice among teachers was low. On the other hand, when policies about a practice were ambiguous, implementation was more variable and teachers' practices were more influenced by teachers' prior experience and the unique interpretations teachers made of the policies. A similar set of findings was reported by Goodrick and Salancik (1996) in the health care domain where organizational variations in the implementation of institutionalized rules were highest when rules were uncertain and ambiguous and lowest when these rules were clear and certain.

These studies suggest that clarity and consistency in institutional rule-making can produce real effects on work activities within the technical core of schools. But institutional effects on teachers' work might also occur even in the fragmented system of educational control in the United States. For example, a great deal of evidence suggests that teaching practices in the United States are surprisingly consistent and numbingly routine. In an early study, Jackson (1968) noted an almost ritual sameness in classroom instruction. Later, Goodlad (1984) described the remarkable (and dreary) sameness of classroom teaching practices, Cuban (1984) noted the persistence of teacher-centered practices in American schools, and Rowan (1995) reported that the majority of high school teachers in his study of teachers' work practices reported that their work was routine.

For institutional theorists, the routine nature of teaching is a strong indication that teaching practices in American schools are institutionalized. Thus an important problem is to uncover the factors that stabilize and institutionalize these practices. The most common argument in research on American schools is that teaching practices are constrained by the organizational structure of schools (Cuban, 1984) and passed down across generations of teachers through an apprenticeship of observation (Lortie, 1975). From the standpoint of institutional theory, this argument makes sense, for it explains quite clearly how social processes are reproduced across generations in a way that is quite consistent with Zucker's (1977) experimental study of these processes and with Berger and Luckmann's (1967) broader discussion of institutionalization processes.

A shortcoming of this explanation, however, is its failure to locate the origins of this institutionalized pattern of teaching practice. In the argument, schools exist as institutionalized structures with embedded routines, people passing through these schools confront these institutionalized routines as objective reality, and thus become habituated to them. Later, as these individuals become teachers, they reproduce the routines they earlier experienced. The question, of course, is what accounts for the original framework?

Decades of research show that teaching practices in the United States are *not* subject to strong regulatory pressure of the sort described by Cohen and colleagues (Cohen and Spillane, 1992; Spillane and Jennings, 1997), so deliberate institution-building by state education agencies and local school districts is an unlikely source for the stability of teaching practices. Moreover, workplace norms of practice are unlikely sources of deep institutionalization, for here too evidence suggests that formal and informal collegial controls over teaching are typically weak in American schools (for a review, see Rowan, 1990).

If explicit regulations and workplace norms do not appear to account for the routine teaching practices found in American schools, perhaps teaching practices are structured by more tacit, cognitive understandings. In fact, Jackson (1968) suggested just such an idea after finding that teachers were unable to articulate any well-developed rationale for their teaching activities. Jackson's work further suggests that these tacit understandings are difficult to surface in the typical study, especially because teachers are largely unaware of the taken-for-granted understandings that structure their activities. What may be required, it seems, is a research design similar to the "breaching experiments" conducted by Garfinkel (1967), in which the tacit understandings and expectations that structure a social situation are violated. As this occurs, tacit understandings are sometimes more easily brought to the surface for study than would be the case in situations where these remain in an assumed form.

In education, an interesting example of a breaching experiment can be found in high schools that are engaged in detracking—reform efforts designed to replace the homogeneous ability grouping so characteristic of U.S. high schools. In a study of 10 racially mixed high schools engaged in such reforms, Oakes and colleagues have begun to demonstrate the powerful ideological and cultural bases of this common instructional practice and, thus, to discover the tacit understandings that shape instructional work in American schools (Oakes, Wells, Jones, and Datnow, 1997). They found that many teachers and parents in the schools under study embraced a commonsense "ideology of intelligence" and a view of social mobility derived from the "American dream." They argued that these views are deeply rooted in American culture and exist as "ruling ideas internalized by a majority of people [that act as] a defining motif of everyday life" (Oakes *et al.*, 1997: 485). In the schools under study, these larger, societal ideologies legitimized tracking and were available to participants as arguments against detracking reforms. Moreover, those who embraced these ideologies were resistant to a rational critique of their views. Thus it appears that tracking and the underlying ideologies which legitimize it are deeply institutionalized and have meaning "far beyond the technical value of the task at hand" (Selznick, 1957: 17).

If the origins of tracking lie in the institution-building of progressive educators and the powerful ideologies institutionalized in American society (Tyack, 1974), it makes sense to see this instructional practice as much more than an efficient and rational solution to the technical problem of individual differences in instruction. Tracking is also a social institution that has important consequences for instructional activities and instructional outcomes. It is well known, for example, that students in different tracks are exposed to different curricular content, that teaching and classroom climates differ across tracks, and that teachers' motivational states are affected by the track of the class they are teaching (Oakes, Gamoran, and Page, 1992; Raudenbush, Rowan, and Cheong, 1992, 1993). A great deal of research shows that these cross-track differences in teaching practice are part of the explanation for the effects of tracking on student achievement. Thus the ideological assumptions about learning, intelligence, and social mobility that rationalize and give legitimacy to tracking also appear to shape the nature of teachers' work in schools, as a variety of studies demonstrate (for a review, see Oakes, Gamoran, and Page, 1992).

The discussion above presents an account of a technical practice in schools that is based on a cognitive conception of institutions, that is, an account of a social institution that focuses on the taken-for-granted assumptions lying behind the institution rather the normative or regulatory bases of the institution. The power of this cognitive view of institutions is also found in recent studies of the effects of academic disciplines on the nature of teachers' work. Jackson (1986: Chapter 6) argued that all subjects within the school curriculum are associated with their own, unique epistemologies, that is, assumptions about the nature of knowledge and how it can be understood. In particular, Jackson (1986) argued that the sciences tend to be grounded in a more structured and paradigmatic view of knowledge and an associated mimetic or transmission-oriented philosophy of learning and teaching. By contrast, he argued that the humanities contain a view of knowledge as fluid and evolving and that the humanities endorse a "transformative" (interactive) strategy of learning and teaching.

An accumulating body of evidence suggests that these epistemological assumptions shape the nature of teachers' work. Stodolsky (1988), for example, studied elementary school teachers as they taught mathematics and history lessons and found that the same teachers used very different teaching strategies when they taught different subjects. Teachers' mathematics lessons were characterized by a more structured approach and involved fewer instructional formats than did social studies lessons, thus confirming Jackson's (1986) views about epistemological differences in the disciplines. More recently, Stodolsky and Grossman (1995) have shown that high school teachers in different disciplines have very different views about the nature of knowledge and engage in different levels of curricular coordination. For example, mathematics teachers tend to see knowledge as highly structured and well-defined, and they tend to work with colleagues to standardize and tightly coordinate the curriculum. English teachers, on the other hand, view knowledge as fluid and less well defined, and they are less likely to attempt to coordinate and standardize the curriculum.

A series of studies of high school teachers conducted by Rowan and colleagues closely parallel and support these findings (Raudenbush, Rowan, and Kang, 1991; Rowan, Raudenbush, and Cheong, 1993; Rowan, Raudenbush, and Kang, 1991). These studies demonstrate strong effects of disciplinary specialization on teachers' views about the nature of their work. Teachers from different disciplines tend to have different views about the extent to which teaching is a routine task, they tend to prefer different teaching strategies, and they have different propensities to engage in collegial relations and participate in school decision-making. Moreover, in the studies conducted by Rowan and colleagues, the effects of disciplinary specialization were found to be much stronger than the effects resulting from within-school variations in the way the "core technology" of instruction was arranged. Thus the discipline in which a teacher is teaching appears to have a much stronger influence in organizing teachers' work than do local, technical circumstances.

To this point, our discussion of institutional effects on teachers' work has concentrated on studies conducted in the United States. However, a growing body of cross-national research suggests how teachers' work is shaped by national cultures and by the institutionalized rules and understandings developed in different countries (for a brief review and relevant citations, see Stedman, 1997). McKnight *et al.* (1987) and Schmidt *et al.* (1996), for example, have shown that the structure and flow of classroom lessons varies significantly across countries. American teachers tend to take a heavily didactic and teacher-centered approach to teaching and focus on a large number of topics. By contrast, Japanese teachers tend to emphasize a smaller number of topics and use a group-centered, discourse-rich teaching strategy that emphasizes problem-solving (see also, Stigler and Stevenson, 1991).

Cross-national differences also are evident in the content covered within the standard school curriculum. Not surprisingly, the U.S. curriculum is often described as fragmented, unfocused, and repetitive, covering a vast range of topics in little depth. Other countries present fewer objectives in more depth (Schmidt *et al.*, 1996; McKnight *et al.*, 1987). Important differences among countries also occur in the ways curricula are sequenced. For example, in the United States, algebra and calculus are introduced later

than in many other countries. There are also enormous differences in tracking systems. The United States maintains a system of comprehensive secondary schools, organized on the basis of local attendance zones, with differentiated curricular tracks occurring within schools. Many other countries have very different systems. In Germany and Denmark, for example, there are many different types of secondary schools offering very different academic and vocational education programs. In Japan, secondary schooling is not compulsory, students are admitted to secondary schools on the basis of examination scores, and there is a clear status ranking among schools.

All of this strongly suggests that cross-national differences in teaching, curriculum, and patterns of academic tracking reflect differences in national culture and ideology. Thus Schmidt *et al.* (1996: 6) argue that teaching is "fundamentally embedded in culture both in its conception and execution." The Japanese emphasis on groupwork in classrooms has been seen as reflecting the general cultural emphasis on the importance of groups in Japan, an emphasis that is seen not only in teaching strategies, but also in promotion policies and instructional grouping practices (McAdams, 1993: 199). In contrast to the United States, students in Japan do not repeat grades and are placed in mixed ability classes throughout primary schooling. Similarly, differences in the curriculum and tracking practices in secondary schools reflect national ideologies, as Turner's (1960) early discussion of contest and sponsored mobility suggests. Differences in curriculum and tracking also appear to reflect the different ways in which national polities are organized. For example, the liberal polity of the United States, with its emphasis on individual responsibility, organizes a system of curricular tracking built around ideologies of choice. By contrast, the corporate polity of Germany, with its emphasis on the representation of private interests at the collective level, gives German businesses a strong role in providing public education and tracks and sorts students early into academic and vocational tracks.

Clearly, much more work is needed to identify the specific aspects of national culture that shape instructional activities in classrooms. But the studies reviewed here illustrate the important point that work in classrooms (the core technology of schooling) is affected in important ways by institutionalized rules. Regulatory conceptions of institutions can be helpful in explaining these effects, but external regulations appear to structure classroom instruction only when they are clear, consistent, and certain (a rare set of conditions in the United States). Workplace norms are also a possible source for the institutional structuring of work, but again such norms appear to be generally weak in American schools. In our view, an important source of work rules is the (often implicit) ideologies held by teachers, students, parents, and administrators in school systems. As our review demonstrates, there is a growing body of evidence on the effects of these ideologies on instructional work in schools.

Institutional Effects on Students

In contrast to the modest attention paid to the effects of institutionalized rules on teachers' work, institutional theorists have given much more attention to the effects of educational institutions on students. What is interesting about this work, however, is the limited attention paid to academic learning. Instead of concentrating on the formal elements of curriculum and instruction in schools and the ways these affect student learning, institutional theorists have tended to pay closer attention to the "hidden" or informal curriculum and the broader ways in which schools socialize students to become members of adult society. This is consistent with the general thrust of institutional theory, which often looks behind the facade of formal structures and manifest functions to identify the real purposes guiding an organization.

An emphasis on the informal or hidden curriculum in schools can be seen in Parsons' (1959) early analysis of the elementary school classroom. For Parsons (1959), schooling in the early grades was about much more than academic achievement. It was also the first step in the long journey toward adulthood and one of the first places where students encountered the important social organizational forms of the larger society. Dreeben (1968) extended this analysis in his discussion of the normative messages transmitted to students through the social organization of classroom activities, showing how the activity structures of classrooms reinforced the broader norms of society. These analyses are important because they view the school, not so much as an organization attempting to maximize academic productivity, but rather as a social institution chartered to socialize students into the norms and values central to adult status.

Another line of analysis in sociology uses labeling theory to address the important sorting and selection function played by schools in the process of status attainment (Rist, 1977). Here emphasis is placed on the ways schools confer status on students through labeling and on the effects that labeling processes have on students. Rist (1977), for example, argued that assignments to an instructional group in early elementary school shape students' self-concepts and teachers expectations about a student's potential for learning. Early labels thus produce self-fulfilling prophesies that lock students into a pattern of instructional treatment that persists through schooling (for more recent evidence on this point, see Pallas et al., 1994). Other classic studies of this process are Cicourel and Kitsuse's (1966) study of high school counselors and Clark's (1960) study of community college counselors, both of which discuss the interaction

rituals employed by education personnel in the labeling process (cf. Rowan, 1982c). Again, labeling theories show that schools are much more than organizations designed to maximize academic performance. They are also social institutions that perform the sometimes tacit function of allocating students to positions in society's stratified division of labor.

In a classic analysis of the role of education in status attainment, Meyer (1977) argued that the statuses conferred by educational organizations give students future access to positions in the political and economic order of society. Furthermore, through a process of diffuse socialization, students learn about and assume the lifestyles, rights, and privileges typically associated with their assigned status. In Meyer's (1977) view, however, the process of status conferral in schools has little effect on what students actually know and are able to do. For example, there is wide variation in the knowledge and skills possessed by individuals with the same education credentials and only a loose relationship between education credentials and the skills needed or used in the workplace. Education credentials remain a central determinant of life chances in modern societies, however, and this occurs because schools function largely to define and confer status, not to socialize students into a specific academic content (cf. Meyer and Rowan, 1978).

Despite institutional theory's useful focus on the non-academic outcomes of schooling, one cannot help but wonder if institutional processes are also at work in the production of *academic* knowledge. Sociocultural theories of learning suggest an affirmative answer to this question, but to date, they have had little impact on the new institutionalism in organization theory (see Moll, 1990 for one overview of this field). This is unfortunate, for sociocultural theories demonstrate how learning is critically dependent on language and culture and how it is strongly shaped by the institutionalized contexts in which it occurs. In particular, Cole (1990) demonstrates that schooling is a particular kind of institutional context for learning that gives rise to a particular type of learning. Compared to other institutional contexts in society, schools are organized around a pattern of discourse that is didactic in form (question/answer/evaluation). Moreover, school work is organized around a distinctive set of tasks that exposes students to a large amount of information that must be committed to memory and used again to access further information. Finally, the tasks of schooling, and the discourse pattern within schools, produce a particular kind of learning. Students who have attended school generally outperform those who have not attended school on tests of memory, classification, and verbal-logical problems (Cole, 1990).

A view of schools as institutions that seek to socialize students into a particular form of knowledge goes a long way in explaining some of the puzzling findings in research on school effectiveness. For example, in a recent analysis of student achievement among high school students in the United States, Richard Snow and colleagues found that variations in instructional processes within schools were more highly associated with student achievement on test items measuring "crystallized" forms of knowledge than with variations in student achievement on test items measuring more "fluid" reasoning abilities (Kuppermintz *et al.*, 1995; Hamilton *et al.*, 1995). Such findings suggest that schools, at least in the United States, are in the business of socializing students into a particular form of institutionalized knowledge, the type of knowledge so aptly described by Cole (1990).

The role of schools as "carriers" of a particular form of knowledge has also been used to explain cross-national differences in the percentages of variance in student achievement explained by typical indices of school quality and resources. Since the 1980s, it has been found that differences in school quality explain a far greater percentage of variance in student achievement in less developed countries than they do in more developed countries, while in more developed countries, differences in social origins tend to explain the largest percentage of variance in student achievement. One explanation for this set of findings is that social class differences in informal (and out-of-school) access to school knowledge is largely absent in less developed countries, while in more developed countries, where universal, mass education has been institutionalized for longer periods of time, informal and out-of-school access to school knowledge tends to be unequally distributed among members of different social classes (Heyneman and Loxley, 1983; Fuller and Clarke, 1994).

Studies of student learning conducted by sociocultural theorists in the United States reinforce these ideas. For example, sociocultural theorists have developed the concept of "cultural congruence," defined as the degree of similarity between the culture of the home and the culture of the school. Research in the United States is beginning to show that when the discourse patterns and activity structures common to schooling differ from the discourse and activity patterns found in homes, children experience difficulty in complying with classroom norms, have difficulty participating successfully in lessons, and are evaluated more negatively. Research also suggests that increasing the congruence between discourse and activity routines in homes and schools can improve student performance (for a review, see Tharp, 1989).

Broader cultural theories also have relevance to the analysis of student academic performance. For example, Ogbu's (1987) work on the ways in which minority group membership affects student participation and success in schooling shows how broader, societal forces affect student attitudes toward and success in school. His work is interesting because it departs from the functionalist accounts of schooling discussed previously, which tend to assume that

students passively conform to the normative framework of schooling (Parsons, 1959). In a series of studies, Ogbu and colleagues have found that students adopt a variety of stances and attitudes toward schools, some of which take the form of resistance to school norms (Ogbu, 1987). Ogbu's work concentrates on differences in student reactions to schooling that occur among students from voluntary and involuntary minority groups. Depending on their migration history, minority groups develop different assessments of their future life chances, hold different folk theories of how to get ahead, develop a distinctive sense of group identity and cultural reference for judging appropriate behavior, and accord different degrees of legitimacy to the dominant institutions of society. Ogbu argues that these processes account for the differences in school outcomes observed among East Asian students (voluntary minorities) and African-American, Hispanic, and Native American students (involuntary minorities).

Resistance theories (Willis, 1977) also suggest that the conformity of students to the normative demands of schooling cannot be assumed and show how student agency plays a role in education productivity. Willis (1977), for example, examined the reactions to schooling among a group of working-class students in England, showing how members of the group developed an assessment of their future life chances that led them to a counter-cultural adaptation to school. Weiss (1988) also describes the counter-cultural formations of students, in this case, a group of high school girls living in an area of the United States with declining economic fortunes. A major theme in resistance theory is the role of social class in shaping students attitudes toward schooling and the effects of these attitudes on successful participation in school.

An important question is whether the patterns of engagement in schooling observed by resistance theorists differ across countries. Fuller and Clarke (1994) suggest that they do. In their view, students from developing nations are less likely than students from developed nations to display patterns of resistance to schooling, in part because education in developing nations is a scarce good and students can uniformly expect that educational attainment will lead to valued occupational outcomes. In more developed nations, by contrast, schooling is often more accessible, and it often has less dramatic effects on occupational attainment. It follows from this reasoning that students in developed nations might display more of a tendency toward disengagement than students from less developed nations.

Other studies suggest that patterns of resistance to schooling differ across highly developed countries. For example, Robinson and Taylor (1989) found that the correlation between low achievement and negative attitudes toward schooling was different in Britain and France, with low achieving students in Britain reporting much lower interest and enjoyment in school work and lower self-esteem than low achieving students in France. Robinson and Taylor

(1989) explained this finding in terms of the different conceptions of student roles found in British and French cultures. In Britain, a student's academic performance was held to reflect a pupil's standing as a person, a possible consequence of the liberal nature of the British polity with its strong emphasis on private responsibility for actions undertaken in a public role like student. Robinson and Taylor reasoned that when a student's *public* role as student is closely intertwined with his or her *private* role as person, performance in the public role can have strong effects on self-assessment. By contrast, Robinson and Taylor (1989) noted that French schools "appear to concentrate on the child as a pupil; [and] a clear separation of the subrole of pupil from that of person means that any evaluations of the subrole [of pupil] need not extend beyond that" (Robinson and Taylor, 1989: 592–593). Thus it appears that broad cultural understandings of the student role, rather than universal psychological processes, may be useful in explaining the connections between low achievement, low self-esteem, and resistance to schooling.

Lees (1994) also compared the British and French school systems and argued that the two countries have created very different learning cultures. She argued that the centrally-controlled French system creates clear, national standards and strong incentives for doing well in school. For example, successful performance in French schools is rewarded from the earliest grades and brings immediate gains in the form of promotion and eligibility for places in elite schools. In Britain, by contrast, standards and incentives are much less clear, and the recent economic climate in the country makes the connection between success in school and later life much less clear. These institutional factors, Lees (1994) believes, create the kind of counterculture among lower social class students noted by Willis (1977), a counterculture that she argues is much less prevalent in France.

Other researchers have called attention to the different incentives for academic performance that exist in various countries. Bishop (1987; 1989), for example, notes the lack of relevance that grades and transcripts have for job placement and enrollment in post-secondary education in the United States, while Rosenbaum and Kiraya (1989) describe the tight institutional linkages between Japanese business firms and schools. In both analyses, it is argued that U.S. schools could secure greater student engagement and higher academic performance by tightening inter-institutional linkages between schools, businesses, and post-secondary institutions. Such linkages would clarify the relationship between student performance in school and future success, and could encourage more explicit monitoring of school achievement by businesses and post-secondary institutions. In fact, there is some evidence to support this view. Using data from the Second International Mathematics Study (SIMS), Bishop (1997) reports

that, after controlling for a variety of relevant variables, average student achievement on the SIMS mathematics tests is higher in countries where curriculum-based examinations determine access to further education than in countries that lack such tests.

The larger point is that there are a number of ways in which institutional arrangements in society can directly affect student engagement in schools *and* student learning. Schools, it seems, are a distinctive type of institution in society. They are organized to socialize students into a particular type of knowledge, and participation in the institution of schooling has real effects on the patterns of knowledge that students acquire. In addition, patterns of ethnic group formation in society, deeply institutionalized ideologies about the role of pupils in society, linkages among institutional sectors in society, and the distinctive institutional characteristics of schooling combine to affect student motivation and engagement in schooling, and through such processes, indirectly affect student achievement.

Conclusion

Having reviewed the varied forms of institutional analysis in the social sciences and education, we conclude by discussing the contributions of institutional analysis to research and practice in the field of educational administration. As an approach to research in the field, we find that the new institutionalism presents a powerful set of explanations for the structure and functioning of educational organizations in modern societies. We have seen, for example, that institutional theory provides a telling account of the rise of large-scale education bureaucracies around the world. It also begins to explain the different patterns of management found in schools located in different states and institutional sectors in the United States and in different nations of the world. Finally, we have argued that institutional theories show increasing promise of producing new explanations for the varying patterns of educational productivity observed in different education systems around the world.

Further development of institutional theory, however, will require a research strategy that is very different from the ones typically used by scholars in educational administration. The work we reviewed here often focused on levels of the social system well beyond the local school and its immediate environment. This stands in sharp contrast to research on educational organizations conducted in the field of educational administration. Studies in educational administration typically focus on processes within a given school or set of schools. In institutional theory, however, the relevant unit of analysis is the broader system within which schools are embedded. Thus research on schools undertaken from an institutional perspective requires attention to organizing processes occurring well above the level of the local organization, and this implies a much greater focus on the broader institutional environment of schools, for example, state education systems within the United States, public and private sectors of schooling, national systems of education, and even the societal context of schooling. Only with a much better knowledge of how these larger systems are organized and function can we gain important insight into the organization and operation of local schools.

Institutional analysis also gives careful attention to historical processes. Because institutionalized patterns of action do not emerge or stabilize quickly, research on education as an institution also requires observation of events over long periods of time. Here too, we find a need for researchers in educational administration to rethink their research practices. For example, analyses of *current* educational reforms are plentiful in the literature on educational administration, and educational researchers frequently draw negative conclusions about the effects of new institutional arrangements on organizational processes after observing events for only a short period of time. Institutional theory, however, shows that conclusions based on short-term analyses of events that occur early in the institutionalization process are often off the mark. Change is pervasive in the American educational system, but studies of current change efforts are best understood as studies of institution building. Only longer periods of time can tell us whether new education reforms will be institutionalized and what effects these reforms will have on the structure of educational organizations and the practices within them.

Apart from these general methodological considerations, we feel that two areas of institutional analysis need immediate attention in the field of educational administration. The first is the application of institutional theory to the study of teaching and learning in schools. Despite an emerging body of work showing that the core technology of schools —the teaching and learning of academic content in classrooms—is vitally affected by larger institutional processes, institutional analysts who study schools have typically ignored issues related to school learning, at least the learning of academic content. We would advocate much more attention to this problem in coming years. The cross-national studies of teaching that we reviewed here, as well as sociocultural theories of learning, suggest that institutional processes are at work in shaping the ways teachers teach and what and how students learn. Identifying these institutional processes should be a high priority for researchers in educational administration, especially those who seek to better understand the conditions under which teaching and learning can be improved in American schools.

A second area that seems underdeveloped is the application of principal-agent theory and transaction cost eco-nomics to problems of schooling. These aspects of the new institutionalism have not entered the educational analysis of schooling as completely as they could. To be sure, a few studies reviewed here applied these perspectives fruitfully to the analysis of schools as organizations, but beyond these we did not find much organizational analysis of schooling using principal-agent theory and transaction cost econom-ics. This is unfortunate because economists and political scientists are at the forefront of a movement to develop a "positive theory of institutions," one that can describe an array of governance arrangements that potentially can improve the efficiency and productivity of educational transac-tions. Many common problems of educational organization can be analyzed from the standpoint of transaction cost eco-nomics and principal agent theory, problems that range from the development of employment contracts with var-ious types of education personnel to the more mundane problems of providing busing and cafeteria services to stu-dents. More importantly, immediate work is needed to see how the common governance mechanisms studied in transaction cost economics and principal agent theory can be applied to the analysis of teachers work and to im-proving the effort and engagement that students put into learning.

Apart from these efforts, there is a continuing need to study the configuration of institutional environments (in different American states and in different countries) and to empirically test the emerging ideas that institutional theo-rists have developed about the effects of such environments on the management of educational organizations. In par-ticular, the studies reviewed here suggest that the institu-tional environment of education is changing in the United States, that there is a greater emphasis on monitoring orga-nizational performance, a growing attempt to develop more coherent education policy, and a growing interest in market-based controls over education. Studies are needed that map the different institutional environments in Amer-ican education and that examine the conditions under which new types of institutional environments develop.

All of this brings us to a final set of observations. If in-stitutional theory is to be useful to the field of educational administration, it must have relevance to educational prac-tice. We have not discussed this problem much here, but we believe that the way institutional theory can make a contribution to practice is for it to develop into a theory of institutional design. As a theory of design, institutional the-ory can present the educational practitioner with a set of tools that has the potential to shape and constrain action within educational organizations. In the theory of institu-tional design that we envision, the tools would consist of various types of institutional rules, regulations, norms, and the taken-for-granted assumptions of those at work in ed-ucational organizations. Institutional theory suggests that fundamental change in education requires much more than changing an organization's formal structure or work practices. In fact, these aspects of organizations are deeply embedded in and defined by complex regulatory, normative, and cognitive constraints. Changing the nature of schools as organizations, and changing the nature of practices within schools, requires attention to changing these institutional constraints.

At one level, a theory of institutional design requires knowledge of current institutions, that is, the tacit ideologies that organize the way we think about and act in educational settings, the norms and values that encourage particular forms of educational practice, and the regulatory constraints that structure schooling. At another level, practitioners also need a vision of alternative institutional arrangements, the kind of knowledge that can only be gained through careful, comparative analysis and theory building. And finally, we need a theory of institutional *change*, that is, a good understanding of how existing institutions are destabilized and new institutions emerge. We think the review of research presented here shows how this kind of knowledge is emerging from studies of education as an institution, but the knowledge we have of these processes is far from complete and has yet to be developed into a positive theory of institutional design. The promise of institutional theory in educational administration, then, is the promise of a theory of institutional design, one that is built from careful, comparative, and historical consideration of the processes by which social institutions affect educational organization and outcomes.

REFERENCES

Abell, P. (1995). The new institutionalism and rational choice theory. In W. R. Scott & T. Christiansen (Eds.), *The Institutional Construction of Organizations: International and Longitudinal Studies*, pp. 3–14. Thousand Oaks, CA: Sage.

Bacharach, S., Masters, B., Frank, W., & Mundell, B. (1995). Institutional theory and the politics of institutionalization: Logics of action in school reform. In R. T. Ogawa (Ed.), *Advances in Research and Theories of School Management and Educational Policy*, Vol. 3, pp. 83–122. Greenwich, CN: JAI Press.

Baker, D. P. (1992). The politics of American Catholic school expansion, 1870–1930. In B. Fuller & R. Rubinson (Eds.), *The Political Construction of Education: The State, School Expansion, and Economics Change*, pp. 189–206. New York: Praeger.

Baum, J. & Oliver, C. (1991). Institutional linkages and organizational mortality. *Administrative Science Quarterly*, 36: 187–218.

Baum, J. & Oliver, C. (1992). Institutional embeddedness and the dynamics of organizational populations. *American Sociological Review*, 57: 540–559.

Berger, P. L. & Luckmann, T. (1967). *The Social Construction of Reality*. New York: Doubleday Anchor.

Bidwell, C. (1965). The school as a formal organization. In J. G. March (Ed.), *Handbook of Research on Organizations*, pp. 972–1019. New York: Rand McNally.

Bill, J. A. & Hardgrave, R. L. (1981). *Comparative Politics: The Quest for Theory*. Washington, DC: University Press of America.

Bishop, J. (1987). *Information externalities and the social payoff to academic achievement*. Ithaca, NY: Cornell University, Center for Advanced Human Resource Studies.

Bishop, J. (1988). *Incentives for learning: Why American high school students compare so poorly to their counterparts overseas*. Ithaca, NY: Cornell University, Center for Advanced Human Resource Studies.

Bishop, J. (1997). The effect of national standards and curriculum-based exams on student achievement. *American Economic Association, Papers and Proceedings*, (May), pp. 260–264.

Blau, P. M. & Schoenherr, R. (1967). *The Structure of Organizations*. New York: Basic Books.

Boli, J., Ramirez, F. O. & Meyer, J. W. (1985). Explaining the origins and expansion of mass education. *Comparative Education Review*, 29: 145–170.

Brint, S. & Karabel, J (1989). *The Diverted Dream: Community Colleges and the Promise of Educational Opportunity in America, 1900–1985*. New York: Oxford University Press.

Burns, L. R. & Wholey, D. R. (1993). Adoption and abandonment of matrix management programs: Effects of organizational characteristics and interorganizational networks. *Academy of Management Journal*, 36: 106–138.

Chubb, J. E. & Moe, T. M. (1990). Politics, markets, and the organization of schools. *American Political Science Review*, 84: 549–567.

Cibulka, J. G. (1995). The institutionalization of public schools: The decline of legitimizing myths and the politics of organizational instability. In R. T. Ogawa (Ed.), *Advances in Research and Theories of School Management and Educational Policy*, Vol. 3, pp. 123–158. Greenwich, CN: JAI Press.

Cicourel, A. V. & Kitsuse, J. I. (1966). *The Educational Decision Makers*. Indianapolis, IN: Bobbs-Merrill.

Clark, B. (1956). *Adult Education in Transition*. Berkeley: University of California Press.

Clark, B. (1960). The cooling out function in higher education. *American Journal of Sociology*, 65: 569–575.

Cohen, D. K. (1996). Rewarding teachers for student performance. In S. H. Fuhrman & J. A. O'Day (Eds.), *Rewards and Reform: Creating Educational Incentives That Work*. San Francisco: Jossey-Bass.

Cohen, D. K. & Spillane, J. P. (1992). Policy and practice: The relations between governance and instruction. In G. Grant (Ed.), *Review of Research in Education*. Washington, DC: American Educational Research Association.

Cole, M. (1990). Cognitive development and formal schooling: The evidence from cross-cultural research. In L. C. Moll (Ed.), *Vygotsky and Education: Instructional Implications and Applications of Socio-historical Psychology*, pp. 89–110. New York: Cambridge University Press.

Crowson, R. L., Boyd, W. L. & Mawhinney, H. B. (Eds.) (1996). *The Politics of Education and the New Institutionalism: Reinventing the American School*. Washington, DC: Falmer Press.

Cuban, L. (1984). *How teachers taught: Constancy and change in American classrooms, 1880–1980*. New York: Longman.

D'Aunno, T., Sutton, R. I. & Price, R. H. (1991). Isomorphism and external support in conflicting institutional environments: A study of drug abuse treatment units. *Academy of Management Journal*, 14: 636–661.

Deavins, N. E. (1989). *Public Values, Private Schools*. London: Falmer Press.

DiMaggio, P. J. & Powell, W. W. (1983). The iron cage revisited: Isomorphism and collective rationality in organizational fields. *American Sociological Review*, 48: 147–160.

DiMaggio, P. J. & Powell, W. W. (Eds.) (1991). *The New Institutionalism in Organizational Analysis*. Chicago: University of Chicago Press.

Dobbin, F. R. (1995). *Forging Industrial Policy: The United States, Britain, and France in the Railway Age*. New York: Cambridge University Press.

Dobbin, F. R., Edelman, L., Meyer, J. W. & Swidler, A. (1988). The expansion of due process in organizations. In L.G. Zucker (Ed.), *Institutional Patterns and Organizations: Culture and Environment*, pp. 71–100. Cambridge, MA: Ballinger.

Douglas, M. (1995). Converging on autonomy: Anthropology and institutional economics. In O. E. Williamson (Ed.), *Organization Theory: From Chester Barnard to the Present and Beyond*, pp. 98–115. New York: Oxford University Press.

Dreeben, R. (1968). *On What Is Learned in School*. Reading, MA: Addison-Wesley.

Firestone, W. A., Rosenblum, S., Bader, B. D. & Massell, D. (1991). *Education reform from 1983 to 1990: State action and district response*. New Brunswick, NJ: Consortium for Policy Research in Education.

Fligstein, N. (1985). The spread of the multidivisional form among large firms, 1919–1979. *American Sociological Review*, 50: 377–391.

Freidlander, R. & Alford, R. R. (1991). Bringing society back in: Symbols, practices, and institutional contradictions. In P. J. DiMaggio & W. W. Powell (Eds.), *The New Institutionalism in Organizational Analysis*, pp. 232–263. Chicago: University of Chicago Press.

Fuhrman, S. H. (Ed.) (1994). *Designing Coherent Education Policy: Improving the System*. San Francisco: Jossey-Bass.

Fuhrman, S. H., Clune, W. & Elmore, R. F. (1988). Research on education reform: Lessons on the implementation of education policy. *Teachers College Record*, 90: 237–258.

Fuller, B. & Clarke, P. (1994). Raising school effects while ignoring culture? Local conditions and the influence of classroom tools, rules, and pedagogy. *Review of Educational Research*, 64: 119–157.

Fuller, B. & Rubinson, R. (Eds.) (1992). *The Political Construction of Education: The State, School Expansion, and Economic Change*. New York: Prager.

Galvin, P. F. & Barrott, J. E. (1995). A national data base for organizations: A proposal for including data from economic theories of organizations. In R. T. Ogawa (Ed.), *Advances in Research and Theories in School Management and Educational Policy*, pp. 21–42. Greenwich, CN: JAI Press.

Garfinkel, H. (1967). *Studies in Ethnomethodology*. Englewood Cliffs, NJ: Prentice-Hall.

Goffman, E. (1967). *Interaction Ritual*. Garden City, NY: Anchor.

Goodlad, J. (1984). *A Place Called School*. New York: McGraw-Hill.

Goodrick, E. & Salancik, G. R. (1996). Organizational discretion in responding to institutional practices: Hospitals and Cesarean births. *Administrative Science Quarterly*, 41: 1–28.

Greenwood, R. & Hinnings, C. R. (1996). Understanding radical organizational change: Bringing together the old and new institutionalism. *Academy of Management Review*, 21: 1022–1054.

Gusfield, J. R. (1955). Social structure and moral reform: A study of the Women's Christian Temperance Union. *American Journal of Sociology*, 61: 221–232.

Hamilton, L. S., Nussbaum, E. M., Kuppermintz, H., Kerkhoven, J. I. M. & Snow, R. E. (1995). Enhancing the validity and usefulness of large-scale educational assessments, II: NELS: 88 science achievement. *American Educational Research Journal*, 32: 555–582.

Hannan, M, T. & Freeman, J. (1977). The population ecology of organizations. *American Journal of Sociology*, 82: 929–964.

Heyneman, S, P. & Loxley, W. A. (1983). The effect of primary school quality on academic achievement across twenty-nine high- and low-income countries. *American Journal of Sociology*, 88: 1162–1194.

House, E. R. (1996). A framework for appraising educational reforms. *Educational Researcher, 25:* 6–14, October.

Jackson, P. W. (1968). *Life in Classrooms*. New York: Holt, Rinehart, and Winston.

Jackson, P. W. (1986). *The Practice of Teaching*. New York: Teachers College Press.

Jensen, M. C. & Meckling, W. C. (1976). Theory of the firm: Managerial behavior, agency costs, and ownership structure. *Journal of Financial Economics*, 3: 305–360.

Jepperson, R. L. (1991). Institutions, institutional effects, and institutionalization. In P. J. DiMaggio & W.W. Powell (Eds.), *The New Institutionalism in Organizational Analysis*, pp. 143–163. Chicago: University of Chicago Press.

Jepperson, R. L. & Meyer, J. W. (1991). The public order and the construction of formal organizations. In P. J. DiMaggio & W. W. Powell (Eds.), *The New Institutionalism in Organizational Analysis*, pp. 204–231. Chicago: University of Chicago Press.

Katz, M. B. (1971). From voluntarism to bureaucracy in American education. *Sociology of Education*, 44: 297–332.

Kuppermintz, H., Ennis, M. M., Hamilton, L. S., Talbert, J. E. & Snow, R. E. (1995). Enhancing the validity and usefulness of large-scale educational assessments, I: NELS: 88 mathematics achievement. *American Educational Research Journal*, 32: 525–554.

Langlois, R. N. (Ed.). (1986). *Economics as a Process: Essays in the New Institutional Economics*. New York: Cambridge University Press.

Lees, L. H. (1994). *Comparative Education Review*, 38.

Levin, H. M. (1989). Education as a public and private good. In N. E. Deavins (Ed.), *Public Values, Private Schools*. London: Falmer Press.

Lortie, D. C. (1975). *Schoolteacher: A Sociological Study*. Chicago: University of Chicago Press.

McAdams, R. P. (1993). *Lessons from Abroad: How Other Countries Educate Their Children*. Lancaster, PA: Technomic Publishing.

McDonnell, L. M. & Elmore, R. F. (1987). Getting the job done: Alternative policy instruments. *Educational Evaluation and Policy Analysis*, 9: 133–152.

McKnight, C. C., et al. (1987). *The Underachieving Curriculum: Assessing U. S. School Mathematics from an International Perspective*. Champaign, IL: Stripes Publishing.

March, J. G. & Olsen, J. P. (1984). The new institutionalism: Organizational factors in political life. *American Political Science Review*, 78: 734–749.

March, J. G. & Olsen, J. P. (1989). *Rediscovering Institutions: The Organizational Basis of Politics*. New York: Free Press.

March, J. G. & Simon, H. A. (1958). *Organizations*. New York: John Wiley.

Meyer, J. W. (1970). The charter: Conditions of diffuse socialization in schools. In W. R. Scott (Ed.), *Social Processes and Social Structure*, pp. 564–578. New York: Holt, Rinehart, and Winston.

Meyer, J. W. (1977). The effects of education as an institution. *American Journal of Education*, 83: 53–77.

Meyer, J. W. (1983a). Institutionalization and the rationality of formal organizational structure. In J. W. Meyer & W. R. Scott, *Organizational Environments: Ritual and Rationality*, pp. 261–282. Beverly Hills, CA: Sage.

Meyer, J. W. (1983b). Centralization of funding and control in educational governance. In J. W. Meyer & W. R. Scott, *Organizational Environments: Ritual and Rationality*, pp. 179–198. Beverly Hills, CA: Sage.

Meyer, J. W. & Rowan, B. (1977). Institutionalized organizations: Formal structure as myth and ceremony. *American Journal of Sociology*, 83: 340–363.

Meyer, J. W. & Rowan, B. (1978). The structure of educational organizations. In M. W. Meyer (Ed.), *Environments and Organizations*, pp. 78–109. San Francisco: Jossey-Bass.

Meyer, J. W. & Scott, W. R. (1983a). *Organizational Environments: Ritual and Rationality*. Beverly Hills, CA: Sage.

Meyer, J. W., Kamens, D. & Benavot, A. (1992). *School Knowledge for the Masses: World Models and National Primary Curriculum Categories in the Twentieth Century*. London: Flamer.

Meyer, J. W., Ramirez, F. O. & Soysal, Y. N. (1992). World expansion of mass education, 1870–1980. *Sociology of Education*, 65: 128–149.

Meyer, J. W., Scott, W. R. & Deal, T. E. (1983). Institutional and technical sources of organizational structure: Explaining the structure of educational organizations. In J. W. Meyer & W. R. Scott, *Organizational Environments: Ritual and Rationality*, pp. 45–67. Beverly Hills: Sage.

Meyer, J. W., Tyack, D., Nagel, J. & Gordon, A. (1979). Public education as nation-building in America: Enrollments and bureaucratization, 1870–1930. *American Journal of Sociology*, 85: 591–613.

Mezias, S. J. (1990). An institutional model of organizational practice: Financial reporting at the Fortune 200. *Administrative Science Quarterly*, 35: 431–457.

Moe, T. M. (1984). The new economics of organization. *The American Political Science Review*, 28: 739–777.

Moe, T. M. (1995). The politics of structural choice: Toward a theory of public bureaucracy. In O. E. Williamson (Ed.), *Organization Theory: From Chester Barnard to the Present and Beyond*, 116–153. New York: Oxford University Press.

Moll, L. C. (Ed.). (1990). *Vygotsky and Education: Instructional Implications and Applications of Sociohistorical Psychology.* New York: Cambridge University Press.

Oakes, J., Gamoran, A. & Page, R. (1992). Curriculum differentiation: opportunities, outcomes, and meanings. In P. W. Jackson (Ed.), *Handbook of Research on Curriculum*, pp. 570–609. New York: Macmillan.

Oakes, J., Wells, A. S., Jones, M. & Datnow, A. (1997). Detracking: The social construction of ability, cultural politics, and resistance to reform. *Teachers' College Record*, 98: 482–510.

Ogawa, R. T. (1994). The institutional sources of education reform: the case of school-based management. *American Educational Research Journal*, 31: 519–548.

Ogbu, J. (1987). *Minority Education and Caste: The American System in Cross-Cultural Perspective.* New York: Academic Press.

Oliver, C. (1991). Strategic responses to institutional responses. *Academy of Management Review*, 16: 145–179.

Organization for Economic Cooperation and Development (OECD). (1996). *Education at a Glance.* Paris: Author.

Pallas, A., Entwisle, D. R., Alexander, K. L. & Slutka, M. F. (1994). Ability group effects: Instructional, social, or institutional? *Sociology of Education*, 67:27–46.

Parsons, T. (1959). The school class as a social system: Some of its functions in American society. *Harvard Education Review*, 29: 297–313.

Parsons, T. (1960). A sociological approach to the theory of organizations. In T. Parsons (Ed.), *Structure and Process in Modern Societies*, pp. 16–58. Glencoe, IL: Free Press.

Perow, C. (1961). The analysis of goals in complex organizations. *American Sociological Review*, 26: 854–866.

Perow, C. (1986). *Complex Organizations: A Critical Essay*, 3rd Edition. New York: Random House.

Powell, W. W. (1991). Expanding the scope of institutional analysis. In P. J. DiMaggio & W. W. Powell (Eds.), *The New Institutionalism in Organizational Analysis*, pp. 183–203. Chicago: University of Chicago Press.

Ramirez, F. O. & Boli, J. (1987). The political construction of mass education: European origins and worldwide institutionalization. *Sociology of Education*, 60: 2–17.

Raudenbush, S. W., Rowan, B. & Cheong, Y. F. (1992). Contextual effects on the self-perceived efficacy of high school teachers. *Sociology of Education*, 65: 150–167.

Raudenbush, S. W., Rowan, B. & Cheong, Y. F. (1993). The pursuit of higher-order instructional goals in secondary schools: Class, teacher, and school influences. *American Educational Research Journal*, 30: 523–553.

Raudenbush, S. W., Rowan, B. & Kang, S. J. (1991) A multilevel, multivariate model for studying school climate with estimation via the EM algorithm and application to U. S. high school data. *Journal of Educational Statistics*, 16: 295–330.

Richardson, J. G. (1994). Common, delinquent, and special: On the formalization of common schooling in the American states. *American Educational Research Journal*, 31: 695–723.

Rist, R. C. (1977). On understanding the processes of schooling: The contributions of labeling theory. In J. Karabel & A. H. Halsey (Eds.), *Power and Ideology in Education*, pp. 292–305. New York: Oxford University Press.

Robinson, W. P. & Taylor, C. A. (1989). Correlates of low academic attainment in three countries. *International Journal of Educational Research*, 13: 592–593.

Rosenbaum, J. E. & Kiraya, T. (1989). From high school to work: Market and institutional mechanisms in Japan. *American Journal of Sociology*, 94: 1334–1365.

Rowan, B. (1981). The effects of institutionalized rules on administrators. In S. B. Bacharach (Ed.), *Organizational behavior in schools and school districts*, pp. 47–75. New York: Praeger.

Rowan, B. (1982a). Organizational structure and the institutional environment: The case of public schools. *Administrative Science Quarterly*, 27: 259–279.

Rowan, B. (1982b). Instructional management in historical perspective. *Educational Administration Quarterly*, 18: 43–59.

Rowan, B. (1982c). The status organizing work of schools. *Social Science Quarterly*, 63: 477–491.

Rowan, B. (1990) Commitment and control: Alternative strategies for the organizational design of schools. In C. Cazden (ed.), *Review of Research in Education*, Vol. 16. Washington, DC: American Educational Research Association.

Rowan, B. (1995). Institutional analysis of educational organizations: Lines of theory and directions for research. In R. T. Ogawa (Ed.), *Advances in Research and Theories of School Management and Educational Policy*, Vol. 3, pp. 1–20. Greenwich, CN: JAI Press.

Rowan, B., Raudenbush, S. W. & Cheong, Y. F. (1993) Teaching as a non-routine task: Implications for the management of schools. *Educational Administration Quarterly*, 29: 479–500.

Rowan, B., Raudenbush, S. W. & Kang, S. J. (1991). Organizational design in high schools: A multilevel analysis. *American Journal of Education*, 99: 238–266.

Schmidt, W. & others. (1996). *A Summary Characterizing pedagogical flow: An Investigation of Science Teaching in Six Countries.* London: Kluwer Academic Publishers.

Schutz, A. (1962). *Collected Papers* (Edited by Maurice Natanson). The Hague, Netherlands: Nijhoff.

Scott, W. R. (1992) . *Organizations: Rational, Natural, and Open Systems.* 3rd Edition. Englewood Cliffs, NJ: Prentice-Hall.

Scott, W. R. (1994). Institutional analysis: Variance and process theory approaches. In W. R. Scott, J. W. Meyer & Associates, *Institutional Environments and Organizations: Structural Complexity and Individualism*, pp. 81–99. Thousand Oaks, CA: Sage.

Scott, W. R. (1995). *Institutions and Organizations.* Thousand Oaks, CA: Sage.

Scott, W. R. & Meyer, J. W. (1991). The organization of societal sectors. In P. J. DiMaggio & W. W. Powell, *The New Institutionalism in Organizational Analysis*, pp. 108–140. Chicago: University of Chicago Press.

Selznick, P. (1948). Foundations of the theory of organizations. *American Sociological Review*, 13: 25–35.

Selznick, P. (1949). *TVA and the Grassroots.* Berkeley: University of California Press.

Selznick, P. (1957). *Leadership in Administration.* New York: Harper and Row.

Shepsle, K. A. & Weingast, B. (1987). The institutional foundations of committee power. *American Political Science Review*, 81: 85–104.

Simon, H. A. (1945). *Administrative Behavior.* New York: Macmillan.

Singh, J. V., Tucker, D. J. & Meinhard, A. G. (1991). Institutional change and ecological dynamics. In P. J. DiMaggio & W. W. Powell (Eds.), *The New Institutionalism in Organizational Analysis*, pp. 390–422. Chicago: University of Chicago Press.

Smith, M. S. & O'Day, J. A. (1990). Systemic school reform. In S. H. Fuhrman & B. Malen (Eds.), *The Politics of Curriculum and Testing.* Bristol, PA: Falmer Press.

Spillane, J. P. & Jennings, N. E. (1997). Aligned instructional policy and ambitious pedagogy: Exploring instructional reform from the classroom perspective. *Teachers College Record*, 98: 449–481.

Stedman, L. C. (1997). International achievement differences: An assessment of a new perspective. *Educational Researcher*, 26: 4–15.

Steinmo, S., Thelen, K. & Longstreth, F. (Eds.). (1992). *Structuring Politics: Historical Institutionalism in Comparative Analysis.* Cambridge, UK: Cambridge University Press.

Stevenson, D. & Baker, D. (1991). State control of the curriculum and classroom instruction. *Sociology of Education*, 64: 1–10.

Stigler, J. & Stevenson, H. (1991). How Asian teachers polish each lesson to perfection. *American Educator*, Spring, 12–20, 43–47.

Stodolsky, S. S. (1988). *The Subject Matters: Classroom activity in math and social studies.* Chicago: University of Chicago Press.

Stodolsky, S. S. & Grossman, P. L. (1995). The impact of subject matter on curricular activity: An analysis of five academic subjects. *American Educational Research Journal*, 32: 227–249.

Strang, D. (1987). The administrative transformation of American education: School district consolidation, 1938–980. *Administrative Science Quarterly*, 32: 352–366.

Tharp, R. G. (1989). Psychocultural variables and constants: Effects on teaching and learning in schools. *American Psychologist*, February, 349–359.

Thompson, J. D. (1967). *Organizations in Action*. New York: McGraw-Hill.

Timar, T. B. & Kirp, D. L. (1988). *Managing Educational Excellence*. New York: Falmer Press.

Tolbert, P. S. & Zucker, L. G. (1983). Institutional sources of change in the formal structure of organizations: The diffusion of civil service reform, 1880–1935. *Administrative Science Quarterly*, 30: 22–39.

Turner, R. (1960). Modes of social ascent through education: Sponsored and contest mobility. *American Sociological Review*, 25: 855–867.

Tyack, D. (1974). *The One Best System*. Cambridge, MA: Harvard University Press.

Tyack, D. & Tobin, W. (1994). The grammar of schooling: Why has it been so hard to change? *American Educational Research Journal*, 31: 453–479.

Tyack, D., James, T. & Benavot, A. (1987). *Law and the Shaping of Public Education*, 1785–1954. Cambridge, MA: Harvard University.

Weber, M. (1947). *The Theory of Social and Economic Organization*, eds. A. H. Henderson and Talcott Parsons. Glencoe, IL: Free Press.

Weick, K. E. (1976). Educational organizations as loosely coupled systems. *Administrative Science Quarterly*, 21: 1–19.

Weimer, D. L. & Vining, A. R. (1989). *Policy Analysis: Concepts and Practice*. Englewood Cliffs, NJ: Prentice-Hall.

Williamson. O. E. (1975). *Markets and Hierarchies: Analysis and Antitrust Implications*. New York: Free Press.

Williamson, O. E. (1985). *The Economic Institutions of Capitalism*. New York: Free Press.

Williamson, O. E. (1995). Transaction cost economics and organization theory. In O. E. Williamson (Ed.), *Organization Theory: From Chester Barnard to the Present and Beyond*, pp. 207–256. New York: Oxford university Press.

Willis, P. (1977). *Learning to Labor*. New York: Columbia University Press.

Woodward, J. (1965). *Industrial Organization: Theory and Practice*. New York: Oxford University Press.

Zald, M. N. & Denton, P. (1963). From evangelism to general service: The transformation of the YMCA. *Administrative Science Quarterly*, 8: 214–234.

Zucker, L. G. (1977). The role of institutionalization in cultural persistence. *American Sociological Review*, 42: 726–743.

CHAPTER 18

The Implications of Social Capital for Schools, Communities, and Cities: Educational Administration As If a Sense of Place Mattered

Mary Erina Driscoll and Charles Taylor Kerchner

Education in a democracy is supported in part because schools help to create a public good from which the whole society benefits. One way of conceptualizing their role in developing that public good may be found by examining the literature on social capital. This chapter uses that literature to frame a discussion of schools as agents of community and of urban development. We emphasize the public benefits of social capital and reinforce the idea that such capital is the product of community interaction, an entity that cannot be produced by an individual, nor be restricted to individual usage. We extend the social capital argument developed by James Coleman and his colleagues (Coleman & Hoffer, 1987; Coleman, 1988; Coleman, 1990) by exploring the ways in which cities can benefit from social capital development as well as the ways in which individuals benefit from activities that produce high levels of social capital. We believe, then, that schools can be seen as *agents* of community and city development as well as the *beneficiaries* of such development.

Throughout this chapter, we will focus on the implications of an understanding of social capital for the practice and study of education and of educational administration. At this point, we present in brief the central plan of our argument as we will develop it below.

In the first part of this chapter, we pose a definition of social capital as a construct that links individual to group action. A critical aspect of this construct is the fact that social capital is available to individuals by virtue of their connection to some larger social group or entity. Although social capital cannot be accrued on an individual basis in the same way that physical or human capital can, membership in a group or organization in which there are high levels of social

capital can have powerful benefits for individuals (Putnam, 1993). We will use this concept to broaden our understanding of how individuals connect to schools and to explore ways in which schools can become vehicles for building the pool of social capital available to the surrounding community and to the city at large.

We will also discuss the chronic undersupply of social capital. The engine of action in traditional human capital theory is individual rational choice. Seldom does one rationalize action that appears to have little *direct* benefit for the individual over time. Despite the fact that high levels of social capital in some organizations appear to have potentially beneficial consequences for all individuals, few people are schooled or socialized to understand the value of this concept. We will suggest some of the ways in which an understanding of these values might point towards new ways of organizing schools and school systems. Here we draw on the contributions of theorists who expand or critique conventional social capital theory. This work addresses imbalances in the power relationships between schools and their constituents and investigates the ways in which institutional barriers fail to address the relative amount of social capital brought into educational institutions by students of different cultures (Bourdieu & Passeron, 1977; Lareau, 1989; Stanton-Salazar, 1997).

In the second part of this chapter, we will focus on the role of schools in building social capital. It is our contention that although schools benefit from the social capital that results from extra-organizational ties among students and their families, they need not be merely passive receptacles of or thoroughfares for the accrued social capital of their student and family constituencies. Schools can also play an important role in building the social capital of the community at large and have a vital part in creating and maintaining social capital in modern cities. By reviewing some signal efforts in this area, we postulate that it is helpful to see schools and educational systems as entities that can build social capital that is then available to the surrounding community and to cities and towns as well.

In the third part of this chapter, we affirm the proposition that one of the core functions of schools is to develop social capital for the polity at large. The traditional mission of schooling has always encompassed the development of human potential on an individual level and has most often been extended to include the development of citizenship qualities in students along with the encouragement of their cognitive and social abilities. In this section, we look at the ways in which the educational system interacts with the urban polity as a critical mechanism in forging the social and economic linkages so vital to modern cities. Here we take seriously this developmental function of schools and schooling and suggest some of the practices that might embody this vision.

Finally, we close with some implications for further research and some intimations of what this larger sense of place might mean for educational administration and educational policy in the future.

Social Capital Theory

First we turn to some of the classic work that posits the existence of social capital as one of the essential conditions of "good" education. The concept of social capital is not new. For many scholars and students of education, however, it is inextricably linked to the studies by James Coleman and his colleagues in which public, private, and Catholic schools were compared. We begin, then, with a review of social capital theory, as developed in the empirical work of James Coleman and some of his colleagues (Coleman, Hoffer & Kilgore, 1982; Coleman & Hoffer, 1987; Schneider & Coleman, 1993). We will then consider in some detail the amplification of this concept by Coleman (Coleman, 1990) in which he focused more narrowly on why this concept is necessary, what constitutes its chief characteristics, and how it is useful in understanding human behavior.

Social Capital and the Comparison between Public and Private Schooling

In 1982, James Coleman and his colleagues published the first of two high-profile studies that examined the national data sample "High School and Beyond" (Coleman, Hoffer, & Kilgore, 1982c). Coleman, Kilgore, and Hoffer's controversial findings that Catholic schools did a "better" job of educating disadvantaged students than did public

schools engendered a lively and provocative national debate, much of which focused on methodological as well as theoretical issues (Alexander & Pallas, 1983; Cain & Goldberger, 1983; Coleman & Hoffer, 1983; Coleman, Hoffer, & Kilgore, 1982a; Coleman, Hoffer, & Kilgore, 1982b; Heyns & Hilton, 1982; Kilgore, 1983; McPartland & McDill, 1982; Morgan, 1983; Murnane, 1984; Salganik & Karweit, 1982; Taueber & James, 1983).

Specifically, Coleman *et al.* claimed to have found a "Catholic school effect" that demonstrated Catholic schools were better at educating disadvantaged poor minority students than the public schools that were historically designed to serve this population. Their research documented a traditional academic environment in Catholic schools that encouraged achievement, in which students encountered a strong press for academic performance and a common curriculum even when the student body was relatively diverse (Coleman *et al.*, 1982c).

Coleman and his colleagues offered several explanations for these results. Most of them, they argued, were not related to students' characteristics, such as race or social class, but rather to items that could be affected by school policy. Among these, for example, were the stricter disciplinary and homework policies of Catholic schools. Coleman *et al.* argued that policies such as these could be instituted in the public sector (Coleman *et al.*, 1982c).

When more data became available on the same students, their families, their teachers, and their schools, these results were linked directly to a theory of social capital (Coleman & Hoffer, 1987). Coleman and Hoffer argued that the kinds of tightly knit social structures found in the small town Middletown, studied by sociologists Lynd and Lynd (1929) in the twenties, were also present in the contemporary Catholic school community. The religious context of the schools and the parish structures in which they were situated produced the same kind of social cohesion as did the overlapping social institutions found in small towns. This degree of cohesion, sustained by parish or religious organizational ties, had much to do with students' success. In a closely knit community students enjoyed a "social capital" that enriched the resources of information and oversight available to them.

Such cohesive supporting social systems (or "functional communities") were absent, argued Coleman and Hoffer, in contemporary public schooling and in the fragmented communities that support it. Most public schools, especially those in urban settings, had no such tightly knit communities. Students and their parents had few connections to other families outside the school and there was little overlap in the worlds students encountered at home and at school. This lack of social capital put public school students at a disadvantage, they suggested (Coleman and Hoffer, 1987).

Social capital also figured in some of the significant critiques of this work. Those who disputed Coleman argued that the results were explained by a far more complex and less clearly defined set of factors (Murnane, 1984). The central argument focused on the fact that non-public schools, unlike public schools, can choose their clientele. Many of Coleman's critics asserted that parents' free choice of schools for their children affected how well those students performed academically. That choice and attention to education, they argued, made those parents and students special, more likely to achieve in school, even if they were matched against public school counterparts who resembled them in race, ethnicity, and economic status. This support from parents made these students truly different, because their families demonstrated a level of interest in education sufficient at least to choose and in many cases to finance a particular type of school. The economic calculus used to determine comparable status among the sectors, which appeared to make students in the public and private sector "equal" except with respect to their in-school experiences, could not account for these added resources; thus (critics argued), students in choice schools began their schooling with substantially more psychic and social resources—in other words, more social capital—than students in non-choice schools.

Ironically, then, both Coleman and his critics focused on the capital residing in home and school relations as a means of explanation for higher achievement in Catholic schools. Although Coleman also pointed to Catholic school policies that fostered achievement (arguing these might be instituted in public schools), both sides of the debate agreed that the communities in and around Catholic schools were different from those in the public sector and were important factors in the success of these institutions.

The research implications of this work were significant. The early findings impelled further exploration of the ways in which we think about the communities surrounding schools and how dense networks of oversight and information to which some students have access can affect educational progress. Coleman and Hoffer's work (1987) also asserted that shared parental knowledge of school programs and policies is a critical resource that can affect whether or not students achieve to their fullest potential. Thus subsequent data collections explored, for example, the role of parents and community supports in the academic achievement of children (see Schneider & Coleman, 1993; Muller, 1993).

An Expanded Formulation of Social Capital

A New Theoretical Context

In his 1990 treatise *Foundations of Social Theory*, Coleman presents a detailed exposition of the theory of social capital as a construct that can help amplify classical understandings of rational behavior. Coleman credits Loury (1977, 1987) with

the introduction of the term "social capital" (Coleman, 1990, p. 300). He cites as well the work of Bourdieu (1980) and Flap and De Graaf (1986), all of whom, he suggests, have used similar terms (Coleman, 1990, p. 300). (In a later section, we will deal with some of the differences between Coleman's concept and that developed by Bourdieu.)

To situate his construct of social capital in a broader theoretical context, Coleman cites the "new institutional economics," remarking in particular on the work of Granovetter (1985). Coleman argues that Granovetter successfully legitimizes the study of "social and organizational relations, not merely as a structure that springs into place to fulfill an economic function, but as a structure with history and continuity that give it an independent impact on the functioning of the system" (Coleman, 1990, p. 302). He notes as well Granovetter's criticisms that even these "new" institutional economics have underestimated the importance of "concrete personal relations and networks of relations—what he calls the embeddedness of economic transactions in social relations—in generating trust, in establishing expectations, and in creating and enforcing norms" (Coleman, 1990, p. 302).

Coleman maintains that the concept of social capital demands that we grapple with the "broadly perpetrated fiction in modern society," namely that "society consists of a set of independent individuals, each of whom acts to achieve goals that are independently arrived at, and the functioning of the social system consists of the combination of these actions of independent individuals. This fiction is expressed in the economic theory of perfect competition in a market, most graphically in Adam Smith's imagery of an 'invisible hand'" (Coleman, 1990, p. 300). But, asserts Coleman, "the fiction is just that—for individuals do not act independently, goals are not independently arrived at, and interests are not wholly selfish" (Coleman, 1990, p. 301).

A Definition of Social Capital

Coleman's definition of social capital is comprehensive:

> Social capital is defined by its function. It is not a single entity, but a variety of different entities having two characteristics in common: They all consist of some aspect of a social structure, and they facilitate certain actions of individuals who are within the structure. Like other forms of capital, social capital is productive, making possible the achievement of certain ends that would not be attainable in its absence. Like physical capital and human capital, social capital is not completely fungible but is fungible with respect to certain activities. A given form of social capital that is valuable in facilitating certain actions may be useless or even harmful for others (Coleman, 1990, p. 302).

The essential characteristic of social capital is the fact that it resides in the relationships within an organization and between individuals. This aspect of social capital has important implications for its creation and maintenance, and accounts in part for the tendency of societies to underinvest in social as opposed to other forms of capital. Despite the fact that it is less tangible than physical capital, however, social capital can still facilitate productivity. For example, a group with high levels of trust will be able to achieve more than a similar group that is characterized by distrust (Coleman, 1990, p. 304).

Forms of Social Capital

There are several forms of social capital. One form is characterized by the reciprocal obligations and expectations of one another held by members of a social group, whereby the favor done for one member by another constitutes a kind of "credit slip" for a favor to be redeemed at some future time. This form is most effective when the level of trust in the organization is such that individuals believe that obligations will be repaid and when the nature of obligations held means that this is likely to happen (Coleman, 1990, p. 304). It is easy to see how the ability to give and return favors in a system over time can expand (or deplete) any one member's resources at any particular interval. And as Coleman notes, the ability to call on or repay obligations may differ significantly according to one's place in the formal hierarchy or commonly understood power structure of any organization (Coleman, 1990, p. 308).

A second form of social capital "is the potential for information that inheres in social relations. Information is important in providing a basis for action." He continues by saying, "But acquisition of information is costly. The minimum it requires is attention, which is always in short supply." Thus social relationships can also be used to augment the information any actor needs to guide action (Coleman, 1990, p. 310). In the case of Catholic schools, for example, Coleman argued that good information networks helped to make expectations on the part of schools and families clear and permitted parents to engage the academic institution armed with both appropriate knowledge and action.

A third form of social capital is the existence of effective norms and sanctions that may encourage some sets of behaviors. These same norms discourage other behaviors. For example, "Strong and effective norms about young persons' behavior in a community can also keep them from having a good time" (Coleman, 1990, p. 311).

Another form of social capital involves the authority relationships within an organization. When individuals transfer the rights to control actions to other individuals, then the person to whom the right is transferred "has available social capital in the form of those rights of control" (Coleman, 1990, p. 311). Sometimes more than one person transfers the right to control actions to the same

person. Then, Coleman argues, "It appears . . . to be precisely the desire to bring unto being the social capital needed to solve common problems that leads persons under certain circumstances to vest authority in a charismatic leader" (Coleman, 1990, p. 311). Being empowered to act on behalf of others for the perceived good of all is thus a potent form of social capital, whether the leader be the head of a religious cult or the Speaker of the House.

Finally, Coleman describes two kinds of organizations that may result in other forms of social capital. In the first case, an organization created for one purpose is made available for other social purposes not envisioned by its founders (Coleman, 1990, p. 312). As examples of this phenomenon, Coleman mentions the study circles of South Korean student radicals who appropriated religious or school organizational ties and used these alliances for political purposes. He also cites perhaps the most widely known of such organizational appropriations—Sills' (1957) description of the manner in which the March of Dimes, organized and supported to fight polio, was able to shift its focus and resources to other diseases once a successful polio vaccine was developed (Coleman, 1990, p. 312; see also Sills, 1957).

A second kind of organization is created in order to invest in public welfare. Such an organization can be a voluntary group that produces a public service, such as a parent-teacher organization. The key element is that those who organize such groups are not the only ones who benefit from them; thus, parents need not be involved in forming a school organization in order to reap some of the positive effects such organizational activity may engender (Coleman, 1990, p. 313).

Social Capital as a Public Good

The "public-good aspect of social capital" explains at least in part the fact that social capital is underestimated, understudied, and for the most part overlooked. In essence, "many of the actions that bring social capital into being are experiences by persons other then the person so acting . . . The result is that most forms of social capital are created or destroyed as a byproduct of other activities. Much social capital arises or disappears without anyone's willing it in or out of being; such capital is therefore even less recognized and taken into account in social research than its intangible character might warrant" (Coleman, 1990, pp. 317–318).

In other words, it is *most* often the case that people who do not directly create social capital benefit from its existence, whether it takes the form of an active parent-teacher association that continues to provide benefits for the school even though not all parents participate, or the protection of a neighborhood from theft because the alarm systems purchased by a small group of neighbors have succeeded in reducing the amount of thieves on the street.

Robert Putnam's study of civic traditions in modern Italy (Putnam, 1993) also emphasizes the ways in which social capital is a public good. He postulates that there are few losers in groups characterized by uniformly high levels of activity or investment in the networks and organizations that promote social capital:

> Stocks of social capital, such as trust, norms, and networks, tend to be self-reinforcing and cumulative. Virtuous circles result in social equilibrium with high levels of cooperation, trust, reciprocity, civic engagements, and collective well-being. These traits define the civic community. Conversely, the absence of these traits in the uncivic community is also self-reinforcing. Defection, distrust, shirking, exploitation, isolation, disorder, and stagnation intensify one another in a suffocating miasma of vicious circles (Putnam, 1993, p. 177).

High levels of social capital, in other words, result in a higher quality of life for those who enjoy membership in the organizations and communities characterized by this state of affairs. But more importantly, the dense networks of civic engagement that Putnam found in some civic organizations had several powerful side-effects. "The denser such networks in a community, the more likely that its citizens will be able to cooperate for mutual benefit." In part, this increased likelihood of cooperation is explained by the fact that such networks foster "robust norms of reciprocity," argues Putnam (Putnam, 1993, pp. 174). Moreover, these networks "facilitate communication and improve the flow of information about trustworthiness of individuals;" likewise, the networks make it easier for participants to cooperate and "embody past success at collaboration" (Putnam, 1993, p. 174).

Thus the "problem of the commons" faced by all individuals in group situations—how to successfully negotiate solutions to problems shared by all—becomes easier to attack when the norms that support high levels of social capital are present.

The Creation of Social Capital

Despite the fact that the formation of social capital can be almost accidental, argues Coleman, there are at least three factors that can have a significant impact on the creation, maintenance, and destruction of social capital. The first of these is the degree of closure in the relationships between different kinds of actors in the same organization. In a school community, for example, parents will have relationships with their own children, and children in the same school may have relationships with other students in the school. In a community with high closure, however, parents also have relationships with one another that carry reciprocal norms and obligations independent of the activities of their children, occurring as a result of business, family, or religious ties.

Second, stability is critical in the formation and maintenance of social capital. When individuals move in and out of the social structure with high degrees of mobility, it disrupts the give and take of relationships in which social capital resides. An individual choice to leave the group has an impact on the social capital available to the group as a whole.

Third, "the very norms held by the group . . . may reinforce the public-good aspect of group relations and indicate the importance of every member to the group as a whole" (Coleman, 1990, p. 321). In explaining the differential performance of students in religious versus public schools described above, for example, Coleman attributes the success of religious school students in part to an ideology that values every student as a member of the school. This reasoning also suggests that a highly competitive, individualistic ideology minimizing commitment to the group can reduce social capital.

Finally, Coleman states, "Like human capital and physical capital, social capital depreciates if it is not renewed. Social relationships die out if not maintained; expectations and obligations wither over time; and norms depend on regular communication" (Coleman, 1990, p. 321).

The implications of this theory for educational practice and policy are complex and will occupy our attention throughout the remainder of this chapter. The early work on comparisons between public and religious schools provides an impetus for a host of proposals intended to reform and improve public schooling. We turn now to a review of some of the suggestions sparked by this early work.

Some Implications of Coleman's Work on Social Capital for Educational Practice and Policy

One of the best-known uses of James Coleman's empirical work on public, private, and Catholic schools in the 1980s was the support of a movement for school choice. Some of these plans focused solely on the ways in which students were allocated to public schools and used the findings on the importance of parent networks and oversight to encourage policies that supported choice systems in the public sector. But others found support in Coleman's work for reform schemes in which families were provided vouchers and permitted to choose the ways in which they used the public dollars provided for education relatively freely. If private and Catholic schools were more efficient in educating children, some advocates argued, then public policy should enable access to these schools by all children. (The extent to which any voucher scheme can truly ensure the ability of poor families to move into private education remains a subject of some debate.)

A second argument for school choice, both within and across sectors of schooling, was linked to the work of Chubb & Moe (1990). In their study of public and private schools that used the longitudinal "High School and Beyond" data, Chubb and Moe argued that the private schools in their sample outperformed the public high schools. Their rationale was twofold: first, the private schools had substantially less district and thus bureaucratic control, which they believed made them inherently more efficient. Like Coleman, however, they also held that the mechanism of school choice maximized social capital. Choice ensured that there was a good "match" between the parent community and the school's administration and teachers. Perhaps, it was argued, only a voluntary community of parents and students can shape and sustain the relationships in which social capital inheres. As was the case with Coleman's earlier work on public and private schools, these studies and the policy recommendations emanating from them provoked serious criticism (see, for example, Lee & Bryk, 1993).

Advocates such as these believe that choice can help to guarantee that the values and beliefs of parents and the community are exemplified by the school and the education activities it embodies. This proposition rests, of course, on the assumption that all schools are *not* created equal and that the particular assumptions, beliefs, and values that characterize teaching and learning in any one school matter a great deal.

The merits of a choice system, especially the variation that encourages greater investment in private education as a means of developing social capital, have been explored extensively elsewhere (see Rasell & Rothstein, 1993, for a thorough discussion of this topic). Restructuring the student allocation system around a set of voluntary mechanisms, however, is by no means the only policy implication of work on social capital. Below we will argue that there are many underexplored and intriguing issues for educators who wish to grapple with the consequences of this work on social capital.

Implications for Creating and Sustaining Social Capital at the School Level

If social capital is valued in the same way that we now consider the import of physical and human capital in schools, for example, then administrators and teachers must learn to construe the school not merely as a physical facility or a collection of professionals, but as a coherent set of relationships. In such a setting, individuals are bound together by more than a random or accidental aggregation of individual characteristics. Coleman's work underscores that these relationships are ordered by trust, knowledge, and authority, rather than mere chance. To link this construct to improved educational performance results in a schoolview for administrators in which interpersonal relationships among all constituencies, as well as the nexus between school and community, gain legitimacy as a focus for at-

tention. We have only begun to ask the kinds of questions that such consideration requires.

Not least important in this framework are notions of how social capital is created and sustained. Each of the mechanisms that Coleman outlines raise interesting questions when translated to a school setting. Trust, for example, is the *sine qua non* of the relationships in which social capital resides. One must have a reasonable expectation that one's claim to an obligation on the part of another will actually be fulfilled. Reciprocal arrangements in which the expectation of a favor to be returned require that all the parties involved have some level of trustworthiness. It is difficult enough to think about this with respect to the relationships among students, among teachers, between teachers and administration, in the connections between school and home, and between education professionals and students and their families. Coleman's work suggests that we must also begin to think about creating an environment in which families trust one another independent of engagement in the school. In this view, the extra-school relationships among students and their families are critical to developing the dense set of ties needed to support relationships that have a high degree of closure. Given our increasingly fragmented environments, this is no mean feat.

Similarly, the role of instability in school and student failure takes on an important new meaning, given these considerations. A highly mobile pattern of school attendance from year to year becomes a critical stumbling block to developing the rich set of relationships that can augment individual resources. Further consideration shows that maintaining some stability of relationships within the school—between teachers and children, for example, or among teaching professionals who share similar challenges—is a crucial part of ensuring the conditions necessary for the best teaching and learning. If the creation of social capital demands a stability in the arrangements through which work and social life are ordered, then administrators must pay serious attention to providing the support necessary for these conditions.

Finally, the notion that ideology plays a part in the creation of social capital cannot be underestimated. A commitment to a larger social entity and the maintenance and support of a set of relationships that undergird the work of the school community flies in the face of a highly individualistic, competitive ethos that privileges some at the expense of others. This ideology can be evident in every aspect of the school, from assessment to resource allocation. We will expand on these themes in a different fashion in subsequent sections.

Alternative Frameworks for Social Capital

The discussion of social capital would not be complete without some consideration of frameworks that posit a different view of the capital resources to which students have access, especially those students who are disadvantaged or who have traditionally had limited success in educational institutions. Chief among these theorists is Pierre Bourdieu (Bourdieu, 1977a, 1977b, 1980; Bourdieu & Passeron, 1977, 1979). His construct of cultural capital highlights the degree to which power and status among social groups who share unequally in critical cultural resources can affect the ways in which disadvantaged parties access the cultural norms, habits, and knowledge necessary for success. Claire Smrekar (1996) notes how Bourdieu's theory emphasizes the ways in which schools affirm and reproduce "the social legitimacy of the habits, objects, and symbols of the dominant class culture." Because more affluent children enter school familiar with these dominant patterns, they are able to transform cultural resources into what Bourdieu calls cultural capital (Smrekar, 1996, p. 3; see also Lareau, 1989). Smrekar makes the helpful distinction that "the concept of cultural capital underscores the *differences in class cultures* and the role of social institutions (schools) in differentially rewarding class cultures. In sharp contrast, the concept of social capital emphasizes the role of organizational (school) relationships in establishing *social ties between members* who share similar attitudes, norms, and values instrumental in promoting a strong sense of obligation, shared expectations, and trust" (Smrekar, 1996, p. 3, italics in original).

Ricardo Stanton-Salazar (Stanton-Salzar, 1997, p. 1) posits that most educational institutions present substantial barriers to minority youth whose stock of social capital is not readily converted into the kinds of understandings and relationships that encourage student success. He suggests that most academic settings are characterized by dominant, middle-class values with which many students are unfamiliar. "Social capital embodies social relationships with agents capable of and oriented toward providing, or negotiating one's access to, institutional support. The possession of social capital does not imply the utilization of support, but rather the potential for such utilization. The process by which individuals convert their social capital into institutional support for the express purpose of reaching certain goals has been termed *instrumental action* by Lin (1982, 1990)."

But current forms of schooling, argues Stanton-Salazar, do not embody or understand the resources that poor and minority children have at their disposal, thereby creating barriers for instrumental action. In order for educational institutions to re-address this deficit, Stanton-Salazar argues, they must become self-conscious about the roles that institutional agents play that can maximize the opportunities for educational success for all children. The forms of institutional support available to them include "1) *the provision of various funds of knowledge* associated with ascension within the educational system; 2) *bridging*, or the process of acting as a human bridge to gatekeepers, to so-

cial networks, and to opportunities for exploring various mainstream institutions . . . 3) *advocacy* . . . 4) *role modeling* . . . and 5) the provision of *emotional* and *moral* support" (Adapted from Stanton-Salazar, 1997, p. 11, italics in original).

It is particularly critical, he notes, for institutional agents to understand that some minority students must develop *bicultural network orientations* (Stanton-Salazar, 1995, p. 25) that permit them to cross cultural borders, successfully negotiating the middle-class institutional environment while maintaining strong sociocultural connections to a home community that may have different, even antithetical, values to the school setting.

Vertical and Horizontal Networks

This perspective on the transformation of social capital into school achievement stresses the difficulty with which such transactions are negotiated by those who come to school unfamiliar with the habits and norms conducive to academic success, much less with ready access to the information sources necessary for effective instrumental action. Putnam (1993) takes a similar position. Like Bourdieu and Stanton-Salazar, Putnam recognizes that many of the relationships in which social capital inheres are characterized by an imbalance of power. He distinguishes, then, between "horizontal" relationships—those among relative equals—and "vertical" relationships—those among individuals with differing status in which one partner is usually clearly advantaged.

> A vertical network, no matter how dense and no matter how important to its participants, cannot sustain social trust and cooperation. Vertical flows of information are often less reliable than horizontal flows, in part because the subordinate husbands information as a hedge against exploitation. More important, sanctions that support norms of reciprocity against the threat of opportunism are less likely to be imposed upwards and less likely to be acceded to, if imposed (Putnam, 1993, p. 175).

The importance of considering power relationships when discussing the social entities that structure relationships cannot be understated. We recognize that vertical networks figure prominently in the relationships between most educational systems and their clients. The effects of this imbalance are important and deserve careful scrutiny.

In the remainder of this chapter, however, we focus on a less-well-examined strategy that draws what we term "developmental implications" from the literature on social capital. We subscribe to Putnam's view: "If horizontal networks of civic engagement help participants solve dilemmas of collective action, then the more horizontally structured an organization, the more it should foster institutional success in the broader community" (Putnam, 1993, p. 175).

We turn next to a consideration of educational initiatives that attempt to even the playing field between educational institutions and communities. We do not mean to suggest that such new arrangements, most of which are systematically focused on developing social capital and, in part, restoring the balance of power, come naturally to any institutions, particularly those of an educational nature. Such transformations do and will continue to require new capacity and new will on the part of schools and those who support them.

The Process of Social Capital Formation Through Community Development

The key to social capital formation lies in its attention to active relationships rather than structures. It is not a question of whether a family, club, church, or association exists; it is a matter of what it does. Some educational institutions are actively engaged in developing social capital that becomes a resource able to serve multiple purposes. These programs and practices are consistent with building the dense set of networks around schools and school systems that can empower the community and also help to support the future of children.

Directed Parent Involvement in the Context of Partnerships

New ways of conceptualizing school and home relations are efforts to build the kind of social capital between home and school that provides a web of support for all children. Rather than constructing these as connections between individual teachers and their students, some theorists have moved to delineating a broad framework in which the parent community and the school work together to build these supportive structures.

Joyce Epstein (1994), for example, asserts that strategies intended to develop and direct academic connections between parent and child are only meaningful when embedded in an understanding of how all the key players in a child's life affect student growth and learning. "The term 'school, family and community partnerships' is a better, broader term than 'parent involvement' to express the shared interests, responsibilities, investments, and the overlapping influences of family, school, and community for the education and development of the children they share across the school years," she writes (Epstein, 1994, p. 39). Epstein argues that naming connections in this fashion appropriately recognizes schools as equals in the partnership and also encompasses the influence of all family members and of the many social and geographical communities that provide a context for the student's academic life. Moreover,

she contends that this broadened understanding also forces consideration of a wider range of student outcomes. "The model assumes that student learning, development, and success, broadly defined, not just achievement test scores, are the main reasons for school and family partnerships" (Epstein, 1994, p. 42).

Epstein's conceptual framework captures six major types of partnership activities, each rooted in a notion of shared responsibility for child welfare. These include: 1) the basic obligations of families; 2) the basic obligations of schools to effectively communicate with families about school programs and children's progress; 3) the involvement of parents at the school building; 4) family involvement in learning activities at home; 5) decision-making, participation, leadership, and school advocacy groups; and 6) collaborations and exchanges with the community (Epstein, 1994, pp. 43–49). Clearly, this approach hearkens back to a Deweyian notion of school and community in that it orients family involvement in academics in a much larger schema of joint care for student learning among the most interested parties.

Site-Based Management Councils

Over the past decade, the direct participation of community in the governance of the school has been advanced through school-based decision models that have been the focus of reform in many states and cities. The central tenet of these reforms is that parents and/or community members are incorporated into the school's governance system via site councils that have some authority over decisions at the site level. Although the major items in the school's budget—such as teachers' salaries—may be under the control of centrally-designed collective bargaining agreements, these site councils most often have some word in how "discretionary" funds, such as Title I moneys, may be spent. In varying degrees, site councils may also have responsibility for school improvement programs, basic policies governing school life, and curricular choices.

There is no need to review the burgeoning literature on the variants of school-based management, as that function has been performed ably elsewhere. (See, for example, Malen, Ogawa & Kranze, 1990; Murphy & Beck, 1995; Wohlstetter & Odden, 1992; Merz & Furman, 1997). Likewise, the Chicago reform in particular has been well documented by independent researchers as well as the Consortium on Chicago School Research (Hess, 1991, 1994, 1995; Easton, Bryk, Driscoll, et al., 1991; Bryk et al., 1993).

We are less concerned, however, with the capability of these arrangements to affect student achievement directly than we are in considering how they might begin to build capacity in the community and to nourish the relationships in which trust, knowledge, and mutual support can reside.

From this perspective, the results of site governance seem mixed. Looking at this literature in sum, for example, Merz and Furman (1997) remark on the efficacy of SBM as a vehicle for community inclusion, given both the reality and the promise of existing reforms:

> Most implemented models of S(chool) B(ased) M(anagement) hold little promise for community connections because they represent simple shifts of decision-making authority within the existing hierarchy . . . Community control models of SBM, though seldom implemented, theoretically hold some promise for community connections. However, even in its most "radical" form, as manifested in Chicago, community-control SBM has had only moderate impact on the bureaucratic, hierarchical structure of the school organization and on the traditional influence relationships among parent/community members and professionals (Merz & Furman, 1997, pp. 55–56).

But the jury may still be out. They continue: "This does not mean that the SBM concept does not have the potential to impact school-community connections over time. There is some evidence that more 'radical' versions of SBM may lead to greater community involvement in school governance over time and to some impact on the school's core program (Blackledge, 1995; Bryk *et al.*, 1993; Hess, 1995)" (Merz & Furman, 1997, pp. 55–56).

Many of the most radical reforms have been promulgated as renewed calls for democratic, nonprofessional control of schools. Seymour Sarason (1995) argues for such community involvement forcefully: "The political principle justifying parental involvement is that when decisions are made affecting you or your possessions, you should have a role, a voice in the process of decision-making" (Sarason, 1995, p. 19). Active community development in this view is not an ancillary result of site governance but an intended and direct effect.

Coordinated Services for Children at Risk: Early Models

There is perhaps no more passionate argument for the restructuring and coordination of social services designed to assist children at risk than *Within Our Reach*, Lisbeth Schorr's 1988 call to arms. Schorr argues persuasively that unless social services are designed to remedy the problems children have with respect to nutrition, medical care, housing conditions, family support, and educational services, then "rotten outcomes," such as poor health, poor performance in school, and even imprisonment, are predictable consequences for poor children.

One of the earliest examples of a strategy for coordinated services that aims to address the needs of the whole child and his or her family is Comer's School Development Program. The first incarnation of the School Development Program in New Haven is documented in the book *School Power* (Comer, 1980). More recent syntheses of the SDP reform document the long-term effects of these efforts (Comer, 1988; Haynes, Comer, & Hamilton-Lee, 1988a, 1988b) and indicate that the Comer School Development Model had expanded to include nearly 1,000 schools by the mid-1990s (Comer, Haynes, Joyner, & Ben-Avie, 1996).

The School Development Program restructures the school in ways that fundamentally alter the notion of school as merely an academic agency. The development of capacity for improved support of education in the parent and the surrounding community are clearly espoused goals of the program. To build this capacity, the activities of the program work on many facets of development in the student and adult populations, as well as in the community itself. The theory of the program is derived from the field of child development and rests on a few key premises: a child's behavior is determined by his or her interaction with the physical, social, and psychological environments; children need positive interactions with adults in order to develop adequately; child-centered planning and collaboration among adults facilitate positive interactions; and all planning for child development should be a collaborative effort between professionals and community members (Emmons, Comer, & Haynes, 1996, p. 29).

These premises result in three guiding principles that are infused throughout the school: consensus, collaboration, and no-fault. These principles are realized in three mechanisms in the school: a school planning and management team, a student and staff support team, and a parent team. Three operations form the agenda for these mechanisms: developing and implementing a comprehensive school plan, engaging in assessment and modification, and engaging in staff development (Emmons, Comer, & Haynes, 1996; Comer, Haynes, & Joyner, 1996).

Building community capacity in and out of the schools becomes central to this philosophy of improving children's lives and education. The School Development Program integrates parent involvement into a radical restructuring of the school that empowers teachers, parents, and students. The program has a coherent and all-encompassing philosophy devoted to the improvement of mental health and the provision of resources essential for teaching and learning. The school takes on far more than an academic mission and addresses key issues of power and collaboration in the process.

Community Development through Coordinated Services: Newer Models

The movement to integrate the services that are delivered to children has moved beyond rhetoric into reality over the past decade; indeed, the National Governors Association 1991 report on the state of the field is entitled *From Rhetoric to Action*. Several states, including California, Oregon, New

Jersey, and Kentucky, have incorporated this strategy for reform either on its own or as a component that is integrated with a restructuring of the state's educational systems (First, Curcio, & Young, 1994). In many cases, the school has become the obvious location for such coordination because it is seen as the central institution in most children's lives. As Louise Adler suggests, "Linking schools and social services has become a nationwide and . . . an international movement" (Adler, 1994, p. 1).

In an attempt to delineate the common elements of most efforts, Adler notes that most definitions include the concept of local access to services at a school or neighborhood institution by families and children: the availability of a variety of services, including health, mental health, employment, childcare, and education; collaboration among all service providers; a developmental, supportive model and a move toward the empowerment of families and community; flexibility in funding; the development of new ways of working among diverse professionals; and some requirements for change at a systemic level (Adler, 1994, p. 1).

As the movement has developed in breadth and scope, an extensive literature has emerged that documents existing efforts and (more recently) critiques the philosophical and conceptual basis for school-linked efforts. (See, for example, Adler & Gardner, 1994; Haertel & Wang, 1997.) Some of this work has highlighted particular issues that make genuine collaboration between school-based professionals and the community difficult. Some studies demonstrate how existing institutional beliefs can result in bureaucratic standard operating procedures that supplant more fragile norms that empower the community (Smylie, Crowson, Chou, & Levin, 1994).

Others, arguing that these problems are more fundamental (Capper, 1994; Chaskin and Richman, 1992), have suggested that more of these programs should be located outside educational institutions and in the community itself, thereby increasing 24-hour access for children and their families and minimizing the status and expertise of educational professionals in these efforts. Still others (McLaughlin, Irby, & Langman, 1994; Heath & McLaughlin, 1994) urge that a new focus on the positive and vital organizations that work well with inner-city youth outside of the educational system might ultimately prove the most instructive activity in the improvement of schools.

The most recent thinking in the policy world about the coordination movement has led to a reexamination of the scope and purpose of models that have been attempted to date. Renewed commitment to these reforms means for some a rededication to the problems found in the community at large in which the school is located (Crowson, 1998). As Adler notes, "We cannot get better childhoods for children unless we build better communities" (Adler,

1994, p. 1). She continues, "If we are serious about prevention, we must focus on how to improve the economic viability of communities. Unless we address issues of economic empowerment, we will never be able to build enough homeless shelters, provide enough compensatory education programs, or move more families off welfare rolls than come onto them" (Adler, 1994, p. 10).

The coordinated service movement continues to argue for more potent and regular mechanisms for connecting families and the institutions that educate and serve their children, moving more forcefully of late towards a stance that argues for greater empowerment of the community at large as the mechanism through which children's lives are likely to be changed for the better.

Restoring a Sense of Place to Educational Administration

Above we argue that educational practices such as school/family partnerships, site governance, and coordinated services are moving actively towards building social capital that benefits children and schools. We also suggest that some educational institutions use these practices effectively by continuing to focus outward towards the community. In these schools, practices make boundaries more permeable and allow parents and community members to engage the school on their own terms. Empowerment is a word that runs through much of this literature, as school bureaucracies relinquish some of their traditional authority and status in an effort to include increasingly more diverse populations in children's education in meaningful, effective ways.

In some ways, this shift outward may be seen as a pragmatic realignment that locates prevention efforts closer to the sources of the problems. We argue, however, that such a shift is consistent with a strategy that deliberately works to build social capital in the relationships between home and school and in the community itself. When educational institutions and their communities come together around a set of activities targeted towards developing this intangible capital, then the knowledge, trust, and obligations that result can have powerful effects. We argue that there is a "breeder" effect—a generation and regeneration of resources that support not only the school community but are available to the greater community for other purposes as well.

Key to understanding how these activities can be fostered is the belief that a sense of place matters. The *particular* connections between people and institutions are what form the strongest ties. Although there may be a set of guiding principles or activities, the blueprint can only indicate the processes through which the best available connections might be made. The implications for the field of educational administration are complex if one believes that administration in one community will look different from administration in another. Such a view runs counter, we argue, to the notions of standardization in outcomes, if not processes, that characterize much of the current educational policy debate. But if social capital has an import for understanding how to improve education, it is to focus on the homely and irregular connections between schools and the families, communities, and cities that sustain them.

Social Capital and the Revitalization of American Cities

The connection between schools and communities is intuitive, attractive, and romantic, but the relationship to city-building seems remote and tangential. We wish to narrow that distance, arguing that social capital production in neighborhoods and communities is instrumental in creating vital cities and that schools are, in fact, basic industries for city development. Understanding this connection between schools and cities begins with examining the productive role of neighborhoods.

Communities as Zones of Production

Since the rise of the Chicago school of urban sociology in the 1920s, cities have been largely analyzed as social spaces: residential areas, shopping districts, gathering places and the like. This analytical framework naturally led to viewing cities in social-problem terms: housing, disease, and crime. Most urban policy has been focused in the same direction, including much of urban educational policy. By the 1970s, urban social problems had been classified into a deficit model of urban life. As a consequence, most urban and educational policy became explicitly redistributive (Peterson, 1981). Money flowed toward areas of identified problems and professional interest groups arose to articulate needs associated with these problems.

Recently, however, there has been renewed attention to communities as zones of production. For example, Scott (1988, 1993) and colleagues demonstrate the spatial clustering of aerospace, women's clothing, and animation industries in Los Angeles. In these places and others, the technical division of labor also produces a social ordering in the surrounding community (Scott, 1988; Scott, 1993; Soja, 1994). Nor is this pattern simply contemporary. Using historical data, Scott (1988, 1993) shows clustering of neighborhoods in Birmingham, England, around the production of guns, in London around footwear, and in Manhattan around making clothing.

Scott (1983) argues that the economies of production for goods and services give rise to significant concentrations of capital and labor and thus become the fundamental condition of large scale urbanization. Because occupational groups that cluster in neighborhoods serve to sustain and reproduce the skills, attitudes, and norms necessary to take up an occupation, neighborhoods become places of acculturation and signifiers of social status and labor market capacity.

Neighborhoods also produce and transmit knowledge. Proximity of one enterprise to another means that specialized expertise is available at relatively low transaction costs and that a supply of young people is available to enter expanding industries. Inter-family social networks bring together people with similar practical experiences about life and work. These "networks function as important communal resources, especially in working-class and ethnic neighborhoods" (Scott, 1988, p. 224). They form a mutual support system transmitting knowledge about how to get a job and the civic obligations and attitudes associated with occupations. Children learn how to gain access to jobs and to a network of individuals that socialized them into adult roles and responsibilities.

The neighborhood knowledge mirrors the local economy. For example, in the Pico-Union district of Los Angeles, an active neighborhood information system shows newly arrived immigrants how to get a first job and housing. On the greater East side of Los Angeles, a region encompassing 31 cities and 1.3 million people, there is embedded knowledge about how to get a job in the hundreds of small family-owned manufacturing industries or increasingly in public employment. The firms involved often involve unglamorous activities, such as food products manufacturing and metal fabrication, but job formation is higher and unemployment lower than the rest of L.A. (Lee, 1994). Housing prices are lower and stable communities exist within reasonable commuting distances, the shortest in the metropolitan area (Valle & Torres, 1994). Cities have a stable and hometown feel. And some communities, such as Monterey Park and Diamond Bar, are becoming targets for capital investment from Asia and sometimes from Mexico.

Understanding how one makes a living in a community is part of what might be called "rice bowl" knowledge, a connection between individual and society that provides insight into how particular industries work. As a colleague recently remarked, "I grew up in an engineer's family in Cupertino. Everyone knew what it would be like to write software, it was something you played at as children, and we had an idea about how you would go about doing that as a living." This worldview of local economies tends to be highly class-stratified and industry-specific. A successful Chinese founder of a scanner company compared Los Angeles to Silicon Valley:

In Silicon Valley, everyone wants to form a firm, and they go to work for someone else only if their venture fails. Everybody wants to control their destiny and have a "golden rice bowl." In Los Angeles, the defense firms generated a culture of the "iron rice bowl:" it might not be golden, but at least it was solid and dependable. Unfortunately, [in the aerospace employment collapse of the 1990s] people who believed in this were betrayed, and now have much less ability to create a living for themselves (Friedman, 1994, pp. iii–27).

Although "rice bowl" knowledge is not part of the formal curriculum, it is surely part of the tacit curriculum by which students construct knowledge of their environments. Each community has a form of rice bowl knowledge, and determining whether local stocks of knowledge will actually flow to students is one of the most important topics in the creation of social capital because, unlike physical capital, social capital only has value when it flows from one individual to another. As Stanton-Salazar (1995, 1997) argues, institutional agents, such as schools, are the keys to connecting social capital flows to racial minority children, and particularly in the case of Mexican-American students, there are significant barriers to the flow of social capital.

Social capital flows are not simply tied to increases in measured cognitive achievement; they have profound developmental effects. They reproduce skills and expectations. They can also contribute to the creation of a new dynamic, lead to a change in expectations, and refresh ideas about civic engagement. Schools are among the most stable and important institutions we have for sustaining and transforming these flows of social capital.

School Administration and Civic Renewal

Understanding neighborhoods as zones of production, rather than understanding them only as social spaces with problems of poverty and violence attached to them, contains implicit threats to school administration but also contains enormous opportunity to regain lost civic leadership.

Since the Progressive Era early in the 20th century, reformers deliberately separated the governance of schools from cities, and they shunned more socially integrated forms of education, such as settlement houses or community centers (Murphy, 1990; Tyack & Hansot, 1982). They also embraced theories that enabled them to separate schools from government conceptually. Early human capital economists predicted large public returns to education and made it possible to view schools as inherently *developmental* (Becker, 1962; Schultz, 1981). Organizationalists offered closed-system efficiency theories of functional specialization that led Progressives to professionalize education and separate its functions from those of families and governments.

By the 1970s, however, it was clear that the developmental assumption had broken down. Policymakers and analysts increasingly focused on socially and economically redistributive activities of big city school systems. Redistributive programs, from desegregation aid to Chapter 1, were expected to be transitory, but suburbanization and deindustrialization overwhelmed the effects of such interventions, leaving central cities increasingly divided between rich and poor (Ehrenreich, 1990).

Not surprisingly, the dominant theories of education and society shifted to match urban reality. Human capital theory moved from its assumptions that more education would automatically translate into prosperity toward something close to cynicism. Economic stratification and reproduction theories seemed a much better explanation of urban development, and these rose to prominence among educational sociologists (Rubinson & Browne, 1994). Even the current organization of educational scholarship reflects this shift. Virtually the entire history of the subfield known as the politics of education is devoted to the politics of distribution: equity, voice, agency, and interest group politics.

We believe we are now at a turning point in both theory and in the organization of city schools in the United States. In the shift from industrial to post-industrial America, which has strong parallels in the earlier transition from an agricultural to an industrial society, Americans have grown increasingly interested in developmental strategies and theories to guide them (Porter, 1995). There is a thirst for open-system and ecological ideas that show how social and economic subsystems interact to produce both growing metropolitan economies and vibrant, livable neighborhoods. Both at the levels of social theory and of education policy, there is a recognition that schools build as well as benefit from good neighborhoods, and that continued legitimacy for public education requires that people believe that the public schools are theirs (Mathews, 1996).

Nowhere is this thirst more evident than in the renewed interest of big city mayors in public education. Among others, the mayors of New York, Chicago, Baltimore, and Los Angeles inserted themselves into school governance and reform efforts (Applebome, 1995). These changes are profoundly threatening to role definition and the authority of school administrators. Fighting with a popular and articulate mayor threatens a superintendent's tenure (Hunter, 1997), but mayors are also vulnerable. In both Baltimore and Chicago, continued perceptions of school failure have brought criticism of the cities' mayors. Increased attention to the developmental capacity of schools holds both danger and opportunity for school administrators.

The potential opportunity for school administrators lies in rethinking leadership and reclaiming lost civic ground. In this century, administrative thought has moved from evangelical fervor to corporate culture (Tyack & Hansot, 1982). Strengthening the public schools' social capital connection provides the opportunity for regaining a sense of vocation associated with school leadership. Schools connect to building neighborhoods and cities in very instrumental ways. Reclaiming lost ground requires first making the case that links school improvement to neighborhood improvement and, second, creating the organizational linkages.

Making the Case: Education as a Basic Industry

Making the case requires seeing schools as basic industries. A renewed awareness that cities cannot economically or socially thrive without excellent schools provides a historic opportunity for school administrators to fashion themselves into leaders of any urban region's basic industries (Kerchner, 1997).

Historically, basic industries occupy central positions in the economy, generate economic surpluses, and ripple wealth through the economy. Mining occupied this role in agricultural societies, steel making and auto manufacturing in industrial societies. Knowledge-generating institutions fill this role in postindustrial cities, and the role of universities is well recognized. The role of Stanford and University of California, Berkeley, in the development of the Silicon Valley, and that of Cal Tech and UCLA in the aerospace industry are part of the literature on economic development (Castells & Hall, 1994; Scott, 1993). The role of schools is less well recognized. Despite the fact that real estate markets value schools highly, the instrumental value of schools in building economies and cities is seldom mentioned, except in the negative.

The case statement for public education argues that attempting to rebuild neighborhoods without a strategy for schooling can have only limited success (Cisneros, 1993). Working-class families who improve their economic status flee, and middle class families don't return to neighborhoods where the schools are in disrepute. For years, this phenomenon was commonly attributed to white flight, but recent work suggests the problem to be as much one of class distinction as racial discrimination. Black and Latino middle class and professional classes also migrated to the suburbs. The results are hollowed-out cities, such as Detroit, where the population approaches half of its 1950 figure, and where the remnant is increasingly that which Wilson calls "the truly disadvantaged" (Wilson, 1987).

Yet schools obviously work in synergistic ways with economies: Good schools attract talented people and give communities the "quality-of-life" label treasured by the mobile and critical professional middle class. Good schools create stability in working-class and poor neighborhoods that allows community organization. A recent economic simulation in Pennsylvania suggests substantial effects on population and regional economics from just a one percent increase in worker productivity, a decline in births to teenage mothers, or an increase in the quality-of-life index (Passmore

& Anderson, 1994). However, by positing schools as basic industries, we wish to explore more instrumental and purposive connections between schools and communities, connections that should be developed and reflected in educational policy.

Mechanism 1: Schools as Magnets

Schools serve as magnets for people and for economic activity. We largely see this in the negative. A recent *Los Angeles Times* article tells the story of Deborah and Les Granow who spent $100,000 *more* to buy a small house in the suburbs, rather than to stay in a larger, nicer one in the city (Kristof, 1994). The deciding factor was the economics of private school tuition. The Granows rejected city public schools for their children, and they calculated that the cost in after-tax dollars of staying in Los Angeles and sending two children to private school would be $200,000; thus, investing more in a suburban house made sense.[1] The irony, of course, is that the government, through the income tax deductibility of mortgage interest and property taxes, interstate highway funds, and mass transit subsidy, provides a very heavy incentive for parents to relocate to towns where they find schools attractive. Public policy contains far fewer incentives for families with financial means to stay and rebuild cities. In the choice between "voice and exit," we are paid to flee (Hirschman, 1970).

However, city schools are not incapable of being attractive. For whatever their association with social stratification, it is clear that magnet schools, vocational specialty schools, and academically elite schools are highly attractive to parents and that students do relatively well in them (Gamoran, 1996a, 1996b). At the same time, the growing development of community-based schools has started to give a boost to the neighborhoods in which they reside. Unfortunately, the data on this last point is still anecdotal, but administrators and teachers at schools such as the Vaughan Next Century Learning Center in Pacomia, California, and the Hoover and the O'Farrell Community Schools in San Diego (Nathan, 1996; Stein, 1996) report that their schools attract people to the neighborhoods and create community stability. In Lynn, Massachusetts, a magnet elementary school creates a microsociety mirroring the school's vision of the best in the surrounding society (Strickland, 1996). In Albuquerque, New Mexico, an elementary school magnet builds on the resources of a local museum and extends science education to whole families (Judd & Judd, 1996).

When education enters the sphere of economic development, the school "magnet" effect becomes much more problematic. Although businesses are attracted to locations because of good schools, they generally don't like to pay for them. Cities and geographic regions are locked in what has been called the "economic war between the states" (Reich,

1996, p. 26). The bidding battles between locations undermine tax bases, and school administrators have largely been unsuccessful in presenting the long-term human capital agenda to a region as an alternative investment to that of manufacturing plants seeking to relocate.

Some particularly poignant examples have resulted. In Cleveland, the school district shared in the tax abatement for new office buildings and a football stadium at the same time that the roof collapsed at one of its elementary schools. Meanwhile, the district contributes about $345,000 a year in tax concessions to the Rock and Roll Hall of Fame. In Anaheim, California, the Walt Disney Co. threatened not to rehab its "happiest place on earth" theme park unless cities and school districts provided tax breaks. As area schools scrambled to find classroom space, Disney got a $546 public works subsidy (Johnston & White, 1997; White & Johnston, 1997).

However, there are some counterexamples. Procter and Gamble, long a civic fixture in Cincinnati, has located a new factory in the city for which it will pay $12 million in school taxes over the next decade. At the same time P & G remains a mainstay of efforts to improve teaching and teacher training in the city (Johnston & White, 1997). In the Seattle area, businesses and local authorities have created a regional economic development organization called Cascadia to build the area's infrastructure, including the schools. Besides attending to hard infrastructure, such as roads and utilities, these organizations are guided by the notion of "soft structure" that includes education and quality of life considerations (Blakely, 1997).

Mechanism 2: Schools as Engines

Schools are big employers with huge budgets. If California's elementary and secondary school system were placed on the *Fortune* 500 list of the largest companies in the United States, it would rank 22nd, just above Metropolitan Life Insurance and just below PepsiCo and Hewlett-Packard. In Los Angeles County alone, the public schools spend nearly $7 billion a year and employ 133,000 people, making it a bigger enterprise than Microsoft, Coca-Cola, or Levi-Strauss (Picus, 1997).

The problem is that in most poor city and suburban neighborhoods, relatively little of the school's funds find their way into the immediate community. The multiplier effect of school expenses on the local micro-economy is severely attenuated and so too are the social capital-generating activities associated with incomes and prosperity.

However, viewing urban communities as assets rather than accumulated deficits provides the means to look at multiplying flows of school funds through such practices as:

- Purchasing goods and services from local producers and suppliers
- Hiring local residents
- Targeting contracts for goods and services to support the creation of new businesses
- Investing resources in local financial institutions, such as credit unions, co-ops, and community development loan funds (McKnight, 1995; McKnight, 1994; McKnight & Kretzmann, 1993)

A mixture of incentives and mandates is capable of directing resource flows in ways that benefit neighborhoods, yet at the same time community-based incentives resurface questions about political graft and corruption, which has been associated with community school boards in New York and other cities, and the balance between professional and populist governance.

One way to multiply the effects of school expenses is to get school employees to live in communities surrounding the school. Mandates have not been particularly successful in this regard, but housing incentives and career ladder plans that allow para-educators, who now represent nearly one in six school staff members, to attend college and become teachers are one of the potentially powerful incentives for connecting community to schools and connecting school resources to community development (Kerchner, Koppich, & Weeres, 1997).

Schools appear most explicitly engine-like when they engage in vocational education. The same industries that seek tax abatements are highly attracted by programs that offer to train their work force. Employer and skill-specific training answers an employer's need for competent entry-level workers and, by using a firm's own equipment for training, targeted education allows training to occur on modern rather than antiquated technology. For educators, the "narrow vocationalism" involved and the apparent movement of benefit from the student to the firm creates an unwarranted public subsidy (Grubb & Stern, 1989). In many cases, school-to-work programs are successful in placing students, but they only boost yearly earnings by $200 to $500 (Grubb, 1996). But if the programs are constructed in ways that allow students to enter the labor market and still have a pathway to higher education, one that has employer encouragement, then an incentive system is created to increase the academic performance of the broad middle range of high school students. These programs work particularly well in cities and use their locational and cultural advantages (Grubb, 1995).

Technology transfer programs and small business development centers provide technical assistance to small and medium-sized firms regarding computer technologies, hardware, budgeting, management skills, and other areas of business. Although these programs most typically involve community colleges, technical institutes, and local universities, business development centers that include public school teachers (on split assignments or summer stipends) would allow teachers to gain a valuable window on the local economy that extends into the schools themselves, rather than being associated solely with a school district's top administrators. Teachers would also gain expertise in their primary linkage to the labor market, that of an intermediary who interprets the economic world to students.

All schools sort their students, whether or not they have an explicit tracking system. In fostering expectations and connecting them to explicit actions, teachers modify the flows of social capital in ways that are, in fact, selectively reproductive. Some aspects of community-rooted cultures are encouraged; others are not. In addition to subject matter and technical knowledge, schools provide the means for students to decode the larger social system. And for students who are not from the dominant culture, schools particularly act as institutional agents providing children with the means to interact with powerful adults and to problem-solve within the context that those adults represent (Stanton-Salazar, 1997). From the choices of classes to expressions in language, the effect of schooling on flows of social capital are quite profound, and these effects are informed by the extent to which teachers and local administrators have knowledge of the pathways and barriers youth in their schools face.

Schools as Training Tracks for Democracy

In his polemic about American democracy, William Greider (1992) attests that Americans need "civic faith" to overcome vast differences among its people. "If these connections between the governed and the government are destroyed, if citizens can no longer believe in the mutuality of the American experience, the country may descend into a new kind of social chaos and political unraveling, unlike anything we have experienced before" (p. 15).

For the past quarter-century, political theory and practice has struggled with the problem of representation and access to school governance. The community control movement and the adoption of community school boards in New York, school site boards in Chicago, and school board elections by district in other cities are testimony to these efforts. So, too, are parent interest groups along racial, neighborhood, or educational interests as diverse as special education parents and band boosters.

However, our experiences in interest group democracy have generally not had the palliative effects of increasing the legitimacy for the institution of public education that supporters of direct participation in governance have forecast. School politics appear increasingly fractured, ideological, and racialized. In much of the country, it has become the politics of distribution.

Social capital formation begs for a retreat from interest-based politics and toward what Mansbridge calls unitary politics, a politics of shared growth and development (Mansbridge, 1983;

Mansbridge, 1990). The basic sense of belonging to something larger than the family and smaller than the nation-state, a sense of multiple citizenships, and a sense of mutual dependency flows from the direct face-to-face politics available only in proximate communities (Bellah, Madsen, Sullivan, Swidler, & Tipton, 1991; Etzioni, 1993; Handy, 1994).

On the one hand, this instinct would appear to call for a romantic return to Tocqueville's description of America's civic virtues and Jefferson's rural republicanism, a virtual denouncement of bureaucracy and modern complexity. Yet Putnam's own work suggests that large, modern institutions are far from antithetical to the creation of civility (Putnam, 1993). In his study, the least civic areas of Italy were the traditional southern villages; the most, the prosperous industrial north. Big institutions can create civility in smaller ones. As we search for points of tangency between what institutions can do to allow schools to become training grounds for democracy, two possibilities can be suggested.

Asset-Based Community Indicators

As we noted earlier, poor communities are traditionally seen in terms of their deficits: violence, crime, disease, and dog bites. To build communities, schools need to be conscious of their community assets. Community developers and activists have come to understand the limits to a disease-based analysis of neighborhoods, and new tools such as the capacity inventory developed at Northwestern University can direct educators' attention to building on assets, rather than counting deficits (McKnight & Kretzmann, 1993; McKnight, 1994). Recent developments in community indicators, a fusion of environmental, civil rights, and economic concepts promote similar interests (Campbell, 1996; Sawicki & Flynn, 1996).

Education indicator systems that view community capacity alongside school goals and outcomes become tools (Bryk & Hermanson, 1993). These tools can be applied to school planning and progress schemes, and they can also be useful in direct instruction. Survey instruments and geographic information systems are capable of being mastered by high school students, and these allow issues studied in history, social studies, economics, or geography to rest on local data.

Neighborliness Creation

Violent crime, spurred by an epidemic of drug use, increased a staggering 367 percent in the decades after the United States declared war on poverty and urban decay (Youngblood, 1993). When individual schools gain greater influence in their curriculum, and when parents are asked about what they want for their children, they talk first about building relationships between children and across generations to teachers. Students want to talk openly about race and racism, often about the emotions and experiences they know because of the color of their skin (Poplin & Weeres, 1992).

When teachers in Pittsburgh, Louisville, and Cincinnati, among other places, negotiated breakthrough union contracts, they used their new influence to start programs in child-to-child dispute resolution (Kerchner & Koppich, 1997). Consensus-building for adults proves no less important than it does for children.

Implications for Further Research

Three research avenues beckon to further exploration into the relationship between education and social capital. The first road leads to further definition and measurement of social capital. The second leads to exploring the chronic problem of undersupply: if social capital is good, why don't we have enough? The third road explores the processes that link individual action and the creation of social capital: what linkages produce social capital under what conditions.

The Measurement of Social Capital

Much of the measurement of social capital relies on essentially opportunistic data elements, principally because large databases already contain them. For example, Kawachi, Kennedy, and Lochner (Kawachi, Kennedy, & Lochner, 1997) report on a positive relationship between social capital and public health. In their study, social capital is measured by a single question in the National Opinion Research Center's General Social Survey: the proportion of respondents in each state who believed that "most people can be trusted." Although trust is central to social capital formation, assessing its presence through opinionaire is a long way from specifying the structure and dynamics of neighborhood formation.

Fortunately, there is a growing instrumentation in community indicators that will provide more fine-grained data on various cities and examples of indicators and how to construct them. The move toward community indicators grows from several perspectives. For example, Hempel describes a "sustainability triangle" that encompasses the quality of human life, civic engagement, and the quality of the biosphere (Hempel, 1996). A handbook for creating community indicators has been written and important research can be done in linking community and educational indicator development at the school and classroom levels (Bryk & Hermanson, 1993; Redefining Progress, Tyler Norris Associates, & Sustainable Seattle, 1997; Sawicki & Flynn, 1996).

The Undersupply of Social Capital

The problem of social capital's undersupply has been linked primarily to the concept of trust and how to en-

courage it through public policy. As Mancur Olson noted more than three decades ago, people have a tendency to ride free on the social streetcar unless compelled to do otherwise (Olson, 1965). Unfortunately, the usual responses to undersupply (creating a market good or a coercive monopoly) undermine social capital formation itself. Most public policy work in this area has taken place at the level of national institutions (Fukuyama, 1995).

There is importance to much more localized research. For example, studies of community schools that seek to find interaction effects between school programs (such as service learning and social service provision) and community characteristics would be most valuable. So, too, would be studies that turned the causal arrow around. For example, Crane's application of epidemic theory to neighborhood effects on school results found that reducing the number of risk factors children faced showed a marked effect on dropping out of school and teenage childbearing (Crane, 1991). McKnight asserts that conventional educational methodology of "needs surveys," once employed in many compensatory education applications, focuses communities on the emptiness, deficiency, and malady, rather than on inherent capacities (McKnight, 1995; McKnight, 1994; McKnight & Kretzmann, 1993). Studies that focus on the community's strengths might provide a welcome change as well as new theoretical insights.

A second social policy approach supplying social capital is found in efforts to create a national accounting for social as well as physical capital. Our current measuring system anchored in the Gross Domestic Product accounts measures money changing hands in the money economy. It makes no distinction between the desirable and undesirable and does not recognize economic or social functions performed by households or the volunteer sector (Cobb, Halstead, & Rowe, 1995). Both economists and theologians have asked whether there is not the need for a better means of social accountability, one that recognizes the good or ill that economic activity does to communities and the environment (Cobb, 1994; Daly & Cobb, 1994). Work on an alternative Genuine Progress Indicator has already begun and includes such factors as the household and volunteer economy, crime expenses to defend against it, the distribution of income, resource depletion, habitat degradation, and the loss of leisure (Cobb, Halstead, & Rowe, 1996).

The Processes Linking Individual and Social Capital

The third research road leads toward understanding which kind of linkage between schools and communities appears productive of social capital indicators: parent engagement and participation and an ethic of caring and support. Unfortunately, the road contains a mass of isolated travelers. Virtually every school district in the country involves itself in some kind of community outreach, and most of them use surveys or other measures of their efficacy. But there is almost no integration or aggregation. For this reason, efforts of organizations, such as the Chicago Consortium on School Reform, that attempt longitudinal tracking of attitudes by neighborhood seem particularly valuable (Bryk & Rollow, 1992).

Social capital is sufficiently important that we need to understand it in its own right, not simply as a vehicle that helps to explain performance on an academic achievement test. Research methodologies that are able to capture important differences among schools and communities with respect to their success at sustaining such capital, and conceptual frameworks that can help make meaning of those differences, must be infused into a literature that too often has focused on a narrow range of outcome measures.

A Sense of Place Revisited

For the last half-century, public education has subordinated a sense of place to other policy issues, in each case for compelling reasons. Desegregation decisions assigned students to schools without regard to historic identities between neighborhood and school. The onset of collective bargaining emphasized uniformity in work rules across school sites and categorical programs classified students into subgroups, rather than connecting them.

Each of these major policy thrusts drew attention away from the embeddedness of schools in communities. Communities were most frequently depicted as a collection of deficits, the chronicling of which was frequently required as a means of attracting categorical and grant funds to the school. Thus even when the location of the school was recognized, it was usually in terms of the school's need to insulate itself from its location or to compensate for its effects.

Social capital theory strongly suggests that schools need to be engrossed in the particular places in which they are located, building up as well as drawing from the community resources that sustain them. Social capital theory also suggests that educational policy acknowledges the role that community resources play in the core mission of schooling. Flows of resources, not just collections of wealth or capacity, show up in measurements of student achievement. Moreover, communities are themselves educative. Just as workplaces concentrate in urban areas, so too do people who work in them, and the craft and cultural knowledge of how to work and how to get work is often locally determined. Beyond the workplace, knowledge about how to navigate life and how to cope with its cruelties is transmitted in neighborhoods. Put simply: Where you live can make you smarter. Living smarter can make your city livable and prosperous. Schools and people who lead them need to attend to these facts.

NOTE

1. The calculations are straightforward. Divide the annual private school tuition by the inverse of your marginal tax rate. The result is how much you would have to earn to pay the tuition. (For example, if you are in the 30% tax bracket, to pay $4,000 in tuition you have to earn $5,714.) Take that result and again divide it by the inverse of your tax rate. Divide that number by 12 to get the amount of added monthly mortgage payments that it would take to equal private school tuition. (In this example the result would be $8,163 or $680 a month. At the traditional real estate rule of thumb of $9/$1,000 in mortgage, the parent(s) in the 30% bracket contemplating $4,000 in private school tuition could afford an extra $75,000 for a house in order to send their children to a desirable public school.)

REFERENCES

Adler, L. (1994). Introduction. In L. S. Adler & S. Gardner (Eds.), *The politics of linking schools and social services* (pp. 1–16). Washington, DC: The Falmer Press.

Adler, L. & Gardner, S. (1994). *The politics of linking schools and social services*. Washington, D. C. & London: The Falmer Press.

Alexander, K. & Pallas, A. (1983). Private schools and public policy: New evidence on cognitive achievement in public and private schools. *Sociology of Education*, 56, 170–182.

Applebome, P. (1995, September 17). Political Hands Reach for The Schools. *New York Times*, p. 14,16.

Becker, G. S. (1962). Investment in human capital: A theoretical analysis. *Journal of Political Economy*, 70 (5, part 2), 9–49.

Bellah, R. N., Madsen, R., Sullivan, W. M., Swidler, A. & Tipton, S. M. (1991). *The Good Society*. New York: Alfred A. Knopf.

Blackledge, A. (1995). Minority parents as school governors in Chicago and Britain: Empowerment or not? *Educational Review* 47, 309–317.

Blakely, E. J. (1997). A New Role for Education Economic Development. *Education and Urban Society*, 29(4), 509–523.

Bourdieu, P. (1977a). Cultural reproduction and social reproduction. In (J. Karabel & A. H. Halsey (Eds.), *Power and ideology in education*. New York: Oxford University Press.

Bourdieu, P. (1977b). *Outline of a theory of practice*. New York: Oxford University Press.

Bourdieu, P. (1980). Le capital social. Notes provisaires. *Actes de la Recherche en Sciences Sociales* 3:2–3

Bourdieu, P. & Passeron, J. C. (1977). *Reproduction in education, society and culture*. Beverly Hills, CA: Sage.

Bourdieu, P. & Passeron, J. C. (1979). *The inheritors: French students and their relation to culture*. Chicago: University of Chicago Press.

Bryk, A. S. & Hermanson, K. L. (1993). Educational Inducator Systems: Observations on Their Structure, Interpretation and Use. In L. Darling-Hammond (Ed.), *Review of Research in Education* (Vol. 19, pp. 405–450). Washington, DC: American Educational Research Assn.

Bryk, A. S. & Rollow, S. G. (1992). *The Chicago Experiment: Enhanced Democratic Participation as a Lever for School Improvement (Issue Report 3)*. Center for Organization and Restructuring of Schools.

Bryk, A. S., Easton, J. Q., Kerbow, D., Rollow, S. G. & Sebring, P. A. (1993). *A view from the elementary schools: The state of reform in Chicago*. Chicago: Consortium on Chicago School Research.

Cain, G. G. & Goldberger, A. (1983). Public and private schools revisited. *Sociology of Education*, 56, 208–218.

Campbell, S. (1996). Green Cities, Growing Cities, Just Cities? *Journal of the American Planning Association*, 62 (3), 296–312.

Capper, C. (1994). We're not housed in an institution, we're housed in the community: Possibilities and consequences of neighborhood-based interagency collaboration. *Educational Administration Quarterly* 30 (3), 257–277.

Castells, M. & Hall, P. (1994). *Technopoles of the World: The making of twenty-first century industrial complexes*. London: Routledge.

Chaskin, R. J. & Richman, H. (1992). Concerns about school-linked services: Institution-based versus community-based models. *Future of Children*, 2 (1), 107–117.

Chubb, J. & Moe, T. (1990). *Politics, markets and America's schools.* Washington, DC: The Brookings Institute.

Cisneros, H. G. (Ed.) (1993). *Interwoven Destinies: Cities and the Nation.* New York: W. W. Norton.

Cobb, J. B. (1994). *Sustaining the Common Good: A Christian Perspective on the Global Economy.* Cleveland, Ohio: Pilgrim Press.

Cobb, C., Halstead, T. & Rowe, J. (1995). If the GDP is Up, Why is America Down? *The Atlantic Monthly,* 276(4), 59–78.

Cobb, C., Halstead, T. & Rowe, J. (1996). *The Genuine Progress Indicator: Summary of Data Methodology.* San Francisco: Redefining Progress.

Coleman, J. (1988). Social capital and the creation of human capital. *American Journal of Sociology 94.* Supplement, S95–S120.

Coleman, J. (1990). *Foundations of Social Theory.* Cambridge, MA and London, England: The Belknap Press of Harvard University Press.

Coleman, J. & Hoffer, T. (1983). Response to Tauber-James, Cain-Goldberger and Morgan. *Sociology of Education,* 56, 219–234.

Coleman, J. & Hoffer, T. (1987). *Public and private schools: The impact of communities.* New York: Basic Books.

Coleman, J., Hoffer, T. & Kilgore, S. (1982a). Achievement and segregation in secondary schools: A further look at public and private school differences. *Sociology of Education,* 55, 162–182.

Coleman, J., Hoffer, T. & Kilgore, S. (1982b). Cognitive outcomes in public and private schools. *Sociology of Education,* 55, 65–76.

Coleman, J., Hoffer, T. & Kilgore, S. (1982c). *High school achievement.* New York: Basic Books.

Comer, J. (1980). *School power: Implications for an intervention project.* New York: The Free Press.

Comer, J. (1988). Educating poor minority children. *Scientific American,* 259(5), 42–48.

Comer, J., Haynes, N. & Joyner, E. (1996). The school development program. In J. Comer, N. Haynes, E. Joyner & M. Ben-Avie (Eds.), *Rallying the whole village: The Comer process for reforming education* (pp. 1–26). New York: Teachers College Press.

Comer, J., Haynes, N, Joyner, E. & Ben-Avie, M. (Eds.). (1996). *Rallying the whole village: The Comer process for reforming education.* New York: Teachers College Press.

Crane, J. (1991). The Epidemic Theory of Ghettos and Neighborhood Effects on Dropping Out and Teenage Childbearing. *American Journal of Sociology,* 96(5), 1226–1259.

Crowson, R. (1998). Community Empowerment and the Public Schools: Can Educational Professionalism Survive? *Peabody Journal of Education.*

Daly, H. E. & Cobb, J. B. J. (1994). *For the Common Good: Directing the Economy Toward Community, The Environment and A Sustainable Future.* Boston: Beacon Press.

Driscoll, M. E. (1993). Choice, achievement and school community. In E. Rasell & R. Rothstein (Eds.), *School Choice: Examining the evidence* (pp. 147–172). Washington, DC: Economic Policy Institute.

Dryfoos, J. (1994). *Full service schools.* San Francisco: Jossey-Bass.

Easton, J., Bryk, A. S., Driscoll, M. E., Kotsakis, J. & van der Ploeg, A. (1991). Charting Reform: The Teachers' Turn (Report No. 1 on a Survey of CPS Elementary School Teachers.) *Catalyst,* 3 (2).

Ehrenreich, B. (1990). *Fear of Falling: The inner life of the middle class.* New York: Harper Perennial

Emmons, C., Comer, J. & Haynes, N. (1996). Translating theory in practice: Comer's theory of school reform. In J. Comer, N. Haynes, E. Joyner & M. Ben-Avie (Eds.), *Rallying the whole village: The Comer process for reforming education* (pp. 27–41). New York: Teachers College Press.

Epstein, J. L. (1992). School and family partnerships. In M. Alkin, (Ed.), *Encyclopedia of Educational Research* (pp. 1139–1151) New York: Macmillan.

Epstein, J. L. (1994). Theory to practice: School and family partnerships lead to school improvement and student success. In C. Fagnano & B. Werber, (Eds.), *School, family and community interaction: A view from the firing lines* (pp. 39–54). Boulder, Co: Westview Press.

Etzioni, A. (1993). *The spirit of community: Rights, responsibilities, and the communitarian agenda.* New York: Crown.

First, P. F., Curcio, J. & Young, D. (1994). State full-service initiatives: new notions of policy development. In L. S. Adler & S. Gardner (Eds.), *The politics of linking schools and social services* (pp. 63–74). Washington, DC: The Falmer Press

Flap, H. D. & De Graaf, N. D. (1986). Social capital and attained occupational status. *The Netherlands' Journal of Sociology* 22:145–161.

Friedman, D. (1994). *The New Economy Project No.* The New Vision Business Council of Southern California.

Fukuyama, F. (1995). *Trust: The Social Virtues and the Creation of Prosperity.* New York: Free Press

Gamoran, A. (1996a). Do Magnet Schools Boost Achievement? *Educational Leadership,* 54(2), 42–46.

Gamoran, A. (1996b). Student Achievement in Public Magnet, Public Comprehensive, and Private City High Schools. *Educational Evaluation & Policy Analysis,* 18(1), 1–18.

Granovetter, M. (1985). Economic action, social structure, and embeddedness. *American Journal of Sociology* 83:1420–1443.

Greider, W. (1992). *Who Will Tell The People: The Betrayal of American Democracy.* New York: Simon & Schuster.

Grubb, W. N. (1995). Reconstructing Urban Schools with Work-Centered Education. *Education & Urban Society,* 27(3), 244–259.

Grubb, W. N. (1996). *Learning to Work: The Case for Reintegrating Job Training and Education.* New York: Russell Sage Foundation.

Grubb, W. N. & Stern, D. (1989). *Separating the Wheat from the Chaff: The Role of Vocational Education in Economic Development No.* National Center for Research in Vocational Education, University of California at Berkeley.

Haertel, G. D. & Wang, M. (Eds.) (1997). *Coordination cooperation collaboration: What we know about school-linked services.* Philadelphia, PA: The Mid-Atlantic Regional Laboratory for Student Success at Temple University.

Handy, C. (1994). *The Age of Paradox.* Boston: Harvard Business School Press.

Haynes, N., Comer, J. & Hamilton-Lee, M. (1988a). The effects of parental involvement on student performance. *Educational and Psychological Research,* 8(4), 291–299.

Haynes, N., Comer, J. & Hamilton-Lee, M. (1988b). The school development program: A model for school improvement. *Journal of Negro Education,* 57(1), 11–21.

Heath, S. B. & McLaughlin, M. (1994) The best of both worlds: Connecting schools and community youth organizations for all-day, all-year learning. *Educational Administration Quarterly,* 30 (3), 278–300.

Hempel, L. C. (1996). *Environmental Governance: The Global Challenge.* Washington, DC: Island Press.

Hess, G. A., Jr. (1991). *School restructuring, Chicago style.* Newbury Park, CA: Corwin.

Hess, G. A., Jr. (Ed.) (1994). Special issue on the Outcomes of Chicago school reform. *Education and Urban Society* 26.

Hess, G. A., Jr. (1995). *Restructuring urban schools: A Chicago perspective.* New York: Teachers College Press.

Heyns, B. L. & Hilton, T. L. (1982). Cognitive tests for High School and Beyond: An assessment. *Sociology of Education,* 55, 89–102.

Hirschman, A. (1970). *Exit, Voice, and Loyalty.* Cambridge, MA: Harvard University Press.

Hunter, R. C. (1997). The mayor versus the school superintendent. *Education and Urban Society,* 29(2), 217–232.

Johnston, R. C. & White, K. A. (1997, March 19). Despite rhetoric, businesses eye bottom line. *Education Week,* Electronic edition: www.edweek.org/ew/vol16/25 tax. h 16.

Judd, M. & Judd, E. (1996). Tradition and technology: A magnet school-museum partnership. *New Schools, New Communities,* 12(2), 39–44.

Kawachi, I., Kennedy, B. B. & Lochner, K. (1997). Long Live Community: Social Capital as Public Health. *The American Prospect,* 35, 56–59.

Kerchner, C. T. (1997). Education as a City's Basic Industry. *Education and Urban Society,* 29(4), 424–441.

Kerchner, C. T., Koppich, J. E. & Weeres, J. G. (1997). *United mind workers: Unions and teaching in the knowledge society.* San Francisco: Jossey-Bass.

Kilgore, S. (1983). Statistical evidence, selectivity effects and program placement: Response to Alexander and Pallas. *Sociology of Education,* 56, 182–186.

Kristof, K. M. (1994, June 5). 3 Keys to Real Estate: Schools, Schools, Schools. *Los Angeles Times*, p. D4.

Lareau, A. (1989). *Home advantage: Social class and parental intervention in elementary education*. London: The Falmer Press.

Lareau, A. (1994). Parent involvement in schooling: A dissenting view. In C. Fagnano & B. Werber (Eds.), *School, family and community interaction: A view from the firing lines* (pp. 61–74). Boulder, Co: Westview Press.

Lee, P. (1994, Aug. 14). San Gabriel Valley: Rising economic star. *Los Angeles Times*, p. D1.

Lee, V. & Bryk, A. S. (1993). Science or policy argument: A review of the quantitative evidence in Chubb & Moe's Politics markets and America's schools. In E. Rasell & R. Rothstein (Eds.), *School choice: Examining the evidence* (pp. 185–208). Washington, DC: Economic Policy Institute.

Lin, N. (1982). Social resources and instrumental action. In P. V. Marsden & N. Lin (Eds.), *Social structure and network analysis* (pp. 131–145). Beverly Hills, CA: Sage.

Lin, N. (1990). Social resources and social mobility: A structural theory of status attainment. In R. Brieger (Ed.), *Social mobility and social structure* (pp. 247–271). Cambridge: Cambridge University Press.

Loury, G. (1977). A dynamic theory of racial income differences. Chapter 8 of *Women, minorities, and employment discrimination*, ed. P. A. Wallace & A. Le Mund. Lexington, MA: Lexington Books.

Loury, G. (1987). Why should we care about group inequality? *Social Philosophy and Policy* 5:249–271.

Lynd, R. & Lynd, H. (1929). *Middletown*. New York: Harcourt.

McKnight, J. L. (1994). Hospitals and Communities Create "Wise" Environments. *Trustee*, 47(2), 22–23.

McKnight, J. L. (1995). *The Careless Society: Community and Its Counterfeits*. New York: Basic Books.

McKnight, J. L. & Kretzmann, J. (1993). *Building Communities From the Inside Out*. Evanston, IL: Northwestern University.

McLaughlin, M., Irby, M. & Langman, J. (1994). *Urban sanctuaries: Neighborhood organizations in the lives and future of inner-city youth*. San Francisco: Jossey-Bass.

McPartland, J. & McDill, E. (1982). Control and differentiation in the structure of American education. *Sociology of Education*, 55, 77–88.

Malen, B. & Ogawa, R. (1988). Professional-patron influences on site-based governance councils: A confounding case study. *Educational Evaluation and Policy Analysis*, 10(4), 251–270.

Malen, B., Ogawa, R. & Kranz, J. (1990). What do we know about school-based management? A case study of the literature and a call for research. In W. Clune & J. Witte (Eds.), *Choice and control in American education, Volume 2: The practice of choice, decentralization and school restructuring* (pp. 289–342). New York: Falmer.

Mansbridge, J. J. (1983). *Beyond Adversary Democracy*. Chicago: University of Chicago Press.

Mansbridge, J. J. (Ed.). (1990). *Beyond Self-Interest*. Chicago: University of Chicago Press.

Mathews, D. (1996). *Is There a Public for Public Schools?* Dayton, OH: Kettering Foundation Press.

Merz, C. & Furman, G. (1997). *Community and schools: Promise and paradox*. New York: Teachers College Press.

Morgan, W. R. (1983). Learning and student life quality of public and private school youth. *Sociology of Education*, 56, 187–202.

Muller, C. (1993). Parent involvement and academic achievement: An analysis of family resources available to the child. In B. Schneider & J. Coleman, (Eds.), *Parents, their children, and schools*. (pp. 77–114). Boulder, Co: Westview Press.

Murnane, R. (1984). Comparisons of public and private schools: Lessons from the uproar. *The Journal of Human Resources*, 19, 263–277.

Murphy, J. & Beck, L. (1995). *School-based management as school reform: Taking stock*. Thousand Oaks, CA: Corwin Press.

Murphy, M. (1990). *Blackboard Unions: The AFT and the NEA, 1900–1980*. Ithaca, NY: Cornell University Press.

Nathan, J. (1996). Early Lessons of the Charter School Movement. *Educational Leadership*, 54(2), 16–20.

Olson, M., Jr. (1965). *The Logic of Collective Action*. Cambridge, MA: Harvard University Press.

Passmore, D. & Anderson, W. (1994). Linking School Reform and the Economy in Pennsylvania. In *Pennsylvania Educational Research Association*, (pp. 10). University Park, PA: Penn State.

Peterson, P. (1981). *City Limits*. Chicago: University of Chicago Press.

Picus, L. O. (1997). The Economic Impact of Public K–12 Education in the Los Angeles Region: A Preliminary Analysis. *Education and Urban Society*, 29(4), 442–452.

Poplin, M. & Weeres, J. (1992). *Voices from the inside* (Project Report 1): The Institute for Education Transformation, The Claremont Graduate School.

Porter, M. E. (1995). The Comparative Advantage of the Inner City. *Harvard Business Review*, 73(3), 55–71.

Putnam, R. D. (1993). *Making Democracy Work: Civic Traditions in Modern Italy*. Princeton, NJ: Princeton University Press.

Rasell, E. & Rothstein, R. (Eds.) (1993). *School choice: Examining the evidence*. Washington, DC: Economic Policy Institute.

Redefining Progress, Tyler Norris Associates & Sustainable Seattle. (1997). *The Community Indicators Handbook*. San Francisco: Authors.

Reich, R. (1996). Bidding Against The Future. Federal Reserve Bank of Minneapolis: *The Region*, 10(2), 26–30.

Rubinson, R. & Browne, I. (1994). Education and the Economy. In N. J. Smelser & R. Swedberg (Eds.), *Handbook of Economic Sociology* (pp. 581–599). Princeton, NJ: Princeton University Press and Russell Sage Foundation.

Salganik, L. & Karweit, N. (1982). Voluntarism and governance in education. *Sociology of Education*, 55, 152–161.

Sarason, Seymour. (1995). *Parental involvement and the political principle: Why the existing governance structure of schools should be abolished*. San Francisco: Jossey-Bass.

Sawicki, D. S. & Flynn, P. (1996). Neighborhood indicators: A review of the literature and an assessment of conceptual and methodological issues. *Journal of the American Planning Association*, 62(2), 165–181.

Schneider, B. & Coleman, J. (Eds.) (1993). *Parents, their children and schools*. Boulder: Westview Press.

Schorr, L. B. (1988). *Within our reach: Breaking the cycle of disadvantage*. New York: Doubleday.

Schultz, T. W. (1963). *The economic value of education*. New York: Columbia University Press.

Schultz, T. W. (1981). *Investing in People*. Berkeley: University of California Press.

Scott, A. J. (1988). *Metropolis: From Division of Labor to Urban Form*. Berkeley: University of California Press.

Scott, A. J. (1993). *Technopolis: High-Technology Industry and Regional Development in Southern California*. Berkeley: University of California Press.

Sills, D. (1957). *The volunteers, means and ends in a national organization*. New York: Free Press.

Smrekar, C. (1996). *The impact of school choice and community*. Albany: State University of New York Press.

Smylie, M., Crowson, R., Chou, V. & Levin. R. (1994). The principal and community-school connections in Chicago's radical reform. *Educational Administration Quarterly* 30, 342–364.

Soja, E. W. (1994). Taking Los Angeles Apart: Toward a Postmodern Geography. *In Postmodern Geographies: The Reassertion of Space in Critical Social Theory* (pp. 222–249). New York: Verso.

Stanton-Salazar, R. D. (1997). A Social Capital Framework for Understanding the Socialization of Racial Minority Children and Youth. *Harvard Educational Review*, 67(1), 1–40.

Stanton-Salazar, R. D., Dornbusch, S. M. (1995). Social Capital and the Reproduction of Inequality: Information Networks Among Mexican-Origin High School Students. *Sociology of Education*, 68(Number 2), 116–35.

Stein, B. (1996). O'Farrell Community School: Center for Advanced Academic Studies. A Charter School Prototype. *Phi Delta Kappan*, 78(1), 28–29.

Strickland, C. S. (1996). The Rainbow Connection: Portrait of a Microsociety Magnet School in Action. *New Schools, New Communities*, 12(3), 60–65.

Taueber, K. E. & James, D. (1983). Racial segregation among public and private schools: A response. *Sociology of Education*, 56, 204–207.

Tyack, D. & Hansot, E. (1982). *Managers of Virtue: Public School Leadership in America, 1820–1980*. New York: Basic Books, Inc.

Valle, V. & Torres, R. D. (1994). Latinos in a 'Postindustrial' Disorder. *Socialist Review*, 23(4), 1–28.

White, K. A. & Johnston, R. C. (1997, Schools' Taxes Bartered Away to Garner Taxes. *Education Week*. Electronic edition: www.edweek.org/ew/vol 16/24 tax. h−16.

Wilson, W. J. (1987). *The Truly Disadvantaged: The Inner City, the Underclass, and Public Policy*. Chicago: University of Chicago Press.

Wohlstetter, P. & Odden, A, (1992). Rethinking school-based management policy and research. *Educational Administration Quarterly* 28, 529–549.

Youngblood, K. (1993). Stopping the hemorrhaging: Human problems at a crisis point. In H. Cisneros (Ed.), *Interwoven Destinies: Cities and the Nation* (pp. 125–146). New York: W. W. Norton.

CHAPTER 19

New Consumerism: Evolving Market Dynamics in the Institutional Dimension of Schooling

Joseph Murphy

Across the nation and across the political spectrum, people concerned about America's schools have come to see the failure of public education as symptomatic of the institutional principles by which it has come to operate (Beers & Ellig, 1994, p. 21).

As fewer and fewer Americans participate in public affairs, more and more public affairs are being relegated to the private sector (Barber, 1984, p. xii).

New perspectives on institutional arrangements in education are emerging—forms that are anchored in consumer- or market-oriented ideologies. These new perspectives take a variety of shapes, ranging from community-controlled models of school-based management on the less vigorous end of the continuum to various forms of privatization, especially vouchers and home schooling, on the more robust end of the scale. These developments in the area of institutional arrangements are viewed quite differently depending on the perspectives one brings to the analysis and the lenses used to examine the phenomena. Many scholars, for example, see consumer-grounded institutional dynamics as antithetical to public meaning and, therefore, as the death knell for public education. Other analysts maintain that what we call "new consumerism" is a natural development in the evolution of control and accountability in public institutions. The logic here is that consumer-based control and accountability are simply a third act in the play known as school governance, an act that follows the professionally controlled governance structures that have dominated education for the past 75 years in the same way that professional control displaced the more democratically based models of school governance that characterized education in its formative years in

the United States (Crowson, 1998; Katz, 1992; Swanson, 1989; Tyack, 1974).

The first objective of our work is to explain why this evolution to consumer-anchored institutional dynamics is occurring. Our guiding framework posits that institutional shifts in education are primarily a response to changes in the larger environment in which schools reside—in the economy, the society, and the polity. In other words, institutional changes in education are economically, socially, and politically determined. Following the lead of Christopher Hood (1994), "the focus is on the broad comparative picture and the general plausibility of the various explanations . . . for why old orthodoxies died out" (pp. 2–3). It is not our intention to provide a normative tincture to the investigation, that is, to explore whether old systems were somehow ethically bankrupt and should have atrophied and whether new institutional approaches are morally superior. We concur with Kettl (1988) that changes in governance structures, although undertaken to alleviate problems and capture benefits, often "simply substitute a new set of difficult problems for the old ones" (p. 513). We also acknowledge that the design that we are employing in our quest for understanding partially masks a central dynamic of change—that new institutional arrangements, even when dominant, often end up sharing the playing field with their predecessors rather than simply replacing them (Cohen, 1989). Finally, we realize that there is overlap between the components of our model—in the domains of both policy extinction and the environment.

In reaching our goal of understanding the evolution to consumer-anchored institutional dynamics, we rely on a framework developed by Hood (1994) to explain the extinction of economic policy structures and the emergence of new policy forms.[1] According to Hood, "Policy reversal is a hybrid of institutional self-destruction, habitat change, and changing interest configurations" (p. 126). More specifically, he maintains that there are four interlinked forces that destroy existing policies and pave the way for new ones:

- The idea that policy reversal comes mainly from the force of new *ideas*, which succeed in upsetting the *status quo* in some way (through experimental evidence, logical force or rhetorical power).
- The idea that policy reversal comes mainly from the pressure of *interests*, which succeed in achieving changes that suit their purposes.
- The idea that policy reversal comes mainly from changes in social '*habitat*,' which makes old policies obsolete in the face of new conditions.
- The idea that policy reversal comes from 'inside,' with policies and institutions *destroying themselves* rather than being destroyed from outside (p. 4).

As seen in Figure 19.1, we have yoked Hood's framework to our own focus on the economic, societal, and political realms of the educational environment to create a rubric to organize our analysis of changing institutional arrangements in education.

The second major goal of the paper is to tie this more global analysis to new perspectives on the governance of education. After reviewing the logic on the self-destruction of education, we turn directly to the goal by describing the dimensions of market-based control that undergird emerging forms of institutional arrangements in education. Finally, we provide a brief overview of some examples of these emerging consumer-grounded governance systems—that is, competitors to the current educational systems. Our initial objective in the section focusing specifically on education is to expose the infrastructure supporting consumer-based models of governance. A further aim is to illustrate how some of the elements of those models—and the principles that undergird them—play out in public schools.

The Changing Environment in Which Education Is Nested

The contest over the meaning and course of the American story is a contest over whose sacred canopy shall prevail. There are recurring attempts to topple one system of meaning and erect another in its place (Heinz, 1983, p. 144).

It is easy to identify turning-points in retrospect, but harder to explain exactly why they took place when they did or what caused the reversal (Hood, 1994, p. 46).

All these factors—political, social, economic, legal, and educational—have converged to create a setting that makes the privatization of public school management very attractive (Richards, Shore, & Sawicky, 1996, p. 54).

The Changing Dimensions of the Economy: Economic Fundamentalism[2]

History can never be over as far as economic policy ideas are concerned. The policy dinosaurs will be back in some form after a generation or two of negative experience with their successors (Hood, 1994, p. 17).

Changes in the economy are integrally linked to emerging views of institutional arrangements in public institutions in general and public schooling in particular (Snauwaert, 1993). At the core of the current economic evolution is a recommitment to a market philosophy, a phenomenon that Thayer (1987) refers to as "economic fundamentalism" (p. 165). In the pages below, we employ Hood's four-part analytical framework (refer to Figure 19.1) to illustrate how the economic environment of education changes under economic fundamentalism.

Changing Habitat

It is almost a fundamental law that the economy is undergoing a significant metamorphosis as we head into the twenty-first century. There is widespread agreement that we have been and continue to be moving from an industrial to a post-industrial economy. Key aspects of the new economy include the globalization of economic activity, the demise of the mass-production economy, a privileging of information technology, an increase in the skills required to be successful, and an emphasis on the service dimensions of the marketplace (Marshall & Tucker, 1992; Murnane & Levy, 1996; Murphy, 1991). It is also becoming clear to many analysts that with the arrival of the post-industrial society, "we are seeing the dissolution of the social structure associated with traditional industrialism" (Hood, 1994, p. 12) and a "habitat that is less hospitable" (p. 101) to government growth. The ascent of the global economy has brought an emphasis on new markets (Lewis, 1993), "a loosening of the constraints of the labor market" (Dahrendorf, 1995, p. 21), and a "break[ing] of the state monopoly on the delivery of human services so that private enterprise can expand" (Lewis, 1993, p. 84). Along with these have come increasing deinstitutionalization, deregulation, and privatization—new forms of consumer-anchored governance, if you will (Lamdin & Mitrom, 1996; Richards *et al.*, 1996).

Self-Destruction

At the same time that the economic policy habitat is evolving, the current foundations of the economy, especially in the public sector, appear to be crumbling. The "economic

Figure 19.1
Framework for Examining Forces Responsible for Changing Governance Structures in Education

		Change Framework			
		New Ideas	Competitors	Changing Habitat	Self-Destruction
Environment	Economy				
	Society				
	Polity				

concepts that have traditionally given legitimacy to government actions have come under growing criticism" (President's Commission on Privatization, 1988, p. 229). The level of public frustration is on the rise (Cronin, 1989). According to many analysts, a "powerful alliance of ideological and commercial interests" (Martin, 1993, p. 2) has turned its guns on the issue of government provision of services.

Reevaluating the rationale for and growth of government sector activity. What accounts for this discontent and skepticism about the public sector of the economy that is helping fuel the quest for new forms of institutional governance? Given the cyclical nature of policy development and other value expressions in American society, some of this rising tide of dissatisfaction with public sector initiatives can be characterized as a response to the nearly unbroken growth of government over the last three-quarters of the twentieth century, a counter-reaction to the Progressive philosophy that has dominated the policy agenda for so long. According to Hood (1994), for example, the growth of the public sector contains the seeds of its own destruction. The public sector model is, in many ways, simply aging and wearing out. Once a major economic model gains ascendancy, "dissatisfaction builds up over time. Unwanted side-effects of the policy [become] more clearly perceived. . . . At the same time, the shortcomings of the alternative orientation—the market in this case—are forgotten, because they have not been recently experienced. Pressure then starts to build for the policy orientation to go over on the other track" (p. 15).

Another piece of the self-destructive puzzle is the widespread perception that "government is doing more than it ought to be doing, that is, it is intruding too much into our lives" (Florestano, 1991, p. 291). Critics note that more and more citizens are chafing under the weight and scope

of government activity (Himmelstein, 1983; Meltzer & Scott, 1978). They characterize a government that has gone too far (Hirsch, 1991)—"public ownership that is more extensive than can be justified in terms of the appropriate role of public enterprises in mixed economies" (Hemming & Mansoor, 1988, p. 3). They argue that "government has become involved in the production of goods and services that do not meet the market failure tests" (Pack, 1991, p. 282) and that government agencies have pushed "themselves into areas well beyond governance. They [have] become involved in the business of business" (President's Commission on Privatization, 1988, p. 3). The results are predictable: Government, it is claimed, "acquires a life of its own" (Savas, 1987, p. 3), welfare loss due to collective consumption increases (Oates, 1972), and citizens experience "a growing desire for more individual self-reliance" (Florestano, 1991, p. 295).

Expanding numbers of citizens have begun to experience "some public sector institutions as controlling rather than enabling, as limiting options rather than expanding them, as wasting rather than making the best use of resources" (Martin, 1993, p. 8). Of particular concern here is the issue of values. On one front, an increasing number of individuals and groups have come to believe that government intrusiveness includes efforts to establish value preferences (Cibulka, 1996; Heinz, 1983; Himmelstein, 1983), values that they believe often undermine their ways of life. Others argue that, at least in some cases, through interest group and bureaucratic capture, some public sector institutions have actually destroyed the values "which they were originally set up to enshrine, guard, and promote" (Hood, 1994, p. 16).

The wearing out of the existing economic environment can also be traced to recent critical analyses of the model of public sector activity developed to support an expanded government presence. The critique here is of three types.

First, when examined as they are put into practice, the assumptions anchoring public sector activity over the last 30 years look much less appealing than they do when viewed in the abstract (that is, conceptually). Indeed, "many of the assumptions and predictions on which the earlier growth of government was based have proved either to be false or at least to be subject to much greater doubt" (President's Commission on Privatization, 1988, pp. 249–250). Thus "part of the account of the retreat of state power since 1979 relies on the way in which its limitations had by then become evident" (Pirie, 1988, p. 16). Foundational propositions such as the non-political nature of public sector economic activities have come under attack as it has been determined that "decisions affecting the economy [are often] made on political grounds instead of economic grounds" (Savas, 1987, p. 8). On the other hand, much of the critique of the market economy upon which public sector growth has been justified, especially market failure, has been weakened with the advent of sociotechnical changes associated with a shift from industrial to post-industrial society (Hood, 1994, p. 48).

Second, as we explain more fully below, "structural weaknesses inherent in the nature of public-sector supply itself . . . which undermine the whole basis on which it is established" (Pirie, 1988, p. 20) have become more visible —visible to the point that, as Martin (1993) notes, some advocates claim that "state ownership and management are intrinsically flawed" (p. 139). Concomitantly, "both the efficiency and effectiveness of public sector activities [have begun] to be questioned seriously" (Hemming & Mansoor, 1988, p. 1).

Third, it is suggested that the reforms that created the large public sector "are themselves sorely in need of reform, as mistakes, excess, waste, and scandals appear[ed] and the inevitable institutional arteriosclerosis set in" (Savas, 1982, p. 2). Reform is increasingly seen in terms of alternatives to rather than the repair of the existing public sector. Changes in governance structures are often privileged in these reform strategies.

Discontent with and expanded skepticism over public sector economic activity are reinforced by a growing suspicion that government intervention is becoming less an instrument to provide services to the general citizenry and more and more a vehicle to establish values and to transfer income and wealth to individuals and groups (Donahue, 1989; Gottfried, 1993). Such transfers are of three types: (1) income and benefit premiums ("rents" in the economics lexicon) available to government employees—that is, additional income and benefits enjoyed by civil servants over that received by employees in comparable jobs in the private sector; (2) affirmative action employment policies that shift wealth in the direction of targeted groups of citizens; and (3) particular programs that are created primarily to redistribute income.

Elshtain (1995) captures one aspect of the concern around income redistribution as follows:

> In the era of declining resources, resentments cluster around government-sponsored efforts that do not seem to solve the problems they were designed to solve (as voters were told when they signed on to the social contract to make provision for those less fortunate). That is, citizens who pay most of the bills no longer see a benefit flowing from such programs to the society as a whole. Instead, they see a growing dependence on welfare, increased inner-city crime, an epidemic of out-of-wedlock births, and the like. They perceive, therefore, a pattern of redistribution through forms of assistance to people who do not seem to be as committed as they are to following the rules of the game by working hard and not expecting the government to shoulder their burdens. This, at least, is the widespread conviction, and it fuels popular anger and perplexity. As a result, programs geared to particular populations have lost . . . legitimacy (pp. 3–4).

Tomlinson (1986) assesses the problem with a different lens:

> Social market theorists argue that the balance of the economy has swung away from the market order towards collectivism. Governments have steadily expanded universal welfare provision . . . and weakened the flexibility and universality of the market (p. 212).

Questioning the performance of the public sector. Central to the rethinking and overhaul of the existing institutional infrastructure are developing beliefs that government is "incompetent and that its inefficiency is a key factor behind the chronic fiscal crisis that plagues the public sector" (Richards *et al.*, 1996, p. 42)—that it is the poor performance of the public sector itself which is leading both to the abandonment of the assumptions used to forge a strong public sector and to calls for more market-oriented governance structures. The sentiment that government is becoming increasingly ineffective and inefficient is expressed along a continuum, from those who read the evidence as a mandate for a reduced public sector to those "advocates [who] want us to think about government as irredeemably incompetent [and prefer] to empty out the portfolio of public responsibilities" altogether (Starr, 1991, p. 35).

The death of public sector economic policy can also be attributed to stories of gross government incompetence or scandal and to a mounting body of evidence that "public enterprises are often inefficient and incur losses" (Hemming & Mansoor, 1988, p. 1) and that it costs more to accomplish tasks in the government than in the private sector. Or, stated alternatively, government is consuming more of the nation's resources than it should: "The government provision and production of many goods and services, including the regulation of market activities, generates substantial deadweight losses" (De Alessi, 1987, p. 24). Although "widespread concern over the increasing costs of government" (Hula, 1990b, p. 4) is an important variable in the algorithm of discontent, especially perceived "waste and inefficiency" (Poole, 1985, p. 46), an even more significant factor is the expanding disillusionment about "the overall effectiveness of government action" (Hula, 1990b, p. 4), particularly the perceived inability of government to meet its goals. Perhaps nowhere is this perception more vivid than in the arena of the large-scale egalitarian programs of the 1960s and 1970s (Hula, 1990b). A number of critics of activist government argue that the conditions that led to the development of these policies have not been ameliorated and that they will "not disappear as a result of having responsibility for them transferred from the private to the public sector" (Savas, 1987, p. 290). In fact, they maintain that such transfers "often aggravate the situation and create even more problems" (p. 290). They go so far as to suggest that many of our social problems are in reality cratogenic, that is, created by the state.

This widespread dissatisfaction with public sector economic activity has led some to question "whether public production . . . is so inherently inefficient that it results in even greater resource misallocation than do the market failures it aims to correct; whether regulation is even more costly to society than the initial resource misallocations" (Pack, 1991, p. 282). In tangible terms, it has helped foster a taxpayer revolt and has given birth to an array of citizen initiatives designed to seize control away from existing government structures (Murphy, 1996). At the core of these reactions is the "feeling that there must be a better way of doing all those things that governments do not do too well" (Savas, 1985, p. 17): "If government is failing in its efforts to provide essential services, should we not reconsider the role we have given government in these areas?" (Carroll, Conant, & Easton, 1987, p. x). For some, especially given the failure of strategies to reform or buttress the public sector, "a more fundamental strategic approach is needed" (Savas, 1987, p. 5). For many in this group, one particular avenue of change—market-based or consumer-based governance approaches—looks especially promising.

New Ideas

According to Hood (1994), major shifts in policy can also be the "result of ideological 'climate change' caused by intellectual developments and changes in the world of ideas" (p. 5). We do not need to search far for evidence that, in the economic domain, the evolution to consumer-anchored views of institutional arrangements is indeed being ideologically powered (Martin, 1993; Starr, 1991). In particular, two lines of thinking support the movement from public to market perspectives on school governance: (1) a bundle of ideas that Himmelstein (1983) labels "economic libertarianism" (p. 15)—a "renewed cultural enthusiasm for private enterprise" (Donahue, 1989, p. 3) in conjunction with "a cooling toward collectivism" (p. 3)—

and (2) a collection of intellectual traditions that have become known as public choice scholarship (Mueller, 1989).

The reemergence of market ideology. In many ways, the discontent and critique of government presented above represents the negative case for the renewed interest in market ideology. It is balanced on the positive side by the growing belief that "free market economics provide the path to prosperous equilibrium" (Thayer, 1987, p. 168)—by "the assumption that, left to itself, economic interaction between rationally self-interested individuals in the market will spontaneously yield broad prosperity, social harmony, and all other manner of public and private good" (Himmelstein, 1983, p. 16). Supported by market theory and theories of the firm and by the public choice literature, there is a "new spirit of enterprise in the air" (Hardin, 1989, p. 16)—a renewed interest in "private market values" (Bailey, 1987, p. 141) and in the "virtues of private property" (Hirsch, 1991, p. 2) and a "promarket trend" (President's Commission on Privatization, 1988, p. 237) in the larger society. A view of individuals as "economic free agents" (Murnane & Levy, 1996, p. 229) is finding widespread acceptance.

Although analysts are quick to point out the fallacy of this emerging belief in the infallibility of markets (Baber, 1987; Hawley, 1995; Martin, 1993), there is little doubt that current shifts in perspectives about control are anchored firmly on a "belief in the superiority of free market forms of social organization over the forms of social organization of the Keynesian welfare state society" (Ian Taylor, cited in Martin, 1993, p. 48). As Starr (1991) notes, this expanding reliance on the market moves individuals in the direction of "exercis[ing] choice as consumers rather than as citizens" (p. 27). It leads organizations to emulate current private sector business practices. Thus according to Ascher (1991), new thinking about governance cannot be viewed as a unique political development but must be seen as part of a larger economic trend.

The expansion of pro-market ideology is powered to a certain extent by the picture painted by some of "a bloated, parasitic public sector blocking the bustle and growth of a more free flowing private economy" (Starr, 1987, p. 124)—of government "interference with the natural working of the market" (Himmelstein, 1983, p. 15). Two beliefs are central to this line of reasoning: (1) that "the structural organization of the public sector itself" (Pirie, 1988, p. 34) is flawed and (2) that public sector decisions "are inherently less trustworthy than free-market decisions" (Savas, 1987, p. 5). Starting from here, we find many analysts adopting an increasingly skeptical stance on the usefulness of government intervention (Tullock, 1988, 1994a, 1994b). In particular, some analysts discern apprehension "about the threat of the state to private enterprise and individualism" (Himmelstein, 1983, p. 19). Their revisiting of the case for public action (Fixler, 1991) "has caused mainstream economists in recent years to narrow significantly the circumstances thought to require government intervention to correct market failings" (President's Commission on Privatization, 1988, p. 237). Accompanying this reconsideration of the case for public action has been a re-analysis of the supposed problems of markets and, according to privatization advocates, a recognition that because "market forces can find ways round or through vested interests" (Seldon, 1987, p. 133), "the regulation which the market imposes in economic activity is superior to any regulation which rulers can devise and operate by law" (Pirie, 1988, p. 10)—a feeling that because "the level of efficiency of government action is apt to be low, and the possibility of damage through erratic, ill-informed decisions is great, government action should be resorted to only when the social cost emanating from the market is quite great" (Tullock, 1988, p. 103).

Public choice theory.   Much of the ideological case for consumer-anchored institutional dynamics, as well as much of the case against government provision of services, can be found in the body of scholarship known as public choice literature. Public choice is concerned with "the politics of bureaucracy" (Tullock, 1965, p. 10) and "the political economy of representative government" (Niskanen, 1971, p. 12). Of central importance is the fact that "a particular approach to economics" (Buchanan, 1989, p. 13) anchors public choice theory—"an analysis of the behavior of individuals . . . in collective activity . . . in terms of an economic calculus" (Buchanan & Tullock, 1962, p. 21). Specifically, "the basic behavioral postulate of public choice . . . is that man is an egoistic, rational, utility maximizer" (Mueller, 1989, p. 2). The central premise of public choice literature is that "the beneficiaries of government monopoly are politicians, bureaucrats, and special interest groups" (Bennett & DiLorenzo, 1987, p. 22)—"that the provision of government services is an incidental effect of the incentives and constraints of voters, politicians, and bureaucrats" (Niskanen, 1994, p. 270). Closer to home, "public choice theory suggests that the obstacles to educational return may be inherent in government delivery of services" (Lieberman, 1989, p. 12).

Public choice analysts maintain that "the behavior of both the executive and the legislature can best be interpreted as the result of maximizing their own personal interests" (Niskanen, 1971, p. 137)—"that decisions are taken with a view of maximizing the probability of electoral success" (Vickers & Yarrow, 1988, p. 30). Thus politicians are said to employ a type of economic algorithm that closely links position-taking and election calculations (Stiglitz, 1986): "Politicians, instead of doing what they thought was in the public interest, would do things which might help them get reelected, or in some cases, might raise their income" (Tullock, 1994b, p. 65). In short, politicians

act in ways that will "win votes for re-election to public office" (Hood, 1994, p. 23), "advance their careers" (Tullock, 1965, p. 29), and "reward themselves and their followers" (Hood, 1994, p. 23).

The logical deduction here, public choice scholars maintain, is that politicians use tax dollars to enhance their own utility by nurturing the support of the other two players in the public choice triangle—public employees and beneficiaries of governmental programs (Bennett & DiLorenzo, 1987; Niskanen, 1971, 1994). Politicians engage in this "hands-on political patronage" (Hood, 1994, p. 43) or tax-funded politics in two main ways: (1) through the creation of programs and the maintenance of existing programs (Lieberman, 1988; Pirie, 1988; Tullock, 1965) and (2) through "payoffs to workers in publicly owned firms" (Vickers & Yarrow, 1988, p. 31) in terms of wages, benefits, and job security (Bennett & Johnson, 1980; Savas, 1982). Niskanen (1994) argues that most of this tax-funded self-promotion centers on the portion of a bureau's discretionary budget that the legislature reclaims for its own use through bargaining with the bureau's managers. The consequence is often "the subordination of the public interest" (Lieberman, 1989, p. 12).

At the heart of the public choice scholarship is a reassessment of the interests of public employees, especially managerial employees well known to us all as government bureaucrats. Central to this reinterpretation is a dismantling or "undermining of the naive faith in the benevolence of governmental bureaucracy" (Buchanan, 1987, p. 206). According to Niskanen (1971), "the beginning of wisdom is the recognition that bureaucrats are people who are, at least, not entirely motivated by the general welfare or the interests of the state" (p. 36). Rather than accepting the assumption that managers of public agencies are "passive agents [who] merely administer and carry out programs" (Bennett & DiLorenzo, 1987, p. 16) with the sole intent of maximizing public interest, public choice analysts advance the belief that these "civil servants often [make] decisions in the interest of their own power or income" (Tullock, 1994b, p. 65). At the most basic level, this results in the notion of the bureaucrat as a public service maximizer giving way to the conception of a manager who attempts to maximize his or her own utility function—a utility function that contains a variety of variables: "salary, perquisites of the office, public reputation, power, patronage, [and] output of the bureau" (Niskanen, 1971, p. 38).

The central claim of the public choice literature is that budget maximization and empire building impose real costs on citizens in terms of public control and overall efficiency of the economy (Bennett & Johnson, 1980). Bureaus are characterized by significant inefficiencies (Hilke, 1992; Niskanen, 1971, 1994; Pack, 1991). Public choice scholarship concludes that "the budget of a bureau is too large, the output . . . may be too low, and the production of this output is uniformly inefficient" (Niskanen, 1994, p. 274), or, more succinctly, "inefficiency in production is the normal condition" (p. 274).

Another strand of public choice discourse focuses on government employees, suggesting that because public employees are, next to transfer payment recipients, "the most direct beneficiaries of government spending" (Savas, 1987, p. 26), they are likely to use the power of the ballot box to promote the objective of government growth (Tullock, 1994a): "Government employees have a vested interest in the growth of government and, because of this interest, are very active politically. Relative to the general public, they vote in greater proportion and have a correspondingly disproportionate impact on political decisions" (Bennett & Johnson, 1980, p. 372). A second line of analysis holds that public-sector unions in particular are key instruments in the growth of bureaus and the concomitant subordination of consumer interests to the objectives of the employees themselves. Ramsey (1987) concludes that when the economic influence of unions is combined with political muscle, public-sector unions have considerable "ability to tax the rest of society" (p. 97). A final slice of the public choice literature focusing on public employees asserts that employee self-interest is nurtured in what might, presented in the best light, be thought of as a symbiotic relationship with the bureau's sponsor—the intersection where "the self-interest of the politician [and] a well-organized union cadre" (p. 97) converge to maximize the utility of both groups. As described above, the well-being of politicians and government employees is often seen to come at the expense of the general citizenry, especially in inefficiencies visible in inappropriate production schedules and unearned rents enjoyed by public servants (Hilke, 1992; Hirsch, 1991; Niskanen, 1971, 1994).

If politicians occupy one point on the public choice triangle and employees (bureaucrats and their subordinates) hold down a second, the third is populated by two related groups that also benefit heavily from government sector expenditures—producers and recipients of specific public services. On the issue of service providers as beneficiaries, Bennett and DiLorenzo (1987) and De Hoog (1984) demonstrate that both politicians and bureaucrats mobilize considerable support for themselves by forging strong relationships with private-sector producers. Concomitantly, "service providers . . . can become powerful advocates for government spending" (Butler, 1987, p. 6).

At the same time, recipients of public services often act as "'rent-seeking' groups that use their competitive advantage in collective action to gain advantages for themselves from government, spreading the cost among a wider group who have lower stakes in the issue and who face higher transaction costs in collective action" (Hood, 1994, p. 96). At the core of this line of reasoning is the proposition that because "groups who, one way or another, get the govern-

ment to provide services for them normally do not pay the full cost, . . . they take advantage of the possibility of imposing part of the cost on other people" (Tullock, 1994b, p. 67). Or, stated less charitably, "interest groups compete in the voting marketplace to redistribute for themselves income plundered through taxation of others" (Fitzgerald, 1988, p. 9). As is the case with politicians and government employees, producer and recipient interest group self-interest generally results in a situation in which production factors are redirected toward political rather than economic purposes (Pirie, 1988), "the amount of service generated is not optimal" (Tullock, 1994b, p. 67), real external costs are imposed (Buchanan & Tullock, 1962), and inefficiencies abound (Niskanen, 1971, 1994; Stiglitz, 1986).

Competitors

Private sector corporations. So far, we have examined three pillars of the economic explanation for the emergence of market-oriented operating principles and models in the public sector. There is still one cornerstone to be considered, however, which is what Hood (1994) refers to as the emergence of competing interest coalitions that stand to gain from the shift in policy. The most salient of these new interests is "commercial pressure" (Savas, 1987, p. 9) to dismantle government initiatives in a wide array of areas. According to this line of analysis, as the United States moves from the industrial to the post-industrial era, corporate growth through traditional paths becomes less and less viable. Expansion in the information age must, perforce, be concentrated in the service areas, "the very areas where public bureaucracies once were unchallenged specialists" (Hood, 1994, p. 99). Analysts perceive that this public service sector "offers lucrative new markets" (Darr, 1991, p. 66) for American corporations. They also "see substantial business opportunities in large capital projects" (Savas, 1987, p. 9) needed to address the infrastructure crisis plaguing the nation. Rationales for market-oriented approaches to service delivery "lie not only in the public sector's own failures but in the pursuit of new markets by large corporations" (Martin, 1993, p. ii); "it is very much a clash between competing producers, both of which want the government's business" (Kolderie, 1991, p. 254).

Education is an especially appealing target for profit-oriented firms for a number of reasons. To begin with, it is a huge market with spending on K–12 education alone approaching $300 billion annually (Garber, 1995, p. 34). Of that amount, $8.3 billion is spent on student transportation, $8 billion on the school food program, $9 billion on cleaning and maintenance, and $10.7 billion on the construction and modernization of school facilities (Beales & O'Leary, 1993). Second, "education is a capital starved industry" (Richards *et al.*, 1996, p. 45). Third, there has been relatively little penetration of the education market by the private sector to date. Finally, for many parts of the educational enterprise, startup costs are far from prohibitive.

Although research on private school parents is only thinly developed to date, a number of reviewers view families currently purchasing private schooling as an important emerging interest coalition (Hawley, 1995). Indeed, analysts such as Jaeger (1992) paint a picture of markets shifting resources "to the schooling of the privileged" (p. 126). On a larger scale, it is possible that market-oriented reforms are being promoted by competitors wishing to rework the welfare state's income transfer algorithm, to shift from the have-nots to the haves.[3]

The Changing Dimensions of Society and the Polity: Libertarianism and Social Traditionalism

> Neither pure traditionalism nor pure libertarianism carries much weight on its own in American culture, while a combination of the two, however paradoxical, speaks to some deeply rooted cultural themes (Himmelstein, 1983, p. 22).

> The dismantling of the welfare state is on the agenda everywhere (Dahrendorf, 1995, p. 26).

> The schools have to function in an environment of declining social and political cohesion (Consortium on Productivity in the Schools, 1995).

In the previous section, we spoke of the decaying economic substructures of the liberal democratic state. In this section, our search for the growth of market-oriented institutional arrangements leads us to the crumbling social and political foundations of the democratic welfare state. As in the earlier analysis, we employ the Hood framework from Figure 19.1 in the following order: changes in the habitat, patterns of self-destruction, the emergence of new ideas, and the presence of competitors.

Changing Habitat

The political and social environment appears to be undergoing two important changes. First, there has been a loosening of the bonds of democracy (Barber, 1984). Thus according to a number of scholars, "our American democracy is faltering" (Elshtain, 1995, p. 1), with a concomitant "loss . . . to our ways of living and working together and to our view of the worth of the individual" (Tomlinson, 1986, p. 211). Second, the infrastructure of civil society has been impaired. Analysts discern fairly significant tears in the fabric known as "modern civil society" (Dahrendorf, 1995, p. 23).

Reviewers of this changing environment are quick to reveal the linkages among the three elements in our model —the economy, the polity, and society. Hood (1994), for example, observes that political change is often perceived to be a product of "contextual . . . social change" (p. 8). More fundamentally, Dahrendorf (1995) discusses how alter-ations in society are nested within environmental shifts in the economy. In particular, he asserts that the values supporting economic fundamentalism—"flexibility, efficiency, productivity, competitiveness, and profitability" (p. 27)—have undermined two essential elements of civil society—stability and security.

As a consequence of these basic shifts—the weakening of democracy and the deterioration of civil society, especially in conjunction with the ideological space that they share with economic fundamentalism—important sociopolitical trends have begun to emerge: (1) "a growing sense of personal insecurity" (Dahrendorf, 1995, p. 26), "unrest in the populace at large" (Liebman & Wuthnow, 1983, p. 3), and a less predictable "worldlife" (Hawley, 1995, pp. 741–742); (2) "the destruction of important features of community life" (Dahrendorf, 1995, p. 26); (3) shifts in the boundaries, both real and symbolic, between the state and alternative sociopolitical structures (Liebman, 1983a); and (4) an expanding belief that the enhancement of social justice through collective action, especially public action, is unlikely (Whitty, 1984).

Self-Destruction

Changes in the sociopolitical habitat are closely linked to what in Hood's framework can be thought of as patterns of self-destruction. In fact, they are so intertwined that in some sense it is appropriate to think of these patterns as fueling alterations in the policy and social environments. The composite picture of self-destruction has been labeled "The Disunity of America" by Dahrendorf (1995, p. 23) and characterized as "the weakening . . . of the world known as democratic civil society" by Elshtain (1995, p. 2).

Discontent with government. One strand of this mosaic is plummeting support for government. In many ways, Americans "have disengaged psychologically from politics and governance" (Putnam, 1995, p. 68): "The growth of cynicism about democratic government shifts America toward, not away from, a more generalized norm of disaffection" (Elshtain, 1995, p. 25). As Hawley (1995) chronicles, "citizens are becoming increasingly alienated from government and politics. They do not trust public officials" (p. 741), and they are skeptical of the bureaucratic quagmire of professional control (Murphy & Beck, 1995). Not surprisingly, "multiple indicators of dissatisfaction and distrust provide ample evidence that something is happening to traditional approaches to public governance" (Bauman, 1996, p. 627).

Critics maintain that government in the United States is troubled and is becoming more so. They discern a sense of hopelessness about civic government (Katz, 1992) and a crisis of confidence in public institutions and representative government (Mathews, 1996; Thomas, Moran, & Resnick, n.d.). They acknowledge that "our distrust of government runs . . . deep" (Marshall & Tucker, 1992, p. 70). They point to surveys revealing "strong mistrust of government" (Hunter, 1995a, p. 140) and opinion polls showing that "Americans are distrustful of government agencies and generally opposed to public sector programs and policies" (Bauman, 1996, p. 625). These polls reveal that: only three in ten citizens believe that government is operated for the benefit of all citizens (Savas, 1987); one in two citizens believes that the federal government has become so large and so influential that it represents a real and immediate danger to the rights and freedoms of citizens (Urschel, 1995); only one in three voters expresses trust in government, down from four in five in the late 1950s (Savas, 1982); and, in 1993, only 13 percent of the citizenry trusted the government "to do what is right most of the time," compared to 62 percent in 1964 (Bauman, 1996, p. 626). Other chroniclers of this unrest speak of a mounting sense of skepticism, "skepticism about public enterprises" (Fitzgerald, 1988, p. 22) in general and "skepticism as to the ability of government to implement social goals" (Hula, 1990a, p. xiii) in particular. They believe that a "philosophy borne of suspicion for big government may underlie this [governance] revolution in America" (Fitzgerald, 1988, p. 20).

Still other reviewers discern a "deeper . . . and much more dangerous" (Savas, 1982, p. 1) cynicism toward (Hula, 1990b), distaste for (Donahue, 1989), or "distrust of government and government officials among Americans" (De Hoog, 1984, p. 1). They describe a "culture of resistance, bitterness, and adversariness" (Bauman, 1996, p. 626). They paint a picture of "'political bankruptcy,' a vaguely defined state of popular alienation and disaffection from government which stops short of revolution" (Hood, 1994, p. 91). These analysts portray "the electorate's disappointment in activist government" (Hirsch, 1991, p. 1) and the rise and spread of an antigovernment philosophy in the 1970s and 1980s, a time during which the "government plumbed new depths of disfavor" (Donahue, 1989, p. 3). They describe a "fundamental concern that government simply 'doesn't work.' Planning is seen as inadequate, bureaucracy as inefficient and outcomes highly problematic" (Hula, 1990a, p. xiii). They go on to argue that the consent of the governed is being withdrawn to a significant degree. In its softest incarnation, this cynicism leads "politicians and citizens alike to argue that government is no longer the solution to everything" (Florestano, 1991, p. 291) and to question the usefulness of much government-initiated activity (Hula, 1990b). At worst, it has nurtured the belief "that government is destined to fail at whatever it does" (Starr, 1991, p. 34). In many cases, it has caused the development of a variety of antigovernment political and social movements (Bauman, 1996). There is little question that this widespread discontent has spilled over into public education (Katz, 1992). As Bauman (1996) notes, "One could argue that people hold a negative view

of the public schools precisely because they are public institutions" (p. 628). We return to the theme of discontent with education below.

Social decay. A second pattern of self-destruction is anchored in issues of poverty. Many analysts, for example, have detailed the "concept and the phenomenon of the underclass" (Dahrendorf, 1995, p. 24) or the "trend toward private wealth and public squalor" (Bauman, 1996, p. 627). According to Dahrendorf (1995), this economically grounded trend represents a new type of social exclusion, the "systematic divergence of the life chances for large social groups" (p. 24). He and others are quick to point out that this condition seriously undermines the health of society: "Poverty and unemployment threaten the very fabric of civil society. . . . Once these [em-ployment and a decent standard of living] are lost by a growing number of people, civil society goes with them" (pp. 25–26).

Consistent with this description of diverging life chances is a body of findings on the declining social welfare of children and their families. These data reveal a society populated increasingly by groups of citizens that historically have not fared well in this nation, especially ethnic minorities and citizens for whom English is a second language. Concomitantly, the percentage of youngsters affected by the ills of the world in which they live, such as poverty, unemployment, illiteracy, crime, drug addiction, malnutrition, and poor physical health, is increasing (Murphy & Beck, 1995).

According to Himmelstein (1983), society is best pictured "as a web of shared values and integrating institutions that bind individuals together and restrain their otherwise selfish, destructive drives" (p. 16). Some reviewers have observed a noticeable attenuation of these social bonds, a failure of social theory (Hood, 1994) or what Elshtain (1995) describes as a "loss of civil society—a kind of evacuation of civic spaces" (p. 5). The splintering of shared values and the accompanying diminution in social cohesiveness have been discussed by Dahrendorf (1995) and Mayberry (1991), among others. Few, however, have devoted as much attention to the topic of changing patterns of civic engagement and political participation as Robert Putnam (1995). According to Putnam, the "democratic disarray" (p. 77) that characterizes society and the polity can be "linked to a broad and continuing erosion of civic engagement that began a quarter-century ago" (p. 77). After examining citizen involvement across a wide array of areas, for example, participation in politics, union membership, volunteerism in civic and fraternal organizations, participation in organized religion, he drew the following conclusion:

By almost every measure, Americans' direct engagement in politics and government has fallen steadily and sharply over the last generation, despite the fact that average levels of education—the best individual-level predictor of political participation—have risen sharply throughout this period. Every year over the last decade or two, millions more have withdrawn from the affairs of their communities (p. 68).

Dahrendorf (1995), in turn, reminds us that citizens "without a sense of belonging or commitment to society . . . [have] no reason to observe the law or the values behind it" (p. 28).

Another piece of the self-destruction story, related to the themes of declining social cohesion and political abstinence but even more difficult to ignore, is the issue of "social breakdown and moral decay" (Himmelstein, 1983 p. 15) or rents in the "sociomoral" (Liebman, 1983b, p. 229) tapestry of society (Boyd, Lugg, & Zahorchak, 1996; Boyd & Lugg, forthcoming; Wuthnow, 1983). Of particular concern is the perception that state actions have contributed to the evolution of social mores that are undermining the adhesiveness that has traditionally held society together (Heinz, 1983; Liebman & Wuthnow, 1983; Mayberry, 1991)—that "the welfare bureaucracy is irreversibly opposed to the established social morality" (Gottfried, 1993, p. 86).

New Ideas

The ideological footings of the emerging sociopolitical infrastructure are only dimly visible at this time. The one piece of the foundation that shines most brightly is what Tomlinson (1986) describes as the "ascendancy of the theory of the social market" (p. 211), a theory that is anchored on the "supreme value [of] individual liberty" (p. 211). This emerging "high regard for personal autonomy, or liberty" (Gottfried, 1993, pp. xiv–xv) is both an honoring of individualization and a discrediting of collective action (Donahue, 1989; Katz, 1971). Social market theory suggests a "reduced role for government, greater consumer control, and a belief in efficiency and individuality over equity and community" (Bauman, 1996, p. 627). According to Whitty (1984), it includes the privileging of private over public delivery and "the restoration of decisions that have been made by professional experts over the last few decades to the individuals whose lives are involved" (p. 53). Although critics of social market theory and glorified individualism foresee "a weakening of democratic participation [and] social cohesion" (Tomlinson, 1986, p. 211), advocates contend that "the individual pursuit of self-interest is not a threat to the social bond, but its very basis" (Himmelstein, 1983, p. 16).

Individualism and anti-collectivism are often joined at the hip to a second ideological trend, "a shift to more conservative social and political values" (Bauman, 1996, p. 627).[4] This conservatism or populism is increasingly marked with a patina of religiosity, especially religious fundamentalism (Himmelstein, 1983; McCarthy, 1996).

Competitors

Insights about alternatives to the sociopolitical structures of the democratic welfare state are speculative at best. Some potential competitors (e.g., voucher systems) adhere closely to the ideology presented above, while others cut across the empirical evidence and the core elements of the ideology of liberty and individualism. In this latter case, for example, the shift from state collective action to private volunteer activity fits neither the data outlined by Putnam (1995) nor the individualistic underpinnings of the liberty ideology laid out by Tomlinson (1986) and others.

Market-Oriented Governance in Education

There is a growing consensus that new governance structures are the key to strengthening schools (Richards *et al.*, 1996, p. 50).

Furthermore, they have seen the best avenue for reform as one which replaces the bureaucratic and democratic control of the school with elements of market control (Beers & Ellig, 1994, p. 21).

After decades and waves of school reform with questionable impacts, there is growing interest in moving the sponsorship of schools from district-level governance systems to a variety of privatized models of school control (Bauman, 1996, p. 640).

In this section, we apply Hood's typology specifically to education. In many ways, important aspects of our task have already been completed because changes in institutional perspectives in education are nested within larger movements in the economy, society, and the polity. Thus we have already captured the altered habitat of educational control. Therefore, we focus our treatment on the remaining three pieces of Hood's framework.

Self-Destruction

As Hood (1994) reminds us, "policies and institutions can often be their own undoing. . . . They can trip over their own feet and dig their own graves" (p. 13). The attraction of more market-oriented forms of school governance can be traced to some extent to internal processes of self-destruction in the educational system. Three patterns of self-destruction are most salient: (1) the perceived failure of public schooling to deliver a quality product; (2) the seeming inability of education to heal itself; and (3) a growing disconnect between the public and public education. The consequence is a significant reinforcement of the "common and widely reiterated observation of a declining confidence in public education . . . [and] the mounting criticisms of the established form and content of publicly-funded educational systems" (Mayberry, 1991, p. 1), along with increasing demands for reforms—reforms that represent an overhaul of current governing arrangements (Murphy, 1996). Whitty (1984) reinforces this latter point, noting that "it is important to recognize that . . . public education fails to serve the majority of its clients and hence makes them potential supporters of reactionary proposals" (p. 54).

Richards and his colleagues (1996) report that "today the public discourse about American education tends to be preoccupied with failure" (p. 15). The most recent decade contains a "raft of hopeless narratives on public education" (Fine, 1993, p. 33). What analysts label "frustration over repeated failures" (Hunter, 1995b, p. 168) or "public concern over the quality of primary and secondary education in the United States" (Beers & Ellig, 1994, p. 19) is a multifaceted phenomenon. Or, stated in an alternate form, the perception[5] "that the level and quality of education in the United States is found lacking" (Hakim, Seidenstat, & Bowman, 1994, p. 1) is buttressed by data on a wide variety of outcomes. Specifically, data assembled in each of the following performance dimensions provide a not-very-reassuring snapshot of the health of the American educational system: (1) academic achievement in basic subject areas, compared to historical data about the United States and to student performance in other countries; (2) functional literacy; (3) preparation for employment; (4) the holding power of schools (dropout rates); (5) knowledge of specific subject areas such as geography and economics; (6) mastery of higher-order skills; and (7) initiative, responsibility, and citizenship (see Murphy, 1990, and Murphy & Beck, 1995, for an extensive compilation of data on each of these dimensions.) Beers and Ellig (1994) provide a summary of the situation:

> A steady stream of reports from the nation's schools has documented a 25 percent national high school dropout rate, high proportions of high school graduates who are functionally illiterate, and three decades of falling test scores. Parents and community leaders have voiced outrage that the public schools are not only failing in their educational mission but are increasingly becoming breeding grounds for drug abuse, violence, and crime. Many in the business world see the decline of primary and secondary education as a major factor behind the nation's eroding productive capacity and faltering competitive position in the world. (p. 19)

Perhaps even more important than the data is "the experience of most Americans tells them that the nation's school system is in trouble and that the problems are getting worse" (Mathews, 1996, p. 1).

Especially damaging to public education is the perceived inability of the schooling industry to reform itself. Questions raised by analysts who take the long-term view on this issue are particularly demoralizing. For example, according to Beers and Ellig (1994):

> [Over the last 40 years,] public school leaders have overseen the implementation of many of the most persistently called-for proposals for school reform. The ever-present call for more funding has been met by tripling real per-pupil expenditures from their 1960 levels. The demand for greater teacher professionalism has motivated a 50 percent increase in average teacher salaries since 1960, adjusted for inflation. Class sizes have fallen by a third since the mid-1960s, and most states have continued to raise graduation requirements (p. 19).

Critics argue that these efforts have resulted not in an increase in educational quality but rather in a proliferation of professional and bureaucratic standards (Hill, Pierce, & Guthrie, 1997; Whitty, 1984), in the creation of subsidies for bureaucracy (Beers & Ellig, 1994), and in the strengthening of a centralized educational system in which "all risks of failure are shifted onto parents, taxpayers, and children" (Payne, 1995, p. 3). Beers and Ellig (1994) make this point dramatically when they claim: "In a very real sense we have tried to run the public schools the same way the Soviets tried to run factories, and now we're paying the price" (p. 20). The effect, critics maintain, is that reform has reinforced the very dynamics that are promoting self-destruction in public education. The natural consequence, they hold, must be the emergence of new forms of educational institutions and new models of school governance (Hakim, Seidenstat, & Bowman, 1994; Lieberman, 1988, 1989).

Also troubling, if not surprising given the analysis just presented, is the feeling that the very substantial efforts to strengthen education over the last 15 years in particular have not produced much in terms of improvement across the seven outcome dimensions listed above. As Richards and his colleagues (1996) document, public interest in alternative governance arrangements for schools reflects a profound disappointment that "the rash of school reform efforts launched over the last decade has failed to turn the tide" (p. 94) and that "despite considerable energy, initial bursts of optimism, and abundant promises, a good many efforts to reform schools, thought not all, are failing in the 1990s" (Mathews, 1996, p. 16). There is expanding agreement on the need to overhaul school-governance systems as well as an emerging belief that conditions in the area of school governance are so bleak that any change could hardly make matters worse (Richards *et al.*, 1996).

Critics aver that at the same time we are discovering that traditional attacks on our problems not only fail to "get at the fundamental causes of the nation's learning malaise" (Beers & Ellig, 1994, p. 20) and may be actually crippling public education, we are witnessing a fundamental disconnect between the public and the public schools. A recent Public Agenda report, for example, asserts that "in the battle over the future of public education, the public is essentially 'up for grabs'" (cited in Bradley, 1995, p. 1). As one indicator of this gulf, Public Agenda researchers report that the public in general and parents in particular see vouchers as an unsurpassed vehicle for helping students who are failing in school (Bradley, 1995).

The most thoughtful and detailed description of society's deepening loss of confidence in public education has been provided by Mathews (1996). He argues that "despite a long tradition of support for public education, Americans today seem to be halfway out the schoolhouse door" (p. 2) and also that "the public and the public schools [are] in fact moving apart, that the historical compact between them [is] in danger of dissolving" (p. i). Mathews documents the decline in public confidence in public schools in a number of ways. He cites data from the National Opinion Research Center that reveal a 40 percent drop (from 37 to 15 percent) from 1973 to 1993 in those expressing confidence in educational institutions. He also cites data showing an increase of 125 percent (from 8 to 18 percent) during this same time frame in citizens expressing low confidence in public institutions (p. 9). Using a more direct measure, he reveals that citizens prefer private schools over public ones: "A virtual chorus said that they would take their children out of public schools if they had that option" (p. 22). Kaufman (1996) adds to this analysis:

> Parents rank private schools higher in 11 of 13 categories, including preparing students for college, safety, and discipline. Public schools rank higher only in serving students with special needs and teaching children how to deal with people of diverse backgrounds (p. 72).

New Ideas

New bundles of ideas are emerging to challenge governance perspectives that have dominated education for the last 75 years. Although not completely isomorphic with the shifting ideologies discussed in earlier sections of this chapter, and in some cases even employing contradictory language, the overlap is considerable. One of the key elements involves a recalibration of the locus of control based on what Ross (1988) describes as "a review and reconsideration of the division of existing responsibilities and functions" (p. 2) among levels of government. Originally called "democratic localism" (p. 305) by Katz (1971), it has more recently come to be known simply as localization or, more commonly, decentralization. Whatever it is called, it represents a backlash against "the thorough triumph of a centralized and bureaucratic form of educational organization" (p. 305) and governance.

A second ideological foundation can best be thought of as a recasting of democracy, a replacement of representative governance with more populist conceptions, especially what Cronin (1989) describes as "direct democracy," Barber (1984) refers to as "strong democracy," and Sarason (1995) labels the "political principle." The perspectives of all three authors share a grounding in (1) the falling fortunes of representative democracy, (2) a "growing distrust of legislative bodies ... [and] a growing suspicion that privileged interests exert far greater influence on the typical politician than does the common voter" (p. 4), and (3) recognition of the claims of its advocates that greater direct voice will produce important benefits for society, that it "could enrich citizenship and replace distrust of government with respect and healthy participation" (Cronin, 1989, p. 48).

Market-oriented models of governance also draw strength from an emerging line of ideology spotlighting the need to rebalance the governance equation in favor of lay citizens while diminishing the power of the state and of educational professionals. This line of ideas emphasizes parental empowerment (McCarthy, 1996) by "recognizing the historic rights of parents in the education of their children" (Gottfried, 1993, p. 109). It is, at times, buttressed by a strong strand of anti-professionalism that subordinates "both efficiency and organizational rationality to an emphasis on responsiveness, close public [citizen] control, and local involvement" (Katz, 1971, p. 306).

The ideology of choice is the fourth pillar supporting emerging conceptions of school governance founded on market-ideology and consumer control (Bauman, 1996). Sharing a good deal of space with the concepts of localism, lay control, and direct democracy, choice is designed to "deregulate the demand side of the education market" (Beers & Ellig, 1994, p. 35) and to "enable parents to become more effectively involved in the way the school is run" (Hakim, Seidenstat, & Bowman, 1994, p. 13). It means that "schools would be forced to attend to student needs and parent preferences, rather than to the requirements of a centralized bureaucracy" (Hill, 1994, p. 76).

Competitors

Consumer-oriented competitors to current school governance systems cover a good deal of ground and take a variety of forms. They all shift responsibility for representing the needs and interests of consumers from others to the consumers themselves. Professional and bureaucratic forms of accountability also are subordinated to the market. Although the distinction is somewhat artificial, it is useful for organizational purposes to group these emerging strategies into two clusters, a group of ideas representing consumer control through governance and an assortment of market-centered competitors.

Although strategies in the first group are designed to enhance the voice of parents in the governance process, the appeal to market forces is relatively weak here. The focus is a rebalancing of control within the current system of educational provision. The three most common forms of these parent-governance alternatives to current control arrangements are community-based models of SBM, parent unions, and work in the area of "parent rights," although none have been widely implemented and the latter two are very recent phenomena indeed. Each takes a somewhat different path to the goal of increased parental control. Community-anchored models of SBM grant parents (and other community members) a dominant position in the formal decision-making processes that shape school activities. Decentralized management in Chicago, where parents and community members are allotted 8 of the 11 council seats, is a good example of community-controlled SBM (Murphy & Beck, 1995). Parent unions embody an attempt to enfranchise and strengthen consumer control in much the same way that the teacher union movement of the 1960s shifted power from school administrators to teachers (Bradley, 1996). Parent rights activities, in turn, encompass an assortment of efforts to ensure that the rights of parents "to direct and control the upbringing, education and discipline of their children" (White, 1996, p. 1) are codified in law (Walsh, 1996).

The strategies that fall into the second cluster strengthen the role of the consumers, not primarily through an enhanced role in governance but rather through more direct exercise of market structures. Choice is the key ingredient here. The logic is that schools compete in the market for customers. Concomitantly, parents are active in selecting the school (a particular bundle of goods and services, if you prefer) that they deem most appropriate. A variety of efforts are underway to create more robust markets for educational services. The most important of these strategies are vouchers, contract schools, charter schools, and home schooling. Significant, if limited, activities are unfolding in each of these areas. Although the jury remains out on the effectiveness of each of these reform vehicles, there is little doubt that collectively they represent an important reconceptualization in school governance, a shift from governmental and professional to consumer control.

NOTES

1. We acknowledge at the outset that we employ the Hood framework to develop hypotheses about changing institutional dynamics in the educational industry. We do not argue that the framework is unassailable but only that it provides a useful vehicle for viewing, probing, and testing propositions about the evolution in institutional arrangements in schooling.

2. The material in this section on the changing economic environment of schooling draws heavily upon our work on privatization, found in Murphy (1996) and Murphy, Gilmer, Weise, and Page (1998).

3. Although it does not fit nicely anywhere in our model, it is worth noting that at least some reviewers have commented on the possibility that government agencies themselves may promote marketization in order to pass accountability to others (Murphy, 1993; Richards et al., 1996) "to exempt themselves from the direct responsibility of quality of the service" (Chen, 1993, p. 14). Thus some scholars suggest that "privatization may be a further step towards minimizing public accountability" (Hood, 1994, p. 50).

4. Cibulka (1996) questions this assertion. He argues that "despite considerable speculation to the contrary, there is little evidence that the American people have drifted to the right politically on social and moral issues, as distinct from economic ones" (pp. 379–380).

5. Whether in "fact" the quality of American education is deteriorating is a hotly debated issue. Using the lens of self-destruction, however, the key issue is the perception of failure.

REFERENCES

Ascher, K. (1991). The business of local government. In R. L. Kemp (Ed.), *Privatization: The provision of public services by the private sector* (pp. 297–304). Jefferson, NC: McFarland.

Baber, W. F. (1987). Privatizing public management: The Grace Commission and its critics. In S. H. Hanke (Ed.), *Prospects for privatization. Proceedings of the Academy of Political Science* (Vol. 36, No. 3; pp. 153–163). Montpelier, VT: Capital City Press.

Bailey, R. W. (1987). Uses and misuses of privatization. In S. H. Hanke (Ed.), *Prospects for privatization. Proceedings of the Academy of Political Science* (Vol. 36, No. 3; pp. 138–152). Montpelier, VT: Capital City Press.

Barber, B. R. (1984). *Strong democracy: Participatory politics for a new age.* Berkeley: University of California Press.

Bauman, P. C. (1996, November). Governing education in an antigovernment environment. *Journal of School Leadership*, 6(6), 625–643.

Beales, J. R. & O'Leary, J. O. (1993, November). *Making schools work: Contracting options for better management.* Los Angeles: Reason Foundation.

Beers, D. & Ellig, J. (1994). An economic view of the effectiveness of public and private schools. In S. Hakim, P. Seidenstat & G. W. Bowman (Eds.), *Privatizing education and educational choice: Concepts, plans, and experiences* (pp. 19–38). Westport, CT: Praeger.

Bennett, J. T. & DiLorenzo, T. J. (1987). In S. H. Hanke (Ed.), *Prospects for privatization. Proceedings of the Academy of Political Science* (Vol. 36, No. 3; pp. 14–23). Montpelier, VT: Capital City Press.

Bennett, J. T. & Johnson, M. H. (1980, October). Tax reduction without sacrifice: Private-public production of public services. *Public Finance Quarterly*, 8(4), 363–396.

Boyd, W. L. & Lugg, C. A. (forthcoming). Markets, choice, and educational reform. In A. Hargreaves, A. Lieberman, M. Fullan & D. Hopkins (Eds.), *International handbook of educational change.* Amsterdam: Kluwer.

Boyd, W. L., Lugg, C. A. & Zahorchak, G. L. (1996, May). Social traditionalists, religious conservatives, and the politics of outcome-based education. *Education and Urban Society*, 28(3), 347–365.

Bradley, A. (1995). Public backing for schools is called tenuous. *Education Week*, 15(7), pp. 1, 13.

Bradley, A. (1996, March 13). Galvanized by strike, parents seek union. *Education Week*, 15(25), 1, 12–13.

Buchanan, J. M. (1987). *Economics: Between predictive science and moral philosophy.* College Station, TX: Texas A&M University Press.

Buchanan, J. M. (1989). *Essays on the political economy.* Honolulu: University of Hawaii Press.

Buchanan, J. M. & Tullock, G. (1962). *The calculus of consent: Logical foundations of constitutional democracy.* Ann Arbor: University of Michigan Press.

Butler, S. M. (1987). Changing the political dynamics of government. In S. H. Hanke (Ed.), *Prospects for privatization. Proceedings of the Academy of Political Science* (Vol. 36, No. 3; pp. 4–13). Montpelier, VT: Capital City Press.

Carroll, B. J., Conant, R. W. & Easton, T. A. (1987). Introduction. In B. J. Carroll, R. W. Conant & T. A. Easton (Eds.), *Private means, public ends: Private business in social service delivery* (pp. ix–xiii). New York: Praeger.

Chen, M. (1993, October). *Sponsored privatization of schooling in a welfare state.* Paper presented at the annual conference of the University Council for Educational Administration, Houston, TX.

Cibulka, J. G. (1996, May). Afterword: Interpreting the religious impulse in American schooling. *Education and Urban Society*, 28(3), 378–387.

Cohen, D. K. (1989, May). *Can decentralization or choice improve public education?* Paper presented at the Conference on Choice and Control in American Education. Madison: University of Wisconsin-Madison.

Consortium on Productivity in the Schools. (1995). *Using what we have to get the schools we need.* New York: Columbia University, Teachers College, The Institute on Education and the Economy.

Cronin, T. E. (1989). *Direct democracy: The politics of initiative, referendum, and recall.* Cambridge: Harvard University Press.

Crowson, R. L. (1998). *School-community relations, under reform* (2nd ed.). Berkeley, CA: McCutchan.

Dahrendorf, R. (1995, Summer). A precarious balance: Economic opportunity, civil society, and political liberty. *The Responsive Community,* 13–39.

Darr, T. B. (1991). Privatization may be good for your government. In R. L. Kemp (Ed.), *Privatization: The provision of public services by the private sector* (pp. 60–68). Jefferson, NC: McFarland.

De Alessi, L. (1987). Property rights and privatization. In S. H. Hanke (Ed.), *Prospects for privatization. Proceedings of the Academy of Political Science* (Vol. 36, No. 3; pp. 24–35). Montpelier, VT: Capital City Press.

De Hoog, R. H. (1984). *Contracting out for human services: Economic, political, and organizational perspectives.* Albany: State University of New York Press.

Donahue, J. D. (1989). *The privatization decision: Public ends, private means.* New York: Basic Books.

Elshtain, J. B. (1995). *Democracy on trial.* New York: Basic Books.

Fine, M. (1993, Winter). A diary on privatization and on public possibilities. *Educational Theory, 43*(1), 33–39.

Fitzgerald, R. (1988). *When government goes private: Successful alternatives to public services.* New York: Universe Books.

Fixler, P. E. (1991). Service shedding—a new option. In R. L. Kemp (Ed.), *Privatization: The provision of public services by the private sector* (pp. 39–52). Jefferson, NC: McFarland.

Florestano, P. S. (1991). Considerations for the future. In R. L. Kemp (Ed.), *Privatization: The provision of public services by the private sector* (pp. 291–296). Jefferson, NC: McFarland.

Garber, M. P. (1995, March 29). Opening the education marketplace. *Education Week, 14*(27), 34, 36.

Gottfried, P. (1993). *The conservative movement* (revised edition). New York: Twayne.

Hakim, S., Seidenstat, P. & Bowman, G. W. (1994). Introduction. In S. Hakim, P. Seidenstat & G. W. Bowman (Eds.), *Privatizing education and educational choice: Concepts, plans, and experiences* (pp. 1–15). Westport, CT: Praeger.

Hardin, H. (1989). *The privatization putsch.* Halifax, Nova Scotia: The Institute for Research on Public Policy.

Hawley, W. D. (1995, Summer). The false premises and false promises of the movement to privatize public education. *Teachers College Record, 96*(4), 735–742.

Heinz, D. (1983). The struggle to define America. In R. C. Liebman & R. Wuthrow (Eds.), *The New Christian Right: Mobilization and legitimation* (pp. 133–148). New York: Aldine.

Hemming, R. & Mansoor, A. M. (1988). *Privatization and public enterprises.* (Occasional Paper No. 56). Washington, DC: International Monetary Fund.

Hilke, J. C. (1992). *Competition in government-financed services.* New York: Quorum Books.

Hill, P. T. (1994). Public schools by contract: An alternative to privatization. In S. Hakim, P. Seidenstat & G. W. Bowman (Eds.), *Privatizing education and educational choice: Concepts, plans, and experiences.* Westport, CT: Praeger.

Hill, P. T., Pierce, L. C. & Guthrie, J. W. (1997). *Reinventing public education: How contracting can transform America's schools.* Chicago: The University of Chicago Press.

Himmelstein, J. L. (1983). The New Right. In R. C. Liebman and R. Wuthrow (Eds.), *The New Christian Right: Mobilization and legitimation* (pp. 13–30). New York: Aldine.

Hirsch, W. Z. (1991). *Privatizing government services: An economic analysis of contracting out by local governments.* Los Angeles: University of California, Institute of Industrial Relations.

Hood, C. (1994). *Explaining economic policy reversals.* Buckingham, England: Open University Press.

Hula, R. C. (1990a). Preface. In R. C. Hula (Ed.), *Market-based public policy* (pp. xiii–xiv). New York: St. Martins Press.

Hula, R. C. (1990b). Using markets to implement public policy. In R. C. Hula (Ed.), *Market-based public policy* (pp. 3–18). New York: St. Martin's Press.

Hunter, R. C. (1995a, February). Private procurement in the public sector in education. *Education and Urban Review, 27*(2), 136–153.

Hunter, R. C. (1995b, February). Privatization of instruction in public education. *Education and Urban Society, 27*(2), 168–194.

Jaeger, R. M. (1992, October). Weak measurement serving presumptive policy. *Phi Delta Kappan, 74*(2), 118–128.

Katz, M. B. (1971, Summer). From voluntarism to bureaucracy in American education. *Sociology of Education, 44*(3), 297–332.

Katz, M. B. (1992). Chicago school reform as history. *Teachers College Record, 94*(1), 56–72.

Kaufman, J. (1996). Suburban parents shun many public schools, even the good ones. *Network News & Views, 14*(5), 72–73.

Kettl, D. F. (1988). Government by proxy and the public service. *International Review of Administrative Sciences, 54*(4), 501–515.

Kolderie, T. (1991). Two different concepts. In R. L. Kemp (Ed.), *Privatization: The provision of public services by the private sector* (pp. 250–261). Jefferson, NC: McFarland.

Lamdin, D. J. & Mintrom, M. (1996). *School choice in theory and practice: Taking stock and looking ahead.* Manuscript in preparation, University of Maryland, Baltimore County.

Lewis, D. A. (1993). Deinstitutionalization and school decentralization: Making the same mistake twice. In J. Hannaway & M. Carnoy (Eds.), *Decentralization and school improvement* (pp. 84–101). San Francisco: Jossey-Bass.

Lieberman, M. (1988, Winter) Efficiency issues in educational contracting. *Government Union Review, 9*, 1–24.

Lieberman, M. (1989). *Privatization and educational choice.* New York: St. Martin's Press.

Liebman, R. C. (1983a). Introduction. In R. C. Liebman & R. Wuthnow (Eds.), *The New Christian Right: Mobilization and legitimation* (pp. 1–9). New York: Aldine.

Liebman, R. C. (1983b). The making of the New Christian Right. In R. C. Liebman & R. Wuthnow (Eds.), *The New Christian Right: Mobilization and legitimation* (pp. 227–238). New York: Aldine.

Liebman, R. C. & Wuthnow, R. (Eds.). (1983). *The New Christian Right: Mobilization and legitimation.* New York: Aldine.

McCarthy, M. M. (1996, May). People of faith as political activists in public schools. *Education and Urban Society, 28*(3), 308–326.

Marshall, R. & Tucker, M. (1992). *Thinking for a living: Work, skills, and the future of the American economy.* New York: Basic Books.

Martin, B. (1993). *In the public interest? Privatization and public sector reform.* London: Zed Books.

Mathews, D. (1996). *Is there a public for public schools?* Dayton, OH: Kettering Foundation Press.

Mayberry, M. (1991, April). *Conflict and social determinism: The reprivatization of education.* Paper presented at the annual meeting of the American Educational Research Association, Chicago, IL.

Meltzer, A. H. & Scott, R. F. (1978, Summer). Why government grows (and grows) in a democracy. *The Public Interest,* (52), 111–118.

Mueller, D. C. (1989). *Public choice II.* New York: Cambridge University Press.

Murnane, R. J. & Levy, F. (1996). *Teaching the new basic skills: Principles for educating children to thrive in a changing economy.* New York: The Free Press.

Murphy, J. (1990). The educational reform movement of the 1980s: A comprehensive analysis. In J. Murphy (Ed.), *The reform of American public education in the 1980s: Perspectives and cases* (pp. 3–55). Berkeley, CA: McCutchan.

Murphy, J. (1991). *Restructuring schools: Capturing and assessing the phenomena.* New York: Teachers College Press.

Murphy, J. (1993). Restructuring: In search of a movement. In J. Murphy & P. Hallinger (Eds.), *Restructuring schooling: Learning from ongoing efforts* (pp. 1–31). Newbury Park, CA: Corwin Press.

Murphy, J. (1996). *The privatization of schooling: Problems and possibilities.* Newbury Park, CA: Corwin Press.

Murphy, J. & Beck, L. G. (1995). *School-based management as school reform: Taking stock.* Newbury Park, CA: Corwin.

Murphy, J., Gilmer, S., Weise, R. & Page, A. (1998). *Pathways to privatization in education.* Norwood, NJ: Ablex.

Niskanen, W. A. (1971). *Bureaucracy and representative government*. Chicago: Aldine-Atherton.

Niskanen, W. A. (1994). *Bureaucracy and public economics*. Brookfield, VT: Edward Elgar Publishing.

Oates, W. E. (1972). *Fiscal federalism*. New York: Harcourt Brace Jovanovich.

Pack, J. R. (1991). The opportunities and constraints of privatization. In W. T. Gormley (Ed.), *Privatization and its alternatives* (pp. 281–306). Madison: The University of Wisconsin Press.

Payne, J. L. (1995, November). *Profiting from education: Incentive issues in contracting out*. Washington, DC: Education Policy Institute.

Pirie, M. (1988). *Privatization*. Hants, England: Wildwood House.

Poole, R. (1985). The politics of privatization. In S. M. Butler (Ed.), *The privatization option: A strategy to shrink the size of government* (pp. 33–50). Washington, DC: The Heritage Foundation.

President's Commission on Privatization. (1988). *Privatization: Toward more effective government*. Washington, DC: U. S. Government.

Putnam, R. D. (1995). Bowling alone: America's declining social capital. *Journal of Democracy, 6*(1), 65–77.

Ramsey, J. B. (1987). Selling the New York City subway: Wild-eyed radicalism or the only feasible solution. In S. H. Hanke (Ed.), *Prospects for privatization. Proceedings of the Academy of Political Science*, (Vol. 36, No. 3; pp. 93–103). Montpelier, VT: Capital City Press.

Richards, C. E., Shore, R. & Sawicky, M. B. (1996). *Risky business: Private management of public schools*. Washington, DC: Economic Policy Institute.

Ross, R. L. (1988). *Government and the private sector: Who should do what?* New York: Crane Russak.

Sarason, S. B. (1995). *Parental involvement and the political principle: Why the existing governance structure of schools should be abolished*. San Francisco: Jossey-Bass.

Savas, E. S. (1982). *Privatizing the public sector: How to shrink government*. Chatham, NJ: Chatham House.

Savas, E. S. (1985). The efficiency of the private sector. In S. M. Butler (Ed.), *The privatization option: A strategy to shrink the size of government* (pp. 15–31). Washington, DC: The Heritage Foundation.

Savas, E. S. (1987). *Privatization: The key to better government*. Chatham, NJ: Chatham House.

Seldon, A. (1987). Public choice and the choices of the public. In C. K. Rowley (Ed.), *Democracy and public choice* (pp. 122–134). New York: Columbia University Press.

Snauwaert, D. T. (1993). *Democracy, education, and governance: A developmental conception*. Albany: State University of New York Press.

Starr, P. (1987). The limits of privatization. In S. H. Hanke (Ed.), *Prospects for privatization. Proceedings of the Academy of Political Science* (Vol. 36, No. 3; pp. 124–137). Montpelier, VT: Capital City Press.

Starr, P. (1991). The case for skepticism. In W. T. Gormley (Ed.), *Privatization and its alternatives* (pp. 25–36). Madison: The University of Wisconsin Press.

Stiglitz, J. E. (1986). *Economics of the public sector* (2nd ed.). New York: W. W. Norton & Co.

Swanson, A. D. (1989, August). Restructuring educational governance: A challenge of the 1990s. *Educational Administration Quarterly, 25*(3), 268–293.

Thayer, F. C. (1987). Privatization: Carnage, chaos, and corruption. In B. J. Carroll, R. W. Conant & T. A. Easton (Eds.), *Private means, public ends: Private business in social service delivery* (pp. 146–170). New York: Praeger.

Thomas, W. B., Moran, K. J. & Resnick, J. (n. d.). *Intentional transformation in a small school district*. Unpublished manuscript, University of Pittsburgh.

Tomlinson, J. (1986). Public education, public good. *Oxford Review of Education, 12*(3), 211–222.

Tullock, G. (1965). *The politics of bureaucracy*. Washington, DC: Public Affairs Press.

Tullock, G. (1988). *Wealth, poverty, and politics*. New York: Basil Blackwell.

Tullock, G. (1994a). Public choice: The new science of politics. In G. L. Brady & R. D. Tollison (Eds.), *On the trail of homo economicus* (pp. 87–100). Fairfax, VA: George Mason Press.

Tullock, G. (1994b). Social cost and government policy. In G. L. Brady & R. D. Tollison (Eds.), *On the trail of homo economicus* (pp. 65–85). Fairfax, VA: George Mason Press.

Tyack, D. B. (1974). *The one best system: A history of American urban education*. Cambridge, MA: Harvard University Press.

Urschel, J. (1995, May 16). Fear, distrust, suspicion of the government. *USA Today*, pp. 1–2.

Vickers, J. & Yarrow, G. (1988). *Privatization: An economic analysis*. Cambridge, MA: MIT Press.

Walsh, M. (1996, April 10). Parent-rights cases against schools fail to make inroads. *Education Week, 15*(29), 11.

White, K. A. (1996, November 13). Colo. voters reject parent-rights measure. *Education Week, 16*(11), 1, 24–25.

Whitty, G. (1984, April). The privatization of education. *Educational Leadership, 41*(7), 51–54.

Wuthnow, R. (1983). The political rebirth of American evangelicals. In R. C. Liebman & R. Wuthnow (Eds.), *The New Christian Right: Mobilization and legitimation* (pp. 167–185). New York: Aldine.

CHAPTER 20

School Leadership for Teacher Learning and Change: A Human and Social Capital Development Perspective

Mark A. Smylie and Ann Weaver Hart

Since the mid-1980s, this nation has engaged in unprecedented efforts to reform its schools. As we have argued about just how troubled our schools are and what steps are necessary to change them (Berliner & Biddle, 1995), it has become increasingly clear that if we want to improve schools for student learning, we must also improve schools for the adults who work within them. We have long understood that student achievement depends fundamentally on the intellectual, dispositional, and ethical capacities of teachers to provide challenging and meaningful classroom learning opportunities. Yet we have only recently come to understand that student learning also depends on the extent to which schools support the ongoing development and productive exercise of teachers' knowledge and skills. As Seymour Sarason (1990) so cogently argued in his book *The Predictable Failure of Educational Reform*, "It is virtually impossible to create and sustain conditions for productive learning for students when they do not exist for teachers" (p. 145).

Our growing recognition of the importance of schools for both student and teacher learning has been accompanied by the emergence of professional community-oriented images that challenge traditional bureaucratic conceptions of schools as organizations (Bacharach & Mundell, 1995; Firestone & Bader, 1992). According to Beck and Murphy (1993),

> The hierarchical, bureaucratic organizational structures that have defined schools for the past 80 years are giving way to more decentralized . . . and more professionally controlled systems . . . Traditional patterns of relationships are altered; authority flows are less hierarchical; role definitions are both more general and more flexible; leadership is connected to competence for needed

tasks rather than to formal position; and independence and isolation are replaced by cooperative work . . . [T]he structural orientation of industrial age schools . . . is being overshadowed by a focus on the human element (p. 187).

Initial efforts to "reform" schools in these images have met with uneven success in improving teaching and learning (Murphy & Beck, 1995; Smylie & Perry, 1998). Mixed outcomes are reported across research examining efforts to establish new team teaching structures (Crow & Pounder, 1997), small schools (Christman & Macpherson, 1996; Levine, 1992; McQuillan & Muncey, 1991), participative decision-making (Murphy & Beck, 1995; Smylie, Lazarus, & Brownlee-Conyers, 1996) and teacher leadership roles and work redesign (Hart, 1995; Smylie, 1994, 1997). Similar outcomes are reported from studies of the most comprehensively reformed schools (Elmore, Peterson, & McCarthey, 1996; Newmann & Associates, 1996).

There are many explanations for these findings that include premature evaluation, implementation failure, and forces of organizational and institutional persistence (Meyer & Rowan, 1977; Scott, 1995; Smylie, 1997). Another significant reason concerns the general ineffectiveness of strategies used in school reform (Sarason, 1990). Efforts to create new, more professional places for teachers to work and students to learn have attended primarily to the structural features of school organizations. In the early 1980s, reform targeted existing educational structures and practices, seeking to make them better through policies of prescription, intensification, and control (Murphy, 1990; Rowan, 1990). Even as the emphasis shifted in the late 1980s and early 1990s toward more comprehensive reforms, the focus remained on the structural dimensions of schools, albeit on their "restructuring" (Elmore *et al.*, 1996; Louis, Marks, & Kruse, 1996b).

The equivocal outcomes of school reform to date could have been predicted. Scholars have consistently pointed to the "slippery and unreliable" relationship between changing organizational structures and improving the performance and productivity of people who work within them (see Elmore, 1995; Murphy, 1991). The reform research strongly suggests that improving teaching and student learning has less to do with structural changes in schools than with changes in what occurs *within* those structures (Elmore *et al.*, 1996). Structures certainly matter. They can present opportunities for, as well as impediments to, teaching and learning. The literature is clear, however, that changing structures is not synonymous with changing the beliefs, habits, knowledge, and skills that undergird teachers' instructional practice (Fullan, 1995; Richardson, 1990). As Newmann & Wehlage (1995) argued, the effectiveness of new forms of school organization will depend ultimately on how well they are able to develop, organize, and support productive teaching and learning. Restructuring may be necessary but certainly not sufficient to bring about significant change.

In light of these findings, empirical and theoretical knowledge of the social factors that nurture productive teaching and learning can provide useful insight into school reform. One particularly valuable perspective comes from human and social capital theory. During the past 10 years, the concepts of human and social capital have gained prominence in discourse about improving the learning and development of children and youth (Coleman, 1987; Furstenberg & Hughes, 1995; Valenzuela & Dornbusch, 1994). Only recently have scholars begun to apply these concepts to teachers and their work in schools (Bryk & Schneider, 1996; Smylie, 1996; Useem, Christman, Gold, & Simon, 1997). Although the social context of schools has long been recognized as a significant factor in teachers' work, increasing attention is now being paid to how social relations among teachers and between teachers and administrators promote or constrain productive teaching. While the concepts of social and human capital seem relevant to teachers' work, the theoretical and empirical arguments for applying them are not well formed. In addition, human and social capital theory provokes new thinking about the nature of school leadership and its relationship to teachers and instructional improvement.

This chapter addresses the implications of a social and human capital development perspective for school leadership and school organization. It explores the mechanisms through which social capital facilitates the development and application of human capital among teachers for the improvement of teaching. The chapter first examines the concepts of social and human capital and their theoretical and empirical relationships. These concepts are then ap-

plied to teacher learning and change in a review of empirical research on teacher-collegial relations, collaboration, and professional community. After examining this research, new views of school leadership and school organization suggested by this analysis are explored. These views include interactional perspectives of principal leadership and leadership as an organizational property. The chapter concludes with a discussion of implications for research and policy.

This analysis proceeds within some parameters. First, it is concerned primarily with sources of social capital available to teachers *within* schools. Important district-level, professional, and non-professional sources of social capital exist for teachers (Elmore *et al.*, 1996; Lieberman & Miller, 1991; Spencer, 1984; Talbert & McLaughlin, 1993); however, examination of these sources is beyond the scope of this chapter. Similarly, this analysis focuses on school-level leadership. District-level leadership can play an important role in developing social capital within schools (Odden & Odden, 1994; Smylie *et al.*, 1996; White, 1992) and leadership in schools can be exercised by many people, including teachers and parents (Heller & Firestone, 1995; Ogawa & Bossert, 1995). We approach the problem of leadership, however, from the perspective of the principal, the administrator who would likely play a crucial role in initiating and supporting social and human capital development among teachers in most schools (Bryk, Easton, Kerbow, Rollow, & Sebring, 1998).

The Concepts of Human and Social Capital

Capital is generally defined as resources available to individuals that can be accumulated and drawn upon to promote productive activity (Bourdieu, 1986). The economic, sociological, and political science literatures distinguish among several forms of capital (Boisjoly, Duncan, & Hofferth, 1995; Bourdieu, 1986; Valenzuela & Dornbusch, 1994). For example, physical capital consists of various material resources or physical implements that may be available to individuals. Financial or economic capital refers to financial resources or resources that can be immediately and directly converted into moneys. Cultural capital is composed of long-lasting theories, dispositions of the mind and body, and goods from cultural and linguistic heritages. Political capital refers to power and influence resources that can be used for coalition building and bargaining.

Two other forms of capital that have received a great deal of attention lately are human capital and social capital. Human capital refers to knowledge, skills, and other attributes that affect a person's capacity to do productive work (Schultz, 1961; Strober, 1990). This form of capital can also be thought of in quantitative terms, as numbers of people engaged in particular work and the amount of time in which they work (Schultz, 1961). Social capital consists of often intangible and abstract resources derived from relationships among individuals and from the social structures that frame those relationships (Bourdieu, 1986; Coleman, 1988, 1990). It is lodged neither in the individuals themselves nor in physical implements of their production. Like other forms of capital, social capital can facilitate certain actions or activities of individuals within social structures. It can also be accumulated and drawn upon to achieve otherwise unattainable objectives (Boisjoly *et al.*, 1995). In sum, social capital is a crucial element in the relationship of individuals to their social groups or organizations.

Elements of Social Capital

Several elements of social capital constitute resources for individuals in their relationships to their social groups or organizations (Coleman, 1988; 1990). These elements include (a) social trust; (b) channels for new information; (c) and norms, expectations, and sanctions.

Social trust concerns confidence in the reliability and integrity of individuals and social relations. According to Bryk and Schneider (1996), trust involves a calculation whereby a person decides whether or not to engage in an action with another individual that incorporates some degree of risk. Trust can be ascribed to persons or institutions in a more or less unquestioning fashion (see Gambetta, 1988). It can be rooted in explicit contractual, legally binding transactions among individuals that define specific relationships and responsibilities among them. Trust can also be a function of mutual understandings that arise out of sustained associations among individuals, each of whom, through discernment of behavior, intentions, and obligations, is expected to behave in normatively appropriate ways. Bryk and Schneider contend that trust is diminished when people perceive that others are not acting in a manner consistent with common understandings and commitments.

Social trust can promote productive behavior in several ways. According to Coleman (1988), trust is the cornerstone of reciprocal action, mutual assistance and accountability, and collective activity. Bryk and Schneider (1996) associate social trust with the predisposition toward cooperation and confidence that individuals have in one another, in leadership, and in the social group as a whole. In high trust organizations, there is less likely to be conflict and fewer issues are likely to be contested. In conjunction with social norms around which it may form, trust can function as an internal social control mechanism that supports some behaviors and discourages others. Finally, social trust can create a context of predictability, stability, assurance, and "safe ground" that can support genuine public conversation and critique, examination of taken-for-

granted assumptions, and risk-taking when individuals and the group are confronted with the need to make change (see also Evans, 1996; Schein, 1988).

A second element of social capital consists of relationships that provide channels for new information that in turn facilitates individual action. According to Coleman (1988), this informational aspect of social relations is not necessarily related to forming obligations, creating social bonds, or establishing trustworthiness among individuals. Rather this element extends a person's access to information that others in the social structure possess. In as much as individuals may be members of multiple social structures, these relations may also provide access to information from outside the immediate group. Such channels can increase productivity by providing new information on which to base specific decisions and actions. And, as we argue later, these channels can be generally educative, fostering the development of knowledge and skills that may be broadly applied to make individual activity more productive.

A third element of social capital consists of norms, expectations, and sanctions (Coleman, 1988). Group norms and expectations can guide and control individual behavior. They can promote certain actions and constrain others. Norms and expectations can be enforced by internal or external sanctions, including the distribution of social support, ostracism, designation of honor and status, conferral of rewards, and expression of disapproval. By providing direction and control, norms, expectations, and sanctions can reduce deviant behavior. At the same time, they can inhibit innovative actions that might be widely beneficial.

Development of Social Capital

Coleman (1988) argued that all social relations facilitate some form of social capital, be it positive or negative, weak or strong. At the same time, certain properties of social structures are more conducive than others for developing strong social capital. Coleman pointed to one particularly important property, the degree of closure of social structures. Closure, in this sense, refers to the extent of interconnectedness among a group's members. Completely closed structures are characterized by full interconnectedness, where all group members are connected to one another and to few if any others outside that immediate group. Open structures are characterized by gaps in interconnectedness, where some group members are not directly connected to one another and where members may be more strongly connected to others outside the group. The importance of closure to social capital rests in the ability of members of a social structure to develop and sustain common norms and effective sanctions that monitor and guide behavior. It also rests in members' ability to exchange information and develop trust through shared expectations and mutual obligations. Closed structures have greater potential for promoting these elements of social capital because members are less likely to engage in external relations that compete or conflict with internal norms, expectations, and obligations. Open structures reduce the possibilities for shared norms, collective sanctions, mutual obligations, and interdependence, but, as noted below, open structures are more likely to provide members access to new information from outside the group.

Another important property is the strength of interpersonal relations within social structures. Granovetter (1973) defined the strength of a relation, or in his words, a "tie," as a combination of the amount of time, emotional intensity, intimacy or mutual confiding, and reciprocal services that characterize the relation. Strong ties are more likely to exist in closed structures, whereas weak ties are more likely to be characteristic of open and diffuse structures. Similarly, strong ties promote cohesion within social structures, whereas weak ties lead to fragmentation within those structures. Granovetter argued paradoxically that weak ties, particularly those linking members of multiple groups, serve a broader integrative function not served by strong ties within social structures. Information can be passed to a larger number of people and traverse greater social distances through weak rather than strong ties. Further, persons to whom individuals are weakly tied are more likely to move in circles different from their own and thus provide access to information different from that which they might otherwise receive. According to Granovetter, weak ties increase informational resources available to individuals and promotes a broader base of social cohesion than could otherwise be achieved within tightly closed structures with strong ties.

Relationship to Human Capital Development

In addition to providing resources and establishing contexts to orient and support productive activity, social capital can also be an important source of human capital development. The development of knowledge, skills, and other individual capacities for productive activity is both a function of planned, structured learning opportunities and a function of interactions among group members. Planned opportunities include formal education (elementary, secondary, post-secondary education), on-the-job training, and study programs for adults (Schultz, 1961). Work experience is also a potential source of knowledge and skills (Strober, 1990).

Social capital enhances human capital in two ways. First, social capital is a mechanism to employ the human capital of some members of a social group in the development of human capital of other members of that group. Second, social capital is grounded in relationships and interactions that themselves are inactively and vicariously educative. The bridging function of social capital is illustrated

by the relationship between parents and their children. The knowledge, skills, and dispositions of educated parents make less difference in the learning and development of their children unless the parents and children have a meaningful social relation (Coleman, 1987). Empirical support for this illustration is found in recent studies indicating that parent presence, support, and involvement in the family increases the impact of parents' education and occupational status on children's academic success in school, educational attainment, and occupation aspirations (Hagan, MacMillan, & Wheaton, 1996; Marjoribanks, 1991; Valenzuela & Dornbusch, 1994).

Insight into the educative function of social capital can be drawn from social learning, incidental learning, and organizational socialization theories. These theoretical perspectives point to aspects of a person's social context that are particularly important for learning. One of the most salient features of social context involves opportunities for individuals to listen to, observe, and interact with others (Argyris & Schön, 1974; Marsick & Watkins, 1990). According to this literature, interaction increases individuals' exposure to new information and to a variety of new ideas and experiences. It provides access to feedback and referrals for assessing one's own ideas, performance, and needs for learning (Bandura, 1986; Van Maanen & Schein, 1979).

Opportunities to observe the performances, successes, and failures of others are very important to developing outcome expectancies—beliefs about relationships between actions and outcomes—and self-efficacy—beliefs in one's own capacity to organize and implement actions necessary to achieve desired outcomes (Bandura, 1986). Both outcome expectancies and self-efficacy are associated with learning and performance (Schunk 1991). People tend to take actions they expect will have positive, valued outcomes. Persons with high self-efficacy are more likely to select complex and challenging tasks, take risks, experiment, expend more energy, persist in the face of difficulty, and be more creative in their thinking and activity. Expectations for what works, and what does not, develop in part by observing others' actions and outcomes. Observation of successful role models tends to enhance self-efficacy, particularly if those models are similar to one's self and are observed dealing successfully with similar problems.

Another way that social capital can promote human capital development is through the particular types and qualities of interactions. These include clear feedback, communication, group work, and a willingness among group members to examine taken-for-granted beliefs and assumptions. Individual learning is enhanced through interactions that provide specific feedback about performance and its consequences (Bandura, 1986). Learning is also enhanced through the communication of expectations or goals against which people can measure their effort, performance, and accomplishments. Further, proactivity, reflection, and creative individual capacities that relate to learning are enhanced by open communication, group-work, and "intellectual play" (Marsick & Watkins, 1990). They are also enhanced by collective examination of taken-for-granted beliefs and assumptions held by individuals and by the group. Opportunities for regular interaction and collective activity with a specific group of people, stability in the social group over time, and mutual responsibility and accountability consequently enhance the quality of relationships (Argyris & Schön, 1974; Jarvis, 1987; Schein, 1969; Van Maanen & Schein, 1979). These conditions provide the greatest opportunities for information exchange and the development of new ideas. They are conducive to the development of trust and a sense of psychological safety for risk-taking, experimentation, and change.

The properties of closure and strength of ties have relevance to the relationship between social capital and human capital development. Closed social structures can intensify the flow of information within a group, create greater potential for learning, and provide a context that promotes the application of that learning in practice. At the same time, closure and strong ties can limit access or receptiveness to new and potentially challenging information from outside the social structure. This condition can reinforce problematic knowledge and assumptions and lead to inferential errors, poor decisions, and unproductive behaviors (Janis, 1983; Nisbett & Ross, 1980). On the other hand, open structures and weak ties to outside individuals can promote greater access to information from a broader range of sources. Granovetter (1973) suggests that these weak external ties are indispensable to individual learning, within-group productivity, and broader social cohesion. He suggests that although strong ties breed group cohesion, they will eventually constrain within-group knowledge and productivity, and lead to overall fragmentation. Without strong internal ties, however, open structures and weak external ties may lack the "potency" required for productive behavior or meaningful change to take place within a social structure. This observation is consistent with theoretical discussions of the "throughput" function of open system organizations, where resources imported into the organization are transformed through member activity into output (see Katz & Kahn, 1978). Thus these different perspectives point to some balance between openness and closure of social structures and between internal and weak external ties (see Scott, 1987; Thompson, 1967).

Teacher Social Relations, Learning, and Change

We have known for some time that social relations in schools, particularly working relationships among teachers and administrators, are crucial factors in promoting student learning (Purkey & Smith, 1983; Rosenholtz, 1989;

see also Bossert, 1988). We have also known that social relations in schools are crucial in teachers' professional learning and development and in change at the school and classroom levels (Lieberman & Miller, 1984; Lortie, 1975). Teachers generally identify one another among their most valuable sources of on-the-job learning (Smylie, 1989). The literature on how teachers learn to teach consistently emphasizes the importance of teaching colleagues as sources of information, feedback, and social support (Carter, 1990; Feiman-Nemser, 1983; Grossman, 1992). Research on planned change routinely recognizes the role of teachers' working relationships and opportunities for collaboration in successful program implementation and change (Fullan, 1991; Little, 1982). Research also reveals that teachers' relations with their principals are an important piece of school social context that supports professional development and change (Goldring & Rallis, 1993; Leithwood & Montgomery, 1982; Rosenblum, Louis, & Rossmiller, 1994).

Although much has been said about the importance of social relations in schools, there is relatively little empirical evidence concerning the particular characteristics and qualities of relations among teachers and between teachers and principals that are most conducive to teacher learning and change. The extant literature can be divided into three general areas of inquiry: (a) studies of teachers' collegial relations in schools, (b) studies of teacher collaboration in improvement initiatives, and (c) studies of teacher professional communities. These studies vary in design and methodology, ranging from longitudinal ethnographic case studies to large-scale cross-sectional survey analyses. They have focused on teachers at both the elementary and secondary grade levels. A growing number of studies are being conducted outside the United States, notably by scholars in Belgium, the Netherlands, and Canada. Even though the empirical literature on teachers' social relations is relatively small and varies by design and methodology, most studies can be considered robust. They are typically well crafted and executed, have carefully chosen samples, and attend to issues of validity and reliability. Their findings are remarkably consistent in their convergence on the concepts of social capital and human capital development.

Teachers' Collegial Relations in Schools

Among the first empirical studies to examine teachers' social relations and learning was Little's (1982) ethnographic study of professional development and instructional change in six western urban elementary and high schools. In general, this study points to the importance of teacher collaboration for creating opportunities for continuous learning on the job. At the same time, it suggests that certain aspects of collaboration are particularly important. These aspects include the extent to which teachers (a) engage in precise and concrete talk about teaching with one another, (b) observe and provide each other with critical feedback about their teaching, (c) help each other prepare teaching materials, and (d) teach each other the practice of teaching. Little's work points to specific characteristics of social relations that undergird productive collaboration. Relations characterized by reciprocity, interdependence, egalitarianism, mutual trust, and common focus on teaching appeared to be the most conducive to teacher learning. It is important to note that while this study focused primarily on teachers, social relations between teachers and their principals were seen as crucial to support and sustain collaborative learning among teachers. The link between teacher collaboration and learning seemed strongest in schools where principals actively endorsed and participated in collegial work.

The role of social relations in teachers' learning was also examined in Rosenholtz's (1989) study of 78 Tennessee public elementary schools. Rosenholtz found statistically significant relations between teachers' reports of opportunities to learn in their schools and their reports of sharing, help-giving and help-receiving, and joint work among teachers. In Rosenholtz's study, these collaborative interactions were grounded in a social context that included the principal and was characterized by common instructional goals, shared norms and expectations for work performance and relationships, and mechanisms for feedback and evaluation based on mutual understanding of and accountability in work. These aspects of context, among others, distinguished schools that Rosenholtz called "learning enriched" from those she called "learning impoverished." And teachers' reports of opportunities to learn were significantly related to gains in student reading and mathematics achievement.

Johnson's (1990) research in 115 public and private elementary, middle, and senior high schools in Massachusetts produced similar findings. Teachers in her study reported substantial benefits of collegial interaction. They believed that it deepened their understanding of both subject matter and pedagogy, supplied them with innovative approaches to teaching, and allowed them to test and compare their practices. Teachers also observed that collegial interaction encouraged cooperative approaches to school improvement, promoted high professional standards, and led to a more coherent instructional experience for students. Like Little (1982) and Rosenholtz (1989), Johnson found that the social contexts and characteristics of collegial interaction made a substantial difference in teacher learning and change. Because of the personal character of teaching, the uncertainties that pervade it, and norms of privacy and autonomy, teachers need a "safe" and supportive social environment in which to interact, open their practice to one another, and subject themselves to others' scrutiny. Johnson's findings suggest that distrust, disrespect, and dissension can undermine social support required for productive interaction, discourage open exchange and cooperation, and thwart opportunities for teacher learning and change.

Teacher Collaboration in Improvement Initiatives

More evidence of the importance of social relations in teacher learning and change can be found in studies of particular school and instructional improvement initiatives. In their analysis of data from a longitudinal study of a three-year staff development project to improve reading instruction in five southwestern intermediate schools (Richardson, 1994), Placier and Hamilton (1994) made two significant and relevant findings. First, they found that cooperative, convivial climates in schools can rest upon shaky social foundations. When these foundations are threatened by demands for true joint work and collaboration, as was the case in this staff development project, dissatisfaction, fear, and distrust can arise and compromise opportunities for teachers to learn and change their practice. Second, however, this study found that new social relations that developed within groups of teachers as part of the staff development process made more of a difference in teachers' learning and change in practice than the social contexts of their schools. The social relations that developed among participating teachers were grounded in new conceptions of instruction and what is best for students, trust, interdependence, and shared accountability in work.

Clift and her colleagues (1995) made similar observations in their study of a three-year collaborative leadership and professional development project involving university-based participants and practitioners from seven midwestern elementary, middle, and high schools. This study found that professional learning reported by teachers, principals, and university faculty and staff related significantly to interaction processes and the social contexts of the project. Among the most important social factors related to participant learning were trust to deal productively with disagreements, mutual obligations for participation and contribution, and subsuming individual needs and interests to agreed-upon goals of the group.

In their study of nine Belgium primary schools participating in the Renewed Primary School project, Vandenberghe and his colleagues (1993) also linked successful implementation of instructional improvement initiatives directly to intensive, ongoing communication among teachers about project activities at the school and classroom levels. Schools that were most successful in the project were schools where faculty interaction provided effective opportunities for teachers to learn. In these schools, teachers created common visions and objectives. They worked together to clarify and solve problems, offered critical assessments of experiences, and explored potential solutions. This study also highlights important aspects of social context that support these interactions. In the group of schools where the most collaboration, learning, and change occurred, social relations were characterized by trust, mutual responsibility, and shared goals and accountability for work. In the group of schools where less learning and change occurred, there was less collaboration among teachers and social relations were more likely to be characterized by differences in goals and perspectives, psychological tension, and defense of individual autonomy and self-interests (see also Staessens, 1993).

In related work conducted in Dutch primary schools, Bakkenes (1996) found that teacher participation in social groups depended significantly on the extent to which those groups provided opportunities for social support, feedback, and learning opportunities related to classroom practice (see also Bakkenes, de Brabander, & Imants, 1993). Similarly, Sleegers, van den Berg, and Geijsel's (1997) analysis of change in Dutch secondary schools found strong positive associations among levels of collaboration, teacher learning, and the innovative capacity of schools.

Case studies of school restructuring in the United States identify many of the same aspects of social relations that are crucial for teacher collaboration, learning, and change. Two sets of case studies illustrate these findings. In their longitudinal cases of three exemplary restructured schools, Elmore, Peterson, and McCarthey (1996) found decided differences among schools in the "deep structure" of social relations. In each of these three schools, there was frequent staff development and active collaboration among principals and teachers on issues of teaching and learning. One school stood out from the others in terms of greater professional learning and more consistently ambitious classroom practice. Social relations in this school were characterized by a common vision among teachers and shared goals and expectations for each other's work. Norms that every teacher should have a particular intellectual interest and that learning and development were part of teachers' professional work pervaded this school. Teachers at this school exhibited a high sense of trust in one another and accepted responsibility for each other's work. Another distinguishing feature of this school was that strong internal relations among teachers were complemented by relations they had developed to external sources of learning and support (see Granovetter, 1973). Although those teachers' external relations did not seem as strong as their internal ones, they nonetheless served as an important link to new information and perspectives that enhanced the learning and effectiveness of this faculty.

In the second set of cases, Lieberman, Darling-Hammond, and Zuckerman (1991a) studied improvement efforts in 12 schools in the "Schools for Tomorrow . . . Today" restructuring program administered by the New York Teacher Centers Consortium of the United Federation of Teachers. Across these cases, Lieberman and her colleagues found that teacher learning and change depended substantially on the strength of social capital in schools. Schools that made the most progress, particularly in the areas of curriculum and instruction, were those where substantial trust existed among teachers, between teachers and administrators, and between school professionals and program facilitators. These schools were places where professional staff held common visions and values about work with students, openly communicated with one another, exchanged "ways of doing things," and shared responsibility and accountability in their work. These schools operated on the basis of consensual decision-making where individuals were first attentive to group goals as opposed to self-interests (see also Ancess, 1995; Lieberman et al., 1991b).

Teacher Professional Community

Some of the most systematic inquiries related to social capital among teachers comes from two lines of research on teacher professional community. The first line of research was conducted during the late 1980s and early 1990s under the auspices of the Center for Research on the Context of Secondary School Teaching at Stanford University and examined teacher professional communities in 16 public and private secondary schools in two states (Cohen, McLaughlin, & Talbert, 1993; Little & McLaughlin, 1993b). This work defined professional community according to three dimensions of teacher social structure and interaction: (a) intensity of relations among teachers with respect to professional practice and commitment, (b) inclusivity of teachers' collegial groups, and (c) orientation, values, and depth of expertise concerning children, teaching, and learning. Embedded in this last dimension are criteria by which teachers can judge one another and set expectations for colleagueship (Little & McLaughlin, 1993a).

According to McLaughlin (1993), cohesive and highly collegial professional communities were settings in which teachers reported a high level of innovativeness, high levels of energy and enthusiasm, and support for personal growth and learning. In schools with weak professional communities, in which teachers reported strong norms of privacy, teachers were less likely to innovate and find support for their own learning. In these latter settings, teachers persisted in prevailing practices despite a lack of student success and despite their own frustration and discouragement. Among the features that distinguished strong from weak professional communities and their relation to teacher learning and innovation were a shared focus on student learning; norms of collective responsibility, mutual support, and obligation for teachers' practice and student learning; and high levels of professional, normative social controls (see also Talbert & McLaughlin, 1994). These characteristics of strong professional community are well illustrated in Talbert's (1993) case of a performing arts magnet high school. This case reveals how daily experiences of working together toward a common goal allowed teachers to develop mutual respect, trust, and joint accountability. Mutual trust and respect served as valuable resources for collective problem solving, learning, and faculty productivity. Joint accountability subjugated individual autonomy to the group's collective mission.

An important contribution of this research is its demonstration that professional community and the social capital that accompanies it may vary substantially among groups of teachers *within* schools (see also Little, 1990b). This research found significant variation among departments within the same high schools (Little, 1993; McLaughlin, 1993). Such variation was related to differences in how teachers set goals for students and constructed their practice (see also Rowan, Raudenbush, & Cheong, 1993).

A second line of research on teacher professional community was initiated by Bryk and his colleagues at the University of Chicago (Bryk & Driscoll, 1988; Bryk, Lee, & Holland, 1993) and expanded as part of a national study of 24 significantly restructured schools conducted under the auspices of the Center for the Organization and Restructuring of Schools at the University of Wisconsin-Madison (Kruse & Louis, 1995; Newmann & Associates, 1996). In this research, professional community was defined by the following elements: (a) shared norms and values, (b) collective focus on student learning, (c) reflective dialog, (d) deprivatization of practice, and (e) collaboration, which involves sharing expertise, joint work to produce materials and activities for curriculum and instruction, and devising new approaches to professional development. In their summary of findings from case studies of six significantly restructured schools, Kruse and Louis (1995) reported that schools exhibiting the highest levels of professional community also had the highest levels of trust and respect among teachers, administrators, and members of the schools communities. These were schools that also exhibited the strongest base of professional knowledge and skill, professional efficacy, and openness to innovation. These findings were replicated in analyses of survey data collected from all 24 schools in the national study (Louis *et al.*, 1996b).

These survey data and accompanying field data revealed that opportunities for teacher professional learning and development were qualitatively different in schools with strong professional communities than in schools with weak professional communities (Louis, Kruse, & Marks, 1996a, Louis, Marks, & Kruse, 1996b). In schools with strong professional communities, opportunities for teacher learning and development were more likely to involve groups of teachers or the whole school than to be pursued independently by individual teachers. These opportunities were more likely to be planned jointly by teachers and administrators and focus on instruction and expanding teachers' repertoires of teaching skills. Although opportunities for teacher learning and development in these schools responded to the special needs of individual teachers, such assistance was likely to be connected to larger, collective purposes. Schools with strong professional communities were more likely to make use of internal as well as external expertise, taking advantage of knowledge and skills within a faculty to share effective practices, conduct peer observations, and teach one another.

Rethinking School Leadership

From our review of the literature on social and human capital among teachers, school leadership can be seen as functioning quite differently from views that have dominated school leadership research and practice. This difference concerns both who school leaders are and how leadership is exercised. Through most of the 20th century, education has modeled its leadership systems on hierarchical, somewhat heroic visions of the school leader, the image of "the man in the principal's office" (Hart, 1995; Wolcott, 1973). These views of leadership are tied historically to structural, bureaucratic conceptions of schools as organizations (see Bacharach & Mundell, 1995). From social and human capital development perspectives, attention is drawn toward relational and interactional aspects of school leadership. These perspectives call for a broader conception of school leadership, one that shifts from a single person, role-oriented view to a view of leadership as an organizational property shared among administrators, teachers, and perhaps others.

These complementary ways to rethink school leadership are discussed below. We look at the particular contributions principals make to social and human capital among teachers. This section first examines the interactional dimension of leadership and then focuses on five aspects of principal leadership particularly conducive to social and human capital development among teachers in schools. These include (a) managing teachers' work, (b) fostering social trust, (c) establishing channels for new information, (d) communicating and enforcing norms and expectations, and (e) balancing internal and external ties. We examine what this discussion implies for the relationship of the individual teacher to the school as an organization and examine leadership as it extends beyond the principal through the school.

Interactional Principal Leadership

The literature on social and human capital development among teachers in schools strongly emphasizes the importance of the interactional dimension of administrative leadership. It points to the role that the principal plays in developing and sustaining productive social relations among teachers. It also identifies interaction generally and particular qualitative elements of interaction as crucial mechanisms of principal leadership. The importance of administrative leadership to develop social and human capital among teachers in schools is illustrated by Burt's (1997) analysis of the role of the manager in bridging "structural holes" in social networks to broker information and promote relations among disconnected groups in ways that may be mutually beneficial.

Interactional perspectives on leadership are not new (Hart, 1995). They echo previously developed views of leadership as a cooperative social system in which leaders are group members validated by others to act on the group's behalf (Blau, 1964; Dornbusch & Scott, 1975; Etzioni, 1964). They also reflect perspectives on leadership that run throughout literature on professional and semiprofessional organizations (Blankenship, 1977a; Etzioni, 1969) and leader succession (Hart, 1993). Interactional leadership is portrayed in the literature not as a unique form of one-way influence. Rather, it derives from the subtle, complex, and mutually-amplifying effects of social relations. In this sense, interactional leadership can be broadly defined as "overt actions, including language, covert deliberations and plans, and physical presence and gesture [that] influence others in a continuing cycle of exchange and communication" (Hart, 1991, p. 91).

The interactional nature of leadership is elucidated by several complementary theoretical perspectives. Exchange theory, for example, suggests that many aspects of social life can be explained in terms of implicit and explicit bargaining and negotiating between individuals and groups (Blau, 1964; Homans, 1958). It assumes that even though individuals may enter into a social relationship with different degrees of relative power, each necessarily must reach accommodation with the other to serve their mutual interests. Bargaining and negotiation involve a calculus of benefits and costs, an analysis of that which can be gained and that which must be expended to achieve that gain. Benefits and costs are defined according to individual and collective normative frameworks. These frameworks incorporate beliefs and assumptions regarding self-interests, the interests of others, goals, and rewards, as well as beliefs and assumptions regarding roles, responsibilities, rights, and obligations in social relationships (see also Jones, 1983). As held by individuals and as grounded in collective contexts, such frameworks suggest which types of social relationships are in individuals' best interests, which are most legitimate, and which are most costly. They also suggest how individuals are to interact with each other and how and in what directions they are to shape their relationships.

As applied in leadership studies, exchange perspectives provide a utilitarian view akin to transactional leadership (Burns, 1978; Hollander, 1979; Jacobs, 1970). In his analysis of leadership as a social exchange process, Yukl (1994) contends that the amount of influence a leader has over group decisions is proportional to the group's evaluation of the leader's demonstrated loyalty, competence, and success in helping the group solve its problems and attain its goals. A leader who demonstrates good judgment and support may accumulate "idiosyncrasy credits" from group members. These credits can later be "spent" to achieve a leader's objectives, particularly in difficult or contentious situations (see also Buchanan, 1974). Hart (1988), following Blau (1964), Dornbusch and Scott (1975), and Burns (1978), interprets the effects of salutary interactions between leaders and followers as a form of social validation through which followers grant to formal and informal leaders the power and right to act on behalf and in the interests of the group.

A second perspective comes from symbolic interaction theory. According to this perspective, a solid and shared understanding, an ontological security, develops among people as they interact over time, interpret the communication they receive from one another, and act in turn (Hart, 1995). In an established group, much of the work of communication diminishes as people come to expect and trust reactions from others, find consistent meanings for words and actions, and come to share values around these meanings and actions. This perspective points to the importance of meaning and symbols communicated through interaction in how people develop self-concepts and assess themselves based on their beliefs about how others see and evaluate them. This view of the social context suggests another dimension of organizational leadership. The meanings ascribed to a leader's messages received through word and deed, the messages sent in return based on their interpretations, the interpretations read into the returned message by the leader, and interactions that lead to new understandings about shared experiences compose the portrait of leadership painted by symbolic interactionism. Schein (1988) asserts that interactions, in their expressive, ideational, and symbolic aspects, form an inseparable bridge between leadership and organizational culture (see also Smircich, 1983). He contends that the deeply held beliefs and assumptions that form an organization's culture are a "learned product of group experience" (p. 7). They can be found only where there is a definable group with a significant history of interaction.

Interactional perspectives do not necessarily conflict with other perspectives on leadership. Indeed, they often complement them. As we discuss later in this section, principal leadership for effective social and human capital development has crucial managerial components. Interactional perspectives also complement recent inspirational and transformational views of leadership. In his analysis of political leadership, for example, Burns (1978) emphasizes the importance of social exchanges or transactions that result in mutual transformation among followers and leaders. From another perspective, Yukl (1994) suggests that the exchange process in transactional leadership does not have to be limited to tangible benefits. The reciprocal influence of transformational leadership can involve an exchange of commitment for meaning. He further suggests that the vision articulated by a transformational leader usually includes "an implicit promise of tangible benefits for followers in addition to an ideological appeal" (p. 367).

Unfortunately, the interactive features of leadership sometimes disappear in the rhetoric of inspirational and transformational perspectives (Bass, 1981). Although leadership qualities revealed from these perspectives may be real, the images of the visionary and inspirational leader they evoke tends to obscure the complicated social nature of leadership in organizations. As Blau (1964) cautioned more than 30 years ago, "There are fundamental differences between the dynamics of power in a collective situation and the power of one individual over another" (p. 17). Collective enterprises, like schools, involve interactive influence processes, beliefs, effort, knowledge, and communication. In these contexts, multi-directional, interactive, and adjustive approaches to leadership provide a more authentic map for educational organizations (Hart, 1995; Lindblom, 1993; Smith & Peterson, 1988).

Overview of Findings

While principals may inspire and transform others' thinking and behavior, their work occurs in large part through a social interactive context. The literature on teachers' social relations, learning, and change consistently refers to the importance of principal leadership. Although much of the literature portrays the principal's role vaguely, many studies identify particular relational aspects of leadership that shape and cultivate qualities of social capital conducive to human capital development among teachers. The implications of the literature seem straightforward, but it should be acknowledged that promoting social and human capital development among teachers in schools can be extremely difficult. As noted later in the conclusion to this chapter, efforts to develop and sustain more productive social relations challenge deeply entrenched patterns of isolation and autonomy that define teachers' work (Johnson, 1990; Lortie, 1975). They implicate long-standing beliefs and practices that define and govern working relationships and leadership in most schools (Feiman-Nemser & Floden, 1986; Little, 1990b).

The research on teacher collegial relations, collaboration, and professional community is consistent in a number of general findings about principal leadership. First, as discussed earlier, this research indicates that principals have substantial influence on the development, nature, and function of teacher social relations, teacher learning, and change. There are substantial differences in patterns of principal leadership between schools with high and low levels of teacher collaboration and between schools with strong and weak professional communities (Louis *et al.*, 1996a, 1996b; Louis & Murphy, 1994; Rosenholtz, 1989; Useem *et al.*, 1997). These differences are not necessarily associated with how principals' roles are formally defined. Nor are they necessarily associated with whether it is the principal or another individual, such as a teacher leader, who performs administrative roles. Rather, these differences are associated with the enactment of those roles, that is, how those roles are performed (Elmore *et al.*, 1996; Louis *et al.*, 1996b).

Second, the research consistently finds that principal leadership is strong and purposive in schools with high levels of collaboration and strong professional communities. Such leadership sees the development of social relationships in pursuit of the school mission and priorities as the "taproot" of high performance and change (Goldring & Rallis, 1993; Louis & Murphy, 1994). Principal leadership in these schools is situated in particular ways with regard to teaching staffs. In Louis' language (Louis *et al.*, 1996a; Louis & Murphy, 1994), it is leadership "from the center" of a school's staff rather than leadership "from the top." In Lieberman's words (Lieberman *et al.*, 1991a), this leadership involves working with, rather than working on, the teaching staff. Further, principal leadership in these schools is based on a balance of emphases. It is supportive and facilitative of expertise and initiative distributed widely across the school. At the same time, it is assertive of the school's collective vision and goals (Louis & Murphy, 1994). It is helpful but not threatening, directive but not overbearing, facilitative but not laissez-faire (Rosenholtz, 1989).

Managing Teachers' Work

The literature consistently points to the importance of certain managerial functions in the development of social and human capital among teachers. Principals in schools with high collaboration and strong professional cultures work actively to create structures, places, and occasions for social relations among teachers to develop and function. They carve out time in and around the daily work schedule for teachers to meet and engage in sustained discussions and joint work (Bryk *et al.*, 1993; Johnson, 1990; Louis *et al.*, 1996a; Useem *et al.*, 1997). Principals in these schools are effective in mobilizing personnel resources to promote the development of teachers' social relations. Several studies point to the principal's role in recruiting and hiring teachers whose philosophical perspectives and pedagogical practices are consistent with the school's (Bryk *et al.*, 1998; Elmore *et al.*, 1996; Stringfield & Teddlie, 1991; Talbert 1993). The research also identifies the importance of principals' actions to reduce turnover and maintain stability within their teaching staffs (Useem *et al.*, 1997). Other studies point to the principal's role in developing teachers' class assignments and work schedules to structure the memberships of teacher workgroups (Elmore *et al.*, 1996; Goldring & Rallis, 1993).

The literature cautions that such managerial actions may generate "contrived" forms of collegiality (Hargreaves, 1989; Hargreaves & Dawe, 1989). These forms consist of social relations that are created administratively or that exist as artifacts of the structural conditions of schools. They are contrasted with more genuine collaborative cultures that consist of relations that are natural and voluntary, and that form around teachers who possess common values, perspectives, and shared purposes (see also Grimmett & Crehan, 1992).

According to Hargreaves (1989), contrived relations are less likely to support meaningful teacher learning and change because they lack the interpersonal foundation of trust, respect, autonomy, and mutual interests and obligations that undergirds more genuine collaborative cultures. While he acknowledged that contrived collegiality can be a useful preliminary phase in the move towards more enduring collaborative relationships among teachers, Hargreaves argued that contrived relations can thwart the development of more genuine relations in several ways. They can fail to recognize existing collaborative conditions and undermine them by imposing administratively-derived structures. Further, contrived relations can lead to a proliferation of unwanted meetings and interactions, causing teachers to experience overload and crowding out the informal camaraderie that is part of more genuine interpersonal relations (Grimmett & Crehan, 1992). The distinction between contrived or induced and more genuine social relations is also noted by Little (1990b), who suggested that the prospects of contrived relations for influencing individuals and organizations productively rest in part on their congruence with established norms of interaction and interpretation among teachers, and on the degree to which they align or conflict with the meaningful reference groups with which teachers associate themselves.

Very little empirical research has compared the nature and function of teachers' social relations under contrived or more genuine circumstances. Nor has research taken into account the different ways that groups and subgroups of teachers can form and function within a school. Yet while some studies caution against breaking up existing groups of teachers that have formed voluntarily or that have functioned well in the past (see Useem *et al.*, 1997), there is little evidence in the empirical research that contrived forms of collegiality are antithetical to or compromise the development and maintenance of productive social relations. This is particularly true if the steps that principals take to establish and shape social groups are accompanied by the relational functions of leadership discussed later. Recall, Placier and Hamilton's (1994) work, reviewed earlier, pointed to the strength of social relations developed within "contrived" teacher professional development groups.

Another managerial function concerns the organization of a broad support system for teachers' social relations. Three elements of this system are particularly salient. The first concerns the provision of formal, ongoing staff development opportunities for teachers and principals' efforts to align those opportunities with school goals (Goldring & Rallis, 1993; Louis & Murphy, 1994). Staff development can help teachers develop the orientations and skills for interacting and working productively together. It can also serve as a source of new information and insight about substantive aspects of work, particularly instruction and student learning.

A second element concerns principals' efforts to buffer their schools and the work of teachers within them from outside pressure and conflicting influence (Talbert, 1993). An important part of buffering is the role that the principal plays in managing relationships between the school and community and between the school and the central office (Louis *et al.*, 1996a; Louis & Murphy, 1994). For example, principals may have to mediate the effects of central office policies that disrupt the stability of social groups within the school or that threaten the time they have to work together (see Useem *et al.*, 1997).

A third element concerns principals' abilities to connect their schools to other external sources of political, economic, and intellectual support (Louis *et al.*, 1996a; Useem *et al.*, 1997). These sources can include other schools, principals, and teachers, membership in school networks or partnerships with external organizations, funders, consultants, universities, and professional organizations. With staff development, these external connections are pursued to bring resources to the school to help achieve its mission and goals. These resources are also pursued to challenge and "check" prevailing assumptions and prevent the school's social structure from simply reinforcing parochial attitudes and practices.

In addition to these managerial functions, the literature places a great deal of emphasis on the interactive and relational nature of administrative leadership (see also Leithwood, 1994). What distinguishes leadership in schools with high levels of collaboration and strong professional communities from schools with low collaboration and weak professional communities are the strategies principals use to foster productive relations and interactions *within* the social structures they may help establish. Of particular importance are the steps they take to foster the primary elements of social capital—social trust, channels for new information, norms, expectations, and sanctions.

Fostering Social Trust

The literature points to a number of different ways that principals can foster social trust among themselves and their teachers. Consistent with the theoretical literature on social capital, their efforts aim to create shared responsibilities, mutual dependence, and mutual obligations. They also aim to engender predictability, dependability, and a climate of stability, respect, assurance, and psychological safety (see Useem *et al.*, 1997).

Research suggests that social trust between principals and teachers emanates from a number of different sources. In large part, it comes from the manner in which principals approach and perform their work. Evans (1996) reasoned that trust in leadership derives from consistency between personal beliefs, organizational aims, and work behavior. It also derives from competence. According to Evans, trust forms from a sense of knowing what leadership stands for, and of being able to count on leadership to know what to do and to do it effectively—to "get the job done." These principles of consistency and competence are well illustrated in Bryk, Lee, and Holland's (1993) analysis of community in Catholic schools (see also Bryk & Driscoll, 1988; Bryk & Schneider, 1996). In that study, principals in schools with strong communities accepted responsibility for the school as a whole and sought to live out school ideals in their work. They performed their tasks effectively. Teachers could count on them to get the job done. These principals adopted a "no job too small" orientation in their work, modeling commitment to and sacrifice for the school community (see also Evans, 1996). They stressed the importance of school vision, and in this case, the spiritual dimension of Catholic schools. They manifested that vision in the language and goals of the school, creating a clear focal point for social bonds among teachers, students, and other members of the school community.

Another way that principals foster social trust between them and their teachers is to provide strong, dependable, and facilitative support of teachers' work. In Bryk and his colleagues' (1993) Catholic school study, principals of schools with strong communities encouraged, supported, and reinforced their teachers. Likewise, in her study of public elementary schools, Rosenholtz (1989) found similar support in schools with strong communities.

Principals can also foster social trust by the steps that they take to manage conflict effectively. Louis and her colleagues (Louis *et al.*, 1996a; Louis & Murphy, 1994) found that principals in schools with strong professional communities practiced in "positive micro-politics." They engaged in "hard listening" to alert themselves to conflict within the school. They actively encouraged individuals to voice their frustrations openly, which included permitting people to criticize the principal's own decisions. These principals were respectful of conflicting opinions, honest in their assessments, and consistent and equitable in the management and rapid resolution of tensions. Importantly, they did not often resolve differences among teachers unilaterally. Instead, they established structures and supportive climates for teachers to resolve them (Louis *et al.*, 1996a). These ac-

tions demonstrated principals' confidence in teachers to address their own problems productively, additionally strengthening the bonds of social trust.

Beyond fostering trust between themselves and their teachers, principals in schools with strong social capital work to develop trust among teachers. Several studies indicate that principals encourage trust among teachers by trying to "deprivatize" or make public classroom instruction, and promote regular teacher interaction around the improvement of practice (Rosenholtz, 1989; Talbert, 1993; Useem *et al.*, 1997). These efforts can involve creating occasions for teachers to observe one another's teaching, engage in reciprocal helping relationships, and participate in joint problem-solving and the development of new programs and practices. Principals can encourage open communication, sharing problems and solutions, challenging taken-for-granted assumptions, and "intellectual play" among teachers. Making teaching and efforts to improve it a public and collective enterprise creates risk for individual teachers. At the same time, it can lead to shared understanding and obligations, conditions conducive to mutual responsibility, respect, and support.

Yet another way that principals can promote social trust is through relinquishing control and sharing authority broadly among teachers. Rosenholtz (1989) found that principals who shared administrative responsibilities with teachers, who made leadership a responsibility for every teacher, communicated trust in teachers' knowledge and creative instincts. Likewise, Louis, Kruse, and Marks (1996a) pointed to delegating authority and taking problems to teachers for joint deliberation and decision-making as ways of promoting social trust. In their analysis of factors associated with strong professional communities, Louis and her colleagues found that the equitable distribution and exercise of power and influence furthered collective responsibility and broadened trust that teachers and principals would act in the best interest of one another. Similar conclusions were reached by Goldring and Rallis (1993) and Elmore and his colleagues (1996) from their respective analyses of participative decision-making in restructured schools.

Establishing Channels for New Information

In addition to establishing conditions for fostering social trust, principals can contribute to the development of social capital by establishing channels for teachers to gain access to new information. The literature points to a number of different ways that principals create these channels. First, in addition to creating structures and occasions for teachers to interact, principals can provide tasks for joint work and encourage helping behavior, both of which establish avenues for exchanging ideas and information (Goldring & Rallis, 1993; Louis *et al.*, 1996a; Rosenholtz, 1989; Talbert, 1993). They can create networks of teachers to share with one another successful instructional practices and help one another experiment with those practices in the classroom (Talbert, 1993). Second, as mentioned above, principals can be instrumental in providing formal staff development opportunities for teachers in their schools (Goldring & Rallis, 1993). These opportunities can also expose teachers to important sources of new information. Finally, principals can create channels for new information through their efforts to link schools to external resources (Louis *et al.*, 1996a). While not as central a concern as developing social relations inside the school, principals in schools with strong professional communities create opportunities for new information to come into the school by establishing relations with other schools, networks, partners, and external organizations (Louis & Murphy, 1994; Talbert, 1993; Useem *et al.*, 1997). These relations are carefully managed and aligned with the mission and priorities of the school.

Communicating and Enforcing Norms and Expectations

The literature finds principals instrumental in communicating and enforcing norms and expectations that support strong social relations in schools. Consistent with social capital theory, these norms and expectations form a basis for how individual teachers relate to and work with one another. They also concern the substantive focus and direction of collective work. As mentioned earlier, principals in schools with high collaboration and strong professional communities function as "keepers" and advocates of their schools' visions (Goldring & Rallis, 1993; Louis *et al.*, 1996a; Louis & Murphy, 1994; Talbert, 1993). They maintain a clear focus on collective goals and discourage the individual pursuit of conflicting goals and interests (Lieberman *et al.*, 1991a). They set a positive value on challenging conventional practices that stand in the way of achieving the school's goals and establish a sense of internal quality for work and innovation (Elmore *et al.*, 1996; Louis *et al.*, 1996b). These principals also communicate a positive value of community and teamwork through public endorsement, modeling their own work, and delegating authority (Bryk *et al.*, 1993). They expect everyone to work as a team and create opportunities to ensure that everyone is a part of the collective enterprise (Rosenholtz, 1989; Talbert, 1993).

In addition to communicating norms and expectations, principals in schools with strong social capital create accountability systems to enforce them. These principals recognize and reward teaching that is consistent with collective norms and expectations, actions that further the mission of the school, and innovations that emerge from collective efforts (Goldring & Rallis, 1993; Louis *et al.*,

1996b). They hold teachers personally accountable for deviant behavior, in both their work with other teachers and with students (Rosenholtz, 1989; Talbert, 1993).

The accountability systems that principals create extend beyond individual sanctions. By creating opportunities for teachers to engage in joint work and decision-making, and by subjugating individual interests to school goals, principals replace individual autonomy and responsibility with collective responsibility and mutual accountability. Under these conditions, teachers are not only accountable to administrative leadership for their actions; they become accountable to their teaching colleagues and subject to group sanctions if they deviate from collective norms and expectations. This shift from individual to collective accountability is illustrated in several studies of collaboration and professional community (Clift *et al.*, 1995; Elmore *et al.*, 1996; Placier & Hamilton, 1994; Talbert, 1993).

Balancing Internal and External Ties

This research indicates that the role of administrative leadership in developing social and human capital among teachers has two complementary foci. The primary focus concerns developing internal cohesiveness and intensity in social relations *within* the school or relevant social structure (see Little & McLaughlin, 1993a). An important aspect of developing the strength of social relations inside a school involves managerial activities to shape and protect the boundaries of the social group from conflicting and threatening external influence.

At the same time, the literature suggests a secondary focus on developing relations to social resources *outside* the school. These external ties perform a crucial function of bringing new information, perspectives, and challenge to teachers inside the school. By creating a combination of internal and external ties, principals are able to enhance the potency of relations among teachers inside a school to work productively and to support change. They are able to enrich internal social relations with external perspectives and counterbalance the possibility that strong internal relations will function only to preserve prevailing knowledge and practice. According to the theoretical and empirical literature, this balance between internal and external ties seems most conducive to teacher learning and productive change.

Toward New Relationships Between Individuals and the Organization

The literature we have reviewed on teacher social relations and interactional principal leadership begins to reveal the dynamics of a new "social physics" implied by emergent conceptions of schools as professional, community-oriented organizations (Beck & Murphy, 1993). These literatures allow us to look inside the images of collaborative workplaces to view the nature, function, and potential outcomes of social relationships within them. They suggest new perspectives on the relationship between schools as organizations and the individuals who work within them. Of particular significance, they suggest that group power and social order of organizations must be examined constantly and balanced in consideration of individual autonomy and discretion, and vice versa. Like views of school leadership that emphasize interaction and social validation, social and human capital development perspectives view individuals and organizations as integrative and reciprocal. They also see individuals and organizations as grounded in integrative and reciprocal ways within their broader environmental contexts. Individuals can retain a substantial amount of autonomy and discretion within their organizations, but the manner in which individual autonomy and discretion is exercised both contributes to and is "bounded" by collective goals, interests, and social accountability.

This balance is illustrated in the literature highlighting the special nature of professional organizations (Bittner, 1977; Etzioni, 1969; Scott, 1987). In this literature, professionals are seen to bring specialized knowledge and expertise from external professional sources to their work in organizations (Benveniste, 1994). In order to apply these resources effectively, individual professionals, such as teachers, require a substantial amount of autonomy (Friedson, 1986; Lipsky, 1980). The picture of work in professional organizations is not one of unbridled individual discretion. Rather, professional work is constrained from two sources. For educators, the first source consists of professional knowledge, norms, and values that transcend the particular school in which an individual professional works (Friedson, 1986; Guy, 1985). The second is the social and normative context of the specific school. While some scholars have argued that professional norms are more powerful than organizational norms (March & Simon, 1958), most acknowledge that the organization is substantially influential (Abrahamson, 1967; see also Hart, 1990). Blankenship (1977b) indicated that professional work in organizations involves attending not only to professional knowledge but to interaction with knowledgeable colleagues within and outside the organization. Colleagues in professional organizations, more than many other forms of social organization, construct work as they interact and work together. This social construction of work intensely influences teachers in schools as well as the nature of the school organization.

The balance between individual teacher autonomy and school organizational needs suggested by the social and human capital development literature is also illustrated in an emerging literature on social communitarianism, which includes extensive discourse on education and schools. Schol-

ars have long pointed to the struggle to balance the rights and interests of the body politic against the rights of individuals within it. Communitarianism, as presented in current scholarly discourse, is a view of public life that seeks a new balance between individual rights and collective responsibilities. According to Etzioni (1996), this balance commits to "voluntary order and bounded autonomy," to a "spirit of community" that consists a set of rights, responsibilities, and commitments that empower and ennoble others. This balance in community spirit recognizes that educators and communities can generate among teachers, administrators, students, and parents a common set of commitments to truth, democratic procedures, solidarity, school, and community (Cooper, 1994). And, while a communitarian perspective limits the "virtues the society favors to a set of core values," it also recognizes legitimate differences on other normative matters (Etzioni, 1996). This perspective seeks to establish new rights-based arguments that transcend the use of individual rights and discretion as trump cards to neutralize all other positions. Accordingly, as applied to schools, rights-based arguments should be established instead on the basis of arguments that weigh the right of an individual teacher, administrator, or student against the rights of those who are affected by the action of that individual. Rather than closing off debate by the simple assertion of individual rights of autonomy and discretion, responsible members of school communities would more carefully and thoughtfully weigh the ways in which their choices and rights interact with and impinge on those of others.

This principle of balance between self-interest and individual rights and collective interests and rights is captured by Etzioni's (1996) articulation of a new societal "golden rule," which has application to organizations:

> The new golden rule . . . [seeks] to greatly reduce the distance between ego's preferred course and the virtuous one, while recognizing that this profound source of social and personal struggle cannot be eliminated. And it seeks a good part of the solution on the . . . societal level rather than merely, or firstly, on the personal one. [T]he new golden rule should read: Respect and uphold society's moral order as you would have society respect and uphold your autonomy (p. viii).

Etzioni (1993) argued that an equilibrium between individual and collective rights is critical for a healthy community or organization to prosper. The responsible citizen or organizational member advocates on behalf of whichever aspect of this delicate mix is least acknowledged at a given time and place. According to Etzioni, this balance results in a "good society . . . that nourishes both social virtues and individual rights" (1994, p. 4).

This communitarian view recasts the political and social spectrum in which school leadership is exerted. Rather than a dichotomy of an autonomous individual teacher versus the school, this perspective focuses attention on "the relationship between the individual and the community, and between freedom and order" (Etzioni, 1996, p. 7). It provides an orientation for leadership that is wholly consistent with theoretical views of social and human capital development in schools. It suggests that school leadership must attend to the relation of individual teachers to their schools in ways that mutually enhance knowledge, skills, and their effective discretionary application in the service of collective organizational goals and priorities.

Leadership as an Organizational Property

The strong surge in interest in communitarian perspectives occurs concurrently with renewed interest in views of school leadership as an organizational property. The literature reviewed earlier in this chapter clearly emphasizes the importance of active principal leadership in social and human capital development among teachers. This contrasts with much of the discourse on teachers' work redesign, leadership, and professional "empowerment," in which the contributions of the principal are largely ignored (Smylie, 1997). At the same time, the literature on social and human capital development does not see leadership as lodged solely in the position of the principal. Rather, this literature sees leadership as infused throughout the school. As discussed earlier, an important contribution that principals play in developing social capital for human capital development is to distribute and cultivate leadership broadly among teachers. Leadership becomes participative and inclusive. It is spread throughout the social system of the school, fostering collective responsibility, mutual trust and obligations, and joint accountability. This perspective signals a shift from leadership as the prerogative of an individual to leadership as an organizational property.

According to Ogawa and Bossert (1995), the idea of leadership as an organizational property can be traced to some of the earliest writings in the modern literature on administration and organizations. They referred to Barnard's (1968) observations that the "authority of leadership" is not confined to those persons in executive positions but can be exerted by anyone in an organization. Similarly, they pointed to Thompson's (1967) assertions that administrative authority is something that exists and flows across hierarchical levels of an organization. They also cited the theoretical and empirical work conducted in the 1950s and 1960s at the University of Michigan that treated leadership as an organizational-level variable, a phenomenon that could be found throughout organizations not just in particular roles (Cartwright, 1965; Katz & Kahn, 1978; Tannenbaum, 1962).

Ogawa and Bossert (1995) argued that the concept of leadership as an organizational property extends beyond

these earlier observations that individuals throughout organizations can lead in formal and informal ways. In a perspective closely related to interactional views of leadership, they suggested that leadership flows broadly through social networks that comprise organizations. Contrasting technical-rational theory with institutional theory of social organization, they argued that the currency of leadership lies in the personal resources of organizational participants and that interaction is the medium through which resources are deployed and influence is exerted. Because leadership affects organizational structure, leadership through interactions influences the system of interactions that constitute the organization. Attention shifts from people's actions to their social interactions. According to Ogawa and Bossert, "The interact, not the act, becomes the basic building block of organizational leadership" (p. 236; see also Lambert *et al.*, 1995; Leithwood & Steinbach, 1995).

Recent empirical support for this concept of leadership as an organizational property of schools can be found in several studies. In their study of academically successful secondary schools, Wilson and Corcoran (1988) found that leadership was dispersed throughout the school organization, that "leaders change with the issue," and that no single individual "provides the answers" (p. 83). They concluded that leadership in these schools was dynamic and changed constantly with the evolving character of school communities.

In a second study, Pounder, Ogawa, and Adams (1995) examined the relationship of the distribution and total amount of leadership at the school level to Parson's (1960) four functions of effective organizations and to several other measures of school effectiveness. Analyzing data from surveys of teachers, administrators, non-teaching professional staff, and clerical and custodial staff from 60 elementary and secondary schools in a large suburban school district, Pounder and her colleagues found that individuals in a variety of roles exert social influence that is associated with different organizational outcomes. They found leadership occurring in both technical and institutional domains of the school organization. For example, they identified significant relations of both principal influence and influence exerted by groups of teachers to organizational loyalty and to the perceived capability of their schools to change. They found principal influence related to job satisfaction and teachers' collective influence related to perceived school effectiveness. Both principal influence and teachers' collective influence were related indirectly to student achievement test scores through job satisfaction and goal achievement respectively. Total organizational leadership, an average of levels of influence from individual sources, was found to directly influence perceived goal achievement and organizational loyalty and indirectly influence perceived school effectiveness, student achievement, student absenteeism, and faculty/staff turnover through these organizational variables.

Heller and Firestone (1995) examined leadership functions related to the institutionalization of a curricular reform in eight elementary schools. From interviews of principals, teachers, district-level informants, and staff of the reform initiative, they found that various leadership functions contributed to change. These functions included sustaining a vision for change, encouraging staff, modifying standard operating procedures, and monitoring progress. What is particularly relevant about this study is that it also found that these functions were performed redundantly by people in a variety of overlapping roles, including central office personnel, principals, teachers, and outside consultants, rather than by any one "heroic leader."

In a final example, Foster's (1997) case study illustrates this broader conception of leadership in an exemplary community-oriented and academically successful high school in Canada. This case shows teachers, administrators, parents, and students engaging in leadership activities within the school community that transcend traditional roles. These activities evolved in a social context that was collaborative, reciprocal, and mutually respectful. Different persons emerged to perform specific leadership functions as the situation required and as their expertise and interest allowed.

The literature on social and human capital development cautions against the more extreme interpretations of the concept of leadership as an organizational property that reduces the principal to being merely "one of the gang." As the empirical literature reviewed in this chapter makes clear, the principal is an integral component of a system of social capital as well as an integral component of organizational leadership. This literature indicates that by virtue of their authority and their formal position, principals' contributions are crucial among the leadership contributions of others in the school in the cultivation and maintenance of social capital among teachers.

Summary and Implications

This chapter has examined how social capital can promote the development and application of human capital among teachers for instructional improvement. It has also analyzed the implications of social and human capital development perspectives for school leadership and organization. The empirical research on teachers' collegial relations, collaboration in improvement initiatives, and professional community provides convergent evidence of the importance of social capital to teachers' professional learning and development. Consistent with the theoretical literature, it identifies specific bases and characteristics of social relations that are most conducive to learning and change. These include common vision, group goals, and shared norms and expectations for teacher interactions and joint work. This

empirical literature also points to reciprocity, mutual responsibility and obligation, trust, and shared accountability as foundation blocks of productive social relations.

Most of the empirical research focuses on the role of social relations in developing teachers' knowledge and skills. A relatively smaller portion focuses on the ways in which social relations can influence teachers' behavior and classroom practice. There is some evidence in the literature that the goals, norms, expectations, and mutual obligations and accountability that define teachers' social relations also form a system of professional social controls that govern the activities of individual teachers in their collegial groups and in their classrooms. Additional evidence of such controls comes from studies of teacher leadership and work redesign, particularly studies of participative decision-making. In these reform contexts, teachers have been found to develop new systems of mutual obligation and accountability to make decisions in the best interest of their colleagues and to act in good faith upon the decisions that are made collectively (Rowan, 1990; Smylie, 1994).

Social and human capital development perspectives suggest different ways to think about school leadership. These views draw attention to relational and interactional aspects of principal leadership. They point beyond a single person, role-oriented concept of leadership to a perspective of leadership as an organizational property. The empirical literature on social and human capital development sees leadership as participative and inclusive, as infused throughout the social system of the school in ways that foster collective responsibility, mutual trust and obligations, and joint accountability. These views signal a shift from leadership that is the prerogative of an individual to leadership that is shared among many.

At the same time, the research is clear that principals play a vital role in the development and maintenance of social capital among teachers. Their contributions come through creating structures and occasions for interaction to take place and for social bonds to form, mobilizing groups for interaction, and establishing broad support systems. Beyond these managerial functions, principals play an active role in fostering productive social relations within the structures they may help create. They foster social trust by exhibiting consistency and competence in their work and by modeling commitment and contribution to the school community. They also foster social trust by providing strong, dependable, and facilitative support of teachers, making teaching public and its improvement a collective enterprise, managing conflict fairly and effectively, and sharing authority and leadership broadly among teachers.

In addition to fostering social trust, principals promote the development of social capital among teachers by creating joint tasks and other avenues for teachers within a school to exchange ideas and information and to form social bonds. They also create channels to obtain new information from outside the school by bringing staff developmental opportunities into the school and by establishing linkages to external resources. Finally, the research shows how principals promote social capital through communicating norms and expectations of community and teamwork that become focal points around which social relations can form and function. Principals in schools with strong social capital enforce these norms and expectations by holding teachers individually accountable for their actions and by promoting collective mechanisms of accountability and collegial control.

Overall, the research shows that principals of schools with strong social capital among teachers work hard to develop social relations within their schools and create enough closure of the social group to sustain its strength and cohesiveness. At the same time, these principals recognize the importance of establishing relations to external resources to evoke new information, challenge, and perspective that will have meaning and contribute to the improvement of their schools. The research suggests that an appropriate balance between internal and external ties is most conducive to learning and improvement.

Finally, our analysis points to new perspectives on the relation of the individual to the organization. The literature suggests the need for a balance between the interests and discretion of individual teachers and the interests and goals of the school. It suggests that attention should be paid to the reciprocal influences between individuals and groups and that efforts to develop one to the neglect of the other will be insufficient to significantly improve teaching, and hopefully, student learning.

Directions for Future Research

Although social and human capital development theory offers a useful framework to explain how and why social relations in schools can function and relate to instructional improvement and school change, our analysis suggests a number of different areas for future research. The first has to do with the content of social and human capital and the value of the goals and behaviors they promote. On one hand, the literature suggests that social capital can support a wide range of goals, norms, and behaviors, both positive and negative (Granovetter, 1973). For example, Putnam (1993) found in his study of modern Italian civic institutions that social capital was similarly important to the effectiveness of democratic community organizations as it was to the effectiveness of hierarchical, authoritative organizations such as the Catholic church and the Mafia. In their analyses of schools, Johnson (1990) and Little (1990b) contend that while strong social relations among teachers can support innovation, they can also spawn and sustain parochial beliefs and unproductive practices. On the other hand, there is evidence that different forms and characteristics of social relations may be associated with

particular types of learning and behavior (Smylie, 1995). Social learning, organizational socialization, and incidental learning theories suggest that social relations characterized by open exchange and critique of ideas and assumptions, multiple referents and sources of information, and equitable distribution of authority are most conducive to creative, innovative, and reflective learning (Bandura, 1986; Jarvis, 1987; Marsick & Watkins, 1990; Van Maanen & Schein, 1979). Indeed, there is some evidence in education literature that social capital in strong teacher professional communities is associated with active, demanding, and authentic forms of classroom instruction (Cohen *et al.*, 1993; Louis *et al.*, 1996a; McLaughlin, 1993). Whether social capital is actually "content neutral" or whether the "hidden curriculum" of its processes can foster particular forms of teacher learning and change remain unexplored. Also left to be examined are the ways in which content in the form of new information and ideas are introduced into social groups, the ways in which it is diffused throughout those groups, and the role leadership plays in these processes.

A second area for inquiry concerns the definition, functions, and relationships among different social groups to which teachers belong within their schools. As we stated earlier, most of the existing research views social capital among teachers from a school-level perspective. However, some research indicates that departments, grade-level teams, or other social structures within schools may be more appropriate units of analysis in the study of social capital than schools (Little, 1993; McLaughlin, 1993; Rowan *et al.*, 1993). This observation is consistent with research on the characteristics and functions of subgroups and subcultures within organizations (Alderfer, 1977; Blake & Mouton, 1961). Other evidence indicates that teachers are connected to professional and non-professional sources of social capital beyond their schools (Lieberman & Miller, 1991; Spencer, 1984). It remains unclear how teachers develop and negotiate multi-group affiliations. It also remains unclear how school leadership can coordinate the relative influences of multi-group affiliations on teachers toward coherent, school-level instructional improvement.

A third area for inquiry concerns the broader professional, cultural, and institutional influences that can mediate the formation and function of social capital among teachers. Perspectives from the emergent body of theoretical literature called the "New Institutionalism" remind us that efforts to develop and sustain more productive social relations among teachers will most likely implicate long-standing, deeply entrenched patterns of belief and practice that define and govern working relationships and leadership in schools (Powell & DiMaggio, 1991; Rossman, Corbett, & Firestone, 1988; Scott, 1995; Zucker, 1987). This is not a new observation. Difficulties in fostering more collaborative and productive working relationships among teachers are consistently noted in the literature (Feiman-Nemser &

Floden, 1986; Little, 1990a, 1990b; Rosenholtz, 1989). None-theless, very little empirical evidence sheds light on these broader institutional influences and how those influences interact with local school cultures and subcultures in shaping the development, function, and outcomes of social capital among teachers (see Hart, 1990).

Finally, while the existing research presents empirical evidence and theoretical arguments that social and human capital development among teachers may be conducive to school and instructional improvement, we have little evidence that such development directly or indirectly benefits students. Very few studies that examine teachers' working relations also include analyses of student outcome data. The studies that do point to very complicated, loose-linked relationships to student learning (Rosenholtz, 1989; Smylie et al., 1996). These relationships should be explored empirically to understand further whether and how benefits that can accrue to teachers from development of their own sources of social capital can also accrue to students through the improvement of classroom opportunities to learn. They should also be explored to understand how teachers can function within a broader system of social capital available to students that can support student learning.

These areas for inquiry suggest different approaches to research that attend concurrently to the capacities of individual teachers, the power and influence of social groups, the development and exercise of leadership as both an individual function and an organizational property, and outcomes for students. Research to date has focused primarily on the individual or the organization, but little work has been conducted to examine these elements together. More complex, multi-level integrative models are needed to understand how teacher capacity, leadership, and social interaction affect students' abilities to develop and learn in school (see Bossert, 1988). Such models call for new longitudinal research designs that can trace the development of these elements over time. They also call for nested data collection and analytic techniques that might use in-depth qualitative inquiries conducted in a small number of sites to document and explain patterns of relationships found in large-scale, cross-site quantitative investigations.

Implications for Policy

Most scholars who consider the development of social capital in schools conclude that policy can do little to establish social capital directly, but it can do much to create contexts that promote and support it (Bryk & Schneider, 1996; Useem et al., 1997). Our analysis calls into question the efficacy of policies that aim to improve teaching and learning through individual as opposed to collective development and accountability mechanisms. It also calls into question policies that focus strictly on the structure of school organization, without due attention to its social processes and contents.

Policies can help reduce the barriers and threats to social and human capital development among teachers in schools. Useem and her colleagues (1997) outline some of the most serious obstacles to overcome. One obstacle is instability in school staffing, particularly principal and teacher attrition, that disrupts the formation and function of social groups. Another consists of work rules in union contracts and central office mandates that constrain productive organization of time and work roles. Useem and her colleagues also point to problems of overload that are often associated with the introduction of collective work and problems of role and task conflicts that result from policies that are not aligned with or support collective activity and its products.

While policies can provide external support, we know that social capital cannot be mandated nor can it be legislated from without the school organization. It must be cultivated and nurtured over time from within. Leadership for social and human capital development among teachers is about changing the nature and function of roles and working relationships in schools. It is about change in the nature and function of leadership itself. As we have suggested, such change will not be easy. In most schools, efforts to develop social capital and the new leadership it demands will run headlong into deeply entrenched patterns of belief and practice. Although it will require long, steady work on the part of principals and teachers, developing social and human capital among teachers represents a potentially powerful approach to school improvement, one that may prove much more effective in enhancing instruction and student opportunities to learn than more structural or political approaches to reform.

NOTE

We are grateful for the assistance of Jill Stein and Han Mi Yoon in identifying and reviewing much of the literature referred to in this chapter. We also thank our reviewers Paul Bredeson, David Clark, and Sharon Conley for their critiques and suggestions.

REFERENCES

Abrahamson, M. (1967). *The professional in the organization.* Chicago: Rand McNally.

Alderfer, C. P. (1977). Group and intergroup relations. In J. R. Hackman & J. L. Suttle (Eds.), *Improving life at work* (pp. 227–296). Santa Monica, CA: Goodyear.

Ancess, J. (1995, March). *An inquiry high school: Learner-centered accountability at the Urban Academy.* New York: National Center on Restructuring Education, Schools, and Teaching, Teachers College, Columbia University.

Argyris, C. & Schön, D. A. (1974). *Theory in practice: Increasing professional effectiveness.* San Francisco: Jossey-Bass.

Bacharach, S. B. & Mundell, B. (Eds.). (1995). *Images of schools: Structures and roles in organizational behavior.* Thousand Oaks, CA: Corwin.

Bakkenes, I. (1996). *Professional isolation of primary school teachers.* Leiden, Belgium: DSWO Press.

Bakkenes, I., de Brabander, C. J. & Imants, J. (1993). Professional isolation in primary schools and teachers task perceptions. In F. K. Kieviet & R. Vandenberghe (Eds.), *School culture, school improvement, and teacher development* (pp. 171–198). Leiden, Belgium: DSWO Press.

Bandura, A. (1986). *Social foundations of thought and action: A social cognitive theory*. Englewood Cliffs, NJ: Prentice-Hall.

Barnard, C. I. (1968). *Functions of the executive*. Cambridge, MA: Harvard University Press.

Bass, B. M. (1981). *Handbook of leadership: A survey of theory and research*. New York: Free Press.

Beck, L. G. & Murphy, J. (1993). *Understanding the principalship: Metaphorical themes 1920s–1990s*. New York: Teachers College Press.

Benveniste, G. (1994). *The 21st century organization: Analyzing current trends imagining the future*. San Francisco: Jossey-Bass.

Berliner, D. C. & Biddle, B. J. (1995). *The manufactured crisis: Myths, fraud, and the attack on America's public schools*. Reading, MA: Addison-Wesley.

Bittner, E. (1977). The concept of organization. In R. L. Blankenship (Ed.), *Colleagues in organization: The social construction of professional work* (pp. 107–120). New York: Wiley.

Blake, R. R. & Mouton, J. S. (1961). Reactions to intergroup competition under win-lose conditions. *Management Science, 7*(4), 420–435.

Blankenship, R. L. (Ed.) (1977a). *Colleagues in organization: The social construction of professional work*. New York: Wiley.

Blankenship, R. L. (1977b). Toward a theory of collegial power and control. In R. L. Blankenship (Ed.), *Colleagues in organization: The social construction of professional work* (pp. 394–416). New York: Wiley.

Blau, P. M. (1964). *Exchange and power in social life*. New York: Wiley.

Boisjoly, J., Duncan, G. J. & Hofferth, S. (1995). Access to social capital. *Journal of Family Issues, 16*, 609–631.

Bolman, L. G. & Deal, T. E. (1991). *Reframing organizations: Artistry, choice, and leadership*. San Francisco: Jossey-Bass.

Bossert, S. T. (1988). School effects. In N. J. Boyan (Ed.), *Handbook of research on educational administration* (pp. 341–352). New York: Longman.

Bourdieu, P. (1986). The forms of capital. In J. G. Richardson (Ed.), *Handbook of theory and research for the sociology of education* (pp. 241–258). New York: Greenwood.

Bryk, A. S. & Driscoll, M. E. (1988, November). *The high school as community: Contextual influences and consequences for students and teachers*. Madison: National Center on Effective Secondary Schools, University of Wisconsin.

Bryk, A. S. & Schneider, B. (1996, June). *Social trust: A moral resource for school improvement*. Chicago: University of Chicago, Center for School Improvement.

Bryk, A. S., Lee, V. E. & Holland, P. B. (1993). *Catholic schools and the common good*. Cambridge, MA: Harvard University Press.

Bryk, A. S., Sebring, P. A., Kerbow, D., Rollow, S. & Easton J. Q. (1998). *Charting Chicago school reform: Democratic localism as a lever for change*. Boulder, CO: Westview.

Buchanan, B. (1974). Building organizational commitment: The socialization of managers in work organizations. *Administrative Science Quarterly, 19*, 533–546.

Burns, J. M. (1978). *Leadership*. New York: Harper & Row.

Burt, R. S. (1997). The contingent value of social capital. *Administrative Science Quarterly, 42*, 339–365.

Carter, K. (1990). Teachers knowledge and learning to teach. In R. W. Houston (Ed.), *Handbook of research on teacher education* (pp. 291–310). New York: Macmillan.

Cartwright, D. (1965). Influence, leadership, control. In J. G. March (Ed.), *Handbook of organizations* (pp. 1–47). Chicago: Rand McNally.

Christman, J. B. & Macpherson, P. (1996). *The five school study: Restructuring Philadelphia's comprehensive high schools*. Philadelphia: Philadelphia Education Fund.

Clift, R., Veal, M. L., Holland, P., Johnson, M. & McCarthy, J. (1995). *Collaborative leadership and shared decision making: Teachers, principals, and university professors*. New York: Teachers College Press.

Cohen, D. K., McLaughlin, M. W. & Talbert, J. E. (Eds.) (1993). *Teaching for understanding: Challenges for policy and practice*. San Francisco: Jossey-Bass.

Coleman, J. S. (1987). Families and schools. *Educational Researcher, 16*(6), 32–38.

Coleman, J. S. (1988). Social capital in the creation of human capital. *American Journal of Sociology, 94* (Supplement), S95–S120.

Coleman, J. S. (1990). *Foundations of social theory*. Cambridge, MA: Harvard University Press.

Cooper, B. (Ed.). (1994). *When teachers lead: Implications for administrators, unions, and school organization*. State College, PA: University Council for Educational Administration.

Crow, G. & Pounder, D. G. (1997, March). *Faculty teams: Work group enhancement as a teacher involvement strategy*. Paper presented at the annual meeting of the American Educational Research Association, Chicago, IL.

Dornbusch, S. M. & Scott, W. R. (1975). *Evaluation and the exercise of authority: A theory of control applied to diverse organizations*. San Francisco: Jossey-Bass.

Elmore, R. F. (1995). Structural reform and educational practice. *Educational Researcher, 24*(9), 23–26.

Elmore, R. F., Peterson, P. L. & McCarthey, S. J. (1996). *Restructuring in the classroom: Teaching, learning, and school organization*. San Francisco: Jossey-Bass.

Etzioni, A. (1964). *Modern organizations*. Englewood Cliffs, NJ: Prentice-Hall.

Etzioni, A. (1969). *The semi-professions and their organization: Teachers, nurses, social workers*. New York: Free Press.

Etzioni, A. (1993). *The spirit of community: Rights, responsibilities, and the communitarian agenda*. New York: Crown.

Etzioni, A. (1996). *The new golden rule: Community and morality in a democratic society*. New York: Basic Books.

Evans, R. (1996). *The human side of change: Reform, resistance, and the real-life problems of innovation*. San Francisco: Jossey-Bass.

Feiman-Nemser, S. (1983). Learning to teach. In L. S. Shulman & G. Sykes (Eds.), *Handbook of teaching and policy* (pp. 150–170). New York: Longman.

Feiman-Nemser, S. & Floden, R. E. (1986). The cultures of teaching. In M. W. Wittrock (Ed.), *Handbook of Research on Teaching* (3rd ed., pp. 505–526). New York: Macmillan.

Firestone, W. & Bader, B. (1992). *Redesigning teaching, professionalism, or bureaucracy?* Albany, NY: State University of New York Press.

Foster, R. (1997, March). *Leadership in a selected exemplary secondary school community*. Paper presented at the annual meeting of the American Educational Research Association, Chicago.

Friedson, E. (1986). *Professional powers: A study of the institutionalization of formal knowledge*. Chicago: University of Chicago Press.

Fullan, M. (1991). *The new meaning of educational change* (2nd ed.). New York: Teachers College Press.

Fullan, M. (1995). The school as a learning organization: Distant dreams. *Theory Into Practice, 34*(4), 230–235.

Furstenberg, F. F., Jr. & Hughes, M. E. (1995). Social capital and successful development among at-risk youth. *Journal of Marriage and the Family, 57*, 580–592.

Gambetta, D. (Ed.) (1988). *Trust: Making and breaking cooperative relations*. New York: B. Blackwell.

Goldring, E. B. & Rallis, S. F. (1993). *Principals of dynamic schools: Taking charge of change*. Newbury Park, CA: Corwin.

Granovetter, M. S. (1973). The strength of weak ties. *American Journal of Sociology, 78*, 1360–1380.

Grimmett, P. P. & Crehan, E. P. (1992). The nature of collegiality in teacher development: The case of clinical supervision. In M. Fullan & A. Hargreaves (Eds.), *Teacher development and educational change* (pp. 56–85). Washington, DC: Falmer.

Grossman, P. L. (1992). Teaching to learn. In A. Lieberman (Ed.), *The changing contexts of teaching* (91st Yearbook of the National Society for the Study of Education, Part I, pp. 179–196). Chicago: University of Chicago Press.

Guy, M. E. (1985). *Professionals in organizations: Debunking a myth*. New York: Praeger.

Hagan, J., MacMillan, R. & Wheaton, B. (1996). New kid in town: Social capital and the life course effects of family migration on children. *American Sociological Review, 61*, 368–385.

Hargreaves, A. (1989). *Contrived collegiality and the culture of teaching*. Paper presented at the meeting of the Canadian Society for the Study of Education, Quebec City.

Hargreaves, A. & Dawe, R. (1989). *Coaching as unreflective practice: Contrived collegiality or collaborative culture?* Paper presented at the meeting of the American Educational Research Association, San Francisco.

Hart, A. W. (1988). A career ladder's effect on teacher career and work attitudes. *American Educational Research Journal, 24,* 479–504.

Hart, A. W. (1990). Impacts of the school social unit on teacher authority during work redesign. *American Educational Research Journal, 27,* 503–532.

Hart, A. W. (1991). Leader succession and socialization. *Review of Educational Research, 61,* 451–474.

Hart, A. W. (1993). *Principal succession: Establishing leadership in schools.* Albany: State University of New York Press.

Hart, A. W. (1995). Reconceiving school leadership: Emergent views. *Elementary School Journal, 96,* 9–28.

Heller, M. F. & Firestone, W. A. (1995). Who's in charge here? Sources for change in eight schools. *Elementary School Journal, 96,* 65–86.

Hollander, E. P. (1979). Leadership and social exchange processes. In K. Gergen, M. S. Greenberg & R. H. Willis (Eds.), *Social exchange: Advances in theory and research.* New York: Winston-John Wiley.

Homans, G. C. (1958). Social behavior as exchange. *American Journal of Sociology, 63,* 597–606.

Jacobs, T. O. (1970). *Leadership and exchange in formal organizations.* Alexandria, VA: Human Resources Research Organization.

Janis, I. L. (1983). *Groupthink: Psychological studies of policy decisions and fiascoes* (2nd ed.). Boston: Houghton Mifflin.

Jarvis, P. (1987). *Adult learning in social context.* London: Croom Helm.

Johnson, S. M. (1990). *Teachers at work: Achieving success in our schools.* New York: Basic Books.

Jones, G. R. (1983). Transaction costs, property rights, and organizational culture: An exchange perspective. *Administrative Science Quarterly, 28,* 454–467.

Katz, D. & Kahn, R. L. (1978). *The social psychology of organizations* (2nd ed.). New York: Wiley.

Kruse, S. & Louis, K. S. (1995). Developing professional community in new and restructuring schools. In K. S. Louis, S. Kruse & Associates, *Professionalism and community: Perspectives on reforming urban schools* (pp. 187–207). Thousand Oaks, CA: Corwin.

Lambert, L., Walker, D., Zimmerman, D. P., Cooper, J. E., Lambert, M. D., Gardner, M. E. & Slack, P. J. (1995). *Constructivist leader.* New York: Teachers College Press.

Leithwood, K. (1994). Leadership for school restructuring. *Educational Administration Quarterly, 30,* 498–518.

Leithwood, K. A. & Montgomery, D. J. (1982). The role of the elementary school principal in program improvement. *Review of Educational Research, 52,* 309–339.

Leithwood, K. A. & Steinbach, R. (1995). *Expert problem solving: Evidence from school and district leaders.* Albany: State University of New York Press.

Levine, D. U. (1992). Implementation of an urban school-within-a-school approach. In H. C. Waxman, J. W. de Felix, J. E. Anderson & H. P. Baptiste, Jr. (Eds.), *Students at risk in at-risk schools* (pp. 233–249). Newbury Park, CA: Corwin.

Lieberman, A. & Miller, L. (1984). *Teachers, their world, and their work.* Alexandria, VA: Association for Supervision and Curriculum Development.

Lieberman, A. & Miller, L. (Eds.) (1991). *Staff development for the 90s.* New York: Teachers College Press.

Lieberman, A., Darling-Hammond, L. & Zuckerman, K. (1991a, August). *Early lessons in restructuring schools.* New York: National Center on Restructuring Education, Schools, and Teaching, Teachers College, Columbia University.

Lieberman, A., Zuckerman, K., Wilkie, A., Smith, E., Barinas, N. & Hegert, L. (1991b, August). *Early lessons in restructuring schools: Case studies of Schools of Tomorrow . . . Today.* New York: National Center on Restructuring Education, Schools, and Teaching, Teachers College, Columbia University.

Lindblom, C. E. (1993). *The science of muddling through.* New York: Irvington.

Lipsky, M. (1980). *Street-level bureaucracy: Dilemmas of the individual in public services.* New York: Russell Sage Foundation.

Little, J. W. (1982). Norms of collegiality and experimentation: Workplace conditions of school success. *American Educational Research Journal, 19,* 325–340.

Little, J. W. (1990a). The mentor phenomenon and the social organization of teaching. *Review of Research in Education, 16,* 297–351.

Little, J. W. (1990b). The persistence of privacy: Autonomy and initiative in teachers professional relations. *Teachers College Record, 91,* 509–536.

Little, J. W. (1993). Professional community in comprehensive high schools: The two worlds of academic and vocational teachers. In J. W. Little & M. W. McLaughlin (Eds.), *Teachers' work: Individuals, colleagues, and contexts* (pp. 137–163). New York: Teachers College Press.

Little, J. W. & McLaughlin, M. W. (1993a). Perspectives on cultures and contexts of teaching. In J. W. Little & M. W. McLaughlin (Eds.), *Teachers' work: Individuals, colleagues, and contexts* (pp. 1–8) New York: Teachers College Press.

Little, J. W. & McLaughlin, M. W. (Eds.) (1993b). *Teachers' work: Individuals, colleagues, and contexts.* New York: Teachers College Press.

Lortie, D. C. (1975). *Schoolteacher.* Chicago: University of Chicago Press.

Louis, K. S. & Murphy, J. (1994). The evolving role of the principal. In J. Murphy & K. S. Louis (Eds.), *Reshaping the principalship: Insights from transformational reform efforts* (pp. 265–281). Thousand Oaks, CA: Corwin.

Louis, K. S., Kruse, S. & Associates. (1995). *Professionalism and community: perspectives on reforming urban schools.* Thousand Oaks, CA: Corwin.

Louis, K. S., Kruse, S. & Marks, H. M. (1996a). School-wide professional community: Teachers work, intellectual quality and commitment. In F. W. Newmann & Associates, *Authentic achievement: Restructuring schools for intellectual quality* (pp. 179–203). San Francisco: Jossey-Bass.

Louis, K. S., Marks, H. M. & Kruse, S. (1996b). Teachers professional community in restructuring schools. *American Educational Research Journal, 33,* 757–798.

McLaughlin, M. W. (1993). What matters most in teachers workplace context? In J. W. Little & M. W. McLaughlin (Eds.), *Teachers' work: Individuals, colleagues, and contexts* (pp. 79–103). New York: Teachers College Press.

McQuillan, P. J. & Muncey, D. E. (1991, May). *School-within-a-school restructuring and faculty divisiveness: Examples from a study of the Coalition of Essential Schools* (Working Paper #6). Providence, RI: School Ethnography Project, Brown University.

March, J. G. & Simon, H. A. (1958). *Organizations.* New York: Wiley.

Marjoribanks, K. (1991). Family human and social capital and young adults educational attainment and occupational aspirations. *Psychological Reports, 69,* 237–238.

Marsick, V. J. & Watkins, K. (1990). *Informal and incidental learning in the workplace.* New York: Routledge.

Meyer, J. W. & Rowan, B. (1977). Institutionalized organizations: Formal structure as myth and ceremony. *American Journal of Sociology, 83,* 340–363.

Murphy, J. (1990). The educational reform movement of the 1980s: A comprehensive analysis. In J. Murphy (Ed.), *The educational reform movement of the 1980s: Perspectives and cases* (pp. 3–55). Berkeley, CA: McCutchan.

Murphy, J. (1991). *Restructuring schools: Capturing and assessing the phenomena.* New York: Teachers College Press.

Murphy, J. & Beck, L. G. (1995). *School-based management as school reform.* Thousand Oaks, CA: Corwin.

Newmann, F. M. & Associates (1996). *Authentic achievement: Restructuring schools for intellectual quality.* San Francisco: Jossey-Bass.

Newmann, F. M. & Wehlage, G. G. (1995). *Successful school restructuring.* Madison: Center on Organization and Restructuring of Schools, University of Wisconsin.

Nisbett, R. & Ross, L. (1980). *Human inference.* Englewood Cliffs, NJ: Prentice-Hall.

Odden, A. & Odden, E. (1994, April). *Applying the high involvement framework to local management of schools in Victoria, Australia.* Paper presented at the annual meeting of the American Educational Research Association, New Orleans, LA.

Ogawa, R. T. & Bossert, S. T. (1995). Leadership as an organizational quality. *Educational Administration Quarterly, 31,* 224–243.

Parsons, T. (1960). *Structure and process in modern societies.* New York: Free Press.

Placier, P. & Hamilton, M. L. (1994). Schools as contexts: A complex relationship. In V. Richardson (Ed.), *Teacher change and the staff development process: A case in reading instruction* (pp. 135–158). New York: Teachers College Press.

Pounder, D. G., Ogawa, R. T. & Adams, E. A. (1995). Leadership as an organization-wide phenomenon: Its impact on school performance. *Educational Administration Quarterly, 31*, 564–588.

Powell, W. W. & DiMaggio, P. J. (Eds.). (1991). *The new institutionalism in organizational analysis.* Chicago: University of Chicago Press.

Purkey, S. C. & Smith, M. S. (1983). Effective schools: A review. *Elementary School Journal, 83*, 427–453.

Putnam, R. (1993). *Making democracy work: Civic traditions in modern Italy.* Princeton, NJ: Princeton University Press.

Richardson, V. (1990). Significant and worthwhile change in teaching practice. *Educational Researcher, 19*(7), 10–18.

Richardson, V. (Ed.) (1994). *Teacher change and the staff development process: A case in reading instruction.* New York: Teachers College Press.

Rosenblum, S., Louis, K. S. & Rossmiller, R. A. (1994). School leadership and teacher quality of work life in restructuring schools. In J. Murphy & K. S. Louis (Eds.), *Reshaping the principalship: Insights from transformational reform efforts* (pp. 99–122). Thousand Oaks, CA: Corwin.

Rosenholtz, S. J. (1989). *Teachers' workplace: The social organization of schools.* New York: Longman.

Rossman, G. B., Corbett, H. D. & Firestone, W. A. (1988). *Change and effectiveness in schools: A cultural perspective.* Albany: State University of New York Press.

Rowan, B. (1990). Commitment and control: Alternative strategies for the organizational design of schools. *Review of Research in Education, 16*, 353–389.

Rowan, B., Raudenbush, S. W. & Cheong, Y. F. (1993). Teaching as a nonroutine task: Implications for the management of schools. *Educational Administration Quarterly, 29*, 479–500.

Sarason, S. B. (1990). *The predictable failure of educational reform.* San Francisco: Jossey-Bass.

Schein, E. H. (1969). The mechanisms of change. In W. G. Bennis, K. D. Benne & R. Chin (Eds.), *The planning of change* (2nd ed., pp. 98–107). New York: Holt, Rinehart & Winston.

Schein, E. H. (1988). *Organizational culture and leadership.* San Francisco: Jossey-Bass.

Schultz, T. W. (1961). Investment in human capital. *American Economic Review, 51*, 1–17.

Schunk, D. (1991). *Learning theories: An educational perspective.* New York: Merrill.

Scott, W. R. (1987). *Organizations: Rational, natural, and open systems* (2nd ed.). Englewood Cliffs, NY: Prentice-Hall.

Scott, W. R. (1995). *Institutions and organizations.* Thousand Oaks, CA: Sage.

Sleegers, P., van den Berg, R. & Geijsel, F. (1997, March). *The innovative capacity of schools and collaboration between teachers.* Paper presented at the annual meeting of the American Educational Research Association, Chicago, IL.

Smircich, L. (1983). Concepts of culture and organizational analysis. *Administrative Science Quarterly, 28*, 339–358.

Smith, P. B. & Peterson, M. F. (1988). *Leadership, organizations, and culture: An event management model.* London: Sage.

Smylie, M. A. (1989). Teachers views of the effectiveness of sources of learning to teach. *Elementary School Journal, 89*, 543–558.

Smylie, M. A. (1994). Redesigning teachers work: Connections to the classroom. *Review of Research in Education, 20*, 129–177.

Smylie, M. A. (1995). Teacher learning in the workplace. In T. R. Guskey & M. Huberman (Eds.), *Professional development in education: New paradigms and practices* (pp. 92–112). New York: Teachers College Press.

Smylie, M. A. (1996). From bureaucratic control to building human capital: The importance of teacher learning in education reform. *Educational Researcher, 25*(9), 9–11.

Smylie, M. A. (1997). Research on teacher leadership: Assessing the state of the art. In B. J. Biddle, T. Good & I. Goodson (Eds.), *International handbook of teachers and teaching.* (pp. 521–592). Dordrecht, The Netherlands: Kluwer.

Smylie, M. A. & Perry, G. S., Jr. (1998). Restructuring schools for improving teaching. In A. Hargreaves, A. Lieberman, M. Fullan & D. Hopkins (Eds.), *International handbook of educational change.* (pp. 976–1005). Dordrecht, The Netherlands: Kluwer.

Smylie, M. A., Lazarus, V. & Brownlee-Conyers, J. (1996). Instructional outcomes of school-based participative decision making. *Educational Evaluation and Policy Analysis, 18*, 181–198.

Spencer, D. A. (1984). The home and school lives of women teachers: Implications for staff development. *Elementary School Journal, 84*, 299–314.

Staessens, K. (1993). The professional relationships among teachers as a core component of school culture. In F. K. Kieviet & R. Vandenberghe (Eds.), *School culture, school improvement, and teacher development* (pp. 39–54). Leiden, Belgium: DSWO Press.

Stringfield, S. & Teddlie, C. (1991). Observers as predictors of schools multiyear outlier status on achievement tests. *Elementary School Journal, 91*, 357–376.

Strober, M. H. (1990). Human capital theory: Implications for HR managers. *Industrial Relations, 29*, 214–239.

Talbert, J. (1993). Constructing a schoolwide professional community: The negotiated order of a performing arts school. In J. W. Little & M. W. McLaughlin (Eds.), *Teachers' work: Individuals, colleagues, and contexts* (pp. 164–184). New York: Teachers College Press.

Talbert, J. E. & McLaughlin, M. W. (1993). Understanding teaching in context. In D. K. Cohen, M. W. McLaughlin & J. E. Talbert (Eds.), *Teaching for understanding: Challenges for policy and practice* (pp. 167–206). San Francisco: Jossey-Bass.

Talbert, J. E. & McLaughlin, M. W. (1994). Teacher professionalism in local school contexts. *American Journal of Education, 102*, 123–153.

Tannenbaum, A. S. (1962). Control in organizations: Individual adjustment and organizational performance. *Administrative Science Quarterly, 7*, 236–257.

Thompson, J. D. (1967). *Organizations in action.* New York: McGraw-Hill.

Useem, E. L., Christman, J. B., Gold, E. & Simon, E. (1997). Reforming alone: Barriers to organizational learning in urban school change initiatives. *Journal of Education for Students Places At Risk, 2*, 55–78.

Valenzuela, A. & Dornbusch, S. M. (1994). Familism and social capital in the academic achievement of Mexican origin and Anglo adolescents. *Social Science Quarterly, 75*, 18–36.

Vandenberghe, R. D., Hertefelt, M. & De Wever, H. (1993). Schools as implementors of an externally proposed improvement program. In F. K. Kieviet & R. Vandenberghe (Eds.), *School culture, school improvement, and teacher development* (pp. 55–76). Leiden, Belgium: DSWO Press.

Van Maanen, J. & Schein, E. H. (1979). Toward a theory of organizational socialization. In B. M. Staw (Ed.), *Research in organizational behavior* (Vol. 1, pp. 209–264). Greenwich, CT: JAI Press.

White, P. A. (1992). Teacher empowerment under ideal school-site autonomy. *Educational Evaluation and Policy Analysis, 14*, 69–82.

Wilson, B. & Corcoran, T. (1988). *Successful secondary schools: Visions of excellence in American public education.* New York: Falmer.

Wolcott, H. (1973). *The man in the principal's office: An ethnographic study.* New York: Holt, Rinehart & Winston.

Yukl, G. (1994). *Leadership in organizations* (3rd ed.). Englewood Cliffs, NJ: Prentice-Hall.

Zucker, L. G. (1987). Institutional theories of organization. *Annual Review of Sociology, 13*, 443–464.

CHAPTER 21

Integrated Services: Challenges in Linking Schools, Families, and Communities

Claire E. Smrekar and Hanne B. Mawhinney

This chapter explores conceptual and empirical work in the area of school-family-community linkages. We address this topic by examining new inter-institutional arrangements between schools and other social institutions that pose critical challenges for educational leaders; these arrangements reflect a growing demand for rethinking and reorganizing schools and the education profession to address evolutionary changes in relationships between educational institutions and society in the 21st century. The purpose is to provide a deep and inclusive overview that includes the most recent conceptual and empirical scholarship from organizational studies, education policy, sociology, political science, and cultural anthropology.

Following a brief overview of school-linked integrated services, we examine the organizational issues that impact these inter-institutional linkages. We analyze the evidence from recent initiatives that suggests that the impressive commitment to consistent and complementary goals (improved service delivery, enhanced student and family functioning) is sometimes undercut by the costs associated with forfeiture of highly valuable organizational assets, including autonomy, authority, and control (Crowson & Boyd, 1993; Cunningham, 1990; Kirst, 1991; Mawhinney & Smrekar, 1996; Melaville & Blank, 1991; Smylie, Crowson, Hare, & Levin, 1993; Wilson, 1989).

The next section explores socio-cultural bridges in coordinated services. The issue of cultural (dis)continuity (Connell, Ashenden, Kessler, & Dowsett, 1982; Delpit, 1995; Heath, 1983) provides the conceptual backdrop for recent work that focuses on governance structures that widen the chasms between socially and ethnically diverse families and schools (Capper, 1996; Delgado-Gaitan,

1991). The issues of authenticity and cultural knowledge are central to the questions: Whose norms, values, and traditions are celebrated in public schools? How do these expectations influence patterns of family-school-community interactions? We examine the conditions that promote strong linkages between parents and schools, including communication networks, shared values and beliefs, a sense of caring, community, and commitment, and collaboration (Delgado-Gaitan, 1991; Driscoll, 1995; Epstein, 1995; Raywid, 1988).

Following this section, we assess the political constraints upon coordinated services that indicate the need to recast inter-institutional and inter-professional collaborations around a community development orientation (Cibulka, 1996; Timpane & Reich, 1997; White & Wehlage, 1995).

We conclude with a set of challenges and dilemmas designed to provoke conversation and creative action among educational leaders around the issue of coordinated services for children.

An Overview of School-Linked Integrated Services

An increasing number of states and localities have recently developed initiatives designed to address fragmentation issues in the delivery of social services for children and their families. Many of these efforts have targeted public schools as the nexus for linkages among education, health, employment, and recreation agencies. The rationale for using schools as the linkage point is found in their unique relationship with students and families. Schools provide the organizational context for the most sustained and ongoing contact with children outside the family setting. This unique position can be utilized to establish a process of problem identification and treatment.

The impetus for greater coordination and collaboration among human service agencies is driven by a growing realization that many children face a complex set of overlapping and interrelated problems. An ecological perspective reinforced by a better understanding of the context of children's lives is expected to result in improved care and enhanced student performance. In addition to these compelling arguments, the notion of using schools as the linchpin for family services resonates with systemic education reform efforts aimed at addressing school, community, and state-level demands and expectations.

Implicit in the discussion and design of school-linked social services is the recognition that changed family patterns, demographics, and economic realities have created discontinuities between the needs of students and the abilities of both schools and families to meet them. Households of two employed parents, single parents, or transient family members predominate across many parts of the nation. Today, one in five children lives in poverty (U.S. Bureau of the Census, 1993). Many of these families are desperately poor, with incomes less than half the federal poverty level (Zill & Nord, 1994). More and more families, dispirited and discouraged by the conditions of their lives, struggle to survive in communities where poverty, unemployment, alienation, and violence are commonplace. These conditions demand new conceptualizations of the integration of systems and services as resources for children and their families.

Although highly variable in program scope and administrative scale, there is a broad and enduring appeal shared among states and local communities for using service and organizational integration as a tool for addressing the multiple needs of students and their families. Illustrative models range from statewide initiatives, to city- and county-led projects, to more modest individual site experiments. The Cities in Schools program is involved in over 200 local school sites and features coordinated health, educational, and social services delivered to students enrolled in public schools. The New Jersey Department of Human Services funds school-based projects that offer employment counseling, drug and alcohol abuse counseling, health services, and recreation services for the 5,000 students enrolled in the New Brunswick Public Schools. Kentucky's Family Resource Centers serve over 500 schools and are based upon a local needs assessment model that provides wide discretion in providing school-linked services to students and their families (Interagency Task Force, 1990). To be sure, the alarming statistics that declared the condition of families and the social systems that serve them in crisis (see Na-

tional Commission on Children, 1991) prompted an emphatic response from policymakers regarding the promise of integrated services.

The next section provides a contemporary context for current debates around school-linked services.[1] The pressing momentum and pace with which local communities, state legislatures, policymakers, and educational leaders are promoting school-linked social services underscore our interest in these issues.

Alarm and Reaction: The Genesis of the Movement

Clustered together with numerous other educational and social reforms of the past decade, the idea of school-linked social services dates back 100 years or more (Tyack, 1992). Conceived during a period of vast social, political, and economic upheaval, the "child-saving" impulses of the Progressive-era philanthropist-reformers coalesced in a broad effort to link schools and social service delivery through a number of targeted initiatives, including health and mental health programs, nutrition and housing assistance, and employment training (Sedlak & Schlossman, 1985). These efforts found their models in the settlement houses of the early 1900s and targeted impoverished immigrant families in urban schools. The schools were considered a natural place to "house" the services because of the sustained contact schools enjoyed with a "captive audience" (Tyack, 1992). Over time, the role and function of school-based social services were transformed as the private organizations that had shepherded the programs were replaced by public bureaucracies. Visiting teachers, who once had enjoyed relative autonomy within the school system by operating as family advocates, were subsumed into the administrative priorities of burgeoning bureaucratic school systems; as reconstituted school social workers, their jobs shifted to enforcing compulsory school attendance and monitoring truancy. Although the Community Schools movement launched in the 1930s (and revived briefly in the 1970s through federal legislation) recalled some of the school-as-community-center focus of earlier periods, this model took hold in only about 10 percent of the nation's schools (Kagan, 1993).

The 1960s and the War on Poverty echoed many of the family-focused efforts of earlier school reforms by establishing new initiatives that targeted particular groups for compensatory aid. These programs included education, health and mental health, nutrition, and counseling, but they were markedly more categorical than coordinated and, by their very bureaucratic nature, failed to deliver services in any comprehensive way.

In the 1970s, the mold was cracked with the Cities in Schools program. Cities in Schools is based on a coordinated and integrated model that views problems of abuse, neglect, undernourishment, and emotional stress as inter-related problems that may occur outside of school but affect in-school performance. Still one of the largest national, school-based, comprehensive delivery models in the country today, this program supports dropout prevention initiatives in over 200 school sites across the U.S. (McLaughlin & Smrekar, 1988).

The Children's Agenda and the Integrated Services Movement

A persistent pattern of "categorical drift" across education and human services toward isolation and division in serving children and families in need prompted an alliance of foundations, policymakers, and service professionals to move aggressively in the late 1980s to remake the system of services for families and children. Armed with an initial grant from the Ford Foundation,[2] the National Association of State Boards of Education (NASBE) launched the "Joining Forces" initiative to build collaborative relationships between education and human service agencies that serve children and families at risk (Levy & Copple, 1989). The kickoff conference at Wingspread in 1988 attracted state policymakers and representatives from several national organizations, including the National Governors Association, the Council of Chief State School Officers, the Education Commission of the States, and the American Public Welfare Association. The Executive Director of NASBE, Gene Wilhoit, issued a call to create a "children's agenda" through a coordinated network of services for children and youth to replace the "seriously flawed" public and private system in place. One year later, the report from the Joining Forces staff indicated a widespread, if measured, response by states, localities, foundations, and professional organizations (the Council of Chief State School Officers [Council, 1992]) to the fledgling coordinated services effort. Interagency agreements, co-located social services, state-level children's commissions, and special legislative committees on children reflected a general interest by policymakers and professional groups to express both symbolically and substantively a concern for children and youth (Smrekar, 1989). NASBE noted the progress with some caution (Levy & Copple, 1989):

> Much of the interagency cooperation and collaboration which is now occurring is relatively small in scale and of a single-venture nature, existing outside normal operations and frequently relying on short-term funding or the strenuous efforts of a few highly motivated individuals. Nonetheless, by building knowledge, trust, and mutual understanding, these efforts show what systems can achieve when they work together, and lay the foundation for future action (p. 8).

Four years later, Yale University researcher Sharon Lynn Kagan (1993) documented the growth of the Integrated Services movement by noting that school-linked social service ventures were "blossoming across the country from Maine to California" (p. 78). Kagan observed:

> More than 800 such efforts have been chronicled by Joining Forces . . . numerous efforts are underway to cross-fertilize information in the field, with the Department of Health and Human Services sponsoring a major technical assistance strategy. How-to volumes are proliferating, as are state-of-the-art reports. What is missing (though in progress) are firm evaluations of the efficacy of school-based and school-linked service integration (p. 78).

The rapid growth in integrated, school-based services (in the absence of documented results) can be measured in the vast dissemination of reports, conference proceedings, and guidelines for state and localities that followed the Wingspread conference in 1988. The movement gained legitimacy and visibility when several states, including New Jersey in 1988,[3] Kentucky in 1990 (Kentucky Education Reform Act, 1990), and California in 1991,[4] established statewide integrated service programs.

Organizational Constraints and Dilemmas

Coordination of services is one of the principal thrusts in the reemergence of interest in improving the working relationships among schools, families, and communities (Cibulka, 1996). Accounts of the history of schooling confirm that there have been numerous reinventions of these relationships over the past century (Tyack, 1992). Along with the impetus to increase coordination with schools of services supporting children and families, the current movement to rethink school, community, and family connections includes contradictory impulses for increased accountability by local principals, parental choice, empowerment, and increased local control. In a recent review of the state of coordinated services, James Cibulka (1996) observes that these impulses are so diverse as to hardly constitute a social movement. It is a movement only in that "it shares in common primarily what it opposes (the status quo) rather than what it stands for" (p. 404). Indeed, efforts to create new links among schools, families, and communities revisit tensions in the "American political system for which historically there has been no clear resolution" (p. 405).

Cibulka identifies four tensions that constrain current coordinated services efforts in education and in other social policy arenas. A tension that impedes clear support for coordinated service models arises between different visions of the proper role of schooling captured in questions like: Should schools acknowledge the ecological nature of child development and fulfill a social role reaching out into community agencies for support, or should schools stick to their academic purposes? A second tension arises over competing conceptions of the appropriate and relative influence of laypersons and professionals: What is the role of lay citizenry in service provision, especially in relation to professional authority and autonomy? The third tension bedeviling school-linked coordinated services initiatives arises over conflicting assumptions about the extent of the specific protection that should be offered to children and families in a modern welfare state: How broad should the safety net be and what mix of public and private provision should define the institutional characteristics of the safety net? A fourth tension, one arising from the competition among values in the larger political culture, fragments the coordinated services movement around the question: Should efficiency be a prime goal in organizing services, or should equality of opportunity or outcome be a paramount goal?

The organizational dilemmas created by the intersection of the competing forces animating all these tensions are complex. In his introduction to a recent comprehensive review of current research, Kritek (1996) illustrates the complexity of the dilemmas evident when initiatives linking schools and community are held out as a means of providing more effective and more efficient services. There is some evidence from research that third wave school-linked collaborative programs may provide effective preventative services (Schorr, 1993). Kritek observes:

> However, coordination itself may have some costs in the form of additional staff and other resources. Further, improved effectiveness and efficiency may lead to greater utilization of services and thus greater total costs. On the other hand, while these services are expensive, it may also be possible to show that programs such as those that have a prevention emphasis reduce the need for additional services in the long run (p. xviii).

The assumption is that collaboration between schools and community agencies will result in more efficient and effective services for children. Researchers who examined efforts undertaken in previous decades to link schools to community agencies are skeptical of claims of increased efficiency and effectiveness. After reviewing policy efforts at service coordination in the 1970s, Townsend (1980) concluded many were "overly abstract, rational, and panacea-minded" (p. 499) initiatives that failed to produce improvements in outcomes such as student success in school. Other researchers concluded that these past efforts showed that sustained collaboration among schools and other organizations will raise complex and subtle organizational dilemmas associated with communication, control, and power (Mawhinney, 1994).

Assessments of the current wave of efforts to link schools confirm these conclusions. Recent reinventions demand a qualitative increase in the extent to which schools become open systems that elicit the support of the community and other service providers (Stefkovich & Guba,

1994). Crowson and Boyd (1993) observe that by the early 1990s proponents of coordinated services for children and families had begun to develop "a growing base of practical savvy about what works and what does not" (p. 141).

Organizational Issues in Collaborative Programs

Practical understanding has not, however, explained "the complexities and deeper organizational issues implicated in collaborative ventures" (Crowson & Boyd, 1993, p. 141). Indeed, one of the concerns of researchers is that practical understanding has preceded the development of a rich knowledge base of research on collaborative initiatives (Crowson & Boyd, 1995). Much of the handbook and guide literature has been characterized as being of an advocacy genre (White & Wehlage, 1995). Michael Knapp's (1995) review of the state of research on collaborative services underscored the need for a new generation of conceptually informed research; this is all the more urgent because the burgeoning advocacy literature threatens to overwhelm policymaking. This problem arises because efforts to create new links between schools and other services have only recently been explored in research focused on organizational issues in educational administration (Adler & Gardner, 1993; Cibulka & Kritek, 1996). Although the *Handbook of Research on Educational Administration* (Boyan, 1988) did offer some scholarly reflection on the organizational dilemmas of school-community links, the organizational issues arising in school-linked, integrated services were not a specific focus of attention. As a result, knowledge about the organizational constraints to school-linked integrated services is relatively incomplete.

Until recently, researchers tended to view the problem of school-community links as one associated with environmental tensions and the need for educators to buffer the school organization from the community. For example, E. Mark Hanson (1979) included among the techniques typically used by educators in buffering the school from its community: "strategic stalling, denying jurisdiction, and strategic ignoring" (pp. 369–370). School organizations were typically viewed as responding to environmental (community) pressures defensively, in ways which isolated the technology of schooling. At the same time, scholars of educational administration acknowledged the profoundly political nature of local school-community relations (Burlingame, 1988). Changes in conceptions of this political nature were noted in a comprehensive examination of school-community relations by Robert Crowson (1992), who observed that:

> While the organizational structures of public schooling reflect environmental pressures, they also influence the nature of those environments and those pressures. At the same time the schools defend a boundary between institution and environment, they

must pay attention to the quality of their fit with that environment (p. 99).

Crowson (1992) concluded that "there is relatively little information on how the internal institutional characteristics of schools can influence their external environments" (p. 97). In their research on school-linked services, Crowson and Boyd (1993) argued that much more must be learned about the complexities and "deeper organizational issues implicated in collaborative ventures" (p. 141). In the intervening years, researchers have built a small but conceptually rich body of research on organizational and managerial issues drawing from institutional theory (Crowson & Boyd, 1993, 1995, 1996; Mawhinney, 1994, 1996; Mawhinney & Smrekar, 1996; Smylie, Crowson, Chou, & Levin, 1996; Smrekar, 1996a), intergovernmental relations (Herrington, 1996), professional and institutional perspectives (Mitchell & Scott, 1994), conceptions of power relations (Corbett, Wilson, & Webb, 1996), sociological theories of community (Furman & Merz, 1996), organizational theory (Shaver, Golan, & Wagner, 1996), critical perspectives (Capper, 1996), and multiple frameworks (McClure, Jones, & Potter, 1996).

Dimensions of Organizational Functioning

The resulting research explores dilemmas that touch the dimensions described by Bolman and Deal (1991) as pivotal to organizational functioning: structures, people, politics, and symbols. The themes and conclusions offered inform understanding of organizational dilemmas at play in each of the key dimensions of service integration identified in a recent Organization for Economic Cooperation and Development (OECD) report (Hurrell & Evans, 1996) on the ways in which many countries are moving towards the coordination and integration of their human services to meet the needs of children and families said to be at risk:

- The structures in place (such as cooperative agreements, coordinating bodies);
- The mechanisms that operate (case conferences);
- The physical location of the actors and structures (inside or outside schools); and
- The actors involved (education, health, or social welfare professionals) (Hurrell & Evans, 1996, pp. 79–80).

Taking a more focused orientation, Crowson and Boyd (1993) regroup these dimensions into exemplars of collaboration differing in:

(a) locus of initiation (such as state-level or local, government, or private foundation);
(b) scope of involvement of agencies (multi-site or single site); and
(c) specificity of targeted services.

Reviewing varieties of contemporary coordinated initiatives produces an array of initiatives ranging from state-level social service coordination, to citywide and countrywide initiatives, to neighborhood and school-site experimentation. A number of paradoxes of scale, hierarchy, deep-structural change, and goal attainment are implied in these dimensions. Crowson and Boyd (1995) suggest, for example:

> One of the many paradoxes (constraints) in children's services coordination is the observation that the comprehensive involvement of a multitude of agencies across a variety of localities and levels has an attractive ring of efficiency and systemic change to it, while more modest projects may more readily attain limited goals but with little basic alteration of the overarching service-delivery "system." The involvement of numerous agencies can make the actual process of collaboration quite cumbersome, inflexible, and hierarchical; but modest projects, less hierarchical and more flexible, can tend to remain on the periphery of deeply structured change (p. 20).

Also paradoxical is the evidence that policy frameworks, regardless of their scope, have not been able to penetrate the organizational structures of schools enough to create the conditions for effective collaboration. Debate over the relative effectiveness of school-based, school-linked, or community-based approaches highlights the importance of consideration of locus of the initiative. Studies examining the organizational implications of the different approaches report that while school-based initiatives tend to be dominated by institutional controls of schools, community-based models incorporate a wider diversity of resources but lose some focus in negotiating among diverse stakeholders (Chaskin & Richman, 1992).

Administrative Problems and Issues

Despite the diversity of the approaches to service integration, many reports have identified commonalties in administrative problems and issues. Crowson and Boyd (1993) observe that the integration of services poses organizational problems associated with the indeterminacies of added funding: the problems of space, facilities management, and differing personnel and salary policies; the negotiation of new roles and relationships; the need to nurture effective leadership; the necessity for careful planning; the challenge of professional preparation programs and professional procedures with few links between them; and the issues of communication, confidentiality, and information retrieval.

Although there is considerable evidence that these problems plague efforts at service integration, there is also evidence of fewer problems in those initiatives that do not attempt to move toward integration but rather maintain parallel programming, effectively maintaining the separate institutional organizations intact. Herrington (1996) found that superintendents and school administrators involved in intergovernmental programming reported no substantial political or public relations problems. She explains that "the professional culture and norms, the standard operating procedures, and the behaviors of the new members to the school community may be tolerated as long as none challenges the existing accommodations negotiated among the core school personnel, i.e., the instructional staff and the school leadership" (p. 217).

One of the important contributions of current research on integrated services is the range of conceptually informed explanations of the lack of reaction to initiatives that do not intrude into the institutional conventions of the schools. In the next section, we examine several dilemmas, which have been raised by research. We examine organizational dilemmas of bureaucratic capture, structures and processes, constraining institutional effects of decoupling structural elements, and professional-lay relationships in school-linked service coordination.

Dilemmas of Bureaucratic Capture

Furman and Merz (1996) argue that one of the paradoxes of the school-linked integrated services movement is that most structures and processes involved reflect the characteristics of bureaucratic responses to problems that have not typically generated the intimacy, trust, and sense of belonging which guidelines for implementing collaborations frequently mention as important indicators of success. Furman and Merz suggest that interagency collaboration will not significantly change the existing, weakened linkages between schools and communities. Further, it is unlikely that collaborations will change the tendency for a bureaucratic, centralized school organization to be alienated from the governance and influence of the local community.

Three themes emerging from research on collaborative initiatives underscore the bureaucratic nature of interagency collaboration. One theme commonly reported is the need for new collaborative initiatives to develop new roles or expand existing ones in the organizations involved. A second theme in research suggests that the formalization of these new roles and new professions through specialized training flows from the demands collaboration places on organizations to engage in strategic planning typically beyond the work assignments of the individuals involved (Crowson & Boyd, 1993). To support these added responsibilities, additional resources and new money must be found (Kirst & McLaughlin, 1990). A third theme in research supports the claim that the bureaucratization of interagency collaboration has resulted in the use of the language of professionalization to define the new roles of professionals and the services that they provide their clients. Furman and Merz (1996) argue that expansion of

bureaucracies by which professionals serve clients is more resonant with ideas of control to ensure social stability than with gemeinschaft values of intimacy, trust, and belonging.

The dilemma is evident. Although successful collaboration initiatives are organized to empower families, actively involving them in identifying their needs, there is nothing in the typically bureaucratic organization of interagency collaborations to ensure a focus on personalization. Researchers concur that coordinated systems can lead to the centralization of services and a focus on organizational goals, constraining choices for clients, while also decreasing financial efficiencies by increasing access and demand for services (Kahne & Kelley, 1993; Capper, 1996). We next outline some of the reasons, suggested by researchers using an institutional frame of analysis, for this bureaucratic capture and some of the dilemmas of structure and processes that integration of services creates for organizations.

Dilemmas of Structure and Processes

In this era of rethinking linkages among schools, families, and communities, it is important to consider that the organizational challenges associated with school-linked services derive from dilemmas of changing institutional structures. Many reports on initial efforts at collaboration conclude that the structures and processes adopted depend on local context. Guthrie and Guthrie (1991) suggest that this reality posed dilemmas for any efforts to identify "effective" models of collaboration because "the strategy that helps collaboration in one community may not apply in the next; and the set of agencies involved, or how they connect with schools, may differ from community to community" (p. 17). The impact of contextual forces raises questions about the viability of identifying models of school-linked services along consistent organizational dimensions. A number of conceptual thrusts have been taken to frame such dimensions. Wang, Haertel, and Walberg (1992) undertook comparative analyses of service coordination efforts that differ in their programmatic goals and program outcomes. Others have examined differences in institutional structures and processes. Hord (1986) and Intriligator (1992) suggest that interagency collaboration can be examined along a continuum of cooperation to collaboration. More recently, Crowson and Boyd (1996) specify that:

> In cooperation, the independence of individual agencies may be little affected, changes in institutional policy and structure are minimal, and "turf" is not a serious issue. Under collaboration (at the other end of the continuum), however, there will be a loss of institutional autonomy, interagency policymaking in place of agency independence, and a need to go beyond turf toward consensus and well-established trust (pp. 140–141).

Using this continuum, Crowson and Boyd (1996) suggest that experiments in children's services coordination can be examined as a point along a continuum from little to no integration of services to a collaborative ideal in the integration of services. They point out, however, that "while a thorough understanding of struggling-toward-collaboration processes is vitally important, it is also vital to understand the complexities of institutional structure that come into play in collaborative ventures" (p. 150). Four interorganizational domains of collaboration are proposed by Crowson and Boyd's (1996) Institutional Continua:

1. Convening processes reflecting a continua from separate institutional goals to shared institutional goals;
2. Institutional interests and reward systems from institutionally separate interests to shared collaborative interests;
3. Institutional environments on a continua from institutionally separate adaptation to a shared environmentalization; and
4. Institutional conventions ranging from institutionally separate conventions to shared collaborative conventions (p. 151).

The Institutional Continua outlined by Crowson and Boyd has provided researchers and policymakers with important benchmarks for analysis and policymaking geared to identifying key institutional constraints such as conflicting reward systems, differing norms and conventions, and professional training differences. At the same time, they conclude that most collaborative efforts involve strategic interventions pragmatically moving toward a goal of coordination and problem-solving as the project unfolds. In the next section, we show how actual strategic interventions can be interpreted using concepts from new institutional theories of organization.

Dilemmas of Constraining Institutional Effects

Researchers, taking an institutional orientation to their analysis, question the assumption of collaborative initiatives that schools are changeable if sufficient support is provided. Institutional theories lead researchers to examine patterns of persistence created by the coherence and structuring of organizational relationships (Scott, 1995). Researchers using this conceptual perspective have found that organizational order is powerfully constructed not only through controls and rewards but also through deep structural patterns of power-relations, norms, symbols, rituals and ceremonies, typical patterns of time-usage, and career paths. They report that the "constant and repetitive quality of much organized life is explicable not simply by reference to individual, maximizing actors, but rather by a view that locates the persistence of practices in both their taken-for-granted quality and their reproduction in structures that are to some extent self-sustaining" (DiMaggio & Powell, 1991, p. 9).

The resistance to changing practices to accommodate the demands of coordination noted by Herrington (1996) and others (Mawhinney, 1996; Mawhinney & Smrekar, 1996) reflects the persistence of existing organizational structures and practices. Smylie, Crowson, Chou, and Levin (1996), reporting on their examination of community-school connections in Chicago's decentralized schools, found that principals play a key role in buffering schools to ensure persistence of institutional arrangements using "tried-and-true administrative devices, such as avoidance, insulation, problem separation, rule and role redefinition, and ambiguity" (p. 179). They report that coordinated services projects created new expectations for schools and introduced new actors into buildings. These changes led to "increased organizational demands, ambiguities, potential loss of control, and indeed greater responsibilities for principals" (p. 184). Principals in their study acted consciously and strategically employed several different control strategies:

> They established communication and reporting systems to stay informed of project activities. They also began to micromanage project activities in their schools. The principals took on the role of gatekeeper to regulate project personnel access and activity in the buildings. Finally, they worked in different ways to influence the agendas of project activities and monitor and influence the work of project staff (p. 185).

Crowson and Boyd (1996) argue that a key task in moving toward collaboration involves overcoming the limitations imposed by the effects of such institutional interests that emphasize protecting jobs, budgets, programs, facilities, "turf," and enrollments. These findings confirm the powerful tendencies to persistence and reproduction of institutional patterns in the face of pressure to collaborate. Order and coherence, derived from institutional conventions, convey meaning and a sense of historical continuity to individuals within an organization. Embedded, taken-for-granted rules and routines are evidenced in the institutional scripts that limit collaborative initiatives to those that fall within a school's zone of acceptable action (Zucker, 1987).

In their exploration of the potential of new institutional theorizing for understanding the paradoxes of coordinated services, Crowson and Boyd (1995) describe the constraining effects of the institutional forces of fragmentation that are unleashed to protect the "technical core" activities of schools. They cite Zucker (1987) in arguing that schools pressured to collaborate will respond by protecting technical activities "through decoupling elements of structure from other activities and from each other, thus reducing their efficiency" (p. 445). Paradoxically, individuals engaged in collaborative efforts may find their initiatives are more loosely coupled with the technical core activities of the school, not less. The decoupling effects described by

Crowson and Boyd are similar to those which Tyack (1992) attributes to the tendency of schools to "pedagogize" any innovations in children's service delivery by absorbing them into the institutional practices of schooling.

Other researchers have found similar fragmentation effects to the services-coordination on the organizational periphery (Crowson & Boyd, 1995). In their study of school-linked programs in schools in Houston and Chicago, Smylie, Crowson, Chou, and Levin (1996) observed the fragmenting and decoupling of the activities of family advocates who, as residents of local communities, were used as outreach personnel. Mawhinney and Smrekar (1996) report that the character and content of family-school interactions in Family Resource Centers (FRCs) in Kentucky show patterns of social distance also reported in research on relationships between teachers and parents (Lightfoot, 1978; McPherson, 1972; Waller, 1932). This social distance between parents and teachers is mediated by FRCs that disconnect the school symbolically and physically in order to establish new and expanded bands of communication with families. Mawhinney and Smrekar (1996) conclude that in the context of schools as places where parents go when there is a problem and, once there, feel uncomfortable or intimidated by school officials, the FRCs work to balance a strategy of disassociation as a way of promoting deep and enduring connections with families.

The dilemmas arise from the scripting processes that Mitchell and Scott (1994) refer to as "typification" and "thematization" (p. 81). Typifications are the taken-for-granted rules that are wound together through "thematization" into a "meaningful story of action, responsibility, and purpose" (p. 81). Thematization often protects the core technical activities of the school from the pressures of disturbances to existing scripts. Crowson and Boyd (1995) describe this effect as one of decoupling elements of structure from each other. Specifying the underlying paradox, they conclude: "It would not be unlikely for us to find that organizations pressed to collaborate will tend to respond by becoming even more fragmented and more loosely coupled, not less" (p. 8).

At the same time, researchers have found that some schools do engage in collaborative initiatives. Despite the constraints imposed by institutional patterns, some schools do change structural elements to facilitate collaboration. Mawhinney (1996) documents movement towards institutionalizing collaborative structures and processes despite the persistence of institutional patterns in her case study of a coordinated service action in a high school. She concludes that the institutional change required to produce collaboration occurs through a broad array of adaptive processes. Structural change depends upon positive feedback from incremental adjustments. However, structural changes required to produce collaborative initiatives can be generated through strategic decisions by educational leaders. Ulti-

mately, however, those decisions are constrained by the institutional environment in which schools are embedded.

Dilemmas of Professional-Lay Relationships in School-Linked Services

The tensions characterizing current professional-lay relationships in coordinated service initiatives are multi-layered. Cibulka (1996) points out that these tensions are rooted in conflicting knowledge bases about children and communities and in the separate role interests of professionals working in an organization designed to support those interests. Professionals typically respond to initiatives to collaborate with a constrained responsiveness defined by the norms of their schools. However, in other research we have reported evidence that suggests that despite institutional pressures for a constrained responsiveness, some teachers and agency personnel do go beyond scripted roles to form tighter links with children and families in their communities (Mawhinney & Smrekar, 1996). We documented the efforts of two professionals who acted as institutional entrepreneurs in transforming the formerly fuzzy boundaries between the private lives of families and the public responsibilities of school professionals. We noted, however, that this transformation is enhanced, in the case of the Kentucky Family Resource Center, by the comprehensive Kentucky policy model that mandates new and expanded roles for schools in addressing the relationship between family functioning and educational success. Under these imperatives, the organizational focus of schools shifts from problem-identification to problem-solving. The roles, rules, and rituals that formerly defined the universe of expectations and experiences for families in their interactions with schools shift in a school culture of advocacy, information exchange, and intervention.

These effects do not rely solely on the impetus provided by organizational imperatives to coordination defined and supported in policy. Local models of school-linked service coordination can enable institutional actors to challenge existing scripts setting out a constrained responsiveness to collaboration. The efforts of institutional entrepreneurs in schools to collaborate with community agencies can define new roles, relationships, and rituals and can create new conceptions of the legitimate scope of school-community links. We conclude that small efforts by such institutional entrepreneurs may "infect other elements in a contagion of legitimacy" (Zucker, 1987, p. 446). However, significant collaboration requires the "infection of legitimacy that develops through state-level coordination, interprofessional university training, some federal attention to services coordination, and an overall thrust nationally (politically and ideologically) towards the service-coordination concept" (Crowson & Boyd, 1995, p. 21).

A review of past efforts, policy debates, and implementation strategies provides a valuable record for assessing the promises and challenges of linking schools and social services. These arrangements may create intraorganizational conflicts that are as intensive as the inter-organizational strife triggered by demands for coordination and support between schools and human service agencies. The saliency of authority and accountability in schooling, coupled with the pressing pace with which states and local communities are moving toward the implementation of school-linked integrated services, underscore the importance of addressing these organizational constraints.

Policy Implications of the Organizational Threats to School-Linked Integrated Services

This review of school-linked service initiatives suggests that the impressive commitment to consistent and complementary goals (improved service delivery, enhanced pupil/family functioning) is sometimes undercut by the political costs associated with forfeiture of highly valuable organizational assets.[5] The politics of inter-organizational linkages involve the redistribution and appropriation of critical organizational resources, including prestige, identity, and status. The competition for power and autonomy and the struggle over turf and program authority create patterns of implementation that are uneven, contested, and often bleak (Crowson & Boyd, 1993; Cunningham, 1990; Kirst, 1991; Wilson, 1989).

A growing consensus among policymakers, educators, and children's advocates indicates the need to recast inter-professional collaborations and service integration initiatives around the following goals: child-focused, family-centered, consumer-guided, and community-development-oriented (Lawson & Hooper-Briar, 1994). The emphasis here rests with relational processes as opposed to our historical leanings toward categorical thinking. This shift has led to exceptional models of interdisciplinary university training programs that should direct future professional development and educational policy efforts.[6] As Knapp, Barnard, Brandon, Gehrke, Smith, & Teather (1994) observe, university programs continue to grapple with problems of collaboration and professional norms. Nevertheless, pre-professional training and education may begin to erode the institutional constraints and organizational barriers highlighted in Kentucky in the direction toward truly integrated professional networks (Mawhinney & Smrekar, 1994).

The final rejoinder to the turf wars and budget battles waged between family resource center directors and school principals can be found in the robust, fully realized alliance between the New York City Children's Aid Society (CAS) and the New York City school system. Intermediate School 218, located in Washington Heights, is the culmination of four years of careful planning, dedication, and trust among the school district personnel and the CAS staff. Chartered in 1992 with an annual budget of about $800,000 to support a family resource center, a medical and dental clinic, extensive before- and after-school programs, and community educational institutes, IS 218 is truly "an excellent example of comprehensive school-based programming" (Dryfoos, 1994, p. 100). But more impressive than the abundant resources available at IS 218 is the absence of insidious intra-organizational hassles noted in earlier reports of other school-linked family resource center programs. Credit for the unbroken spirit of coordination and cooperation between the family resource center director and the principal rests with their intensive involvement over four years of planning that laid the conceptual foundation for the school. The partnership model established at IS 218 unites the principal and the family resource center director (a CAS staff member) in a complex leadership arrangement that relies upon shared goals, mutual respect, and regular, open communication to resolve an array of anticipated conflicts and problems. Notable for its uncompromising sentiment of making schools the center of community life, IS 218 gives point and direction to the other initiatives that have strayed from this central goal in the pursuit of less cooperative and communal aims.

Socio-Cultural Bridges in School-Linked Integrated Services

The importance of addressing issues of socio-cultural congruence rests with a set of sweeping assumptions regarding the roles of administrators, teachers, and parents under the model of school-linked integrated services. Programs aimed at enhancing students' abilities to succeed in school by providing them and their families with greater access to social services are linked to certain expectations regarding enhanced levels of understanding, trust, familiarity, and communication between parents and school officials. A traditional school asks teachers to also think about what happens to their students in the *classroom*; a school linked to a social service delivery system asks teachers and administrators to think about what happens to their students when they go *home*. Linking schools with social services demands a reorientation for both families and schools to a set of relationships that exceeds the tenuous, negotiated parameters demarcating professional and private spheres.

The implications of these expanded roles and relationships for schools and families include a shift from a model of education based upon separate spheres with blurry boundaries to an ecological perspective of family life that considers the human context of need and locates the school as the nexus for expanded interventions. The rationale for this effort is clear. Students and their families do not live in social isolation; rather, they function within cultural, economic, and geographical communities that are intersected by schools. Against the backdrop of a social distance between parents and schools, integrated social services represent a potential organizational force for bridging the worlds of families and schools.

Disconnections

Patterns of family-school interactions are neither trivial nor distinct from the objectives of the integrated services movement and the larger goals of school improvement. Under conditions in which teachers do not regularly communicate with parents or in which the levels of trust and familiarity between families and schools is thin and brittle, the goals implied in the integrated services movement can be difficult to reach. To the degree that the family resource centers and other integrated services models fail to fundamentally reorder the character and content of family-school interactions in terms of deeper interactions between parents and teachers, it may be interpreted as a missed opportunity to develop the partnerships crucial for student growth and success.

This section on socio-cultural bridges underscores the need to connect the dialog on integrated social services to the impulses of reform in school-family-community networks. The images emerging from early research document the serious and negative implications of integrated services programs that ignore the social distance, cultural conflict, and anonymity associated with family-school-community interactions. As Crowson and Boyd (1996) note, the most valuable rewards associated with the school-linked social services movement can be found in "reshaping the priorities and practices of schools toward a closer understanding of, and even partnership with, the families served" (p. 6). Our interest here rests with making explicit the importance of socio-cultural continuity in home-school relationships to the central aims of improving the lives of students and their families embraced within a school-linked services model. We begin this effort by examining the influence of cultural capital and social class on patterns of family-school interactions.

Cultural Capital

A pattern of direct contact between families and schools increases understanding and promotes greater cooperation, commitment, and trust between parents and teachers (see Booth & Dunn, 1996; Epstein, 1996; Fagnano & Werber, 1994; Rioux & Berla, 1993; Ryan, Adams, Gullotta, Weissberg, & Hampton, 1995). The integrated services model is anchored to an enhanced pattern of interactions between families and schools, which makes greater involvement and intervention possible. Recent research, however, has documented the ways in which these processes are often undercut by different levels of "cultural capital" associated with the social class position of school parents.

According to French sociologist Pierre Bourdieu (1977a, 1977b), schools function as the primary institution for affirming and reproducing the social legitimacy of the habits, objects, and symbols of the dominant class culture. This analysis is central to the work on the importance of class and culture in parents' interactions with schools (see Baker & Stevenson, 1986; Connell *et al.*, 1982; Ogbu, 1974; Wilcox, 1978). In applying Bourdieu's concept to studies of parent-school interactions, Annette Lareau (1989) concludes that higher social class provides parents with more resources to bind families into tighter connections with social institutions than are available to working-class or low-income families. These resources are derived from parents' education, income and material resources, occupational status, style of work, and social networks. As examples, higher social status allows parents to approach school officials as equals and provides a sense of confidence in the educational setting, higher incomes make it possible for parents to obtain child care services and transportation to attend school-based events, and upper-income parents are more likely to be members of social networks that provide information on school processes and practices. Lareau's study of family-school relationships in two different school settings, one a working-class community and the other a middle-class community, raises critical issues for school leaders and educational policymakers regarding the cultural resources rendered by social class position in American schools and society. As Lareau notes:

> Middle-class culture provides parents with more information about schooling and promotes social ties among parents in the school community. This furthers the interdependence between home and school. Working-class culture, on the other hand, emphasizes kinship and promotes independence between the spheres of family life and schooling (p. 82).

Lower-income parents' position of independence raises serious dilemmas for coordinated social service initiatives grafted to an ideal of *interdependence* between families and schools. To the degree that distance and distrust characterize relationships between families and schools, the integrated social services movement faces serious obstacles in promoting new linkages that locate the school as the nexus for expanded interventions in family life. Consequently, school-linked integrated services proposals must be accompanied by a set of strategies that take into account the pervasive social distance between lower-income families and schools.

The research on school programs designed to develop family-school linkages is particularly promising and helpful here. School-based projects such as Family Math, Funds of Knowledge, Schools Reaching Out, and the Yale Child Study Center programs have recorded strong and positive responses from both families and schools (see Comer, 1980; Davies, Burch, & Johnson, 1992; Diaz, Moll, & Mehan, 1986; Epstein, 1992). Other strategies flow directly from research on school-linked social services. In findings from a three-year ethnographic study of the Kentucky Family Resource Center initiative, Smrekar (1994) argues for a three-pronged approach aimed at restructuring family-school interactions in an integrated social services setting. The strategy includes three elements: (1) a network of communication channels to facilitate sustained information exchange between families and schools; (2) home visits to expand teachers' understanding of the challenges that face families in poverty and despair, and to begin the process of working with families and human service agencies to ensure that those needs are met effectively; and (3) teacher teams to provide a "continuity of care" to students over a three-year period to ensure sustained, continuous interactions built upon familiarity, understanding, and trust.

Although these strategies reflect the laudable goals of enhanced family-school relationships in an educational environment pegged to improved family functioning and student performance, the integrated services movement raises deep and enduring issues regarding family autonomy and school authority. These issues are embedded in the politics of social class, urban education, and social service collaboration.

Social Class, Urban Education, and Service Collaboration

A cautionary flag raised early in the integrated services movement called into question proponents' claims of emancipation from inefficient, fragmented, and bureaucratic service delivery systems (Capper, 1996). The promises of coordination in state and local school-linked service initiatives continue to be scrutinized with specific concerns regarding centralized services that lead to constrained consumer choices and shifts in goals and priorities that lead away from clients' needs to larger organizational imperatives. Kahne and Kelley (1993) note:

> Coordination can also centralize and strengthen the authority of service providers, limiting the ability of parents and children to guide the direction of their care and creating problems associated with confidentiality and expectations. What some view as local, intimate, and supportive settings may be experienced by others as coercive, intrusive, and constraining (p. 189).

In a context in which families may be unfamiliar or uncomfortable with schools and school officials, such a location for the delivery of needed services appears wrongheaded. This critical view of integrative services provokes a response that

encompasses more than a set of prescriptive guidelines for "good practices." As a school reform designed to "bring parents in," Michelle Fine (1993) argues that such remedies are oversold as a panacea for school and social ills and distract from reforms aimed at larger, more entrenched issues of unequal power, authority, and control in urban schools. Based on her involvement in the Baltimore "With and For Parents" program, Fine concludes that community-based family resource programs aimed at collaboration tend to erode into individually itemized, deficit-focused services for parents at the expense of real reform. She writes:

> Rich and real parental involvement requires a three-way commitment, to organizing parents, to restructuring schools and communities toward enriched educational and economic outcomes, and to inventing rich visions of educational democracies of difference. Unless parents are organized as a political body, parental involvement projects will devolve into a swamp of crisis intervention, leaving neither a legacy of empowerment nor a hint a systemic change (p. 707).

According to Fine (1993), without restructured schools and communities that involve families and educators "working across lines of power, class, race, gender, status, and politics" (p. 708), there will be no transformative communities in schools, even in those schools that offer a so-called "full service" orientation. To be sure, the call for "real reform" resonates with the argument outlined by Crowson and Boyd (1997) to move beyond full service models to a concerted strategy in which schools play "an active and even more complex and socially involved role in the empowerment and economic revitalization of their communities" (p. 17). This argument, in turn, raises new challenges for educational leaders to develop new social structures that connect schools to the goals of empowerment and community development.

Integrated Services and the Ideal School Community

The ideal of empowerment through collaborative structures in schools rests upon a classic concept of community, Gemeinschaft, developed by German sociologist Ferdinand Tonnies (1855–1936) that is characterized by trust, belongingness, and security (Bender, 1978; Newmann & Oliver, 1968). Tonnies' distinction between Gemeinschaft (community) and Gesellschaft (society) underscores the nature of relationships in society that ranges from more natural and organic to more mechanical or rational. Relationships within a Gemeinschaft community are rooted in familiarity and interdependence, whereas relationships within a Gesellschaft community reflect formal, contractual relations found in legal and commercial institutions and bureaucratic organizations characterized by independence and logic (Bender, 1978). Rather than an association with physical or geographical boundaries, the concept of community, or Gemeinschaft, is grounded in social structures and social relations that are characterized by a shared commitment to a common purpose.

The challenge for educational leaders invested in efforts aimed at collaboration and community development is to adjust for social trends that have transformed relatively stable, familiar, and rooted communities of earlier periods to contemporary arrangements that are marked by fragmentation, anonymity, and transience (Bellah, Madsen, Sullivan, Swidler, & Tipton, 1991). Amidst these social upheavals, the shifts in school character toward greater bureaucracy and centralization have further alienated local communities from their schools by creating more legalistic, formal relationships between families and schools (Henry, 1996). The nature and function of school communities have clearly shifted along the continuum from the values of Gemeinschaft to the structures of Gesellschaft. This swing has profound implications for the architects of new collaborative relationships among families, schools, and their communities. As Furman and Merz (1996) note, "The role of the school in relation to community has become troubled and ambiguous . . . Can schools shape a new mission that will both serve the larger society and be understood and accepted by local communities?" (p. 332).

We now turn to issues of ethnic and cultural diversity as a missing link in the movement toward new and deeper connections among schools, families, and communities.

Ethnic and Cultural Continuity

Thus far, educational leaders, researchers, and policymakers have paid greater attention to the organizational constraints and budget battles associated with the integrated services movement than to issues related to socio-cultural diversity. While calls for "valuing differences" and "seeing culture and color" headline a new line of research findings in teacher education and classroom culture (see Delpit, 1995; Foster, 1997; Ladson-Billings, 1994), these critical concerns remain relatively absent in the research on new family-school-community linkages. In this section, we draw together the emergent lines of inquiry from the research literature on cultural differences in education in order to consider the saliency and centrality of these concerns to the integrated services movement.

In a report issued jointly by the U.S. Department of Education and the American Educational Research Association (1995), a series of questions provide an outline to assess the quality and character of cultural congruence in school-linked integrated programs. The queries include:

How does cultural competence of staff affect services and the development of collaboration? What strategies work best in transforming the attitudes of current staff toward greater acceptance and response to the cultural diversity of their clients? What strategies work best for the active inclusion of children and families from different cultures in the designing of agendas, setting of priorities, and evaluation of services? (p. 18).

These themes provide a useful heuristic for designing and implementing school-linked services and are articulated in the policies and practices at the Walbridge Caring Communities Program in St. Louis, Missouri.

Walbridge was developed in 1989 through a partnership between the Danforth Foundation and the Missouri Departments of Education, Mental Health, Social Services, and Health to provide an array of preventive and early intervention services through an elementary school-based integrated services system (Waheed, 1993). Four key elements outlined by Blank and Lombardi (1992) form the conceptual foundation for the Walbridge program:

- Children must be seen in the context of families, and families in the context of communities in which they live.
- Comprehensive services must be provided in a way that respects the individual needs and cultures of the families and communities.
- Program services must go beyond the provision of goods and services and must nurture relationships that help people grow.
- Services must be "democratic." That is, the people most directly affected must have some control over the types of services provided and the ways they are delivered (p. 6).

The issue of cultural competence is central in the design of Walbridge and the training of staff members; it is outlined as "a set of congruent behaviors, attitudes, and policies that come together in a system, agency, or amongst professionals and they enable that system, agency, or the professionals to work effectively in cross-cultural situations" (Isaacs & Benjamin, 1991, p. 6). The tendency to dismiss racial differences and cultural variations is explicitly rejected here. As Khatib Waheed (1993), the Director of the Walbridge program, argues:

The more that professionals and service providers attempt through culturally incompetent systems to ignore and thus invalidate the cultural differences of minority children, families, and communities, the more adverse the effect can be on children's success in school and families prospects of advancing socially (p. 106).

The principle of cultural congruence with the predominantly African-American population in the Walbridge community is affirmed by emphasizing Afrocentricity, operationalized here to include "using both positive and practical African and African-American concepts and philosophies as the focus for defining the individual and collective lifestyles of the children and families" (Waheed, 1993, p. 107).

The Walbridge Caring Communities Program embraces the imperatives outlined in recent research literature that focuses on teachers and teaching in culturally diverse settings. In a call for educators "to see color and to see culture," Gloria Ladson-Billings (1994, p. 31) echoes eloquently the principle of cultural congruence and cultural relevance in educational settings. Her argument to acknowledge and embrace racial and ethnic differences as a positive force in developing richer repertoires for increased understanding and deeper relationships between families and schools has immediate and obvious applications to school-linked integrated service designs. Specifically, this research suggests a template for designing new school-community linkages that build upon exposure to cultural differences in ways that are affirming to self-identity for students and families, and that promote cultural competence for educators, service providers, policymakers, and researchers.

Not surprisingly, many of the most relevant conceptual cues central to the notion of cultural congruence in school-linked integrated services flow from research studies in bilingual education. Home-school connections in ethnically and linguistically diverse settings form the core concern for a set of accommodations set out by Claude Goldenberg (1993). In an extension of Joyce Epstein's (1992) six types of family-school partnerships (parenting, communicating, volunteering, learning at home, decision-making, collaborating with community), Goldenberg suggests a seventh model of partnership that utilizes the students' home culture in terms of social-interactional patterns, linguistic styles, family/community knowledge and resources, and social networks. In an application of Goldenberg's partnership model to the school-linked integrated services system, parents' home language would be incorporated in family resource center programs to encourage and sustain deeper home-school-community linkages.

Undergirding these policies and practices is a recognition that schools have traditionally viewed socio-cultural differences as *deficits* and ignored and invalidated the opportunities and resources represented in ethnically diverse communities (Chaskin, 1993; Delgado-Gaitan, 1991; Delpit, 1995). These arguments resonate with Jim Cummins' (1986) theoretical framework for examining the institutional practices in schools that disempower minority communities. In this seminal work, Cummins considers cultural/linguistic incorporation in schools along an "additive-subtractive" continuum and community participation along a "collaborative-exclusionary" scale. Cummins argues that schools can adopt an array of communication strategies that embrace, rather

than exclude, minority culture and language. This may or may not include bilingual classes for parents but should involve incorporation and appreciation of linguistic *differences* in education programs.

In a school-linked integrated services arrangement, a set of culturally additive and collaborative school-level policies anchored to these principles includes the use of family-school liaisons who are multilingual and indigenous to the community. This strategy involves tapping into the lines of trust and communication already established by community-based organizations, including civic and labor groups and religious and volunteer organizations, in an effort to broaden information exchange between families and schools (Smrekar, 1996b). Building a bridge through existing social networks formed among families and community members offers schools a new channel for the coordination of services, but it also demands a reorientation to a new cluster of social structures and relationships (Cibulka, 1996). As Delgado-Gaitan and Trueba (1991) argue, "crossing cultural borders" between families and schools requires rethinking the institutionalized practices that disempower the very groups of people that the new and expanded programs are designed to reach.

Professional Norms, Communication, and the Context of Community

The axis of ethnic diversity and expanded school-family-community linkages turns on the patterns of communication established by educators. The challenge rests with rethinking the institutionalized policies and practices that bracket family-school interactions around formal, scripted, rule-driven information exchanges. The special education system provides a useful example of the problems posed by traditional relationships between education professionals and families and of the implications of these institutionalized patterns of communication for school-linked integrated services. A pattern of social distance and professional discourse is common in the highly categorized and intensely rigid special education system (Harry, 1992). Barriers to collaboration and parental empowerment in this system include the traditional norms of professionals bound by a commitment to compliance with codified rules and regulations. Issues of cultural diversity exacerbate strained relationships between families and schools under these conditions. The most compelling evidence of these constraints is found in an extensive ethnographic study of cross-cultural communication patterns between Puerto Rican-American parents and schools. Beth Harry (1992) found that passive participation patterns among parents in the special education programs were directly influenced by the legalistic and authoritarian characteristics of the special education system. The types of parent behavior viewed by professionals as "apathetic" and "disinterested" can be explained by the nature of highly structured interactions between educators and families. Harry suggests:

> Assumptions concerning the importance of objectivity, as well as the need for legal accountability, have led to a form of home-school discourse that is impersonal and decontextualized in nature. This has resulted in the exclusion rather than inclusion of many parents, in particular, parents from diverse cultural backgrounds whose styles of interaction are often distinctly personalistic and reliant on highly contextualized communication (p. 472).

Rather than simply enhancing the types of information made available to parents or improving the level of logistical support, these findings argue for new participation structures that move from a model of exclusion to one of inclusion in the decision-making process around services for children. In this structure, the parent assumes a central role, not a supporting one, and the patterns of communication reflect a concern for the total ecology of the student, not merely the imperatives of an Individual Education Plan (IEP). The change agents in this process of empowerment must demonstrate a commitment to cultural congruence, community knowledge, and the context of children's lives. The challenge demands a conceptual reorientation for educators and policymakers. As Harry (1992) writes:

> We must ask whether we believe that culturally different parents who are poor and have little formal education have a valuable contribution to make to our understanding of their children . . . [and] whether our systems are designed for communication or for control, for questions or only for answers, to empower or to disempower students and their families (p. 493).

The implications of this research and its underlying concepts for school-linked integrated services are immediate and unmistakable. In many ways, the integrated services model is merely an expanded version of the IEP process that brings together professional service providers in an effort to meet the interrelated needs of students and their families. From this view, the challenges and tasks for educational leaders are unambiguous. The new participation structure constructed under the umbrella of school-linked integrated services demands seamless collaboration between families, schools, and their communities and a new covenant with reconstructed systems that are "designed for communication, not for control" (Harry, 1992, p. 493).

The Political Constraints: An Emerging Consensus View

Beyond the persistent problems of organizational conflict and socio-cultural chasms, some compelling evidence from recent evaluations of prominent, integrated services initia-

tives suggests an ambivalence regarding the public priority of family and children's services and the scope of the welfare state (Cibulka, 1996). The first note of caution and alarm was sounded by the June, 1994, announcement that the Pew Charitable Trust was terminating a $60 million commitment to support comprehensive family policies and school-linked family centers. Pew had invested two years in the Children's Initiative at a cost of over $5 million to assist five states with a 10-year process of institutional change and improved service delivery. Some observers found fault with the leadership and internal management of the project (Cohen, 1994). However, statements by Carolyn Asbury, Pew's director of health and human services program, illustrate a far more intractable concern pegged to Pew's determination "that the goals could not be accomplished within the time and resources anticipated" (Sommerfeld, 1994, p. 9). Pew withdrew because it believed that the broad changes envisioned by the Children's Initiative required fundamental reforms in a wide array of social policy areas, including housing, employment, and drug abuse prevention (Cohen, 1994). Further doubts about "the political feasibility of proceeding if the plan did not produce strong evaluation results" (p. 1) suggest a public acknowledgment of the political climate marked by a general skepticism and impatience with new programs in the absence of tangible and substantial indicators of "success." The risks associated with the goals of remaking policy for children and families (time, costs, improved outcomes) provoked a certain degree of "failure" that the Pew Charitable Trust found troubling and, ultimately, untenable. Although other large foundations, states, and professional organizations remain committed to school-linked integrated services, the abrupt withdrawal of the Pew initiative and the problems of legitimacy in the Casey Foundation's efforts underscore the movement's tenuous position as essentially a professionally driven and controlled reform effort without a solid populist base (Cibulka, 1996).

Institutional Reform and the Problems of People Served

The Annie E. Casey Foundation described their New Futures initiative at the 1988 Wingspread conference as a challenge to communities to "come together around a crisis, the crisis of the loss of a third of a generation" (Levy & Copple, 1989, p. 27). The Foundation targeted dropout prevention, youth employment, and teen pregnancy prevention and made grants to individual communities, rather than a single agency or system. Casey eventually selected six cities: Dayton, Ohio; Lawrence Massachusetts; Little Rock, Arkansas; Pittsburgh, Pennsylvania; Savannah, Georgia; and Bridgeport, Connecticut, to develop an integrated services approach to the administration, finance, and delivery of youth services. The Foundation expected to spend about $15 million each year over a five-year period (White & Wehlage, 1995).

The New Futures evaluation released in 1995 confirms the doubts associated with the Pew project's demise. An examination of data gathered over five years across all six of the New Futures cities was made by University of Wisconsin evaluators, Julie White and Gary Wehlage. The evaluators cited policy conflicts, gaps between policy design and implementation, and a lack of knowledge about the conditions of the communities served as the fatal flaws that undermined the legitimacy and effectiveness of the initiative (White & Wehlage, 1995).[7] To be sure, the dismal evaluation of the New Futures Initiative dealt a deep blow to the spirit of optimism and the unwavering support that have underwritten the efforts of state and local officials since 1988. As a centerpiece of the movement's institutional collaboration strategy, the New Futures findings argue for a fundamental reconsideration of largely top-down efforts supported by large amounts of money and an elevated degree of intervention authority. In a direct challenge to the approach adopted by many integrated services conference reports and blueprint papers, the New Futures evaluation cautioned that "collaboration should not be seen primarily as a problem of getting professionals and human service agencies to work together more efficiently and effectively" (p. 36). Evaluators White and Wehlage concluded:

> The major issue is how to get whole communities, the *haves* and the *have-nots*, to engage in the difficult task of community development. Rather than start with a view of collaboration focusing on professionals and programs, collaboratives might begin with the political strategy of getting organizations and groups to reallocate resources for disadvantaged communities. Public and private resources need to go directly into targeted communities as forms of social capital and economic capital investment. Such investments would give community collaboration new meaning and greater political legitimacy as it seeks to strengthen the social infrastructure of families, groups, neighborhoods, and communities (p. 37).

The need to address fundamental social conditions that characterize whole urban neighborhoods and communities was underscored early on in the New Futures initiative. Otis S. Johnson, the Executive Director of the Chatham-Savannah Youth Futures Authority, urged policymakers to address systemic causes of youth problems in a paper commissioned by the Council of Chief State School Officers 1992 Summer Institute. Johnson (1992) prodded participating cities to "develop a sense of community urgency and a sense of public accountability for the problems and dilemmas facing their institutions—then collaborate, plan, fund, and deliver services to youth" (p. 89). Although Johnson (1992) was generally optimistic regarding the potential impact of institutional collaboration, he framed the dilemma facing policymakers this way:

> A dandelion continues to reappear until you get to the roots. Often social service systems do a fine job of meeting temporary needs of children and youth; however, if we are to "solve" the problems of children at risk, we need to address the roots of the problem (p. 89).

The increasingly vocal response to this challenge includes a redefinition of schools from the integrated services movement model of "full-service schools" to the new call for fully transformed "enterprise schools" (Crowson & Boyd, 1996). The new concept means moving schools beyond the traditional development needs of children to a deep involvement with the more entrenched issues of community revitalization. The model includes new economic partners, including banks and retail businesses, as well as the social service providers involved in full-service schools. As Michael Timpane of the Carnegie Foundation and Rob Reich of Stanford University (1997) argue:

> At its heart, community development constitutes a philosophical change in the way schooling is conceived. Community development changes the core identity from isolated, independent agencies to institutions enmeshed with other community agencies in an interconnected landscape of support for the well being of students and learners (p. 466).

Community development initiatives are the cornerstone of President Clinton's urban policy agenda, with a $3.8 billion package of tax incentives and grants pegged to urban revitalization under the Empowerment Zones (EZ) and Enterprise Communities (EC) Program (Empowerment, 1995). Under this federal program, 105 communities in 42 states will receive assistance (Cohen, 1996). The focus of these programs rests with the economic improvement of poor neighborhoods through a strengthening of indigenous community institutions. This strong community-level emphasis is anchored to employment, job-training, and private-public partnerships designed to stimulate economic activity and improve the quality of life (better housing, upgraded education, anti-crime initiatives).

The notion of "empowerment" is central to the design, planning, and implementation strategies involved in community development. The model's prominent affirmation of neighborhood investment, involvement, and control is based upon the assumption that without a sense of ownership, sustainable change cannot occur. Community development programs emphasize communities' *demands* for assistance, while the full-service schooling model focuses on the providers' *supply* of services to a community. In this sense, community development, as envisioned through programs such as the EZ/EC initiative, marks a radical departure from a social intervention model pegged to satisfy the immediate needs of city residents through income, food, and housing support systems.

Community development is part of current reform efforts designed to fundamentally alter the traditional distancing between city schools and their neighborhood environments (Lawson & Hooper-Briar, 1997). These reforms argue for a transition to family supportive-community schools that embrace John Dewey's notion of schools as the centers of social and cultural life of communities. Under this model and consistent with community development thrusts, schools are expected to shift from the broker of social services and the locus of crisis intervention to full partnership in a compact with local community members, nonprofit organizations, government agencies, and corporations. In pursuit of a set of more cooperative and communal aims leading to economic revitalization, this model moves schooling to the center of community life with the addition of after-school programs, adult literacy and job training, and expanded health and dental services.

Conclusion

A consensus is growing within the integrated services movement regarding the need to emphasize improving the lives of children and families in conjunction with the narrower goal of enhancing the effectiveness and efficiency of the delivery systems that serve them (Cibulka, 1996). While some foundations[8] move forward to embrace this imperative (such as a refocused New Futures), action among policymakers at the federal and state levels offers little optimism. Response at the federal level appears limited to the devolution of the authority to manage (or cut) welfare benefits and to provide modest child care and employment training programs, a formula that is focused on the *systems* that serve children and families.

The increasing signs of elevated self-interest, social and residential isolationism, and racial segregation in America have led some scholars to suggest that the social ties that once connected Americans have violently eroded over the past decade in a convulsion of crass consumerism and individualism (see Bellah, Madsen, Sullivan, Swidler, & Tipton, 1985; Elshtain, 1995; Lasch, 1995). According to this view, the perceived decline of communal associations, including such social institutions as families, churches, unions, and civic groups, has silenced the political discourse that enjoins individuals of different ethnic, class, and religious lines to common action. The spirit and activities of Americans, notes political scientist Jean Elshtain (1995), suggest a "culture of distrust" that displaces a sense of shared interests, collective commitments, and mutual interdependence:

> In an era of declining resources, resentments cluster around government-sponsored efforts that do not seem to solve the problems they were designed to solve. That is, citizens who pay most

of the bills no longer see a benefit flowing from such programs to the society as a whole. Instead, they see a growing dependence on welfare, increased inner-city crime, an epidemic of out-of-wedlock births, and the like. They perceive, therefore, a pattern of redistribution through forms of assistance to people who do not seem to be as committed as they are to following the rules of the game by working hard and not expecting the government to shoulder their burdens. This is the perceived conviction, and it fuels popular anger and perplexity (p. 4).

A public policy for children and families is tethered to this frayed line of public obligation by the sentiment that protects private advantages in economic life. Kozol (1995) argues that these advantages are most prominent in our schools, health care and juvenile justice systems, and housing arrangements. At the same time, the line of public obligation is undercut by professionals and private organizations who are consumed with "clientizing" communities in an effort to deliver services that sustain the institutions rather than the individuals. As Elshtain (1995) notes, "When professionals move in on communities to 'solve a problem,' what happens is that people grow weaker, not stronger, for their 'needs' are authoritatively defined by sources outside themselves" (p. 18). This is the problem of legitimacy that the New Futures initiative evidenced so pointedly.

The abrupt cancellation of the Pew Children's Initiative and the devastating evaluations of the Casey Foundation New Futures project raise critical questions for educational leaders beyond the familiar issues of organizational conflict in school-linked integrated services. These questions probe whether or not children and families can be "saved" without more attention paid to community economic development and job creation; they require policymakers to explain what "ending welfare as we know it" will mean for children first and the systems that serve them second; and they involve leaders in a discourse on the loss of community bonds and the erosion of civic engagement. These questions force educational leaders and policymakers to penetrate the veneer that has helped slide the issue of children's services to the center of the policy table on the naive and narrow assumption that integrated services will produce more economical and efficient systems for families. Their responses will require a movement beyond the erratic and irregular child-saving impulses that have marked earlier actions, toward efforts that take into account the complexity of the lives of children and their families and the persistence of the dandelions that grow beside them.

NOTES

1. The terms "school-based integrated services," "school-linked integrated services," and "full-service schools" are related but not necessarily interchangeable. "School-based integrated services" describes arrangements in which schools serve as the central organization for the location, management, and integration of social services. "School-linked integrated services" describes programs in which schools are

equal partners along with other human service agencies involved in the collaborative arrangement; services can be delivered at the school or at a site located near the school. "Full-service schools" describes integrated services that are provided within the school, with the school serving as the central partner in the collaborative effort.

2. Other foundations sponsoring the Joining Forces effort include the Joyce Foundation, the Prudential Foundation, and the Johnson Foundation.

3. The School-Based Youth Services Program (SBYSP) was launched in 1988 to develop a "one-stop shopping" model for health and social service programs in schools (Dryfoos, 1994; U.S. General Accounting Office, 1993). All 29 sites funded under the program provide health care, mental health and family counseling, substance abuse services, employment counseling, and recreation (Levy & Copple, 1989).

4. California's Healthy Start initiative was established in 1991 in an effort to restructure the state's fragmented systems of education, health, mental health, and social services for children and families. Three-year grants were awarded to 40 collaboratives to implement comprehensive, school-linked integrated services (Wagner, Golan, Shaver, Newman, Wechsler, & Kelley, 1994).

5. Evaluations of inter-organizational collaboration have provided the material for numerous handbooks on the challenges of coordinated social services. Beginning in 1971, an evaluation of nine school-linked social service programs across six states by Syracuse University concluded that the initiatives suffered from an array of micro-political problems including "bureaucratic immobility," concerns related to a possible loss of control and discretion among school and service agency personnel, and inadequate communication and cooperation among different professional groups (Crowson & Boyd, 1993).

6. The programs at Ohio State and Miami University (Ohio) avoid merely adding on to prescribed professional core curricula; rather, the models embrace true interdisciplinary and interprofessional experiences by bringing together students from nursing, law, education, and social work to address problems of professional practice within an ecological model of family functioning.

7. It is instructive to contrast these unsuccessful foundation efforts with the Carnegie Corporation's Middle Grade School State Policy Initiative. This program funds a network of schools involved in adopting changes in middle school organization and teaching (including a focus on the health and social well-being of adolescents) that were outlined in the 1989 Carnegie report, *Turning Points: Preparing American Youth for the 21st Century*. The program is noteworthy for its holistic, integrated approach to organizational change, a well-established system of technical support and monitoring, and a strong investment in a longitudinal assessment of the implementation of the program and its impact across 75 schools in 15 states. The early evaluation of the Carnegie middle school reform program indicates the critical role of "mature and comprehensive" implementation of the broad array of structural changes, changes in norms, and increases in resources for at-risk adolescents outlined in the Carnegie plan (Felner, Jackson, Kasak, Mulhall, Brand, & Flowers, 1996). These initial findings suggest that this type of long-term investment in comprehensive school transformation will produce gains in achievement and enhance the mental health and socio-behavioral functioning of young adults hoped for in the *Turning Points* initiative.

8. The important role of foundations in nationwide efforts to enhance the lives of students and their families through expanded community-based social and health services is best represented by the Robert Wood Johnson Foundation (RWJ), which has supported school-based health clinics since 1986 by providing the funding and programmatic direction for these and other initiatives. The original 24 school-based clinics funded by RWJ were designed to improve health care for poor children by making services more accessible. School systems subcontracted with community health care providers in order to ensure high quality health care and to institutionalize school-based care as a core element in community health care systems (Lear, Gleicher, St. Germaine, & Porter, 1991). Today over 700 school-based health clinics are in operation, with support from an array of foundation and state government programs.

REFERENCES

Adler, L. & Gardner, S. (1993). *The politics of linking schools and social services.* Washington, DC: Falmer Press.

Baker, D. & Stevenson, D. (1986). Mothers' strategies for children's school achievement. *Sociology of Education, 59,* 155–166.

Bellah, R., Madsen, R., Sullivan, W., Swidler, A. & Tipton, S. (1985). *Habits of the heart.* Berkeley, CA: University of California press.

Bellah, R., Madsen, R., Sullivan, W., Swidler, A. & Tipton, S. (1991). *The good society.* New York: Vintage Books.

Bender, T. (1978). *Community and social change in America.* New Brunswick, NJ: Rutgers University Press.

Blank, M. & Lombardi, J. (1992). *Towards improved services for children and families: Forging new relationships through collaboration* (Policy brief presented at the Eighth Annual Symposium). Washington, DC: A. L. Mailman Family Foundation, Institute for Educational Leadership.

Bolman, L. G. & Deal, T. E. (1991). *Reframing organizations: Artistry, choice, and leadership.* San Francisco: Jossey-Bass.

Booth, A. & Dunn, J. (1996). *Family-school links.* Mahwah, NJ: Lawrence Erlbaum.

Bourdieu, P. (1977a). Cultural reproduction and social reproduction. In J. Karabel & A. H. Halsey (Eds.), *Power and ideology in education* (pp. 487–511). New York: Oxford University Press.

Bourdieu, P. (1977b). *Outline of a theory of practice.* New York: Cambridge University Press.

Boyan, N. J. (Ed.). (1988). *Handbook of research on educational administration.* New York: Longman.

Burlingame, M. (1988). The politics of education and educational policy: The local level. In N. J. Boyan (Ed.), *Handbook of research on educational administration* (pp. 439–451). New York: Longman.

Capper, C. (1996). We're not housed in an institution, we're housed in the community: Possibilities and consequences of neighborhood-based interagency collaboration. In J. Cibulka & W. Kritek (Eds.), *Coordination among schools, families, and communities: Prospects for educational reform* (pp. 299–322). Albany, NY: State University of New York Press.

Carnegie Council on Adolescent Development. (1989). *Turning points: Preparing American youth for the 21st century.* New York: Carnegie Corporation of New York.

Chaskin, N. F. (1993). *Families and schools in a pluralistic society.* Albany, NY: State University of New York Press.

Chaskin, R. J. & Richman, H. A. (1992). Concerns about school-linked services: Institution-based versus community-based models. In *The future of children, 2(1)* (107–117). Los Altos, CA: The David and Lucile Packard Foundation.

Cibulka, J. (1996). Toward an interpretation of school, family, and community connections: Policy challenges. In J. Cibulka & W. Kritek (Eds.), *Coordination among schools, families, and communities: Prospects for educational reform* (pp. 403–435). Albany, NY: State University of New York Press.

Cibulka, J. & Kritek, W. (Eds.) (1996). *Coordination among schools, families, and communities: Prospects for educational reform.* Albany, NY: State University of New York Press.

Cohen, D. (1994, June 1). Demise of Pew project offers lessons to funders. *Education Week, 13*(36), 1, 9.

Cohen, D. (1996, May 1). In the Zone: Effort aims to link economic gains, school reform. *Education Week, 15*(32), 1, 8–9.

Comer, J. (1980). *School power.* New York: University Press.

Connell, R. W., Ashenden, D. J., Kessler, S. & Dowsett, G. W. (1982). *Making the difference: Schools, families, and social divisions.* Sydney, Australia: Geo. Allen and Unwin.

Coontz, S. (1992). *The way we never were.* New York: Basic Books.

Corbett, H. D., Wilson, B. & Webb, J. (1996). Visible differences and unseen commonalities: Viewing students as the connections between schools and communities. In J. Cibulka & W. Kritek (Eds.), *Coordination among schools, families, and communities: Prospects for educational reform* (pp. 27–48). Albany, NY: State University of New York Press.

Council of Chief State School Officers. (1992). *Ensuring student success through collaboration.* Washington, DC: Author.

Crowson, R. L. (1992). *School-community relations: Under reform.* Berkeley, CA: McCutchan.

Crowson, R. L. & Boyd, W. (1993). Coordinated services for children: Designing arks for storms and seas unknown. *American Journal of Education, 101*(2), 140–179.

Crowson, R. L. & Boyd, W. (1995, April). *The constraints to coordinating services for children: A new institutionalism perspective.* Paper presented at the annual meeting of the American Educational Research Association, San Francisco, CA.

Crowson, R. L. & Boyd, W. (1996). Structure and strategies: Toward an understanding of alternative models for coordinated children's services. In J. Cibulka & W. Kritek (Eds.), *Coordination among schools, families, and communities: Prospects for educational reform* (pp. 137–169). Albany, NY: State University of New York Press.

Crowson, R. L. & Boyd, W. (in press). New roles for community services in educational reform. In A. Hargreaves (Ed.), *International handbook of educational change.* Dordrecht, The Netherlands: Kluwer Academic Publishers.

Cummins, J. (1986, February). Empowering minority students: A framework for intervention. *Harvard Educational Review, 56*(1), 18–36.

Cunningham, L. (1990). Reconstituting local government for well-being and education. In B. Mitchell & L. Cunningham (Eds.), *Educational leadership and changing contexts of families, communities, and schools* (Eighty-Ninth Yearbook of the National Society for the Study of Education, pp. 1–18). Chicago: University of Chicago Press.

Davies, D., Burch, P. & Johnson, V. (1992). *A portrait of schools reaching out* (Report No. 1). Boston, MA: Center on Families, Communities, Schools, and Children's Learning.

Delgado-Gaitan, C. (1991). Involving parents in the schools: A process of empowerment. *American Journal of Education, 100,* 20–46.

Delgado-Gaitan, C. & Trueba, H. (1991). *Crossing cultural borders.* Bristol, PA: Falmer Press.

Delpit, L. (1995). *Other people's children: Cultural conflict in the classroom.* New York: New Press.

Diaz, S., Moll, L. & Mehan, H. (1986). Sociocultural resources in instruction: A context-specific approach. In *Beyond language: Social and cultural factors in schooling language minority students.* Los Angeles: California State University, Evaluation, Dissemination, and Assessment Center.

DiMaggio, P. J. & Powell, W. W. (1991). Introduction. In W. W. Powell & P. J. DiMaggio (Eds.) *The new institutionalism in organizational analysis* (pp. 1–38). Chicago: University of Chicago Press.

Driscoll, M. E. (1995). *Thinking like a fish: The implication of the image of school community for connections between parents and schools.* In B. Schneider & P. Cookson (Eds.), Creating School Policy. Greenwood Press, 209–236.

Dryfoos, J. (1994). *Full-service schools.* San Francisco: Jossey-Bass.

Elshtain, J. (1995). *Democracy on trial.* New York: Basic Books.

Empowerment. A new covenant with America's communities: President Clinton's national urban policy report. (1995). Washington, DC: U.S. Department of Housing and Urban Development, Office of Policy Development and Research.

Epstein, J. (1992). School and family partnerships. In M. Alkin (Ed.), *Encyclopedia of educational research* (pp. 1139–1151). New York: Macmillan.

Epstein, J. (1995, May). School/family/community partnerships: Caring for the children we share. *Phi Delta Kappan, 76*(9), 701–712.

Epstein, J. (1996). Perspectives and previews on research and policy for school, family, and community partnerships. In A. Booth & J. Dunn (Eds.), *Family-school links* (pp. 209–246) Mahwah, NJ: Lawrence Erlbaum.

Fagnano, C. & Werber, B. (1994). *School, family, and community interaction: A view from the firing lines.* Boulder, CO: Westview.

Felner, R., Jackson, A., Kasak, D., Mulhall, P., Brand, S. & Flowers, N. (1996). The impact of school reform for the middle years: A longitudinal study of a network engaged in *Turning Points*-based comprehensive school transformation. In R. Takanishi and D. Hamburg, (Eds.,), *Preparing adolescents for the twenty-first century.* New York: Cambridge University Press.

Fine, M. (1993). [Ap]parent involvement: Reflections on parents, power, and urban public schools. *Teachers College Record, 94*(4), 682–710.

Foster, M. (1997). *Black teachers on teaching.* New York: New Press.

Furman, G. & Merz, C. (1996). Schools and community connections: Applying a sociological framework. In J. Cibulka & W. Kritek (Eds.), *Coordination among schools, families, and communities: Prospects for educational reform* (pp. 323–348). Albany, NY: State University of New York Press.

Goldenberg, C. (1993). The home-school connection in bilingual education. In M. B. Arias & U. Casanova (Eds.), *Bilingual education: Politics, practice, and research* (Ninety-Second Yearbook of the National Society for the Study of Education, pp. 225–250). Chicago: University of Chicago Press.

Guthrie, G. P. & Guthrie, L. F. (1991). Streamlining interagency collaboration for youth at risk. *Educational Leadership, 49*(1), 17–22.

Hanson, E. M. (1979). *Educational administration and organizational behavior.* Boston: Allyn & Bacon.

Harry, B. (1992). *Cultural diversity, families, and the special education system: Communication and empowerment.* New York: Teachers College Press.

Heath, S. B. (1983). *Ways with words.* New York: Cambridge University Press.

Henry, M. (1996). *Parent-school collaboration.* Albany, NY: State University of New York Press.

Herrington, C. (1996). Schools as intergovernmental partners: Administrator perceptions of expanded programming for children. In J. Cibulka & W. Kritek (Eds.), *Coordination among schools, families, and communities: Prospects for educational reform* (pp. 197–222). Albany, NY: State University of New York Press.

Hord, S. M. (1986). A synthesis of research on organizational collaboration. *Educational Leadership, 43*(5), 22–26.

Hurrell, P. & Evans, P. (1996). Strategic, operational and field levels: The theoretical and practical dimensions of integrated services. In *Successful services for our children and families at risk* (Report prepared by the Organization for Economic Cooperation and Development, pp. 79–86). Paris: Organization for Economic Cooperation and Development.

Interagency Task Force on Family Resource and Youth Services Center. (1990). *Final report.* Frankfort: Kentucky Cabinet for Human Resources.

Intriligator, P. A. (1992, October). *Designing effective inter-organizational networks.* Paper presented at the annual meeting of the University Council for Educational Administration (UCEA), Minneapolis, MN.

Isaacs, M. R. & Benjamin, M. P. (1991). *Towards a culturally competent system of care.* Washington, DC: Child and Adolescent Service System Program.

Johnson, O. (1992). Savannah's new futures initiative: Getting to the root of the dandelion. *Ensuring student success through collaboration* (pp. 89–100). Washington, DC: Council of Chief State School Officers.

Kagan, S. L. (1993). *Integrating services for children and families: Understanding the past to shape the future.* New Haven: Yale University Press.

Kahne, J. & Kelley, C. (1993, February). Assessing the coordination of children's services. *Education and Urban Society, 25*(3), 187–200.

Kentucky Education Reform Act. (1990). Frankfort: Commonwealth of Kentucky.

Kirst, M. W. (1991). Improving children's services: Overcoming barriers, creating new opportunities. *Phi Delta Kappan, 72*(8), 615–618.

Kirst, M. W. & McLaughlin, M. (1990). Rethinking policy for children: Implications for educational administration. In B. Mitchell & L. L. Cunningham (Eds.). *Educational leadership and changing contexts of families, communities, and schools* (Eighty-Ninth Yearbook of the National Society for the Study of Education, Part II (pp. 69–90). Chicago: University of Chicago Press.

Knapp, M. S. (1995). How shall we study comprehensive services for children and families? *Educational Researcher, 24*(4), 5–16.

Knapp, M., Barnard, K., Brandon, R., Gehrke, N., Smith, A. & Teather, E. (1994). University-based preparation for collaborative interprofessional practice. In L. Adler & S. Gardner (Eds.,), *The politics of linking schools and social services* (pp. 137–152). Washington, DC: Falmer Press.

Kozol, J. (1995). *Amazing grace.* New York: Crown.

Kritek, W. J. (1996). Introduction. In J. Cibulka & W. Kritek (Eds.), *Coordination among schools, families, and communities: Prospects for educational reform* (pp. ix–xxv). Albany, NY: State University of New York Press.

Ladson-Billings, G. (1994). *The dreamkeepers.* San Francisco: Jossey-Bass.

Lareau, A. (1989). *Home advantage.* New York: Falmer Press.

Lasch, C. (1995). *The revolt of the elites and the betrayal of democracy.* New York: W. W. Norton & Co.

Lawson, H. & Hooper-Briar, K. (1994). *Expanding partnerships: Involving colleges and universities in interprofessional collaboration and service inte-*

gration. Oxford, OH: The Danforth Foundation and Miami University, The Institute for Educational Renewal.

Lawson, H. & Hooper-Briar, K. (1997). *Connecting the dots: Progress toward the integration of school reform, school-linked services, parent involvement and community schools.* Oxford, OH: The Danforth Foundation and Miami University, The Institute for Educational Renewal.

Lear, J., Gleicher, H., St. Germaine, A. & Porter, P. (1991). Reorganizing health care for adolescents: The experience of the school-based adolescent health care program. *Journal of Adolescent Health, 12,* 450–458.

Levy, J. & Copple, C. (1989). *Joining forces: A report from the first year.* Alexandria, VA: National Association of State Boards of Education.

Lightfoot, S. L. (1978). *Worlds apart.* New York: Basic Books.

McClure, M. W., Jones, B. A. & Potter, E. (1996). Beyond consensus: Mapping divergent views of systems and power in collaboratives. In J. Cibulka & W. Kritek (Eds.), *Coordination among schools, families, and communities: Prospects for educational reform* (pp. 379–401). Albany, NY: State University of New York Press.

McLaughlin, M. & Smrekar, C. (1988). *School-linked comprehensive service delivery programs for middle schools.* New York: Carnegie Corporation Council on Adolescent Development.

McPherson, G. (1972). *Small town teacher.* Cambridge, MA: Harvard University Press.

Mawhinney, H. B. (1994). Discovering shared values: Ecological models to support interagency collaboration. In L. Adler & S. Gardner (Eds.). *The politics of linking schools and social services* (pp. 33–47). Washington: Falmer Press.

Mawhinney, H. B. (1996). Institutional effects of strategic efforts at community enrichment. In J. Cibulka & W. Kritek (Eds.), *Coordination among schools, families, and communities: Prospects for educational reform* (pp. 223–243). Albany, NY: State University of New York Press.

Mawhinney, H. B. & Smrekar, C. (1994, October). *Professional ethics, child advocacy, and institutional constraints in school-community collaboration: An international perspective.* Paper presented at the annual conference of the University Council for Educational Administration, Philadelphia, PA.

Mawhinney, H. B. & Smrekar, C. (1996). Institutional constraints to advocacy in collaborative services. *Educational Policy, 10*(4), 480–501.

Melaville, A. & Blank, M. (1991). *What it takes: Structuring interagency partnerships to connect children and families with comprehensive services.* Washington, DC: Education and Human Services Consortium.

Mitchell, D. E. & Scott, L. D. (1994). Professional and institutional perspectives on interagency collaboration. In L. Adler & S. Gardner (Eds.), *The politics of linking schools and social services* (pp. 75–91). Washington, DC: Falmer Press.

National Commission on Children. (1991). *Beyond rhetoric.* Washington, DC: U.S. Government Printing Office.

Newmann, F. & Oliver, D. (1968, Winter). Education and community. *Harvard Educational Review, 37,* 61–106.

Ogbu, J. (1974). *The next generation.* New York: Academic Press.

Raywid, M. A. (1988). Community and schools: A prolegomenon. *Teachers College Record, 90,* 198–210.

Rioux, W. & Berla, N. (1993). *Innovations in parent and family involvement.* Princeton Junction, NJ: Eye on Education.

Ryan, B., Adams, G., Gullotta, T., Weissberg, R. & Hampton, R. (1995). *The family-school connection.* Thousand Oaks, CA: Sage.

Schorr, L. B. (1993). What works: Applying what we already know about successful social policy. *The American Prospect, 13,* 44–45.

Scott, W. R. (1995). *Institutions and organizations: Theory and research.* Thousand Oaks, CA: Sage.

Sedlak, M. & Schlossman, S. (1985). The public school and social services: Reassessing the progressive legacy. *Educational Theory, 35*(4), 371–383.

Shaver, D., Golan, S. & Wagner, M. (1996). Connecting schools and communities through interagency collaboration for school-linked services. In J. Cibulka & W. Kritek (Eds.), *Coordination among schools, families, and communities: Prospects for educational reform* (pp. 379–401). Albany, NY: State University of New York Press.

Smrekar, C. (1989). State policy making for children. In M. Kirst (Ed.), *The condition of children in California* (pp. 321–332). Berkeley, CA: Policy Analysis for California Education (PACE).

Smrekar, C. (1994, Winter). The missing link in school-linked social service programs. *Educational Evaluation and Policy Analysis, 16*(4), 422–433.

Smrekar, C. (1996a). The Kentucky Family Resource Centers: The challenges of remaking family-school interactions. In J. Cibulka & W. Kritek (Eds.), *Coordination among schools, families, and communities: Prospects for educational reform* (pp. 3–25). Albany, NY: State University of New York Press.

Smrekar, C. (1996b, April). *The social context of school choice.* Paper presented at the annual meeting of the American Educational Research Association, New York, NY.

Smylie, M. A., Crowson, R. L., Chou, V. & Levin, R. A. (1996). The principal and community-school connections in Chicago's radical reform. In J. Cibulka & W. Kritek (Eds.), *Coordination among schools, families, and communities: Prospects for educational reform* (pp. 171–195). Albany, NY: State University of New York Press.

Smylie, M. A., Crowson, R., Hare, V. & Levin, R. (1993). The principal and community-school connections in Chicago's radical reform. Paper presented at the annual meeting of the American Educational Research Association, Atlanta, GA.

Sommerfeld, M. (1994, April 6). Pew abandons its ambitious 10-year 'Children's Initiative.' *Education Week, 13*(28), 9.

Stefkovich, J. A. & Guba, G. J. (1994). Using public policy to impact local practice: Can it work? In L. Adler & S. Gardner (Eds.), *The politics of linking schools and social services* (pp. 107–109). Washington, DC: Falmer Press.

Timpane, M. & Reich, R. (1997, February). Revitalizing the ecosystem for youth. *Phi Delta Kappan, 78*(6), 464–470.

Townsend, R. G. (1980). Is the local community an ecology of games? The case of schools relating to city agencies. *Education and Urban Society, 12*(4), 486–507.

Tyack, D. (1992). Health and social services in public schools: Historical perspectives. In *The Future of children: School-linked services* (pp. 19–31). Los Altos, CA: The Center for the Future of Children.

U. S. Bureau of the Census. (1993). *Poverty in the United States: 1992* (CPR P–60–185). Washington, DC: U.S. Government Printing Office.

U. S. Department of Education. (1995). *School-linked comprehensive services for children and families: What we know and what we need to know.* Washington, DC: Office of Educational Research and Improvement and the American Educational Research Association.

U. S. General Accounting Office. (1993). *School-linked human services: A comprehensive strategy for aiding students at risk of school failure.* Washington, DC: Author.

Wagner, M., Golan, S., Shaver, D., Newman, L., Wechsler, M. & Kelley, F. (1994). *A healthy start for California's children and families: Early findings from a statewide evaluation of school-linked services.* Menlo Park, CA: SRI International.

Waheed, K. (1993). The Walbridge Caring Communities Program. In *Ensuring student success through collaboration* (pp. 101–122). Washington, DC: Council of Chief State School Officers.

Waller, W. (1932). *The sociology of teaching.* New York: Wiley.

Wang, M. C., Haertel, G. & Walberg, J. J. (1992, October). *The effectiveness of collaborative school-linked services.* Paper presented at the Invitational Conference on School/Community Connections, National Center on Education in the Inner Cities, Washington, DC.

White, J. & Wehlage, G. (1995). Community collaboration: If it is such a good idea, why is it so hard to do? *Educational Evaluation and Policy Analysis, 17*(1), 23–38.

Wilcox, K. (1978). *Schooling and socialization for work: A structural inquiry into cultural transmission in an urban American community.* Unpublished doctoral dissertation, Harvard University, Department of Anthropology, Cambridge, MA.

Wilson, J. Q. (1989). *Bureaucracy: What government agencies do and why they do it.* New York: Basic Books.

Zill, N. & Nord, C. W. (1994). *Running in place: How American families are faring in a changing economy and an individualistic society.* Washington, DC: Child Trends.

Zucker, L. G. (1987). Institutional theories of organization. *American Review of Sociology, 13,* 443–464.

CHAPTER 22

New Demands and Concepts for Educational Accountability: Striving for Results in an Era of Excellence

Jacob E. Adams, Jr., and Michael W. Kirst

Citizens, through their elected representatives, periodically call on schools to provide an accounting of their activities. In the past, these accounts have dealt with the money schools spent, students they served, and professionals they hired, as well as with the programs schools offered, curriculum they taught, and steps they took to comply with federal or state regulations. Beginning in the mid-1980s, the account citizens increasingly demanded revolved around the academic performance of America's schools: what and how much students were learning. This rising salience of quality concerns came to drive a new generation of educational expectations and policies. The "excellence movement" was launched, and in its wake followed an evolution in the notion of educational accountability commensurate with the movement's challenge to obtain better student performance.

From the mid-1980s through the 1990s, new demands for educational accountability symbolized the nation's commitment to educational quality. Accountability figured prominently, for example, in major presidential initiatives. President Bush's America 2000 strategy defined national educational goals and called for national and state report cards to track student achievement. President Clinton's Goals 2000: Educate America Act promoted content and performance standards and student assessments to measure progress toward those standards. These high-profile initiatives signaled the nation that the policy and business communities viewed accountability as a springboard to school improvement.

The sheer volume of state-level accountability activity also heralded accountability's ascendance. By mid-decade, 46 states were collecting and reporting information on the status of public education (Council of Chief State School Officers, 1995). Moreover, states and localities were experimenting with new accountability mechanisms such as benchmarking, school performance planning, performance reporting, and composite school indices, as well as site councils, vouchers, quality and program reviews, and professional certification.

In addition to being active and inventive, states and localities were more serious, too, raising the stakes of educational accountability by attaching consequences to school performance. Kentucky, South Carolina, and Dallas, Texas, for example, paid cash bonuses to schools that improved student achievement. In other locations, failure to meet performance goals led, by design, to various degrees of state intervention, from mandatory school improvement planning processes to outright takeover (as in Maryland, Illinois, New Jersey, Texas, and California), loss of school accreditation (Mississippi), and school closure (Kentucky).

Educational accountability garnered still more attention as states implemented novel forms of student assessment (such as portfolios, performance events, and criterion-referenced tests aligned with challenging state standards), as state courts began to define constitutional standards for adequacy in terms of academic outcomes (see *Rose v. Council for Better Education, Inc.*, 1989), and as scholars began to report findings from research on new accountability systems (for example, Ladd, 1996). In the private sector, foundations launched the National Board for Professional Teaching Standards, the nation's premier initiative in teacher professionalization, certification, and accountability. Such attention to accountability in education mirrored developments in other public sectors, efforts captured under the popular banner "reinventing government" (Osborne & Gaebler, 1992; U. S. Advisory Commission on

Intergovernmental Relations, 1996), and in business, with its regard for total quality management (Hradesky, 1995). Truly, accountability became a defining theme of the period, engaging politicians and technicians, legislators and judges, leaders in government and business, bureaucrats and professionals, and parents.

Extensive and novel efforts notwithstanding, what made educational accountability particularly notable in the closing years of the 20th century was its primary focus on student performance. In the mid-1990s, 43 states were actively engaged in redesigning accountability systems to focus on student performance (Elmore, Abelmann, & Fuhrman, 1996). Rewards and sanctions were triggered by diverging levels of student performance. Standard setting activities among the states and academic disciplines scripted expectations for student performance. In fact, performance-based accountability represented a new political consensus that schooling should be challenging and that results matter. Academic success became the preferred strategy to produce competent workers, engaged citizens, and happier individuals.

At one level, of course, public education has always focused on student performance: teachers and parents have routinely concerned themselves with students' academic success. Beginning in the mid-1980s, however, whole political systems, at state and national levels, adopted student performance as the primary social objective of schooling. Throughout the preceding quarter-century, the macro-level politics of education concentrated on values such as desegregation, compensation for perceived socioeconomic disadvantages, inclusion of handicapped and limited–English-proficient populations, resource equity, and service delivery. In other words, society focused on the clients, resources, and processes of schooling but not on its outcomes. Against this backdrop, the nation's growing attention to accountability for educational performance marks a major shift in public expectations, educational policies, and administrative challenges, a shift neatly captured by the title of the National Governors' Association report, *Time for Results* (1986).

How does accountability promote academic achievement? In an ideal system, performance-based accountability focuses educational policy, administration, and practice directly on teaching and learning. Accountability accomplishes this alignment, in principle, by defining goals, allocating authority, managing incentives, building capacity, measuring progress, reporting results, and enforcing consequences, all related to student performance. As such, educational accountability represents not only a movement to improve student achievement but also a mechanism to secure the relationship between public schools and their communities, grounding the relationship in explicit expectations and demonstrated performance as the basis of public support.

Whether states and schools develop operational patterns of accountability commensurate with this potential remains an open question. No superintendent or princi-

pal, elected official or teacher, works in an ideal system. The reality of educational accountability at the close of the 20th century involves contested standards, a problematic distribution of authority, weak incentives, variable capacity, and rudimentary technology. Accountability is further complicated by operating across levels of government and by engaging both public agencies and private associations. The theme of accountability for results ties these agents and activities together. Political and technical achievements push accountability designs forward, but no educational accountability system in the United States is fully developed. Most systems represent vast experiments. Neither are system designs sufficiently sophisticated to fully acknowledge or to forcefully address the competing conceptions and operational complexities of accountability. Sorting out the details of accountability; managing its political, organizational, and technical turbulence; and seeking its practical effect are tasks awaiting educational leaders as new demands for educational accountability move forward.

Chapter Overview

Our purpose in this chapter is to examine policy trends and cross-cutting themes in educational accountability and to identify important accountability challenges for school leadership and research. We oriented the analysis around the potential of accountability mechanisms to elevate student performance, and so to enhance teaching and learning. This narrow, instrumental performance bias represents our own interests. More importantly, it reflects trends in the field, and it reinforces teaching and learning as the core mission of schooling and the important focus of educational administration. We readily acknowledge, however, that accountability holds broader meaning in normative democratic theory and that accountability is a defining characteristic of representative democracy, whether or not it serves any instrumental purpose. By omitting this larger discussion, we are not rejecting broader political notions of accountability. We are simply limiting our analysis of accountability to late 20th century political demands for improved student performance.

We develop the analysis in four parts. First, we note the long search for educational accountability and describe new demands that are shaping this search. Then, using conceptual and descriptive lenses, we review accountability policy developments during the excellence era in educational reform, beginning in 1983. The dual perspectives enable us to present a typology of accountability systems and to assess tradeoffs and problems associated with these systems.

In the second part of the analysis, we identify six cross-cutting themes in educational accountability: identifying principals and agents, authorizing action, managing agent productivity, defining accounts, ensuring causal responsibility, and promoting agent compliance. These themes represent fundamental operations of accountability systems, no matter the type. Readers will see how the emerging state-school accountability relationship harbors reciprocal responsibilities for accomplishing accountability goals.

Next, we use the cross-cutting themes to flag eight challenges for school leadership and research, challenges associated with the still-evolving nature of performance-oriented accountability systems. In order to pursue accountability goals effectively, educational administrators must navigate problems of principal-agent ambiguity, contested standards, conflicting policies, ill-fitting management practices, rudimentary accounts, inadequate technology, unmotivated staffs, and uncertain causal theories.

We conclude the chapter by highlighting conflicts between so-called internal (school) and external (system) accountability standards and structures. This internal-external dichotomy raises questions about whether prevailing modes of performance-based educational accountability—designs rooted in external controls and bureaucratic relationships—are inconsistent with important attributes of teaching and teachers' motivation and, therefore, whether external standards alone limit the potential of accountability to stimulate substantially higher levels of student learning. The questions are provocative and lead us to argue that the next advances in accountability design, practice, and research must address fundamental conflicts between external and internal modes of educational accountability. Perhaps alignment between these poles of accountability can better motivate teachers; perhaps it can promote accountability mechanisms that serve instructional needs at the same time as they satisfy political or managerial demands for accounts. From our vantage, the next era of accountability policy, practice, and research must examine issues of congruence and conflict between external and internal accountability mechanisms.

In building this argument, we draw on existing empirical studies and refer to contemporary accountability experiments. The contribution of the chapter lies in its organization of accountability policies, analysis of accountability challenges, and vision of accountability roles for educational administrators, who establish the conditions and manage the processes of learning.

Evolving Search for Educational Accountability

Notions of educational accountability have evolved along with public schools themselves. As one scholar remarked, "Policymakers' search for greater accountability in public school performance has been constant from the beginning of publicly funded schools" (Herrington, 1993, p. 37). The

search, however, has not been steady in pace or consistent in strategy. Accountability developments have followed larger economic and political movements (scientific management, program planning, and reinventing government, for example), and policies have variously targeted educational resources, processes, and outputs.

Nor has the search for educational accountability been trouble-free. On this point, Kirst (1990) argued that the history of educational accountability is one of "use, misuse, and controversy" (p. 3). As early evidence, he cited the mid-19th century English "payment by results" scheme, which drew criticism for narrowing the curriculum. School administrators dropped geography and history courses in order to focus on the reading, writing, and arithmetic skills measured by school inspectors. Similarly, the scientific management movement that swept the U.S. in the early 20th century drew fire on the grounds that efficiency reforms ignored the substance of education, attended to trivial matters, and created factory-like school facilities; critics also argued that efficiency experts subordinated educational questions to business considerations, trained administrators as managers rather than educators, introduced suspect methods, and reinforced the nation's anti-intellectual climate (Callahan, 1962).

A half-century later, accountability again captured policy and professional attention, propelled by Leon Lessinger's book, *Every Kid a Winner: Accountability in Education* (1970). Lessinger promoted accountability grounded in performance measurements, incentives, results linked to resources, and capacity-building; in short, accountability through better management and fiscal procedures (Pipho, 1989). His scheme was consistent with public administration trends of the 1960s and 1970s, the era of planning, programming, budgeting systems (PPBS), management by objectives (MBO), management information systems (MIS), uniform accounting systems, program evaluation, and zero-based budgeting (ZBB).

Policy and professional attention to educational accountability during this program planning era was widespread. Thirty-five states enacted accountability statutes, and two federal projects chronicled the burgeoning activity: the Cooperative Accountability Project, a consortium of seven state departments of education, and the State Education Accountability Repository, managed by the Wisconsin Department of Education (Pipho, 1989). In fact, few educational concepts of the time gained the rapid acceptance and approbation of accountability (Leight, 1973). Observers heralded "the time has come for accountability—educational accountability" (Browder, 1973), and proclaimed that "the accountability movement is here to stay" (Barbee & Bouck, 1974, p. 14).

Accountability's popularity and wide chronicling notwithstanding, the management and financial accountability strategies of this era faded away. According to Kirst (1990), "All of these budget techniques were resisted by school boards and local educators and have disappeared with barely any residue" (p. 3). Accountability during this period may have secured a grip on the culture and practice of public administration, but its form would soon change.

New Demands for Educational Accountability

The tremendous amount of policy attention devoted to elementary and secondary education during the 1980s and 1990s, the substance of the excellence movement, is routinely traced to the watershed federal report, *A Nation at Risk: The Imperative for Educational Reform* (National Commission on Excellence in Education, 1983). In drafting this report to the nation, the National Commission on Excellence in Education attributed the success of America's schools, that is, their capability to promote the nation's prosperity, security, and civility, to their academic performance. In fact, the commission defined excellence in education for individuals as performance on the boundary of individual ability in ways that expand personal limits; for schools, as setting high expectations for all learners and working to help students achieve them; and for society, as adopting policies supporting excellence. Commission members wrote that the nation "must demand the best effort and performance from all students, whether they are gifted or less able, affluent or disadvantaged, whether destined for college, the farm, or industry" (p. 24).

Among a set of recommendations regarding curriculum, high expectations, rigorous and measurable standards, time on task, and teaching quality, the commission also recommended that citizens hold educators responsible for schools' success, with the caveat that citizens themselves provide resources and stability necessary to the educational reform task. This recommendation signaled the need for performance-based accountability to complement the move toward excellence in America's schools.

A call for excellence and accountability presupposes a broad perception that both attributes are lacking from schools. In fact, behind the national report and public pronouncements lay the judgment that America's schools were declining. Notwithstanding recognized pockets of excellence, the general perception of America's schools was of "a vast mass shaped by tensions and pressures that inhibit systematic academic and vocational achievement for the majority of students . . . [Furthermore, that] the ideal of academic excellence as the primary goal of schooling seems to be fading across the board in American education" (National Commission on Excellence in Education, 1983, p. 14). The National Commission on Excellence in Education presented Americans with a threefold message: education is declining, it is important, and schools must be held accountable for improvements.

As the excellence movement developed, policy makers, business and school leaders, and researchers elaborated conditions of education that fueled the press for performance-based accountability. For example, the National Assessment of Educational Progress (NAEP), a set of standardized tests measuring the math and reading skills of U.S. 9- and 17-year-olds, demonstrated some improvement in student performance over the 1982–1992 period but also that half of all 17-year-olds in 1992 could not read or count at the level needed to get a job in a modern automobile plant (Murnane & Levy, 1996a). At the same time, analyses of the emerging global economy identified "new basics" for schooling, including high levels of mathematics, reading, and problem-solving skills, the ability to work in groups and to make effective oral and written presentations, and the ability to use personal computers (Murnane & Levy, 1996a). Courts likewise began to shift their attention from the distribution of educational resources (equity) to student outcomes (adequacy) (Heise, 1995), and experts called for greater school productivity as a precursor to better outcomes (Consortium on Productivity in the Schools, 1995). Policy makers opened a discussion of national educational goals, curriculum, and tests as the basis for school improvements and accountability (Ravitch, 1995). In short, governmental and civic actors recognized the need for improved student performance, and accountability became their preferred mechanism to attain it.

Accountability in an Era of Excellence

Accountability policies in the 1980s and 1990s evolved beyond their policy forebears of the preceding decades. In the context of the excellence movement, accountability focused increasingly on student achievement with ties to instruction. Attention turned to measuring student performance (or the lack of it) and assigning responsibility for improving it (Pipho, 1989). Decision makers relied increasingly on statutory mandates and incentives to get the job done. However, no strategy was completely abandoned. Policy makers, educational leaders, practitioners, and parents also continued to seek better student performance and accountability through management practices, professional standards, teacher commitment, democratic processes, and parent choice. In the aggregate, these attempts indicate a dense and varied landscape of educational accountability, one marked by numerous policies, causal theories, and policy instruments. Separately, these attempts represent different types of accountability systems.

Types of Educational Accountability

Educational accountability systems can be categorized in six types: bureaucratic, legal, professional, political, moral, and market. Different types of accountability systems represent different ways of managing public expectations regarding what should be accomplished, by whom it should be accomplished, and who establishes the agenda (Romzek & Dubnick, 1987). Types of accountability are distinguished by four attributes. First, accountability systems express different relationships between principals and agents. Principals are those who establish an expectation (regarding a task to be accomplished) and to whom an account is owed; agents are those of whom performance is expected (in accomplishing the task) (Stiglitz, 1987). The second, third, and fourth attributes of accountability systems indicate the nature of the accountability relationship, or what is expected of agents, the type of mechanism employed to ensure accountability, and the nature of the incentive used to compel agents' actions (Table 22.1). Accountability systems are further distinguished by whether an accountability expectation originates outside or inside an accountable agency, introducing the element of external versus internal control and the extent of control under which agents operate (Light, 1993; Romzek & Dubnick, 1987).

Bureaucratic Accountability

Bureaucratic accountability ensures that the preferences and decisions of organizational leaders govern the work of employees throughout an organization. It is based on the relationship between superiors and subordinates and operates through a system of supervisory control characterized by hierarchical structure, standard operating procedures, and rewards and punishments (Gortner, Mahler, & Nicholson, 1989; Romzek & Dubnick, 1987). As such, bureaucratic systems exert a high degree of control over employees, who are expected to carry out their accountable tasks by applying established rules and procedures. Bureaucratic accountability is widely used in public administration.

In educational agencies, bureaucratic accountability operates where state departments of education or school district central offices promulgate rules and regulations to ensure that schooling occurs according to set standards (Darling-Hammond & Ascher, 1991). Such standards specify course offerings, textbook selection, curriculum scope and se-

quence, class schedules, student assignment, and the like. In a bureaucratic system, schools are divisions of larger organizations, administered through hierarchical decision-making, which educate children through standardized programs.

Over time, organizational rules and standard operating procedures, personnel evaluations, and local educational planning have supported bureaucratic accountability systems at an operational level. Local planning around issues of school improvement and student performance continue to play supporting roles in excellence era accountability systems. In the 1980s, California's School Improvement program provided money to schools to develop and implement school improvement plans, which state officials then approved. In the 1990s, Kentucky's School Transformation plans accomplished similar purposes in the context of that state's reform requirements. State officials also routinely track school district expenditures through fiscal audits, just as state and federal officials oversee educational practices through compliance audits, such as those employed in federal compensatory and special education programs.

Legal Accountability

Like its bureaucratic counterpart, legal accountability involves the enforcement of rules and a high degree of control over agents. Control in a legal context, however, originates outside the agencies that must account for their actions. The legal accountability expectation is that individuals or agencies fulfill their fiduciary or contractual obligations. In this manner, a state legislature passes a law and monitors state or local educational agencies' implementation of the law, or a court orders a school district to desegregate and oversees the implementation of that order. Similarly, parents might seek relief in court because a state failed to provide equal educational opportunity for their child. In these illustrations, legislatures and courts hold educational agencies accountable through the oversight of agency operations and the threat or imposition of legal sanctions. The principal-agent relationship exists between relatively autonomous parties and involves a formal or implied fiduciary agreement between a public agency

Table 22.1
Types and Attributes of Accountability Systems

Type of accountability system	Nature of principal-agent relationship	Nature of accountability expectation	Accountability mechanism	Incentive
Bureaucratic	Superior/subordinate	Compliance with organizational rules	Supervision	Reward/punishment
Legal	Policymaker/implementer	Complicance with legal mandates	Oversight	Legal sanction
Professional	Layperson/expert	Special knowledge	Training	Discretion
Political	Constituent/representative	Responsiveness	Election	Support
Moral	Group/individual	Effort	Obligation	Affirmation
Marker	Customer/provider	Service provision	Choice	Patronage

Note: Adapted from Henig, 1994; Romzek & Dubnick, 1987; and Wagner, 1989.

and its legal overseer (Romzek & Dubnick, 1987). Schools are viewed as autonomous actors that, nevertheless, are legally obligated to carry out certain duties or to meet specified standards.

Because of the intergovernmental nature of state school systems, state policy makers often rely on legal mandates to structure educational accountability. The history of policy activity in this domain is not only rich but conceptually varied, with accountability policies targeting educational resources, processes, and performance. For instance, policy mechanisms such as school funding formulas, state teacher certification, school accreditation, and program standards affect the resources and program structures available to schools. Wisconsin's school district standards illustrate the point. As a condition of state approval, these standards (Wisconsin School Laws, Section 121.02) require each school board to ensure, for example, professional certification for all teaching, supervisory, and administrative staff; professional development planning; remedial reading services; kindergarten; counseling services; 180 days of instruction; adequate instructional materials; safe and healthful facilities; health, physical education, art, and music instruction; curriculum scope and sequences; graduation standards; and planning for at-risk students.

In contrast, other legal mandates have targeted the processes of schooling, touching on issues of resource allocation, governance, and school organization. For example, union contracts dictate the organization and working conditions of schools, such as who can teach what, when, and for how long, and other process issues. Desegregation orders prescribe attendance policies and transportation services, while state graduation requirements specify courses students must study. Decentralization policies shift authority within educational systems. Chicago's School Reform Act, for example, replaced bureaucratic control of schools with control by individual school councils composed of parents, teachers, community representatives, and the principal (Hess, 1993). Kentucky incorporated a similar provision in the Kentucky Education Reform Act of 1990, devolving authority for school practices to school councils composed of teachers, parents, and the principal (Adams, 1993b).

A third group of legal mandates focused on the outputs of schooling, namely, student performance. Excellence era accountability policies related to student performance appeared in two waves. The first wave arrived early, in the mid-1980s, and centered on performance reporting. California's Performance Report for California Schools, for example, developed in the aftermath of the state's omnibus educational reform legislation, Senate Bill 813, reported results of the California Assessment Program achievement tests in reading, writing, and mathematics, enrollment in academic courses, dropout rates, and SAT and AP scores. In a section of the document devoted to local data, districts reported on the strength of school curricula, school cli-

mate, the amount and quality of students' homework, and the amount and quality of students' writing, as well as the books read by students, community support for schools, awards received by faculty and students, support for special needs students, and student participation in extracurricular activities.

Similarly, the Southern Regional Education Board (SREB) has issued periodic report cards on progress toward 12 educational goals set for the region. The *Educational Benchmarks* series reports performance indicators ranging from readiness for first grade to high school graduation. Individual state reports vary within the SREB region. They are required variously by state legislatures, state departments of education, or gubernatorial commissions. Responsibility for reporting rests with state commissioners, state boards of education, or school districts. Reporting occurs at the level of state, district, school, region, or nation. Early reports focused on inputs such as degrees earned, teacher salaries, and number of certified staff. Over time, however, reports have come to focus on student performance, announcing results of state tests; nationally formed tests; SAT, AP, and ACT tests; and dropout rates. Reports are distributed to policy makers, parents, educators, and the public (Gaines, 1991).

President Bush's America 2000 strategy called for national and state report cards to track student performance. By 1995, 46 states produced at least one annual performance report, and 25 states produced two or more reports. (Exceptions include Minnesota, Montana, South Dakota, and Wyoming.) Of the states with reports, 42 publish at least one report providing statistics at the district level and 35 states report statistics at the school level; 37 states produce reports as a result of state mandates (Council of Chief State School Officers, 1995).

The theory of action underlying performance reporting asserts that provision of information and comparison among schools or districts will stimulate improvement efforts in relatively weaker schools. Little systematic information is available to support or refute this contention. Performance reporting failed to induce improvement efforts in Illinois, but it did stimulate positive changes in policy and practice in South Carolina (Cibulka, 1991). On the whole, however, the effectiveness of school report cards to improve student school practices and student leaning has been questioned (Herrington, 1993).

The second wave of excellence era accountability policies related to student performance arrived generally around 1990 and introduced high-stakes performance assessment tied to rewards and sanctions. Kentucky, for example, enacted the Kentucky Instructional Results Information System (KIRIS), which holds schools accountable for student achievement measured on state tests tied to new state curricula. Schools that meet or exceed their performance targets qualify for monetary rewards that can be used for any purpose, including salary bonuses; schools that don't meet their performance goals suffer various sanctions, ranging from mandatory improvement planning, loss of control over key decisions, even school closure (Petrosko, 1997).

Tennessee implemented a value-added assessment system that purports to measure district, school, and teacher effects on student achievement gains. The accountability system uses performance data from the Tennessee Comprehensive Assessment Program (Baker & Xu, 1995). Similarly, South Carolina and Dallas, Texas, launched incentive-based assessment programs. South Carolina educators compete for school rewards through the state's School Incentive Reward program, the first of the nation's incentive and reward systems, with rewards based on student achievement gains, teacher attendance, and student attendance (Richards & Sheu, 1992). Dallas tests students using the Texas Assessment of Academic Skills and the Iowa Test of Basic Skills, then supplements test scores with measures of student attendance, promotion rates, dropout rates, and course enrollments. Both South Carolina and Dallas provide financial rewards to schools based on schools relative rankings (Clotfelter & Ladd, 1996).

Other innovations included Mississippi's performance-based state accreditation of school districts, with districts ranked across five levels based on a combination of performance and process variables (Elmore, Abelmann, & Fuhrman, 1996); and Vermont's portfolio assessment strategy (Murnane & Levy, 1996b). Also, charter schools began spreading rapidly across the states and probably will reach 1,000 school in a few years. A charter school trades increased autonomy for increased accountability. Charters contain clear, measurable, and consequential accountability provisions. Scholars have begun to explore the accountability components of charters school laws (see Millot, 1996, for example).

Another emerging trend involves the probation and reconstitution of schools, which seem to be spreading from initial locations in San Francisco, Houston, and Chicago. School reconstitution is different from the state takeover of local school systems that is part of the New Jersey and Kentucky reforms. These system takeovers resulted in a fiscal cleanup but not much impact on schools and classrooms (Fuhrman & Elmore, 1992). In contrast, school reconstitution is a state or central system intervention of last resort for failing schools that removes all staff from a school. Only San Francisco has taken over many schools, but Chicago had more than 100 schools on probation in 1997. One accountability consideration with reconstitution concerns the appropriate criteria for identifying "failing" schools. What are the implications, tradeoffs of varying processes, instruments, indicators, and standards for identifying when a school is beyond repair. There are complex validity and reliability issues here including training of evaluators and duration of the process.

Accountability systems based on rewards and sanctions for student performance depend on educational standards to direct what students should know and be able to do. Beginning in the late 1980s, educational reformers dedicated substantial attention to the articulation and adoption of content, opportunity-to-learn (Porter, 1991), and performance standards for student achievement. The "standards movement" was born. Efforts to construct disciplinary, state, and national standards blossomed. Federal Goals 2000 legislation created a National Education Standards and Improvement Council to review existing state and local standards. Professional organizations, led by the National Council of Teachers of Mathematics, crafted curriculum and evaluation standards. In concert with the U.S. Department of Education, foundations started the New Standards Project, a consortium of states and major school districts dedicated to designing student assessments based on common standards of performance (Resnick & Nolan, 1995). Content-focused standards and performance-based accountability became the twin screws propelling the excellence movement. Content and performance standards represent external-legal forms of educational accountability.

Professional Accountability

In contrast to the high degree of agent control associated with bureaucratic and legal accountability systems, professional models devolve authority for accountability tasks to the agents (street-level bureaucrats, à la Lipsky, 1980) who deliver the services or perform the tasks for which an agency is accountable. Professional systems assume that services are nonroutine and that knowledgeable professionals must tailor their activities to accommodate clients' needs. Thus while professional accountability can operate within organizations, the relationship between principals and agents is more akin to that between laypersons and experts insofar as laypersons employ experts to perform tasks or produce results. They assume that experts possess the specialized knowledge and skills to do so. Deference to expertise constitutes the operating dynamic. Control over professionals' discretion, however, operates on both sides of their activities. Beforehand, the training and socialization professionals experience in graduate schools, internships, and professional associations orient them to standards of professional practice and clients' needs (see, for example, Kaufman, 1960); afterwards, clients or agency managers terminate or continue professionals' employment based on their performance.

In educational settings, professional accountability means that administrators and teachers acquire specialized knowledge, pass certification exams, and uphold professional standards of practice (Darling-Hammond & Ascher, 1991). These professionals then orient their work toward student needs, focusing on outcomes rather than processes, and utilizing discretion rather than standard procedures. On behalf of students, educational managers—school principals, program directors, superintendents—hold teachers accountable for results but without prescribing the route they take to achieve those results. In a professional context, schools become client-oriented firms that utilize specialized knowledge and seasoned judgment to address students' educational needs.

At an operational level, then, accountability can be approached from the perspective of professionals' specialized knowledge and training. Professionalism receives lots of attention in educational policy but little action in terms of accountability. O'Reilly (1996) noted that

> rarely do current state and local accountability systems incorporate professional accountability approaches. To be sure, many states set aside funds for and have even increased requirements for professional development activities, but these policies are not necessarily linked to accountability or to efforts to increase the professionalization of teaching (p. 33).

Exceptions include New York's School Quality Review Initiative, in which teachers participate in internal school self-reviews, and New Mexico's World Class Teacher Project, which involves school-university collaboration and encourages certification from the National Board for Professional Teaching Standards (O'Reilly, 1996).

Peer review constitutes the primary policy mechanism regarding professional approaches to educational accountability. Kerchner, Koppich, and Weeres (1997) described peer review as "probably the most powerful demonstration that teachers create and display a knowledge of practice" (p. 87) and credited peer review with bringing higher standards to teaching. As an accountability mechanism, peer review influences decisions regarding hiring, promotion, tenure, discipline, and dismissal, and thus influences the gamut of professional practices in schools. But peer review has been tried in less than two dozen school districts nationwide (Kerchner, Koppich, & Weeres, 1997).

In the late 1990s, the most notable policy development in the area of professional accountability centered around national certification from the National Board for Professional Teaching Standards. National Board certification requires peer-reviewed, performance-based demonstrations of professional competence and promises to be a powerful, long-term school improvement strategy.

There is another dimension to professional modes of educational accountability, one that emanates from professional communities in individual schools and that is organized by professional knowledge, autonomy to act, commitment to clear standards of student learning, and peer pressure to meet performance goals. Later in the chapter, we will contrast this internal-professional mode of accountability to the external-legal mechanisms that dominated educational policy in the late 1990s. The point we will make is that these internal-professional mechanisms substantially govern practice, are more easily aligned with teaching and learning, and thus are more likely to improve student performance. The management question regarding school-based professional communities becomes how to support school-based modes of accountability while aligning them with demands from schools' bureaucratic or political superordinates.

Political Accountability

Political accountability involves constituents' expectations that their elected or appointed representatives will respond to their value preferences. After all, politics is about allocating values through government, and educational concerns are not exempt (Wirt & Kirst, 1997). Whether the issue involves tax rates, multiculturalism, or mainstreaming, or outcomes-based assessments, creationism, and sex education, organized groups press their representatives to "do the right thing," allocating the group's preferences across whole school systems. Constituents hold their representatives accountable by proffering or withdrawing support, primarily at the ballot box, as state legislators and school board members periodically stand for election. But political accountability exists in any situation where one party expects another to be responsive to his or her interests. The parents, business officials, publishers, union members, and interest group leaders who cast ballots also promote their interests directly with state, district, and school staffs. In the midst of this lobbying, the critical accountability question becomes, Whom does the educator represent? As the object of political activity, schools are transformed into fields of competition where organized interests vie to promote their value preferences regarding education.

Political accountability manifests most directly and dramatically as elected bodies convert interest group demands and voter preferences into educational policies. Conversion encompasses issues of basic state and local support, dictating who pays and who benefits. It defines expectations for educational principals and agents. It allocates group preferences for programs, accountability structures, and other artifacts. It mediates shifts in basic values such as equality, efficiency, and choice (Guthrie, Garms, & Pierce, 1988; Stone, 1988). Conversion processes have resulted in omnibus school reform plans, such as California's Hughes-Hart Educational Reform Act of 1983 and the Kentucky Education Reform Act of 1990. In the latter case, school reform launched a major experiment in performance-based accountability.

Moral Accountability

Moral accountability derives from agents' personal obligations or senses of duty. In other words, moral accountability operates where agents' actions are conditioned by conscience and loyalty to the work-based principles and values they deem to be important (Wagner, 1989). Obligations originate in social customs, entangle agents in the interests of others, and define expectations between individuals and the groups they join, extending from peers to society. Among the six types of accountability examined here, professional and moral models are the only ones in which agents' obligations are assumed rather than assigned.

The moral basis of accountability manifests inside accountable agencies at the level of individual agents. Though the degree of operational control over these agents is low, the assumed obligation, and the threat of remorse or ostracism that results from failing to fulfill one's obligation, are themselves powerful forces of accountability. Of course, society routinely invests certain expectations with legal status to discourage the variation in agent compliance that might otherwise ensue. Still, the primary response of many agents to social or employment obligations emanates from a moral standard of behavior they apply to their jobs. Moral accountability in schools, therefore, leads teachers, principals, counselors, and others to faithfully discharge their educational responsibilities. So teachers make a good faith effort to instruct students, principals support instruction by ensuring a school climate conducive to learning, counselors seek appropriate remedies for troubled students, and so forth across the range of roles found in schools. Schools operate as learning centers in which moral individuals make faithful efforts to fulfill the expectations they and others hold for educators.

Educational policy treats moral dimensions of educational accountability as individual idiosyncrasy, thus not worth addressing. As a result, this mode of accountability garners little attention, except as a rhetorical target. However, to the extent that teachers' commitment and constructions of professional obligation originate in social customs and norms of practice, obligation can be influenced through policies shaping teacher preparation, induction, and professional development. As they relate specifically to issues of individual-level accountability, teacher preparation, induction, and development activities received little policy attention in the 1990s. Professional development policies focused on capacity building, thus playing only a supporting role in accountability designs.

In contrast, one professional development structure has been shown to positively affect teachers' attitudes toward work, subject matter, and students, namely, teacher networks (Adams, 1993a; Lieberman & Grolnick, 1996; Lieberman & McLaughlin, 1992). The positive role of teacher networks in crafting professional community demonstrates the potential of policy incentives, administrative practices, and professional structures together to foster a deeper sense of professional obligation and individual accountability.

Market Accountability

Accountability in markets begins in customers' expectations that providers will offer a product or service of sufficient utility and quality to merit its use. Customer choice operates as the accountability mechanism. Customers define their needs in relation to particular services or products, and then select among alternatives based on factors such as quality and convenience. In education, market accountability means that parents select the schools their children attend without regard to attendance zones (Chubb & Moe, 1990; Henig, 1994).[1] Although choice operates outside schools, it is based on the performance of the school, a product of students, teachers, administrators, and others who work in schools. Parents as customers not only select schools for their children to attend, they also maintain their relationship with schools based on their satisfaction with the results they observe. And while the degree of direct agent control is low, the consequences of parents' choices for schools are high, as schools' very existence depends on their capability to attract customers. Theoretically, schools will alter their operations to satisfy parents' preferences for programs and quality. Under the market metaphor, schools become shops that tailor the selection and quality of services to attract the families upon whose patronage they depend.

The voluntary market exchanges that match customers to educational services is symbolized best by vouchers. In a voucher system, governments subsidize students' education directly by distributing vouchers that parents then use to purchase educational services, much as the federal government subsidizes nutrition through the use of food stamps. Consistent with much of American political culture, vouchers have nevertheless received a cool public response (Henig, 1994). Alum Rock, CA, conducted a limited experiment with vouchers in the 1970s with mixed results. Vouchers constitute one mechanism of school choice.

East Harlem in New York City, Minnesota, and Milwaukee offer other examples of choice in public education. In East Harlem, students apply for enrollment in one of the district's alternative schools, all of which are organized by program specialty, such as performing arts, science and math, or maritime studies. Choice extends to schools within a single district. The Minnesota plan allows open enrollment across district boundaries within the state, with state money following the students who cross those boundaries. Milwaukee's Parental Choice Program goes farther still, allowing choice among public and private schools. State support of $2,500 follows students into private schools. Implementation of these market-based experiments has been challenging as legal, procedural, and public relations problems have arisen in each case (Henig, 1994).

Magnet schools constitute another form of choice. Traditionally, magnet schools use additional resources and special programs (the magnets) to attract a diverse student population to a high-minority school, hence accomplishing voluntary desegregation. Magnet schools spread widely during the 1970s and 1980s.

Contracting offers another kind of choice and accountability in public education. A contract school replaces existing bureaucratic controls over school programs with an agreement that defines the school's mission, guarantee of public funding, and grounds for accountability (Hill, Pierce, & Guthrie, 1997). The contract binds a school board and a party the board engages to operate a particular school. In the 1990s, contractors such as Educational Alternatives, Inc., Edison, and Alternative Public Schools captured public attention with attempts to operate schools on a contract basis.

Accountability Trends in the 1990s

Educational accountability gained importance during the 1990s just as it became more consequential. As the excellence movement continued into its second decade, new forms of educational accountability appeared. The advent of performance standards, performance accreditation, value-added assessment, portfolio assessment, and high stakes testing associated with rewards and sanctions represented political systems' new demands for better student performance. Charter, magnet, and contract schools emerged as alternative means to secure performance. National teacher certification arose as a potentially powerful long-term strategy to ensure performance. In contrast, the management and fiscal process innovations of the 1960s and 1970s faded. Policy makers' concerns with resource allocation and program requirements as stand-alone accountability measures diminished. Intensification strategies, such as raising graduation requirements, which dominated early excellence-era policy agendas, remained, but their potential to spur widespread improvements in student achievement all but vanished.

The performance-oriented "new educational accountability" (Elmore, Abelmann, & Fuhrman, 1996) introduced several important shifts in the nature of public school accountability (Elmore, Abelmann, and Fuhrman, 1996). First, governors and state legislatures played more prominent roles in education, driving policy making and displacing educational interest groups as the primary instigators of educational policies. Second, states focused their role increasingly on promoting higher standards for education, initially through intensification of existing efforts, then through accountability systems designed around indicators of student performance. Third, states tightened accountability links between states, districts, and schools through consequences for performance. Fourth, states focused attention on school-level accountability by reporting student test performance and by creating school site councils to enhance site performance. In short, educational accountability in the 1990s shifted from districts to schools, from compliance regarding inputs and practices to student performance, from comparative performance to performance against a standard of achievement (Fuhrman, 1994; Hansen, 1993;

O'Reilly, 1996). "What's new about the new educational accountability is its increasing emphasis on student performance as the touchstone for state and district governance" (Elmore, Abelmann, & Fuhrman, 1996, p. 1).

Being new, performance-based accountability systems also exhibited problems of design, implementation, and acceptance. Technical problems involving validity and reliability of measures, fairness of comparisons, student transfers, and the like still affect the complex systems created during the 1990s (Baker & Xu, 1995; Evaluation Center, 1995). Implementation issues have arisen around incentives for students, operation of incentives, perceptions of fairness, and states' capacity to deliver (Elmore, Abelmann, & Fuhrman, 1996). Likewise, conflicts over performance-based assessments arose in California, Kentucky, Vermont, Virginia, Arizona, and Connecticut (Kirst & Mazzeo, 1996; Newmann & Wehlage, 1995). Political issues have encompassed constituency pressures, resource constraints, political stability, public and educator understanding, and the persistence of input and process standards (Elmore, Abelmann, & Fuhrman, 1996). Technical and political problems such as these, however, do not set education apart from other public endeavors. Accountability is a fundamental but underdeveloped concept in American public administration generally (Romzek & Dubnick, 1987).

Development, implementation, and practice problems notwithstanding, two factors militate against a pessimistic assessment of performance-based accountability systems. First, as Elmore (1996a) noted, there is a tremendous amount of learning occurring in states and localities around accountability issues related to standard setting, assessment design, interpreting performance data, and use of incentives. These lessons will bolster future efforts in accountability design. Second, early evidence on performance-based systems indicates that using student test scores on prescribed tests to make judgments about the quality of education in particular schools has evoked changes in what happens in the classroom (Murnane & Levy, 1996a). We conclude from these developments that emerging problems must be interpreted in the context of expected research and development issues, implementation constraints, and sketchy though promising results. Critical reviews of nascent performance accountability systems are needed not only to evaluate system operations but also to ensure that accountability designs effectively support the teaching and learning practices upon which student achievement depends.

Tradeoffs Among Accountability Systems

The accountability systems and strategies we have discussed so far reflect different relationships between principals and agents and contrasting roles for principals and agents. They utilize various mechanisms for ensuring agent compliance, and they rely upon distinctive incentives to stimulate that compliance. In addition simply to arraying types and strategies of accountability systems and their salient attributes, this comparative analysis also enables important insights regarding accountability system design.

For instance, the summary overviews of accountability attributes in Tables 22.1 and 22.2 (upcoming) confront policy makers with more than 50 dimensions of accountability. Such complexity highlights the need to ensure internal consistency in accountability designs, such that the alignment among incentives, accountability mechanisms, principal-agent relationships, and the like is logically reinforcing. Misalignment among design factors, such as tight supervisory control over professionals, introduces internal contradictions that draw attention away from important accountability goals.

Similarly, because accountability systems define relationships between principals and agents and establish the nature of agents' work, accountability designs can be used to transform relationships within or across organizations. The professionalization of teaching presents such a case. Kerchner, Koppich, and Weeres (1997) argued that, in keeping with society's evolution from an industrial to a knowledge base, teachers' work must be reorganized around their knowledge of learning and professional community, with teachers held accountable for student achievement. The reorganization could be facilitated through professional mechanisms of educational accountability, or impeded by an overreliance on bureaucratic supervision. In general terms, accountability systems imply value choices about principal-agent relationships; thus, system designs should be advanced recognizing these implications.

Accountability systems pose tradeoffs between operational values, too, particularly as bureaucratic orientations set up artificial tensions between accountability and values such as creativity and innovation (Light, 1993). As one analyst remarked,

> I begin with the premise that accountability, anymore than any other single value, is not an absolute. If everyone were held accountable for everything he did or tried or thought or imagined, this would be a pretty sterile, dull, and static world. Accountability is not commonly associated with invention or novelty or serendipity, but rather with carrying out assignments, which are more or less specifically defined, honestly, efficiently, effectively, and at minimal cost. Thus at the very outset, there is a conflict between the value associated with accountability and the values of originality, experimentation, inventiveness, and risk-taking (Mosher, 1982, quoted in Light, 1993, p. 13).

Accordingly, designers must be explicit about the values their accountability systems advance, if only to ensure that these are the values they intend to advance.

Accountability designs also express tradeoffs between political and institutional goals. For example, Light (1993) argued that the federal government's preference for compliance monitoring, which produces more findings, less expensive recommendations, cleaner jurisdictional lines, and easier implementation, has to do more with ease of operations and Congressmen's penchant for credit claiming (Mayhew, 1974) than it does with enhancing government's effectiveness. To achieve institutional goals, accountability designs must support the goals directly, rather than the narrower interests of system participants.

Finally, options among accountability designs raise a question about the need to match accountability systems to the circumstances in which they will operate. Strengths and weaknesses of any system will manifest to the extent that the match between system and task makes sense. For example, tight supervisory control is incompatible with situations in which lower-level workers are expected to exercise discretion (Lipsky, 1980). Similarly, legislative oversight of school programs is inconsistent with school systems based on parent choice. Incompatible design elements, stitched together, reduce accountability's effectiveness. Alignment of accountability situations and systems, therefore, emerges as an important factor in system success. The balance of responsibilities between principals and agents, and the degree to which principal-agent actions are mutually reinforcing, constitute another factor in system success. Parceling responsibilities across principals and agents, however, adds another layer of complexity to the framework supporting educational accountability.

Cross-Cutting Themes in Educational Accountability

Accountability is an enduring theme in public education. It serves many purposes, involves sundry policies, and operates through mechanisms as varied as legal mandates, management practices, professional knowledge, democratic processes, individual commitment, and parent choice. The "new educational accountability" elevates public education's commitment to performance, promulgating content standards, performance assessments, and schools as the locus of learning.

It is important to understand accountability trends to track the changing expectations society holds for schools. But trends alone provide little insight into the operations of accountability systems or the administrative and research challenges that accompany new accountability demands. Neither do trends enable one to assess theories of accountability, or design better policies, or fix implementation problems, or explain accountability results. To approach these tasks, administrators and researchers need a perspective on accountability that bridges policy and administration, that frames the functions of educational accountability so as to open them to scrutiny and practice.

We find this useful perspective in a set of themes common to all types of accountability systems. By theme, we mean a central problem or function that circumscribes the operations of accountability systems. We recognize six such themes here: identifying principals and agents, authorizing action, managing agents' productivity, defining accounts, ensuring causal responsibility, and promoting agent compliance. Examining these themes gives educational administrators and researchers some purchase on the operations of accountability systems, hence on the challenges of school leadership for accountability.

Identifying Principals and Agents

Accountability as a policy strategy for improving student performance poses the question: Who is accountable to whom? In terms of the economics of organizations (Moe, 1984), the question refers to a relationship in which one party, the principal, engages another party, the agent, to produce outcomes desired by the principal. In the context of new demands for educational accountability, principals seek improved student performance and agents are expected to produce it. Thus the principal-agent relationship stands at the center of accountability design.

Who are the agents of student performance? Students, teachers, school principals, school site councils, schools, elected school boards, and school districts variously can be designated as agents of student performance, and held accountable accordingly. The "new educational accountability" increasingly targets schools as the locus of accountability. This designation is appropriate insofar as schools organize and deliver educational services. But "school" encompasses many individuals, and accountability designs must distinguish between schools as a unit of organization and school principals, teachers, and students as key operatives in achieving accountability goals.

The cast of principals who make accountability demands is long, too, comprising electorates, politicians (legislators, governors, mayors), educational politicians (chief state school officers, state boards of education, school boards), judges, bureaucrats, business and professional associations, interest groups, textbook and test publishers, educational administrators, teachers, and parents. Multiply this list by federal, state, and local levels, and recognize that principal-agent roles in education shift depending on the context of the interaction—electorate-school board, school board-superintendent, superintendent-school principal, school principal-teacher, teacher-student, even student-parent—and the complexity of principal-agent relations in education becomes apparent.

Once defined, principals and agents become parties to an accountability agreement. Principals commission agents to act on their behalf; agents accept and act on the commission. Because principals hold agents responsible for these actions, principals represent the locus of control in accountability systems. The "new educational accountability" focuses on state legislatures as key principals in performance-oriented accountability systems. States possess constitutional authority for education, authorize schools, and contribute most extensively to their support. States also are driving forces in contemporary calls for educational accountability.

In the conventional political organization or schooling, states vest school districts with the responsibility to educate children, hence establish school districts as agents for accountability purposes. However, this state-district alignment is waning. School site councils, charter schools, contract schools, site-based budgeting, and the bodies of law and research that support these policy developments are altering perceptions of the appropriate locus of control over student learning, elevating schools at the expense of school districts. Moreover, through mandated school performance reporting, states reinforce schools as centers of learning, thus agents for accountability purposes. By shifting performance expectations from districts to schools, policy makers assign responsibility for results to agents lower in the educational system, closer to the point of service delivery.

In short, to the degree that principals and agents are clearly specified, accountability systems establish certainly who is accountable to whom.

Authorizing Action

Once principals and agents are known, a transaction occurs: a principal commissions an agent to perform a task. The commission represents a delegation of authority; it authorizes action on behalf of the principal. Authorizing action expresses a second function of accountability systems. School districts have been the usual recipients of this authority. However, as this arrangement becomes unsatisfactory, new delegations of authority will result. Charter schools, site councils, and various forms of privatization represent encroachments on the state-district arrangement.

Principals authorize agents because it is impractical for principals to act directly. Authority in democratic regimes resides in citizens. In political communities of any size, however, citizens cannot effectively exercise their authority across the range of public responsibilities. Even in small communities, New England townships, for example, where voters consider public problems and craft policy solutions, citizens must delegate authority to agents in order to accomplish basic public functions such as collecting taxes, removing garbage, maintaining order, and educating children. As community size increases and government responsibilities expand, public administration grows in kind. In authorizing public administrators and the bureaus in which they work, citizens create a set of official actors, giving them the right to act on behalf of society and to commit collective resources (March & Olsen, 1995).

In articulating student performance as the goal of educational accountability, and by authorizing agents to pursue this goal, citizens establish their interests and expectations. Accountability goals define society's collective interests vis-à-vis the self-interests of its agents or the narrower interests of the groups that lobby them. Accountability, therefore, informs and reorients the behavior of agents, directing what they should accomplish (Benveniste, 1985). It also provides an agreed language about agents' conduct and performance, and the criteria that should be used in assessing them (Day & Klein, 1987). In so doing, accountability delegates authority, conveys expectations, and orients the behavior of agents.

In creating agents who act and spend on society's behalf, citizens do not simply cede authority and then hope for the best. They maintain control through systems of accountability. Indeed, democratic authority means the right to exercise discretion, subject to being held accountable (March & Olsen, 1995). The accounting is necessary to protect citizens against the flaws of their agents, against implementation of bureaucratic preferences contrary to those authorized by elected officials, and against outright abuses of power that threaten citizens or the democratic government they embody.

In the first instance, accountability constrains agents' tendencies to slacken efforts, lose focus, or promote their own or others' special interests. Accountability systems thus extend to public agents the checks and balances that exist among the branches of government (Gortner, Mahler, & Nicholson, 1989).

In the second instance, responsible agents possess considerable discretion in shaping public policies during implementation, even to the extent of blurring distinctions between policy formulation and execution (Lindblom & Woodhouse, 1993). Accountability affects this process by circumscribing implementation options, ensuring a measure of fidelity between elected officials' intentions and bureaucrats' actions.

In the third instance, unaccountable power forms the seedbed of public abuses (Knott & Miller, 1987). Control is important in this circumstance not only because public agents use resources but also because they affect the way government serves or regulates citizens (Gruber, 1987). Moreover,

> controlling bureaucracies . . . takes on special urgency in democracies because unaccountable power flies in the face of the central norms of such political systems. When legitimacy of a government derives from the consent of the governed, the problem becomes not merely an inability to get the governmental apparatus to act in ways the leaders or citizens wish but also a challenge to the fundamental nature of that government (Gruber, 1987, p. 5).

In protecting against agents' flaws, preferences, and usurpations, accountability links democracy and bureaucracy (Lipsky, 1980), creating agents to carry out declared policies and mechanisms to ensure their responsiveness to legitimate authority. Accountability thus creates and controls autonomy in public agencies. Through clear mandates, development of agency expertise, and known indicators of performance, accountability enables autonomous agency action; by enforcing performance commensurate with official expectations, accountability balances this autonomy (Khademian, 1996). Accountability thus authorizes and limits the discretion of public agents, keeping their actions within defined boundaries, checking their exercise of power. This emphasis on restraint is common to all conceptions of accountability (Gruber, 1987).

Managing Agents' Productivity

Bureaucratic, legal, professional, political, moral, and market conceptions of accountability draw one's attention to types of relationships between principals and agents and to the incentives and controls that govern these relationships. A variation on this perspective highlights a third function of accountability systems: managing agents' productivity. In this regard, accountability systems are distinguished by their focus, respectively, on agent behavior, agent performance, and agent capacity (Light, 1993). From a strategic standpoint, then, accountability systems can specify how agents are to accomplish their tasks, how much discretion (hence, authority) they may exercise, and how much principals invest in agents' activities. To illustrate, imagine a state legislature deciding that schools must educate students to world-class standards in mathematics. The legislature can, alternatively, prescribe the procedures schools must use in pursuing this goal; define world-class performance goals and provide incentives for schools to seek this level of performance; or invest in the human, material, and technological resources schools need to perform at world-class levels. Different strategies dictate different design requirements for accountability systems, alter roles for educational administrators, and influence a state's long-term capability to seek and maintain world-class performances in mathematics.

Attributes of these accountability strategies differ in important ways depending on whether the strategy focuses on agent behavior, agent performance, or agent capacity (Table 22.2). For instance, principals can intervene with agents at different points in the latter's activity. Principals focused on agent behavior examine agents' activities after the fact to assess whether rules and procedures were followed. To wit, did the curriculum committee include a parent representative? In contrast, principals focused on agent performance intervene both before and after agents act, steering their activities with incentives *and* rewarding success, such as a school board providing release time for professional development and awarding salary bonuses to teachers for reaching a school's

Table 22.2

Types and Attributes of Accountability Strategies

	Accountability Strategies		
Attribute	Focus on agent behavior	Focus on agent performance	Focus on agent capacity
Point of intervention	Post-activity	Mixed pre- and post-activity	Pre-activity
Primary mechanism	Rules	Incentives	Technologies
Role of sanctions	Negative	Positive	Positive
Role of management	Supervision and discipline	Goal setting and reinforcement	Advocacy and stewardship
Role of oversight	Detection and enforcement	Evaluation and bench marking	Analysis and design
Complexity of strategy	Simple	More complex	Most complex
Durability of effects	Short-term	Intermediate	Long-term

Note: Adapted from Light, 1993.

mathematics performance goal. Principals focused on agent capacity invest resources in agencies before they act in order to enhance their ability to act, such as linking math teachers and university mathematics experts via Internet connections.

Accountability mechanisms and the nature of sanctions function differently across these behavior, performance, and capacity strategies. Behavior-oriented systems operate through rules, and rule-breakers are reprimanded, fined, or otherwise punished. Sanctions are negative and crafted to deter future noncompliance. In contrast, the incentives associated with performance-oriented systems, and the training opportunities and technologies that enhance capacity-building efforts, influence agents through positive means.

Administration functions differently, too, across accountability strategies. In a rule-driven, behavior-oriented system, to administer means to supervise and discipline workers, enforcing standard practices and punishing breaches where they occur. Alternatively, administrators in performance-based systems establish or reinforce performance goals and promote workers' efforts to attain them. Administrators frequently accomplish these tasks through personnel or program evaluations and bench marking, a process of setting performance goals to meet or exceed a high standard of practice (the bench mark) and tracking progress relative either to one's present position or to the bench mark itself (U.S. Advisory Commission on Intergovernmental Relations, 1996). Goal setting and bench marking constitute different roles still from those of administrators charged with building an organization's capacity. In a capacity-focused context, administrators analyze deficiencies in organizational capacity, design remedies, and secure technologies necessary to close the gap. In capacity-oriented accountability systems, administrators function more as stewards of their organizations, managing community resources to achieve desired ends.

Finally, behavior, performance, and capacity strategies vary in terms of their complexity and durability. Behavior-

oriented systems, for instance, are relatively simple to design and to administer. However, as accountability in these systems resides in rules that need constant reinforcing, their effects are short-lived (Light, 1993). Performance-oriented systems are more durable, as accountability resides in agents who assume responsibility for an organization's performance. But individuals come and go, and with them goes part of an organization's performance base. In capacity-focused systems, accountability resides in an agency itself. Organizational capacity is tended over time, such that accountability goals become embedded in an organization's conception of work. Though more enduring, capacity-oriented systems are more complex to design and costly to operate. They also require longer-term maintenance across generations of policy makers.

In sum, principals can pursue accountability using different strategies to manage agents' productivity; they can even mix strategies. At the same time, they must be mindful of the principal and agent commitments implied by each strategy and the probability that any one strategy will accomplish the specific task for which it was selected.

Defining Accounts

The democratic emphasis on informed consent as the basis of authority requires that accounts be given and that accountability be enforced (March & Olsen, 1995). "Those who act on behalf of the political community by virtue of holding an office, and on the basis of authority and resources derived from that community, are accountable to the judgments of ordinary citizens informed by such accounts" (March & Olsen, 1995, p. 150). Therefore, in addition to identifying principals and agents, delegating authority, and managing agents' productivity, accountability systems provide methods of accounting and consequences for results, a fourth function. Such an account reports, explains, and justifies actions taken and the consequences of these actions (Wagner, 1989). In the educational arena, accounts provide a way of knowing and judging schools (Wilson, 1996).

In specifying the accounts that must be rendered, state legislatures articulate their particular interest in student performance. Basics or critical thinking? Academics only? Core subjects or others? What resulting skills? What level of accomplishment? All students or a select group? These and similar decisions are represented in requirements for schools. Through these requirements, states specify the indicators (test scores or other measures) that will measure performance and standardize discussions of student learning.

Over time, educational accounts have taken many forms, including fiscal audits, accreditation reports, school inspections, test results, personnel evaluations, program evaluations, and performance reporting. All are useful for some purpose. With the growing orientation of educational accountability toward student performance, particularly at the school level, performance reporting continues to gain importance as a method of tracking educational progress and communicating results to school boards, legislatures, and voters.

All states collect performance data about schools (OERI, 1988), but the data are generally weak. In 1991, prominent researchers concluded that "ideas about how to both stimulate and measure school improvement are still in their infancy" (Darling-Hammond & Ascher, 1991, p. 13); in 1997, analysts noted how school performance data were insufficient to use as the basis of a comprehensive educational-indicator information system (Education Week, 1997). Still, performance reporting relies on statistical indicators of school quality.

In terms of shaping the accounts of educational performance, several points are relevant (OERI, 1988). To begin, the selection of indicators largely determines who will be held accountable, to whom, and for what. Indicators therefore have a defining influence on accountability systems, thus warranting careful consideration. Furthermore, because the choice of indicators ultimately determines the utility of an accountability system, indicators should be selected that measure the central features of schooling, measure what is actually taught or considered important for students to know, provide information that is policy-relevant, focus on schools, allow for fair comparisons, and balance information's usefulness against the burden of collecting it. Indicators also should be valid, measuring what they purport to measure, and reliable, operating free from errors of measurement and data collection. In addition to selecting indicators, system designers must also decide at what level data will be collected, the level at which it will be reported, mechanisms for reporting, and how schools will be compared. In other words, choices among indicators are consequential in defining the character and the utility of educational accountability systems.

Accountability designs also must consider the scope of the account that conveys the most useful information

about school performance. As the OERI State Accountability Study Group posed this issue,

> Accountability is a blunt tool unless policymakers, educators, and the public have information that allows them to determine the likely sources of a problem and find clues about how to fix it. Consequently, accountability systems should do more than simply collect testing data. They should provide an integrated picture of the schooling environment and include data on fiscal and other resources, teachers, school organization, curriculum, and the distribution of various student outcomes (achievement, participation) across different types of students and schools (OERI, 1988, p. 7).

Similarly, March and Olsen (1995) conceived of accounts in terms of "stories that bring order to the obscurities of political causality" (p. 149). Applying this notion to public schools, educational accounts must be broad enough to explain the experience of schooling. The task is difficult. School processes and outcomes are often ambiguous, obfuscated by scale, constrained by technology, clouded by shared responsibilities, and diminished through competing expectations. In this context, educational accounts that explain and interpret school performance can make important contributions to knowing and judging schools. Such accounts would relate results to actions of agents, outside influences, adequacy of resources, and engagement of students. They would range beyond simple compilations of statistical indicators. And though they would explain performance better, they also would make accounting more difficult. Accounts that included indicators *and* explanations would, however, more readily allow for political consensus about the needs and potential of public schools, and thus form the basis of action among agents and stakeholders who use and support public schools.

In sum, accountability systems organize public resources to promote publicly agreed ends (Knott & Miller, 1987). Educational accounts in the late 1990s do not do this well. They have not settled on valid and reliable indicators, nor have they offered compelling explanations of outcomes. They do not even yet reflect clearly agreed ends. Tough developmental work lies ahead, and the quest for accurate and robust indicators and explanations will drive it.

Ensuring Causal Responsibility

Responsibility is a fundamental construct in accountability systems. In democratic theory, within which questions of governmental accountability reside, the meaning of responsibility encompasses accountability, causation, and obligation (Spiro, 1964).

Responsibility as accountability means being answerable to someone else and having to account for one's actions or inaction and their consequences (Browder, 1973; March & Olsen, 1995). In this sense, if we say that school superintendents are responsible for student achievement, we mean that superintendents must give an account of the manner in which they addressed student achievement, with the account rendered most likely to a school board.

Responsibility as causation means that, through action or inaction, one causes a particular result. Superintendents who are responsible for student achievement, in this sense, actually caused the level of student achievement which resulted, perhaps by allocating a district's resources in particular ways or by hiring unusually strong teachers. For superintendents to be causally responsible, they must possess resources required by the task, foreknowledge sufficient to predict the consequences of their actions, discretion to act, and resolution to act (Spiro, 1964). They also must be situated to cause a result.

Responsibility as obligation refers to a person's sense of purpose. In this regard, superintendents who are responsible for student achievement assume an obligation to act in ways that influence student achievement. The obligation can arise via a school board directive, state program advisory, legislative reform, or intrinsic construction of a superintendent's role related to student achievement. Whatever the source, the sense of purpose needs to be sufficiently strong to oblige superintendents either to follow a prescribed course of action or to exert their capacity for causal responsibility in order to accomplish the performance for which an account must be rendered. Obligation and motivation are interchangeable constructs in this context, as they both animate agents' actions.

The notion of responsibility broadens discussions regarding accountability by identifying causal responsibility as the complement to accountability. Whereas accountability focuses on the performance of agents, causal responsibility highlights the relative contribution of principals and agents to the outcome.

Importantly, being held accountable creates a presumption of capability and discretion (March & Olsen, 1995). More to the point, "to be accountable for something, one must have control over it in some way" (Sarlos, 1973, p. 74). However, causal responsibility occurs in varying degrees (see Table 22.3). Explicit causal responsibility operates when agents are aware of their obligation to act; when they exercise full discretion in selecting among possible courses of action; when they possess sufficient operational knowledge to predict the consequences of these various courses of action; when they possess the material, human, and other resources necessary to accomplish the task; and when acting directly influences the result. Conversely, causal responsibility is implicit to the extent that any of these factors is missing. Under this condition, principals' assumptions of causality would be invalid, but principals—legislatures, for example —often do not recognize the problem and so do not adjust their expectations.

Accountability systems must strike a balance between principals' expectations and agents' causal responsibility. Oth-

Table 22.3
Factors of Causal Responsibility

Factor	Explicit[a]	Implicit[b]
Expectation[c]	Clear	Unknown
Causality[d]	Direct	Indirect
Knowledge[e]	Certain	Uncertain
Resources[f]	Adequate	Inadequate
Discretion[g]	Unlimited	Limited

[a] Causal responsibility is explicit to the extent that principals assume causality and factors that support causality are present. Explicit causal responsibility expressed an agent's ability to act in accord with accountability expectations and the degree to which he or she can be held accountable fairly for a result.

[b] Causal responsibility is implicit to the extent that principals assume causality but one or more factors that support causality are lacking. Under this condition, principals' assumptions of causality would be invalid, but principals often do not recognize the problem and so do not adjust their expectations. Implicit causal responsibility constrains an agent's actions and the degree to which he or she can be held accountable fairly for a result.

[c] Awareness of obligation to carry out specific task.

[d] Degree of agent control over result.

[e] Foreknowledge of consequences of actions, for self and others.

[f] Material, human, financial, other.

[g] Freedom to select among all available courses of action.

Note: Adapted from Spiro, 1969.

erwise agents will be held accountable for results they cannot control. To the extent that principals create the conditions under which agents carry out their tasks—by influencing resources, knowledge, choices, or purposes—principals assume an obligation to enhance the causal responsibility of those who must act. Clients, for example, do not determine the capacity of the professionals who serve them, nor do they expect to. On the other hand, through promulgation of policies related to tax levels, teacher certification, curriculum frameworks, and the like, state legislatures do influence the capacity of teachers, school principals, superintendents, and educational agencies to educate students. Thus accountability systems that define states' expectations for student performance also must assume an appropriate state burden to develop educators' or educational agencies' causal responsibility, and accordingly adjust the standard of accountability to which these agents are held. In the connections between principals' expectations and agents' causal responsibility, one begins to see the complexity and potential in accountability designs.

Promoting Agent Compliance

The central problem in principal-agent relations regards incentives that motivate agents to act in the interests of their principals (Stiglitz, 1987). Accountability systems perform a sixth function insofar as they structure incentives that promote agent compliance. Promoting agent compliance is a matter of enhancing the motivation and capacity of agents to attain accountability goals. As schools become the primary agents of performance accountability, the aggregate effort of school principals, teachers, and students comprises the range of agent actions that must be motivated.

Motivation animates activity; it encompasses individuals' goals, their assessments of what they can accomplish, and whether the contexts in which they work will support or condemn them for making the attempt (Ford, 1992). This analysis of motivation as goal attainment complements claims in expectancy theory that behavior is need-driven and that individuals are motivated to try to achieve a certain performance if they believe it is attainable and if attaining the performance will lead to outcomes they value (Mohrman & Lawler, 1996). In either construction, motivation underlies individuals' attempts to perform in particular ways and to reach particular levels of accomplishment. Thus the challenge to accountability systems is to structure incentives that effectively motivate school staffs (and others) to pursue accountability goals.

What do we know about the effects of incentives and accountability on individual behavior? We know, for example, that incentives come in many forms and that the details matter a lot (Hanushek, 1996). That is, individuals do not respond similarly to the same incentives (Elmore, 1996b). Moreover, being responsible for one's own actions makes a difference both to behavior and to the way individuals justify their behavior: being accountable accentuates deliberateness in decision making but also increases caution about change and risk-taking (March & Olsen, 1995). Furthermore, many questions regarding incentives do not involve policy but larger issues of culture and norms (Fuhrman, 1996). We know that rewards and extrinsic reinforcement do not reduce one's intrinsic motivation (Cameron & Pierce, 1994),[2] that individual merit and incentive pay programs do not work, but that competency-based pay and group performance rewards can reinforce learning goals (Odden & Kelley, 1997). Furthermore, teachers are motivated by helping students achieve, by collaborating with colleagues on issues of teaching and learning, and by high quality professional development; thus, school systems organized to increase student achievement can themselves motivate teachers (Odden & Kelley, 1997).

Furthermore, we know that teachers are skeptical about change and reluctant to engage new reforms (Mohrman & Lawler, 1996). Also, accountability systems can generate unintended and corrupting consequences (teaching to the test) (Clotfelter & Ladd, 1996), and that the validity and comprehensibility of accountability measures affect teachers' attitudes (Elmore, Abelmann, & Fuhrman, 1996). In addition, there is little evidence that the incentives embedded in the current educational accountability system work

(Hanushek, 1996). We know enough, that is, to find promise and caution in the incentives embedded in new systems of educational accountability, and to encourage the search for better incentives.

But even the notion of grounding accountability in student performance recalls the problem of scale, as seeking and inducing higher performance requires more and better effort from all those involved. In Susan Fuhrman's words,

> If reform is about changing teaching and learning to focus more on understanding and applying knowledge, then all those involved in the educational enterprise must learn how to promote those goals. Teachers must learn to teach in much more ambitious ways; students must take greater responsibility for their own learning; educators and policymakers must learn how to organize and manage schools and systems to support such improvements in teaching and learning (Fuhrman, 1996, p. 330).

These challenges are not to be understated. American education has had little success getting to scale with improvements in the core of educational practice, namely, how teachers understand the nature of knowledge, the student's role in learning, and how these ideas about learning are manifested in teaching and classwork (Elmore, 1996b). Accountability contributes to the solution, however, by focusing expectations, structuring incentives to reinforce those expectations, developing capacity, and requiring an account. Because student achievement both anchors performance-based accountability systems and motivates classroom teachers, educational systems can expect some progress on this basis alone. Further developments depend on the varying capacities of school staffs and different levels of student engagement.

Insofar as directing agents' actions, motivation and capacity are mutually reinforcing. Capacity provides the wherewithal behind causal responsibility. Narrowly defined, capacity encompasses the skills and knowledge required to carry out assigned or assumed tasks (Ford, 1992). However, researchers are beginning to broaden the concept as it is applied to schools and targeted at student performance. Newmann, King, and Rigdon (1997), for example, defined capacity as professional knowledge and skills, effective leadership, technical and financial resources, and organizational autonomy to act, but also as the degree to which human, technical, and social resources of schools are organized into an effective collective enterprise. Guthrie and Hill (this volume) introduced the notion of "integrative capacity" to refer to the strategic and effective application of a school's financial, human, social, and political capitals to affect student learning. Spillane and Thompson (1997) likewise defined a broad view of local agency capacity, including knowledge, skills, and dispositions of leaders within a district; social links within and outside a district, together with norms and trust to support open communication; and dollars as allocated to staffing, time, and materials. Corcoran and Goertz (1995) refer to capacity in terms of the intellectual skills, quality and quantity of resources, and social organization of instruction or instructional culture. In effect, research is beginning to support a focus on school capacity in much the same way as policy developments are beginning to focus on school responsibility in promoting student achievement.

Because schools increasingly are assigned the role of accountable agent regarding student performance, accountability systems must enhance schools' capacities to perform as expected, organizing those capacities they possess and securing others from outside, whether that means brokering expertise, providing professional development, securing material resources, or the like. Schools then must act to enhance student learning in ways commensurate with state expectations, and they must account to the state, describing the results they achieved and perhaps the strategies and activities they undertook in doing so. The state's supporting role comes in providing incentives (including authority and resources) sufficient to counteract competing expectations or insufficient causal responsibility.

Themes for Accountability Design and Research

These six cross-cutting themes in educational accountability provide insights into the operations of accountability systems. These systems specify who is accountable to whom, they commission specific work on behalf of principals through limited grants of authority, and they structure the context in which agents conduct their work. By defining the nature of the account that must be rendered, accountability systems also define expectations for the type, amount, and quality of the result that agents must accomplish. In addition, accountability systems distribute responsibility among principals and agents. Recognizing joint responsibilities is important in the public domain, where public agencies, including school districts and schools, depend on political superordinates for the lion's share of resources they need to pursue accountability goals. In public education particularly, state legislatures enhance or constrain student performance through myriad policies regarding finance, facilities, governance, organization, personnel, curriculum, and assessment. The same sense of causal responsibility that reveals a legislature's role in achieving accountability results also opens the question of who influences student achievement and in what degree. To the extent that students themselves are responsible for their own performance, then educational accountability systems must either recognize performance factors that operate beyond educators' control, and adjust sanctions in kind, or affirm students as accountable agents and craft incentives to promote their compliance.

This thematic or functional perspective on accountability raises a series of questions pertinent to accountabil-

ity design, implementation, and evaluation. A beginning list includes the following:

- Are principals and agents clearly and fairly specified?
- Is the authorization adequate to focus agents actions?
- Is the work context consistent with accountability goals? (Avoiding, for example, bureaucratic controls when accountability goals depend on the exercise of professional discretion.)
- Are design elements reinforcing or conflicting?
- Are accounts defined using meaningful, valid, and reliable data?
- Are indicators useful to principals and agents?
- Are accounts able to judge schools?
- Is accountability technology sufficient for rewards and sanctions?
- Do agents have discretion to act?
- Do agents have resources to act?
- Are agents capable of acting?
- Is the principal providing support?
- Are sanctions commensurate with causal responsibility?
- Do incentives motivate agents?

To the degree that these questions are addressed, accountability systems, logically, gain efficacy. Future practice and research must determine the extent to which this is the case. Embedded in these questions, however, lie challenges for school leadership.

Challenges for School Leadership

The challenge of educational accountability in the late 1990s is one of scale, conceptualization, and commitment. School reformers want accountability to improve the academic performance of students across whole school systems. Kentucky and Maryland are good examples (Education Week, 1997). This large-scale ambition triggers attributes of accountability related to incentives and support that are more complex than policy makers or educational leaders are used to addressing. Moreover, a weak conceptualization of accountability exacerbates the problem, limiting the efficacy of performance-based accountability systems and mitigating policy and administrative efforts to attain accountability goals. As we argued earlier, performance-based accountability requires complementary commitments on the part of policy makers and educators that reach beyond the simple articulation of performance expectations on one hand and business-as-usual responses on the other. In a more ambitious system, principals and agents alike must act on their respective obligations to build capacity and perform responsibly. Such a relationship distributes assignments across policy and administration while (perhaps) constraining expectations for what accountability can accomplish in educational settings. In this light, educational accountability appears more complex and costly than reformers envision and more appropriate and useful than practitioners acknowledge.

When observers describe accountability mechanisms as problematic (Darling-Hammond, 1989), invalid and trivial (Sagor, 1996), or ineffective (Wilson, 1996), one wonders whether education's growing preoccupation with accountability might be counterproductive to the goals of school improvement. Though perhaps reasonable at first glance, that conclusion would be premature. Consider, for instance, the efficacy of educational accountability mechanisms to ensure probity in school district accounts, depth of program offerings, equity in resource distribution, or progress on desegregation. Similarly, accountability mechanisms have opened educational governance to public scrutiny and secured due process in personnel actions, better training for school professionals, even structural safety of school buildings.

Acknowledging the utility of accountability mechanisms in these circumstances is not logically incompatible with observers' criticisms of accountability reforms. In fact, the applications of accountability in these two contexts are fundamentally different. Among the now-standard operating practices of schools, such as how they handle money, structure programs, or implement regulations, accountability features limited purposes, clear responsibilities, and a focus on resource provision or organizational process. In the context of excellence era reforms, with academic performance driving school improvement, accountability encompasses ambitious but contested purposes, overlapping responsibilities, and a focus on organizational outcomes. School reformers have ratcheted up expectations for educational accountability but have not yet developed accountability systems commensurate with these demands.

Because of the diversity of accountability systems (OERI, 1988), complexity of the accountability task (Sarlos, 1973; Wagner, 1989), and evolving nature of accountability expectations (Elmore, Abelmann, & Fuhrman, 1996), challenges associated with accountability practice are numerous and substantial.

One can summarize the challenges of educational accountability at the close of the 20th century by imagining a group of citizens setting out to tour the terrain. What would they encounter?

The tour would begin at the launching pad of the excellence movement, where the political system selected student performance as the preferred waypoint along the route toward a strong economy, vibrant democracy, and satisfied citizenry. This point, by convention, is delineated by the publication of *A Nation at Risk* (National Commission on Excellence in Education, 1983). Nevertheless, from this point forward, our tourists would confront a confusing array of alternative routes, varying road conditions, and conflicting directions.

Their first impression would register vast activity, with dozens of construction companies surveying possible routes, clearing land, paving roadbeds, and erecting signposts. Closer inspection would reveal that not all roads received equal attention. Several roads were older, abandoned or in need of repair, and ended short of the waypoint. Others were newer, were presumed to be headed in the desired direction, but were under construction, so were still impassable. Even in the most active construction zones, our tourists would observe foremen and crews arguing about who should do what for whom, crews forging ahead with poorly specified blueprints, crews slowed for lack of equipment, roadbeds unfinished for want of paving crews, and crews disgruntled over assigned tasks. At intervals, our tourists would note travel agents debating the choice of routes, citizens protesting construction at various sites, and traffic cops monitoring interchanges where roads looped off toward alternative destinations. After a trip like this, our tourists might bemoan the absence of a good map to show them logical connections among the routes and to help them track progress toward their goal.

Such observations would be consistent with a more literal assessment of late 20th century accountability efforts. From this vantage, observers would see federal, state, and local agents serially promulgating mechanisms of accountability. They would watch policy makers launch major accountability initiatives (standards), tinker with others (choice), bypass earlier efforts (graduation requirements), or make repairs as support dictated (certification). Observers also would see elected officials, professionals, and parents vying to define accountability standards; performance-based accountability policies layered onto resource distribution and program standards; competing theories of accountability; principal-agent problems; tentative professional commitment; and accountability designs outpacing available technologies. In other words, as the preferred solution to low student achievement (and to the economic, civic, and social outcomes it inhibits), the "new educational accountability" quickly translates into a set of political, managerial, and technical problems for educational leaders. Eight of these problems particularly define the context of accountability for educational leaders at the turn of the millennium.

Problem 1: Principal-Agent Ambiguity

Earlier we introduced the principal-agent relationship which underlies all accountability systems. This relationship answers the question: who is accountable to whom? We raise the issue again in the context of challenges to educational administration to note that the political and intergovernmental character of education, and the dispersion of responsibility for learning, make it difficult to know certainly who is accountable to whom.

Principal-agent ambiguity arises from a context characterized by numerous, vague goals (Sizer, 1984); multiple authorities and conflicts of interest (Spring, 1993); inadequate and inequitably distributed resources (Guthrie, 1997); absence of a "production function" to effectively steer resources toward student performance (Monk, 1992); policy incoherence and fragmented attempts at improvement (Fuhrman, Elmore, & Massell, 1993); and student values that frequently do not support learning (Steinberg, 1996). Such a context invites ambiguous specifications of purposes, principals, and agents.

Even when focused on the central goal of raising student performance, with state legislatures asserting their prerogatives to establish performance expectations, "agents" still beg definition. The usual candidates include school districts, schools, school principals, teachers, students, and, perhaps, parents. Through targeted incentives and sanctions, accountability systems should resolve the ambiguity. Kentucky's performance award system, for example, holds schools accountable for student performance. Tennessee's valued-added assessment focuses responsibility on teachers. But no system in the United States holds students accountable for learning through a system of high-stakes exams in the European style. Yet student performance ultimately depends on students. Perhaps future accountability designs will specifically recognize multiple agents of student performance, holding each to a fair measure of accountability.

The challenge to educational administrators amidst such ambiguity is to remain responsive to political superordinates while simultaneously assuming appropriate responsibility for performance goals, and to shield school faculties from demands that mitigate the focus on performance and the central work of teaching and learning. Research can support this endeavor by examining the relationship between competing demands and schools' assumptions of responsibility. In addition, research can identify the interests behind competing demands, and it can explore the allocation of responsibilities and resources that define agents of student performance.

Problem 2: Contested Standards

In the diverse setting of American education, the standards that drive educational accountability have not been easy to establish. Portraying the status of the standards movement in the mid-1990s, Resnick and Nolan noted that

> Several years after the initial grants were made for developing standards in English, history, science, and geography, educators and, more important, the public at large are not sure what stan-

dards are, and doubts are arising about whether they are needed or wanted (1995, p. 99).

Resnick and Nolan also chronicled conflicts within academic disciplines, between political parties, and among local constituencies that believed standards were a way of promoting social values rather than academic rigor. Thus the second problem educational administrators confront is a political one: how to press ahead in the face of goals and standards that are actively contested; particularly, how to mediate the contest while simultaneously shaping schools' responses to new accountability demands. It is the problem represented in the question: accountable for what? The corresponding research task is to describe the content and evolution of emerging performance standards and to explain the factors that shape these public expectations.

Problem 3: Ill-Fitting Management Practices

Leadership is essential to ensure accountability in public organizations. The political, legal, and appropriations-driven environments of public agencies, including schools, provide many opportunities for workers to lose sight of accountability goals, and few or perverse incentives to pursue those goals. Educational leaders must capture and focus the attention of the professional and public communities in which they operate, and they must stimulate the imagination of their faculties and staffs with effective communication regarding their visions of good practice and performance (Kearns, 1996).

In educational accountability systems focused on resource allocation or process requirements, leadership is less important to accountability results than good management, and few people need to be involved. In the excellence era of school reform, with performance accountability gaining prominence, leadership becomes central to accountability results as leadership is needed to focus and motivate the range of individuals who influence student learning.

The leadership challenge to educational administrators is to shift educational management away from bureaucratic modes of supervision and discipline toward professional models based on goal-setting, reinforcement, advocacy, and stewardship in building school capacity to achieve accountability goals over time. The center of this effort may lie in reconciling school versus system expectations of accountability (a theme we develop later in the chapter). In this construction, administrators' primary responsibilities involve gaining agreement on performance goals, communicating goals constantly, and fostering commitment to goals throughout school communities, as well as aligning resources with goals, analyzing performance, and fixing problems. Research can facilitate this transformation by identifying barriers to performance in personnel, regulations, standard operating procedures, and resources, and by evaluating management structures and procedures to learn which best facilitate staff and student performance.

Problem 4: Rudimentary Accounts

As new demands for educational accountability appeared, new accountability policies translated these demands into requirements for practice. Typical in these cases, however, new policies were layered onto older ones, creating a complex web of accountability expectations. The diversity of accountability policies promulgated during this period also reflected policy makers' search for accounts anchored in student performance. The question, How can we hold schools accountable for results?, was answered initially by policy broadsides, which, in the case of Kentucky, required administrators to manage and track simultaneous changes in curriculum, assessment, finance, and governance, a phenomenon Kentucky educators referred to as "rebuilding the airplane while flying it." Policy makers have addressed the complementary question, Which indicators capture emerging performance expectations?, by requiring reports on student achievement, competency, course-taking, college-going, attendance, dropouts, and the like. Such indicators are usually available but represent only weak proxies for school quality and system effort. Accountability systems have yet to craft accounts that reflect the experience of schooling.

The problem here is that performance indicators, though rudimentary, still form the basis of school comparisons, even rewards and sanctions. In this light, rudimentary does not mean inconsequential. As standards and tests become better aligned, achievement indicators will become more useful in conveying what students know and are able to do. Meanwhile, the challenge to educational administrators is to integrate performance indicators into schools' own assessments of performance and practice, interpreting and acting on the same information used by districts and states. Educational leaders also must assume the task of shaping indicators that better reflect school experiences and more directly support teaching and learning. Research can improve the utility of performance indicators by examining the relationship between various indicators and teachers' assessments and alterations of practice.

Problem 5: Inadequate Technology

Educational administrators confront a fifth problem insofar as the tests used to hold schools accountable are technically not adequate to the task. It is the problem related to the question: How will we hold agents accountable? Koretz (1995) noted the limitations of assessment as a tool of accountability, arguing that test scores can be inflated, tests can narrow (fewer subjects) and degrade (focus on drill) instruction, tests cannot distinguish educational quality from other factors such as students' backgrounds, and tests cannot simultaneously serve monitoring and accountability goals. Koretz concluded that testing expectations are too high, that testing technology is limited, and that more needs to be learned about the contributions of tests to educational accountability. In examining Kentucky's Instructional Results Information System (KIRIS), analysts from the Kentucky Institute for Educational Research similarly concluded that two of the three components of the KIRIS accountability index were not sufficiently reliable to be used in a high stakes assessment system (Evaluation Center, 1995). In short, the technology of testing is not yet commensurate with the political system's desire for test-based accountability. Nevertheless, accountability systems press ahead using available technology, even assigning rewards and sanctions.

The imperative for administration is to align school resources in curriculum, professional development, and leadership with new assessment tools so as to produce the greatest positive result, while monitoring and limiting unintended and degrading effects of accountability assessments on instruction. Researchers can assess the impact of accountability testing on instruction and school climate, support test development, and inform policy makers regarding the need for improved tests or alternative technologies.

Problem 6: Limited Causal Responsibility

Who is causally responsible for student performance? Responsibility is shared across students, teachers, parents, and others, complicating design issues in educational accountability. As Brown concluded,

> Despite the elaborate system of rules and regulations produced by . . . various accountability mechanisms, there is little belief that the outcomes of education are under anyone's control . . . The sheer complexity of the mission and the environment impose limits on our ability to hold public education accountable. In education, the normal complexity of a public agency is compounded by the fact that we are trying to educate human beings with their different skills, interests, and resources, instead of making robots or processing tax forms (Brown, 1990, p. 2).

Causal responsibility poses a fundamental challenge to performance-based accountability systems. The construct represents an agent's ability to act in accord with accountability expectations and the degree to which that agent can be held accountable. It requires a knowledge base relating effective means of accomplishing accountability goals. In the resource-dependent environment of public education, causal responsibility also recognizes the obligations of principals to state expectations clearly and to provide resources and discretion sufficient for agents to carry out their responsibilities. The causal responsibility challenge is grounded in expectations, knowledge, resources, discretion, and causality.

Knowledge supports an agent's capacity to pursue accountability goals. Performance-based accountability requires that teachers develop the capacity to teach high standards. The capacity problem for educational administrators leads them to broker the resources needed to improve teachers' abilities to teach the new standards, whether this involves securing materials, information, or technology; manipulating schedules or release time to create opportunities to practice; facilitating professional networks; or creating a school culture that supports change. It also means lobbying for the discretion needed to act in ways that school staffs deem effective and professionally responsible. The research issue here lies in defining adequate resources and in exploring the relationship between increased local, probably school, discretion and professional efforts directed at accountability goals.

Problem 7: Unmotivated Staffs

Higher standards and new forms of educational accountability portend changes in curriculum, instruction, and assessment—changes, that is, in teaching and learning. The history of school reform, however, indicates that innovations in teaching and learning seldom penetrate more than a small fraction of classrooms and seldom last long when they do (Elmore, 1996b). Innovations frequently fail because the individuals who make it happen, those directly responsible for changes, are not committed to the effort (McLaughlin, 1987). They lack motivation. Agents are motivated to change when their personal goals are aligned with change, when they are confident in their ability to change, and when they feel supported in attempting the change (Ford, 1992).

Accountability can facilitate motivation by narrowing system expectations, focusing educators' attention and responsibilities, and compelling policies that support performance and counteract competing interests. In this regard, educational accountability can structure policy supports for public schools and enhance the motivation and capacity of school staffs to get the right job done.

Because the commitment of teachers and students is central to performance-based accountability, educational leaders must increase teachers' and students' commitments to performance goals by identifying and applying incentives that motivate teachers and students to pursue those goals. On this dimension, the central challenge for educational administrators is to create a demand for performance

goals, to build teacher and student will, and to promote school cultures that reward achievement. The research task involves examining the relationship between types and levels of incentives and faculty and student performance.

Problem 8: Uncertain Causal Theories

Variations in accountability policy represent either a range of preferences among designs or uncertainty regarding which designs are relatively more efficacious. The latter choice poses the question: which accountability designs work? Accountability goals are more likely to be achieved through designs based on valid causal theories about the problematic teaching or learning behaviors that inhibit performance and about the relationship between accountability instruments and these behaviors (Winter, 1990). In other words, poor accountability designs well implemented still will not improve student performance. The challenge to educational administrators and researchers alike lies in understanding how accountability designs are supposed to work, assessing how they actually work, and communicating these results to policy makers to facilitate policy redesign.

Toward School-Based Accountability for the 21st Century

New demands for educational accountability highlight a major shift in accountability expectations and a problem. The shift from resource and process concerns to a performance orientation establishes accountability as an instrument of teaching and learning. Performance goals depend on good teaching and student engagement. Yet current accountability efforts inadequately support teaching and learning, convey negative connotations, and lack face validity with some teachers. The following comments illustrate these points.

> Most of what states and localities are doing in the name of performance accountability in schools has nothing to do with helping educators know how to do the right things. Setting standards and changing organizational and governance arrangements does not, by itself, address the problem of knowing how to do the right things (Elmore, 1996a, p. 10).

> For too many educators, [accountability] carries connotations of power being exerted over them by external quality control officers. We are reminded of politicians, administrators, or demagogues promising to hold others accountable for the results of their performance (Sagor, 1996, p. vii).

> Our accountability schemes provide inappropriate information based on measures that are widely viewed as invalid. Many practitioners see our systems as controlling, not supportive. Many re-

formers experience them as hurdles. Many policymakers see them as trivial (Wilson, 1996, p. 225).

Moreover, early analyses of school-based, internal accountability standards indicate that educators rarely use accountability data to make decisions related to practice; it is used mostly for compliance purposes (Consortium for Policy Research in Education, 1997). And while system-wide, external accountability standards cannot reinforce practice, they can be harmful. As Leithwood and Atkin (1995) argued,

> The consequences of tightening the accountability "screws" often are a narrowing and trivializing of the school curriculum and the creation of work cultures that reduce, rather than increase, professional commitments and circumscribe the full use of existing teacher and administrator capacities (p. 3).

A corollary problem arises in external accountability's implied assumption that "one accountability model will be sufficient across all school contexts and that the capacity to respond is shared equally by schools" (Elmore, Abelmann, & Fuhrman, 1996, p. 1). In other words, state-mandated, performance-based accountability mechanisms may shift system attention to student performance, but they may not motivate teachers to teach or students to learn; neither may they provide a mechanism that effectively builds the capacity of schools to respond to state performance standards.

Early research on performance accountability systems has begun to build a contrasting case that external accountability and instruction can be reinforcing. Research on Vermont's portfolio assessment, for example, demonstrated how teachers' attention to portfolio development could encourage good educational practice and provide a focus for professional development for teachers and how it could encourage local initiatives in developing curricula and effective approaches to teaching (Murnane & Levy, 1996b). Similarly, research on Kentucky's school-based performance award program indicated how external accountability standards can motivate teachers to change practice to improve student performance (Kelley, 1997).

Logically, the efficacy of performance accountability derives from its use in practice and its contribution to improved student achievement. Therefore,

> It is critical for legislators to understand that, by itself, a statewide accountability system is insufficient to make a significant impact on improving student learning. The problem is that the vast majority of schools in California, and across the nation, are not organized so that they can use standards and test results in ways which help them make improvements in teaching and learning. We need high standards and a statewide assessment system. But even more than that, we need schools with the habit of collaborative, results-oriented practices that are likely to use this data to improve student learning. It is time to shift away from *accountability as "accounting"*—the gathering, organizing and reporting of information about student performance—and toward *ac-*

countability as a local "system of use" for interpreting and acting on information (*Summary of remarks*, 1997, p. 1).

By implication, accountability designers need to retool their standards- and test-based performance systems in order to ensure that they enhance system efforts to promote greater student achievement.

Implications for Educational Leadership and Research

Assessing new demands of educational accountability involves attention to issues of conceptualization and practice. Because policy makers intend performance accountability to promote greater student achievement, the standard for evaluating an accountability system must be that system's ability to support teaching and learning practices which raise student performance. This standard necessitates a design linkage, through consensus or appropriate incentives, between external accountability standards and the predispositions of the administrators, teachers, and students who are responsible for meeting those standards.

The accountability perspective we have developed enables a comparison between external-policy and internal-school orientations on accountability (see Table 22.4). For instance, school-based accountability systems develop around professionally negotiated standards for school performance and are site-specific.[3] Teachers' motivation originates inside the school, where their collaboration can affect teaching directly. Yet schools have few resources for capacity building and make no public accounting of performance. Alignment between school and system standards is possible but not necessary. Empirical support for the image of school-based accountability presented in Table 22.4 comes from Newmann, King, and Rigdon's (1997) study of school restructuring.

In contrast, state accountability systems develop from politically negotiated standards for school performance and apply across whole school systems. Motivation originates outside schools, and external demands have problematic connections to practice. States possess the resources to develop teacher skills needed to promote new performance standards, but they rarely include such provisions in their accountability designs. Public accounts are required, and alignment between school and system standards is expected but not verified.

Based on this comparison, neither internal-professional nor external-legal accountability models, as currently rendered, effectively combine high performance standards linked to student needs with attention to the street-level motivation and capacity required to attain performance goals. The requisite components are spread across the different models. Policy and practice both could benefit from

Table 22.4
Internal and External Models of Educational
Accountability Compared

Factor	Internal	External
Locus of performance standard	Site	System
Construction of performance standard	Professionally negotiated	Politically negotiated
Source and effect on agent motivation	Internal, effective	External, problematic
Alignment between site and system standards	Possible, not necessary	Expected, not verified
Impact on teaching	Direct	Indirect
Capacity building	Site needs known, resources limited	Site needs not known, resources available
Public accounting	No	Yes

accountability designs that better link public expectations and school standards, accountability and classroom practice, and responsibility and resources. When these linkages occur, student achievement can improve. Successful schools in Kentucky, for example, aligned school resources—curriculum, professional development, and school leadership—with state accountability demands; lower performing schools did not (Kelley, 1997).

Research on internal accountability is much less developed than external policies and practices. Consequently, it is very difficult to make precise or generalizable statements concerning internal versus external conflict, congruence, or effects. We do know that federal and state legislators do not tailor their external policies to account for schools' internal accountability practices. Consequently, implementation will be difficult to predict because local context can be crucial in shaping responses to standardized external accountability mandates or inducements. Moreover, the lack of capacity-building accompanying most external accountability policies will blunt their intended local impact.

We believe the next era of accountability research should examine issues of external-internal congruence and conflict. The impact and response of the same external policy will be different in a college prep-oriented high school as contrasted to an inner-city high school with low achievement. What accountability policies work best in these different contexts? What mixture of mandates, inducements, and capacity building is optimal? When is radical system-changing accountability, like that implied by vouchers, warranted?

State policy analysts have learned that there is no uniform local effect from the same accountability policies, but they know little else about differential local internal effects. The limited impact of many accountability policies discussed in this review suggests that internal accountability research will be useful. Moreover, if internal accountability systems were better known to policy makers and utilized, there may be less need for external interventions. Perhaps also the local internal policies are more attuned to local de-

mocratic concerns that conflict with federal and state interventions and that encourage higher and different pupil attainment standards. At this stage, we do not know enough to answer these vital questions.

School administrators face major challenges in reconciling external and internal accountability concepts. They need to blend these different signals about accountability in order to formulate coherent local policies. The key task for educational administrators is to create common expectations among teachers concerning what they are accountable for—that is, educational leaders need to raise the collective sense of teachers about accountability's specific standards and measures. Leaders then must work to ensure that these collective teacher academic expectations are aligned with external state accountability criteria. Furthermore, leaders need to break up the atomistic accountability of teachers operating behind classroom doors. Isolated teachers do not discuss what teachers are collectively accountable for, thus they cannot participate responsibly in school (and state) efforts to improve student performance.

Leaders can accomplish these tasks through a variety of capacity-building techniques that link internal and external accountability at the site. Newmann, King, and Rigdon (1997) suggested several based on their study of restructuring schools. They include setting clear school performance standards and a responsible reporting system, supporting staff development opportunities for teachers within schools, and collaborative opportunities to formulate performance goals and ways to implement them.

Finally, as policy makers review and refine state accountability systems, they will recognize the need to ground their designs in a public and professional consensus regarding performance standards, a consensus that allows ownership on the part of educators, parents, business representatives, and communities (Gaines & Cornett, 1992). The standards should be congruent with teachers' values and teachers' sense of effective teaching and learning (Murnane & Levy, 1996b). Importantly, policy makers can facilitate effective accountability practices and stronger teaching and learning by promulgating policies that support teacher and administrator understanding, competence, and use of the performance standards that drive state accountability systems. Fostering useful standards of internal accountability, and aligning internal and external standards, will be key to educational leadership in the opening decade of the 21st century. Explicitly linking accountability and responsibility, and balancing public expectations with supports for practice, will better enable accountability systems to play their intended role in promoting stronger student performance.

NOTES

1. Other market mechanisms operate in education agencies today through the private provision of services which range from janitorial services to whole-school or district management. See Hill, Pierce, and Guthrie, 1997; and Murphy, 1996.

2. Though this point is not without critics. See Kohn, 1996; Lepper, Keavney & Drake, 1996; and Ryan & Deci, 1996.

3. We recognize that professional standards exist outside schools, too, in professional organizations and certification procedures. But these external professional standards indirectly influence the day-to-day actions of administrators and teachers, and may not express a consistent view of professional practice across administrators and teachers. Our concern here is the direct, professionally negotiated responses of school staffs which are specific to school communities.

REFERENCES

Adams, J. E., Jr. (1993a). *Curriculum implementation through teacher professional networks.* Paper presented at the annual meeting of the American Educational Research Association, Atlanta.

Adams, J. E., Jr. (1993b). School finance reform and systemic school change: Reconstituting Kentucky's public schools. *Journal of Education Finance, 18,* 318–345.

Baker, A. P. & Xu, D. (1995). *The measure of education: A review of the Tennessee value added assessment system.* Nashville: Comptroller of the Treasure, Office of Education Accountability.

Barbee, D. E. & Bouck, A. J. (1974). *Accountability in education.* New York: Petrocelli Books.

Benveniste, G. (1985). The design of school accountability systems. *Educational Evaluation and Policy Analysis, 7,* 261–279.

Browder, L. H. (1973). *An administrator's handbook on educational accountability.* Arlington, VA: American Association of School Administrators.

Brown, P. R. (1990). *Accountability in public education* (Policy Briefs No. 14). San Francisco: Far West Laboratory.

Callahan, R. (1962). *Education and the cult of efficiency.* Chicago: University of Chicago Press.

Cameron, J. & Pierce, W. D. (1994). Reinforcement, reward, and intrinsic motivation: A meta-analysis. *Review of Educational Research, 64,* 363–423.

Chubb, J. E. & Moe, T. M. (1990). *Politics, markets & America's schools.* Washington, DC: The Brookings Institution.

Cibulka, J. G. (1991). Educational accountability reforms: Performance information and political power. In S. H. Fuhrman & B. Malen (Eds.), *The politics of curriculum and testing* (pp. 181–201). New York: The Falmer Press.

Clotfelter, C. T. & Ladd, H. F. (1996). Recognizing and rewarding success in public schools. In H. F. Ladd (Ed.), *Holding schools accountable: Performance-based reform in education* (pp. 23–63). Washington, DC: The Brookings Institution.

Consortium for Policy Research in Education. (1997, August 11). [Accountability/incentive structures discussion]. Unpublished project memorandum.

Consortium on Productivity in the Schools. (1995). *Using what we have to get the schools we need: A productivity focus for American education.* New York: Institute on Education and the Economy, Teachers College, Columbia University.

Corcoran, T. & Goertz, M. (1995). Instructional capacity and high performance schools. *Educational Researcher, 24,* 27–31.

Council of Chief State School Officers. (1995). *Moving toward accountability for results: A look at ten states' efforts.* Washington, DC: Author. (ERIC Document Reproduction Service No. ED 390 123)

Darling-Hammond, L. (1989). Accountability for professional practice. *Teachers College Record, 91,* 59–80.

Darling-Hammond, L. & Ascher, C. (1991). *Creating accountability in big city school systems.* New York: National Center for Restructuring Education, Schools, and Teaching. (ERIC Document Reproduction Service No. ED 334–339)

Day, P. & Klein, R. (1987). *Accountabilities.* London: Tavistock.

Education Week. (1997, January 22). *Quality counts* [Special supplement].

Elmore, R. F. (1996a). *Accountability in local school districts: Learning to do the right things.* Cambridge, MA: Harvard University, Consortium for Policy Research in Education.

Elmore, R. F. (1996b). Getting to scale with successful educational practices. In S. H. Fuhrman & J. A. O'Day (Eds.), *Rewards and reform: Creating educational incentives that work* (pp. 294–329). San Francisco: Jossey-Bass Publishers.

Elmore, R. F., Abelmann, C. H. & Fuhrman, S. H. (1996). The New accountability in state education reform: From process to performance. In H. F. Ladd (Ed.), *Holding schools accountable: Performance-based reform in education* (pp. 65–98). Washington, DC: The Brookings Institution.

Evaluation Center. (1995). *An independent evaluation of the Kentucky Instructional Results Information System (KIRIS).* Frankfort, KY: Kentucky Institute for Education Research.

Ford, M. E. (1992). *Motivating humans.* Newbury Park, CA: Sage Publications.

Fuhrman, S. H. (1994). *Evaluation of performance in the United States: Changes in accountability.* New Brunswick, NJ: Rutgers University, Consortium for Policy Research in Education.

Fuhrman, S. H. (1996). Conclusion: Building a better system of incentives. In S. H. Fuhrman & J. A. O'Day (Eds.), *Rewards and reform: Creating educational incentives that work* (pp. 330–341). San Francisco: Jossey-Bass Publishers.

Fuhrman, S. H. & Elmore, R. F. (1992). *Takeover and deregulation: Working models of new state and local regulatory relationships.* New Brunswick, NJ: Rutgers University, Consortium for Policy Research in Education.

Fuhrman, S. H., Elmore, R. F. & Massell, D. (1993). School reform in the United States: Putting it into context. In S. L. Jacobson & R. Berne (Eds.), *Reforming education: The emerging systemic approach* (pp. 3–27). Thousand Oaks, CA: Corwin Press.

Gaines, G. F. (1991). *Report cards for education: Accountability reporting in SREB states.* Atlanta: Southern Regional Education Board.

Gaines, G. F. & Cornett, L. M. (1992). *School accountability reports: Lessons learned from SREB states.* Atlanta: Southern Regional Education Board.

Gortner, H. F., Mahler, J. & Nicholson, J. B. (1989). *Organization theory: A public perspective.* Pacific Grove, CA: Brooks/Cole Publishing Company.

Gruber, J. E. (1987). *Controlling bureaucracies: Dilemmas in democratic governance.* Berkeley: University of California Press.

Guthrie, J. W. (1997). School finance: Fifty years of expansion. *The Future of Children, 7* (3), 24–38.

Guthrie, J. W., Garms, W. I. & Pierce, L. C. (1988). *School finance and education policy* (2nd ed.). Englewood Cliffs, NJ: Prentice Hall.

Hansen, J. B. (1993). Is educational reform through mandated accountability an oxymoron? *Measurement and Evaluation in Counseling and Development, 16,* 11–21.

Hanushek, E. A. (1996). Comments on chapters two, three, and four. In H. F. Ladd (Ed.), *Holding schools accountable: Performance-based reform in education* (128–136). Washington, DC: The Brookings Institution.

Heise, M. (1995). State constitutions, school finance litigation, and the third wave: From equity to adequacy. *Temple Law Review, 68,* 1151–1176.

Henig, J. R. (1994). *Rethinking school choice.* Princeton, NJ: Princeton University Press.

Herrington, C. D. (1993). Accountability, invisibility and the politics of numbers: School report cards and race. In C. Marshall (Ed.), *The new politics of race and gender* (pp. 36–47). Washington, DC: The Falmer Press.

Hess, G. A., Jr. (1993). Race and the liberal perspective in Chicago school reform. In C. Marshall (Ed.), *The new politics of race and gender* (pp. 85–96). Washington, DC: The Falmer Press.

Hill, P. T., Pierce, L. C. & Guthrie, J. W. (1997). *Reinventing public education*. Chicago: University of Chicago Press.

Hradesky, J. (1995). *Total quality management handbook*. New York: McGraw-Hill.

Kaufman, H. (1960). *The forest ranger: A study in administrative behavior*. Baltimore: Johns Hopkins Press.

Kearns, K. P. (1996). *Managing for accountability*. San Francisco: Jossey-Bass Publishers.

Kelley, C. (1997). *The Kentucky school-based performance award program: School-level effects*. Manuscript submitted for review. University of Wisconsin-Madison.

Kerchner, C. T., Koppich, J. E. & Weeres, J. G. (1997). *United mind workers: Unions and teaching in the knowledge society*. San Francisco: Jossey-Bass Publishers.

Khademian, A. M. (1996). *Checking on banks: Autonomy and accountability in three federal agencies*. Washington, DC: The Brookings Institution.

Kirst, M. W. (1990). *Accountability: Implications for state and local policymakers*. Washington, DC: U. S. Government Printing Office.

Kirst, M. W. & Mazzeo, C. (1996). The rise, fall, and rise of state assessment in California, 1993–96. *Phi Delta Kappan, 78*, 319–323.

Knott, J. H. & Miller, G. J. (1987). *Reforming bureaucracy: The politics of institutional choice*. Englewood Cliffs, NJ: Prentice-Hall, Inc.

Kohn, A. (1996). By all available means: Cameron and Pierce's defense of extrinsic motivators. *Review of Educational Research, 66*, 1–4.

Koretz, D. M. (1995). Sometimes a cigar is only a cigar, and often a test is only a test. In D. Ravitch (Ed.), *Debating the future of American education* (pp. 154–166). Washington, DC: The Brookings Institution.

Ladd, H. F. (Ed.). (1996). *Holding schools accountable: Performance-based reform in education*. Washington, DC: The Brookings Institution.

Leight, R. L. (1973). *Philosophers speak on accountability in education*. Danville, IL: The Interstate Printers & Publishers, Inc.

Leithwood, K. & Atkin, K. A. (1995). *Making schools smarter: A system for monitoring school and district progress*. Thousand Oaks, CA: Corwin Press.

Lepper, M. R., Keavney, M. & Drake, M. (1996). Intrinsic motivation and extrinsic rewards: A commentary on Cameron and Pierce's meta-analysis. *Review of Educational Research, 66*, 5–32.

Lessinger, L. (1970). *Every kid a winner*. Palo Alto, CA: Science Research Associates.

Lieberman, A. & Grolnick, M. (1996). *Networks and reform in American education*. New York: The National Center for Restructuring Education, Schools, and Teaching (NCREST), Teachers College, Columbia University.

Lieberman, A. & McLaughlin, M. W. (1992). Networks for educational change: Powerful and problematic. *Phi Delta Kappan, 73*, 673–677.

Light, P. C. (1993). *Monitoring government: Inspectors general and the search for accountability*. Washington, DC: The Brookings Institution.

Lindblom, C. E. & Woodhouse, E. J. (1993). *The policy-making process* (3rd ed.). Englewood Cliffs, NJ: Prentice Hall.

Lipsky, M. (1980). *Street-level bureaucracy*. New York: Russell Sage Foundation.

McLaughlin, M. W. (1987). Learning from experience: Lessons from policy implementation. *Educational Evaluation and Policy Analysis, 9*, 171–178.

March, J. G. & Olsen, J. P. (1995). *Democratic governance*. New York: Free Press.

Mayhew, D. R. (1974). *Congress: The electoral connection*. New Haven, CT: Yale University Press.

Millot, M. D. (1996). *Autonomy, accountability, and the values of public education: A comparative assessment of charter school statutes leading to model legislation*. Seattle, WA: Program on Reinventing Public Education, Institute for Public Policy and Management, University of Washington.

Moe, T. M. (1984). The new economics of organization. *American Journal of Political Science, 28*, 739–777.

Mohrman, S. A. & Lawler, E. E. III. (1996). Motivation for school reform. In S. H. Fuhrman & J. A. O'Day (Eds.), *Rewards and reform: Creating educational incentives that work* (pp. 115–143). San Francisco: Jossey-Bass Publishers.

Monk, D. H. (1992). Education productivity research: An update and assessment of its role in education finance reform. *Educational Evaluation and Policy Analysis, 14*, 307–322.

Mosher, F. C. (1982). Comment by Frederick C. Mosher. In B. Smith & J. Carroll (Eds.), *Improving the accountability and performance of government* (pp. 71–74). Washington, DC: The Brookings Institution.

Murnane, R. J. & Levy, F. (1996a). *Teaching the new basic skills*. New York: The Free Press.

Murnane, R. J. & Levy, F. (1996b). Teaching to new standards. In S. H. Fuhrman & J. A. O'Day (Eds.), *Rewards and reform: Creating educational incentives that work* (pp. 257–293). San Francisco: Jossey-Bass Publishers.

Murphy, J. (1996). *The privatization of schooling: Problems and possibilities*. Thousand Oaks, CA: Corwin Press.

National Commission on Excellence in Education. (1983). *A nation at risk: The imperative for educational reform*. Washington, DC: U. S. Government Printing Office.

National Governors' Association. (1986). *Time for results*. Washington, DC: Author.

Newmann, F. M. & Wehlage, G. G. (1995). *Successful school restructuring*. Madison, WI: University of Wisconsin, Center on Organization and Restructuring of Schools.

Newmann, F. M., King, M. B. & Rigdon, M. (1997). Accountability and school performance: Implications from restructuring schools. *Harvard Educational Review, 67*, 41–74.

Odden, A. & Kelley, C. (1997). *Paying teachers for what they know and do*. Thousand Oaks, CA: Corwin Press.

OERI (Office of Educational Research and Improvement). (1988). *Creating responsible and responsive accountability systems: Report to the OERI study group on state accountability systems*. Washington, DC: Department of Education. (ERIC Document Reproduction No. ED 299 706)

O'Reilly, F. E. (1996). *Educational accountability: Current practices and theories in use*. Cambridge, MA: Harvard University, Consortium for Policy Research in Education.

Osborne, D. & Gaebler, T. (1992). *Reinventing government*. Reading, MA: Addison-Wesley Publishing Company, Inc.

Petrosko, J. M. (1997). Assessment and accountability. In J. C. Lindle, J. Petrosko & R. Pankratz (Eds.), *1996 Review of research on the Kentucky Education Reform Act*. Frankfort, KY: Kentucky Institute for Education Research.

Pipho, C. (1989, May). Accountability comes around again. *Phi Delta Kappan, 70* (9), 662–663.

Porter, A. (1991). Creating a system of school process indicators. *Educational Evaluation and Policy Analysis, 13*, 13–29.

Ravitch, D. (Ed.) (1995). *Debating the future of American education: Do we need national standards and assessments?* Washington, DC: The Brookings Institution.

Resnick, L. B. & Nolan, K. J. (1995). Standards for education. In D. Ravitch (Ed.), *Debating the future of American education: Do we need national standards and assessments?* (pp. 94–119). Washington, DC: The Brookings Institution.

Richards, C. E. & Sheu, T. M. (1992). The South Carolina School Incentive Reward Program: A policy analysis. Economics of *Education Review, 11*, 71–86.

Romzek, B. S. & Dubnick, M. J. (1987, May/June). Accountability in the public sector: Lessons from the Challenger tragedy. *Public Administration Review, 47*, 227–238.

Rose v. Council for Better Education, Inc. 790 S. W. 2d 186 (Ky. 1989).

Ryan, R. M. & Deci, E. L. (1996). When paradigms clash: Comments on Cameron and Pierce's claim that rewards do not undermine intrinsic motivation. *Review of Educational Research, 66*, 33–38.

Sagor, R. (1996). *Local control and accountability: How to get it, keep it, and improve school performance*. Thousand Oaks, CA: Corwin Press.

Sarlos, B. (1973). The complexity of the concept accountability in the context of American education. In R. L. Leight (Ed.), *Philosophers speak on accountability in education* (pp. 65–81). Danville, IL: The Interstate Printers and Publishers, Inc.

Sizer, T. R. (1984). *Horace's compromise*. Boston: Houghton Mifflin Company.

Spillane, J. P. & Thompson, C. L. (1997). Reconstructing conceptions of local capacity: The local education agency's capacity for ambitious instructional reform. *Educational Evaluation and Policy Analysis, 19*, 185–203.

Spiro, H. J. (1964). *Responsibility in government: Theory and practice*. New York: Van Nostrand Reinhold Company.

Spring, J. (1993). *Conflict of interests: The politics of American education* (2nd ed.). New York: Longman.

Steinberg, L. (1996). *Beyond the classroom*. New York: Simon & Schuster.

Stiglitz, J. E. (1987). Principal and agent. In J. Eatwell, M. Milgate & P. Newman (Eds.), *The new Palgrave: A dictionary of economics* (pp. 966–972). New York: The Stockton Press.

Stone, D. A. (1988). *Policy paradox and political reason*. Glenview, IL: Harper Collins Publishers.

Summary of remarks by Maggie Szabo: An accountability system that matters: The devil is in the local details. California State Assembly, Education Committee, Hearing on Accountability (1997, March 19) (Testimony of Maggie Szabo).

U. S. Advisory Commission on Intergovernmental Relations. (1996, May). *Intergovernmental accountability* (SR–21). Washington, DC: Author.

Wagner, R. B. (1989). *Accountability in education: A philosophical inquiry*. New York: Routledge.

Wilson, T. A. (1996). *Reaching for a better standard: English school inspection and the dilemma of accountability for American schools*. New York: Teachers College Press.

Winter, S. (1990). Integrating implementation research. In D. J. Palumbo & D. J. Calista (Eds.), *Implementation and the policy process: Opening up the black box* (pp. 19–38). New York: Greenwood Press.

Wirt, F. & Kirst, M. (1997). *The political dynamics of American education*. Berkeley, CA: McCutchan Press.

CHAPTER 23

Generating and Managing Resources for School Improvement

David H. Monk and Margaret L. Plecki

Significant amounts of financial resources enter the U.S. public schools each year. The National Center for Education Statistics (1996) estimates that in 1993–94, $260.1 billion were spent on public schools. In the mid-1980s, U.S. spending on K–12 education amounted to 4.1 percent of its gross domestic product (Ram, 1995). Concerns have existed for many years about the origins of these resources and their management. Escalating expectations for the schooling system in the face of limited growth in the available resource base, thanks in part to increased competition for alternative social services like health care, are promoting even higher levels of scrutiny and new proposals for sometimes sweeping reform. In this chapter, we examine both the sources and utilization/management of these resources and provide an update on what has been learned about the prospects for reform. Because all the topics we examine are directly related to either a concern for equity, efficiency, or adequacy in education, we begin the chapter with an overview of these important topics. The balance of the chapter is divided into three major sections and begins with a discussion about the major sources of revenue for the public schools. Most of this section focuses on the advantages and disadvantages of various tax instruments that are in use for education, but we also examine what appears to be the rising use of "non-traditional" revenue sources, such as the proceeds of user fees. We turn next to an assessment of how resources are currently being allocated for education and trace resource flows across several levels of governance. Interest in recent years has been growing in studies of what has come to be known as "micro-level" resource allocation, and we provide a review of this emerging work.

Having mapped the origins and allocations of education resources, we shift attention next to recent research dealing with management and utilization of resources. Our emphasis here is on the process through which resources are transformed into desired outcomes with a focus on the tradeoffs and tensions that can exist between commitments to efficiency, equity, and adequacy.

The chapter concludes with an examination of strategies for school improvement through reforms of how resources are either generated, allocated, or utilized within schooling systems.

Evolving Notions of Equity, Efficiency, and Adequacy

There have been long-standing concerns about both equity and efficiency in the allocation of resources for education, and it is useful at the outset to reach a common understanding about what these social goals entail. Equity is broadly concerned with fairness in the distribution of resources, while efficiency places emphasis on consequence and benefit relative to cost. In recent years, interest has grown in ensuring that the system also operates at a level that is adequate to meet long-term social goals.

Equity

Traditionally, two types of equity have been at issue in the debate over how best to finance public education. On the one hand, there has been a concern over inequality in the level of resources entering schooling units. The underlying premise here is that students are equal with respect to certain fundamental rights and that each should be treated equally by the public with respect to the education that is made available. The further presumption is that the supply of resources is an important part of how the public treats its students and that inequalities in resource shares are potentially worrisome from an equity perspective.

On the other hand, there has been a willingness to recognize that students differ from one another in important ways that may have bearing on the nature and perhaps even the level of resources that are appropriate. For example, some students may have certain disabilities that have important implications for how many resources they will need to realize for certain learning goals. Or, some students may live in an area where the cost of living is relatively high. Under these circumstances, a concern over equity can dictate a willingness to tolerate and even encourage inequality in the distribution of resources.

There has been an important strand of this second type of equity concern that gives rise to certain prohibitions on resource allocation practices. In particular, there have emerged a series of "suspect" structural characteristics whose connection to resource distribution has been disturbing from an equity perspective. A good example of a suspect structural characteristic is the fiscal capacity of an individual schooling unit. A "negative" standard of equity has developed in this context suggesting that the fiscal capacity of an individual schooling unit ought *not* to be related to the quality of the education being provided (Wise, 1967). Evidence of positive relationships between measures of fiscal capacity and the quality of educational programs has been a traditional concern for equity advocates.

Efficiency

The idea of efficiency or productivity in education deals explicitly with the relationship between the supply of resources and their subsequent transformation into desired outcomes like gains in learning or improved social and/or economic results. Conceived of in this way, it is easy to see that both types of equity introduced above have elements of efficiency intertwined. The concern over inequality is animated in part by a belief that resources committed to education make a difference in the acquisition of some important benefit. The willingness to entertain the possibility of differences in treatment as a means of achieving equity grows out of an underlying belief that different sorts of resources have different kinds of effects on different types of students. In recent years, researchers have made progress toward looking more systematically at the nature of relationships between resources and learning outcomes (cf. Hanushek, 1989, 1996; Laine, Greenwald, *et al.*, 1996; and Monk, 1992), as well as at the impact of educational attainment on subsequent economic well-being (Card and Krueger, 1992; and Ashenfelter and

Krueger, 1994). We provide an overview of research examining the connection between resources and learning gains later in this chapter.

Adequacy

The term "adequacy" is surfacing with increasing frequency in the debate about the allocation and utilization of resources for education. Critics note that even if a schooling system operates efficiently in the sense that it is realizing the greatest possible outcome from the inputs being supplied, it may still fall short of producing the kinds of social and economic results that are needed for the broader society's well-being. Thus in addition to the "input-learning outcome" relationships that tend to be the focus of efficiency analyses, there are questions about the overall level at which the system should function. This latter question lies at the core of the debate over school system adequacy and efforts are being made to derive the implications for education finance (Clune, 1994; Underwood, 1995). This is a particularly difficult standard to develop because inefficiencies can also contribute to needs for resources. As a general rule, reformers are less interested in providing resources to cover inefficiencies in the operation of the schools than they are in ensuring that the system operates at adequate levels.

Policy Responses

States have responded in various ways to the call for financing education in ways that enhance equity, efficiency, and adequacy. An overview of each state's approach has been published by the American Education Finance Association in cooperation with the Center for the Study of the States (1995). Foundation approaches are common wherein states make it possible for individual school districts to spend at a pre-specified minimal level per pupil, regardless of how impoverished an individual district might be. Foundation approaches are designed to build a floor that helps to limit the amount of spending variation that can exist among school districts. An alternative approach is built around matching grants in aid that are designed to reduce the influence of individual school district's fiscal capacity on spending decisions. The matching grant approach provides greater local autonomy with respect to decision-making about how much to spend on the schools. In contrast, a strict foundation plan specifies a minimum spending level per pupil below which no district can fall.

Neither approach deals explicitly with the transformation of spending levels into learning gains for students, and in recent years efforts have been made to shift education finance systems in this direction (see Berne and Picus, 1994 and Clune, 1994). As we have seen, the term adequacy is used to make an explicit link between the provision of resources and the realization of desirable or at least acceptable results. Just because a state makes it possible for each school district to spend at some minimum level per pupil begs the question of whether the chosen spending level is *adequate* to accomplish the state's aims with its public schools. A new class of school finance suits has arisen that is structured around adequacy rather than conventional equity notions. (For a good example of a modern adequacy-based decision, see Campbell v. State of Wyoming, 1995; for an overview, see Benson, 1991). We will return to this topic later in the chapter when we examine the progress being made toward understanding the impact of resources on learning outcome gains.

Origins of Education Resources for the Public Schools

Nature of the Existing Resource Base[2]

As we indicated in our introduction, the United States raised more than $260 billion of revenue for its public elementary and secondary schools in 1993–94. Almost all these resources were generated by taxes imposed by various levels of government, but state and local units of government contributed the largest shares (93 percent) with the Federal government contributing the balance (National Center for Education Statistics, 1996). This distribution of governmental responsibility for generating public education revenues has been changing. For many years, the share contributed by local governments declined in favor of increased shares for other levels of government. The Federal percentage share peaked in the 1980s and has been steady in recent years. In the 1990s, the state share began to decline and this has begun to place greater fiscal responsibility on units of local government. The tax on real property is the primary means by which local governments raise tax revenues, and rising tax burdens at the local level have sparked taxpayer protests that are frequently focused on the property tax (Lankford and Wyckoff, 1995).

Changes have also been occurring in the absolute magnitude of the resource base for education in the United States. Evidence suggests that the level of investment has been increasing in real terms, although the precise magnitude of the increase is in some dispute (cf. Rothstein with Miles, 1995, and Odden *et al.*, 1995). Odden estimates the increase at 200 percent in real terms per pupil over 30 years; according to Rothstein and Miles, estimates such as Odden's overstate the real growth by a factor of 40 percent. Much of the dispute over the precise magnitude centers around questions about changes in the needs of students and resulting changes in the nature of educational opportunities. If the public schools are delivering a significantly

different product today than 20 years ago, it is clear that simple comparisons between what was spent then and now may be very misleading.

Current Revenue Raising Practices

The states use various tax instruments to raise revenues and on average in 1991 they collected 32.8 percent of their revenues from sales taxes, 31.8 percent from personal incomes taxes, 6.6 percent from corporate income taxes, and 16.7 percent from excise taxes (Center for the Study of the States, 1995). At the local level, revenues for education are almost exclusively raised by the tax on real property. In 1991, there were only four states where the property tax totaled less than 98 percent of the local tax revenue of school districts (Center for the Study of the States, 1995).

The property tax is widely perceived to be a highly inequitable and unacceptable means of providing revenue for the schools. Criticisms of the tax include the allegation that it fails to treat equals equally so that two identically situated taxpayers can find themselves paying significantly different amounts of tax. Similarly, the tax is criticized for how it distinguishes among taxpayers with differing abilities to bear taxes. Specifically, the property tax is widely assumed to be a "regressive" type of tax that imposes higher rates of tax on lower income taxpayers. Among economists, the matter is not so straightforward, and the actual incidence of the tax across persons with differing abilities to pay is quite sensitive to the rules and practices that pertain to how the tax is administered in particular localities. Berne and Netzer (1995) observed that in New York state the prevailing practices contributed significantly to the regressivity of the tax.

Tax Limitation Efforts

Despite these shortcomings, the property tax remains the single most important source of revenue for the nation's public schools. The heavy reliance on the property tax as a source of revenue for the schools can be explained in part by the fact that the property tax has the advantage of providing a dependable and relatively stable source of revenue and is well suited as a source of revenue for local units of government like school districts.

Nevertheless, public dissatisfaction with the cost of education in general and the property tax in particular has prompted noteworthy attempts to restrict the use of this tax. Proposition 13 in California and Proposition 2 ¹/₂ in Massachusetts are perhaps the most visible tax limitation efforts, but related efforts can be found in many parts of the nation (Ladd, 1985; Picus, 1991). Indeed, according to data collected by the U.S. Census Bureau, only four states (Connecticut, Maine, New Hampshire, and Vermont) do not have any provisions that limit the capability of property-taxing jurisdictions to raise revenue. The four most common types of limitations are a) property tax rate limits that can be exceeded only with a popular vote;[1] b) property tax levy limits that place restrictions on the total revenue that can be raised from the property tax, regardless of the tax rate; c) limits on the growth of property assessment levels; and d) requirements for full disclosure and truth in taxation that require public discussion and explicit legislative votes on tax rate or levy increases (Advisory Commission on Intergovernmental Relations, 1995).

Reforms of the Property Tax Instrument

Reform efforts can be divided into three broad categories. First, there are efforts to improve the administrative management of existing property tax systems. Berne and Netzer (1995) were particularly critical of how New York state administers its property tax and called for reforms that would decrease the number of separate taxing jurisdictions, further professionalize the methods in use to assign value to property, and conduct more frequent reevaluations of property.

Second, there are attempts to provide property tax relief for low-income persons who own relatively valuable parcels of property. These provisions take the form of devices known as homestead exemptions or "circuit breakers." In 1994, 35 states offered circuit breakers of some kind (Lankford and Wyckoff, 1995). Progress is also being made with devices known as reverse equity mortgages, which are designed to permit elderly persons to draw down the value of assets like owned housing as a means of meeting day-to-day expenses. When coupled with annuity features, a reverse equity mortgage in principle has several important equity-enhancing features. (For more detail on reverse equity approaches, see Monk and Brent, 1997.)

Third, there are reform proposals for the consolidation of tax bases for the purpose of raising revenues for education. These initiatives come in many versions and can be thought of as part of a long-standing effort to consolidate small units of government into larger units. The rationale for these consolidations can stem from concerns over inequities as well as over inefficiencies that are believed to accompany small units. The smaller the unit, the greater the inequality tends to be from one unit to the next. Smaller units can also suffer from diseconomies of small scale that erode the efficiency of the operation.

Much of the current interest in tax base consolidation reforms centers around the treatment of non-residential properties. These include commercial properties like shopping malls and power plants that account for significant amounts of the inequality across school districts in the distribution of fiscal capacity. There have been proposals to shift these non-residential properties to either regional units or to the state as a whole, tax the property at a common rate, and distribute the proceeds back in an equalizing

fashion (Brent, 1997; Ladd, 1976; Ladd and Harris, 1995). Findings suggest that these reforms can enhance equity within the school finance system without requiring the addition of new state dollars. The research also suggests that a regional approach has important advantages over a statewide approach given the adverse impact the statewide approach can have for urban districts (Brent, 1997).

Shifts Away from the Tax on Real Property

Given the dissatisfaction that exists with the property tax, it is not surprising to discover efforts to rely on alternative sources of revenue for the schools. These alternative revenue sources can include conventional taxes like sales or income, lottery revenues, or non-traditional mechanisms like user fees.

Sales and Income Taxes

In Michigan, for example, the state significantly reduced its reliance on local property taxes and shifted toward a higher state sales tax as a means of supporting public education (Kearney, 1995). The initial reform in Michigan involved a reduction in the local property tax rate from an average of 34 mills to a state-mandated levy of six mills on all property and a local levy (if authorized by voters) of up to 18 mills on eligible property. This reduction in property taxes was accompanied by an increase of two percentage points in the state sales tax (from four percent to six percent).

Interest has also surfaced in relying more heavily on local income taxes as a source of revenue for the schools. Strauss (1995) simulated the effects of a shift away from the local property tax towards a local income tax in New York and found that on average the local income tax rate necessary to support the schools at the existing level of spending was on the order of six to seven percent.

Lotteries

New Hampshire, beginning in 1964, was the first state to use a lottery to help finance public services. By 1992, 37 states and the District of Columbia had a lottery in place to help finance public services, and 12 of these states earmarked at least some portion of the proceeds for education (Advisory Commission on Intergovernmental Relations, 1994). Nine states reported lottery revenues in excess of $1 billion in 1992, and Florida's lottery proved to be the largest revenue producer by generating in excess of $2 billion.

Lottery-based sources of revenue for education have been criticized on equity as well other grounds (Borg et al., 1991; Monk and Brent, 1997). It has also been found that lottery revenues tend not to constitute "add-on" revenues for the schools. Instead, even when the revenues are earmarked for education, lottery dollars have been found to supplant previously allocated resources and do not constitute a significant source of new spending (Borg *et al*, 1991).

Non-Traditional Revenues

The rise of taxpayer frustration with the burden they carry for the support of the existing schools is also prompting efforts to explore "non-traditional" sources of revenues (Monk and Pijanowski, 1996). In particular, interest is growing in revenues taking the form of user fees, proceeds of fund-raising, and grants from private groups such as businesses, foundations, and booster clubs. In most places, these new kinds of revenues are playing only marginal roles (typically on the order of less than one percent of revenues), but some public schools are beginning to raise significant sums of money in these unorthodox ways. Swanson and King (1997) report instances where school districts have been charging significant user fees—on the order of $1,000 for a technical studies course, $1,500 for extra-curricular activities, and $12,000 for an international program. It is difficult to estimate the true magnitude of these resource flows for entire states or for the nation because it is possible for the accounts to exist outside of regulated accounting systems for the schools. One of the challenges facing those with interests in accounting for school revenues is the development of common practices within as well as across the states with respect to accounting for these revenue streams.

Allocations of Education Resources Across Levels of Governance

Overall Spending for K–12 Public Schools[2]

There are a number of important questions to answer about how these education revenues are being spent. For example, one might reasonably wonder about how much is spent on a typical pupil in the public schools. The answer for 1993–94 was $5,325 according to the National Center for Education Statistics (1996). However, this answer can be misleading because the figure alone does not reveal the tremendous amount of variation that occurs across individually-organized schooling units. Some of this variation exists at the state level. For example, the highest spending state that year was New Jersey at $9,075 and the lowest spending state was Utah at $3,206 (a difference of better than 2.8 to 1). Significant variation can also exist within the individual states. For example, in New York during the 1993–94 school year, the district at the 90th percentile of the spending distribution spent close to twice as much as the district at the 10th percentile. Much larger spending discrepancies occur if districts in the respective tails of the New York spending distribution are compared.

The clear lesson to learn from these figures is that states as well as individual schooling units vary substantially in terms of the level of resources being invested in education. Some of the variation is due to factors such as differences in the cost of living (Chambers and Fowler, 1995) and geographically-based differences in fiscal capacity.

Spending by Function

Schooling systems provide a vast array of services, including some that are only tangentially related to instruction (such as food and transportation services). Overall, we now know that 60 percent of the education dollar (nationwide) is spent on instructional services. The 60 percent figure is remarkably consistent across different types of schooling units. It holds across school districts of different size, wealth, spending level, region, incidence of minority populations, and incidence of children living in poverty (Odden *et al.*, 1995). Thus it appears that although districts have significantly different levels of resources to spend, they apportion their resources in much the same way. It also appears that the 60 percent figure has remained steady during the past 35 years.

Research has also shown that the remaining 40 percent of the education dollar is divided as follows across the remaining budget categories: 8 percent–10 percent to instructional support (curriculum development, professional development, student services, and so on); 9 percent–11 percent to operation and maintenance of the physical plant; 4 percent–6 percent to transportation and food services; and 9 percent–11 percent on administrative services (Odden *et al.*, 1995).

There has been a contentious debate in recent years over the level of spending on administrative services. Critics of the public schools have been known to talk about an "administrative bloat" that is drawing resources away from the instructional core of the schools, particularly in large city schools. Researchers have responded to these allegations by developing accounting models that can distinguish between funds going to individual schools from those being spent elsewhere within the larger system. Coopers & Lybrand, in particular, developed this kind of model (Speakman *et al.*, 1996a) and have used it to study microlevel resource allocation practices in a series of school districts around the nation (Speakman *et al.*, 1996b). One of the districts that has been studied is New York City (Coopers & Lybrand L.L.P., 1994), where the results suggest that 81.4 percent of all budgeted funds go to the school sites. This accounting model has also been used to generate insight into differences in spending by school type within the New York City schools. In particular, the firm found that per pupil spending is higher in elementary and middle schools than it is in high schools, a surprising finding that made headlines in the *New York Times* when it was confirmed by an internal New York City school district study (Steinberg, 1996).

Researchers have also dealt with the "administrative bloat" issue by looking directly at expenditures earmarked for specific administrative functions including central, school, special education, and subject administration. The emerging results of these efforts did not support allegations about extravagant spending on administration. As indicated earlier, the estimated percentage for administration is on the order of 9–11 percent, with the largest share going to special education administration (Monk, 1996).

Spending by Program

Some important progress has been made toward breaking out district expenditures according to program and the type of student being served. Interest has grown in knowing more about existing levels of investment in special education programs, in particular. Lankford and Wyckoff (1996) approached this issue by examining changes in spending for special education using data from New York state. They found that additional expenditures for disabled students between 1980 and 1993 comprised more than one-third of the increase in real per pupil expenditures in districts other than New York City. The data from New York City suggested that the special education increase was more than one-half of the total growth in real spending. This rapid growth could be traced to two sources: (1) growth in the number of students classified with one or more disabilities; and (2) growth in the real expenditure levels per classified student. More specifically, the number of classified students in New York State grew at a rate of 65 percent from 1980 to 1993 (compared to a national average of 24 percent). Real spending per classified student also reached high levels and the magnitude was estimated at $22,000. One of the policy issues addressed directly by Lankford and Wyckoff concerned the degree to which the growth in spending on special education has come at the expense of spending for regular education. They found no clear evidence to support or reject the view that investments in "regular" education have suffered as a byproduct of the growth in special education. Rothstein with Miles (1995) also found growth in spending for special education between 1967 and 1991 in nine nationally representative school districts. Special education spending increased from four to 18 percent in these districts while spending on "regular" education declined by 21 percent of total per pupil spending.

Speakman et al. (1996a) conducted a cross-sectional analysis of spending differences between special and "regular" students in the New York City school district. They found that spending on full-time special education programs was $23,598 per pupil in 1993–94, or 298 percent of the average spending level. They estimated the total cost for full-time special education students at one-fourth of the total education expenditures for the district.

Spending by Curricular Area

Researchers have begun to make progress at measuring allocations of teacher resources across subject areas of the secondary school curriculum (Monk et al, 1996; Picus et al. 1995; Nakib, 1995). For example, Table 23.1 reports teacher staffing levels on average within New York state districts on a subject-by-subject basis. As the table makes clear, the academic portion of the secondary curriculum in New York received approximately 80% of the total professional staffing resource that was available within the secondary schools, with English and mathematics receiving the largest shares.

Attention has also been paid to the allocation of teacher resources between remedial, "regular," and advanced science and mathematics courses, and significantly different resource allocation practices have been found across these two subject areas. Specifically, a greater degree of curricular differentiation of this kind was found in New York for mathematics compared to science. In mathematics, 69.9 percent of New York teacher assignments were categorized as "regular;" in science, the comparable figure was 90.8. Moreover, whatever differentiation that occurred in science

Table 23.1

Professional Secondary School Staffing Levels for New York State School Districts 1991–1992*

Subject	Professional Staff per 1,000 district pupils	% Share
Academic		
English	5.48	15.8
Mathematics	4.65	13.4
Social Studies	4.19	12.1
Science	4.23	12.2
Foreign Language	2.55	7.4
Music and Art	2.93	8.5
Phys. Ed. and Health	2.56	7.4
Other Academic	.98	2.8
Vocational		
Trade	2.28	6.6
Business	1.17	3.4
Other	.34	1.0
Special		
Resource Rooms	1.29	3.7
Special Classes	1.67	4.8
ESL	.16	.5
Other	.11	.3
Total	34.59	99.9

* Regular K–12 school districts excluding the Big Five city districts (n=645).

Source: Adapted from Monk (1996).

took the form of more advanced (rather than remedial) offerings. For example, in science, the proportion of remedial courses was 1.18 percent while the comparable figure for mathematics was 20.65 percent (Monk, 1996).

The New York research also included analyses of relationships between school district structural characteristics like the incidence of poverty and the allocation of resources to the science and mathematics areas of the curriculum. One of the remarkable findings is that school district characteristics like wealth and per pupil spending levels are largely unrelated to the internal allocation of teacher resources to science and mathematics areas of the curriculum. Indeed, it is only among the wealthiest and highest spending districts in the state that there is any evidence at all of an infusion of additional professional staff into these key areas of the academic curriculum. The research shows that science and mathematics are not unique in this regard. The supply of additional teacher resources into the academic area of the curriculum is remarkably insensitive to differences in districts' wealth and overall spending levels.

According to the New York data, allocations of teacher resources into key academic areas like science and mathematics have been increasing. Between 1982–83 and 1991–92, the teacher supply per pupil grew by 6.02 percent in science and 4.31 percent in mathematics. The longitudinal results regarding curricular differentiation are also of interest. Across all academic subjects there was growth in both advanced and remedial offerings that significantly outpaced growth in the allocation of resources to the "regular" area of the curriculum. Teacher resources being devoted to the advanced area of the curriculum increased from 1.21 to 1.55 teachers per 1,000 district pupils (or 28.10 percent) between 1982–83 and 1991–92, while the increase registered for remedial courses was from 1.64 to 1.96 (or 19.51 percent). Growth in staff support for "regular" courses was relatively flat during the period (17.29 to 17.60 or 1.79 percent). It is clear that most of the new staff going into the academic curriculum during this period of reform was directed away from the so-called "regular" offerings (Roellke, 1996).

Spending by Type of Teacher Input

We will deal with research on teacher compensation in the section devoted to the management of educational resources. The focus here will be on research that has examined investments in alternative types of teacher inputs. One of the most significant studies of this type was conducted by Karen Hawley Miles (1995) and dealt with how the Boston school district divides resources across different types of teacher inputs. Specifically, Miles was concerned with spending on classroom teachers in contrast to spending on more specialized teachers, such as those who provide

testing, counseling, and remedial services to either individual students or small groups of students. Miles found that the Boston school district employed one teacher for every 13.2 students. She contrasted this teacher pupil ratio with the fact that most classes in the district operated with more than 23 students per teacher. The discrepancy could be explained in terms of a) the classification of students and teachers; b) the provision of time for teacher professional development; and c) the assignment of students to schools, grades, and programs. More specifically, she found that more than 40 percent of teachers in Boston worked in areas other than general (regular classroom) teaching. She also found that contract provisions such as caps on class size and rules regarding involuntary teacher transfers led to significant unevenness across schools, grades, and programs in the allocation of teacher resources. These differences translated directly into variation in class sizes. Miles estimated that the integration of Title I and special education students into the regular classroom could bring average class sizes down from 23 to something on the order of 16. The wisdom of such a policy depends heavily on the comparative productivity of the teacher resources in these alternative uses.

Management of Education Resources

Educational leaders have the responsibility for the equitable and productive management of resources. Frequently, educational leaders must address questions related to resource management such as: Are education dollars being used efficiently? Are human resources being managed effectively? What is the optimum size for our schools and school district organizations? How can we best allocate resources to students with differing educational needs? How can we better focus resources on the improvement of student performance?

This section focuses on what research tells us about the management of educational resources. We will discuss both productivity and equity concerns and we will specifically address matters concerned with the management of human resources, resources for special populations, organizational scale, and assessing the costs of educational reform. We will examine these issues at district, school, and classroom levels.

Productivity

School administrators are often faced with addressing the issue of educational productivity. With increasing frequency, policymakers are asking the question: Are we getting the most for our educational dollar? Moreover, in recent years, decisions about increases in education budgets are often being tied to increased expectations for higher educational performance. The current climate of fiscal conservatism in funding governmental services further emphasizes the need to better understand whether or not we are utilizing educational resources in the most efficient manner.

What does the research say about the relationship between the allocation of education dollars and improved performance? A historical review of the literature indicates that there has been considerable debate in the research community about the manner in which increased spending on education may or may not be related to improved performance. For the most part, studies of educational productivity have examined the relationship between the amount of money spent on various educational "inputs" and the resultant student achievement. These studies are typically referred to as education production function research and share a good portion of their conceptual framework with the microeconomic theory of the firm. The production function model attempts to analyze the relationship between inputs and outputs. The goal of this inquiry is to investigate the changes in output (typically measured by student achievement test scores) associated with changes in the levels or mix of educational inputs (often measured in terms such as per pupil expenditures, teacher characteristics, and teacher-student ratios, with some statistical controls for variations in student background and family characteristics).

Several significant conceptual and technical problems surface when attempting to apply a production function theory to educational productivity. The lack of agreement about the elements of a theoretically sound theory of production in education plagues the research in this area. An additional problem in the literature is in the variability of the unit of analysis. Some studies have used aggregate measures of student performance outcomes at the national, state, district, or individual school level. Other studies have focused on individual student performance. Some studies examine variations within a single system while others analyze variations across units, as in interdistrict, interstate, and international comparisons.

A set of technical problems that exist in analyzing and applying lessons learned from research on educational productivity centers around the specification of variables. Production function researchers choose certain particular input or output measures either because information is readily available, the variable has some policy relevance, and/or because the variable is intuitively plausible (Monk, 1990). Other criticisms of the specification of variables include the heavy reliance on test scores as the sole measure of student achievement.

A seminal article on the subject of educational productivity (Hanushek, 1981) claimed that after reviewing 130 studies of educational productivity, no consistent, positive, significant relationships could be uncovered between increased spending on education and improved student achievement. Additional review of this subject by the same author (Hanushek, 1986, 1989, 1991) yielded the same general result. These studies have been central pieces in the "dollars do/dollars don't matter" debate. A reexamination of Hanushek's analysis of the literature was conducted by Hedges, Laine, and Greenwald (1994). These researchers arrived at a different conclusion: that certain input measures do have a significant relationship to student outcomes. The authors explain that the difference in results is due to the use of a different methodology for conducting the meta-analysis of the same literature. Others claim (Ferguson and Ladd, 1996) that prior analyses of production function research did not critically sort out the methodologically weak studies from consideration, thus casting doubt on the validity of the conclusions being drawn.

Over the past two decades, there have been waves of productivity studies that have employed a more micro-analytic approach using disaggregated data (Murnane, 1975; Summers and Wolfe, 1977; Thomas and Kemmerer, 1983; Brown and Saks, 1975; Rossmiller, 1986) rather than the more typical studies, which have used more global measures. Results from the micro-analytic studies revealed a similar pattern of mixed results. However, several production function studies have demonstrated positive relationships between teachers' ability levels (usually a measure of verbal aptitude) and student achievement (Ehrenberg and Brewer, 1995; Summers and Wolfe, 1977).

In recent years, researchers have conducted additional production function studies regarding the empirical relationship between inputs and outputs. Ferguson (1991) examined school districts in Texas and concluded that there are systematic relationships between educational inputs and student outcomes that he estimated to account for between one-quarter and one-third of student achievement differences. In a more recent study, Ferguson and Ladd (1996) examined Alabama schools and concluded that there is evidence that the input variables of teacher's test scores, the percentage of teachers with master's degrees, and class size are positively associated with student test scores. The authors assert that the use of more methodologically sound analytic techniques (value-added specification) combined with a more disaggregated analysis can address some of the perplexing problems that have been associated with production function research.

Other researchers have cast a number of doubts about the utility of the production function literature. Some argue that even when significant relationships are found between input variables and student outcomes, these results do not have useful policy implications (Witte, 1990; Murnane, 1991). Others question the appropriateness of the specific variables being used and the limitations imposed by an almost exclusive focus on test scores as the measure of student outcomes (Smith, Scott, and Link, 1995).

It is also important to note that results from the production function research studies that do not uncover a significant relationship between increased spending and increased student outcomes collide with the widely held, rather commonsense belief shared by practicing educators and some members of the public that increased dollars spent on education do make an important difference. Some researchers assert that insufficient attention has been paid to how additional dollars have been spent on education inputs. As previously discussed, in an analysis of school district spending in New York state (Lankford and Wyckoff, 1995), researchers found that a sizable portion of the increased resources were allocated to special education programs for the disabled. Given that student outcome measures for disabled students are often unavailable or excluded from aggregate data sets, it is likely that this aspect of increased spending is not accounted for in the production function studies.

Alternatives to the input-output predictive model for assessing educational productivity have been noted in the literature. Barnett (1994) suggests that embedding production function and cost function studies in the theoretical model of private firms may not be appropriate for understanding how resources are allocated. He suggests models derived from theories about bureaucratic behavior (Niskanen, 1971) may more appropriately explain how resource allocation decisions are made. In this alternate view, the unit cost of the school is determined by the available revenue, not by the most effective way to allocate, and school administrators strive to maximize revenues and allocate resources to keep employees responsive and cooperative and maintain the school's reputation. Hughes *et al.* (1993) finds that resource allocation is more closely linked to funding those factors presumed to be related to quality or general school goals, rather than those factors that are directly linked to improved educational outcomes. Monk (1992) calls for a line of inquiry in educational productivity research that elevates the importance of classroom-level analysis and complements the school-based studies. Elmore (1994) offers the observation that traditional budgeting practices in schools and school districts are not centered on determining the actual costs of educational inputs, but they rather focus on either adding or subtracting dollars from a baseline budget. He also notes that educators typically do not have any special training or background designed to assist them with the complex problems embedded in budgeting and improving productivity. Odden and Clune (1995) discuss several factors related to low productivity, including an highly uneven distribution of resources across states, schools, districts, and students; unimaginative uses of dollars that do not translate into improved perfor-

mance; and a focus on additional programs rather than results. The authors cite several areas where additional productivity research might be extended: research on increased course-taking at the secondary level, examination of organizational strategies associated with improved performance, and research on high-poverty schools.

Human Resource Development

Research regarding the effective and efficient use of human resources in education can be seen as a critically important area to investigate. The bulk of operating expenditures in education is allocated to pay for the cost of employing school personnel with the largest portion of those expenditures allocated to classroom teachers. The quality of education is highly dependent on the classroom teacher to produce educational outcomes. Consequently, research examining the utility of various strategies designed to improve the quality of the teaching force may provide useful insights and policy recommendations. In the discussion which follows, we will focus on three areas of interest in teacher resource development: the ongoing professional development of teachers, the preparation of individuals entering the teaching profession, and teacher compensation systems.

Ongoing Professional Development

Professional development for teachers has consisted of a myriad of activities and programs that are financed in a variety of ways from all levels of government. Several studies about the costs of staff development have been conducted (Moore and Hyde, 1981; Lytle, 1983; Stern, Gerritz, and Little, 1989), but an analysis of the available research indicates that there is little generalizable information about the range of resources allocated for professional development (Orlich and Evans, 1990). However, one study found that teachers are two to three times more likely to be participants in district-provided staff development than enrolled in a college or university course (Little, 1989). The same study also calculated that more than four-fifths of state dollars for staff development were controlled by the local district. It is significant to note that most districts, somewhat due to the requirements of the bargained contracts with teachers, compensate teachers for staff development activities through an increase in salary, thus representing a "hidden" cost of traditionally-delivered staff development.

Professional development activities have been dominated by a training-based delivery system that offers teachers a variety of workshops targeted on special projects or narrowly defined aspects of reform (Little, 1993). This type of packaged professional development is not well suited to current educational reform purposes and ignores the opportunities to learn that are part of the school organization (Hargreaves, 1990, 1993). An increased focus has been placed on the need to have professional development practices more crucially linked to the improvement of student performance (Darling-Hammond and McLaughlin, 1995).

The systemic reform initiatives during the past 10 years emphasize the importance of high standards for all students, a thinking-oriented curriculum, and performance-based student assessments linked to the standards (Resnick, 1993). Educational reform based on standards and performance-based assessment implies a focus on the development of new professional knowledge and skills that teachers will need to produce an elevated level of student outcomes. The particular set of required knowledge and skills would vary by the context and conditions of the individual school setting (Cohen, McLaughlin, and Talbert, 1993). Efforts underway by the National Board for Professional Teaching Standards and the National Commission on Teaching and America's Future are two examples of the types of efforts underway to improve teacher recruitment, retention, preparation, and continual development. The Interstate School Leaders Licensure Consortium is a parallel initiative to improve the preparation and professional development of school administrators.

Identifying resources to fund new directions in ongoing teacher professional development will most likely have to result from the redirection of resources that are currently devoted to this task. Some efforts have been made to calculate the costs of resources currently being devoted to the continuing education of teachers. Miller, Lord and Dorney's (1994) estimates range between 1.8 percent and 2.8 percent of the district's operating budget. The cost per regular classroom teacher ranged between $1,755 and 3,259. Their study was based on a series of intensive case studies in four districts located in different regions in the U.S., ranging in size from 9,500 to 125,000 students. The estimates are based on direct costs, such as the salaries of district and school administrators, and substitute teachers, as well as on the direct costs of materials and supplies. The observation has been made for years that a school district with more than one percent of its budget allocated to professional development is an exception (Darling-Hammond, 1994; Houston and Freiberg, 1979). A study of spending on professional development in the Los Angeles Unified School District (Ross, 1994) found that the district spent $1,153 million in teacher salaries in 1991–92, and that 22 percent of this figure could be attributed to salary point credits that were earned because of courses or other approved professional development activities on the part of teachers. The analysis goes on to call several of the features of the salary point credit system into question and makes proposals for improving the current investment being made in teachers' professional development.

Teacher Preparation

The need to better prepare teachers entering the profession has been a central concern of education reformers. Since the publication of *A Nation at Risk* in 1983, a number of reforms in teacher education have been implemented, many of which added components to the traditional four-year teacher preparation programs, including requirements to add a major in a subject-related field, a master's degree, or a fifth year of additional study (Clark and Plecki, 1997). Hawley (1987) estimated the private and social costs of the fifth year of study nationwide to be approximately seven billion dollars per year. Another cost analysis for the fifth year of study (Lewis, 1990) was estimated to be $30,754 per teacher education candidate. These costs included the candidate's foregone wages, school tuition, and social costs.

The establishment of professional development schools represents an additional approach to improving teacher preparation, along with ongoing professional development of educators, school renewal, and research. The professional development school model has the potential to take better advantage of complementaries that can exist between institutions of higher education and local schools as senior teachers can function as clinical faculty, and a dependable supply of interns at the school level can provide opportunities for reallocation of the local teaching talent for other uses. Research on the costs of professional development schools is limited. Theobald (1990) offers some models for estimating student and staffing arrangements that could be used in estimating costs. Using data from 28 sites in 10 states, Clark (1996) estimated the range of costs of professional development schools from the institution of higher education's perspective to be between $3,000 and $7,000 per participating student teacher.

Teacher Compensation

Historically, teachers have been compensated for their efforts through a system based on an entry-level salary. The base salary is then augmented by increments on an established salary schedule based primarily on years of teaching experience and levels of additional education (such as advanced degrees or credit for professional development activities). However, one can reasonably assert that the two simple factors of years of experience and levels of education and training do not provide the formula for producing the very best teachers. Consequently, one focus in the research on teacher compensation is characterized as an attempt to uncover the types of incentive systems that are more closely linked to improved quality of teaching and student learning.

In the past two decades, varieties of reforms to the traditional system of teacher compensation have been attempted. During the early 1980s, merit pay was reintroduced as a policy alternative. In principle, merit pay individually rewards teachers based on the performance of their duties. Some merit pay plans provide for an individual financial bonus on a yearly basis, while other plans call for a permanent advancement on the salary schedule (Darling-Hammond and Berry, 1988). In many instances where merit pay systems have been tried, merit pay has been abandoned, primarily due to internal dissension and problems determining who would receive the additional pay (Murnane and Cohen, 1986; Robinson, 1983). In addition to merit pay proposals, the idea of teacher career ladders was put forth as another type of alternative compensation strategy. Career ladder programs have met with a similar lack of success (Freiberg and Knight, 1991; Bellon *et al*, 1989, Southern Regional Education Board, 1994).

Why have the various attempts at altering teacher compensation borne so few fruitful results? One possible explanation is that the traditional salary structure provides for horizontal equity. That is, teachers are treated as equals on the salary schedule regardless of their gender, race, or teaching assignment (Protsik, 1996). Others assert that teachers are primarily motivated by intrinsic rewards that result from the process of working as a teacher (Lortie, 1975; Conley and Levinson, 1993; Richardson, 1990). Firestone (1991) offers the view that research on merit pay has not sufficiently considered the relationship between money and teacher motivation. Firestone distinguishes between merit pay systems (which reward some teachers for doing essentially the same work better than other teachers) and job enlargement reforms (which provide additional compensation to teachers for doing different work) and agues that job enlargement is more closely linked to teachers' intrinsic motivations.

Another explanation is that prior reforms in compensation have focused on individually-based rewards, rather than rewards for group performance. An alternative approach to teacher compensation suggested by Mohrman, Mohrman, and Odden (1996) includes group-based performance rewards as well as skill-based and competency-based pay. The authors emphasize that the basis for determining the specific skills, competencies, and group rewards must be that the rewards support the central educational purposes of the school and are well-suited to the type of organizational arrangements that define the particular site.

Research has been conducted regarding the alignment of compensation strategies with various education organizational designs. In a recent article, Kelley (1997) notes that historically teacher compensation has been viewed as separate from other aspects of reforming educational organizations. The author analyzes how compensation systems differ under four types of organizational models—scientific management, effective schools, content-driven, and high standards/high involvement—and recommends that the design of teacher compensation systems should be better fitted to the type of organizational design that represents the school setting in which teachers work, including the organization's structure, values, and goals.

Currently, there are school systems in the process of implementing alternative compensation plans, including Kentucky, South Carolina, Dallas, and the Charlotte-Mecklenburg school district in North Carolina. Places where alternative compensation plans have been developed and implemented have relied on participation by educational administrators, teacher unions and community members in the plan's design (Odden and Kelley, 1997).

Resources for Special Populations

The Chapter 1 program is sponsored by the federal government and provides resources to meet the instructional needs of educationally disadvantaged children. An aim of the program is to direct resources to high-poverty school districts and schools, mostly at the elementary level. The program has undergone a number of evaluations and policy changes in recent years, including an examination of resource allocation issues by Moskowitz, Stullich, and Deng (1993). A primary focus of this study was examining whether or not Chapter 1 funds have been targeted to the highest-poverty communities. The authors concluded that Chapter 1 services were not provided in 14 percent of elementary schools that served a student population in which more than 50% of students were eligible for subsidized school lunches. At the same time, Chapter 1 funds were provided to almost half of elementary schools that served a student population in which less than 10% of students were eligible for subsidized lunches. The authors present alternative ways to design the Chapter 1 funding formula that might increase the targeting of funds to the highest poverty school communities.

As previously discussed in this chapter, the nature and extent of rising costs of special education programs have been a focus of recent research and debate. Some analysts note an increasing conflict between regular and special education that displays itself in part as a competition for scarce dollars, but it is mostly due to dramatic philosophical, pedagogical, and legal differences between the two groups (Meredith and Underwood, 1996). The financing of programs for special education students served under Part B of the federal Individuals with Disabilities Education Act (IDEA) has come from a combination of federal, state, and local resources and is estimated to account for approximately 12 percent of public education budgets (Parrish and Chambers, 1996). During the 1993–94 year, 5.3 million children were served by special education programs nationwide, and growth in the special education population is expected to continue in the future.

In recent years, most states have either altered or are considering major changes in special education finance policies. Based on a survey of all states completed by Parrish and Chambers (1996), changes in special education finance policies are being driven primarily by the need for greater flexibility in providing services and the desire to remove existing fiscal disincentives for placing students in the least restrictive setting. Other related issues include increased fiscal stress on state and local agencies, increased accountability, the need for less complicated funding formulas, the current inadequacy of some services, and the improvement of equity. Parrish and Chambers observe that at least six states have recently adopted a census-based funding system for special education, rather than the traditional system of funding based on the number of identified students. The authors note proponents of this change argue that census-based funding provides for greater flexibility in use of funds, a reduction in the costs for referral and assessment, and a reduction in over-identification of students, while still maintaining the procedural safeguards of IDEA. Opponents of census-based funding believe it would place funding and procedural safeguards in jeopardy, create inequities in states or districts with higher identification rates, and diminish accountability.

Organizational Scale

The issue of optimum size of schools and school districts has been debated for decades. Much of the research on school and school district size examines the nature of returns to organizational scale. The benefits, or returns, being examined in the literature generally fall into two categories: reduction of costs in providing the same level of educational services and increased quality of educational services available to students. We will begin with a look at examinations of cost savings associated with school and school district size. We then discuss the research on organization size and student achievement at both school and classroom levels.

Size and Cost Savings

Initial studies in scale economies assumed that a parabolic, or U-shaped, curve best describe the relationship between cost and school or school district size (Riew, 1986; Cohn, 1968). Cohn (1975) looked for an equation designed to define the "optimal" school size—that is, the enrollment level at which the average per pupil costs are at a minimum. Cohn noted two fundamental difficulties associated with determining the relationship between cost and size. One problem was that the parabolic function was not always the appropriate model for analysis. He further discovered that the choice of the unit of analysis was highly variable—whether it was the individual school, the school district, or the individual educational programs being offered.

When Fox (1981) reviewed 35 studies of economies of size in education, he noted that the computations of educational costs in most of the research on scale economies were incomplete. He pointed out that many of the 35 studies underestimated the administrative and support service costs of larger schools because these costs were typically absorbed by the district, rather than the school. Fox concluded that the existence of size economies is supported by most of the research, but he added, "The theoretical underpinnings of nearly all of the interpretable studies are deficient and some may suffer from data difficulties." He stated that a variety of weaknesses that he identified in his review of the literature "raise doubts about the exact size of any economies."

A study of scale economies conducted by Kenny (1982) disaggregated the costs of providing educational services into two components: transportation costs and instructional costs. He hypothesized that the returns to scale for any instructional costs caused by increased school size should be offset by additional transportation costs caused by increased enrollments. He noted that most studies of scale economies do not adequately address transportation costs. Riew (1986) compared scale economies in elementary and secondary school settings in a Maryland school district. He concluded that savings due to economies of scale are greater for secondary schools than they are for elementary schools. Specifically, cost savings due to scale economies existed in the range from 600–900 pupils for secondary schools and from 200–300 pupils for elementary schools. Riew also noted that most studies of cost savings associated with school size did not account for capital outlay expenditures. Monk (1990) made an additional observation regarding the incomplete accounting for costs in economy of scale studies. He stated that studies which examine cost savings do not track the level or the manner in which savings can be distributed to individual school sites.

The results of a study on the internal allocation of resources within districts and within schools (Monk, 1984) suggest that school and school district size are negatively related to the proportion of resources allocated to instruction.

Size and Student Achievement

Perhaps a more important aspect of the research on organizational size is focused on understanding the relationship between size and student achievement. Some early research suggested that school size is positively related to achievement (Coleman, 1966; Summers and Wolfe, 1977). However, research efforts in this area are limited and results are mixed with regard to the type of relationship between school and/or school district size and educational outcomes. Several studies point to the possibility that large institutions are not consistently associated with improved student performance. Kiesling (1967) examined the relationship of high school size and student achievement, while holding measures of student ability and socioeconomic status constant. He found a negative relationship between school size and school quality, and concluded that the evidence suggested caution regarding the massive school consolidation movement underway when the research was conducted. On the other hand, another study of high schools during the same period (Burkehead, Fox, and Holland, 1967) found no statistically significant relationship between school size and measures of test scores, dropout rates, and post-high school educational intentions.

In their 1967 book, *Big School, Small School—High School Size and Student Behavior*, Barker and Gump examine the relationships between high school size and the scope of academic program offerings. They concluded that "the smaller schools were deficient, in comparison, with the larger schools, with respect to specialized mathematics, specialized social and behavioral sciences, foreign languages, and specialized business classes." However, they also found some of the curricular content of the specialized classes being covered in other related courses in smaller schools. The two researchers also concluded that increased extent of curricular scope was not nearly proportional to increased high school size. Their study also compared the participation and satisfaction levels of students attending large and small high schools. They concluded that students in smaller schools participate more in a wider variety of school activities than students in larger schools. It was also noted that the educationally disadvantaged student in a smaller school experienced as much incentive to participate as the non-disadvantaged student. In research conducted 20 years after the Barker and Gump investigation, Monk (1987) drew a similar conclusion. He noted that gains made in curriculum comprehensiveness due to increased high school size beyond a modest level of enrollment are minimal. He concluded that "the case for maintaining secondary school enrollments at the 400 pupil level is convincing; the case for maintaining secondary school enrollments beyond 400 is more problematic."

In a study of all New Jersey school districts, Walberg and Fowler (1987) examined the relationship of district size on per pupil expenditure and on student achievement. Although they found a positive correlation between district size and per pupil expenditure, they also found a moderate, negative correlation between district size and achievement.

Early studies examining the relationship between school or school district size and educational outcomes at the elementary school level yield mixed results. One 1968 study (Alkin, Benson, and Gustafson) found no statistically significant relationship between school district size and achievement in elementary grades one through three. Michelson (1972) analyzed the relationship between elementary school size and sixth grade reading scores. He found a negative, but statistically insignificant relationship in his sample. Edington and Martellaro (1984) examined

four years of data from New Mexico elementary and secondary schools and found no significant relationship between size and achievement. However, Eberts, *et al.* (1984), using a nationwide sample of 338 elementary schools, studied the relationship between school size and student achievement in mathematics. He found that the difference in student mathematics achievement between small schools (enrollment under 200 students) and medium size schools (enrollment between 200–800 students) is not significant, but real differences in achievement exist when comparing medium size school with large schools (enrollment above 800 students). Eberts found a strong negative association between large schools and student performance and suggested additional investigation into other factors, which may account for differences in achievement in schools with enrollment over 800 pupils. A study of 50 London elementary schools (Mortimer *et al.*, 1988) revealed no positive relationship between larger schools (enrollment over 160 pupils) and student progress. The researchers found a positive relationship between elementary schools of 160 enrollment or less and pupil progress in cognitive areas. The study concludes that there is "no evidence from the Project's findings that larger schools were associated with better progress in any area." A study of all elementary schools in California (Plecki, 1991) found that the negative relationship between school size and student achievement was most pronounced in the urban areas of the state and for schools serving high concentrations (more than 25 percent of total enrollment) of students in poverty. A recent study of high school size (Lee and Smith, 1996) concluded that learning is maximized in high schools whose size ranges from 600–900 students, and that the effect of size is stronger in schools serving high concentrations of minority students.

Some research seems to indicate that larger schools do not necessarily take advantage of the benefits possible given returns to specialization. In a discussion of scale economy research, Monk (1990) drew the distinction between economies of scale that are theoretically possible and those that are actually realized by schools and/or school districts. Monk's assertion is that many schools do not take advantage of the economy of scale opportunities and, as a result, actual differences due to size are minimal.

Class Size

Two decades ago, a meta-analysis of class size research conducted by Glass and Smith (1978) demonstrated a relationship between class size and student achievement. The authors found that students learned more in smaller classes, particularly in the early grades, and recommended that class size be reduced to less than 20 students, preferably at least to 15 students. As was the case with the meta-analysis of productivity research discussed earlier in this chapter, criticism of the Glass and Smith study has centered around the methodology for conducting the meta-analysis, especially concerning the inclusion of studies that are methodologically weak. Odden (1990) reviewed the research on class size and concluded that (1) much of the positive effect on student achievement associated with reduced class size can be accounted for by individual or small group (2–3 students) tutoring and (2) the greatest benefit derived by class sizes of 15 students are in the reading and language arts areas.

A longitudinal, experimental study of class size reduction, Project STAR (Student Teacher Achievement Ratio), was conducted in Tennessee between 1984 and 1990. Results from this study showed that students in smaller classes (13–17 students) achieved more in reading and math in grades K–3, and that the effects were greatest for minority students (Finn and Achilles, 1990; Achilles, 1994; Bracey, 1995). Follow-up analyses have been conducted on a portion of the students who were in Project Star's small classes. Results reported for eighth graders who were in small classes in grades K–3 indicate that they "remain significantly ahead of those who were in regular classes" (Achilles, 1996).

Site-Based Management

One popular trend in school reform activities has been an increase in the allocation of decision-making authority to individuals who are located at the school site level. A number of terms have been used to describe this strategy, including site-based management, school-based decision-making, school-based management, and participative decision-making. The site-based decision-making teams typically include classroom teachers and school staff, the school principal, and parents and/or community members.

In a case study of the literature on site-based management, Malen, Ogawa, and Kranz (1990) conclude that site-based management is widespread and seems to occur in times of intense pressure on schools, that there is great variability in the ways in which schools arrange their formal decision-making systems, and that the study of site-based management is "empirically elusive." Although numerous studies of site-based management exist, a relatively small proportion of the existing literature examines the relationship between site-based management and changes in resource allocation. Malen, Ogawa, and Kranz's review indicated that site-based management teams had little influence over core budget, personnel, or program decisions.

Other studies of site-based management have focused on the participation of teachers in the site-based decision-making process (Conley, Schmidle, and Shedd, 1990; Conley, 1991; Little, 1988, 1990). There is evidence to suggest that teachers are more willing to participate in decisions about curriculum, instruction, and staff development than in decisions about personnel and general administration (Smylie, 1992). Teachers' willingness to participate in all areas of decision-making is strongly influenced by the nature of the teacher-principal relationships. That is, teachers are more willing to participate when the teacher-principal relationship is characterized as open, collaborative, and/or supportive (Smylie et al. 1996; Johnson, 1990; Malen and Ogawa, 1988; Rothschild and Whitt, 1986). Additional research indicates that participative decision-making processes are quite difficult to develop, even under favorable conditions (White, 1992; Murphy and Beck, 1995). However, a longitudinal study of the instructional outcomes of participative decision-making (Smylie, Lazarus, and Brownlee-Conyers, 1996) concludes that teacher participation in site decision-making is positively related to instructional improvement and student outcomes.

Management of Classroom Resources

The management of classroom resources is primarily determined by the classroom teacher. Classroom teachers make numerous instructional decisions about the use of curriculum materials, the type of instructional activities, the amount of time spent on each activity, the arrangement of space and the use of instructional equipment, and the number and type of individual, small group, and large group teacher-student interactions. Teachers also must manage other elements of a classroom that are not directly related to instruction, such as classroom discipline, participation in school routines and activities, and compliance with procedural and record-keeping expectations.

Carroll (1963) advanced the notion that how students' time is used is an important element in understanding the learning process. Carroll discussed how the amount of time a student spends "on-task," that is, productively engaged in learning activities, along with a student's ability and the quality of instruction are principle determinants of student achievement levels.

A three-year longitudinal study of resource use and student achievement in four elementary schools in Wisconsin (Rossmiller, 1986) examined the relationship between time on-task in different types of instructional settings and performance in reading and mathematics. The author concluded that while student time on-task is important, "it is quite clear that merely increasing time on-task is not a panacea." This study also concluded that classroom teachers' attitudes and beliefs were more important predictors of student achievement than the traditional teacher input variables such as education level and years of experience.

In a recent set of case studies of resource allocation in secondary schools, Brent and Monk (1996) found remarkably high proportions of the day of secondary school teachers being devoted to non-classroom assignments such as preparation periods. These ranged from 14 percent to 41 percent depending on the subject being taught and the social and economic characteristics of the school and district.

School Improvement and Resources

Knowledge about the costs of educational reform strategies for school improvement are crucial to decision-making about the types of strategies to be implemented and the level of resources that will be devoted to any particular set of reform efforts. However, a number of problems are posed for the researcher attempting to develop cost estimates of improvement policies, including difficulties associated with assessing costs of a new program that has limited data, the importance of determining the net effect of a reform, and the estimation of avoided future costs resulting from more successful outcomes related to the reform.

Central to a number of school improvement strategies has been the development of performance-based assessment for students. A recent study (Stecher and Klein, 1997) of the costs of a large-scale, science performance assessment was based on data from a field trial of more than 2,000 students in the fifth and sixth grades. The cost estimates examined the resources involved with test development, administration, and scoring. As one might expect, the cost of performance-based measures are substantially more expensive than traditional multiple-choice methods. The researchers also found that the science performance assessment was three times more expensive than open-ended writing assessments. The authors suggest several alternatives to reducing costs of a large-scale performance assessment, such as combining performance-based items with multiple-choice items, the use of sampling techniques such as matrix sampling, and realizing economies of scale by pooling resources for assessment costs across broad jurisdictions.

School-Based Analysis

Understanding the effects of current reform initiatives at the individual school level has become particularly important because these reforms have often been associated with increased decision-making discretion and autonomy at the school site level. A long-standing problem for researchers attempting to study the interactions between fiscal and educational improvement policies and individual school performance has been the lack of uniform school-based data, particularly financial data. This lack of school-based data creates an information void for policymakers. For example, the recent establishment of charter schools in many states has raised important questions about state-level mechanisms for funding individual schools that are difficult to resolve due to the lack of existing school-level information.

Several researchers have recently discussed ways in which school-level fiscal data could be helpful in analyzing important questions about productivity, adequacy, and equity in the distribution and use of educational resources. Some argue that real progress in understanding productivity questions can only be made when researchers can accurately portray how dollars are translated into the educational resources, which are available at the school site, and how the purchased resources affect instructional practices and student outcomes (Berne, Stiefel, and Moser, 1997; Monk, 1997; Picus, 1997). A key equity question particularly relevant for urban districts is the nature and level of inequities among schools within the same district. School-level data would allow for more comprehensive and detailed analysis of intra-district equity (Goertz, 1997; Monk, 1997). Farland (1997) notes that school-level data could assist in developing better cost estimates for proposed new programs. School-level data also has the potential to improve the management of school-level resources and in developing better accountability systems at the state level that are more closely linked to student performance (Berne, Moser, and Steifel, 1997; Goertz, 1997).

Developing and implementing a new information system that is centered around the school as the unit of analysis requires an alteration in how school finance has been typically construed. One set of recommendations for accomplishing the necessary changes in information systems calls for a rethinking of school finance with a focus on providing timely, user-friendly financial information relevant to school site planning, budgeting, and local accountability (Speakman *et al.*, 1997). One example of the way in which school-level fiscal data can be developed can be found in the Finance Analysis Model, a computer software program that tracks resource flows to the classroom and student level (Speakman *et al.*, 1996a) and uses a relational database that provides for analyses by function (instruction, operations, and so on), location (central or school site), type of school (elementary, secondary, or alternative schools), and program (special education, vocational, Chapter 1).

Concluding Remarks

In this chapter we have explored numerous perspectives and issues related to resource allocation for school improvement. Dominant themes in the research discussed in this chapter have been the critical values of equity, efficiency, and adequacy. Recent research on how resources impact school improvement reflect the evolving nature of these values. Policy discussions that attempt to identify and implement strategies for school improvement often must weigh the relative commitments to equity, efficiency, and adequacy for each policy initiative under consideration.

Often, research on school improvement does not include investigations regarding the level and type of resources necessary for successful implementation of a particular set of reforms. In particular, research is lacking regarding how existing resources are reallocated or how existing commitments to activities are altered when an improvement strategy is undertaken. It is important to improve our understanding of how dollars are translated into the array of educational resources and consequently how the utilization of those purchased resources affect educational practice and educational outcomes. Some of the most promising work on this topic is being focused on the management of resources at points that are close to where educational improvement actually occurs. We have been particularly impressed with the importance of resource allocation analyses that are focused at both the school and classroom levels of school organizations. We expect to see policymakers' interest in achieving and sustaining school improvement to foster a further expansion of this kind of research in the near future.

NOTES

1. The limits may apply in general to property taxes or be defined more narrowly for certain types of services like education.
2. This section draws on materials that were prepared by one of the authors for the American Association for the Advancement of Science Blueprint for Reform project. The text is used with permission.

REFERENCES

Achilles, C. M. (1996, February). Students achieve more in smaller classes. *Educational Leadership*: 76–77.

Achilles, C. M., *et al.* (1994, November). *The multiple benefits of class-size research: a review of STAR's legacy, subsidiary and ancillary studies.* Paper presented at the Mid-South Educational Research Association, Nashville, TN.

Advisory Commission on Intergovernmental Relations (1994). *Significant Features of Fiscal Federalism, Volume 1–2.* Washington, DC: Author.

Advisory Commission on Intergovernmental Relations (1995). *Tax and Expenditure Limits on Local Governments.* Washington, DC: Author.

Alkin, M. C., Benson, C. S. & Gustafson, R. H. (1968, February). *Economy of scale in the production of selected educational outcomes.* Paper prepared for the annual meeting of the American Educational Research Association, Chicago, IL.

American Association for the Advancement of Science (in press). *Blueprints for Reform.* Washington, DC: Author.

Ashenfelter, O. & Krueger, A. B. (1994). Estimates of the economic return to schooling from a new sample of twins. *American Economic Review* 84, 5: 1157–1173.

Barker, R. G. & Gump, P. V. (1964). *Big School, Small School: High School Size and Student Behavior.* Palo Alto: Stanford University Press.

Barnett, W. S. (December 1994). Obstacles and opportunities: Some simple economics of school finance reform. *Educational Policy* 8, 4: 436–452.

Bellon, E. C., Bellon, J. J., Blank, M. A., Brian, D. J. G. & Kershaw, C. A. (1989, March). *Alternative incentive programs for school based reform.* Paper presented at the annual meeting of the American Educational Research Association, San Francisco, CA.

Benson, C. S. (1991). Definitions of equity in school finance in Texas, New Jersey, and Kentucky. *Harvard Journal on Legislation 28*,2: 401–422.

Berne, R. & Netzer, D. (1995). Discrepancies between ideal characteristics of a property tax system and current practice in New York. *Journal of Education Finance* 21,1: 39–56.

Berne, R. & Picus, L. O. (Eds.) (1994). *Outcome Equity in Education.* Thousand Oaks, CA: Corwin Press.

Berne, R., Stiefel, L. & Moser, M. (1997). The coming of age of school-level finance data. *Journal of Education Finance* 22, 3: 246–254.

Borg, M. O., Mason, P. M. & Shapiro, S. L. (1991). *The Economic Consequences of State Lotteries.* New York: Praeger.

Bracey, G. C. (1995, September). Research oozes into practice: The case of class size. *Phi Delta Kappan*: 89–90.

Brent, B. O. (1997). *Student and Taxpayer Equity in Education Finance: An Analysis of Nonresidential Expanded Tax Base Approaches to Funding Public K–12 School Systems.* Doctoral dissertation in progress, Department of Education, Cornell University.

Brent, B. O. & Monk, D. H. (1996, March). *How are teacher resources used? A micro-level analysis.* Paper presented at the annual conference of the American Education Finance Association, Salt Lake City, Utah.

Brown, B. W. & Saks, D. H. (1975). The production and distribution of cognitive skills in schools. *Journal of Political Economy* 83, 3: 571–593.

Burkehead, J., Fox, T. & Holland, J. (1967). *Input and Output in Large City Schools.* Syracuse, NY: Syracuse University Press.

Campbell v. State of Wyoming, 907 p. 2d 1238 (Wyo. 1995).

Card, D. & Krueger, A. B. (1992). Does school quality matter? Returns to education and the characteristics of public schools in the United States. *Journal of Political Economy 100*,1: 1–40.

Carroll, J. (1963). A model for school learning. *Teachers College Record* 64: 723–733.

Center for the Study of the States (1995). *Public School Finance Programs of the United States and Canada, 1993–94.* Albany, NY: Author.

Chambers, J. & Fowler, W. J., Jr. (1995). *Public School Teacher Cost Differences Across the United States.* National Center for Education Statistics, Analysis/Methodology Report, October, NCES 95–758.

Clark, R. C. (1996). *Professional development schools: Costs and finances.* A working paper for review and study by NNER, NCREST, and the NCATE Standards Project. Center for Educational Renewal, University of Washington, Seattle, WA.

Clark, R. C. & Plecki, M. L. (1997). Professional development schools: Their costs and financing. In M. Levine & R. Trachtman (Eds.) *Making Professional Development Schools Work.* New York: Teachers College Press.

Clune, W. H. (1994). The Shift from Equity to Adequacy in School Finance. *Educational Policy* 8,4: 376–394.

Cohen, D. K., McLaughlin, M. & Talbert, J. (Eds.) (1993). *Teaching for Understanding: Challenges for Policy and Practice.* San Francisco: Jossey-Bass.

Cohn, E. (1968). Economies of scale in Iowa school operations, *Journal of Human Resources* 3: 422–434.

Cohn, E. (1975). A proposal for school size incentives in state aid to education. *Journal of Education Finance 1*, 2: 216–225.

Coleman, J. S. (1966). *Equality of Educational Opportunity.* Washington, DC: U. S. Government Printing Office.

Conley, S. C. (1991). Review of research on teacher participation in school decision making, *Review of Research in Education* 17: 225–266.

Conley, S. C. & Levinson, R. (1993). Teacher work redesign and job satisfaction. *Educational Administration Quarterly* 29, 4: 453–478.

Conley, S. C., Schmidle, T. & Shedd, J. B. (1990). Teacher participation in the management of school systems. *Teachers College Record* 90: 259–280.

Coopers & Lybrand, L. L. P. (1994). *Resource Allocations in the New York City Public Schools.* Special Counsel for Fiscal Oversight of Education.

Darling-Hammond, L. (1994). *The current status of teaching and teacher development in the United States.* Background paper prepared for the National Commission on Teaching and America's Future.

Darling-Hammond, L. & Berry, B. (1988). *The Evolution of Teacher Policy.* Santa Monica, CA: RAND.

Darling-Hammond, L. & McLaughlin, M. W. (1995, April). Policies that reform professional development in an era of reform. *Phi Delta Kappan* 76, 8: 597–604.

Eberts, R. W., Kehoe, E. & Stone, Joe A. (1984). *The effect of school size on student outcomes.* Center for Educational Policy and Management, University of Oregon, Eugene, OR.

Edington, E. D. & Martellaro, H. C. (1984). *Variables affecting academic achievement in New Mexico schools.* Paper presented at the annual meeting of the American Educational Research Association, New Orleans, LA.

Ehrenberg, R. G. & Brewer, D. J. (1995). Did teacher's race and verbal ability matter in the 1960s? Coleman revisited. *Economics of Education Review* 14: 291–299.

Elmore, R. (1994). Thoughts on program equity: Productivity and incentives for performance in education. *Educational Policy* 8, 4: 453–459.

Farland, G. (1997). Collection of fiscal and staffing data at the school-site level. *Journal of Education Finance* 22, 3: 280–290.

Ferguson, R. F. (1991). Paying for public education: New evidence on how and why money matters. *Harvard Journal on Legislation* 28, 2: 465–497.

Ferguson, R. F. & Ladd, H. F. (1996). How and why money matters: An analysis of Alabama schools. In H. F. Ladd (Ed.), *Holding Schools Accountable* (pp. 265–298). Washington, DC: Brookings Institution.

Finn, J. D. & Achilles, C. M. (1990, Fall). Answers and questions about class size: A statewide experiment. *American Education Research Journal* 27, 3: 557–577.

Firestone, W. A. (1991). Merit pay and job enlargement as reforms: Incentives, implementation, and teacher response. *Educational Evaluation and Policy Analysis* 13, 3: 269–288.

Fox, W. F. (1981). Reviewing economies of size in education. *Journal of Education Finance* 6, No. 3: 273–96.

Freiberg, J. & Knight, S. (1991). Career ladder programs as incentives for teachers. In S. C. Conley & B. S. Cooper (Eds.), *The School as a Work Environment: Implications for Reform.* Boston, MA: Allyn and Bacon.

Glass, G. V. & Smith, M. L. (1978). *Meta-Analysis of Research on the Relationship of Class Size and Achievement.* San Francisco: Far West Laboratory for Educational Research and Development.

Goertz, M. E. (1997). The challenges of collecting school-based data. *Journal of Education Finance* 22, 3: 291–302.

Hanushek, E. A. (1981). Throwing money at schools. *Journal of Policy Analysis and Management* 1, No. 1: 19–41.

Hanushek, E. A. (1986). The economics of schooling: Production and efficiency in public schools. *Journal of Economic Literature* 24: 1141–1177.

Hanushek, E. A. (1989). The impact of differential expenditures on school performance. *Educational Researcher* 18, 4: 45–51.

Hanushek, E. A. (1991). When school finance reform may not be good policy. *Harvard Journal on Legislation* 28, 2: 423–456.

Hanushek, E. A. (1996). The quest for equalized mediocrity: School finance reform without consideration of school performance. In L. O. Picus & J. L. Wattenbarger (Eds.), *Where Does the Money Go? Resource Allocation in Elementary and Secondary Schools* (pp. 20–43). Thousand Oaks, CA: Corwin Press, Inc.

Hargreaves, A. (1990). Teachers' work and the politics of time and space. *Qualitative Studies in Education* 3: 303–320.

Hargreaves, A. (1993). Individualism and individuality: Reinterpreting the teacher culture. In J. W. Little & M. W. McLaughlin (Eds.), *Teachers' Work: Individuals, Colleagues, and Contexts.* New York: Teachers College Press.

Hawley, W. D. (1987). The high costs and doubtful efficacy of extended teacher-preparation programs: An invitation to more basic reform. *American Journal of Education* 45, 2: 275–298.

Hedges, L. V., Laine, R. D. & Greenwald, R. (1994, April). Does money matter? A meta-analysis of studies of the effects of differential school inputs on student outcomes. *Educational Researcher* 23, 3: 5–14.

Houston, R. W. & Freiberg, J. H. (1979). Perpetual motion, blindman's bluff, and in-service education. *Journal of Teacher Education,* 30, 1: 7–9.

Hughes, J., Moon, C. G. & Barnett, W. S. (1993, October). *Revenue-driven costs: The case of resource allocation in public primary and secondary education.* Paper presented at the annual meeting of the Atlantic Economic Society, Philadelphia, PA.

Johnson, S. M. (1990). Redesigning teachers' work. in R. F. Elmore & Associates, *Restructuring Schools: The Next Generation of Educational Reform.* San Francisco: Jossey-Bass.

Kearney, C. P. (1995). Reducing local school property taxes: Recent experiences in Michigan. *Journal of Education Finance* 21,1: 165–185.

Kelley, C. (1997). Teacher compensation and organization. *Educational Evaluation and Policy Analysis* 19, 1: 15–28.

Kenny, L. W. (1982). Economies of scale in schooling. *Economics of Education Review* 2, 1: 1–24.

Kiesling, H. J. (1967). Measuring a local government service: A study of school districts in New York State. *Review of Economics and Statistics* 49: 356–367.

Ladd, H. F. (1976). Statewide taxation of commercial and industrial property for education. *National Tax Journal* 29: 143–153.

Ladd, H. F. (1985). Education and tax limitations: Evidence from Massachusetts. *Journal of Education Finance* 10: 281–296.

Ladd, H. F. & Harris, E. W. (1995). Statewide taxation of nonresidential property for education. *Journal of Education Finance* 21,1: 39–56.

Laine, R. D., Greenwald, R., *et al.* (1996). Money does matter: A research synthesis of a new universe of education production function studies. In L. O. Picus & J. L. Wattenbarger (Eds.), *Where Does the Money Go: Resource Allocation in Elementary and Secondary Schools* (pp. 44–70). Thousand Oaks, CA: Corwin Press, Inc.

Lankford, H. & Wyckoff, J. (1995). Property taxation, taxpayer burden, and local educational finance in New York. *Journal of Education Finance* 21, 1: 57–86.

Lankford, H. & Wyckoff, J. (1996). The allocation of resources to special education and regular instruction. In H. F. Ladd (Ed.), *Holding Schools Accountable* (pp. 221–262). Washington, DC: Brookings Institution.

Lee, V. E. & Smith, J. B. (1996). *High school size: Which works best, and for whom?* Paper presented at the annual meeting of the American Educational Research Association, Washington, DC.

Lewis, D. R. (1990). Estimating the economic worth of a 5th year licenser program for teachers. *Educational Evaluation and Policy Analysis* 12, 1: 25–39.

Little, J. W. (1988). Assessing the prospects for teacher leadership. In A. Lieberman (Ed.), *Building a Professional Culture in Schools.* New York: Teachers College Press.

Little, J. W. (1989). District policy choices and teacher's professional development opportunities. *Educational Evaluation and Policy Analysis* 11, 2: 165–179.

Little, J. W. (1990). The persistence of privacy: Autonomy and initiative in teachers' professional relations. *Teachers College Record* 91: 509–536.

Little, J. W. (1993). Teachers' professional development in a climate of educational reform. *Educational Evaluation and Policy Analysis* 15, 2: 129–151.

Lortie, D. C. (1975). *Schoolteacher.* Chicago: University of Chicago Press.

Lytle, J. H. (1983). Investment options for in-service teacher training. *Journal of Teacher Education* 34, 1: 28–31.

Malen, B. & Ogawa, R. T. (1988). Professional-patron influence on site-based governance councils: A confounding case study. *Educational Evaluation and Policy Analysis* 10: 251–270.

Malen, B., Ogawa, R. T. & Kranz, J. (1990). What do we know about school-based management? A case study of the literature—A call for research. In W. H. Clune & J. F. Witte (Eds.), *Choice and Control in American Education, Vol. 2: The Practice of Choice, Decentralization, and School Restructuring.* New York: Falmer Press.

Meredith, B. & Underwood, J. (1996). Irreconcilable differences? Defining the rising conflict between regular and special education. *Journal of Law and Education* 24, 2: 195–226.

Michelson, S. (1972). For the plaintiffs: equal school resource allocation. *Journal of Human Resources* 7, 3: 283–306.

Miles, K. H. (1995). Freeing resources for improving schools: A case study of teacher allocation in Boston Public Schools. *Educational Evaluation and Policy Analysis* 17,4 : 476–493.

Miller, B., Lord, B. & Dorney, J. (1994). *Staff Development for Teachers: A Study of Configurations and Costs in Four Districts*. Newtonville, MA: Education Development Center.

Mohrman, A. M., Mohrman, S. A. & Odden, A. R. (1996). Aligning teacher compensation with systemic school reform: Skill-based and group-based performance rewards. *Educational Evaluation and Policy Analysis* 18, 1: 51–71.

Monk, D. H. (1984). The conception of size and the internal allocation of school district resources. *Educational Administration Quarterly* 20, 1: 39–67.

Monk, D. H. (1987). Secondary school size and curriculum comprehensiveness. *Economics of Education Review* 6, 2: 137–150.

Monk, D. H., (1990). *Educational Finance: An Economic Approach*. New York: McGraw-Hill.

Monk, D. H. (1992). Education productivity research: An update and assessment of its role in education finance reform. *Educational Evaluation and Policy Analysis* 14,4: 307–332.

Monk, D. H. (1996). Resource allocation for education: An evolving and promising base for policy-oriented research. *Journal of School Leadership* 6: 216–241.

Monk, D. H. (1997). Challenges surrounding the collection and use of data for the study of finance and productivity. *Journal of Education Finance* 22, 3: 303–316.

Monk, D. H. & Brent, B. O. (1997). *Raising Money for Education: A Guide to the Property Tax*. Thousand Oaks, CA: Corwin Press.

Monk, D. H. & Pijanowski, J. (1996). Alternative school revenue sources. *School Business Affairs* (July): 4–10.

Monk, D. H., Roellke, C. F. & Brent, B. O. (1996). *What Education Dollars Buy: An Examination of Resource Allocation Patterns in New York State Public School Systems*. Final Report to the Finance Center, Consortium for Policy Research in Education (CPRE). Ithaca, New York: Cornell University, Department of Education.

Moore, D. & Hyde, A. (1981). *Making Sense of Staff Development: An Analysis of Staff Development Programs and Their Costs in Three Urban School Districts*. Chicago: Designs for Change.

Mortimer, P., Sammons, P. Stoll, L. Lewis, D. & Ecob, R. (1988). *School Matters*. Berkeley, CA: University of California Press.

Moskowitz, J., Stullich, S. & Deng, B. (1993). *Targeting, Formula, and Resource Allocation Issues: Focusing Federal Funds Where the Needs Are Greatest*. Washington, DC: U. S. Department of Education.

Murnane, R. J. (1975). *The Impact of School Resources on the Learning of Inner City Children*. Cambridge, MA: Ballinger.

Murnane, R. J. (1991). Interpreting the evidence on 'Does Money Matter,' *Harvard Journal on Legislation* 28: 457–464.

Murnane, R. J. & Cohen, D. K. (1986). Merit pay and the evaluation problem. *Harvard Educational Review* 56, 1: 1–17.

Murphy, J. & Beck, L. G. (1995). *School-Based Management as School Reform: Taking Stock*. ERIC Reproduction Services Document Accession No. ED 385 912.

Nakib, Y. A. (1995). *Beyond district level expenditures: Resource allocation and use in Florida's public schools*. Paper presented at the annual meeting of the American Education Finance Association, Savannah, GA.

National Center for Education Statistics (1996). *Statistics in Brief: Revenues and Expenditures for Public Elementary and Secondary Education: School Year 1993–94*. Washington, DC: U. S. Department of Education, Author. NCES 96–303.

Nikansen, W. A. (1971). *Bureaucracy and representative government*. Chicago: Aldine Atherton.

Odden, A. (1990). Class size and student achievement: Research-based policy alternatives. *Educational Evaluation and Policy Analysis* 12, 2: 213–227.

Odden, A. & Clune, W. (1995). Improving educational productivity and school finance. *Educational Researcher* 24, 9: 6–10, 22.

Odden, A. & Kelley, C. (1997). *Paying Teachers for What They Know and Do: New and Smarter Compensation Strategies to Improve Schools*. Thousand Oaks, CA: Corwin Press.

Odden, A., Monk, D., Nakib, Y. & Picus, L. O. (1995). The story of the education dollar: No Academy Awards and no fiscal smoking guns. *Phi Delta Kappan* (October): 161–168.

Orlich, D. C. & Evans, A. (1990). *Regression Analysis: A Novel Way to Examine Staff Development Cost Factors*. Unpublished manuscript. ERIC Reproduction Service Document No. ED 331 808.

Parrish, T. B. & Chambers, J. G. (1996). Financing special education. *The Future of Children* 6, 1: 121–138.

Picus, L. O. (1991). Cadillacs or Chevrolets?: The evolution of state control over school finance in California. *Journal of Education Finance* 17,1: 33–59.

Picus, L. O. (1997). Using school-level finance data: Endless opportunity or bottomless pit? *Journal of Education Finance* 22, 3: 317–330.

Picus, L. O., Tetreault, D. & Hertert, L. (1995). *The allocation and use of education dollars at the district and school level in California*. Paper presented at the annual meeting of the American Education Finance Association, Savannah, GA.

Plecki, M. L. (1991). *The relationship between elementary school size and student achievement*. Paper presented at the annual meeting of the American Educational Research Association, San Francisco, CA.

Protsik, J. (1996). History of teacher pay and incentive reforms. *Journal of School Leadership* 6, 3: 265–289.

Ram, R. (1995). Public educational expenditures in the United States: An analytical comparison with other industrialized countries. *Economics of Education Review* 14,1: 53–61.

Resnick, L. B. (1993). Standards, assessment, and educational quality. *Stanford Law and Policy Review* 4: 53–59.

Richardson, V. (1990). Significant and worthwhile change in teaching practice. *Educational Researcher* 19, 7: 10–18.

Riew, J. (1986). Scale economies, capacity utilization, and school costs: A comparative analysis of secondary and elementary schools. *Journal of Education Finance* 11, 4: 399–415.

Robinson, G. (1983). *Paying Teachers for Performance and Productivity: Learning from Experience*. Arlington, VA: Educational Research Service.

Roellke, C. F. (1996). *The Local Response to State Initiated Education Reform: Changes in the Allocation of Human Resources in New York State Schooling Systems, 1983–1995*. Unpublished Ph.D. dissertation, Department of Education, Cornell University.

Ross, R. (1994). *Effective Teacher Development Through Salary Incentives (An Exploratory Analysis)*. RAND, Institute on Education and Training.

Rossmiller, R. A. (1986). *Resource Allocation in Schools and Classrooms: Final Report*. Madison, WI: University of Wisconsin-Madison, Wisconsin Center for Education Research, School of Education.

Rothschild, J. & Whitt, J. A. (1986). *The Cooperative Workplace: Potentials and Dilemmas of Organizational Democracy and Participation*. New York: Cambridge University Press.

Rothstein, R. & Miles, K. H. (with). (1995). *Where's the Money Gone? Changes in the Level and Composition of Education Spending*. Washington, DC: Economic Policy Institute.

Smith, M. S., Scott, B. W. & Link, J. (1995). The growing importance of cognitive skills in wage determination. *Review of Economics and Statistics* 77: 251–266.

Smylie, M. A. (1992). Teacher participation in school decision making: Assessing willingness to participate, *Educational Evaluation and Policy Analysis* 14, 1: 53–67.

Smylie, M. A., Lazarus, V. & Brownlee-Conyers, J. (1996). Instructional outcomes of school-based participative decision making. *Educational Evaluation and Policy Analysis* 18, No. 3, 181–198.

Southern Regional Education Board (1994). *Reflecting on Ten Years of Incentive Programs: The 1993 SREB Career Ladder Clearinghouse Survey*. Atlanta, GA: Author.

Speakman, S. T., *et al.* (1996a). Bringing money to the classroom: A systemic resource allocation model applied to the New York City Public Schools. In L. O. Picus & J. L. Wattenbarger (Eds.), *Where Does the Money Go? Resource Allocations in Elementary and Secondary Schools* (pp. 106–132). Thousand Oaks, CA: Corwin Press.

Speakman, S. T., *et al.* (1996b). Tracing school-site expenditures: Equity, policy, and legal implications. In B. S. Cooper & S. T. Speakman (Eds.), *Optimizing Education Resources* (pp. 149–193). Greenwich, CT: JAI Press Inc.

Speakman, S. T., *et al.* (1997). The three Rs of education finance reform: Rethinking, retooling and reevaluating school-site information. *Journal of Education Finance* 22, 4: 337–367.

Stecher, B. M. & Klein, S. P. (1997). The cost of science performance assessments in large-scale testing programs. *Educational Evaluation and Policy Analysis* 19, 1: 1–14.

Steinberg, J. (1996). High Schools Get Less Aid than Elementary and Middle Ones. *New York Times*, November 24.

Stern, D. S., Gerritz, W. & Little, J. W. (1989). Making the most of the district's two (or five) cents: Accounting for investment in teachers' professional development. *Journal of Education Finance* 14, 4: 19–26.

Strauss, R. P. (1995). Reducing reliance on the school property tax: Rationales and first results. *Journal of Education Finance* 21,1: 123–164.

Summers, A. & Wolfe, B. (1977). Do schools make a difference? *American Economic Review* 67, 4: 639–652.

Swanson, A. D. & King, R. A. (1997). *School Finance: Its Economics and Politics*. New York: Longman.

Theobald, N. (1990). *Allocating Resources to Renew Teacher Education*. Occasional Paper No. 14, Seattle: University of Washington, College of Education, Center for Educational Renewal.

Thomas, J. A. & Kemmerer, F. (1983). *Money, Time, and Learning*. Albany, NY : State University of New York at Albany, School of Education.

Underwood, J. (1995). School finance adequacy as vertical equity, *University of Michigan J. L. Ref.* 28: 493.

Walberg, H. J. & Fowler, W. J. (1987). Expenditure and size efficiencies of public school districts. *Educational Researcher* 16, 7: 5–13.

White, P. A. (1992). Teacher empowerment under ideal school-site autonomy. *Educational Evaluation and Policy Analysis* 14: 69–82.

Wise, A. E. (1967). *Rich Schools Poor Schools*. Chicago: University of Chicago Press.

Witte, J. F. (1990, August). *Understanding high school achievement: After a decade of research, do we have any confident policy recommendations?* Paper presented at the annual meeting of the American Political Science Association, San Francisco.

CHAPTER 24

A New Research Paradigm for Understanding (And Improving) Twenty-First Century Schooling

Paul T. Hill and James W. Guthrie

A dramatic and global change in economic and technological conditions is fundamentally altering personal relationships, work, and education. Thanks to jet transportation and worldwide computer linkages, members of today's adult generation have friends, relatives, collaborators, and competitors in many places other than their home towns. The organizations they work in are also likely to have partners and competitors from all parts of the world. In their work, as in their private lives, individuals are continually required to learn new ideas and skills, and to be alert for developments—everything from competitors' business tactics to new threats to personal health—to which they must adapt.

When the readers of this volume were in school, few people could have fully anticipated today's world. Many people of our generation have been able to build on their basic educations and adapt to constant change in society and the economy, but many have not. Aside from unaccountable differences in personality, what distinguishes people who can adapt to change from those who cannot is the habit of mental mastery of their environment. People who master the basic skills of information access and analysis, who know how to learn new skills and assess the risks and opportunities posed by changes in context, and who expect to adapt continuously are far more likely than people without those traits to support themselves and retain their personal independence.

These realities underline the importance of effective schooling. Though education must be lifelong, individuals' habits and mental capacities are strongly influenced by what they learn as children and young adults. That said, however, the requirements of effective schooling are hard to describe in detail. Just as educators in 1940 could not fully anticipate the challenges that their students would face today, so today's educators cannot anticipate everything their students must be able to do tomorrow. As Peter Drucker argued in his November 1994 *Atlantic* article, "The Age of Social Transformation," we are at the end of an unprecedented era in which people with only a minimal level of schooling could get high-wage jobs and maintain a high standard of living. This comfortable condition is changing dramatically. In the near future, there will be few if any secure, well-paying jobs for people who lack extensive education and adaptable skills.

Educational leaders thus face the certainty of continued change and great uncertainty about where those changes will lead. Our students' futures depend heavily on the quality of schooling they receive, but we cannot know exactly what quality will mean in an unknown future. Some things are clear, however: schools must use students' time well, help students form their mental capacities and habits of attention to work, link students to the challenging world outside the academic enterprise, and provide students with facts and methods of analysis that allow them to interpret events and understand their own stakes in the economic, social, and political changes that will occur in their lifetimes.

How can today's leaders create schools that will accomplish these ends, and for all students rather than just a few? No one can truthfully claim to know the whole answer. Clearly, schools constructed around a narrow vision of the needs of today's adults assuredly will not met the needs of tomorrow's. Just as clearly, there are too many uncertainties about what students need to know and exactly what educational experience is most productive to justify any effort to create a uniform model of the "one best school." However, uncertainty does not absolve educators and researchers from trying to learn as much as possible about what makes schools productive and putting it into practice.

This chapter makes a bold claim: that the traditional approaches to research on education policy do not fully recognize the facts discussed above. The dominant policy research paradigm treats the school as a sum of responses to politically-created mandates. Other paradigms that lead to policy-relevant conclusions regard schools as gathering places for teachers or for separate instructional programs, and they assume that school productivity is the sum of teachers' or programs' individual performance. These paradigms do not regard the school as a problem-solving entity that must both ground students in the shared facts and values of today's society and equip them for a mentally challenging future. We propose a new research paradigm that considers a school as a productive, problem-solving organization, whose links to public authorities and parents are defined by accountability for performance and by the school's vision of students' possible futures and its specific approach to instruction.

The Need for a Paradigm for Productive Schooling

Given the global economic transformation and its likely consequences for formal education, it is essential that educational research and policy focus on what makes schools flexible, responsive to change, and effective. What is needed is a paradigm or a model that guides research and policy directly to issues that bear on school productivity.

What is a paradigm? In the seminal American Educational Research Association–sponsored initial *Handbook of Research on Teaching*, editor Nathan L. Gage (1963) contributed a chapter entitled "Paradigms for Research on Teaching." Gage describes paradigms as " . . . models, patterns, or schemata . . . which . . . often represent variables and their relationships in some graphic or outline form. Events or phenomena that have various temporal, spatial, causal, or logical relationships are portrayed in these relationships by boxes, connecting lines, and positions on vertical and horizontal dimensions."

Paradigms are descriptive, analytic, and normative. They are descriptive in that they identify the main components of a set of relationships, analytic because they show how the components interact with one another, and normative because they imply that certain actions and relationships are more important than others.

As Gage (1963) writes, "Paradigms, like theories, can be either explicit or implicit. . . . Choice of a paradigm, whether deliberate or unthinking, determines much about the research that will be done. The style, design, and approach of a research undertaking, indeed, the likelihood that it will bear fruit, are conditioned in large part by the paradigm with which a researcher begins. . . . "

A succession of different paradigms has informed the recent history of educational research. The period from 1951 to 1966 was a remarkably fertile time for research in educational administration. Scholars such as Andrew Halpin (1966), Jacob Getzels (1968), Egon Guba (1990), and Daniel Griffiths (1962) stood on the intellectual shoulders of Talcott Parsons and Robert Merton and constructed theories and paradigms that spawned literally thousands of empirical studies of schooling and its management. Judged by conventional criteria of scientific success, this period contributed much to understanding but little to prediction or control. Scholars of the period sought truth, not necessary improved performance; their studies provided a rich understanding of the operational and organizational dynamics of schools and schooling systems, but they did little to guide school improvement. Andrew Halpin's paradigm, for example, focused on administrative behavior, but it did not ask either how public policy affected administrative actions or how those actions affected student learning.

The Policy Research Paradigm

The struggle for school desegregation and President Lyndon Johnson's war on poverty inspired another new research paradigm, which regards the school as an implementer of formal policies enacted by general government. During the early struggle for desegregation, schools came under court orders and government regulations about how students should be assigned to schools and classes and how teachers should act toward students, especially members of racial minority groups. The Great Society broke through the long prohibition against federal aid to K–12 education with a program designed to provide extra money for the education of disadvantaged children. The premise of this program, still known today as Title I, is that core school programs are good, but the school systems do not take the needs of poor and minority children seriously enough. Title I provided federal funds to provide extra services for such children and introduced a new regime of federal regulation that defined disadvantaged children's access to both regular and federally-funded instructional programs. These regulations also created new classifications of federally-paid teachers and governed the ways they and regular classroom teachers could work together.

Throughout the 1970s, Congress and state legislatures created additional funding and regulatory programs, all on the premise that schools were essentially sound, but that the needs of some group—racial minorities, refugees, limited-English speaking children, and many categories of handicapped and gifted children—were not being met. Those programs created new separate categories of funds, new rules on how children with particular characteristics were to be treated, and new regulations on how different groups of teachers could work and with whom (Kimbrough and Hill, 1980).

The Great Society also stimulated an immense growth in social program evaluations, many of which showed that programs were not working as intended. Berman and McLaughlin (1979) were the first among many to show that schools do not simply comply with new requirements imposed from the outside. To the contrary, schools convert external pressures in their own ways, reflecting teachers and principals' values, priorities, and professional role definitions. These insights stimulated a major policy research enterprise that continues to this day. Its purpose is to help policymakers—legislators, governors, judges, and school board members—understand three things: how they can influence schools, how externally-prescribed policies affect the operation of schools, and how schools internal structures and values limit what can be accomplished by policy initiatives. Major exemplars of this mode of research are McDonnell and Elmore (1987), Elmore and McLaughlin (1988), and Hill and Marks (1982).

In its simplest form, the policy research paradigm regards a policymaker (a legislator, government executive, or judge) as a legitimate overseer of schools who nonetheless has an limited array of very crude tools. It also regards the school as a recipient and converter of impulses from the outside. The goal of policy research is to help policymakers understand the strengths and limitations of the tools they have (mandates, regulations, subsidies, and so on), so that government's aspirations will be realistic and official actions can be designed to have desired effects and avoid harmful unintended consequences. The best thought-through expression of this paradigm is provided by McDonnell and Elmore (1987).

This paradigm has dominated federally-funded research and evaluation from the 1970s until the present. However, as research evidence created under the paradigm accumulated, it became clear that schools do more than process and divert impulses from the external policy system; they are changed by such impulses, and often not for the better. Analysts following the policy research paradigm first considered whether particular policies were changing schools in ways that made them less able to provide effective instruction (see, for example, Hill and Madey, 1983); analysts later asked whether separate policy initiatives compete with one another for the time and attention of teachers and students (see, for example, Kimbrough and Hill, 1983; Knapp *et al.*, 1983; and Hannaway, 1985). These latter analyses argued that the aggregate result of many programs and policies,

each intended to leave the school's core untouched but to introduce new benefits or services for disadvantaged groups, was a dramatic reduction in the integrity of public schools as organizations. Thus the aggregate effects of the actions taken in pursuit of those ends was to undermine the basic assumption behind the policies themselves; many schools were no longer essentially sound.

Today's most prominent users of the policy research paradigm, represented by the federally-funded Center for Policy Research in Education, have recognized the dangers of successive unrelated programs and incentives. Without changing the basic form of the policy research paradigm, they have introduced the concern for policy *alignment* (Fuhrman, 1994). The alignment perspective recognizes that schools cannot respond well to a series of unrelated mandates that take no account of one another. Alignment analysts argue that remote government institutions can have good effects on schools—protecting the rights of particular groups while promoting, not reducing, the schools overall effectiveness—only if all policies are carefully coordinated. The alignment theory, as represented by proposals for systemic reform, calls for careful joint design of student performance standards, testing, curriculum, instructional methods, allocation of funds, pre-service teacher training, in-service teacher training, principal training and selection, parent participation, rewards and penalties for educators and students, employers hiring standards, and higher education admissions requirements.

The policy research paradigm has great strengths, but it has the weaknesses of those strengths. It inherently regards a school as a resultant of outside forces, rather than as an entity guided by permanent goals, responsible for serving a particular population or pursuing a defined theory of teaching and learning. Like all the foregoing paradigms, policy research has its uses and implications. In the foregoing section we propose yet another paradigm that also has its normative aspects and its limitations. We present the new paradigm because it points to important lines of research that other paradigms neglect.

Other Paradigms with Implications for Policy

The classic policy research paradigm is not the only one used to derive prescriptions about how society might improve existing schools. One common framework is the *teacher qualities paradigm*. It assumes that a school is essentially a collection of classrooms run by teachers. A school is good and productive to the degree that the individual teachers are well-educated, well-motivated, and in command of a wide repertoire of effective teaching techniques (Darling-Hammond, 1997). The most important mechanism for promoting school quality is teacher training, both in-service and pre-service.

Another common framework is the *resident programs paradigm*. It assumes that a school is essentially a collection of specific instructional programs (math labs, art sequences, reading exercises, computer-aided instruction routines) to which students are assigned according to their needs and interests (Powell *et al.*, 1985). A school is good and productive to the degree that individual instructional programs are of high quality and students are assigned to them appropriately. Holding program quality constant, a school with many different programs is more likely to be effective for a given set of students than a school with fewer programs.

Unlike the policy research paradigm, these assume that schools are productive when they are assembled out of the right components. Like the policy research paradigm, they assume that the actions of people on the outside fundamentally determine a school's effectiveness. The policy research paradigm assumes that productive schools depend on the right combinations of goals and rules set by public officials. The teacher qualities and resident programs paradigms, on the other hand, assume that people outside the school—who train and assign teachers, or who design and place programs—fundamentally determine school productivity.

In the following section we propose a new paradigm that assumes school productivity depends on how people inside the school work together and how they manage the school's collective external relationships. The new paradigm tries to make explicit what has for some time been implicit in work by Newmann *et al.* (1997), Bryk, Lee, and Holland (1993), Hill *et al.* (1990), and others, which focuses on schools as productive organizations.

A New Paradigm Focused on School Productivity

In working to create a new program of research and experimentation on productive schools, the authors and other members of the Consortium on Renewing Education (CORE) found that none of the existing paradigms embodied a set of ideas about how schools operate as productive organizations and how productive schools relate to their environments. We sought, and ultimately developed, a new paradigm that meets these requirements. Our new paradigm is based on four central propositions:

1. The essential product of any system of elementary and secondary education is student learning, and for these purposes the school is the fundamental unit of production.
2. To be the fundamental unit of production, schools need to be both true organizations and true communities.
3. Each school is uniquely defined by the ways in which it controls and uses five forms of capital: integrative, financial, human, social, and political.

4. The roles of external institutions that influence schools —including government agencies, labor markets, and professional organizations—are to promote and support school productivity.

This section explains our assumptions in detail and then shows how they combine into a productivity-oriented paradigm for research and policymaking.

The School as the Fundamental Unit of Production

Our central proposition is that the school, not the individual classroom nor the broader education system, is the principle locus of student learning.

Though students learn particular bits of information in individual classrooms, the sum of their knowledge—the information, skills, habits and values that they take to the next level of schooling or into their adult lives—depends on the ways in which their separate classroom experiences build on or conflict with one another. Teachers often work alone in closed classrooms, but their effectiveness depends heavily on the quality of students' prior preparation and on whether other classes reinforce or conflict with what is taught. Exceptional teachers can motivate and discipline students they have before them, but students' overall attitudes and effort reflect the sum of their experiences in the entire school context.

Similarly, the direct source of a student's learning is not the broader school system's capabilities or the performance of schools other than the one the student attends. A student succeeds or fails because of the quality and coherency of instruction she or he receives directly and the reinforcement for consistent effort experienced in a particular school.

The School as Organization and Community

An organization produces something, controls resources necessary to fulfill its purposes, prospers if it is productive, and languishes if it is not. A school that is an organization is based on specific ideas about how instruction can be organized to meet the needs of a particular group of students; it is an active agent, not a passive barometer driven entirely by external forces.

An organization has clear goals and the capacity to organize and adapt its own activities in order to meet them. Such a school can invest in its own future by hiring, training, and developing teachers to operate effectively within its specific context. It can operate on adult personal responsibility, ensuring that every teacher and administrator is rewarded for contribution to students' instructional success, and it does not burden students with adults who cannot or will not help students learn. Such a school can also say forthrightly what it requires of students and their families, and it will not allow a few students to disrupt other students' learning or destroy the school's educational effectiveness.

The CORE paradigm treats schools as if they were analogous to firms. Though schools are seldom profit-seeking organizations, they are, as described in the economic theory of the firm, groups of individuals coordinating the use of their complementary skills toward a common end. Groups attempting to produce a joint product are more effective than groups in which people disagree on what is to be produced and how. Groups that cannot combine their efforts effectively often dissolve, in part because other organizations can produce better results, and in part because group members who truly care about the task to be done depart for other, more productive groups.

What does it mean for schools to be communities? A community is a bridge between the most fundamental unit of society, the family, and the broader society, as defined by city, state, and nation. Schools assume responsibility for a family's most precious asset, its children. They also act on behalf of the broader society to ensure that children learn sufficiently to become informed voters, decent citizens, productive taxpayers, and full participants in a future economy. Because the hopes of parents and the broader society are not always identical, schools must cope with conflicting needs and expectations. They must do so with great competence and sensitivity, simultaneously maintaining parental trust and public confidence.

Communities build unity without destroying individuality by developing basic agreements in principle about values, norms of behavior, and bases of reciprocal obligation. Though they cannot satisfy the needs of all members at all times, communities thrive by maintaining members' confidence that members' shared norms and concerns are more important than their differences. To be a community, a school must be free to engage parents and other adults about values, sometimes following and sometimes leading, but never automatically imposing formulas based on extraneous political settlements reached outside the school community.

Schools must be highly competent at recognizing the different desires of parents and the state, devising instructional programs that serve both parties purposes whenever possible, and resisting demands from either parents or the broader society that needlessly or callously override preferences of the other. To perform these functions, a school probably needs to have its own conception of the child's interests, one that is richer than a mere vector sum of the demands of parents and the state.

The School as a Combination of Capitals—Integrative, Human, Financial, Social and Political

To promote a fine-grained understanding of schools as hybrids of firm and community, the CORE paradigm reduces the main ingredients of every school to a set of *capitals*—assets that when deployed or engaged contribute to the production of an outcome (Carlton and Perloff, 1990). Schools can be seen as having five forms of capital:

- *Integrative capital:* The glue that holds a school together, its shared understanding of how financial, social, intellectual, human, and political capital can be used together successfully in a purposeful and consistent instructional program.
- *Human capital:* What adults who operate in the school know (or know how to access from the stock of knowledge available to society as a whole) and can impart to students, and what they know about how students learn.
- *Financial capital:* Funding that allows the school both to operate on a current basis and to invest in improvements.
- *Social capital:* The bonds of trust and habit that define the school as a community. These bonds exist among staff members, between the staff and parents, among parents, and between students and the adult members of the school community.
- *Political capital:* The basis of the school's legitimate authority to educate children on behalf of the state, to confer credentials on graduates, and, in the case of public schools, to receive public funds.

Schools hold and use all five forms of capital, but integrative capital, the school's specific theory of how the other forms of capitals are to be combined to product effective instruction and student learning, is the master of all the others. A school's integrative capital determines which forms of the other capitals it needs and how they are to be used.

Figure 24.1 illustrates the relationships among the five forms of capital. It shows that every school incorporates human, social, intellectual, and political capitals, but that individual schools are defined and differentiated by their integrative capital. (In the figure, the differences in schools integrative capital are represented by their shapes—circular, square, and triangular). Figure 24.1 also shows that the relationships between schools and external institutions are defined by the school's integrative capital. Thus schools' relationships with outside support agencies, like teacher labor suppliers and authorizing agencies, are "shaped" differently by each schools' integrative capital.

What the figure does not show is our ultimate hypothesis. We assert that schools that have a definite approach to instruction and internal management—integrative capital, and are supported in ways consistent with their integrative capital—are highly productive. Conversely, we assume that

Figure 24.1

Legend: Every school incorporates human, social, financial, and political capital but is defined by its integrative capital.

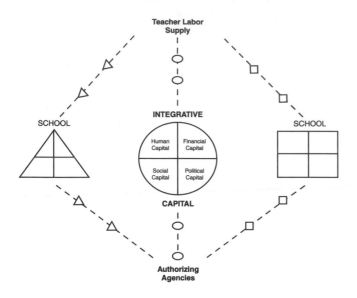

schools lacking in integrative capital—that have vague goals or lack a clear understanding of how financial, social, intellectual, human, and political capital can be used together successfully in a purposeful and consistent instructional program—are less productive.

Every school's relationship with outside agencies is defined by its integrative capital, such as the school selects teachers to fit its approach to instruction. The school's relationships with authorizing agencies are also shaped by its goals and approach.

Integrative Capital

The concept of integrative capital is grounded in a simple observation: People who visit many schools know that some are united, disciplined, and consistent in what they expect of adults and offer students, and others are not. Similarly, some schools are united and collaborative and others are fragmented. Schools also vary tremendously on how much responsibility they take for students' learning. Some schools do not expect to have much influence on what a student values or on the choices a student will make in her or his life, and many are resigned to the limitations imposed by poverty, low parental education, and racial minority status.

But other schools expect to make a great deal of difference in a child's knowledge and abilities. Schools that expect to mold and transform children have very clear goals and definite methods for pursuing those goals. These schools goals and methods color every transaction among faculty and between faculty, students, and parents. Such schools have definite approaches to motivating students. They also ensure that students' learning is cumulative over

time. They show students the connections among subjects, and they make sure that every succeeding teacher builds on what earlier teachers have taught.

Schools that have ambitious goals for students, and discipline the work of students and faculty to make sure those goals are met, have high degrees of integrative capital.

Integrative capital is the glue that holds a school together —it is what distinguishes a school in which everyone considers themselves united in a common enterprise from a school in which everyone goes their own way, working according to their own lights without particular efforts to contribute to or build on what others do. A school's integrative capital is an educational philosophy translated into organizing principles that focus all the activities of a school. It defines:

- The ideas, facts, and habits the school intends to help students learn;
- The learning experiences the school intends to offer students and how the school intends to provide those experiences in order to ensure that students do learn;
- The characteristics of students the school intends to serve (defined by age groups, prior education, and other attributes); and
- The school's relationships to parents and the public officials responsible to act in the children's interests.[1]

Schools high in integrative capital are different from one another in many ways: some are private and some public, some are in rich neighborhoods and some in poor, and some use modern technology and up-to-date instructional methods while others are old-fashioned. What they have in common is commitment to learning, personal attention to students, and disciplined collaboration among adults.

Brief descriptions of two schools studied in the course of the senior author's ongoing study of integrative capital illustrate the concept's meaning, both of which are listed below. The first school is high in integrative capital because its central philosophy of education and goals for students unite all aspects of the school and structure the work of every person, adult, and child. The second school is lower in integrative capital because its intentions do not translate into disciplined action, and though adults care about students learning, much is left to chance.

A public elementary school that serves immigrant children from many countries has devoted itself to making children literate and skillful in English as quickly as possible. Teachers devote half of every day to literacy—half the morning in grade-level groups of mixed ability and half the morning in smaller groups to allow teachers to work closely with small groups of children with similar levels of English proficiency. Every teacher in the school works with small groups. To make sure that the large and small groups reinforce one another, the regular classroom teachers have agreed to use a common set of reading materials and to closely coordinate their schedules. In hopes of creating a common experience for students from different language groups, the school uses visual arts in all its teaching, encouraging children to express themselves in art and to discuss one another's art in English. The school also expressly teaches students' self-control, both to ensure that students respect others and take their work seriously, and to make it possible to run a productive school in a potentially noisy open-plan building. The school has maintained this approach for many years, despite changes in principal, staff, and ethnic groups served. In this school with high integrative capital, student achievement greatly exceeds the average for schools serving similar demographic groups.

A private K–8 school serves minority families who want their children to have a disciplined, safe environment. The school is a model of decorum: students wear uniforms, teachers dress well, classrooms are orderly and the halls are quiet. Parents are proud of the school and students are happy: the price of orderliness is not repression. The school's mostly-minority staff are united on issues of respect and decorum, but they are left on their own about instructional planning. Many teachers have weak academic preparation, but the school relies on them to identify materials and plan classes. Many students in this school with low integrative capital learn to read on schedule but fall behind national norms after the third grade. By the upper grades, student achievement levels are mixed but on average low, and the more desirable public and private high schools, though eager to accept minority students, are skeptical about the school's graduates.

Another way to illustrate the meaning of a school's integrative capital is to suggest how parents and lay people can make their own assessment of it. A school is high in integrative capital if:

- Teachers can describe how their class fits with other classes at a particular grade level, and that students who come to them from earlier grades are well prepared.
- Students can explain how one class connects with what is taught in other classes.
- Parents of students attending the school can give comparable accounts of what the school's goals are and believe that the school keeps its promises.
- The principal can explain teacher hiring in terms of the school's overall goals (instead of saying that teachers are assigned by someone else or that they just have to take whomever comes along).
- Faculty and staff can give similar answers in describing the desired graduate of the school.

Integrative capital is an amalgam of educational philosophy and organizing principles, a combination of ideas and process, around which all activities of a school are focused. Schools high in integrative capital are not all radically innovative or totally original. They contain many imitated ideas and methods found elsewhere, but they are devoted to pursuing those ideas rigorously and to avoiding the kind of eclecticism that allows everyone to dash off in different directions. However, despite their dedication to putting specific ideas into practice, schools high in integrative capital are living organizations: each constantly adapts its core ideas to fit a specific time and place, and to reflect student needs and faculty capacities.

Schools high in integrative capital arise from particular philosophies of education, but they require process as well. The adults who work in a school must work together to learn many things: how to put basic ideas into practice, how to judge whether students are progressing satisfactorily, how to adapt the instructional program when students are not learning all they should, or when society demands that students learn new things. Adults in schools must also learn when to collaborate, when to work independently, when to compromise, and when to allow dissidents to split off.

What Integrative Capital Looks Like in Practice

Table 24.1 summarizes the key attributes of schools high in integrative capital. Such schools are ambitious and demanding in what they aim for and what they demand. They expect to provide information but also expect to form students attitudes and values—to mark them for life. Given these goals, schools high in integrative capital try to use every part of a student's experience to teach and influence. Such schools also expect to influence students activities outside of class, both during and after regular school hours. Extracurricular activities are not extra at all but are tightly integrated into students' overall activities.

Schools high in integrative capital are not authoritarian: they can make demands on students because they work constantly to show students that the school offers them a route to something valuable. Such schools use their traditions and their links to alumni to demonstrate links to desirable adult lives. The schools also use external validators —colleges, universities, and desirable employers that seek the school's graduates, high-status alumni, and students and faculty from schools with similar goals and methods— to assure students and parents that the school's offerings and demands make sense. The orientation to external validators sharply distinguishes schools high and low in integrative capital. Schools that are not highly coherent and disciplined rely on individual teachers and students to assign meaning to what they do. Individual faculty members can teach excellent courses and show students why they are important, but the school takes no responsibility for ensuring that every faculty member does this, or that students can make sense of their overall school experience.[2]

Table 24.1 also shows that the adults in schools high in integrative capital put heavy demands on themselves and one another. Teachers in schools high in integrative capital

Table 24.1

How Schools High in Integrative Capital Function

Importance of unifying goals for students and agreement on essential student experiences	Everone focuses on ideas and habits to be learned, how teachers should perform in classes, forms of work done by students, and teachers' responsibilities to struggling students. Uses extracurricular activities as well as formal courses to teach skills, habits, and values.
Scope of school's goals (re: students)	Goals emphasize knowledge and mental skills, as well as values, habits, and future community roles.
Basis of leadership authority	Expertise in the school's core ideas and methods, link to tradition.
Formality of decision-making processes	Leader has clear authority in some areas, consults in others, and defers to committee work in others.
Importance of tradition	School takes care to maintain continuity with past even as it adapts to changes in society and student needs
Differentiation of teaching and leadership roles	Most administrators also teach. Teaching experience is a precondition to leadership.
Basis of teacher recruitment	Commitment to the school's goals and training and experience (re. the school's specific approach to instruction).
Teacher socialization practices	Concerted effort to familiarize teachers with school's traditions and methods; direct supervision by top school leaders.
Basis of student recruitment	Family choice based on understanding of the school, matching with student needs and family values.
Roles of parents	Choosers, partners, volunteers
Internal standards for student and teacher performance (internal accountability)	Defined in light of desired student characteristics, expected student milestones and performances, expectations of receiving institutions.
Importance of external validators (alumni, receiving schools, employers)	Linkages with networks of similar schools (and advisory organizations built for those networks) are essential to school's quality control and financial survival; they also provide role models for student socialization.

are selected for their ability to contribute to all facets of the school's mission, and they are carefully socialized and supported for the same purpose. School leaders are "keepers" of the flame of the school's history and traditions; they also buttress this authority by teaching classes and knowing the names and personalities of students.

Human Capital

Human capital is the knowledge and skill embodied in individuals who are employed or otherwise operate in a school and the broader society's store of knowledge.[3] Teachers are almost always a school's most important holders of human capital in the form of subject matter knowledge and repertoires of teaching skills and techniques. Administrators also have relevant knowledge and skill, some parts of which may overlap with that of teachers and other parts of which (adult leadership, accounting, marketing, and so on) might not.

Another vital source of human capital is students. What they already know determines what and how they should be taught. Knowledgeable students can also contribute to the instructional process, through peer tutoring, and so on. Also, the social characteristics of students may shape the collective human capital of a school. Students learn from one another, both formally and informally. A school comprised of students from high socioeconomic households can have an advantage in terms of academic learning transmitted from student to student.

Depending on how a school organizes and coordinates instruction (its integrative capital), there might be other relevant holders of human capital. Parents who tutor students, assist teachers, or handle instructional duties on a volunteer basis are important sources of human capital for some schools. Contractors who provide services (such as vendors of special or remedial education, or teacher collaboratives that contract to provide regular instruction in specialized fields like art, science, and math) are also parts of a school's human capital.

A school gains access to human capital in many ways: it employs individuals who have certain knowledge and skills, it helps employees with deficient training obtain added knowledge, and it can obtain donated or fee-based services from individuals who know things that school employees do not. In the absence of external rules that limit the school's access to human capital, a school might also stop employing people whose knowledge and skills are weak or redundant and strengthen its human capital by employing others.

Financial Capital

Financial capital is the stock of fungible and tangible assets (in other words, money) upon which a school can draw. These assets are available to be converted into or contribute to other forms of capital. Financial capital translates into the physical components of a school, such as buildings, buses, and books. It also shapes operational components of a less enduring nature, such as purchasing employee time or utilities and services.

Financial capital is essential to a school's capacity to function as a true organization. However, it is a component that America's individual public schools have virtually had no discretion over throughout the major portion of this century. By specifying the use of resources from a position external to the school, most modern district allocation rules have deprived schools of decision-making capacities. They cannot formulate their own "production function;" they cannot select and develop staff in support of a specific instructional strategy. The "capital's" paradigm directs research and development toward understanding how funds can be allocated to schools to support school productivity.

Social Capital

Social capital consists of the habits or trust, mutual reliance, and reciprocity among members of an organization or community.[4] Various parties—teachers, administrators, non-instructional staff, students, parents, and community members—must be able to rely upon one another. Without a sense of trust, a school is deeply, perhaps fatally, weakened.

Trust is the willingness to accept the risk of social interaction, to be willing to believe others' statements, and to take actions in confidence that others will also act as they have promised. Trust is also a sense of personal and social obligation to those with whom one frequently interacts. Institutions regarded as trustworthy are characterized by low incidence of conflict and are able to resolve issues and make decisions efficiently. Institutions that enjoy high degrees of social capital do not need to monitor their members' actions in detail. They can expect that people will do whatever is necessary, not just what their job descriptions of the school rules absolutely require. With a broad base of norms held in common, incidence of "shirking" and "free rider" problems are less prevalent.

Social capital leads to recognition of interdependency and mutual obligation. Collective actions—efforts to solve problems of low performance or to adapt a school to changing student needs—are easier and more productive when trust is high. When trust is low, problem-solving can be impeded by efforts to defend turf or by demands to be compensated for changing habitual and convenient patterns of work.

Where does social capital come from? It is in part a natural product of habit and familiarity, especially in the course of a productive collaboration. But it is also a result of organizational clarity—explicit goals, overt shared commitment, and habits of disciplined and predictable action. Schools that have definite goals and methods can attract people who want to work and learn in them. This can mean that professionals and parents come together on the basis of agreement on fundamental principles, and thus have some ready basis for mutual trust. Similarly, schools

can lose social capital if they fail to live up to their promises, or if their goals become unclear due to personnel turnover or new external mandates and constraints.

Political Capital

Political capital is the school's legitimacy as an agent of the broader community. A school has political capital to the degree that public officials who can authorize the school to receive public funds and instruct the public's children have confidence that the school will act in the public interest.

All schools depend upon legitimate authority, even private schools. For example, a private religious school could be closed by state authorities under some extreme conditions. A public school that is about to be closed and reconstituted because of low performance or a record of abuse of children or theft of money has low political capital. A school that has an unblemished record has more freedom of action and has a better chance of surviving a crisis than a school that is frequently accused of abuses or low performance.[4]

Different schools have different forms of political capital. Some have blanket permission to do almost anything as long as they achieve decent results and do not condone criminal acts by faculty. Others have permission to operate as long as they do specific things: they can come to the attention of public authorities if they deviate from quite specific rules, such as how a handicapped child's program gets planned or how a piece of equipment is used.

Thus political capital has two dimensions: type (the requirements contained in the school's license to operate) and amount (the trust that public authorities have in the school, given its record of performance). Private schools, charter schools, and regular public schools all have political capital, though in different forms and degrees.

Tying the Capitals Together

Each school's integrative capital determines how the other four capitals (human, financial, social, and political) are built, sustained, and used. Integrative capital is the architecture that makes the other capitals of the school—the money the school has to spend on staff, equipment, and adult learning, and the knowledge of the professionals and others who contribute time and effort to the school—work together. The dynamic relationships among these forms of capital are highly complex, and it is not always easy to disentangle the forms of capital in practice. For example:

- A teacher's actions in one class on one day reflect both her own knowledge of the subject to be taught (her own part of the school's human capital), the availability of instructional materials and equipment (the results of financial capital), and her understanding of how the knowledge she is trying to impart contributes to the school's overall goals and learning plans for students (integrative capital).

- A school's decisions about how to invest the money (financial capital) set aside for staff retraining and recruitment (human capital) reflect a set of priorities derived from its overall instructional priorities and assessment of its own current capabilities (integrative capital).

- A school's relationships of trust and confidence with parents and the wider community (social capital) and its ability to maintain stable relationships with government authorizers (political capital) depend in part on whether it can give a clear account of its goals, methods, and performance expectations (integrative capital) and whether the teachers and administrators are up to the tasks they have set for themselves (human capital).

- A school's ability to adopt and rigorously pursue a curriculum and method of instruction (integrative capital) depends on the willingness of staff to cooperate in a common undertaking (social capital), on the school's ability to invest (financial capital) in appropriate instructional resources and teacher training, and in teachers' knowledge and skill (human capital).

- A staff member might internalize her school's integrative capital and carry it with her elsewhere. When it is only personal knowledge, information about how to put a theory of instruction into operation is human capital, but when it is shared and used to organize the work of students and teachers, the same information is best understood as the school's integrative capital.

The Roles of External Institutions as Supporting Structures

Treating schools as organizations and communities affects the ways we regard external institutions that govern, provide resources for, and assist schools. In order to be organizations and communities, schools cannot be regarded as subordinate nodes in a complex local district or state-level bureaucracy. They must have the capacity to adapt to meet their members' needs and, accordingly, to differ from one another. The fundamental challenge of public policy for K–12 education is to determine the means by which individual schools can accept government funding and yet remain the primary loci of production. Under the CORE paradigm, external institutions are not justified by traditions, historical practices, political arrangements, or even laws. Their purpose and operation is understood only in terms of what they contribute to school productivity. The CORE paradigm leads to research questions of the form, "How can policy be arranged to sustain and reinforce the effectiveness of individual schools?" This is significantly different than the conventional paradigm of current school operation; the conventional paradigm assumes the individual school is an instrument or object of the policy system.

The Difference a Paradigm Makes

The CORE paradigm is clearly different from the others presented earlier, but are the differences important? The only test of a paradigm's contribution is whether it opens up lines of analysis or action that others do not open. The CORE paradigm certainly meets this test. By viewing the school as an agent able to initiate actions, determine its own priorities, make decisions that affect its future capacities and obligations, and respond to changes in its environment, the CORE paradigm suggests important new roles for key institutions and new avenues for research.

The CORE paradigm regards schools as:

- *Whole organizations informed by a theory of how the parts fit together to help students learn.* Seeing schools in this way raises questions about how schools come to be informed by such theories, what can prevent or impede schoolwide integration, how thoroughly everyone in the school must accept such a theory before it can be effective, and whether some theories or sources of assistance are more likely than others to create coherent and effective schools.

- *Choosers, trainers, evaluators, and socializers of staff.* Seeing schools in this way focuses attention on questions about how schools with different theories of instruction value specific teacher knowledge and undertake, find, or develop teacher expertise, and how a system in which schools employ teachers affects the supply of would-be teachers, the skills demanded, and teacher salary structures.

- *Purchasers, priority-setters, investors in their own capabilities, and makers of conscious tradeoffs between instructional and other services as well as between current services and performance-enhancing investments.* Seeing schools as holders and users of financial capital leads to questions about how schools can manage money and risks, evaluate potential purchases of equipment and services, and determine how much to save for contingencies.

- *Makers and keepers of commitments, as priority-setters that decide whose needs and expectations will and will not be met, and as communities that build or lose members' trust depending on performance.* Seeing schools in this way focuses attention on questions about how schools define their clienteles and determine how to manage differences among groups of parents on instructional emphases, how to improve facets of the school that are not performing as expected and help students who are not benefiting from the school's regular instructional program, and how to deal with student behavior that threatens the school climate.

- *Managers of their own reputations in the broader community, as entities calculating which external demands it will satisfy and which ones it will ignore.* Seeing schools as creators and users of political capital leads to questions about how individual schools can build and keep the confidence of funders and voters, how a school can ensure that the public and policymakers understand the limits of its mission, and how schools can keep others' expectations focused on performance rather than compliance (Newmann, King, and Rigdon, 1997).

Table 24.2 shows how differently the policy research and CORE paradigms define the roles of key actors external to the schools.

A researcher or policymaker interested in school improvement would explore very different questions, depending on whether she adopted the policy research or the CORE paradigms, as Table 24.3 demonstrates.

The questions raised by the CORE paradigm are very different from those derived from the traditional policy research paradigm, which starts with policymakers' tools and asks how they can be used to change schools in ways desired by public officials (Hill and Marks, 1982; McDonnell and Elmore, 1987). The conventional policy research framework regards a school as a receiver of assets created elsewhere and as an implementer of decisions made and priorities set by a central school board.

Conclusion

Our paradigm does not necessarily eliminate the need for other research and policy discussions structured by other paradigms. As long as schools are publicly funded and subject to oversight by public officials; there will be some need for the policy research paradigm. However, a new framework like the CORE paradigm described above is required to structure research on how to strengthen schools as active

agents and problem-solvers, rather than as passive responders to outside forces.

Much current educational policy and research treats the school as a black box: things are done to or for the school, not by it. Assets (staff members, equipment) are added to or subtracted from schools. Constraints in the form of new goals, performance quotas, testing programs, and regulations are imposed on schools by school boards and funding agencies. New curricula and staff-training programs are selected for whole districts and then infused into schools. Budget shortfalls are met by mandated district-wide reductions in school staffing or services. Such policies are always intended to make schools better, stronger, or fairer places. But, as decades of research in education and other areas of public service have shown, productive schools are communities that take their own initiatives and assume responsibility for children's learning; they are not passive material ready to be molded.

In order to create a new understanding of schools as productive organizations, the CORE paradigm starts with a new conception of the school. We see the school as a unique hybrid organization like a firm in that it is composed of fungible resources and specific people with definite skills and knowledge, all tied together by some overall conception of how the people, money, and equipment combine to deliver instruction and help students learn and develop skills, habits, and values. We see the school as a community in that it requires and develops bonds of trust and confidence, among the people who work within it and between the school and parents, neighbors, and the broader society. The school is productive because it has the incentive and the capacity to adapt its educational program to changing needs, both those of its students and of the society and economy that students will someday enter.

Table 24.2

Roles of Key Actors Under Two Paradigms

	Policy Research Paradigm	*CORE Paradigm*
School Boards	Create a policy framework for all schools that reflects results of community-wide deliberation and incorporates settlements of political conflicts. Hold schools accountable for compliance.	Authorize individual schools to operate with clear, specific goals and approaches to instruction. Hold schools accountable for performance.
Teacher suppliers (training institutions and local personnel offices)	Provide teachers who approximate a generic vision of quality and assign teachers to jobs in ways that respect their contractual rights.	Prepare teachers who can work effectively in highly-focused schools and help schools find teachers that meet their needs.
Funding sources	Use funds to purchase assets needed by schools (teachers, books, equipment) and allocate to schools according to formulas set by the funding sources.	Allocate funds directly to schools, expecting schools to hire and purchase assets according to their goals, instructional approaches, and needs.
Parents	Support the school program defined by the district board and take part in shared school governance.	Choose schools that fit parents' views of childrens' needs, insist that the school keep its promises, and in turn live up to the family's promises to the school.

Table 24.3
Different Paradigms Identify Different Questions About How to Improve School Performance

	Policy Research Paradigm	*CORE Paradigm*
School purposes and productivity (integrative capital)	How shall public officials define schools' goals and ensure that every school pursues priorities set by public deliberation?	How can a school adopt and implement a clear theory of teaching and learning that meets the needs of its students; what can impede schoolwide integration, what sources of help are available to help schools choose and implement integrating theories of instruction?
Sources and uses of funds (financial capital)	How shall public officials determine the proper amounts and uses of funds for schools and ensure that schools use funds as intended?	How can schools stabilize income and manage money and risks; how can they make prudent tradeoffs between current services and future performance?
Sources, quality, and effectiveness of teachers (human capital)	How shall public officials determine what skills teachers need, ensure that schools have access to properly-prepared teachers, and invest in in-service programs to ensure teacher quality?	How can schools define their staff needs, choose between alternatives of hiring new staff and training existing staff, and find qualified people to hire? How can public officials ensure that schools have a wide range of high-quality choices?
Parental and community support (social capital)	What rules should public officials enact to ensure that school staff take parental and community views and aspirations seriously?	How can a school clarify its promises and demands so that teachers and parents can know what to expect; how can school leaders balance personalization and responsiveness to parents with the need to keep promises about academic and behavioral standards; how diverse a set of expectations can a school meet?
School's legitimacy as a public institution (political capital)	What rules must all schools follow if they are to be considered public? How should public officials respond to a school's failure to comply with basic rules?	How can schools build and keep the confidence of public officials and voters, while maintaining the freedom of action necessary for self-improvement?

NOTES

1. The concept of integrative capital is original to CORE, but it draws from many sources, including the work of Newmann *et al.*, Lee and Smith, Bryk and Lee, and Hill *et al.* It goes beyond the "effective schools" literature, which lists attributes of productive schools but does not explain how they come about or are sustained. It is consistent with Newmann's work on schools' organizational capital, which he defines as "a school's ability to organize itself as a collective enterprise, uniting the use of human, social, and technical resources." Integrative capital looks beneath the phenomenon of collaboration to the ideas about teaching and learning that underlay it. The concept of integrative capital, in short, sees leadership, shared commitment, and collaboration as results of something deeper—in goals for students and a strategy of teaching and learning that can help students reach those goals.

2. Our ongoing study of schools' integrative capital has shown that what can look to teachers like a stimulating environment that permits individual self-expression can look to students like an unmotivated chaos. In high schools, students' ability to explain the school's instructional agenda was the best single index of integrative capital: if students understood the school as a whole and could explain it to us, we found most or all of the other features in Table 24.1; if students could not explain the school, we found few of the features in Table 24.1.

3. Here we refer to the stock of knowledge and understanding existing within a society that is capable of being distilled by decision-makers as the substance to be transmitted to students. Some societies are rich in intellectual capital, others less so. Increasingly, as a consequence of global communication and electronic information storage technology, the stock of intellectual capital upon which a school can draw is the planet's total understanding. However, the widespread availability of virtually all human knowledge in a manner never before possible does not render the school's job of distillation any easier. Increasingly, decisions must be made regarding what knowledge is of most value. Also, a school's integrative capital can play a limiting function on the selection of intellectual capital to be presented to students. For example, a religious view regarding the appropriateness of Darwin's theory of evolution might restrict the flow of ideas available to some students. Thus intellectual capital is a function both of what is available to be transmitted and the judgments that are made regarding which components are of value to be transmitted.

4. Anthony Bryk made important contributions to early drafts of this section.

REFERENCES

Berman, P. & McLaughlin, M. W. (1979). *Federal Programs Supporting Educational Change, Vol. 4*: The Findings in Review. Santa Monica, CA: RAND.

Bryk, A. S., Lee, V. E. & Holland, P. B. (1993). *Catholic Schools and the Common Good.* Cambridge, MA: Harvard University Press.

Carlton, D. W. & Perloff, J. M. (1990). *Modern Industrial Organization.* Chp. 13. Glenview, IL: Scott, Foresman.

Darling-Hammond, L. (1997). *The Right to Learn*, San Francisco: Jossey-Bass.

Elmore, R. F. & McLaughlin, M. W. (1988). *Steady Work. Policy, Practice, and the Reform of American Education.* Santa Monica, CA: RAND.

Fuhrman, S. (1994). *Politics and Systemic Education Reform, CPRE Policy Briefs.* New Brunswick: Consortium for Policy Research in Education.

Gage, N. L. (1963). *Handbook of Research on Teaching; A Project of the American Educational Research Association.* Chicago: Rand McNally.

Getzels, J. W., Lipham, J. M. & Campbell, R. F. (1968). *Educational Administration as a Social Process: Theory, Research, Practice*. New York: Harper & Row.

Griffiths, D. E., *et al.* (1962). *Organizing Schools for Effective Education*. Danville, IL: The Interstate Printers & Publishers.

Guba, E. G. (Ed.) (1990). *The Paradigm Dialog*. Newbury Park, CA: Sage Publications.

Halpin, A. (1966). *Theory and Research in Administration*. New York: Macmillan, 1966.

Hannaway, J. (1985). Administrative Costs and Administrative Behavior Associated with Categorical Programs, *Educational Evaluation and Policy Analysis*; Vol. 7, No. 1, pp. 57–64.

Hill, P. T. & Madey, D. L. (1983). *Educational Policy-Making Through the Civil Justice System*. Santa Monica, CA: RAND.

Hill, P. T. & Marks, E. L. (1982). *Federal Influence over State and Local Government: The Case of Nondiscrimination in Education*. Santa Monica, CA: RAND.

Hill, P. T., Foster, G. E. & Gendler, T. (1990). *High Schools with Character*. Santa Monica, CA: RAND.

Kimbrough, J. & Hill, P. T (1980). *The Aggregate Effects of Federal Education Programs*. Santa Monica, CA: RAND.

Kimbrough, J. & Hill, P. T. (1983). *Problems of Implementing Multiple Categorical Education Programs*. Santa Monica, CA: RAND.

Knapp, M. S, *et al.* (1983). *Cumulative Effects of Federal Education Policies on Schools and Districts: Summary Report of a Congressionally Mandated Study*. Menlo Park, CA: SRI International.

Lee, V. E. & Smith, J. B. (1997). High School Size: Which Works Best and for Whom? *Educational Evaluation and Policy Analysis, 19* (3), 205–227.

McDonnell, L. M. & Elmore, R. F. (1987). Getting the Job Done: Alternative Policy Instruments, *Educational Evaluation and Policy Analysis*; Vol. 9, No. 2, pp. 133–152.

Newmann, F. M., *et al.* (1997). *Authentic Achievement*. San Francisco: Jossey-Bass.

Newmann, F. M, Rigdon, M. & King, M. B. (1997). Accountability and School Performance: Implications from Restructuring Schools, *Harvard Educational Review*; Vol. 67, No. 1, pp. 41–74.

Powell, A. G., Farrar, E. & Cohen, D. K. (1985). *The Shopping Mall High School: Winners and Losers in the Educational Marketplace*. Boston: Houghton Mifflin.

NAME INDEX

SUBJECT INDEX

A

ABT Associates, 37, 40

Academies, preparation in, 120

Accelerated Schools, 246, 332

Accountability: accounts in, 476–477, 483; aspects of, 463–489; authority in, 474–475; background on, 463–464; bureaucratic, 467; and causal responsibility, 477–478, 483–484; and causal theories, 484; collective, 433; and consumerism, 417; demands for, 466; efficacy of, 481; and excellence, 466–473; external and internal, 485–486; in future, 484–485; history of, 465–466; implications of, 485–487; and internationalization, 81–82; and leadership, 52, 480–484; legal, 467–469; market, 471–472; moral, 470–471; and motivation, 478–480, 484; overview of, 464–465; policy and practice on, 81–82; political, 470; and principal-agent relationship, 467, 474, 481–482; professional, 469–470; for reform, 176; research needed on, 480, 486; as social force, 197; strategies for, 475–476; themes in, 473–480; tradeoffs in, 472–473; trends in, 472; types of, 466–472

Accreditation, for preparation programs, 234

Action, and culture, 299

Action research, and internationalization, 91–92

Activities: and organizational boundaries, 288; practical, 208–210; and situated learning, 209; teleological or symbolic, 212–213; as units of analysis, 206–208

Adams Avenue Middle School, culture of, 304, 306

Adams School System, 17

Adequacy, of resources, 492–493

Administrative bloat, and resources, 495–496

Administrators: and accountability, 476, 486; and culture, 314–317; and integrated services, 447–448; rethinking and reacting by, 351–355; role reorientation for, 352–353

Administrators Notebook, 8

Adults: and school cultures, 304–306; subcultures of, 306–308

Advisory Commission on Intergovernmental Relations, 494, 506

Affirmative action, and women, 112

Agency, scene versus, 213–214

Agreement, dialog versus, 213–214

Alabama, resources in, 498

Alberta, University of: Department of Educational Administration at, 87; Project Decide at, 18

Albuquerque: mentoring in, 220; social capital in, 397

Alignment theory, and policy research paradigm, 513

Alternative Public Schools, 472

Alum Rock, California, accountability in, 471

America 2000, 84, 190, 346, 463, 468

American Association for the Advancement of Science, 506

American Association of Colleges for Teacher Education, 136

American Association of School Administrators (AASA): and history of research, 2, 4, 17, 19, 20; and preparation programs, 121, 122, 123, 129, 136, 137; and women, 110, 114, 116

American Association of Supervision and Curriculum Development, 352

American Association of University Women (AAUW), 309, 319

American Education Finance Administration, 129, 492

American Educational Research Association (AERA): and community, 352; and history of research, 4, 7, 18; and integrated services, 454; and internationalization, 87, 92; and knowledge base, 25, 39; and paradigm, 512; and preparation programs, 119, 122, 130, 131, 132; and research methods, 142; and social constructivism, 221

American Federation of Teachers, 233, 240, 246

American Psychological Association, 27

American Public Welfare Association, 445

Amtrak, 364

Anaheim, and social capital, 398

Anomie, and civil order, 329–330

Annie E. Casey Foundation, 456–457, 458

Anthropology: and culture, 297; knowledge base for, 28, 32

A+ Coalition, 196, 197, 199

Apprenticeship learning: in classroom, 219–220; by observation, in teaching, 230, 311, 373; and school administration, 219–220; and social constructivism, 206–207, 214

Architecture, organizations as, 261–262

Arizona, accountability in, 472

Asia-Pacific Economic Cooperation (APEC) Forum, 77

Assertiveness, as value, 303

Association for Supervision and Curriculum Development (ASCD), 63, 136

Association of School Business Officers, 136

Associations. *See* Professional organizations

Aston studies, 91

Atlanta, women in, 105, 108

Atlanta University, 105

ATLAS, 259–260

Australia: and internationalization of policy, 73, 75, 78, 79, 80, 81–82, 83; and internationalization of theory, 86–87, 91, 92; leadership studies in, 46, 60; polity in, 329; women in, 115

Australian Council of Educational Administration, 87

Austria, and culture, 302, 303

Authority: in accountability, 474–475; sources of, for leadership, 55–64; of teachers, 237–238

B

Bakke case, 199

Baltimore: integrated services in, 453; school reform in, 197; social capital in, 396

Barbados, and internationalization, 87

Behavioral theory, and leadership, 57, 58

Belgium: and culture, 301, 302, 303; human capital studies in, 425, 426–427; leadership studies in, 60; women in, 101

Bellevue School District, and compliance, 290

Bethune-Cookman College, 105

Bilingual Education Act of 1968, 187

Board of Education, Brown v., 185, 186, 187, 199

Boards of education, and boundary dilemma, 289

Boston, resources in, 497

Botswana, women in, 101

Boundaries, dilemma of organizational, 287–289

Brains, organization as, 263–265

Bridgeport, Connecticut, integrated services in, 456

British Education Management and Administration Society, 87

Brookings Institution, 83, 189

Brown University, 268

Brown v. Board of Education, 185, 186, 187, 199

Brunei, women in, 101

Buffalo, University of, 17

Bureaucracy: and accountability, 467; criticisms of, xxiii; and ideologies, 172–173; and institutional theory, 361, 363, 369–372; and integrated services, 448; and leadership, 61; and organizational dilemmas, 281–282, 284–285; and public choice theory, 410; and school community, 345–346, 351, 352; studies on, 91; and women, 107–108, 109

Business activism, and ideologies, 170, 173

Business Coalition for Education, 190

Business interests, as social force, 189–190, 194

Business Roundtable, 120, 170, 190

C

California: accountability in, 463, 467, 468, 470, 472, 485; compliance in, 290; culture in, 314; integrated services in, 445, 459; personnel categories in, 368; professionalism in, 234, 240, 241; Proposition 13 in, 493; resources in, 493, 503; social capital in, 393–394, 398

California Assessment Program, 468

California at Berkeley, University of, 397

California at Los Angeles, University of, 397

California at San Diego, University of, 208

California Institute of Technology, 397

California Learning Assessment System, 221

Cambridge, school choice in, 242

Campbell v. State of Wyoming, 493, 506

Canada: cultural studies in, 150; human capital studies in, 425, 436; and internationalization, 73, 78, 81, 86, 87; leadership studies in, 60, 315; preparation in, 122, 129, 131; women in, 115

Canadian Administrator, The, 87

Canadian Society for the Study of Educational Administration, 87

Caring: and history of research, 13; and school community, 343, 347–348, 353–354

Index